SOURCES
CONCERNING THE HOSPITALLERS OF
ST JOHN IN THE NETHERLANDS
14TH-18TH CENTURIES

STUDIES IN THE HISTORY
OF
CHRISTIAN THOUGHT

EDITED BY

HEIKO A. OBERMAN, Tucson, Arizona

IN COOPERATION WITH

HENRY CHADWICK, Cambridge
JAROSLAV PELIKAN, New Haven, Connecticut
BRIAN TIERNEY, Ithaca, New York
ARJO VANDERJAGT, Groningen

VOLUME LXXX

JOHANNA MARIA VAN WINTER

SOURCES
CONCERNING THE HOSPITALLERS OF
ST JOHN IN THE NETHERLANDS
14TH-18TH CENTURIES

SOURCES CONCERNING THE HOSPITALLERS OF ST JOHN IN THE NETHERLANDS 14TH-18TH CENTURIES

BY

JOHANNA MARIA VAN WINTER

BRILL
LEIDEN · BOSTON · KÖLN
1998

This book is printed on acid-free paper.

Library of Congress Cataloging-in-Publication Data

Sources concerning the Hospitallers of St. John in the Netherlands,
14th-18th centuries / [compiled] by Johanna Maria van Winter.
  p. cm. — (Studies in the history of Christian thought, ISSN
0081-8607 ; v. 80)
  Includes bibliographical references and indexes.
  ISBN 9004108033 (cloth : alk. paper)
  1. Knights of Malta—Netherlands—History—Sources.
  2. Netherlands—Church history—Sources.   3. Netherlands—Charters,
grants, privileges.   4. Civilization, Medieval—Sources.
  I. Winter, J. M. van (Johanna Maria)   II. Series.
BX4220.N4S68   1998
271'.79120492—dc21   97-40116
                                                                CIP

Die Deutsche Bibliothek - CIP-Einheitsaufnahme

Winter, Johanna Maria van:
Sources concerning the Hospitallers of St. John in the Netherlands,
14th - 18th centuries / by Johanna Maria van Winter. – Leiden ;
Boston ; Köln : Brill, 1998
  (Studies in the history of Christian thought ; Vol. 80)
  ISBN 90-04-10803-3

ISSN   0081-8607
ISBN   90 04 10803 3

CONTENTS

ACKNOWLEDGEMENTS

After almost 35 years of more or less intensive research on the sources of the Hospitallers of St John in the Netherlands I wish to express my sincere gratitude for the opportunity given me by Prof.Dr.Heiko A.Oberman to publish a large selection of them in one of his Brill series, Studies in the History of Christian Thought. I started my investigations on Hospitaller sources concerning the Netherlands in January 1963, on demand of both branches of the modern Hospitallers in the Netherlands: the Roman Catholic 'afdeling Nederland van de Soevereine en Militaire Orde van Malta' and the Protestant 'Johanniter Orde in Nederland'. The Organization for Scientific Research ZWO (nowadays NWO) sponsored my travels to Malta, Karlsruhe and Mons, where I visited the Archives of the Order of Malta at Valletta during the months January 1963 and April 1965, the Badisches Generallandesarchiv at Karlsruhe in June/July 1963, and the Archives de L'Etat at Mons in August 1963. The keepers of these archives deserve my warmest thanks for their kind helpfulness. The same is true for the staff of several state and town archives in the Netherlands, such as the Rijksarchief and Gemeentelijke Archiefdienst at Utrecht, the Rijksarchief in Gelderland at Arnhem, the Stadsarchief of Haarlem, and the Algemeen Rijksarchief at The Hague. For although the bulk of my material is derived from foreign archives, there are letters and other documents concerning the international interests of the Order to be found in Dutch archives as well.

Occasionally in the course of 1980 or 1981 a rent-roll of St Catherine's at Utrecht from the 14th century turned up in the Stadsarchief at Ghent, Belgium. Fortunately its existence came to my knowledge in due time, and in June 1982 I spent some days at Ghent in transcribing the first pages of it. However, because of its scope and the corroded state of most of its leaves, which made the reading very difficult and time consuming, I quickly understood the impossibility of doing all that labour there and then. So I was very glad to get the archivist's permission to take this volume with me to Utrecht for a long term of loan and deposit in the safe of our History Department. There it remained until 1986, when I brought it back for restoration. In the meantime a group of students in history under my supervision (and correction) had made a full transcription of the volume in the academic term 1982-'83, and one of them, Willem van 't Geloof, wrote his masters thesis about it. Especially the many increases in the lease sums in the course of about thirty years at the end of the 14th century aroused his curiosity and sense of statistics, which were sharpened by ingenious computer software programming that was done for this purpose by my then assistant Leen Breure. This man, now a database specialist at the Artes Faculty in Utrecht, deserves my utmost gratitude for his help and advice at my own essays in computing: without his textbase software I hardly could have made the registers of this source edition.

In the beginning the shape and format of this work were not clear to me at all. I conceived the thought of making on-line entrances by computer only, without printed texts, but dropped the idea in the course of time. A printed book keeps its advantages even in our computer era. But then the printed texts should have the qualities of different kinds of source editing, because a charterbook (part A of this edition) is neither the same as a rent-roll (part B) nor as visitation acts (part C) nor as a list of pamphlets (part D). For his advice at the making of part A, I want to sincerely thank Bas de Melker, member of the staff of the Gemeentelijke Archiefdienst Amsterdam and an expert in editing charters.

Many other colleagues at home and abroad crossed my path during the many years that I worked on this subject, and mentioning the one would seemingly mean forgetting the other. Therefore I pass over their names in silence, hoping nevertheless that they will be convinced of my gratitude to all of them.

Utrecht, May 1997   Johanna Maria van Winter

INTRODUCTION

In the first half of the twelfth century, the Order of St John arose in the Holy Land as the continuation of a fraternity of hospitallers that was already present in Jerusalem in the middle of the eleventh century. This fraternity, founded by merchants from Amalfi, Italy, took care of diseased pilgrims and other western European travellers, even before crusaders made their way to Jerusalem. When in 1099 Godfrey of Bouillon led the crusaders to the successful conquest of Jerusalem from the Moslems, resulting in a terrible massacre, the brothers and sisters hospitallers of St John did their utmost to minister to the numerous wounded. Gratefully, Godfrey of Bouillon bestowed on them a knightly manor and two ovens in Jerusalem.[1]

Although they could not dispose of goods in the Holy Land but rather of possessions in their home countries, mainly Italy and France, this example was soon followed by other knights of the Cross. Thus, the fraternity had to administer possessions scattered across Europe, necessitating the establishing of an organization in order to enjoy the yields. Revenues thus obtained were used partly to found hospitals in situ, but for the largest part they were used for the maintenance of the Jerusalem hospital, which had to be expanded considerably. It became the headquarters of a group whose character gradually developed into that of an order, first consisting of religious only, especially men, but since c.1130 including knights as well.

Religious military orders were quite a novelty in twelfth-century Christianity, for religious brothers and sisters were in principle expected to live defenceless lives and not stain their hands with blood. To protect themselves, they recruited laymen, knights, who accepted this task, partly out of piety, partly out of ambition or profit seeking. However, soon it appeared more appropriate to admit these protectors themselves into the fraternity and have them take the same vows

---

[1] J.Delaville le Roulx, *Cartulaire général de l'Ordre des Hospitaliers de St. Jean de Jerusalem*, 4 volumes, Paris, 1894-1906; I nr.1, without date [1099-1100], with reference to its confirmation in I nr.20, dd. 28 September 1110. See about the early history of the Hospitallers: C.H.C.Flugi van Aspermont, *De Johanniter-Orde in het Heilige Land (1100-1292)*, Assen 1957 (Van Gorcum's Historische Bibliotheek, deel 54); Jonathan Riley-Smith, *The Knights of St John in Jerusalem and Cyprus, 1050-1310*, London 1967; Rudolf Hiestand, 'Die Anfänge der Johanniter', in: Josef Fleckenstein & Manfred Hellmann (eds), *Die geistlichen Ritterorden Europas*, Sigmaringen 1980 (Vorträge und Forschungen, Bd.26), pp.31-80.

of obedience, poverty and unmarried status that the religious took. This transformed the fraternity into a religious military order, not living in accordance with Benedict's Rule—prescribing *stabilitas loci,* the permanent dwelling in one place, in addition to the three vows mentioned—but an order living in accordance with Augustine's Rule. This was such a general guideline, that it could be subjected to various interpretations, which in the course of time was indeed done by a succession of spiritual institutions. In any case it permitted the change of location which was a prerequisite for the accompanying and defending of pilgrims.

The Hospitallers and their double task: caring for the sick and fighting for the faith[2]

a. Caring for the sick

The transformation from a fraternity of hospitallers into a religious military order did not imply that all its members became knights. Furthermore, it did not mean that its membership exclusively consisted of noblemen. The original division of tasks between nurses and protectors was maintained in the two main classes of the Order: that of the knights (*milites*) and that of the chaplains or priests (*cappellani*). In addition, a third class, that of the sergeants at arms and serving brethren (*(armorum) servientes*) was introduced that could be deployed both in the defense of the strongholds and in the hospital. The original fraternity of hospitallers had also included sisters, whose position in the newly formed military order was that of nuns in the women's department of a double monastery or in convents of their own. Although they were a small minority, the visitation of 1495 shows that women's houses of hospitallers in The Netherlands could be found on the isle of Walcheren and in Warffum, Wijtwerd and Oosterwierum in the province of Groningen[3]. The Order was also familiar with associated knights who would join its battles (*confratres*), and benefactors who could share in the Order's religious merits on account of their donations (*donats*).

As early as 1113, Pope Pascal II placed the Hospitaller fraternity of St John in Jerusalem under his protection in a bull that confirmed

---

[2] This subtitle has been inspired by the name of the volume *The Military Orders. Fighting for the faith and caring for the sick.* The papers from the International Conference on Military Orders held at Clerkenwell, September 1992, edited by Malcolm Barber, Aldershot, Hampshire, U.K., 1994 (Variorum, Ashgate Publishing Ltd.).

[3] See below, in C.2.

its rightful possession of goods that had been or would be given to it. Furthermore, it granted the fraternity the right to elect its own Grand Master[4]. In 1135, the Pope confirmed and further elaborated this privilege by the stipulation that no bishop could place the Hospitaller churches under the interdict, *i.e.* the ecclesiastical ban. If the ban was posed on a city or an entire region in which the Hospitaller church stood, it would still be allowed to celebrate mass behind closed doors for its own members[5]. In 1137 the Pope added another bull which stated that the interdict would not interfere with the members' right to an ecclesiastical funeral. Moreover, the Hospitallers would still be allowed to open their churches once a year for communal services and collections[6]. The Order's benefactors were also included in the membership and especially the prospect of an ecclesiastical funeral with all the appropriate sacraments and the care for the salvation of the soul motivated many laymen to donate to the religious military order[7].

Visiting the sick was among the biblical works of charity. Christ had said that whoever did these things to the least of his brothers, would do them to Him as well (Matthew XXV, 31-46). During the Last Judgment the just would be on his right side as sheeps, whereas the unjust would be on his left side as goats. Thus, visiting the sick was a moral obligation which accrued spiritual merits. It is remarkable that the biblical text does not mention nursing or even the ministering to the sick; this put the emphasis in medieval Christian nursing on spiritual care by way of taking confessions and administering sacraments.

The Near East under Moslem rule had different priorities that were mostly determined by the writings of Greek physicians such as Hippocrates (c. 400 BC) and Galenos (2nd century AD). These texts were translated from Greek into Syrian and from Syrian into Arabic and provided the Islamic world with the basic conceptions of illness, health and medical treatment for the latter's preservation and recuperation[8]. It was almost inevitable that the fraternity of hospitallers in Jerusalem, which had been there since the eleventh century, was influenced by such thought and practice.

---

[4] Delaville, *Cartulaire*, I nr.30, dd. 15 February 1113.
[5] Ibidem, I nr.113, dd. 16 June 1135.
[6] Ibidem, I nr.122, dd. 7 February 1137.
[7] Cf. Berthold Waldstein-Wartenberg, 'Beiträge zur mittelalterlichen Liturgie des Johanniterordens, II, Das Totengedächtnis', in: *Annales de l'Ordre souverain militaire de Malte* 30 (1972), pp.84-91.

This also emerges from a comparison of the various statutes of the Hospitaller Order in the twelfth century. The first rule, undated but issued under the sway of Grand Master Raymond du Puy (1125-1153), states in its 3rd article with respect to the sick that they should be visited by a priest in white vestment, reverently holding the host in both hands, who should be preceded by a deacon, a subdeacon or an acolyte carrying both a lantern with a lit candle and a spunge with holy water. Article 16 further stipulates that a sick person who is newly admitted should first confess and receive the Holy Communion and then be put to bed. Every day he should have a fine meal before the brothers eat; every Sunday the house should hear songs from the Epistles and the Gospel and be sprinkled with holy water during a procession[9]. The rule makes no mention of medical treatment and details of physical care are not given.

This is different in the second rule, issued under Grand Master Roger de Molins: it decrees that four learned physicians will be appointed in the service of the poor in Jerusalem, who will be able to discern between different sorts of urine and various illnesses and can advise the sick to the preparation of their medicine as well [2]. It also states that standard measures will be introduced for the length and width of hospital beds and that each bed should have its own mattress and two clean sheets [3]. Furthermore, the sick should have fur cloaks, boots and woollen hoods at their disposal for visiting the toilet [4], one set for every two patients [*pars secunda*, 2]. Equally remarkable is the provision that cradles should be available for babies who are born out of women pelgrims in the hospital, so that they can be set apart and will not be troubled by their mothers [5]. The hospital also admits children who have been abandoned by their parents (foundlings) [*pars secunda*, 3]. It also turns out that district nursing existed in some form, as the General Chapter added the stipulation

---

[8] See e.g. Donald Campbell, *Arabian Medicine and its influence on the Middle Ages. Origin and development of Arab medical science and its subsequent cultivation among the Arabistae of the Latin West.* 2 vols, London, 1926; reprint in 1 vol., Amsterdam, 1974 - F.Rofail Farag, 'Why Europe responded to the Muslims' medical achievements in the Middle Ages' in: *Arabica, Revue d'Etudes Arabes*, 25 (1978) pp.292-309 - Max Meyerhof, *Studies in medieval Arabic Medicine: Theory and Practice*, ed. by Penelope Johnstone, Variorum Reprints 1984 (Collected Studies 204) - Franz Rosenthal, *Science and Medicine in Islam. A collection of essays.* Variorum Reprints 1991 (Collected Studies 330) - Heinrich Schipperges, *Die Assimilation der arabischen Medizin durch das lateinische Mittelalter.* Wiesbaden, 1964 (Sudhoffs Archiv, Beiheft 3) -
Manfred Ullmann, *Die Medizin im Islam.* Handbuch der Orientalistik, I.Abteilung, Ergänzungsband VI, 1.Abschnitt, Leiden (Brill) 1970 - M.Ullmann, *Islamic Medicine.* Edinburgh 1978.

[9] Delaville, *Cartulaire*, I nr.70, without date [1125-1153].

that nine *servientes* should be sent to every street where sick people lived in order to wash their heads and feet, dry them with cloth, tidy their beds and prepare their food and drink[10]. In his confirmation of these statutes in 1184 or 1185 Pope Lucius III summarized all this by stating that four physicians and as many surgeons should be present in the hospital at all times. Everything necessary for the sick should be at their disposal[11].

At the beginning of the twelfth century, when the Hospitaller fraternity of St John (John the Baptist) had not yet become a military order but had already acquired possessions in Europe, the obligation to minister to the sick in all probability was practised in the new hospitals. In his bull from 1113 Pope Pascal II used the formula *xenodochia sive ptochia in occidentis partibus* to indicate that the following places fell under the authority of the Hospitaller fraternity: St Gilles, Asti, Pisa, Bari, Otranto, Tarente and Messina. According to a literal interpretation, the words *xenodochia sive ptochia* need not refer to health care, since they literally allude to 'houses where strangers or beggars are received'. However, in the Byzantine Empire the Greek word *xenodochia* usually pertained to hospitals, and perhaps alternative descriptions were unfamiliar to the Pope. In Hospitaller settlements of later date the obligation of hospitability toward the poor and strangers was reduced to the admission of transients instead of the bedridden sick. Further down, we shall see that the St Catherine's Convent in Utrecht formed an exception to this.

b. Fighting for the faith

Around 1130 the Hospitaller fraternity of St John was transformed into a religious military order, a novelty in the Christianity of that time. The knightly element was not mentioned in its statutes, but in this it followed the example of another group who cared for pilgrims in the Holy Land: the Order of the Knights Templar. This Order had no antecedents pre-dating the First Crusade and was not the result of the need to minister to the sick. It were the necessities to protect both the newly annexed territories against Moslim raids and the pilgrims on their way to the sacred places that moved Hugues de Payens, a crusader from Champagne, and seven companions to take the three monastic vows of obedience, poverty and chastity under the auspices of the patriarch of Jerusalem. Baldwin II, King of Jerusalem,

---

[10] Ibidem, I nr.627, dd. 14 March 1182.
[11] Ibidem, I nr.690, dd. 4 November 1184 or 1185.

provided them with quarters by way of a wing of his palace that had previously been used as a mosque. Because the Christians believed that the mosque occupied the grounds where Solomon's temple once stood, they henceforth called themselves *fratres militiae Templi* or Knights Templar. Their original task was purely military and they lived in accordance with an oral code that supported their military goals. However, when after some years the need arose to put this code into writing, Hugues de Payens submitted it in 1128 to the Council of Troyes which had gathered on the initiative of Bernard of Clairvaux and was attended by all the ecclesiastical leaders of the period. At that time Bernard, abbot of Clairvaux, stood at the head of the relatively young Cistercian Order, a monastic order that wanted to follow Benedict's Rule with renewed sternness. Our crusaders did not join the Cistercian Order that consisted of unarmed monks who practised the Benedictine principle of *stabilitas loci* and were thus unfit to escort pilgrims. However, on authority of the Council Bernard wrote them a rule which in many ways was inspired by that of the Cistercians. Next, he lent them his moral support by means of the tract *De laude novae militiae*, in which he presented an image of truly Christian chivalry[12].

The actions of wordly knights, he wrote, could better be characterized as *malitia* than as *militia*, as instances more exemplary of malevolence than of knighthood. Moreover, it brought them nothing: who died in battle lost his life, who won lost his soul. If the battle was not fought for Christ's cause, they would commit manslaughter and thus forfeit salvation. "On the other hand, the knights of Christ safely conduct their Lord's battle, wholly unafraid of sin induced by the killing of their enemies and the hazard lain in their own deaths: for when death has to be endured or inflicted for the sake of Christ, it bears no resemblance to crime but all resemblance to great glory. (...) The death of a pagan glorifies a Christian, because Christ himself is glorified; the death of a Christian proves the King's generosity, when the knight is rewarded with his demise." Such was the reward of Christian knighthood: glory on this earth and heavenly bliss afterwards.

The new rule of the Knights Templar did not include any allusion to ministering to the sick, and although in imitation of the Hospitallers they would have guest rooms with their houses later on, their main concern remained the crusaders' military tasks: the escort-

---

[12] S.Bernardi abbatis Clarae-Vallensis, De laude novae militiae, ad milites Templi liber, in: J.P.Migne (ed.), *Patrologia Latina* tomus 182 (Paris 1854), kolom 921-939.

ing of pilgrims through hazardous areas, the building and defending of strongholds, and their fight against the infidels. Like the Hospitallers, they had the same three classes of knights, chaplains and serving brethren as well as associated knights and benefactors; part of their activities was not mentioned in their rule, too. For the Knights Templar the part left out concerned caring tasks, for the Hospitallers it concerned military tasks.

The first Order to combine both caring and military goals in its rule was the third religious military order of the Holy Land, the Teutonic Order. This Order came into being during the Third Crusade (1189-1192) in the army camp near Acre, where merchants from Bremen and Lübeck constructed a field hospital for their fellow countrymen from the sails of a cog. Many Germans partook in the crusade, which among others was led by their Emperor Frederick Barbarossa. If they were wounded, they felt the need to confess in their native language. Most of the Hospitaller and Templar priests were of Italian or French origin and could not provide that kind of spiritual care. As early as 1191, the field hospital was placed under protection of the Pope and soon was allotted a permanent stand in Acre. When after the fall of Acre in 1291 the Holy Land definitely became a lost cause for the crusaders, the Teutonic Order largely moved its field of operation to Prussia, where its main objective was the submission and conversion of the Slavonic peoples. Its new headquarters became Marienburg on the Weichsel near Danzig. The Teutonic Order founded hospitals in many towns throughout the German Empire; however, one could perhaps better refer to them as guest houses, since their health care was soon only extended to transients[13].

Thus three religious military orders were present in the Holy Land at the end of the twelfth century that all had the double tasks of fighting and nursing (albeit with varying emphasis on either element)

---

[13] See about the Teutonic Order, e.g.: Marian Tumler, *Der Deutsche Orden in Werden, Wachsen und Wirken bis 1400*, Wien 1955; Udo Arnold, 'Entstehung und Frühzeit des Deutschen Ordens', in: Josef Fleckenstein & Manfred Hellmann (eds), *Die geistlichen Ritterorden Europas*, Sigmaringen 1980 (Vorträge und Forschungen, Bd.26), pp.81-108; Hartmut Boockmann, *Der Deutsche Orden. Zwölf Kapitel aus seiner Geschichte*, München, 1981 (Beck'sche Sonderausgaben); U.Arnold & G.Bott (eds), *800 Jahre Deutscher Orden*. Ausstellungskatalog des Germanischen Nationalmuseums Nürnberg in Zusammenarbeit mit der Internationalen Kommission zur Erforschung des Deutschen Ordens, Gütersloh-München, 1990; U.Arnold (ed.) *Kreuz und Schwert. Der Deutsche Orden in Südwestdeutschland, in der Schweiz und im Elsaß*, Ausstellungskatalog, Mainau, 1991; U.Arnold e.a. (eds), *Ritter und Priester. Acht Jahrhunderte Deutscher Orden in Nordwesteuropa / Ridders en Priesters. Acht eeuwen Duitse Orde in Noordwest-Europa*, Ausstellungskatalog / Tentoonstelling van de Landcommanderij Alden Biesen, 1992.

and all consisted of various social classes. Of these, the knights were held in the highest regard, followed by the priests. However, it would be a mistake to think of all these knights as high nobility, although some of them indeed were of the highest birth. This case is further complicated by the different criteria of nobility that existed in Europe; by crossing a boundary, a nobleman's blood did not necessarily remain the deepest shade of blue. The one thing they all had in common was their gentle birth, signifying that they were born in a family of knights and squires; but these were not regarded as nobility everywhere.

Nobles or knights

Knighthood came into being during the eleventh century in France. It was constituted by the able-bodied servants of a lord and more or less rooted in the lower strata[14]. The knights were led by noblemen, but at first these did not bear the knightly title *miles* or *chevalier*, because it implied servitude. The Latin word *miles* merely meant 'soldier' and did not acquire its connotation of chivalry until the eleventh and twelfth century. The Christian Church was a major contributor to the creation of this halo as it among other things developed the crusading ideology and propagated knighthood in tracts such as Bernard of Clairvaux wrote for the Knights Templar. Knightly ideals were ideals of duty, in which the service of a vassal to his lord and the service of the crusaders to Christ fulfilled exemplary functions. Since the Gospel lets service prevail over lordship (Matthew XX, 20-28, Mark X, 35-45), the propaganda of the Church improved the image of the subordinate knights. This and their successes in battle gave such prestige to their title that it became more appealing to noblemen. In France, the nobles started calling themselves knights with

---

[14] The following is a summary of my own viewpoints; see *e.g.* Johanna Maria van Winter, *Ridderschap, ideaal en werkelijkheid*, Bussum, 1965 (Fibulareeks 11); 4th edition, Bussum, 1982; German translation: *Rittertum, Ideal und Wirklichkeit*, München, 1969; 2nd edition, München, 1979; eadem, "Uxorem de militari ordine, sibi imparem", in: *Miscellanea Mediaevalia in memoriam Jan Frederik Niermeyer*, Groningen 1967, pp.113-124 (in French); eadem, "Cingulum Militiae', Schwertleite en 'miles'-terminologie als spiegel van veranderend menselijk gedrag' (avec résumé français), in: *Tijdschrift voor Rechtsgeschiedenis / Revue d'Histoire du Droit* 44 (1976), pp.1-92; eadem, 'Knighthood and nobility in the Netherlands', in: *Gentry and lesser nobility in late medieval Europe*, edited by Michael Jones, Gloucester-New York, 1986, pp.81-94.

These viewpoints are shared, among others, by Jean Flori, *L'Essor de la chevalerie, XIe-XIIe siècles*, Genève (Librairie Droz), 1986; idem, *La première croisade. L'Occident chrétien contre l'Islam*, Bruxelles (Editions Complexe), 1992; idem, *La chevalerie en France au Moyen Age*, Paris, 1995 (Que sais-je?).

increasing frequency during the second half of the eleventh century. This resulted in an assimilation between noble and lowly born knights around 1100, which gave the whole of knighthood in France the hallmark of nobility. The crusaders who joined the young Hospitaller and Templar Orders may thus be referred to as nobility inasfar as they came from France.

Outside France this assimilation process lasted much longer and began much later as well. In the German Empire, which included The Netherlands, knighthood was formed in the twelfth century out of unfree servants or *ministeriales* of princes and bishops. In the service of their lord they were allotted certain responsible tasks on the domains, at court and in the strongholds. The better they performed these tasks, the more prestige and influence they received in addition to material rewards in the form of fiefs. This enabled them to procure horses and armament which made them employable in their lord's armed cavalry. These people were *milites* in the real meaning of the word, since they fought under noble commanders who considered the knightly title to be below them. This gradually changed during the thirteenth century in a process that can be followed from West to East. In those regions closest to France, such as Flanders (which for the largest part was a feud to the French King) and Brabant (belonging to the German Empire), noblemen sooner bore the knightly title than in those territories that lay farther East, such as Bavaria and Austria. In the Dutch regions, the phenomenon of nobility bearing a knightly title occurred since about 1225.

This did not mean that the *nobiles* in the German Empire fused with the *ministeriales* bearing a knightly title to form one nobility, however. Together, the two groups constituted knighthood and thus the upperlayer of society, but both stuck to their own legal rank. Nobility remained free by birth, the *ministeriales* remained unfree servants who in court appealed to their ministerial law and could still be exchanged by their lord for another lord's *ministeriales*, even during the late Middle Ages. Notwithstanding the fact that this never occurred without their approval, it still indicates a fundamental difference in legal status between noble and non-noble knights and squires. However, both were of gentle birth, *i.e.* born into a family of knights and squires, and enjoyed the possible prospect of receiving the accolade themselves one day. The knights from the German and Dutch regions that during the late Middle Ages made part of the Hospitaller and Teutonic Orders could descend very well from an ancestry of gentle *ministeriales*. The French thought was followed only by the coastal regions of Holland and Zeeland that since the second half of the thirteenth century considered all of gentry to be nobility.

It was not until the Modern Time, when many ancient noble families had died out, that outside Holland and Zeeland an assimilation occurred that transformed the entire knighthood into nobility. For this reason, knights from both Orders in the sixteenth, seventeenth and eighteenth century can safely be called nobles, even if their progenitors may have been *ministeriales*.

The precondition of gentle birth did not apply to the other classes of the Orders, the chaplains and the serving brethren, so that most of the inhabitants of the St Catherine's Convent in Utrecht and its subordinate *membra* did not descend from families of knights and squires and most certainly did not have noble backgrounds. The Utrecht bailiwick and its subordinate *membra* had always been destined for chaplains, not knights—a distinction that the Order maintained as strictly as possible insofar as headquarters were abreast of the local situation[15].

There never were many Templars in the German Empire, but after the Order had been disbanded as the result of a controversial trial in 1312, its goods outside France were largely allocated to the Hospitallers. In The Netherlands this only concerned the bailiwick Ter Brake under Alphen in the province Noord-Brabant, which came to fall under the French tongue, the *langue de France*.

---

[15] see below, A.nr.82, dd. 5 August 1493, partition of the preceptories of the Priorate of Germany between knights and chaplains & serving brethren. Perhaps this decree was caused by uncertainty about the status of some preceptories, like Arnhem with *membrum* Nimwegen. Although in 1493 it was marked as a preceptory for a knight, before that date most of its commanders seem to have been chaplains; *e.g.* frater Arnoldus Groenewoud, who had been treasurer of the bailiwick of Utrecht in 1404, March 27 (J. Loeff, *Het archief der Commanderij van St Jan te Arnhem*, Rijksarchief in Gelderland, The Hague 1950, pp.189/190, regest nr.296), before becoming commander at Arnhem (see below, A.nr.24, dd. 4 July 1421, when he was succeeded by frater Simon van Bracht, who also was a chaplain). The successor of frater Simon van Bracht, frater Johann von Swalbach, probably was a knight (A.nrs.32, 33 & 35, dd. 1, 3 & 28 July 1432, A.nr.53, dd. 1 September 1451, and A.nr.65, dd. 29 May 1462). After his death in 1462 headquarters appointed frater Bertold Stehelin as his successor, probably a knight, however forgetting that already in 1453, October 12, frater Steven van Gruuthusen was the head of the preceptory of Arnhem (A.nr.54). This man probably was a chaplain; cf. Loeff, *Archief*, inventaris nr.58, regest nr. 362, dd. 1 May 1447. Frater Bertold Stehelin almost immediately resigned in 1462 and was succeeded by frater Philips von Reiffenberg, probably a knight (A.nr.66, dd.6 July 1462), who also resigned after a short time (cf. A.nr.70, dd. 23 July 1466). Then on 12 June 1467 Arnhem and Nimwegen were given to frater Dirk Wolf, a chaplain of the Order (A.nr.72). Not before c.1494-1496, after the decree of 1493, with certainty a knight was commander at Arnhem: frater Johann von Hatstein, who resigned in 1496 (A.nr.83, dd. 10 October 1496) and was succeeded by frater Thomas van Rothusen, also a knight. After his death, however, again a chaplain was appointed as his successor: frater Laurens von Adenau (A.nr.90, dd. 14 December 1503).

The organization of the Hospitallers[16]

As said before, the Hospitaller fraternity in Jerusalem, which was to become the military Order of St John, received real properties in the Holy Land and Europe since the First Crusade, whose revenues in the first place should go to headquarters. This necessitated the founding of an organization which made it possible to manage the goods in situ and make regular payments (*responsiones*) to the central treasury. Furthermore, the origanization should safeguard a resolute policy of the Order as a whole while taking into account local circumstances in the countries where the goods remained.

To this end one developed a system of bailiwicks, priorates and tongues, each headed by its own incumbent who was responsible to the Grand Master and the General Chapter. The Grand Master was the head of the Order and resided in headquarters. Every member of the Order owed him absolute obedience. In his turn he himself was subjected to the supervision and the decisions of the General Chapter, even though this body consisted of men who again depended on him. This reciprocal principle of obedience was intended to improve the members' discipline and the leadership's decisiveness as well as to create the conditions for a certain democratic involvement. The General Chapter consisted of dignitaries from headquarters, heads of priorates and a number of important bailiwicks who assembled once every five years. These men were called the 'grand crosses' after the large white eight-point crosses on their black cloaks. The eight points of the cross referred to the Beatitudes from the Sermon on the Mount (Matthew V, 3-10). After the fifteenth century, when the Order had come to include eight tongues, they also referred to these language fields.

For advice pertaining to current affairs, the Grand Master was assisted by a council that consisted of the dignitaries from headquarters and representatives from the eight tongues. These tongues (Latin: *linguae*, French: *langues*) were the following, more or less matching the Order's eight language fields and given in order of seniority and prestige: *Provence* (in the surroundings of Toulouse), *Auvergne* (in the surroundings of Lyons), *France* (North, Central and West France and Belgium), *Italia* (Italy), *Aragon* (Aragon, Catalonia and Navarre),

---

[16] Besides the information given by the late chevalier Josef Galea, who was the keeper of the AOM in the years I visited them (1963-1970), this paragraph has mainly been based upon the 18th-century classic by the abbot De Vertot, who got acquainted with the Order as it still functioned in Malta with all its Grand Crosses and elaborate international connections: L'Abbé De Vertot, *Histoire des Chevaliers Hospitaliers de S.Jean de Jerusalem, appellez depuis les Chevaliers de Rhodes, et aujourd'hui les Chevaliers de Malte*, 4 vols., Paris, 1726.

Angleterre (England, Scotland and Ireland), *Alemagne* (the German Empire, Bohemia, Hungary and Scandinavia) and *Castilia* (Castilia, Leon and Portugal, which did not secede from the originally undivided Spanish tongue until 1462). Of old, most knights came from the three French tongues, which were therefore limited geographically in order to keep their number balanced with those tongues with fewer members.

The knights did not live on their bailiwicks. Instead, they lived together with the other members of their tongue at headquarters in a large house, a so-called *Auberge*, of which some still stand on Rhodes and Malta today. Each *Auberge* was headed by a dignitary or *Grand Bailli Conventuel* who was elected by the knights of the tongue and thus received the right to sit in on both the Grand Master's council and the General Chapter. The positions were distributed per tongue as follows: the *Langue de Provence* was headed by the Grand Commander, who functioned as chief treasurer; *Auvergne* furnished the Marshal, who commanded the army; *France* filled the position of *Grand-Hospitalier*, head of the hospital; *Italia* put in the Admiral, commander of the fleet; *Aragon* took care of the *Drapier*, or the Grand Conservator, who supervised clothing; *Angleterre* delivered the *Turcopilier*, the head of the cavalry; *Alemagne* came up with the Grand Bailiff, who was entrusted with the fortifications of the stronghold *Château de St Pierre* in Asia Minor near Halicarnassus, an outpost of Rhodes (this position was created in 1428, when the Order resided on Rhodes); finally, *Castilia* produced the Grand Chancellor, head of the chancery, whose job description specifically required him to be able to read and write.

In order to manage the goods in Europe, every tongue was divided into one or more priorates under supervision of a prior. He did not live at headquarters, but in the priorate itself, so that he would be better able to inspect those bailiwicks under him. Some important bailiwicks stood under the command of a *bailli capitulaire, i.e.* a bailiff who wore the grand cross like the priors and the eight *Grand Baillis Conventuels* and had a seat on the General Chapter. One of these *baillis capitulaires* was the bailiff of Brandenburg, usually referred to as the *Herrenmeister*, who made part of the German tongue. In addition to its own *Grand Bailli Conventuel*, this tongue comprised the following grand crosses: the priors of Germany, Bohemia, Hungary and *Dacia* (Denmark) and the bailiff of Brandenburg. Every five years, these five men made their way to headquarters to attend a General Chapter, and otherwise only if business required it. For the rest of the time, they resided elsewhere in Europe. On the other hand, the ordinary knights and commanders could hardly ever be found on their bailiwicks. Instead, they remained at headquarters, in the field, or on the galleys.

After some years' service a young knight without bailiwick would eventually deserve the right to command one. Another few years of loyal service in this position would earn him *antianitas* or seniority[17] which made him a candidate for a better bailiwick within his own tongue. This he would place in the care of a manager, after which he could only visit and inspect it with the approval of the Grand Master. Such a visit required a *licentia recedendi et redeundi*[18]. It was his concern to see to it that improvements were implemented regularly and that the payments to the treasury were duly made. His own livelihood and armour he paid from the revenues of his bailiwick. Once sufficient improvements had been made and he had become eligible for promotion, Grand Master and council could allot him a richer bailiwick within his tongue. An exceptional improvement of position was to be appointed as a prior, which meant that one could remain on one's favourite bailiwick in Europe. This seems to have had quite an appeal on older men.

Next to bailiwicks for knights every tongue also had bailiwicks for chaplains or serving brethren. We already have pointed out the uncertainty that could exist with regard to the status of a bailiwick, which necessitated a fixation of statuses in the German priorate in 1493[19]. Chaplains as well as serving brethren were allowed to live on their bailiwick and manage it themselves, but like the knights they had to make payments to the treasury. This implied that they could put more money and energy into their bailiwick and that their presence had more meaning for the local population. The St Catherine's Convent of Utrecht (not to be mistaken for a nunnery), which has always been the seat of a chaplain's bailiwick, serves as a good example of this.

The first crusaders came from the Romanic regions: Lorrainers such as Godfrey of Bouillon and furthermore especially French and Italian people. German, Dutch and Flemish people did not show an interest in the movement before the Second Crusade took place in 1147-1149. Therefore it is all the more remarkable that in 1122, there were several brethren in Utrecht who were referred to as *Jerosolimitani* and with great probability may be assumed to have belonged to the Jeru-

---

[17] Cf. below, A.nr.91, dd. 16 January 1504, about the *antianitas* of frater Laurens von Adenau.
[18] Cf. below, A.nr.14, dd. 5 January 1414; A.nr.21, dd. 27 September 1420; A.nr.25, dd. 10 July 1421; A.nr.35, dd. 28 July 1432; A.nr.38, dd. 4 August 1433: *licentia recedendi et redeundi*.
[19] See before, note 15, about the partition of 1493.

salem hospitallers of St John the Baptist. They acted as witnesses to the charter whereby the Emperor Henry V confirmed the privileges that Bishop Godebald had shortly before given to the citizens of Utrecht and Muiden, declaring that all those who worked on an earthen wall to secure Utrecht would be exempted from tollage[20]. Their names were *Godeschalcus, Vscherus, Algerus, Petrus, Tanco, Gerardus, Robertus*, thus apparently foreign in part, and their presence in this list of witnesses becomes significant when we consider that the wall that was built at that time cuts across the terrain on which the Hospitallers' St Catharine's Convent later had its hospital and churchyard: the present Vredenburg and the area opposite the Catharijnesingel. The tufa stone foundations of their church, which must date back to the twelfth century, have been excavated on the Vredenburg site[21].

So even before the Jerusalem fraternity of hospitallers had been transformed into a religious military order, it was most probably already represented in the town of Utrecht by a piece of land on which a house with a church and a churchyard could be built, the last of which was baptised the 'piteous churchyard': the churchyard of poor strangers. In this place, later sources tell us, the Hospitallers ran a hospital with 24 beds in which sufferers of all diseases were nursed, even those suffering from the plague, with the sole exception of lepers[22]. Hypothetically, the founding of the hospital could be envisaged as a gift from Bishop Godebald to the citizens of his town, perhaps to compensate them for the inconvenience he caused in 1122, when the

---

[20] *Oorkondenboek van het Sticht Utrecht tot 1301*, I, eds S. Muller and A.C. Bouman, Utrecht, 1920; II, ed. K. Heeringa, The Hague, 1940 (*OSU*); I nr.308, 1122, June 2; cf. Johanna Maria van Winter, 'De heren van Sint-Catharijne te Utrecht', in: *Bewogen en bewegen. Liber amicorum aangeboden aan Prof. dr. H.F.J.M. van den Eerenbeemt*, Tilburg, 1986, pp.349-364, and in French translation: Johanna Maria van Winter, 'Les seigneurs de Sainte-Catherine à Utrecht, les premiers Hospitaliers au Nord des Alpes', in: *Autour de la Première Croisade*. Actes du Colloque de la Society for the Study of the Crusades and the Latin East (Clermont-Ferrand, 22-25 juin 1995), réunis par Michel Balard, Paris 1996 (Série Byzantina Sorbonensia, 14), pp.239-246.

[21] T.J. Hoekstra, 'Vredenburg, Archeologische Kroniek van de gemeente Utrecht over 1967-1977', *Maandblad Oud-Utrecht*, 53 (1980), 24-31 (especially 25); T.J. Hoekstra, 'Utrecht, Vredenburg', *Bulletin KNOB* (1977), pp.39-45.

[22] P.Q. Brondgeest, *Bijdragen tot de geschiedenis van het gasthuis, het klooster en de balije van St.Catharina der Johanniter-ridders en van het Driekoningengasthuis te Utrecht*, Hilversum, 1901, p.100, Appendix V, and below, A.nr.79, copy of a letter by Pope Sixtus IV dated 1472, June 12, in which the St Catharine's Convent receives or maintains permission to choose its own bailiff, partly owing to its managing a hospital for all diseases. The exception of lepers appears from the visitation of 1495, *Archives de L'Ordre de Malte* (AOM) 45, fol.199v (below, in C.2), and 'Visitatie-verslagen' (note 29 below), p. 158. That the hospital contained 24 beds appears from Brondgeest p.6 and Appendix VI, p.104, Memorandum of 1561.

Kromme Rijn was dammed at Wijk bij Duurstede and they had to dig the Vaartse Rijn to create another outlet to the Lek, the Lower Rhine and the German hinterland. The bishop had the Kromme Rijn dammed because he wanted to reclaim and cultivate the surrounding morass lands. The idea made part of a comprehensive project that he and his successors largely completed during the twelfth century[23].

The first Hospitallers in the Netherlands.

It is not the deeds of gift, but a statement by the head or 'balijer' (bailiff) of the Utrecht bailiwick in a visitation report from 1540[24], that shows us that the Bishop of Utrecht was one of the great patrons of the St Catharine's Convent. At the time he did not say what the gifts were, but a rent-roll of St Catharine's from the second half of the fourteenth century reveals the extensiveness of its estate. Especially the Hof ter Weide at Vleuten, which never became a separate *membrum* but was always directed from the main house in Utrecht, formed a sizeable estate complex of well over 300 acres (150 *iugera*)[25]. Nobody but the bishop could have had so many adjacent domains at his disposal, and not even he after the first quarter of the twelfth century: ecclesiastical goods were divided amongst the bishop and the great urban chapters, of which Utrecht had gained three in the eleventh century: St Peter's, St John's and Our Lady's in addition to the existent chapters of the cathedral and Oldminster. Thus, the pasture lands to the West of the town of Utrecht must have been the last big estate at the bishop's disposal in the twelfth century; presumably, he split it between the town, which was given the Hoge and Lage Weide, and the St Catharine's Convent of the Hospitallers, which received the Hof ter Weide.

The Order and its archives
As previously mentioned, the alleged donation of the Hof ter Weide is not known from an official document, but indirectly from a somewhat obscure statement by the bailiff in 1540. It is further supplemented by a fourteenth-century rent-roll which, to everyone's

---

[23] C.Dekker, *Het Kromme Rijngebied in de Middeleeuwen. Een institutioneel-geografische studie*, [Zutphen] 1983 (De Walburg Pers, Stichtse Historische Reeks, 9), p.266.

[24] Visitation of 1540, AOM 6340, fol.9r (below, in C.3).

[25] Ghent City Archive, Surmont de Volsberghe family funds, rent-roll of the St Catharine's Convent of the Order of St John in Utrecht, fol.60r.

amazement, was found in a family archive, kept in the City Archive in Ghent, Belgium. Unlike the archives of the Teutonic Knights in Utrecht, which are still kept by knights of this Order in their own filing safe, accommodated in their recently restored ancient housing on the Springweg, the old archives of the St Catharine's Convent were lost for the greatest part[26]. But then again, the Utrecht bailiwick of the Teutonic Order was not disbanded and its goods were not confiscated as a result of the Reformation, as happened to the Hospitallers' possessions; firstly, the Utrecht bailiwick of the Teutonic Order was a knightly house, contrary to the St Catharine's Convent of the Hospitallers, which was a clerics' house, and secondly, the bailiwick withdrew from the central association of the Teutonic Order and converted to Calvinism in time. Therefore, the Estates of the various Dutch provinces in which its subordinate preceptories resided had no reason or pretext to confiscate these goods *ad pios usus*, as was the custom with spiritual goods. Because of this, the archives of the Teutonic House in Utrecht date back to the beginning of the thirteenth century and contain among other things a deed from 1219 by which Sweder van Dingede, in the army camp at Damiate, Egypt, bestowed on the Teutonic Order some goods near Dieren, which were later to fall under the Utrecht bailiwick[27].

The knowledge we still have about the Hospitallers before the Reformation is partly due to the fact that elsewhere in The Netherlands, especially in Haarlem, Arnhem and Leeuwarden[28], more of

---

[26] The loss may be accounted for by the fire in the St Catharine's Convent in 1518: AOM 6340, Visitation of 1540, fol.11v, and the Utrecht Municipal Archive (GA Utrecht), Buurspraakboek van Utrecht 1518, fol.194v., 1518, February 19; two days after the fire had raged through the St Catharine's Convent. For further information G.C.M. van Dijck, *Inventaris van het archief van de Balije van Utrecht der Johanniterorde 1251-1851*, second, completely revised edition by E.T. Suir, Rijksarchief Utrecht, Inventaris I, Utrecht, 1985 (abbreviated as Suir, *Balije*).

[27] *OSU* II nr.668, A.D. 1219; P.J.C.G. van Hinsbergen, *Inventaris van het archief van de Ridderlijke Duitsche Orde Balije van Utrecht 1200-1811*, Utrecht, 1955-1982, nr.1.718.

[28] Only the archive of the Order of St John in Arnhem has a printed inventory: J. Loeff, *Het archief der Commanderij van St Jan te Arnhem*, Rijksarchief in Gelderland, The Hague 1950. Haarlem and Leeuwarden only keep typographical inventories, of the preceptories of Haarlem and Sneek respectively, both originally included under the bailiwick of Utrecht. The Groningen State Archive has a small file on the Order of St John, which has been described in a printed inventory: S. Hiddema and C. Tromp, *Inventaris van archieven van kloosters in de provincie Groningen*, Publikaties van het Rijksarchief in Groningen nr.7, Groningen, 1989, pp.49-68, pertaining to the convents of the Order of St John of Warffum, Oosterwierum and Wijtwerd, included under the Burgsteinfurt bailiwick. The houses in the province of Zeeland at Kerkwerve (near Domburg), Middelburg and Wemeldinge have hardly been recorded in archivalia. Cf. J.A.Mol, 'De Johannieter Commanderij van Wemeldinge', in: *Historia. Jaarboek van Zuid- en Noord-Beveland* 10 (1984), pp.35-56.

their medieval and sixteenth-century archivalia have been preserved than in Utrecht. However, much is also owed to the Order's international character from the beginning, which did much to stimulate the central filing in the headquarters of the Grand Master and the Prior of Germany. Thus, the 1540 visitation report concerning Utrecht is only known from the Order's central archive on Malta, the AOM (Archives de l'Ordre de Malte). The contemporaneous copy of this visitation report in the State Archive in the province of Gelderland at Arnhem does not contain the section concerning Utrecht[29].

In the following, we will mainly focus on the archivalia of the Dutch Hospitallers in foreign archives, putting more stress on the connections with the Grand Master and the Prior of Germany than on the internal affairs of the various houses in The Netherlands. As said before, since its earliest days the Order had been an international institution, managing goods in the Holy Land and Europe, its primary object being the nursing of pilgrims and the sick, and its secondary object the armed struggle against the infidels. Initially, headquarters were located in Jerusalem, but after 1291, when the crusaders' last stronghold in the Holy Land, Acre, had to be given up, they were temporarily moved to Cyprus. They subsequently moved to Rhodes in 1309, where they remained until the Hospitallers were driven away after a siege by the Turkish Sultan Suleiman the Magnificent in 1522[30]. For eight years, the Hospitallers' galleys drifted through the Mediterranean without a harbour of their own, until the Emperor Charles V gave them the isle of Malta out of his Aragonese possessions, in 1530. There they built their new headquarters on a peninsula in a large bay, which were strengthened as a fortress, the Birgu. After they defended this successfully against the Turks in 1565, it was named Vittoriosa, as it is still called today. In the same bay, on a larger peninsula opposite the Birgu, they next built a new, much larger town for their headquarters, Valletta, named after the Grand Master who had led them during the siege: Jean de la Vallette. This remained their seat until Napoleonic troops made them flee to Rome.

---

[29] E. Wiersum and A. Le Cosquino de Bussy, eds., 'Visitatie-verslagen van de Johanniter-kloosters in Nederland (1495, 1540, 1594)', in: *Bijdragen en Mededeelingen van het Historisch Genootschap*, 48 (1927) pp.146-340.

[30] For further information about the Cyprus and Rhodes eras, see J. Delaville le Roulx, *Les Hospitaliers à Rhodes, 1310-1425*, Paris, 1913, Variorum Reprints 1974, and further Anthony Luttrell, *The Hospitallers in Cyprus, Rhodes, Greece and the West (1291-1440)*, Variorum Reprints, Collected Studies 77, 1978; idem, *Latin Greece, The Hospitallers and the Crusades, 1291-1440*, Variorum Reprints, Collected Studies 158, 1982; idem, *The Hospitallers of Rhodes and their Mediterranean World*, Variorum Reprints, Collected Studies 360, Aldershot, Hampshire, U.K., 1992.

Valletta still keeps their old archives from before the French Revolution, the AOM.

Considering that the Hospitallers drifted at sea from 1522 to 1530, having no safe haven and taking their documents with them in galleys, the number of medieval documents that survived the storms is remarkable. The older documents have been published in Delaville le Roulx's four-volume *Cartulaire*, which runs from 1100 to 1310[31], but many more have been preserved. Especially the *Libri Bullarum*, folio volumes written on paper in parchment covers, containing copies of outgoing bulls, are of great importance for the Dutch preceptories. They start in 1346, when the Order resided on Rhodes, subsequently contain the years 1347, 1351, 1358, 1365, 1374 and then commence an almost uninterrupted sequence with the years 1381-1382 up to 1798.

In these *libri bullarum*, the outgoing bulls have been organized per priorate, and all priorates have been grouped per *lingua*, which means in accordance with the eight language fields or tongues, known to the Order. All the Dutch preceptories except one belonged to the Priorate of Germany, led by the later so-called 'Grand Prior of Heitersheim', who was one of the Grand Crosses of the German tongue. The only exception was the former preceptory of the Knights Templar Ter Brake near Alphen (in the province Noord-Brabant), which belonged to the Priorate of France within the French tongue.

Unlike the Grand Master with his dignitaries, the priors did not reside in headquarters but in one of their *camerae priorales*, from which, in the case of the Prior of Germany, Heitersheim near Freiburg im Breisgau became the most important one in the sixteenth century. Originally every prior had four *camerae priorales* at his disposal, *i.e.* preceptories from which he obtained a large part of the yields, except for a contribution to the central treasury. However, in 1367 it was decided to grant every prior a fifth *camera* to compensate him for the loss of certain dues from the goods of deceased brethren in his priorate[32]. Amongst priors, the *camerae* could vary, but after 1506 Freiburg, combined with its *membrum* Heitersheim in 1547[33], always formed the fifth *camera* of the Prior of Germany[34]. Since the fifteenth century, the bailiwick Utrecht with all its *membra* formed one of the

---

[31] See before, note 1.

[32] General Chapter in Avignon, March 1367, Statutes nr.9, summarized in J. Delaville le Roulx, *Les Hospitaliers à Rhodes*, p.162 with note 7.

[33] AOM 209, *Decreta concilii* 1473-1560, fol.235v-236v, 1547, February 28 (below, A.nr.112).

[34] AOM 397, *libri bullarum* 1505-1506, fol.147r-149r, 1506, February 25 (below, A.nr.94).

other four *camerae* of this prior and was to remain so formally until the end of the eighteenth century[35].

Because Heitersheim was the Prior of Germany's permanent seat since the middle of the sixteenth century, this was also the place where the archive of the priorate was formed; nowadays, it is kept in the *Generallandesarchiv* in Karlsruhe (GLA)[36]. Its inventorial system is badly organized and hardly manageable, but it contains among other things many documents pertaining to attempts made to recover the goods, once confiscated in The Netherlands. It may be perceived to embody the complement to the seventeenth-century correspondence on this matter in the State Archive at Arnhem, Gelderland, which was made accessible by Loeff's inventory[37].

Summarizing, the most important foreign archives in which documents can be found concerning the Hospitallers in The Netherlands are the AOM in Valletta, the GLA in Karlsruhe and the Ghent City Archive. The last one contains a valuable—although corrosion of the parchment by the ink has damaged it severely—fourteenth-century rent-roll made in 1368, pertaining to the St Catharine's Convent in Utrecht. In contrast to what the AOM and GLA offer, one does not find anything concerning the Order's central organization here, but only information about the internal administration of the Utrecht bailiwick and some of its subordinate *membra*. It is unknown how this document ended up in Ghent, and it is not even sure if it really belongs to the Surmont de Volsberghe family funds, into whose inventory it was entered. As a hypothesis one could imagine that in the sixteenth century, at the time of the confiscation of the goods, one of the brethren's friends took it with him to secure it in anticipation of better times. Of course, it could substantiate claims to recover illegitemately expropriated possessions. When these better times did not arrive, the folio probably became part of this friend's and his descendants' legacy.

---

[35] AOM 334, *libri bullarum* 1407-1408, fol.112v, 1408, November 5 (below, A.nr.9); last time in 1777, August 21, GLA Karlsruhe, 20/168, original bull on parchment (below, A.nr.205).

[36] See M. Krebs, *Gesamtübersicht der Bestände des Generallandesarchivs Karlsruhe*, 1.Teil, Veröffentlichungen der Staatlichen Archivverwaltung Baden Württemberg, Heft 1, Stuttgart, 1954. Of these, especially the files 20 'Johanniter-Archive' (pp.67-68), 89 'Akten Heitersheim Generalia' (p.260) and 90 'Akten Heitersheim, Reichs- und Kreissachen' (p.260) are significant. Of file 90 a typographical repertory is available, edited by A. Maisch, U. Nieß, C. Rehm, U. Schäfer, Karlsruhe, 1991, without a list of summarized records and with a merely general indication of the contents of the often highly voluminous convolutions.

[37] See before, note 28.

This rent-roll was made in 1368 under the auspices of frater Hugo van Coudenkerc, *dispensator* (administrator) of the St Catharine's Convent, and contains the goods of the convent in the town of Utrecht and the Nedersticht as well as the borderland with the County of Holland, ordered per parish. One folio page usually contains the description of only two goods, their adjoining properties, leaseholder, term, rent and date of maturity, with the idea that all these data would be regularly adjusted. In many instances this was indeed done, often after ten years or as long as the term lasted, and sometimes it was repeated up·to three times. This occasion usually coincided with a raise in rent, so that the inflation in that period can be monitored quite closely. Dues in kind, such as chicken, wax and one's obligation to transport peat, usually stayed at the same level. Because many brethren seem to have been entrusted with the supervision of these lease extensions and they extend over a considerable period of time, many different handwritings appear, that sometimes cannot be distinguished from one another. Furthermore, reading is made very difficult by the ink that has more or less eaten into the parchment pages and has burnt through the folio's. It is only thanks to the use of many standard formulae that a large part of the text can still be reconstructed. In any case this is a valuable source that teaches us many new things about the medieval possessions of the St Catharine's Convent and their management.

The documents from the AOM and GLA are of a completely different kind. From the AOM we already mentioned the *libri bullarum*, organized per tongue and subsequently per priorate. They contain copies of all the outgoing bulls by the Grand Master and headquarters as well as chancery notes pertaining to their practical elaboration. The heads of the European preceptories were usually appointed by a bull from the Grand Master and the Grand Council. For this occasion, future heads of preceptories were expected to be present at headquarters to receive their bulls in person. Next, they had to receive explicit permission to leave for their preceptories and inspect them. In the case of a preceptory for a priest, he need not return, but a knight had to return to headquarters after the obligatory inspection and resume his duties on the galleys or in the fortresses. This permission to leave and return was called a *licentia recedendi et redeundi* and was recorded in the relevant *liber bullarum* by the chancery. For the medieval period they can mostly be found for the Arnhem preceptory with *membrum* Nimwegen and Mechelen (in South Limburg) with *membrum* Aachen.

Utrecht and all its subordinate preceptories became a *camera prioralis* at an early date, which destined it for inspections by the Prior of Germany without being recorded in the files at headquarters. However, when Utrecht and headquarters were at loggerheads about a *membrum*, as was the case with the Sint Jansdal near Harderwijk in 1448-1460, the *libri bullarum* do mention it[38]. They also mention a complaint by the procurator of the German tongue in 1466, concerning the fact that the head of the preceptory of Haarlem, a mere administrator of a Utrecht *membrum*, had seceded from the mother bailiwick and had declared Haarlem an autonomous preceptory, all to the disadvantage of the Prior of Germany[39].

The Prior of Germany's power to dispose of Utrecht as one of his *camerae priorales*, in practice consisted of his approving of the new bailiff, chosen by the convent's brethren in Utrecht. However, sometimes the prior or others would question the rightfulness of this practice, necessitating many a negotiation to have the ancient custom recognised. An instance of this from 1472 is found in the State Archive of Utrecht, involving the Pope finally acting as a mediator on behalf of the bailiff[40]. In 1603 the issue reappears or simply is recorded again, but in this case the Grand Master himself ruled in favour of the bailiff[41]. This had been preceded by a decision of the General Chapter of the Order in 1588, admitting a brother of the German tongue from outside the St Catharine's Convent to become a resident of this house in order to keep the bailiwick out of heretical hands[42]. Moreover, the Chapter had decided that the appointment of a new bailiff in the houses of Strassbourg, Cologne, Wesel and Utrecht should be approved of by headquarters, which was an un-

---

[38] AOM 361, *libri bullarum* 1447-1449, fol.205r, 1448, February 28; AOM 364, *libri bullarum* 1453-1454, fol.106v-107r, 1453, October 12 and November 18; AOM 370, *libri bullarum* 1460, fol.139r, 1460, November 2. Towards Rhodes, Utrecht maintained that Sint Jansdal was a *membrum* of the St Catharine's Convent and not an autonomous preceptory, and seems to have been proven right; in 1460, the person who had been appointed by headquarters resigned (below, A.nrs.44, 54, 55, 61).

[39] AOM 376, *libri bullarum* 1466, fol.132r-v, 1466, c. December 22 (below, A.nr.71).

[40] Utrecht State Archive (RA Utrecht), Collection Buchel-Booth, nr.134, 1472, June 12, edited in Brondgeest, *Bijdragen*, pp.99-101, Appendix V and below, A.nr.79; also above, note 22.

[41] RA Utrecht, Statenarchief, nr.487, 1603, August 18, October 26 and 28, November 15, edited in Brondgeest, pp.105-111, Appendices VII, VIII and IX; RA Utrecht, Suir, *Balije*, inventory nr.1, 1603, December 28, below, A.nr.136.

[42] AOM 444, *libri bullarum* 1588-1589, fol.208r-209r, 1588, March 30 (below, A.nr.131).

precedented infringement on the rights of these houses, against which they filed an appeal[43].

As regards the centuries during which the Dutch preceptories were threatened to be or actually were expropriated as a result of the Reformation, the *libri bullarum* state which persons were charged with the recovering of lost possessions and under which conditions. One may conclude that the chancery relied increasingly heavily on rhetorics and the use of long-winded formulae, which were appropriately abbreviated in the copies. Sometimes the GLA contains an original bull for comparison, yet its contents, though unimpaired, have nothing additional to offer. As a matter of fact, the AOM contain a large compilation of seventeenth-century correspondence and pamphlets dealing with the goods that were seized in the Republic, thus supplementing the GLA documents[44].

Surprisingly, the AOM further contain seventeenth-century letters from The Netherlands requesting the release of seamen, captured from Barbary pirates by the Maltese fleet and subsequently placed on the Order's galleys. Sometimes, these letters were written at the orders of the Prince of Orange, Frederick Henry, and sometimes they bear his signature[45]. In these and in the GLA one also finds deliberations considering the advantages and disadvantages of retaliations against the Republic's merchants and ships in the Rhineland and the Mediterranean[46].

That connections with The Netherlands still existed in the eighteenth century appears from a compilation of payments made by preceptories in the Priorate of Germany, in which Arnhem and Nimwegen remarkably enough function as tributary houses[47].

---

[43] AOM 291, *Sacrum Capitulum Generale* 1588, fol.79v-80r, 1588, June 24 (below, A.nr.132); RA Utrecht, Suir, *Balije*, inventory nr.1, 1588, December 1 (below, A.nr.133).

[44] AOM 2198, fol.138-516v. The pamphlets from this compilation are recorded in part D.

[45] AOM 57, *Liber epistolarum*, fol.180r, dd.1622, February 13; fol.166r-v, dd.1626, March 3; fol.167r-v, dd.1626, October 11; fol.181r-v, dd.1629, February 3; fol.182r-v, dd.1629, February 5; fol.186r-v, 1629, February 15 (below, A.nrs.149, 150, 152, 153, 154, 155).

[46] AOM 58, *Lettere di Francia*, fol.302r-v, dd.1647, December 27; AOM 57, *Liber epistolarum*, fol.351r-352r, undated, after 1652, May 12; GLA 89/325, dd.1652, November 12 and 14, and December 20; GLA 90/462, fol.29r-v, dd.1661, December 16; fol.28r-v, dd.1662, March 18 (below, A.nrs.159, 169, 165, 166, 167, 170, 171).

[47] AOM 893 and 894, *Risponsioni Alemagne*, 1777-1796 and 1761-1780 (below, A.nr.209).

The most interesting information about Dutch houses in the Order from a local point of view is to be found in the visitation acts, whose contemporaneous, incomplete copies of 1495 and 1540 are also kept in the Gelderland State Archive and have been published verbatim in the same, incomplete form[48]. Especially the visitation of 1540 is more comprehensively covered in the AOM files than in the Gelderland files, which lack a description of Arnhem, Nimwegen, Utrecht, Haarlem and several other *membra* of Utrecht, which the AOM files do describe[49].

The Grand Master and his Council ordered a visitation for an entire priorate or an even larger area, because they were mainly concerned for the central treasury to receive and keep as many revenues as possible. This inspection of moveables and immoveables had to be conducted every five years, but not so many records have been preserved, either because they were lost or because the visitations never were conducted. Therefore, it was quite surprising when a visitation act from 1732 of the Priorate of Germany, including Arnhem, was found in the AOM, proving that this preceptory, even though severly damaged, to some extent still functioned as the Order's property and still regularly held Roman-Catholic services[50].

As previously mentioned, the GLA in Karlsruhe contains a comprehensive correspondence concerning Arnhem and Nimwegen, which forms a supplement to that in the Gelderland State Archive. The GLA further keeps documents pertaining to the redemption of the Haarlem preceptory in 1667, for which the Order received 150,000 florins, through mediation of the Grand Pensionary Johan

---

[48] See above, note 29.

[49] The visitation of 1495 is in AOM 45, *Visitatio Commendarum Superioris et Inferioris Alemaniae Anno Domini 1495*. The Dutch houses are on fol.176r-178r (Mechelen and Aachen), fol.191v-223v (Utrecht, Ingen, Buren, Sint Jansdal, Oudewater, Waarder, Harmelen, Wemeldinge, Kerkwerve, Middelburg, Sneek, Haarlem) and fol.234r-235v (Warffum, Wijtwerd, Oosterwierum) (below, C.2). The visitation of 1540 can be found in AOM 6340, *Descriptio visitationis preceptariarum, beneficiorum et domorum ordinis sancti Johannis Hierosolimitani per Germaniam*. The Dutch houses are on fol.8v-12v (Utrecht), fol.31r-35v (Haarlem), 126v-129r (Mechelen and Aachen), fol.147r-152r (Warffum, Wijtwerd, Oosterwierum), fol.158v-162v (Arnhem and Nijmegen), fol.162v-173r (the *membra* of Utrecht: Buren, Ingen, Sint Jansdal, Oudewater, Waarder, Harmelen, Wemeldinge, Middelburg, Kerkwerve, Sneek) (below, C.3). In 1544 Utrecht received another *membrum* in Montfoort, which of course was not involved in the visitations of 1495 and 1540, but was involved in that of 1594; see Wiersum and Le Cosquino de Bussy (above, note 29), pp.322-324 and below, C.4.

[50] AOM 6339, *Priorato d'Alemagna, Visite 1733*. Nr.25 contains the 'Visitatio prioralis der Commenden Arnheim', conducted on 6-9 October 1732 (below, C.9).

de Witt[51]. Years of negotations on the Order's behalf had been conducted by Reinier Kempinck, delegate of Grand Prior Frederick
Prince-Cardinal Landgrave of Hessen, who showed great diligence
and perseverence in the process. Even though the redemption also
appears from the files in the Haarlem Municipal Archive, most information about the preceding struggle is to be found in the AOM and
the GLA.

The aftermath of this redemption proved rather an embarrass-
ment for the Order. Instead of rewarding Reinier Kempinck gener-
ously by reserving a share of the redemption money for his pension,
the Grand Master and the Maltese Council earmarked the entire sum
for the central treasury and thought it appropriate for the Prince-
Cardinal Landgrave to reward his delegate out of his own pocket.
The official reasoning was, that a brother of the Order who had
recovered an expropriated commodity could enjoy its fructuary for
life. However, the fact that Haarlem had not returned into the Order's lap, but had been sold instead, rendered this stipulation
invalid[52]. It was also of no avail that Johan de Witt and the Estates of
Holland intervened in the interests of Reinier Kempinck with Prince-
Cardinal Landgrave of Hessen, offered him a £1,000 gold chain and
promised him a bonus of 3,000 Carolus guilders[53].

In the seventeenth and the eighteenth centuries, the Maltese Order more or less lived on its past merits and occupied itself mainly
with the privateering of the Mediterranean to fight pirates. However,
the status of the sovereign power could not stop the decay and it hit
rockbottom when the Napoleonic wars made it without fighting
abandon headquarters, which had precisely been built after a heroic
siege in 1565. Still, it should not be forgotten that particularly in the
first centuries of its existence, the Order played an important role in
the Holy Land and Europe with its double task of nursing and fighting. To achieve this, a central organization had to be created, that
could both fulfil its duties as headquarters and see to a sensible management of the preceptories all over Europe. The fact that this net-

---

[51] GLA Karlsruhe, 90/472, fol.nr.2r-9r, confirmation by the Prince-Cardinal
Landgrave of Hessen dd.1668, December 8 of the bull by Grand Master Nicolas
Cotoner dd.1668, December 5 to redeem Haarlem, including the contract text itself
(below, A.nr.187).

[52] Letters concerning Reinier Kempinck's reward from Grand Master Nicolas
Cotoner in AOM 1443, dd.1667, October 15 and November 17, and 1668, February 22 (without folio numbers) (below, A.nrs.182, 183, 185, 186).

[53] Letter from the Estates of Holland dd.1669, October 10, in GLA, 90/473,
fol.214r (below, A.nr.189).

work included Dutch houses as well is most clearly shown by foreign archives.

Although a minor part of The Netherlands as they are today fell under the French tongue, namely the former Templar preceptory of Ter Brake near Alphen in the province Noord-Brabant and some goods in Zeeuws-Vlaanderen that belonged to the preceptory of Slype-Caestre in the diocese Terwaan[54], it was decided to limit this book to the German tongue. Ter Brake's most historical moment in the Order's general existence was its head Amador de la Porte exchanging the preceptory, which lay in the front line between Spanish troops and those of the Dutch Republic, for 7,600 florins interest out of the goods of Prince Philip William of Orange in Burgundy in 1616[55].

About this edition

The text edition presented here consists of four parts:
A. bulls and letters to and from the Grand Master and the Prior of Germany, ranging from 1319 to 1797, and largely from the AOM and the GLA (the comprehensiveness and varying significance of the available files made a selection necessary);

---

[54] Insofar as the archives of these preceptories were kept in the *Archives de l'Etat* in Mono (Belgium), they were largely lost during the acts of war in 1940. They have been described by L. Devillers in *Inventaire analytique des archives des commanderies belges de l'Ordre de Saint-Jean de Jérusalem ou de Malte*, Mons, 1876. Further, see E. Mannier, *Ordre de Malte. Les commanderies du Grand-Prieuré de France d'après les documents inédits conservés aux Archives Nationales à Paris*, Paris, 1872, and A. Wauters, 'Exploration des chartes et des cartulaires belges existants à la Bibliothèque Nationale à Paris', in: *Compte rendu des séances de la Commission Royale d'Histoire, ou Recueil de ses Bulletins*, 4e série tome II, Bruxelles, 1875, p.78 sqq; pertaining to the Knights Hospitallers pp.155-198, and especially concerning the preceptory of Chantraine to which Ter Brake belonged, pp.170-177.
For Belgian preceptories in the AOM, see: Andrée Scufflaire, 'Les archives de l'Ordre de Saint-Jean de Jérusalem à la Royal Malta Library, La Valette. Rapport de mission', in: *Bulletin de la Commission Royale d'Histoire*, 129 (1963), pp.lxix-lxxiv and pp.cccxxxii-ccclxxii, and Andrée Scufflaire, 'De Hospitaalbroeders op Malta belicht vanuit hun archief', in: Marleen Forrier (ed.), *De Orde van Malta in de Zuidelijke Nederlanden (12de-18de eeuw)*, Brussels, 1993 (General State Archive and State Archive in the Provinces, Educational Services, Dossiers 2nd series 7; Dossier with the exhibition of the same name in the General State Archive in Brussels), pp.41-48.
[55] This entire affair with all the necessary approvals can be found in the AOM 459, *libri bullarum* 1615-1619, fol.12r-16v, and in the General State Archive (ARA) in The Hague, Archief Nassause Domeinraad Folio, inventory 1.08.15, fol.518v-521r.

B. the rent-roll of the St Catharine's Convent in Utrecht, made in 1368 and kept in the Ghent City Archive (Belgium);

C. visitation acts and inquiries from one, some or all of the Dutch preceptories from 1495, 1540, 1603, 1700, 1704, 1719 and 1732, largely from the AOM and the GLA, for purposes of comparison supplemented by a inquiry that was published before and pertained to Mechelen in South Limburg, in 1373, and the visitation acts of Utrecht and Arnhem with their *membra* from 1594;

D. titles of pamphlets, printed or written in the sixteenth, seventeenth and eighteenth centuries, concerning the Order's expropriated goods and its attempts to recover them; the pamphlets themselves are in the AOM, the GLA and several Dutch archives and libraries.

All documents are included in their original language or translation—some pamphlets were, shortly after their publication, translated from Dutch into German or French—and are unchanged as far as punctuation and spelling are concerned. Thus, the Maltese inclination to double the 't' in words such as *legittimus* and the sixteenth-century abundant interspersion of comma's have both been respected. Some modest punctuation has been added to documents pre-dating this period to render some long-winded Latin sentences more comprehensible. Some uniformity was introduced into the texts insofar as the use of 'j' instead of 'i' in Latin words was concerned, even if the handwriting has a letter that bears closer resemblance to a 'j'; *e.g.*, *iuxta* instead of *juxta*. Proper names of non-Latin origin, such as Johannes and Jerusalem, have kept their 'J' in Latin texts. The undifferentiated use of 'i', 'j', 'ij' or 'y' in non-Latin texts has been maintained. The use of 'u' and 'v' has been formalized in accordance with their pronunciation in, *e.g.*, *usus* and *verbum*. The letter 'w' is rendered as it is pronounced: as 'w', 'vu' or 'uu'. Furthermore, the monogram of Christ has been preserved in its standard abbreviations *Xpo (Christo)* and *Xpi (Christi)* in the copies of Grand Masters' bulls, since they may be regarded as the chancery's hallmarks. The use of capitals has been treated with some reserve, partly owing to the fact that some letters cannot be specified as particularly small or capital writing.

In dating its bulls and other official documents, the Order used the Annunciation-style, meaning that a new year did not begin until 25 March, Annunciation Day. From about the middle of the fifteenth century this custom occurs in the formulation of the date: pieces that are issued after 25 March are dated *anno incarnationis Domini*, whereas pieces from before that date have the formula: *anno ab incarnatione Domini*. Before the middle of the fifteenth century the chancery was not yet quite consistent in using this terminology and showed divergences, *e.g.* A.nr.2, dd.12 January 1323, A.nr.7, dd.23 January 1391, A.nr.13, dd.5 January 1414, and A.nr.76, dd.19 October 1469. Afterwards we do not find these inconsistencies any more.

Grand Master Nicolas Cotoner explained this custom quite clearly to his correspondents in a bull dd.28 August 1664, as it seemed to cause some confusion at the time. This writing ended up in the Order's preceptory of Arnhem and thence moved to the State Archive in Gelderland, where it still remains today; it has been rendered in part A as nr.180. The headnotes accompanying the bulls in question in this edition always indicate whether they have been dated in the Annunciation-style and its exact wording has been added wherever possible, even if the bull is only rendered in summarized form.

PART A

BULLS AND LETTERS, 1319-1795

General remark: the series *libri bullarum* in the AOM has two or even more foliations: older and newer ones, partly disintegrated. Here the clearest or most legible foliation is referred to, which in some volumes may be the older and in others the newer one. Although this may be very confusing, it was impossible to maintain one system for all the different eras.

1. 1319, April 12 – *Frater Fulco de Vilaret, Grand Master, orders frater Jacob Bishop of Zuden, head of the houses at Utrecht and Haarlem, to pay 3,000 florins to frater Paolo de Modena, who will also receive responsions and other payments from frater Ulrich von Rechberg, head of the preceptory of Colmar, and others, in order to pay Brutio Carucii, merchant of Florence, to redeem the pledge given by frater Leonardo de Tibertia, Prior of Venice and procurator at the papal curia.*

Original charter on parchment: AOM 16 = bullae magistrales, nr.10; writing in many places faded; file with seal lost.

Venerabili in Xpo padri domino fratri Jacobo Dei gratia episcopo Zudensi preceptori domorum Traiectensis et [Hairlemensis]ᵃ, frater Fulco de Vilareto Dei gratia sancte domus hospitalis sancti Johannis Jerosolimitani magister humilis et pauperum Xpi custos, salutem et sinceram in Domino caritatem.

Quia dilectum in Xpo nobis carissimum fratrem Paulum de Mutina domus eiusdem vicepriorem per Saxoniam, Thuringiam, Marchiam et Slaviam, de [cuius] fid[e] et sollicitudine et circumspectione plene confidimus, fecimus et constituimus ac ordinavimus nostrum verum et legitimum procuratorem, sindicum, negociorum gestorem, yconomum, petoremᵃ et nuncium specialem ad recipiendum, petendum et exigendum a vobis et singulis vestrum usque ad summam trium milium florenorum auri de Florencia necnon a fratre Ulrico de Rechberc preceptor[e] Columbarie ac aliis quibuscumque nostris procuratoribus alias ordinatis per nos in partibus ipsis ad petendum, exigendum et recipiendum a vobis et singulis vestrum nobis debitas [re]sp[on]siones et subvenciones, quos tria milia florenos idem frater Paulus de mandato nostro solvere habet Brutio Carucii, mercatori de

Florencia, qui a fratre Leonardo de Tibertis priore Veneciarum et procuratore in Romana curia, propterea recepit quedam vasa et iocalia nostra in pignore, volumus et vobis auctoritate presencium permittimus, quatenus responsionem ad quam nobis tenemini et dicto hospitali, dicto fratri Paulo vel eius speciali nuncio persolvatis, ut de dictis tribus milibus florenis possit satisfacere mercatori supradicto, [b] recipientes ab ipso fratre Paulo de hiis que ei solveritis, vel eius [in - neam] apodixam vel literas quitancie de hiis quo solutis ad cautelam.

In cuius rei testimonium et certitudinem pleniorem b[ulla] nostra [plum]bea presentibus est appensa.

Datum Arelate die duodecima mensis Aprilis anno Domini millesimo trecentesimo decimo nono.

---

[a] *uncertain reading ms.* [b] [-]per *cancelled ms.*

2. 1323, January 12 – *Frater Olivier von Sayn, head of the house at Arnhem, and others ask frater Helion de Villeneuve, Grand Master, to replace frater Paolo de Modena as head of the preceptories of Thüringen, Saxony and the March by frater Albrecht von Schwarzburg, recently appointed Prior of Germany and visitator of Bohemia and Denmark.*

Original charter on parchment: AOM 16 = bullae magistrales, *nr.15, with the spurs of five lost seals. In case of Annunciation-style the date is* 1324, January 11.

Magno religionis viro domino fratri Eliono de Villa Nova sacre domus hospitalis sancti Johannis Jerosolimitani magistro summo fratres Oliverius de Seina in Arnheim, Gerhardus de Hamerstein in Briseke, frater Eberhardus de Kestenburg in Frankenvort, Johannes de Grunbach de Herbipoli, Rudolfus de Masemunster domorum commendatores *[point out that]* frater Albertus de Nigro Castro prior noster et ex parte vestra visitator regionum Bohemie et Dacie *[has deserved very well overseas and ask]* quare paterna pensacione non respexeritis, dummodo vobis constiterit, ut preceptoriam Duringie, Saxonie et Marchie, quam frater Paulus de Mutina tenet, eidem domino fratri Alberto non duxeritis committendam, cum infra terminos eiusdem preceptorie idem dominus frater Albertus de clariori sanguine principum, comitum et nobilium traxerit originem, qui hodierno tempore dictas partes dominio regunt et potencia defendunt *[also because this preceptory is in a state of disrepair for lack of direction from the outsider frater Paolo de Modena.]*

In cuius rei testimonium sigilla nostra presentibus sunt appensa.

Datum anno Domini M° CCC° XX° III, die Mercurii post Epiphaniam eiusdem.

3. 1358, August 1 – *Frater Roger des Pins, Grand Master, notifies frater Conrad von Braunsberg, head of the bailiwick Utrecht, that he is appointed over this bailiwick for another ten years, beginning at the next St John's day.*
Registration: AOM 316 = libri bullarum 1346-1358, *fol.219r.*

Frater Rogerius [de Pinibus] etc. religioso etc. fratri Cunrado de Brunsperg domus eiusdem preceptori seu bailivo Tragetensi salutem etc. Propter probitatis vestre merita et administrationem accomodam quam in comissis vobis regiminibus in nostro ordine sicut testimonio fidedigno accepimus habuistis, illa vobis libenter annuimus que conservationem vestri status concernere dignoscuntur. Igitur preceptoriam seu baiuliam Tragetensem seu in Traiecto prioratus nostri Alamanie cum omnibus et singulis suis membris, iuribus et pertinenciis universis ad eam spectantibus et pertinentibus quoquomodo et cum quibus eam tenetis et presencialiter possidetis, habendam, tenendam, regendam, gubernandam, augmentandam et meliorandam in spiritualibus et temporalibus tam in capite quam in membris sub annua responsione et aliis oneribus impositis et imponendis rationabiliter secundum communem cursum aliarum baiuliarum prioratus nostri Alamanie supradicti in capitulo provinciali dicti prioratus annis singulis exolvendis et nisi feceritis destituendi vos de dicta baiulia et illam ad manus suas ponendi iuxta statutum priori et receptori responsionum dicti prioratus, hac serie plenam concedimus potestatem huiusmodi facta vobis gratia in aliquo non obstante, hinc adinstans festum nativitatis sancti Johannis Baptiste et ab eodem festo inantea ad annos decem continuos et completos de nostrorum procerum concilio auctoritate presencium de nostra certa sciencia et speciali gratia vobis confirmamus benefaciendo in eadem, comitentes etc. Quocirca etc. Inhibentes etc.
In cuius etc.
Data Rodi die prima mensis Agusti anno LVIII.

4. 1383, April 10 – *Frater Conrad von Braunsberg, Prior of Germany, is ordered to send four armed knights to headquarters.*
Chancery note: AOM 322 = libri bullarum 1382-1384, *fol.199r, referring to a letter from frater Juan Ferdinando d'Heredia, Grand Master, to the Prior of Bohemia dd. 10 April 1383 in the same source, same folio.*
Sub eisdem dato, modo et forma prescriptis scriptum fuit fratri Conradi de Brunsperg priori Alamanie seu ipsius prioratus regimini presidenti et mandatum ut supra ut quatuor fratres milites eligendos per ipsum et fratrem Hessonem mictat ad conventum termino prescripto et ipsis ut accedant cum equis et armis ut in forma prescripta.

5. 1384, April 3 – *Frater Ricardo Carracciolo, Grand Master, and the brethren of the General Chapter nominate frater Symon dux Tassinensis, Prior of Bohemia and Poland as* nostrum et nostre dicte domus locumtenentem, visitatorem, correctorem et privatorem secundum statuta nostre religionis in prioratibus Alamannie, Saxonie et Brabantzie procuratorem, actorem, syndicum, yconomum, responsionum petitorem et certum nuncium specialem —.

Data Neapoli durante nostro predicto capitulo generali die tertia mensis Aprilis in anno incarnacionis Domini millesimo trecentesimo ottuagesimoquarto.

Copy: AOM 281 = liber actorum capituli generalis 1384, *fol.26v. Frater Ricardo Carracciolo was a counter-Grand Master, appointed by the Pope in Rome, Urbanus VI, whereas the rightful Grand Master frater Juan Ferdinando d'Heredia and the Convent supported the Avignon Pope Clemens VII.*

6. 1385, May 17 – *Frater Juan Ferdinando d'Heredia, Grand Master, and Convent grant* Heimerino de Mastricht *the sustenance and attire of a donat for his lifetime* in domo nostra de Heutershem membro baiulie de Friburgo.

Datum Avinione die XVII^{ma} Maii anno incarnacionis Domini M^o CCC^o LXXXV^{to}.

Registration: AOM 323 = libri bullarum 1385-1386, *fol.149r.*

7. 1391, January 23 – *Frater Juan Ferdinando d'Heredia, Grand Master, grants the Priorate of Germany, vacant by the death of* fratris Cunradi de Brunsperg, *to frater* Friderico de Zolra *(von Zollern), as the Grand Master's* locutenentem.

Data Avinione die XXIII^{ma} mensis Ianuarii anno incarnacionis Domini M^o CCC^{mo} nonagesimo.

Registration: AOM 325 = libri bullarum 1391, *fol.134r-v. Annunciationstyle, but not yet dated as such.*

8. 1400, July 6 – *Frater Philibert de Naillac, Grand Master, and Convent assign the preceptories of Frankfurt and Mosbach as a fifth prioral chamber to frater Hesso Slegelholtz, Prior of Germany.*

Registration: AOM 330 = libri bullarum 1399-1400, *fol.82r-v. The institution of a fifth* camera prioralis *dates from the General Chapter in Avignon, March 1367, Statutes nr.9, summarized in Delaville le Roulx, Les Hospitaliers, p.162 with note 7.*

Frater Philibertus etc. et nos conventus etc. religioso in Xpo nobis carissimo fratri Hessoni Slegelholtz priori Alamanie et preceptori Lengoni dicte domus salutem, etc.

Sequentes ut tenemur nostre religionis statuta secundum que dicte domus fratres priores et castellani omnes et singuli in ipsorum prioratibus et castellaniis pro statu et oneribus suis supportandis quatuor baiulias pro suis cameris ipsorum iure ordinario et quintam baiuliam eorum tamen collacioni pertinentem debent habere in recompensationem certorum iurium que ipsi solebant percipere et habere de bonis fratrum preceptorum prioratuum et castellaniarum suarum decedencium, quodque quintam baiuliam ut prefertur vobis debitam in dicto prioratu nondum fueritis assecutus — *[and since both the vacant preceptories of Frankfurt and Mosbach fall under the collated properties of the Grand Master, the preceptories are assigned to him as his fifth chamber].*

Data Rodi die sexta mensis Iullii anno incarnationis Domini millesimo quatercentesimo.

9. 1408, November 5 – *Frater Philibert de Naillac, Grand Master, and Convent appoint frater Hamman zu Rhein as Prior of Germany after the resignation of frater Hesso Schlegelholtz, with Klingnau, Rheinfelden, Utrecht and Cologne as his four prioral chambers.*

Registration: AOM 334 = libri bullarum 1407-1408, *fol.112v.*

Frater Philibertus etc. et nos conventus Rodi domus eiusdem religioso etc. fratri Hanmano ze Ryn dicte domus salutem etc.

— Igitur prioratum nostrum Alamanie per resignacionem per dicte domus fratrem Hessonem Schlegelholtz[a], preceptorem Langoni et dicti prioratus priorem ultimum, de eo sua spontanea voluntate in manibus nostris factam et per nos acceptam vacantem presencialiter et ad nostram disposicionem racionabiliter propterea devolutum cum omnibus et singulis suis membris, pertinentiis et iuribus ad prioratum ipsum spectantibus et pertinentibus ac spectare et pertinere debentibus quoquomodo cum omni onere, emolumentis et honore et cum preceptoriis de Clingenow, R[hein]velden, Traiectensis et Coloniensis cameris suis et quas vobis pro cameris assignamus cum omnibus et singulis earum et cuiuslibet earum membris, pertinentiis et iuribus universis habendum, tenendum, regendum, gubernandum, augmentandum et meliorandum in spiritualibus et temporalibus tam in capite quam in membris vobis tanquam digno et benemerito invicem deliberato consilio auctoritate presencium sub responsione annua .. florenorum auri de Florencia et boni ponderis per vos, prout pro cameris vestris vos continget, et per preceptores preceptoriarum dicti prioratus, prout pro preceptoriis suis pro rata eis pertinebit, receptoribus deputatis vel deputandis per nos ad recipiendum responsiones in prioratu prefato aut alii vel aliis, quibus et ubi ordinaverimus et mandaverimus, in festo nativitatis sancti Johannis Baptiste annis singulis ex pacto expresso infallibiliter exsolvenda et quibuscumque aliis oneribus dicto prioratui qualitercumque et quomodocumque incumbentibus et incumbendis, impositis et imponendis per vos et dictos preceptores, ut predicitur, ex pacto eciam ultra responsionem predictam supportandis de nostra certa scientia et speciali gratia benefaciendo in eodem conferimus, concedimus et donamus ad annos decem continuos et completos salvo iure communis thesauri ratione vacantie pro una annata retento nobis et specialiter reservato etc. —

Data Rodi die quinta mensis Novembris anno incarnacionis Domini millesimo CCCC° octavo.

---

^a Schlegeolhtz *ms.*

---

10. 1410, May 12 – *The three lieutenants of Grand Master frater Philibert de Naillac, residing at the chapter general in Aix-en-Provence, give confirmation of position to* fratri Johanni Cruze baiulo seu preceptori baiulie seu preceptorie Westphale.

Registration: AOM 336 = libri bullarum 1410, fol.142v. The fact that the Grand Master has three locumtenentes *at the same time is the result of the Conciliar Movement in the period between Pisa and Konstanz, which included three popes at the same time.*

It may be questioned how far the area of this bailiwick Westphalia extended. Did the houses in Burgsteinfurt, East-Frisia and Groningen fall under its command as well?

---

11. 1413, January 21 – *Frater Johan Cruze, bailiff of Westphalia and head of the preceptory of Wesel, and the St John's house at Wesel acknowledge their agreement with frater Arnold van Donen, bailiff of the house at Utrecht, about an exchange of landed property between these two houses.*

Registration (by Arnout van Buchell, 16th/17th century): RA Utrecht, Collectie Buchel-Booth nr.51 (old ms.352), fol.104r-v; at the top: ut supra abr.; at the bottom: onder hangen 3 groene wasse segelkens der geenre hier genampt, waer inne dese wapenen, with drawings of three seals. In case of Annunciation-style the date is 1414, January 21.

Wy broeder Johan Cruze balyer toe Westphalen ende commanduer des huses te Wesel s.Johans ordre ende wy gemeene Convents broeders des huses voorss. bekennen voor ons ende onse nakomelingen dat wy metten eerbaren broder Arnold van Donen Belier ende commander tot Utrecht etc. eens wessels overcomen syn met goeden beraede, ende om nutticheit onser huser den wij vastelicken holden sullen, to beyden zyden, Alsoe dat het huys tot Utrecht hebben sal alsodane erffenisse ende goede als onse huse leggende heeft inden gestichte ende in Hollant in wat enden die gelegen syn, daer het huse tUtrecht mede geervet syn sal, ende hebben de balyer ende commanduer ende den convent tUtrecht weder voor bewiset ende overgegeven alsodanig erffenisse ende goede als daer sy den huse te Wesel aen *[fol.104v]* gevestiget heeft gelegen inden karspel van Ingen na uuytwijsen haerder brieve etc.

Alle dese poincten beloven wij etc.

In orcunde heb ic broder Jan Balier ende commendur voor mij ende dat gemeene convent mynen segel aen desen brief doen hangen, ende want het gemeen convent jegenwoirdich geen segel en hevet, so hebben wi omme de meere vestenisse gebeden broder Kaerl van Malden prior, Henric Jordens scaffener des voorss. huses to Wesel eer segelen mede daer an te hangen, des wy etc. Gegeven int jaer ons Heeren 1413 op s. Agneten dach der hilger joncfrouwen.

12. 1413, November 5 – *Frater Philibert de Naillac, Grand Master, and Convent, issue a bull in which they mention* frater Hugo comes de Montfort *as Prior of Germany.*

Registration: AOM 337 = libri bullarum 1408-1416, *fol.77r.*

13. 1414, January 5 – *Frater Arnold van Doenen, bailiff of the convent at Utrecht and chaplain, is admitted as the Grand Master's domestic chaplain.*

Chancery note: AOM 338 = libri bullarum 1413-1415, *fol.140r, Annunciation-style, but not yet dated as such.*

Die Vᵃ Ianuarii anno incarnationis Domini Mᵒ CCCCᵒ XIIIᵒ Lugduno admissus fuit in cappellanum et familiarem domini magistri frater Aelnardus de Doenen, preceptor et bailhivus baiulie Traiectensis, cappellanus domus nostre, ut in forma.

14. 1414, January 5 – *Frater Lambert van Moerdijk, chaplain in the St Catharine's Convent at Utrecht, is licensed to leave for the headquarters at Rhodos.*

Chancery note: AOM 338 = libri bullarum 1413-1415, *fol.140r.*

Anno, die et loco predictis data fuit licentia fratri Lamberto Wan Murdic in sancta Katharina de Utric commoranti cappellano domus

eiusdem recedendi de prioratu nostro Alamanie et eundi ad nostrum
Rodi conventum quando voluerit Deo et nostre religioni servituro a
suo superiore requisita licencia.

15. 1414, October 18 – *Frater* Lucius de Vallinis, *marshal and lieutenant
of the Grand Master, and Convent appoint frater* Symon de Berntvelde *as
head of the preceptory of Lage after the death of its last head frater* Hermanus de
Bruntlicht.
  Registration: AOM 339 = libri bullarum 1409-1416, *fol.158v.*

16. 1414, December 8 – *Frater Philibert de Naillac, Grand Master, confirms
frater* Symon de Berntvelde *as* preceptor baiulie de Laghe. —
Data Constancie die octava mensis Decembris anno incarnationis
M° CCC° XIIII°.
  Registration: AOM 338 = libri bullarum 1413-1415, *fol.144v. In AOM
349* = libri bullarum 1432-1433, *fol.70v, dd. 28 July 1432,* Simon
Berntvelde *is mentioned as* preceptor Monasternensis.

17. 1415, April 11 – *Frater Philibert de Naillac, Grand Master, and Council
grant the Priorate of Germany* ad vitam *to frater Hugo Count of Montfort.*
  Registration: AOM 338 = libri bullarum 1413-1415, *fol.147v-148r. In
margin:* Refecta fuit hec confirmatio de mandato domini propter inde-
signationem camerarum prius declarari obmissarum per me Michaelem Paquanti etc. et prima extitit cancellata.
  Granting ad vitam *was a favour, bestowed by Grand Master and Council; it
meant that the favoured person was allowed to stay in his preceptory without
having to return to headquarters. Normally a preceptory was granted for 5 or 10
years, and a priorate for 2 years.*

Frater Philibertus de Nailhaco etc. religioso in Xpo nobis carissimo
fratri Hugoni comiti de Montfort priori prioratus nostri Alamanie
dicte domus salutem etc.
  [Deserving brothers must be rewarded.] Attendentes itaque quod in administracione prioratus nostri Alamanie predicti estis fructuosus utiliter comprobatus, prioratum ipsum cum omnibus et singulis suis
membris, iuribus et pertinenciis universis ad prioratum ipsum spectantibus et pertinentibus ac spectare et pertinere debentibus quoquomodo cum omni onere emolumentis et honore et cum preceptoriis
ᵃsive Baiuliis Traiectensi, Coloniensi, Klingnawie et Bubikonᵃ cameris
suis pro cameris assignatis cum omnibus et singulis earum et cuiusli-

bet earum membris, iuribus et pertinenciis, habendum, tenendum, regendum, gubernandum, augmentandum et meliorandum in spiritualibus et temporalibus tam in capite quam in membris vobis tamquam digno et benemerito — ad vitam vestram confirmamus et ad uberiorem vestram cautellam de novo conferimus, concedimus et donamus. —

Data Constantie die undecima mensis Aprilis anno incarnationis Domini millesimo CCCC° decimoquinto.

———————

ª sive — Bubikon *in margin ms.*

18. 1419, December 10 — *Frater Philibert de Naillac, Grand Master, and Convent renew* fratri Johanni Cruze baiulo seu preceptori baiulie seu preceptorie Westphalie *the grant of this preceptory, and because of his merits* ad vitam.

Registration: AOM 342 = libri bullarum 1418-1419, *fol.144r.*

19. 1420, September 19 — *Frater Philibert de Naillac, Grand Master, and General Chapter approve a nomination by frater Hugo von Montfort, Prior of Germany.*

Registration: AOM 345 = libri bullarum 1420, *fol.140r.*

Frater Philibertus etc. et nos conventus Rhodi domus eiusdem capitulum generale celebrantes, *[approve a nomination]* per religiosum in Xpo nobis carissimum fratrem Hugonem Montisfortensem prefati prioratus priorem, ad annos decem —.

Datum Rhodi durante nostro prefato generali capitulo die decima nona mensis Septembris anno incarnationis Domini millesimo CCCC^mo XX^mo.

20. 1420, September 19 — *Frater Philibert de Naillac, Grand Master, and Convent appoint visitators of the Priorate of Germany.*

Chancery note: AOM 345 = libri bullarum 1420, *fol.140r. The full text, only with other names, is to be found in AOM 345, fol.165, under the Priorate of Rome.*

Frater Henricus de Bye *in 1415 was* sancti Johannis Parisiensis preceptor, *as appears from AOM 338* = libri bullarum 1413-1415, *fol.147v dd. 11 April 1415;* frater Johannes de Monreal *was* preceptor Colonie, *AOM 345 fol.145v, dd. 25 October 1420 and AOM 348* = libri bullarum 1428, *fol.129v, dd. 25 August 1428.*

Die XIX^a fuerunt constituti ad visitandum in prioratu Alamaniae fratres Henricus de Bye et Johannes de Monreall prout in prioratu Urbis continent mutatis mutandis folio CLXV^o.

21. 1420, September 27 – *Frater Philibert de Naillac, Grand Master, and Convent license frater Hugo von Montfort, Prior of Germany,* — de nostro Rhodi conventu recedendi et vos transferendi ad partes vestras visitaturus ac gubernaturus dictum vestrum prioratum, ne in ruina quod absit deveniat, et deinde ad dictum conventum redeundi —.

Registration: AOM 345 = libri bullarum 1420, *fol.141r. This kind of license is called a* licentia recedendi et redeundi.

22. 1420, October 4 – *Frater Philibert de Naillac, Grand Master, and Convent give orders to* religioso in Xpo nobis carissimo fratri baillivio Westfalie [Johanni Cruze] *to appear the next St John's day for a provincial chapter of Germany* cum omnibus et singulis preceptoribus in vestra baiulia commorantibus —.

Registration: AOM 34 = libri bullarum 1420, *fol.144r-v.*

23. 1420, October 25 – *The German tongue grants the seniority in the bailiwicks Cologne, Utrecht and Westphalia to frater Johann von Monreal, head of the preceptories of Cologne and Adenau, as is granted to other ambassadors.*

Chancery notice: AOM 345 = libri bullarum 1420, *fol.145v.*

Anno Domini millesimo CCCC^o XX° die XXV^a mensis Octobris ipso die cum licencia reverendissimi domini magistri congregata et in unum convocata extitit lingua Alamanie, in qua quidem convocacione una voce nemine discrepante concessa extitit venerabili fratri Johanni de Monreal, Colonie et Denhune^a preceptori, sua ancianitas sive antiquitas ad petendum, postulandum commendarias, beneficia, officia et per sua[m] dictam ancianitatem in baiulis scilicet Colonie, Traiectensi et Westfalie ipso exeunte in legacione, servicio et ambassarie ex magistri et conventus in modo et forma quibus aliis ambassiatoribus est concessum, quod eciam domino nostro recitavimus more solito conventus, qui suam voluntatem et consensum omnibus supradictis exhibuit. Datum —

---

^{a} *i.e.:* Adenau.

24. 1421, July 4 – *Frater Antoine Fluvian, Grand Master, and Convent grant the vacant preceptory of Arnhem to frater Simon van Bracht, chaplain of the Priorate of Germany.*
Registration: AOM 346 = libri bullarum 1421-1422, *fol.122r-v.*

Frater Anthonius Fluviani — et nos conventus Rodi domus eiusdem religioso in Xpo nobis carissimo fratri Simoni de Bracht[a] cappellano prioratus nostri Almanie dicte domus salutem et sinceram in dominum caritatem.

Vestris exposcencibus mentis paterna benevolencia proscequentes baiuliam seu preceptoriam de Arnheym dicti prioratus vacantem per mortem dicte domus quondam fratris Arnoldi de Groenhem[b] dicti prioratus ultimi eiusdem preceptoris et propterea ad nostram collacionem et dispositionem racionabiliter devolutam cum omnibus et singulis suis membris, iuribus et pertinenciis universis ad eam spectantibus et pertinentibus ac spectare *[fol.122v]* et pertinere debentibus quoquomodo et cum quibus illam hactenus tenuit et possedit dominus quondam frater Arnoldus, habendam, tenendam, regendam etc. invicem etc. ad decem annos etc. committentes etc. —

In cuius rei testimonium bulla nostra plumbea presentibus est appensa.

Datum Rhodi in nostro conventu die quarta mensis Iulii anno incarnationis Domini millesimo quadringentesimo vicesimo primo.

---

[a] Brachi *ms.* [b] *i.e.:* Groenewoud.

25. 1421, July 10 – *Frater Simon van Bracht, head of the preceptory of Arnhem, is licensed to leave Rhodos for his preceptory.*
Chancery note: AOM 346 = libri bullarum 1421-1422, *fol.122v.*
Data fuit licentia fratri Symoni de Bracht preceptori de Arnheym recedendi a conventu et iterum redeundi ad dictum conventum, prius tamen habita licentia a suo superiori. Die decima mensis Iulii anno incarnationis Domini M° CCCC° vigesimo primo.

26. 1421, July 12 – *Grand Master and Convent assign to frater Simon van Bracht an income of 104 Rhineland florins in the Priorate of Germany.*
Chancery note: AOM 346 = libri bullarum 1421-1422, *fol.122v.*
Die duodecima mensis Iulii anno ut supra fuit facta dicto fratri Simoni assignacio centum quatuor cum dimidio florenorum Renensium in prioratu Almanie.

27. 1421, July 13 – *Frater Simon van Bracht, head of the preceptory of Arnhem, is licensed to promote two chaplains of the Order to the position of sergeant at arms.*

Chancery note: AOM 346 = libri bullarum 1421-1422, *fol.122v.*

Die XIII mensis Iulii anno ut supra data fuit licentia fratri Simoni preceptori de Arnheym prioratus Alamannie faciendi duos fratres cappellanos armorum servientes ut moris est.

28. 1422, May 31 – *Frater Antoine Fluvian, Grand Master, sends a letter to the brethren of the bailiwick of Utrecht, admonishing them to be obedient in their quarrel with the treasury about an unnamed house.*

Copy: AOM 346 = libri bullarum 1421-1422, *fol.124v.*

The house at stake is the preceptory of Arnhem, assigned to the chaplain Simon van Bracht, cf. the preceding nrs.24, 25, 26, 27. During its vacancy Arnt Zeuwelkin, priest, functioned as its locumtenens; *cf. Loeff, Archief, p.198-199, regesta nrs.330, 332 & 333, dd. 27 March, 25 June & 5 July 1422.*

Frater Anthonius Fluviani sacre domus hospitalis sancti Johannis Hierosolymitani humilis magister et pauperum Xpi custos religiosis in Xpisto nobis carissimis fratribus Zandro de Helwick ballivo domus nostre Traiecti, Arnaldo Zeuwelkin ac priori conventus dicte domus necnon fratribus conventualibus domus eiusdem salutem in Domino et nostris firmiter obedire mandatis.

Ad nostram presentiam olim ex veris et manifestis litterarum nostrorum procuratorum relacionibus pervenit quod dudum nostros responsionum receptores mortuaria, vacantia et alia iura nostro communi thesauro pro defensione catholice fidei spectancia et pertinencia exhigentes repulistis sub umbra cuiusdam frivole excusacionis dictam domum membrum Traiectensis camere asserentes, super quo nullam fidedignam probacionem non obstante termino ab ipsis receptoribus dato in capitulo provinciali demonstrastis; insuper vos novissime visitari a nostris procuratoribus, visitatoribus et correctoribus quibusdam interpositis reprobandis allegacionibus minime permisistis, secularesque personas contra nostre religionis statuta et consuetudines laudabiles procuratoribus nostris iam dictis minas et terrores incucientes introduxistis; et quoniam nemo suo dolo et fraude debet gaudere, vobis et unicuique vestrum in virtute sacre obediencie districte precipiendo mandamus quatenus emendacionis spiritum resuperii[a] procuratoribus nostris predictis dicta iura nostro dicto thesauro pertinencia et possessiones dicte domus omni contradictioni pos[t]posita assignetis, Taliter vos in predictis exhibentes ut debita obediencia apud nos recommendari valeatis. Valete in Xpisto.

Datum in nostro Rodi conventu die ultima mensis Maii M°
CCCC° XXII°.

ª *uncertain reading ms, perhaps* = resipiti, *from* resipiscere, *to repent.*

29. 1428, June 1 – *Frater Antoine Fluvian, Grand Master, and Convent grant*
fratri Ricardo de Norchg — domum seu baiuliam Steinfort situatam
in Westvalia.
Registration: AOM 348 = libri bullarum 1428, *fol.126v.*

30. 1428, August 16 – *Frater Antoine Fluvian, Grand Master, and Convent
grant* fratri Ghirardo Butterman — domum sive preceptoriam Vesa-
liensem baiulie Westfalie —, *vacant by resignation of* fratris Johannis
Cruxe, baiulivi Westfalie —.
Registration: AOM 348 = libri bullarum 1428, *fol. 130v.*

31. 1428, August 16 – *Frater Antoine Fluvian, Grand Master, and Convent
grant* fratri Gherardo Vuyst, commendatori nostre domus in Duys-
borgh — *for advancement of his position* — preceptoriam seu domum in
Walscheim in baiulia Westphalie —.
Registration: AOM 348 = libri bullarum 1428, *fol.130v. In another
extract on the same fol.130v, dd. 2 November 1428, frater Gerard Vuyst is called*
Gerardus de Werthusen dictus Vuyst, capellanus, preceptor domorum nostrorum Steynfordie, Duysburg ac Walshem.

32. 1432, July 1 – *Frater Antoine Fluvian, Grand Master, and Convent grant
to frater* Johannes de Swalbach *in addition to the* baiuliam Wyssel *(=
Niederweisel), which he already possesses,* baiulias seu preceptorias de Arnhem et Novomagio, *vacant by the death of frater* Simon Bracht, *the ad-
vowson of which belongs to Grand Master and Convent, for 10 years.*
Registration: AOM 349 = libri bullarum 1432-1433, *fol.70r.*

33. 1432, July 3 – *Frater Antoine Fluvian, Grand Master, acquits frater
Johann von Swalbach, the new head of the preceptories of Arnhem and Nimwegen,
of his obligations regarding the annates of the said preceptories to the amount of
133 gold Venetian ducats and 12 aspers, for which amount, including the annual
contributions* (responsiones), *these two preceptories were assigned to him; with
the stipulation that should the annates accrue a surplus value to an amount of 20*

florins, the additional revenues would be settled with the Grand Master; and includes order to the central and prioral treasuries to allot Johann the usufruct of these annates without further charge.

Registration: AOM 349 = libri bullarum 1432-1433, fol. 70r.

Frater Anthonius Fluviani etc. habens regimen etc. universis et singulis presentes recognicionis et quictancie litteras visuris et audituris salutem in Domino sempiternam. Notum facimus quod de religioso in Xpo nobis carissimo fratre Johanne de Swalbach preceptore domorum seu baiuliarum supradictarum prioratus predicti habuimus ac manualiter, realiter et de facto recepimus ducatos Venetos auri boni et iusti ponderis centum triginta tres et asperos duodecim pro duabus annatis vacantibus iam dictarum preceptoriarum quas sibi arrendavimus pro precio dictorum cxxxiii ducatorum et asperorum xii inclusis responsionibus, tali condictione et pacto quod si informati fuerimus quod plus valeant et ascendant dicte due annate vacantes de viginti florenis ultra dictos cxxxiii ducatos et asperos xii nobis reffundere et solvere quod plus erit ultra dictos cxxxiii ducatos asperos xii tenebitur, de quibuscumque ducatis cxxxiii asperis xii nos tenemur contentos ac integrales solutos et satisfactos, mandantes harum serie thesaurario generali nostre religionis et receptoribus dicti prioratus presentibus et futuris ut dictum fratrem Johannem de dictis duabus annatis utifrui promictant, nichil sibi petentes vel aliqualiter ipsum predicta causa molestantes, precipientes ecciam universis et singulis domus nostre fratribus presentibus et futuris cuiuscumque gradus, status, condicionis vel preheminencie existantibus ne contra presentem nostram quictanciam veniant, quinymo eundem fratrem Johannem in eadem deffendere et observare[a].

In cuius rei testimonio etc.

Datum Rhodi die III mensis Iulii anno quo supra.

---

[a] deffendare et observere *ms.*

34. 1432, July 20 – *The heads of the preceptories of Vallterre and Mainz are ordered to place frater* Rutgerus de Juede *in the peaceful possession of the preceptory of Mechelen.*

Chancery note: AOM 349 = libri bullarum 1432-1433, fol.70v.

35. 1432, July 28 – *Frater Johann von Swalbach, head of the preceptories of Niederweisel, Arnhem and Nimwegen, is licensed to leave Rhodos for his preceptories.*

Chancery note: AOM 349 = libri bullarum 1432-1433, *fol. 70r.*
Die XXVIII mensis julii Anno domino millesimo CCCC⁰ XXXII⁰
fuit data licentia fratri Johanni de Swalbach preceptori domorum seu
baiuliarum nostrarum in Wyssel, Arnhem et Novomagio prioratus
Alamanie dicte domus recedendi de conventu et redeundi quando
voluit etc. ut in forma.

36. 1433, June 20 – *The* Preceptori Brabancie et cuilibet alteri fratri
prioratus Almanie *is ordered to place frater Rutger de Juede in the peaceful
possession of the preceptory of Mechelen.*
Chancery note: AOM 349 = libri bullarum 1432-1433, *fol. 70v.*

37. 1433, July 10 – *Frater Antoine Fluvian, Grand Master, and Convent,
appoint frater Rutger de Juede, head of the preceptory of Mechelen, as their special
proxy and nuncio.*
Registration: AOM 350 = libri bullarum 1433, *fol. 176r-v.*

Noverint universi has presentes litteras procurationis inspecturi, quod
nos frater Anthonius Fluvianus etc. et nos conventus Rhodi domus
eiusdem, confisi de probitate et legalitate religiosi in Christo nobis
carissimi fratris Rogerii Jude dicte domus preceptoris de Mechlen
prioratus nostre Alemanie, quibus altissimus fuit gratia dotavit eundem, ex nostra certa scientia, invicem deliberato consilio omnibus
melioribus via, modo et forma quibus melius et aptius valemus et
scimus de iure facimus, constituimus et solempniter citra revocationem aliorum nostrorum procuratorum in diversis mundi partibus
ordinatorum tenore presentium ordinamus nostrum et dicte domus
nostre procuratorem, actorem, factorem, sindicum et yconomum, ac
negociorum nostrorum infrascriptorum gestorem et nuncium specialem et generalem. —.
    Datum Rhodi in nostro conventu die X Iulii Anno in carnationi-
bus Domini M CCCC XXXIII⁰.

38. 1433, August 4 – *Frater Rutger de Juede, head of the preceptory of
Mechelen, is licensed to leave Rhodos for his preceptory.*
Chancery note: AOM 350 = libri bullarum 1433, *fol. 176v.*
Die IIII mensis Augusti M⁰ CCCC⁰ XXXIII⁰ fuit data licentia fratri
Rutghero Jude preceptori Mechlem etc. recedendi de conventu et
revertendi ut in forma.

39. 1439-1440, *undated* – *Frater Johannes de Lastico, Grand Master, and Convent order frater* Rogerius de Jude in Mechelinie, *as well as the heads of the preceptories of Herford, Lage, Würzburg, Neuenburg, Überlingen, Rohrdorf and Sulz,* — ut reperietur in Castellanie Emposte —.

Registration: AOM 354 = libri bullarum 1439-1440, *fol.182v. This text has been abbreviated to such an extent, that its contents and date seem to have been left out.*

40. 1441, October 7 – *Frater Johannes de Lastico, Grand Master, and Convent grant frater* Rogerius de Jude, *head of the preceptories of Mechelen and Herford, in order to advance his position,* — baiulliam nostram de Rhod et Rhodenburg —, *which is vacant. He remains the head of Mechelen and Herford.*

Registration: AOM 355 = libri bullarum 1441-1442, *fol.153r.*

41. 1442, May 11 – *Johannes Geminger,* officialis curie Basiliensis, *declares that he has made an official German translation of some Latin statutes of the Order for frater Bertold Stehelin, head of the preceptory of Neuenburg, and frater Heinrich Scaler [?], proxy of the house at Villingen, both in the diocese of Konstanz.*

Official charter on parchment with wax seal in wooden casing on hemp string: GLA Karlsruhe, 20/115. Legend of the seal: SIGILVM CVRIE BASILIENSIS. *This item has been inserted here because frater Bertold Stehelin later became head of the preceptories of Arnhem and Nimwegen; cf.nr.65.*

The translated statutes contain the following sentences:
Post vero magister seu baylivi aut quisquam frater hospitalis nichil debent penitus mutuare nec pro aliquo ullam causam assumere nec hereditates neque possessiones domus hospitalis alienare sine consilio capituli generalis[1]

&

Secundum fuit statutum olim quod si aliquis frater ullam empcionem seu aquestum faciat illudque sic emit seu acquisivit per magistrum et conventum est sibi ad vitam recommendatum; si vero nonnullus frater quitquam emat seu acquirat illud ipse frater non valeat rendere nec impignerare neque alienare sine magistri et conventus licencia speciali[2].

[1] *Margat 1204-1206, Statuts promulgués par le chapitre général de l'ordre sous le magistère d'Alphonse de Portugal, ed. Delaville le Roulx,* Cartulaire II *nr.1193, p.38.*
[2] *Limisso, 1295, September 12, Statuts promulgués par le chapitre général sous le magistère d'Eudes des Pins,* Cartulaire III *nr.4295 sub 2, p.674, French and Latin*

texts. The Latin text from AOM is dated 1295, December 12. It is slightly different from the above text and runs as follows in the Cartulaire:

Secundum quod fuit statutum olim, si aliquis frater ullam empcionem seu aquestum faciat, illud, quod sic emit vel acquisivit per magistrum et conventum, est sibi ad vitam recommendatum. Si vero nonnullus frater quidquid emat seu acquirat, illud ipse frater non valeat vendere, nec impignorare, neque alienare, sine magistri et conventus licencia speciali; et si emptio seu acquestus sint franci et liberi, quod frater emptor seu acquisitor illam vel illum nulli domino recognoscere valeat, sine magistri et conventus licencia speciali.

42. 1444, October 1 – *Frater Johannes de Lastico, Grand Master, reproaches the brethren of the house in Utrecht for their renewed inobedience, because they have not asked the approval of the Prior of Germany for the election of their new bailiff, and orders them to have this election approved as yet.*

Registration: AOM 356 = libri bullarum 1444, fol.124r-v. This text has been abbreviated to such an extent, that I am not sure about its contents.

43. 1448, January 23 – *Frater Johannes de Lastico, Grand Master, and Convent order a visitation* in prioratibus nostris Alamanie, Ungarie et Boemie —. Datum etc. 23 Ianuarii anno ab incarnatione 1447.

Registration: AOM 361 = libri bullarum 1447-49, fol.201r-v, dated in Annunciation-style.

44. 1448, February 28 – *Frater Johannes de Lastico, Grand Master, and Convent appoint frater Johan van Wychflit as head of the vacant house Sint Jansdal near Harderwijk, which has been occupied by some inobedient brethren.*

Registration: AOM 361 = libri bullarum 1447-1449, fol.205r, dated in Annunciation-style.

Frater Johannes de Lastico etc. et nos conventus Rhodi domus eiusdem, religioso in Xpo nobis carissimo fratri Johanni de Wychflit dicte domus prioratus nostri Alemanie salutem in Domino sempiternam.

Religionis decor, morum honestas, et alia virtutum vestrarum comendabilia merita, quibus apud nos fidedigno testimonio comprobamini animum nostrum inducunt, ut vobis merito reddamur, ad gratias liberales, sperantes igitur, quod in comisso vobis regimine effectus administrationis utilis favente Domino vos commendet, domum seu baiulliam nostram Vallis Sancti Johannis prope villam de Ardnuk[a] dicti prioratus, nunc a quibusdam, ut nobis relatum est, inobedientibus fratribus, sive personis occupatam et detentam, per

mortem quorumvis dicte domus fratrum eiusdem baiullie legittimo-
rum preceptorum sive hoc, sive alio quovis modo vacantem presentialiter, et ad nostram collationem, ordinationem, donationem et
dispositionem propterea rationabiliter et legittime devolutum, cum
omnibus et singulis suis membris, iuribus et pertinentiis universis ad
eam spectantibus et pertinentibus seu spectare et pertinere debentibus
quoquo modo et cum quibus illam ipsius baiullie quondam legittimi
preceptores, dicte nostre domus fratres, habuerunt, tenuerunt et possiderunt, seu habere, tenere et possidere quomodolibet debuerunt;
habendam, tenendam, regendam, gubernandam, augmentandam et
meliorandam in spiritualibus et temporalibus tam in capite quam in
menbris sub annua responsione sive solutione impositionis et taxe
nuper imposite et ordinate ac etiam imponende et dicto prioratui
incumbentis, prout videlicet vobis pro rata dicte preceptorie tanget et
pertinebit; et aliis oneribus impositis et imponendis etc. Alias secundum continentiam et seriem statuti etc. Puta fratri alicui etc. in aliquo
non obstante, ex nostra certa scientia, et speciali gratia, ad annos
decem continuos et completos, vobis auctoritate presentium conferimus, concedimus et donamus, vosque preceptorem etc., committentes vobis fiducialiter etc. —.

In cuius rei testimonium bulla nostra communis plumbea presentibus est appensa.

Datum Rhodi in nostro conventu die XXII mensis Februarii anno
ab incarnatione Domini nostri MCCCCXLVII, magisterii vero nostri prefati magistri anno XI°.

ª *i.e.* Harderwijk.

---

45. 1448, March 28 – *Frater Johannes de Lastico, Grand Master, and
Convent authorize frater Michael d'Castellario, visitator of Germany etc., to appoint several priors in Low Germany and one 'bailiff by chapter' or Prior in Frisia
'as was the custom there', and to appoint four or five sons of noblemen from these
regions as knights of the Order.*
    Registration: AOM 361 = libri bullarum 1447-1449, *fol.205v.*
*With respect to the question if the Order really was accustomed to have a Prior of
Frisia, it may be remarked that as early as 5 October 1240, the head of the
preceptory of Burgsteinfurt already called himself:* Frater Heinricus de Stein-
vordia, prior hospitalis beati Iohannis per dyocesem Traiectinam, *in
an agreement with the Count of Guelders on the market toll at Arnhem, with this
legend on his seal:* S.H.PRIORIS STEVERDIE [ET F]RISIE;
L.A.J.W.Sloet (ed.), Oorkondenboek der graafschappen Gelre en Zutfen *('s-Gravenhage 1872-1876) nr.621, and H.Brugmans & K.Heeringa (ed.),*

Corpus sigillorum Neerlandicorum, *2 vols ('s-Gravenhage 1937-1940) nr.375.*

Frater Johannes de Lastico Dei gracia etc. et nos conventus Rhodi domus eiusdem, religioso in Xpo nobis precarissimo fratri Michaeli d'Castellario utriusque iuris doctori iudicique appellationis nostre urbis Rhodi ac visitatori nostrorum prioratuum Alamanie, Hungarie et Boemie nuper ordinato, salutem in Domino, et diligentiam in comissis.

Non discedentes in quoquam a mandato generali de dicta visitacione, prioratuum prefatorum vobis dato, nichilominus considerantes esse valde necessarium et expediens particulariter in Alamania Bassa et Frisia rebus nostris nostreque religionis providere, ex nostra certa sciencia ac matura prius deliberatione habita, consentientibus ad hoc religiosis in Xpo nobis carissimis fratribus venerabilis lingue Alamanie in nostro conventu residentibus, tenore presencium vobis comitimus licenciamque atque facultatem damus, ut auctoritate nostra in dicta Alamania Bassa possitis creare unum vel duos vel tres et plures si necessarium erunt, priores, et in Frisia unum baiulivum per capitulum sive priorem, sicut illic in Frisia fuit consuetum; item in illis partibus facere quatuor vel quinque filios nobilium virorum, si erunt ydonei, secundum formam stabilimentorum nostrorum bonorumque morum nostre religionis, fratres milites nostri ordinis, dumtamen dicti priores et baiulivus per capitulum, ac fratres milites per vos eligendi et faciendi promittant et iurent sollemniter quod erunt obedientes nobis et nostre religioni prefate, et solvent annuatim infallibiliter responsiones consuetas et alia onera imposita et imponenda rationabiliter nostro comuni thesauro sicut faciunt alii priores, preceptores et fratres nostre dicte religionis.

In cuius rei testimonium bulla nostra comunis plumbea presentibus est appensa.

Datum Rhodi in nostro conventu die XXVIII mensis Marcii anno ab incarnatione Domini nostri millesimo CCCC XLVIII, magisterii vero nostri magistri anno undecimo.

46. 1449, December ? – *Frater Johannes de Lastico, Grand Master, orders frater Steven van Gruuthusen, head of the preceptory of Arnhem, to appear in the Convent at Rhodos to account for his inobedience towards frater Johann Loesel, Prior of Germany.*

Registration: AOM 361 = libri bullarum 1447-1449, *fol.213v.*

Frater Johannes de Lastico *[gives order to]* — fratri Stephano de Gruthusen domus sive baiulie in Arnhem arrendatori vel possessori — *[to appear in Rhodos personally:]* — quantum temporibus retroactis te ipsum ab omni vera obedientia et humilitati atque mandatorum venerabilis in Xpo nobis precarissimi fratris Johannis Loesel prioratus nostri Alamanie prioris et ceterorum ordinis nostri officialium retracxeris et alienum prestiteris in grave anime tuum detrimentum etc.

47. 1449, December 29 – *Frater Johannes de Lastico, Grand Master, and Convent appoint frater Hendrik Oesterzel, chaplain, as head of the preceptory of Kattendijke, vacant because of its usurpation by the lord of Kattendijke, with an annual contribution of 50,000 florins.*

   Registration: AOM 361 = libri bullarum 1447-1449, *fol.214v.*

Frater Johannes de Lastico etc. et nos conventus Rhodi domus eiusdem religioso in Xpo nobis carissimo fratri Henrico Oesterzel dicte domus cappellano prioratus nostri Alamanie salutem in domino sempiternam.

   Inter alia que a nostris maioribus probatissimis religiosis pro conservacione domorum, iurium et bonorum dicte sacre domus salubriter stabilita noscuntur, illud maxima diligenter statuerunt ne domus, preceptorie, res et bona in fidei christiane tutelam et pauperum custodiam dedicata in aliorum manibus et potestate quam illorum qui nostram religionem professi sunt per ignariam et desideriam diucius consistere pro viribus permittamus; quinymo ad illarum et illorum reparacionem utilem et directam, omne studium, curam et diligenciam adhibere per veram compellimur obedienciam, ut ex nostrorum stabilimentorum lege diffusius noscitur apparere. Cum igitur ad nostram sepe sepius noticiam fidedignorum domus nostre fratrum relacione pervenerit, domum sive baiulliam nostram de Cattendick prioratus nostri Alamanie, noscitur quibus tamen id acciderit modis, causis, vel rationibus, ad manus et potestatem magnifici et honorabilis in Xpo nobis amantissimi domini eiusdem loci de Cattendick a pluribus citra temporibus pervenisse, et ab ipso domino in eandem preceptoriam rectores, gubernatores et alterius ordinis religiosos in grave detrimentum iurium, dignitatum et auctoritatum nostre, pro sue voluntatis arbitrio pro tempore collocari, ideo nos imitari volentes quantum cum Deo possumus predecessorum nostrorum laudanda vestigia et parere tamquam veri obedientes his que a nostris stabilimentis iniuncta existunt intendentes, de laudabili probitate ac religionis vestre laudanda observacione et sperantes vos pro optima futura operacione domum ipsam et sua membra ac iura in spiritualibus et temporalibus recuperari, bene dirigi et utilius gubernari, ideo eandem

preceptoriam sive domum nostram de Cattendick quovismodo religionis nostre fratre seu per obitum aut privacionem vel deposicionem
ultimi illius immediate preteriti preceptoris sive alio quovismodo vacantem ad nostram collacionem et provisionem legittime devolutam
ac pertinentem et expectantem, cum omnibus et singulis suis membris, iuribus et pertinentiis universis ad eandem spectantibus et pertinentibus ac spectare et pertinere debentibus quoquomodo et quibus
eandem preteriti eiusdem preceptores legittimi habuerunt, tenuerunt
et possiderunt, sive habere, tenere et possidere quomodolibet debuerunt, habendam, tenendam, regendam, gubernandam, augmentandam et meliorandam in spiritualibus et temporalibus tam in capite
quam in membris sub annua responsione etc. de summa florenorum
quinquaginta millium nuper in nostro proximi generali celebrato capitulo usque ad aliud proximum futurum generale capitulum imposita et aliis omnibus etc. Alias secundum seriem et continenciam statuti
etc. et qui illius etc. invicem deliberato consilio etc. ad annos decem
continuos et completos vobis auctoritate presentium conferimus, concedimus et donamus benefaciendo in eadem, vosque preceptorem et
comendatorem etc. comittentes etc. Quocirca ac hominibus et vassallis etc. precipimus et mandamus ut vobis tamquam eorum superiori
etc. vobisque suum prebeant etc. necnon universis et singulis fratribus
domus nostre quacumque dignitate etc. ne contra presentem nostram
collacionem etc. quinymo eam studeant etc. ac priori etc. amoto
abinde etc. inhibentes etc. ne pretextu etc. et si quod absit etc. illud et
illa etc.

In cuius rei testimonium bulla nostra comunis plumbea presentibus est apponoa.

Datum Rhodi in nostro conventu die vicesimonono mensis Decembris ab incarnato Xpo Ihesu domino Deo nostro anno millesimo
CCCC quadragesimonono.

48. 1449, December 31 − *Frater* Aymundus de Emechoten *of Vallterre,*
[Rutgerus] de Juoede *of Mechelen,* Johannes de Wifflett *of* Vallis sancti
Johannis *and some anonymous brethren are ordered to place frater* Henricus
Oesterzel *in the peaceful possession of* Cattendick.
Chancery note: AOM 361 = libri bullarum 1447-1449, *fol.215r.*

49. 1450, May 7 − *Frater* Henricus Oesterzel *is licensed to leave Rhodos*
for his preceptory of Cattendick.
Chancery note: AOM 362 = libri bullarum 1450-1451, *fol.112r.*

50. 1450, May 8 – *Frater Johannes de Lastico, Grand Master, and Convent appoint frater* Theodericus de Ullfft *as head of the preceptory of Lage.*

    Registration: AOM 362 = libri bullarum 1450-1451, *fol.112r. In 1482 the preceptory of Walsum appears to be vacant by the death of brother* Theodericus de Uuolfft, *AOM 388,* libri bullarum 1481-1482, *fol.126v. This man must not be mistaken for the head of the preceptory of Arnhem Dirk Wolf, appointed in 1467; below, nr.72.*

51. 1450, June 12 – *Frater Johannes de Lastico, Grand Master, and Convent give frater Hendrik Oesterzel the right of* stagia, *i.e. of residence, in the house of Middelburg until the time that he can take possession of his preceptory at Kattendijke.*

    Registration: AOM 362 = libri bullarum 1450-1451, *fol.113v.*

Frater Johannes de Lastico etc. religioso in Xpo nobis carissimo fratri Henrico Oesterzel domus sive baiullie nostre de Cattendick prioratus nostri Alamanie preceptori salutem in Domino sempiternam.

    Odor ac laudabilis religiose vestre vite cum aliorum comendabilium suffragancia meritorum usque ad nos fide dignorum relacione perductus vobis ad graciam liberales nos inducens, ab illa die qua in partibus et loco infra scripte domus sive preceptorie nostre applicueritis donec et quousque pacificam possessionem supradicte domus de Cattendick per vos vel procuratores vestros fueritis assecutus, in domum sive preceptoriam nostram de Middelburg dicti prioratus auctoritate presentium de nostra certa sciencia et speciali gratia stagiam assignamus, mandantes sub virtute sancte obedientie firmiter et districte religioso in Xpo nobis carissimo fratri domus eiusdem de Middelburg preceptori moderno aut successoribus suis vel cuivus quovis alio titulo premisse preceptorie nostre nunc vel in posterum regimini presidenti, ut vos ad dictam preceptoriam venientem moraturum pro stagia usque ad tempus prefixum ad stagiam ipsam benigne admittant et caritative pertractent, vobisque dicto durante tempore in ipsa preceptoria in vestris necessariis provideant secundum bonos usus et laudabiles consuetudines dicte nostre domus. Quocirca universis et singulis domus nostre fratribus presentibus et futuris cuiuscumque status, gradus, vel condicionis existant sub virtute sancte obedientie predicta districte precipimus et mandamus ne contra predictam nostram stagie assignacionem aliqualiter dicto vel facto publice vel occulte per se vel interpositas personas facere vel venire presumant, quinymo illam studeant efficaciter et inviolabiliter observare.

    In quorum testimonium bulla nostra magistralis in cera nigra presentibus est impressa.

Datum Rhodi in nostro conventu XII mensis Iunii ab incarnato salvatore Xpo Ihesu domino Deo nostro anno M° CCCC° quinquagesimo.

52. 1450, June 12 – *Frater Johannes de Lastico, Grand Master, orders all brethren of the Order to support frater Hendrik Oesterzel in recovering his usurped preceptory of Kattendijke.*
Registration: AOM 362 = libri bullarum 1450-1451, *fol.113v-114r.*

Frater Johannes etc. —
Tenore presencium notum facimus qualiter domus sive baiullia nostra de Cattendick prioratus nostri Alamanie diucius contra et preter voluntatem nostram et in grave dampnum et preiudicium nostre religionis per nonnullas seculares et alias extra ordinem nostrum personas violenter et indebite occupata periter et detenta, per nos — collata fuit — fratri Henrico Oesterzel, *[and orders all brethren of the Order to support him with help and counsel if he should need these for the recovery of his preceptory.]*

53. 1451, September 1 – *Frater Johannes de Lastico, Grand Master and Convent confirm the Latin translation dd. 7 May 1450 of a German charter dd. 9 February 1449 by* Frater Johannes Lösel prior partium Alamanie generalis, *together with* fratres – Johannes de Swalbach balivus et commendator Coloniensis, – Berchtoldus Stechelly in Friburgo Brisgaudie, – Philippus de Riffenberg in Rüdikheim – commendatores.
Registration: AOM 363 = libri bullarum 1451-1452, *fol.149r-151r.*

54. 1453, October 12 – *Frater Johannes de Lastico, Grand Master, confirms the allocation of the preceptory of Sint Jansdal to frater Johan van Withflit and orders frater Steven van Gruuthusen, head of the preceptory of Arnhem, to place him in the physical possession of his preceptory.*
Registration: AOM 364 = libri bullarum 1453-1454, *fol.106v-107r.*

Frater Johannes etc. — fratri Stefano de Gruthusen, domus nostre de Arnam prioratus nostri Alamanie preceptori —.
Serie presencium vobis et cuilibet vestrum duximus fore notificandum, quod alias et nunc de novo contulimus et confirmavimus per nostras bullas secundum morem nostri conventus religioso in Xpo nobis carissimo fratri Johanni de Withflit dicti nostri prioratus preceptoriam nostram Vallis sancti Johannis prefati prioratus, sicut in

bullis nostris super huiusmodi collationibus confectis late comprehenditur. — *[Now orders are given to place him in the possession of his preceptory].*

55. 1453, November 18 – *Frater Johannes de Lastico orders frater Engelbert van Foreest, head of the preceptory of Utrecht, and the other brethren of his house, to place frater Johan van Withflit in the possession of his preceptory of Sint Jansdal within a fortnight. Should they pretend to have some rights to this preceptory, then they are asked to appear at the Convent at Rhodos within nine months, so that justice be done to them.*
Registration: AOM 364 = libri bullarum 1453-1454, *fol.107r.*

Frater Johannes de Lastico etc. religioso in Xpo nobis carissimo fratri Engbert de Forese preceptori de Utrach et quibuscumque aliis dicte domus nostre fratribus, tam militibus quam secularibus et capellanis, nobis et nostre religioni subditis, occupatori vel occupatoribus ac detentori sive detentoribus domus sive preceptorie nostre Vallis sancti Johannis prioratus nostri Alamanie, salutem in Domino et nostris firmiter obedire mandatis.

Tenore presentium vobis et cuilibet vestrum duximus fore notificandum quod iamdudum et nunc de novo contulimus et confirmavimus religioso in Xpo nobis carissimo fratri Johanni de Withflit dicti nostri prioratus tamquam idoneo et benemerenti dictam nostram preceptoriam Vallis sancti Johannis sicut bullis nostris super huiusmodi collatione confectis latissime apparet; a quo nobis querulenter expositum fuit per vos dictam nostram preceptoriam indebite et iniuste et in sui maximum damnum et interesse, occupari et detineri, quod nobis molestissimum fuit, quare nobis humiliter supplicavit ut super hoc de remedio opportuno providere dignaremur.

Nos itaque volentes sicut iuris est dicto fratri Johanni de Withflit in collatione nostra eidem facta favere ut laborum suorum premia consequatur, harum serie ex nostra certa scientia vos supradictum et unumquemque vestrum monemus, et si opus est vobis et cuilibet vestrum in virtute sancte obediencie et damnate rebellionis[a] pena precipimus et mandamus quatenus dicto legittimo preceptori sive eius procuratori in termino quindicim dierum, computandorum a die presentationis presentium facte, consignetis effectualiter dictam nostram preceptoriam liberam et expeditam, omni exceptione et contradictione remota. Si vero quod non credimus hec nostra mandata iusta et sancta non adimpleveritis, pretendentes in ea fortasse aliquod ius habere, sub eadem virtute sancte obedientie vobis precipimus et expresse mandamus quatenus in termino novem mensium computandorum a die presentationis harum vobis facte, quorum tres pro primo, tres pro secundo et tres pro tercio et ultimo peremptorio termino et canonica monitione assignant, personaliter sive per procuratorem sufficienter[b] instructum in hoc nostro Rhodi conventu compareatis, dicturus et alegiturus iura vestra si qua in dicta nostra preceptoria habere pretenditis, quia vos audiemus et vobis et parti vestre adverse administrabimus iusticie nostri ordinis complementum. Transacto vero dicto termino et vobis neque personaliter neque per procuratorem comparente, contra vos tamquam contra inobedientem et rebellem sive inobedientes et rebelles procedemus procedique faciemus secundum formam stabilimentorum nostrorum bonorumque morum et consuetudinum dicte nostre religionis. Taliter ergo in premissis vos inhibeatis ut de vera valeatis apud nos obedientia commendari.

In cuius rei testimonium bulla nostra magistralis[c] in cera nigra presentibus est impressa.

Datum Rhodi in nostro conventu die **XVIII** mensis Novembris anno ab incarnato Xpo Jesu domino nostro MCCCCLIII.

---

[a] rebelionis *ms.* [b] suffitienter *ms.* [c] magistrali *ms.*

56. 1454, December 10 – *Frater Jacques de Milly, Grand Master, successor of frater Johannes de Lastico, gives notice to frater Engelbert van Foreest, bailiff of Utrecht, that the Prior of Germany has been ordered by the chapter general to hold a provincial chapter. Therefore, the Grand Master orders Engelbert to appear personally at this chapter together with two fully empowered heads of houses in his bailiwick as soon as the Prior summons him.*

Registration: AOM 365 = libri bullarum 1454-1455, *fol.197r-v.*

Frater Jacobus de Milli etc. — fratri Engelberto de Forest domus seu baiullie nostre Traiectensis prioratus nostri Almanie baiullio sive preceptori —.

— quatenus ad omnem instanciam, inquisicionem et vocacionem *[fol.197v]* dicti venerabilis prioris in capitulo sive capitulis provincialibus per eum tenendis sive convocandis in prefato nostro prioratu personaliter cum duobus eiusdem baiullie preceptoribus qui habent potestatem plenissimam ab omnibus preceptoribus prefate baiullie ipsis comissam comparendi, concludendi et firmandi omnia que in hoc capitulo sive capitulis provincialibus agenda erunt et ferant secundum verum valorem preceptoriorum dicte baiullie sumptum et habitum medio et solempni iuramento ab omnibus preceptoribus ipsius baiullie vobis personaliter prefato, ita ut unicuique equalitas ponderis et oneris ac taxacionis fieri queat secundum ordinaciones capitulorum generalium antedictorum, omnibus exceptione, contradictione et impedimento summis abscantibus, taliter [er]go in premissis vos exhibeatis ut de vera valeatis apud nos obediencia merita commendari.

In cuius rei testimonium bulla nostra magistralis in cera nigra presentibus est impressa.

Datum Rhodi in nostro conventu durante nostro capitulo generali die X mensis Decembris anno ab incarnato Xpo Ihesu domino nostro M° CCCC LIIII°.

57. 1454, December 22 – *Frater Jacques de Milly, Grand Master, orders frater Rutger de Juede, head of the preceptory of Mechelen, to remove the unworthy curate of Wahlwiller, frater Herman Holt, from the parish church under the collation of his preceptory in order to send him back to his convent.*
Registration: AOM 365 = libri bullarum 1454-1455, *fol.198r.*

Frater Jacobus de Milly etc. religioso in Xpo nobis carissimo fratri Rogerio Joede domus seu baiullie nostre de Mechelen prioratus nostri Almanie preceptori salutem in Domino et nostris firmiter obedire mandatis.

Ad aures nostras pervenit vos quendam religiosum nostri ordinis nominatum fratrem Hermannum Holt fecisse pastorem sive curatum in quadam parochia sive ecclesia nominata Willre dominationis dicte nostre preceptorie, quiquidem frater ut audimus est scandalosus rixas movens et inhoneste vivens in obprobrium nostre religionis et dicte ecclesie et eciam vestri preceptoris.

Quocircha ex nostra certa sciencia volentes providere honestati nostrorum religiosorum vobis committimus et si opus est in virtute sancte obediencie precipiendo mandamus quatenus sine aliqua dilacione dictum fratrem Hermannum removeatis a cura sive parochia et regimine dicte ecclesie, et sibi iubeatis et eum cogatis ad redeundum et revertendum ad suum conventum sive stagiam ubi primitus morabatur; et casu quo dictus frater Hermannus nollet exire dictam ecclesiam et obedire mandatis vestris, vobis auctoritatem et facultatem damus eum capiendi, detinendi, incarcerandi et puniendi tamquam inobedientem et rebellem secundum formam stabilimentorum nostrorum bonorumque morum et consuetudinum nostre religionis. Taliter ergo in premissis vos exhibeatis ut de vera valeatis aput nos obediencia comendari.

In cuius rei testimonium bulla nostra magistralis in cera nigra presentibus est impressa.

Datum Rhodi in nostro conventu die XXII Decembris anno MCCCCLIIII.

ªNon obstante quacumque investitura sive confirmatione facta a quocumque ordinario dicto fratri Hermano.ª

ª *in smaller writing.*

58. 1458, August 1 – *Frater Bernard Schedelich, bailiff of Westphalia, is ordered to place frater Anton Racht in the peaceful possession of the preceptory of Wesel.*
Chancery note: AOM 367 = libri bullarum 1457-1458, *fol.230v.*
Die prima mensis Augusti M IIIIC LVIII fuit data commissio fratri Bernardo Schedelich domus seu baiullie de Westphalie prioratus nostri Alamanie preceptori et cuicumque fratri super hoc primitus requisito ut ponat in possessionem pacifficam fratrem Anthonium Racht preceptorie Wesalie etc. in forma cancellarie consueta.

59. 1458, November 12 – *Frater Jacques de Milly, Grand Master, and Convent give full powers to* fratri Bernardo Schedelich Westphalie baiullivo ac preceptorie nostre in Steinfort prioratus nostri Alamanie preceptori, *to convoke frater* Theodericus de Ulfft, *head of the preceptory of Lage, before the regional congregation to account for the reception of large sums of money in the past, which have not been accounted for.*
Registration: AOM 367 = libri bullarum 1457-1458, *fol.234v.*

60. 1460, October 10 – *Frater Jacques de Milly, Grand Master, and Convent appoint frater* Johannes de Wifflicht *as head of the preceptory of Velden.*
Registration: AOM 370 = libri bullarum 1460, *fol.137v.*

61. 1460, November 2 – *The vice-chancellor registers the formal abdication by frater Johan van Withflit, head of the preceptory of Velden, of the preceptory of Sint Jansdal.*
Chancery notice: AOM 370 = libri bullarum 1460, *fol.139r.*

Registrata in presenti registro ad futuram rei memoriam de mandata reverendissimi domini magistri instantibus infrascriptis qui super hiis licenciam et congiectum impartitus est pro firmiori cautela infrascriptorum.
Die secunda mensis Novembris anni ab incarnacione millesimi CCCC LX constitutus in cancellaria sacri conventus Rhodi persona-

liter in presencia mei vicecancellarii et testium infrascriptorum dominus frater Johannes de Wifflicht preceptor de Velden prioratus Alamanie de sua pura et spontanea voluntate de licencia et congiecto ipsius Reverendissimi domini magistri sibi gratis datis et concessis iuravit ponendo manum dexteram super crucem sui habitus more solito religiosorum ordinis Iherosolymitani atque promisit bona fide dare suas probaciones bonas et auctenticas et presentare se personaliter seu per procuratorem legittimum coram capitulo provinciali sive assemblea dicti prioratus quibus commissum est per ipsum reverendissimum dominum magistrum et conventum, ut videre habeant dictas probaciones super facto dampnorum affectorum illatorum preceptorie Vallis sancti Johannis, sicut ample apparet in bullis commissionis super hoc confectis, infra terminum duorum annorum completorum a die predicta in antea computandorum. Insuper promisit solvere seu solvi facere in termino predicto taxam quam debet lingue Alamanie racione preceptorie predicte sibi cabimento date et concesse sub obligacione omnium bonorum suorum ac dicte preceptorie. Et casu quo idem frater Johannes in predictis deficet aut in aliquo eorundem, fuit et est contentus quod eo ipso et incontinenti absque alia citacione et monicione privetur dicta preceptoria et quod contra eum procedatur tamquam contra inobedientem et rebellem secundum formam stabilimentorum nostrorum dicte religionis, renuncians omnibus et singulis stabilimentis, consuetudinibus, et usibus dicti ordinis que pro eo in hac causa faceri possent quovismodo.

Presentibus reverendo domino fratre Petro Raffini magno preceptore dicti conventus Rhodi et fratre Raymundo de Solier ac Bertrando de Boussignach.

62. 1460, December 10 – *Frater* Rodericus Jude preceptor in Mechel *is ordered to place frater* Johannes de Wifflicht *in the peaceful possession of the preceptory of Velden.*
Chancery note: AOM 370 = libri bullarum 1460, fol.139r.

63. 1460, December 11 – *Frater* Johannes de Wifflicht *is licensed to leave Rhodos for his preceptory of Velden.*
Chancery note: AOM 370 = libri bullarum 1460, fol.139r.

64. 1461, July 6 – *Grand Master and Convent grant the preceptory of Mechelen, vacant by the death of frater* Rutgerius Jude, *to frater* Hermannus Schult, *head of the preceptory of* Columbaria *(Colmar).*
Registration: AOM 371 = libri bullarum 1461, fol.134v.

65. 1462, May 29 – *Frater Pietro Raffini, Grand Commander, acting as Grand Master during the vacancy of the Grand Master's seat, and Convent bestow the preceptories of Nimwegen and Arnhem, vacant after the death of their last head frater Johann von Swalbach, on frater Bertold Stehelin, with an annual contribution of 51,000 florins a year.*

Registration: AOM 372 = libri bullarum 1462, fol.132v. The chancery was not quite up to date in this case, because it was not frater Johann von Swalbach, but frater Steven van Gruuthusen, who was the last head of the preceptory of Arnhem, e.g. 1453, October 12; see above, nr.54.

Frater Petrus Raffini etc. et nos etc. religioso in Xpo nobis carissimo fratri Betholdo Stehelin dicte domus et prioratus nostri Alamanie etc. salutem in Domino etc.

Religionis decor etc. Baiullias seu preceptorias nostras de Numegen et Arnheim dicti nostri prioratus per obitum quondam religiosi venerandi in Xpo nobis precarissimi fratris Johannis de Swalbach earumdem preceptoriarum ultimi legittimi preceptoris et possessoris ac nostri conventus Rhodi magni baiullivi, sive hoc sive alio quovismodo vacantes presencialiter et ad nostram etc. cum omnibus et singulis earundem membris, iuribus etc. et cum quibus illas dictus quondam venerandus frater Johannes habuit etc. sive prefati dicte domus fratres earundem preceptoriarum habuerunt etc. sub annua responsione prout pro rata dictis preceptoriis pertinebit de summa florenorum quinquaginta unius millium etc. imposita et aliis omnibus etc. Alias etc.

Datum die XXIX Maii M IIII^C LXII.

66. 1462, July 6 – *Frater Pedro Raymundo Zacosta, Grand Master, and Convent grant the preceptories of Nimwegen and Arnhem, vacant through resignation of their last head frater Bertold Stehelin, to frater Philips von Reiffenberg.*

Registration: AOM 372 = libri bullarum 1462, fol.134r-v.

Frater Petrus Raymundus Zacosta etc. et nos etc. religioso in Xpo nobis carissimo fratri Philippo de Riffenberg dicte domus et prioratus nostri Alamanie etc. salutem etc.

Religionis decor etc. Baiullias seu preceptorias nostras Numegen et Arnheim dicti nostri prioratus per puram simplicem et spontaneam resignacionem sive renunciacionem de eisdem factam in manibus nostri prelibati magistri a religioso in Xpo nobis carissimo fratre Betholdo Stehelin earumdem preceptoriarum ultimo legittimo preceptore sive hoc sive alio quovismodo vacantes presencialiter et ad nostram collacionem etc. cum omnibus et singulis earum membris etc. et cum quibus illas dictus frater Betholdus etc. sive hoc sive alio quovismodo

etc. habendas, tenendas, regendas etc. sub annua responsione et ceteris quibusvis omnibus impositis et in futuris quolibet imponendis racionabiliter secundum communem cursum etc. Alias etc. puta etc.
invicem deliberato consilio de nostra certa sciencia et speciali gratia
ad annos decem continuos et completos pro vestro cabimento vobis
auctoritate presencium confecimus, concedimus et donamus benefaciendo in eisdem vosque preceptorem in dictis baiulliis constituimus
etc. committentes etc. Quocirca etc. necnon etc. ac priori etc. amota
etc. inhibentes etc.

In cuius etc. bulla communis plumbea etc.

Datum die VI Iullii M IIII^c LXII.

67. 1462, July 6 – *The lieutenant of the Grand Bailiff and proxies of the Prior
of Germany state the principle of certain advowsons, held by this Prior, notwithstanding his abdication of them in a given case.*
   Chancery notice: AOM 372 = libri bullarum 1462, *fol.138r.*

Cum die VI Iullii M IIII^c LXII facta esset provisio de preceptoriis
Numegen, Arnheim, Franckfordia Prioratus Alamanie per vene-
randam linguam Alamanie pro resignacione iuris collacionum reverendi prioris dicti prioratus, dominus frater Betz de Hechtenberg
locumtenens reverendi magni baiullivi et ceteri procuratores ipsius
domini prioris protestati sunt, quod si pro futuro compertum fuerit
quod aliqua dictarum preceptoriarum pertinet collacioni ipsius domini prioris, quod non obstante provisione facta de eisdem possit facere
suam collacionem.
   Registrata ad futuram memoriam anno, die et mense quibus supra.

68. 1462, November 4 – *Frater Raymundo Ricardi, Prior of Saint Gilles and
lieutenant of Grand Master frater Pedro Raymundo Zacosta, declares that the
acquired possessions of the Order must be preserved and orders to see to it that they
remain beneficial to the Order in the future, especially referring to the properties in
High and Low Germany.*
   Registration: AOM 372 = libri bullarum 1462, *fol.140v.*

— Cum igitur sicuti plurimorum relatibus accepimus in provinciis
Alamanie tam alte quam inferioris nonnulli dicte domus baiulliatus,
preceptorie, loca, domus, membra et iurisdictiones existant ut pote
baiulliatus Westphalie, preceptoria de Steinforden, baiulliatus Stirie,
prioratus sive baiulliatus Dacie, baiulliatus Frisie ac preceptorie, loca,

domus, membra et iurisdictiones eorundem, que malignitate et contemptu possidencium, votorum per eos emissorum inmemorum, parum utilitatis ordini nostro reddunt in dedecus ac vilipendium ordinis ipsius et damnum nostri communis thesauri qui de proventibus et emolumentis beneficiorum et locorum religionis nostre subventionem suscipere solet, ideo volentes —.

Datum Rhodi — die IIII novembris M IIII^C LXII.

69. 1465, June 20 – *Frater Pedro Raymundo Zacosta, Grand Master, confirms the gift of 10,000 new gold French shields from Philip Duke of Burgundy through his treasurer Jacques de Brigiles for the building of a tower on Rhodos on the location of the former church of St Nicolas, which will serve as the most important defensive stronghold for the harbour and the town of Rhodos. He declares he will have this tower erected within two years, its bulwark decorated with a marble sculpture signifying the coat of arms of the duke and the upper parts with those of his provinces.*

Registration: AOM 375 = libri bullarum 1465, *fol.160r.*

— faciemusque corpori dicte turris valloque eius sive bolenerdo vulgariter nuncupato affigere plena atque inclita arma ipsius clarissimi principis lapide marmoreo sculpta excellencius quam fieri poterit; in munimentis autem superioribus ipsius turris sive in machicollis vulgariter nuncupatis afficta erunt arma suarum provinciarum pariformiter lapide marmoreo incisa in monimentam dignam et celebrem memoriam ipsius inclitissimi principis benefactoris quidem optimi et specialissimi huiusce ordinis. —.

Datum in conventu Rhodi die XX mensis Iunii M IIII^C LXV.

70. 1466, July 23 – *The registration office issues a statement in favour of frater Philips von Reiffenberg concerning his disputed abdication of his preceptories Nimwegen and Arnhem.*

Chancery notice: AOM 375 = libri bullarum 1465-1466, *fol.93v. Sguardio* = *register.*

Die XXIII Iullii M IIII^C LXVI per dominum fratrem Bernardum Myron preceptorem de Sousterres caput sguardii ac nonnullos fratres dicti sguardii fuit relatum quod per eum sguardium fratrum datum super differentia vertente inter dominos fratres Echardum de Heringen et Fridericum zum Stein nomine lingue Alamanie agentes ex una ac Philippum de Riffenberg inite nunc se defendentem partibus ex altera, racione et causa resignacionis preceptorie de Numegen et Arn-

heim, asserentes predicti quod idem frater Philippus non poterat re-
signare preceptoriam de Numegen et Arnheim quia non fecerat suam
diligenciam in persecucione habende possessionis dicte preceptorie, et
idem frater Philippus ostendit probaciones et instrumenta auctentica
secundum formam stabilimentorum qualiter fecit suam diligenciam.

Itaque auditis dictis partibus et eorum racionibus visisque proba-
cionibus auctenticis et productis fuit iudicatum et firmatum quod
idem frater Philippus probavit autentica qualiter fecit suam diligenciam debitam in prosecucione dicte possessionis preceptorie prefate
de Numegen etc.

71. 1466, [circa December 22] – Fr. Erhardo de Heringen procura-
dor de la laingue d'Almaigne del vestro conventu de Rhodo *issues a
petition concerning:*
1. the bailiwick of Brandenburg,
2. the Priorate of Hungary,
*3. the preceptory of Haarlem, a member of the prioral chamber Utrecht, which is
nonetheless maintained by frater Pieter van Schoten to the disadvantage of the Prior
of Germany, who cannot ask for an alternative member or prioral chamber.*

Chancery notice: AOM 376 = libri bullarum 1466, *fol.132r-v. Cf. below,
nr.76.*

[fol.132v] Ulterimo expone el dicto supplicante che non obstante che
la vostra Reverenda Signorìa et el vostro sacro capittolo habia data
audituri supra certa controversia e infra lo conmendatore de Trayec-
to et frar Petro de Schotten el qual tien la commanda de Harlem per
forza, la quale e membro de Traiecto che e camera del prior de
Lamaigna, contra ogni rason et iusticia, pro tanto el dicto supplicante
se presente davanti la vostra Reverenda Signorìa e non obstante che
devanti li prefati audituri habia protestato con licencia de vostra Reverenda Signorìa iterum et de novo protesta et fa sua protestacion
davanti vostro general capitulo, qualche non obstante dicta commissione che ava abuti li prefati seignori audituri che tute sentencie inter-
locutorie over diffinitive sianno dati per li supraditti audituri deputati
in preiudicio de la laingue dAlmaigne, non posse demandar aultre
membre en loco del supradicto membro de Harlem overa aultra
camera priorale si non tenire a questa de Uctrecht et presertim que lo
prior deldicto priorat era present etc.

72. 1467, June 12 – *The lieutenant of frater Giovanni-Baptista de Orsinis, Grand Master, and Convent grant the preceptory of Arnhem and Nimwegen to frater Dirk Wolf.*
Registration: AOM 377 = libri bullarum 1467-1468, *fol.132r.*

Frater Jacobus de Lialtrin, locumtenens — religioso in Xpo nobis carissimo fratri Theodorico Wolleff decretorum licenciato dicte domus et prioratus nostri Almanie capelano —.
— preceptoriam sive baiulliam nostram de Arnhem et Numaghem dicti nostri prioratus —, *[vacant through resignation by]* fratre Philipo de Riffenberch *[and the death of]* fratris Johannis Swalbach, — pro vestro cabimento —.
Datum Rodi in nostro conventu die XII Iunii M IIII^C LXVII.

73. 1467, June 19 – *Frater* Theodericus Wolef *is licensed to leave for his preceptory* de Arnahem et Numaghem.
Chancery note: AOM 377 = libri bullarum 1467-1468, *fol.133r.*

74. 1467, June 19 – *Order is given to place frater Dirk Wolf in the possession of his preceptory.*
Chancery note: AOM 377 = libri bullarum 1467-1468, *fol.133v.*
Die XIX Iunii M IIII^C LXVII fuit directa executoria fratribus Engilleberto de Forest preceptori Trayectensi et Herrico de Barsdonch capelano prioratus Almanie, ut ponant in possessionem dicte preceptorie eundem fratrem Theodoricum, quam ipse habuit pro suo cabimento etc. in forma consueta.

75. 1469, July 28 – *Frater Giovanni-Baptista de Orsinis, Grand Master, and Convent grant some houses in Frisia to frater Peter Madur.*
Registration: AOM 378 = libri bullarum 1469, *fol.139v-140r. Names of predecessors are not mentioned, nor is any mention made of the existence of a vacancy 'per cessum vel decessum'. Frater Peter Madur is probably a knight of the Order, since he is not alluded to by the title of chaplain.*

Frater Baptista de Ursinis etc. — fratri Petro Madur dicte domus et prioratus Alamanie —.
— preceptorias itaque nostras Wermer, Snick et quascumque alias baiullias quorum nomina volumus hic haberi pro sufficienter expressis, sitas et positas in provincia et dicione Frisie nostre religioni spectantes et ad nostram collacionem, donacionem, ordinacionem et

disposicionem pertinentes *[fol.140r]* cum omnibus et singulis earum et cuiuslibet ipsarum domibus, locis, iurisdictionibus, membris, claustris fratrum et sororum, pertinenciis, fructibus et redditibus universis — in dicta patria Frisia — spectantibus et pertinentibus —, *[in the same way their legitimate heads have possessed them before]*.

Datum Rhodi die XXVIII Iullii M IIII^c LXVIIII.

76. 1469, October 19 – *Frater Giovanni-Baptista de Orsinis, Grand Master, authorizes the fratres Jean de Chalby and Jacques Calliot to do justice in the case of frater Johann von Ono [?], Prior of Germany, versus frater Engelbert van Foreest, Bailiff of Utrecht, who refuses to pay his full duties to the treasury and has not yet appeared at the Convent, in person or by proxies, to defend his case.*

Notarial copy: AOM 46 = Miscellanea. *In this volume a parchment with a notarial copy of two letters of the Grand Master is included, the second of which is referred to here.*

In AOM 375 = libri bullarum 1465-1466, *fol.160r, anno 1465, mention is made of* fratris Johannis de Chally preceptoriarum nostrarum de Fieffes, Beaunoyr, Auxoirre etc. preceptoris nostri procuratoris et consiliarii.

In AOM 378 = libri bullarum 1469, *fol.144r-145v, 1469, October 5, a bull of Grand Master and Convent has been registered in which the preceptory of Haarlem, hitherto a member of the prioral chamber of Utrecht, becomes an independent prioral chamber for which the bailiwick Utrecht no longer has to pay (cf.the difficulties in 1466, nr.71 above). The full text of this bull is to be found in AOM 45, Visitation of Germany, fol.220v-222r, where the Prior is named* Johannis de Ors. *The original bull in Stadsarchief Haarlem,* Inventaris Enschede, I *nr.1789, has* Johannis de Orv *or* Ow. *For the full text of the Visitation of Germany of 1495, see Part C.2 in this edition.*

Frater Baptista de Orsinis Dei gratia sacre domus hospitalis sancti Johannis Hierosolimitani magister humilis et pauperum Ihesu Christi custos et nos conventus Rhodi domus eiusdem, religiosis in Christo nobis precarissimis fratribus Johanni de Chalby preceptoriarum nostrarum de Fieffes etc. et Jacobo Calliot Brabantie prioratus nostri Francie preceptoribus salutem in Domino et diligentiam in commissis.

Coram nobis nostroque venerando consilio tam pro parte nostri communis thesauri quam etiam venerandi religiosi in Christo nobis precarissimi fratris Johannis de Ono^a prioratus nostri Alamanie prioris querolose fuit expositum, qualiter religiosus in Christo nobis carissimus frater Engelbertus de Forest preceptor Traiactensis camere

prioralis dicti prioratus Alamanie dare tenetur et obligatus est nonnullas summas et quantitates pecuniarum eidem nostro communi thesauro prout legittimi procuratores ipsius thesauri vel qui eius nomine
agere intendunt probare. Etiam quod idem venerabilis prior frater
Johannes de Ono[a] pretendit sano iure nonnulle debere habere ab
eodem fratre Engelberto et contra eum agere in nonnullis suis causis,
de quibus hactenus de eodem fratre Engelberto satisfactio non est
habita ymo semper facere debitum renuit et neglexit in non mediocre
dedecus et incommodum religionis nostre et dicti communis thesauri
pariter et ipsius venerandi prioris. Quorum nominibus super hiis de
oportuno iustitie remedio provideri instantissime nobis extitit postula-
tum et eos autem qui indemnitati ipsius nostri ordinis et fratrum
nostrorum consulere peroptamus cupimusque neminem in suo iure
ledere. Idcirco iussimus in primis secundum consuetudinem nostri
conventus Rhodi vocari et citari procuratores ipsius fratris Engelberti
si qui hic essent quo responderent pro suo principali, nomine cuius
nullus hactenus comparuit. Eapropter considerantes viarum distan-
ciam et nonnullis personarum atque parcium qualitatibus pensatis
serie presentium invicem maturo et deliberato consilio vobis et utrique vestrum casu quo alteri legittime —[b] causa hinc nostre commissarii [dare] —[b] posset alioquin ambo simul hanc commissionem
exequi teneantur, duximus committendum et committimus, ut ad
omnem instanciam et requisicionem tam procuratorum ipsius communis thesauri vel receptoris Inferioris Alamanie aut alterius ab eis
commissi vel committendi quam venerandi prefati prioris Alamanie
fratris Johannis de Oro[a] vel eius procuratoris tam coniunctim[c] quam
divisim eodem aut diversis temporibus vocatis, monitis et citatis tam
predicto fratre Engelberto per se aut per procuratorem et aliis qui
vocandi et citandi fuerint auditis ad plenum iuribus, racionibus, expli-
cationibus, scripturis testium quoque deposicionibus ab utraque parcium semel et quociens necessarium et vobis benevisum fuerit et
oportunum pro cognicione iurium[d] utriusque partis super questioni-
bus motis aut movendis iudicetur, sentencietis et diffumatis[e] secundum   formam   stabilimentorum   bonorumque   morum   et
consuetudinum religionis nostre, facientes quod per nos iudicatum et
sentenciatum fuerit in vim obediencie et sub pena solita secundum
formam dictorum stabilimentorum et consuetudinum execucioni de-
bite omni contradictione cessante demandare, dantes et concedentes
vobis et utrique vestrum casu premisso in predictis plenariam auctoritatem, facultatem et potestatem totaliter vices quemadmodum in
premissis agere possemus si personaliter interessemus.

In cuius rei testimonium bulla nostra communis plumbea presentibus est appensa.

Datum Rhodi in nostro conventu die decima nona mensis Octobris anno ab incarnatione Domini millesimo quadringentesimo sexagesimo nono.

Super premissis omnibus et singulis dictis bullis taliter ut premissis etc. *[goes on about the correctness of the notarial copy.]*

ᵃ *uncertain reading ms.* ᵇ *illegible because of damaged parchment.* ᶜ coniuctum *ms.* ᵈ iurum *ms.* ᵉ = diffundatis?

77. 1471, September 17 – *Frater Giovanni-Baptista de Orsinis, Grand Master, grants to* fratri Hermanno Schult preceptoriarum nostrarum Mechel et Columbarie prioratus nostri Alamanie preceptori — *an annual rent of 40 gold Rhineland guilders from the revenues of the* camera magistralis Buchs.

Registration: AOM 379 = libri bullarum 1470-1471, *fol.127r.*

78. 1471, December 5 – *License is given to* fratri Hermano Schult preceptori de Mechel, *to leave Rhodos for his preceptory.*

Chancery note: AOM 380 = libri bullarum 1471, *fol.132r.*

79. 1472, June 12 – *Pope Sixtus IV orders the provost of the chapter of St John in Utrecht to grant papal consent, if he thinks the demand reasonable, to the St Catharine's Convent in Utrecht in electing its own head and having the election confirmed by the Prior of Germany afterwards, as was the habit under the last prior.*

Copy: RA Utrecht, Collectie Buchel-Booth *nr.134, double leaf doublesided, pp.1-2-3 written on. Page 1 begins with the word* Copia. *Under the text on p.3 is written:*

Onder op de plike stondt getekend: Timotheus /
ende was bezegeld med een zegel van lood beneden uyt-hangende aen een geklost koordeken.

Accordeert med zijn origineel
In kennisse van mij
I.Berck

The copy has been edited before by P.Q.Brondgeest, Bijdragen, *p.99-101, Bijlage V.*

Sixtus episcopus servus servorum Dei dilecto filio preposito ecclesie sancti Johannis Traiectensis salutem et apostolicam benedictionem.

Votis illis nos decet prestare assensum per que loca religiosa que-

cunque feliciter et utiliter possint gubernari. Sane pro parte venerabilis fratris nostri Davidis episcopi Traiectensis ac dilectorum filiorum
burgimag[ist]rorum et consulum civitatis Traiectensis nec non preceptoris domus sancte Catherine Traiectensis Hospitalis sancti Johannis Ierosolimitani nobis nuper exhibita petitio continebat quod licet
dudum dilecti filii fratres et conventus eiusdem domus dilectum filium
Engelbertum de Foreest fratrem domus et hospitalis predictorum ad
preceptoriam ipsam tunc certo modo vacantem pro illius regimine
magis ydoneum in ip[s]orum ac domus predicte preceptorem elege-
rint ac ipsa eorum electio tanquam canonice celebrata per priorem
Alamanie secundum morem dicti hospitalis confirmata fuerit et illarum obtentu dictus Engelbertus domum prefatam annis triginta et
ultra possederit prout possidet de presenti pacifice et quiete. Nichilominus quia ab aliquibus asseritur quod dictus prior Alamanie pro
tempore existens superioribus temporibus preceptorem domus prefate illius vacationis tempore occurrente pro nutu suo ponere consuevit,
non habito respectu an domui ipsi pro illius *[p.2]* regimine utilis foret
cum in longinquis habitans mores patrie illius ignoret ac penitus sibi
incognite existant, valde dubitandum est quod si hoc fieret "domus
ipsa in qua hore canonice diurne et nocturne quotidie decantantur et
hospitalitas magna ibidem servatur et quilibet infirmus quocumque
morbo etiam peste epidimia gravatus ad eandem domum declinans
benivolum sibi in eadem reperit receptorem", ad ruinam prout alias
propter incuriam et malum regimen preceptorum pro tempore olim
per dictum priorem Alamanie deputatorum sepenumero minata fuit
et in ea hospitalitates neglecte et divinus cultus diminutus fuere, pro-
hdolor deveniat. Quare pro parte episcopi, burgimag[ist]rorum, consulum, preceptoris et fratrum predictorum nobis fuit humiliter
supplicatum ut indemnitati dicte domus super hoc oportune providere de benignitate apostolica dignaremur.

Nos itaque de premissis certam notitiam non habentes huiusmodi
supplicationibus inclinati discretioni tue per apostolica scripta mandamus quatinus si vocatis quorum interest tibi de premissis legitime
constiterit auctoritate nostra perpetuo statuas et ordines quod fratres
et conventus domus predicte qui melius norunt quis domui ipsi pro
illius regimine utilior sit de preceptore pro tempore utili et ydoneo
eidem preceptorie providere valeant *[p.3]* quotiens illius vacationem
pro tempore occurrere contingeret servatis solemnitatibus in talibus
consuetis unum ex fratribus dicte vel alterius domus hospitalis predicti quem ad hoc magis ydoneum noverint eligere possint, quem prior
Alamanie pro tempore existens confirmare teneatur sicut predecessor
immediatus moderni prioris Alamanie huiusmodi ultimam electionem per dictos fratres et conventum factam confirmavit. Non obstan-

tibus premissis ac constitutionibus et ordinationibus apostolicis nec non statutis, stabilimentis et consuetudinibus hospitalis et domus predictorum iuramento, confirmatione apostolica vel quavis firmitate alia roboratis ceterisque contrariis^a quibuscunque.

Datum Rome apud sanctum Petrum anno incarnationis dominice millesimo quadringentesimo septuagesimo secundo, pridie Idus Iunii pontificatus nostri anno primo.

---

^a contariis *ms.*

80. 1472, August 25 – *Frater Giovanni-Baptista de Orsinis, Grand Master, and Convent grant the preceptory of Mechelen with member at Aachen, vacant by the decease of frater Hermann Schult, to frater Peter Madur, head of the preceptory of Frisia, on account of his merits.*

Registration: AOM 381 = libri bullarum 1472-73, *fol.125v-126r. The vacancy of frater Schult's other preceptory, Colmar, is registered on fol.124v.*

Frater Baptista de Ursinis etc. — fratri Petro Madur preceptoriarum nostrarum tocius provincie Frisie prioratus nostri Alamanie preceptori —.

— non obstante igitur quod dictas preceptorias nostras noscamini presencialiter obtinere, baiulliam itaque seu preceptoriam nostram de Mechel cum membro de Aquis prefati prioratus per obitum quondam religiosi in Xpo nobis carissimi fratris Hermanni Schult eiusdem preceptorie ultimi legittimi preceptoris et possessoris — vacantem —.

Datum Rhodi in nostro conventu die XXV Augusti M IIII^c LXXII.

81. 1481, January 22 – *Frater Giovanni de Cardona, lieutenant of the Grand Master, orders the convents at Haarlem, Arnhem and Nimwegen to be obedient to the bailiff of Utrecht, because they fall under his jurisdiction.*

Copy: RA Utrecht, Collectie Buchel-Booth *nr.134, double leaf single-sided, written on p.1; dated in Annunciation-style. Above the text is written:* Copije; *under the text:* was onderteykend
Johannes Lutius dictus Visso,
ende bezegeld med een beneden uythangend zegel van groen wasch, aen een dubbeld geklost koordeken in een houten napjen.
Concordat.
*Cf.*Inventaris Oud Archief Nijmegen *regest nr.276, 1463 May 17: declaration that the house at Nimwegen of old falls under the command of the bailiff of Utrecht.*

1480.[a]

Frater Johannes de Cardona baiulius Maioricarum reverendissimi domini magistri senescalcus et locumtenens, ac sanctissimi domini nostri pape comissarius, venerabilibus religiosis in Xpo nobis precarissimis fratribus preceptoribus, et conventualibus domorum Harlemensis[b], Aernhemmensis et Novomagensis salutem in Domino sempiternam.

Quoniam nobis significatum est vos[c] esse sub iurisdictione baiuli[v]atus Traiectensis ideo serie presentium vigore et auctoritate locum tenentie nostre vobis et cuilibet vestrum sub virtute sancte obedientie rebellionis, privationis et excommunicationis penis districte precipimus et mandamus quatenus omni prorsus mora et contradictione cessante debeatis parere et obsequi venerando baiulivo Traiectensi presenti et successoribus suis, et subiicere vos visitationi, reformationi et correctioni ipsius baiulivi, nec possitis et valeatis aliquem vel aliquos ad ordinem nostrum recipere et in eo investire absque consensu, licentia et mandato eiusdem baiulivi Traiectensis, et omnia alia et singula facere, observare et adimplere, que hactenus de more et consuetudine solita sunt et antiquitus laudabiliter observata. Taliter ergo in premissis vos geretis ut in religione nostra et apud nos de vera obedientia valeatis merito comendari.

In cuius rei testimonium sigillum nostrum presentibus est appensum.

Datum Colonie die vigesima secunda mensis Ianuarii anno ab incarnatione Domini millesimo quatringentesimo octuagesimo.

---

[a] in the left margin. [b] Harlensis ms. [c] nos ms.

82. 1493, August 5 − Frater Pierre d'Aubusson, Grand Master, and the General Chapter at Rhodos confirm a letter concerning the division of the preceptories of the Priorate of Germany amongst knights and chaplains & serving brethren. Preceptories for knights are among others Burgsteinfurt and Arnhem; for chaplains among others Mechelen; Utrecht is not mentioned.

Copy: AOM 391 = libri bullarum 1492-1493, fol.96r-97r.

Partitio commendarum inter fratres milites, et cappellanos ac servientes prioratus Alemaniae.

— Series ordinis et particionis talis est. In nomine Domini amen. Anno incarnacionis eiusdem MCCCCLXXXXIII die vero quinta mensis Augusti reverendi domini domini fratres Petrus Stolz magnus baiulivus sacri conventus Rhodi et Karolus [fol.96v] de Jesualdo prior

Ungarie atque Johannes Reccrot preceptor de Honrem prioratus Alamanie cappellanus electi et depputati arbitri arbitratores et amicabiles compositores cum auctoritate et licencia reverendissimi domini cardinalis et magni magistri ac reverendi capituli generalis per honorandos dominos fratres milites ex una et capellanos servientesque parte ex altera venerande lingue Alamanie ad ordinandum, parciandum, dividandum ac depputandum in vim capituli generalis omnes et singulas preceptorias dicti prioratus tam Inferioris quam Superioris Alamanie determinarunt, deliberarunt, arbitrati sunt, concordarunt et ordinarunt unanimi consensu et voto pro quitte predictarum partium religionisque utilitate preceptorias ex quibus fratres milites dicte lingue habere provisionem possunt et debent titulo cabimenti, melioramenti seu aliter et etiam illas de quibus dicti fratres capellani et servientes provideri possunt et habere sub predictis titulis, intellectis tamen quod fuit salva iura thesauri imposita et imponenda et quod huiusmodi determinacio atque particio non fit in preiudicium preeminenciarum magistralium et venerandi prioris Alamanie, in conferendis preceptoriis de gratia sed de his possint libere uti non obstante huiusmodi particione que talis est.

Primo declararunt, ordinarunt et partiti sunt quod preceptorie que secuntur, intelliguntur et sunt depputate pro fratribus militibus dicti prioratus Alamanie tam Inferioris quam Superioris, videlicet Hoenreym, Basilia, Emendorff, Villingen, Magoncia, Heymbach, Torleschem, Sulcz, Ffriburg, Tobel, Rodorff, Rotwill, Uberlingen, Castrim, Adenaue, Treveris, Steymffurt, Dusperg, Walsheim, Loige, Rotemburg, Erlingen, Hall, Wibourg, Rudigheim cum membro Nida quod per huiusmodi particionem intelligitur esse unitum ipsi preceptorie, Mergetheim, Ffrancffurdia, Wycsella, Arnnheim, cum suis membris et pertinenciis consuetis. Preceptorie autem deputate fratribus *[fol.97r]* capellanis et servientibus sequuntur: Columbaria, Ratispona, Schlussingen, Wysensehe, Wormasia, Prisich cum membro Mergenheim quod etiam per dictam particionem intelligitur esse unitum cum preceptoria[a], Velden, Mecheln, Herforden, Burhem cum suis membris et pertinenciis consuetis, quamquam particionem, divisionem et deputacionem predicte partes tam milites quam capellani et servientes solemni iuramento prestito de licencia Reverendissimi domini cardinalis et magni magistri acceptarunt et gratam ratamque habuerunt promiseruntque nullo umquam tempore contrafacere, dicere seu contravenire clam vel palam sub pena periurii et inhabilitatis ad obtinendas preceptorias.

In cuius rei testimonium bulla nostra communis plumbea presentibus est appensa.

Datum Rhodi durante nostro generali capitulo die quinta mensis augusti anno ab incarnato Xpo Ihesu domino nostro millesimo quadringentesimo nonagesimo tercio.

---

^a preceptorie *ms.*

83. 1496, October 10 – *Frater Pierre d'Aubusson, Grand Master, and Convent appoint frater Thomas van Rothusen, knight of the Order in the Priorate of Germany, as head of the preceptory of Arnhem and Nimwegen after resignation by its last head frater Johann von Hatstein.*
  Registration: AOM 392 = libri bullarum 1494-1496, *fol.95r; cf. formulary in AOM 372* = libri bullarum 1462, *fol.134, dd. 6 July 1462 (see nr.66 above). Frater Johann von Hatstein appears to be the head of the preceptory of Heimbach in AOM 394* = libri bullarum 1502-1503, *fol.152v, dd. 24 November 1503.*

Frater Petrus etc. et nos etc. religioso etc. fratri Thome de Rothusen dicte domus et prioratus nostri Alamanie militi salutem etc.
  Virtutum merita quibus prefulgere nosimini postulant ut vobis reddamur ad gratias liberales baiuliam itaque seu preceptoriam nostram de Arnen et Nomeghe dicti nostri prioratus per resignationem sive renuntiationem facitam de eadem in manibus nostri prelibati magistri a religioso etc. fratre Joanne Atsteym eiusdem preceptorie ultimo legitimo preceptore sive hoc sive alio quovismodo vacantem presentialiter etc.
  Datum etc. die X^{ma} mensis Octobris anno 1496.

84. 1496, October 22 – *Order is given to* fratri Petro Stoltz, magno bailivo *and head of the preceptories of Frankfurt and Mainz, and* fratri Joanni de Usterwich baiulivo Coloniensi *and head of the preceptories of Wesel and Borken* ac baiulio in Traiecto Inferiori, *to introduce frater Thomas van Rothusen in his preceptory of Arnhem and Nimwegen.*
  Chancery note: AOM 392 = libri bullarum 1494-1496, *fol.96v.*

85. 1500, March 26 – *Frater Rudolph Graf von Werdenberg, Prior of Germany, and the bailiffs and heads of preceptories, celebrating a chapter assembly in Worms, declare on complaint of frater Thomas van Rothusen, head of the houses at Arnhem and Nimwegen, that the maintenance of frater Nicolaus van Schoten must be paid for by the head of the preceptory of Haarlem, because this house has been assigned as his residence.*
  Original charter on parchment with a fragment of the Prior's seal in red wax

on a folded slip (double tail) of parchment: RA Gelderland, Loeff, Archief, *inventory nr.34, regest nr.442.*
On the backside: Mandaet van den Hr. Groot Balij, aenden Hr. Commanduer van Haerlem

Frater Rudolfus comes de Werdennberg prior, baiulivi et preceptores ordinis sancti Johannis Jerosolimitani etc.

Recognoscimus per presentes quod coram nobis die datorum presentium in provinciali Wormatie celebrato capitulo comparuit frater Thomas de Rothusenn commendator domorum prefati nostri ordinis in Arnheim et Numagen, exponens non sine gravi querela, quod licet frater Nicolaus de Schotten suo stagio in Harlem lenie provisus fuerit et esse debeat, nicholominus tamen in domo prefati fratris Thome commendatoris in Arnheim alimenta recipiat sine refusione huiusmodi sibi in Harlem provisum sit de duodecim aureis Renensibus sibi subvenientibus ubicumque alimenta recipiat, petens sibi in hiis de aliquo remedio subvenire ne dictus frater Nicolaus in sua alimentorum provisione defraudetur, attento quod sibi duodecim anni extant insoluti et restant exolvendi. Nos quoque attendentes prefati fratris Thome petitionem fore iustam et necessariam ordinavimus nec non per presentes ordinamus quod nunc et in antea singulis annis in quolibet festo Nativitatis sancti Johannis Baptiste a commendatore sive possessore domus Harlem prefati duodecim auri Renenses prefato fratri Thome commendatori in Arnheim et Numagen presententur ad sustentationem vite fratris Nicolai de Scotten. Quod si predictus commendator Harlemensis secusfecerit tunc frater Thomas eundem fratrem Nicolaum sine ᵃ contradictione prefati commendatoris in Harlem ad conventum suum remittere habeat et debeat alimenta et vite necessaria recipiendum.

Datum sub sigillo nostri prioratus presentibus appenso die vicesima sexta mensis Marcii anni millesimi quingentesimi.

ᵃ *beginning of a word erased in ms.*

86. 1500, September 1 – *Frater* Petrus Daubusson, *Grand Master, sends a summons to* fratri Rudolpho de Werdenberg, *Prior of Germany, for a meeting at Rhodos concerning the combat against the Turks and appropriate financial measures, ordering him to pass the message to several heads of preceptories, amongst them frater* Thomas de Rothusen, *head at Arnhem.*

Collated copy from the chancery at Rhodos, with damaged folds and margins: RA Gelderland, Loeff, Archief, *inventory nr.11, regest nr.443; cf. Loeff,* Archief, *inventory nr.11, regest nr.447, 1501 January 11, original letter in Ger-*

man from the Meister in Tutschen Landen *(= Prior of Germany) to frater*
Thomas van Rothusen *with summons for a meeting at Friburg in Breisgau;*
and Loeff, inventory nr.10, regest nr.448, 1501 February 6, notarial copy of a
letter in German from the Meister in Tutschen Landen *to frater* Thomas
van Rothusen *concerning the demand of the Grand Master as regards financial*
support for the fight against the enemy, propounded at the provincial chapter at
Freiburg im Breisgau.

87. 1501, August 26 – *Frater Pierre d'Aubusson, Grand Master, and Convent*
summon frater Otto van Haeften, chaplain of the Order and holder of the member
Nimwegen of the preceptory Arnhem, to appear at Rhodos within nine month on
accusation of disobedience and refusal to pay duties by frater Thomas van Rothu-
sen, head of the houses at Arnhem and Nimwegen.

Registration: AOM 393, libri bullarum 1501, *fol.104v-105r; copy: RA*
Gelderland, Loeff, Archief, *inventory nr.504, regest nr.456. The text in AOM*
has been followed. The text was used again by the chancery in 1504 with the
name of Laurentius de Adinau; *see below, nr.92.*

^a Frater Petrus etc. religioso etc. fratri Otto de Hasten nostri ordinis
et prioratus Alemanie capellano salutem in domino et nostris firmiter
obedire mandatis.

Comparuit eoram nobis et nostroque generali capitulo religiosus in
Xpo nobis charissimus frater Thomas de Rothusen preceptor preceptorie nostre de Arnheim, querelose exponens qualiter vos indebite et
preter formam stabilimentorum nostrorum occupatis membrum ipsius preceptorie nominatum Neumagen in grave eius preiudicium,
preterea quod insolencia ductus recusatis in signum recognitionis su-
perioritatis dare et solvere eidem pensionem annuam secundum universalem stilum religionis; Item quod contra formam stabilimentorum
predictorum hactenus renuistis dicto preceptori solvere annuatim iura
thesauri pro rata ipsum membrum tangentem ut ipse postea pro
membro et tota preceptoria nostro communi thesauro debitas solutiones faciat secundum imposiciones capitulorum generalium, etiam
quod peius est audetis contra ipsum preceptorem vestrum superiorem
damnate superbie cornua erigere et eo spreto uti prerogativa preceptoris, super quibus multum se gravatum asserit, quare a nobis nostroque generali^b capitulo^b de opportuno iusticie remedio providere
instanter postulavit. Nos itaque unicuique fratrum nostrorum iusti-
ciam ministrare cupientes serie presentium cum deliberatione dicti
capituli^b vos monemus, hortamur, et si opus sit in vim vere obedientie
iniungimus et mandamus ut in termino none mensium a die presentationis harum nostrarum litterarum computandorum, quorum tres

pro primo, tres pro secundo, tres pro tertio, quarto ultimo et peremptorio termino assignamus, compareatis hic in Rhodo coram nobis
nostroque venerando consilio personaliter vel per procuratorem legitimum de iuribus vestris sufficienter instructum responsurus predictis
contra vos per dictum fratrem Thomam^c obiectis, quando vobis et
ipsi preceptori parati sumus ministrare iusticie complementum. Aliter
dicto termino elapso et vobis ut prefertur non comparente contra vos
procedemus procedique faciemus ad privationem pretensi iuris per
vos super dicto membro de Neumangen vestra contumacia. In aliquo
non obstante, taliter etc.

In cuius etc. bulla nostra magistralis in cera nigra.

Datum etc. die XXVI mensis Augusti durante nostro generale
capitulo Anno M° VC^mo primo.

---

^a *in margine:* ✠
^b *in margin replaced by:* venerando consilio, *c.q.* venerandi consilii.
^c *in margin replaced by:* Laurentium.

88. 1501, October 1 − *Frater Pierre d'Aubusson, Grand Master, informs the
Prior of Germany, the Grand Bailiff and all the heads of preceptories in High
Germany how much each preceptory has to pay to the treasury.*

Registration: AOM 393 = libri bullarum 1501, *fol.133v-134r. Both
items render the amounts in florins (*flor. or f°), whites (*alb.) and doits (d.). The
bull begins on fol.133v and continues on:*

[*fol.134r*] Sequuntur nomina preceptoriarum et summe cuilibet
preceptorie per supradictos imposite et descripte. Et primo

Camere priorales

preceptoria Vucbutensis	flor.LV alb.XX	
preceptoria Wedeschwil	flor.LXXI	
preceptoria Luckern	f° XLIX alb.XIX	
preceptoria Biberstein	f° X alb.IIII	
Summa	f° I^c LXXXVI alb.XVI	
preceptoria Hohenreym	flor. XXII	
preceptoria Raden	f° XV	
preceptoria Freyburg in Briszgaw	f° CX alb.II	
preceptoria Basel	f° LXXX	
preceptoria Hemmendorff	f° LXX	
preceptoria Vilingen^a	f° XLIIII alb.XII	
preceptoria Meinz	f° XL alb.XX d.I	
preceptoria Heimbach	f° CI alb.V d.I	
preceptoria Buchs	f° LXXXIIII	

preceptoria Colmar f° xxviii
preceptoria Torlossim f° lxv alb.x
preceptoria Stroszburg f° cx alb.xxi d.iii
preceptoria Sletstat f° lv alb.v
preceptoria Sulcz f° lx alb.viii
preceptoria Friburg in Yechtlandt f° xxvi alb.xii
preceptoria Tobel f° xcix alb.x
preceptoria Rodorff f° ci alb.xxi d.ii
preceptoria Rottwil f° xxxvi alb.xii
preceptoria Uberlingen f° xliii
preceptoria Wermes f° vii alb.iiii
preceptoria Meyfenbeym f° xv alb.xiiii
preceptoria Sobernheim^b f° vii alb.xv
preceptoria Kusnach f° xx alb.iiii
preceptoria Wiell f° v alb.iii d.i

Summa mil iiii^c lvii f° xxv alb.

In cuius etc. bulla nostra communis plumbea etc. .
Datum etc. die prima Octobris anno M° V^Cmo primo.

---

^a Silingen ms. ^b Ubernheim ms.

89. 1501, October 1 — *Frater Pierre d'Aubusson, Grand Master, informs the heads of preceptories in Low Germany how much each preceptory has to pay to the treasury.*

  Registration: AOM 393 = libri bullarum 1501, *fol.134v.*

Sequuntur nomina preceptoriarum et summe cuillbet preceptorle per supradictos imposite et descripte. Et primo
Preceptoria de Colonia f° lix alb.ii d.ii
preceptoria Mergenheim flor.iiii
preceptoria Novacastra f° xx alb.iiii
preceptoria Stron f° vii alb.xv
preceptoria Mecheln f° xxiiii
preceptoria Nychdecken f° vii alb.xv
preceptoria Velden f° xii alb.xx d.ii
preceptoria Adenow f° xviii
preceptoria Treveris f° x alb.iiii
preceptoria Kiringen f° vii alb.xv
preceptoria Rode f° vii alb.xv
preceptoria Cronberg f° vii alb.xv
preceptoria Brisig f° xxi alb.vii
preceptoria Steinfurt f° xii alb.v
preceptoria Monster f° iii

preceptoria Lage	f⁰ L alb.v
preceptoria Duschspurg	f⁰ VII alb.XV
preceptoria Walsheim	f⁰ X alb.VI
preceptoria Burchheim	f⁰ XIII alb.IIII
preceptoria Wiesel	f⁰ XLV alb.XIIII
preceptoria Herferden	f⁰ X alb.IIII d.IIII
preceptoria Arnem	f⁰ X alb.XII
preceptoria Nimienheim	f⁰ L
preceptoria Rotemburgh	f⁰ LXIII alb.XVII
preceptoria Erlingen	f⁰ XCV alb.IIII
Item nunc dabitur	f⁰ XLVIII
preceptoria Schlysingen	f⁰ VII alb.XV
preceptoria Hal	f⁰ XXXVIII
preceptoria Vuerzburg	f⁰ LXXXVII alb.XXIIII
preceptoria Ruedicken	f⁰ LVII alb.II d.IIII
preceptoria Grestnow	f⁰ V
preceptoria Regenspurg	f⁰ XV
preceptoria Monster	f⁰ VI alb.X
preceptoria Mengetheim	f⁰ XXIIII alb.IX d.VIII
preceptoria Wisense	f⁰ XIX alb.XX
preceptoria Franckfurt	f⁰ LXVIII alb.IX
preceptoria Bassel	f⁰ LXIII alb.VII d.II
preceptoria Wissentfeldt	f⁰ X alb.XIIII
preceptoria Uetricht	f⁰ II^C XXVIII
Summa mil II^C LXXXI flor.	alb.XIII d.II.

In cuius etc. bulla nostra communis plumbea etc.
Datum etc. die et anno predictis.

90. 1503, December 14 − *Frater Ludwig von Schalingen, Admiral of the Order, and Convent, grant to frater Laurens von Adenau, chaplain of the Order, the preceptory of [Arnhem] with member Nimwegen for a period of ten years after the death of its last head frater Thomas van Rothusen.*

Registration: AOM 394 = libri bullarum 1502-1503, *fol.153v.*

Frater Ludovicus etc. [de Schalingen, humilis admiralis] et nos etc. religioso etc. fratri Laurentio de Adinau prioratus nostri Alemanie cappellano salutem etc.

Zelus quem in cultum divinum habere noscimini nos inducunt ut vobis reddamur ad gratias liberales atque personam vestram favore prosequamur in compensationem laudabilium obsequiorum per vos nostre religioni in orientem prestitorum, baiuliam itaque seu preceptoriam nostram de Harleem^a dicti prioratus per obitum quondam fratris Thome de Rothuseem eiusdem preceptorie ultimi legitimi preceptoris et possessoris sive hoc etc. cum membro de Nimagium et aliis omnibus et singulis suis membris, iuribus etc. invicem maturo et deliberato consilio de nostra certa scientia ad annos decem continuos et completos de gratia venerande lingue Alemanie et titulo solutionis debitorum dicte preceptorie nostro communi thesauro vobis auctoritate presentium confecimus, concedimus, et donamus bene faciendo in eadem, vosque preceptorem etc.

In cuius etc. bulla nostra communis plumbea etc.

Datum etc. die XIIII Decembris 1503.

ᵃ *i.e.* Arnhem.

91. 1504, January 16 — *Frater Ludwig von Schalingen, admiral of the Order, and Convent make known, that they grant to frater Laurens von Adenau, chaplain of the Order and head of the preceptory of [Arnhem], the seniority and the right to succeed as the head of the preceptories Mechelen and Velden [?] should they become vacant.*

Registration: AOM 394 = libri bullarum 1502-1503, *fol.155r, dated in Annunciation-style.*

Frater Ludovicus — et nos conventus —

— considerantes virtutibus et meritis religiosi etc. fratris Laurentii de Adinau dicte venerande lingue cappellani preceptoris de Herleemᵃ dederunt, tradiderunt et concesserunt eidem fratri Laurentio antianitatem, declarantes hoc modo videlicet quod non obstante dictus frater Laurentius obtineat prefatam preceptoriam existens tam in conventu Rhodi quam extra conventum ipsum et in partibus occiduis, possit et valeat de preceptoriis de Mechellen et Fedem quas nunc possidet religiosus etc. frater Ulricus Witel dicti prioratus, pro suo cabimento, quocienscumque eas per cessum vel decessum dicti fratris Ulrici vel alio quovismodo vacare contigerit, et cum semel se cabitus de dictis preceptoriis fuerit, si se meliorare voluerit, presens in nostro Rhodi conventu adesse teneatur — etc.

Datum etc. die XVIᵗᵃ Ianuarii 1503 ab incarnatione.

ᵃ *i.e.* Arnhem.

92. 1504, March 9 — *Frater Ludwig von Schalingen, admiral of the Order, and Convent summon frater Otto van Haeften, chaplain of the Order, to Rhodos on accusation by frater Laurens von Adenau, head of the preceptory of [Arnhem].*

Registration: AOM 394 = libri bullarum 1502-1503, *fol.155v, dated in Annunciation-style; cf. AOM 393* = libri bullarum 1501, *fol.104v, 1501 August 26; see nr.87 above.*

Ludovicus etc. religioso etc. fratri Otto Hasten nostri ordinis et prioratus Alemanie cappellano salutem in domino et nostris firmiter obedire mandatis.

Comparuit coram nobis nostroque venerando consilio religiosus etc. frater Laurentius de Adinau legitimus preceptor preceptorie nostre de Hasten[a] querelose exponens qualiter vos etc.

Sume reliquum ex registro 1501 fol.104 ubi est tale signum ✠ usque Taliter ergo etc.

In cuius etc. bulla armorum nostrorum qua uti consuevimus in cera nigra etc.

Datum etc. die nona Marcii 1503 ab incarnatione.

---

[a] *i.e.* Arnhem.

93. 1504, March 10 – *Frater Emery d'Amboise, Grand Master, and Convent grant by letter of frater Ludwig von Schalingen to frater Laurens von Adenau, head of the preceptory of [Arnhem], the possession called Tanasi on Rhodos at the foot of Mount Philermos, vacant by the decease of frater Pietro Coroca, for life.*
    Registration: AOM 394 = libri bullarum 1502-1503, *fol.156r, dated in Annunciation-style.* [1] Collachus = Conventus.

Frater Ludovicus — fratri Laurentio de Adinau — preceptori de Harlehem[a] — predium seu possessionem dictam Tanasi sitam in castellania nostra Triande ad radices montis Philermi predicte, datam in dotem cuiusdam cappelle erecte ad altare sancti Blasii in ecclesia sancti Johannis Collachi[1] Rhodi vacantem per resignationem factam in favorem et commodum tuum a quondam fratre Petro Coroca eiusdem predii legitimo possessore et dicti capelli capellano tua vita durante – etc. non obstante quod in futurum alia beneficia nostri ordinis consequeris et in partibus occiduis moram faceres – etc.

Datum etc. die decima mensis Marcii anno M°CCCCC^mo tercio ab incarnacione.

---

[a] *i.e.* Arnhem.

94. 1506, February 10 – *Frater Emery d'Amboise, Grand Master, and Convent grant the Priorate of Germany, vacant by the death of frater Rudolf von*

Werdenberg, to frater Johann Heggenzer, with five prioral chambers, among which Utrecht.

Registration: AOM 397 = libri bullarum 1505-1506, fol.147r-149r, dated in Annunciation-style; cf. nr.97 below.

Frater Emericus — et nos conventus — fratri Joanni Heggenzer, magno baiulio conventuali ac preceptoriarum nostrarum de Torleschen, de Uberlina Dembniz, de Colnmar ac Rotuil prioratus nostri Alamanie preceptori —.

[He receives the Priorate of Germany with the following five prioral chambers: fol.147v] — videlicet Utrecht, Colonie, Torloschen loco Lucernensis, et Bubeshem necnon preceptoriam de Friburg in Presigayr pro quinta vestra camera —.

Datum etc. 10 Februarii 1505 ab incarnacione.

95. 1510, June 22 — *The proxies of the Common Treasury have concluded an agreement with frater Guillaume Quinon that he will receive the preceptory of Arnhem for his lifetime, although he does not belong to the German tongue. All the preceptory's debts to the treasury will be remitted until 24 June 1511 and no duties will be levied for five years until 23 June 1516. These stipulations were included because none of the brethren of the German tongue wanted to accept the preceptory, which was impoverished by war and mismanagement. After those five years two men from the German tongue will come to see the improvements he has made and will decide on the real value of the preceptory.*

Chancery notice: AOM 399 = libri bullarum 1508-1510, fol.153r-v.

In nomine domini Amen. Die vigesima secunda Iunii 1510 constituti in cancellaria Rhodi Reverendi domini procuratores communis thesauri, auditores computorum et locumtenens Reverendi domini magni preceptoris fecerunt infrascriptam concordiam, concessionem, et pactum cum domino fratre Guillelmo Quinon helemosinario secretario Reverendissimi domini magni magistri domini fratris Emeri d'Amboise super preceptoria de Arnem prioratus Alamanie cum suis iuribus et pertinentiis, videlicet quod attento quod dicta preceptoria de Arnem tam in capite quam in membris occasione guerrarum et inutilis regiminis pro preterito tempore in ea impensi est redacta ad terminum et conditionem quod nullus fratrum prioratus Alamanie eam voluit acceptare neque de cabimento neque de gratia, confidentes de fidei probitate et diligentia predicti domini fratris Guillelmi eidem eam de gratia speciali sua vita durante concesserunt, non obstante quod de alio prioratu fit, hoc tamen sine preiudicio venerabilis lingue Alamanie, quoniam sibi reservarunt et Reverendus dominus

magnus baiulivus inter prefatos Reverendos dominos incorporatus in
prefata cancellaria reservavit quod post cessum vel decessum antedic-
ti domini fratris Guillelmi pure, mere et simpliciter prefata preceptoria revertatur ad dispositionem prefate lingue Alamanie et non
alterius; concordaruntque cum dicto domino fratri Guillelmo, de quo
specialem fiduciam habent, ut eam tam in spiritualibus quam temporalibus pro suo posse et facultate reparet, augeat et ad pristinum
statum reducat, et quia antedicta preceptoria est debitarum comuni
thesauro in magna pecuniarum quantitate, prefati reverendi domini
procuratores et auditores ad hoc ut idem dominus frater Guillelmus
melius possit dictis reparationibus vacare relaxaverunt et elargiti sunt
liberaliter et sine aliqua reservatione omnia et singula arreragia per
preteritos preceptores in dicta preceptoria contracta ob solutiones
iurium comunis thesauri non factas usque ad festum sancti Joannis
Baptiste de mense Iunii anni millesimi quingentesimi undecimi.

Preterea ordinaverunt quod dictus dominus frater Guillelmus habeat, teneat, et possideat dictam preceptoriam ex nunc et eius sit
verus et legitimus preceptor et de eadem sibi conficiantur littere in
ampla forma per magistrum et conventum secundum stilum religionis, reservato quod pro quinquennio non erit obligatus neque tenebitur solvere aut dare comuni thesauro antedicto ratione premisse
preceptorie aliquam summam pecuniarum et hoc quia sperant quod
dictus dominus frater Guillelmus adhibebit suam omnem industriam
ad relevandum dictam preceptoriam, et prefatum quinquennium initium capiet in festo sancti Joannis Baptiste de mense Iunii 1511 et
finiet in vigilia eiusdem festi anni millesimi quingentesimi decimi sexti, et hic annus non computatur propter absentiam dicti fratris Guillelmi a prefata preceptoria, non obstante quod si accesserit infra
annum ad prefatam preceptoriam et fructus recollegerit, pro ipsis in
nichilo tenebitur erga dictum thesaurum.

[After those five years, the real value of the preceptory will be assessed.]

96. 1510, July 3 – *Frater Emery d'Amboise, Grand Master, and Convent grant
frater* Guillelmus Quinon *the function of head of the preceptories Arnhem and
Nimwegen.*
    Registration: AOM 400 = libri bullarum 1510-1511, *fol.151r.*

97. 1512, July 3 – *Frater Emery d'Amboise, Grand Master, and Convent
appoint frater Johann von Hatstein as Prior of Germany, with five prioral chambers, among which Utrecht.*
    Original bull on parchment, with holes of lost string and seal of Grand Master

and Convent: GLA Karlsruhe, 20/159. Registration: AOM 2198 = lingua di Alemagna, *fol.18r-v, and AOM 401* = libri bullarum 1512, *fol.175v. The text from AOM 2198 has been followed, some references are made to GLA.*
[1]*AOM 397* = libri bullarum 1505-1506, *fol.147r-149r, dd. 10 February 1505 ab incarnacione (1506); see before, nr.94.*
[2]*AOM 401* = libri bullarum 1512, *fol.175v, dd. 3 July 1512.*

Frater Emericus etc. et nos etc. venerando etc. fratri Joanni Haisten[a] praeceptoriarum nostrarum de Hombach et Francfort prioratus Alemaniae praeceptori ac ordinis nostri magno baiulivo conventuali salutem etc.

Duce rationis agere arbitramur si quos etc. Sume hanc bullam ex libro bullarum MDV et VI fol.cxlvii[1] usque: resignatis igitur prius per vos in manibus nostri praelibati magistri secundum formam statutorum nostrorum dicto magno baiulivatu ac praeceptoria de Francfort, et per nos magistrum dicta resignatione suscepta si tamen et aliter non cum infrascripti prioratus possessionem pacificam et quietam fueris assecutus, nec non resignata similiter per vos praeceptoria nostra de Torlezehen pridem camera priorali, et loco ipsius secundum[b] tenorem stabilimentorum nostrorum retenta nostra dicta praeceptoria de Hombach pro una camerarum priorialium, et per nos magistrum ipsa resignatione suscepta, prioratum itaque nostrum Alemaniae per obitum quondam fratris Joannis Heggezer eiusdem prioratus ultimi legitimi prioris et possessoris, sive hoc sive alio etc. quoquomodo etc. et cum omni honore, praerogativis et emolumentis atque suis quatuor cameris prioralibus prioratus ipsius, et vobis priori eiusdem assignamus videlicet Utrecht, Coloniae, Hombach[c] nec non praeceptoria de Friburg in Praesigaro[d] pro quinta vestra camera, consentientibus adhoc fratribus nostrae venerandae linguae Alemaniae Rhodi ad Dei et religionis nostrae obsequia residentibus, quibus huiusmodi negotium particulariter spectat, cum omnibus earundem camerarum membris, iuribus et pertinentiis universis ad ipsas et ipsarum qualibet spectantibus et pertinentibus etc. prout in eadem.

In cuius rei etc. communis etc.

Datum etc. die tertia Iulii M° D° XII°.

Ex libro bullarum[2]. Frater Johannes Otho Bosius Vicecancelarius.

---

[a] Johannes de Haesten *GLA.* [b] silicet *ms.* [c] Hembach loco Tolesehen predicte Lucernensis et Bubekem, *GLA; the fourth camera prioralis Bubikon has mistakenly been left out in AOM 2198.* [d] Presigayr *GLA.*

---

98. 1527, January 19 – *Frater Philippe de Villiers l'Isle-Adam, Grand Master, and Convent, grant to frater Jean Quinon, head of the preceptory of Du*

Bourgault in the Priorate of France, the preceptory of Arnhem, vacant by resignation of its last head frater Guillaume Quinon, sibling of Jean.
Registration: AOM 412 = libri bullarum 1526-1528, *fol.183v, dated in Annunciation-style.*

Frater Philippus etc. et nos conventus etc. religioso etc. fratri Joanni Quineo preceptorie nostre Du Burgault prioratus Francie preceptori salutem etc.

Morum et vite honestas, divini cultus observantia aliaque probatis et virtutum tuarum merita quibus apud nos commendaris necnon laudabilia obsequia per te religioni nostre prestita et que ardentius te prestiturum speramus nos inducunt ut te quibus possumus favoribus et gratias prosequamur, non obstante igitur quod de prenominato prioratu esse dignosceris, preceptoriam nostram de Arnem Gheldrensi prioratus Alemanie per liberam resignationem in manibus nostri prelibati magistri de eadem factam a legitimis procuratoribus religiosi etc. fratris Guillermi Quineo tui secundum carnem fratris dicte preceptorie de Arnem Gheldrensi ultimi legitimi preceptoris et possessoris, adhoc specialiter constitutis, ut nobis legitime apparuit sive hoc sive alio quovismodo vacante, presentialiter et ad nostram collationem, donationem, et omnimodam dispositionem spectantem et devolutam cum omnibus et singulis etc. et cum quibus illam dictus frater Guillermus Quineus ceterique ordinis nostri fratres habuerunt etc. —.

Datum Viterbii etc., die XVIIII Ianuarii anno ab incarnacione domenica 1526.

99. 1530, March 18 – *Frater Philippe de Villiers l'Isle-Adam, Grand Master, and Convent grant to frater Georg von Hohenheim, knight of the German tongue, the preceptory of [Arnhem], vacant by the death of frater Jean Quinon.*
Registration: AOM 414 = libri bullarum 1528-1530, *fol.186v, dated in Annunciation-style.*

Frater Philippus de Villers Lisleadam etc. et nos etc. Religioso etc. fratri Georgio de Hohenheim nostre dicte domus venerande lingue Allemanie militi salutem etc.

Virtutum tuorum merita — promerentur ut te ad commoda ordinis nostri promoveamus bayliam itaque seu preceptoriam nostram de Arläm^a prioratus Alemanie per obitum quondam fratris Joannis Quynon ultimi legitimi eiusdem preceptorie de Arläm preceptoris et possessoris sive hoc sive alio quovismodo vacantem —.

Datum Syracusis etc. die XVIII Martii anno ab incarnatione dominica MDXXVIIII.

ª *i.e.* Arnhem.

100. 1531, January 7 – *Frater Philippe de Villiers l'Isle-Adam, Grand Master, allows frater Georg von Hohenheim to trade his preceptory of [Arnhem] for the preceptories of Sulz and Dorlisheim.*
Registration: AOM 414 = libri bullarum 1528-1530, fol.187r, dated in Annunciation-style.

— Georgius de Hohenheim *[is allowed to trade his]* preceptoriam de Harlaimª — cum preceptoriis de Sulcz et Dorlasteyn quas tenet et possidet religiosus etc. frater Philippus Scheling venerandi magni baiulivi locumtenens. —.
Datum in conventu nostro Melite etc. die VII mensis Ianuarii anno ab incarnatione dominica MDXXX.

ª *i.e.* Arnhem.

101. 1531, January 7 – *Frater Philippe de Villiers l'Isle-Adam, Grand Master, allows frater* Philippus Scling *[= Schilling] to trade his preceptories of* Sulcz et Dorlasteim *for* Arlaimª.
Registration: AOM 414 = libri bullarum 15281530, fol.187rv, dated in Annunciationstyle; see the previous item.

ª *i.e.* Arnhem.

102. 1534, December 14 – *Frater Pietro del Ponte, Grand Master, orders frater Johann von Hatstein, Prior of Germany, to appoint a small committee to examine if frater Hendrik Bushoff, cleric of the diocese of Utrecht and former Black Friar, meets the condition of legal birth and other conditions of admittance to the rank of chaplain of the Order.*
Registration: AOM 415 = libri bullarum 1531-34, fol.176r.

Frater Petrus de Ponte etc. venerando religioso etc. fratri Joanni de Hatsteyn prioratus nostre Alemanie priori salutem in Domino et diligentiam in commissis etc.
Serie presentium tibi significamus qualiter religiosus etc. frater Henricus Bushoff clericus Traiectensis diocesis ex dispensatione apos-

tolica ab ordine sancti Dominici ad nostram translatus nuper receptus fuit in nostra veneranda lingua Alemanie sub gradu fratris capellani non ostensis sue legitimitatis probationibus de quibus constare se facturus in certo termino promisit, quapropter eius petitionibus annuentes cum deliberatione nostri venerandi consilii tibi comittimus et mandamus, ut duobus nostri ordinis fratribus quo idoneos et propinquiores loco unde sit oriundus cognoveris auctoritate nostra committas quatenus testes fide dignos coram eis producendos examinent si dictus frater Henricus est de legitimo matrimonio intra limites dicti prioratus natus et procreatus, bonis moribus constitutus, ac denique si est talis qualem ordinis nostri stabilimenta pro fratre capellano postulant et requirunt, quorumquidem testium sacramento adactorum depositiones per notarium publicum in scriptis auctenticis redactas manibus eorundem commissariorum abs te deputatorum seu tuis subscriptas et sigillis obsignatas ad nos et dictam linguam mitti curabis; taliter ergo in premissis te exhibeas ut tua apud nos mereatur comendari sedulitas.

In cuius rei etc. in cera etc.

Datum Melite etc. die XIIII Decembris 1534.

103. 1542, April 27 – *Frater* Johan van Hatsteijn Sanct Johans Ordens Maister in Teutsch Landen *sends a letter concerning the decision of the Reichstag in Speyer on the share of the Order of St John in the anti-Turks tax.*

Contemporaneous copy: RA Gelderland, Loeff, Archief, inventory nr.8, regest nr.507.

104. 1542, June 3 – *Frater Philips Schilling, head of the preceptory of Arnhem, asks the administrator of this house, frater Joannes Beltghen, to pay one tenth of its yearly income to the head of the preceptory in Cologne for the fight against the Turks.*

Original letter: RA Gelderland, Loeff, Archief, inventory nr.8, regest nr.508, single leaf, double-sided, damaged folds and margins, signed by the writer, addressed at the backside, with superimposed little seal for closing, causing a piece of the paper to tear in the act of opening.

Mein freuntlichen grus unnd alles gut zuvor. Lieber herr Schafner, mir hat verganger tag der hochwerdig mein gnediger herr, meister Sanct Johans ordens in Teutschen Landen ainen abtruck des abschieds wes sich konigliche Maiestat mit sampt den Churfursten und Stenden des Reichs der anlag halben wider den turcken uff den hor-

zug verglichen und verainiget mich darauff gantz ernstlichen verma-
net, mich bey meiner Conscientz zu bewerdigen was und wievil meiner jerlichen nutzung meiner hewser und Comethereyen zu
Rotemburg und Arnheim sey, und darauff Je von zehen gulden jer-
lichs einkomens ain gulden zu Schatzung und anlag gelt seinen gnaden uffs scherst zu zu schicken, das ich dan aus schuldiger gehorsam
zu thon bewilligt. Nach dem mir aber abgefallen was und wievil des
ordens haws Arnheim jerlicher einkomender nutzung sein mag, So ist
an euch mein freuntlich begeren, Ir wollet des hawes Registra für die
hendt nemen und daraus alle nutzung uffs vleissigst und getreulichst
uff ain Prima gelts anschlagung und rechner, und darnach je von
zehen gulden ainen gulden, So vil die rechnung des einkomens be-
trifft in zwayen wochen, Nach dem euch dieser briff uberantwort
wurdt, meinem heren Comether Sant Johans ordens gem Colen zu
handen antworten, damit er solches gelt furter meinem gnedigen heren dem meister uber antwort, und wir als die gehorsamen erfunden
und des ordens und desselben hewser ferrer schad furkomen werde,
und euch in dem gehorsamlichen erzaigen. War es d[em] betreffen
wurdt will ich euch zu negster rech- *[verso]* nung gutlichen abziehen,
thut wie ich euch vertrawe, lieber herr Schaffner. Ich hab lengst zu
euch schicken und mit euch die verwaltung des haws Arnheim han-
delen wollen, So hab ich j[e]ner doer vermeint das Capitel solt fur-
gangen sein, So ist es doch bishero des gehalten reichstag und andere
ursachen halben unterlassen. Bet euch demnach, Ir wollet euch das
haws mit getrewen vleis bevolhen sein lassen, und mit dem anleg gelt
gefast sein und dasselbig wie abgemelt dem Comether zu Colen zu
schicken, das wil ich gegen euch als dem ich alles guten vertrau
freuntlich beschulden.

Datum eylend Rotemburg uff der Thawber Sambstag den dritten
Iunii Anno *[XV^c]* xlij.

Philips Schilling Sant Johan ordens Comether zu Rotenburg und
Arnheim

[the address of the letter, in the same handwriting:]
Dem Werdigen heren Joanni Beltghen
Sant Johans ordens Convent bruder
und Schafner Im Johanniter Gang zu
Arnheim, meinem lieben heren und ordens Bruder

*[under this, another hand has added in different ink some abbreviations in what
appears to be Latin, ending with:]* D-B
    anno 1542

105. 1543, March 15 – *Grand Master and Council have decided, on demand of the grand bailiff of Germany, that the chaplain frater Jacob Vandeslaher must be admitted to the Council until the galleys return, because there are not enough knights of the German tongue to assist at the Council.*
 Chancery notice: AOM 209 = Decreta concilii 1473-1560, *fol.190r, dated in Annunciation-style.*

Die XV mensis Martii 1542 ab incarnatione. Audita petione domini locumtenentis venerandi magni baiulivi Alemanie petentis dominum fratrem Jacobum Vandeslaher dicte lingue cappellanum in consiliis admitti, attento quod ex fratribus militibus prefate lingue ad presens sufficiens numerus non reperitur qui interesse possit et hoc in dicta lingua ob causam predictam, non semel sic consuetum, reverendissimus dominus magnus magister et venerandum consilium ordinaverunt dictum fratrem Jacobum usque ad eventum triremium in consiliis admitti debere ut tunc ea res maturius declaretur et terminetur.

106. 1543, April 3 – *Grand Master and Council have decided that a chaplain may be admitted to the Council with the consent of the German tongue.*
 Chancery note: AOM 209 = Decreta concilii 1473-1560, *fol.190r-v.*
Die tertia mensis Aprilis 1543. Per reverendissimum dominum magnum magistrum et venerandum consilium cum scruttinio ballotarum fuit declaratum quod pro veneranda lingua Alemanie frater cappellanus eiusdem lingue accedente voluntate et consentu dicte *[fol.190v]* lingue in consiliis completis admittatur.

107. 1543, October 6 – *Frater Juan de Homedes, Grand Master, informs frater Joseph von Cambian, head of the preceptories of Hohenrain and Mechelen, that the Prior of Germany, frater Johann von Hatstein, has appointed him head of the preceptories Mechelen and Aachen by bull of 23 May 1542, issued at Speyer. The preceptories had become vacant after renunciation by their last head frater Johann von Sirich; the Grand Master now confirms this appointment by bull of 6 October 1543, issued on Malta, into which the text of the prioral bull has been inserted.*
 Registration: AOM 419 = libri bullarum 1543-1545, *fol.180 r-v.*
[The bull of the Prior is addressed to] religioso in Christo nobis charissimo fratri Josepho de Cambianis eiusdem nostri ordinis militi et per Germaniam et Bohemiam visitatori generali — *[and grants him, on account of his merits]* beneficia itaque seu domos de Mechlin et Aquisgrano ordini nostro spectantia, que modo per spontaneam et meram cessionem et renunciationem religiosi fratris Joannis de Sirich vacant, qui infirmi-

tate et senectute gravatus ipsas domos et omne ius suum in manibus collatione et dispositione nostra remisit et sponte renunciavit —.

108. 1545, June 18 – *Mary, dowager queen of Hungary and Governess of the Netherlands on behalf of her brother the Emperor Charles V, writes a letter to Grand Master frater Juan de Homedes, asking his help in the case of the son of the noble Reinald, lord of Brederode and Vianen, who has joined the troops that rebel against the emperor.*

Copy: AOM 420 = libri bullarum 1545-1547, *fol.202 r-v.*

Reverendo et Illustri principi Dilectioni Vestre[a] de Homedes ordinis militaris divi Joannis Hyerosolimitani magno magistro Amico nostro syncere dilecto.

Maria Dei gratia Hungarie, Bohemie et etc. regina vidua archidux[b] Austrie et cn.[c] Cessaree magestatis in Germania Inferiore locuntenens et etc. Reverendo et illustri principi Dilectioni Vestre[a] de Homedes ordinis militaris divi Joannis Hierosolimitani magno magistro amico nostro syncere dilecto. Salutem et synceri amoris affectum.

Reverende et illustris princeps amice syncere dilecte,

Qui has nostras Dilectioni Vestre exhibiturus est litteras, patre natus est Raginaldo domino a Brederoode et Viana ordinis Aurei Velleris equite ex illustri et antique nobilitatis familia, is quum partim etatis vitio partim facinosorum aliquot et perversorum consilio magis quam ex determinato iuditio, quod illi etati raro inesse solet, sese sub initium huius belli illis copiis adiunxisset, que adversus Cesaream magestatem dominum et fratrem nostrum ab ipsius adversariis parabantur, graviter fereque implacabiliter prefatam ipsius magestatem offendit. Quare illius criminis eluendi culpeque expiande causa consultum visum est iis, qui iuvenem funditus perire nolent, ut sese militie alicui sancte addicat, in eaque tractanda talem sese prestet ut quam imbecillitate etatis gratiam amisit, eam militari virtute recuperet, quam ad rem inventus est omnium commodissimus sacer ordo militaris divi Joannis Hierosolimitani, ut pote qui severitate discipline et gloria militari longe plurimos antecessat. Proinde si quando venire illum ad Dilectionem Vestram[a] contigerit eandem rogamus ut ad se venientem recipiat, eumque in militie laboribus exerceat talibusque in locis constituat, ubi virtutis specimen maius edere possit, quandoquidem bona in spe versamur illum maiorum suorum vestigiis inhesurum, et in frugi virum aliquando evasurum esse. Factura in hoc prefata Dilectio Vestra[a] rem nobis preterquam gratam, debito officiorum gratie a nobis recognoscendam: quam etiam feliciter valere optamus. Datum Daventrie die XVIII mensis Iunii MDXXXXV. Maria Regina.

---

^a Dilectio Vestra *with inflexions abbreviated as* D.V. *ms.*
^b *sic, ms.* ^c *unknown abbreviation ms:* cⁿ.

109. 1546, August 23 – *The Council decides to give frater Jacob Vandeslahert one year to settle his dispute with the proxy of the German tongue about the surrendering of the preceptories of Mechelen, Velden and Niederbreisig into the hands of the Prior of Germany and the alleged rights frater Jacob Vandeslahert has to them, in order to prove the renunciation of those preceptories by frater Johann von Syrich, sergeant at arms of the Order;*
the Council rules in favour of frater Johannes Vandeslahert in his dispute with frater Jean Picart concerning the seniority in the French tongue.
Chancery notice: AOM 87 = libri conciliorum 1543-1548, fol. 67v-68r.

Die XX tertia mensis Augusti M D XLVI. —.
^aterminus transmarinus concessus.^a
Eodem die cum dominus frater Jacobus Vandeslaher primo coram reverendissimo domino magno magistro et venerando consilio, deinde coram commissariis ab eo deputatis pretendisset quod frater Joannes Syrich eiusdem lingue serviens armorum in privationem preceptoriarum de Mechel, Velden et Brisac incurrisset, eo quod preceptoriam premissam de Mechel contra formam stabilimentorum scilicet in manibus venerandi prioris Alemanie renunciasset, dictasque preceptorias sibi tanquam antiano et in presentiarum capaci in suo gradu deberi et spectari petiisset, comparuit denuo idem Vandeslaher dicens quod etsi credat dictam renunciationem et cessionem satis probasse per bullam venerandi prioris Alemanie qui hoc asserit clarissime et non teneri ad aliam probationem, tamen pro potiori cautela, volens cautius agere, petiit terminum ac dilationem transmarinam ad probandum auctentice dictam renunciationem sibi concedi; cui contradixit procurator eiusdem lingue, petens quod dictus frater Jacobus in dicta pretensa petitione non audiatur, sed ei silentium imponatur, tum quia etsi stabilimentis caveatur, quod preceptorie vacantes cuius nullus est capax conferri debeant fratribus in conventu existentibus, hoc debere esse ex libera gratia lingue et non ex iustitia ut dictus frater Jacobus petiit, quam gratiam dicta lingua ei facere non vult, tum quia non constat de renunciatione nisi per bullam prioris, cui quo ad hoc adhibenda non est fides. Cum ad aliud se referat, contradixit etiam ei procurator fratris Asmi Haciel idem asserens, ac petens, casu quo declaretur dictum fratrem Joannem Syrich incidisse in penam privationis preceptoriarum secundum formam stabilimenti

XXV de collationibus suo principali antianiori dictas preceptorias vel alteram illarum conferri.

Quibus auditis ad plenum ac earum rationibus allegationibus et *[fol.68r]* productionibus mature perpensis, ac insuper habita relatione commissariorum super id ad audiendum et referendum deputatorum reverendum consilium cum scrutinio ballotarum nemine discrepante dederunt et concesserunt eidem fratri Jacobo Vandeslahert terminum ac dilationem transmarinam unius anni ad probandum dictam renuntiationem in partibus occiduis.

[a]In favorem fratris Joannis Vandeslahert.[a]

Eodem die super discordia vertente inter procuratorem fratris Joannis Picart, pretendentem esse de passagio fratris Joannis Vandeslahert cum aliis de causis tum maxime quia etsi prefatus Joannes Vandeslahert fuit prius receptus tamen fuit cum hac condictione quod esset de passagio illorum qui committati fuerunt reverendissimum quondam fratrem Philippum de Villers Lisleadam de cuius committina ipse Picart erat, nihilque obstet quod lingua post eius receptionem abstulerit et deleverit ex libro lingue illam conditionem, cum illud non poterat facere in suum preiudicium, nec revocare quod ipsamet prius concesserat ex una, ac procuratorem prefati Joannis Vandeslahert contradicentem ac pretendentem suum principalem esse antianum prefati Picart, tum quia primo presentatus fuit in lingua ut ex libro lingue constat, tum quia talis conditio et moderatio a lingua poni et prefigi non poterat, cum esset idoneus, et qualem stabilimenta requirunt, tum etiam quia quando lingua quod esset iustum et equum delevit illam conditionem dictus Picart erat presens et non contradixit, immo consensit, ac ideo pretendentem et petentem iudicari esse antianum prefati Joannis Picart partibus ex altera, reverendum consilium auditis partibus et earum rationibus et allegationibus mature perpensis, ac examinatis, ac insuper habita relatione commissariorum super id ad audiendum et referendum deputatorum cum scrutinio ballotarum nemine discrepante iudicaverunt dictum fratrem Joannem Vandeslahert esse antianum prefati fratris Joannis Picart pro antianoque eius habendum, et reputandum.

---

[a] *in margin ms.*

110. 1546, August 26 – *Frater Juan de Homedes, Grand Master, and Convent grant to* fratri Joanni Vandeslaer nostre dicte domus prioratus Francie capellano — *in order to advance his position,* bayliam seu preceptoriam et commendam nostram Sansoir et Baudelu —.

Registration: AOM 420 = libri bullarum 1545-1547, *fol.7v.*

111. 1547, January 4 – *Frater* Joannes Vandeslahert *is permitted to leave for his preceptory.*
Chancery note: AOM 420 = libri bullarum 1545-1547, *fol.11r, dated in Annunciation-style.*

112. 1547, February 28 – *The Council decides on the union of Freiburg with Heitersheim as the fifth prioral chamber of Germany in addition to Utrecht, Cologne, Heimbach and Bubikon.*
Chancery notice: AOM 209 = decreta concilii 1473-1560, *fol.235v-236v, dated in Annunciation-style.* Dehisterhent *should be* Heitersheim; *this already was a member of the preceptory of Freiburg as early as 1385, May 17: AOM 323* = libri bullarum 1385-1386, *fol.149r; see before, nr.6.*

28 Februario 1546 ab incarnatione.
Super differentia vertente inter procuratorem venerandi domini fratris Georgii Schilingh pro eo petentem prioratum Alemanie cum suis quatuor cameris, scilicet Utrech, Colonia, Hembac et praeceptoria de Bobequm, necnon preceptoria de Dehisterhent pro quinta camera, unita cum preceptoria de Friburg, et aliis membris, iuribus et pertinentiis ut sui predecessores presertim venerandus quondam frater Joannes Hastent habuerunt et possederunt — *[on the other hand, the proxy of the German tongue pretended that this union was but valid during the life of the last prior, because rich preceptories like these could not be united, only poor ones. In this matter, the lieutenant of the Grand Master and the Venerable Council decided that frater Georg Schilling as Prior of Germany should have the same rights as his predecessor.]*

113. 1547, February 28 – *Frater Juan de Homedes, Grand Master, and Convent appoint frater* Georgius Schilingh *after the decease of frater Johann von Hatstein as Prior of Germany, with the prioral chambers* videlicet Traiectum, Colonia, Hembach et Bobeguem necnon preceptoria de Friburgh in Presigay pro quinta tua camera —.
Registration: AOM 420 = libri bullarum 1545-1547, *fol.164r, dated in Annunciation-style.*

114. 1547 October 17 – *Frater Juan de Homedes, Grand Master, authorizes frater Georg Schilling, Prior of Germany, to install a small commission to collect all evidence concerning the dispute between frater Jacob Vandeslahert and the proxies of the German tongue concerning the claim of frater Vandeslahert to the preceptories of Mechelen, Velden and Niederbreisig, since frater Vandeslahert has* *not been able to give evidence in the Convent within a year after 23 August 1546 by circumstances beyond his control and is therefore allowed nine months extra to support his cause.*

Registration: *AOM 421* = libri bullarum 1547-1549, *fol.167r-v*. See before, *nr.109*.

Frater Joannes de Homedes etc. venerando religioso etc. fratri Georgio Schiling prioratus nostri Alemanie priori salutem in domino et diligentiam in commissis.

Noveris qualiter super lite et causa vertente inter religiosum nostrum fratrem Jacobum Vandeslahert ex una ac procuratorem venerande lingue Alemanie necnon procuratores religiosi nostri fratris Asmi Haciel occasione preceptoriarum de Mechel, Velden et Prisac quas idem Vandeslahert sibi deberi et spectare certo modo asserebat partibus ex altera, per nos nostramque venerandum consilium volentes ad ulteriora procedere, promulgatum et interlocutum fuit in modum qui sequitur: Die XXIII mensis Augusti M D XLVI. Cum dominus frater Jacobus Vandeslahert etc. et inseratur ad longum prout est in libro consiliorum et postea dicatur, in quo quidem termino ut premittitur assignato, cum idem Vandeslaher, non tamen culpa sua sed iniuria temporum ac bellorum inter Catholicam magestatem et principes Lutheranos exortorum ac aliis de causis nihil probare potuisset, eidem ad id probandum alios novem menses concessimus et prorogavimus. Quapropter cum equum et consentaneum sit ut quilibet de suo iure et iustitia docere possit, tenore presentium tibi committimus et mandamus, ut ad instantiam et requisitionem prefati de Vandeslahert, seu sui legitimi procuratoris, deputes unum vel duos commissarios ordinis nostri fratres qui vocato predicto fratre Joanne Sirich seu eius legitimo procuratore omnes et quoscumque testes quos ipse de Vandeslahert seu alius suo nomine producere voluerit ad probandum *[fol.167v]* predictam renunciationem, examinent et examinari curent instrumenta et alia acta ad id facienda recipiant et admittant, quorum quidem testium depositiones unacum instrumentorum huiusmodi tenore in scriptis auctenticis per notarium publicum et legalem redactas manibus eorum subscriptas et sigillis obsignatas, prefato Jacobo Vandeslahert assignabis, seu assignabunt, ut cognita veritate quod iustum fuerit decernere valeamus.

In cuius rei etc. bulla nostra ad arma etc.

Datum Melite etc. die XVII mensis Octobris M D XXXXVII.

115. 1547, October 17 – *Frater Jacob Vandeslahert, head of the preceptory of Herford, is licensed to leave for his preceptory.*

Chancery note: AOM 421 = libri bullarum 1547-1549, *fol.167v.*
Die XVII mensis Octobris M D XLVII concessa fuit licentia fratri
Jacobo Vandeslahert preceptori de Herfort discedendi de conventu et
eundi ad dictam preceptoriam.

116. 1553, January 20 – *Frater Johann Schmeling, head of the preceptory in
Cologne, asks frater* Johan Beltgen, Schaffner *(administrator) of the houses at
Arnhem and Nimwegen, to pay his contribution arrears and chapter costs; however,
the amounts are not mentioned.*
    *Original letter in German: RA Gelderland, Loeff, Archief, inventory nr.12,
regest nr.527, double leaf double-sided, pp.1-2 written, dated and undersigned by
the writer on p.2:*
Datum 20ten Januarij Anno 53.
Johan Schmeling Ordens S.Johans Compthuir zu Collen, Receptor
address on p.4: Ehrwürdiger herrn Johan Beltgen S.Johans Ordens
Schaffner beider häuser, Arnheim und Newmagen, Mainem lieben
herrn und guten freundt.

117. 1570, May 29 – *Frater Pietro del Monte, Grand Master, gives instructions concerning many matters to frater Antonio Maldonado, head of the preceptory
of Fresno in Leon and ambassador to the King of Spain. Some of these instructions
pertain to the Dutch bailiwick of Utrecht, prioral chamber of Germany, which
refuses to pay the treasury its annual contributions and other dues that are fixed
proportional to its real value.*
    Registration: AOM 433 = libri bullarum 1570-1571, *fol.245r.*

Nella Bassa Alemagnia è posta in paese delli stati di sua Maesta la
commenda di Utrecth, seu Traiecto in Holandia camera priorale del
priorato d'Alemagnia, la quale è d'entrata importante et è possessa et
goduta da certi preti che non riconoscono la religione et commun
Thesoro salvo d'una miseria che si po dire niente rispetto la valuta, et
per che non è di raggione ne di mente delli fundatori. Il principale
intento delli quali fu che li beni se impiegassero nella hospitalità la-
quale exercemo et nella militia della quale facemo professione contra
infideli. Per ciò procurarete ottener da sua Maesta proviggione expressa et valida che non ostante qual si voglià privileggio che li detti
preti havessero ò potessero allegare, dobbino et siano obligati come è
di guistitia, riconoscer et pagare la Religione nostra delle responsioni
et impositioni alla rata che sogliono pagar' le altre commende
d'Alemagna. Et di più venendo à vacar possi il commun Thesoro
godere le despoglie delli defuntti et l'annata del mortuario et vacate,

conforme li nostri statuti, et se per facilitar il negotio fosse necessario qualche proviggione da sua Serenita ce ne avisarete ottenendo tra tanto il consenso di sua Maesta che siamo certi ch'il Papa lo confirmara subito, et bisognando vene mandaremo le provigioni. Et si sua Maesta rimettesse il detta negotio al suo consiglio di stato in Bassa Alemagnia, in tal caso ne scriverete all'illustrissimo et eccelentissimo signor Duca d'Alba et al prior Don Ferdinando accio faccino che de la le informationi venghino in favor di nostra religione.

In cuius rei etc. bulla nostra magistralis in cera nigra etc.

Datum Melite etc. die XXIX mensis Maij M D LXX.

118. 1571, December 20 — *Frater Adam von Swalbach, Prior of Germany, summons frater Joachim Krabbe, former administrator of the houses at Arnhem and Nimwegen, to the provincial chapter on 5 May 1572 on account of his administration.*

Contemporaneous copy: RA Gelderland, Loeff, Archief, inventory nr.14, regest nr.561, double leaf double-sided, written on pp.1-2, note on p.4, in the same handwriting:

In Zaecke van H.Jochum Crabbe van S.Johans orden binnen Arnhem

Cf.Loeff, Archief, inventory nr.14, regesta nrs.562, 563 and 564, dd. 15, 22 and 24 April 1572, containing declarations of good behaviour as administrator and priest of St John's houses at Arnhem and Nimwegen, as prior at Arnhem and as citizen of Nimwegen for Joachim Crab or Krabbe from mayors, eschevins and council of Arnhem, chancellor and councillors of the duchy of Guelders, and mayors, eschevins and council of Nimwegen.

Nos Adamus a Schwalbach ordinis sancti Johannis Hijerosolymitani magister per Alemaniam devoto nobis dilecto fratri Joachimo Krabe presbitero ordinis nostri salutem in Domino et obedientiam in mandatis.

Cum iam sepius a fide dignis nobis relatum sit, vos post obitum honorandi quondam fratris Johannis Schmeijsings comendatoris in Arnemia ac Noviomago officio procuratoris ac oeconomi negotiorumque gestoris in predictis comendis ac domibus functum esse et preter spem que de vobis tanquam ordinis presbitero concepta erat magis privato lucri studio inhaerens quam comendarum comoditatem et utilitatem (pro ut debebatis) invigilans, simulaveritis vos a quibusdam vestris cognatis, noningentos thaleros in mutuum recepisse eandemque summam (quod tamen minime factum est) in ordinis ac comendarum usum et utilitatem translatam ac collatam esse fingens et pro nunc tempore existenti comendatori ut fertur imposuistis ut literas in quibus debitum praedictum noningentorum thalorum confi-

teretur, conscriberet et curiam seu praedium rusticum Holanderpruch ad ordinem et comendam spectans atque pertinens in hijpothecam obligaret. Que si ita in veritatis substantia se haberent pro ut
nobis de ea re fides facta est, certe res fratre ac praesbitero ordinis
nostri esset indignissima. Cumque etiam hactenus vos nostris nostro-
rumque comendatoriorum mandata que eis iniunximus ut tenemini
minime obtemperastis, nos vigore ac virtute nostri ordinis laudandae
consuetudinis ac iuris nec non stabilimentorum hactenus observato-
rum nullo modo eiusmodi nostri ordinis *[p.2]* detestandam maculam
absque animadversione ferre ac absque correctione dimittere quinius,
itaque cum maturo habita consultatione statuerimus secundum ordinis nostri allegatam laudandam consuetudinem provintialem capitulum proximum futurum, die Lune post Dominicam Cantate quinta
mensis Maij anno proximo septuagesimo secundo celebrare atque
omnes et singulos nostri ordinis baiulivos, comendatores atque fratres
convocare, vos tenore presentium citamus atque monemus, primo,
secundo, tertio ac peremptorie quatenus vos in propria persona omni
exceptione remoratione postposita ad praenominatum capitulum,
nempe diae Lunae post Dominicam Cantate quinta mensis Maij anni
futuri septuagesimi secundi Spirae in curia nostra ac capitulari loco
ibidem consueto mane compareatis ac presto sitis vestra comissa de-
licta de quibus infamati estis adeoque vestram hactenus perpetratam
contumatiam purgaturi ibidemque usque ad finem ac exitum capituli
perseveraturi nostrisque decisionibus atque mandatis pareturi ac satis
facturi. Alias vobis non comparentibus atque in contumatia perma-
nentibus ad declarationem paenarum per ordinis statuta apostolica-
que indulta contra inobedientes mandatisque suorum superiorum
rebelles inflictarum usque ad privationem habitus et beneficiorum
procedi efficiemus, contumatia vestra in aliquo non obstante, que
vobis hisce patentibus literis intimare atque significare intermittere
noluimus.

Datum Haitershaim Brisgoiae domo residentie nostre, vigilia sancte Thomae apostoli XX Decembris Anno M D LXXI.

119. 1572, May 9 – *Frater Adam von Swalbach, Prior of Germany, the Grand
Bailiff, proxies and heads of preceptories of the provincial chapter decide that frater
Philips von Rosenbach, head of the preceptories of Arnhem and Nimwegen, must
stop the annuity of frater Joachim Krabbe until his debts have been paid.*

*Original letter: RA Gelderland, Loeff, Archief, inventory nr.14, regest
nr.565; single leaf single-sided, the superimpressed seal is lost.*

Nos Adamus a Schwalbach, magister, nec non magnus baiulivus, procuratores et comendatarii provincialis capituli religionis sancti Johannis per Alemaniam.

Notum facimus universis et singulis has literas visuris, lecturisve, quod coram nobis comparaverunt, strenuus ac devotus nobis singulariter dilectus, Philippus a Rosenbach comendator in Arnemia[a] et Noviomago ex una, et frater Joachimus Krabe nostri ordinis praesbiter ex altera parte, cumque ipsis super controversia hinc inde auditis percipissemus ac cognoverimus, quatenus dudum elapso tempore, praedictus Joachimus Krabe, cum[b] procuratoris ac aeconomi vices in comenda Arnemiae sustineret, simulaverit, se a quibusdam suis cognatis noningentos thaleros in mutuum recipisse, insuper praedicto Philippo a Rosenbach cum primitus tanquam comendator: possessionem comendae Arnemiae adeptus esset, persuasit, ut literis in hoc negotio scriptis, debitum noningentorum thalerum confiteret, et curiam seu praedium Holanderpruch, ad comendam iam nominatam pertinens, in hijpothecam ea propter obligaret. Inde eventum cum quidam Guilielmus Göms [?] literas obligatorias noningentorum thalerum penes se ac in potestate haberet, ac propter suspicionem haeresis ac Lutherane sectae, fugitivus factus, una cum reliquis suis bonis etiam literae obligatoriae noningentorum thalerum a fiscali Catholicae regis maiestatis Hispaniarum Inferioris Germaniae confiscatae, ac praedictum praedium, seu curia Holanderpruch ad comendam Arnemiam pertinens, per eundem fiscalem arestatum est. Quae quidem omnia, sive incuria, dole seu culpa praenominati fratris Joachimi Kraben, ordini ac comendae Arnemiae erepta atque alienata sunt.

Ne autem in futurum in detrimentum, ac iacturam ordinis eiusmodi eveniant, ac exemplum in eos statuatur qui culpa atque incuria ordinis nostri facultates, bona atque iura amittunt atque alienant, nos vigore ordinis nostri privilegiorum ac stabilimentorum ac matura desuper habita deliberatione, capitulum provinciale celebrantes, decrevimus, statuimus, et declaramus, cum hactenus praedictus frater Philippus a Rosenbach comendator in Arnemia et Noviomago, sepius nominato fratri Joachimo Kraben annuatim ex debita pensione triginta sex thaleros hactenus numeraverit ac persolverit, in futurum eandem pensionem retineat ac in alios comendae Arnemiae usus ac emolumenta convertat praecipimus, donec et tam diu saepe nominatus Joachimus Krabe suis propriis sumptibus et pecunia praelibatam curiam seu praedium Holanderpruch ab omni onere, obligatione, et debitis exoneravit, et in libertatem priorem ordini restituerit, iniungentes fratri Philippo a Rosenbach nostris obtemperare mandatis, alias sciat se inobedientiae notum et desuper statutis paenis incursurum.

Datum in nostro provinciali capitulo Spirae, Veneris nona mensis

Maij, anno salutis millesimo, quingentesimo septuagesimo secundo.

_____

ª Armenia *ms.* ᵇ *is missing in ms.*

120. 1573, March 3 – *Frater Henrick Berck, Bailiff of Utrecht, writes a concept-letter to frater Adam von Swalbach, Prior of Germany, asking him for remission of his annual contributions for one year on account of the state of war in his region.*

Original concept letter: RA Utrecht, Collectie Buchel-Booth *nr.18 (old ms.356 I), fol.79r-v with address on fol.84v:*

Reverendissimo domino ac illustrissimo principi D.Adamo a Swallbach ordinis domini Johannis Hyerozolimitani per Alª Germaniam magistro, domino meo clementissimo.

This nr.18 is a volume of documents, written on paper, 134 folia, in several handwritings, with a charter on parchment from 1581 added at the back; the blank pages contain notes in the handwriting of Arnoud van Büchel, with an index in his hand at the end.

Reverendissime domine, ac illustrissime princeps, post obsequii mei assiduam commendationem omni qua possim modestia celsitudini vestrae renuntio, literas celsitudinis vestrae die vigesimo primo Decembris proximo praeteriti scriptas, non ita dudum per me receptas, quibus me ad capitulum certo quodam et designato die Friburgi celebrandum vocas debitis pensionibus et responsionibus instructum. Est quod (proh dolor) in hisce regionibus tantis aerumnis et calamitatibus undique praemimur, quod omnia nostra pecora et mobilia extra civitatem Traiectensem existentia ab immanibus hostibus sunt occupata et direpta, adeoque ordinis nostri commendatarii bonis et possessionibus funditus nudati, domibusque expulsi quae partim igno sunt consumptae, partim penitus demolitae, ita ut tamquam exules ad baiuliarii Traiectensis suum habuere et adhuc de praesenti habent refugiu̱m, quibus omnia victui necessaria subministrare proᵇ offitioᵇ debeo. In summa hostibus undique cingimur, et viarum tanta sunt discrimina quod ne quidem in unius anni spatio pedem extra muros civitatis ponere ausus fui, ipsorum quoque hostium immanitas indies intrudescit ita ut rustici et coloni maxime ecclesiasticorum bonorum tam dire vexantur, et excoriantur, quod ne unum aureum intra anni spatium acceperim et proinde in re tam tenui sum ut ne —ᵈ solidum quidamᶜ impendere in mea sit *[fol.79v]* potestate. Quapropter celsitudinem vestram suppliciter etª peramanterª oratum velim quatenus praesentium calamitatum ratione habita, meam hanc excusationem iustam et legitimam aequi bonique consulere, nec non huiusᵇ anniᵇ

pensionem cessam^a una cum responso pro^a hac vice gratiose remittere dignetur. Quantum^c ad me quod^a attinet ubi haec secula exelcera-
ta cessaverint, et in re aliquanto meliori fuero offitii mei debitum (ut
obedientem ordinis fratrem decet et qualem semper se domus Traiec-
tensis erga celsitudinem vestram praestitit) quantum^a fieri^a poterit^a
Deo annuente adimplere totis viribus conabor, novit ipse Deus qui
celsitudinem vestram in multos annos felicem et sanum conservet.

Raptim ex conventu Traiectensi —^d tertia Martii anno millesimo
quingentesimo septuagesimo tertio.

Celsitudinis vestrae ad omnia obedientissimus
    f.Henricus Barck
missa sunt hae literae ex Traiecto 9na Martii.

---

^a *crossed out.* ^b *added in the margin.* ^c *inserted in the text.* ^d *made illegible by deletion.*

121. 1573, October 3 – *Frater Jean Levesque de la Cassière, Grand Master,
and Convent appoint frater Philips Flach,* commendatarius *of* Trieres et
Turlesheim, *as Prior of Germany and successor of frater Adam von Swalbach.
The origin of the fifth prioral chamber is explained.*

*Original bull on parchment: GLA Karlsruhe, 20/160, with holes of lost string
with seal of Grand Master and Convent.*
*The chapter which is referred to, is the one from Avignon, March 1367. It
concerns its statutes no.9, summarized in J.Delaville le Roulx, Les Hospitaliers, p.162 with note 7. The explanation of the need for a fifth camera
prioralis appears as early as 1400, July 6, AOM 330 fol.82r-v, in the
appointment bull for frater Hesso Schlegelholtz; see nr.8 above.*

*[Frater Philips Flach receives the Priorate of Germany with its prioral cham-
bers]* videlicet Traiectum, Coloniam, Hembach et Boboquem necnon
commendam de Friburg et Preisgaw pro quinta tua camera.

— Rursus cum retroactis temporibus priores nostre dicte domus
super bonis et harnesiis commendatariorum in dies decedentium haberent et reciperent certa iura que per ordinationem in memorato
capitulo promulgatam communi erario applicata fuerunt et reservata,
in compensationem premissorum iurium concessum fuerit et permissum prefatis Prioribus ultra quatuor Cameras ordinarias unam aliam
commendam cum vacabit in eodem prioratu ad collationem prioris
pertinentem accipere, tibi quoque pro quinta Camera predictam
Commendam de Friburg in Preisgaw prout supra narratur assignamus eamque accipiendi potestatem, facultatem ac licentiam impartimur. —

122. 1575, March 5 – *Frater Jean Levesque de la Cassière, Grand Master, and Convent grant the preceptory of Mechelen with its members at Aachen and Heideck, vacant by the decease of its last head frater Joseph von Cambian, to frater Michel Olivier, chaplain of the German tongue.*
    Registration: AOM 435 = libri bullarum 1574-1575, *fol.198v, dated in Annunciation-style.*

Frater Joannes Levesque dela Cassiere etc. custos et nos conventus etc. religioso etc. fratri Michaeli Oliverio nostrae dictae domus venerandae linguae Alemaniae capellano salutem etc.

    Morum et vitae honestas, cultus divini peritia et observantia multiplicesque animi tui dotes, nec non laudabilia obsequia per te ordini nostro prestita et quae in dies sedulo prestare non desinis, promerentur ut te ad commoda bonorumque ordinis nostri regimina promoveamus. Bailiam itaque seu commendam nostram de Mechlin prioratus Alemaniae per obitum venerandi quondam fratris Josephi Cambiani ultimi legitimi dictae commendae de Mechlin commendatarii et possessoris sive hoc sive alio quovismodo vacantem presentialiter et ad nostram collationem, donationem etc. cum omnibus et singulis suis membris et presertim de Auch et Heidech nec non prediis, iuribus etc. et cum quibus illam dictus quondam venerandus frater Josephus Cambianus habuit, tenuit etc. —.

    Datùm Melitae etc. die quinta mensis Martii 1574 ab incarnatione.

123. 1575, December 10 – *Frater Philips Flach von Schwartzenburg, Prior of Germany, summons frater Philips von Rosenbach, head of the preceptories at Arnhem and Nimwegen, to the provincial chapter at Freiburg on 2 February 1576 and informs him of the Grand Master's appeal next March to go to Malta because of the Turkish threat.*
    Original letter: RA Gelderland, Loeff, Archief, inventory nr.11, regest nr.570; double leaf double-sided, written pp.1-2-3, undersigned with autograph, address on p.4: Dem Würdigen unnd gestrengen unnserm lieben besonndern Br. Philipsen von Rosenbach Sant Johanns Ordenns Comenthur zu Arnheim unnd Newmegen Receptor in Nider Deutsch-Landen,
    Arnheim oder Newmegen

[p.1, beginning:] Philips Flach von Schwartzenburg Sannt Johanns Ordens Meister in Deutschlanden.
[p.3] Datum Spire den IV Decembris Anno 75.
    Philips Flach   Meister rs

124. 1577/1578 [date?] – *Frater Jean Levesque de la Cassière, Grand Master, gives instructions to frater Bernardino Scaglia, ambassador of the Order to the Imperial Majesty. These instructions concern among other things the need to prevent the German preceptories of the Empire from seceding from the Order of Malta, under the pretext that fighting the Turks in Hungary together with the Teutonic Order would be preferable to being useless to Christianity and the Empire in the capacity of members of the Order of Malta with its remote headquarters.*
Registration: AOM 437 = libri bullarum 1577-1578, *fol.241r.*

125. 1579, August 19 – *Frater Jean Levesque de la Cassière, Grand Master, and Convent order frater* Joannes Georgius Schomborn magnus baiulivus linguae Alemaniae *and frater* Philippus Riedesel commendatarius in Erlinghen, *to introduce frater* Michael Oliver capellanus *in his preceptory* Mechlin *and to place him in possession of it.*
Registration: AOM 438 = libri bullarum 1578-1579, *fol.198r.*

126. 1586, May 13 – *Frater Hugues de Loubenx Verdala, Grand Master, lends his ear to frater* Michael Oliverius, *head of the preceptories of* Mechlin et Kiringhen, *as proxy of frater* Philippus de Riedesel, *head of the preceptory of* Erlinghen.
Registration: AOM 443 = libri bullarum 1586-1587, *fol.204r.*

127. 1586, September 20 – *Frater Hugues de Loubenx Verdala, Grand Master, gives instructions to frater* Philippus Riedesel, *head of the preceptory of* Erlingen, *and frater* Wipertus de Rosembach, *head of the preceptories of* Basel *and* Hohenrhein, *about a visitation of* Alemagna, Ungaria & Dacia, *recommending them among others to be discrete in those places where the churches are in Protestant hands, but to refurnish and sequester the income of the churches of preceptories in Catholic regions, which are neglected by their heads.*
Registration: AOM 443 = libri bullarum 1586-1587, *fol.248v.*

Item perche alcune commende di detto priorato sono sottoposte al dominio di principi Lutherani, Zuingliani et altri heretici dove non se ponno mantenere le chiese et culto divino come si conviene secondo i tempi e luoghi; usarete in cio destrezza et discrettione pero essendo che molte altre commende che sono in luoghi Catholici et dove a commendatori conviene per l'honor d'Iddio quanto per la intentione del fundatore di detta commenda intratenere la chiesa con suoi giogali, paramenti, sacerdoti et altri cose che e necessario, et che nondimeno al contrario per la avantia loro con grande scandalo di quelli popoli et vilipendio di nostra Religione lasceramo andare la chiesa et ogn'altra cosa in ruina, essendo in quella citta et lochi ogni altro tempio aperto et administrato di divini officii fuori di quello di nostra religione, il quale serve d'albergo piu d'animali brutti che d'altrecose, perquesto vi commettemo et in virtu di sancta obedienza commandamo che trovando l'errore sudetto, ipso fatto habbi a sequestrare l'intrate di dette commende, dandovi potesta di fare le chiese di novo con paramenti, ornamenti di sacerdoti et altra cosa consueta conforme l'ordine del fundatore, et che habbi a mandare il processo de tali, qua in conventu nostro per essequire che le leggi commandino.

128. 1587, March 20 − *Frater Hugues de Loubenx Verdala, Grand Master, and Convent grant to frater* Michael Oliverius, *head of the preceptory of* Mechlin, *the right of receiving, after his abdication of Mechelen,* — bailiam seu commendam nostram de Wormatia, *vacant by the decease of its last head frater* Johannes Georgius Schomborn.
Registration: AOM 443 = libri bullarum 1586-1587, *fol.207v, dated in Annunciation-style; see next item.*

129. 1587, March 20 − *Frater Hugues de Loubenx Verdala, Grand Master, and Convent grant to the knight frater Walther von Orspach, by lack of a vacant knight's preceptory, the chaplain's preceptory of Kieringen, vacant through renunciation by frater Michel Olivier, which will be united with Mechelen.*
Registration: AOM 443 = libri bullarum 1586-1587, *fol.211r, dated in Annunciation style. Cf. A.nr.134 below.*

Frater Hugo Verdala etc. — fratri Gualthero de Orspach militi —.
— commendam nostram de Kiringhen eiusdem prioratus ad statum fratrum capellanorum et servientium armorum spectantem vacantem per renuntiationem religiosi etc. fratris Michaelis Oliverii, interim et usque quo commendam status fratrum militum habueris et in redditu fueris, tunc vero quod dicta commenda de Kiringhen vacare censeatur ac commenda de Mechlin dicti prioratus uniatur et incorporetur. Hinc est quod bailiam seu commendam prefatam de Kiringhen predicti prioratus Alemanie per liberam renuntiationem dicti fratri Michaelis Oliverii (ut prefertur) ad commendam nostram de Wormatia pro suo melioramento promoti ultimi legitimi dictae commendae de Kiringhen commendarii et possessoris sive hoc, sive alio quovismodo vacantem — sub eisdem supradictis pactis, modis, legibus vel — ad decem annos continuos et completas et ultra ad nostrum beneplacitum, ac cum conditionibus quibus tibi constituta

fuit, conferimus, concedimus et donamus benefaciendo in eadem.
—.

Datum Melita etc. die XX^{ma} mensis Martii MDLXXXVI ab incarnatione.

130. 1587, August 21 − *Frater Hugues de Loubenx Verdala, Grand Master, and Convent grant to frater* Philippus Lucius Snouck, *head of the preceptories of* Slusingh et Weisen[see] et Mechlin, *an annual rent of 50 gold shields from the preceptory of Erlingen.*
    Registration: AOM 443 = libri bullarum 1586-1587, *fol.210r. This is repeated in AOM 444* = libri bullarum 1588-1589, *fol.211r, dd. 21 February 1588* ab incarnatione *(1589, February 21).*

131. 1588, March 30 − *Frater Hugues de Loubenx Verdala, Grand Master, and the General Chapter appoint frater Philips Lucius Snouck, head of the preceptories of Weissensee, Mechelen and Aachen, as convent chaplain of the bailiwick of Utrecht with the right to regain this bailiwick from heretical hands and enjoy its yields during his lifetime.*
    Registration: AOM 444 = libri bullarum 1588-1589, *fol.208r-209r.*

Frater Hugo etc. cardinalis etc. custos et nos baiulivi, priores etc. capitulum generale etc. religioso etc. fratri Philippo Lucio Snouch commendarum nostrarum de Weisensche, Mechelen et Aquasgrana prioratus Alemaniae commendatario salutem in Domino sempiternam.
Virtutum tuarum merita multiplicesque animi tui dotes laudabiliaque obsequia per te ordini nostro praestita et quae in dies sedulo prestare non desinis promerentur et nos inducunt ut tuis votis facilem prebeamus assensum.
[fol.208v] Supplicatio siquidem tua nobis porrecta erat tenoris sequentis:
    Illustrissimo et Reverendissimo Monsignor et sacro general capitulo. Il commendator fra Philippo Lucio Snouck humilissimo religioso della sua veneranda lingua d'Alemagna et servitor di Vestra Signorìa Illustrissima a quello et sacro general capitulo espone che la commenda de Utricht della religione Hierosolimitana posta nella provintia di Olanda estata sempre et al presente e posseduta dal stato de fra capellani li quali ordinariamente sono residenti sopra la detta commenda da dieci o dodeci in circa et sono chiamati conventuali, et si come colui il quale vuole intrare in detta commenda o convento é electo dal priore o commendatore et deli altri capellani conventuali

cosi anchora succedendo la morte del detto commendatore loro elig-
nio un altro della loro comitiva estimandosi exempto di venir in Convento et di pagare li carrichi, responsioni et impositioni della
religione; et perche il commendatore della detta commenda tiene la
collatione di altre diece comende che li sono sotoposte cio e Harlem,
Engen, Buren, Vallis Sancti Joannis, Aldewater, Hermelen, Wemlingen, Richwerff[a], Midelburg et Chenek[b] comprese quelle che sono in
Olanda, Zelanda et Gheldria, le quali provintie essendo hoggi ribelle
dalla Maesta Cattholica loro natural signore consequentemente dette
commende o alcune di quelle sono cascate in mano di Lutaerani,
Sguinquylani[c] et altri heretici in grandissimo damno et pregiuditio
della religione nostra, per tanto supplica Vestra Signorìa Illustrissima
et sacro general capitulo si degnino restar serviti in virtu della lor
supprema auctorita ricevere per fratre conventuale di detto convento
et commenda de Utricht al supplicante et che in esso possa havere
voto attivo et passivo et goder tutte le dignita, preeminentiae, offitii et
benefitii di detto convento accioche per quella via et favor del prenci-
pe di Parma o lucotenente del re Cattholico in quelle parte ritornan-
do (come si spera) detta provintia alla devotion del loro natural
signore possa ricuperar lo expectante le dette commende et redurle
alla obedientia et devotione della religione; derogando per questa
volta tantum alle fondatione, privilegii, prerogativi, exemptioni, stabilimenti et qualsivoglia legge, uso et costume in contrario dictante, et
restara di continuo apregar nostro signor Dio per la longa vita pros-
pero et felicissimo stato di Vestra Signorìa Illustrissima et di sua sacra
religione Et ita supplicat ut altissimus

Hinc est quod premissorum meritorum tuorum intuitu et contemplatione suasi supplicationibusque tuis inclinati invicem maturo et
deliberato concilio de nostra certa scientia et speciali gratia te fratrem
Philippum Lucium presentem et acceptantem in fratrem conventualem praedictae commendae et conventus de Utricht prout petis et
supplicas recipimus et cooptamus receptumque et cooptatum in
eadem esse volumus [fol.209r] et declaramus cum omnibus et quibuscunque praerogativis, praeeminentiis, privilegiis, immunitatibus offi-
ciisque et beneficiis, honoribus et oneribus quibus ceteri fratres dictae
commendae et conventus de Utricht utuntur, fruuntur et gaudent
fruique et gaudere consueverunt; non obstantibus quibuscumque statutis, privilegiis, usibus et aliis contrarium dictantibus quibus pro hac
vice dumtaxat derogamus ac derogatum esse volumus; membraque
sive commendas, predia et possessiones a predicta commenda de
Utricht dependentia et per quoscumque contra formam nostrorum
statutorum, privilegiorum apostolicorum et indultorum detenta, videlicet Harlen, Engen, Buren, Vallis Sancti Joannis, Aldewater, Herme-

len, Wemelingen, Kirchwerff, Myddelburgt, Schnecse[b] prout in dicta
supplicatione continetur ad petendum et tuis expensis recuperandum
in iusque et dominium nostrae religionis restituendum dictisque
membris sive commendis, praediis et possessionibus tuis expensis et
industria recuperatis vita tua perdurante fruendum ac gaudendum ac
in tuos usus convertendum. Iuxta prefatorum nostrorum statutorum
ac consuetudinem nostri ordinis et pro his et horum ratione in iuditio
et extra coram quibuscumque tribunalibus ecclesiasticis vel temporalibus comparendum, agendum et experiendum et omnes iuridicos
actus faciendum tibi indulgemus et facultatem damus ac liberaliter
impartimur, praecipientes omnibus et singulis dictae domus nostrae
fratribus quacumque auctoritate, dignitate officioque fungentibus
presentibus et futuris, et praesertim fratribus nostris dictae commendae et conventus de Utrecht in virtute sanctae obedientiae ne contra
presentes nostras receptionis et provisionis literas aliquatenus facere
vel venire presumant sed eas studeant inviolabiliter observare.

In cuius rei etc. bulla nostra communis plumbea etc.

Datum Melitae etc. durante nostro generali capitulo die penultima
mensis Martii MDLXXXVIII.

---

[a] *i.e.* Kerkwerve. [b] *i.e.* Sneek. [c] *i.e.* Zwingliani.

132. 1588, June 24 sq. – *The General Chapter decrees, that brethren who are
appointed by Grand Master and Convent or by the General Chapter as convent
members of the houses at Strassburg, Cologne, Wesel, and Utrecht, will have the
same rights as the other members of those houses and that newly elected heads of
those houses must ask the consent of Grand Master and Convent at Malta within
six months. All privileges pertaining to charges or duties of those houses are
annulled.*

Copies: AOM 291 = Sacrum Capitulum Generale, *1588, fol.79v-80r;
RA Utrecht,* Collectie Buchel-Booth *nr.18, fol.82r-83r. See about this volume nr.18: before, nr.120. The text of RA Utrecht has been followed although
fol.80-81, containing the beginnings and the date, are missing. The date has been
added from AOM 291. By the looks of the handwriting, the ms. in RA Utrecht
seems to be a copy from the chancery at Malta.*

[fol.82r] Reverendi domini XVI illustrissimo et reverendissimo domino cardinali magno magistro.

Item cum conventus sive domus Argentinensis, Coloniensis, Vesaliensis, et Ultraiactensis, pariter cum commendis suis, tam annexis,
quam connexis, sint quasi extra obedientiam ordinis nostri sub prae-
textu multorum privilegiorum ac unionum, quas habere se affirmant,

ab ipso ordine nostro, ac etiam a summis pontificibus et imperatoribus, et quod peius est, non exolvant passagia, responsiones, vacantia, mortuaria, nec quascunque alias impositiones, taliter, quod nec receptores ordinis nostri, et eius communis aerarii fratrum defunctorum spolia audeant contrectare, atque etiam praetendant, se non astrictos ad veniendum in Conventum, et reliqua officia, prout veri religiosi dicti nostri ordinis facere tenentur. Itaque status rerum eiusdem ordinis, in dictis conventibus et domibus, ad pessimam sit reductus conditionem, ultraque valde timendum sit, ne propter bella intestina, quae multo iam tempore in illis partibus flagrarunt, et adhuc durant, dicti conventus et domus, ac bona dicti ordinis, ad extremum penitus redigantur interitum, nisi oportunis remediis mature huic negotio consulatur. Idcirco reverendi domini XVI capitulares, suprema aucthoritate, in ordine nostro fungentes, revocantes prius, et annulantes, ac abrogantes omnia et singula pri-*[fol.82v]*vilegia, exemptiones, concessiones, uniones, et gratias ac alia quaecunque indulta, dictis conventibus et domibus, eorumque commendatariis, per praeterita capitula generalia dicti ordinis, vel bonae memoriae magnos magistros, et conventum, vel aliter per religionem nostram concessa, quoquomodo, et ex quavis causa etiam incognita, statuerunt et ordinaverunt, quod nullus possit esse commendatarius dictorum conventuum et domorum, nisi prius resederit hic Melitae in Conventu nostro, et quod fratres venerandae linguae Alemaniae, qui a magno magistro et conventu, vel a capitulo generali, in quovis dictorum conventuum et domorum Argentinensis, Coloniensis, Vesaliensis et Ultraiactensis recepti fuerint, sint, atque intelligantur esse veri conventuales eorundem conventuum et domorum, ac etiam possunt semper concurrere ad electionem commendatarii, cum voce activa, et passiva, fruique emolumentis ac praerogativis ipsis, quibus caeteri conventuales, in dictis conventibus et domibus fruuntur et gaudent. Ipsi vero qui in Commendatarios electi fuerint, teneantur in termino sex mensium petere et obtinere confirmationem a magno magistro et conventu: alioquin talis electio sit *[fol.83r]* nulla, et eidem magno magistro et conventui liberum sit, alium vel alios in locum electorum eligere et cooptare. Quiquidem commendatarii astricti et obligati sint, ad persolvendum dicto ordini, et eius communi aerario, omne id, quod antiquitus solitum et consuetum fuit persolvere, tam de responsionibus, quam aliis quibusvis impositionibus et iuribus dicti aerarii. Et ut praemissa suum debitum sortiantur effectum, iidem reverendi domini XVI remisserunt illustrissimo et reverendissimo domino cardinali, magno magistro, ut vices suas interponat, cum sanctissimo domino nostro Syxto, papa quinto, sanctaque sede Apostolica, ac cum maiestate caesarea imperatoris, et aliis regibus et principibus, ut praesentem constitutionem, quae vim statuti habere voluerunt, confirmare dignentur, cum derogatione privilegiorum, immunitatum, exemptionum, confirmationum, et aliorum quorumcunque per dictam sedem Apostolicam, suamque caesaream maiestatem, et alios sacros imperatores, reges, et principes suos predecessores, dictis conventibus et domibus Argentinensi, Coloniensi, Vesaliensi et Ultraiactensi eorumque fratribus et commendatariis concessorum.

133. 1588, December 1 – *Frater Andreas Wilhelm, head of the preceptory of Straßburg, informs his colleague at Utrecht about the Chapter decision at Malta concerning the appointment of new heads in several German preceptories and advises him to appeal against it at the papal court.*

Original letter: RA Utrecht, Suir, Balije, inventory nr.1, double leaf double-sided, written pp.1-2-3, undersigned by autograph, address on p.4: Reverendo ac Religioso Domino N.N. Ordinis Sancti Joannis Ultraiectensi Commendatori, Domino et Confratri suo. *Underneath, in different handwriting:* ontffangen in Januario 89.

Recte Reverende ac Religiose Domine Commendator, Confrater charissime, Cicero inquit literarum usum eum potissimum in finem esse adinventum, ut si quid habeamus, quod amicum intervallo locorum a nobis disiunctum scire velimus, id perscribamus. Cum itaque reverendissimus in Christo pater, ac dominus, dominus Philippus Flach a Schwartzenburg, nostri ordinis per Germaniam magister princeps noster clementissimus, proxime praeterita septimana mihi significari fecerit, bullam quandam a generali capitulo Melitensi, suae reverendissimae gratiae transmissam, nuper in generali colloquio Spirensi (quod propter minus prosperam valetudinem visitare non potui) publicatam, atque in eadem inter reliqua contenta introclusae huius schedae compraehensa esse; Ego vero eadem legens liquido cognoverim, praedictum capitulum, non modo meae et Reverentiae Vestrae sed et aliarum commendatoriarum et conventuum privilegia, exemptiones, concessiones, uniones, gratias, et indulta revocasse sed insuper etiam statuisse, quod in eisdem posthac nullus in commendatorem eligi, neque pro tali electus reputari debeat, nisi primum Melitae in ipsorum conventu aliquandiu resederit, *[p.2]* post electionem de se factam, intra spacium sex mensium a magno domino magistro et conventu confirmationem obtinuerit, et praeterea omnibus suis privilegiis et indultis neglectis, quasvis responsiones, impositiones, et iura communis aerarii persolvat. Deinde quod quilibet Germanus, nobis etiam incognitus et improbatus, pro vero membro nostrorum conventuum haberi debeat, qui a magno magistro et conventu, vel

etiam generali capitulo Melitensi, pro conventuali receptus fuerit, ti-
muerimque ne si talis revocatio et ordinatio respective ad effectum
deducerentur, perpetuus interitus meae commendatoriae et conventus sequatur, ante lapsum decem dierum a tempore notitiae, ad
cautelam, a contentis huiusmodi schedae et bullae, coram notario et
testibus, ad summum pontificem in scriptis appellavi. Verum quia
haec causa admodum ardua, non minus Reverentiae Vestrae quam
mei conventus salutem concernat, magnaque deliberatione, et maturo consilio egeat, distantia vero locorum, ut de illa coram cum eadem
conferam, non admittat, me operae pretium facturum, existimavi, si
illam Reverentiae Vestrae perscriberem, si-*[p.3]*mulque peterem scire, quid ipsa de eadem sentiat, et agendum statuat. Putarem quidem
ego non inconveniens esse, ut quemadmodum nos quatuor neque
auditi, neque citati, in praescripta scheda simul sumus gravati: ita
quoque coniunctis animis, et communibus sumptibus per viam appellationis, in Romana curia, pro cassatione et sublatione inflictorum
gravaminum laboraremus. Quod non quidem ideo scribo, ut meam
qualemcunque opinionem Vestrae Reverentiae eliminato iudicio, et
solido consilio antiponam, sed illam eo citius commoveam, ad mihi
vicissim communicandum, quid nobis omnibus in hac difficultate facto opus iudicet.

Deus optimus maximus Reverentiam Vestram cum eiusdem conventu, quibus ego et mei fratres, quaevis gratissima nostra officia,
prompto offerimus animo, quam diutissime conservet incolumes.

Datum Argentinae, prima Decembris, stylo correcto, anno 88.
Reverentiae Vestrae
Ad quaevis paratissimus
Andreas Wilhelm Ordinis sancti Joannis in viridi insula Argentinae
Commendator.

134. 1589, March 23 – *Frater Hugues de Loubenx Verdala, Grand Master,
and the General Chapter rule in favour of frater Philips Lucius Snouck, head of the
preceptory of Mechelen, ruined by war, that his preceptory will be united with
Kieringen as soon as frater Walther von Orsbach, knight, is compensated for his
loss with the yields of a knightly preceptory.*

Registration: AOM 444 = libri bullarum 1588-1589, *fol.212v-213v,
dated in Annunciation-style.*

Frater Hugo etc. cardinalis etc. custos et nos baiulivi, priores, commendatarii etc. concilium completum retentionum capituli generalis
etc. religioso etc. fratri Philippo Lucio Snouch commendae nostrae de
Mechlin prioratus Alemaniae commendatario salutem in Domino
sempiternam.

Morum et vitae honestas multiplicesque animi tui dotes necnon laudabilia obsequia per te religioni nostri prestita et quae in dies sedulo prestare *[fol.213r]* non desinis promerentur ut ea quae tibi tuis commoditatibus et exigentibus meritis concessa sunt rathificemus, confirmemus, et alias prout securitati tuae convenire dignoscuntur provideamus. Supplicatio si quidem tua nobis dicto generali capitulo porrecta erat tenoris sequentis:

Illustrissimo et Reverendissimo Monsignor et sacro general capitulo, fra Filippo Lucio Snouck humilissimo servitore et religioso de Vestra Serenità Illustrissima aquella et a suo sacro general capitulo espone che hebbe de gratia della veneranda lenga d'Alemagna la commenda de Mechlen con le suoi appartenenti et del suo venerando consiglio ha optenuto le bulle; et perche la detta commenda di parechi anni in qua per le guerre di Fiandra (chancora durano) e stata brusciato la casa grangia et altri edificii per dove detta commenda si trova di puoco vallor, la veneranda lenga d'Allemagna accio che il commendator habbia meglior modo di ristaurarlo hanno incorporato et annexato alla detta commenda de Mechelen la commenda o ver membro de Kiringen del stato di fra serventi, laquel fu data al cavaglier fra Gualthero di Orsbach con conditione come appare per l'estratto della detta lenga che la dovisse goder fin tanto che fusse cabito de commenda de cavaglier et che all'hora fusse et s'intendisse incorporato et annexato in detta commenda de Mechelen; per tanto supplica a Vestra Serenità Illustrissima et suo sacro generale capitulo restanno servitto degnarsi confirmar detta gratia et si opus fuerit di nova concederlo approbando l'incorporatione et annexatione sopradetto, derogando per questa volta tanto a tutti li statuti, ordinatione, leggi, usi, et costumi che in contrario vi fosse, supplendo il tutto con lor suprema authorita et non cessara di pregar Iddio per il felice estato de Vestra Serenità Illustrissima et sua sacra religione, humilissimo et obedientissimo religioso et servitor de Vestra Serenità Illustrissima et suo sacro generale capitulo fra Philippo Lucio Snouck.

Hinc est quod premissorum meritorum tuorum intuitu et contemplatione suasi, invicem maturo et deliberato concilio, de nostra certa scientia et speciali gratia, auctoritate, et decreto ac in vim capituli generalis predictam commendam de Mechelen omniaque et singula in dicta supplicatione contenta et inde sequuta quaecumque laudamus, approbamus, et confirmamus unionemque, incorporationem, et annexationem predictam dictae commendae sive membri de Kirhingen cum commenda predicta de Mechelen prout petis et supplicas rathificamus et quatenus opus est de novo illud eidem unimus et annectimus, supplentes omnes et singulos defectus si qui forsam intervenerint in unione huiusmodi, nonobstantibus quibuscumque statutis,

ordinationibus, et consuetudinibus in contrarium dictantibus; decernentes praeterea et declarantes quod contingente (ut premittitur)
vacatione dictae commendae sive membri de Kiringhen per cessum
vel decessum religiosi etc. fratris Gualtherii de Orsbach, qui eam vel
illud de presenti tenet et possidet sive verius per adeptionem fructuum
et reddituum consequutionem et perceptionem commendae status
fratrum militum iuxta concessionem de dicta commenda sive membro de Kiringhen eidem fratri Gualthero de Orbasch per veneran-
dam linguam Alemaniae factam, possis et valeas per te sive per tuum
legitimum procuratorem possessionem eiusdem commendae sive
membri de Kiringhen cum suis prediis, iuribus et pertinentiis universis ad illam seu illud spectantibus et pertinentibus intrare, apprehen-
dere, et tenere fructusque, redditus, ac proventus ipsius colligere
[fol.213v] et percipere nulla aliunde requisita licentia, auctoritate, vel
concensu; Precipientes omnibus et singulis dictae domus nostrae fratribus quacumque auctoritate, dignitate, officioque fungentibus presentibus et futuris in virtute sanctae obedientiae ne contra presentes
nostras confirmationis et novae aanexationis et incorporationis litteras aliquatenus facere vel venire presumant, sed eas studeant inviolabiliter observare.

In cuius rei etc. bulla nostra communis plumbea etc.

Datum Melitae etc. durantibus retentionibus capituli generalis die
vigesima tertia mensis Martii MDLXXXVIII ab incarnatione.

135. 1594, November 4 — *The deputies of the Prior of Germany and visitators of the Dutch preceptories render an account of their address to the (vice-)
chancellor and councillors of the principality of Guelders at Arnhem on 2 August
1594 (should be: 12 August 1594) concerning the restitution of the lost properties
of the Order in this province.*

*Original report: GLA Karlsruhe 90/82, fol.12r-13r, with covering letter on
fol.14r-15r, dd. 4 November 1594, to the chancellor of the Order in Germany.
Cf. C.4. below, Visitation of 1594, especially Arnhem, 12 August 1594, and
D.nr.7.*

[fol.12r] Propositio des Herrn Maisters St. Johans Ordens in teutschen Landen abgefertigten Commissarius an die Herren des Gubernammts in Gellerlandt. Anno 94 2. Augusti.

Anno 1594 am 2. Augusti.
Van wegen des Hochwürdigen Fürsten und Herrn, Herren Philippen
Riedessell, St. Johans Ordens Meisteren in teutschen Landen, Römi-
sches Kaijserlichen Maijestäts Rath, und derselben General uber die

Armada uf dem Thünawstraum, haben die Ehrwürdige, Wollgeborene, Gestrenge und Edle Herrn, Herr Augustin freiher zu Mörszberg und Beffort, Commenthur zu St. Johan Paszell, Dorleszheim und Hemmendorff, und Herr Arnoldt von Lulstorff Commenthur zu Herrnstrunden, Burg, Deuszburg und Velden, alsz zu hochgemelten Ordens Personen und Gueteren in Niderteutschlanden zu Arnheim, Neumegen, Utricht und Harlem gelegen, und dero membra abgefertigte Visitatores und Commissarien, dem Wolledlen, Ehrenvesten und hochgelerthen Herrn Cantzler und hochweiszen Rathen des Fürstentumbs Gelder und Graveschafft Zutphen, alles liebs, freundlich grusz, guten willen, und dabei angetzeigt,

Das inen von Hochgemelten Fürsten irem gnedige herren uferlegt, in Krafft inen gelieferten Commission und befehls, des ordens Personen und Guetere, in diesen Niderlandischen orthern gelegen, zu visitiren, derselben beschaffenhait einzunhemen, und darin befindende mengell, nach möglicher gelegenhait, bei der obrigkeit eines jeden orths ins best zu verwenden.–

Deme gehorsamblich nachkomende, die im werck gespuertt, welcher maszen alhier, nach abscheide des herren Philippen von Rossenbach (welchen diese ritterliche Gueter in administration befohlen, und er gleichwoll, ohn geheiss, verlassen) und daruff gefolgten schwärlichen kriegswesen, bei zeiten, dho gute Policei, nit, wie jetzo, Gott lob, geachtet werden konnen, des ordens gueter in Gelderschem gebiete und statt Arnheim gelegen, vast in frembde hende auszgetheilt, verpachtet und die ufkimpst darab angehalten.

[fol.12v] Daruf den hochweisen herrn Canzlern und Räthen zu gemueth gefhuert, welcher maszen der Ritterlicher orden St. Johans von Jerusalem, numehr in Maltha residerendt, von allen innerlichen und civil kriegen, die sich ehrtzeits in Christenhait, zwischen Christlichen Potentaten erraiget, gantz unpartheisch und neutral ertzeiget, und noch also verhalten, allein aber, ihr profession widder den Erbfeindt Christlichen nhamens, der gantzen Christenhait zu schutz und besten, gerichtet stehe. Dawidder sie sich immerse bei tag und nacht und ohn alle underlasz, mit ansetzung leibs, guts und blutts, dapfferlich ufhalten.–

Denwegen nit allein ihr person und gueter, who und wie sie gelegen, von Römischen Kaijsern, Koenigen, und allen Christlichen Potentaten hoch privilegiijrt und begnadet, sonderen auch noch bisz anhero, in allen Christlichen landeren, who gute Policei vorhanden, sonderlichen im Reich Teutscher Nation, under allen Chur- und Fursten, Standen und Stäten des Reichs, von was Religion sie auch seien. Darzu aber in diesen Niderlendischen Vrijnten Provincien, bei ufgerichter, und an jetzo, Gott lob, restaurirter, vigirender Policei, vermoeg und nach gefolge underscheidtlichen Pacificationn recesz und abscheidt, wie hiebej mit :A:/– zu allem guten respettirt, und so viel die zeiten erleiden konnen, beschoenet und verdedigt worden –. Und das umb desthomehr, sijtemall ein Meister des Ordens St. Johans in Teutschen Landen, *[fol.13r]* ein Furst und ungemittelt Glidt des Reichs ist, und darvor, so von Iren Römischen Kaijserlichen Mayestät alsz allen anderen angehoerigen des Reichs Potentaten recognoscirt und gehalten wirdet, under welches Magisterio diese gueter gehoerigh seint.

Demnach von Iren fürstlichen Gnaden wegen, dero abgesanten Commissarien gentzlich trawen, vor ire person, sie fleiszig und empsig gepetten haben wollen, die herrn Cantzler und Räthe, dem Ritterlichen orden sein alhie gelegenes Ritterhaus, mit seinen Pertinentien, angehoerigen, und sonst demselben Orden zustehenden im Furstenthumb Geller gelegenen gueteren, gunstlichen zu restitueren, zu gefolgen und einzuantwurtten; wasz dan die Administration derselben gueter, in zukunfftige Zeit anlangt, soll hiehin, von Irer fürstlichen Gnaden ufs allerehrst ein Commenthur und Ritter Bruder verordnet werden, so des adelsz, und, ohne zweifell dergestalt qualificirt sein, auch sich also nachparlichen verhalten; das die herrn Cantzler, Räthe und jeder meuglich daran ein gefallens tragen werden -.

Daran geschehe, was an ime selbsen recht und pillig, und zu erhaltung des hochnoetigen Ritterlichen Ordens, auch dieser landen loblicher Ritterschafft (die uf begeren, zu solchen orden komen moegen) zu allem besten erschlieszlich.

So wiridts hochgedachter Furst, und dessen adliche Ritter Brudere umb ein jeden, mit gunsten und zimblichen diensten inderzeit beschulden, und die herren Commissarien wollens bei Irer fürstlichen Gnaden und sambtlicher Ritterschaft hochlich rhuemen, daruber erklerung gewartig.

Also ist zu Nemmegen wie Utricht und Harlem ongforlich noch gelegenheit ende sach furgebracht worden (den parlemente).

[fol.14r] Mein freündtlich dienst unnd gruoss zuvor, ehrnvester, Hochgelerther, insonders lieber Herr und Freündt.

Demnach ich ausz bewegenden Ursachen den IX. nechst abgeloffene Monats octobris ins Schwoben Landt verreijszen müeszen, hab ich doch zuvor, nachdem mein Schreijber wider von Haijtterscheim khommen, gegenwertig schreijben ahn meinen gnädigen Fürst und herrn abgeben unnd verferttigen laszen, und meinem Diener alhir alhes alszbaldt zu überschickhen bevohlen. Allsz aber ich diszer tagen wider zu hausz khommen, so hab ich dasselbig wider meinen willen und bevelch ausz vergeszenheitt ahn uberschickht noch alhir befunden, daroche mir ein grosz miszfallen beschehen. Derwegen belangt unnd ist mein freündtlich bitt, Ihr wöllend beij Iro fürstlichen Gnaden so albernith wie ich bericht worden wider glückhlich ankhommen, mich dessen, wie auch desz Tituli, do Iro fürstlicher Gnaden desselben nicht mehr gebrauchen hochlich endtschuldigen. Fürs erst.

Zum anderen, So werden ihr die beschaffenheitt der Niderländischen Commission, in Iro fürstlichen Gnaden schreijben zum theil weithläüffig vernehmen, unnd schickhe euch auch hiemit, zum mehreren bericht, ettliche Acta so mit dem A.b.s.[a] signiert, ausz welchen ihr meinen gnädigen Fürst und herrn, mündlich oder schriftlich, was der enden proponiert und tractiert worden —.
[fol.15r] —

Datum Bischnicu den 4.Novembris Stylo Novo Anno 1594.
Sein dienstwilliger freindt
Augustin freiherr zu Mörsperg, Ritter und Camthur

---

[a] *unknown abbreviation; it also may be:* A.b.5.

136. 1603, December 28 – *Frater Alof de Wignacourt, Grand Master, announces to the convent brethren at Utrecht, that he will write a letter to the Estates of the province of Utrecht and the citizens of the town of Utrecht about the brethren's disputed rights to choose their own new bailiff after the death of the last one.*

Original letter from Malta: RA Utrecht, Suir, Balije, inventory nr.1 (old number: Kleine Kapittels en kloosters nr.284), double leaf double-sided, written pp.1-2, undersigned by autograph, address on p.4, with superimpressed paper seal bearing the coat of arms of the Grand Master. Gift from the Estates of the province of Friesland, from the Gabbema-archief; underneath on the left side of p.1 a round imprint with: . Gabbema archief . Leeuwarden. Under this:*
Aux Relligieulx d'Utrech

This letter from the Grand Master had been preceded by letters and negotiations between the Prior of Germany Weybert and the Estates of the province of Utrecht that also involved the stadtholder Prince Maurits van Nassau and the Estates General of the Dutch Republic. The negotiations concerned the rights of the bailiwick of Utrecht to choose its own bailiff after the decease of the last one; pieces pertaining to this matter dd. 18 August, 26 and 28 October, and 15 November 1603 from the RA Utrecht, Statenarchief nr.487, have been edited as Bijlagen VII, VIII & IX in P.Q.Brondgeest, Bijdragen, pp.105-111. Cf. also Brondgeest, Bijlage VI and below, D.nr.1., c.1561.

Magister hospitalis Iherosolymitani

Noz chers et bien amez Relligieulx, Nous avons par vostre lettre du
2e Aoust, et celle de nostre Receveur frere Theodore Dattenberg,
entendu, que par la mort du dernier commandeur de vostre convent
(a qui Dieu face pais), les estatz d'Olende ce sont voullu entremettre
en l'administration des bien d'icelluy, et y auroient a cest effect commis et depputé ung oeconome particulier, qui est contrevenir aux
antiens privilleiges qui ont esté conceddez a nostre ordre, de tous les
princes dela chrestienté, chose que nous avons eue aultant a deplaisir,
que le resentiment vous en peult estre fascheux et dommageable. Cest
pourquoy nous en escripvons avec beaucoup d'affection ausdits seigneurs des estatz, et encores aux citoyens dela ville d'Utrech, a ce que
suyvant et conformement a nos privilleiges, et a l'entienne coustume
observee en vostre dit couvent, ilz vous laissent librement et sans
contredict procedder a la nouvelle eslection d'un commandeur, affin
que par ce moyen vous ayez subiect de faire ce qui est de vostre
debvoir en luy obeyssant, mais nous voullons bien vous faire resouve-
nir par ceste cy, que comme le premier et principal fondement de
nostre Relligion, a esté en intention de servir a Dieu, aymer et sustan-
ter les pauvres de Jhesus Crist, et randre en cela noz actions ediffica-
tives a ceulx qui en ont la congnoissance, il faut aussy que vous *[p.2]*
mettiez peyne de vous en acquicter en sorte que les citoyens deladite
ville d'Utrech et lesdits seigneurs des estatz par leur rapport, puissent
estre plustost disposez a vous maintenir en Noz previlleiges, qu'a vous
y apporter des nouveautez. Cela estant vous y serez maintenuz par la
grace de Dieu qui convertira leurs vollontez a vous honnorer et che-
rir, et nous, qui aurons plus de subiect de vous avoir en particulliere
recommandation, et de prier la divine Magesté qu'elle vous veille
maintenir soubz sa tressaincte et digne garde. A Malte le 28 decembre 1603.

Wignacourt

[p.4, address:] A Nos chers et bien amez les Relligieulx de nostre convent en la ville d'Utrech
A Utrech
[superimpressed paper seal of the Grand Master]

ªAdolfus Vignacourtius anno 1602. Princeps Melitensis et Gozensis,
post Martinum Garces factus est 54. magnus magister ordinis Johan-
nitarum, eique defuncto successit Joannes de Vasconcellis.
De Melita insula videlicet Turcograciam Mar.Crusii foll.528.

Item de insula Gaulo, vulgo Gozzo et altera Camon nomine.
Item Thomas Fazellus de rebus Siculis decade 1. liber I. caput 1.ᵃ

ᵃ Adolfus — caput 1. *in a later hand.*

137. 1603, December 28 – *Frater Alof de Wignacourt, Grand Master, announces to the brethren at Haarlem that he will write a letter to the Estates of Holland requesting them to respect the property and privileges of the Order and especially the rights of the Haarlem brethren in choosing their own head.*

Original letter from Malta: GA Haarlem, Stads Archief loketkas 7-7-6 *without further numbering or pages, double leaf double-sided, written pp.1-2, undersigned by autograph, p.4 sealed with the superimpressed paper seal bearing the coat of arms of the Grand Master and the address:* A nostre cher et bien amé Relligieulx le Commandeur Conventuel de la Commanderie d'Harlem
A Harlem
interspersed in different Maltese handwriting:
Rec. 28.decembris 1603.

[p.1]   Magister hospitalis Iherosolymitani

Tres cher et bien amé Relligieulx, Nous avons entendu par la lettre que nous escript le commandeur Dattemberg nostre receveur dela Basse Allemagne, comme avec beaucoup de soing et de devotion, vous vous acquictez du gouvernement et administration du bien de vostre Commanderie d'Arlem, dont nous avons eu ung grand contentement, cela nous a disposé avec plus d'affection, d'escripre aux Seigneurs des Estatz d'Hollande, et les prier qu'ilz vous laissent jouir plainement et paisiblement de vos biens, previlleiges, et immunitez, et particullierement de ceulx qui ont esté conceddez a tous ceulx de nostre ordre, par les princes chrestiens et desquelz nous jouyssons encores de presant sans contredict; Non seullement en France, Espagne et Ytallie, mais encores parmy les terres des Suisses, Conte Palatin et autres princes et protestans d'Allemaigne; Comme aussy appares que vous aurez faict votre cours en ce monde et passe en l'autre, de ne voulloir troubler les relligieulx de vostre commanderie, proceddans par eulx a nouvelle eslection d'un commandeur, comme nous avons sceu qu'ilz veullent faire en celle d'Utrech, et de ny mettre aultre administrateur que celluy qui sera esleu du commun consentement des *[p.2]* relligieulx, et affin qu'ilz soyent encores plus stimullez a l'entretenement de voz entiennes coustumes, vous aviserez de les y convincre par une bonne et saincte vie, affin qu'a vostre exemple, ceulx qui viendront apres se rendent agreables premierement a Dieu et puis au peuple; et alors nous serons tant plus disposez de vous prendre en nostre protexion et a prier la divine Majesté qu'elle vous veille maintenir et conserver soubz sa tressainte et tres digne garde. A Malte le 28. decembre 1603.

Wignacourt
[address on p.1, below left:]
Au C.d'Harlem

138. 1603, December 28 – *Frater Alof de Wignacourt, Grand Master, requests the Estates of the province of Holland to respect the property and privileges of the Order at Haarlem.*
   Original letter from Malta: GA Haarlem, Stads Archief loketkas 7-7-6 *without further numbering or pages, double leaf double-sided, written pp.1-2, undersigned by autograph, p.4 sealed with the superimpressed paper seal bearing the coat of arms of the Grand Master and the address:* A Messieurs
Messieurs les deputez des Estatz d'Hollande
interspersed by a second Maltese hand:
Rec. 28.decembris 1603.
   This letter is accompanied by a duplicate without seal or signature, with on p.4 in yet another hand:
Magnus Magister scribit Deputatis Statuum Holandiae in favorem commendae in Harlem
underneath, in the same second Maltese hand:
Rec. 28.decembris 1603

[p.1] Messieurs si bien je vous ay aujourdhuy escript et prie de voulloir vous departir de l'administration des biens de la Commanderie d' Utrech deppendant de nostre ordre et permettre aux relligieulx d'icelle de procedder a la nouvelle eslection d'un commandeur suyvant et conformement ce qu'ilz avoyent accoustumé faire antiennement, je vous ay bien encores voullu prier par ceste cy de voulloir departir vostre auctorité et faveur au commandeur dela Commanderie d'Harlem a ce que par le moyen d'icelle il ce puisse et les biens de sa commanderie garentir des oraiges dela guerre et des entreprises de ceulx qui les en voudroyent despouiller, comme aussy avenant le decedz dudict commandeur, ne pouir permettre que les relligieulx d'icelle, soyent troublez ou empeschez en la jouyssance des biens qui en deppendent, ny d'eslire ung nouveau commandeur pour l'administration d'iceulx, comme ils ont acoustumé faire entiennement, attendu mesmes que les biens de nostre relligion et la relligion mesme, sont membres de l'empire; c'est la cause pourquoy les Suisses, le conte Pallatin et les aultres princes protestans d'Allemaigne, ne s'en sont jamais voullu emparer, et encores moings les princes de France; car mesmes pendant les *[p.2]* guerres civilles ilz nous en ont tousiours laissé la libre et enthiere disposition de nos biens et personnes, iugeant aussy que nous estions establiz pour la deffentive de l'ennemy commun du nom Crestien, vous ne vouldrez je m'assure non plus qu'eulx nous faire ceste consequence. C'est ce qui me faict encores vous en prier et vous promettre en recompence tous les services que vous pouvez esperer de moy qui suis

Messieurs

le bien humble et affaictionné a vous fere service, le grand maistre

Wignacourt

A Malte le 28 decembre 1603

139. 1603, December 28 − *Frater Alof de Wignacourt, Grand Master, requests the mayor and citizens of Haarlem to respect the property and privileges of the Order at Haarlem and promises to correct misconduct of the brethren.*

Original letter from Malta: GA Haarlem, Stads Archief loketkas 7-7-6 *without further numbering or pages, double leaf double-sided, written pp.1-2, undersigned by autograph, p.4 sealed with the superimpressed paper seal bearing the coat of arms of the Grand Master and the address:* A Messieurs

Messieurs les Bourgmaistre et citoyens de la ville d'Harlem

A Harlem

interspersed in a second Maltese hand:

Recepta 28.decembris 1603.

This letter is accompanied by a duplicate without seal or signature, with on p.4 in yet a different hand:

Magnus Magister scribit Burgimaestro et senioribus in Harlem

underneath, in the second Maltese handwriting:

Rec. 28.decembris 1603

[p.1] Messieurs si j'avois aultant de moyen de m'employer pour vostre service que j'en ay de vollonté je m'asseurerois que mes prieres auroyent quelque efficace en vostre endroit, je ne laisseray touteffois de les employer pour nostre baiulive, commanderie, couvent et relligieulx, de vostre ville d'Harlem, a ce qu'il vous plaise les proteger maintenir et conserver en leurs biens, dignitez, honneurs, previlleiges, droictz de nouvelle eslection, et en touttes aultres choses dont ilz auroient besoing de vostre ayde faveur et assistance. Vous n'obligerez pas seullement eulx, mais aussi toutte ceste relligion et moy particullierement quy vous prometz de m'en revencher par touttes les occasions que

vous iugerez que je le pourray faire, je leur en escriptz, et l'enjoinctz
de ce gouverner si sagement en leurs actions, qu'elles puissent estre
premierement agreables a Dieu, et puis au public. Cela estant je
m'asseure que vous serez encores plus disposez a vous employer pour
leur conservation, et neantmoings s'il ce commettoit quelque desor-
dre, ou mauvais exemplaire de vie parmy eulx (Ce que je ne say pas)
nous mandons a nostre grand prieur d'Allemaigne qu'il aye de faire
procedder a la visitte dudict couvent et corriger ses faultes qui si *[p.2]*
pourroient commettre, separer les membres infectez d'avec les aultres
et faire en sorte que vous puissiez en avoir le contentement que vous
en debuez attendre. Ce que voullant croire prierons Dieu, Messieurs
vous maintenir et conserver en sa garde. A Malte le 28 decembre
1603

Vostre affaictionné vous fere service, le grand maistre
   Wignacourt

[address on p.1, below left:]
Aux Citoyens de la ville d'Arlem

140. 1604, June 21 – *The German tongue has decided to grant the preceptory
of Aachen with its members, vacant by the decease of its last head frater Wilhelm
Bellersehm, knight, to the chaplain frater Jean Blanchard.*
   Chancery notice: AOM 2198 = lingua di Alemagna, *fol.3r. This Italian
statement must have been written by a Maltese, as is apparent, according to the
late Joseph Galea, conservator of the AOM until c.1980, from spellings such as*
dritti *instead of 'diritti',* capimento *instead of 'cabimento',* partenga *instead of
'appartenga', and* ansiano *instead of 'anziano' (= ancianitas, seniority).*

A di 21. di Giugno 1604: Con licenza di monsignore illustrissimo
gran maestro fra Alosio de Vignacourt é 'tenuta la veneranda lingua
d'Alemagna (della quale fu capo il molto illustro fra Arbogasto de
Andlau gran ballio d'Alemagna) nella quale anco conparsero li reverendissimi fra Giováni Blanchard capellano dell'ordine di detta lingua, et domandó la commenda de Aquisgrano ed sue membri et
giurisditioni per il suo capimento, come anziano et benemerente,
quale commenda vacó per la morte del nobili signore cavalliero fra
Guglielmo Bellersehm, et la have dato di gratia priorale il maestro di
Alemagna Riedesel; et anco il reverendo fra Pompilio Minucci[a] diacono di san Giováni, quale há pretenduto et pretende la commenda
di Friburg in Ichlandia per lo suo capimento, quale commenda fú
data al detto fra Giováni Blanchard giá cinque anni sono per recupe-

rarne, et gratia speciale, quale commenda detto fra Giovàni Blanchard non have ancora recuperata secondo li statuti e tempo; per occasione, che detto maestro d'Alemagna la haveva data ad un prete d'obedienza, a'chi havea dato lo habito et la commenda insieme nominato fra Claudio Fallio, che la tiene fin'hora in possessione; per il che detto fra Pompilio pretende detta commenda non esser piu di detto di Blanchard, ma che li partenga per il suo capimento, et la dimanda de giustitia, con dire che detto di Blanchard non possa havere due commende; et ladetta veneranda lingua intese le raggioni dell'uno et dell'altro, tenuto discorso fra loro, finalmente hanno dato detta commenda di Aquisgrano al detto fra Giovàni Branchard come ansiano, capace et bene merente si come teneva prima il detto commendatore fra Guglielmo et non altrimenti et questo fú nemine discrepante de iustitia; quanto alla commenda di Friburgh, la detta veneranda lingua have dato al detto fra Pompilio per suo capimento de iustitia per occasione che detto di Blanchard non have recuperato detta commenda secondo li statuti et il tempo, reservandosi detta lingua li soi dritti et pertinentie.

---

a Minicucci ms.

141. 1605, October 29 – *Frater Alof de Wignacourt, Grand Master, and Convent, give the right to regain the preceptories Arnhem and Nimwegen to frater Dietrich Rolman von Dattembergh, head of the preceptories of Trier and Adenau.*
Registration: AOM 455 = libri bullarum 1603-1606, fol.216v-217r. A copy of this bull can be found in RA Gelderland, Loeff, Archief, inventory nr.59, und from this copy edited as Bijlage III in F.A.Hoefer & J.S.van Veen, 'De commanderieën der orde van St.Jan in Gelderland', in: Bijdragen en Mededeelingen van Gelre, 13 (1910) pp.277-332, especially pp.325-327.

Frater Alofius de Wignacourt etc. custos, et nos conventus etc. religioso etc. fratri Theodorico Rolman de Dattembergh commendae nostrae de Treveri et Adnau prioratus nostri Alemaniae commendatario salutem etc.

Morum et vitae honestas, multiplicesque animi tui dotes aliaque virtutum tuarum merita quibus insignitus dinosceris, nec non laudabilia obsequia per te ordini nostro praestita et quam in futurum te praestiturum confidimus, nos hortantur, ut ea tibi liberaliter concedamus, quae ad recuperationem bonorum nostrorum tuamque commoditatem facere dinoscuntur.

Cum igitur commenda nostra de Arnem et Nimmegen dicti prioratus nostri Alemaniae sicut accepimus a quibusdam personis a reli-

gione nostra alienis iamdudum occupata detineatur in grave nostri
ordinis vilipendium et damnum, nostraque intersit ut illa de iure evincatur vel alias recuperetur; volentes nobis ipsis onerique nostro satisfacere, dictam commendam de Arnem et Nimmegen cum omnibus et
singulis suis membris, praediis, iuribus, et pertinentiis universis ad
ipsam spectantibus et pertinentibus seu spectare et pertinere debentibus quoquomodo recuperandam a manibus eius vel eorum qui eam
nunc detinent, cuius vel quorum nomina et cognomina hic volumus
haberi pro sufficienter expressis, ac si de ipsis et quolibet eorum particularis et distincta mentio fieret, habendam, tenendam, possidendam, regendam, administrandam, augmentandam, et meliorandam
in spiritualibus et temporalibus tam in capite quam in membris, sub
annua solutione etc. salvo etiam etc. alias in defectu etc. invicem
maturo et deliberato consilio de nostra certa scientia nostraque et
dictae linguae speciali gratia tenore presentium ad annos decem continuos et completos et ultra ad nostrum beneplacitum tibi conferimus,
concedimus, et donamus benefaciendo in eadem, teque commendatarium in illa constituimus et ordinamus, committentes tibi circa recuperationem, curam, regimen, et administrationem ac omnimodam
dictae commendae bonorumque et iurium eius defensionem tam in
agendo quam defendendo harum serie vices nostras.

Quocirca universis et singulis fratribus, sororibus, et donatis in
virtute sanctae obedientiae, ac hominibus vassallis et quibuscumque
aliis nobis subditis in dicta commenda constitutis presentibus et futuris sub sacramento fidelitatis et homagii, quo nobis et religioni nostrae
sunt astricti, praecipimus et mandamus ut tibi tamquam eorum superiori et commendatario reverenter pareant, obediant, et intendant
tibique praebeant auxilium, consilium, et favorem in omnibus concernentibus recuperationem et utilitatem dictae commendae quotien-
scunque opus fuerit et eos duxeris requirendos, necnon universis et
singulis etc. atque cuicunque fratri etc. amoto ab eadem quolibet alio
etc. inhibentes etc.

In cuius rei etc. bulla nostra communis plumbea etc.

Datum Melitae etc. die XXIX mensis Octobris 1605.

142. 1606, January 20 – *Frater Weypert, Prior of Germany, summons the
bailiff of Utrecht to a chapter meeting at Speyer on 17 April 1606, ordering him
to have with him the taxation arrears.*

*Original letter from Freiburg: RA Utrecht, Suir, Balije, inventory nr.5, double
leaf double-sided, written pp.1-2-3, p.4 with remnants of a superimpressed red
seal and address:* Denn würdigen Unsernn lieben andächtigen und be-
sondern Prior und Convent St.Johann Ordens zu Uttrecht.

Uttricht. Cito
   Cito
   Citissime
written with one and the same capital C,
with four appendices that are, like the letter itself, followed on separate leaves by a
Copia translata. *The* Copia translata *of the letter, in 17th-century Dutch,*
without the appendices, has been edited as Bijlage X in P.Q.Brondgeest, Bijdragen, *pp.111-113. The date of the chapter meeting at Speyer in the heading by*
Brondgeest mistakenly mentions 17 April 1603 instead of 1606; the date of the
letter mentions 30 January 1606 instead of 20 January 1606.

Weypert von Gottes genaden St.Johan Ordens Meister in Teüschen
Landen.
Unnsern gnedigen gruess zuvor, Würdiger Lieber Andächtiger und
besonderer, demnach unns sowol unnsers Ritterlicher Ordens Statuten gemess, als auch altem loblichem brauch und gewohnheit nach,
jährlich ein gemeine zusamenkhunfft zuhalten obligt, Unns auch selbige unvermeijdenlicher notturfft halben fürderlich anzustellen jetzt-
mals angelegen ist, derhalben wihr dann in der wochen Jubilate
nechsstkhommendt abermal ein Provincial Capitul, vermittelsst Göttlicher genaden angesehen, und zuhalten entschlossen, zu deme ende
auch einen jeden Commenthurn daselbe in zeiten, zur nachricht wis-
sendt zumachen ein notturft erachtet. Alss bestimen Wihr solches, auf
Montag den 17. schierist khünfftigen Aprilis Neuwen Calenders, widerumb, und auss erheblichen Ursachen zu Speijr, und verkhünden
Euch daselbe hiemit gleig andern, tragenden ambtshalben, beij der
obedientz gnediglich befehlendt, dass Ir Sontags Jubilate den 16. ermelts Monats Aprilis zuvor zu Speijr gewiss, und bej straff den Statuten einverleibt gehorsamblich einkhommen, volgenden Montag, in
Unnsern hous daselbsten, bej Unnss erscheinen, dem Capitul aigner
Persohns bejwohnen, wie auch biss zu erlangtem Endt beflissenlich
ausswarten und Euch sonsten allermassen wie sichs wol bezeimt, und
wihr Unns gnedig thuen versehen, verhalten sollet und wollet, da Ir
dann Ewerer anbefohlnen Comenthureijen halber, gravamina und
beschwerden auf solch Capitul fürzubringen hetten, die werden und
sollen Ir zuvor Unnser *[p.2]* Canzleij zu zeitlicher berathschlagung
der ordnung gemess überschickhen, dessgleichen, auf bestimpte zeit
mit gelt also gefasst erscheinen, damit Unnss sowol die restierende
Posten der alten Reichs und Craisshilfen, alss auch die letste Termin
zur Türckhen Contribution, vermög bejkhommenden Designation
Numero .1. Ewertwegen unfahlbar erlegt werden, dann Ir auss bej
geschlossenen Copijs zweijer ernstlichen Kaijserlichen Schreibens mit
Nr. 2. und 3. bezeichnet, wol abzunemmen, mit was ungenaden die

Römisch Kaijserliche Majestät unsser Allergenedigister herr, zum fahl nicht zahlens, gegen dem Orden bewegt, bejnebens der Kaijserliche Fisscal seine process auch schon gescherpfft und starckh procediert, also abermahl höchlich zubesorgen, das es entlichen zur privation Unnsers Ordens uralter herrlicher Privilegien, zusambt der Regalien gerathen möchte. Wass Euch dann Unnsers Ordens Receptorn, und eines Ehrwürdigen Provincial Capituls Einnemmern zuerlegen angebeüren thuet, weiln sonderlich das Capituls einkhommen und gefäll, über ermelts Einnemmers starckhes urgirn, so gemach und ringlich eingebracht werden, das besorglich die Advocaten und Procuratorn bej weitem nicht ausszalt werden mögen, also die höhe notturfft erfordert älle Capituls Extantzen nach möglichheit einzufordern. Unnd dann Ir auch vermög bejligender Verzeichnuss No.4. und denselbigen in hinderresst verbliben, derhalben Ir ermelte Ewere Extantzen zu bezahlung gemelter Advocaten, Procuratorn und andern Notturfft, so gewisser zuerlegen haben sollet.

[p.3] So hat auch herr Landtgrave Moritzen Landgrave zu Hessen, beij jüngstem Craisstag zu Wormbs in verscheinen Septembri[a] gehalten, abermal und uber die vorigen Anno 98 bewilligte 12. Monaten, noch 12. und also in summa 24. Monatn vor sein Kriegs Verlag per maiora und durch aufgemelten Abschidt erhalten, doch also dass ein jeder Craiss standt, so die ersten in Anno 98. bewilligte 12. Monat noch nicht erlegt, dieselb sobald unverzuglich erstatten, die uberigen 12. Monaten aber, im nechsst volgenden 606, 607, 608 jahren, jedes jahrs 4. Monat in der Franckhfurter herbstmess entrichten sollen. Dieweil dann die obgemelten zwölf erste Monat Ewern theils noch nicht erlegt worden, alss solt Ir auch ebenmässig ainetzo damit gefasst erscheinen und Unnserm Einnemer, unfahlbar entrichten lassen, aufdass nicht etwa desswegen Unnserm Orden und Euch selbsten besorgendt Preiuditz und nachtheil daraus entstehen und bej wachsen mogen. Welches Wihr Euch, deme also haben nach zu setzen und gehorsame volge zuleisten gnediglicher meinung unangefüegt nicht lassen wollen. Unnd verbleiben Euch mit gnediglichen willen wolgewogten. Datum Freijburg den 20en Januarij Anno 606.

Weiprecht Meister

---

[a] 7bri *ms.*

Appendix nr.1, single leaf single-sided:
Vertzeichnuss
Was das Cammer Magistral Hauss Uttrecht an Türggenhülffen unnd andern Contributionen schuldig.
Erstens soll bemelt hauss an den 80 Monatlichen in Anno 94 bewillig-

ten Türggenhülff 800 R[eichsthaler]
Item an den 60 Monatlichen Türggenhülff Anno 98 bewilligt   350 R.
An der auf dem Oberreinischen Kreisstag zu Wormbs Anno 601 bewilligter Monatlichen eijllenden Türggenhülff 200 R.
Item an der in Anno 99 zu Sucurs dess Westphalischen Creisses Landtgraff Moritzen zu Hessen bewilligten 12 Monatlichen hülff 120 R.
Uber vorgesezte Summa, restirt das hauss Uttrecht, noch an den 1400 R. so noch an der in Anno 97 Extraordinari bewilligten Creisshülff zu bezaln zu seiner gebür 58 R. 5 bz.[batzen]
Mer belaufft dem hauss Uttrecht von den ferndrigen 42 Monaten in abschlag der 86 Monaten, auf jüngstem Reichs Tag bewilligt 420 R.
Und dan von den heürigen 22 Monaten selbiger hülff 220 R.
Mer für die bede letste zil diser hülff 220 R.
So dan für die 8 Monat Creisshülff disses 605 jars zu Wormbs bewilligt 80 R.

Summa Summarum aller ausstendiger alten und newen Reichs und Creisshülffen, so beim hauss Uttrecht aussteen 2468 R.

Appendix nr.2, double leaf double-sided, on p.4:
Copia kaijserlichen Schreibens an den Hochwürdigen Unsern genedigen Fürsten und Herrn St.Johann Ordens Meister in Teütschlanden No.2 *[dd. 7 October 1605, according to the text on p.2].*

Appendix nr.3, double leaf double-sided, on p.4:
Copia Kaijserlichen Schreibens No.3 *[dd. 1 December 1605, according to the text on p.2].*

Appendix nr.4, single leaf single-sided:
Capituls Exstantien No.4
Beij der Commenden Uttrecht unnd Harlem steet von vilen jarn Capitulcosten, als järlichen 8 R[eichsthaler] in Reichswärung auss, solchen aber allein von 1601 biss auf 1°. Maij 1605 jars gerechnet, belaufft sie den ausstandt von 5 jarn Reichswärung, in allem 40 R. die machen gemeiner wärung, als auf jeden gulden 2 bz.[batzen] gerechnet, in allem 45 R. 5 bz.
Mer Capitul Costen Anno 605: 8 R.

143. 1613, May 10 – *Frater Alof de Wignacourt, Grand Master, and Council grant the right to regain all preceptories in the Dutch Republic to frater Eugène d'Arembergh, knight of the Priorate of France.*
Registration: AOM 458 = libri bullarum 1612-1615, fol.265v.

Frater Alofius etc. custos, et nos baiulivi, priores, comendatarii et fratres concilium in Domino celebrantes, nobili Eugenio de Aremberghe filio illustrissimi comitis de Aremberghe, nostrae dictae domus prioratus nostri Franciae in gradum fratrum militum recepto, salutem in Domino et prosperos ad vota successus.

Ad ea solerti animo aciem mentis nostrae dirigeri tenemur, et debemus, quae recuperationem et conservationem commendarum, beneficiorum, et omnium bonorum, praediorum, et possessionum stabilium pro tuitione fidei etc. dignoscuntur. Cum igitur in partibus Hollandiae et provintiis ac statibus cum Hollandensibus confederatis, multae commendae, membra, praedia, territoria, possessiones, redditus, proventus, beneficia, et bona, ad nos nostramque religionem spectantia etc. oportet nos aliquam personam disputare, qui dicta nostra bona, commendas, membra, praedia, territoria, stabilia, possessiones, et quaecunque beneficia, et alia in dictis confinibus Hollandiae, et provinciis ac statibus cum Hollandensibus confederatis unitis, et dependentibus existentia, occupata etc. reducere possit et debeat.

Hinc est quod consideratis per nos quamplurimis virtutum tuarum meritis, confisi de tua diligentia, industria, fide, probitate ac sedulitate, attento consensu pariter, et assentu locumtenentis venerandi magni baiulivi commendatariorumque et fratrum nostrae venerandae linguae Alemaniae hic Melite ad Dei et ordinis nostri obsequia residentium, super id more et loco solito legitime et serie congregatorum, praedictas commendas, membra, praedia, territoria, stabilia, possessiones, redditus, proventus, et quaecunque beneficia ac bona ad nos etc. a quibuscunque personis a religione nostra alienis etc. et usurpata in dictis partibus Hollandiae et provinciis ac statibus cum Hollandensibus confederatis unitis et dependentibus existentia, cum omnibus et singulis iuribus etc. quoquomodo tuis expensis recuperandum, in iusque et dominium nostrum etc. restituendum, dictisque commendis, membris, bonis, beneficiis, praediis, et possessionibus stabilibus, et aliis quibuscunque sic recuperatis, et ad obedientiam nostram dictaeque nostrae religionis Deo favente reintegratis, et redactis per te gaudendum, usufructuandum vita tua durante duntaxat, sub eadem tantummodo solutione nostro communi aerario fieri consueta per dictas personas ab ordine nostro alienas a quarum manibus recuperabuntur, et iuxta dispositionem statuti quinquagesimi quinti de commendis et sub declarationibus, conditionibus, et pactis in deliberationibus dictae venerandae linguae expressis; hoc adiecto quod post tuum obitum commendae et praedicta bona (ut praemittitur[a]) recuperata, redeant ad linguas et commendas ad quas spectant et a quibus respective dependent; scilicet vel Franciae, vel Alemaniae iuxta limites earundem venerandarum linguarum. Item omnes et quoslibet detentores illicitos dictarum commendarum et bonorum nostrorum quorum nomina etc. et compellendum ad praedictas commendas et bona, una cum eorum fructibus etc. et tradendum. Item omnes et quascunque lites etc. Nec non etc. ratione coram sacra Caesarea maiestate, illustrissimis dominis proregibus, principibus etc. comparendum, agendum etc. unique vel plures procuratores etc. ad lites tamen substituendum etc. Et generaliter etc. Promittentes etc. quicquid perte, et substituendos a te modo premisso actum etc.

In cuius rei etc. bulla nostra communis plumbea etc.

Datum Melitae etc. die X mensis Maij 1613.

ª *uncertain rendition of abbreviation ms.*

144. 1614, October 22 − *Frater Alof de Wignacourt, Grand Master, and Convent give the right to regain the preceptory of Arnhem & Nimwegen to frater Bernhard von Goldstein.*

Registration: AOM 458 = libri bullarum 1612-1615, *fol.247v-248r. For a more complete formulary, cf. AOM 455, fol.216v-217r, similar bull for frater Dietrich Rolman von Dattembergh dd. 29 October 1605, nr.141 above; a copy of the bull of 1614 can also be found in RA Gelderland, Loeff,* Archief, *inventory nr.60.*

Frater Alofius etc. custos, et nos conventus etc. religioso etc. fratri Bernardo de Golsten nostrae dictae domus venerandae linguae Alemaniae militi salutem etc.

Morum et vitae honestas — promerentur, ut ea tibi liberaliter concedamus, quae ad recuperationem bonorum nostrorum tuamque commoditatem facere dinoscuntur.

Cum igitur commenda nostra de Arnhem et Niemegen cum suis membris et dependentiis prioratus nostri Alemaniae (sicut accepimus) a quibusdam personis a religione nostra alienis iamdudum occupata et usurpata detineatur in grave nostri ordinis vilipendium et damnum damnationemque animarum occupantium, usurpantium, et detinentium, nostraque intersit ut illa de iure evincatur vel alias recuperetur; hinc est quod volentes nobis ipsis onerique nostro satisfacere dictam commendam de Arnhem et Niemegen cum omnibus et singulis suis membris, praediis, iuribus, et pertinentiis ac dependentiis universis ad ipsam spectantibus et pertinentibus seu spectare et pertinere debentibus quoquomodo recuperandam a manibus eius vel eorum qui eam nunc detinent, —, recuperandam, habendam, tenendam, possidendam, regendam, administrandam, augmentandam, et meliorandam in spiritualibus et temporalibus tam in capite quam in membris, sub annua solutione etc. —.

Datum Melitie etc. die XXII mensis Octobris 1614.

145. 1614, November 18 – *Frater Hartmann von Thun is allowed to let his preceptory of Aachen for a period of three years.*

Chancery note: AOM 458 = libri bullarum 1613-1615, *fol.248r.*

Die XVIII mensis Novembris 1614. Venerandus dominus frater Hartemanus de Thun prioratus Daciae prior et commendae de Aquisgrano prioratus Alemaniae commendarius propter residentiam suam etc. habuit licentiam locandi et arrendandi dictam commendam pro tribus annis et tribus recollectis tantum incipiendo a die festo sanctorum Philippi et Jacobi proxime futuro.

146. 1614, November 22 – *Frater* Hartemanus de Thun *Prior of* Dacia *and head of the preceptories of Sulz, Colmar and Aachen is allowed to leave for his preceptories and to return to Malta afterwards.*

Chancery note: AOM 458 = libri bullarum 1613-1615, *fol.248r.*

147. 1614, November 26 – *Frater Bernhard von Goldstein is allowed to leave for his preceptories of Arnhem and Nimwegen.*

Chancery note: AOM 458 = libri bullarum 1613-1615, *fol.248v.*

Die XXVI mensis Novembris 1614 dominus frater Bernardus de Golstein commendae de Arnhem et Niemegen prioratus Alemaniae commendarius habuit licentiam eundi ad regendam dictam commendam.

148. 1617, August 24 – *Frater Johann Friedrich Hundt von Saulheim, Prior of Germany, confirms the* facultas recuperandi *of all the Order's possessions in the seventeen Dutch provinces for frater Franciscus de Soria and his colleagues frater Jacques de Bolleux & frater Jean Baptist Lambert.*

Copy: GLA Karlsruhe, 90/474, fol.2r-3r, with note on fol.3v: Bulla pro Don Francisco Soria de recuperandis commendis et bonis in Alemania Inferiori. 24. Augusti 617.; *copy of a* prioral *instrumentum in confirmation of a Grand Master's bull dd. 14 January 1617, dated in Annunciation-style.*

Nos Frater Johannes Fredericus Dei gratia sacre domus hospitalis sancti Johannis Hierosolymitani per Alemaniam magister et prior sacrique imperii princeps; Universis et singulis presentes nostras litteras visuris, lecturis et audituris salutem in Domino.

Comparuit coram nobis nobilis nobisque charissimus frater don Franciscus de Soria, ordinis nostri religiosus; nobisque exposuit quatenus illustrissimus et reverendissimus dominus magnus magister, baiulivi, priores, et commendatarii concilium Melite celebrantes, sub die decima quarta mensis Ianuarii anno millesimo sexcentesimo decimo sexto ab incarnatione, ipsi et fratribus Jacobo de Bolleux, et Johanni Baptiste Lambert, collateralibus, et consortibus suis liberum consensum et plenam facultatem dederint, bona mobilia, et immobilia, predia, territoria, domos, possessiones, iura, redditus, proventus, baiulivatus, commendas, beneficia, et membra quecunque sita et posita in Bassa seu Inferiori Alemania et in decem et septem provinciis Belgii, hoc est tam in confinibus territoriis et dominiis, serenissimi archiducis Alberti, quam illustrium dominorum Statuum Generalium, Holandie, Zelandie, Frisie, Geldrie, Harlem, Utrecht, ac omnium aliarum provinciarum seu dominiorum eisdem subditorum, confinium et unitorum, non solum per ipsosmet illustres dominos Status Generales supradictos, verum etiam per multas, et diversas alias *[fol.2v]* personas, publicas et privatas tam ecclesiasticas, seu religiosas quam seculares et ab ordine nostro alienas, reperiantur occupata, usurpata, distracta indebite detenta, et absque titulo et promotione legittima nostra, nostrique ordinis, possessa, et contra formam nostrorum stabilimentorum, ac privilegiorum dispositionem in grave damnum ac preiudicium et interesse dicti nostri ordinis, nostrique communis erarii, et in damnationem animarum detinentium et occupantium recuperandi et in pristinum ordinis nostri statum reducendi, omniumque prelatorum bonorum possessionem actualem et corporalem petendi, et capiendi, a nobis humiliter petens, ut pariter nos authorisationem, consensum, et assensum adiungere velimus.

Cum igitur ipsius petitio non modo honesta, et equa, verum etiam necessaria nobis visa fuit, idcirco libenter annuimus, et hoc publico instrumento consensum nostrum sic declaramus, damus, et ex nostra parte authorizamus ita ut prefatus don Franciscus de Soria et ipsius supradicti collaterales et consortes iam et imposterum, coniunctim placide et quiete ius suum recuperationis, vigore bulle, prefati illustrissimi domini magni magistri impetrate, et huius instrumenti nostri exercere, et omnia que ad ordinis nostri commodum et utilitatem spectant, pertractare et expedire, bonisque taliter acquisitis, vita sua respective durante (cum condicionibus expressis in publico instrumento in dicta bulla mentionato, quod hic pro inserto *[fol.3r]* haberi et teneri volumus) uti, ac frui, libere possint ac valeant, omniaque ad eundem effectum facere et exercere, que quilibet procurator legittimus facere, pertractare et adimplere posset et deberet, atque nosmet facere, et adimplere possemus, etiamsi talia essent, que magis speciale mandatum exigerent quam presentibus sit expressum, denique omnia facere que ad dictam recuperationem reperient utilia et necessaria, promittentes sub bona fide habere ratum, gratum et firmum quicquid per supranominatum don Franciscum de Soria eiusque collaterales tanquam nuntios nostros generales, et speciales, procuratores, et sijndicos, vel quoscunque ab iis substituendos ad predictum effectum, actum, factum, recuperatum, procuratumve fuerit.

In cuius rei testimonium [a]nos propria manu subscripsimus[a] sigillumque nostrum consuetum presentibus est appensum, Heiterhemii ex residentia nostra die vigesima[a] quarta[a] 24 mensis Augusti [b]anno millesimo sexcentesimo decimo septimo[b] anno 1617.

---

[a] nos — subscripsimus *and* vigesima quarta *added in the margin in a different hand.* [b] anno — septimo *added under the text in a different hand.*

149. 1622, February 13 – *Mr.*Pijnacker, consiliarius illustrissimi principis Auraniae, *addresses a petition in Latin to the Grand Master [frater Louis de Vasconcelos] to ask the liberation of some subjects of the Estates of Holland who are still enchained on galleys that were captured by the Order from Tunesian pirates.*

Original letter: AOM 57 = Liber epistolarum, *fol.180r.*

Hagae comitatus Holandiae ipsis Idibus Februarii anni Jesu[a] Christi[a] Theanthropou[a] Messiae MDCXXII.

---

[a] *in Greek characters, partly abbreviated.*

150. 1626, March 3 – *The Estates General of the Dutch Republic address a petition in French to the Grand Master frater Antonio de Paula for the restitution of the cargo vessel* Le Soleil *under captain* Theodore Cornelle, *which was loaded in Livorno by the Dutchmen* Jean Maurique *and* Isaac Keijser *and was heading for Algiers, but deviated from its course, escaped to Malta and was sequestered there.*

Original letter: AOM 57 = Liber epistolarum, *fol.166r-v.*

151. 1626 August 24 – *Frater Antonio de Paula, Grand Master, exhorts the Prior of Germany, frater Johann Friedrich Hundt von Saulheim, to undertake a visitation of his four prioral chambers, starting with those that lie outside war regions, within six month after reception of this letter.*

Copy: AOM 1405, letters of the Grand Master to ambassadors and others, without page or folio numbers. In the next letter, with the same date, the Grand Master orders frater Giovanni Vernero de Rattenau *to carry out this visitation.*

152. 1626, October 11 – *Mr.*Pijnacker, *counsellor of the Prince of Orange and envoy in Tunis and Algiers, addresses a petition to the Grand Master [frater Antonio de Paula] for the restitution of the cargo vessel* Peregrinus *to its owner* Giovan Eeuwouds van der Meulen *from Schiedam, although the vessel was captured from an Algerian.*

Original letter: AOM 57 = Liber epistolarum, *fol.167r-v.*

[Jan Eeuwouds still claims ownership]
— Nam etsi dicta navis sit erepta Argierensi, non tamen fuerat ea facta Argirensium eam ob causam quod iuste nostri hostes non essent eo tempore quo clientulum nostrum piratice privarunt ea. —.

Lutetiae Parisiorum ad XI Octobris anni nostri Redemptoris Theanthropou[a] M D CXXVI.

---

[a] *in Greek characters.*

153. 1629, February 3 – *The Prince stadtholder* Frederic Henderic *sends a petition to the Grand Master [frater Antonio de Paula] on behalf of the parents of* Jean Nicolas *from Edam, who left more than two years ago on a vessel under captain* Nicolas Lambert *from Delft, was led captive to Tunis after an exchange of fire with three Turkish pirate vessels in the Mediterranean, sent to sea again in October 1628 as a galley slave and captured by Maltese galleys, on one of which he is enchained as a galley slave.*

Original letter: AOM 57 = Liber epistolarum, *fol.181r-v.*

[The petition for his release is willingly supported by the stadtholder Frederik Hendrik because] — qu'elle est faicte pour un subject de cet Estat lequel de tout temps a entretenu bonne correspondence *[fol.181v]* amitié et neutralité avec Vostre Ordre outre que la notoire innocence du prisonnier accompaignié d'une continuelle et insupportable misere doit trouver quelque lieu à la compassion et faveur de ceux qui font profession de sauver et soulager les affligez —.

La Haye, ce 3me de Febvrier 1629.

154. 1629, February 5 – *The Prince stadtholder* Frederic Henderic *addresses a petition in French to Grand Master frater Antonio de Paula for the release of* Henrij Roeloffs, *citizen of Hoorn, who was taken prisoner by Turks aboard the vessel under captain* Simon Hillings *and has been enchained as a galley slave; although the ship has meanwhile been captured by galleys of the Order, he still is forced to work as a galley slave.*
    Original letter: AOM 57 = Liber epistolarum, *fol.182r-v.*

155. 1629, February 15 – *The Estates General of the Dutch Republic address a petition in French to the Grand Master [frater Antonio de Paula] on behalf of the mayors of Amsterdam for the release of* Jan Janssen, *citizen of Amsterdam, who was taken prisoner by Tunesian pirates five years ago aboard a vessel under a captain from Medemblik and was enchained on a galley that has been captured by the Order afterwards.*
    Original letter: AOM 57 = Liber epistolarum, *fol.186r-v.*

156. 1635, May 9 – *Frater Antonio de Paula, Grand Master, and Convent appoint frater Archimann von Jhann as Prior of Germany, as the successor of frater Friedrich Hundt von Saulheim, with five prioral chambers, among which Utrecht.*
    Original bull on parchment: GLA Karlsruhe, 20/163, with holes of lost string with seal of Grand Master and Convent.

Frater Antonius de Paula — fratri Archemano de Jhann prioratus nostri Ungarie priori ac commendarum nostrarum de Sultz, Colmar et Uberlinghen prioratus Alemaniae commendatario —,
    [Frater Archimann receives the Priorate of Germany with its prioral chambers] videlicet Traiectum, Coloniam, Hembach, et Boboquem, necnon Commendam de Friburg et Bresgaw pro quinta tua camera —.

157. 1636, August 12 – *Frater Jean Paul Lascaris Castellar, Grand Master, and Convent appoint frater Walram Scheiffart van Merode as general receiver in Low Germany instead of frater Bernhard von Goldstein.*
    2 identical copies of a bull from Malta: RA Gelderland, Loeff, Archief, inventory nr.534.

Frater Johannes Paulus Lascaris Castellar — et nos conventus domus eiusdem — *[on account of the merits of]* religiosi in Xpo nobis carissimi fratris Walrami Scheffardt de Merode commendae nostrae de Maguntia prioratus Alemaniae commendatarii —, revocantes prius pro-

curationem receptoriae infra-scriptae in personam religiosi in Xpo
nobis carissimi fratris Bernardi de Goltsteijn alias emanatam — eundem fratrem Walramum Scheiffart de Merode presentem — tenore
presentium facimus, creamus, constituimus & solemniter ordinamus
nostrum, nostrique ordinis & iurium eiusdem communis erarii, receptorem, collectorem, procuratorem, actorem, negotiorumque nostrorum gestorem, syndicum, aeconomum ac nuntium nostrum
specialem et generalem — in Inferiori seu Bassa Alemania —.

Datum Melitae in conventu nostro die duodecimo mensis Augusti
millesimo sexcentesimo, trigesimo sexto.

158. 1644, July 28 — *Frater Jean Paul Lascaris Castellar, Grand Master, and
Council grant the right to regain the Order's possessions in Utrecht, Haarlem and
elsewhere in the provinces of the Estates General and in Low Germany, with the
exception of the preceptories of Wesel, Borken, Arnhem and Nimwegen, Burgsteinfurt, Münster, Lage and Herford, and Herrenstrunden, to frater Jacques de Souvré.*

Copy of a Maltese chancery copy: Herzog-August-Bibliothek, Wolfenbüttel,
Die Handschriften der herzoglichen Bibliothek zu Wolfenbüttel, *be-
schrieben von Otto von Heinemann, 2.Abt.II (Wolfenbüttel 1895), p.19:
Kat.Nr.2137 sub 153, fol.388r-391r. In the upper left corner of fol.388r:*
Bulla Magni Magistri Ordinis s[ti] Joannis in Jerusalem. *On fol.391r:*
Signatum
Il gran Canciller Fr. Don Antonio de Loncina Centreraij
Registrata in Cancellaria
  In plica
Frater Lucas Bonus Coadiutor Vicecancellarius

Frater Joannes Paulus Lascaris Castellar Dei gratia sacrae domus
hospitalis sancti Johannis Hierosolymitani et militaris ordinis sancti
Sepulchri dominus magister humilis pauperumque Jesu Christi
custos; et nos baiulivi priores commendatarii et fratres concilium ordinarium celebrantes venerando religiose in Christo nobis perclarissi-
mo fratri Jacobo de Souvraij ordinis nostri baiulius ac commendae de
Valleurae prioratus nostri Campaniae commissario salutem in Domino et diligentiam in commissis.

Ad ea studiose atque libenter intendimus, aciemque mentis nostrae
dirigimus, quae recuperationem et conservationem commendarum,
bonorum, praediorum, possessionum et iurium ordinis nostri concernere dinoscuntur.

Cum itaque commendae nostrae de Utrecht et de Haerlem, mul-
taque bona mobilia et immobilia, praedia, territoria, domus, posses-

siones, iura, reditus, proventus, baiulivatus, commendae et membra
sita et posita in provinciis, confinibus, territoriis et dominiis illustrissimorum et excellentissimorum dominorum Statuum Generalium nuncupatorum, non modo sicut accepimus ab ipsismet illustrissimis et
excellentissimis dominis Statibus Generalibus, verum etiam a quibusdam aliis personis ab ordine nostro alienis occupata detineantur, nostraque intersit, ut illa de iure evincantur [fol.388v] seu alias
recuperentur. Hinc est, quod volentes nobis ipsis onerique nostro
satisfacere, ac consideratis praeclaris virtutum tuarum meritis, laudabilibusque obsequiis per te praedicto nostro ordini summa cum fidei
probitate praestitis, confisi de tua industria, cura, ac in rebus peragendis dexteritate, iuxta decretum in nostro concilio hodierna die desuper emanatum, invicem maturo et deliberato consilio de nostra certa
scientia, te venerandum fratrem Jacobum de Souvraij absentem tanquam praesentem, omnibus melioribus via, modo, iure et forma, quibus melius et validius facere possumus et debemus, revocantes prius
nullasque declarantes similes commissiones recuperandi dicta bona in
favorem quarumvis personarum hactenus emanatas, tenore praesentium facimus, creamus, constituimus et solemniter ordinamus
nostrum totiusque ordinis nostri, ac eius communis aerarii nuntium
generalem et specialem, procuratorem, actorem, syndicum, oecono-
mum, negotiorum praedictorum et infrascriptorum gestorem: ita tamen, quod specialiter generalitati non deroget; nec e contra, videlicet
specialiter et expresse ad, nostro, praedictique aerarii et ordinis nomine praenominatas commendas de Utrecht et de Haerlem, omniaque
et quaecumque alia bona, mobilia et immobilia, praedia, possessiones, domos, iura, beneficia, baiulivatus, [fol.389r] commendas et
membra in Bassa seu Inferiori Alemania et in praefatis provinciis sita
et posita una cum omnibus et singulis iurisdictionibus pertinentiis
membris fructibus reditibus ac proventibus decursis et decurrendis a
praenominatis personis (ut praefertur) usurpata, detenta, et absque
titulo et legitima provisione nostra occupata petendum, ac praedic-
tarum commendarum de Utrecht et de Haerlem, bonorumque omnium huiusmodi possessionem actualem et corporalem capiendum;
exceptis tamen et expresse reservatis commendis de Wesel, Borkum,
Aernheim et Nimwegen cum suis membris et dependentiis universis,
nec non omnibus bonis et iuribus quibuscumque ad comendas de
Steinfurt, Munster, Laghen, Herforden[a] et Herenstrunden, quomodolibet spectantibus, quorum bonorum et iurium huiusmodi recuperatio (si quae in illis partibus usurpata reperiuntur) ad praefatarum
commendarum praeceptores sive commendatarios pertinet.

    Decernentes, ut omnibus praedictis bonis per te, ut praefertur,
recuperandis iuxta formam statutorum nostrorum vita tua perdurante

uti, frui, et gaudere in tuosque usus ac utilitatem convertere libere et licite possis ac valeas; et post obitum tuum transactisque terminis in praecalendato nostri venerandi consilii decreto expressis commendae et bona praefata remaneant et esse intelligantur iuxta eorundem statutorum et ordinationum capi-*[fol.389v]*tularium formam et dispositionem; salvis insuper et reservatis quibuscumque iuribus, impositionibus et responsionibus nostri communis aerarii declarandis et imponendis statim secuta huiusmodi recuperatione, licet antea alius fuissent naturae, praefatisque iuribus et impositionibus ac responsionibus minime obnoxia et non aliter, nec alio modo.

Atque ut omnia praemissa suum plenarium sortiantur effectum, te nuntium nostrum, negotiorumque gestorem habilitamus, virtuteque praesentium nostrarum literarum authorisamus ad omnes et quascumque lites activas et passivas, motas et movendas, super omnibus et singulis huiusmodi bonis prosequendum, mediandum et terminandum, seu prosequi, mediari, finiri et determinari curandum atque ad definitivam sententiam ac corporalem possessionem. Nec non in et super praemissis omnibus et singulis, et eorum ratione non modo coram praedictis illustrissimis et excellentissimis dominis Statibus Generalibus, verum etiam coram Imperatoria et regum maiestatibus, serenissimis archiducibus Austriae, Germaniae, Hispaniae, Franciae et Flandriae potentibus, principibus[b], ducibus, comitibus, locatenentibus, praesidentibus, assessoribus, aliisque magistratibus, tam ecclesiastica, quam mundana auctoritate fungentibus, praesentibus *[fol.390r]* et futuris; etiam coram sanctissimo domino nostro pontifice, illustrissimis cardinalibus, archiepiscopis, episcopis et quibuscumque aliis personis in ecclesiastica dignitate constitutis, quatenus expedire videbitur comparendum, agendum, et defendendum fora, loca et Iudices declinandum et recusandum, de iudicibus et locis conveniendum, restitutionem in integrum petendum, libellum seu libellos et petitiones verbo vel in scriptis dandum et faciendum, exceptiones declinatorias[c] allegandum, litem seu lites contestandum, de calumnia seu malitia vetanda in animam nostram iurandum petendum et articulandum, petitionibus et articulis respondendum, testes, literas, acta et instrumenta producendum, et contra producta dicendum, replicandum, triplicandum, et si opus fuerit quadruplicandum, exemptiones peremptorias et alias quascumque allegandum, in causis concludendum ius, ordinationes, et sententias interlocutorias vel definitivas dici, dari et pronuntiari videndum, petendum et audiendum, ab ipsis et quolibet alio gravamine appellandum et reclamandum semel vel pluries, et appellationem seu appellationes, aut reclamationes relevandum et prosequendum, apostilos cum debita instantia petendum et obtinendum, super expensis iurandum, ipsasque *[fol.390v]* taxari petendum, auxilium quoque brachii secularis implorandum pro conservatione iurium et indemnitatis nostrae, nostraeque religionis unum, vel plures procuratores cum pari vel limitata potestate ad lites tantum substituendum, et eum vel eos revocandum, quoties opus fuerit, praesenti procuratorio mandato nihilominus in suo robore duraturo. Et generaliter in praemissis et quolibet praemissorum omnia et singula adimplendum et faciendum, quae quilibet legitimus procurator facere et adimplere posset et deberet, et quae nosmet facere et adimplere possemus; etiam si talia forent, quae magis speciale mandatum exigerent, quam praesentibus expressum, ac denique omnia facere, qui ad huiusmodi recuperationem reperies utilia et necessaria; promittentes bona fide habere ratum gratum et firmum, quicquid per te et substituendos abs te modo praemisso actum factum recuperatum procuratumve fuerit sub hypotheca et obligatione omnium bonorum nostrorum, nostrique religionis praesentium et futurorum.

In cuius rei testimonium bulla nostra communis plumbea praesentibus est appensa.

Datum Melitae in conventu nostro die vigesima octava mensis Iulii millesimo sexcentesimo, quadragesimo quarto.

ᵃ Steinforden *ms.* ᵇ principibus *ms.* ᶜ declatorias *ms.*

159. 1647, December 27 – *Frater Jacques de Souvré informs Grand Master frater Jean Paul Lascaris of his intention to negotiate the restitution of the Order's sequestered goods with the Estates of Holland.*
Original letter: AOM 58 = Lettere di Francia, fol.302r-v.

Monseigneur
Comme je ne pers pas un moment de temps sans penser aux occasions qui peuvent apporter quelque utilité et avantage à la Religion, je croy estre obligé de descouvrir à Vostre Eminence une pensée que iay dans l'esprit il y a quelque temps, laquelle peult estre elle ne desaprouvera pas. Cet que voyant les grandes dificultez que lon faict a Malte il y a si long temps d'envoyer quelqu'un a Munster, je me suis resolu de faire un petit voiage moymesme en Hollande a ce mois de May prochain lorsque la Cour sera a Amiens, si Vostre Eminence le trouve bon et avec lettres du Roy et de Monseigneur le Cardinal agir envers Messieurs les Estats a ce quils laissent a la Religion la libre et paisible jouissance du bien quelle a dans l'estendue de leur domination; j'estime qu'ils escouteront ma proposition en leur remonstrant que tous les jours leurs vaisseaux sont a Malte pour les radouber et y prendre tous les raffreschissemens et aultres choses dont ils ont be-

soing, quils y ont tousiours trouvé un favorable accueil et toute l'assistance quils peuvent souhaitter et que on auroit peu a bon droict user de quelque droict de represaille voyant le peu destat que lon a faict jusques a present de restituer le dict bien a lordre, mais qu'on a voulu attendre avec patience le temps pour ne pas rompre la bonne intelligence qui a tousiours esté avec eux, et a present que la Religion est obérée de debtes et en tresgrande nécessité, elle cherche toute [fol.302v] sorte de moyens pour s'acquiter, ce qui ne peult estre en facon quelconque si elle ne jouist de tous ses biens, et ainsy je croys quils termineront les longueurs quils ont apporté a la restitution desdicts biens quils ne tiennent que par usurpation et en cas quils apportent de la dificulté, y joindre quelque sorte de menaces et leur faire entendre que la Religion ne pouvant plus vivre dans cette oppression se resoudra a rechercher quelque aultre voye pour reprendre son bien partout où elle pourra par droict de represailles, en quoy on ne peult trouver aucune chose a redire, et si Vostre Eminence et le Conseil trouvent cela bon, je la supplie tres humblement de m'envoyer un pouvoir absolu et toutes despesches necessaires pour negotier cette affaire. Cependant je ne juge pas a propos quil soit necessaire d'envoyer Monsieur de la Rouviere a Munster ny pas un aultre, qui sera aultant de despense espargnée, pretendant faire ce voiage la a mes coustes et despens. Jattendray la response de Vostre Eminence sur ce subiect avec impatience et demeureray a jamais
Monseigneur
Vostre tres humble et tres obeissant serviteur et religieux
   Jacques de Souvré
Paris le 27. decembre 1647

160. 1648, January 31 – *Frater Jean Paul Lascaris, Grand Master, and Convent grant the right to regain the Order's possessions in the United Provinces of the Netherlands to frater Jacques de Souvré and empower him to negotiate with the Estates of those provinces.*
   Registration: AOM 472 = libri bullarum 1647-1649, fol.229r, dated in Annunciation-style.

Frater Joannes Paulus Lascaris etc. et militaris etc. custos, et nos conventus etc. venerando fratri Jacobo de Souvre ordinis nostri baiulivo, ac oratori nostro ordinario apud Maiestatem Christianissimam salutem in Domino, et diligentiam in commissis.
   Cum apud illustrissimos et prepotentes dominos Status Provinciarum foederatarum Belgii multa, variaque negotia occurrant, quibus propter absentiam nostram commode prospicere non possumus,

necessarium duximus aliquem ex nostris illuc mittere, qui ea curare, et peragere valeat.

Confidentes igitur de tua fide, probitate, et prudentia, ac in rebus agendis dexteritate, et solertia, citra tamen revocationem aliorum nostrorum procuratorum, oratorum, sive ambasciatorum in diversis mundi partibus constitutorum, te venerandum fratrem Jacobum de Souvray absentem tamquam presentem invicem maturo, et delibera-to consilio de nostra certa scientia eligimus, constituimus, et deputa-mus, oratorem sive ambasciatorem nostrum extraordinarium, atque legatum, procuratorem, et nuncium nostrum specialem et generalem tenore presentium creamus, et solemniter ordinamus ad nostro dicti-que militaris ordinis nostri nomine coram dictis dominis Statibus, et alias ubicunque opus fuerit comparendum et supplicandum, ut res nostras suo favore prosequantur, et ab eisdem impetrandum, peten-dum, et obtinendum omnia, et singula, que pro honore, et commodo dicti ordinis, tibique visa fuerint necessaria, et opportuna, et a nobis habueris in mandatis; et precipue recuperationem, et restitutionem omnium, et singulorum bonorum, et commendarum ad predictum nostrum militarem ordinem in predictis provinciis spectantium, et a personis ab eo alienis occupatorum, amotis quibuscunque dictorum bonorum, et commendarum detentoribus, et occupatoribus. Et pro huiusmodi recuperatione et restitutione coram predictis dominis Sta-tibus, et quibuscunque iudicibus, si opus fuerit, comparendum, ac iustitie complementum, privilegiaque, immunitates, et libertates mili-taris ordinis nostri observari petendum, et procurandum, ac ea impe-trandum, que pro tempore nobis, tibique visa fuerint necessaria, et opportuna. Committentes tibi in premissis, et circa recuperationem, et restitutionem predictam totaliter vices nostras, quarum vigore ea possis, et valeas, que nosmet facere possemus, si presentes essemus, etiam si talia forent, que magis speciale mandatum exigerent, quam in presentibus sit expressum. Dantes, et concedentes tibi facultatem, et potestatem tenore presentium necessariam, et opportunam ad no-mine nostro aliquem probum virum sufficientem, et idoneum tibi benevisum eligendum, et deputandum, illumque constituendum, et sollemniter ordinandum nostrum, nostrique militaris ordinis apud predictos dominos Status Provinciarum factorem, actorem, et sollici-tatorem ad premissa, et predictam recuperationem, et restitutionem sollicitandum, procurandum, et prosequendum. Cauto tamen quod huiusmodi factor, actor, et sollicitator transactionem aliquam super premissis concludere non possit, nisi consultis nobis, et obtento nostro speciali mandato. Promittentes bona fide habere ratum, gratum, et firmum quicquid per te in premissis, et circa premissa actum, gestum-ve fuerit, sub obligatione bonorum nostrorum, nostrique ordinis pre-

sentium, et futurorum.   In cuius rei etc. bulla nostra communis
plumbea etc.
  Datum Melite etc. die ultima mensis Ianuarii 1647 ab incarnatione.

161. 1648, August 31 — *Frater Jean Paul Lascaris, Grand Master, answers
the letters of the Prince Landgraf von Hessen [Prior of Germany] of 30 May and
4 July 1648, sending him an enclosed copy of the instructions to the nuncio Chigi
for the peace negotiations in Münster. As regards the prince's desire to obtain the
right to regain the Order's possessions in the Dutch Republic, which have been
given to the bailiff Souvré, the Grand Master advises him to take it up with Souvré
himself.*

*Copy: AOM 1426 = Copies of letters of Grand Master frater Jean Paul
Lascaris to ambassadors etc., 1648, without page or folio numbers.*

*Fabio Chigi was inquisitor on Malta from 1634 to 1639, apostolic nuncio in
Switzerland and Germany, and later became known as Pope Alexander VII. For
Chigi's role as a protector of the Jesuits and the rapid career of the Prince Landgraf
von Hessen within the Order of Malta as a converted Lutheran with a Jesuit
confessor, see: D.F.Allen, 'Anti-Jesuit rioting by knights of St John during the
Malta carnival of 1639', in:* Archivum Historicum Societatis Jesu, *65
(1996) pp.3-30, especially pp.24-27.*

Principe Landravio a di 31 Agosto 1648
Havendo risposto à 2 del cadente à molto lettere di Vostra Eccelenza
rispondiamo hoggi con questa all' altre due delli 30. di Maggio e 4. di
Luglio, sopra giunteci insieme quattro giorni sono, dicendole in primo luogo di mandarle qui annesso un Duplicato dell'instructione, e
delle littere scritte à Monsignor Nuntio Chigi ed altri, sopra
gl'interessi di nostra Religione da trattarsi in Munster nel congresso
della Pace Universale, che piaccia à Dio di concederci ed haver dati
gl'ordini opportuni, perche anche dalle corone si incarichi stretta-
mente à loro Plenipotentiarii di non consentir in modo alcuno alli
nostri pregiuditii. Ond'altro non rimane in questa parte, che di sentire à suo tempo il buon ricapito di questi Dispacci, é che l'Eccelenza
Vostra se ne sia valsa nel continuare le buone diligente incaminate,
guista il tenore della detta Instruttione.
Molto prima ch'ella ci esprimesse il desiderio suo intorno alla ricuperatione delli Beni e Commende occupati alla nostra Religione nelle
Provincie e Stati d'Olanda, si era in cio conceduta da noi, e dal
nostro Venerando Consiglio la facolta necessaria e la permissione di
goderne in vita sua al Venerando Balio di Souvré[a] nostro Ambasciadore in corte di Francia, che ne fece l'instanza. In riguardo però di

questa preventione non resta hora altro campo che di suggerire à Vostra Eccelenza che trovandosi il detto Balio in cotesti Paesi venuto-vi, per tal'effetto, potra ella trattar seco, e vedere s'egli ne le vuol cedere alcuna parte, assicurandola in tanto, che in questo caso con-correremo molto volentieri nella sodisfatione di lei.

[the remainder of the letter concerns the preceptory of Tobel]

ª Souré *ms.*

162. 1648, October 27 – *Frater Johann Gobet, head of the preceptory of Aachen, is licensed to make up a will concerning one-fifth of his moveables and money, and is granted the free disposal of his patrimony during and after his lifetime.*
   Chancery notes: AOM 472 = libri bullarum *1647-1649, fol.215r.*

Die XXVII mensis Octobris 1648 frater Joannes Gobet commendae de Aquisgrana prioratus Alemanie commendarius habuit lecentiam testandi de quinta parte suorum bonorum mobilium et pecunie nu-merate; ita tamen quod relique quatuor partes integre ad commune erarium perveniant etc. cum clausula; reservato etiam statu predicte commende pro futuris commendariis, ac sub bulla magistrali plum-bea in forma etc.

Die eadem. Idem commendarius frater Joannes Gobet habuit licen-tiam disponendi de suis bonis patrimonialibus tam in vita, quam in mortis articulo etc. dummodo etc.

163. 1649, May 26 – *Frater Jean Paul Lascaris, Grand Master, and Convent grant the right to regain the Order's possessions in Utrecht, Haarlem and elsewhere in the provinces of the Estates General and in Low Germany, with the exception of the preceptories of Wesel, Borken, Arnhem and Nimwegen, Burgsteinfurt, Mün-ster, Lage and Herford, and Herrenstrunden, to Prince Friedrich Landgraf von Hessen, Prior of Germany, instead of frater Jacques de Souvré, who was given this right in 1644, July 28; see nr.158 above. Souvré ended his mission under protest: see below, D.nrs. 22-23, dd. 23 September 1648. Registration: AOM 472* = libri bullarum 1647-1649, *fol.217v-218r.*

Frater Iohannes Paulus Lascaris etc. et militaris etc. custos et nos baiulivi, priores, commendatarii et fratres consilium ordinarium in Domino celebrantes illustrissimo ac venerando principi Federico

Landgravio Hassiae Darmstaden prioratus nostri Alemaniae priori salutem etc.

Ad ea studiose atque libenter intendimus etc. que recuperationem et conservationem commendarum, bonorum, prediorum, iurium, et possessionum etc. ordini nostro pie concessorum concernere dignoscuntur.

Cum itaque baiulivatus noster de Utrecht, et commenda de Harlem, earumque membra et dependentiae, aliaeque commendae et bona mobilia etc. sita et posita in Bassa seu Inferiori Alemania, et in provinciis, confinibus, territoriis, ac dominiis illustrissimorum et excellentissimorum dominorum Statuum Generalium nuncupatorum non modo (sicut accepimus) ab ipsismet illustrissimis et excellentissimis dominis Statibus Generalibus, verum etiam a quibusdam aliis personis ab ordine nostro alienis occupata detineantur, nostraque intersit, ut illa de iure evincantur, seu alias recuperentur, hinc est quod volentes nobis ipsis, onerique nostro satisfacere, ac consideratis amplissimis tuis meritis *[fol.218r]* laudabilibusque et preclaris obsequiis per te eidem ordini nostro summa cum fidei probitate prestitis, iuxta decretum in nostro concilio hodierna die editum, ac deliberationem nostrae venerandae linguae Alemaniae in ipso decreto insertam, confisi de tua industria, cura, et in rebus peragendis dexteritate, revocantes prius, nullasque declarantes omnes, et singulas similes concessiones recuperandi supradictum baiulivatum, commendas, et bona in favorem quarumvis personarum hactenus emanatas, et presertim illas in favorem venerandi fratris Jacobi de Souvray dicti ordinis nostri baiulivi sub die XXVIII mensis Iulii 1644 e cancellaria nostra expeditas, invicem maturo, et deliberato consilio de nostra certa scientia te illustrissimum ac venerandum principem Federicum Landgravium absentem tanquam presentem omnibus melioribus via, modo etc. et debemus, tenore presentium cum ampla auctoritate facimus, constituimus etc. procuratorem etc. videlicet specialiter et expresse ad nostro predictique erarii et ordinis nomine prenominatum baiulivatum de Utrecht, et commendam de Harlem, eorumque membra, et dependentias, omnesque alias commendas, et quecunque bona mobilia etc. in Bassa, seu Inferiori Alemania, et in prefatis provinciis sita et posita una cum omnibus, et singulis earum iurisdictionibus, pertinentiis, membris, fructibus etc. petendum, ac predictarum commendarum de Utrecht, et Harlem, aliarumque commendarum et bonorum omnium huiusmodi possessionem etc. capiendum. Exceptis tamen, et expresse reservatis bonis ad commendas de Vesel, Borken, Arnheim et Nimmeghen, Steinfort, Munster, Laghen, et Hervorderen, et Herenstrunden quomodolibet spectantibus, quorum bonorum, et iurium huiusmodi recuperatio ad preceptores, seu commendatarios de ipsis commendis iam provisos pertinet, et reservata censeatur.

Decernentes, ut omnibus predictis baiulivatu, commendis, et bonis per te propriis expensis recuperandis iuxta formam statutorum nostrorum vita tua perdurante uti, frui, et gaudere, in tuosque usus, et utilitatem convertere libere, et licite possis, et valeas, cum hoc tamen, et non alias quod in quolibet anno quintam partem fructuum, reddituum et proventuum, quos ex eisdem baiulivatu, ac commendis, et bonis ut supra recuperandis percipies pro rata eorum, quae in dies recuperabis predicto nostro communi erario pro responsionibus cum effectu persolvere tenearis, et post tuum obitum baiulivatus, et commende ac bona huiusmodi remaneant, et esse intelligantur iuxta eorumdem statutorum et ordinationum capitularium dispositionem.

Atque ut omnia premissa suum plenarium sortiantur effectum te nuntium nostrum etc. habilitamus etc. Nec non etc. et generaliter etc. Promittentes etc.

In cuius rei etc. bulla nostra communis plumbea etc.

Datum Melitae etc. die XXVI mensis Maii 1649.

164. 1650, August 4 & September 4 – *Frater Jean Paul Lascaris, Grand Master, sends a letter dd. 4 August to the Prince Landgraf von Hessen [Prior of Germany], in addition to some letters from Malta concerning the recovery of the Order's possessions in the province of Holland, advising him to show these letters to the Archduke [of Austria] to get his approval before using them in his negotiations with the Estates of Holland; and a letter dd. 4 September to the same in reaction to his letter dd. 2 July 1650 concerning the same matter.*

Copies: AOM 1428 = Copies of letters of Grand Master Jean Paul Lascaris to ambassadors etc., 1650, without page or folio numbers.

Principe Landgravio a di detto [4 Agosto 1650]
Essendosi finalmente superati le difficolta, che da persona del nostro Venerando Consiglio si facevano alle lettere domandati da Vostra Eminenza sopra la ricuperatione delle Commende occupateci in Olanda si sono spediti da noi, e quì allegati se l'enviano, acciò possa valersene, e' procurare di raccorne' il desiderato frutto à benefitio di nostra Religione e di lei stessa. Ma perche' la persona medisima insiste sempre nel dire, ch'elleno possono essere di qualche preguiditio agl'interessi di Vostra Altezza Cattholica, il che non e preveduto, ne creduto da noi, nè da altri, e sarebbe ciò fuori d'ogni nostra intentione, rivolta sempre alle cose di servitio della Altezza Vostra, sará bene in ogni modo che prima di presentarle, si contenti l'Eccellenza Vostra di farle vedere al Serenissimo Arciduca, per sentire sopra di esse il sentimento di Sua Altezza, e per ricevere in caso

d'esser approvate, come speriamo, l'accompagnamento de suoi effica-
cissimi e benignissimi uffici dall' autorità de quali non può aspettarsi,
che vantaggi et agevolezza maggiore in questo si importante negotio.
Ch'è quanto potiamo dirle in risposta dello scrittoci con più sue in
questa materia. E senza più baciamo à Vostra Eccelenza le mani, e le
preghiamo dal Signor Iddio continua prosperità e salute etc.

1650, September 4, same address:
—. Dopo la detto ci e sopragiunta l'altra sua delli 2 di Luglio in
materia della ricuperatione della Commenda d'Arlem in Olanda. Ma
perche in cio ci troviamo d'haver già sodisfatto al desiderio
dell'Eccelenza Vostra con le lettere inviatele per quelli stati, altro per
hora non occorre di soggiugnerle, se non che staremo aspettando si
sentire il ritratto dalla presentatione di esse, per venir poi consideran-
do quel più che in caso di bisogno possa e debba eseguirsi in affare di
questa sorte. E col fine baciando a Vostra Eccelenza le mane le
preghiamo dal Signor Iddio prosperita continua etc.

165, 166, 167. 1652, November 12 & 14, & December 20 – *Letters
concerning the sequestration of Dutch merchandise passing Heitersheim as a repri-
sal for the Order's confiscated possessions in the Dutch Republic.*
    Convolution of three original letters: GLA Karlsruhe, 89/325, titled:
Von dem Herrn Fürste Johannitermeister Cardinal von Hessen, gegen die Republik Holland, wegen dem Orden vorenthaltenen Gütern
und besitzungen, vorgehabte regreßirung mittelst anhaltung und ar-
retirung der beij Heitersheim fürüber führenden Holländischen
waaren, und desswegen angehaltene Fuhrwägen.
    Welches aber die Vorder Österreichische Regierung als einen Ter-
ritorial-Eingriff nicht gestattet, und dem Heitersheimischen Herrn
Amtmann verbothen hat.

165. 1652, November 12 – *The agents of the Archduke of Austria prohibit
Hans Kaspar Kuentzer, official at Heitersheim, the further sequestration of Dutch
merchants' goods passing through his country.*
    *Original letter which is the first in a convolution of three original letters: GLA
Karlsruhe, 89/325.*

Den Ehrsamben unserem lieben und gueten freündt Hannß Caspar
Kuentzeren, Ambtman zue Heiterßheimb.
Unnßer grueß tuewr Ehrsamber lieber unndt gueter freündt,
Wür haben auß deinem schreiben die ursachen vernommen, warum-

ben du ein Zeit herein, die das Landt herauf, undt abfahrende Güetter fuhren anhalten, und die fuhrleüth für dich führen, und dero
selben Brief zue ersuechen, auch ein solches für baß zue continuieren
dich anmaßen wollest. Wann dann dergleichen begünnen der Fürstlich durchlauchtester Ferdinand Carln Erzherzogen zue Össterreich
unßers gnedigsten Herren, undt Landtsfürstens dis orths habenden
hochen Regalien und geleijdtlichen Juribus zue wider laufft und aber
unns solche in Salvo zue erhalten obligt, Alß ist innammen höchstgedachter unßerer gnedigsten herrschafft hiemit unszer nachmahlegir
ernstlicher bevelch, das du dich aller angedeüter attentaten genzlichen enthalten sollest. Widrigen falls, und auf ferner einlangende
clagdten wir andre müttel wider dich vorzunemmen nicht underlas-
ßen werden, gestalten wir unß zu dir alß versehen. Datum Freijburg
den 12. Novembris[a] 1652.

Fürstlich durchlauchtester Ferdinand Carls Erzhertog zu Ostereichs
Statthalter Regenten und Räthe Vorder Österreichischer Landen.

[undersigned with two illegible names, something like]
Speredessen *[and]* Zellerdr

---

[a] 9bris *ms.*

166. 1652, November 14 − *Hans Kaspar Kuentzer informs the Prince-
Cardinal Landgraf von Hessen, his lord at Heitersheim, that his order to impound
the goods of Dutch merchants to retaliate for the occupation of the Order's posses-
sions in the Dutch Republic will be followed and is approved of by the King of
France; however, most merchants fail to produce the required commercial letters
showing the origin of their cargo and must be dismissed.*
*Original letter which is the second in a convolution of three original letters:
GLA Karlsruhe, 89/325.*
The abbreviation bz. means batzen, small part of a florin.

Hochwürdigster, durchluüegtig − und hochgeborene Fürst Gnedigster Herr.

Ihro Hoch Fürstlicher Eminenz beede vom 19. undt 27. jüngsthin
verwichenen monats octobris auß Prag ahn mich gnedigst abgebene
schreiben habe sampt dem Einschluß mit underthänigster reverenz
empfangen: solle deren Inhalt in ein- und anderem soviel möglich,
insonderheit wider Mr. Capitain Doncourt (so zwahr noch nicht alhier, aber Herrn Canonici Verelchs[a] bericht nach täglich erwartet
würdet) beij dessen ankhunfft gehorsambist volzogen werden.

Ihro Hoch Fürstlicher Eminenz schreiben ahn Herrn General Audi-
teur Völcker in Preisach, habe demselben mit ablegung behöriger
Curialien gehorsambist eingeliffert, thuet Ihro hoch Fürstlicher Eminenz: derselbe neben gehorsambister seiner recommendation, daß
ahn seiten der Königlichen Regierung zue Preisßach mit arrestierung
der holländischen güetter nichts ermanglen solle underthänigst versi-
cheren; mit ahndeüten mann auf französischer seiten nichts anderß
sueche, als den Holländeren eintrag zue thuen und dieselbe derdurch
zue einer newen Allianz mit der Cron Franckhreich zuebringen,
maßen dann auf ahnhalten Herrn obristen Dubadels so vor dießem
gewüßen Holländeren 8000 Reichsdahler hehrgeschosßen, aber zue
seiner bezahlung nicht widerumb gelangen möchte, dergleichen arrest auff Holländische güetter auch gesuecht, und da einicher angelegt werden khöndte, selbiger sicherlich zuevorderist Ihro Hoch
Fürstlicher Eminenz zue guetem amploijiret werden solte.

Dieser Tagen seündt die Vorder Österreichische Landtständt aber-
mahlen zue Freijburg zuesammen – alhiesige herrschaft aber dabeij
nicht beschriben worden, was eijgentlich tractiert, oder biszhero eingewilliget worden saijn möchten, hat mann noch nichts gewüsses ver-
nemen mögen, aussert was der scheffner zue Sankt Johann in
Freijburg berichtet das beij deren deselbsten durch den Herrn von
Puochenberg beschehenen proposition den ständen nachfolgende 5
Puncten vorgetragen werden seijen.
Erstens werden die zulängst auf den saltz handell geschlage und gelter ad jedem sester salz 2 bz. gefordert.
2. ist befelch ertheijlt, die Contribution etwas gleichers abzutheijlen,
und da solches von den ständen nicht beschehe mueste eß ein hoch-
lobliche[a] Regierung vernemmen.
3. dahin zusehen damit die Freijburgische Guarnison fleisßiger alß
bißhero bezalt und da einiche quitanzen ahnstehen, alßbalden die
wünschliche execution vorgenommen und zuemahlen ein magazin
aufgerichtet werden solte.
4. der Preijsachische achtell oder die jenige gelter so die ständ in
Elsasß schuldig, werden in gleichen von desszeits Reics Ständen gefordert.
5. weijlen unter Österreich kheine fridumbgelter bezalt werden, als
würdt zue Ihro Erz Fürstlicher Herzoglicher[b] Reijß nachh Regen-
spurg ein Tuckhgelt (dessen quantum noch ohnbenambset) sodann
zue besserer nußpringung der Vorder Österreichischen Regierung
ein beijtrag erfordert. Es sollen aber die gesambte standt bis ahnhero
ahnnung gahr wenig eingewilliget haben.
Was sonsten von der Vorder Österreichischen Regierung wider
hisige herrschafft bishero vorgenommen worden, werden Ihro hoch

Ehrsambiste Eminenz auß meiner vorher gegangenen gehorsambisten relation gnedigst vernommen haben.

Alhir würdt die wacht umb arrestierung holländischer güetter fleisßig continuiert; ist aber zuebesorgen, weijlen die aichl[a] brieff (wie sije von den kauffleuthen genennt werden) den fuehrleüthen nicht auffgeben, sonderen durch die ordinari posten übersandt, und auß den vrocht zedelen nichts anders alß die quantitet der wahren neben beijgesezten ohnbekhanten marquen, wehre aber selbige zuestendig, daß geringste vernommen werden khann, dis orths alhir wenig zue richten seijn werde. Unnd ihnen damit in erwartung weiterer gnedigster ordre Ihro Hoch Fürstlicher Eminenz zue allem gnedigsten wohl ergehen unnd zue dero behahrlichen hochfürstlichen Gnaden mich underthänigst empfehlen.

Ihro Hoch Fürstlicher Eminenz
underthänigst trew gehorsambister
Johann Caspar Kuontzer
    propria manu
dathieret Heijttersheim
den 14. Novembris[c] 1652

---

[a] *uncertain reading ms.* [b] *uncertain abbreviation ms.:* Erz Fr.H. [c] 9bris *ms.*

167. 1652, December 20 − *The agents of the Archduke of Austria request the chancellor and councillors at Heitersheim to desist from impounding the goods of Dutch merchants, lest they should avoid the archduke's lands for the transportation of their goods, to the detriment of this country.*

Original letter which is the third in a convolution of three original letters: GLA Karlsruhe, 89/325. The letter is undersigned by the same persons as nr.165.

Dem hochgelehrten unndt ehrsamben, unsrem lieben gueten freündt unndt besondren N.N. Canzler unndt Räthen zue Heijterszheimb. Heijterszheim den 20 Decembris[a] 1652.

Unnßer freündtlich dienst unndt grueß tuewr hochgelehter auch ehrsamber, lieber und gueter freundt, undt besonderer,
Wür haben dier dem ambtman vom 8. Novembris[b] jüngsthin wegen beij Heiterszheimb anhaltender fuohrleüthen, so mit kaufmans wahren das lanndt auf und abfahren, unndt das man denselben ihre Brieff eröfne, anbefohlen, desßen genzlichen zuebemüesßigen, nit gezweiflet, er ambtman wurde deme gehorsamet haben; Wür müesßen aber des widrig, unndt sovil vernemmen das noch ieweils zue

angedeütem enndt bestelte wächter auf dergleichen fuohrleüth pas-
ßen, unndt ihnen mithin anlaß geben, die straß zue enderen, und
den weeg durch das Elßäs auf unndt abzuenemmen, so unserer gnedigsten herrschafft zue Össterreichs nit allein zue schaden, sondern
auch schmelerung Ihrer Landtsfürstlichen Hochait, und gelaidts ge-
rechtigheit geräichen wurde, so wür kheines weegs gestatten khön-
den, dergleichen repressalien auch im Römischen Reich verbotten,
und gar nit zue gelaßen werden; Alß ist in höchstgedachter unßerer
gnedigsten Herrschafft zue Össterreichs nammen hiemit unßer nach-
mahliger bevelch, das Ihr die auf- und ab pasßierende fuohren ohn-
angefochten führfahren laßen sollendt, sonsten widrigen
unverhofenden fall wurde unnß an müttel nit ermanglen, so wohl
mehr höchstgedachter unßerer gnedigsten herrschafft gerechtsamben
zue erhalten, alß auch die verursachende schäden, und cössten, an
Euch widerumben zue erhollen, darnach Ihr Euch zue richten, unndt
selbsten vor ungelegenheit zue sein, unndt unnß Euwer Erclärung
hierüber einzuschiekhen wisßen werden.
Datum Freijburg den 16. Decembris Anno 1652.

Fürstlich durchlauchtester Ferdinand Carls Erzherzogen zue Össterreichs Statthalter, Regenten und Räthe Vorder Österreichischer Landen.

[undersigned with two illegible names]

---

^a Xbris *ms.* ^b 9bris *ms.*

168. 17th century, undated – *Specification of some possessions of the Order.*
Chancery notice from Heitersheim: GLA Karlsruhe, 89/326; this rather small
volume contains among others a document in threefold with a list of the bailiwicks,
preceptories and possessions of the Order of St John in the Dutch Republic:

Specification
der von denen Herren Staaten der Vereinigten Provincien würcklich
besisender den ritterlichen Johanniter orden und dessen obristmeisterthumb in teütschen Landen gehöriger Bajulivaten, Commenden und gütheren.
Das grosse Bajulivat von Utrecht mit der Residenz und zugehörigen
ahnsehnlichen haüseren und dorffschafften auch commenden.
   Das Bajulivat und ahnsehnlich haus Harlem mit seinen haüsern
und commenden, Schineck, Kirchwerff, Hardewick, Midelburg,
Harmelen, Engen, Büren, Oldewater, Werder, Wemenick, Mont-

forth, Ummeren, Binnerwick, Embtskirch, Suderwau, Kasterwau, Lanwold, Hasselt, zum theil Benningum, Dumbroch, Bassamenicum, Worgsum, Witwort, Osterwierumb, Arnheim, Nimwegen.

Nebst diesen obspecificirten Baiulivaten, Commenden und gütteren seijnd ferners seith einigen saeculis von den riterlichen orden und dessen obristmeisterthumb separiret worden

alle in denen erzherzoglichen österreichischen erbländeren gelegene wohlgediehenen[a] ordens commenden und güther, welche dem böheimischen Priorat incorporirt seijnd;

die jenige, so in Brandenburg, Preüszen, Pommeren, Mecklenburg, und Hollstein sich befinden, diese constituiren ein separates corpo und recognosciren das Johanniter obristmeijsterthumb nur certo modo;

das ganse Priorat Datia, so allein den Titul und dignität noch heütiges tags führet, ist völlig, und dar nebst diesem seind auch so wohl die in der Schweitserischen aijdgenoszenschafft als in des Römischen Reichs unterschiedlich ahnsehnliche Commenden und güether entzogen worden.

---

[a] *uncertain abbreviation ms.:* wohlgedn.

169. 17th century – *Concept, presumably meant for discussion in the Venerable Council, concerning reprisals against Dutch vessels.*
Original concept: AOM 57 = Liber epistolarum, *fol.351r-352r; undated document without addressee and undersigning.*

The mentioning of the support from the King of Denmark alludes to a letter from Frederic III, King of Denmark, dd. 12 May 1652, whose Italian and German translations can be found in AOM 57, fol.218r-v, 375r-v, 376r-v; printed Latin version in Recueil 1750 *nr.15.*

Resposta alle difficultadi che sofferiamo sopra le Reprisaglie delli vascelli Hollandesi por la restitutione delli beni della Sacra Religione usurpati in quelli Paesi.

Illustrissimi Signori

Gia sono le Signorie Illustrissime loro pienamente informati da diverse lettere e scritture presentate e lette nel Venerando Consiglio del torto fatto à questa Sacra Religione da parecchie città delli Paesi Bassi, in usurpare e ritenere per più di trenta millia scudi d'entrata di beni spettanti ad essa, come anco del modo che è stato molte volte proposto e particolarmente da qualche tempo in quà dall'Eminentissimo Signore Cardinale Lantgravio d'Assia e Gran Priore d'Alemagna per ricuperatione di essi appoggiato da Sua Maestà di

Danemarca, e di molti altri Principi e Potentati, anzi desiderato da diverse persone principali del proprio Paese interessati nel trafico di Levante, e di questi mari, havendo già un pezzo fà li Borgomaestri della Città d'Amesterdam presentato alli stati generali un memoriale in favore della Sacra Religione protestando che in caso che ci sarebbe illato qualche danno alli loro vascelli si ripigliarebbono sopra li detenta delli nostri beni di modo che non bisogna tediare le Signorie Illustrissime loro con nuova informatione sopra il fatto, ma di rispondere brevemente alle obiettioni che (come si intende) vengono ò potrebbono venir fatte.

Primo non si fa torto alle usurpationi cominciando (dopò tante amichevole instanze vanamente fatte) per la esecutione in sequestrar de fatto alcuni vascelli loro senza dargliene aviso, non havendo essi mai avisato la Sacra Religione dalle violenze usate da loro in levarle il suo, e perciò non haveranno occasione di lamentarsi di sopresa tenendosi da parte della Religione il camino mostrato da loro medesimi, quanto più che già sanno che la Sacra Religione è sempre stata in questa giusta pretensione di restitutione.

Secondo non osta la ragione che si potrebbe allegare con dire che mentre li Signori Francesi che all'hora erano in Consiglio si hanno opposto quando il medesimo si ha procurato da Don Luiggi di Portugallo in tempo che la corona di Francia era confederata con li stati d'Olanda, Adesso non si deve permettere stante che quelli sono amici della Maesta Cattholica [a] . In questo particolar si vede una grandissima differenza perche in quel tempo la corona di Francia haveva lega offensiva e defensiva con li stati d'Olanda, dove che adesso quella di Spagna ha solamente una pace semplice con li detti stati senza alcuna confederazione [fol.351v] di che si può giudicare che quella non può havere interesse veruno d'impedire la Sacra Religione nella giusta recuperatione del suo, e tanto di più che il Serenissimo Arciduca Leopoldo che comanda l'armi di detta Maesta in Fiandra et altri ministri Spagnoli hanno più volte detto à Sua Eminenza il Gran Priore che si maravigliavano che la Sacra Religione non si servi contro l'Olandesi delli mezzi che ne ha nelle mani con detener li loro vascelli.

Terzo si confessa che d'alcuni anni in qua particolarmente dopò la pace fatta con la Corona di Spagna son capitati pochi vascelli Olandesi in questo porto godendo quelli di Napoli, Sicilia, Sardegna, e che quelli che vi sono venuti sono stati caricati in parte di robba, e mercantia spettante ad Italiani, e cittadini Hansiatiche, e che di simile incontro potrebbe nascere un grande interesse alla Religione se si trattasse di smaltire senza distinctione delli Padroni la robba presa, ma sequestrandola solamente e salvandola in utile delli veri proprieta-

ri non si potrebbe correre nuovi risico di sodisfattione rilevanti ad esse
che del tempo che li vascelli sarebbono stati arrestati, anzi apparendo
che fossero del tutto ò in parte caricati di mercantia appartenente ad
altri, che di quelli Paesi si potrebbono subito rilasciare, ritenendo
quello che sarebbe giudicato di buona presa, e salvarlo per represag-
lie fino alla restitutione delli beni.

Quarto non si niega, che essendo l'Olandesi avisati d'una tale
risolutione, evitaranno questo porto, ma non potranno fuggire
l'incontro delle Galere in mare, le quali saranno sempre bastanti ad
impedire la navigatione loro, e di pigliarne quanti vascelli troveranno,
essendo certo che non combatteranno non trovandogli à conto
d'andare con convogli di vascelli di guerra per la grossa spesa, che
bisognarebbe fare, e se à caso alcuni andassero tanto accompagnati,
che non se gli potrebbe far danno sarebbe almanco la Religione
sicura di non esserne assalita, ne forzata à combattere, facendo
guerra offensiva secondo che più ò meno il partito sarebbe proporzio-
nato alle forze sue.

Quinto nel canale non ci è niente da temere dalli vascelli di guerra
che hoggi di si trovano in questo mare contro gl'Inglesi, perche una
volta ritornati à casa, il che forse sarà più presto, che si pensa, non
potendo la guerra contro detti Inglesi durar tanto, non torneranno
mai più, non meritando [fol.352r] negotio il trattener una Armata
appostà contro la Religione e mentre vi sono hanno tanto à fare per
difendersi contro li detti inimici, che non ardiscono di separare la
squadra loro, e manco d'impiegarla tutta contro di noi è tanto più se
si donasse licenza alli Corsali nostri di combatterli, il che temono più
che niuna cosa.

Sesto è vero che risolvendosi le Galere, ò li corsali à combattere
uno ò più vascelli in mare e mettendoli à fondo con mercantia spettante ad Italiani ò altri la Religione sarebbe obbligata à rifarne il
danno alli Padroni, ma incontra è certissimo che subito, che si inten-
dera la risolutione, nessuno delli sopradetti mercanti si servirà più
delli vascelli Olandesi, il che loro farà gran danno per la parte, che
hanno ordinariamente in simili trafichi e per utile che cavano da
simili noliti.

Settimo non pare che la consideratione dell'Isola di San Christo-
foro sia così relevante come alcuni pensano, essendo in ogni modo
meglio di ricuperarne quello che si è perso, che d'acquistar beni novi,
di che non si sà ancora ne la vera valuta ne l'effetto, che ha di
seguirne.

Ultimo che li beni usurpati siano in alcune parti applicati al trat-
tentimento d'Hospitali, Scole, e Ministri è vero, ma non è anco vero,
che molti particolari ne godono bona portione, e che queste applica-

tioni son fatte senza il consenso del vero Padrone, e per consequenza nulle.

Si supplica pertanto che le Signorie Illustrissime loro si vogliano compiacere à pigliare una risolutione adequata al bisogno, è di crede-re per certo, che con la minima dimostratione si verrà se non alla totale restitutione almanco ad un avantagiosissimo accordo per la Sacra Religione essendo certo, che li stati d'Olanda non lascieranno mai arrivare la cosa, che loro poco importa al termine di forza d'arme, e che venendosi à questro estremo tutti li Potentati della Christianità l'approveranno per giusta, e fondata in ragione.

ᵃ *blank space ms.*

170. 1661, December 16 – *Frater Rafael Cotoner, Grand Master, answers a letter from the Prince-Cardinal Landgraf von Hessen dd. 23 September 1661 in which he asks for a final decision on the reprisals against Dutch vessels. The Grand Master has received his letter on 10 December 1661, with deep concern. He also declares that the possible recovery of the Dutch possessions of the Order of St John is due to the Prince-Cardinal and not to Souvré, notwithstanding the latter's pretensions in this matter, which will be discussed in the Venerable Council.*
    Original letter: GLA Karlsruhe, 90/462, fol.29r-v, undersigned by autograph by the Grand Master.

171. 1662, March 18 – *Frater Rafael Cotoner, Grand Master, writes to the Prince-Cardinal Landgraf von Hessen concerning the difficulty of taking reprisals against Dutch vessels.*
    Original letter: GLA Karlsruhe, 90/462, fol.28r-v, undersigned by autograph by the Grand Master.

Monseigneur le Cardinal Landgrave de Hesse.
Monsieur
Le memoire instructif quil a plu a Votre Eminence de m'envoier fait bien voir que Messieurs les Estats ont plus de connoissance du tort quilz nous font que de volonté de le reparer. Il est iustement arrivé dans le temps que ie venois de nommer quatre Commissaires pour examiner et nous raporter tout ce qui s'est fait iusques a present en intention de parvenir a cette pretendue restitution, et comme il est cappable de leurs donner plusieurs lumieres du passé, Je leur ay aussy tost fait consigner, esperant quil leur aidera a decider plus prompte-ment le point de represaille que Votre Eminence me donne pour

facile et que ie ne trouve pas sans difficulté, c'est adire en matiere d'execution, car pour la resolution, elle sera fort aisée a prendre.

Il est question quil y a fort peu d'holandois qui naviguent aujourd-huy en cette Mer et que ceux que lon y voit une fois l'année, sont tous noligez pour le tiers et pour le quart en façon que nostre represaille ne peut estre que d'un corps de vaisseau sur lequel il nous faudra dedomager ceux ausquelz les marchandises appartiendront; Votre Eminence iuge apres cela sy ce grain imaginaire nous doit mettre en hazard de recevoir quelque perte notable et beaucoup de déplaisir ainsy quil Nous seroit desia arrivé, sy nous eussions commancé les actes d'hostilité depuis le temps que l'on nous en presse, l'admiral Ruyter estant venu le Mois passé, mouiller avec quinze Vaisseaux de Guerre devant ce port et aiant premierement trouvé cinq de nos Galeres sur le corps desquelles ilz auroient pu mil fois passer veu le vent frais qui reignoit pour lors. Je dis de mon Chef ces raisons a Votre Eminence afin qu'elle connoisse la nécessité que Nous avons de nous bien prevaloir des assistances que les Princes Chrestiens nous donnent, estant le plus court et le plus asseuré chemin pour parvenir a nostre satisfaction. Ce n'est pas a dire que si lesdits Commissaires, au deffaut de celuy là, nous en ouvrent quelqu'autre qui nous donne moien de pouvoir monstrer nostre ressentiment, que Nous ne nous y portions avec plaisir, et moy sur tous les autres, desirant de faire connoitre a Votre Eminence combien ie deffere a ses sentimens estant de coeur et d'affection.

Monsieur
Son tres affectioné Serviteur
Le Grand Maistre
    Cotoner
Malte ce 18me Mars 1662

172. 1663, May 20 – *The deputies of the Prince-Cardinal Landgraf von Hessen, Prior of Germany, declare that the Order will accept the redemption of the preceptory of Haarlem by the Estates of Holland for the prize of 150,000 florins on condition that the Estates of the other provinces will redeem the Order's goods within their territories for a reasonable price as well; the preceptories of Arnheim and Nimwegen will be left out of these transactions.*
    Copy: GLA Karlsruhe, 90/280, fol.2r-3r.

Nous soubsignés Députés de son Altesse Monseigneur le Prince Cardinal et Lant Grave de Hesse, Grand Prieur de l'ordre de Malthe en Allemagne, promettons et declarons par ces presentes, qu'au cas que les Nobles Grands et Puissants Estats de la Province d'Hollande et

Westfrise vueillent promettre par un bon et raisonnable contract de payer pour les biens de la Commanderie de Haerlem dans le temps de six mois prochains, la somme de cent cinquante mille florins de vingt sols chacun, et de disposer dans le mesme temps de six mois ou environ a compter du jour de la date des presentes, les autres provinces leurs alliés, qui possedent aussy des biens de l'ordre a ce qu'elles promettent aussy de payer dans peu de temps, pour le rachat desdits biens, telle somme de deniers qui sera trouvée raisonnable sur le pied et a proportion du revenu des biens qu'elles possedent, qu'en ce cas la nous soubsignés en la qualité susdite, si lesdites provinces font en effect ladite promesse, tascherons de disposer nos superieurs, a ce qu'ils se contentent pour le rachat des [fol.2v] biens de ladite Commanderie de Haerlem, de la somme de cent cinquante mille florins, pour la part que la Province d'Hollande doit en toute la masse. Toutesfois avec cette condition et reserve expresse qu'en cas que Messieurs les Estats d'Hollande ne puissent pas disposer les autres provinces dans[a] ledit temps de six mois, plus ou moins, a promettre et a payer une somme de deniers a proportion des revenus annuels desdits biens, ou telle autre somme dont ledit ordre se puisse contenter, cette proposition, et ce qui s'en sera ensuivy, sera tenue comme non faite, nulle et sans effect, et que ledit ordre de Malthe se reserverà ses droits et pretensions sur les biens situés dans les Provinces Unies, comme lesdites provinces de leur costé leurs pretenduës raisons au contraire, l'affaire demeurant de part et d'autre en l'Estat ou elle est presentement. Avec cette reserve expresse, que la Commanderie d'Arnheim, dont l'ordre joüit paisiblement et la Commanderie de Nimmegen qui a esté adjugée par sentence solemnelle de l'année 1646. a l'Ordre ne seront point compris audit rachapt general des [fol.3r] biens de l'ordre, mais en demeureront exemtes. Et en cas que les autres provinces puissent estre disposees a suivre la bonne intention de Messeigneurs les Estats d'Hollande, et a payer une somme de deniers, dont l'ordre se puisse contenter, l'on n'inserera point au contract que l'on fera pour cela, des conditions fascheuses et qui ne seroient pas agreables a l'ordre. Les Deputés soubsignés se promettans que l'on fera aussy reflexion sur la grande despense et sur les frais qui ont esté faictes pendant la poursuitte de plusjeurs années pour la recouvrement des biens de l'ordre. Faict a la Haye le 20 Maij 1663, estoit signé

Le Commandeur de Pallandt

R.Kempinck

---

[a] dan *ms.*

173. 1663, June 23 – *Frater Rafael Cotoner, Grand Master, informs the Prince-Cardinal Landgraf von Hessen that he has authorized him to negotiate with the Estates General in order to recover the Order's property in the best way possible, either in kind or in money. The same authorization has been given to Jacques de Souvré and the head of preceptory De* Villeneufve, *agent of the Order in Flanders.*

Original letter: GLA Karlsruhe, 90/462, fol.19r.

The authorization for the other two men is to be found in RA Gelderland, Loeff, Archief, inventory nr.149: *certificate in which* Don Raphael Cotoner, *Grand Master of the Hospital of St John of Jerusalem, authorizes* Jacobus de Souvré, *bailiff of Morea and Cury, and* Leonettus de Villanova, *head of the preceptory of Montbrison, to negotiate restitution of the Order's property with the Estates; 1663, June 5.*

174. 1664, January 28 – *Chancellor and councillors of the Order of St John in Germany assess the amount of the yearly contributions due by the bailiwick of Utrecht with its preceptories and members, which is a prioral chamber of the prior of Germany.*

Original: RA Gelderland, Loeff, Archief, inventory nr.525, *document from the chancery at Heitersheim, single leaf double-sided, with superimpressed seal of red wax under a four-pointed wafer cartouche. Legend of the seal:* IOANNIS ...ERMANNI.

Wir des fürstlichen Johannitermeisterthumbs in Teütschen landenn Cantzler unndt Räthe, thuen kundt, zeugen undt bekhennen in krafft dises allenn und jedermanniglichenn, das wir in hochermelten Johannitermeisterthum haubt Archivo, unndt darin verwahrtenn der löblichen Cammer zue Malta Receptoraths büechernn, Visitations Libelln, Provincial Capituls abschreiben, alten rechnung undt andernn Documenten finden ausgestelt die Balleij Utrecht sambt zugehörigen Commenden unndt Membris, dem Ritterlichen Maltheser orden aigenthumblich zuestehet, undt eines zeitlichen desselben Grand Prioris in Teütschenlandenn Cammera Magistralis seij, dannentscher in recognitionem nachfolgende gebühr schuldig, als der Cammer zu Malta iährlichen undt alle jahr auff 1 Maij ahn ordinari responsiones fünff und sibenzig goldtgülden welche nach erheissender noth ijffers zweij-, dreij- unndt vierfach bezahlt werden müessen, heissen alstan Impositiones, zum anderen einem zeitlichen Grand Priorn iährlichen und alle iahr auff Joannis Baptistae zweijhundert goldtgülden, unndt wahn ein Commenthur zue Utrecht mit thot abgehet, und ein ander erwählt, von hochgedachten Hern Grand Priorn confirmirt wirt, noch einmahl so viel – als als in selbigem iahre

vierhundert goldtgülden – zu die *[verso]* die reichs ahnlagen so viel
Römermonathen aingewilliget werden, so viel zwölff und ainen halben goldtgülden, machen zu hundert Römermonathenn 1250 goldtgülden iährlichen unnd alle iahr auff Philippi unnd Jacobi. Einem
hochwürdigen mehrermelten Ritterlichen ordens Provincial Capitull
in Teutschenlandenn zehen goldtgülden bestendiger Capituls lasten,
visitations kosten, undt andere schuldigkaiten mehr.

Los[a] deme als bezeugen wir vermiddels hierunden getrückten
hochermelten fürstlichen Johannitermeisterthumbs in Teutschenlandenn hierunden getruckten Cantzleij Imsigell. Is gegeben den acht
undt zwanzigsten Januarij Anno Ein tausendt sechshundert vier
unndt sechszig.

---

[a]*uncertain reading ms.*

French translation of the said document.
   *Copy: GA Gelderland, Loeff, Archief, inventory nr.525, single leaf single-
sided.*

Nous Chancelier et Conseillers de l'illustre Maistrise de l'ordre de
St.Jean en Allemagne scavoir faisons, reconnoissons et tesmoignons
en vertu des presentes a tous et a un chacun, que nous trouvons dans
les archives principales de ladite maistrise de St.Jean, et dans les livres
de la Chambre de la recepte de Malthe, dans les procés verbaux des
visites, dans les recés des chapitres provinciaux, en des vieux comptes,
et en plusjeurs autres actes, que le baillage d'Utrecht, avec les commanderies et membres qui en dependent, appartient en proprieté a
l'ordre des chevalliers de Malthe, et qu'il est de la Chambre Magis-
trale du Grand Prieur en Allemagne, qui est pour lors, et qu'il recon-
noist sa superiorité, en payant les devoirs suivants: scavoir a la
Chambre de Malthe tous les ans, au premier jour de May, en rede-
vances ordinaires, soixante quinze florins d'or, qui bien souvent, selon
l'estat des affaires, sont doublées, triplées et quadruplées, et alors on
leur donne le nom d'impositions. Secondement au Grand Prieur, qui
vit pour lors, tous les ans, au jour de St.Jean Baptiste, deux cens
florins d'or, et lors qu'un commandeur d'Utrecht meurt, et qu'un
autre est esleu en la place du defunct, et confirmé par ledit Seigneur
Grand Prieur, celuicy paye encore la mesme somme, en sorte qu'en
la mesme année il reçoit quatre cens florins d'or. Pour autant de mois
de contributions, que l'Empire accorde a l'Empereur, le bailly
d'Utrecht paye douze florins d'or et demy par mois, tellement que si

l'Empire consent a cent mois, le bailly payera 1250 florins d'or tous les ans, au jour de St.Philippe et de St.Jaques. Au reverend chapitre provincial de l'ordre en Allemagne dix florins d'or, pour les frais des chapitres et des visites, et pour d'autres devoirs.

En tesmoin de la verité de ce que dessus nous avons fait apposer icy le sceau de la Chancellerie deladite illustre Maistrise de St.Jean en Allemagne. Donné ainsy le 28 Janvier 1664.

175. 1664, February 4 – *Frater Nicolas Cotoner, Grand Master, thanks the Prince-Cardinal Landgraf von Hessen for his support at the Grand Master's nomination [23 October 1663]. He also alludes to the role of the pope in negotiations with the province of Zeeland.*

Original letter: GLA Karlsruhe, 90/462, double leaf double-sided, only written fol.18r-v.

Je suis fort aise de voir que les negociations de Votre Eminence aient porté la Province de Zelande a suivre l'exemple de celle de Hollande, mais je ne scay comme Nous pourrons passer sous silence le nom de Nostre St.Pere dans la nouvelle procure que vous desirez. Il est vray que ceux lequels Nous avons a traitter y ont aversion, mais il est aussy bien certain qu'encore que Nous soions Religieux Militaires Nous ne laissons d'estre soumis a la saineteté —. *[He promises to take it up with the Venerable Council.]*

176. 1664, April 16 – *Frater Nicolas Cotoner, Grand Master, writes to the Estates General concerning the capture of the Dutch vessel 'Den Keijser Octaviaen' by Corsair ships under the command of Maltese knights.*

Original letter: ARA 's-Gravenhage, Archief van de Staten Generaal, Lias Barbarije, *nr.6909 omslag 1664 [= cover 1664] I, Double leaf double-sided, written pp.1-2, undersigned by autograph by the Grand Master. At the bottom of p.1:* Messieurs les Estats Generaulx des Provinces Unies; *in the upper right hand corner of p.1, in another hand, which also has drawn the underlining:* d[epeché] 16 april 1664, r[eçu] 22 may 1664.

As appears from the Resoluties van de Staten Generaal 1664, *nr.3270 fol.554v-555r, this letter concerning the vessel 'den Keijser Octaviaen' was not received on 22 May but on 22 July 1664 and was sent for notice to the Direction of the Levantine Commerce.*

Messieurs

Il est tres certain que mes predecesseurs, de glorieuse memoire, ont tousiours asseuré Vos Tres puissantes et tres Illustres Seigneuries que Nos galeres, vaisseaux, et tout ce qui seroit au pouvoir de leur Ordre contribueroit de tres grand coeur à faciliter le commerce que leurs navires font en cette mer. C'est aussy ce quilz ont en tout temps fort punctuellement executé et ce que ie promet a Vos Tres puissantes et tres Illustres Seigneuries de vouloir fort exactement continuer (ainsy plût il a Dieu que Nous fussions correspondues. Il est question maintenant qu' un Navire nommé L'Empereur Octavian aiant esté abordé et deschargé par six Vaisseaux Corsaires dont les trois estoient commandez par de nos chevaliers et que Nous songions a desdomager les interesses a la perte qui sy est faitte attendu que le Grand Turc a fait paier aux directeurs du Commerce de Levant tout ce qui s'est pris dans ledit navires; A quoy, Messieurs, je dois respondre qu'il Nous a de tout temps esté permis de prendre ce qui appartient a nos ennemis en quelque lieu que nous le rencontrions et que Nous l'avons tousiours fait ainsy sans qu'aucun Prince en aie jamais reclamé si ce n'est lors que les navires, ou marchands ennemis ce sont trouvez chargez de leur passeport. Ce que Nous ne pouvons pas dire avoir esté dans le presant rencontre d'autant que Nous n'avons que des advis confus de cette prise, la pluspart aiant escrit que le navire a esté pris [p.2] a l'ancre, fort proche d'Alexandrie, et que les Turcs ce sont fait rembourser de leurs marchandises attendu que le capitaine au lieu de ce tirer, comme il pouvoit facilement, sous le canon de la forteresse, a plustot songé à aller negocier avec les Corsaires lorsqu'il les a apperceuz, et s'est prevalu par ce moien d'une bonne partie de la prise; Voila, Messieurs, ce que j'en ay jusques a presant apris et ce qui ne m'empeschera pas lorsque lesdits vaisseaux reviendront dedans Nos ports de faire toutte sorte de diligence pour connoître la verité du fait et en cas qu'il ce soit commis quelque chose d'extraordinaire en ce procedé Vos Tres puissantes et Tres Illustres Seigneuries soient asseurées que Nous ferons tout nostre possible pour rendre justice à qui elle appartiendra afin de faire connoître que les inclinations de mon Ordre n'ont point changé et que je ne suis pas moins que mes predecesseurs,
Messieurs,
Vostre tres affectionné Ami et Serviteur
Le Grand Maistre
    Cotoner
A Malte ce 16e Apvril 1664

177. 1664, April 17 — *Report of the Deputies for the affairs of Malta to the Estates General of the United Provinces, requesting them to urge the Provincial Estates whose territory comprises landed property of the Order of Malta to either end the disagreement about these goods peacefully or procure the goods, since strong pressure is practised by several allied potentates.*

Original report: ARA 's-Gravenhage, Archief van de Staten Generaal, Resoluties van de Staten Generaal 1664, nr.3270, fol.251v-252v, inserted in a resolution of the Estates General; copy: GLA Karlsruhe, 90/462, fol.17r-v.

[fol.252r] – – omme verscheijdene respecten, ende in sonderheijt in consideratie vande krachtige interressien van verscheijden Hooge Potentaten goede vrunden ende geallieerden van desen staet, mitsgaders de ouvertures ende aensoecken in derselver namen gedaen omme voorsz. differenten bij amicable wegen ter neder te leggen – – .

178. 1664, May 4 & 6 — *Frater Nicolas Cotoner, Grand Master, confirms the amount of 532 gold florins as the yearly contribution due by the convent in Utrecht to the Order's treasury.*

Authorized copy: RA Gelderland, Loeff, Archief, inventory nr.525, authentic document from the chancery at Malta, single leaf double-sided, undersigned by autograph by frater Raffael Spinola and the vice-chancellor, with superimpressed seal of black wax with round wafer on it. The faded seal seems to bear the same image as nr.180 below.

Copy: ARA 's-Gravenhage, Archief van de Staten Generaal, Loketkas Malta, nr.12578.47.

Constat ex vera valutatione omnium prioratuum baiulivatuum et commendarum sacrae relligionis Hierosolymitanae secundum aestimationem factam in generali capitulo anno Domini 1583 ab eminentissimo domino dictae sacrae relligionis magno magistro fratre Ugone De Loubenx^a Verdalla celebrato, Ultraiectensem conventum in limitibus magni prioratus Inferioris Germaniae positum taxatum fuisse pro oneribus sive solitis responsionibus communi aerario annuatim debitis in summam quingentorum et triginta duorum aureorum florenorum. Dico 532.

Datum Melitae in venerabili camera computorum communis aerarii die 4 mensis Maii 1664.

[undersigned:]

Com. frater Raffael Spinola Comunis Aerarij a Secretis

Frater Don Nicolaus Cotoner Dei gratia sacrae domus Hospitalis sancti Johannis Hierosolymitani et militaris ordinis sancti Sepulchri dominus magister humilis pauperumque Jesu Xpi custos: Universis et singulis presentes nostras litteras visuris lecturis et audituris salutem.

Notum facimus et in verbo veritatis attestamur qualiter religiosus in Xpo nobis charissimus frater Raphael Spinola qui suprascriptis se subscripsit fuit et de presenti est nostri communis aerarii secretarius [verso] cuius subscriptionibus in similibus scripturis ubique tam in iudicio quam extra semper adhibita fuit, et in dies adhibiet plena et indubitata fides.

In cuius rei testimonium bulla nostra magistralis in cera nigra presentibus est impressa.

Data Melitae in conventu nostro die sexto mensis Maii millesimo sexcentesimo sexagesimo quarto.

[undersigned:]
F.D.Emmanuel Arias Vicecancellarius
[superimpressed seal]

---

[a] Boubenx *ms. in both copies.*

179. 1664, June 25 – *Frater Nicolas Cotoner, Grand Master, expresses his gratitude towards the Estates General about their resolution to send a fleet to the Mediterranean against the Corsairs.*

Original letter: ARA 's-Gravenhage, Archief van de Staten Generaal, *Lias Barbarije, nr.6909 omslag 1664 [= cover 1664] II, double leaf doublesided, written pp.1-2, undersigned by autograph by the Grand Master; at the bottom of p.1.* Messieurs les Estats Generaux des Provinces Unies. *copy:* GLA Karlsruhe, 90/462, fol.16r. *The text of the original letter has been followed here, although some spelling errors have been corrected in the copy. The reception of this letter is recorded in the* Resoluties van de Staten Generaal *dd. 5 September 1664, nr.3270 fol.664v.*

The letter was the reply to a letter from the Estates General dd. 20 February 1664 (in draft and in copy in Lias Barbarije, nr.6909 omslag 1664 [= cover 1664] I), addressed *Au Grand Maistre de l'Ordre de Malthe, in which they informed him of their resolution to send a fleet to the Mediterranean against* les Corsaires de Barbarie, *but not without his consent.*

Messieurs
Si i'avois plustost receu l'advis, que Vos Tres puissantes et Tres Illustres Seigneuries ont bien voulu me donner de l'armée qu'elles desirent faire passer en cette Mer, Je me serois a l'instant expliquée, comme je fais a presant, de la joie que cette glorieuse et necessaire

resolution m'a faitte concevoir. Il est vray Messieurs qu'elle est autant digne de nostre pieté que de nostre puissance et que si toutte la Chrestienté n'est en estat de la seconder, elle la doit pour le moins regarder dans un esprit de gratitude; pour ce qui est de mon Ordre, Vos Tres puissantes et Tres Illustres Seigneuries ce peuvent asseurer qu'il est tousiours porté du mesme desir en ce qui regarde la bonne et cordialle amitié dont Vos navires tant de guerre que de marchandise ce sont en tous rencontres prevaluz, et en des temps mesme qu'il sembloit que quelques unes de Vos provinces faisoient gloire de nous dépouïller de nos biens, ce qu'estant aujourdhuy bien different, veu que l'on Nous asseure que vos ªTres puissantes et Tres Illustres Seigneuriesª traittent serieusement de nous faire faire raison et reconnoitre nostre justice, il est a croire quil ny a rien que Nous ne fassions pour tesmoigner nostre correspondance, et que l'esperance de voir bien tost donner une favorable conclusion sur touttes nos pretensions, augmentera, sil ce peut, le zele que Nous devons avoir [p.2] pour tout ce qui regarde le bien et advantage de la Chrestienté, c'est sur quoy, Messieurs, Vous pouvez faire un fondement tres asseuré et qu'en mon particulier Je recevray tout ce qui viendra de la part de Vos Tres puissantes et Tres Illustres Seigneuries avec touttes les marques de bonne volonté que l'on doit attendre

Messieurs

D'un tres affectionné Ami et Serviteur

Le Grand Maistre

   Cotoner

Malte ce 25 Juin 1664

ª Tres — Seigneuries *abbreviated* T.P. et T.Ill.S. *ms.*

180. 1664, August 28 – *Frater Nicolas Cotoner, Grand Master, attests and repeats a bull of his predecessor frater Hugo de Loubenx Verdala from 3 March 1583 ab incarnatione, i.e. 3 March 1584 in Nativity-style, explaining that all writings from the Order's chancery use the Annunciation date of 25 March as the beginning of the year.*

Authorized copy: RA Gelderland, Loeff, Archief, inventory nr.598, single leaf double-sided, authentic document from the chancery at Malta, with superimpressed paper seal with portrait of the Grand Master; legend of the seal: F[rater] D[ominus] NICOLAUS COTONER MAG[ister] HOSP[italis] & [sancti] SEP[ulchri] HIER[osolymitani].

Frater Don Nicolaus Cotoner Dei gratia sanctae domus Hospitalis sancti Johannis Hierosolymitani et militaris ordinis sancti Sepulchri

Dominici magister humilis, pauperumque Jesu Christi custos universis et singulis presentes nostras litteras visuris, lecturis, et audituris
salutem.

Notum facimus, et in verbo veritatis attestamur, qualiter infrascripta attestatio extracta fuit ex libro bullarum in cancellaria nostra
conservato, quam quidem in hanc publicam formam extrahi, et redigi iussimus, ut ubique tam in iudicio, quam extra eidem plena, et
indubitata fides adhibeatur, cuius tenor est qui sequitur videlicet:

Frater Hugo de Loubenx Verdala Dei gratia sanctae domus Hospitalis sancti Johannis Hierosolymitani magister humilis, pauperumque Jesu Christi custos, et nos conventus domus eiusdem universis et
singulis presentes nostras litteras visuris, lecturis, et audituris salutem.

Decet veritati testimonium adhibere, ne propter rerum ignoran-
tiam alicui generetur preiudicium. Eapropter tenore presentium notum facimus, et in verbo veritatis attestamur, fidemque facimus
indubiam, qualiter in omnibus actis, provisionibus, et bullis, aliisque
scripturis a nostra cancellaria expeditis ab antiquo usque in presentem diem, annus numeratur ab incarnatione, non autem a nativitate,
et incipit, principiumque habet a festo Annunciationis beate Virginis
Marie die vigesima quinta mensis Martii, et sic a die nativitatis Domini nostri Jesu Christi usque ad dictum festum Annunciationis additur
verbum hoc: ab incarnatione, ut verbi gratia in data presentium dicitur: anno 1583 ab incarnatione, numerando a nativitate diceretur 84.
Et sic de ceteris. Et quia semper in dicta nostra cancellaria ita fuit
observatum, et est, ideo in huius rei testimonium bulla nostra communis plumbea presentibus est appensa. Datum Melitae in conventu
nostro die tertia mensis Martii 1583 ab incarnatione.

Et quia ita se habet veritas, tactaque fideli [verso] cum originali
collatione concordare comperimus, ideo in huius rei testimonium
bulla nostra magistralis in cera nigra presentibus est impressa.

Datum Melitae in conventu nostro die XXVIII mensis Augusti
millesimo sexcentesimo sexagesimo quarto.

Registrata in cancellaria   [superimpressed paper seal
Frater Dom Emmanuel Arias   of the Grand Master]
    Vicecancellarius

181. 1664, November 24 − *Frater Nicolas Cotoner, Grand Master, urges the
Estates General to restitute the Order's usurped possessions.*
Original Letter: ARA 's-Gravenhage, Archief van de Staten Generaal,
Loketkas Malta, *nr.12578.47, double leaf double-sided, written pp.1-2, un-
dersigned by autograph by the Grand Master; at the bottom of p.1:* Messieurs les

Estats Generaulx des Provinces Unies.

This letter was received together with a letter of Le Comte Destrades ambassadeur extraordinaire de France *dd. 11 February 1665, read by the Estates General at the same day and after deliberation handed over to* de Heeren van Ommeren, ende andere hare Ho: Mo: Gedeputeerden tot de saecken van Maltha, *as appears from the Extract of their resolutions dd. 11 February 1665 in the same* Loketkas Malta, *nr.12578.47.*

Messieurs

L'advis que l'on nous a donné que Vos Tres puissantes et Tres Illustres Seigneuries differoient de nous rendre justice presuposant que Nous n'estimions pour rien les biens qui nous ont esté usurpez dans Vos Estats, puisque Nous nous contentions de laisser agir tous les potentats de la Chrestienté sans que personne parut de Nostre part et que bien loin de nous ressentir du retardement que Vous apportiez a cette juste restitution Nous avions fait toutte sorte de bon accueil au Vice Admiral Ruyter et ne cessions jamais de bien traitter tous les navires que les mauvais temps obligeoient a chercher du secours dedans Nos ports; Cet advis dis je qui n'est pas moins surprenant que difficile a concevoir, m'obligeroit a remettre en advant touttes les instances que Nous avons faittes par le passé quand je serois asseuré qu'elles deussent estre plus considerables que celles qui ce font aujourdhuy par les susdits potentats et quand quelq'un pourroit mettre en doutte que l'Eminentissime Cardinal Landgrave d'Hesse et le Bailly de Souvré Nostre ambassadeur pres Sa Maiesté Tres Chrestienne, ce fussent en quelque temps que ce soit portez a pretendre ny negocier aucune chose concernante laditte restitution, sans estre bien et deüement pourveux de Nos procures et commissions; Cette verité, Messieurs, qui ce peut facilement prouver, et qui doit avec raison faire cesser tous ces petits pretextes, *[p.2]* me fait esperer que Vos Tres puissantes et Tres Illustres Seigneuries ne tarderons pas davantage en vertu de cette nouvelle instance que je joints a touttes les precedantes, a prendre une juste et prompte resolution, sur laquelle Nous puissions regler les nostres et faire connoître a touttes les puissances du Christianisme que le refus qui leur seroit fait nous toucheroit plus vivement que Nostre propre perte, c'est a quoy je me persuade que Nous n'arriverons pas et que vous ne me priverez point du contentement que je reçois en pouvant avec honneur me dire
Messieurs
Vostre tres affectionné Ami et Serviteur
Le Grand Maistre
    Cotoner
A Malte ce 24e Novembre 1664

182. 1667, October 15 – *Frater Nicolas Cotoner, Grand Master, writes to the Prince-Cardinal Landgraf von Hessen concerning the remuneration of Reynier Kempinck, which cannot be paid in money, since the Order's only reward for the recovery of possessions is the lifelong usufruct of those goods by the knight who regained them at his own expense.*

Copy: AOM 1443 = Copies of letters of Grand Master Nicolas Cotoner to ambassadors etc., 1667-1668, without folio numbers.

Al Cardinale d'Hassia à di 15 Octobre[a] 1667

Essendosi compiacciuta Vestra Eminenza di rinovarmi l'istanza à favore di Reynier Kemping, io devo renderla certa d'essersi rinovato anche in me il desiderio di servirla in tal congiuntura, come sommamente ambisco di fare in qualunque altra cosi in riguardo del suo singular merito, come per mia stretta obligatione e natural' inclinatione. Devo però informare Vestra Eminenza non esser cosi sufficientemente commoda la Religione che possa caricarsi di nuovi stipendii, mentre non gli bastano le sue entrati ordinarie per la meta delle spese, che necessariamente gli conviene di fare ogni anno; per il che sempre andiamo studiando di scemar qualche parte delle dette spese annuali, con andar anche ristretti al possibile nelle straordinarie, affinche possiamo almeno supplire con le piu inescusabili. E per questa cagione trovandosi la Religione molti, e molti beni occupati e usurpati da diversi potentati, e altre persone aliene, e non potendo ella stessa far le spese necessarie per la ricuperatione di essi, ne concede la facoltà a'i Cavalieri che la ricercano, con obligo di far la spesa del proprio, et in riguardo di essa, gli concede il privilegio di godere lor vita durante di quanto haveranno ricuperato: et à molti succede di far grosse spese per la ricuperatione di qualche bene, per la speranza di doverlo godere, e non sortendo l'effetto restar' anche perdenti nella spesa, che non segli fà buona in conto alcuno dalla Religione. Se dunque il Reynier Kemping è stato impiegato da quelli, che ne havevano la facoltà alla ricuperatione di qualche bene dell'ordine, non è tenuta di sodisfarlo la Religione la quale ne meno può farlo. Perilche proponendosi questo negotio in Consiglio, mentre non cade sotto la mia facoltà, restarebbe infallibilmente escluso con mortificatione di chi ve lo fà proporre. Pero supplico la benignità di Vostra Eminenza compiacersi di far riflessione à tutti questi motivi e veder la mia impossibilità di servirla in questa congiuntura; assicurandosi, che mi troverà sempre pronto in ogni altra, ovevorrà favorirmi de' suoi comandi, e bacio per fine à Vostra Eminenza affettamente le mani.

---

[a] 8bre *ms.*

183. 1667, November 17 – *Frater Nicolas Cotoner, Grand Master, writes to the Prince-Cardinal Landgraf von Hessen concerning the remuneration of Reynier Kempinck.*

Copy: AOM 1443 = Copies of letters of Grand Master Nicolas Cotoner to ambassadors etc., 1667-1668, without folio numbers.

Al Cardinale d'Hassia à di 17 Novembre 1667

Trovandomi haver già detto à Vostra Eminenza quanto mi occorreva intorno alle pretensioni di Reynier Kempink, non hò però ora da soggiungerle altro in risposta dell' humanissima sua dei 16 Septembre[a], se non che pretendendo tuttavia quegli d'haver attione contro la Religione per la sua sodisfatione potrà costituir qui Procuratore che in consiglio, o dove sarà di bisogno rappresenti le sue ragioni, eporti le sue istanze. Assicurando Vostra Eminenza che per quanto toccherà à me, io non lascero (in riguardo dei di lei comandi) di procurare vivamente che gli sia amministrata compita giustitia. E qui resto bacio à Vestra Eminenza affettamente le mani.

---

[a] 7bre *ms.*

184. 1668, February 18 – *Frater Nicolas Cotoner, Grand Master, writes a letter to the Estates of Holland about the ratification of the treaty concerning the redemption of the preceptory of Haarlem, further requiring them to practise some pressure on the other provinces to follow their example.*

Copy: GLA Karlsruhe, 90/473, fol.215r-v.

Messieurs

J'aij appris par Monsieur le Prince Cardinal Landgrave que Vos Tres Nobles, Tres Illustres et Grandes Puissances ont pris à la fin resolution de nous donner l'esquivalant de Nostre Commanderie de Harlem, dont je voij une acte passé du quel j'envoij la ratification en bonne forme affin q'un chascun puisse connoistre que des le moment que Vos Tres Nobles, Tres Illustres et Grandes Puissances ont incliné a nous rendre cette justice, Nous avons faict tout ce qui a esté en noistre pouvoir pour contribuer promptement à la gloire que cette noble et vertueuse action doit produire à leur gouvernement. Mais Messieurs comme il est en Vostre pouvoir de rendre de jour à autre cette gloire plus esclatante, je veux esperer que Vostre generosité portera Vos Tres Nobles, Tres Illustres et Grandes Puissances à nous vouloir donner une seconde marque de leur affectueuse integrité emploiant leur credit et aucthorité pres des autres Provinces Unies, pour les obliger à suivre une si belle resolution, permettant en cas de refus qu'on puisse saisir leurs biens qui se trouveront scitueer sous

Vostre gouvernement et faisant pour conclusion executer la sentence rendue l'an 1646 contre la ville de Nimeghen. Voila Messieurs demander beaucoup tout à la fois, et demander fort peu de chose au respect de la *[fol.215v]* grandeur de Vos Tres Nobles, Tres Illustres et Grandes Puissances, pour l'action presante des quelles et pour celles que Nous attendons encore à l'advenir, je proteste que j'auraij tous jours toutte la reconnoissance qu'on doit attendre de la gratitude plus accomplie,
Messieurs,
D'un tres affectionné Amij et Serviteur,
Le Grand Maistre
     Cotoner
à Malte ce 18 Feb.1668.

185. 1668, February 22 – *Frater Nicolas Cotoner, Grand Master, writes to the ambassador Caumons about the ratification of the agreement between Johan de Witt, Grand Pensionary of the Estates of Holland, and Reynier Kempinck, proxy of the Prince-Cardinal Landgraf von Hessen, concerning the redemption of the preceptory of Haarlem for 150,000 florins, instructing him to inquire if the pope has given his consent in this matter before transmitting the text to the Prince-Cardinal; to transfer the authorization to receive the money to the Prior of Dacia; and to inform the Prince-Cardinal of the decision of the Venerable Council that he has to remunerate Reynier Kempinck himself.*
     Copy: AOM 1443 = Copies of letters of Grand Master Nicolas Cotoner to ambassadors etc., 1667-1668, without folio numbers.

All'Imbasciadore Caumons à di 22 Febraro 1668.
Essendo seguita nel nostro Venerando Consiglio la ratifica dell'accordo passato tra il Signor Giovanni de Wibtt Consigliario pensionario de Signori Stati d'Olanda e Westfrise e Reynier Kemnpink come Procuratore dell'Eminentissimo Signor Cardinale d'Hassia ve ne mandiamo pero qui annesse le speditioni e in conformita di quanto ha deliberato il Venerando Consiglio vi ordiniamo che prima^a di consegnarle a Sua Eminenza presentiate da lei se ha ottenuto da Nostro Signore la sua confirmatione apostolica, e quanto gli sia passato con Sua Santità sopra la materia. Doppo di che in qualunque maniera che vi risponda Sua Eminenza doverete voi pur dar parte del tutto a Sua Beatitudine, significandogli essersi lasciato di riservar' espressamente nell'atto della ratifica, com'era di dovere, il beneplacito Apostolico, perche nell'anno 1663 non han voluto li stati Generali delle Provincie unite dar'orecchio a i trattati, che all'ora si proponevano con simile conditione. Di che s'è data parte in quel tempo dalla

Religione per mezzo del suo imbasciadore alla Santità d'Alessandro VII[b]. Ma che non intende la Religione, che vaglia nulla tutto quello che ora s'è fatto, senza che preceda espressamente la sua licenza e volontà: anzi che vi è stato ordinato (come precisamente v'ordiniamo) che se la Santità Sua non si compiacerà di concederci tal licenza ò consenso, non dobbiate consegnare al Signor Cardinale le dette speditioni mà di doverle rimandare in Convento. Supplicarete nulladimeno sua Beatitudine che si degni si concederlo, ò per Breve secreto ò in voce ò in quella maniera, che la sua somma prudenza stimerà, che non sia per disturbare la ricuperatione che può far l'ordine in questo modo di qualche parte de' suoi beni persi et occupati in quelle Provincie. Et ottenuto tale consenso in qualunque forma, consegnarete all'ora, e non prima le speditioni al Signor Cardinale contiene l'accordo in sostanza, che noi rinunciamo à tutte le pretensioni, che habbiamo sopra li beni della commenda di Harlem, mediante il pagamento di 150 mille fiorini di 20 soldi.

L'atto della ratifica vi si manda fuori del piego del Signor Cardinale affinche possiate farlo vedere a Nostro Signore quando havesse talgusto et havuto il suo consenso, lo consegnarete insieme con il detto piego al Signor Cardinale.

Quello che vien diretto al Venerando Prior di Datia, non lo consegnarete à Sua Eminenza, ma doppo haver ottenuto il consenso di Sua Santità, lo incaminarete voi medesimo per quella via, che stimarete più breve e sicura, senza dir'altro à Sua Eminenza se non che nel medesimo atto della ratifica và inserita la deputatione del Prior di Datia per l'essatione del denaro, e che noi non havremo lasciato d'inviargli gli ordini necessarii. Il che direte essendo ricercato.

Significarete al Signor Cardinale, che dalla Religione si stima ben meritevole di una generosa rimuneratione il Reynier Kempink per le fruttuose diligenze da lui impiegate in quest'affare, e per animarlo a proseguirle con ogni maggior affetto; mà che non può la Religione scemar' il denaro, che stà per ricuperarsi, mentre si doverà applicare in compra d'altri beni da sostituirsi in luogo delli rinuntiati. Ne meno può, ne suole in simili occasioni pagar col proprio denaro, onde hà giudicato il Venerando Consiglio che la rimuneratione più propria, che possa darsi al detto Kempink, è l'assegnamento di quella pensione, che parerà più adeguata alle sue fatiche et alla generosità di Sua Eminenza sopra i frutti, che produranno i danari ricuperati ò li beni da comprarsi con quelli esibendosi pronto il medesimo consiglio di spedirgliene le bolle, doppo che da sua Eminenza gli sarà constituita, con fargli intendere, che l'istessa gratitudine si userà seco, sempre che col mezzo delle sue diligenze se ne farà altra ricuperatione soggiungendo voi a Sua Eminenza che prevedendosi dalla Religione fin dal tempo, che fu concessa la facoltà di ricuperar questi beni d'Olanda al Venerando Prior de Souvré, ch'egli havrebbe necessità di valersi di mezzi e dell'opera d'altri, fù all'ora deliberato, che questi tali fussero rimunerati in questa medesima forma, cioé coll'assignatione d'alcuna pensione sopra i beni ricuperandi: e con le conditioni ch'era stata conceduta al detto Venerando Priore, fù poi anche dimandata e concessa à sua Eminenza.

E finalmente v'avvertiamo, benche non sia di bisogno, che se non amicarete à terminar questo negotio prima di finir la vostra imbasciata, consegnarete il tutto al vostro successore, etiandio la presente, con dargli in oltre tutte le informationi che saranno necessarie, cosi nel presente, come in tutti gli altri affari; giache noi presentemente gli mandiamo le lettere credentiali, per poter a' suo tempo entrare nell'essercitio della carica. E Nostro Signor Iddio vi conservi etc.

---

a *abbreviated* p.ma *ms.* b7 *ms.*

---

186. 1668, February 22 – *Frater Nicolaus Cotoner, Grand Master, informs frater Jan Jacob van Pallandt, Prior of Dacia (= Denmark), that the Venerable Council has appointed him as the Order's special deputy to receive the sum of 150,000 florins in redemption of the preceptory of Haarlem.*
    Copy: AOM 1443 = Copies of letters of Grand Master Nicolaus Cotoner to ambassadors etc., 1667-1668, without folio numbers; same page as the preceding letter.

Al Prior di Datia fra Giovanni Giacomo de Pallandt à di 22 Febraro 1668.
Essendo seguito accordo trà il signor Giovanni de Wibt Consiliario pensionario delli Signori Stati d'Olanda e Westfrise, e Reinier Kempink Procuratore dell' Eminentissimo Signor Lantgravio d'Hassia sopra la commenda di Harlem, cedendo da parte nostra tutte le pretensioni, che habbiamo sopra di quella e suoi beni, mediante lo sborso di 150 mille fiorini, è stato ratificato il medesimo accordo dal nostro Venerando Consiglio il quale confidando molto nella vostra puntualità e prudenza, vi hà deputato special procuratore per l'esatione e conservatione di detta somma. Nel che dovendo voi governarvi in comformità delle instruttioni, che vi mandiamo qui annesse, à noi non rimane di dirvi altro nella presente, che d'incaricarvi la puntual' essecutione di quanto nelle medesime instruttione si contiene, e di avvisarci poi con tutta diligenza di quanto haverete operato, e di quello, che anderà accadendo in tal materia; e senza più restiamo preghando il Signor Iddio. etc.

187. 1668, December 8 − *The Prince-Cardinal Landgraf von Hessen confirms the bull of Grand Master Nicolas Cotoner dd. 17 February 1668, in ratification of the treaty concerning the redemption of the Order's possessions at Haarlem for 150,000 florins, dd. 6 December 1667 (meant is: 5 December 1667).*

Vidimus: GLA Karlsruhe, 90/472, fol.2r-5v, dd. 1668, December 31.
The treaty of redemption itself, dd. 5 December 1667, is to be found in copy in GLA, 90/472, fol.6r-9r; and in GA Haarlem, Stads Archief loketkas 7-12-5-7, letter p-2, *without folio numbers, inserted in the* Extract uyt de resolutien vande heeren Staeten van Hollant ende Westvrieslandt, in haer Ed.Gr.Mo.vergaderingh genomen op Vrydagh den 9 December 1667; *the Grand Master's bull dd.17 February 1668, including the treaty dd. 6 December 1667 (meant is: 5 December 1667), has been printed in* Recueil 1750, *No. 28, pp.32-34. Some spelling mistakes have been corrected in accordance with these pieces, but the original spelling has been left unchanged. The imprinted seal of the chancery at Heitersheim, mentioned on fol.4r, is missing and no room has been spared for it; it may be that this is only a copy of the vidimus.*

Frere Dom Nicolas Cotoner, Grand Maistre de l'Ordre de St.Jean de Hierusalem, et du St.Sepulchre, et nous baillis, prieurs, commandeurs et freres, tenants le conseil du dict Ordre, ayant veu le traitté, et accord, fait à La Haye le sixiesme du mois de Decembre, mille six cent soissante sept entre le Sieur Jean de Wit, Conseiller pensionaire des Messieurs les estats de la Province d'Hollande, et Westphrise, et le Sieur Reinier Kempingk, comme ayant pouvoir de l'Eminentissimé Cardinal, et Prince Landgrave d'Hessen, sous le bon plaisir neantmoins, et approbation des dicts Estats, et la nostre, au sujet du recouvrement, et restitution par nous pretendue des biens, situez dans la dicte province appartenantes à nostre dict Ordre, duquel traitté la teneur suit de mot à mot.
  D'autant que despuis plusieurs annees l'on a faict des grandes, et reiterees instances, tant au nom de feu Monsieur Vualrave Scheiffert de Merode de la part de l'Ordre des Chevaliers de St.Jean de Hierusalem, establi à Malte, qu'au nom et de la part de son Altesse Serenissime Monsieur le Prince Cardinal & Landgrave de Hessen, comme Maistre Provincial du dict Ordre de Malte en Allemagne, en vertu de la bulle et commission, datée de Malte le 26. May 1649 tant aupres des hauts, et puissants Seigneurs les Estats generaux des Provinces Uniees des Pays-bas, qu'aupres des Messieurs les Estats d'Hollandes, et Westphrise, tendantes à ce, qu'on restituat audict Ordre plusieurs biens situés en ces pays, et particulierement en ceste province, le revenu, et le fond, desquels l'Ordre a cydevant possedé, et pretend encore, luy appartenir, pour en estre par luy disposé suivant les sta-

tuts, et ordonnances, sans que neantmoins l'on a ayt encor peu regler cette affaire, parce que leurs illustres, et grandes puissances comme aussi quelques autres des Provinces Unies sustenoient, qu'elles possedoient ces biens à bon, et juste titre, contre lesquelles le dict Ordre de son costé a aussi produit ses pretensions, auxquelles il se rapporte encore. Donques pour prevenir une plus grande alienation d'esprits, et une plus grande aigreur, que la contestation pour ces biens pourroit causer; comme aussi pour d'autres bonnes raisons, et considerations, et particulierement en esgard à la resolution prise par leurs hautes puissances le 17.me Juillet 1654, par laquelle elles renvoyoient les ministres du dict Sieur le Prince Cardinal, en la dicte qualité à Messieurs les Estats des provinces particulieres, ou ses biens sont situez, en declarant, que c'est à eux, à qui appartient la disposition souveraine des dicts biens, non obstant les raisons, qui ont esté alleguees au contraire de la part du dict Ordre, auxquelles le dict Ordre persiste encore presentement; En fin par l'entremise et mediation de Monsieur le Comte d'Estrades Ambassadeur extraordinaire de France auprez de leur hautes puissances, et apres plusieurs conferances, tenues sur ce sujet entre le Sieur Jean de Wit, Conseiller pensionaire des dicts Seigneurs d'Estats d'Hollande, et Westphrise &cetera en vertu de son pouvoir du 3.me Aoust 1663 d'une part, et le Sieur Renier Kempingk, comme ayant pouvoir du dict Sieur le Prince Cardinal et Landgrave d'Hessen, en vertu des deux differants pouvoirs de son Altesse [fol.2v] dateez du 3.me Juillet de la mesme année 1663 et du 30.me[a] May dernier respectivement, d'autre, pour l'abolition et extinction de toutes les actions et pretensions, que ledict Ordre pourroit avoir sur les biens situez en cette province dependants de la Commanderie de Harlem, l'on est convenu et accordé sous l'adveu et approbation de leurs superieurs de part et d'autre, en la maniere suivante:

Scavoir que les dicts Seigneurs Estats d'Hollande et Westphrise payeront, ou fairont payer à Ambsterdam, en argent conptant et incontinent apres l'echange des ratifications, audict Seigneur Prince Cardinal en la qualité que dessous ou bien à celuy ou à ceux, qui sera, ou qui seront souffisement autorisez par son Altesse, ou par le dict Ordre tout à la fois, la somme de cent cinquante mille florins, vingt souls la piece, scavoir cinquante mille florins pour les fruicts, qui peuvent avoir esté par ceux des dicts biens despuis le dict jour 26.May 1649 en vertu de la dicte commission des dicts jour et an, jusque au jour de la date des presentes, et les autres cent mille florins pour la proprieté des dicts biens de la Commanderie de Harlem, faisant ensemble la dicte somme de cent cinquante mille florins. Et le dict Sieur Kempingk au nom, et de la part que dessous, a promis,

ainsi qu'il promet par ces presentes, que devant le payement de ladicte somme de cent cinquante mille florins[b] son Altesse obtiendra, et
faira expedier le plustot que faire se pourra et au plus tard dans cinq
mois à compter du jour de la signature des presentes un acte de son
Eminence Monsieur le Grand Maistre du dict Ordre de St.Jean de
Hierusalem par lequel il approuve et ratifie en bonne et deüe forme le
present accord avec renonciation de tous les droicts et pretensions,
que ledict Ordre pourroit avoir eu, ou soustenir avoir encore, tant sur
les dicts biens de la Commanderie de Harlem ou sur leurs possesseurs
que sur leurs illustres et grandes puissances, ou quelques membres
particuliers ou habitants de cette province, en sorte que ni le dict
Ordre ni Monsieur le Grand Maistre, ses successeurs ou quelque
autre personne du dict Ordre, ne pourront jamais faire aucune instance à l'esgard et occasion des dicts biens de la Commanderie de
Harlem, se reserver, ni intenter en justice ou autrement aucune action ou pretension, l'encontre de la Province d'Hollande et Westphrise, ou aucunes de ses villes et membres sans en excepter aucun en
general ou en particulier, ou contre ceux, qui pourroient posseder les
dicts biens, mais qu'ils en sont et demeureront descheux et frustrez
pour à jamais, bien entendu, que ceste renonciation ne sortira pas son
effect, qu'apres que ladicte somme de cent cinquante mille florins
aura esté payé tout à la fois en la maniere sousdicte, sans qu'apres
cela l'on ait besoing d'autre chose pour accomplissement de ce que
dessous.

Deplus il a esté bien expressement stipulé, qu'en cas que quelques
des autres Provinces Unies, dans lesquelles quelques biens apparte-
nants au dict Ordre sont aussi situez, et dont les dictes provinces
jouissent, ou qu'elles possedent encore, ne poussent pas estre portees
à traicter avec sa dicte Altesse en la qualité que dessous à propor-
[fol.3r]tion de la valeur des biens et des commanderies du dict Ordre,
en sorte qu'il en peust demeurer satisfaict, à quoy leurs illustres et
grandes puissances contribueront leurs bons offices, cette accord ne
prejudiciera aucunement aux pretensions que le dict Ordre des Chevaliers pourra former contre ces provinces la au sujet de ces biens de
l'Ordre, mais ces pretensions luy seront conservees toutes entieres,
tout ainsi, que si ce present accord n'eust point esté faict.

Avec ceste condition expresse, afin que le dict Ordre n'ait pas sujet
de se plaindre, qu'en ces Provinces Uniees on ne luy faict pas justice
de mesme qu'aux autres que leurs illustres et grandes puissances pro-
mettront, ainsi qu'elles promettent par ces presentes, qu'elles fairont
rendre en tout temps bonne et briefve justice audict Ordre contre
tous ceux qu'il pourra, ou voudra legitimement convenir par devant
la cour de justice, ou par devant quelques autres juges de ceste Pro-

vince d'Hollande, et que leurs illustres et grandes puissances promettent aussi par ces presentes, qu'elles employeront leurs bonnes et fortes recommendations et autres offices convenables et autant qu'en eux est, tiendront la main a ce que conformement à l'union les sentences, que le dict Ordre a desja legitimement obtenues à son advantage, en quelques cours de justice de ces Provinces Unies, ou pourra encore legitimement obtenir à l'advenir, soient executees la et ainsi qu'il appartiendra sans aucun delay ou remise.

Finalement il a esté stipulé et accordé comme l'on stipule et accorde par ces presentes, qu'en cas que contre l'esperance que l'on a, cette accord ne soit point ratifié par le dict Ordre, il sera aussi tenu pour nul, et de nulle valeur, tout ainsi que s'il n'avoit jamais esté faict, sans qu'aucune des deux parties en puisse rien tirer à son advantage, et sans qu'on y puisse fonder aucun droict ou pretension directement, ou indirectement, mais chacun conservera les pretensions et droicts sur les dicts biens au mesme estat qu'elles estoient au paravant la conclusion de cest accord et sans qu'aucune des parties interessees soit obligée d'executer ce que dessous, ou estre convenu pour raison de cella en justice ou ailleurs. Ainsi faict, et accordé

à La Haye en Hollande le 6. Decembre 1667.
Signé D'Estrades, Jean de With, R.Kempingk.

Ayant d'oncques nous Grand Maistre et Conseill susdicts bien et deuement consideré le contenu au susdict traitté avec toutes les clauses et conditions en desirans entretenir la bonne correspondance, qui a tousiours esté entre les susdictes Estats de la Province d'Hollande et Westphrise et nous et nostre dict Ordre, et pour plusieurs autres bonnes et justes considerations à ce nous mouvantes, avons approuvé, confirmé et ratifié et par ces presentes nous approuvons, confirmons, et ratifions en la meilleure forme que faire se peust, le susdict traitté et accord, ainsi et en la maniere, qu'il est [fol.3v] couché cy devant sans y rien changer, augmenter, ou diminuer, renonçants, moyennant l'effectif payement, en une seule fois comme cy dessous, de cent cinquante mille florins à vingt souls la piece, à touts les droicts et pretensions que nous, et nostre dict Ordre avons eu, pouvons avoir, ou pourrions soustenir avoir encore, tant pour et contre les biens de la Commanderie d'Harlem, ou sur les possesseurs d'iceux, que sur les illustres et grandes puissances des dicts Estats, touts les membres particuliers, ou habitants de la dicte province quelles qu'ils soient, ou puissent estre, en sorte, que nous dict Grand Maistre, nostre susdict Ordre, ou nos successeurs, ni aucune autre personne du mesme Ordre, pouissions jamais faire et intenter en justice, ou autrement aucune instance, demande ou poursuite à l'esgard et pour raison des dicts biens de la Commanderie de Harlem situez dans la dicte Province d'Hollande et Westphrise, à l'encontre de la dicte province ou aucune de ses villes et membres sans en excepter aucun en general ou en particulier, ni enfin contre ceux, qui pourroient posseder les dicts biens. Voulons et entendons en demeurer dechaux et frustrez à jamais moyennant, comme dict est, l'effectif, et reel payement des dicts cent cinquante mille florins et non autrement sans qu'apres cella il soit plus besoing d'autre chose pour l'accomplissement de ce que dessous.

Et comme ladicte renonciation ne doit avoir lieu par le moyen, ni estre d'aucune valeur, qu'apres le payement des dicts cent cinquante mille florins, nous avons esleu, commis, et deputé, elisons, commettons, et deputons, le venerable Prieur de Dace, frere Jean Jacque Paland pour nostre particulier, expres, et special procureur aux fins de recevoir en nostre nom et de nostre dict Ordre de la part des dicts Seigneurs les Estats de la Province d'Hollande et Westphrise, et de toute autre personne que besoing sera, la sousdicte somme de cent cinquante mille florins à vingt souls la piece et luy avons donné, et donnons par ces presentes plein et entier pouvoir d'en bien et deuement quitter, absoudre et decharger les dicts Estats et touts autres qu'il appartiendra, passer pour cest effect et pour tousjours les descharges, quitances et contracts necessaires avec les clauses, et conditions aussi necessaires et convenables, promettants de ne leurs en faire jamais aucune recherche, ni demande, en foy de quoy nous avons fait mettre et appendre à celle cy nostre commune bulle de plomb en laes de corde.

Donné à Malte le dix septiesme jour de Fevrier mille sixcent soisante sept de l'incarnation de nostre Seigneur Jesus Christ selon le stile de nostre chancellerie et de sa nativité mille six cents soisante wict.

estoit signé
Il luogot[enen]te del Gran Cancelliero
    Alo[y]s[i]o Munez St Sigecourz
Reg[istra]ta in Cancellario
fr. Dehimanuel Arias Vicecan[cellarius]ᶜ

[fol. 4r]
Nous Frideric par la grace de Dieu Cardinal Landgrave d'Hessen, Grand Prieur d'Allemagne, pour l'Ordre de St.Jean de Hierusalem, Prince de Hirsfeld, Comte de Cazenelnbogen, Diez, Nidda, Scauembourg, Ziegenheim, Isenbourg et Budingen, Protetteur d'Allemagne

et de la Couronne d'Arragon; Ayans leu le traitté et accord escrit de l'autre costé faict à La Haye le 6.de Decembre 1667 entre Monsieur Jean de Wit Commissaire et Pensionaire de Messieurs les Estats de la Province d'Hollande et de Westphrise et le Sieur Reinier Kempingk nostre Agent en vertu des pouvoirs, que l'un et l'autre en avayent de leurs superieurs et le tout sous la ratification de nostre dict Ordre et la nostre aussi et du recouvrement et de la restitution des biens, qui nous appartiennent dans ladicte province, comme aussi la ratification que nostre dict Ordre en a faict, Nous pour les mesmes raisons, qu'il y ont esmeu, avons bien voulu en tant que nous peut toucher comme Grand Prieur ou qu'il peut estre necessaire et convenir, nous conformer audict traitté et accord et pareillement à la ratification, l'approuvant, confirmant, et ratifiant, aussi par ces presentes en la meilleure forme, que faire se peut et en la maniere, que l'un et l'autre sont couchez sans y rien changer, augmenter, ou diminuer et ce moyennant le payement de la somme de cent et cinquante mille florins, dont l'on est convenu pour la redemption des biens qui sont situez dans la dicte Province d'Hollande et dependent de la commenderie de Harlem, et pour la reception de la dicte somme, nostre dict Ordre ayant nominé Monsieur le Prieur de Dace de sa part et nous de la nostre ledict Kempingk, nous luy donnons, le mesme plein pouvoir par ceste d'en bien et deuement quitter, absoudre et decharger les dicts Seigneurs Estats de ladicte province et tous autres, qu'il appartiendra, que nostre dict Ordre a donné audict Sieur Prieur de Dacie. En foy de quoy non seulement avons bien voulu signer ces presentes de madicte main, faire registrer dans la chancellerie de nostre dict Grand Prieuré et y avons faict apposer le cachet ordinaire de nos armes. à Rome le 0.de Decembre 1660.

L.S.   Le Cardinal de Hessen

Quod hacce copia bene auscultata et collationata cum suo originali in omnibus et per omnia concordet, attestatur vi infrapressi sigilli cancellariae Heitersheimensis ibidem 31.Decembris[d] 1668.

[fol.5v]
Copia Vidimata Recuperationis factae pro Commenda Harlem in pecunia numerata.
Et desuper ex Malta et a supremo Allemaniae Magistro subsecutae Ratificationis.

---

[a] 3.me May *ms, but according to the copy in GLA Karlsruhe, 90/472, fol.6-9, especially fol.6v, the copy in GA Haarlem and Recueil 1750 p.33, this must be 30 May.*

^b livvres *ms, and in the copy on fol.7v:* Livres, *but in GA Haarlem and Recueil 1750:* florins.
  ^c *here the undersigning from GA Haarlem is given, because this one is less corrupted than the one in GLA Karlsruhe.*
  ^d 10bris *ms.*

188. 1669, July 12 – *The Prince-Cardinal Landgraf von Hessen confirms the treaty concerning the redemption of the preceptory of Haarlem; copy of the same Grand Master's bull dd. 17 February 1668, but with confirmation by the Prince-Cardinal Landgraf von Hessen in different words and bearing another date.*

Copy: GA Haarlem, Stads Archief loketkas 7-12-5-7, letter p-2, *without page or folio numbers, double leaves double-sided, with note on the last page (verso):* Rakende de goederen van de Commanderye van St.Jan en hoe die aen dese stadt gekomen syn. 12.Julij 1669
6.Dec.1667
17.Febr.1668
12.Jul.1669
Under the letter itself is written:
Accordeert met het Origineel
  Herbert van Beaumont
  1669

[3rd last page, verso] Nous Frederic par la Grace de Dieu Cardinal Landgrave de Hesse, Grand prieur d'Allemagne pour l'Ordre de St.Jean de Hierusalem, Prince de Hirsfelt, Compte de Catzenelleboge, Dietz, Nidda, Schaussenbourg, Isembourg, et Andruchen, Ambassadeur de Sa Majesté Impériale^a aupres de l'St.Pere, protecteur d'Almagne et des Royaumes d'Aragon, et de Sardaigne etc.

Ayant veu le traitté et accord cij joinct de l'autre costé faict a la Haije le 6e Decembre 1667 entre le Sieur Jean de Witt Conseiller et pensionnaire de Messieurs les Estats de la Province de Hollande et de Westfrise et le Sieur Reijnier Kempingk nostre agent, en vertu des pouvoirs que nous lui en avions donnés, et le tout sous nostre ratification et de nostre Ordre, au sujet de nostre recouvrement et de la restitution des biens qui nous appartienent dans ladicte province comme aussij la ratification que nostre dit Ordre en a faict, Nous pour les mesmes raisons qu'il ij ont esmeu, avons bien voulu, en tant qu'il nous peut toucher, comme Grand Prieur, ou puisse estre necessaire et convenir nous confirmer audit traitté et accord, et a sa ratification, l'approuvant, confirmant, *[2nd last page, recto]* et ratifiant aussij ces presentes en la mellieure forme que faire se peut, et en la maniere que l'un et l'autre sont couchez sans ij rien changer ou diminuer, et

cest moijennant le paijemant entiere de la somme des cent et cinquante mil florins dont l'on est convenu pour la redemption des biens
quij sont scitues dans ladite province de Hollande et de Westfrise et
dependant de la Commanderie de Haerlem, appartenante a nostre
dit Ordre et dependance de nostre dit Grand Prieur, et pour la reception de laquelle somme nostre dit Ordre aijant nommé le Sr.Prieur de
Dacia Baron de Pallandt, nous avons aussij nommé de nostre part le
Sr.Reijnier Kempingk et auquel donnons le mesme plein pouvoir par
ceste presantes, d'en bien et d'heuement quitter et absoudre et decharger lesdits Sieurs Estats, et tous autres qu'il appartiendra, que
nostre dit Ordre donne audit Sr.Prieur de Dacia. En foij de quoij
nous avons signé les presantes de nostre main, fait registrer en la
chancellerie de nostre dit Grand Prieuré et q'avons faict apposer le
cachet ordinaire de nos armes a Rome le 12e de Juillet 1669
      estoit signé Le Cardinal de Hessen

---

a S.M.I. *abbreviated ms.*

189. 1669, October 10 − *The Estates of Holland write to the Prince-
Cardinal Landgraf von Hessen about the remuneration of Reynier Kempinck.*
    Copy: GLA Karlsruhe, 90/473, fol.214r.
*The Estates of Holland had remunerated Reynier Kempinck and the Baron van
Pallandt with the sum of 6,000 livres and a gold chain worth 1,000 livres; in
addition, Johan de Witt had declared that a gratification of 3,000 Carolus
guilders would be paid to Reynier Kempinck for his conduct in the negotiations:
GA Haarlem, Stads Archief loketkas 7-12-5-7, letter p-2, without folio
numbers, resolution dd. 9 December 1667, see also Allan, Geschiedenis van
Haarlem II p.385.*

Au Cardinal Landtgrave de Hessen
Serenissime Prince
Apres avoir eschangé les ratifications de l'accord qui fust fait, il ij aura
bien tost deux ans pour les biens, que l'ordre de Malthe pretendoit
luij appartenir, et aupres avoir par ce moijen mis la derniere main à
cest ouvrage, pour ce qui regarde cette Province, Nous estimons ne
devoir pas laisser partir le Sr. Kempinck, avec le quel cest accord a
esté conclu de la part de Vostre Altesse Serenissime, sans le tesmoignage que nous devons au zele, qu'il a pour le service de l'ordre, et
pour Vos interest[s] particuliers, il ij a plus de trante ans, qu'il [a]
travaillé icij à la poursuitte des affaires de l'ordre, avec une affection,
application, et patience qui merite une reconnoissance extraordinai-

re, et nous luij devons rendre ce tesmoignage, que jamais ministre n'a donné tant de preuves extraordinaires d'une fidelité, et assiduité sans exemple. Nous ne doutons point, que Vostre Altesse Serenissime ne les considere comme il faut, et ne suive en cecij les mouvements de sa generosité, et comme cette lettre ne sert à autre fin, Nous prions Dieu, Serenissime Prince de vouloir garder la personne de Vostre Altesse Serenissime en sa saincte protection.

De Vostre Altesse Serenissime tres affectionnés Amis,
    Les Estats de Hollande et Westfrise,
De l'ordonnance des dits Estats estoit signé
    Herbert de Beaumont
A la Haije 10 octobre 1669.

Au Serenissime Prince Monsieur le Cardinal, Landtgrave d'Hessen, Maistre Provincial de l'ordre de St.Jean de Jerusalem en Allemagne, Prince de Hirtsfelt, Comte de Catzen Elleboegen, Dietst, Siegenheim, Nidda, Schauwenburgh, Isenburgh, et Budingen.

190. 1672 – *The provincial chapter of the Order of St John in Germany declares that, although the right to recover the preceptories of Arnhem and Nimwegen has been given to frater* Godfried Drost in Vischering *by Grand Master's bull, he himself has requested to assign the recovery of the Nimwegen properties in Niel and the Duffelt to* baro de Wachtendung; *the chapter gladly agrees with his request (in Latin).*

Copy: GLA Karlsruhe, 90/462, double leaf double-sided, written fol.12r-v-13r, anno 1672.

191. 1682, November 29 – *Frater Gregorio Carafa, Grand Master, and Convent appoint frater Herman baron van Wachtendonck as Convent bailiff of the German tongue.*

Registration: AOM 489 = libri bullarum 1681-1682, fol.235v.

Frater Gregorius Carafa — et nos conventus etc. — fratri Hermanno baroni de Wactendonck, commendatario de Hemmendorff —. *[He receives]* — baiulivatum nostrum conventualem venerandae linguae Alemaniae per renuntiationem venerandi religiosi etc. fratris Gothifredi Drost de Wischering ad dictum prioratum nostrum Alemaniae promoti, ultimi legitimi dicti magni baiulivatus baiulivi et possessoris —.

192. 1683, January 16 – *Frater Gregorio Carafa, Grand Master, and Convent appoint frater Herman baron van Wachtendonck as Prior of Germany with five prioral chambers, among which Utrecht.*

Original bull on parchment, with holes of lost string with seal of Grand Master and Convent: GLA Karlsruhe, 20/164, dated in Annunciation-style; with extract in AOM 489 = libri bullarum 1681-1682, fol.236r, 1683 January 26 in Annunciation-style. The extract mistakenly mentions 26 January, but from the original bull it clearly appears that the correct date is 16 January.

Frater Gregorius Carafa — et nos conventus — fratri Hermanno baroni de Wachtendonck ordinis nostri magno baiulivo Alemaniae ac commendae nostrae de Leugheren prioratus nostri Alemaniae commendatario —.

[He receives the dignity of Prior of Germany, vacant by the death of frater Gothefredus Drost de Wischering, after he has resigned his function of Grand Bailiff and his preceptory Leuggern in the hands of the Grand Master], quam pro tuo melioramento obtines, aliisque bonis quae iuxta formam stabilimentorum nostrorum simul cum dicto prioratu tenere non potes —.

[He will possess the priorate the same way its last real possessor, the Prince-Cardinal Friedrich Landgraf von Hessen-Darmstadt, had it] cum suis quatuor cameris prioralibus infrascriptis sibique assignatis, et quas pro cameris prioralibus etiam tibi venerando priori assignamus, videlicet Traiectum, Coloniam, Haimbach et Bugiken necnon commendam de Friburg et Bresgau pro quinta tua camera —.

Datum Melitae in conventu nostro die decima sexta mensis Ianuarii millesimo sexcentesimo octuagesimo secundo ab incarnatione.

193. 1687, January 23 – *Frater Gregorio Carafa, Grand Master, and Convent grant the right to recover the prioral chamber of Utrecht to frater Herman baron van Wachtendonk, Prior of Germany.*

Original bull on parchment: GLA Karlsruhe, 20/3, with lead seal on hemp string of Grand Master and Convent. Legend of the seal, front: BVLLA MAGISTRI ET CONVENTUS; back: HOSPITALIS HIERVSALEM; on the frontside are six brethren. The bull is dated in Annunciation-style.

Copy: GLA Karlsruhe, 90/279, fol.2r-3v, chancery document from Malta dd. 2 October 1693.

The formulary of this bull is almost the same as Wolfenbüttel Kat.Nr.2137 sub 153, dd. 28 July 1644 for frater Jacques de Souvré (see nr.158 above), and AOM 472 = libri bullarum 1647-1649, fol.217v-218r, dd. 26 May 1649, for Prince Friedrich Landgraf von Hessen-Darmstadt, Prior of Germany (see nr.163 above), without abbreviations.

The content differs from that of the bull of 1649 on the following points: in the first place, no mention is made of Haarlem, secondly, no earlier concession is revoked, and thirdly, this grant is restricted to the prioral chamber Utrecht and does not concern the entire region of the Low Countries:

[1687:] Cum itaque commenda nostra de Utrecht camera prioralis dicti prioratus nostri Alemanie eiusque membra — *[instead of 1649:]* Cum itaque baiulivatus noster de Utrecht, et commenda de Harlem, earumque membra —;

[the following sentence from 1649 is cancelled:] Revocantes prius, nullasque declarantes omnes, et singulas similes concessiones recuperandi supradictum baiulivatum, commendas, et bona in favorem quarumvis personarum hactenus emanatas, et presertim illas in favorem venerandi fratris Jacobi de Souvray dicti ordinis nostri baiulivi sub die XXVIII mensis Iulii 1644 e cancellaria nostra expeditas, —;

[1687:] — te praefatum venerandum priorem fratrem Hermannum baronem de Vachtendonc presentem, et onus huiusmodi acceptantem — *[instead of 1649:]* — te illustrissimum ac venerandum principem Federicum Landgravium absentem tanquam presentem —;

[1687:] — ad nostro dictique ordinis nomine praenominatam commendam cameram prioralem de Utrecht eiusque membra, et dependentias — *[instead of 1649:]* — ad nostro predictique erarii et ordinis nomine prenominatum baiulivatum de Utrecht, et commendam de Harlem, eorumque membra, et dependentias —;

[the following sentences from 1649 are cancelled:] Exceptis tamen, et expresse reservatis bonis — iam provisos pertinet, et reservata censeatur. *[and:]* — cum hoc tamen, et non alias quod in quolibet anno quintam partem fructuum, — pro responsionibus cum effectu persolvere tenearis, — .

Datum Melitae in conventu nostro die vicesima tertia mensis Ianuarii millesimo sexcentesimo octuagesimo sexto ab incarnatione iuxta stylum nostrae cancellariae, secundum vero cursum ordinarium millesimo sexcentesimo octuagesimo septimo.

194. 1693, May 30 — *The provincial chapter of Germany authorizes frater* van Merveldt *to dispose the goods of the preceptory of Arnhem at his discretion. Original* Extractus *from the German chancery: RA Gelderland, Loeff, Ar-*

chief, *inventory nr.15, with the superimpressed paper seal of the provincial chapter, representing the baptism of Christ by St John the Baptist. Legend of the seal:* SIGILLVM PROVINCIALIS CAPITVLI ORDINIS S.IOANNIS PER ALEMANIAM. *Frater* Goswiin Herman Otto van Merveldt *is mentioned already in 1691 as head of the preceptory of Arnhem: RA Gelderland, Loeff,* Archief, *inventory nr.26.*

195. 1695, June 18 – *Order is given to inspect the improvements made by frater Herman Otto baron van Merveldt in his preceptory of Rothenburg.*
Chancery note: AOM 499 = libri bullarum 1695, *fol.85r.*

Die eadem fuit expedita similis commissio ad visitandum melioramenta facta per fratrem Ermannum Othonem baronem de Merveldt in commenda de Rotenburg prioratus Alemaniae, quam titulo cabimenti possidet etc. directa venerandis priori Ungariae fratri Carolo Philippo comiti de Fridach, de Tobel, Herrenstronden et Rottveil, et priori Daciae fratri Teodoro Enrico de Pallandt de Lagen, et fratribus Johanni de Rol de Hohenrein, Raiden, Bux, Basel et Dorlsceim, fratri Philippo baroni de Schombornh, de Wirtzburg et Emendorff, Bernardo de Metternich de Francfort, Roth et Vianden, fratri Arnoldo baronis de Wacktendonck de Rordorff et Schwabishal, Maximiliano de Westrem de Treviri, fratri Sigismondo baroni de Schasberg, de Willingen et Hasselt, fratri Fiderico de Schenck de Staufenberg, de Basilea, Enrico Ferdinando baroni de Stain a Rechtenstein de Sultz, et Ermanno baroni de Beveren d'Uberslingen commendarum prioratus Alemaniae commendatariis etc.

196. 1695, June 18 – *Order is given to inspect the improvements made by frater Jacob Dudingh in his preceptory of Aachen, followed by a similar order concerning his preceptory of Regensburg and Altmühlmünster.*
Chancery notes: AOM 499 = libri bullarum 1695, *fol.85v.*

Die eadem fuit expedita similis commissio ad visitandum melioramenta facta per fratrem Jacobum Dudingh in commenda de Aquisgrana prioratus Alemaniae, quam titulo melioramenti possidet etc. directa venerandis priori Alemaniae fratri Ermanno baroni de Waktendonck, ac supradictis priori Ungariae, priori Daciae et commendatariis etc. de Metternik, de Waktendonck, de Merveldt, de Westrem, de Sciasberg et de Beveren.
Die eadem fuit expedita commissio similis ad visitandum melioramenta facta per fratrem Jacobum Dudingh in commenda de Ratisbo-

na et Althmunmunser prioratus Alemaniae, quam titulo gratiae linguae possidet etc. directa supradictis commendatariis de Rol, de
Schombour, de Merveldt, de Westrem, de Staufenberg, de Rechenstein, de Waktendonk, de Sciasberg et de Beveren.

197. 1695, August 3 – *Frater Adrien de Wignacourt, Grand Master, asks for
the registration of a letter from Pope Innocentius XII dd. 18 June 1695, in favour
of frater Johan Arnold baron van Wachtendonk.*
   Chancery notice: AOM 499 = libri bullarum 1695, *fol.85v-86r.*

— commendatario fratri Ioanni Arnoldo baroni de Wachtendonk
venerandi prioratus Alemaniae militi, ut si contingat eum ad magnum prioratum Alemaniae promoveri, ipse nihilominus unam tantum
quam maluerit ex praeceptoriis seu commendis per eum de presenti
obtentis seu in futurum obtinendis una cum eodem prioratu, quoad
vixerit, retinere illiusque fructus, redditus et proventus percipere, exi-
gere et levare ac in suos usus et usitatem convertere libere et licite
possit et valeat in omnibus et omnia, perinde ac si prioratum Alemaniae huiusmodi non obtineret, iuxta dictarum litterarum Apostoli-
carum formam concessit et indulsit. —

198. 1698, January 7 – *An unnamed representative of the Order expresses
some claims to the revenues of the house at Nimwegen.*
   *Original draft: GLA Karlsruhe, 90/279, fol.31, undated, inserted in a piece
dd. 7 January 1698 concerning the recovery of the house at Nimwegen. Cf. below,
nr.199,* Proiect van Accoort *[dd. 18 May 1700].*

Dat die Magistraet van Nijmwegen die vruchten van den Jahren
1638, 39 ende 1640 verschenen souden proffiteren mits wat van ons
gebuert daer van mochte zijn, niiet gerepeteert sall worden, waer-
mede oock die gagie van predicanten tot soe feer sullen vergeten zijn.

Dat die predicanten gagie geaugumenteert soude worden ende in
plaets dat vierhondert gulden jaerlix waeren betaelt geweest 600 gulden jaerlix betaelt souden worden, en dat alsoe den eijsch vanden
heeren van Nijmwegen den 3 ende 4 Februarii 1691 is geweest acht
honderd gulden jaerlix, sall het different van zes tot acht hondert
gulden tot uuttspraeck van het hoff verblijven.

Dat die affgeparste pennongen van hr. Dr. de Jongc cort ende schae-
deloes souden worden gerembourseert.

Dat alle andere vruchten sedert den jaere 1690 verschenen, ende bij die Magistraet van Nijmwegen ontfangen souden moeten worden gerestitueert.

Dat het dispuijt tegens Sander van Mumste[a] sall verblijven tot decisie vanden Hoeve.

Dat het huys der residentie binnen Nijmwegen uutterlijck ende ten langsten noch 3 jaeren in huijr sullen behouden tegens 200 gulden jaerlix.

Dat die reparatien soe gedaen zijn sullen blijven tot last van de voornoemde Magistraet, ende geen nuwe meer mogen maecken dan noetsaeckelik ende met kennis van die volmachtigers.

Dat alle chartres ende mobilien getrouwlick sullen worden gerestitueert alles tot behoeff van Orden.

Dat, bij transactie van alle pretensie sullen renuntieeren, sonder in toe commende tijden, nuwe disputen dees aengaende te moegen movieren, dit alles onder submissie vande Hove van Gelderlant.

---

[a] *uncertain reading ms.*

199. c.1700 – *The Prior of Germany and chapter present a treaty for the restitution of part of the Order's properties belonging to the house at Nimwegen.*
   Original draft. GLA Karlsruhe, 90/337, fol.51r–54v, undated; see full text of 2° under C.6.
   Cf. below, nr.204, according to which this treaty was dated 18 May 1700, but never was ratified.

[note on fol.54v:]
Proiect van Accoort door sijn Hooghvorstelijcke Genade van Heitersheim en t'Illustre Capittel gemaeckt aengaende de restitutie der goederen gehoorende tot de Commendeurie van St.Jans binnen Nijmegen, en sulcx naer het proiect van deselve stadt deswegen overgelevert.

[fol.51r] Alsoe veele, en verscheidene jaeren achter malcanderen disputen en oneenigheden sijn ontstaen, ende proceduren gevoert tussen de Heeren Ridderen, en Commendeurs van d'Illustre Ordre van St.Jan tot Maltha Requiranten ter eenre, ende de Heeren Burger-

meesteren, Schepenen, ende Raaden der Stadt Nijmegen Gerequireerdens ter anderen zijde, waerbij de Heeren Requiranten hebben gesustineert ende alnoch sustineren dat aen d'Illustre Ordre van St.Jan tot Maltha souden moeten gerestitueert worden alle de goederen, renten, en effecten, tot de Commendeurie binnen de Stadt Nijmegen gelegen gehoorende, En aen zijde van de Heeren Gerequireerdens, dat Haer Ed: en Achtb: tot onderhoudt ofte verpleginge van kerck, en schooldienaren souden gerechtight, oft bevoeght sijn deselve te behouden, soo is naer verscheide onderhandelingen ende bijeenkomsten tusschen den Hoogh Welgebooren Heere Gooswijn Herman Otto Vrijheer van Merveldt des Illustre Ordens Ridder, en Commendeur van Rotenburgh, Reichersraet, Arnhem, en Nijmegen etc. in qualiteit als Volmachtiger van sijn Hoogh Vorstelijcke Genaden van Heitersheim, etc. volgens procuratie, verthoont, geexamineert, ende van waerden gehouden en erkent ter eenre, en de Welgemelte Heeren Burgermeesteren, Schepenen, ende Raet der Stadt Nijmegen ter anderen zijde, opgericht het naervolgende Accoort, in Transactie, ende daer bij onverbreeckelijck, edoch op approbatie van Hooghgemelte Ordre geconditioneert, en overkomen,

1º. Dat de Magistraet der Stadt Nijmegen aenstonts naer de ratificatie, en uijtwisselen van dit Contract aen den Heere Commendeur off aen de voorgenoemde Illustre St.Jans Ordre sall restitueeren, en inruimen dese hier naer gespecificeerde goederen ende renten, soo, ende gelijck deselve voorheens, ende van oudts geweest sijn, met welcke welgemelte St.Jans Ordre sall bemachtight sijn te disponeren, ende te laeten, te verkopen, ende te doen, als andere met haere eijgendommelijcke goederen.

2º. Volght hier naer de specificatie der Bouwhoven, Renten, en Effecten soo de Stadt Nijmegen bij dese restitueert, en overgeeft *[fol.51v-52r, see C.6.]*

[fol.52v]
3º. Dan wijders ten derden sal de voorschreve Stadt de voornoemde goederen ontlasten van alle Capitalen, en daer op verlopene Interesse indien boven vermoeden mochte bevonden worden, dat door de Stadt daer op eenige Capitalen genegotieert off veronderpandt sijn, sullende de Stadt dan oock niet te doen hebben met die penningen, die bij het quartier, mitsgaeders d'ampten, en Dorpen waer onder de goederen respective sijn gelegen daer op nevens andere erven genegotieert sijn.

4º. Dat den Vrijheer van Merveldt als tijdelijcken Commendeur van St.Jan tot Nijmegen in naeme van sijne Ridderlijcke Ordre d'op-komsten van de voors. goederen op Martini 1698 verschenen, sal trecken, en proffijteren, ende daertegens d'ongelden, en lasten in het selve jaer daerop verlopen, draegen.

ªNB. Dewiele de Stadt in mora is gebleven dat dit Contract niet geperfecteert is geworden, dat in September oft October 1698 had konnen geschieden.ª

5º. Dat de respective pachters van de voorschreve goederen haere respective pachtsiaeren sullen uijtgehouden worden tot expiratie van de gestipuleerde jaeren.

6º. Dat aenstonts naer het uijtleveren van de ratificatie van dit Con-tract aen den Heere Commendeur sall uijtgegeven worden een au-thenticque Copie van de respective pachtscedullen mitsgaeders alle originale chartres, en papieren die onder de Stadt, off desselfs Rent-meester sullen mogen berusten, aengaende de voorschreve Commen-deurie goederen.

7º. Dat de Magistraet voor haer, ende haere Successeuren, mits deses afstandt doet van alle pretense vorderingen op de goederen, die uijt cracht van dit Contract aen de St.Jans Ridder Ordre ende den tijdelijcken Commendeur sullen ingeruimt worden sonder dat de Regeringe van deselve Stadt Nijmegen oijt, off immermeer dese gerestitueerde goederen, en effecten, noch den persoon van den tegenwoordigen, off toekomenden Heere Commendeur, off Succes-seurs, en Inhebberen deser goederen hoger sall belasten, off beswae-ren, als goederen van andere personen, uijt wat hooffde off pretext het selve soude mogen sijn, en selfs niet wegens onderhoudt, off ali-mentatie van kercke, off schooldienaren.

8º. Dat de Stadt Nijmegen sall lasten, ende draegen alle impositien, en ongelden, soo eenige wegen dit accoort soude moeten betaelt wor-den, oock soo veel doendelijck behulpsaem wesen, en goede officie doen, dat desere Commendeurie goederen niet anders sullen worden beswaert, en in de belastinge geconsidereert, als goederen inheimse toebehoorende.

[fol.53r] 9º. Dat de voorschreve Illustre St.Jans Ordre ingevolge van dit Contract renuntieert niet alleen op het gedeelte van het Veer, maer oock op alle andere goederen, huijsen, renten, thijnsen, dewel-cke hier boven niet gespecificeert sijn, ende den Ridderlijcken Orden

toebehooren, (welcke alle aen de Stadt eijgendommelijck verblijven sullen, sonder dat dese Stadt, off eenige particulieren t'eeniger tijdt sullen mogen geinquieteert worden wegens eenige landerien, erven, renten, erfpachten, thijnsen, en andere recognitien, effecten, off goederen van de voors. Commendeurie dewelcke voor primo Maij 1698. door de voorgemelte Stadt vercoft, weghgegeven, off andersints veralieneert moghten sijn, ofte oock wegens eenige penningen, off andere effecten van de voorseijde Commendeurie, die bij de Stadt ontfangen, off geproffiteert sijn, waer tegens oock den tijdelijcken Heer Commendeur, en desselfs Successeurs met haere bijhebbende Domesticques, Dienaren, peerden, koetsen, en ander gespan, en bagagie deser Stadts Veer passeerende, en repasserende toties quoties vrij, en exempt sullen sijn van de betaelinge van het veergeldt.

10°. Dat de Ridderlijcke Ordre van St.Jan gelijckfals renuntieert op de vrughten die de Stadt van deser Commendeurie goederen tot primo Maij 1698 genoten heeft, en voorders ingevolge van dit Contract van de goederen, die deselve behouden, genieten sal, gelijck d'emolumenten van d'affgebroockene Kerck van St.Jan, mitsgaeders op alle aengewende gerichtelijcke en ongerichtelijcke kosten, en voorts generalijck op alle andere pretensien geene uijtgesondert, die den Heere Commendeur, sijne Predecesseurs, en de meergemelte sijne Illustre Ordre uijt hooffde van de Sententie, en het aenslaen van de Commendeurie goederen, als anders, eenighsints soude mogen hebben tegens dese Stadt off tegens eenige particulieren aen dewelcke eenige van de voorschreve goederen, off effecten door de Stadt mochten vercoft, gegeven, off andersints veralieneert sijn, off die aen de Stadt eenige penningen mogen betaelt hebben, waervoor den Heere Commendeur, ende Hooghgedachte Ordre sigh stormaechen, Renuntierende parthijen van beijde sijden op alle bedenckelijcke Exceptien, die dit accoort eenighsints soude konnen praeiudiceren, en in specie op het beneficio [fol.53v] van rescissie wegens laesie over de helfte, ofte oock propter enormissimam laesionem, et utilitatis publicae.

11°. Sall meergemelte Heere Commendeur Vrijheer van Merveldt van dit tegenwoordigh accoort in den tijdt van [-]ᵇ uijtbrengen beheerlijcke ratificatie, en approbatie niet alleen van sijn Hooghvorstelijcke Genade Oversten Meester in Duijtslandt, maer oock van Sijn Eminents den Heere Grootmeester der Ridderlijcke St.Jans Maltheser Ordre.

12°. Tot naerkominge van alle het geene voorschreve, hebben beijde parthijen Contrahenten sigh, en haere Successeuren gesubmitteert aen allen Heeren Hoven, Richteren, ende Gerichten, en in specie den WelEd: Hove van Gelderlandt, welcke sullen bemachtight sijn den geene, soo dit Contract in eenige deelen niet naerkomt, tot het volvoeren van dien, en hersettinge van allen affganck, en schaeden per viam executionis nullo paenitus iuris ordine servato, en sonder eenigh tegenspreecken aen te houden, en te constringeren. Dies ter warer oirconde is dit accoort in triplo^c uijtgevaerdight, en van den Vrijheer van Merveldt, als tijdelijcken Commendeur names hooghgedachte Ridderlijcke Ordre beteeckent en met het aengebooren Vrijadelijcke pitschaft becrachtight, en van wegen Heeren Burgermeesteren, Schepenen, Raaden, en samentlijcke Gemeensluijden der Stadt Nijmegen door derselver Secretaris onderteeckent, en met des Stadts Segel besegelt, soo geschiet binnen Nijmegen den [–]^b.

---

^a *in the left margin.* ^b *not filled in.* ^c *corrected from* duplo.

200. 1704, March 4 – *Frater Ramon Perellos, Grand Master, and Council grant the right to negotiate the properties of the house at Nimwegen to frater Herman Goswin baron van Merveldt.*
  Original bull on parchment: GLA Karlsruhe, 20/2525, with a small piece of hemp string of the lost seal of Grand Master and Convent, dated in Annunciation-style.

Don Raymundus de Perellos — et nos baiulivi, priores, praeceptores caeterique equites concilium ordinarium domus praedictae in Domino celebrantes *[grant]* facultatem transigendi super bonis membri de Nimwegen pro commendatario Hermanno Gosuino libero barone de Merveldt *[with the right to sell them for the minimal price of]* 40,000 plastris. —.
  Die quarta mensis Martii 1703 ab incarnatione iuxta stylum nostrae cancellariae vero cursum ordinarium 1704.

201. 1709, March 16 – *Frater Ramon Perellos, Grand Master, and Convent grant the right to regain the preceptories of Arnhem and Nimwegen to frater Gosuinus Ermannus baro de Mervelt, because he has the intention to make some attempts to that purpose at the peace conference at Utrecht.*
  Authorized copy: GLA Karlsruhe, 90/282, fol.14r-v-15r, chancery document from Malta dd. 5 May 1709. The bull itself is dated in Annunciation-style:
  Die 16. mensis Martii 1708 ab incarnatione.

202. 1712, March 16 – *Frater Ramon Perellos, Grand Master, issues a letter of credence for frater Goswin Herman baron van Merveldt.*
   Copy: GLA Karlsruhe, 90/282, fol.18.

Messieurs
Le Commandeur Gosuin Herman baron de Merveld qui rendra cette Lettre de Créance a Vos Excellences, a esté nommé par Moy et mon Conseil en qualité d'Envoyé Extraordinaire a l'assemblée Generale de la Paix, pour Vous representer les droits de mon Ordre sur plusieurs biens usurpés et occupés dans les états de divers princes d'Alemagne, et des Provinces-Unies des Pays-Bas; je me flate Messieurs, que je seray protégé dans mes intentions par toutes les puissances qui interviendront dans Vôtre assemblée, je leur en ay fait faire mes instances par mes ambassadeurs; Et dans la confiance que Vos Excellences auront des ordres particuliers pour que mes justes demandes entrent en ligne de compte, je les assureray que je conserveray une parfaitte reconnoissance de tout ce qu'elles feront en faveur de mon Ordre, et que je suis en mon particulier, avec une parfaitte estime pour leurs personnes.
a Malte ce 16me Mars 1712
   Messieurs
de Vos Excellences
le tres affectionné Serviteur
   Le Grand Maitre
   Perellos

203. 1721, November 6 – *Frater Marcantonio Zondadari, Grand Master, and Convent appoint frater Goswin Herman baron van Merveldt as Prior of Germany, with five prioral chambers, among which Utrecht.*
   Authorized copy: GLA Karlsruhe, 20/165, chancery document from Malta.

Frater Marcus Antonius Condadari — et nos conventus — fratri Gosuino Hermanno baroni De Merveldt, prioratus nostri Datie priori ac commendae nostrae de Tobel prioratus Alemaniae commendatario —.
   [He receives the dignity of Prior of Germany after the death of] fratris Bernardi Ernesti baronis de Reede, *[with five prioral chambers]* videlicet Traiectum, Coloniam, Haimbach et Bugikem, nec non Commendam de Fribourg et Bresgau pro quinta tua camera —.

204. 1746, May 26 – J.J.Van Wanray I[uris] V[triusque] Doctor, *gives an account of his visits to Nimwegen in order to present a petition by his lord frater Dietrich Hermann baron von Schade, head of the preceptories Arnhem and Nimwegen, adding the text of this petition.*
    Authorized German translations of a Dutch petition with covering letter dd.17 May 1746: GLA Karlsruhe, 90/460, fol.8r-13v, the petition on fol.9r-11v is folded in the covering letter on fol.8r-v and 13r-v.
    An undated copy of the Dutch version of this petition is to be found in GLA Karlsruhe, 90/337, fol.7r-9r.

[fol.8r] Copia sive Traductio.
    Son Excellence
Umb auff das von Ihro Excellence an mir gnädigst erlassenes anschreiben sehr unterthänig zu berichten, auf was manier ich die sachen wegen restitution der commendarije Nimwegen auff ordres von Ihro Excellence nahmens meines vatters verrichtet und befunden habe, so ist zu wissen, dass nachdem ich empfangen habe das beijgehörige request oder Memoriale, alswelches von Ihro Hochw. Excellence eigenhändig unterzeichnet war:/ immediatè mich nach Nimwegen verfüget, und alda beij den Stabtrager von wohlgemelte stadt geaddressiret habe, bevorab auch zu grösserer versicherung/: ehe ich an denselben das original request mit der copia habe übergeben, von ihm versucht ein attestatum auff gemelte copia zu schreiben, das nahmentlich darvon das original den 9.Martij dieses jahrs durch mich ihm zu handen gestellet wäre, und er dasselbe an den Magistrat der Stadt Nimwegen auff einen darzu bestimmten tag sölte praesentiren; solches habe ich nöthig zu seijn geurtheilet zu dem ende, damit ich mich könte justificiren und beweisen, das ich die ordres von Ihro Hochw. Excellence in allen stucken observirt hätte, in fall ich hernach kein appointement oder resolution auf das original request unverhoffentlich erlangen mögte. Jedoch gemelte Stabtrager, weil Er sich darbeij beschwert befande, indem selbiges request gegen den Magistrat, wie er vorgabe, eingerichtet war, hat er solches auff allerleij weise gesucht zu decliniren, dannoch endtlich auf mein starckes *[fol.8v]* anhalten, wendete er für, das er unpässlich und nicht im stand wäre solches zu verrichten, derowegen ersuchte er mich, ich möchte über einige zeit wiederkommen, wan er nemlich mit seinen confrater daruber würde gesprochen haben, alsdan würde er mir nach befindung der sachen eine positivè antwort geben; endlich liess er sich verstehen, das er das attestatum, nicht ohne gefahr sein ambt zu verlieren, oder zum wenigsten sich in grossen hass beij der Regirung zu setzen, mir geben könte; diese forcht war beij ihm so gross, das er gemeltes request dem Magistrat nicht hat wollen überreichen, weswegen ich

genöthiget wurde, mich zu den Secretarium der gemelten stadt zu
verfügen, und ihn zu ersuchen, das er das request denen Herrn von
den Magistrat einhändigen mögte, und mir ein attestat darvon geben;
das erste hat gemelter Secretarius mir versprochen beij erster zusah-
menkunfft nachzukommen, das zweite aber hat er mir abgeschlagen;
nachdehm ich nun alles mündlich recommendiret, und, so viel mir
möglig war, wohl besorget hatte, bin ich nach Arnheim zu ruck ge-
kehret, aber den 18 Martij bin ich wieder auff Nimwegen gereiset,
umb zu vernehmen, ob auff gemeltes request etwas mögte disponiret
seijn, habe aber mit grossen leidwesen verstanden, das noch keine
resolution darauff erfolget wäre, als welches mich in zweiffel gesetzet
hat, alswan selbiges request durch gemelten Secretarium nicht mögte
überreichet, sondern von ihm untergeschlagen seijn; umb von diesen
versichert zu seijn, habe ich mich beij den gerichtsdien[ern] informi-
ren lassen, [fol.13r] welche mir bezeugten, das das request von Ihro
Excellence eingehändiget wäre, und das bisweilen wohl mehrmahlen
sich zutragte, das auff die eingehändigte requaesten in 14 tagen keine
resolution würde gegeben, wodurch ich einen theils völlig versichert
wurde, das das request wäre überreichet, und anderen theils noch in
hoffnung stunde, einige resolution zu erhalten, habe es also darbeij
lassen bewenden, und mich auff den 25ten Martij wieder auff Nimwegen begeben, zu der zeit erfuhre ich auch, das auf das requaest
noch nichtes resolviret wäre, derowegen bin ich zu etlichen Herrn
von den Magistrat gangen und habe remonstriret alles was ich in
diesem stuck angewendet habe; allein aus der ursach, damit ich auff
gemeltes requaest resolution erhalten mögte. Zu diesem ende habe
ich auch allegiret die grosse mühe und fleiss, welchen Ihro Excellence
im jahr 1731 zu Nimwegen in person gegenwärtig dessentha[l]ben
haben angewendet, ersuchte also darbeij das sie mir doch einiges
responsum mögten geben, es wurde mir aber gesagt, das annoch
keine resolution vorhanden wäre, könten auch nicht sagen, ob jetz
darvon sölte disponiret werden. Diesem unangesehen habe ich mich
nach kurzer zeit wiederum nach Nimwegen begeben, und vorgestellet
die nachtheilige gefolgen, die aus verweigeren einer auff aequität und
gerechtigkeit gegründeten sache könten entspringen, dan noch wurde
eben so wenig auf das eine als auf das andere reflexion gemacht, also
hat es das ansehen nicht, das ins zukünfftige [fol.13v] jemahls darvon
etwas sölle disponiret werden; unterdessen werde ich nicht unterlassen, die aüsserste devoir anzuwenden, und meine schuldige pfligt zu
observiren, zu welchen mich obligirend mit aller unterthänigkeit ver-
bleibe

Son Excellence
Arnheim, den 17ten Maij 1746 ./.

Dinstschuldiger diener
J.J.Van Wanray   I[uris] V[triusque] Doctor

Das hievorgesezte Relation oder bericht aus seinem Originale in
hochteutsch vertiret, Von Uns beyden collationiret und gleichlau-
thendt befunden worden, wärd unter aigenhändiger subscription und
pettschaftliche beytewdchung[a] hiemit attestiret. Geschehen auff das
Commentchen zu Steinfurt den 26ten Maij 1746.
     Lucas Becker Zentemeister[a] dahie
     Ludwig Albert Bingelius Secretarius

[fol.9r] Copia sive Traductio.
     Ahn die wohl-Edele, Achtbahre Herrn Bürgermeister der Stadt
Nimwegen.

     Wohl-Edele und Achtbahre Herrn:
Es gibt sehr ehrbietsamb zu erkennen Dieterich Herman Freyherr
von Schade der Maltheser Ritter ordens Gros-Creutz und Commen-
dor über die gütter zu Arnheim und Nimwegen als wo anders gelegen
und zu vorgemelte Commendarien gehörende, wie das die Ritter von
den Maltheser orden in Euer WohlEdelen achtbahre stadt und Bur-
germeisterthumb als wo anders verschiedene gütter liegen haben,
deren einige von euch WohlEdelen und Achtbahren Herrn in besitz
genommen seijnd.
     Das Hochgemelte Ritters oder der in tempore würcklicher Com-
mendor zur acquisition von ihrer rechtmässigen praetension darüber
viele instantien gemacht haben, ja das in soweit vorgemelter orden
sich nolens volens hat verpflichtet gefunden gegen die Stadt Nimwegen den process vor dem Hoff von Gelderland zu instituiren, als
welcher auch von einem solchen success gewesen ist: das im jahr
1646 den 19 Decembris beij wohlgemelten Hoff nebst achten durch
Ihro Edelmögende Herrn darzu expressè ersuchten Commissarien
eine Sententz gegen wohlgemelte stadt ist pronuntiiret worden,
[fol.9v] vermög welcher der Commendarie diverse gütter von Euch
WohlEdelen und Achtbahren Herrn bis zu jetziger stund annoch
possidiret worden mit deroselben genossenen früchten nebst denen
auch angewendeten unkösten seijnd adjudiciret worden, relatio sen-
tentiae darüber ergangen ist.
     Obwohlen nun diese sentenz ihren effect hätte müssen erlangen,
ist jedoch bis dato nicht das gringste darauf erfolget, bis dass endlich
im jahr 1700 18 Maij zwischen die Herrn des Magistrats der Stadt
Nimwegen und den Freijherrn von Mervelt als dero Commendarien
zeitlichen Commendören ein accord oder transactio ist eingegangen,

geschlossen und gezeichnet, vermög welchen accords die zu vorgemelten orden gehörende gütter gegens einem sicheren aequivalent
sölten restituiret werden, zu welchen ende auch im jahr 1731 der
supplicant sich nach Nimwegen verfüget, und zu selbiger zeit so wohl
grosse requisition als auch viele andere sollicitation gethan hat, ohne
das darauff ein appointement oder die gringste resolution von Euch
Wohl-Edelen und achtbahren Herrn hat mögen erlangen, dass auch
bis dato die vorgemelte transactio noch keinen effect erreichet hat, da
doch dieselbige durch die allerkräfftigste approbation nicht allein von
seiner Hochfürstlichen Gnaden von Heitersheim als zeitlichen Gross-
Prioren von Teutschland sambt dessen Hochwürdigen Capital, sondern auch von Seiner Hochfürstlichen Eminenz als Gross Meister des
gantzen Maltheser Ritter ordens, und dessen Hochwürdigen *[fol.10r]*
Senat zu Maltha als eine des Hohen Ritterlichen Maltheser ordens
Souveraine in forma solemnissima ist ratificiret worden.

Als welches dan desto grösseren effect in diesem fall müsste aus-
wircken, so Ewr Wohl-Edele und Achtbahre herrn considerirten, wie
das dieser Ritterlicher Maltheser Orden publicâ Authoritate ist einge-
setzet um das commercium der Christlichen potentaten fur die bar-
barische zee-räubereijen, so viel als möglich, freij und in sicherheit zu
halten, wobeij die eingesessenen der vereinigten Niederlanden in specie sonderlich interessirt seijnd, und des ordens hülff und beijstand
tägligs geniessen, angesehen sie nicht allein in den haven und festun-
gen des Maltheser Ordens ihren freijen eingang haben und auff ersuchen, mit vivres und allen nothwendigkeiten versehen, sondern auch
mit ihren schiffen und gütteren aus der macht deren barbarischen
zee-räuberen, wobeij die Maltheser Ritter ihro leib und leben auffset-
zen und perielitiren, befreijet und erlöset werden.

Das der Maltheser Ritter orden keine eigenschafft habe mit denen
kirchlichen oder geistlichen stands-Personen sondern das desselben
ordens militaire Herren Ritters in eigener person gegen den Erbfeind
des Christenthumbs streiten, in qualität eines Officires oder Generals
den degen tragen und den krieg befördern, als welches geistliche
personen, um ihre function licitè zu verrichten, *[fol.10v]* inhabiles
machen würde.

Obschon man nun gegen die wahrheit sölte sustiniren wöllen das
vorgemelte Maltheser Ritter etlichermassen für geistliche personen
könten gehalten werden, so müssten sie dannoch von keiner schlech-
teren condition seijn, als die jenige welchen zum reguard die concordata dieser landen statuiren: das alle Geistliche personen, deren
fundation und Residenz ausserhalb dieser Provincen gelegen, und
dannoch in dieselbige begütteret seijn, wiederum sollen kommen zum
eigenthum, und genuss ihrer gütteren. Das des Ritterlichen Maltheser

Ordens von St.Joann zu Jerusalem Corpus fundationis, Residentia und Gouvernement anjetzo zu Maltha seij, also das alle häuser und gütter, so binnen diese landen und wo anders gelegen seijnd, incorporirt und vereiniget seijn mit dem vorgeschriebene corpus und den Ritterlichen Maltheser Orden zu Maltha und gehören unter das eigenthumb desselbigen ordens, welche gütter von den zeitlichen Commendören nicht anders possidiret werden als zum dinst und nutzen des vorgemelten ordens, und darvon nicht mehr haben als das Dominium utile, so doch das sie nebst ihren persönlichen dinsten jährlichs sichere responsa oder contributiones von denen ihnen anbefohlenen Commendarijen /: welche nach gelegenheit des ewig daurenden krieges gegen den erbfeindt des gantzen Christenthumbs vermehret werden :/ müssen subministriren, und das ihre hinterlassenschafft [fol.11r] und alles, was sonsten von denen Commendören zeit lebens nicht consumiret ist, an vorgemelten orden müsse gelieffert werden.

Man supponirt nun, das der Magistrat von Arnheim es habe verstanden, als wanehr von Euch WohlEdelen und Achtbahren Herrn effectivè seijn restituiret und von vorgemelten orden bis zu jetziger zeit hin alle die gütter sambt ihren ap- und dependentien besessen werden.

Hierauf ist auch fundiret das von allen unter der Maltheser Commendarije zu Arnheim gehörenden gütteren vor einige jahren das Collateral, als welches allein von dependent-einheimischen gütteren geforderet wird, habe müssen bezahlt werden.

Es ist auch aus dem deducirten Manifesto bekant, das der Ritterliche Maltheser Orden wegen verschiedenen ursachen zu vorgemelten gütteren eine billige und rechtmässige praetension habe, also nimbt der Supplicant die freijheit, weil Er vermittels sowohl durch den request als durch an die Herrn von den Magistrat geschriebenen briefen nicht das gringste hat können effectuiren noch einige antwort oder resolution darauf mögen erlangen, Also thuet nahmens des gantzen ordens so wohl als für sich selbst sehr inständig ersuchen, damir Ewr WohlEdele und achtbahre Herrn den Supplicanten zum effect der gemelten transaction oder gemachten accords sich wollen gefallen lassen zu gelangen.

Solches Supplicirend

Loco Sigilli

Le Baili Barone de Schade
Chevalier de la Grand Croix et Commendeur de l'ordre du St.Jean de Malthe

[fol.11v] Das hievorgesezte Supplic aus seinem Originale in hochteutsch vertiret, Von Uns beiden Collationiret und gleichlauthend
befunden worden, wärd unter aigenhändiger Unterschrifft und pettschaftliche beytewtchung[a] hiemit attestiret. Es geschehen auf das
Commentchen Steinfurt den 26ten Maij 1746.

> Lucas Becker Zentemeister[a] dahier
> Ludwig Albert Bingelius Secretarius

---

[a] *uncertain reading ms.*

205. 1755, February 15 − *Frater Emmanuel Pinto, Grand Master, and
Convent appoint frater Jean-Baptiste Baron von Schauenburg as Prior of Germany, with five prioral chambers, among which Utrecht.*

*Original bull on parchment: GLA Karlsruhe, 20/167, with silk string with
lead seal of Grand Master and Convent, and elaborately decorated margins; legend
of the seal, front:* BVLLA MAGISTRI ET CONVENTVS; *back:* HOS-
PITALIS HIERVSALEM; *on the frontside are eight brethren. The bull is
dated in Annunciation-style.*

Frater Emmanuel Pinto — fratri Joanni Baptistae baroni de Scha-
wenburg ordinis nostri magno baiulivo ac commendarum nostrarum
de Cronweissemburg, et Brüxall, et de Villinghen prioratus nostrae
Alemaniae commendatario —.

[He receives the dignity of Prior of Germany after the death of fratris Philippi
Joachimi baronis de Prasperg, *[with five prioral chambers]* videlicet
Traiectum, Coloniam, Haimbach et Bugiken, necnon commendam
de Friburg, et Bresgaw pro quinta tua[a] camera —.

Datum Melitae in conventu nostro die XV mensis Februarii 1754
ab incarnatione iuxta stylum nostrae cancellariae, secundum vero
cursum ordinarium 1755.

---

[a] sua *ms.*

206. 1777, August 21 − *Frater Emmanuel de Rohan, Grand Master, and
Convent appoint frater Joseph Benedikt Graf von Reinach as Prior of Germany,
with five prioral chambers, among which Utrecht.*

*Original bull on parchment: GLA Karlsruhe, 20/168, with holes of lost string
with seal of Grand Master and Convent and elaborately decorated margins.*

Frater Emmanuel de Rohan — et nos conventus — fratri Josepho
Benedicto comiti de Reinach prioratus nostri Hunghariae priori, ac

commendae nostrae de Villingen prioratus nostri Alemaniae commendatario —.

[He receives the dignity of Prior of Germany after the death of fratris Francisci Sebastiani baronis de Remching *[with five prioral chambers]* videlicet Traiectum, Coloniam, Heimbach et Bubiken, nec non commenda de Friburg et Bresgau pro quinta tua[a] camera —.

---

[a] sua *ms.*

---

207. 1778, August 22 − *The treasurer at Malta writes to frater Franz Konrad Freiherr von Truchseß concerning the difficulty of collecting payments from the preceptories of Arnhem and Nimwegen.*

Copy: AOM 1610 = Letters from the treasurer to the collector in Germany, p.63. This letter first deals with Wesel and Borken, then with Regensburg, and finally with Arnhem/Nimwegen. The addressee is probably not Franz Konrad but Franz Heinrich Freiherr von Truchseß; cf.nr.211. The letters referred to date from 5 July 1778.

Al Commendatore fratre Francesco Corrado barone de Truchsses, 22 Agosto 1778. Coll'ultimo ordinario abbiam ricevuto un grosso plico del vostro antecessore, contenente il suo terzo annuale conto, con altri documenti, accompagnati da due sue lettere, segnate li 5. del trascorso Luglio.

Con sommo rammarico poi scorgiamo l'irregolare operato del venerando Bali Principe de Hohenlohe rapporto alla Commenda di Arnheim e Nimwegen. Farem noi le nostre considerazioni sulle memorie rimessui sopra tal evento dallo stesso vostro antecessore; e intanto testiam soddisfatti del zelo con cui il venerando Capitolo ha preso il partito di scriverne al venerando Bali de Breteuil nostro ambasciatore in Parigi, e di deputare il venerando Bali de Flachssanden, e il Cancelliere per trasportarsi in Olanda per riconoscere lo stato delle cose, e preservare la commenda da qualche cattiva conseguenza. Sol giudichiamo dovervi avvertire, che le spese, che per tale commissione occorreranno, dovra il venerando Capitolo rimborsarsele dalla stessa Commenda di Arnheim e Nimwegen, e dell'altra di Tobel. Attenderemo sopra tal delicato assunto gli ulteriori riscontri, el'esito di quanto pratticherà il venerando ambasciatore Bali de Breteuil per prender quelle piu spedienti risoluzioni, che converranno. —.

208. 1778, September 5 – *The treasurer at Malta writes to the* Baron de Truchssess, *(thanking him for the payment of his predecessor for the period of May 1774 to April 1775, and) referring to a letter dd. 1 July 1778 of the Order's ambassador in Paris concerning the difficulties with the preceptory of Arnhem.*
  Copy: AOM 1610 = Letters from the treasurer at Malta to the collector in Germany, p.65.

— Da un'altra acclusa copia poi della lettera del primo Luglio scritta dal venerando bali nostro ambasciadore in Parigi allo stesso vostro antecessore scorgiamo il vero attuale stato dell'affitto della Commenda di Arnheim tra'il venerando bali Principe de Hohenlohe col signore Caumartin, e come si spera, che il contratto sarà rescisso per ciò, che assicura il venerando ambasciatore, cosi attenderemo gli ulteriori risconti, approvando il partito preso di sospendere la commissione capitolare. —.

209. 1778, November 21 – *The treasurer at Malta expresses his satisfaction towards the* Baron de Truchssess, *that the sequestration of the property of the preceptories of Arnhem and Nimwegen has been annulled.*
  Copy: AOM 1610 = Letters from the treasurer at Malta to the collector in Germany, p.69.

— Apprendiamo con piacere, che siasi tolto il sequestro imposto da magistrati alla Commenda di Anrheim e Nimwergen, e resa cosi non necessaria la commissione capitolare del venerando Bali Flaxanden. Altro per or non ci occorre, che manifestarvi vieppiù la nostra soddisfazione, ed augurarvi ogni bene. —.

210. 1777 sqq. – *Checks and balances of the Priorate of Germany, 1777-1796, beginning with the decision of the Venerable Council that in addition to the usual annual payments to the treasury at Malta, a payment in imperial florins must be made.*
  Original: AOM 893 = Risponsioni Alemagna 1777-1796.
  The preceding book to which is referred, is AOM 894 = Risponsioni Alemagna 1761-1777. The scudi are abbreviated as @.

[fol.1, double page; left:] Deveo [right:] Avereo

marginal note on the left page:]

Anzi. Il Venerando Consiglio con suo decreto di 20 Marzo 1779 ordinò, che alle risponsioni antiche, che solevano pagare, come nel precedente libro si aggiungono fiorini imperiali, o siano usuali 7205, corrispondenti in moneta di Malta scudi 6550 da ripartirsi al priorato e commende d'Alemagna Alta e Bassa. E cio da regularsi dal primo Maggio 1777.

[crosswise in the length of the left margin:]

Risponsioni antiche e carichi f.d'oro 1182 – 7 – 3

Aumento f.imperiali, o siano usuali   1178 – 53 – 1

Il fiorino imperiale, o sia usuale in conformità della dicontro proporzione riviene in moneta di Malta scudi 10-18-1 131

$$\overline{\qquad\qquad}$$

1441

[fol.31, double page, left: Deveo   right: Avereo

left page:] Deveo

Commenda Arnheim e Nimeguen

Il venerando barone fr. Carlo Principe di Hohenlohe

Dal primo Maggio 1777 all'Aprile 1778 fiorini d'oro   33 – 4 – 3

E per aumento fiorini imperiali   141 – 27 – 2

[etc. yearly to and including April 1797]

[at the top of the left margin:]

483. 8. 67

$$\overline{\qquad\qquad}$$

Scudi   Anzi.

[crosswise in the left margin:]

Risponsioni antiche e carichi   F 33 – 4 – 3 d'oro

Aumento f.imp. o siano usuali   141 – 27 – 2

[right page:] Avereo

1778	E col primo conto d'Alemagna all'Aprile 1779		@ 1	33. 4. 3.
	E col bil. di Dicembre^a 1779 control.		@ 278	33. 4. 3.
	E col bilancio di Marzo 1780	ff. 141. 27. 2.	@ 280	
1779	Liu.	ff. 141. 27. 2.	@ detto	
1780	E col bilancio di Maggio 1780	ff. 141. 27. 2.	@ 281	33. 4. 3.
1781	E col bilancio d'Agosto 1781	ff. 141. 27. 2.	@ 288	33. 4. 3.
1782	E col bilancio di Settembre 1782	ff. 141. 27. 2.	@ 293	33. 4. 3.
1783	E col bilancio d'Ottobre 1783	ff. 141. 27. 2.	@ 298	33. 4. 3.
1784	E col bilancio di Luglio 1785	ff. 141. 27. 2.	@ 193	33. 4. 3.
1785	E piu	ff. 141. 27. 2.	@ detto	33. 4. 3.
1786	E col carro a rutto [?] Apr.1777	ff. 141. 27. 2.	@ 8+12	33. 4. 3.
1787	E col bilancio di Settembre 1787	ff. 141. 27. 2.	@ 200	33. 4. 3.
1788	E col bilancio di Luglio 1788	ff. 141. 27. 2.	@ 203	33. 4. 3.
1789	E col bilancio di Settembre 1789	ff. 141. 27. 2.	@ 206	33. 4. 3.
1790	E col bilancio di Novembre 1790	ff. 141. 27. 2.	@ 207	33. 4. 3.
1791	E col bilancio di Luglio 1791	ff. 141. 27. 2.	@ 211	33. 4. 3.
1792	Giugno 1792	ff. 141. 27. 2.	@ 213	33. 4. 3.
1793	Luglio 1793	ff. 141. 27. 2.	@ 217	33. 4. 3.
1794	Novembre 1797	ff. 141. 27. 2.	@ 229	33. 4. 3.
1795	Suddetto	ff. 141. 27. 2.	@ detto	33. 4. 3.

[fol.35, double page, left: Deveo   right: Avereo
left page:] Deveo

Commenda Aquisgrana do sia Aix la Chapelle
Il sacerdote commendatore fr.Claudio Giuseppe Duding

Dal primo Maggio 1777 all'Aprile 1778	ff. 113.10. -	fiorini d'oro 101. 29. 7	
E per aumento fiorini imperiali			
[etc. yearly to and including April 1788]			
E piu sino li 2.Settembre seguente, che mori	ff. 38. 21. -,	ff.[d'oro]	34. 17. 2
	ff. 1283.11. -	ff.[d'oro]	1155. 25. 7

Il sacerdote commendatore fr.Carlo Luigi barone de Gaza

ff.[d'oro] 101. 29. 7

[at the top of the left margin:]

Scudi   435. 3. 10

Anzi.

[crosswise in the left margin:]

Risponsioni antiche e carichi   ff 101. 29. 7 d'oro
Aumento f.imp. o siano usuali   113. 10. -

[right page] Avereo

	E col primo conto d'Alemagna a tutto Aprile 1779	@ 2	ff. 101. 29. 7
1778 {	E col bilancio di Giugno 1779	@ 276.	ff. 101. 29. 7
{	E col bilanzio di Settembre[b] 1780	@ 284.	ff. 101. 29. 7
1779 1780	E col sudetto bilancio per l'aumento all Aprile 1778, 1779, e 1780 ff 339.30 —		
1781	E col bilancio d'Agosto 1781 ff. 113.10.-	@ 284	ff. 101. 29. 7
1782	E col bilancio di Giugno 1782 ff. 113.10.-	@ 288	ff. 101. 29. 7
1783	E col bilancio di Luglio 1783 ff. 113.10.-	@ 291	ff. 101. 29. 7
1784	E col bilancio di Giugno 1784 ff. 113.10.-	@ 297	ff. 101. 29. 7
{	E col bilancio di Febrajo 1785	@ 191	
1785	E col bilancio di Giugno 1785 ff. 113.10.-	@ 193	ff. 101. 29. 7
1786	E col bilancio di Settembre 1786 ff. 113.10.-	@ 194	ff. 101. 29. 7
1787	E col bilancio di Giugno 1787 ff. 113.10.-	@ 198	ff. 101. 29. 7
1788	E col bilancio di Giugno 1788 ff. 113.10.-	@ 199 / @ 202	ff. 101. 29. 7

Ed in tanti che per saldo si passano in suo debito
nel brogliardo di spogli B @ 91   ff. 38. 21.-   ff. 34. 17. 2

    ff 1283.11.-   ff 1155. 25. 7

Anno		@	ff	ff
1791	E col bilancio di Giugno 1791	@ 210	ff. 113.10.-	ff. 101. 29. 7
1792	„ „ „ Giugno 1792	@ 213	ff. 113.10.-	ff. 101. 29. 7
1793	„ „ „ Giugno 1793	@ 216	ff. 113.10.-	ff. 101. 29. 7
1794	„ „ „ Giugno 1794	@ 219	ff. 113.10.-	ff. 101. 29. 7

[a] Xmbre ms.   [b] 7mbre ms.

211. after 1784 – *Alphabetical/chronological listing of the names, first of the knights and then of the chaplains, of the Priorate of Germany, c. 1500-1800, with the dates of their proofs; from fol.65 onwards, followed by a list of all preceptories with their improvements, rent-rolls (=* cabrei) *etc.*

Original listings: AOM 2199 = Lingua di Alemagna. *The rolls and other pieces to which these listings refer are not to be found there.*

[fol.73v:] Arnheim e Nimwegen
Miglioramenti fatti
1. dal commendatore fra Gotifrido Drost nel 1678
2. dal commendatore fra Teodoro Ermanno barone de Schade nel 1742
3. dal commendatore fra Francesco Enrico barone de Truchssess nel 1755
4. dal venerando bali fra Filippo principe di Hohenlohe nel 1784

[fol.74r:]
Cabrei della commenda Arnheim e Nimwegen.
Documenti diversi relativi ai cabrei di questa commenda prodotti dal commendatore fra Francesco Enrico barone de Truchsess, in prova dell'impossibilità di rinovare li cabrei suddetti. Degli anni 1761 al 1766.
[fol.74v:]
Carte relative alla commenda Arnheim e Nimwegen.
Varie lettere e scritture concernenti la ricuperazione del membro Nimwegen, di anni diversi.

[fol.118r:] Aquisgrana
Miglioramenti fatti
1. dal commendatore fra Alessandro Watz nel 1670
2. dal commendatore fra Giacomo Duding nel 1698
3. dal commendatore fra Claudio Duding nel 1736

[fol.118v:]
Cabrei della commenda Aquisgrana
1. Attestato di cabrei rinovati e spedito nel 1670
2. Attestato di cabrei rinovati negli anni 1695 e 1696

[fol.119r:]
Carte relative alla commenda Aquisgrana.

PART B

RENT-ROLL OF ST CATHARINE'S CONVENT AT UTRECHT, 14TH CENTURY

Municipal Archives, Ghent (Belgium), family fund Surmont de Volsberghe. *Rent-roll of the landed property of the St Catharine's Convent of the St John's Order in Utrecht, 1368 sqq., made by frater Thomas van Ghore, clerk of St Catharine's Convent, on order of frater Hugo van Coudenkerc, dispensator (= administrator) of this house.*

Parchment, 151 folios, 31x21 cm, double-sided, highly corroded by oxidation of the ink, especially in the upper parts of the leaves. The original covering in brownish leather has disintegrated largely, but its inner structure that consists of oakboards with binding-thongs in the spine and a metal clasp is still preserved.

   The text has been written in Latin by several hands, mostly from the second half of the 14th century, with the exception of some scattered passages, some inserted loose leaves and fol.134r+v, which have been written in Dutch in yet different hands. We have tried to distinguish all the different Latin hands by means of characters, hand A, hand B and so on, but to little avail. Next to the basic hand A with its different writings (smaller in the margins and in some later additions), only clearly discernable hands have been characterized: hand B dates from c.1370-1375, hand C from c. 1370-1380, hand D from c.1376-1385, and hand E from c.1381-1386. Unless indicated otherwise, the hand referred to is the basic hand.

One inserted paper leaf that seems to originate from a cash-book, reads in an 18th-century handwriting:
eenen bouck op francijn comt uyt den onbekenden koffer, item noch eenen op pampier uyt den selfven koffer.

On the second flyleaf, verso, in a 15th-century handwriting:
Int Jaer ons heren M IIIIC ende **XXXVII** *[1437]* doe wert die aef-docht ghemaect uuten kelre onder den dorpel van der doer vanden reventer doert velt voert vrouwenhuys ende vergadert mitter koken aefdocht bider knechten stille[a] neffens die aefdocht die uuter stille inder stat graft gaet ende inden kelre plach alte groet ghebrec van water te wesen datmen in natten weder altoes osen most ende dese aefdocht is ruym ende hoech datter 1 man wel in knyelen mach dit is daer om ghescreven ofter ghebrec in viel datmense dan de bet vijn-den mocht

---

[a] *in the ms. corrected from* stylle *ms.*

in another 15th-century hand:

Int Jaer ons heren M IIII^C XLVII *[1447]* doe ghinghen die koeyen ende beest so langhe te weyden dat men te midwinter graesde botter at daer die koeyen doe noch inden graes of ghinghen midwinter XLVIII *[1448]*; item inden selven jaer ghinghen die koeyen also vroe weder te weyden datmen op sunte Gheertruden dach anno XLVIII *[1448]* die doe opten Palmdach wat ^a nye graesde botter hadde te-ghen den Paeschen ende inden selven winter wast so goeden droghen weder dat daer veel beest int velt bleven die niet te stal en quamen.

---

^a grae *cancelled ms.*

On the third flyleaf, verso, in 18th-century hand:

Hugo de Kauderkerck dispensator qui scripsit hunc librum per Tho-mam de Ghore a° 1368 fuit tertius commendator domus Haerlemen-sis & postea pastor in Haserwoude.

On the fourth flyleaf, recto, in the 14th-century hand of a large part of the ms, is a table of contents, red-lined, with headings, paraphs (¶) and folia-indications in red, partly corroded:

Redditus nostre domus sancte Katerine, quem sub numero sequenti. Primo intra Civitatem Traiectensem

Parrochia Civilis ecclesie	.I.II.III.IIII.V.
Parrochia sancti Nycolai	.VI.
Parrochia sancti Jacobi intra Civitatem	.VII.VIII.IX.X.

[Extra] Civitatem Traiectensem

Parrochia sancti Jacobi extra Civitatem supra Venum	.XI.XII.etc.
Ameronghen.	.XXIX.XXX.
Doerne.	.XXXI.
Tule.	.XXXII.
Ravenswade.	.XXXIII.
Langhebroec.	.XXXIIII.
Overlanghebroec.	.XXXV.
Wike.	.XXXVI.
Tulle.	.XXXVI.
Coten.	.XXXVII.XXXVIII.etc.
Werconden.	.XL.

Odijc.	.XL.
Houten.	.XLI.
Scalcwijc.	.XLI.
Culenborch.	.XLII.
Wale.	.XLII.
Parrochia sancti Nycolai. extra Civitatem supra Raven.	.XLIII.
Parrochia sancte Ghertrudis supra Raven.	.XLIII.

On the fourth flyleaf, verso:

Parrochia sancte Ghertrudis in Galicop et Gheno.	.XLV.
In Jutfaes.	.XLVI.
Parrochia Civilis ecclesie extra Civitatem, in Heyencop.	.XLIX.
Vloten.	.LIII.LIIII.LV.LVI.LVII.etc.
¶ Curtis de Weyda.	.LIX.LX.
Maersen.	.LXI.LXII.
Broeclede.	.LXIII.LXIIII.LXV.LXVI.
Lonen.	.LXVII.
Loesdrecht.	.LXVIII.
Apcoude.	.LXIX.
Nichtvecht.	.LXX.
Horstweerde.	.LXX.
Wesepe.	.LXX.
Cokangen.	.LXX.
Hermalen.	.LXXI.LXXII.LXXIII.etc.
¶ Curtis in Reynerscop.	.LXXIX.LXXX.etc.
¶ Curtis in Hermalen.	.LXXXVI.LXXXVII.
Lynschoten.	.LXXXVIII.
Cameric.	.LXXXIX.
Woerden.	.XC.XCI.
Weyrder.	.XCII.XCIII.etc.
¶ Curtis in Weyder.	.XCVIII.

On the fifth flyleaf, recto:

Bodegraven.	.XCIX.
Oudewater.	.C.CI.CII.etc.
¶ Curtis seu domus in Oudewater.	.CVII.
Infra oppidum Oudewater.	.CIX.etc.

Montfoerde.	.C.XII.
Yselsteyne.	.C.XIIII.
Benscop.	.C.XV.etc.
Pulsbroec.	.C.XXI.etc.
Lopic.	.C.XXIII.etc.
Jaersvelt.	.C.XXVII.
Yselmunde.	.C.XXVII.
Ammers.	.C.XXVIII.
Langherake.	.C.XXVIII.
Molnersgrave.	.C.XXIX.
Ameyda.	.C.XXIX.
Merkerke.	.C.XXX.
Gasperde.	.C.XXXI.
Nyeland.	.C.XXXI.
Nyelanderkerke.	.C.XXXI.
Lederbroec.	.C.XXXI.
Goudrian.	.C.XXXII.
Almekerke	.C.XXXII.

verso:

Rewijc.	.C.XXXIII.
cancelled: Slupic	
Middelborch.	.C.XXXIII.
Suademerdam.	.C.XXXIIII.
Nyencop.	.C.XXXIIII.
Gheervliet.	.C.XXXIIII.
Slupic.	.C.XXXIII.

fol.1r,   In parrochia Civilis Ecclesie [intra] Civitatem   I
The first lines are highly corroded:

Redditus domus sancte Katerine Traiectensis hospitalis [—] prove-
nientes/ annuatim [—] domibus et areis intra/ civitatem [—] diver/
sis terrarum iugeribus agris et peciis extra civitatem in diversiis paro-
chiis/ [—] et locis [—] infertus per ordinem in hoc libro prout in
[-] situationes eorum [—]/[—] poterant et invenire distincte notatis
ex/ commissione discreti viri fratris Hugonis de Coudenkerc/ [—]
dispensatoris domus prenominate non sine gravi labore per Thomam
de Ghore dicte domus clericum in anno domini/ MCCCLXVIII
tempore ieiunii quadragesimalis et ulterius in eodem anno diligenter
conscripti.
[a]Hugo de Kouderkerck dispensator Sanctae Catharinae conscribi

hunc librum fecit per Thomam de Ghore dictae domus clericum aᵒ Domini 1368.ᵃ

Primo. In parrochia Civilis ecclesie Traiectensis intra civitatem habet domus sancte Katherine tres domos lapideas cum areis et terris attinenciis et edificiis seu stabulis ibidem retro stantibus recte ex opposito chori ecclesie dicte domus sancte Katerine situatas insimul et constructas, quarum unam scilicet maiorem, Hamersteyne nuncupatam pro nunc titulo emptionis possidet ᵇJohannes de Ameronghen filius Arnoldi Rieme ad vitam suam absque pensioneᵇ. Sub condicione quod ipsam domum cum suis attinenciis tenebit sanis in edificiis et tegminibus congruis suis sumptibus et expensis, et omnia edificia immobilia clavis lapidibus aut in terris firmata per ipsum in eadem domo constructa pariter et construenda post eius obitum in eadem illesa remanebunt, et cetera secundum tenorem littere super hoc optente. ᶜModo possidet ᵈ

Item ibidem mediam domum lapideam dictarum trium, Landscrone appellatam cum suis attinenciis, quam modo ᵇJohannes de Hamersteyne ad V annosᵇ possidet ab anno LXVIIIᵒ *[1368]* Pasche pro XIIj *[12.5]* antiquis scudatis annuatim monete Cesaris aut Francie aut pagamento equivalenti, Victoris et Pasche solvendis, sub condicione quod dictam domum suis sumptibus sanis in structuris et edificiis retinebit. Nec aliquid edificii in eadem construere aut frangere valebit absque commendatoris aut dispensatoris consensu, et cetera prout littera exinde tenet.
ᶜModo possidet Ghis[bertus] Albertiᶜ
1360.ᵃ

ᵃ *in the right margin, in an 18th-century hand.* ᵇ *cancelled.* ᶜ *added in different writing of hand A.* ᵈ *not filled in.*

fol.1v,   [—]
the first part is heavily corroded:

Item [ibidem — Walenborgh ap]/[pellatam — modo possidet Tidemannus]/ [Meus ad X annos ab anno — pro XVI libris —]/ [Victoris et Pasche solvendis. Sub condicionibus quod dictam —]/ [sanis in edificiis et tegminibus — servabit —]/ [concurendo sed ubicumque poterit meliorando —]/ [alius concedet — ad inhabitandum absque commendatoris et dispensatoris consensu.]
Etiam providebit ne mansiones nostre et aree retro [dictas nostras]/

domos et suas attinencias situate quas nunc Rodolphus de/ Vuren et Hildegondis eius uxor a nobis [possident occasione me]/atus aquarum plumalis de dicta domo lapidea [descendentium]/ aliquid evidens nocumentum patiantur. Et est prout [littera exinde opten]/ta tenet.

aTydemannus Meus.a

Item ibidem domum et aream cum suis attinenciis in duas mansiones distinctam prout iacet retro dictas tres domos nostras lapideas et attinencias earundem in vico dicto Viesteghe, inter domum et aream heredum Reyneri Fabri a parte superiori, et domum et aream Johannis Pillen a parte inferiori, quas modo possidet Rodolphus de Vuren et Hildegondis eius uxor ad vitam eorum, manente et optenta dictis tribus domibus nostris lapideis huiusmodi porta per medium dicte domus exeundo per commorantes in eisdem et intrando in vicum prenarratum, dictamque domum in sanis structuris servabunt et meliorabunt, et constructa per eosdem et construenda post eorum obitum integre remanebunt in eadem. Et dabunt annuatim exinde <u>VII libras XVI solidos denariorum</u> Traiectensium Victoris et Pasche.

Ipsis vero defunctis Aleydis eorum filia, si tunc supervixerit dictam domum ulterius possidere potest si perpetualiter habitare voluerit in eadem pro X libris annuatim quoad vixerit sub condicionibus supradictis in littera super hoc optenta contentis.

aRodolphus de Vuren bet Hildegondis eius uxorb ad vitama
obiitc

---

a *in the left margin.* b *cancelled.* c *in a different hand in the left margin.*

On a loose parchment leaf between fol.1v and 2r, a bit smaller in size, in an earlier 14th-century hand,
recto:
In sent Jacobs
In sent Jacobs kerspel

Int eerst sent Jacobs kerke van I hofstat die Willem van Hovelaken plach te hebben XII solidos XVI denarios siaers.

Item die selve kerke van I hofstat die Henric van Dorsschen plach te hebben XVI solidos siaers.

Item opten Camp Jacob Pauwels zone Uten Broeke van I hofstat daer aen die over zide naest gheland is her Johan sanctus vicarijs tsente Marien tUtrecht ende aen die neder zide wi zelve met I hofstat die Ghisebert van Papendorp heeft X solidos siaers.

Item daer naest gheleghen I hofstat die Ghisebert van Papendorp voers. van ons in pacht heeft om V solidos siaers.

Item daer alre naest gheleghen I hofstat die half ons is onderdeelt metter kerke van Buerkerc die Ghisebrecht van Papendorp voers. van ons in pacht heeft om V solidos siaers.

verso:
Item in die selve Viesteghe Rodolphus van Vuren en Hildegond sijn wijf van onsen II cameren ende hofsteden die wi daer hebben achter onsen drien steenhusen daer si inne wonen VIII libras siaers minus III groot tot hoerre beider live.

fol. 2r,   <u>Intra Civitatem</u>   II
the upper part is highly corroded:

[Item ibidem aream propius inter domum et aream dicte nostre]/
[domus quam pronunc Wilhelmus Corthoze a nobis]/ [possidet a parte superiori et dictas tres domos nostras lapi]/[deas a parte inferiori, quam modo possident heredes]/ [Reyneri Fabri perpetue sub annua pensione <u>XXV librarum.</u>]/ [an—]
[a]Modo possidet dictus Batenborch[a]
[b]Heredes Reyneri Fabri perpetue[b]
Batenborch[c]

Item ibidem propius domum et aream que quondam fuit Nycolai Frisonis, qua superius propius iacet Communis Platea civitatis; item inferius heredes Reyneri Fabri predicti cum huiusmodi area predicta quam a nobis hereditarie possident. Quam domum cum area modo titulo emptionis possident Wilhelmus Corthoze et Belia eius uxor ad vitam eorum, sub annua pensione <u>IIII librarum denariorum Traiectensium</u> annuatim Victoris et Pasche solvenda, sub condicione quod dictam domum sanis in edificiis eandem in structuris meliorando [-]/ omnia per eosdem in eadem constructa et construenda [-]/ integre remanebunt. Non ulterius locare seu concedere poterint alicui ad inhabitandum ante nec retro absque consensu commendatoris et conventus et cetera secundum tenorem littere super hoc optente.
[d]Willem Corthoze [b]et Belia eius uxor[b] ad vitam[d]

Item ibidem recte ex opposito iam dicte domus et aree ultra Plateam

domum et aream per Hermannum Scade et Wendelmodim de Spijc
eius uxorem nostre domui precollatam sub annuo censu trium librarum et duorum pullorum prout iacet in fine et posteriori parte
magne domus lapidee et aree heredum Ade Zoudenbalchs, inter domum et aream heredum Jacobi Henrici de Alrehorst a parte aquilonis
et portam posteriorem dictorum heredum Ade a parte meridionali
prout eandem modo dicta Wendelmodis inhabit, et ulterius possidebit a nobis ad vitam eius absque pensione nobis exinde danda. Sed
ipsa dictum annuum censum ex area eiusdem domus quoad vixerit
suis sumptibus solvet. Et nos eandem domum nostris sumptibus in
tegminibus et structuris congruis retinere tenemur et cetera. Inde
habet litteram a nobis et nos e converso exinde instrumenta et litteram censualem habemus.

^eModo dicta domus ex certis causis et controversiis cum Ernesto
Taetze habitis de manibus eius ad pietanciam nostre domus devenit,
ita quod magister pietancie ulterius se de dicta domo habet intro-
mittere ad locandum, et redditus exinde recipiendum et exponendum
et cetera cum ea faciendum quod fuerit faciendum.^e

^bWendelmodis de Spijc, ad vitam^b
obiit^f

---

^a *in a different hand.* ^b *in the right margin, cancelled.* ^c *in the right margin, in the*
same hand as ^a*.* ^d *in the right margin.* ^e *under the text in a different hand, abbreviated*
to such an extent that the reading is uncertain. ^f *in the right margin, in the same hand*
as ^e*.*

fol.2v,   Civilis Ecclesie
with a hole in the parchment, caused by corrosion:

Item ibidem, in Vico sancte Katerine domum longam [———] sub/
uno tegmine in sex cameras distinguatam et constructam, quarum
unam et primam in angulo Communis Platee stantem proviso possidet Aleydis Ruyschen ad VII annos ab anno LXV *[1365]* Pasche pro
VII libris annuatim Victoris et Pasche solvendis.

^aModo possident Johannes filius Bernardi et Aleydis eius uxor.^a
^bAleyd Ruyschen^b
^cJohannes filius Bernardi^c

Item secundam cameram primam ibidem ascendendo pronunc possi-
det/ [dominus Egidius Pijl] presbyter ad X annos ab anno LXXVI
[1376] Victoris/ pro XVI libris annuatim Pasche et Victoris solvendis. ^aPer fratrem Johannem Gaude.^a
^cdominus Egidius Pijl^c

Item tertiam cameram pronunc possidet Johannes Vrenke <u>pro III</u>
<u>libris</u> annuatim Victoris et Pasche solvendis.
^c<u>Johannes Vrenke</u> ad vitam eius^c

Item quartam cameram ibidem modo possidet domicella Katherina
uten Weyrde pro <u>III libris X solidis</u> annuatim Victoris et Pasche
solvendis. ^dModo possidet eam Aleydis Pawen ad V annos ab anno
LXXXV *[1385]* Victoris pro XII libris quo pactus solvuntur in
Traiecto. Per fratrem Johannem de Arnem dispensatorem.^d
^bKaterina uten Werde^b

---

^a *in a different hand.* ^b *in the left margin, cancelled.* ^c *in the left margin.* ^d *in another*
hand (D).

fol.3r.   <u>Intra Civitatem</u>   III

Item quintam cameram ibidem modo possidet Agatha Hermanni
Frisonis ad vitam suam absque annua pensione.
^aModo possidet Jacobus Hollander ad X annos ab anno LXXV
[1375] Victoris pro XI libris annuatim Victoris et Pasche solvendis.^a
^bAgatha Hermanni ad vitam^b
^cJacobus Hollander^c

Item sextam cameram habitacionis modo possidet et inhabitat
Thomas de Ghore, clericus nostre domus, absque pensione annua,
^dquamdiu est in servicio domus; videlicet servicio cessante dabit IIII
libras solidorum annuatim ad vitam suam; habet litteram.^d
^e<u>Thomas de Ghore</u> ad vitam eius^e

Item ibidem propius, domum et aream cum orto et stabulo ad eandem pertinentibus, quas modo titulo emptionis possidet Belya de
Zeyst ad vitam eius absque annua pensione, sub condicione quod
huiusmodi domum cum stabulo suis propriis sumptibus servabit congruis et sanis in edificiis et tegminibus, eandem cum suis attinenciis
non peiorando, sed ubi poterit meliorando. Ac per ipsam in eisdem
domo et stabulo seu orto constructa et construenda post eius decessum ibidem integre remanebunt. Etiam si per incendium quod absit
devastarentur, area tamen sibi ad reedificandum remaneret et reedifi-
cata per eandem in huiusmodi area nobis post eius obitum remane-
rent. Et est prout in littera super hoc optenta continetur.
^e<u>Belya de Zeyst ad vitam</u>^e

Item ibidem vicinius, aream in dicto vico situatam, qua exterius et interius cum domibus et areis nostris iacemus, quam modo possident heredes Ade Zoudenbalch ad quinquaginta annos ab anno XLIIII *[1344]* Nicolai pro II libris annuatim Victoris et Pasche solvendis, quibus finitis ad nos secundum tenorem littere super hoc optente libere revertetur.
^eHeredes Ade Zoudenbalch^e

---

^a *in a different hand.* ^b *in the right margin, cancelled.* ^c *in the right margin, in the same hand as* ^a. ^d *added in different writing.* ^e *in the right margin, in the basic hand.*

fol.3v.   <u>Civilis Ecclesie</u>

Item ibidem vicinius ascendendo supra fossatum dictum Graft, duas domos cum areis, scilicet domum dictam Magnum Lilium cum suis attinenciis stabulo scilicet et orto, et aliam dictam Parvum Lilium cum suo cellario, prout ambe iacent a parte occidentali eiusdem fossati aquarum, inter domum et aream heredum Ade Zoudenbalch a parte aquilonis, et vicum dictum Sente Katherinen Steghe a parte meridionali, retrograde se extendentes versus occidentem usque ad aream nostram predictam quam dicti heredes Ade a nobis possident. Quas duas domos cum areis, magno tamen cellario subtus Magnum Lilium cum suis meatibus et accessibus ante et retro, una cum parvo cellario dicto Cluze excepto, modo titulo emptionis possident ^aCristina de Speculo, et Aleydis eius soror ad vitam earum^a absque annua pensione, sub condicionibus in litteris contentis et hinc inde super hoc datis et optentis.
^bModo possident Johannes Wicke filius Henrici et eius uxor Margareta filia Frankonis Vreden ad vitam eorum, pro XII antiquis scudatis annuatim Victoris et Pasche solvendis.
^cJan die Wicke Henrix zoon et eius uxor Margareta^c

Item ibidem ultra fossatum recte ex opposito pontis dicti Her Jans Brugge a parte orientali, duas domos dictas Lelienbergh, cum areis et pomerio suisque attinenciis ibidem retro constructis, extendentes se a dicto fossato usque ad plateam seu locum dictum Noede, prout situate sunt inter domum et aream Godscalci Vrencken a parte aquilonis, et Petri filii Yden anterius, et Ghiseberti de Ruweel posterius a parte meridionali. Quas domos cum areis modo possidet <u>Jacobus Hawe</u> ad vitam eius, absque annua pensione, excepto et nobis optento huiusmodi parvo cellario subtus pontem predictam a parte orientali situato, sub condicionibus in littera quam super hoc habemus plenarie contentis.

^dJacobus Hawe ad vitam eius ^aet uxoris sue^{a d}

---

^a *cancelled.* ^b *in a different hand.* ^c *in the left margin in the same hand as* ^b. ^d *in the left margin, in the basic hand.*

---

fol.4r,   Intra Civitatem   IV
the first lines are highly corroded:

[Item ibidem parvum cellarium subtus ponte] domini Johannis predicto a/ [parte orientali — modo possidet Hermannus Lineman.] ^aHermannus Lineman^a

Item super Oudwicam sancti Johannis, domum et aream cum pomerio prout iacent super Oudwicam predictam, inter domum et aream domini Ghiseberti de Lonen presbyteri a parte meridionali, et domum et aream domicelle Heylewigis de Scalcwiic a parte aquiloni, extendentes se a Communi Platea civitatis versus orientem usque ad domum et aream domicelle Machtildis de Rodenborch prout modo possident dominus Gerardus de Hermalen presbyter, necnon Fya, Machteldis et Katherina eius sorores de Beyarden, ad vitam eorum, sub annua pensione <u>VI librarum denariorum</u> Traiectensium Victoris et Pasche solvendarum, sub condicionibus quod huiusmodi edificia in dicta area constructa et construenda sub eorum expensis in tegminibus et aliis structuris sanis et congruis servabunt, constructaque et construenda in eadem area post earum obitum nostros ad usus ibidem illesa remanebunt. Et est secundum tenorem littere qua utimur super illo
^b<u>Dominus Gerardus et eius sorores de Beyarden ad vitam</u>^b

Item in fine pomerii nostri, iuxta locum dictum Scupstoel, habet dicta domus beate Katherine quatuor domos cum areis insimul constructas, quibus nostrum pomerium propius iacet a parte aquilonis et Jacobus filius Hugonis Eren cum una domo et area a parte meridionali, extendentes se a Communi Platea versus occidentem usque ad nostrum ortum olerum. Quarum domorum unam cum eius area, nostro pomerio a latere aquilonis vicinius et contiguam modo possidet ^cdomicella Aleydis Taetzen pro^c ^dModo possidet Gouda ad vitam eius pro VII libris annuatim sub condicionibus prout littera tenet.^d Gouda^e

---

^a *in the right margin, cancelled.* ^b *in the right margin.* ^c *added in smaller writing over an erased line, cancelled.* ^d *in another hand (D).* ^e *in the right margin, in the same hand as d.*

fol.4v,   Civilis Ecclesie
starts with two corroded lines:

[Item secundam domum — pronunc possidet]/ [-——]/ Pasche.
ᵃLubbargis de Davantriaᵃ

Item tertiam domum ibidem cum suis attinenciis modo possidet
Henricus de Speculo ad IIII annos ab anno LXVII *[1367]* Pasche
pro VIII libris X solidis/ annuatim Victoris et Pasche solvendis.
ᵇUlterius dabit X libras ad X annos ab anno LXX *[1370]* Victoris.ᵇ
ᵃHenricus de Speculo.ᵃ

Item ibidem quartam domum cum suis attinenciis modo possidet
Aleydis de Damme pro   ᶜ
ᵃAleydis de Dammeᵃ

ᵈItem in Vico Pistorum, aream qua superius propius cum proprietate
iacent heredes Petri Mauricii, et inferius heredes aut successores Ely-
zabet de Colonia, quam modo possident Wilhelmus filius Wilhelmi
de Loesdrecht et Henricus Kroec pro VII solidis annuatim Victoris et
Pasche solvendis.ᵈ ᵉdit is qwiit ghecoftᵉ
ᶠWilhelmus Wilhelmi et Henricus Kroecᶠ

Item ibidem aream, qua superius vicinius iacent successores Elysabeth de Colonia et inferius heredes aut successores Hugonis de
Hundswijc, quam modo possidet Gherburgis de Lexsmunde, solvendis X solidis annuatim Victoris et Pasche.
ᶠGherburgis de Lexsmundeᶠ

ᵃ *in the left margin, cancelled.* ᵇ *in another hand (B).* ᶜ *not filled in.* ᵈ *cancelled.*
ᵉ *in a different hand.* ᶠ *in the left margin, in the basic hand.*

fol.5r,   Intra Civitatem   V
the first lines are heavily corroded:

[Item ibidem propius aream — quam -]/ [—]
ᵃheredes Hugonis de Hundswijcᵃ

Item ibidem propius aream etiam iam supradicte aree contiguam,
quam modo possidet Dietmarus Pawe pro IIII solidis annuatim Victoris et Pasche solvendis. Quam aream una cum duabus precedenti-
bus areis dedit nostre domui Otto de Zulen pro perpetua memoria
nutricisᵇ sue Odilie.
ᵃDietmarus Paweᵃ

Item <u>In die Linemarct</u>, dimidiam aream, quam dedit soror nostra
Machteldis Schiven, situatam supra vicum dictum Vuelsteghe inter
eundem vicum a parte meridionali, et aream in qua nunc manet
Ghisebertus Backer filius Gerardi Weddeloep a parte aquilonis.
ᶜQuam sub hereditario pactu XX grossorum annuatim possidemus.ᶜ
Exinde domus nostra habebit VIII libras annuatim denariorum
Traiectensium perpetuo Victoris et Pasche. Inde habemus litteram
civitatis, tali signo ⊔ ᵈ signatam.
ᵉdictus Coeldou modo possidet et solvet annuatimᵉ
Coeldouᶠ

Item <u>In die oude Sprincwijc</u>, iuxta locum dictum Scupstoel, iacet una
area qua superius propius iacet Communis Platea qua itur versus
murum civitatis et inferius area Petri uten Leene, cuius aree medietas
ex donacione legitima sororis nostre Machteldis Schiven ad dictam
domum nostram pertinet et devenit. Ex qua medietate domus habet
annuatim <u>III libras</u> denariorum Traiectensium perpetue Victoris et
Pasche. Reliquam vero medietatem dicte aree pro nunc possident
Otto de Yselsteyne cum eius uxore filia Alberti Alvekin et eiusdem
uxoris senior filius quem genuit apud Theodericum Schive eiŭs mari-
tum.
ᵉYda de Hokelem et Heylewigis de Vuchten modo possident et solvent de nostra medietate aree annuatimᵉ ᵍ
ᶠYda de Hokelem et Heylewigis de Vuchtenᶠ

ᵃ *in the right margin.* ᵇ *uncertain reading ms.* ᶜ *cancelled.* ᵈ *kind of a coat of arms
with a perpendicular line in the middle.* ᵉ *added in smaller writing under the text.* ᶠ *in
the right margin, in the same hand as* ᵉ. ᵍ *not filled in*

fol.5v,   <u>Civilis Ecclesie et sancti Nicolai</u>
the first lines are rather corroded:

Item <u>In die</u> [Linepad extra muros civitatis aream situatam recte] ex
op/posito [ecclesie sancte Marie inter aream Johannis Liebaerd. a
parte superiori et aream]/ heredum Gerardi Gulden a parte inferiori,
quam idem Gerardus possidebat ad vitam eius <u>pro VIII grossis an-
nuatim</u> Victoris et Pasche. Modo possidet eandem ᵃ
ᵇ<u>Gerardus Gulden</u>ᵇ

Item ibidem Aream quam mater Ernesti quondam possidebat, solventem annuatim <u>I libram</u> denariorum Traiectensium dandam ad
vinum in Pascha.
ᵇ<u>mater Ernesti</u>ᵇ

Item <u>Apud Ameydam Fabrorum</u>, aream iacentem in Vico Fabrorum a parte aquilonis iuxta Ameydam Fabrorum, qua superius et inferius moniales sancti Servacii propius sunt situate. Quam nunc possident Fredericus filius Conradi et Agneza eius uxor pro XX grossis annuatim Victoris et Pasche, ad vitam eorum.
^bFredericus Conradi et eius uxor ad vitam^b

Item aream situatam inter fabros, inter aream Gerardi Homboud a parte superiori, et aream heredum Arnoldi de Velde a parte inferiori, quam modo possidet Henricus de Wesel pro XX grossis annuatim Victoris et Pasche.
^bHenricus de Wesel^b

Item in die Twistrate, aream iacentem inter aream Gerardi Coman a parte superiori, et aream Tidemanni Pampoys a parte inferiori, quam possidebat quondam Dankardus. Modo possidet eandem Lodewicus de Zanctis <u>pro XXIIII grossis annuatim</u>, Victoris et Pasche.
^bLodewicus de Zanctis^b

---

^a *not filled in.* ^b *in the left margin.*

fol.6r.   <u>Intra Civitatem, Civilis Ecclesie</u>   VI

Item <u>onder die Scutemakers</u>, duas areas collatas quondam a fratre Becekino, prout iacent inter aream heredum Herbordi de Palaes a parte superiori, et aream Johannis Homboud a parte inferiori, quas modo possidet idem Johannes Homboud <u>pro XL grossis</u> annuatim Victoris et Pasche.
^aJohannes Homboud^a

Item in Vico Straminum, aream situatam inter aream Jacobi Cloyer a parte superiori et aream quam Wilhelmus Ghele a nobis hereditarie possidet a parte inferiori, quam modo possidet Everardus Trindo <u>pro XX grossis annuatim</u>, Victoris et Pasche et II pullis.
^aEverardus Trindo^a

Item ibidem, aream, in eodem vico situatam inter predictam aream quam Everardus Trindo nunc possidet a nobis a parte superiori, et aream Johannis Jacobi Houtschemaker a parte inferiori, quam modo possidet Wilhelmus Ghele <u>pro XX grossis annuatim</u> Victoris et Pasche, perpetue. Inde est littera.
^aWilhelmus Ghele^a

Item In die Gaerde, aream sitam ad litus aquarum fossati, super quam nunc parva domus est constructa, solventem nobis annuatim XVI solidos VII denarios Victoris et Pasche, perpetue. Henricus Ramkin nunc solvet. ᵇModo possidet Stephanus de Rietvelt.ᵇ
ᶜHenricus Ramkinᶜ
ᵈStephanus de Rietveltᵈ

Item iuxta Pontem Urbis seu Castri, aream in qua domus sancti Spiritus nunc est constructa, solventem annuatim XXVI grossos. Sed inde recipiunt canonici sancti Salvatoris annuatim X grossos, et nos partem residuam scilicet XVI grossos annuatim Victoris et Pasche, perpetue
ᵃprocurator domus sancti Spiritusᵃ

ᵃ *in the right margin.* ᵇ *in a different hand.* ᶜ *in the right margin, cancelled.* ᵈ *in the right margin, in the same hand as b.*

fol.6v.   Civilis Ecclesie, intra Civitatem

Item ibidem, in Foro Salis, aream, quam quondam possidebat Lyza Gherlaci, ad vitam suam pro X grossis annuatim. Modo autem ᵃ
Notaᵇ

In Veteri Cimiterio, aream, situatam inter aream Johannis et Gerardi Pot fratrum a parte orientali et aream ᵃ a parte occidentali, quam modo possidet Wilhelmus Werloep pro V grossis annuatim Victoris et Pasche.
ᵇWilhelmus Werloepᵇ

Item ibidem, aream, solventem annuatim I libram bonorum denariorum pro qua heredes domini Johannis Vrenken solent dare vinum fratribus et infirmis in Nativitate Domini.

In Platea Fratrum Minorum, aream, sitam inter domum et aream Jacobi de Jutfaes a parte superiori, et domum et aream domini Johannis de Bosynchem a parte inferiori, quam nunc possidet dominus Fredericus Richardi presbyter, solvens exinde nobis V grossis annuatim Victoris et Pasche.
ᵇdominus Fredericus Richardiᵇ

ᵃ *not filled in.* ᵇ *in the left margin.*

fol.7r,   In parrochia Sancti Jacobi, intra Civitatem   VII
the first lines are rather corroded:

[In parrochia sancti Jacobi in loco dicto Boventorp in platea ducan-
te]/ ab ecclesia Predicatorum versus Curtim Baghinarum, [aream
situatam inter]/ domum et aream Johannis Lisse [—] a parte superiori et aream ^{a} / ^{a} a parte inferiori, solventem nobis annuatim [XX]
grossos Victoris et Pasche/ de quibus nunc solvent quedam bagute
commorantes super eandem ex anteriori parte eiusdem aree XVIII
grossos annuatim, necnon Elisabet, Fya, et Aleydis van der Meer II
grossos annuatim, de posteriori parte aree predicte.
^{b}Quedam bagute et sorores^b

Item ibidem Boventorp, onder die Louwers, aream, qua nunc a superiori parte Hermannus de Vinne et inferius heredes Arnoldi Proys
propius cum areis sunt situati, quam quondam possidebat dictus Mi-
zeler et eius uxor. Nunc autem possidet Matheus filius Gerardi de
Molendino. Solvet X grossos annuatim Victoris et Pasche.
^{b}Matheus Gerardi de Molendino^b

Item in Vico Predicatorum, aream, quam tenemus a capitulo sancti
Johannis Traiectensis, sub annua pensione X solidorum. Que divisa
est ita quod super maiorem partem huius aree a parte occidentali
versus fossatum aquarum habemus domum constructam, quam
modo una cum area possidet Wilhelmus Passard et Ghertrudis eius
uxor filia Arnoldi Noyden ad vitam eorum pro XII loet argenti aut
pagamento equivalenti annuatim Victoris et Pasche. Sub condicione
quod dictam domum in omnibus suis structuris sanam et integram
servabunt, acsi domus eadem ad ipsos personaliter spectaret sub eorum expensis, et constructa et construenda ibidem post eorum obitum nobis integre remanebunt. Et si deficerent in solucione et
condicionibus caderint ab omni iure, secundum tenorem littere qua
utimur super illis. ^{c}Modo possidet dictam aream Ghertrudis predicta
hereditarie pro VI loet argenti annuatim sub condicionibus in littera
exinde contentis.^{c}
^{d}Wilhelmus Passard et eius uxor ad vitam^d
^{e}Ghertrudis eius uxor modo possidet hereditarie^e

^{f}Item ibidem propius minor pars de predicta area a parte orientali
dictarum domus et aree situata, quam pronunc una cum domo super
eandem constructa possidet Hubertus Mandemaker pro X solidis
annuatim, Victoris et Pasche.
^{b}Hubertus Mandemaker^b

^gcaret annis^g

---

^a *not filled in.* ^b *in the right margin.* ^c *in a different hand (C).* ^d *in the right margin, cancelled.* ^e *in the right margin, in the same hand as c.* ^f *linked with brace to the foregoing item.* ^g *in the left margin, in another hand (D).*

fol.7v,   Sancti Jacobi
the first lines are heavily corroded, the fourth item only to some extent:

[Item in Cimiterio sancti Jacobi —]/ [———]/ [de quibus areis nunc — eius solvent nobis]/ [annuatim XXII grossos Victoris et Pasche perpetue.]
^aProcuratores ecclesie sancti Jacobi^a

Item in Vico Aquarum, aream situatam iuxta Cimiterium sancti Jacobi a parte aquilonis inter aream Johannis de Clarenborch a parte superiori, et aream dicte ecclesie sancti Jacobi a parte inferiori, quam nunc possidet Johannes de Endoven solvens XX grossos annuatim Victoris et Pasche.
^aJohannes de Eyndoven^a

Item Super Harenam, aream quam superius propius iacet area heredum Hermanni Capellani et inferius Bernardus Spronc cum una area quam tenet ab una capellania in ecclesia sancti Jacobi fundata. Hanc prescriptam aream possidebant Johannes Albus filius Henrici Ralof et Bernardus Spronc. Modo possidet eandem Johannes Meye, solvens exinde II grossos annuatim
^aJohannes Meye^a

Item supra Campum dictum Op sent Jacobs velt, aream, qua a superiori/ parte propius iacet area ^b et inferius domus nostra parrochialis cum/ una area [quam nunc Theodericus de Weyda possidet,] solvens annuatim X solidos.
^aTheodericus de Weyda^a

Item ibidem propius unam partem de area prescripta quam Ghisebertus de Papendorp a nobis possidebat, et quam nunc possidet Theodericus de Weyda, solvens exinde V solidos annuatim Victoris et Pasche.
^aTheodericus de Weyda^a

---

^a *in the left margin.* ^b *not filled in.*

fol.8r,   <u>Intra Civitatem</u>   VIII
the first lines are highly corroded:

Item [ibidem propius medietatem unius aree, cuius] reliqua medietas
ad/ [Ecclesiam Civilem pertinet — et possidebat Ghisebertus de]
Papendorp./ [Nunc — Theodericus de Weyda] possidet eandem pro
VI solidis VIII denariis/ annuatim [Victoris et Pasche.]
^a<u>Theodericus de Weyda</u>^a

Item ibidem aream, continens XII virgatas et I quartale virgate in
longitudine et IIII virgatas et quartale unius virgate in anteriori parte
a parte meridionali, et tres virgatas in posteriori parte a parte aquilonis in latitudine continens, prout sita est inter aream quondam Wilhelmi Koken a parte superiori et aream quondam Clementie filie
Frederici Honichs, et eandem quondam possidebat Hermannus
Vrencke. Modo possident Gerardus de Reno et Johannes frater eius,
sub annua pensione <u>XXVI solidorum VIII denariorum</u> pagamenti
Traiectensis Victoris et Pasche. Quod si possessor dicte aree in solucione defecerit, tenebitur extunc in primis ad duplicatam^b pensionem.
Quam si tunc non solveret primo termino sequenti cum pacto principali caderet ab omni iure secundum tenorem littere qua utimur super
illo.
^a<u>Gerardus de Reno</u>^a

Item ibidem, aream, quam quondam una cum area immediate
subscripta frater Arnoldus Ghiselmar contulit domui nostre, qua superius Loef Herbord et inferius custos ecclesie sancte Ghertrudis propius cum areis iacent, quam Fredericus de Woert possidebat. Modo
possidet Gerardus Pijl filius eius <u>pro I libra annuatim</u> Victoris et
Pasche.
^a<u>Gerardus Pijl</u>^a

^cItem ibidem retro aream iam dictam, unam aream, qua superius
heredes Huberti Sutoris, et inferius heredes Frederici predicti vicinius
iacent, quam quondam Ghisebertus Textor possidebat. Modo possidet Gerardus Pijl predictus <u>pro X grossis annuatim</u>, Victoris et Pasche.
^a<u>Gerardus Pijl</u>^a

---

^a *in the right margin.* ^b duplatam *ms.* ^c *linked with brace to the foregoing item.*

fol.8v, <u>Sancti Jacobi, intra Civitatem</u>
the first four lines are highly corroded:

Item <u>Opten Camp</u>, aream [sitam in parte meridionali platee]/ qua
superius Boudewinus Witte, et inferius [— Gerardus Bole cum]/
areis iacent. Quam modo possident [heredes —]/ et Gerardi Bolen
pro <u>V grossis annuatim</u>, Victoris [et Pasche.]
^a<u>heredes Gerardi Bole</u>^a

Item ibidem, duas areas, sitas inter aream Bartholomei de Campo a
parte superiori et aream ecclesie sancti Jacobi a parte inferiori, quas
Wilhelmus Vuylvoet a nobis possidebat ad vitam suam. Modo pos-
sidebit easdem Aleydis Bouwers ad X annos ab anno LXVIII *[1368]*
Pasche <u>pro VI libris denariorum</u> Traiectensium annuatim, Victoris et
Pasche.
^aAleydis Bouwers^a

Item ibidem magnam et amplam aream quondam orti nostri olerum,
et domum desuper constructam prout iacet prope murum civitatis ex
opposito turris dicte vulgariter Bollardstoern infra aream capituli
sancte Marie a parte orientali et infra viam communem civitatis iuxta
murum circuiens. Quam una cum domo modo possidet Gerardus
Taetze ad XII annos ab anno LXI *[1361]* Victoris <u>pro XV libris XV</u>
<u>solidis</u> denariorum Traiectensium annuatim, Pasche et Victoris, sub
condicionibus in littera quam super hoc habemus contentis.
^b¶ Modo dictam aream possident Wilhelmus Gardener et Benedicta
eius uxor ad X annos ab anno LXX *[1370]* Victoris pro XXVI libris
denariorum Traiectensium et VI caponibus annuatim absque defalcatione. Non ulterius locabunt alicui absque consensu et solvent Pasche et Victoris vel cadent ab omni iure, et cetera prout littera tenet.
Per fratrem Thomam.^b
^c¶ Modo possidet Wilhelmus de Eyc ad XXV annos ab anno LXXIX
[1379] Pasche pro XXXIII libris denariorum Traiectensium et VI
caponibus annuatim absque defalcatione. Solvet Victoris et Pasche
vel cadet ab omni iure et cetera prout littera tenet.^c
^dGerardus Taetze^d
^eWilhelmus Gardener^e
^fWillem van Eyc^f

---

^a *in the left margin.* ^b *in a different hand (B).* ^c *in another hand (C).* ^d *in the left
margin, cancelled.* ^e *in the left margin, in the same hand as* ^b. ^f *in the left margin, in yet
another hand.*

fol.9r.   <u>Sancti Jacobi, intra Civitatem</u>   IX

^adie voers. hofstede heeft Willem van Eyc ten erfpacht elx jaers om XXXIIII lb. Stat paye ende VI capoenen te betalen die ene helfte vanden ghelde ende die capoenen Victoris ende die ander helfte tot Pasche vel infra mensem vel cadet ab omni iure et cetera.^a

Item ibidem, aream, cum domo desuper constructa, quam superius Henricus Witte et inferius Petrus Zoudenbalch^b seu eius successores cum areis propius iacent, qua etiam a parte meridionali Communis Platea civitatis propius et a parte aquilonis communis via et murus civitatis, quam una cum domo quondam possidebat frater Johannes Ouderman. Modo possident easdem Cristina filia Hermanni Pistoris uten Weerde, et Margareta filia Hermanni, que fuit ancilla quondam dicti fratris Johannis ad vitam earum pro XXXII solidis annuatim denariorum Traiectensium solvendis infra quindenam post Victoris et Pasche, vel cadent ab omni iure et cetera sub condicionibus in littera super hoc optenta contentis.
^cCristina filia Hermanni Pistoris et Margareta ad vitam earum^c

---

   ^a *in a different hand.* ^b Zoudenbach *ms.* ^c *in the right margin, in the basic hand.*

fol.9v.   <u>Sancti Jacobi, in den Weyrde</u>

<u>In den Weyrde extra muros civitatis</u> a latere orientali aream situatam inter aream Symonis de Loesden a parte superiori, et aream Jacobi filii Conradi a parte inferiori. Cuius aree medietatem nunc possidet Johannes Mant filius Ecberti et Bertradis eius uxor <u>pro II grossis annuatim.</u>
^aJohannes Mant et eius uxor Bertradis^a

^bReliquam vero medietatem dicte aree, quam quondam Godefridus Stephani possidebat pronunc possidet Adam Dorrinc, et Cristina uxor eius pro <u>II grossis annuatim.</u>
^aAdam Dorrinc et Cristina eius uxor^a

Item ibidem, aream, qua superius Johannis filius Symonis, et inferius Henricus Pawe cum areis propius iacent. Quam modo possidet dictus Bronijs filius Gerardi pro <u>IIII grossis annuatim,</u> Victoris et Pasche.
^a<u>Bronijs filius Gerardi</u>^a

Item ibidem, aream, qua canonici sancti Johannis Traiectensis a superiori parte, et Fya filia Thome a parte inferiori cum area de qua
XII grossos habemus annuatim propius iacent. Quam modo possidet
Gerardus de Veno pro VIII grossis annuatim Victoris et Pasche.
ªGerardus de Venoª

Item ibidem propius, aream, qua superius Gerardus de Veno, et inferius heredes Jacobi van den Herte cum areis vicinius iacent. Quam
modo possidet Petrus Bonteroc pro XII grossis annuatim, Victoris et
Pasche.
ªPetrus Bonteroc
ᶜdit is vercoftᶜ

ª *in the left margin.* ᵇ *linked with brace to the foregoing item.* ᶜ *in a different hand.*

fol.10r.   In den Weyrde   X

Item ibidem, tres areas insimul situatas, inter aream Henrici de Otterspoer a parte superiori, et aream Hermanni Pellificis a parte inferiori, quarum unam nunc possidet Albertus filius Scillinxs et Aleydis
eius uxor pro V grossis annuatim.
ªAlbertus filius Scillinxsª

ᵇReliquam vero aream nunc possidet Jacobus Snider filius Godefridi
pro V grossis annuatim Victoris et Pasche.
ªJacobus Snider filius Godefridiª

ᵇTerciam vero aream de tribus areis predictis, modo possidet Johannes filius Wolteri Lutifiguli ad vitam Ottonis Potter pro VIII grossis
annuatim, Victoris et Pasche.
ªJohannes filius Wolteriª

ª *in the right margin.* ᵇ *linked with braces to the foregoing item.*

fol.10v.   *is blank.*

fol.11r.   ¶ In parrochia sancti Jacobi extra Civitatem   XI

In parrochia sancti Jacobi, extra civitatem, primo apud Zulen, quartale terre prout iacet in iurisdictione domini de Zulen, quo nunc

superius Wolterus de Colen et Hermannus de Vinen cives Traiectenses et inferius dominus de Zulen cum dimidio manso propius iacent.
Quod modo possidet Lubbertus filius Nycolai ad vitam eius pro <u>VII
libris denariorum Traiectensium II talentis cere et IIII caponibus</u>
annuatim, infra quindenam post Petri et Martini solvendis absque
defalcatione. Et erit nostre domui et nobis fidelis amicus in omnibus
quibus poterit vel cadet ab omni iure. Habet litteram exinde et nos e
converso. Per fratrem Johannem de Via Lapidea commendatorem,
sub data anni LI *[1351]* Valentini.
[a]¶ Post mortem [b]fratris[b] dicti Lubberti possidet dictam terram Nicolaus de Wiel frater eius ad XV annos pro XV libris pagamenti
Traiectensis cum ceteris superius notatis.[a]
[c]¶ Modo possidet Ghisbertus Alberti.[c]
[d]Lubbertus filius Nycolai ad vitam[d]
[e]<u>Ghisbert Albertzn</u>[e]

Item ibidem <u>unum iuger</u> prout iacet in eadem iurisdictione domini de
Zulen, iuxta monasterium Vallis Sancte Marie, quod possident moniales eiusdem monasterii <u>pro XX grossis annuatim,</u> Martini et Petri
solvendis.
[f]<u>Moniales Vallis Sancte Marie</u>[f]

---

[a] *in a different hand (D).* [b] *cancelled.* [c] *in another hand.* [d] *in the right margin,
cancelled.* [e] *in the right margin, in the same hand as* [c]. [f] *in the right margin, in the basic
hand.*

fol.11v.   <u>Sancti Jacobi extra Civitatem</u>

Item ibidem, quatuor iugera cum dimidio, prout iacent in iurisdictione domini de Zulen, inter terram Theoderici Bole a parte superiori,
et terram Johannis de Landscrone civium Traiectensium a parte inferiori. Que vero iugera modo possidet Johannes Benscop filius Gerardi
<u>ad X annos</u> ab anno LXV *[1365]* Epiphanie Domini, pro <u>X libris
XVII solidis et IIII pullis</u> annuatim, absque defalcatione infra quindenam post Martini et Petri solvendis vel cadet ab omni iure. Habet
litteram et nos e converso per fratrem Hugonem de Coudenkerc
dispensatorem.
[a]¶ Item Johannes ulterius possidebit dictam terram prout iacet ad X
annos ab anno LXXV *[1375]* Petri pro XVIII libris IIII pullis
annuatim.[a]
[b]¶ Modo predictam terram possidebit ulterius Ghisebertus de Middach ad X annos ab anno LXXXV *[1385]* Purificacio sancte Marie
pro IIII antiquis scudatis monete Cesaris aut Francie vel pro equiva-

lenti pagamento et IIII pullis annuatim, solvendis Martini et Petri, vel
cadet ab omni iure. Non ulterius locabit vel segregabit dictam terram
absque licencia commendatoris vel dispensatoris. Habet litteram et
nos e converso, per fratrem Johannem de Arnem dispensatorem.[b]
[c]Ulterius dictam terram possidebit Rutgher filius Petri ad X annos ab
anno XCIIII *[1394]* Lamberti pro VI antiquis scudatis in forma ut
supra.
[d]Johannes Benscop[d]
[e]Ghisebert van Middach[e]

---

[a] *in a different hand (B).* [b] *in another hand (E).* [c] *in still another hand.* [d] *in the left margin, cancelled.* [e] *in the left margin, in the same hand as* [b].

fol.12r.   Sancti Jacobi extra Civitatem, supra vhenum   XII

Item In den Achtienhoven, in iurisdictione temporali prepositi sancti
Johannis Traiectensis, quartale terre prout iacet inter terram monialium monasterii Vallis Sancte Marie a parte inferiori, quod modo
possident Machteldis relicta Henrici Bilen et Nella eius filia ad vitam
earum pro VI libris denariorum Traiectensium II talentis cere et IIII
pullis annuatim, infra XIIII dies post Martini et Petri solvendis, vel
cadent ab omni iure. Inde habent litteram per fratrem Johannem de
Via Lapidea commendatorem.
[a]¶ post obitum dicte Machteldis possidebit Nicolaus de Wiel dictam
terram ad XVI annos una cum duobus quartalibus terre sequentibus
ab alia parte huius folii, pro XLVIII libris pagamenti Traiectensis
cum ceteris superius et inferius signatis.[a]
[b]Machtildis relicta Henrici Bilen[b]

---

[a] *in a different hand.* [b] *in the right margin.*

fol.12v.   Sancti Jacobi extra Civitatem, supra venum

Item ibidem duo quartalia prout iacent In den XVIII Hoeven in
dicta iurisdictione prepositi sancti Johannis, inter terram monasterii
Albarum Dominarum in Traiecto a parte orientali, et terram heredum Arnoldi Gunters a parte occidentali, prout illam quondam Bernardus nostre domus famulus et eius liberi possidebant. Que duo
quartalia modo possident Machteldis relicta Henrici Bilen et Nella
eius filia ad vitam earum pro XVI libris denariorum Traiectensium et
VIII caponibus. Et vehent II hont cespitum annuatim absque defalcatione, solvendis infra XIIII dies post Martini et Petri vel possunt

expandari in omnibus bonis eorum ubicumque situatis. Et constituent fideiussores pro pacto si requiritur ab eis, secundum tenorem littere quam super hoc habemus. Per fratrem Johannem de Via Lapidea commendatorem.

^a¶ Post obitum dicte Machteldis possidebit dictam terram una cum uno quartali superius ab alio latere signato ad XVI annos pro annua pensione ab alio latere signata.^a

^bMachteldis relicta <u>Henrici Bilen</u>^b

---

^a *in a different hand (C).* ^b *in the left margin.*

fol.13r,   <u>Sancti Jacobi extra Civitatem, supra venum</u>   XIII
the first lines are rather corroded.

Item ibidem [<u>dimidium mansum</u> prout iacet in eadem iurisdictione prepositi sancti]/ Johannis In den XVIII hoeven, [quo Tidemannus de Luttekenhuys et]/ Hermannus [Brunt propius iacent cum uno quartali communiter] a parte superiori et/ [Wiburgis relicta Stephani Monbar cum dimidio manso a] parte inferio/ri. Quem dimidium mansum pronunc possident dicta Wiburgis et Johannes Monbaer et dictus Beer Monbar eius filius ad vitam eorum trium, pro <u>VIII libris denariorum Traiectensium annuatim</u> absque defalcatione, solvendis Martini et Petri. Per fratrem W. de Oerschoten dispensatorem.

^a¶ Modo ulterius possidebunt dictam terram prout iacet inter terram relicte Hermanni Brunt et suorum heredum a parte superiori et terram dicti Beer Monbar a parte inferiori, dictus Beer Monbaer et eius uxor Fya filia domini Ghisberti de Nyenrode, et Splinterus et Johannes Monbar eorum liberi, ad vitam eorum quatuor, pro VIII libris denariorum Traiectensium annuatim absque defalcatione solvendis Martini et Petri. Per commendatorem.^a

^bWiburgis relicta Stephani Monbar et cetera^b
^cBeer Monbar <u>et Fia eius uxor</u> et cetera^c

---

^a *in a different hand.* ^b *in the right margin, cancelled.* ^c *in the right margin in the same hand as* ^a.

fol.13v,   <u>Sancti Jacobi extra Civitatem, supra venum</u>
the first lines are rather corroded.

Item [ibidem <u>dimidium mansum</u> prout iacet in eadem iuridictione] prepositi sancti Johannis/ [extendentem se superius a communi via ibidem versus vhenum inter terram]/ [dominorum sancti Johannis Traiectensis a] parte superiori, et terram heredum Stephani Monbar/ a parte inferiori, super quem nunc moratur Margareta infrascripta,/ et quem eadem Margareta cum liberis suis subscriptis una cum quartali/ terre immediate [sequenti] sub annua pensione subscripta possidebit/ ad vitam eius et puerorum suorum inferius nominatorum.

Item ibidem <u>quartale</u> quod seminari potest, prout iacet extra viam inter locum dictum Hoeftdijc et inter viam ducentem et transeuntem per XVIII mansos dictos vulgariter Achtienhoeven, quo superius Johannes Crane et inferius heredes Wilhelmi Vlamync propius cum terris eorum sunt situati. Quod quartale una cum dimidio manso prescripto modo possident Margareta relicta Heynonis filii Machteldis ad vitam eius et ad vitam puerorum suorum, scilicet Jacobi, Machtildis, Hugonis, Griete, Elzebele, et Griete, quos ab Heynone eius quondam marito genuit <u>pro VIII libris VI solidis VIII denariis denariorum Traiectensium et XII pullis annuatim,</u> et vehent II hont cespitum annuatim absque defalcatione. Solvent infra XIIII dies post Martini et Petri, vel cadent ab omni iure. Inde est littera. Per fratrem Hugonem dispensatorem.
^aMargareta Heyno<u>nis et pueri sui</u>^a

---

^a *in the left margin.*

fol.14r.   <u>Sancti Jacobi extra Civitatem, supra venum</u>   XIIII

Item ibidem <u>dimidium mansum,</u> prout iacet in dicta iurisdictione prepositi sancti Johannis In den Achtienhoven inter terram Hermanni Hoghelant seu eius heredum a parte superiori et terram monialium monasterii Vallis Sancte Marie a parte inferiori. Quem modo possident Hildebrandus Ghisonis, Jacobus eius filius, et Ymma filia Ernesti eiusdem Jacobi uxor, ad vitam eorum trium, <u>pro XIIII libris X grossis, VIII caponibus, VI talentis cere</u> annuatim, absque defalcatione. Et vehent II hont cespitum annuatim. Solvent infra XIIII dies post Martini et Petri, vel cadent ab omni iure. Etiam si dicta Ymma ceteris prescriptis mortuis sola superstes remaneret, et extunc aliud matrimonium contraxerit, extunc nichil iuris ulterius in dicto dimidio manso optineret, nisi de voluntate commendatoris et conventus nostri id ulterius tunc cum suo tutore posset adipisci, secundum tenorem littere quam habemus exinde. Per fratrem Johannem de Via Lapidea commendatorem.

fol.14v.   Sancti Jacobi extra Civitatem, supra vhenum

Item ibidem <u>dimidium mansum,</u> prout iacet in iurisdictione prepositi
sancti Johannis In den XVIII Hoeven, inter terram Johannis Vlaminc
a parte superiori et terram capituli sancti Salvatoris Traiectensis a
parte inferiori, quem modo possidet Albertus Kiviet ad vitam eius <u>pro</u>
<u>XIII libris VI solidis VIII denariis denariorum Traiectensium, IIII</u>
<u>talentis cere et VIII caponibus.</u> Et vehet IIII hont cespitum annuatim
absque defalcatione infra XIIII dies post Martini et Petri solvendis,
vel cadet ab omni iure. Erit nobis et nostre domui fidelis amicus in
omnibus quibus poterit. Et singulis annis constituet fideiussores pro
pacto si requiritur ab eo. Habemus inde litteram. Per fratrem Johannem de Via Lapidea commendatorem.

[a]¶ Modo possident dictam terram iuvenis Albertus Kiviet et Albertus
filius Theodorici eius fratris ad vitam eorum pro XXVII libris denariorum Traiectensium et IIII talentis cere et VIII caponibus. Et vehent quatuor hont cespitum annuatim absque defalcatione, sub
condicionibus prout in littera continetur. Per fratrem Thomam.[a]
[b]Albertus Kiviet[b]
[c]Iuvenis Albertus Kiviet et Albertus <u>filius Theoderici eius fratris</u>[c]

---

[a] *in a different hand (B).* [b] *in the left margin, cancelled.* [c] *in the left margin, in the*
same hand as [a].

fol.15r.   Sancti Jacobi extra Civitatem, supra vhenum   XV

Item ibidem <u>quartale terre cum dimidio quartali,</u> in dicta iurisdictione sancti Johannis prepositi situatum, quo nostra domus personaliter
propius iacet cum uno quartali quod Wilhelmus Merendoc nunc a
nobis possidet a parte superiori, et capitulum sancti Johannis
Traiectensis etiam cum uno quartali, quod nunc colit Vastradus filius
Gerardi uten Enge. Quod quartale cum dimidio modo possidet
Machtildis de Roden, relicta Alberti filii Matte, ad vitam eius <u>pro X</u>
<u>libris et IIII pullis, et vehet IIII hont cespitum annuatim,</u> absque
defalcatione solvendis infra XIIII dies post Martini et Petri, vel cadet
ab omni iure, secundum tenorem littere qua utimur super illo. Per
fratrem Hugonem dispensatorem.

[a]¶ Ulterius possidebit Johannes Splinter Aelberts soen ad vitam ab
anno LXXXVII [1387] Petri pro V oude scilde ende I quartier IIII
hoenre IIII hont mennens. Per fratrem Johannem Haze.[a]
[b]<u>Machteldis de Roden relicta Alberti Matte</u>[b]

---

[a] *in a different hand.* [b] *in the right margin, in the basic hand.*

fol.15v,   Sancti Jacobi extra Civitatem, supra vhenum
the first lines are rather corroded:

Item ibidem quartale vheni prout iacet in dicta iurisdictione preposi-
ti/ [sancti Johannis, inter terram monialium monasterii Albarum
Dominarum] in Traiecto a parte superiori/ [et terram nostre domus
sancte Katerine quam pronunc Machteldis] relicta Alberti/ [filii
Matte a nobis possidet a parte inferiori. Quod quartale quondam
Godefridus]/ [filius Stephani[a] et Elisabet eius neptis a nobis possidebant.] [b]Et postea Wilhelmus Merendoc. Modo possident illud Johannes filius Everardi et Elizabet eius uxor filia Petri Hellinxs ad vitam
eorum pro XXIII loet boni argenti aut pro pagamento equivalenti in
Traiecto et VI pullis annuatim infra quindenam post Martini et Petri
solvendis. Et vehent VI hont cespitum annuatim consuetis temporibus cum requisiti super hoc fuerint, aut cadent ab omni iure, et cetera
prout littera exinde tenet. Per fratrem Hugonem dispensatorem.[b]
[c]Johannes filius Everardi et Elysabet eius uxor ad vitam[c]

---

[a] *uncertain reading ms.* [b] *added in different writing.* [c] *in the left margin.*

fol.16r.   Sancti Jacobi extra Civitatem, supra vhenum   XVI

Item ibidem mansum terre, prout iacet in eadem iurisdictione prepositi sancti Johannis Traiectensis In den Achtienhoven, extendentem se
a communi via usque ad clausuram dictam vulgariter Hecke super
aqueductum seu meatum aquarum stantem, situatum inter terram
Godscalci Vrenken et relicte Nycolai Sloyer Indivisim a parte superiori, et terram Johannis de Vheno a parte inferiori, super quem
mansum modo Rodolphus Mathie et Wendelmodis eius uxor moran-
tur. Et possidebunt eundem una cum quinque virgatis terre postea in
iurisdictione prepositi Traiectensis notatis et situatis, ad vitam eorum,
pro IIII libris denariorum Traiectensium et V pullis annuatim absque
defalcatione Martini et Petri solvendis, sub condicionibus diversis in
litteris quibus super hoc utimus contentis. Post eorum vero obitum
dictus mansus terre, una cum quinque virgatis ad nos libere devolven-
tur. Dummodo tunc statim ad monitionem heredum eorum ipsis he-
redibus satisfecerimus de Ij C *[150]* libris, in quibus ipsis tunc solvere
tenemur, secundum tenorem littere super hoc obtente. Ad cuius in-
spectionem statim post eorum obitum recurratur ad evitandum nocumentum quod exinde domui nostre posset oriri. Per fratrem
Godefridum de Clivis commendatorem et W. de Orschoten dispensatorem actum.

^a¶ Post obitum vero dictorum Rodolphi et eius uxoris, Rodolphus eorum filius possidebit, unum mansum terre predictum ad X annos a die obitus eorum conquirendum. Et dabit tunc exinde XII libras et V pullas annuatim. Per fratrem Jo Gaude commendatorem.^a
<u>^bRodolphus Mathie et Wendelmodis eius uxor</u>^b

---

^a *in a different hand (C).* ^b *in the right margin, in the basic hand.*

fol. 16v.   <u>Sancti Jacobi extra Civitatem, supra vhenum</u>

Item ibidem mansum magni vheni nostri, prout iacet in iurisdictione dicti prepositi sancti Johannis In den XVIII Hoeven, quo nunc superius Johannes Crane et Albertus die Diker, et inferius Johannes de Veno propius iacent, quem mansum modo domus nostra personaliter possidet.
<u>^adomus personaliter possidet</u>^a

Item ibidem, <u>terram dictam Heetvelt</u> ^b-iacentem pro uno manso-^b eiusdem magni vheni nostri prescripti, prout iacet in dicta iurisdictione prepositi sancti Johannis In den Achtienhoven, que quidem terra incipit in fine huiusmodi terre quam Rodolphus Mathie et eius uxor nunc a nobis possident, et extendit se ulterius usque ad locum in quo domus nostra ibidem supra venum est constructa. Quam terram modo possidet Wilhelmus Merendoc familiaris noster et custodiet suis sub sumptibus et expensis, ad vitam suam, absque annua pensione sibi concessa, sub condicionibus in littera qua utimur exinde contentis. Per fratrem Johannem de Via Lapidea commendatorem. ^cModo dictam terram una cum duobus dimidiis mansis inferius signatis possidebunt ulterius Johannes Snellart et Elisabet eius uxor ad X annos ab anno LXIX *[1369]* Petri. Et solvent annuatim tam de hanc terram quam de aliis sequentibus in universo XX loet argenti aut pagamentum equivalens in Traiecto tempore solucionis infra quindenam post Martini et Petri, aut cadent ab omni iure, et cetera prout littera exinde tenet. Per fratrem ^dHugonem^d ^eJohannem Gaude commendatorem.^{e c}
^f¶ Ulterius idem Johannes et Elisabet eius uxor possidebunt dictam terram una cum duobus dimidiis mansis subsequentibus ad XXII annos ab anno LXXXIII *[1383]* Petri, et solvent annuatim tam de hac terra quam de aliis sequentibus in universo XX loet argenti aut pagamentum equivalens, et vehent II hont cespitum et cetera prout littera tenet. Per fratrem Johannem Gaude.^f
<u>^gJohannes Snellert et Elisabet eius uxor</u>^g

^hItem vehet II hont^h

---

^a *in the left margin.* ^b *in smaller writing above the underlined name.* ^c *added in the same smaller writing.* ^d *cancelled.* ^e *corrected in another hand.* ^f *in a different hand.* ^g *in the left margin in the same hand as* ^{bc}. ^h *in the left margin, in the same hand as* ^e.

fol.17r,   <u>Sancti Jacobi extra Civitatem, supra vhenum</u>   XVII
the first line is somewhat corroded:

Item <u>dimidium mansum</u>, prout iacet ibidem [supra vhenum in iuris-
dictione]/ temporali domini prepositi Traiectensis, quo iuvenis
Rodolphus Mathie a superiori parte, et Johannes Crane et Albertus
Diker ab inferiori parte propius pronunc sunt situati, prout eundem
dimidium mansum modo possidet domus nostra personaliter. ¶^a
^b<u>domus personaliter possidet</u>^b

Item ibidem <u>terram dictam Heetvelt</u> ^c-iacentem pro dimidio manso-^c
eiusdem parvi vheni nostri prout iacet in eadem iurisdictione preposi-
ti Traiectensis, extendentem se a novo meatu aquarum ibidem usque
ad locum dictum Cloestede quo terminatur die Wijc. Quam terram
modo possidet etiam Wilhelmus Merendoc familiaris noster, et custodiet eandem sub suis expensis, ad vitam suam, absque annua pensione sibi concessa, salvo domui nostre loco quo cespites accumulari
possint pro dicte nostre domus commodo et utilitate, et ceteris sub
condicionibus in littera quam super hoc habemus notatis. Per fratrem
Johannem de Via Lapidea commendatorem. ^dModo hanc terram
possidebunt ulterius Johannes Snellart et eius uxor ad XXII annos ab
anno ^eLXXXIII *[1383]*^e Petri, una cum terra superius et eciam inferius super eosdem signata, sub eadem annua pensione superius signa-
ta, et cetera prout littera tenet. Per fratrem ^fHugonem^{fd} ^gJohannem
Gaude commendatorem.^g
^h<u>Johannes Snellert et eius uxor</u>^h

---

^a *two fully erased lines in a later hand.* ^b *in the right margin, cancelled.* ^c *added in smaller writing above the underlined name.* ^d *added in the same smaller writing.* ^e *written over an erased year.* ^f *cancelled.* ^g *corrected in another hand.* ^h *in the right margin in the hand of* ^{cd}.

fol.17v.   <u>Sancti Jacobi, supra vhenum</u>

Item ibidem <u>terram dictam Heetvelt</u>, dictam Popelers land, prout
iacet pro dimidio manso terre in iurisdictione prepositi sancti Johan-

nis Traiectensis, extendentem se a communi via transeunti per vhenum sursum versus locum dictum Drienscoten ab antiquo meatu aquarum usque ad novum meatum. Qua terra pronunc propius iacet a superiori parte dominus Fredericus Richardi presbyter, et a parte inferiori Nycolaus Sloyer cum suis liberis, prout illam possidebat a nobis Wilhelmus Merendoc. Modo possidebunt eandem Johannes Snellart et eius uxor, una cum alia terra superius super eosdem signata ad X annos ab anno LXIX *[1369]* Petri, sub eadem annua pensione superius notata et sub condicionibus prout littera exinde tenet. Per fratrem Hugonem.

[a]¶ Ulterius possidebunt dictam terram[b] ad XXII annos ab anno LXXXIII *[1383]* Petri sub eadem annua pensione superius signata et sub condicionibus ut littera tenet. Per fratrem Johannem Gaude.[a] [c]Johannes Snellart et eius uxor.[c]

---

[a] *in a different hand* [b] *missing in ms.* [c] *in the left margin.*

fol.18r,   Sancti Jacobi supra vhenum   XVIII
the first line is somewhat corroded:

Item IX iugera, prout iacent [in eadem iurisdictione prepositi Traiectensis ab]/ aqueductu seu meatu aquarum dicto vulgariter Hoeftweteringhe ulterius se extendentia usque ad iter dictum Venewech, iacentia inter terram Boudewini Witten iuxta dictum aquameatum, et terram Petri uten Lene apud iter predictum a parte superiori, et inter Ghiseberti Grawert et Gerardi Jepel terram a parte inferiori. Que modo possident a nobis heredes Alphardi de Lichtenberch ad XII annos ab anno LXII *[1362]* Circumcisione Domini pro XII libris denariorum Traiectensium annuatim absque defalcatione Martini et Petri solvendis et cetera, secundum tenorem littere quam inde habemus. Per fratrem Hugonem dispensatorem.

[a]¶ Modo ulterius possidebunt predictam terram Ghisbertus et Nicolaus filii Theodorici Boumans ad X annos ab anno LXXV *[1375]* Agnetis pro XXXVI libris denariorum annuatim Martini et Petri solvendis vel cadent ab omni iure. Et vehent II hont cespitum annuatim cum requisiti fuerint. Habent litteram et nos e converso per fratrem Johannem Gaude vicecommendatorem.[a]

[b]¶ Ulterius dictus Ghisbertus solus possidebit dictam terram ad X annos ab anno LXXXVI *[1386]* Petri pro XLVI libris pagamenti quo pactus solvuntur in Traiecto, Martini et Petri solvendis. Et vehet[c] II hont cespitum annuatim et cetera prout littera tenet. Per fratrem Johannem de Arnhem.[b]

^dAlphardus de Lichtenbergh^d
^eGhisbertus ^fet Nycolaus^f Bouman^fs^{fe}

---

^a *in a different hand (C).* ^b *in another hand (E).* ^c vehent ms. ^d *in the right margin, cancelled.* ^e *in the right margin, in the hand of* ^a. ^f *erased.*

fol.18v, <u>Sancti Jacobi extra Civitatem, supra venum</u>
the first lines are rather corroded:

[Item ibidem <u>quatuor campos continentes dimidium mansum</u>]/
[prout iacet quem Godefridus filius Stephani et Elisabet eius neptis
pos]/[sidebant, quibus quatuor campis superius propius iacet terra
quam Johannes]/ [Crane nunc possidet, que quondam fuit domini de
Apcoude.] Et inferius/ [iacet terra quam Nycolaus Sloyer nunc possidet, nuncupata Sy/mons Viertel. Cuius dimidii mansi medietatem
scilicet duos/ campos vertentes seu extendentes se cum uno fine ad
aggerem/ dictum Smalendijc, et cum alio fine ad reliquos duos campos nostre domus ibidem adiacentes, modo possidet Theodericus
Zasse <u>ad/ X annos ab anno LXIIII *[1364]*</u> Petri <u>pro IX libris et XIIII
solidis denariorum Traiectensium</u>/
annuatim absque defalcatione. Et vehet II hont cespitum annuatim.
Solvet/ Martini et Petri vel cadet ab omni iure. Habet litteram exinde
et nos e converso./ Per fratrem Hugonem dispensatorem.
^aTheodericus Zasse^a

---

^a *in the left margin.*

fol.19r. <u>Sancti Jacobi extra Civitatem, supra venum</u> XIX

Item ibidem reliquam <u>medietatem prescripti dimidii mansi,</u> scilicet
duos campos de quatuor campis predictis prout iacent. Modo possidet Wilhelmus Merendoc ad VIII annos ab anno LXVI *[1366]* Petri
<u>pro X libris denariorum</u> Traiectensium annuatim Martini et Petri
solvendis, vel cadet ab omni iure. Inde habemus litteram. Per fratrem
Hugonem dispensatorem.
^aWillem Merendoc^a

---

^a *in the right margin.*

fol.19v.   Sancti Jacobi extra Civitatem, supra vhenum

Item ibidem <u>mansum terre</u> ᵃ-continentem XVIII iugera-ᵃ prout iacet in iurisdictione prepositi Traiectensis inter terram Margarete Kale-wards a parte superiori et terram quam pronunc Nycolaus de Leyden tenet a domino de Apcoude a parte inferiori, quem quondam a nobis possidebat Theodericus van der Maet. Modo vero medietatem dicti mansi possidet domicella Adelissa de Vloten relicta Tydemanni Zou-debalchs ad vitam eius titulo vendicionis sibi ad vitam eius facte, nichil pensionis inde dans.

ᵇ¶ Modo predictam terram possidet ulterius Theodericus van der Maet ad X annos ab anno LXXIII *[1373]* Petri pro XXXV libris denariorum Traiectensium annuatim Martini et Petri solvendis, vel cadet ab omni iure et cetera prout littera tenet. Per fratrem Thomam.ᵇ

obiitᶜ

ᵈ<u>domicella Adelissa de Vloten</u>ᵈ

ᶜ<u>Dirc van der Maet</u>ᶜ

ᵃ *in smaller writing above the underlined text.* ᵇ *in a different hand (B).* ᶜ *in the left margin, in the same hand as* ᵇ. ᵈ *in the left margin, cancelled.*

fol.20r.   Sancti Jacobi extra Civitatem, supra vhenum   XX

Item <u>reliquam medietatem eiusdem mansi</u> prescripti ᵃscilicet IX iuge-raᵃ modo possident heredes Ghiseberti de Reno ad <u>XII annos</u> ab anno LXII *[1362]* Petri pro <u>XXII libris denariorum Traiectensium et IX pullis</u> annuatim absque defalcatione Martini et Petri solvendis vel cadent ab omni iure.

ᵇUlterius dictam terram possidebunt Johannes filius Goude et Hildebrandus Gansecoper ad X annos ab anno LXX *[1370]* Petri ad Cathedram pro III marcis argenti et IX pullis annuatim, absque de-falcatione solvendis Martini et Petri, vel cadent ab omni iure, secun-dum litteram quam inde habemus. Per fratrem Hugonem dispensatorem.ᵇ

ᶜ<u>Heredes Ghisberti de Reno</u>ᶜ

ᵈ<u>Johannes filius Goude et Hildebrandus Gansecoper</u>ᵈ

ᵃ *added in smaller writing above the underlined text.* ᵇ *added in smaller writing.* ᶜ *in the right margin, cancelled.* ᵈ *in the right margin.*

fol.20v.   Sancti Jacobi extra Civitatem, supra vhenum

Item ibidem binnen weechs, <u>tria quartalia prout iacent</u> in iurisdictione preposition prepositi Traiectensis, inter terram Petri uten Lene a parte superiori, et terram Ghiselberti Grawert a parte inferiori.

Item ibidem <u>quinque virgate terre</u>, prout iacent in eadem iurisdictione inter terram seu vhenum monialium Vallis sancte Marie a parte superiori et inter vhenum nostre domus sancte Katerine a parte inferiori. Que tria quartalia una cum quinque virgatis huiusmodi modo possident ᵃTheodericus Boumanᵃ, Grieta eius uxor, ᵃet Wilhelmus eorum filiusᵃ ad vitam eorum <u>pro VI libris denariorum Traiectensium IIII talentis cere VI caponibus absque</u> defalcatione, et vehent IIII hont cespitum annuatim, solvendis Martini et Petri, vel cadent ab omni iure, sub ceteris condicionibus in littera quam super hoc habemus contentis. Per fratrem Johannem de Via Lapidea commendatorem.
ᵇ<u>Theodericus Bouman</u>ᵇ
ᶜ<u>Grieta eius uxor</u>ᶜ

ᵃ *cancelled.* ᵇ *in the left margin, cancelled.* ᶜ *in the left margin.*

fol.21r.   Sancti Jacobi extra Civitatem, supra vhenum   XXI

Item ibidem <u>quinque virgate terre</u> prout iacent, quibus domus nostra personaliter propius iacet a superiori parte cum prescriptis quinque virgatis quas modo colunt Theodericus Bouman cum eius uxore et filio predictis, et inferius Henricus filius Pelegrimi civis Traiectensis cum uno quartale vheni. Que quinque virgate modo possidet Nicolaus filius Theodericus Bouman ad vitam eius <u>pro VIII libris denariorum Traiectensium</u> annuatim, et <u>vehet IIII hont</u> cespitum annuatim debitis temporibus, solvendis Martini et Petri, vel cadet ab omni iure. Habemus inde litteram. Per fratrem Hugonem dispensatorem.
ᵃ<u>Nicolaus Bouman</u>ᵃ

ᵃ *in the right margin.*

fol.21v.   Sancti Jacobi, supra vhenum

Item ibidem quartale vheni, prout iacet in eadem iurisdictione prepositi Traiectensis, inter terram nostre domus quam modo possidet Johannes Starke a parte superiori, et terram domicelle Hildegondis de Veno, relicte Loef Hazaerds a parte inferiori. Quod modo possident Hugo filius Arnoldi et Matheus filius Hugonis eius cognatus, ad vitam eorum, una cum alio quodam quartali inferius ultra sex folia conscripto, pro *XXVI* loet boni argenti et IIII pullis aut cum pagamento equivalenti, solvendis Martini et Petri, vel cadet ab omni iure et cetera secundum litteram quam inde habemus. Per fratrem Hugonem dispensatorem.
ªHugo filius Arnoldi et Matheus Hugonisª

ª *in the left margin.*

fol.22r,   Sancti Jacobi, supra vhenum   XXII
the first lines are rather corroded:

Item ibidem [quartale vheni, cuius medietas pertinet ad]/ pietanciam [nostram, prout iacet in iurisdictione prepositi Traiectensis,]/ inter terram monialium monasterii Vallis sancte Marie a parte superiori/ et terram nostre domus sancte Katerine a parte inferiori. Quod quartale/ modo possident a nobis Johannes Starke et Stephania eius uxor filia Henrici Maechlem, ad vitam eorum pro X libris/ denariorum Traiectensium annuatim absque defalcatione. Et vehent IIII hont cespitum/ annuatim abª. Inde habebit pietancia nostra V libras annuatim. Solvent/ Martini et Petri, vel cadent ab omni iure. Habemus litteram. Per fratrem Hugonem.
ᵇModo dictam terram ulterius possidebunt Wilhelmus Roede filius Johannis, et Barbara eius uxor filia Gerardi de Wurze ad vitam eorum, pro XXXII libris annuatim pagamenti Traiectensis et vehent IIII hont cespitum. Inde habebit pietancia XVI libras annuatim. Solvent Martini et Petri vel cadent ab omni iure et cetera prout littera tenet.ᵇ
ᶜJohannes Starke et Stephania eius uxorᶜ
ᵈWilhelmus die Rode et Barbara eius uxorᵈ

ª *cancelled.* ᵇ *in a different hand (D).* ᶜ *in the right margin, cancelled.* ᵈ *in the right margin, in the same hand as* ᵇ.

fol.22v,   Sancti Jacobi, supra vhenum
the first lines are highly corroded:

[Item ibidem <u>quartale terre</u> prout iacet inter terram —]/ [— a parte superiori, et terram monialium] monasterii Vallis[a]]/ [in Oudwica a parte inferiori,] quod modo possidet Gerardus filius/ [Johannis Alberni] et Aleydis eius uxor <u>ad X</u> <u>annos</u> ab anno LXV *[1365]*/ Agnetis, <u>pro XV libris denariorum Traiectensium et IIII caponibus, et vehent IIII/ hont cespitum annuatim,</u> absque defalcatione solvendis Martini et Petri/ vel cadent ab omni iure et cetera prout in littera quam inde habemus continetur. Per fratrem/ Hugonem dispensatorem.
[b]Ulterius idem Gerardus et Aleydis eius uxor possidebunt dictam terram ad X annos ab anno LXXV *[1375]* Petri pro XXXII libris denariorum Traiectensium et IIII caponibus annuatim, solvendis Martini et Petri, vel cadent ab omni iure, prout littera tenet. Per fratrem Thomam dispensatorem.[b]
[c]Gerardus filius Jo. Alberni[c]

---

^a *cancelled.* ^b *in a different hand (B).* ^c *in the left margin.*

fol.23r,   Sancti Jacobi supra vhenum   XXIII
the first lines are highly corroded:

Item ibidem [<u>dimidium mansum</u> — prout iacet in]/ iurisdictione predicta [temporali prepositi —]/ in Traiecto et domicella Engela [—]/ a parte superiori, et capitulum sancti Johannis Traiectensis a parte [inferiori, quem modo]/ possidet Godefridus filius Heynonis <u>ad X annos</u> [ab anno LXVIII *[1368]*]/ Valentini pro <u>XIII antiquis scudatis</u> boni auri monete Cesaris aut Francie aut pagamentum equivalens pro eisdem, <u>necnon III talentis cere et VIII pullis, et vehet IIII hont cespitum</u> annuatim, absque defalcatione Martini et Petri solvendis, vel cadet ab omni iure et cetera prout littera continet exinde optenta. Per fratrem Hugonem dispensatorem.
^a<u>Godefridus filius Heynonis</u>^a

---

^a *in the right margin.*

fol.23v,   <u>Sancti Jacobi supra vhenum</u>
the first lines are highly corroded:

Item [ibidem <u>quartale terre</u> prout iacet in iurisdictione] prepositi
Traiectensis inter/ [terram capituli sancte Marie a parte superiori,] et
terram monialium monasterii/ Albarum [Dominarum in Traiecto a
parte inferiori.] Quod modo possidet Johannes/ Haec ad X annos ab
anno LXI *[1361]* Petri <u>pro VI libris et X grossis</u> pagamenti Traiectensis et <u>IIII caponibus.</u> Et vehet <u>IIII hont</u> cespitum annuatim absque
defalcatione. Solvet Martini et Petri vel cadet ab omni iure. Per fratrem Hugonem dispensatorem.
[a]¶ Ulterius possidebit dictam terram Aleydis relicta Johannis Haec ad
X annos ab anno LXXI *[1371]* Petri pro XVI libris denariorum
Traiectensium et IIII caponibus. Et vehet IIII hont cespitum annuatim absque omni defalcatione, sub condicionibus in littera contentis.
Per fratrem Johannem Gaude.[a]
[b]¶ Ulterius possidebit Johannes filius Hermanni ad X annos ab anno
LXXXIX *[1389]* Petri pro XXII libris IIII capoen et vehet IIII hont
cespitum annuatim absque omni defalcatione.[b]
[c]Johannes Haec[c]
[d]<u>Aleydis relicta eius</u>[d]

---

   [a] *in a different hand (C).* [b] *in another hand.* [c] *in the left margin, cancelled.* [d] *in the left margin, in the same hand as* [a].

fol.24r.   <u>Sancti Jacobi, supra vhenum</u>   XXIV

Item ibidem <u>quartale vheni</u> prout iacet in iurisdictione predicta inter
terram monialium monasterii sancti Servacii Traiectensis a parte superiori, et terram capituli sancte Marie Traiectensis a parte inferiori.

Item ibidem <u>duo iugera,</u> versus vhenum se extendentia de quibus
quondam Jacobus de Nyendael habuit annuatim a nobis XIIj *[12.5]*
galinas et I pullam. Quos redditus quitos emimus ab Alphardo de
Nyendal eius germano et a relicta dicti Jacobi uxore Johannis de
Speculo. Que duo iugera una cum quartale predicto modo possident
Godefridus filius Arnoldi et Johannes eius frater pro <u>VI libris VIII</u>
<u>denariis, VI caponibus et I pulla</u> annuatim. Et vehent annis singulis
<u>IIII hont</u> cespitum absque defalcatione ad vitam eorum, Martini et
Petri solvendis, vel cadent ab omni iure, secundum litteram quam
inde habemus. Per fratrem Johannem de Via Lapidea commendato-
rem.

^aGodefridus filius Arnoldi et Johannes frater eius^a

---

^a *in the right margin.*

fol.24v, Sancti Jacobi supra vhenum
the first lines are somewhat corroded:

[Item ibidem] quartale terre, prout iacet in iurisdictione prepositi Traiectensis, inter [terram monialium monasterii in] Oudwica a parte superiori et terram monialium monasterii sancti Servacii Traiectensis a parte inferiori, quod olim possidebat a nobis Marsilius pistor. Modo vero possidet Johannes Swan ad X annos ab anno LX *[1360]* Petri pro X libris pagamenti Traiectensis et IIII pullis annuatim absque defalcatione Martini et Petri solvendis vel cadent ab omni iure et cetera secundum [tenorem littere] qua utimur exinde. Per fratrem Hugonem dispensatorem. ^a¶ Ulterius idem Johannes Swan possidebit dictam terram prout iacet ad X annos ab anno LXX *[1370]* Valentini pro XXV loet argenti aut pro pagamento equivalenti in Traiecto et IIII pullis annuatim, absque defalcatione infra quindenam post Martini et Petri solvendis, aut cadet ab omni iure, prout littera exinde tenet. Per fratrem Hugonem dispensatorem.^a
^bJohannes Swan^b

---

^a *added in smaller writing.* ^b *in the left margin.*

fol.25r. Sancti Jacobi, supra vhenum XXV

Item ibidem, tria quartalia vheni, prout iacent in iurisdictione prepositi Traiectensis, ab Aquemeatu Episcopi extendentia se ad locum dictum Hoeftdiic inter terram nostre domus sancte Katherine a parte superiori, et terram capituli sancti Johannis Traiectensis a parte inferiori, prout illa quondam senior Jacobus Orvilie possidebat. Modo vero possident eadem Jacobus Wigheler, Jordanus et Stephanus eius filii, ad vitam eorum pro XIII libris denariorum Traiectensium et IIII talentis cere, IIII caponibus, IIII pullis annuatim absque defalcatione. Et vehent IIII hont cespitum singulis annis. Martini et Petri solvent vel cadent ab omni iure et cetera prout littera tenet exinde optenta. Per fratrem Johannem de Via Lapidea commendatorem.
^a¶ Modo predictam terram possident Jacobus filius Jacobi, Johannes eius filius et Elisabet neptis eius, ad vitam eorum, pro XIII libris denariorum Traiectensium et IIII talentis cere, IIII caponibus et

vehent IIII hont cespitum annuatim, sub condicionibus in littera contentis. Per fratrem Thomam.[a]
[b]Jacobus Wegheler et ceteri[b]
[c]Jacobus filius Iacobi, Johannes eius filius et Elisabet neptis eius[c]

---

[a] *in a different hand (B).* [b] *in the right margin, cancelled.* [c] *in the right margin, in the same hand as* [a].

fol.25v. Sancti Jacobi, supra vhenum

Item ibidem dimidium mansum vheni, prout iacet in iurisdictione prepositi Traiectensis, inter terram heredum Alardi de Veno a parte superiori et terram domini Nicolai Proys presbyteri a parte inferiori. Quem modo una cum quartali immediate sequenti possident a nobis Hermannus Wolf Zonderland, iuvenis Jacobus Veliken et Erenbertus eius frater, ad vitam eorum, pro XV libris denariorum Traiectensium annuatim et VI talentis cere. Et vehent IIII hont cespitum singulis annis debitis temporibus. Solvent Martini et Petri vel cadent ab omni iure et cetera prout littera quam habemus inde continet. Per fratrem Johannem de Via Lapidea commendatorem.
[a]Wolf Zonderland et ceteri[a]

---

[a] *in the left margin.*

fol.26r. Sancti Jacobi, supra vhenum   XXVI

Item ibidem quartale vheni, prout iacet inter terram Huberti de Wulven a parte superiori, et terram nostre domus sancte Katerine, qua sunt tria quartalia a parte inferiori, prout illud una cum dimidio manso prescripto modo possident Hermannus Wolf Zonderland, iuvenis Jacobus Veliken, et Erenbertus eius frater, ad vitam eorum, pro huiusmodo annua pensione superius signata et sub eisdem condicionibus prout littera exinde tenet. Per fratrem Johannem de Via Lapidea commendatorem.
[a]Wolf Zonderland et ceteri[a]

---

[a] *in the right margin.*

fol.26v. Sancti Jacobi, supra vhenum

Item ibidem quartale vheni, prout iacet in iurisdictione prepositi Traiectensis, quod quondam possidebant a nobis Nycolaus filius Henrici dicti Ymme et Nycolaus filius eius quo pronunc propius iacet Henricus filius Pelegrimi a superiori parte, et priorissa et conventus monasterii Albarum Dominarum in Traiecto a parte inferiori. Quam terram vheni modo possident dicta priorissa et conventus Albarum Dominarum perpetue, solventes nobis exinde XI loet boni argenti annuatim aut pagamentum equivalens in Traiecto, Martini et Petri, sub condicionibus in littera quam inde habemus contentis, signo tali desuper signata . M . Actum per commendatorem et conventum.
ᵃConventus Albarum Dominarum perpetueᵃ

ᵃ *in the left margin.*

fol.27r. Sancti Jacobi, supra vhenum XXVII

Item ibidem quinque virgatas vheni, prescripto quartali propius adiacentes in eadem iurisdictione prepositi Traiectensis, supra Vhenum Orientale, extendentes se ab Aquemeatu Episcopi versus locum dictum Dryenscoten, quibus a superiori parte nunc vicinius iacet Hughe filius Arnoldi, et inferius domus nostra sancte Katerine personaliter, prout easdem modo una cum manso terre superius in iurisdictione prepositi sancti Johannis notato possident Rodolphus Mathie et Wendelmodis eius uxor, ad vitam eorum, pro huiusmodi annua pensione superius iuxta eundem mansum signata. Quibus defunctis, conventus Albarum Dominarum ulterius easdem quinque virgatas a nobis, una cum quartale vheni inmediate prescripto si voluerit perpetue possidebit, pro annua pensione tunc per duos peritos viros ad hoc per eundem et nos deputandos declaranda et pronuncianda.
ᵃRodolphus Mathie et Wendelmodis eius uxorᵃ

ᵃ *in the right margin.*

fol.27v. Sancti Jacobi, supra vhenum

Item ibidem dimidium mansum vheni, emptum quondam erga Hermannum de Stella, prout iacet in iurisdictione prepositi Traiectensis, inter terram domicelle Engele Scorren de Speculo et suorum liberorum a parte superiori, et terram Bernardi filii Bernardi Proys et dicti

Wolf Zonderland partitim, a parte inferiori. Cuius dimidii mansi medietatem superiorem scilicet <u>quartale</u> possidebat Vastradus filius iuvenis Jacobi Velekini. Modo possidebit illud ulterius Jacobus filius Bernardi ad vitam suam pro IIII loet argenti annuatim aut pro pagamento equivalenti tempore solucionis in Traiecto infra quindenam post Martini et Petri solvendis, aut cadent ab omni iure et cetera prout littera exinde tenet. Per fratrem Hugonem.
^a<u>Jacob Bernds zoen</u>^a

---

^a *in the left margin.*

fol.28r.   <u>Sancti Jacobi, supra vhenum</u>   XXVIII

Item <u>reliquam vero medietatem</u> prescripti dimidii mansi, scilicet <u>quartale</u>, prout iacet, una cum quodam alio quartali superius conscripto, modo possidebunt a nobis Hugo filius Arnoldi et Matheus filius Hugonis ad vitam eorum, pro annua pactu superius iuxta aliud quartale signato. Inde habemus litteram. Per fratrem Hugonem dispensatorem.
^aHugo filius Arnoldi et Matheus Hugonis^a

---

^a *in the right margin.*

fol.28v.   <u>Sancti Jacobi, supra vhenum</u>

Item ibidem <u>agrum terre</u> prout iacet inter terram Werneri de Drakenborch a parte superiori et terram Arnoldi Steel a parte inferiori, quondam domui nostre datum per uxorem Symonis de Amersfordia. Quem agrum modo possidet dictus Arnoldus Steel <u>pro XXVI solidis VII denariis pagamenti</u> Traiectensis annuatim, Martini et Petri solvendis.
^aArnoldus Steel^a

---

^a *in the left margin.*

fol.29r.   <u>In parrochia Ameronghen</u>   XXIX

<u>In parrochia de Ameronghen, in Ghinkel, domum et aream</u> cum agriculturis et suis attinenciis prout iacet pro uno manso terre quondam domui nostre per Ricoldum de Ghinkel, Cristinam eius uxorem

et Machteldim eorum unicam filiam secundum seriem littere quam
inde habemus pie collato. Que bona prout iacent modo possidet
Ricoldus Velync ad X annos, ab anno LX *[1360]* Petri pro VI modiis
siliginis mensure Traiectensis et I talento cere annuatim absque
defalcatione Martini et Petri solvendis, vel cadet ab omni iure. Optento nostre domui magno secatu lignorum ibidem dicto vulgariter
'grote holthou' quem nobis reservavimus, cum ceteris condicionibus
in littera quam inde habemus contentis. Per fratrem Hugonem dispensatorem.
ᵃRicoldus Velincᵃ

ᵃ *in the right margin.*

fol.29v.   In Ameronghen

Item ibidem dimidium mansum quem quondam emimus erga filios
Godefridi de Tienhoeven, cuius situationem et possessorem ad presens ignoramus.

Item ibidem in Ameronghen habet domus de quadam petia terre
unum antiquum sterlingnum annuatim, quem solvent modo heredes
Theoderici de Brunchorst.

Item ibidem de alia quadam petia terre I antiquum sterlingnum annuatim, quem Aleydis de Vliete solebat solvere. Modo solvet ᵃ

⁊ *not filled in.*

fol.30r.   In Ameronghen   XXX

Item ibidem duo iugera terre et I hont, prout iacent, cuius terre VIII
hont cum dimidio iacent vulgariter dicendo binnen diix, inter terram
Johannis Borre a parte aquilonis, et terram Suederi de Vianen a parte
meridionali. Et reliqui IIII hont terre iacent buten diix, inter terram
Johannis Borre a parte superiori, et terram Suederi de Vianen a parte
inferiori, quam terram Henricus de Dypenem a nobis possidebat.
Modo possidet eandem Theodericus de Zulen ad X annos ab anno
LXVIII *[1368]* Petri pro IX libris X solidis denariorum Traiectensium annuatim absque defalcatione Martini et Petri solvendis, vel
cadet ab omni iure. Per fratrem Ottonem Gronerᵃ vicecommendatorem.

^bDirc van Zulen^b

^cItem soe heeft ons huys in Ameronghen een stuck veens dat lanck is achthondert roeyen ende viertich ende drieentwyntich roeyen breet ter guder maten, daer bonwen naest leet myt veen dat dat convente van Arnhem toe behoert onser oirden ende beneden Derck Borrenz. myt synen veen.

Item noch hebben wy een boss ende velt ghelegen inder voers. parrochien streckende an onss ghenedigen heren van Utricht inder tijt veen te Ginkel totten Harden toe daer ons voers. here bonwen leet ende wy beneden ende Derck Borrenz. beneden ons ende hier was dividracht om tussen ons heren ghenaden ende ons als biscop David van Burgondien anno LXXVIII *[1478]* alsoe dat dat voers. boss opgheradet wart vanden ousten vanden voers. dorpe in thegenwordigheyt synre ghenaden raden ende scaffeners ons convents daert alsoe bewonden is als voers. steet byder opradynghe ende heeft ons daer nae onghemaeyt ghelaten.^c

---

^a *uncertain reading ms.* ^b *in the right margin.* ^c *in a much later writing, end of the 15th century?*

On a loose paper leaf, with papermark P under a quatrefoil, in a 16th or 17th-century hand,
recto:

Item vant bosche te Amerongen ghelegen, uyt ghemeten met Willem die Beer daer boven oostwerts die Keyser naest ghelegen is ende westwaert die kerck van Amerongen ende is breet tsamen ses ende dertich royen daer die helfft off ons toecoemt, te wesen achtien royen, ende strect vant lant behorende die kerck tot sint Joosten wech toe off als zommige sich laten duncken tot an onse veenen; dit is ondersocht by Jan Janz. ende Huych Ruys, welck twee Willem die Beer zijn bosche vercofft hadde.

verso, partly illegible:

besceyt vant bosch te Ameronghen — gegeven ende — op rekening X s.

fol.30v.   In parrochia Doerne

Item iuxta Leersum, unum agrum, solventem dimidium modium siliginis annuatim prout eundem agrum quondam Hugo filius Bodekini
et post eum Ghisekinus de Voerde possidebant. Modo vero eundem
prout iacent ^a
nota^b

Item in parrochia Doerne in der Dertheze habet domus predicta
quedam bona censualia dicta ten Berghe, prout iacent pro uno manso
terre, que bona nunc possidet et tenet a nobis Gerardus Bole filius
Gerardi, sub annuo censu *XX* denariorum bonorum, singulis annis in
die beati Lebuini hyemalis absque longiori mora solvendorum. Quod
si non fecerit tenebitur ad solutionem duplicis census. Hec huiusmodi
bona non^c debent dividi, sed semper a vero herede in heredem integre possideri. Et quociens a nobis de dictis bonis alicui sub annuo
censu predicto providi continget tociens inde habebimus duplicem I
takam boni vini, pro novis litteris tunc inde sigillandis, et cetera secundum tenorem littere super hoc tradite. Per commandatorem et
conventum.
^ddit goet heeft dat convent van Sinte Johans Dale gecoft^d
^eGerardus Bole hereditarie^e

---

^a *not filled in.* ^b *in the left margin, in smaller writing.* ^c non *is missing in ms.* ^d *in
a different hand.* ^e *in the left margin.*

fol.31r.   In Doerne,   in Tule   XXXI

Item ibidem dimidium mansum, quem nunc possident a nobis heredes domini Johannis de Broechusen sub annua censu XV denariorum
bonorum.
hereditarie^a
^bFlorencius de Broechusen^b

Item ibidem duos agros, necnon unum agrum qui dicitur Gravel eis
propius adiacentem, prout iacent inter terram Johannis de Voerde a
superiori et inferiori parte, quos tres agros insimul iacentes modo
possidet Johannes Pawe pro II modiis siliginis mensure Traiectensis,
IIII pullis et I talento cere annuatim exinde infra^c XIIII dies post
Martini solvendis.
^dModo dictam terram Petrus de Baren pro II malderis siliginis IIII

pullis I libra cere ad X annos a festo Petri anno LXXXIIII *[1384]*
absque defalcatione.[d]
[b]Johannes Pawe[b]

Item ibidem aream prout iacet inter terram domini Ghiseberti de
Starkenborch a superiori parte, et terram heredum Johannis Gerardi,
civis Traiectensis a parte inferiori, quam quondam possidebat Elyas
uten Biezen. Modo possidet eandem Volquinus Sutor pro I scepelino
siliginis annuatim, aut V solidis denariorum traiectensium annuatim
pro eodem. [e]Ulterius possidebit dictam aream Arnoldus de Velpen et
Elisabet eius uxor, ad X annos ab anno LXX *[1370]* pro X solidis
denariorium Traiectensium annuatim.[e]
[f]Volquinus Sutor[f]
[b]Arnoldus de Velpen et eius uxor[b]

---

  [a] *in the left margin.* [b] *in the right margin.* [c] infra infra *ms.* [d] *in a different hand.*
[e] *added in a different writing.* [f] *in the right margin, cancelled.*

fol.31v.   In parrochia Doerne, in Tule

Item in Tule mansum cum dimidio et domum et XV iugera in Tuel-
rebroec prout iacent et ea quondam possidebat Albertus de Schoenoerde. Modo possidet Johannes de Voerde una cum terra
subsequenti, pro annuo pacto [a]XXIIII modiorum siliginis annuatim.
¶ Ulterius predictam terram, una cum bonis et terris inferius signatis,
possidebunt Arnoldus de Velpen et Elisabet eius uxor, pro eodem
annuo pacto XXIIII modiorum siliginis ad X annos, ab anno LXX
[1370].[a]
[b]¶ Ulterius predictam terram una cum bonis et terris inferius signatis
possidebunt Jonghe Jan van Velpen ende Ghisebert van Velpen Ghi-
seberts zoon, pro eodem annuo pacto XXIIII mud rogghe ad X
annos, ab anno LXXXVII *[1387]* Lamberti.[b]
[c]Johannis de Voerde[c]
[d]Arnoldus de Velpen et eius uxor[d]

Item ibidem dimidium mansum eyghens lands, qui quondam fuit
Helye van den Oerde, prout iacet et eundem etiam Albertus de
Schoenoerde quondam possidebat. Modo possidet eundem Johannes
de Voerde ad annos infrascriptos, una cum ceteris bonis in hoc folio
notatis. [a]Ulterius possidebunt Arnoldus de Velpen et eius uxor ad
annos predictos.[a]
[c]Johannis de Voerde[c]

^dArnoldus de Velpen <u>et eius uxor</u>^d

^aItem ibidem <u>domum et aream</u> et edificia super eandem constructa, ende een cot land tinsgoeds, mit zinen broeclande, dat daer toe behoert, prout iacent et ea quondam possidebant a nobis Ruthgerus Smale et eius uxor, postea Arnoldus de Broechusen et Johannes de Voerde possidebant, una cum ceteris bonis prescriptis. Modo possident Arnoldus de Velpen et eius uxor, ad annos et sub annua pensione predictis.^a

^dArnoldus de Velpen <u>et eius uxor</u>^d

^a<u>Hanc prescriptam terrarum agriculturam in diversis agrorum peciis situatam invenies hic postea, particulariter et distincte, prout sequitur signatam.</u>^a

---

^a *in different writing.* ^b *in a different hand.* ^c *in the left margin, cancelled.* ^d *in the left margin.*

fol.32r.   <u>In Tule</u>   XXXII

^aItem ibidem <u>unum agrum terre</u>, qui vocatur die Rampslaer, situatum inter terram Wilhelmi Vivien vel suorum heredum, a parte superiori, et terram domini de Apcoude et Everardi Wize, a parte inferiori.

Item Opten Braem Stripen, <u>unum agrum terre</u>, iacentem inter terram Theoderici de Weeden a parte superiori, et terram domini Symonis de Haerlem a parte inferiori.

Item ibidem <u>unum agrum terre</u>, qui vocatur Clotcken, inter terra Ghiseberti de Velpen, a superiori, et etiam inferiori parte iacentem.

Item ibidem <u>unum agrum</u>, qui vocatur die Stelt, inter terram domini Symonis de Haerlem a parte superiori, et terram domini Ghiseberti de Starkenborch a parte inferiori situatum.

Item op Aen den Berch, <u>unum agrum</u>, qui vocatur Teygen, inter terram Ghiseberti de Velpen a parte superiori, et terram domini Ghiseberti de Starkenborch a parte inferiori situatum.

Item ibidem An den Berch, beneden der houtsteghen, <u>unum agrum terre</u>, situatum inter terram Theoderici de Weeden a parte superiori, et terram domini de Apcoude a parte inferiori.

Summa terrarum prescripte agriculture LXVIII agros II iugera IIII campos terre, necnon domum et aream, una cum terra eis in una pecia circumiacente, prout eandem modo possident a nobis Arnoldus de Velpen et Elisabeth eius uxor, pro XXIIII modiis siliginis annuatim, ad X annos, ab anno LXXI *[1371]* solvendis, secundum tenorem littere quam inde habemus.[a]

---

[a] *in the same smaller writing as* [a] *on the foregoing folio.*

fol.32v.   In Ravenswade

In Ravenswade habet domus tria iugera dicta Gheer iacentia inter terram domini de Culenborch a superiori parte et terram communitatis de Zelmonde a parte inferiori.
[a]Alardus filius Zuermonds[a]

Item ibidem XIIII hont terre supra Ridenbergh sita in maelscap in loco dicto Maet, quibus nunc superius et inferius dominus de Culenborch iacet propius.

Item ibidem VIII hont terre in loco qui dicitur Boencamp, prout iacent modo inter terram domini Arnoldi Vischer a superiori et etiam inferiori parte.

Item ibidem aream Quints cum suis attinenciis, super quam nunc moratur dictus Coman Zuermond, quam superius propius iacet vicus dictus Ravenswader Steghe, et inferius Guydo de Weyda. Quam aream una cum terra prescripta, prout ea quondam Alardus de Ravenswade possidebat a nobis et ea tenemus a decano et capitulo sancte Walburgis in Aernhem, sub annuo censu VIII denariorum per possessores dicte terre, annuatim nomine nostro solvendorum. Modo possidet Alardus filius Zuermonds, perpetue de herede in heredem, et semper seniori heredi manendo, pro V libris, quemlibet bonum grossum Turonensem pro XIIII denariis computandum, aut pro pagamento equivalenti, pro quibus nunc temporis solvet nobis VI libras X grossos pagamenti Traiectensis annis singulis infra quindenam post Martini et Petri solvendo, vel cadet ab omni iure nisi legitimum et evidens impedimentum obstaret, et cetera secundum tenorem littere super hoc optente, desuper signate signo tali . H .
perpetue[a]

---

[a] *in the left margin.*

fol.33r.   Ravenswade   XXXIII

Item in loco dicto Zelmonder Maet, <u>tria iugera</u> terre, prout iacent in tribus peciis distincta, quibus duabus peciis pro nunc propius iacent heredes Lamberti de Buren a superiori parte, et sancti Nycolai terra a parte inferiori. Et huiusmodi tercia pecia iacet inter terram pronunc Arnoldi Zuermond a parte superiori, et terram Florencii filii divitis Florencii a parte inferiori.

Tercium vero iuger exinde iacet in Ravenswade in loco dicto Up die Gheweren, inter terram pronunc heredum domini Huberti Schenken de Culenborch a parte superiori, et terram dicti Arnoldi Zuermond a parte inferiori. Que tria iugera prescripta prout iacent modo iure feodali possidet et tenet a nobis Arnoldus predictus iure Zutphaniensi <u>cum XX</u> grossis pro herghewade dandis cum evenerit a nobis optinenda. Inde habemus litteram in anno LVII *[1357]* ultimo optentam, querendam iuxta signum tale . G .
^a<u>bona feodalia</u>^a
^b<u>Aernd Zuermond</u>^b

---

^a *in the left margin.* ^b *in the right margin.*

fol.33v.   In parrochia de Langebroec

In Langhebroec <u>tria iugera cum dimidio</u> prout iacent inter terram Helye van den Oerde a superiori, et etiam ab inferiori parte, que modo possidet a nobis dictus Helyas van den Oerde, ad X annos ab anno LXIII *[1363]* Petri, pro <u>V libris X solidis</u> denariorum Traiectensium annuatim Martini et Petri solvendis, vel cadet ab omni iure, secundum tenorem littere quam inde habemus. Per fratrem Hugonem dispensatorem.
^a<u>Helyas van den Oerde</u>^a

---

^a *in the left margin.*

fol.34r.   In Langhebroec   XXXIIII

Item ibidem in Overlanghebroec, <u>mansum terre cum dimidio</u> prout iacet in iurisdictione prepositi Traiectensis, cuius terre videlicet ab una parte aquemeatus ibidem ten Goyewerts per se iacet inter terram Wolteri filii <u>domicelle</u> Ermegardis a superiori parte, et terram Henrici

filii Symonis uter Koken a parte inferiori. Reliquus vero dimidius
mansus iacet ab alia inferiori   parte aquemeatus ibidem te Reyne-
werds, inter terram Wolteri de Zulen a parte superiori, et terram
Wilhelmi de Venemael et Theoderici filii Volquini a parte inferiori,
quam terram prescriptam quondam possidebat a nobis Volquinus de
Derthesen, postea dominus Johannes de Broechusen. Modo vero possidet eandem   ᵃ

ᵇModo prescriptam terram prout iacet, possidebit ulterius Symon
uter Koken, ad X annos ab anno LXXXI *[1381]* Lamberti, et dabit
annuatim XX antiquos scudatos vel pagamentum equivalens, et XII
capones et XII pullas Martini et Petri absque defalcatione, vel cadet
ab omni iure. Habet litteram   et nos e converso. Per commendato-
remᵇ ᶜvendita est hec terraᶜ
ᵈSymon uter Kokenᵈ

ᵃ *not filled in.* ᵇ *in a different hand (E).* ᶜ *in another hand behind the text, which has
crossed out the whole item with pale ink.* ᵈ *in the right margin, in the same hand as* ᵇ.

fol.34v.   In Overlanghebroec

In parrochia de Overlanghebroec, mansum terre, prout iacet inter
propietatem terrarum domini Symonis de Haerlem militis a superiori
et etiam ab inferiori parte.
ᵃWolterus de Zulenᵃ

Item ibidem tria iugera terre, iacentia inter terram Wolteri de Zulen
a parte superiori, et terram domini Symonis de Haerlem a parte
inferiori, que tria iugera una cum manso terre iamdicto, modo possidet Wolterus de Zulen predictus *ad X* annos ab anno LXVII *[1367]*
Petri pro XLVII libris X solidis denariorum Traiectensium VI talentis cere et XIX pullis annuatim absque defalcatione, Martini et Petri
solvendis, vel cadet ab omni iure. In fine annorum medietatem dicte
terre incultam resignabit, secundum tenorem littere quam habemus
inde. Per fratrem Hugonem dispensatorem.

ᵃ *in the left margin.*

fol.35r.   Overlangebroec   XXXV
Item ibidem twe strepen lands, prout iacent in palude, in temporali
iurisdictione de Derthesen in Langelare inter terram puerorum Ade
de Derthezen a parte superiori et terram Gerardi Pawe a parte infe-

riori, prout eandem terram possidebat quondam Henricus filius
Symonis uter Koken. Modo possident eam Wolterus de Colonia civis
Traiectensis, et Nycolaus Pawe filius Gerardi, hereditarie pro III libris
seu talentis cere annuatim, infra quindenam post Martini solvendis.
perpetue^a
^bWolterus de Colonia et Nicolaus Pawe^b

---

^a *in the left margin.* ^b *in the right margin.*

fol.35v. In Wike

Item iuxta Wyc dimidium iuger et unam aream prout iacent inter
terram prepositi sancti Salvatoris Traiectensis a parte aquilonis, et
terram Wolteri de Ponte a parte meridionali, quam terram una cum
area modo possidet Heyno filius Sammels ad *X* annos ab anno LXIII
[1363] Purificatione Marie, pro XXV solidis annuatim pagamenti
Traiectensis, Martini et Petri solvendis, vel cadet ab omni iure, prout
littera exinde tenet. Per fratrem Hugonem dispensatorem.
^aHeyne Sammels zoen^a

---

^a *in the left margin.*

fol.36r. In Tulle XXXVI

In Tulle, in eo loco ubi quondam fuit aggeris ruptio habet domus
quandam terram iacentem communiter cum terra curati ecclesie de
Tulle et custodis ibidem, prout eandem terram modo possident a
nobis Jacobus Spruyt et Diliana eius uxor, ad *XXX* annos ab anno
XLII *[1342]* pro X solidis denariorum Traiectensium annuatim,
Martini vel infra XIIII dies postea solvendis vel cadent ab omni iure.
Habemus inde litteram. Per fratrem Jacobum Ridder dispensatorem.
^aJacobus Spruyt^a
^bTheodericus filius eius nunc possidet.^b

---

^a *in the right margin, cancelled.* ^b *in the right margin.*

fol.36v. In Coten

^aItem in parrochia de Coten habet dicta domus beate Katerine duo
iugera terre dicta Spijc prout iacent, que quondam possidebat Wige-

rus die Witte. Modo possidet ea domicella Belya filia Ghiseberti de Wijc, pro <u>XXVI solidis VIII denariis</u> pagamenti Traiectensis. Dicta II iugera iacent inter terram dicti Zuermond de Hyndersteyne a parte superiori, et terram Richardi filii Johannis Stultinxs a parte inferiori. Solvet Martini et Petri, perpetue.[a]

[b]Deze voerscreven renten zijn vercoft om dat si op tinsghoet stonden want het mit recht gheweert wart dat wi gheen renten daer of crighen en conden ende gout[c] die penninc siaers XX, dat hebbe wi weder beleyt.[b]

[d]Belya filia Ghiselberti de Wijc[d]

[e]Item ibidem <u>dimidium iuger</u>, prout iacet inter terram Capelle in Wijc de qua domina Beerta de Ysendoern nunc habet usufructum suum a parte superiori, et terram capituli sancti Martini Traiectensis a parte inferiori, quod modo possidet Gerardus de Reno seu de Speghelberch ad <u>X annos ab anno LXVII</u> *[1367]* Lamberti pro <u>XXXVII solidis IIII denariis</u>, annuatim absque defalcatione, Martini et Petri solvendis, vel cadet ad omni iure. Habemus inde litteram. Per fratrem Hugonem.[e]

[f]vendita est[f]

[d]Gerardus de Reno[d]

---

[a] *crossed out with dark ink.* [b] *in a different hand.* [c] *uncertain reading ms.* [d] *in the left margin.* [e] *crossed out with pale ink.* [f] *with the same pale ink under the text, in a different hand.*

fol.37r.   <u>In Coten</u>   XXXVII

Item ibidem <u>aream</u> dictam Riisbrugghen Hoffstede, prout iacet infra molendinum et communitatem, prout eandem nunc possidet Rodolphus uten Broeke, pro <u>XXVI</u> solidis <u>VIII denariis</u> pagamenti Traiectensis.

[a]Rodolphus uten Broke[a]

nota[b]

Item ibidem <u>XVIII iugera</u>, prout iacent inter terram capituli sancti Johannis Traiectensis et Marsilii filii Gerardi Monts a parte superiori, et terram Gerardi de Reno filii Johannis a parte inferiori.

[a]Ghisebertus de Blomenwerde[a]

Item ibidem <u>unum iuger</u> dictam Molenacker, iacentem in eadem parrochia, quod quondam fuit Gerardi Zomer.

Item ibidem IIj *[2.5]* iugera terre, prout iacent in Wikerbroec In den Brync, in parrochia de Wijc, que XXIj *[21.5]* iugera predicta modo possidet Ghisebertus de Blomenweerde ad X annos ab anno LXVIII *[1368]* Jacobi apostoli Maioris, pro XX pullis et IIII marcis et V loet boni argenti, aut cum pagamento annuali equivalenti solvendis absque defalcatione Martini et Petri, vel cadet ab omni iure. Habemus inde litteram. Per fratrem Hugonem dispensatorem.

c¶ Ulterius idem Ghisebertus possidebit dictam terram ad XII annos, ab anno LXXV *[1375]* Lamberti pro summa pecunie superius expressata.c

---

a *in the right margin.* b *in the left margin.* c *in a different hand (C).*

fol.37v.   In Coten

Item ibidem XVIII iugera terre, prout iacent in dicta parrochia de Coten inter terram capituli sancti Johannis Traiectensis a parte superiori, et terram pronunc Johannis de Reno a parte inferiori.
aGhisebertus de Blomenwerdea

Item ibidem VII hont terre, prout iacent in eadem parrochia Int Middelvelt, qui quondam fuerunt Gerardi Zomers.

Item ibidem duo iugera iacentia in Wikerbroc inter terram Theoderici filii Wilhelmi a parte superiori, et terram Johannis de Reno predicti a parte inferiori, quam terram prescriptam insimul quondam possidebat Ghisebertus de Roemst. Modo possidet eandem a nobis Ghisebertus de Blomenwerde ad XX annos ab anno LXI *[1361]* Laurencii pro III marcis et IIj *[2.5]* loet argenti aut proinde pagamentum equivalens, et XX pullis, solvendis absque defalcatione Martini et Petri, vel cadet ab omni iure. Inde est littera. Per fratrem Johannem de Via Lapidea commendatorem.
bUlterius idem Ghisebertus possidebit dictam terram ad XII annos ab anno LXXV *[1375]* Lamberti pro annuo pactu superius expressato.b

---

a *in the left margin.* b *in a different hand (C).*

fol.38r.   In Coten   XXXVIII

Item ibidem XX iugera terre prout iacent, quibus terra decani et capituli Maioris ecclesie Traiectensis a superiori et inferiori parte pro-

pius iacet, et prout illa quondam Ermegardis Monts a nobis possidebat. Modo possidet ea Stephanus de Blomenwerde ad X annos ab
anno LXV *[1365]* Petri pro XXIII antiquis scudatis boni auri et
ponderis aut pagamento equivalente in Traiecto, et XX pullis annuatim absque defalcatione Martini et Petri solvendis vel cadet ab
omni iure, secundum litteram quam inde habemus. Per fratrem Hugonem dispensatorem.
[a]Modo possidebit ulterius Roelof uten Broec ad X annos ab anno
LXXXVI *[1386]* Lamberti pro XXIII [b]antiquis scudatis[b] et XX pullis annuatim sub condicione predicta. Per fratrem Johannem Haze.
[c]Stephanus de Blomenwerde[c]

---

[a] *in a different hand.* [b] antiqua scudata *ms.* [c] *in the right margin.*

fol.38v.   In Coten

Item ibidem VIII iugera prout iacent inter terram capituli sancti
Martini Traiectensis a parte superiori et terram nostre domus sancte
Katherine quam pronunc Theodericus Goes a nobis possidebat a
parte inferiori, que VIII iugera quondam Theodericus de Muden a
nobis possidebat. Modo possidet ea Ghisebertus de Blomenwerde ad
X annos ab anno LXVII *[1367]* Lamberti, solvendo nobis exinde IIj
[2.5] marcas argenti aut pagamentum equivalens in Traiecto et VII
pullas annuatim absque defalcatione Martini et Petri solvenda, vel
cadet ab omni iure. Inde est littera. Per fratrem Hugonem dispensatorem.
[a]Ulterius possidebit dictam terram ad XII annos ab anno LXXV
[1375] Lamberti pro annua pensione superius expressata.[a]
[b]Ghisebertus de Blomenwerde.[b]

---

[a] *in a different hand (C).* [b] *in the left margin.*

fol.39r.   In Coten   XXXIX

Item ibidem VII iugera prout iacent inter VIII iugera supradicta, que
modo Ghisebertus de Blomenwerde a nobis possidet a parte superiori, et terram Theoderici Goes a parte inferiori, prout illa possidebat a
nobis Theodericus Goes hucusque. Modo vero possidebit ea Ghisebertus de Blomenwerde una cum quinque iugeribus inmediate sequentibus pro annuo pacto subscripto ad X annos ab anno LXVIII
[1368] Lamberti.
[a]Ghisebertus de Blomenwerde[a]

Item ibidem <u>quinque iugera</u> prout iacent inter terram domine de
Ema a parte superiori, et terram domus nostre sancte Katerine quam
Stephanus de Blomenwerde possidet modo a parte inferiori, prout illa
Johannes de Reno filius Heinrici Clotinx a nobis possidebat. Modo
vero possidebit ea una cum VII iugeribus predictis Ghisebertus de
Blomenwerde <u>ad X annos</u> ab anno LXVIII *[1368]* Lamberti, pro
<u>quatuor marcis cum dimidia boni</u> argenti aut pagamento equivalente,
<u>et XII</u> pullis annuatim, Martini et Petri solvendis absque defalcatione,
vel cadet ab omni iure, secundum tenorem littere quam inde habemus. Per fratrem Hugonem dispensatorem.
[b]Ulterius idem Ghisebertus possidebit dictam terram, scilicet VII iugera et V iugera ad XII annos ab anno LXXV *[1375]* Lamberti sub
annuo pactu prenarrato.[b]
[a]<u>Ghisebertus de Blomenwerde</u>[a]

---

[a] *in the right margin.* [b] *in a different hand (C).*

fol.39v.   In Werconden

In <u>parrochia Werconden</u> habet domus <u>XII iugera terre</u>, empta quondam erga dominum Ghisebertum de Wijc, prout iacent inter terram
decani et capituli sancti Martini Traiectensis a parte superiori, et
terram Ade Over die Vechte a parte inferiori, prout illa prius possidebat a nobis Gerardus de Reno seu de Speghelberch. Modo possidet
ea Ghisebertus de Blomenwerde <u>ad X</u> annos ab anno <u>LXVIII</u> *[1368]*
Jacobi Maioris, pro <u>duabus marcis et quatuor loet argenti</u> vel pro eis
pagamentum equivalens in Traiecto, <u>et XII</u> pullis annuatim absque
defalcatione Martini et Petri solvendis, vel cadet ab omni iure, et
cetera prout littera exinde tenet. Per fratrem Hugonem dispensatorem.
[a]Ulterius idem Ghisebertus possidebit istam terram ad XII annos ab
anno LXXV *[1375]* Lamberti pro annua pensione predicta.[a]
[b]<u>Ghisebertus de Blomenwerde</u>[b]

---

[a] *in a different hand (C).* [b] *in the left margin.*

fol.40r.   In Odijc   XL
In <u>parrochia Odijc</u> habet domus <u>quatuor iugera terre</u> minus II hont
prout iacent inter terram Ghiseberti de Scaedwic a parte superiori, et
terram Ghiseberti filii Trudonis de Scaedwic et Johannis dicti Breye a
parte inferiori, prout illa modo possidebit a nobis Henricus Buddync
ad X annos ab anno LXIX *[1369]* Petri pro XI libris denariorium

Traiectensium et III pullis annuatim absque defalcatione infra quatuor ebdomadas post Martini et Petri solvendis, aut cadet ab omni
iure, et cetera prout littera exinde tenet. Per fratrem Hugonem.
ªUlterius possidebit predictam terram Gherit Andries zoon pro IIII
antiquis scudatis ad X annos ab anno LXXXVIII *[1388]* Lamberti in
parrochia predicta.ª
ᵇHenricus Buddincᵇ

Item in parrochia de Houten habet domus aream quam dedit dominus uten Goyen solvendam annuatim II libras X grossos, prout illam
quondam possidebat a nobis Wilhelmus filius Heinrici Buddincs.
notaᶜ

ª *in a different hand.* ᵇ *in the left margin.* ᶜ *in smaller writing in the right margin.*

fol.40v.   In Houten

In parrochia de Houten, in Westongeren, habet domus *VII hont* terre,
prout iacent in Loric inter terram ecclesie de Houten a parte superiori, et terram Henrici Buddinc a parte inferiori.

ªItem ibidem medietatem unius aree, continentem Vj *[5.5]* hont
terre, super quam Ghisebertus Scade de Quedinchoven pronunc
habitat, qua idem Ghisebertus propius iacet cum reliqua medietate
eiusdem aree a parte inferiori, et dominus uten Goye a parte superiori, prout eandem medietatem aree una cum VII hont terre prescripte
insimul modo possidet dictus Ghisebertus Scade hereditarie pro V
libris denariorum Traiectensium annuatim solvendis infra mensem
post Martini et Petri, et si tunc monitus non solverit, potest expandari. Quod si tunc non sustinuerit aut si non satisfecerit tunc cadet ab
omni iure, secundum tenorem littere quam inde habemus, signo tali
foris signate .I.
ᵇModo possidet dictam terram Otto filius eius.ᵇ
ᶜGhisebertus Scade hereditarie.ᶜ

Item ibidem int Goy IIj *[2.5]* hont terre prout iacent et ea quondam
possidebat dominus Ghisebertus Scade presbyter. Modo vero possidet
Nicolaus de Oestrum frater eius pro IIII solidis annuatim, perpetue.
ᶜNicolaus de Oestrum perpetueᶜ
notaᵈ

Item ibidem IIII iugera cum dimidio prout iacent et ea quondam

possidebat Ghisebertus Faber. Modo possidet dominus uten Goye, annuatim exinde solvendus <u>VI solidos VIII denarios</u> perpetue. Dicta terra iacet inter terram domini episcopi Traiectensis a parte orientali, et terram domini de Vianen a parte occidentali.
^c<u>dominus uten Goye, perpetue</u>^c

---

^a *with accolade linked with the foregoing item.* ^b *in a different hand.* ^c *in the left margin.* ^d *in smaller writing in the left margin.*

fol.41r.   In Scalcwijc   XLI

<u>In parrochia Scalcwijc habet domus dimidium mansum</u> prout iacet in iurisdictione temporali domini de Culenborch inter terram unius altaris fundati in ecclesia de Langebroec et Nycolai de Canebroec a superiori parte, et terram domini de Culenborch quam nunc possidet Johannes de Blochoven a parte inferiori. Quem dimidium mansum modo possidet Albertus van den Zile filius Alberti van den Zile hereditarie, pro XXXVj *[35.5]* loet argenti aut cum pagamento equivalenti in Traiecto, solvendo annuatim infra quindenam post Martini et Petri. Quod si non fecerit extunc ulterius solutionem dicti pacti differre potest sub pena unius libre domui nostre tunc solvende absque maiori dampno, sed si infra quinque septimanas post quemlibet dictorum terminorum non solverit, extunc cadet ab omni iure et hereditario pactu sibi in dicta terra competenti, secundum tenorem littere quam inde habemus, signato signo tali . L .
^aSupradicto Alberto mortuo eius unica filia etatis ultra XV annorum tamquam unicus et verus heres eiusdem, huiusmodi hereditarium pactum cum littera inde a nobis optenta ad usus Bernardi Buc avunculi sui ibidem presentis in manus fratris Hugonis de Coudekerke dispensatoris nostri et conventus libere resignavit. Cui Bernardo tunc ulterius eundem hereditarium pactum in supradicto dimidio manso concessimus sub conditionibus premissis et in litteris hinc inde datis contentis. Actum in refectorio nostro sub anno domini M.CCC.LXVIII *[1368]* Willibrordi, presentibus ibidem Thome de Ghore clerico, notario publico, Theoderico Bole et Hermanno de Coppel, civibus Traiectensibus testibus ad premissa vocatis.^a
^b¶ Modo prescriptum hereditarium pactum in predicta terra possidebit ulterius <u>Gerardus filius</u> Heynonis ex libera resignatione supradicti Bernardi Buc in manus dicti dispensatoris ad usus eiusdem Gerardi libere facta. Cui Gerardo idem dispensator huiusmodi hereditarium pactum in supradicto dimidio manso nomine totius conventus concessit sub conditionibus superius notatis et in litteris inde confectis

contentis. Actum in dispensatoria sub anno Domini M.CCC.LXIX
[1369] in die beati Ambrosii, presentibus Thome de Goer notario
publico, Theoderico Bole, Frederico eius filio civibus Traiectensibus,
et aliis quam pluribus.[b]
hereditarie[c]
[d]Albertus de Zilo[d]
[e]Gerardus filius Heynonis[e]

Item ibidem <u>unum iuger terre</u> prout iacet et illud quondam possidebant heredes Wilhelmi de Bertangen.

---

[a] *added in different writing.* [b] *continued in different ink.* [c] *in the left margin.* [d] *in the right margin, cancelled.* [e] *in the right margin.*

fol.41v.   In Culenborch . In Wale

In <u>parrochia Culenborch</u> [a]
[b]Johannes de Wale[b]

In <u>parrochia de Wale quartale terre</u> prout iacet in iurisdictione temporali domini de Culenborch inter terram [c]Goetscalci dicti Vrenken a
parte superiori, et a parte inferiori Goetscalci dicti Vrieze, quod
modo possidebit Gerardus dictus Lyl pro tribus antiquis scudatis et
IIII pullis Martini et Petri solvendis, vel cadet ab omni iure prout
littera exinde tenet, ad X annos ab anno LXXXIX *[1389]* Lamberti.[c]
[b]Bernardus Snoye[b]

---

[a] *not continued.* [b] *in the left margin.* [c] *continued in a different hand.*

fol.42r.   In Wale   XLII
Item ibidem <u>quartale terre</u> prout iacet in iurisdictione temporali de
Scalcwiic, quo Johannes de Landscrone civis Traiectensis propius iacet cum uno quartali terre [a]a parte[a] quod tenet a preposito sancti
Petri Traiectensis a parte superiori, et inferius [b] , quod modo possidet
idem Johannes de Landscrone perpetue de herede in heredem pro V
libris denariorum Traiectensium annuatim grosso Turonensi regio
pro XVI denariis computato, Martini et Petri aut infra quindenam
postea solvendis, vel ipse et sui heredes cadent ab omni iure, secundum tenorem littere inde optentam querendam signo tali . K .[c]
[d]Johannes de Landscrone[d]
hereditarie[e]

Item ibidem <u>quartale terre</u> quod quondam dedit frater Bartolomeus Goeswini de Werconden, prout iacet in iurisdictione domini de Culenborg inter terram Ludolphi filii Ode a parte superiori, et terram heredum seu successorum domini Wilhelmi de Duvenvoerde militis quondam domini de Vianen a parte inferiori, prout illud quartale quondam possidebat Johannes Conradi. Modo possidet idem Ghiselbertus filius Bartholomei de Weyda pro V libris denariorum Traiectensium annuatim, Martini et Petri solvendis. Inde habemus instrumentum sub sigillo officialis Traiectensis cum huiusmodi littera . F . exterius signatum.
^f<u>Ghisebertus Bartholomei</u>^f
^d<u>Jan van Wael</u>^d

---

^a *cancelled.* ^b *not filled in.* ^c *The book contains a torn piece of paper, verso signed* . K . *with the heading:* Littera Johannis de Lanzcrone, *continued in other writing:* hereditario pactu in parrochia Wale, *continued in yet another writing, cancelled:* In Scalcwijc. *This piece of paper contains recto the last part of the said letter, ending with:* Ghegheven int jaer ons Heren dusent driehondert ende neghen ende dertich des anderen daghes na des helichen sacramens dach *[1339 May 28].* ^d *in the right margin.* ^e *in the left margin.* ^f *in the right margin, cancelled.*

fol.42v.   In parrochia sancti Nycolai, supra Raven

In parrochia sancti Nycolai Traiectensis <u>dimidium mansum terre</u>, prout iacet supra Hoghe Raven in orientali parte Reni inter terram domus sancti Spiritus a parte superiori, et terram heredum Maechelmi de Busco Ducis a parte inferiori. Quem dimidium mansum una cum dimidio quartali seu duobus iugeribus in parrochia de Juttaes signatis, necnon cum duobus hont terre subscriptis modo possident Hermannus de Coppel et Gerardus Ever <u>ad X annos</u> ab anno LXVII *[1367]* Petri pro <u>XVj</u> *[15.5]* <u>antiquis scudatis</u> auri aut pro pagamento equivalenti in Traiecto, <u>et I talento cere et X pullis</u> annuatim, absque defalcatione Martini et Petri solvendis, vel cadent ab omni iure, sub ceteris condicionibus in littera quam inde habemus contentis. Per fratrem Hugonem dispensatorem.
^aHermannus Coppel et Gerardus Ever^a

Item ibidem <u>duo hont terre</u> prout iacent tot Weden in dicta parrochia, quibus propius iacet a parte orientali et aquilonis terra spectans ad quoddam altare fundatum in ecclesia sancti Nycolai, et a parte occidentali et meridionali propius iacet die Middelweteringe circueundo. Que modo possident Hermanus Coppel et Gerardus

Ever una cum X iugeribus predictis pro annua pensione et sub condicionibus superius signatis.
^aCoppel et Gerardus Ever^a

---

^a *in the left margin.*

fol.43r,   In parrochia sancti Nicolai, supra Raven   XLIII
the first lines are rather corroded.

Item ibidem <u>quartale terre</u> prout iacet supra Raven inter terram mo/
[nialium sancti Servacii Traiectensis a parte superiori et terram]
Everardo/ uten Weyrde a parte inferiori, quod modo possidet Everardus uten Weyrde/ <u>ad X annos ab anno LXI</u> *[1361]* Petri [et pro
XX libris denariorum Traiectensium]/ IIII talentis cere IIII caponibus annuatim absque [defalcatione solvendis]/ Petri vel cadet ab
omni iure. Inde est littera. Per fratrem [Hugonem].
^aModo/ possident dictam terram moniales sancti Servacii ad X annos
ab anno LXXI *[1371]* Agnetis pro XXII libris denariorum Traiectensium et IIII talentis cere et IIII caponibus annuatim absque defalcatione ^b Martini et Petri solvendis aut cadent ab omni iure. Per
fratrem Thomam.^a
^cItem dese heel hoeff lants gheheten sinter Niclaes camp is ghemeten
ende hout XVIII mergen III hont ende XC roden; hier off so sel
hebben die kerc tsinter Niclaes tUtrecht IX mergen mit dyck, weteringe, slobbe ende sloet die hem off gemeten syn anden oesteren
egge, ende die van sinte Servaes sellen hebben vijff mergen gemetens
lants. So blijft ons dan voir ons viertell IIIIj *[4.5]* mergen XC roden
op die westsyde mit die van sinte Servaes in gemengeder voer; dit
heeft gedadynct^d Heinric de Witte ende Willem van Gent des vrida-
ges voir Cathedra Petri anno een ende vijftich *[1451 February 19]* bij
wille ende consent der drier pertien voirscreven.^c
^eEvert uten Werde^e
^fConventus sancti Servacij^f

Item ibidem <u>IIIj</u> *[3.5]* <u>hont terre</u> prout iacent solventes annuatim <u>X
grossos</u>, que nunc possidet Everardus uten Weyrde, perpetue.
^fEverd uten Werde^f
nota^g

---

^a *in a different hand (B).* ^b solvendis *ms.* ^c *in a later hand, 15th century.*
^d gedaynct *ms.* ^e *in the right margin, cancelled.* ^f *in the right margin.* ^g *in the left
margin, in the basic hand.*

fol.43v,   In parrochia sancte Ghertrudis, supra Raven
the first lines are somewhat corroded:

In parrochia sancte Ghertrudis habet domus IIII iugera, prout
iacent/ supra [Laghe Raven] a parte occidentali [Reni] inter terram/
[pronunc domicelle] Engelen Scorren de Speculo et heredum Lau-
rencii/ uten Gruythuys Onderdeel a parte aquilonis et meridionali/
que nunc una cum quatuor iugeribus immediate subscriptis possidet/
Hermannus [de Coppel] pro XVIII libris III solidis IIII denariis annuatim absque defalcatione ad XI annos ab anno LXV *[1365]* Petri
solvendis Martini et Petri, vel cadet ab omni iure. Inde est littera. Per
fratrem Hugonem dispensatorem.
Coppel[a]

Item ibidem IIII iugera prout iacent inter terram dominorum Theutonicorum a superiori parte, et terram Johannis et Gerardi Pot
fratrum a parte inferiori, que una cum quatuor iugeribus predictis
modo possidet Hermannus de Coppel pro annua pensione supradicta.
Coppel[a]

---

[a] *in the left margin.*

fol.44r,   Sancte Ghertrudis, supra Raven   XLIIII
the first lines are highly corroded:

Item ibidem novem iugera prout iacent [supra Raven iuxta villam]/
de Jutfaes et [locum —]/ [—][a parte meridionali et terram —]/ a
parte aquilonis, que modo possident [Johannes filius Petri et Wil]/
helmus Noddert ad X annos ab anno LXVIII *[1368]* Petri pro Vj
[5.5]/ marcis et II loet argenti aut pagamento equivalenti in Traiecto
solvendis Martini et Petri, vel cadent ab omni iure. Inde est littera.
Per fratrem Hugonem dispensatorem.
[a]Ulterius possidebit Wilhelmus Noddert ad IX annos ab anno
LXXVII *[1377]* Petri, una cum duobus iugeribus sequentibus pro
LXXXIIII libris, XI talentis cere, XI caponibus solvendis ut supra.
Per fratrem Johannem Gaude commendatorem.[a]
[b]Johannes filius Petri[b]
[c]et Wilhelmus Noddert[c]

Item ibidem duo iugera prout iacent supra Raven communia cum
terra Gerardi Witten civis Traiectensis, inter terram Johannis de

Speculo a parte superiori, et terram capituli sancti Martini Traiectensis a parte inferiori, que modo possidet Amilius filius Ernesti <u>ad X
annos ab anno LXVI [1366] Petri pro VII libris denariorum Traiectensium, II talentis cere et II caponibus annuatim</u>, absque defalcatione Martini et Petri solvendis vel cadet ab omni iure, et cetera prout
littera tenet. Per fratrem Hugonem dispensatorem.
^aModo possidebit Wilhelmus Noddert una cum IX iugeribus supra-
dictis sub annua pensione prescripta.^a
^b<u>Amilius filius Ernesti</u>^b
^c<u>Wilhelmus Noddert</u>^c

----

^a *in a different hand (C).* ^b *in the right margin, cancelled.* ^c *in the right margin, in the
same hand as* ^a.

fol.44v,   <u>Sancte Ghertrudis, in Galicop</u>
the first lines are highly corroded:

[Item ibidem domus nostra habet] <u>quinque iug[era] et unam [are-
am]</u>/ [inter terram heredum] magistri [Hugonis -]/ [a parte meridionali et terram] Johannis de Groenewoude a/ parte [aquilonis, prout
illa una cum] area possidebat a nobis/ S[—.] Modo vero dictam
terram una cum area/ [possidebit a nobis Gerardus] Piil filius Tydemanni in Galicop/ ad VIII annos ab anno LXX *[1370]* Petri ad
Cathedram, pro ^aXXXV libris denariorum in Traiecto dativorum^a
^bparvorum vel pagamento equivalenti tempore solucionis in Traiec-
to^b et XIII pullis et dimidio modio hanepzaeds et II bindel haneps
annuatim Martini et Petri solvendis vel cadet ab omni iure, secundum
tenorem littere quam inde habemus. Per fratrem ^cJohannem Gaude
dispensatorem.^c
^d<u>Gerardus Piil</u>^d

<u>In parrochia de Gheno</u> habet domus tres <u>areas</u> in villa de Gheno
insimul iacentes, solventes annuatim <u>IIII solidos denariorum Traiec-
tensium</u>, quas quondam possidebat Martinus filius Martini. Modo
possidet easdem Alardus dictus van den Doeme civis Traiectensis,
prout iacent inter terram ecclesie de Gheyne a parte orientali et terram seu aream Elisabet relicte Ghiseberti Muys a parte occidentali.
^d<u>Alardus van den Doem hereditarie</u>^d

----

^a *in a different hand.* ^b *in the basic hand, cancelled.* ^c *in the hand of* ^a *written on an
erased line.* ^d *in the left margin in the basic hand.*

fol.45r, In Jutfaes XLV
the first lines are rather corroded:

In parrochia de Jutfaes habet domus [quinque iugera prout iacent]/
[inter terram dictum Gronewech] a parte superiori [—]/ a parte
[inferiori prout illa possidet Hermannus Wolf filius]/ Wolfs de [Jut-
faes ad X annos ab anno LXI *[1361]* Petri]/ pro XII libris denariorum Traiectensium annuatim [et V pullis absque defalcatione
Martini]/ et Petri solvendis, vel cadet ab omni iure, et cetera prout
littera [exinde]/ tenet. Per fratrem Hugonem dispensatorem.
[a]Modo possidet dictam terram prout iacet Wilhelmus Bartholomei.[a]
[b]Hermannus Wolf[b]
[c]Wilhelmus Bartholomei[c]

---

[a] *in a different hand.* [b] *in the right margin.* [c] *in the right margin, in the same hand
as* [a].

fol.45v, In Jutfaes
the first lines are somewhat corroded:

Item ibidem Ij *[1.5]* iugera continentia VIII hont terre prout iacent/
[retro ecclesiam] de Jutfaes inter terram relicte Alberti Keysers/ [a
parte superiori] et terram heredum Gerardi Homboud civis Traiec/
tensis [a parte inferiori], que [modo] possidet dominus Egidius Piil/
de Jutfaes presbyter ad X annos ab anno LXVII *[1367]* Petri pro IIII
libris denariorum Traiectensium annuatim Martini et Petri solvendis,
vel potest expandari in paratioribus bonis suis ubicumque locorum
sitis et cetera secundum litteram quam exinde habemus. Per fratrem
Hugonem.
[a]Dominus Egidius Piil[a]

---

[a] *in the left margin.*

fol.46r, In Jutfaes XLVI
the first lines are highly corroded:

Item ibidem dimidium [mansum] prout iacet [in iurisdictione temporali — domini]/ de Vianen, quo [superius et inferius —]/ Homboud
[civis Traiectensis] prout [——]/ [—] a nobis possidebat. Modo possidet [Gerardus Oudecalle]/ ad X annos ab anno [LXVII *[1367]*
Purificatione Marie pro — libris denariorum] Traiectensium et VIII

pullis [annuatim absque defalcatione Martini et Petri solvendis]/ vel cadet ab omni iure et cetera prout littera tenet. Per fratrem Hugonem dispensatorem.

^aGerid Oudecalle^a

---

   ^a *in the right margin.*

fol.46v,   In Jutfaes
the first lines are rather corroded:

[Item ibidem <u>decem iugera</u> prout iacent iuxta] Yselam apud Kipperd[s]/ [— in Jutfaes prout —]/ [— et inferius — domus]/ [— nunc possident heredes Hermanni] Keyser/ [que X iugera quondam colebat] Gerardus Philippi. Modo possidet ea/ [Ghisebertus filius Mathie] ad X annos ab anno LXIII *[1363]* Petri/ [pro <u>XXXII libris denariorum Traiectensium et]</u> X pullis annuatim absque defalcatione Martini et/ Petri solvendis vel cadet ab omni iure. Dictam terram non ulterius locabit alicui nec edificia super eandem constructa non ammovebit nec alienabit absque consensu commendatoris vel dispensatoris et cetera secundum tenorem littere quam inde habemus. Per fratrem Hugonem dispensatorem.

^aUlterius idem Ghisebertus possidebit dictam terram ad X annos ab anno LXXIII *[1373]* Petri pro XLVI libris denariorum Traiectensium et X pullis annuatim absque defalcatione Martini et Petri solvendis, aut cadet ab omni iure et cetera prout littera tenet. Per fratrem Johannem Gaude.^a

^bUlterius possidebit Weyndelmodis Giselberti Mathie ad X annos ab anno LXXXIIII *[1384]* Petri pro L libris monete Traiectensis qua pactus persolvantur et X pullis annuatim absque defalcatione Martini et Petri solvendis aut cadet ab omni iure et cetera. Per me fratrem Gerardum.^b

^cGhisebertus Mathie^c

---

   ^a *in a different hand (C).* ^b *in another hand.* ^c *in the left margin, in the basic hand (A).*

fol.47r,   In Jutfaes   XLVII
the first lines are rather corroded:

Item ibidem <u>unum iuger cum dimidio</u> prout [insimul] iacent exten/ dentia se a iurisdictione temporali de Jutfaes [ad locum dictum Yseldic in]/ iurisdictionem domini^a de Yselsteyne, inter [locum dictum

Heyenco]per [—]/ a parte superiori et terram ecclesie de Yselsteyne
a parte inferiori.
ᵇHeredes Hermanni Keyserᵇ

ᶜItem ibidem <u>duo iugera</u> insimul communi sulcu in uno agro iacentia,
quorum una medietas ad domum nostram sancte Katerine, reliqua
vero ad leprosos pertinet. Quam terram prescriptam insimul, scilicet
triaᵈ iugera cum dimidio, modo possident heredes Hermanni Keyser
<u>ad XII annos</u> ab anno LXVI *[1366]* Petri pro <u>VIII libris X solidis et
IIII pullis</u> annuatim, absque defalcatione Martini et Petri solvendis,
vel cadent ab omni iure et cetera prout littera tenet. Per fratrem
Hugonem.

ᵃ *dominii ms.* ᵇ *in the right margin.* ᶜ *linked with brace to the foregoing item.*
ᵈ *with different ink on an erased spot.*

fol.47v,   In Jutfaes
the first lines are somewhat corroded:

Item ibidem <u>dimidium mansum</u>, prout iacet supra Laghe Raven ab
[orientali parte Reni] inter terram monasterii sancti Pauli Traiectensis a parte aqui[lonis et terram heredum] Maechelmi de Busco Ducis
a parte meridionali, quem dimidium mansum una cum dimidio quartali proxime sequenti modo possidet Johannes filius Johannis Lizen
<u>ad X annos</u> ab anno LXVII *[1367]* Petri pro <u>XXIIII antiquis</u> scudatis
auri, aut pro pagamento equivalenti <u>et X solidis et V talentis cere et
X pullis</u> annuatim absque defalcatione Martini et Petri solvendis, vel
cadet ab omni iure, sub ceteris condicionibus in littera quam inde
habemus contentis. Per fratrem Hugonem dispensatorem.
ᵃJohannes filius Johannis Lizenᵃ

ᵃ *in the left margin.*

fol.48r,   In Jutfaes   XLVIII
the first lines are highly corroded:

Item ibidem <u>quartale terre prout</u> iacet [supra Laghe Raven inter]
terram/ curati ecclesie sancti Nycolai a [parte superiori — filii]/
Alardi uten Weyrde a parte inferiori [—]/ duo iugera modo possidet
una cum [dimidio manso supradicto Johannes]/ filius Johannis Lizen
ad annos et pro annua pen[sione superius signata]. Reliquam vero

medietatem, scilicet II iugera, modo possident Hermannus de/
Coppel et Gerardus Ever, una cum quadam alia terra [superius] in
parro/chia sancti Nycolai signata ad annos et sub eadem annua
pensione/ ibidem signata.
^aJohannes filius Johannis Lizen^a
^aCoppel et Gerardus Ever^a

---

  ^a *in the right margin.*

fol.48v,　　In parrochia Civilis Ecclesie, in Heyencop
the first lines are highly corroded:

Item [in parrochia Civilis] ecclesie habet dicta nostra domus VIII
iugera/ [— inter terram] monasterii sancti Pauli Traiectensis/ [a
parte superiori — dominorum] sancti Petri Traiectensis a parte inferiori,/ [que VIII — iugeribus] iacentibus in parrochia de Vloten/ [—
] sunt. Modo possidebunt Hugho de Bredae/ civis [Traiectensis et
Johannes] Wedighe filius Ghiseberti ad X annos ab anno/ LXIX
[1369] Petri pro IIII marcis et IIII loet argenti et XI pullis annuatim,
absque defalcatione Martini et Petri solvendis vel cadent ab omni
iure, et cetera prout littera tenet. Per fratrem Hugonem dispensatorem.
^aHugo de Bredae et Johannes Wedighe^a

---

  ^a *in the left margin.*

fol.49r,　　Civilis Ecclesie, in Heyencop　　　　　　　　XLIX
the first lines are highly corroded:

Item ibidem in Heyencop unum mansum [dictum —]/ hoeve, prout
iacet apud [Antiquum Rhenum — Ghi]/seberti Vastraed a parte
superiori [—]/den civis Traiectensis a parte inferiori, quem modo
[possidet Ghise]/bertus de Roeden ad XII annos ab anno LXVII
[1367] Petri pro XXXII libris denariorum Traiectensium et XVI
pullis et I loep salis annuatim absque defalcatione Martini et Petri
solvendis, vel cadet ab omni iure et cetera secundum tenorem littere
quam inde habemus. Per fratrem Hugonem dispensatorem.
^aGhiselbertus de Roeden^a

---

  ^a *in the right margin.*

fol.49v, <u>Civilis Ecclesie</u>
the first lines are somewhat corroded:

Item ibidem [<u>XX^{ti} iugera</u>] prout iacent inter terram domini Frederici uten/ [Hamme militis a parte superiori] et terram nostre domus sancte Ka/[therine] a parte inferiori, quam pronunc colit Jacobus Loze, que XX iugera modo possidet Nicolaus de Wiel ad X annos ab anno LXIX *[1369]* Lamberti, <u>pro Vj *[5.5]* marcis et VI loet argenti et III solidis IX denariis</u> aut pagamento equivalenti et <u>IIII talentis cere et X caponibus X pullis</u> annuatim, absque defalcatione Martini et Petri solvendis vel cadet ab omni iure, et cetera, prout littera exinde quam habemus tenet. Per fratrem Hugonem dispensatorem.
^aUlterius idem Nicolaus possidebit dictam terram ad X annos ab anno LXXVIII *[1378]* Petri pro XCV libris cum ceteris suprascriptis absque defalcatione Martini et Petri solvendis vel cadet ab omni iure.^a
^bUlterius Johannes filius eius possidebit predictam terram ad X annos ab anno LXXXVIII *[1388]* Petri pro XCV libris cum ceteris suprascriptis absque defalcatione.^b
^cNicolaus de Wiel^c

---

^a *in a different hand (C).* ^b *in another hand.* ^c *in the left margin in the basic hand.*

fol.50r. <u>Civilis Ecclesie</u> L

Item ibidem <u>quatuor iugera terre</u>, paulo plus, prout iacent inter terram nostre domus sancte Katerine quam nunc possidet Nicolaus de Wiel a parte superiori, et terram heredum Henrici Plaetzard a parte inferiori, que modo possidet Jacobus Loze <u>ad X annos</u> ab anno LXII *[1362]* Petri pro <u>X libris V solidis denariorum Traiectensium et V pullis</u> annuatim absque defalcatione Martini et Petri solvendis, vel cadet ab omni iure et cetera prout littera exinde tenet. Per fratrem Hugonem dispensatorem.
^aModo dictam terram possident ulterius Wolterus Loze et Aleidis soror eius, ad X annos ab anno LXXII *[1372]* Petri pro XVIII libris denariorum Traiectensium et V pullis Martini et Petri, et dimidium quarti butiri annuatim in fine May solvendis absque defalcatione, sub condicionibus ut littera tenet. Per fratrem Thomam.^a
^bJacobus Loze^b
^cWolterus Loze et Aleidis eius soror^c

---

^a *in a different hand (B).* ^b *in the right margin, cancelled.* ^c *in the right margin, in the same hand as* ^a.

fol.50v.   <u>Civilis Ecclesie</u>

Item ibidem <u>XIIII iugera</u> prout iacent inter terram nostre domus sancte Katerine a parte superiori et terram heredum Richardi Vernoeghen a parte inferiori, prout illa quondam a nobis possidebat Ghisebertus Vastradi. Modo possidet ea Jacobus filius Johannis <u>ad X annos</u> ab anno LXVIII *[1368]* Petri pro <u>LII libris X solidis denariorum Traiectensium et II talentis piperis et VII caponibus VII pullis</u> annuatim absque defalcatione Martini et Petri solvendis, vel cadet ab omni iure. Non ulterius locabit nec dividet terram absque consensu et omnia plantata super dictam terram tam in salicibus quam aliis arboribus non evellet. Sed salices potest denudare a ramis more solito debitis temporibus et cetera prout littera exinde tenet. Per fratrem Hugonem dispensatorem.
^aJacobus filius Johannis^a

---

  ^a *in the left margin.*

fol.51r.   <u>Civilis Ecclesie</u>   LI

Item ibidem <u>duo iugera et Ij *[1.5]* hont terre</u> prout iacent communi sulcu cum terris capituli sancti Martini Traiectensis necnon Johannis Lyebard et Aleydis relicte Bernardi Proys, quam terram modo possidet Bernardus Creyt filius Erkenradis <u>ad X annos</u> ab anno LXV *[1365]* <u>Lamberti pro V libris XII solidis VI denariis, II talentis cere</u> et II caponibus annuatim absque defalcatione Martini et Petri solvendis, vel cadet ab omni iure et cetera, prout littera exinde optenta tenet. Per fratrem Hugonem.
^a<u>Bernardus Creyt filius Erkenradis</u>^a

---

  ^a *in the right margin.*

fol.51v.   <u>Civilis Ecclesie</u>

Item ibidem <u>duo iugera cum dimidio</u>, empta quondam erga Theodericum de Weyde, prout iacent in dicta parrochia inter terram nostre domus sancte Katerine quam nunc colit Ghisekinus Alberti a parte superiori et terram Ghiseberti de Weyda a parte inferiori.

^aItem ibidem <u>XI iugera terre</u> prout iacent inter terram domini Frederici Utenhamme militis a parte superiori, et terram Ghiseberti de

Ruweel filii Jacobi de Puteo a parte inferiori, que XIIIj *[13.5]* iugera insimul prescripta una cum quadam alia terra et areis inferius in parrochia de Vloten sitis et signatis modo possidet Rotardus Ansem <u>ad X annos</u> ab anno LXVI *[1366]* <u>Petri pro LVII libris denariorum Traiectensium et VI caponibus et XV pullis</u> annuatim absque defalcatione Martini et Petri solvendis, vel cadet ab omni iure, et cetera prout littera exinde optenta tenet. Per fratrem Hugonem dispensatorem.

[b]Ulterius possidebit dictam terram Wilhelmus filius Helye una cum quadam alia terra et areis inferius in parrochia de Vloten signatis pro LXXXVI libris denariorum Traiectensium et XIIj *[12.5]* solidis et VI caponibus et XV pullis annuatim absque defalcatione et cetera prout littera tenet. Per fratrem Johannem Gaude commendatorem.[b]

[c]Ulterius possidebit predictam terram Wilhelmus filius Helye una cum quadam alia terra et areis inferius in parrochia de Vloten signatis pro XC libris denariorum Traiectensium ende XIIj *[12.5]* solidis ende VI caponibus ende XV pullis annuatim absque defalcatione et cetera prout littera tenet. Per fratrem Johannem Haeze.[c]

[d]Rotardus Ansem, Wolterus filius eius[d]

[e]Wilhelmus filius Helye[e]

---

[a] *linked with brace to the foregoing item.* [b] *in a different hand (C).* [c] *in another hand.* [d] *in the left margin, cancelled.* [e] *in the left margin, in the same hand as* [b].

fol.52r,   <u>Civilis Ecclesie, iuxta Mernam</u>   LII
the first lines are highly corroded:

Item ibidem [<u>dimidium mansum</u> prout iacet in dicta Civili parro]/ [chia andie Meerne inter terram dominorum Theutonicorum a parte]/ [superiori et terram domus nostre sancte Katerine quam —]/ [[a] a parte inferiori prout eundem dimidium mansum] una cum/ quadam alia terra quondam a nobis possidebat Johannes Zuerbier. Modo possidet eundem Theodericus Edelkint una cum uno manso et VIIj *[7.5]* hont terre in parrochia de Vloten iacentibus et ibidem inferius scriptis et notatis ad <u>quinque annos</u> ab anno LXVII *[1367]* Petri sub eadem annua pensione et condicionibus ibidem iuxta aliam terram in parrochia de Vloten expressatis. Per fratrem Hugonem.

[b]Ulterius idem Theodericus possidebit dictam terram una cum uno manso et uno agro et VIIj *[7.5]* hont terre in parrochia de Vloten situatis, ad annos et sub eadem annua pensione inferius iuxta aliam terram signatis, ut littera exinde tenet. Per fratrem Johannem Gaude.[b]

^cUlterius possidebit ad X annos ab anno LXXIX *[1379]* Petri pro C.XIX libris denariorum Traiectensium cum ceteris suprascriptis.^c
^dUlterius possidebit Petrus dictus Koel predictam terram ad X annos ab anno LXXXIX *[1389]* Petri pro C.XIX libris. Per fratrem Johannem Haze.
^eDirc Edelkint^e

---

^a *not filled in.* ^b *in a different hand (C).* ^c *in another hand (D).* ^d *in yet another hand.* ^e *in the right margin in the basic hand.*

On a loose leaf in a 14th-century hand:

<u>In parochia Civilis Ecclesie in Galicop et apud Antiquum Renum habet domus hanc</u> terram subscriptam: primo VIII iugera, que possidebat Hugho de Bredae et Johannes Wedighe.

Item ibidem unum mansum qui dicitur Schaets hove, quem nunc possidet Ghisebertus de Roden.

Item ibidem XX iugera que nunc possidet Johannes de Wiel.

Item ibidem IIII iugera, que possident Wolterus Loze et Aleydis eius uxor.

Item ibidem XIIII iugera, que possidebat Jacobus filius Johannis.

Item ibidem duo iugera Ij *[1.5]* hont, que possidet Bernardus Creyt filius Erkenradis.

Item ibidem XIIIj *[13.5]* iugera, que possidet Wilhelmus filius Helye.

Item ibidem dimidium mansum quem possidet Theodericus Edelkint.

Summa LXXXVj *[85.5]* iugera, Ij *[1.5]* hont.

++

On a small piece of paper, elsewhere in the book, late 15th- or early 16th-century, recto:
Item dat stueck dair die moelen op staet uut die Wecht in die waterganck, IIIj *[3.5]* merghen ende II hont

Item dat stueck over die weterynge die moellen op staet, III merghen ende II hont minus XXV roeyen facit VII merghen ende een hont minus XXV roeyen.

Item onsen acker dair aen van Griete Spykers, VIII hont ende XXII roeyen.

Item dat stueck van sinte Berberen gaesthuys lant, dair boven Aert Wernertsz ende beneden die heren van sinte Peter.

verso:

Item dat stueck beneden den bogert, XIII hont ende XVI roeyen.

Item dat stueck uuten bogert aenden hoeck toe, XVI hont.

Item dat stueck inden hoeck by Aert Evertsz, XVj *[15.5]* hont ende II roeyen.

Item dat stueck beneden by Aert voirscreven, XX hont XXI roeyen.

   Somma van deser syden X merghen ende V hont minus IX roeyen.

   Somma XVIII merghen minus XXXIIII roeyen nae mynre reke-nynge.

          ++++++++++++++++++++++++++++++++++++

On a sheet of paper, folded vertically, partly the same statements in a 16th-century hand,
outside:
Dit is alsuelke lant als Coernelis Goeyerszoon gebruuct heeft ende ghemeten is.

Item III acker houdende ghemeten lants III mergen, dair boven die heren van sinte Meyren naest gelant syn ende beneden Ghisbert Branszoon naest ghelant, streckende mitten enen eynde aen den Aellenderpschen wech ende mitten anderen eynde aen Ghisbert Branszoon lant.

Item noch VIII acker streckende mitten eenren eynde aen den Aellenderpschen wech ende mitten anderen eynde aen die Boerch

Wleyt, houdende ghemeten lants Ij *[1.5]* mergen ende XII roeyen, dair boven die kapel van die Merrel ende die joeffer van Witte Wrouen ªende beneden aenª naest ghelant syn ende beneden die heren van sinte Meyren naest ghelant syn.

Item noch dat stueck vanden Alendorpª Alenderpschen wech aen Coernelys hoefstede, houdende IIIIj *[4.5]* mergen, dair boven naest gelant die heren van Oudemoenster ende Erst van Drakenboerch ende benede die joefferen van Wytte Wrouen.

Item noch dat stueck mitten boegert ende hoefstede aen Baeynis boeghert toe, houdende XX hont, dair wij ende Aert Taest boven naest ghelant syn ende beneden die joefferen van Wytte Wrouen naest ghelant syn.

Item noch III ackeren by dat croeys aen beyden syden van den wech te Statwert aen, houdende VIII hont ende XX roeyen, dair boven Aert Taest naest ghelant is ende beneden sinte Berberen ghesthuys.

Item dat stueck dair die moelen op staet uut die Wecht in die water-ganck, hout IIIj *[3.5]* mergen ende II hont.

Item dat stueck dair tegens aen, hout III mergen ende II hont minus XXV roeyen,
facit VII mergen ende een hont minus XXV roeyen.

Item onsen acker van Griete Spijkers dair besyden aen, hout VIII hont ende XXII roeyen.

Item dat stueck beneden den boeghert, XIII hont ende XVI roeyen.

Item dat stueck mitten boghert aenden hoeck toe, XVI hont.

Item dat stueck inden hoeck by Aert Everszoon, XVI hont ende II roeyen.

Item dat stueck beneden by Aert Everszoon voirscreven, XX hont en XXI roeyen.

Somma XVIII mergen endeª minus XXXIIII roeyen nae mynre re-kenynghe.

inside:

Item noch enen acker streckende vanden aefteren dick totten ouden Rynschen dieck toe, houdende VII hont ende X roeyen, dair boven naest ghelant syn die heren van Oudemoenster ende beneden Ghisbert van Lichtenberch naest ghelant is.

Item noch in dat overste stueck in Gherit van Rijnen lant in Langg-heraech enen smalen acker, houdende IIII hont lants ende XIXj *[19.5]* roey.

Item noch enen acker op die kae teynden Langheraech, II hont mi-nus V roeyen, dair boven naest ghelant sinte Berberen ghesthuys ᵃende benedenᵃ ende beneden naest ghelant is Gherit van Rijn.

Somma tsamen van dit voirscreven lant XV mergen ende Vj *[5.5]* hont ende VIj *[6.5]* roey.

Item noch ghemeten lants VIII mergen ende II roeyen in dat Rynlant in Boerkerker kerspel, dair boven die heren van Oudemoenster ende beneden Heycmier Wleyt.

Somma van dit voirscreven lant tesamen XXIII mergen ende Vj *[5.5]* hont ende VIIIj *[8.5]* roey.

Item myn wrou te Witte Wrouwen heeft IIII mergen lants aen die Merrel, dair boven naest ghelant die heren van sinte Katerynen ende beneden naest ghelant die kapel van die Merrel.

Item noch heeft myn vrou voirscreven IIII mergen lants, dair boven Jan Zoerbier ende beneden naest ghelant Wouter die Budeyn.

ᵃ *cancelled.*

fol.52v.   In Vloten

Item ibidem in parrochia de Vloten habet dicta domus tria iugera terre paulo minus aut plus prout iacent apud Antiquum Renum inter terram Huberti de Uulven a parte superiori et terram liberorum Sca-de de Welle a parte inferiori, que modo possident una cum VIII iugeribus in parrochia Civilis ecclesie superius scriptis et signatis Hug-ho de Bredae civis Traiectensis et Johannes Wedighe ad X annos ab anno LXIX *[1369]* Petri sub eadem annua pensione ibidem iuxta

aliam terram superius expressata. Per fratrem Hugonem.
ªHugo de Bredae et Johannes Wedigheª

ᵇItem ibidem dimidium iuger prout iacet iuxta Mernam inter terram
heredum domicelle Elisabet de Puteo a parte superiori et terram VIII
agris nostre domus a parte inferiori, prout illud modo possidet Gerardus Hollander ad vitam suam pro XIII solidos et IIII denarios annuatim Martini et Petri solvendis vel cadet ab omni iure. Inde est littera.
Per fratrem Hugonem.ᵇ ᶜvendita est hec terra.ᶜ

ª *in the left margin.* ᵇ *cancelled.* ᶜ *in a different hand.*

fol.53r.   In Vloten   LIII

Item ibidem iuxta Mernam <u>unam aream</u> prout iacet inter terram
heredum Gerardi Zuerbier a parte superiori et terram monasterii
Albarum Dominarum in Traiecto a parte inferiori, quam modo possidet Wilhelmus filius Petri <u>ad X annos</u> ab anno LXI *[1361]* Petri pro
<u>II libris</u> denariorum Traiectensium et <u>X iuvenis</u> pullis annuatim Mar-
tini et Petri solvendis vel cadet ab omni iure. Inde habemus litteram.
Per fratrem Hugonem.
ªWillem Peterszoenª

Item ibidem <u>VIII iugera terre</u> prout iacent in Alendorp inter terram
Theoderici Heye a parte superiori et terram heredum Frederici Heye
a parte inferiori, que quondam possidebat Hermannus Heye. Modo
possidet ea Henricus Heye <u>ad X annos</u> ab anno LX *[1360]* Valentini
<u>pro XX libris denariorum Traiectensium, IIII talentis cere, VIII
caponibus</u> annuatim absque defalcatione Martini et Petri solvendis
vel cadet ab omni iure. Inde est littera. Per fratrem Hugonem.
ªHenricus Heyeª

ª *in the right margin.*

fol.53v.   In Vloten

Item ibidem <u>X iugera terre</u> prout iacent in die Nederslaghe inter
terram Mauricii filii Meng de Heynen a parte superiori et terram
Werneri de Lonen a parte inferiori.
ªTheodericus Heyeª
ᵇNella eius uxorᵇ

^cItem ibidem <u>VII iugera terre</u> dicta Zantcamp quibus domus nostra personaliter propius iacet ex utraque parte, que XVII iugera insimul prescripta quondam possidebat Henricus Badeloghe. Modo possidet ea Theodericus Heye <u>ad VII annos</u> ab anno LXV *[1365]* Lamberti, <u>pro XXVII libris denariorum Traiectensium et XVII pullis</u> annuatim absque defalcatione Martini et Petri solvendis vel cadet ab omni iure et cetera, prout littera exinde tenet. Per fratrem Hugonem.

^dUlterius possidebit dictam terram Nella relicta Theoderici Heye cum suis pueris ad X annos ab anno LXXIII *[1373]* Petri pro XXXVI libris denariorum Traiectensium et XVII pullis annuatim absque defalcatione Martini et Petri solvendis aut cadet ab omni iure et cetera, prout littera tenet. Per fratrem Thomam.^d

^aTheodericus Heye^a
^bNella eius uxor^b

---

^a *in the left margin, cancelled.* ^b *in the left margin, in the same hand as* ^d. ^c *linked with brace to the foregoing item.* ^d *in a different hand (B).*

fol.54r. <u>In Vloten</u> LIIII

Item ibidem <u>unum mansum et unum agrum</u> continentem VII hont terre prout iacet supra Hoghewoert in iurisdictione temporali prepositi sancti Salvatoris Traiectensis, inter terram capituli sancte Marie et fratrum domus Theutonicorum in Traiecto, Nicolai de Puteo, Theoderici Heye et Johannis Zuerbier a parte superiori, et terram conventus monasterii Albarum Dominarum in Traiecto a parte inferiori. Quam terram prescriptam una cum dimidio manso superius in parrochia Civilis ecclesie sito et signato Johannes Zuerbier possidebat. Modo possidet eandem Theodericus Edelkint ad quinque annos ab anno LXVII *[1367]* Petri <u>pro LVI libris denariorum Traiectensium, XII talentis cere, XII caponibus, XII pullis</u> annuatim absque defalcatione Martini et Petri solvendis vel cadet ab omni iure sub ceteris condicionibus in littera quam inde habemus contentis. Per fratrem Hugonem.

^aUlterius idem Theodericus possidebit dictam terram una cum dimidio manso superius in parochia Civilis ecclesie sito ad XII annos ab anno LXX *[1370]* Petri. Et dabit tam de hiis quam de aliis VII marcas et XI loet argenti et XII talenta cere, XII capones et XII pullas annuatim solvendas Martini et Petri aut cadet ab omni iure et cetera, prout littera tenet. Per fratrem Johannem Gaude.^a

^bTheodericus Edelkint^b

---

^a *in a different hand (C).* ^b *in the right margin.*

fol.54v.   In Vloten

Item ibidem <u>aream et IIII iugera</u> terre paulo plus aut minus, prout iacent inter terram heredum Henrici Plaetzard a parte superiori et terram domicelle Aleydis filie Wilhelmi van der Weyde a parte inferiori, quam quondam possidebat Lubbertus Vos. Modo possidet Ghisekinus filius Alberti <u>ad X annos</u> ab anno LXV *[1365]* Lamberti <u>pro VI libris X solidis II caponibus</u> annuatim absque defalcatione Martini et Petri solvendis vel cadet ab omni iure. Inde est littera. Per fratrem Hugonem.

[a]¶ Modo dictam terram possidebit ulterius idem Ghisekinus ad X annos ab anno LXXV *[1375]* Petri pro XIIII libris denariorum Traiectensium et II caponibus annuatim Martini et Petri solvendis vel cadet ab omni iure et cetera, prout littera tenet. Per fratrem Johannem Gaude vicecommendatorem.[a]

[b]Ghisekinus filius Alberti[b]

Item ibidem <u>duo iugera</u> prout iacent et ea quondam possidebat Johannes Loze. Modo possident ea Elzebela relicta Johannis Lozen pro una medietate et Machteldis relicta Hugonis uten Gaerde pro alia. Solventur exinde annuatim <u>VIII grossi</u> perpetue.

[b]relicta Johannis Lozen hereditarie[b]

nota[c]

---

[a] *in a different hand (C).* [b] *in the left margin, in the basic hand.* [c] *in the right margin, probably in the basic hand.*

fol.55r.   In Vloten   LV

Item ibidem <u>XXII iugera terre</u> prout iacent, quibus a superiori parte propius iacet Bernardus Creyt cum V iugeribus terre que tenet a Wernero van der Hare et ab inferiori parte dominus Bertoldus perpetuus vicarius in ecclesia sancti Johannis Traiectensis cum tribus iugeribus spectantibus ad suum altare in eadem ecclesia fundatum. Que XXII iugera modo possidet Ghisebertus van der Hare <u>ad X annos</u> ab anno LXV *[1365]* Pontiani pro <u>XLIII libris denariorum Traiectensium et XXI pullis</u> annuatim absque defalcatione Martini et Petri solvendis vel cadet ab omni iure et cetera, prout littera tenet. Per fratrem Hugonem dispensatorem.

[a]Modo dictam terram possidebunt Ghisebertus van der Hare et Alpharus uten Ham ad X annos ab anno LXXV *[1375]* Petri pro LVIII libris V solidis, XXI pullis, per fratrem Johannem Gaude com-

mendatorem, annuatim Martini et Petri solvendis vel cadent ab omni iure et cetera, prout littera tenet.^a

^bGhisebertus van der Hare^b

---

^a *in a different hand.* ^b *in the right margin, in the basic hand.*

fol.55v.   In Vloten

Item ibidem aream continentem VII hont terre prout iacet inter terram Alberti Alvekin civis Traiectensis a parte superiori et terram nostre domus quam Rotardus Ansem nunc possidet a parte inferiori. ^aModo possidet Wilhelmus filius Helye una cum terra superius signata.^a

^bRotardus Ansem^b

^cWilhelmus filius Helye^c

^dItem ibidem aream et Vj *[5.5]* iugera terre, quibus prescripta area nostre domus de VII hont terre propius iacet a parte superiori et terra Wilhelmi de Weyda a parte inferiori. Quas duas areas et Vj *[5.5]* iugera terre prescriptas una cum quadam alia terra superius in parrochia Civilis ecclesie sita et signata, modo possidet Rotardus Ansem *ad* X annos ab anno LXVI *[1366]* Petri sub eadem annua pensione et sub condicionibus superius iuxta aliam terram signatis. Per fratrem Hugonem.

^aModo possidet Wilhelmus Helye una cum alia terra superius in parochia Civilis ecclesie signata.^a

^bRotardus Ansem^b

^cWilhelmus filius Helye^c

---

^a *in a different hand (C).* ^b *in the left margin, cancelled.* ^c *in the left margin, in the same hand as ^a.* ^d *linked with brace to the foregoing item.*

fol.56r,   In Vloten   LVI
the first lines are somewhat corroded:

Item ibidem decem iugera terre prout iacent supra H[eynxstmade]/ inter terram nostre domus a parte superiori et terram [Wilhelmi de Weyda] a/ parte inferiori, prout illa modo possidet Gerardus Coliin ad X annos ab anno LXVII *[1367]* Petri pro XXVIII libris V grossis denariorum Traiectensium, V caponibus V pullis absque defalcatione Martini et Petri solvendis vel cadet ab omni iure et cetera, prout littera exinde tenet. Per fratrem Hugonem dispensatorem.

^aUlterius ad X annos ab anno LXXVII *[1377]* Petri pro LXXXII libris XVII solidis IIII denariis, V caponibus V pullis, per fratrem Johannem Gaude commendatorem, annuatim Martini et Petri solvendis vel cadet ab omni iure prout littera tenet.^a
^bGherid Coliin^b

Item in eadem parochia IIII iugera terre prout illa quondam possidebat a nobis Nicolaus Jagher, iacentia inter terram domini Frederici uten Hamme militis a parte superiori et terram monasterii Albarum Dominarum et etiam bagutarum in Traiecto, nuncupatam die Helle, a parte inferiori. Que modo possidet Nicolaus Boudewini ad X annos ab anno LXVI *[1366]* Petri pro IX libris denariorum Traiectensium annuatim absque defalcatione Martini et Petri solvendis vel cadet ab omni iure et cetera, prout littera tenet. Per fratrem Hugonem.
^aUlterius ad X annos ab anno LXXV *[1375]* Petri pro XIIII libris, per fratrem Johannem Gaude commendatorem, annuatim Martini et Petri solvendis aut cadet ab omni iure sine defalcatione.^a
^bNicolaus Boudewin^b

---

^a *in a different hand.* ^b *in the right margin, in the basic hand.*

fol.56v,   In Vloten
the first lines are highly corroded:

Item ibidem [supra Heynxst]made <u>XII iugera terre</u>, quibus cetera/ [terra nostre domus sancte Katerine propius iacet a parte superiori et − terra]/ [Wilhelmi de Weyda] a parte inferiori, que Johannes [Longus] modo possidet/ una cum ceteris terrarum iugeribus infrascriptis sub una et eadem annua/ pensione inferius signata.
^aJohannes Longus^a
^bGherid Coliin^b

^cItem ibidem supra Heynxstmade <u>tria iugera terre</u>, quibus terra Wilhelmi de Weyda propius iacet a parte superiori et terra unius altaris in Civili ecclesia Traiectensi fundati, a parte inferiori.
^aJohannes Longus^a
^bGherid Coliin^b

^cItem ibidem supra Heynxstmade <u>lj *[1.5]* iugera terre</u>, iacentia inter terram heredum Gerardi Bole a parte superiori et terram Ghiseberti de Yselsteyne a parte inferiori.

---

^a *in the left margin, cancelled.* ^b *in the left margin, in the same hand as* ∫ *on the next folio (C).* ^c *linked with brace to the foregoing item.*

fol.57r,   In Vloten   LVII
the first lines are highly corroded:

[Item ibidem supra Heynxstmade —]/ propius [iacet a parte superiori et terra ᵃ ᵇWilhelmi filii Hasenᵇ a parte inferiori.
ᶜJohannes Longusᶜ
ᵈGherid Coliinᵈ

ᵉItem ibidem <u>unum iuger</u> nuncupatum vulgariter Kiifacker, quo
superius et inferius terra Wilhelmi de Weyda propius iacet. Ista prescripta XXVII iugera terre cum dimidio modo possidet insimul Johannes Longus ad quinque annos <u>ab anno LXVI</u> *[1366]* Lamberti <u>pro
LXXX libris V solidis denariorum Traiectensium et XIII caponibus
et XIIII pullis</u> annuatim absque defalcatione Martini et Petri solvendis vel cadet ab omni iure. In fine annorum Lamberti resignabit
libere de dicta terra XVIIj *[17.5]* iugera. Cetera vero X iugera supra
Themat iacentia resignabit inculta Petri ad Cathedram deinde proxime sequenti, et cetera prout littera tenet quam inde habemus. Per
fratrem Hugonem dispensatorem.
ᶠModo prescripta XXVIIj *[27.5]* iugera possidebit ulterius Gerardus
Coliin ad X annos ab anno LXXII *[1372]* Petri et solvet annuatim
inde C.IX libras et X solidos denariorum Traiectensium et XIII
capones et XIIII pullas annuatim absque defalcatione Martini et Petri
solvendas vel cadet ab omni iure, et cetera prout littera exinde
confecta tenet. Per fratrem Johannem Gaude.ᶠ

ᵃ *corroded and cancelled.* ᵇ *in different writing under the cancelled part.* ᶜ *in the right
margin, cancelled.* ᵈ *in the right margin, in the same hand as* ʲ. ᵉ *linked with brace to the
foregoing item.* ᶠ *in a different hand (C).*

fol.57v,   In Vloten
the first lines are highly corroded:

Item [ibidem —]/ iacet unum iuger terre [—] ad Wilhelmum filium
Haessen iacentem/ inter terram capituli sancti Salvatoris Traiectensis
quam Johannes die Wale hereditarie possidet a parte superiori et
terram domicelli de Zulen a parte inferiori, que V iugera terre una
cum IIII hont terre sequentibus modo possidet a nobis Wilhelmus
custos ecclesie in Vloten ad X annos ab anno LXV *[1365]* Petri et
solvet tam de hiis quam de IIII hont sequentibus <u>XI libras XV solidos
et V capones</u> annuatim Martini et Petri vel cadet ab omni iure. Per
fratrem Hugonem dispensatorem.
ᵃWilhelmus custos in Vlotenᵃ

ᵇItem ibidem <u>IIII hont terre</u> prout iacent inter terram ecclesie de
Vloten a parte superiori et terram monialium Vallis sancte Marie a
parte inferiori, que modo possidet Wilhelmus custos in Vloten una
cum V iugeribus supradictis ad annos et sub annua pensione predicta. Per Hugonem.
ᵃWilhelmus custos in Vlotenᵃ

ᵃ *in the left margin.* ᵇ *linked with brace to the foregoing item.*

fol.58r, <u>In Vloten</u>   LVIII
the first part is heavily corroded:

Item [ibidem aream pro nunc — supra —]/ [———] de Weyda qua
[—]/ [cum terra circumiacente, quam aream Yda Vedinx possidebat
—]/ [Modo possidebit eandem Gerardus Stoep ad X annos ab an/
no LXIX *[1369]* Petri pro V libris denariorum Traiectensium annuatim absque defalcatione]/ [Martini et Petri solvendis vel cadet ab
omni iure —]/ alias arbores in huiusmodi area plantatas aut [—]/
una cum ipsa area meliorabit nec ammovebit easdem sed debito tempore salices a ramis denudare valebit ut moris est et cetera, sub condicionibus in littera quam inde habemus contentis. Per fratrem
Hugonem dispensatorem.
ᵃGerardus Stoepᵃ

ᵃ *in the right margin.*

fol.58v,   ¶ In Vloten, [curtis] de Weyda
the first part is heavily corroded:

[———]/ [———]/ [———]/ [———]/ [— hospitali – prout iacent inter
terram]/ [— septentrionali] et terram nostre domus a parte/ [meridi-
onali.]ˑ
Weydaᵃ

Item ibidem Op die hoeven <u>XII iugera et IIII hont</u>, quibus a parte
septentrionali propius iacet domus nostra personaliter cum terra prescripta dicta Spitael et a parte meridionali communis agger.
Weydaᵃ
oud sciltᵇ

Item op dat Goy <u>VIII iugera et IIj *[2.5]* hont</u> prout iacent inter aream

nostre domus quam pronunc Gerardus Stoep possidet a parte septentrionali et terram Werneri de Lonen a parte meridionali.
Weyda[a]
florenis[b]

---

[a] *in the left margin.* [b] *in the left margin, in a different hand.*

fol.59r.   Curtis de Weyda   LIX
the first lines are heavily corroded:

Item [— XXII iugera et IIII hont —]/ [———]/ a parte orientali [et
— a parte occidentali —]/ Calvercamp.
Weyda[a]
florenis[b]

Item ibidem aream dictam Cuelmans hofstat, continentem V hont et
LXXV virgatas terre.
Weyda[a]

Item ibidem terram dictam Calvercamp cum tribus parvis campis
continentem VIII iugera et IIj *[2.5]* hont prout iacent inter terram
dictam die Hare a parte orientali et terram dictam die Nesse a parte
occidentali.
Weyda[a]
florenis[b]

---

[a] *in the right margin.* [b] *in the right margin, in a different hand.*

fol.59v,   In Vloten [Curtis]
the first lines are heavily corroded:

Item [— XIIIj *[13.5]* iugera — terram]/ [— a parte orientali]/ [—]
Vloten/ a parte occidentali.
Weyda[a]
oud scilt[b]

Item op Heynxstmaede LVj *[55.5]* iugera terre prout iacent inter
terram civitatis Traiectensis a parte orientali et terram nostre domus
quam nunc Johannes Longus colit a parte occidentali.
Weyda[a]
[b]oud scilt florenis[b]

Item op Themat XI iugera et IIj *[2.5]* hont terre, quibus dominus
Bernardus uten Enge miles propius iacet cum terra a parte orientali
et domus nostra personaliter cum uno manso terre a parte occidentali. ^cDe hiis modo possidet Albertus van der Eme Ij *[1.5]* iugera ad X
annos ab anno LXVII *[1367]* Petri pro VI libris annuatim denariorum Traiectensium possessori curtis de Weyda solvendis.^c
Weyda^a
II florenis^b

---

^a *in the left margin.* ^b *in the left margin, in a different hand.* ^c *added in different
writing.*

fol.60r,   De Weyda   LX
the first lines are highly corroded:

Item op Themat XVI iugera [—]/ nostra domus quam nunc colit
Albertus [— a parte]/ orientali et terram nostre domus quam [nunc
possidet —]/ a parte occidentali.
Weyda^a
II florenis^b

¶ Summa iugerum predictorum que pronunc colonus dicte nostre
curtis de Weyda possidet C.LII iugera IIIj *[3.5]* hont et LXXV virgatas terre prout mensurata sunt, preter aream et ortum eiusdem curtis
continentem forsitan I iuger aut plus ut mensura dederit de eisdem.
^cHanc curtim nostram cum huiusmodi terrarum iugeribus modo pos-
sidet titulo locationis Ghisekinus filius Alberti ad X annos ab anno ^d
sub condicionibus in littera quam inde habemus contentis, et solvet
domui nostre annuatim exinde: Primo II.C *[200]* libras denariorum
Traiectensium. Item C modios tritici. Item C modios avene. Item IIII
modios pisarum albarum. Item III modios ordei. Item I aprum ma-
crum. Item I vas butyri. Item C caseos oviles. Item I iuger virentium
wickarum.^c

---

^a *in the right margin.* ^b *in the right margin, in a different hand.* ^c *added in different
writing.* ^d *not filled in.*

fol.60v,   ¶ In Maersen
the first lines are somewhat corroded:

Item [habet domus in parrochi]a de Maersen iuxta [Civitatem IX
iugera et] II hont terre prout iacent, opstreckende van die Vechte an

den Broydiic, inter terram heredum Spikeri Benscop a parte superiori et terram curati ecclesie de Maersen a parte inferiori, prout illa possidebat a nobis Johannes Taetze. Modo possident ea Gerardus filius Hermanni et Wendelmodis eius uxor ad X annos ab anno LXVIII *[1368]* Lamberti et dabunt tam de hiis quam de aliis IX iugeribus et II hont sequentibus in universo VII marcas et IX loet argenti et III solidos annuatim et VIII talenta cere et XVIII capones annuatim absque defalcatione Martini et Petri solvendos aut cadent ab omni iure. Non ulterius locabunt absque consensu et cetera, prout littera exinde tenet. Per fratrem Hugonem.
ᵃGherid Hermanszoen ende Wendelmoed siin wijfᵃ

ᵇItem ibidem IX iugera et II hont prout iacent inter terram heredum Spikeri Benscop a parte superiori, quam nunc possidet Haza van der Grotenhuys relicta eiusdem Spikeri, et inter terram curati ecclesie de Maersen a parte inferiori, prout illa possidebat a nobis Gerardus Slechte. Modo possidet ea Gerardus filius Hermanni et Wendelmodis eius uxor una cum IX iugeribus et II hont supradictis ad X annos ab anno LXIX *[1369]* Petri, sub eadem annua pensione superius signata et sub condicionibus in littera exinde contentis. Per fratrem Hugonem.
ᶜ¶ Ulterius possidebunt suprascripta XVIII iugera et IIII hont terre ad X annos ab anno LXXIX *[1379]* Petri et solvent tunc ulterius XC libras denariorum Traiectensium cum ceteris superius signatis et cetera prout littera tenet.ᶜ
ᵃGherid Hermanszoen ende Wendelmoed ziin wijfᵃ

ᵃ *in the left margin.* ᵇ *linked with brace to the foregoing item.* ᶜ *in a different hand (C).*

fol.61r, <u>In Maersen</u> LXI
the first lines are somewhat corroded:

Item ibidem XX iugera terre prout iacent [inter terram Arnoldi van der Oy et Wilhelmi filii Hugonis civium in Traiecto a parte superiori et terram Suederi filii Spikeri Benscop a parte inferiori,] que modo possidet una cum quartali terre sequenti Arnoldus filius Machteldis relicte Wendekini ad X annos ab anno LXX *[1370]* Agnetis pro VII marcis et XIII loet argenti, XII talentis cere, XXIIII caponibus annuatim Martini et Petri solvendis absque defalcatione vel cadet ab omni iure, et cetera sub condicionibus in littera qua fruimur inde contentis. Per fratrem Hugonem.

^aUlterius possidebunt Theodericus Drubbel et Machteldis eius uxor
ad X annos ab anno LXXIX *[1379]* Lamberti pro C.XXXII libris,
XXIIII caponibus, XII talentis cere, pagamenti Traiectensis solvendis
Martini et Petri vel cadet ab omni iure. Per commendatorem.^a
^bUlterius possidebunt idem Theodericus et Henricus filius eius ad X
annos ab anno ^cLXXVII Lambe^c LXXXVII *[1387]* Lamberti pro
C.XXXII libris, XII talentis cere, XXIIII caponibus pagamenti
Traiectensis solvendis Martini et Petri vel cadet ab omni iure. Per
fratrem Johannem de Arnhem.^b
^dArnoldus filius Machteldis^d
^eTheodericus Drubbel^e

^fItem ibidem quartale terre prout iacet in Marsenbroec in dicta par-
rochia inter terram Frederici filii Theoderici Bole a parte superiori et
terram domicelli de Zulen, quam nunc ipso tenet in feodo Hubertus
filius Ghiseberti Colentyer de Jutfaes a parte inferiori. Quod quartale
una cum XX iugeribus terre prescriptis modo possidet a nobis Arnoldus filius Machteldis ad annos et sub annua pensione superius signatis
et cetera, prout littera exinde tenet. Per fratrem Hugonem.
^bUlterius possidebunt idem Theodericus et Henricus filius eius una
cum XX iugeribus suprascriptis in eodem pactu superius expressato
ad X annos ab anno LXXXVII *[1387]* Lamberti.^b
^dArnoldus filius Machteldis^d
^eDirc Drubbel^e

---

^a *in a different hand.* ^b *in another hand.* ^c *cancelled.* ^d *in the right margin, cancelled.*
^e *in the right margin, in the same hand as* ^a. ^f *linked with brace to the foregoing item.*

fol.61v,   In Maersen
the first lines are heavily corroded:

[Item in Marsebroec dimidium quartalis terre —]/ [— prout iacet
inter terram capituli]/ [sancti Johannis Traiectensis a parte superiori
et terram heredum —]/ [a parte inferiori,] quod modo possidet Johannes [filius Johannis]/ [Hermanni pro VI] solidis annuatim perpetuo.
^aJohannes filius Johannis Hermanni hereditarie^a

Item ibidem ex uno quartali terre, eens zeysdeils min, prout iacet in
die X hoven, in iurisdictione temporali dominorum sancti Petri
Traiectensis inter terram abbatisse de Oudwica a parte superiori et
terram heredum Ade de Blomenwerde a parte inferiori, I libram

Traiectensem solvendam annuatim in Nativitate Domini et in Nativitate beati Johannis Baptiste. Modo possidet Jacobus filius Hermanni perpetuo.
^aJacobus filius Hermanni hereditarie^a

Item in villa de Maersen I aream quam contulit quondam Elisabet soror Johannis quondam curati in Maersen, prout iacet inter terram seu aream Brunonis filii Mondeyen a parte superiori et aream Aleydis relicte Henrici ^bHenrici^b de Slike quam nunc possidet Henricus Piirs a parte inferiori. Aleydis de Slike modo possidet pro I libra annuatim perpetuo.
^aAleydis de Slike hereditarie^a

---

^a *in the left margin.* ^b *cancelled.*

fol.62r, <u>In Maersen</u> LXII
the first lines are rather corroded:

[Item ibidem unum iuger prout iacet inter terram prepositi sancti Johannis Traiectensis]/ [a parte superiori et terram domini de Zulen a parte inferiori prout illud]/ [quondam possidebat a nobis Ghisebertus van de Grotenhuys. Modo]/ [possidet Hasa van den Grotenhuys ad X annos ab anno LXII *[1362]*/ [Petri pro XXXII solidis denariorum Traiectensium annuatim Martini et Petri solvendis. Per Hugonem.]
^aUlterius possidebit Swederus de Opburen filius eius ad X annos ab anno LXXIII *[1373]* Petri pro XL solidos.^a
^bUlterius possidebit Henric Zwederssoen ad X annos ab anno XCIIII *[1394]* Petri pro IIIj *[3.5]* libris. Modo Willem van Opbueren.^b
^cHasa van den Grotenhuys^c

Item ibidem in Marsenbroec <u>VIj *[6.5]* iugera terre</u> prout iacent inter terram Johannis de Byndelmaer a parte superiori et terram domini de Zulen a parte inferiori et ante et retro domus nostra personaliter propius iacet cum terra quam nunc possidet a nobis Suederus van der Meer. Que VIj *[6.5]* iugera modo possidet a nobis Theodericus Drubbel ad VIII annos ab anno LXIX *[1369]* Agnetis pro <u>X antiquis scudatis auri aut pagamento equivalenti et II talentis cere et VII caponibus</u> absque defalcatione Martini et Petri solvendis annuatim vel cadet ab omni iure. Non conburet, non ulterius locabit et cetera sub condicionibus in littera contentis. Per fratrem Hugonem.
^dUlterius possidebunt Theodericus Drubbel et Heynricus filius eius

ad X annos ab anno LXXXVI *[1386]* Petri una cum VIII igu^e iuge-
ribus^f sequentibus pro LX libris pagamenti quo pactu solvuntur in
Traiecto vel sub condicionibus prout littera tenet. Per fratrem de
Arnhem.^d
^cTheodericus Drubbel^c

---

^a *in a different hand.* ^b *in another hand.* ^c *in the right margin, in the basic hand.*
^d *in yet another hand.* ^e *cancelled.* ^f iugegeribus *ms.*

fol.62v,   In Maersen
the first lines are rather corroded:

[Item ibidem VIII iugera terre prout iacent in Marsenbroec inter
terram]/ [Johannis de Byndelmaer a parte superiori et terram domini
de Zulen a parte]/ [inferiori] prout illa a nobis Arnoldus de Snellenberch. Modo possidet ea ^aSuederus van der Meer ad X annos ab
[anno LXXII *[1372]*]/ Martini pro tribus marcis argenti aut pagamento equivalenti et VIII^a pullis annuatim absque defalcatione Martini et Petri solvendis sub condicionibus in littera quam inde habemus
contentis. Per fratrem Hugonem dispensatorem.
^bTheodericus Drubbel et eius uxor modo possident hanc terram.^b
^c¶ Ulterius possidebunt Theodericus Drubbel et Heynricus filius eius
ad X annos ab anno LXXXVII *[1387]* Petri una cum VIj *[6.5]*
iugeribus prescriptis sub eadem annua pensione superius ab alio la-
tera signata.^c
^dSuederus van der Meer^d
^eTheodericus Drubbel^e

Item ibidem mansum terre qui vocatur Crauwelshoeve prout iacet
inter terram domini de Zulen a parte superiori et terram prepositure
sancti Johannis Traiectensis a parte inferiori, quem modo possidet a
nobis Hermannus Loze ad X annos ab anno LXI *[1361]* Agnetis pro
XXX libris denariorum Traiectensium, IIII talentis cere et XVI pullis
annuatim solvendis Martini et Petri sub condicionibus in littera contentis. Per fratrem Hugonem dispensatorem.
^f¶ Ulterius dictam terram possidebit Ecbertus Loze ad X annos ab
anno LXXI *[1371]* Purificatione Marie pro LIII libris denariorum
Traiectensium annuatim et IIII talentis cere et XVI pullis absque
defalcatione Martini et Petri solvendis aut cadet ab omni iure et
cetera, prout littera tenet. Per fratrem Tho^g Johannem Gaude.^f
^dHerman die Loze^d

^hEcbert die Loze^h

---

^a *cancelled.* ^b *added in different writing.* ^c *in a different hand.* ^d *in the left margin, cancelled.* ^e *in the left margin, in the basic hand.* ^f *in yet another hand (C).* ^g *cancelled.* ^h *in the left margin, in the same hand as* ^f*.*

fol.63r,   ¶ <u>In Broeclede</u>   LXIII
the upper part is blank.

¶ <u>Item habet domus in parrochia</u> de Broeclede aream solventem annuatim <u>II grossos,</u> quam nunc possidet Albertus filius Tydemanni.
^aAlbertus filius Tidemanni^a

---

^a *in the right margin.*

fol.63v,   <u>In Broeclede</u>
the first lines are rather corroded:

[Item ibidem in Otterspoerbroec dimidium mansum prout iacet]/
[cui domus nostra personaliter propius iacet cum IX iugeribus que
nunc possidet a]/ [nobis Gerardus Pape a parte septentrionali et
moniales Vallis sancte]/ [Marie a parte meridionali, prout eundem
modo possident a nobis]/ Johannes Lieve et Ghertrudis eius uxor una
cum area et duobus/ iugeribus sequentibus, ad X annos ab anno
LXVIII *[1368]* Lamberti/ et dabunt tam de hiis quam de aliis II
iugeribus in [universo trias]/ [marcas] et IIII loet argenti aut pagamentum [equivalens] et/ X pullas annuatim Martini et Petri et cetera
prout littera tenet. Per Hugonem.
^aJohannes Lieve et Ghertrudis eius uxor^a

^bItem ibidem <u>I aream et II iugera</u> prout iacent inter terram monia-
lium Vallis sancte Marie a parte meridionali et terram liberorum
Johannis Scarpen a parte septentrionali, que una cum dimidio manso
prescripto modo possident Johannes Lieve et Ghertrudis eius uxor
sub eadem annua pensione et ad annos superius notatos. Per Hugonem.
^aJohannis Lieve et Ghertrudis^a

---

^a *in the left margin.* ^b *linked with brace to the foregoing item.*

fol.64r,   In Broeclede   LXIIII
the first lines are somewhat corroded:

Item ibidem IX [iugera] in Otterspoerbroec iacentia inter terram/
nostre domus quam [nunc colit] Johannes/ Lieve et eius uxor a parte
[superiori]/ et terram Aleidis Henrici Spikers et suorum liberorum a
parte inferiori, prout illa modo possidet Gerardus Pape ad IX annos
ab anno LXVIII *[1368]* Valentini et dabit annuatim II marcas argenti et IIj *[2.5]* loet aut pagamentum equivalens et IX pullas absque
defalcatione Martini et Petri et cetera, prout littera tenet. Per fratrem
Hugonem.
ªGerardus Papeª

Item ibidem Xj *[10.5]* iugera terre prout iacent inter terram Hermanni Herbord a parte superiori et terram Alberti filii Wouteri a parte
inferiori, prout illa modo possidet ᵇ
ªAlbert Wouterszoenª

    ª *in the right margin.* ᵇ *not filled in.*

fol.64v,   Broeclede
the first lines are a bit corroded:

Item ibidem VII iugera in Otterspoerbroec prout iacent inter terram
domini Ghiseberti de Nyenrode militis a parte superiori et terram
Ghiseberti filii Egidii a parte inferiori. Johannes filius Hermanni Yen
nunc possidet una cum terra infrascripta sub annis et annuo pacto
inferius signatis.

ªItem ibidem duo iugera prout iacent inter quatuor iugera terre que
iure feodali tenentur a domino de Apcoude a superiori parte et inter
tria iugera que tenentur a domino de Vianen a parte inferiori. Johannes filius Hermanni Yen nunc possidet ad annos infrascriptos. ᵇ¶
Modo ᵇ

ªItem ibidem III iugera prout iacent in Otterspoer inter terram domini Ghiseberti de Nyenrode a superiori parte et terram Johannis filii
Hermanni Yen a parte inferiori, que idem Johannes modo possidet
cum ceteris iugeribus in hoc latere signatis.
ᶜModo possidebit Henricus filius Ghisonis ad X annos ab anno
LXXVII *[1377]* Petri una cum XII iugeribus alio latere signatis sub
annua pensione ibidem signata.ᶜ

^aItem ibidem <u>unum</u> iuger prout iacet inter terram monialium Vallis
sancte Marie a parte superiori et terram liberorum Johannis Scarpen
a parte inferiori, quod quidem iuger una cum ceteris XII iugeribus
supra particulariter signatis modo possidet idem Johannes filius Hermanni predictus ad X annos ab anno LXVII *[1367]* Petri <u>pro XIII</u>
<u>antiquis scudatis auri minus IIII solidis</u> aut pagamento equivalenti et
<u>VI talentis cere et XIII pullis</u> annuatim Martini et Petri et cetera, sub
condicionibus in littera contentis. Per fratrem Hugonem.
^dJohannes filius Hermanni Yen^d

---

^a *linked with brace to the foregoing item.* ^b *cancelled, more than the entire following line*
erased. ^c *in a different hand (C).* ^d *in the left margin, in the basic hand.*

fol.65r,   In Broeclede   LXV
the first lines are somewhat corroded:

Item ibidem <u>tria iugera terre</u> super quibus [nunc moratur Henricus
filius Wilhelmi]/ prout illa iacent inter terram dominorum sancti [Pe-
tri Traiectensis a parte superiori et terram]/ monialium Vallis sancte
Marie a parte inferiori. Que idem Henricus et/ Hermannus eius
frater nunc possident una cum quatuor et quinque iugeribus
sequentibus sub annis et annua pensione inferius signatis.
^a¶ Modo dictam terram una cum quatuor et quinque iugeribus se-
quentibus possidebit ulterius Henricus filius Ghisonis sub annis et
annua pensione inferius signatis.^a

^bItem ibidem *IIII* iugera iacentia in Otterspoerbroec inter terram
domini de Apcoude a parte superiori et terram domini de Vianen a
parte inferiori, que eciam dicti Hermannus et Henricus nunc possident.
^a¶ Modo possidet Henricus filius Ghisonis.^a

^bItem ibidem <u>quinque iugera terre</u> super quibus nunc moratur Her-
mannus filius Wilhelmi predictus, prout iacet inter terram   domini
Ghiseberti de Nyenroede a parte superiori et terram Johannes filii
Hermanni Yen a parte inferiori, que XII iugera prescripta nunc insimul possident idem Hermannus et Henricus prescripti ad X annos ab
anno LXVII *[1367]* Petri pro <u>XII antiquis scudatis auri</u> ^cquarta parte
unius scudati minus^c aut pagamento equivalenti et VI talentis cere et
XII pullis annuatim Martini et Petri solvendis sub condicionibus in
littera contentis. Per fratrem Hugonem.
^a¶ Modo prescripta XII iugera una cum duobus^c tribus^d iugeribus

superius in alio latere signatis possidebit ulterius Henricus filius
Ghisonis ad X annos ab anno LXXVI^a ^{e}I *[1376/77]* Petri pro ^{f}XLI
libris V solidis^f ^{c}XXXVIII libris X solidis^c, scilicet quodlibet iuger pro
II libris et XV solidis pagamenti Traiectensis necnon XIIII pullis et
VII talentis cere Martini et Petri solvendis absque defalcatione sub
condicionibus in littera contentis. Per fratrem Johannem Gaude commendatorem.

¶ Modo possidet ulterius Jacobus van der Hoerne ad VIII annos ab
anno LXXVIII *[1378]* Petri in eodem pactu ut superius dictum est.^{e}
^{g}¶ Ulterius idem Jacobus possidebit dictam terram ad X annos ab
anno LXXXVI *[1386]* Petri pro XLI libris denariorum quibus pactus
solvuntur in Traiecto, VII talentis cere, XIIII pullis absque defalcatione. Per fratrem Johannes de Aernem.^{g}
^{h}Hermannus et Henricus filii Wilhelmi^h
^{i}Henric Ghizen zone^i
^{j}Jacobus van der Hoerne^j

---

^{a} *in a different hand.* ^{b} *linked with brace to the foregoing item.* ^{c} *cancelled.* ^{d} *written
above the cancelled text.* ^{e} *in another hand (C).* ^{f} *in the left margin, in the same hand
as* ^{e}. ^{g} *in yet another hand.* ^{h} *in the right margin, in the basic hand, cancelled.* ^{i} *in the
right margin, in the same hand as* ^{a}, *cancelled.* ^{j} *in the right margin, in the same hand
as* ^{e}.

fol.65v,   In Broeclede
the first lines are rather corroded:

Item ibidem [dimidium mansum prout iacet inter terram] dominorum sancte/ Marie [Traiectensis a parte superiori] et terram [iuvenis
Johannis et] Johannis Meye/ et aliorum quorum terra [communi]
sulcu iacet a parte inferiori, quem modo/ possidet Hermannus filius
Splinteri de Otterspoer ad X annos ab anno LXI *[1361]* Petri pro X
libris X solidis, V caponibus, V pullis annuatim, sub condicionibus in
littera contentis quam inde habemus. Per fratrem Hugonem.
^{a}¶ Ulterius idem Hermannus possidebit dictam terram ad X annos ab
anno LXXI *[1371]* Valentini pro XX libris denariorum Traiectensium et V caponibus et V pullis annuatim Martini et Petri et dimidium quarti butyri in fine May vel Lamberti solvendis absque
defalcatione et cetera, prout littera tenet. Per fratrem Thomam.^{a}
^{b}¶ Ulterius Ghijsbertus Cruysberch possidebit dictam terram ad X
annos ab anno XCII *[1392]* Petri pro IIII oud scilde, IIII caponibus,
IIII pullis.^{b}
^{c}Hermannus filius Splinteri de Otterspoer^c

Item ibidem IIIj *[3.5]* iugera terre prout iacent inter terram Johannis de Rietvelt a parte superiori et terram Petri Croniken civis Traiectensis a parte inferiori, prout illa modo possident Gerardus Pape et Stephania eius uxor pro III libris IIII solidis annuatim Martini et Petri solvendis ad vitam eorum. ^dHabent litteram exinde.^d
^cGherid Pape et Stephania eius uxor^c

---

^a *in a different hand (B).* ^b *in another hand.* ^c *in the left margin, in the basic hand.*
^d *added in different writing.*

fol.66r,   [In Broeclede]   LXVI
the first lines are heavily corroded:

[Item ibidem — hont terre —]/ [— per Otterspoer—]/ Vallis sancte Marie cum duobus iugeribus, quam terram una cum terra immediate subscripta modo possidet Gerardus Pape ad X annos ab anno LXVI *[1366]* Petri pro VIII libris XVI solidis IIII denariis et III pullis annuatim solvendis Martini et Petri sub condicionibus in littera contentis. Per Hugonem.

^aItem ibidem VI hont terre prout iacent inter terram Gerardi Pape ambabus partibus. Idem Gerardus modo possidet ad annos predictos.

^aItem ibidem VI hont terre prout iacent inter terram monialium Vallis sancte Marie a parte superiori et terram dominorum sancti Petri Traiectensis a parte inferiori. Dictus Gerardus Pape nunc etiam possidet ad annos et sub annua pensione supradicta.
^bGherid Pape^b

---

^a *Linked with the previous item by brace in the left margin and pen stroke in the right margin.* ^b *in the right margin.*

on a loose leaf of paper in a 15th-century hand:

VI iugera in Otterspoer inter terram Werneri Lubb^a Louwenssoon boven et terram commendatorum sancte Katharine beneden

V iugera in Otterspoer inter terram IJsbrandi filii Henrici Zwarten boven et terram commendatorum sancte Katharine beneden

VI iugera inter terram abbatisse van den Dael ab una parte et terram commendatorum ab alia parte a Brodijck usque inden Vecht

V iugera inter terram heredum Johannis Scerpe ab una parte et inter terram commendatorum ab alia parte a Brodijck usque inden Vecht

Item beneden leet Henric Spiker myt 1j *[1.5]* morghen ende bowen die joffren van den Dael

---

^a *cancelled.*

++++++++++++++++++++++++++++++

fol.66v,   ¶ <u>In Lonen</u>
the first lines are highly corroded:

[Item — Lonen] habet domus quartale [terre prout iacet]/ [— posside]bat a nobis Lambertus Frederici [dicti] Corte/ ^aWelk viertel lants ghelegen is op gront oever biden huys te Minden daer die grave van Hollant naest ghelant is aen die noertside ende her Wouter van Minden an die zuytzide.^a
^bNicolaus Cuper^b

Item ibidem <u>duo iugera terre</u> que dedit Gerardus de Palaes prout iacent communi sulcu cum terra Nycolai Hellinc, inter terram here-dum domini Amilii de Mynden a parte meridionali ^cet terram^c Ghise-kini van der Cluze, que duo iugera nunc possidet idem Nycolaus Hellinc <u>ad X annos</u> ab anno LXVIII *[1368]* Petri pro <u>IIj *[2.5]*</u> anti-quis scudatis auri <u>minus XII denariis</u> aut pagamento equivalenti et II caponibus annuatim solvendis Martini et Petri et cetera sub condicio-nibus in littera contentis. Per fratrem Hugonem.
^dModo possidet Wilhelmus filius Ghiselberti ad X annos ab anno LXXXIX *[1389]* Petri pro VIII libris X solidis II caponibus et iacet inter terram   Gerardi van der A ex utroque latere.^d
^bNicolaus Hellinc^b

---

^a *in a different hand.* ^b *in the left margin, in the basic hand.* ^c *in terra ms.* ^d *in another hand.*

fol.67r,   <u>In Lonen</u>   LXVII
the first part is heavily corroded:

[——]/ [——]/ [——]/ [-] perpetuo, quos[—]/ [—] Johannis pro perpetua sui memor[ia —]/ [—] Ecberto defuncto dabuntur[—]/ libris annuatim perpetuo et cetera sub condicionibus [—]/ quod super hoc habemus contentis.

ᵃEcbertus [—]igheᵃ

Item ibidem ex dimidio iugere terre iacenti inter terram Wilhelmi de Cronenborch a parte superiori et terram Henrici de Damme a parte inferiori, III antiquos grossos annuatim perpetuo, quos legavit Henricus Botterman.
ᵇJohannes Bottermanᵇ
perpetueᶜ

ᵃ *in the right margin, torn.* ᵇ *in the right margin.* ᶜ *in the left margin.*

fol.67v, [In Loesdrecht]
the first part is heavily corroded:

[Item ibidem —]/ [————]/ [————]/ [—]bluclane[—]/ [—] X annos ab anno LXVI *[1366]* [-]/ [—] III talenta cere et VI pullas annuatim/ [—]Petri sub condicionibus in littera contentis. Per fratrem Hugonem.
ᵃJacobus Ploysᵃ

Item ibidem in Loesdrecht a parte septentrionali ex uno agro terre sito iuxta terram Johannis dicti Scoute a parte superiori et iuxta terram Johannis dicti Cleyne a parte inferiori XVI antiquos grossos annuatim solvendos infra quindenam post Martinum hyemalem vel possessor eiusdem agri cadet ab omni iure. Quem agrum quondam possidebat Wilhelmus de Barinchem. Modo possidet Henricus Scutter perpetuo. Habemus inde litteram sub data M.CCC.XLIX *[1349]*.
ᵃHenricus Scutter
¶ perpetueᵃ

ᵃ *in the left margin.*

fol.68r, In Loesdrecht LXVIII
the first lines are highly corroded:

[Item ibidem op die Loesdrecht unum agrum propius iacentem inter]/ [terram Johannis Cliis — a parte superiori —]/ne a parte inferiori, ex quo agro [Meylan— Conradusᵃ]/ Callen legavit quondam ordini nostro XVI solidos bonorum annuatim perpetuo. Quem agrum modo possidet Nicolaus Kippinc perpetuo sub annua pensione predicta nobis annuatim infra quindenam post Petri ad Cathe-

dram solvenda vel cadet ab omni iure. Habemus inde litteram.
^b[Nicolaus] Kippinc^b
¶ perpetue^c

Item ter Ouder A duo iugera que quondam contulit Gerardus Friso
prout iacent. ^bGhertrudis relicta Johannis de Ven^b

Item ibidem ex uno agro terre, quem nunc possidet Johannes filius
Alberti, II solidos bonorum denariorum perpetuo.
^bJohannes filius Alberti^b
¶ perpetue^c

---

^a *uncertain reading ms, possibly Gerardus.* ^b *in the right margin.* ^c *in the left margin.*

fol.68v,   ¶ In Apcoude
the first lines are rather corroded:

¶[Item in parrochia de Apcoude] Vj *[5.5]* iugera terre quorum [per]
se iacent [in]/ [alio loco] VI hont terre inter terram A[rnoldi filii
Petri] a parte su/[per]iori et terram Johannis des Couden a parte
inferiori.
^aJacobus [Engelraed]^a

^bItem de eisdem in alio loco duo iugera prout iacent int Cleyne Mo-
lenland

^bItem de eisdem V hunt terre prout iacent retro dicta II iugera
ibidem ultra viam in des Cupers Nesse.

^bItem de eisdem duo iugera iacentia int Grote Molenland inter ter-
ram Johannis filii Ottonis a parte septentrionali et terram Alberti filii
Lyzen a parte meridionali, quam terram prescriptam prout iacet pro
Vj *[5.5]* iugeribus insimul nunc possidet a nobis Jacobus Engelraed
ad X annos ab anno LXV *[1365]* Petri pro X libris denariorum
Traiectensium et VI aucis annuatim absque defalcatione solvendis
Martini et Petri vel cadet ab omni iure et cetera, prout littera tenet.
Per fratrem Hugonem.

---

^a *in the left margin.* ^b *linked with brace to the foregoing item.*

fol.69r,   <u>In Apcoude</u>   LXIX
the first line are somewhat corroded:

Item ibidem <u>ex dimidio iugere</u> annuatim [Vj^a *[5.5]* grossos quod
nunc possidet]/ filius Hermanni de Busco prout iacet.
^bfilius Hermanni de Busco^b
¶ perpetue^c

^dItem ibidem ex uno iugere terre iacenti in Borchardsweer V grossos
annuatim, quod quidem iuger nunc possidet Hermannus filius Bor-
chardi perpetuo, quorum reddituum medietatem idem Hermannus
contulit. Reliquam vero medietatem Borchardus eius pater dedit. ^edit
heeft Jan Snoec qwiit ghecoft.^e ^d
^fHermannus Borchardi^f
¶ perpetue^c

Item ibidem <u>lj *[1.5]* iugera</u> iuxta castrum de Loenresloet annuatim
XX grossos et I ghifte butiri Theodericus Splinter possidebat. Quis
modo possidet ignoratur adhuc et nichil inde habemus.
nota^c

Item ibidem <u>II huont</u> terre parum plus annuatim IIII solidos Johannes Werburgis quondam possidebat. Quis modo possidet et ubi terra
iacet adhuc ignoratur et nichil inde habemus.
nota^c

---

^a *cancelled.* ^b *in the right margin.* ^c *in the left margin.* ^d *crossed out.* ^e *in a different*
hand. ^f *in the right margin, cancelled.*

fol.69v,   ¶ <u>In Nichtvecht</u>   ¶ <u>In Horstwerde</u>
the first line is somewhat corroded:

¶[In Nichtvecht <u>unum iuger</u> quod] quondam contulit Rissendis/ de
Wesepe prout iacet nunc ^ainter terram Henrici bastaert de Loenresloet a superiori parte et inter terram Gerardi filii Lubberti a parte
inferiori. Modo possidebit Johannes de Dorschen filius Henrici
Rampoys ad X annos ab anno LXXXIX *[1389]* Petri pro II loet
argenti annuatim Martini et^b Petri vel cadet ab omni iure. Per fratrem Johannem Hase.^a
^cHenricus Rampoys^c
nota^d

¶ <u>Item in parrochia de Horstwerde unum iuger</u> prout id quondam possidebat Johannes Ricoldi et modo possidet eundem Theodericus Hermanni, solvens annuatim VIII grossos, prout illud iuger nunc iacet.
^eLubbertus Vos possidet [ac—]^e
^cTheodericus Hermanni^c
nota^d

^fItem Alfaer van der Horst uut j *[0.5]* morghen lants ghelegen inden kerspel vanden Horst in heren Eersts broec, daer Alfer zelve mit III morghen in ghemengder voer naest ghelant is ande overside ende Onser Vrouwen outaer in der kerke ter Horst an die nederside, III vierendel van een lode goets fiins zulvers te betalen alle jaer Petri vel infra mensem. Ende deden sijs niet so siin zi dubbelen pacht sculdich, ende hier mede is qwiit gheseyt alle aensprake die wi hadden an II morghen lants in Horstweerde die Korstiaen Janssoen brukede.^f
perpetue^g

Item ibidem <u>lj *[1.5]* iugera</u> terre et in Cortehoven unum veenacker prout illam terram quondam possidebat Johannes Ricoldi. Modo possidet eandem Cristianus Johannis, solvens annuatim exinde Xj *[10.5]* grossos. ^hLubbert Vos heeft de veenacker ut trede.^h
^cCristianus Johannis^c

ⁱItem Peter Kibbe uut j *[0.5]* morghen lants ghelegen inden kerspel vander Horst in heren Eerst broec, daer die here van Apcoude boven naest ghelant is met II morghen lants die Peter Kibbe van hem hout ende Wouter van den Berghe mit IIIj *[3.5]* morghen beneden, j *[0.5]* loet goets fiins zulver erfliken te renten te betalen alle jaer Petri vel infra mensem. Dede hiis niet, so is hi van dien tormiin dubbelen pacht sculdich ende hier mede is qwiit gheseyt zulke aensprake als wi hadden an IIIj *[3.5]* morghen lants ghelegen in Horstweerde die Jan Ryqwiinssoen voortijds te bruken plach. Inde habemus litteram.ⁱ ^hdit is qwiit gecoft^h
perpetue^g

---

^a *in a different hand.* ^b *et missing in ms.* ^c *in the left margin, in the basic hand.* ^d *in the right margin, probably in the basic hand.* ^e *in another hand, cancelled.* ^f *in yet a different hand.* ^g *in the left margin, in the same hand as* ^f*.* ^h *in yet another hand.* ⁱ *in the same hand as* ^f*, cancelled.*

fol.70r.   ¶ <u>In Wesepe</u>   ¶ <u>In Cokangen</u>   LXX

In Wesepe ex uno agro terre quem possidet Ghisebertus Brunt annuatim XVIII denarios bonorum denariorum.
ªGhisebertus Bruntª
notaᵇ

Item ibidem ex duobus iugeribus que quondam possidebat Tidemannus filius Godeldis, modo possidet ea Henricus Scutter aut eius successor, annuatim II solidos bonorum denariorum.
ªHenricus Scutterª
notaᵇ

Item ibidem ex uno hont terre annuatim XVIII denarios bonorum denariorum prout iacet et illud modo possidet heres seu successor Meynardi.
Meynardusª
notaᵇ

Item ibidem unum iuger terre quod contulit nostre domui Tydemannus filius Jacobi Autenis prout iacet in dicta parrochia de Wesepe ultra Vechtam in VII iugeribus terre, spectantibus nunc ad Tidemannum filium Nycolai, inter terram dicti Fyekerdi filii Petri a parte meridionali et terram Tidemanni Wolf a parte septentrionali situatis. Quod quidem iuger nunc possidet a nobis idem Tidemannus filius Jacobi sub hereditario pactu trium librarum denariorum communiter in Traiecto tempore solucionis dativorum annuatim in festo beati Petri ad Cathedram aut infra quindenam postea solvendarum aut cadet qualibet die postea in penam unius grossi et cetera, prout littera a nobis super hoc optenta tenet. De dicto iugere terre habemus litteram scabinorum in Wesepe foris signatam signo tali . ᶜ .
ᵈModo possidet Roelof Trudenzoen per violenciam.ᵈ
ªTidemannus filius Jacobiª
perpetueᵇ

¶ In <u>parrochia de Cokangen dimidium quartale terre</u> quod contulit quondam Godefridus de Bertangen, solvendos annuatim <u>XII solidos bonorom denariorum</u>. Ecbertus filius eiusdem Godefridi et Lambertus Cronekin gener eius possidebant. Quis modo possidet ignoramus ad presens. Nichil inde habemus.
notaᵇ

ª *in the right margin.* ᵇ *in the left margin.* ᶜ *a coat of arms with a cross.* ᵈ *in a different hand.*

fol.70v.   ¶ <u>In Hermalen</u>

¶ <u>Item habet domus predicta in parrochia de Hermalen hanc terram infrascriptam.</u>
Primo in <u>Rosweyda VII iugera terre</u> prout iacent communia cum tribus nostre domus iugeribus infrascriptis pronunc Bernardo Creyt locatis, que VII iugera modo possidet a nobis Hugo Roede una cum reliquis terrarum iugeribus his sequentibus ad annos et sub annua pensione infra notatis. Et hec X iugera insimul extendunt se cum uno fine ad locum dictum Jutfaescher Landscheydinghe et cum alio fine ad aggerem dictam Marendiic, quibus an die zuytwestzide propius iacet dominus Stephanus de Zulen miles ende aen die noertwestzide Jans erfnamen van den Speghel.
ªHughe die Roedeª

ᵇItem ibidem an die ander zide van der Maernediic in Batua <u>unum campum</u> terre continentem <u>VII hont terre</u> prout iacet ab inferiori parte eiusdem aggeris et est hec terra quondam separata a X iugeribus predictis per dictum aggerem ibidem transpositum. Hugo Roede modo possidet cum ceteris hic signatis.
ªHughe die Roedeª

ᵇItem ibidem <u>in Batua IIII hont</u> terre prout iacent communia cum aliis nostre domus IIIj *[3.5]* hont terre pronunc locatis Bernardo Creyt inferius notatis, quibus ab uno fine propius iacet die Maerndiic et ab alio fine a parte superiori vicinius iacet terra Johannis Homboud et a parte inferiori terra Wilhelmi Scepen. Hugo Roede modo possidet cum ceteris ad annos et sub condicionibus infra notatis.
ªHughe Roedeª

ª *in the left margin.* ᵇ *linked with brace to the foregoing item.*

fol.71r.   <u>In Hermalen</u>   LXXI

Item ibidem <u>in Velthusen XV iugera terre</u> prout iacent communia cum aliis nostre domus XV iugeribus infra notatis pronunc Bernardo Creyt locatis, que XXX iugera extendunt se cum uno fine ad Antiquum Renum et cum alio fine ad Aqueductum in Reynerscop, quibus etiam propius iacet pro nunc terra domini Frederici uten Hamme militis a parte superiori et terra Werneri de Drakenborgh a parte inferiori. Que XV iugera prescripta modo possidet a nobis Hugo Roede una cum terra suprasignata et solvet tam de hiis quam de aliis annuatim X marcas et X loet argenti et III talenta cere, V capones et XVIII pullas ad *X* annos ab anno LXX *[1370]* Petri ad Cathedram, Martini et Petri, vel cadet ab omni iure et cetera, prout littera exinde tenet. Per fratrem Hugonem dispensatorem.

^aUlterius prescriptam terram possidebit ^b ad X annos ab anno LXXV *[1375]* Petri pro XXVIII libris, III talentis cere, V caponibus et XVIII pullis. Solvet Martini et Petri vel cadet ab omni iure et cetera, prout littera tenet. Per fratrem Johannem Gaude commendatorum.^a

^cHughe die Roede^c

---

^a *in a different hand (C).* ^b *not filled in.* ^c *in the right margin, in the basic hand.*

fol.71v,   In Hermalen
the first lines are somewhat corroded:

[Item ibidem tria iugera iacentia] in Rosweyde communia cum VII [nostre domus iugeribus suprasignatis] pronunc Hugoni den Roeden locatis, et hec X iugera insimul se extendunt cum uno fine ad dictum Jutfaescher Landscheydinghe et cum alio fine ad aggerem dictum Marendijc et cetera, prout supra signatum est. Que tria iugera modo possidet Bernardus Creyt una cum ceteris terrarum iugeribus sequentibus sub annis et condicionibus infra notatis.

^aBernardus Creyt^a

^bItem ibidem in Velthusen XV iugera prout iacent communia cum aliis nostre domus XV iugeribus supra notatis pronunc Hugoni.Roeden locatis, et insimul situata sunt ut superius ab alio latere istius folii est expressum. Que XV iugera modo possidet Bernardus Creyt filius Henrici cum ceteris iugeribus super eundem signatis et sibi locatis ad annos et sub annua pensione inferius insimul signatis.

^aBernardus Creyt^a

^bItem ibidem in Batua XII iugera terre prout iacent et extendunt se cum superiori fine ad aggerem de Reynerscop et cum inferiori fine ad aggerem dictum Maerndiic, quibus a superiori parte propius iacet terra heredum Hermanni et Henrici Creyt et inferius dominus Stephanus de Nijenvelt et cetera, prout illa Bernardus Creyt modo possidet cum ceteris hic signatis.

^aBernardus Creyt^a

---

^a *in the left margin.* ^b *linked with brace to the foregoing item.*

fol.72r,   In Hermalen   LXXII
the whole page is more or less heavily corroded:

Item [— IIIj *[3.5]* hont —]/ [——]/ [signatis et pronunc locatis
Hugoni den Roeden —]/ terre propius iacet ab uno fine die [Maern-
diic et ab alio fine a parte]/ superiori propius iacet terra Johannis
Homboud [et a parte inferiori terra]/ Wilhelmi Scepen. Que IIIj
hont terre modo possidet Bernardus/ Creyt supradictus una cum
terra [superius notata ad X annos]/ ab anno LXVII *[1367]* Agathe et
[solvet in universo tam de hiis quam]/ de aliis iugeribus prescriptis
XCII libras V grossos denariorum Traiectensium et [XXIX]/ pullas
annuatim absque defalcatione solvendas Martini et Petri vel cadet ab
omni iure/ et cetera sub condicionibus in littera contentis. Per fratrem Hugonem.
[ᵃBernardus Creytᵃ]

Item ibidem in Liesvelt Ij *[1.5]* hont terre
ᵇcredo quod supradictus Bernardus Creyt/ possidet una cum terra
supradicta, [que Hugo Roede ne]scit ubi/ iacent ut dicit et sic inter
hos duos [latitur hec terra].ᵇ
notaᶜ

ᵃ *in the right margin.* ᵇ *added in different writing.* ᶜ *in the left margin.*

fol.72v,   In Hermalen
the whole page is more or less heavily corroded:

[— XX iugera —]/ [——]/ [— Gerardus Galicop una cum IIIj
[3.5] iugeribus terre]/ [— situatis et signatis ad *IX* annos ab anno
LXVIII *[1368]* / [Valentini] et solvet annuatim tam de hiis quam de
aliis in universo/ [—] marcas et XV loet argenti aut pagamentum
equivalens in Traiecto/ [et XV pullas et vehet II hont] cespitum
annuatim debito tempore. Solvet/ [Martini et Petri vel cadet ab omni
iure et cetera] sub condicionibus in littera contentis. Per fratrem/
Hugonem.
ᵃ[Gerardus Galicop]ᵃ

Item ibidem XIX iugera terre iacentia supra Bilenvelt tusschen die
twe/ [Ziitwinden inter terram nostre domus] ex omni parte prout illa
modo possidet/ Henricus filius [Theoderici] ad X annos ᵇab annoᵇ
LXVIII *[1368]* Petri pro XXXVII libris denariorum Traiectensium
et XIX pullis annuatim solvendis Martini et Petri vel cadet ab omni

iure et cetera sub condicionibus in littera quam inde habemus contentis. Per fratrem Hugonem.
^aHenric Dirix zoen^a

---

^a *in the left margin.* ^b *written above the text.*

on a loose leaf of paper, in a 15th-century hand:

Alsoe als dat ghelegen is in landen Giesbert van Scaedwic aen die overside ende landen Giesbert Truden soen van Scadewic ende Jan Breyen aen die nedersyde alsoe dat Henric Buddync gebruckten inden jaere van LXIX *[1469]* ende daer na heeft dat ghebrucket Gerijt Andrieszoen vanden jaere van LXXXVIII *[1488]*.

fol.73r.   In Hermalen   LXXIII

Item ibidem VII iugera terre prout iacent inter terram nostre domus sancte Katerine ex omni parte prout illa nunc possidet Ricoldus Bokeler ad XI annos ab anno LX *[1360]* Petri pro VI libris denariorum Traiectensium et VII pullis annuatim solvendis Martini et Petri vel cadet ab omni iure et cetera prout littera exinde tenet. Per fratrem Hugonem.
^aUlterius idem Ricoldus possidebit dictam terram ad VI annos ab anno LXXI *[1371]* Petri una cum IX iugeribus postea in Reynerscop situatis et signatis et dabit tam de hiis quam de aliis in universo III marcas argenti aut pagamentum equivalens et XVI pullas annuatim Martini et Petri solvendas aut cadet ab omni iure et cetera ut littera tenet. Per fratrem Johannem Gaude.^a
^bUlterius possidebunt dictam terram Reynerus Johannis et Johannes de Nesse ad X annos Petri LXXXIIII *[1384]* pro annua pensione videlicet quodlibet anno XXVI libris V solidis et VII pullis secundum monetam qua pactus in civitate Traiectensi persolvuntur libere et in defalcatione. Per me fratrem G.^b
^cRicoldus Bokeler^c
^dReynerus Johannis et Johannes Nesse^d

Item ibidem V iugera terre prout iacent inter terram nostre domus quam nunc possidet Everardus Godekini a parte superiori et terram nostre domus dictam Ziitwinde a parte inferiori, que modo possidet Johannes Yoie filius Petri ad X annos ab anno LXVIII *[1368]* Petri pro XXI loet argenti aut pro pagamento equivalenti ^eet III solidis^e

denariorum Traiectensium et IIII pullis annuatim solvendis Martini
et Petri aut cadet ab omni iure et cetera. Per fratrem Hugonem.
ᶠModo istam terram possidebunt ulterius Wilhelmus filius Trudonis et
Johannes de Delf ad X annos ab anno LXXV *[1375]* Petri pro XX
libris V solidis V pullis Martini et Petri solvendis vel cadet ab omni
iure et cetera prout littera tenet.ᶠ
ᶜJohannes Yoie filius Petriᶜ
ᵍWillem Truden zoen en Jan van Delfᵍ

ᵃ *in a different hand (C).* ᵇ *in another hand.* ᶜ *in the right margin, cancelled.* ᵈ *in the right margin, in the same hand as* ᵇ. ᵉ *cancelled.* ᶠ *in yet another hand (B).* ᵍ *in the right margin, in the same hand as* ᶠ.

fol.73v,,   In Hermalen
the whole page is more or less corroded:

[Item ibidem VIII iugera terre prout iacent tusschen onse twe Ziit-
winden]/ [Inter terram domus nostre circumiacentem ab omni parte
prout illa modo possidet]/ [Everardus filius Godekini una cum IIj
[2.5] iugeribus immediate sequentibus]/ [ad X annos ab anno
LXVIII *[1368]* Valentini et dabit tam de hiis quam de]/ [aliis IIj
[2.5] iugeribus duas marcas et IIII loet argenti] aut pagamentum/
[equivalens in Traiecto et X pullas annuatim absque defalcatione
Martini] et Petri solvendas/ [vel cadet ab] omni iure et cetera prout
littera tenet. Per fratrem Hugonem.
ᵃEverd Godekins zoenᵃ

ᵇItem ibidem IIj *[2.5]* iugera terre iacentis tusschen onse twe Ziitwin-
den/ inter terram nostre domus circumiacentem propius ab omni
parte prout illa modo/ una cum VIII iugeribus predictis possidet
Everardus Godekini ad annos/ et [sub condicionibus supradictis]
ᵃEverd Godikens zoneᵃ

ᵃ *in the left margin.* ᵇ *linked with brace to the foregoing item.*

fol.74r,   In Hermalen   LXXIIII
the first part is heavily corroded:

Item ibidem [VI iugera terre prout iacent aen die] Ziitwinde inter/
[terram Petri — a parte superiori —]/ [— a parte inferio]/[ri, que
VI iugera modo possidet Trude relicta Wilhelmi Ghiseberti ad]/ [X

annos ab anno LXVIII *[1368]* Petri pro XVIII libris denariorum
Traiectensium, II talentis]/ cere et VIII pullis [solvendis annuatim
Martini et Petri absque defalcatione et cetera]/ prout littera tenet.
Per fratrem Hugonem.
^aTrude Wilhelmi^a

Item ibidem aream continentem circa VIII hont prout iacent inter
terram nostre domus quam nunc possidet Trude Wilhelmi supradicta
a parte superiori et terram nostre domus quam nunc possidet Johannes Yoie filius Petri a parte inferiori, quam aream modo possidet
^bJohannes filius Lubberti Yoien seu^b Aleidis filia Coppen ad X annos
ab anno LXXI *[1371]* pro VIj *[6.5]* libris et I pulla annuatim solvendis Martini et Petri et cetera. Per fratrem Hugonem.
^cJohannes Lubberti Yoien^c
^dAleydis Coppen^d
^aWendelmoed Coppen^a

---

^a *in the right margin.* ^b *cancelled.* ^c *in the right margin, cancelled.* ^d *in the right
margin, erased.*

fol.74v, In Hermalen ^aReynerscop^a
the first lines are somewhat corroded:

[Item ibidem supra Reynerscop decem iugera terre, prout illa Her-
mannus]/ [— Spengard quondam possidebat et prout modo iacent
inter terram dominorum sancti]/ [Petri] Traiectensis a parte orientali
et terram Henrici Cyriken a parte/ occidentali, que modo possidet
Henricus de Oerscoten una cum aliis terrarum iugeribus subscriptis
et solvet in universo tam de hiis quam de aliis XXV iugeribus sequentibus XLVI libras X grossos et XXXV pullas annuatim absque defalcatione Martini et Petri solvendas vel cadet ab omni iure, ad XVI
annos ab anno LVII *[1357]* Epiphanie et cetera sub condicionibus in
littera contentis. Per fratrem Joannem de Via Lapidea commendatorem.
^bHenricus de Oerscoten^b

^cItem ibidem XVIII iugera prout iacent inter terram Ghiseberti filii
Hugonis et eius uxoris a parte orientali et terram liberorum Bertholdi
de Haghenouwe a parte inferiori seu occidentali. Henricus de Oerscoten modo possidet ad [annos prescriptos] et sub eadem annua pensione predicta.

^bHenricus de Orscoten^b J.^d

---

^a *added in different writing.* ^b *in the left margin.* ^c *linked with brace to the foregoing item.* ^d *in the right lower corner of the page, as a quire indication, corresponding with a K. in the left lower corner of fol.75r.*

fol.75r,   In Hermalen ^ain Reynerscop^a   LXXV
the first lines are heavily corroded, the second part only to some extent:

Item ibidem in [Reynerscop tria iugera terre prout iacent communia]/ [cum aliis scilicet — pronunc – Henricum]/ [de Oerscoten III — borchgravium de Montforde]/ [et hec sex iugera — inter terram eiusdem borchgravii] a parte [orientali et terram monasterii sancti Pauli Traiectensis a parte occidentali.]/ Que tria iugera dictus Henricus de Orscoten modo possidet a nobis et moratur super eisdem ad annos et sub annua pensione ut supra dictum est.
^bHenricus de Oerscoten^b

^cItem in eadem parrochia in Cattenbroec quartale terre prout iacet commune cum terra monasterii sancti Servacii Traiectensis prout illud modo pos/sidet a nobis [una cum terris suprascriptis dictus Henricus de Oerscoten]/ ^dmodo possidet^d ad annos et sub annua [pensione superius signatis].
^bHenricus de Oerscoten^b

K.^e

---

^a *added in different writing.* ^b *in the right margin.* ^c *linked with brace to the foregoing item.* ^d *cancelled.* ^e *in the left lower corner of the page, as a quire indication, corresponding with a J. in the right lower corner of fol.74v.*

fol.75v,   In Hermalen ^aReynerscop^a
the first part is rather corroded, the second part a bit:

[Item in Reynerscop XXII iugera terre prout iacent] inter terram nostre/ [domus — Wilhelmus] Corthoze/ [ad X annos ab anno LXVIII *[1368]* Petri — libris Traiectensibus et V solidis]/ [denariorum Traiectensium et XXII pullis annuatim absque defalcatione] Martini et Petri solvendis/ [vel cadet ab omni iure et cetera sub condicionibus in littera quam inde habemus] contentis./ Per fratrem Hugonem.
^bWilhelmus Corthoze^b

Item ibidem in Reynerscop [dimidium] mansum prout iacet inter terram borchgravii de [Montfoerde] a parte superiori et terram nostre domus ᶜa parteᶜ quam nunc possidet Wilhelmus Corthoze a parte inferiori prout eundem dimidium mansum modo possidet Henricus filius Tydemanni ad X annos ab anno LXVII *[1367]* Purificatione Marie pro XVIII libris XVIII solidi denariorum Traiectensium et VII pullis annuatim absque defalcatione solvendis Martini et Petri vel cadet ab omni iure et cetera prout littera exinde tenet. Per fratrem Hugonem.

ᵈUlterius possidebit Fredericus Jacobs zoen ad X annos ab anno LXXXVII *[1387]* Petri pro XXXIII libris ende VII pullis sub condicione prescripta. Per fratrem Joannem Haze.ᵈ

ᵇHenric Tydemans zoenᵇ

ᵃ *added in different writing.* ᵇ *in the left margin.* ᶜ *cancelled.* ᵈ *in a different hand.*

fol.76r, In Hermalen ᵃReynerscopᵃ LXXVI
the first lines are somewhat corroded:

Item ibidem in Reynerscop mansum et VII iugera terre [quibus a] su/periori parte [propius iacent] Ghisebertus filius Hugonis [et Hugo die Roede]/ communi sulcu [et a parte] occidentali [borgravius] de Montfoerde et Jo/hannes filius Hermanni communi sulcu. Quam terram modo possidet Gerardus Starke una cum terra proxime sequenti ad X annos ab anno LXIX *[1369]* Petri et solvet tam de hiis quam de aliis iugeribus subscriptis annuatim IX marcas et VI loet argenti aut pagamentum equivalens et XXX pullas annuatim absque defalcatione Martini et Petri aut cadet ab omni iure et cetera prout littera tenet. Per fratrem Hugonem.

ᵇUlterius possidebit Herman Janszoen ad X annos ab anno LXXXVIII *[1388]* Petri pro CXV libris XVII solidis III denariis ende XXII pullis sub omni condicione prescripta. Per fratrem Joannem Haze.ᵇ

ᶜGerardus Starkeᶜ

ᵈItem ibidem VII iugera II hont minus prout iacent In een gheweer lands van Xj *[10.5]* marghen in quibus Xj iugeribus dominus Stephanus de Zulen habet I iuger, dominus Bernardus uten Enge V hont, ecclesia et custos ecclesie in Hermalen I iuger et moniales Vallis sancte Marie I iuger terre et domus nostra cetera VII iugera II hont minus prescripta. Quibus Xj *[10.5]* iugeribus propius iacet terra monasterii sancti Pauli Traiectensis a parte superiori et terra Ghiseberti filii Hugonis et Hugonis Roede a parte inferiori. Que VII iugera minus II hont modo possidet Gerardus Starke una cum terra superius notata ad annos et sub eadem annua pensione superius signatis. ᶜGerardus Starkeᶜ

ᵃ *added in different writing.* ᵇ *in a different hand.* ᶜ *in the right margin, in the basic hand.* ᵈ *linked with brace to the foregoing item.*

fol.76v,   In Hermalen ᵃReynerscopᵃ
the first lines are rather corroded:

[Item ibidem in Reynerscop XIIII [iugera terre] iuxta terram nostre domus]/ [a superiori parte —]/ [— Ghisekinus Alberti ad]/ [X annos ab anno LXVII *[1367]* — pro XXVIII libris V solidis]/ [denariorum Traiectensium et XIIII pullis annuatim solvendis infra quindenam post Martini et]/ [Petri vel cadet ab omni iure et cetera] sub condicionibus in littera contentis. Per/ [fratrem Hugonem]. ᵇ*Ghisekinus Alberti*ᵇ

Item ibidem in Reynerscop IX iugera prout iacent inter terram nostre domus dictam Ziitwinde a parte superiori et alias ab omni parte inter terram nostre domus prout illa modo possidet Ricoldus Bokeler ad XI annos ab anno LXI *[1361]* Petri pro XII libris denariorum Traiectensium et IX pullis annuatim solvendis Martini et Petri vel cadet ab omni iure et cetera prout littera exinde tenet. Per commendatorem.
ᶜUlterius idem Ricoldus possidebit dictam terram una cum VII iugeribus superius signatis ad VI annos ab anno LXXI *[1371]* Petri proᵈ subᵉ eadem annua pensione superius iuxta aliam terram signata, sub condicionibus in littera contentis. Per fratrem Johannem Gaude.ᶜ
ᶠUlterius possidebit Everardus Breide ab anno LXXXIIII *[1384]* Petri ad X annos pro annua pensione videlicet pro XXXVI libris secundum solutionem pactus in Traiecto currentem et pro IX pullis secundum modum et formam prout fieri est consuetum. Per me fratrem Gerardum.ᶠ
ᵍRicoldus Bokelerᵍ
ʰEverardus Breideʰ

ᵃ *added in different writing.* ᵇ *in the left margin.* ᶜ *in a different hand (C).* ᵈ *cancelled.* ᵉ *written above the cancelled word.* ᶠ *in another hand, with pale ink.* ᵍ *in the left margin, cancelled.* ʰ *in the left margin with pale ink, in the same hand as* ᶠ.

fol.77r,   In Hermalen ^aReynerscop^a   LXXVII
the first part is heavily corroded:

[Item ibidem ——]/ [——]/ [——]/ [annua pensione superius in universo iuxta alia XV iugera sig]/natis.
[^bGhisekinus Alberti^b]

Item ibidem V iugera prout iacent in Reynerscop aen den Vliet quibus terra nostre domus ex omni latere propius iacet et prout illa modo possidet Henricus filius Theoderici ad X annos ab anno LXVIII *[1368]* Petri pro XIII libris et V pullis solvendis Martini et Petri annuatim et sub condicionibus in littera contentis vel cadet ab omni iure. Per Hugonem.
^bHenric Dirixzoen^b

---

^a *added in different writing.* ^b *in the right margin.*

fol.77v,   In Hermalen ^aReynerscop^a
the first part is heavily corroded:

[——]/ [——]/ [— ad X an]/[nos ab anno LXIX *[1369]* Valentini pro IIII marcis et XIIj *[12.5]* loet]/ argenti et XIX denariis, VII caponibus, VII pullis annuatim absque defalcatione solvendis infra quindenam post Martini et Petri vel cadet ab omni iure et cetera prout littera tenet. Per fratrem Hugonem.
^b[Henric van den Velde ende] Aleyd siin wiif^b

Item ibidem IIII iugera prout iacent inter terram Maioris ecclesie Traiectensis a [superiori] et inferiori parte, que modo possidet Johannes Spronc filius Theoderici ad X annos ab anno LXVIII *[1368]* Purificatione Marie pro XV loet argenti et IIII caponibus annuatim absque defalcatione solvendis infra quindenam post Martini et Petri vel cadet ab omni iure et cetera sub condicionibus in littera contentis. Per fratrem Hugonem.
^bJohannes Spronc^b

---

^a *added in different writing.* ^b *in the left margin.*

fol. 78r,   In Hermalen ªReynerscopª   LXXVIII
the first lines of both items are rather corroded:

[Item ibidem XI iugera —]/ [per — inter terram]/ nostre domus a parte superiori et terram Wilhelmi Pape a parte [inferiori, que]/ modo possidet Aleydis relicta Alberni Riclandi ad X annos ab anno LXIX *[1369]* Petri pro IIII marcis argenti aut pagamento equivalenti et V caponibus VI pullis annuatim absque defalcatione solvendis Martini et Petri vel cadet ab omni iure et cetera prout littera exinde tenet. Per fratrem Hugonem.
ᵇAleydis relicta [Alberni Ric]landiᵇ

Item ibidem V iugera iacentia [inter terram nostre domus quam nunc possidet]/ Wilhelmus Corthoze a parte superiori et terram nostre domus quam nunc possidet/ provisor curtis nostre in Reynerscop [— nunc possidet] ᶜHen/ricus Scatterᶜ ad X annos ab anno LXIX *[1369]* Agnetis [pro XXIX loet]/ argenti aut pagamento equivalenti et [— pullis annuatim absque defalcatione] / solvendis Martini et Petri vel cadet ab omni iure et cetera [prout littera exinde]/ tenet. Per fratrem Hugonem.
ªModo possidet Aleydis relicta Wilhelmi Riclandi et Gerardus Spronc eius filius ad annos et sub annua pensione prout supra et sub condicionibus prout littera exinde tenet. Per fratrem Hugonem.ª
ᵇAleydis relicta Wilhelmi Riclandi et Gerardus Spronc eius filiusᵇ

ª *added in different writing.* ᵇ *in the right margin.* ᶜ *cancelled.*

fol. 78v,   In Hermalen ªReynerscopª
the first lines of both items are somewhat corroded:

[Item ibidem VIII iugera quibus a superiori parte propius iacet terra dicta]/ [Ziitwinde et a parte inferiori terra domus nostre sancte Katerine quam]/ nunc possidet curtis in Reynerscop dicta Coecamp prout illa modo possidet a nobis Jacobus Spengard ad X annos ab anno LXVIII *[1368]* Valentini pro XXVI libris denariorum Traiectensium et VIII pullis annuatim absque defalcatione infra quindenam post Martini et Petri solvendis aut cadet ab omni iure et cetera prout littera tenet. Per fratrem Hugonem.
ᵇUlterius possidebit dictam terram ad X annos ab anno LXXVI *[1376]* Petri pro XXXVI libris denariorum et VIII pullis et cetera prout littera tenet.ᵇ
ᶜUlterius possidebit predictam terram Hugo Pot ad X annos ab anno

LXXXVI *[1386]* Petri pro XXXVI libris ende VIII pullis sub condicione prescripta. Per fratrem Johannem Haze.ᶜ
ᵈJacob Spengardᵈ

Item ibidem I campum terre continentem VIII iugera extendentem se cum uno/ fine ad locum dictum Dwersweteringhe prout iacet inter viam dictam/ [die Blindeweg a parte orientali] et terram borgravii de Mont/[foerde et Wolteri Gherardi van] den Polle a parte occidentali./ [Quem campum modo possident Nicolaus] filius Symonis et Wilhelmus de Holten/ ad X annos ab anno LXII *[1362]* Petri pro XX libris denariorum Traiectensium et VIII/ pullis [annuatim absque defalcatione solvendis Martini] et Petri vel cadet ab omni iure et cetera/ in littera. Per fratrem Hugonem.
ᵉModo dictam terram possidet Jacobus ᶠfilius [Symonis]ᶠ ad X annos ab anno LXXII *[1372]* Petri pro XXXII libris denariorum Traiectensium et VIII pullis annuatim absque defalcatione solvendis Martini et Petri vel cadet ab omni iure et cetera prout littera tenet. Per fratrem Thomam dispensatorem.ᵉ
ᵍUlterius idem possidebit dictam terram prout iacet ad X annos ab anno LXXXII *[1382]* Petri pro XL libris denariorum Traiectensium et VIII pullis solvendis Martini et Petri vel cadet ab omni iure. Per commendatorem.ᵍ
ʰNicolaus Symonis et Wilhelmus de Holtenʰ
ⁱJacob Symons zoenⁱ

ᵃ *added in different writing.* ᵇ *in a different hand (C).* ᶜ *in another hand.* ᵈ *in the left margin, in the basic hand.* ᵉ *in another hand (B).* ᶠ *filius filius ms.* ᵍ *in yet another hand (D).* ʰ *in the left margin, cancelled.* ⁱ *in the left margin, in the hand of* ᵉ.

fol.79r, In Hermalen ᵃcurtis in Reynerscopᵃ LXXIX
the first lines are somewhat corroded:

Item ibidem supra Reynerscop [habet domus hanc terram infrascriptam quam nunc]/ possidet provisor [curtis nostre ibidem sub annua responsione inferius notatam]

Primo XXXI iugera terre prout iacent ab ista parte curtis nostre ibidem versus Renum, quibus a parte orientali propius iacet domus nostra cum VIII iugeribus que nunc possidet Jacobus Spengard et a parte occidentali etiam domus nostra cum terra iugeribusᵇ quam nunc colit Gerardus Galicop. Hanc terram nunc possidet frater Wilhelmus de Orscoten provisor curtis nostre ibidem.
ᶜcurtis Reynerscopᶜ

^dItem ibidem ab alia parte curtis nostre ibidem versus Yslam <u>XXXIII iugera terre</u>, in quorum medio domus nostra iacet cum V iugeribus que nunc possidet a nobis Henricus filius Theoderici et eciam cum IIIj *[3.5]* iugeribus que nunc possidet a nobis Gerardus Galicop. Et a superiori parte dictorum XXXIII iugeribus propius iacet iter dictam Blindeweg et inferius capitulum seu collegium sancti Petri Traiectensis. ^aFrater Wilhelmus de Oerscoten nunc possidet ad annos et sub annua responsione inferius signatis.^a
^c<u>Curtis Reynerscop</u>^c

---

^a *added in different writing.* ^b *cancelled.* ^c *in the right margin in the same writing as* ^a.
^d *linked with brace to the foregoing item.*

fol.79v,   In Hermalen ^a<u>curtis Reynerscop</u>^a
the first lines are somewhat corroded:

Item [ibidem per <u>unum campum</u> continentem <u>XI</u> hont terre] quibus a su/[periori parte propius] iacet [domus nostra cum —] iugeribus, que nunc possidet Hen/ricus Scatter et ab inferiori parte propius iacet die Blindewech. Et/ [hec terra] extendit se cum uno fine an die Dwersweteringhe die/ midden doert land gaet. Predictus frater Wilhelmus una cum ceteris modo possidet ad annos infrascriptos.
^b<u>curtis Reynerscop</u>^b

<u>Item opt hoghe land III iugera terre</u>, quibus canonici regulares in Traiecto propius iacent a superiori parte versus Renum ab ambabus partibus, et a parte posteriori versus finem orientalem propius iacet terra domini de Apcoude et versus finem occidentalem eiusdem terre propius iacet terra domus nostre sancte Katerine. ^aProvisor curtis in Reynerscop modo possidet una cum ceteris suprascriptis.^a
^b<u>curtis in Reynerscop</u>^b

^c<u>Summa prescriptorum iugerum terre pronunc pertinentium ad curtim nostram in Reynerscop LXIX iugera et I hont exceptis area et orto in quibus domus eiusdem curtis est constructa.</u>^c
^aQuam curtim cum huiusmodi terrarum iugeribus prescriptis modo possidet frater Wilhelmus de Orscoten ad X annos ab anno LXV *[1365]* Petri sub annua responsione C et XV librarum denariorum Traiectensium Martini et Petri solvendarum sub ceteris condicionibus in littera quam inde habemus contentis. Per magistrum de Brunsberch locumtenentem et commendatorem.^a

---

^a *added in a different writing.* ^b *in the left margin in the same writing as* ^a. ^c *indent with decorated capital letter.*

fol.80r,   In Hermalen ªSupra Hanewycª   LXXX
the first lines are heavily corroded:

[Item ibidem —]/ [———]/ Everardus Godekini a parte septentrionali
et [terram nostre domus]/ scilicet Eyndelinge daer aen streckende
quam nunc possidet Curtis in Reynerscop a parte meridionali prout
ea possidebat Johannes Abelini. Modo possidebit ea una cum ceteris
terrarum iugeribus hic proxime sequentibus Johannes Yoie filius Petri
ad X annos ab anno LXVIII *[1368]* Petri Et solvet tam de hiis quam
de aliis in universo IIII marcas V loet argenti aut pagamentum equivalens in Traiecto et XVIII denarios et XVII pullas annuatim absque
defalcatione Martini et Petri solvendas aut cadet ab omni iure et
cetera prout littera exinde tenet. Per fratrem Hugonem.
ᵇUlterius possidebit istam terram una cum terra sequenti Johannes de
Attevelt ad X annos ab anno LXXV *[1375]* Petri et solvet in universo
tam de ista terra quam de alia inferius super eundem signat, inclusis
quatuor iugeribus que curtis in Hermalen possidebat, LXXXVI libras XXI pullas denariorum Traiectensium absque defalcatione et
cetera   prout   littera   tenet.   Per   fratrem   Johannem   Gaude
commendatorem.ᵇ
ᶜJohannes Yoie filius Petriᶜ
ᵈJohannes de Atteveltᵈ

Item in eadem parrochia supra Hanewiic VI iugera que fuerunt
quondam Henrici Helenburgis prout iacent inter terram domini
Theoderici de Zulen militis a parte superiori et terram capituli sancti
Salvatoris Traiectensis a parte inferiori. Johannes Abelini possidebat.
Modo possidebit ea una cum ceteris Johannes Yoie filius Petri ad
annos et sub annua pensione in universo superius signatis.
ᶜJohannes Yoieᶜ
ᵈJohannes de Atteveltᵈ

ª *added in different writing.* ᵇ *in a different hand (C).* ᶜ *in the right margin, cancelled.*
ᵈ *in the right margin, in the same hand as* ᵇ.

fol.80v,   In Hermalen ªsupra Hanewycª
the first lines are heavily corroded:

[———]/ [parte superiori et terram domini Theoderici de Zulen a
parte inferiori]/ [prout illa Johannes A]belini possidebat. M[odo]
possidet ea Johannes Yoie filius/ [Petri cum] ceteris iugeribus in hoc
folio signatis. Sub condicionibus quibus supra.
ᵇJohannes Yoieᵇ
ᶜJohannes de Atteveltᶜ

^dItem ibidem III iugera empta quondam erga Arnoldum Duerhant iacentia inter terram capituli sancti Salvatoris Traiectensis a parte superiori et terram domini Theoderici de Zulen a parte inferiori, que Johannes Abelini possidebat. Modo possidet ea Johannes Yoie predictus sub annis et condicionibus quibus supra.
^bJohannes Yoie^b
^cJohannes de Attevelt^c

^dItem ibidem ^asupra Oudeland^a IIj *[2.5]* iugera terre streckende van de Broydiic, quibus ab ambabus partibus propius iacet terra Constancii Scottelvoet. Johannes Abelini possidebat. Modo possidet ea Johannes Yoie supradictus una cum ceteris iugeribus super eundem superius signatis ad X annos ab anno LXVIII *[1368]* Petri sub condicionibus superius signatis.
^bJohannes Yoie^b
^cJohannes de Attevelt^c

---

^a *added in different writing.* ^b *in the left margin, cancelled.* ^c *in the left margin, in a different hand (C).* ^d *linked with brace to the foregoing item.*

fol.81r,   In Hermalen   LXXXI
the first lines are heavily corroded:

Item [ibidem unum iuger terre iacens —]/ [———]/ iacet a superiori [parte idem dominus Theodericus de Zulen et inferius domus]/ nostra cum terra quam nunc possidet a nobis Johannes Yoie filius [Petri]. Quod quidem iuger qondam possidebat a nobis [Machteldis relicta Quints] ad vitam suam pro V solidis bonorum annuatim. Modo dictus dominus Theodericus possidet ulterius sub eadem annua pensione.
^aQuam asserit esse hereditarie. Perscrutetur inde veritas. Credo [enim] quod idem iuger ex obitu dicte Machtildis ad nos sit libere devolutum.^a
^bdominus Theodericus de Zulen^b

Item ibidem I iuger prout illa possidebat a nobis Hilwaris Antonii de Cattenbroec ad vitam suam pro VI solidis bonorum denariorum annuatim. Que ^adiu defuncta est et quis modo istud iuger possideat aut ubi situm sit ignoratur ad huc.^a
^bHilwaris Antonij^b

Item ibidem in Cattenbroec Ij *[1.5]* quartalia iacentia inter terram

nostre domus quam nunc possidet Gerardus filius Johannis a parte superiori et terram Petri custodis ecclesie in Hermalen a parte inferiori, que modo possidet Johannes filius Ghiseberti Hunenberch <u>ad X annos</u> ab anno <u>LXVIII</u> *[1368]* Valentini et solvet annuatim II marcas et I loet argenti annuatim minus II solidis et VII pullis absque defalcatione Martini et Petri vel cadet ab omni iure et cetera sub condicionibus in littera contentis. Per Hugonem.
^b<u>Johannes filius Ghiseberti</u>^b

---

^a *added in different writing.* ^b *in the right margin in the same writing as* ^a

fol.81v.   ^a<u>In Hermalen supra Cattenbroec</u>^a

Item ibidem <u>dimidium mansum et Ij *[1.5]* quartalia</u> prout iacent inter terram monialium sancti Servacii Traiectensis a parte superiori et terram nostre domus quam nunc possidet Johannes filius Ghiseberti Hunneberch a parte inferiori. Modo dictam terram prout iacet possidet Gerardus filius Johannis <u>ad X annos</u> ab anno LXVIII *[1368]* Valentini <u>pro V marcis et II loet argenti et XV denariis</u> aut cum pagamento equivalenti in Traiecto et <u>VI talentis cere, VII caponibus, VII pullis</u> annuatim solvendis absque defalcatione Martini et Petri vel cadet ab omni iure et cetera sub condicionibus in littera exinde contentis. Per fratrem Hugonem.
^b<u>Gerardus filius Johannis</u>^b

Item ibidem <u>dimidium mansum terre</u> prout iacet inter terram Wilhelmi Svaggerd a parte superiori et terram Stelle de Montforde a parte inferiori, que modo possidet Gerardus Wiichman <u>ad X annos</u> ab anno <u>LXVII</u> *[1367]* Petri. Et solvet nobis annuatim <u>XI antiquos scudatos auri et XXVI solidos III denarios et IX pullas</u> absque defalcatione Martini et Petri vel cadet ab omni iure et cetera prout littera exinde tenet. Per fratrem Hugonem.
^cUlterius possidebit Johannes Veer tot Montforde ad X annos ab anno LXXVII *[1377]* Petri pro XI antiquis scudatis auri aut pagamento equivalenti et VI talentis cere et VII caponibus absque defalcatione solvendis Martini et Petri vel cadet ab omni iure. Per fratrem Johannem commendatorem.^c
^d<u>Gerardus Wijchman</u>^d
^e<u>Johan die Veer</u>^e

---

^a *added in different writing.* ^b *in the left margin.* ^c *in a different hand (C).* ^d *in the left margin, cancelled.* ^e *in the left margin in the same hand as* ^c.

fol.82r, ᵃIn Hermalen, supra Cattenbroecᵃ LXXXII
the first part is somewhat corroded:

Item ibidem supra Cattenbroec V [iugera terre prout iacent inter terram]/ [Hermanni filii Gerardi de Cattenbroec a parte superiori et terram]/ Henrici Pellencussen a parte inferiori. [Idem Hermannus modo pos]/sidet ad X annos ad anno LXX *[1370]* Petri una cum XIIj *[12.5]* iugeribus et [—]/ iugeribus hic sequentibus et solvet tam de hiis quam de aliis in [universo] IIj *[2.5]*/ marcas argenti, IIII talenta cere, V capones, IIII pullas annuatim absque/ defalcatione Martini et Petri vel cadet ab omni iure et cetera prout [littera tenet. Per fratrem Hugonem.] Non conburet et medietatem terre in fine annorum incultam resignabit ac pro dictis IIII talentis cere solvere potest XII grossos Traiectensis pagamenti annuatim.
ᵇHermannus filius [Gerardi]ᵇ

ᶜItem ibidem IIIj *[3.5]* iugera terre quibus terra nostre domus una cum terra Hermanni filii Gerardi communi sulcu propius iacet a parte superiori et terra eiusdem Hermanni a parte inferiori, que idem Hermannus possidet.
ᵇHermannus filius Gerardiᵇ

ᶜItem ibidem Ij *[1.5]* iugera iacentia inter terram collegii sancti Petri Traiectensis a parte superiori et terram dicti Hermanni filii Gerardi a parte inferiori, que etiam idem Hermannus modo possidet una cum ceteris iugeribus supradictis.
ᵇHermannus filius Gerardiᵇ

ᵃ *added in different writing.* ᵇ *in the right margin in the same writing as* ᵃ. ᶜ *linked with brace to the foregoing item.*

fol.82v, In Hermalen
the first part is rather corroded:

[Item ibidem supra Blocland XIIII iugera terre prout iacent inter] terram/ [— et terram domini]/ [Theoderici de Zulen a parte inferiori, que modo possidet A]rnoldus/ [filius Wendelmodis ad X annos ab anno LXIX *[1369]*] Petri. Solvet/ exinde XVII antiquos scudatos et I quartale unius scudati auri aut/ [pagamentum equivalens], IIII talenta cere, XII capones, VI pullas annuatim/ [absque defalcatione Martini] et Petri vel cadet ab omni iure et cetera prout littera exinde tenet. Per fratrem Hugonem.

^aModo dictam terram possidebit Ghisebertus de Crimpen ad X annos ab anno LXXIII *[1373]* Petri pro II marcis et XIII loet argenti, IIII talentis cere, VI caponibus, VII pullis annuatim absque defalcatione Martini et Petri solvendis vel cadet ab omni iure. Duos campos non conburet sed de ceteris potest conburere medietatem semel si voluerit et cetera prout littera exinde tenet. Per fratrem Thomam.^a
^b<u>Arnoldus filius Wendelmodis</u>^b
^c<u>Ghisebertus de Crimpen</u>^c

Item ibidem in Gherwerscop <u>VI iugera terre</u> prout iacent in I gheweerscop de XV iugeribus vel circiter, quibus VI iugeribus propius iacent Jacobus filius Arnoldi, Ghisebertus Blome, Johannes filius Ysebrandi et Ysebrandus filius Heynonis Svarten cum terra eorum communi sulcu a parte orientali et terra Henrici filii Ludolphi et Petri Erlewini etiam communi sulcu propius iacent a parte occidentali. Que modo possidet Petrus filius Erlewini ad X annos ab anno LXI *[1361]* Petri pro <u>IX libris, VI pullis annuatim.</u>
^aUlterius idem Petrus possidet dictam terram ad X annos ab anno LXXI *[1371]* Valentini pro XXI libris denariorum Traiectensium et dimidium quartale butiri et VI pullis annuatim absque defalcatione Martini et Petri vel cadet ab omni iure et cetera prout littera tenet. Per fratrem Thomam de Doesborch. Butyrum solvet in fine May.^a
^d<u>Petrus Erlewini</u>^d

---

^a *in a different hand (B).* ^b *in the left margin, cancelled.* ^c *in the left margin in the same hand as* ^a. ^d *in the left margin.*

fol.83r,   In Hermalen   LXXXIII
the first lines are heavily corroded:

Item ibidem <u>duo iugera [terre</u> iacentia inter terram Hermanni Antiqui Cla]/[wen filii [Ferencii a superiori parte et —]/ [a parte inferiori.]
^a<u>Bartholomeus filius Wilhelmi</u>^a

^bItem ibidem <u>unum iuger</u> emptum quondam erga Wilhelmum Sweertvegher prout iacet communi sulcu in VIII iugeribus terre. Quibus VIII iugeribus propius iacent hec duo iugera nostre domus prescripta a superiori parte et inferius iacet ene kae. Quod quidem iuger una cum II iugeribus prescriptis modo possidet Bartholomeus filius Wilhelmi ad <u>X annos</u> ab anno LXX *[1370]* Petri. Et solvet tam de hiis tribus iugeribus prescriptis insimul <u>XII loet argenti aut</u> paga-

mentum equivalens in Traiecto et III pullas annuatim, infra quindenam post Martini et Petri solvendis aut cadet ab omni iure et cetera
prout littera exinde tenet. Per fratrem Hugonem.
^aBartholomeus filius Wilhelmi^a

---

^a *in the right margin.* ^b *linked with brace to the foregoing item.*

fol.83v.   In Hermalen
the first lines are rather corroded:

Item ibidem aen [den Broydijc dimidium campum terre] continentem II/ iugera, [dimidium thyrintum et —] unius thyrinti terre
prout/ iacet inter terram domini Frederici uten Hamme militis a
parte superiori, et terram Wilhelmi Duerkant a parte inferiori.
^aHaza relicta Johannis van der Koken modo possidet una cum XII
iugeribus sequentibus.^a
^bModo possident Magnus Reynerus et Aleidis eius uxor filia Johannis
dicti Dogheden una cum XII iugeribus sequentibus sub annuo pactu
infra notatis.^b
^cHaza relicta Johannis van der Koken^c
^dMagnus Reynerus et Aleidis eius uxor^d

^eIdem ibidem XII iugera terre dimidium hont et quartam partem
unius hont prout iacent inter terram domini Frederici uten Hamme a
parte superiori et terram Wilhelmi Duerkant a parte inferiori, prout
illa modo possidet una cum dimidio campo terre prescripto Haza
relicta Johannis van der Koken ad X annos ab anno LXVIII *[1368]*
Valentini. Et solvet annuatim tam de hiis quam de aliis in universo
XXXI antiquos scudatos et unum quartale unius scudati auri aut
pagamentum equivalens et V talenta cere et XIIII pullas Martini et
Petri vel cadet ab omni iure et cetera prout littera exinde tenet. Per
fratrem Hugonem.
^fModo possidebit dictam terram Magnus Reynerus ad XI annos a
festo Petri anno LXXXIII *[1383]* pro LXXXIIII libris monete qua
pactus solvuntur absque defalcatione. Per fratrem Johannem Gaude
et XIIII pullis.^f
^gMagnus Reynerus et Aleidis eius uxor^g

---

^a *added in different writing.* ^b *in a different hand (D).* ^c *in the left margin, cancelled.*
^d *in the left margin, in the same hand as* ^b. ^e *linked with brace to the foregoing item.* ^f *in
another hand.* ^g *in the left margin, in the same hand as* ^f.

fol.84r, In Hermalen LXXXIIII
the first lines are rather corroded:

Item ibidem an den Broydijc XVII [iugera terre inter terram domi-
ni]/ [Frederici uten Hamme militis a parte superiori et terram —
uut]/ den Enge militis a parte inferiori [prout illa modo possident
Johannes filius]/ Ysebrandi et Ghisebertus Blome [ad X annos ab
anno LXVIII *[1368]* Va]/lentini pro V marcis et [XIII loet argenti
aut pagamento equi]/valenti in Traiecto et IIII talentis cere, VIII
caponibus et IX pullis annuatim solvendis infra quindenam post
Martini et Petri vel cadet ab omni iure et cetera prout in littera
exinde continetur. Per fratrem Hugonem.
ᵃUlterius possidebunt Ghisebertus filius Alberti et Nycolaus de Wiel
et Ghisebertus Otte ad X annos ab anno LXXVII *[1377]* Petri pro
LXIIII libris, IIII talentis cere, VIII caponibus, IX pullis et cetera
prout littera tenet. Per commendatorem fratrem Johannem Gaude.ᵃ
ᵇJohannes filius Ysebrandi et Ghisebertus Blomeᵇ
ᶜGhisebertus Alberti Nycolaus de Wiel et Ghisebertus Otteᶜ

Item ibidem supra Bilenvelt VIII iugera et plus ut credo iacentia inter
terram monasterii Albarum Dominarum in Traiecto a parte superiori
et terram nostre domus quam nunc possidet ᵈ a parte inferiori, prout
illa modo possidet iuvenis Johannes Brabant ad X annos ab anno
LXVII *[1367]* Petri pro XXII libris denariorum Traiectensium, VIII
solidis et VIII pullis annuatim absque defalcatione solvendis infra
quindenam post Martini et Petri vel cadet ab omni iure et cetera sub
condicionibus in littera contentis. Per fratrem Hugonem.
ᵉJunge Jan Brabantᵉ

ᵃ *in a different hand (C).* ᵇ *in the right margin, cancelled.* ᶜ *in the right margin in the
same hand as* ᵃ. ᵈ *not filled in.* ᵉ *in the right margin in the basic hand.*

fol.84v, In Hermalen
the first part are rather corroded:

Item ibidem XIIj *[12.5]* iugera terre prout iacent iuxta/ [communia
— a parte o]rientali et inter terram heredum/ [—] a parte occidentali. Quorum unam me/[dietatem scilicet VI iugera et Ij *[1.5]* hont]
modo possidet frater Henricus Wit/tiken curatus in Hermalen ad X
annos ab anno ᵃ
ᵇfrater Henricus Wittikenᵇ

Reliquam vero [medietatem dictorum] XIIj *[12.5]* iugerum terre scilicet VI iugera et Ij *[1.5]* hont modo possidet senior Johannes Brabant
ad X annos ab anno LXII *[1362]* Petri pro XII libris denariorum
Traiectensium, II talentis cere et VI pullis annuatim absque defalcatione infra quindenam post Martini et Petri solvendis vel cadet ab
omni iure et cetera secundum tenorem littere qua utimur exinde. Per
fratrem Hugonem.
ᵇJohannes Brabant seniorᵇ

ᵃ *not filled in.* ᵇ *in the left margin.*

fol.85r,   In Hermalen   LXXXV
the whole page is more or less corroded:

Item ibidem III iugera [— inter terram nostre]/ [domus quam modo
possidet —]/ inter terram [Heinrici de Hermalen a parte inferiori,
prout illa modo]/ possidet Petrus custos una cum ceteris iugeribus
[sub —]
ᵃ[Petrus custos]ᵃ

Item ibidem V iugera iacentia inter terram nostre domus quam modo
possidet ᵇ a parte superiori et inter viam communem ecclesie de
Hermalen a parte inferiori. Petrus custos nunc possidet cum ceteris
hic super eundem signatis. ᵃPetrus custosᵃ

Item ibidem IIIj *[3.5]* iugera prout iacent inter terram heredum Hugonis de/ Vloten a parte [superiori et terram collegii Maioris ecclesie
Traiectensis a]/ parte inferiori, que modo [possidet Petrus custos una
cum ceteris]/ iugeribus superius super eundem [signatis ad X annos
ab anno LXI *[1361]*]/ Petri. Et solvet tam de hiis quam de aliis in
universo [XX libras denariorum]/ Traiectensium et VI talenta cere
annuatim absque defalcatione Martini et Petri [vel cadet ab]/ omni
iure et cetera. Per fratrem Hugonem.
ᵃPetrus custosᵃ

ᵃ *in the right margin.* ᵇ *not filled in.*

fol.85v.   In Hermalen

Item ibidem VIII iugera cum dimidio prout iacent inter terram Wilhelmi de Vloten a parte superiori et terram pertinentem ad quoddam

altare fundatum in ecclesia Traiectensi a parte inferiori, prout illa modo possidet Franco de Denemarken ad X annos ab anno LXIX *[1369]* Petri pro II marcis et XI loet argenti minus VIII denariis et IIII talentis cere et VIII caponibus annuatim absque defalcatione solvendis Martini et Petri vel cadet ab omni iure et cetera prout littera exinde tenet. Per fratrem Hugonem.
[a]Vranke van Denemarken[a]

Item ibidem in Hermaler Weyrt Ij *[1.5]* iugera prout iacent communi sulcu cum terra Theoderici Bolen, daer an den nederen egge naest gheland is her Dirc van Zulen, prout illa modo possidet Johannes uten Nesse ad X annos ab anno LXIII *[1363]* Purificatione Marie pro III libris, VIIj *[7.5]* solidis et II pullis annuatim Martini et Petri solvendis. Per fratrem Hugonem.
[a]Johannes uten Nesse[a]

---

[a] *in the left margin.*

fol.86r,   In Hermalen [curtis] in Hermalen   LXXXVI
the first lines are rather corroded:

Item ibidem in eadem [parrochia de Hermalen habet domus nostra – terram subscriptam quam nunc]/ possidet [provisor curtis nostre sub annos et annua pensione infra]/ notatis.

Primo XLV iugera terre super que domus et edificia dicte curtis ibidem sunt constructa prout iacent inter terram collegii sancti Martini Traiectensis a parte orientali et inter viam communem ecclesie de Hermalen a parte occidentali.
[a]Frater Henricus Wittiken provisor curtis eiusdem modo possidet.[a]
[b]curtis in Hermalen[b]

Item ibidem II petias terre nuncupatas vulgariter II werve in quibus crescunt rame scilicet weyrt twigher, continentes circa II iugera prout iacent inter viam communem ecclesie ibidem a parte orientali et terram Henrici de Hermalen a parte occidentali.
[a]Frater Henricus provisor curtis modo possidet.[a]
[b]curtis in Hermalen[b]

Item ibidem opt Hogheland IIII iugera terre, empta quondam erga dominum Thomas Petri aurifabrum commensalem nostrum, prout iacent inter terram domini Theoderici de Zulen a parte orientali et

terram monialium Claustri Dominarum a parte occidentali.
^aIdem provisor curtis modo possidet.^a
^bcurtis in Hermalen^b

---

^a *added in different writing.* ^b *in the right margin, in the same writing as* ^a.

fol.86v, [In Hermalen curtis ibidem]
the first lines are somewhat corroded:

Item ibidem I iuger [ex Reno transiens] ad locum dictum Loesloet/
cui ab ambabus partibus terra [domini Theoderici de Zulen] propius
iacet.
^aProcurator pronunc possidet.^a
^bcurtis ibidem^b

Item ibidem IV iugera terre, quibus a superiori parte propius iacet
virida via dicta Gronewech et a parte inferiori domus nostra cum
terra quam nunc idem provisor curtis possidet.
^aProcurator curtis modo possidet.^a
^bProvisor curtis ibidem^b

Item ibidem V iugera remeantia ex Reno prout iacent inter terram
domini Theoderici de Zulen a parte orientali, eyndelinge daer aen
streckende, et terram Petri Mauriken a parte occidentali.
^aProcurator curtis modo possidet.^a
^bProcurator curtis^b

Item ibidem I iuger prout iacet in die Lange Maet inter terram custodis ecclesie in Hermalen a parte orientali et terram domini de Apcoude a parte occidentali.
^aIdem procurator possidet.^a
^bProcurator curtis^b

---

^a *added in different writing.* ^b *in the left margin, in the same writing as* ^a.

fol.87r, In [Hermalen curtis ibidem] LXXXVII
the third item is rather corroded:

Item ibidem op die Hoghe Loe IX hont terre, quibus terra domini de
Apcoude propius iacet ab ambabus partibus.
^aIdem procurator possidet.^a

^bProvisor curtis ibidem^b

Item ibidem op die Laghe Loe VIII hont terre prout iacent inter terram domini de Apcoude a parte orientali et terram conventus bagutarum in Traiecto a latere occidentali.
^aProcurator curtis possidet.^a
^bProcurator curtis ibidem^b

Item ibidem III iugera ex Reno [remeantia] ad locum dictum Loesloet/ prout iacent inter terram [Johannis Yoie filii Petri] a latere orientali et/ terram Suederi de Zulen [a parte occidentali.]
^cIdem procurator curtis possidet.^c
^dModo possidet Johannes de Attevelt una cum terra superius signata et una cum uno iugere subscripto ad decem annos ab anno LXXV [1375] Petri et cetera prout littera tenet.^d
^bProcurator curtis ibidem^b
^eJohannes de Attevelt^e

Item ibidem I iuger ab aggere Reni ibidem transiens ad locum dictum Loesloet prout iacet inter terram sancti Dyonisii a parte orientali et terram Johannis Yoie filii Petri a parte occidentali.
^cIdem procurator curtis modo possidet una cum ceteris supra signatis.^c
^dJohannes de Attevelt possidet modo.^d
^fProcurator curtis ibidem^f
^eJohannes de Attevelt^e

Summa prescriptorum iugerum terre ad curtim in Hermalen pertinentium LXVI iugera et V hont.

^aQuam curtis cum huiusmodi terrarum iugeribus modo possidet frater Henricus Wittiken ad X annos ab anno LXVI [1366] Johannis Baptiste sub annua pensione C et XXV librarum Martini et Petri solvenda sub ceteris conditionibus in littera exinde contentis. Per magistrum Alamanie et commendatorem huius domus actum et locatum.^a

---

^a *added in different writing.* ^b *in the right margin, in the same writing as* ^a. ^c *added in the same writing as* ^a *but cancelled.* ^d *in a different hand (C).* ^e *in the right margin, in the same hand as* ^d. ^f *in the right margin, like* ^b, *but cancelled.*

fol.87v, In [Lynschoten]
the first lines are rather corroded:

Item habet domus in parrochia de Lynschoten in Mastwijc *duo/* quartalia terre [prout iacent inter terram] Hermanni Blankart a parte/ superiori et terram [—] a parte inferiori, prout/ illa modo possidet [Engelbertus Vinke] ad X annos ab anno LXII *[1362]/* [Petri pro XIIII] libris denariorum Traiectensium et VI caponibus annuatim absque defalcatione Martini et Petri/ solvendis vel cadet ab omni iure et cetera prout littera exinde tenet. Per fratrem Hugonem. ªUlterius idem Engelbertus possidebit dictam terram ad X annos ab anno LXXII *[1372]* Petri pro XXII libris denariorum Traiectensium et VI caponibus absque defalcatione, nisi si contigerit dari de consensu ecclesie Traiectensis domino episcopo Traiectensi communem exactionem dictam merghenghelt, ad illam solvere deberet II grossos de quolibet iugere et residuum nostra domus et cetera sub condicionibus in littere quam inde habemus contentis. Per fratrem Thomam.ª
ᵇEngelbertus Vinkeᵇ

ª *in a different hand (B).* ᵇ *in the left margin.*

fol.88r, In Lynschoten LXXXVIII
the first part is somewhat corroded:

Item ibidem IX iugera terre iacentia inter terram dicti Rover Yen zoen/ a parte superiori et terram [Johannis Trindo a] parte inferiori prout/ illa modo possidet Everardus filius [Johannis] van den [Polle] ad VII/ annos ab anno LXX *[1370]* Petri [pro XXV.] libris denariorum Traiectensium et IX/ pullis annuatim solvendis Martini et Petri vel cadet ab omni iure et cetera secundum tenorem littere super hoc optente. Per fratrem Hugonem.
ªUlterius possidebit dictam terram Gerardus Spronc filius Wilhelmi Ricklandi pro LIIII libris, IX pullis ad X annos ab anno LXXVI *[1376]* Petri solvendis Martini et Petri vel cadet ab omni iure et cetera prout littera tenet. Per fratrem Johannem de Gaude commendatorem.ª
ᵇUlterius possidebit idem Gerardus dictam terram ad X annos ab anno LXXXVIII *[1388]* Petri pro LIIII libris, IX pullis. Per fratrem Johannes Haze.ᵇ
ᶜEverd Janszoneᶜ

Item ibidem dimidium quartale terre, nuncupatum In den Ketel-

acker, prout iacet communi sulcu cum alio dimidio quartali pertinenti pro nunc ad Johannem den Coster, cui integro quartali propius iacet terra Laurencii Zonderland quam tenet a Ghiseberto de Lynschoten a parte superiori et terra monialium in Oudwica a parte inferiori, prout illud dimidium quartale modo possidet a nobis Henricus de Zoetgraft hereditarie pro XXX solidus bonorum denariorum annuatim infra quindenam post Martini et Petri solvendis vel cadet ab omni iure prout littera exinde tenet.
^dQuod invenietur signa tali △ ^e
grosso regio Turonensi pro XII denariis conputato.^d
^cHenricus de Zoetgraft^c
hereditarie^f

Item ibidem Ij [1.5] iugera de quibus Jutta de Wedda habuit usufructum prout iacet.
^dIgnoratur adhuc quis possidet et ubi iacet.^d
nota^f

---

^a *in a different hand (C).* ^b *in another hand.* ^c *in the right margin, in the same writing as* ^d. ^d *added in different writing.* ^e *the sign looks like a triangle on its base with a handle.* ^f *in the left margin in the same writing as* ^d.

fol.88v,   In [Cameric]
the first lines are heavily corroded:

[Item habet domus in parrochia de Cameric iuxta Nijevelt]/ [— et XX — prout iacent inter]/ [— a parte meridionali et terram Martini filii Nycolai a parte aquilonali prout eundem] mansum/ [modo possidet Wilhelmus Ghisekini ad X annos] ab anno/ LX [1360] Petri [pro XVI libris denariorum Traiectensium, VI talentis cere et XXIIII anetas]/ [absque defalcatione Martini et Petri solvendis] vel cadet ab omni iure et cetera prout littera/ exinde tenet. Per fratrem Hugonem.
^aUlterius idem Wilhelmus possidebit dictam terram ad X annos ab anno LXXIII [1373] Petri pro XXXVIII libris denariorum Traiectensium, VI talentis cere, XXIIII anetas et duo quartalia butyri annuatim absque defalcatione solvendis Martini et Petri et cetera prout littera tenet vel cadet ab omni iure. Per fratrem Thomam dispensatorem.^a
^bUlterius possidebit dictam terram Theodericus filius Wilhelmi ad VIII annos ab anno LXXIX [1379] Petri pro XLVIII libris pagamenti Traiectensis, VI talentis cere vel III libris pro eis et XXIIII anetas vel XXIIII plaggas pro eis.^b

^cUlterius possidebit dictam terram Johannes filius Ghisberti ad X annos ab anno LXXXVII *[1387]* Petri pro XLVIII libris pagamenti Traiectensis, VI talentis cere vel III libris pro eis et XXIIII anetas vel XXIIII plaggas pro eis. Per fratrem Johannem Haze.^c

^dWilhelmus [Ghisekini]^d

^eEvert Dircsoen^e

---

^a *in a different hand (B).* ^b *in another hand (C).* ^c *in yet another hand.* ^d *in the left margin, in the basic hand.* ^e *in the left margin in later writing.*

fol.89r,   In [Cameric]   LXXXIX

the first lines are heavily corroded:

Item [ibidem V —]/ [——]/ [— et ter—]/nis [prout illa quondam possidebat a nobis —]/ment. Modo [possidet ea Nicolaus filius —]/ annos ab anno LXVI *[1366]* Petri pro <u>XXXVIIj</u> *[37.5]* libris [dena- riorum Traiectensium et —]/ anetas aut pro [qualibet I grossum annuatim absque defalcatione Martini et]/ Petri solvendis vel cadet ab omni iure et cetera [prout in littera exinde continetur]. Per fra- trem Hugonem.

^aUlterius idem possidebit dictam terram ad X annos ab anno LXXVIII *[1378]* Petri pro L libris denariorum Traiectensium et VI ancis solvendis Martini et Petri vel cadet ab omni iure et cetera ut littera tenet.^a

^bNicolaus filius Nicolai^b

Item ibidem ex uno manso terre quondam Theoderici Bistal et Machtildis eius uxoris IIj *[2.5]* solidos bonorum ^ddenariorum^d annua- tim prout iacet inter terram capituli ecclesie sancte Maria Traiecten- sis a parte meridionali et terram Gerardi de Malche, Florencii filii Jacobi de Jutfaes et Heynekini Zalenzoen a parte septentrionali, quem mansum modo possidet Heynekinus filius Heynekini Zalen hereditarie.

^bHeynekinus Zalen^b

perpetue^c

---

^a *in a different hand.* ^b *in the right margin, in the basic hand.* ^c *in the left margin, in the basic hand.* ^d *missing in ms.*

fol.89v, In [Woerden]
the first part is heavily corroded:

[— —etevelt quatuor]/ [———] Oudwica/ [—] cum uno quartali
terre/ [— possidebat] a nobis. Modo possidet/ [— Corthoze ad X
annos ab anno LXIX *[1369]* Petri et]/ [solvet annuatim exinde Ij
[1.5] marcas argenti] aut pagamentum equivalens in Tra/[iecto et —
solidos et IIII pullas absque defalcatione Martini et] Petri solvendas
vel/ [cadet ab omni iure et cetera prout] littera exinde tenet. Per
fratrem Hugonem.
ªModo possidebit illam terram ab anno LXXXIIII *[1384]* ad X annos Herman van Eyke Martini et Petri solvendis pro XIIII libris et X
solidis qua pactus solventur absque defalcatione ut in formula.ª ᵇIIII
pullas. Per fratrem Gerardum Rijk.ᵇ
ᶜReynerus [Corthoze]ᶜ
ᵈHermannus de Eykeᵈ

Item ibidem iuxta Putkuep VII iugera terre, iacentia inter terram
comitis Hollandie a parte superiori et terram domini de Yselsteijne a
parte inferiori prout illa possidebat a nobis Albertus Cosini. Modo
possidet ea Albertus filius Hugonis [Uten Gaerde] ad X annos ab
anno LXVI *[1366]* Petri pro VIII libris denariorum Traiectensium
et VII pullis annuatim Martini et Petri solvendis vel cadet ab omni
iure et cetera secundum tenorem littere quam inde habemus. Per
fratrem Hugonem.
ᵉModo ulterius possidebit dictam terram Wouter Dirkszoen ad X
annos ab anno LXXXVII *[1387]* Petri pro XXV libris, VII pullis in
formula predicta. Per fratrem Johannem Haze.ᵉ
ᶜAlbertus filius Hugonisᶜ

ª *in a different hand.* ᵇ *added in a different hand.* ᶜ *in the left margin, in the basic
hand.* ᵈ *in the left margin in later writing.* ᵉ *in yet another hand.*

fol.90r, In [Woerden] XC
the first part is heavily corroded:

[Item ibidem IX iugera — hont —]/ propius iacet [— a parte]/
[Henrici Cyriken prout illa possidebat a nobis Wilhelmus —]/ Modo
[possidebit ea Henricus Cyriken ad] X annos ab anno LXIX *[1369]*/
Agathe virginis [et solvet annuatim exinde] III marcas et Vj *[5.5]* loet
argenti/ aut [pagamentum equivalens in Traiecto minus] XII denariis et IX pullis absque/ defalcatione Martini et Petri solvendis aut

cadet ab omni iure et cetera prout in/ littera quam inde habemus continetur. Per fratrem Hugonem.
ᵃModo possidet Wolterus filius Theoderici ad X annos ab anno LXXXIIII *[1384]* Petri pro decem antiquis scudatis, IX pullis.ᵃ
ᵇHenricus Cyrikenᵇ

Item ibidem XXI iugera terre, prout iacent inter terram domini de Yselsteine a parte superiori et terram nostre domus quam nunc possidet Jacobus Speyard a parte inferiori, prout illa modo possidet a nobis Johannes Meynard ad X annos ab anno LXII *[1362]* Petri pro XXIIII libris denariorum Traiectensium, X caponibus, X pullis annuatim solvendis Martini et Petri aut cadet ab omni iure et cetera sub condicionibus in littera contentis. Per fratrem Hugonem.
ᶜModo dictam terram possidebit ulterius Vivien filius Johannis Meynardi ad X annos ab anno LXXII *[1372]* Petri et solvet annuatim exinde LXIII libras denariorum Traiectensium et X capones et X pullas annuatim absque defalcatione solvendas Martini et Petri vel cadet ab omni iure prout littera continet. Per fratrem Johannem Gaude.
Ulterius idem Vivien possidebit dictam terram ad XII annos ab anno LXXXIII *[1383]* Petri. Et solvet annuatim exinde LXV libras denariorum Traiectensium quibus pactus solvuntur et X capones et X pullas absque defalcatione Martini et Petri vel cadet ab omni iure. Per fratrem Johannem Gaude.ᶜ
ᵈJohannes Meynertᵈ
ᵉVivien ziin zoneᵉ

ᵃ *in a different hand.* ᵇ *in the right margin, in the basic hand.* ᶜ *in another hand (C).* ᵈ *in the right margin, cancelled.* ᵉ *in the right margin, in the same hand as* ᶜ.

fol.90v,   [In Woerden]
the first lines are rather corroded:

[Item — terre quibus a superiori parte propius iacet terra]/ [— sancti —] a parte inferiori ᵃBoudewini/ filii Theoderici prout ille a nobis possidebat Johannes Meye. Modo possidet ea Wolterus filius Theoderici ad X annos ab anno LXXI *[1371]* Petri pro LII libris X solidis et IIII talentis cere, IX caponibus, IX pullis absque defalcatione solvendis Martini et Petri vel cadet ab omni iure et cetera prout littera exinde tenet. Per fratrem Thomam.ᵃ
ᵇJohannes Meyeᵇ
ᶜWolter Dirkszoenᶜ

^d¶ Medietatem prescripte terre scilicet VIII iugera V hont modo possidet Johannes^e Vivien Jan Meynards zoon ad X annos ab anno LXXXVII *[1387]* Petri pro XXVII libris, V solidis, IX pullis annuatim pagamenti Traiectensis absque defalcatione Martini et Petri solvendis. Per fratrem Johannem de Arnhem.^d
^fVivien Jan Meynards zoon^f

^g¶ Reliquam vero medietatem prescripte terre scilicet VIII iugera et V hont possidebit ulterius modo Henricus filius Jacobi ad X annos ab anno LXXXII *[1382]* Petri pro XXIX libris V solidis, Ij *[1.5]* talentis cere, IIII caponibus et V pullis annuatim Martini et Petri solvendis absque defalcatione vel cadet ab omni iure prout littera tenet.^g
^bRotards zoon^b
^hHenric Jacobs zoon^h

Item ibidem X iugera terre ⁱin Diirmodebroecⁱ inter terram domini Gerardi de Pollanen militis a parte superiori et terram abbatis et conventi monasterii sancti Pauli Traiectensis a parte inferiori situata prout illa modo possidet a nobis Petrus filius Johannis ad X annos ab anno LXIX *[1369]* Purificatione Marie pro VI marcis et IXj *[9.5]* loet argenti aut cum pagamento equivalenti solvendis et X pullis annuatim Martini et Petri absque defalcatione aut cadet ab omni iure et cetera prout littera exinde tenet. Per fratrem Hugonem.
^jModo possidet Theodericus filius Agathe ad X annos ab anno LXXXIX *[1389]* Petri pro XIIII oude vrancken et X pullis.^j
^kPetrus filius Johannis^k

---

^a *in a different hand (B).* ^b *in the left margin, cancelled.* ^c *in the left margin, in the same hand as* ^a. ^d *in another hand (D).* ^e *cancelled; from here onwards the whole passage, including the marginal note, has been written over erased words.* ^f *in the left margin, in the same hand as* ^d. ^g *in yet another hand (E).* ^h *in the left margin, in the same hand as* ^g. ⁱ *written above the text.* ^j *in yet another hand.* ^k *in the left margin, in the basic hand, not cancelled.*

fol.91r, [In Woerden] XCI
the first lines are rather corroded:

Item ibidem VIII iugera terre, iacentia [—] inter Renum [—]/dem a parte orientali et [—] terram filie Jacobi Speyard [—]/ eiusdem Jacobi a parte occidentali, prout illa modo possidet idem Jacobus Speyard ad X annos ab anno LXIII *[1363]* Petri pro VIII libris denariorum Traiectensium annuatim Martini et Petri solvendis aut cadet ab omni

iure et cetera sub condicionibus in littera contentis quam inde habemus. Per fratrem Hugonem.

ᵃUlterius possidebit dictam terram Hermannus Speyard ad X annos
ab anno LXXIII *[1373]* Ponciani pro XXII libris XVIII solidis denariorum Traiectensium annuatim absque defalcatione Martini et Petri
solvendis aut cadet ab omni iure, et semper ad biennium constituet
bonos fideiussores pro pacto predicto et cetera prout littera tenet. Per
fratrem Thomam.ᵃ

ᵇJacobus Speyardᵇ
ᶜHerman Speyardᶜ

Item ibidem <u>XVIII iugera</u> prout iacent inter terram nostre domus
quam nunc possidet Johannes Meynard a superiori parte et terram
Hermanni Speyard a parte inferiori, que modo possidet Jacobus
Speyard ad XI annos ab anno LXI *[1361]* Petri pro <u>XVIII libris</u>
<u>denariorum Traiectensium et XVIII pullis</u> annuatim Martini et Petri
solvendis vel cadet ab omni iure et cetera prout littera exinde tenet.
Per fratrem Hugonem.

ᵃUlterius possidebit dictam terram Hermannus Speyard ad XI annos
ab anno LXXII *[1372]* Ponciani. Et solvet inde annuatim LI libras et
XII solidos denariorum Traiectensium et unum quartale butyri et
XVIII pullas annuatim absque defalcatione Martini et Petri vel cadet
ab omni iure. Butyrum solvet in fine May, et constituet semper ad
biennium bonos fideiussores pro pensione predicta et cetera prout
littera tenet. Per fratrem Thomam.ᵃ

ᵈModo possidet Hermanus Rotardi.ᵈ
ᵉJacobus Speyardᵉ
ᶜHerman Speyardᶜ

ᵃ *in a different hand (B).* ᵇ *in the right margin, in the basic hand.* ᶜ *in the right*
margin, in the same hand as ᵃ. ᵈ *in another hand.* ᵉ *in the right margin, cancelled.*

fol.91v,   <u>In Woerden</u>
the first lines are somewhat corroded:

Item ibidem [<u>supra Rietveld</u>] VI <u>virgas</u> terre, nuncupatas die/ [Kijf-
acker] prout iacent inter terram domicelli de Vliete quam/ heredes
Arnoldi de Buscho nunc ab ipso tenent in feodo a parte orientali et
terram domicelle Ghertrudis filie Wolfs a parte occidentali, prout
dictam terram possidebat a nobis quondam Theodericus Belyard.
Modo possidet eandem Conegondis relicta Arnoldi de Buscho <u>pro X</u>

solidis bonorum denariorum hereditarie Petri ad Cathedram solvendis annuatim.

ªConegondis Arnoldi de Busco perpetueª

ª *in the left margin.*

fol.92r,   In Weyrder   XCII
the first lines are somewhat corroded:

Item habet domus in parrochia de Weyrder [XVII iugera terre
prout]/ iacent inter terram capituli sancti Petri Traiectensis a parte
superiori [— et terram Hey]/nonis Ghiselman a parte inferiori, prout
illa modo possident Hermannus et Johannes filii Johannis Gerardi ad
X annos ab anno LXV *[1365]* Epiphanie Domini pro XLVII libris,
XII solidis denariorum Traiectensium et IX caponibus et VIII pullis
annuatim absque defalcatione solvendis Martini et Petri vel cadent
ab omni iure. Non comburent nisi tria iugera semel et cetera sub
condicionibus in littera exinde contentis. Per Hugonem.
ªUlterius possidebunt dictam terram Baldewinus filius Johannis et
Johannes frater eius ad X annos ab anno LXXV *[1375]* Petri pro
LXXXIX libris, V solidis et IX caponibus, IX pullis et cetera prout
littera tenet. Per fratrem Johannem commendatorem.ª
ᵇUlterius idem Baldewinus solus possidebit dictam terram ad X annos
ab anno LXXXVI *[1386]* Petri pro LXXXVI libris pagamenti quo
pactus solvuntur in Traiecto et IX caponibus, VIII pullis solvendis
Martini et Petri vel cadet ab omni iure et cetera prout littera tenet.
Per fratrem Johannem de Aernhem.ᵇ
ᶜHermannus filius Johannis Gerardi et Johannes eius fraterᶜ
ᵈBoldewinus filius Johannisᵈ

Item ibidem II iugera et IIIj *[3.5]* hont terre, prout iacent inter aque
meatum de Berwerdsweyrde a parte superiori et terram Johannis de
Denemarken a parte inferiori, que modo possident a nobis Theodericus Sluseman et Wilhelmus de Roden ad X annos ab anno LXVI
[1366] Petri pro XI libris denariorum Traiectensium annuatim absque defalcatione solvendis Martini et Petri vel cadet ab omni iure et
cetera prout littera exinde tenet. Per fratrem Hugonem. ᵉDirc Sluseman ende W.van Rodenᵉ

ª *in a different hand (C).* ᵇ *in another hand (E).* ᶜ *in the right margin, cancelled.* ᵈ *in
the right margin, in the same hand as* ª. ᵉ *in the right margin, in the same hand as* ᶜ.

fol.92v,   [In Weyrder]
the first lines are rather corroded:

[Item ibidem — prout iacent inter terram Jacobi filii Jacobi]/ [a
parte superiori et terram Hugonis filii Jacobi Agathe a parte]/ [infe-
riori, prout illa nunc possidet Johannes filius Petri de Osse ad IX]/
[annos ab anno LXII *[1362]* Petri pro XXIII libris denariorum
Traiectensium et VI caponibus et]/ [VI pullis annuatim absque de-
falcatione] Martini et Petri solvendis aut cadet ab omni iure. Me/
[dietatem dicte terre] semel conburere potest et cetera prout in littera exinde continetur. Per/ fratrem Hugonem.
ᵃUlterius dictam terram possidebunt dictus Johannes filius Petri et
eius mater ad X annos ab anno LXXI *[1371]* Valentini pro XLV
libris denariorum Traiectensium et VI caponibus et V pullis annuatim Martini et Petri solvendis et quartali butyri infra octo dies ante
Lamberti solvendis absque defalcatione aut cadet ab omni iure et
cetera prout littera tenet. Per fratrem Thomam. Medietatem conburere possunt.ᵃ
ᵇJohannes filius Petri de Osse et Katerina eius materᵇ

Item ibidem XII iugera terre prout iacent inter terram Agathe filie
Jacobi a parte superiori et terram Wilhelmi filii Jacobi a parte inferiori, prout illa modo possidet Theodericus Sluseman filius Lize ad IX
annos ab anno LXII *[1362]* Petri pro XXX libris, XII caponibus
annuatim absque defalcatione Martini et Petri solvendis vel cadet ab
omni iure. Quatuor iugera potest conburere semel et cetera prout
littera exinde tenet. Per fratrem Hugonem.
ᶜUlterius dictus Theodericus possidebit dictam terram ad X annos ab
anno LXXI *[1371]* Petri pro LXIX libris denariorum Traiectensium,
XII caponibus et I quartali butyri annuatim solvendis Martini et Petri
vel cadet ab omni iure et cetera sub condicionibus prescriptis et prout
littera exinde tenet. Per fratrem Johannem Gaude dispensatorem.ᶜ

ᵃ *in a different hand (B).* ᵇ *in the left margin, in the basic hand.* ᶜ *in another hand*
(C).

fol.93r,   [In Weyrder]   XCIII
the first part is heavily corroded, the second part only a bit:

Item ibidem X iugera [terre —]/ terram capituli sancti Petri [Traiec-
tensis a parte superiori —]/ne a parte inferiori [— Henricus de Osse
et Fredericus]/ eius frater ad X [annos ab anno LXII *[1362]* Petri

pro XX- libris, -]/ caponibus [annuatim absque defalcatione Martini et Petri solvendis vel cadent ab omni iure.]/ Constituerunt [fideiussores pro pacto annuatim solvendo –]/ et ceteris [condicionibus prout in littera exinde fit mentio. Per fratrem Hugonem.]
ªUlterius possidebunt dictam terram ad X annos ab anno LXXI *[1371]* Valentini pro XLV libris denariorum Traiectensium et X caponibus annuatim Martini et Petri et I quartale butyri infra octo dies ante Lamberti solvendis absque defalcatione. Medietatem conburet et cetera prout in littera continetur. Per fratrem Thomam.ª
ᵇHenricus de Osse et Fredericus eius fraterᵇ

Item ibidem X iugera terre dicta vulgariter des Papenland prout iacent inter terram [nostre] domus quam modo possident liberi Henrici de Osse a superiori parte et terram [Hugonis] filii Jacobi a parte inferiori, prout illa modo possidet Jacobus filius [Johannis Ludolphi] ad X annos ab anno LXI *[1361]* Petri pro XXI libris, X caponibus annuatim absque defalcatione solvendis Martini et. Petri vel cadet ab omni iure. Medietatem dicte terre semel conburere potest et cetera prout littera exinde tenet. Per fratrem Hugonem.
ªUlterius idem Jacobus possidebit dictam terram ad X annos ab anno LXXI *[1371]* Valentini pro LV libris denariorum Traiectensium, X caponibus Martini et Petri et unum quartale butyri Lamberti solvendis annuatim absque defalcatione et cetera prout in littera continetur. Medietatem conburere potest semel. Per fratrem Thomam.ª
ᵇJacobus Johannis Ludolphiᵇ

ª *in a different hand (B).* ᵇ *in the right margin, in the basic hand.*

fol.93v, In Weyrder
the first lines are rather corroded:

[Item ibidem dimidium] iuger prout iacet communi sulcu cum uno/ [— alio dimidio iugere pertinenti] ad Ludolphum filium Hugonis daar/ [aen] den oesteren egge naest gheland is Hughe Ghisebertszoen/ ende an den westeren egge Ludolf Hughen zone, prout illud/ [modo] possidet Ghisebertus Hughe ad X annos ab anno LXV *[1365]*/ Agnetis pro XXXII solidus denariorum Traiectensium annuatim solvendis Martini et Petri aut cadet ab omni iure. Et si moriretur infra dictos annos, eius pueri supplebunt annos et nullus alter et cetera prout littera exinde tenet. Per Hugonem.
ªGhisebertus Hugheª

Item ibidem XII iugera terre, prout iacent inter terram nostre domus a parte septentrionali et terram capituli sancti Petri Traiectensis a parte meridionali, prout illa possidebat a nobis Friso van den Werve. Modo possidet ea Wilhelmus filius Petri ad X annos ab anno LXII *[1362]* Petri pro XL libris denariorum Traiectensium annuatim absque defalcatione Martini et Petri aut cadet ab omni iure. Tertiam partem dicte terre semel conburere potest et cetera prout littera exinde tenet. Per fratrem Hugonem.

^bIdem Wilhelmus ulterius dictam terram possidebit ad X annos ab anno LXX *[1370]* Petri pro VI marcis argenti aut pro pagamento equivalenti in Traiecto tempore solucionis annuatim infra quindenam post Martini et Petri solvendis aut cadet ab omni iure. Duo iugera conburere potest et cetera prout littera exinde tenet. Per fratrem Hugonem.^b

^cModo ulterius possidebunt Jacob oud Wyllemszoen ende Aelbertus van der Hoghe predictam terram ad X annos ab anno LXXXVII *[1387]* Petri pro LXVI libris in forma predicta. Per fratrem Johannem Haze.^c

^aWillem Peters zoen^a

---

^a *in the left margin.* ^b *added in different writing.* ^c *in another hand.*

fol.94r, [In Weyrder] XCIIII
the first part is heavily corroded:

Item ibidem [XIII —]/ [———]/ [———]/ illa ab [— possident Johannes —]/ [annos ab anno LXVII *[1367]* Purificatione Marie pro X —]/ auri Francie [regis monete aut pagamento equivalenti et XX —]/ caponibus annuatim absque [defalcatione Martini et Petri solvendis aut cadet ab omni iure]/ et cetera sub condicionibus in littera exinde contentis. Per fratrem H[ugonem.]

^aModo medietatem dicte terre scilicet VIj *[6.5]* iugera terre possidebit ulterius Arnoldus Sluzeman, prout ea solebat colere Johannes filius Petri, quibus proprius iacet domus nostra personaliter cum terra quam Wilhelmus filius Petri solebat colere a parte superiori et etiam a parte inferiori domus nostra personaliter cum terra quam Poncianus filius Petri solebat colere, ad X annos ab anno LXXXVI *[1386]* Petri pro XXXIII libris denariorum quibus pactus solvuntur in Traiecto et II caponibus et I pulla annuatim absque defalcatione Martini et Petri solvendis vel cadet ab omni iure. Per fratrem Johannem de Aernhem.

¶ Reliquam vero medietatem supradicte scilicet VIj *[6.5]* iugera

modo possidebit ulterius Coppardus filius Ponciani prout ea pater
eius colebat et iacent inter terram domus nostre quam colebat Johannes filius Petri a parte superiori et terram domus dictam Crelingsland
a parte inferiori ad X annos ab anno LXXXVI *[1386]* Petri pro
XXXIII libris denariorum Traiectensium quibus pactus solvitur in
Traiecto, II caponibus, I pulla absque defalcatione Martini et Petri
solvendis. Per fratrem Johannem de Aernhem.^a
^bJan Pons^b
^cAernd Sluzeman^c
^cCoppard Poncianszoen^c

Item ibidem apud ecclesiam XII iugera prout iacent inter terram
nostre domus quam nunc possidet Ludolphus filius Petri a parte superiori et terram domini Alemanni militis a parte inferiori quam tenet
in feodo a comite Hollandie, prout illa modo possident a nobis Gerardus filius Eufemie et Machteldis eius uxor ad X annos ab anno
LXIII *[1363]* Petri pro XXXI libris denariorum Traiectensium, XII
caponibus annuatim absque defalcatione Martini et Petri solvendis
aut cadet ab omni iure. Medietatem dicte terre semel conburere possunt infra annos prescriptos et cetera in littera. Per fratrem Hugonem.
^dGerardus filius Eufemie^d

---

 ^a *in a different hand (E).* ^b *in the right margin, cancelled.* ^c *in the right margin, in the*
same hand as ^a. ^d *in the right margin, in the basic hand.*

fol.94v, [In Weyrder]
the whole page is heavily corroded:

[Item ibidem — Weyrder —]/ [——]/ [——]/ [——]/ [— filio]/
[ad X annos ab anno LXII *[1362]* Petri pro — XII]/ [pullis solvendis Martini et Petri vel cadet ab omni iure]. Tria/ iugera de predictis
iacentia op die Weteringe [conburere possunt semel et cetera prout]
littera exinde tenet. Per fratrem Hugonem.
^a¶ Ulterius possidebunt dictam terram ad X annos ab anno LXXII
[1372] Petri et solvent annuatim LV libras denariorum Traiectensium et unum quartale butyri et XII pullas absque defalcatione Martini et Petri solvendas aut cadet ab omni iure. Butyrum solvet in fine
Maii et cetera prout littera tenet. Per fratrem Thomam.^a
^b[Johannes filius Petri, Juta] eius uxor [et —]^b

[Item ibidem IIII iugera terre, iacentia an den] hoeke communi sulcu
cum/ [— iugeribus nostre domus. Quodlibet colit provisor curtis]

nostre ibidem, quibus/ [a parte meridionali propius iacet terra nostre] domus dicta vulgariter Vrie/[viertel — provisor] curtis possidet, prout illa IIII iugera/ [modo possidet Johannes filius Petri ad X annos ab] anno LXII *[1362]* Petri/ pro <u>XI libris denariorum Traiectensium, — et IIII pullis annuatim</u> absque defalcatione Martini et Petri/ solvendis aut cadet ab omni iure et cetera prout littera exinde tenet. Per fratrem Hugonem.
^bJohannes filius Petri^b

---

^a *in a different hand (B).* ^b *in the left margin, in the basic hand.*

fol.95r, [In Weyrder] XCV
the whole page is heavily corroded:

Item ibidem in [—]/ terram liberorum [Herberti — pro —]/ci filii [Nicolai et Johannis — a parte inferiori pro —]/ Wilhelmus filii [Theoderici Reynburgis — annos ab —]/ Agnetis pro [<u>LXIII libris X solidis et XI caponibus, – pullis</u>]/ annuatim absque defalcatione [Martini et Petri solvendis aut cadet ab omni iure. Non conburet]/ nisi VIII [iugera de predictis infra decem annos — et cetera prout]/ littera exinde tenet. Per fratrem Hugonem.
^aModo dictam terram possidebit ulterius Nicolaus filius Wilhelmi Ghiben ad X annos ab anno LXXXVI *[1386]* Petri pro C.XXXVIIj *[137.5]* libris denariorum quibus pactus solvuntur in Traiecto, XI caponibus, XI pullis absque defalcatione. Per fratrem Johannem de Arnhem.^a
^bReynburgis Wilhelmus^b
^cClaes Willem Ghibenzoens^c

<u>Item ibidem I campum terre [et aream cum aggere et cum kae prout insimul]/ iacent pro IIIIj *[4.5]* iugeribus,</u> quibus propius [iacet terra]/ ecclesie ibidem a superiori parte et terra collegii sancti [Petri Traiectensis a parte inferi]/ori, prout eundem campum cum [area et ceteris possidebat [—]/ Clare^d. Modo possidet Henricus [Sluseman —an]/nos ab anno LXVI *[1366]* Petri [pro XVIII libris — absque defalcatione]/ solvendis infra quindenam post Martini et Petri aut cadet ab [omni iure et cetera sub] / condicionibus in littera exinde contentis. Per fratrem Hugonem.
^eHenricus Sluzeman filius Petri^e

---

^a *in a different hand (E).* ^b *in the right margin, cancelled.* ^c *in the right margin, in the same hand as* ^a. ^d *uncertain reading ms.* ^e *in the right margin, in the basic hand.*

fol.95v,   [In Weyrder]
the whole page is more or less corroded:

[Item ibidem X iugera terre, iacentia op dat] Hoghe Land inter/ [—
inter terram nostre domus quam nunc possidet provisor curtis nostre
ibidem]/ [— et terram Amilii filii Wilhelmi] Hagonis a parte/ [infe-
riori, prout illa modo possidet Johannes] filius^a Petri ad X/ [annos ab
anno LXI *[1361]* Petri pro XXIII] libris, XV solidis denariorum/
[Traiectensium et – caponibus et] V pullis [annuatim absque] defalcatione Martini/ [et Petri solvendis aut cadet ab omni iure et cetera
prout]/ littera tenet. Per fratrem Hugonem.
^bJohannes filius Petri^b

[Item ibidem VI iugera terre int] Kervelant iacentia, quibus/ [—
iacet terra dicta die Barchhove]/ [— meridionali terra domus] nostre
quam nunc possidet provisor/ [curtis —], prout illa modo possidet
Nicolaus/ [filius Petri —] ad X annos ab anno ^cLXXVII *[1377]*
[Petri]/ [pro — libris denariorum Traiectensium] annuatim absque
defalcatione solvendis/ [Martini et Petri aut cadet ab omni iure] et
cetera prout littera tenet./ Per fratrem Johannem Gaude.^c
^d¶ Ulterius idem Nycolaus possidebit dictam terram prout iacet ad X
annos ab anno LXXXVI *[1386]* Petri pro XXXI libris pachtgelds
absque defalcatione solvendis Martini et Petri aut cadet ab omni iure
prout littera tenet. Per fratrem Johannem de Arnhem.^d
^bNicolaus filius Petri^b

---

^a filii *ms.* ^b *in the left margin.* ^c *in a different hand (C).* ^d *in another hand.*

fol.96r,   in Weyrder   XCVI
the first lines are somewhat corroded:

Item ibidem [XIIII iugera terre paulo plus aut minus prout iacent]/
[inter terram nostre domus quam nunc colit provisor curtis nostre
ibidem a]/ superiori parte et terram Hagonis Zoeten a parte inferiori,
prout illa]/ modo possidet [Theodericus Utendike ad X annos ab
anno LXIII *[1363]*]/ Petri pro XXXVII libris denariorum Traiectensium et XII pullis annuatim absque defalcatione/ Martini et Petri
solvendis [aut cadet ab omni iure. Non conburet nisi unum cam]/
pum de dicta terra [per se distincte situm ultra aquaductum] ibidem
et cetera prout in/ littera exinde continetur. Per fratrem Hugonem.
^a¶ Ulterius idem Theodericus possidebit dictam terram ad X annos
ab anno LXXIII *[1373]* Petri pro LIIII libris dicte monete et XII

pullis et unum quartale butyri annuatim solvendis prout littera exinde
tenet aut cadet ab omni iure. Per fratrem Thomam dispensatorem.ᵃ
ᵇUlterius possidebit dictam terram predictus Theodericus ad X annos
ᶜin omni modo et forma prout in litteris continetur super hoc confectis a festo Petri LXXXIIII *[1384]*ᶜ ᵇ ᵈab anno LXXXIIII *[1384]* Petri
pro LII libris, I viertel butyri et XII pullis absque defalcatione et
cetera prout littera tenet.ᵈ
ᵉ[Dirc uten Dike]ᵉ
ᶠDirk uten Dyke per me fratrem G[erardum]ᶠ

Item ibidem IIII iugera iacentia prope vadam inter terram Johannis
filii Henrici Zalen et suorum liberorum a parte orientali et terram
Gerardi Rampe a parte occidentali, que modo possidet idem Gerardus Rampe hereditarie sub annua pensione II librarum bonorum
denariorum Martini et Petri solvendis.
ᵉGherid Rampeᵉ
perpetueᵍ

ᵃ *in a different hand (B).* ᵇ *in another hand.* ᶜ *cancelled.* ᵈ *in yet another hand (D).*
ᵉ *in the right margin, in the basic hand.* ᶠ *in the right margin, in the same hand as* ᵇ*.*
ᵍ *in the left margin, in the basic hand.*

fol.96v, In Weyrder
the first part is somewhat corroded:

[Item ibidem XXIIII iugera terre prout iacent inter terram] nostre
domus/ [quam modo possidet] provisor [curtis] nostre ibidem [a par-
te] septentrionali/ et terram custodis ecclesie [ibidem pro tempore
existentis a] parte meridionali/ [prout] illa modo [possident Vriterus]
et Elisabet uxor eius et super/ [quibus] nunc [mansionem] habent, ad
VII annos ab anno LXVII *[1367]* Petri/ pro XXVI libris denariorum
Traiectensium et [XII] caponibus annuatim absque defalcatione/
infra quindenam post Martini et Petri solvendis aut cadet ab omni
iure. Non/ conburent nisi duo iugera de predictis [semel] et cetera
prout littera exinde tenet. Per fratrem Hugonem.
ᵃ¶ Modo dictam terram possidet Henricus Sluseman filius Ghiseberti
ad X annos ab anno LXXIIII *[1374]* Petri et solvet exinde CXX
libros denariorum Traiectensium et XII capones Martini et Petri et
duo quartalia butyri in fine Maii et Lamberti solvenda annuatim
ᵇabsque defalcationeᵇ. Medietatem semel conburere potest et cetera
prout littera tenet. Per fratrem Thomam.ᵃ
ᶜ[Vriterus et] eius uxorᶜ
ᵈHenricus Sluseman filius Ghibertiᵈ

Item ibidem <u>IIII iugera terre</u> prout iacent inter terram nostre domus ab ambabus partibus scilicet a parte septentrionali cum terra quam nunc possidet provisor curtis nostre ibidem et a parte meridionali terra nostra supradicta quam nunc Vriterus possidet, prout illa IIII iugera modo possidet Amilius filius Wilhelmi Hagonis ad X annos ab anno LXVII *[1367]* Petri pro <u>XVI libris denariorum Traiectensium annuatim</u> absque defalcatione Martini et Petri solvendis aut cadet ab omni iure et cetera prout littera tenet. Per fratrem Hugonem.
^eAmilius Wilhelmi Hagonis^e

---

^a *in a different hand (B).* ^b *written twice ms.* ^c *in the left margin, cancelled.* ^d *in the left margin, in the same hand as* ^a. ^e *in the left margin, in the basic hand.*

fol.97r.   <u>In Weyrder</u>   XCVII

Item ibidem <u>dimidium iuger</u> solvens annuatim <u>III solidos IX denarios</u> bonorum perpetuo. Baldewinus filius Johannis possidebat.
^anota
perpetue^a

---

^a *in the left margin.*

fol.97v.   <u>In Weyrder Curtis ibidem</u>

<u>Item in eadem parrochia de Weyrder habet domus hanc terram sub-scriptam quam modo possidet provisor curtis nostre ibidem ad annos et pro annua pensione</u> infra signatos

Primo <u>XXIII iugera terre</u>, quibus a parte orientali propius iacet agger ibidem vulgariter dicendo die Dijc et a parte occidentali terra domus nostre quam nunc possidet Theodericus uten Dijke.
Frater Henricus de Bredae provisor eiusdem curtis modo possidet.
^aProvisor curtis^a

Item ibidem opt Hogheland <u>XVIII iugera terre, prout iacent</u> inter terram Gerardi Rampe a parte orientali et terram nostre domus quam nunc possidet Johannes filius Petri a parte occidentali.
Dictus provisor curtis modo possidet.
^a<u>Provisor curtis</u>^a

---

^a *in the left margin.*

fol.98r,   In Weyrder   XCVIII
the first line is somewhat corroded:

Item ibidem in dat [Kerveland] XXIX iugera terre prout iacent in-
ter/ terram nostre domus quam nunc possidet Vriterus a parte meridionali et terram nostre domus quam nunc possident Nicolaus filius
Petri et Johannes die Coninc a parte septentrionali.
Idem provisor curtis modo possidet.
ᵃProvisor curtisᵃ

ᵇItem ibidem int Kerveland II iugera prout iacent inter terram liberorum Agathe Theoderici Foyen a parte meridionali et terram Gerardi Rampe a parte septentrionali.
Idem provisor curtis modo possidet.ᵇ
ᵃProvisor curtisᵃ

ᶜDit erve hebben wi den hospitael t sinte Johan te Wezel vercoft ende
hebben dat ghelt weder beleyt anden rente die wi hebben buten opter
stede graft van Oudewater an de Zuijtside van den stede alse uut den
hofsteden die wi teghens Herman Vranckenzoen cofte.ᶜ

ᵃ *in the right margin.* ᵇ *cancelled.* ᶜ *in a different hand.*

fol.98v,   In Weyrder
the first line is somewhat corroded:

Item ibidem VII iugera dicta Vrie[viertel prout iacent inter] terram
nostre do/mus quam nunc possidet Ludolphus filius Petri a parte
meridionali et terram nostre domus quam nunc possidet Johannes
filius Petri a parte septentrionali.
Idem provisor curtis modo possidet.
ᵃProvisor curtisᵃ

Item ibidem aen den Gronen Dijc Ij *[1.5]* iugera prout iacent inter
terram ecclesie ibidem a parte meridionali et terram domini Aelmanni militis a parte septentrionali.
Idem provisor curtis modo possidet.
ᵃProvisor curtisᵃ

Item in den Groten Hoeke I iuger terre prout iacet communi sulcu
cum aliis quatuor nostris iugeribus que nunc possidet Johannes filius
Petri superius ultra quattuor folia signatis.

Idem provisor curtis modo possidet una cum ceteris iugeribus prescriptis.
ªProvisor curtisª

Summa prescriptorum iugerum terre pro nunc ad curtim nostram in
Werder pertinentium LXXXIj *[81.5]* iugera, excepta area cum suis
attinenciis in qua domus curtis ibidem est constructa.
ᵇQuam curtis cum huiusmodi terrarum iugeribus modo possidet frater Henricus de Bredae ad X annos ab anno ᶜ sub annua pensione
seu responsione XCV librarum Martini et Petri solvendarum et
cetera prout in littera inde continetur. Per magistrum Alamannie
commendatorem huius domus actum et locatum.ᵇ

ª *in the left margin.* ᵇ *added in different writing.* ᶜ *not filled in.*

on a loose leaf of paper, 15th century:

Anno LXXIII *[1473].* Item op Paeschen gehat XIII ghewaren soute
voegelen, elk ghewaer VIII witt, facit XVII stuver II witt.

Item LXIIII gansen, elc gans III stuver facit XII Arnhemse gulden
ende XII stuver.

Item XXIII gans croes, elc croes I stuver facit XXIII stuver.

Summarum faciunt XV Arnhemse gulden VII stuver II witt.
Dit is betaald in die Visitationis Marie anno LXXIII *[1473].*

Item IIII galinas. Item LXIIII gansen.

Item Jan Peterszoen.

on another loose leaf of paper, 15th century, stuck between fol.110v and 111r, but
more appropriately placed here:
Heer Hilbrant [curatus] in Zeyst [ende] heer Jan Bloc vice[curatus]
in [Zwamerdam] tusschen Dirc Luytgerensz. Luytgen sinen zoen,
opte een sijde ende den heren opte ander zijde vanden lande dat
Peter Jan Negelszoen te bruken plach, dats te verstaen van XªVII
stuver, dair Dirc voirsz. ende sijn erfgenamen off betalen sollen XIX
gulden X witte stuvers voir elken gulden, dach Lamberti over een
jaer. Dit geschiede altera die Decollacionis Johannis Baptiste anno
XLVII *[30 August 1447].*

Item [sel] meister Willem gegeven VII Rijnse gulden IIII post[ulaets] gulden voer III Rijnse gulden. Dirc Ludikenszoen solvet III post[ulaets] gulden myn IIIIj *[4.5]* wit, Dirc Ludiken sijn soen, Bartholomei.

^bItem acht hont lants^b

---

^a X *cancelled.* ^b *on the backside.*

fol.99r.   <u>In Bodegraven</u>   XCIX

Item in parochia Bodegraven habet domus ex terra dicta Meynards weer an die Ziitwinde <u>III solidos IX denarios</u> parvorum denariorum perpetuo.

perpetue^a

^bDit heeft Deric Ludekins zoen quiit ghecoft want men daer in XLI jaren niet of gheboert en hadde ende men daer niet of krijgen en konde, ghesciet bi rade des commenduers van Werder wantet al verloren was anno XXXIIII *[1434].*^b

^cItem heeft Dirc Lukens zoen voirscreven noch qwyt gecoft die VII solidi jaerlix die Peter Jan Nagelsoen te voeren te gheven plach ende menich jaar verloeren gheweest heeft ende hier heeft hi voer gegheven XVII Arnhemse gulden van consciencien weghen anno XLVIII *[1448]* op sinte Victordach.^c

Item in parrochia de Bodegraven habet domus ex terra quondam dicti Slach int Ryet <u>V solidos III denarios</u> annuatim bonorum denariorum hereditarie.

^anota
perpetue^a
^dheredes Slach int Riet^d

Item apud Leijden ex quadam petia terre dicta die Darch, iacenti in officio de Wermonde <u>VI antiquos Hollandenses</u> annuatim perpetuo. Johannes filius Trude modo possidet.

perpetue^a
^dJohannes filius Trude^d

---

^a *in the left margin.* ^b *in a different hand, 15th century.* ^c *in another 15th-century hand.* ^d *in the right margin.*

fol.99v.   In Oudewater

Item habet dicta domus in parochia de Oudewater bi der Linschoten
XXV iugera terre nuncupata Wilghen haghe, quibus pronunc a superiori latere propius iacent quatuor iugera terre spectancia pronunc ad
Reynerum et Johannem filios dicti Vivien, et ab inferiori latere II
iugera pronunc spectancia ad liberos Jacobi de Ghiesen, prout dictam
terram quondam possidebat a nobis Theodericus Ploye. Modo vero
unam medietatem dicte terre possidet a nobis Florencius filius Hugonis ad X annos ab anno LXIIII [1364] Petri pro L libris denariorum
Traiectensium, VI talentis cere et XII caponibus annuatim absque
defalcatione solvendis Martini et Petri vel cadet ab omni iure et cetera prout littera exinde tenet.
[a]Modo ulterius predictam medietatem possidet Gerardus Ruysche ad
X annos ab anno LXXXIIII [1384] Petri pro XXIIII antiquis scudatis vel [b]pagamento equivalenti[b], VI talentis cere et XII caponibus
absque defalcatione.[a]
[c]Florencius filius Hugonis[c]
[d]Gerardus Ruysche[d]

Reliquam vero medietatem prescriptorum iugerum modo possidet a
nobis Hugo filius Ployen ad VI annos ab anno LXVIII [1368] Pontiani pro XLI libris denariorum Traiectensium annuatim absque defalcatione et VI talentis cere et XII caponibus Martini et Petri solvendis
aut cadet ab omni iure. Non conburet et cetera sub condicionibus in
littera exinde contentis. Per fratrem Hugonem. [e]Predictus Hugo dictam terram resignavit ad usus Ponciani filii Petri et Henrici Sluseman
filii Ghiseberti, qui modo dictam terram possidebunt in eodem pactu
prescripto ad IIII annos ab anno LXX [1370] Ponciani et cetera sub
condicionibus in littera contentis. Per fratrem Johannem Gaude
dispensatorem.[e]
[f]¶ Ulterius predicti Poncianus et Henricus possidebunt dictam terram
ad X annos ab anno LXXIIII [1374] Petri pro IIII marcis, VIII loet
argenti, VI talentis cere, VIII caponibus annuatim absque defalcatione Martini et Petri solvendis aut cadent ab omni iure et cetera prout
littera tenet. Per fratrem Thomam dispensatorem.[f]
[c]Hugho Ployen[c]
[g]Pons Peterszoen ende Henric Sluseman[g]

---

[a] *in a different hand (D).* [b] pagamentum equivalens *ms.* [c] *in the left margin,
cancelled.* [d] *in the left margin in the same hand as* [a]. [e] *in another hand (C).* [f] *in yet
another hand (B).* [g] *in the left margin in the same hand as* [e].

fol.100r. In Oudewater   C

Item ibidem <u>quartale terre</u> prout iacet inter terram pronunc liberorum Jacobi de Ghiesen a parte superiori et terram heredum Wilhelmi uten Gaerde senioris a parte inferiori, prout illud possidebat a nobis Arnoldus filius Cleyninxs. Modo vero possidet ulterius Gerardus Rampoys ad X annos ab anno LXVII *[1367]* Petri <u>pro IX cum dimidio antiquis scudatis auri et VIIj *[7.5]* solidis</u> aut cum pagamento equivalenti in Traiecto solvendis annuatim absque defalcatione Martini et Petri vel cadet ab omni iure et cetera sub condicionibus ut littera exinde tenet. Per fratrem Hugonem.
ᵃGherid Rampoysᵃ

Item ibidem <u>VII iugera IIj *[2.5]* hont et VI eencloperscacht</u> prout iacent inter terram nuncupatam der Lewingher hoeve a parte superiori et terram nostre domus quam nunc possidet provisor domus nostre in Oudewater et Jacobus Ver ulterius ab eodem a parte inferiori, prout illa modo possidet a nobis Nicolaus Rampoys ad <u>X</u> annos ab anno <u>LXVIII *[1368]*</u> Petri pro <u>XXj *[20.5]* antiquis scudatis auri annuatim</u> aut cum pagamento equivalenti solvendis Martini et Petri vel cadet ab omni iure et cetera prout littera tenet. Per Hugonem.
ᵇ¶ Ulterius possidebit dictam terram Jacobus Wesemaker ad X annos ab anno LXXVI *[1376]* Petri pro LXVIII libris pagamenti Traiectensis Martini et Petri solvendis vel cadet ab omni iure. Per commendatorem fratrem Johannem Gaude.ᵇ ᶜcommendatorem.
¶ Ulterius idem Jacobus possidebit dictam terram ad X annos ab anno LXXXVI *[1386]* Petri pro XLVIII libris pagamenti Traiectensis Martini et Petri solvendis vel cadetᵈ ab omni iure. Per fratrem Gerardum Rijc dispensatorem.ᶜ
ᶜNicolaus Rampoysᶜ
ᶠJacobus Wezemakerᶠ

ᵃ *in the right margin.* ᵇ *in a different hand (C).* ᶜ *in another hand (E).* ᵈ cadent ms. ᵉ *in the right margin, cancelled.* ᶠ *in the right margin, in the same hand as* ᵈ.

fol.100v. In Oudewater

Item ibidem in <u>Keynoxhoeve dimidium quartale</u>, prout iacet aen die noertzide van der Linscoten inter terram collegii sancti Salvatoris Traiectensis ab utroque latere scilicet superiori et inferiori, prout illud quondam possidebat a nobis Oude Clawe. Modo possidet Johannes filius Viveens ad X annos ab anno LXIIII *[1364]* Epiphanie Domini

pro IX libris denariorum Traiectensium et VIII pullis annuatim absque defalcatione Martini et Petri, vel cadet ab omni iure et cetera
prout littera exinde tenet. Per fratrem Hugonem.
[a]Johan Vivienszoens[a]
[b]Jacob Weesmakers erfnaem[b]

Item ibidem quartale terre prout iacet pronunc inter terram Wilhelmi
Roede a parte orientali et terram Symonis dicti Wezemaker a parte
occidentali, prout illud possidebat a nobis Johannes Coutmont. Modo
possidet Wilhelmus dictus Roede pro II libris bonorum denariorum
annuatim Martini et Petri solvendis hereditarie.
[c]hereditarie
Willem die Roede[c]

---

[a] *in the left margin, cancelled.* [b] *in the left margin in later writing.* [c] *in the left margin
in the basic hand.*

fol.101r,   In Oudewater   CI
the first part is heavily corroded:

Item ibidem [dimidium quartale terre, iacens — inter]/ terram domus [nostre quam modo possidet — a parte]/ orientali et [terram
Wilhelmi die Roede, qui cum dimidio quartali]/ propius iacet a parte
occidentali, [prout Wilhelmus dictus Roede modo possidet]/ sub annua pensione II librarum bonorum denariorum   Martini et Petri
solvendarum hereditarie.
hereditarie[a]
[b]Willem die Rode[b]

Item ibidem dimidium mansum terre prout iacet inter terram nostre
domus quam nunc possident heredes Wilhelmi uten Gaerde iunioris
a parte superiori et terram Wilhelmi Roede a parte inferiori, prout
eundem possidebat a nobis Johannes Visscher. Modo possidet illum
Symon die Wezemaker ad *X* annos ab anno LXIX *[1369]* Petri et
solvet annuatim[c] exinde quattuor marcas et XIIII loet boni argenti
annuatim[d] absque defalcatione infra quindenam post Martini et Petri
aut cadet ab omni iure et cetera prout littera tenet. Per fratrem Hugonem.
[e]¶ Ulterius dictam terram possidebit Wolterus Velliken ad X annos
ab anno LXXIX *[1379]* Petri pro LXIIII libris absque defalcatione
solvendis Martini et Petri vel cadet ab omni iure et cetera prout littera
tenet.[e]

^fSymon Wezemaker^f
^gWolter Velliken^g

Item ibidem <u>ex quartali</u> quod dominus Petrus de Crabbendyc quondam emit erga Godefridum filium Wendelmodis, prout iacet inter terram nostre domus quam nunc possidet Johannes die Lewe a parte occidentali, et terram borgravii de Montfoerde a parte orientali, annuatim <u>I libram bonorum denariorum</u>, quam dictus dominus Petrus contulit nobis pro memoria sua. ^h<u>Ex eodem quartali habent fratres domus Theutonice I libram</u> et <u>fratres dicti Kalanderbroders I libram bonorum annuatim</u>, quas eciam idem dominus Petrus dedit. Philippus die Crane modo possidet hereditarie. Solvet Martini et Petri.^h
¶ perpetue^a
^bPhilips die Crane^b

---

^a *in the left margin.* ^b *in the right margin.* ^c *cancelled.* ^d anuatim *ms.* ^e *in a different hand (C).* ^f *in the right margin, cancelled.* ^g *in the right margin, in the same hand as* ^e. ^h *added in different writing.*

fol.101v,   In Oudewater
the first lines are somewhat corroded:

[Item ibidem <u>IV iugera terre</u> prout iacent inter terram Johannis] filii Jacobi/ [de Zeyst a parte superiori et terram nostre domus quam modo possidet] Nico/[laus filius Wolteri, prout illa possidebat a] nobis Zuwa relicta Wilhelmi./ Modo possident [ea heredes Wilhelmi filii Wilhelmi] uten Gaerde ad XI an/nos ab anno *LXV [1365]* Circumcisio Domini pro XVIII libris denariorum Traiectensium, <u>VI talentis cere et VI caponibus annuatim</u> absque defalcatione solvendis Martini et Petri aut cadent ab omni iure et cetera prout littera exinde tenet. Per fratrem Hugonem.
^a¶ Ulterius possidebit Wolterus Velliken dictam terram ad X annos ab anno ^bab LXXX^b LXXIX *[1379]* Petri pro XXXVI libris cum ceteris suprascriptis solvendis Martini et Petri vel cadet ab omni iure.^a
^cWillem uten Gaerde^c
^dWolter Velliken^d

Item ibidem <u>X iugera terre</u> empta quondam erga Reynerum Vinke, prout iacent inter terram pronunc Hermanni filii Ghisonis et suorum liberorum a parte superiori et terram nostre domus sancte Katerine, quam nunc possidet Laurencius Baldewini a parte inferiori, prout illa modo possident Johannes die Lewe et pueri Nicolai Alardi ad <u>X</u>

annos ab anno LXIII *[1363]* Ponciani pro <u>XXIX libris denariorum</u>
<u>Traiectensium et X caponibus annuatim</u> absque defalcatione solven-
dis Martini et Petri aut cadet ab omni iure et cetera prout littera
exinde tenet. Per fratrem Hugonem.

^c¶ Modo possidet Henricus filius Lubberti ad X annos ab anno
LXXIII *[1373]* Petri pro III marcis et Vj *[5.5]* loet argenti et X
caponibus annuatim absque defalcatione sub condicionibus ut littera
tenet. Per fratrem Thomam.^e

^f¶ Ulterius idem possidebit^g dictam terram prout modo iacet inter
terram Philippi de Craen a parte superiori et terram Rodolphi filii
Constancii a parte inferiori una cum tribus quartalibus terre sequentibus ad decem annos ab anno LXXXV *[1385]* Petri et solvet annuatim tam de ista terra quam de tribus quartalibus sequentibus C.XVIII
libras pagamenti Traiectensis, IIII pont was, XXII capones absque
defalcatione solvendas Martini et Petri aut cadet ab omni iure et
cetera prout littera tenet. Per fratrem Johannem de Arnhem
dispensatorem.^f

^h<u>Johan die Lewe ende Claes Alards kinderen</u>^h
ⁱ<u>Henricus filius Lubberti</u>ⁱ

---

^a *in a different hand.* ^b *cancelled.* ^c *in the left margin, in the basic hand.* ^d *in the left*
margin in the same hand as ^a. ^e *in another hand (B).* ^f *in yet another hand.*
^g poscidebit *ms.* ^h *in the left margin, cancelled.* ⁱ *in the left margin, in the same hand*
as ^e.

fol.102r. <u>In Oudewater</u> CII

Item ibidem <u>tria quartalia terre</u> prout iacent inter terram Philippi
dicti Crane a superiori parte et terram Ghisekini filii Gherwardi et
Andree fratris sui a parte inferiori, prout illa modo possidet Laurencius Boudewini ad X annos ab anno LXI *[1361]* Conversio Pauli pro
<u>XXX libris denariorum Traiectensium, IIII talentis cere et XII capo-</u>
<u>nibus</u> annuatim absque defalcatione solvendis Martini et Petri aut
cadet ab omni iure et cetera secundum tenorem littere quam inde
habemus. Per fratrem Hugonem.

^a¶ Modo dictam terram possidet Henricus Lubberti ad X annos ab
anno LXXIII *[1373]* Petri pro LX libris denariorum Traiectensium
et IIII talentis cere et XII caponibus annuatim absque omni defalcatione, sub condicionibus in littera contentis. Per fratrem Thomam.
Solvet etiam j *[0.5]* viertel boni butyri Martini annuatim.^a

^b¶ Ulterius possidebit^c dictam terram una cum decem iugeribus su-
prascriptis, prout modo iacet inter terram presbiterorum Civilis Ec-

clesie Traiectensis a parte superiori et terram h^d liberorum Hermanni Gisonis a parte inferiori, solvendis tam de ista terra quam de decem iugeribus prescriptis, prout superius est signatum.^b

^eLouwe Boudewins^e
^fHenricus filius Luberti^f

Item ibidem an die Lynscoten, quartale terre, emptum quondam erga Katerinam de Beyarden, prout iacet inter terram capituli sancti Salvatoris Traiectensis a parte superiori et terram Machteldis relicte Andree filii Gherwardi a parte inferiori, prout illud modo possidet Johannes filius Berinxs ad X annos ab anno LXIIII *[1364]* Petri <u>pro IX libris XV solidis denariorum Traiectensium et IIII talentis cere et IIII caponibus</u> annuatim absque defalcatione solvendis Martini et Petri aut cadet ab omni iure et cetera prout littera exinde continet. Per fratrem Hugonem.

^gUlterius ad X annos ab anno LXXVI *[1376]* Petri pro XV libris cum ceteris.^g
^hJohannes filius Berinxs^h

---

^a *in a different hand (B).* ^b *in another hand.* ^c poscidebit *ms.* ^d *cancelled.* ^e *in the right margin, cancelled.* ^f *in the right margin, in the same hand as* ^a. ^g *in yet another hand (D).* ^h *in the right margin, in the basic hand.*

fol.102v,   In Oudewater
the whole page is somewhat corroded:

[Item ibidem an die Linscoten] <u>III iugera terre</u> prout iacent inter terram domini/ [Jacobi Scrodekin] presbiteri Traiectensis a parte superiori et terram [heredum] domini Gerardi/ de Vliete militis quam [Antiquus Jacobus et Hermannus Coutmont]/ [tenent] ab eisdem a parte inferiori, prout illa modo possidet a nobis/ Theodericus Torriken ad <u>X</u> annos ab anno <u>LXII</u> *[1362]* Petri pro/ <u>X libris IIII solidis et III pullis</u> annuatim absque defalcatione Martini et Petri solvendis/ aut cadet ab omni iure et cetera prout littera [exinde tenet.] Per fratrem Hugonem.

^aUlterius dictus Theodericus possidebit dictam terram ad X annos ab anno LXXII *[1372]* Ponciani pro ^bXVIII libris monete Traiectensis tempore solucionis^b in Traiecto et III pullis annuatim absque defalcatione Martini et Petri solvendis aut cadet ab omni iure et cetera prout littera tenet. Per fratrem Johannem Gaude dispensatorem.^a ¶ Modo^c d

^eDirc Torriken^e

Item ibidem <u>XV iugera</u> empta quondam erga Johannem de Baten-
borch/ prout iacent inter VII iugera nostre domus que nunc possidet
Wil/helmus Roede a parte orientali et [terram quatuor iugerum nos-
tre] domus quam/ nunc possidet ^d a parte occidentali, prout illa/
quondam possidebat a nobis Rolandus [Bloc.] Modo possidet ea
Theodericus/ Torriken ad *X* annos ab anno <u>LXVII</u> *[1367]* Petri <u>pro</u>
<u>XXXVI libris</u> denariorum Traiectensium <u>et XV pullis annuatim</u> ab-
sque defalcatione solvendis Martini et Petri aut cadet ab omni iure et
cetera prout littera exinde tenet. Per fratrem Hugonem.
^f¶ Ulterius possidebit idem Theodericus dicta XV iugera terre prout
iacent ad X annos ab anno LXXX *[1380]* Petri pro LXXXII libris
VII solidis pagamenti Traiectensis et XII pullis solvendis Martini et
Petri vel cadet ab omni iure. Per commendatorem.^f
^g¶ Modo dictam terram possidebit ulterius Danyel Briens zoen ad X
annos ab anno LXXXVII *[1387]* Petri pro LXXXIIII libris pagamenti Traiectensis et XV pullis Martini et Petri solvendis vel cadet ab
omni iure. Per fratrem Johannem de Arnem.^g
<u>obiit</u>^h
ⁱ<u>Dirc Torriken</u>ⁱ
^j<u>Danyel Bryens zoen</u>^j

---

   ^a *in a different hand (C).* ^b *written over erased words.* ^c *in another hand.* ^d *not filled
in.* ^e *In the left margin, in the basic hand.* ^f *in yet another hand.* ^g *in yet a different
hand (E).* ^h *in the left margin, in a later hand.* ⁱ *in the left margin, cancelled.* ^j *in the
left margin, in the same hand as* ^g.

fol.103r,   In Oudewater   CIII
the first lines are somewhat corroded:

Item ibidem <u>VII iugera</u> empta quondam una cum XV [iugeribus
prescriptis er]/ga Johannem de [Batenborch,] prout iacent inter terram heredum [domini Gerardi de]/ Vliete militis a parte superiori et
terram nostre domus quam nunc possidet The/odericus [Torriken] a
parte inferiori, prout illa quondam possidebat a nobis/ Theodericus
[Geel.] Modo possidet ea Wilhelmus Roede ad X annos/ ab anno
LXIIII *[1364]* Valentini <u>pro XX libris denariorum Traiectensium et</u>
<u>VII pullis ann</u>/uatim absque defalcatione Martini et Petri solvendis
aut cadet ab omni iure et cetera prout littera exinde tenet. Per fratrem Hugonem.
^a<u>Willem die Roede</u>^a

Item <u>in Hedekedorp quartale terre</u> prout iacet inter terram collegii

sancte Marie Traiectensis quam nunc hereditarie possidet Wilhelmus dictus Roede a parte superiori et terram comitis Hollandie quam nunc Theodericus de Gouda tenet ab eodem in feodo a parte inferiori, prout illud possidebat a nobis Albertus Witte filius Theoderici de Maersen. Modo possidet et ulterius possidebit a nobis Johannes filius Hille ad X annos ab anno LXX *[1370]* Petri pro II marcis et IIj *[2.5]* loet argenti minus XV denariis aut pro pagamento equivalenti tempore solutionis in Traiecto et IIII pullis annuatim infra quindenam post Martini et Petri solvendis aut cadet ab omni iure et cetera prout littera tenet. Per fratrem Hugonem.
^b¶ Ulterius possidebit Jacobus filius eius ad X annos ab anno LXXXIX *[1389]* Petri pro XXXII libris et IIII pullis sub condicione predicta. Per fratrem Johannem Haze.^b
^aJohan Hillen zoen^a

---

^a *in the right margin.* ^b *in a different hand.*

fol.103v,   In Oudewater
the first lines are slightly corroded:

Item ibidem dimidium mansum terre, op streckende mitten overen egge/ an den Ysel dijc ende mitten nederen egge [aen] Papencop, cui/ [ab utroque latere] scilicet a latere orientali et [eciam] occidentali propius/ iacet terra Leyde relicte Constancii filii iunioris Rodolphi et puerorum suorum, prout eundem modo possident eadem Leyda et pueri sui ad X annos ab anno LXII *[1362]* Lucie pro XVIII libris denariorum Traiectensium annuatim absque ^adefalcatione^a infra quindenam post Martini et Petri solvendis aut cadet ab omni iure et cetera prout littera exinde tenet. Per fratrem Hugonem.
^b¶ Ulterius dictam terram possidebit Rodolphus filius Constancii ad X annos ab anno LXXII *[1372]* Valentini pro L libris denariorum annuatim absque defalcatione solvendis Martini et Petri aut cadet ab omni iure et cetera prout littera exinde tenet. Per fratrem Johannem Gaude.^b
^cLeyda relicta Constancii^c
^dRodolphus eius filius^d

Item ibidem in Hedekedorp quartale terre prout iacet in iurisdictione temporali comitis Hollandie, receptum quondam a domino Gerardo de Vliete milite nomine permutacionis seu concambii pro dimidio manso terre, iacenti prope castrum de Vliete olim ad nos pertinente, quod quidem quartale extendit se a flumine Ysele ad aggerem dictum

Ruweyderdijc iacetque communi sulcu cum uno quartali terre pronunc ad Fredericum filium Johannis Lewen spectanti, inter terram
Hermanni filii Hugonis de Bilwijc a parte superiori et terram Magorii
et liberorum iuvenis Johannis Myen a parte inferiori, quod idem
dominus Gerardus a nobis possidebat. Modo possident filius seu heredes eiusdem pro IX libris denariorum Traiectensium annuatim hereditarie infra quindenam post Martini et Petri solvendis, aut potest
expandari de dicta terra nostra aut de bonis super eandem existentibus et cetera prout in littera quam inde habemus plenius continetur.
^edit punt is doet mit enen dedinghe ende verleyt an II merghen lants
in Polsbroec die Dirc Den bruket.^e
^fheredes domini Gerardi de Vliete ¶ perpetue^f

---

^a *missing in ms.* ^b *in a different hand (C).* ^c *in the left margin, cancelled.* ^d *in the left margin, in the same hand as* ^b. ^e *in another hand.* ^f *in the left margin in the basic hand.*

fol.104r, In Oudewater CIIII
the whole page is more or less corroded:

Item ibidem dimidium quartale emptum ut credo erga Georgium in
[Scho]/enhoven et [Margaretam] eius sororem, prout iacet inter
viam [communem bi]/ der Langer Weyde a parte orientali et terram
Aleyd[is Alardi et liberorum]/ suorum a parte [occidentali, quod
modo possidet eadem Aleydis Alardi]/ perpetuo pro XXX solidis
bonorum [denariorum annuatim] Martini et Petri solvendis.
¶ perpetuo^a
^bAleydis Alardi^b

Item ibidem [dimidium quartale —]/ a parte [orientali et aquemea-
tum dictum — weteringhe] a parte occidentali, [quem modo possident Henricus et Johannes Gruter] hereditarie/ pro IIII libris
bonorum denariorum annuatim Martini et Petri solvendis.
^cHier of heeft Vrederic de Gruter ziin helft qwiit ghecoft.^c
¶ perpetuo^a
^bHenric ende Jan die Gruter^b

Item ibidem IIII iugera [prout iacent inter terram Johannis] filii Ni-
colai/ a parte orientali et terram [Johannis de Linschoten a] parte
occidentali,/ que modo possidet Theodericus [Craker hereditarie
pro] XX solidis/ bonorum denariorum Martini et Petri solvendis
[annuatim.]
¶ perpetuo^a

ᵇDirc die Crakerᵇ

ᵃ *in the left margin.* ᵇ *in the right margin.* ᶜ *in a different hand.*

fol.104v, In Oudewater

the first half of the page is rather corroded:

Item ibidem <u>dimidium quartale terre</u> prout iacet inter terram Engelberti/ [de Woude a parte orientali] et terram domine de Holensteyne quam/ [nunc tenet ab eadem in feodo] Jacobus Speyard a parte occidentali,/ [quod modo possidet idem Jacobus] Speyard <u>pro III libris/ bonorum denariorum</u> annuatim [Martini et Petri] solvendis hereditarie.

ᵃ<u>Jacobus Speyard</u>ᵃ

¶ perpetuoᵃ

[Item ibidem — prout] iacet inter/ Magorii [et Wil— oppidanorum in Oudewater a parte] superiori et/ terram [Johannis de Gheyne in Montfoerde a parte] inferiori, prout/ eundem [possidebat a nobis Aleydis relicta Rutgheri]. Modo possidet/ eum Speyard filius Ruthgeri ad <u>X annos ab anno *LXVII [1367]* Petri pro XVII libris XV solidis denariorum Traiectensium et V pullis</u> annuatim absque defalcatione infra quindenam post Martini et Petri solvendis aut cadet ab omni iure et cetera prout littera exinde tenet. Per fratrem Hugonem. ᵇ¶ Modo possidebit ulterius hanc terram Ruthgerus die Merseman ad X annos ab anno LXXVII *[1377]* Petri pro XL libris pagamenti Traiectensis et XV pullis annuatim absque defalcatione solvendis Martini et Petri vel cadet ab omni iure et cetera prout littera tenet. Per fratrem Johannem Gaude commendatorem.ᵇ

ᶜ¶ Ulterius possidebit Ghisebertus Reynekens zoen ad X annos ab anno LXXXVIII *[1388]* Petri.ᶜ

ᵈ<u>Speyard filius Rutgheri</u>ᵈ

ᵉ<u>Rutgher die Merseman</u>ᵉ

ᶠItem ibidem in Hekendorp III iugera terre empta per fratrem Hugonem de Coudenkerc erga Petrum, Wilhelmum et Egidium filios seniores Rodolphi Moliaerd, prout iacent communi sulcu cum tribus iugeribus spectantibus ad Willekinum filium Tydemanni et Elisabet eius uxorem matrem dictorum trium filiorum, quibus VI iugeribus insimul propius iacet terra Heynekini Versoyen et liberi Clemencie van der Hoghe a parte superiori et iuniores pueri Rodolphi Moliard a parte inferiori. Que tria iugera modo possidet Jacobus die Veer

Matten zoen ad annos Petri ab anno LXXIIII *[1374]* pro III nobel
XIII. quart annuatim. Per fratrem Johannem Gaude.^f
^g¶ Modo dictam terram prout iacet possidebit ulterius Jacobus de^g ^h
^idese III morghen lants ziin verwesselt om IIIj *[3.5]* morghen lants
ghelegen te Weerder int Kervelant die Wouter Ludolfs zoens plaghen
te wesen.^i
Jacob^j

---

^a *in the left margin.* ^b *in a different hand (C).* ^c *in another hand.* ^d *in the left margin, cancelled.* ^e *in the left margin, in the same hand as* ^b. ^f *in yet another hand (E).*
^g *added in different writing (E).* ^h *not filled in.* ^i *in later writing.* ^j *in the left margin, in the same hand as* ^f.

fol.105r, In Oudewater CV
the first lines are somewhat corroded:

Item ibidem dimidium quartale continens IIj *[2.5]* iugera terre |prout
iacet inter]/ terram Nycolai filii Symonis a parte orientali et terram
[domine de Hol]/steyne a parte occidentali, prout illud modo possidet idem [Nicolaus]/ filius Symonis de Vliderhoven sub annua pensione [II librarum bonorum]/ denariorum Martini et Petri solvendis
hereditarie.
¶ perpetuo^a
^bNicolaus filius Symonis^b

Item ibidem dimidium mansum terre quem Henricus filius Hermanni
Ghisonis nu ter tijt beleghen heeft mit lande an den [oesteren] egge,
et Jacobus Plonijs an den westerenegge. ^cIdem Jacobus modo possidet
una cum quartali sequenti.^c

^dItem ibidem quartale terre, cui ab utroque latere propius iacet terra
pronunc Jacobi Plonijs et prout iacet an den westeren egge van dies
zelven Jacobs weer, daer hi nu op woent. Quod quidem quartale una
cum dimidio manso prescripto modo possidet a nobis idem Jacobus
Plonijs ad X annos ab anno LXVII *[1367]* Petri pro XVIII libris
denariorum Traiectensium annuatim absque defalcatione Martini et
Petri solvendis aut cadet ab omni iure et cetera prout littera exinde
tenet. Per fratrem Hugonem.
^bJacobus Plonijs^b

---

^a *in the left margin.* ^b *in the right margin.* ^c *added in different writing.* ^d *linked with brace to the foregoing item.*

fol.105v.   In Oudewater

Item ibidem IIIj *[3.5]* iugera terre prout iacent inter terram Theoderici dicti Sutor filii Gerardi Sutor a parte orientali et terram Gerardi dicti Vierscoten a parte occidentali, prout illa modo possidet domicella Blidradis pro II libris bonorum denariorum annuatim Martini et Petri solvendis hereditarie aut infra VIII dies postea vel caderet ab omni iure. Inde dabuntur XV solidos bonorum ad secundam lampadem in hospitali.
ᵃdomicella Blidradis
¶ perpetuoᵃ

Item ibidem in Snodelreweyrt octo hont terre vel circiter cum tribus virgatis aggerum, empta erga Hermannum filium Vrouwini, prout iacent inter terram Gerardi filii Symonis de Vliderhoven a parte superiori et terram bagutarum in Traiecto a parte inferiori. Idem Gerardus filius Simonis modo possidet ad X annos ab anno LXI *[1361]* Petri pro XXXII solidis pagamenti Traiectensis annuatim absque defalcatione Martini et Petri solvendis aut cadet ab omni iure et cetera ut littera tenet. Per fratrem Hugonem.
ᵇ¶ Ulterius possidebit Nicolaus filius Symonis ad XII annos ab anno LXXIX *[1379]* Petri pro Ij *[1.5]* antiquis scudatis solvendis Martini et Petri vel cadet ab omni iure.ᵇ
ᵃGerardus filius Symonisᵃ

ᵃ *in the left margin.* ᵇ *in a different hand (C).*

fol.106r.   In Oudewater   CVI

Item ibidem in Hoencop ultra Yselam dimidium mansum prout iacet inter terram domicelli de Vliete filii domini Gerardi de Vliete a parte orientali et terram Gerardi filii Jacobi a parte occidentali, prout eundem quondam possidebat a nobis Hannekinus van der Hoghe. Modo possidet eum ᵃGerardus Wassenburchᵃ hereditarie pro III libris bonorum denariorum annuatim exinde solvendis Martini et Petri et cetera prout littera nostra exinde tenet.
ᵇModo possidet Johannes filius Theoderici in Pulsbroec.ᵇ
perpetuoᶜ
ᵈGherid Wassenberchᵈ
ᵉJan Dirix zoenᵉ

Item ibidem in Hoencop XIIII iugera terre, quibus a superiori parte
propius iacent domicellus de Vliete filius domini Gerardi et borgra-
vius de Montfoerde, quivis eorum cum uno iugere, et inferius Gerardus filius Werneri de Vliete cum uno manso terre quem tenet in
feodo a domino Ghiseberto de Nyenroede. Que iugera modo possidet
a nobis Johannes Hoebroec ad X annos ab anno LXVI *[1366]* Petri
pro XL libris denariorum Traiectensium et XIIII caponibus annuatim absque defalcatione Martini et Petri solvendis aut cadet ab omni
iure et cetera prout littera exinde tenet. Per fratrem Hugonem.
ᵉJohannes Hoebroecᵉ

ᵃ *cancelled.* ᵇ *added in different writing.* ᶜ *in the left margin, in the basic hand.* ᵈ *in
the right margin, cancelled.* ᵉ *in the right margin, in the basic hand, not cancelled.*

fol.106v.   In Oudewater

Item ibidem in Hoencop ex X iugeribus terre, quibus propius iacet
Stephanus de Boechout cum Vj *[5.5]* iugeribus terre a parte orientali
et terra Ghiseberti de Vliete a parte occidentali, XXVI solidos VIII
denarios hereditarie. Jacoba filia Wyrici nunc possidet et solvet Martini et Petri annuatim.
ᵃJacob Wirix dochter
¶ hereditarieᵃ

Item an die Lynschoten ex quadam pecia terre V solidos perpetue.
¶ perpetueᵃ

ᵇItem V iugera terre, empta per fratrem Hugonem de Coudenkerc
dispensatorem, iacentia pro nunc inter terram Elburgis Nycolai filii
Hugonis et puerorum eius a parte superiori et terram Johannis Wolfard et eius uxoris filie Florencii Vischer, que possidebat quondam
Speyardus filius Rutgheri. Modo possidet ea Johannes Donre ad X
annos ab anno LXXVI *[1376]* Petri pro XXVIII libris pagamenti
Traiectensis Martini et Petri solvendis vel cadet ab omni iure prout
littera tenet. Per fratrem Johannem de Arnhem. Modo dicta terra
iacet inter terram Wilhelmi de Haestricht a parte superiori et terram
Johannis Wolfard a parte inferiori.ᵇ
ᵃJan Donreᵃ

ᵃ *in the left margin.* ᵇ *in a different hand (E).*

fol.107r,   In Oudewater domus ibidem   CVII
the first lines are slightly corroded:

Item in eadem parrochia de Oudewater habet [domus hanc terram subscriptam]/ quam modo possidet provisor domus nostre in Oudewater frater Johannes [de Leyden]/ ad vitam suam.

Primo in Papencop duos mansos terre quos nunc Jacobus Butendiix colit, prout iacent inter terram liberorum Ghisekini filii Gherwardi a parte septentrionali et terram liberorum Nycolai filii Rodolphi a parte meridionali. ^aFrater Johannes de Leyden possidet.^a
^bfrater Johannes de Leyden^b

Item an die Linscoten unum mansum terre quem nunc colit Jacobus Ver, prout iacet inter terram nostre domus quam modo possidet Nicolaus Rampoys a parte orientali et terram domini Aelmanni militis a parte occidentali. ^aFrater Johannes de Leyden modo possidet.^a
^bfrater Johannes de Leyden^b

---

^a *added in different writing.* ^b *in the right margin.*

fol.107v,   In Oudewater
the first lines are slightly corroded:

Item ibidem an die Linscoten unum mansum terre nuncupatum vulgariter [Verlinne hoeve prout iacet inter terram] capituli sancti Salvatoris Traiectensis a latere orientali et terram Johannis Pensternaech a parte occidentali. ^aFrater Johannes de Leyden modo possidet.^a
^bfrater Johannes de Leyden^b

Item ibidem aen die zuytzide van der Linscoten XIIII hont prout iacent inter terram Nicolai filii Jacobi [doorgestreept: ^cet terram^c a parte orientali et terram domicelle Blidradis et Splinteri uten Hamme a parte occidentali. ^aFrater Johannes de Leyden modo possidet.^a
^bfrater Johannes de Leyden^b

---

^a *added in different writing.* ^b *in the left margin.*

fol.108r, In Oudewater CVIII
the first lines and the second item are somewhat corroded:

Item ibidem IIII^{or} iugera [terre que nunc colunt Nicolaus Rampoys]
et Copitte [eius frater, prout iacent inter terram nostre domus
quam]/ nunc a nobis possidet [Theodericus Torriken a parte orienta-
li]/ et terram Boudewini [filii Henrici Versoyen ^{a}a parte occiden]/
tali^a et Nycolai [Rampoys et Copitte fratris] eius communi sulcu/ a
parte occidentali. ^{b}Frater Johannes de Leyden modo possidet unacum
iugeribus prescriptis.^{b}
^{c}frater Johannes de Leyden^c

Item ibidem prope [muros oppidi de Oudewater twe cingelen]/ lands
prout iacent a [−, inter terram]/ dictam Cost[verloren — -ier der]/
Buerland scheydet. Heredes Ghiseberti filii Jacobi modo colunt/ pro
IIIj [3.5] libris denariorum annuatim ad X annos ab anno LXII
[1362] Petri et cetera sub condicionibus in littera quam inde habemus
contentis. Per fratrem Hugonem. ^{b}Frater Johannes de Leyden modo
recipit redditus.^{b}

^{b}Summa prescriptorum iugerum terre que modo possidet frater Johannes de Leyden provisor domus nostre in Oudewater ad vitam
suam LXX iugera et II hont et II cingelen terre, sub annua pensione
XXXII libris denariorum Traiectensium et sub condicionibus in littera exinde contentis. Per dominum magistrum Alamanie actum.^{b}

---

^{a} *cancelled.* ^{b} *added in different writing.* ^{c} *in the right margin.*

fol.108v, Infra oppidum [Oudewater]
the whole page is rather corroded:

[Item infra muros oppidi de Oudewater aream] prout iacet inter/
[aream quam nunc possidet a nobis — a fratre Johanne de Leyden]/
a parte [occidentali et aream Gerardi Boechout] a parte ^{a} / prout
[eandem modo possident heredes domini Gerardi] de Vliete perpe-
tuo/ pro III libris et IX [grossis antiquis annuatim].
^{b}heredes domini Gerardi de Vliete^b

Item ibidem aream quam dominus Henricus Sluseman dedit, situatam inter aream Petri filii Rotardi a parte meridionali et aream liberorum dicti Ployen a parte septentrionali, quam modo possidet
Hermannus Teyghelaer perpetuo pro XL grossis annuatim.

^bHerman Teyghelar^b

Item de <u>area</u> [situata inter aream et domum predictorum] dictam Wanthuys/ a parte orientali et [aquemeatum —] a parte occidentali/ <u>XXVIII solidos VIII</u> denarios. [Petrus Wayschilt modo possidet] hereditarie.
^bPeter Wayschilt^b

Item de <u>area</u> iacenti inter aream Korstancii a parte occidentali et aream Ghertrudis dicte Properzalve a parte septentrionali <u>V grossos annuatim</u>. Johannes Vischer modo possidet hereditarie.
^bJohannes Visscher^b

---

^a *not filled in.* ^b *in the left margin.*

fol.109r,   [Infra oppidum Oudewater]   CIX
the whole page is rather corroded:

[Item ibidem *aream* quam uxor — prout iacet inter aream]/ [pronunc – filii — Johannis van der]/ [-ieze a parte occidentali, prout — possidebat a nobis dominus]/ Gerardus Quattelar. [Modo possidet eam Heynemannus Snyder pro]/ <u>I libra annuatim</u> hereditarie.
^aHeynemannus Snider^a

Item <u>de area iacenti</u> pronunc inter aream Wilhelmi Visscher filii Johannis/ a parte [meridionali et terram – Wilhelmi — a parte septentrionali]/ VII grossos annuatim. [Theodericus Schilt modo possidet eandem hereditarie].
^aTheodericus Schilt^a

Item <u>de area</u> iacenti pronunc [inter aream Wilhelmi Visscher filii Johannis]/ a parte meridionali et inter aquefossatum [dictum Weteringhe] a/ parte septentrionali <u>IX grossos</u> [annuatim. Theodericus Schilt modo possidet]/ hereditarie.
^aTheodericus Schilt^a

Item de <u>area</u> qua propius iacet area pronunc Theoderici Rampoyse a parte/ meridionali et die Weteringhe a parte [septentrionali <u>II solidos</u>]/ annuatim. Modo [possident eandem Theodericus Schilt et Theodericus]/ Wolter hereditarie. ^a<u>Theodericus Schilt et Theodericus Wolter</u>^a

---

^a *in the right margin.*

fol.109v,   [Infra oppidum Oudewater]
the whole page is slightly to heavily corroded:

[Item ibidem <u>aream</u> —]/ [- a parte meridionali —]/ [parte septentrionali —]/ [<u>XX</u> grossos annuatim perpetuo.]
ᵃWilhelmus van Loenᵃ

[Item ibidem <u>ex una area</u> prout iacet et eandem modo possidet]
Wolterus/ filius [Jacobi Melijs XI grossos annuatim] perpetuo.
ᵃ<u>Wolter Jacob Melijs zoen</u>ᵃ

[Item ex <u>area</u> iacenti inter aream] Wilhelmi de Beydentziden a par-
te/ [meridionali et aream Theoderici] filii Everardi a parte septen-
trio/[nali <u>VIII grossos</u> annuatim hereditarie. Modo possidet Wolterus
die/ Rike.
ᵃ<u>Wolter die Rike</u>ᵃ

[Item ex <u>area</u> iacenti inter aream domini Coman] Aernd a parte
meridio/nali [et aream Hugonis filii Florencii a parte] septentrionali/
<u>II grossos annuatim</u> perpetuo. Modo possidet Theodericus filius
Gheyen.
ᵃ<u>Dirc Gheyen zoen</u>ᵃ

ᵃ *in the left margin.*

fol.110r,   [Infra oppidum Oudewater]   CX
the whole page is heavily corroded:

[Item <u>ex area</u> — pronunc -]/ [——]/ [——]/
ᵃJan die [—]ᵃ

Item ex <u>domo et area</u> [oppidi ibidem dicta Wanthuys situata inter]/
communem plateam [a parte orientali et aream Petri Wayscilt a parte
occi]/dentali [XXXV solidos IIII denarios. Oppidani in Oudewater
possident]/ perpetuo.
ᵃ<u>magister civium ibidem</u>ᵃ

Item <u>ex area</u> [— iam dicte domus et aree dicte]/ Wanthuys [a parte
septentrionali et aream Spikeri a parte meridio]/nali <u>VI solidos</u> [VIIj
[7.5] <u>denarios</u> annuatim perpetuo. Agatha Templiers modo pos]/
sidet.
ᵃ<u>Agatha Templiers</u>ᵃ

Item de <u>domo et area</u> Jacobi [van den Vliete prout iacent] inter are/
am Henrici de Bosynchem [a parte meridionali et aream Johannis
Vischer]/ a parte septentrionali [<u>XVIII solidos VIII denarios annua-
tim</u>. Modo possidet]/ Cristianus hereditarie.
<u>Cristianus</u>ᵃ

ᵃ *in the right margin.*

fol.110v,   [<u>Infra oppidum Oudewater</u>]
the first half is heavily corroded:

[Item <u>ex area</u> iacenti inter aream Aleydis Arnoldi a parte meridio]/
[nali et aream —]/ [de Honthorst — possidet]/ Jacobus Vlisman
hereditarie.
ᵃ[Jacob Vlisman]ᵃ

Item <u>ex area iacenti</u> inter vicum extendentem se a Platea Capelle
ibidem/ versus murum oppidi a parte meridionali et aream Jacobi
Vlisman/ a parte septentrionali, [prout eandem] modo possidet Aleydis Aerni/[kini <u>I libram annuatim</u> hereditarie].
ᵃ<u>Aleyd Aernikins</u>ᵃ

Item <u>ex area iacenti</u> inter cimiterium nostre capelle ibidem a latere/
meridionali et inter vicum iam supradictum a parte septentrionali/
<u>XXIIII solidos</u> annuatim. [Modo possidet — Philippus] die/ Monic
hereditarie.
ᵃ<u>Philips die Monic</u>ᵃ

Item <u>ex area</u> iacenti inter aream Henrici ᵇHermanniᵇ filii Hermanni
Ghisonis a parte meridionali et aream Johannis dicti die Elsche a
parte septentrionali <u>IX solidos IIII denarios annuatim</u>. Albertus filius
Woudradis modo possidet perpetuo.
ᵃ<u>Albertus Woudrade zoen</u>ᵃ

Item ibidem <u>aream</u> iacentem inter aream nostre domus in Oudewater quam nunc possidet frater Johannes de Leyden a parte meridionali et aream Johannis dicti Olislagher a parte septentrionali <u>XXXII
solidos annuatim</u>. Idem frater Johannes de Leyden modo possidet.
ᵃ<u>frater Johannes de Leyden</u>ᵃ

ᵃ *in the left margin.* ᵇ *cancelled.*

fol. 111r, [Infra oppidum Oudewater]
the first lines are heavily corroded:

Item <u>aream</u> [iacentem — Laghen Eynde]/ a parte [meridionali et — quam nunc possidet frater Johannes]/ de Leyden a parte [septentrionali, prout eandem modo possidet Henricus]/ filius Petri Blomen pro <u>XVI solidis</u> annuatim [hereditarie].
[a]<u>Henric Peter Blomen</u> zoen[a]

Item <u>ex area</u> dicta Rossemolenwerf iacenti inter aream nostre domus quam nunc possidet a nobis frater Johannes de Leyden a parte meridionali et aream Alberti Rampoyse a parte septentrionali <u>XXVI</u> solidos annuatim. Idem Albertus Rampoys modo possidet perpetuo.
[a]<u>Albertus Rampoys</u>[a]

Item <u>aream</u> iacentem inter aream Iuvenis Johannis filii Petri a parte orientali et murum circumeuntem oppidum Oudewater a parte occidentali, prout eandem nunc possident heredes Florencii Hugonis <u>pro II libris annuatim.</u>
[a]<u>Florens Hughen</u> zoen[a]

Item ibidem <u>aream</u> situatam [inter] murum nostre domus in Oudewater circui/entem domum et curtim ibidem a parte meridionali et vicum quo itur a Platea Capelle versum murum oppidi a parte septentrionali, prout eandem modo possidet a nobis Amilius filius Wilhelmi Hagonis <u>pro IIII libris annuatim.</u> [b]infra XIIII dies post Martini et Petri solvendis vel cadet ab omni iure.
[a]<u>Amilius Wilhelmi Hagonis</u>[a]
<u>nota</u>[c]
[d]<u>caret annis</u>[d]

---

[a] *in the right margin.* [b] *added in different writing.* [c] *in the left margin.* [d] *in a different hand.*

fol. 111v, [In Montfoerde]
the whole page is somewhat corroded:

[Item habet domus nostra in parrochia de Montfoerde primo in Willenscop]/ [tria <u>quartalia terre</u>, prout iacent inter terram capituli sancti] Salvatoris/ Traiectensis a parte [superiori et terram heredum Jacobi] Golen a parte inferiori,/ que quondam possidebat a nobis Theodericus Boechout. Modo possidet ea Henricus de Otterspoer ad

X annos ab anno <u>LXVI</u> *[1366]* Petri pro <u>XLVIII libris denariorum</u>
<u>Traiectensium et XII pullis</u> annuatim absque defalcatione infra XIIII
dies post Martini et Petri solvendis aut cadet ab omni iure et cetera
prout littera exinde tenet. Per fratrem Hugonem.
^a¶ Ulterius possidebunt dictam terram Splinterus filius Henrici Otter-
spoer et Bya eius mater ad X annos ab anno LXXXII *[1382]* pro
XCVI libris denariorum Traiectensium, IIII talentis cere, IIII caponibus, XII pullis absque defalcatione solvendis Martini et Petri vel cadent ab omni iure. Una cum terra infrascripta.^a
^bHenricus de Otterspoer^b
^cSplinterus filius eius et Bya mater eius^c

Item ibidem <u>quartale terre</u> dictum Kaeviertel, prout iacet inter terram Agathe filie Frisonis a parte superiori et terram Johannis filii
Louwen a parte inferiori, prout illud quondam possidebat a nobis
dictus Screvel filius Ghertrudis. Modo possidet illud Henricus de Otterspoer ad X annos ab anno <u>LXV</u> *[1365]* Petri <u>pro XVIII libris</u>
<u>denariorum</u> Traiectensium et IIII/ [talentis cere et IIII caponibus
annuatim absque <u>defalcatione Martini et</u>] Petri solvendis aut/ [cadet
ab omni iure et cetera prout littera exinde tenet. Per fratrem Hugonem.
^a¶ Ulterius possidebunt hanc terram una cum tribus quartalibus su-
prascriptis Splinterus predictus et Bya eius mater ad annos supradictos pro pacto annuo superius signato.^a
^bHenricus de Otterspoer^b
^cSplinterus filius eius et Bya mater eius.^c

---

^a *in a different hand (D).* ^b *in the left margin, cancelled.* ^c *in the left margin in the*
same hand as ^a.

fol.112r,   [In Montfoerde]   CXII
the first lines are heavily corroded:

[Item ibidem —] inter terram borchgravii de/ Montforde quam nunc
Amilius Johannis ab ipso tenet in feodo a parte orientali et terram
Jacobi Coyfas et Alberti Coyfas a parte occidentali, prout illud modo
possidet a nobis Amilius filius Johannis ad XX annos ab anno LIIII
[1354] Conversio Pauli pro IX libris denariorum Traiectensium absque defalcatione Martini et Petri solvendis annuatim. Habet exinde
litteram per fratrem Fredericum Ruter.
^aUlterius idem Amilius possidebit dictam terram prout iacet ad X
annos ab anno LXXVIII *[1378]* Petri pro XX libris denariorum

Traiectensium absque defalcatione. Per commendatorem fratren Johannem Gaude.[a]

[b]Ulterius idem Amilius possidebit dictam terram prout iacet ad X annos ab anno LXXXVIII *[1388]* Petri pro V oud scilde ende I quartier et quatuor pullis vel VI plak pro pulla sub condicione predicta. Per fratrem Johannem Haze.[b]

[c]Amilius Johannis[c]

Item ibidem <u>III iugera terre</u> iacentia inter terram heredum Elzebele Scorren a parte occidentali et terram heredum Wilhelmi Vlamync de Botternesse a parte occidentali, prout illam modo possidet Beerta relicta Ghiseberti Hugonis Cornekini ad X annos ab anno LXVIII *[1368]* Valentini pro <u>VII libris denariorum Traiectensium et III caponibus annuatim</u> absque defalcatione Martini et Petri solvendis aut cadet ab omni iure et cetera prout littera tenet. Per fratrem Hugonem.

[b]Ulterius possidebit predictam terram Maes Spronc ad X annos ab anno LXXXVIII *[1388]* Petri pro XX libris denariorum Traiectensium absque defalcatione aut cadet ab omni iure ende III capoenen. Per fratrem Johannem Haze.[b]

[c]<u>Beerta relicta Ghiseberti filii Hugonis Corniken</u>[c]

---

[a] *in a different hand (C).* [b] *in another hand.* [c] *in the right margin, in the basic hand.*

fol.112v,   <u>In Montfoerde</u>
the first lines are somewhat corroded:

Item ibidem <u>IIII iugera terre</u> [prout iacent inter terram pronunc] Johannis filii/ Scouten a parte superiori et terram Johannis Wittinc a parte inferiori, prout illam possidebat a nobis Nycolaus Wittinc. Modo possidet ea Johannes Wittinc perpetuo pro <u>V libris V grossis denariorum Traiectensium</u> annuatim Martini et Petri solvendis.

perpetuo[a]

[b]Hector Janszoon[b]

[c]Johan Wittinc[c] ·

Item in Hesewijc in eadem parrochia <u>quartale terre</u> prout iacet in uno manso terre nuncupato die Molenhoeve, inter terram Johannis dicti Veer ab utroque latere, prout illud quartale modo possidet Jacobus Cuper hereditarie pro IIII libris denariorum Traiectensium annuatim Martini et Petri aut infra quindenam postea solvendis.

[a]<u>Jacob die Cuper</u>

perpetuo[a]

Item in den Achtersloet dicte parrochie [d]
[e]Wilhelmus filius Arnoldi[e]
perpetuo[a]

---

[a] *in the left margin.* [b] *in the left margin, in a different hand.* [c] *in the left margin in the basic hand, cancelled.* [d] *not continued.* [e] *in the left margin, in a different writing from the basic hand.*

fol.113r,   In Montfoerde   CXIII
the first lines are heavily corroded:

Item [in eadem parrochia —]/ [–] prout [iacet —]/ri et terram [Hermanni dicti D— et —] prout illud modo/ possidet Ockerus filius Johannis hereditarie pro XXX [solidis denariorum Traiectensium]/ Martini et Petri solvendis.
perpetuo[a]
[b]Ocker Janszoen[b]

Item in eadem parrochia in Willescop [c]ex quadam pecia terre X grossos. Ignoratur adhuc terra et quis possidet.[c]
perpetuo[a]
Righeland[d]

Item ibidem an den Tiendwech [c]ex quadam petia terre II solidos. Ignoratur adhuc terra et possessor eius.[c]
perpetuo[a]
[d]Jan Hoebroec[d]

---

[a] *in the left margin.* [b] *in the right margin.* [c] *in different writing.* [d] *in the right margin, in the same different hand.*

fol.113v,   In Yselsteyne
the whole page is rather corroded:

[Item habet dicta domus in parrochia de Yselsteyne – in]/ [-lant XII iugera —] prout iacent/ [inter terram capituli sancti Salvatoris Traiectensis a latere superiori] et terram/ [domus sancti] Spiritus in Traiecto [a latere inferiori, prout illa] possi/debat a nobis Gerardus Goeswini. [Modo possidet] ea Henricus/ filius eiusdem Gerardi ad X annos ab anno LXVIII *[1368]* Petri/ pro XXIIj *[22.5]* antiquis scudatis auri [aut pagamento equivalenti] in Traiecto/ et XVII pullis annuatim absque defalcatione Martini et Petri solvendis aut cadet ab omni iure et cetera prout littera exinde tenet. Per fratrem Hugonem. ᵃ[Henricus filius Gerardi]ᵃ

Item ibidem opt Oudeland XII iugera terre prout iacent inter/ terram Cosini de Ysselt a parte superiori et terram heredum/ [domini Johannis de Lewenberch a parte inferiori, prout] illa/ modo possidet a [nobis Nicolaus] Olislagher ad X annos/ ab anno LXIX *[1369]* Petri pro XXIX antiquis scudatis auri aut/ pro pagamento [equivalenti in Traiecto] et XII pullis annuatim absque/ defalcatione Martini et Petri solvendis aut cadet ab omni iure et cetera prout littera exinde tenet. Per fratrem Hugonem. ᵃClaes Olislagherᵃ

ᵃ *in the left margin.*

fol.114r,   In Yselsteyne   CXIIII
the whole page is somewhat corroded:

Item ibidem [opt Oudeland VIII iugera terre prout iacent] inter/ XII iugera nostre [domus prescripta que nunc possidet Nicolaus Olislagher] a parte/ superiori et terra [comitis Hollandie a parte inferiori, que quondam] possi/debant a nobis [Nycolaus Weldighe et Egidius. Modo] possident ea Johannes/ Koeze et Egidius Wolteri adᵃ una cum dimidio manso et quatuor/ iugeribus proxime sequentibus [ad IX annos ab] anno LXI *[1361]* Pontiani et/ dabunt tam de hiis quam de aliis in universo XL libras denariorum Traiectensium et XII pullas annuatim absque defalcatione Martini et Petri solvendas aut cadent ab omni iure et cetera prout littera exinde tenet. Per fratrem Hugonem.
ᵇModo predicta VIII iugera possidebit ulterius Petrus de Muden pro IIIj *[3.5]* marc ende VIj *[6.5]* loet argenti aut pagamento equivalenti in Traiecto et II solidis et XII caponibus ad X annos ab anno LXX *[1370]* Petri. Solvet Martini et Petri aut cadet ab omni iure et cetera prout littera tenet. Per fratrem Johannem Gaude, una cum quartali ab alio latere sequenti in eodem pactu.ᵇ ᶜet post istos annos habebit X annos pro IIII marcis et XII caponibus.ᶜ
ᵈJohannes Koze et Egidius Wolteriᵈ
ᵉPetrus de Mudenᵉ

Item ibidem In die Hoghe Biezen dimidium [mansum] quem [contulerunt ordini] nostro una cum/ XII et VIII iugeribus iam proxime prescriptis frater Theodericus de A et domina Hasekina uxor eius, prout iacet inter terram Godscalci Vrenken civis Traiectensis a parte superiori et aream domine de Yselsteyne a parte inferiori, quem Nycolaus Weldighe possidebat a nobis. Modo possident eundem Johannes Koze et Egidius Wolteri una cum ceteris ad annos et sub annua pensione prescripta.

ᵇModo dictum dimidium mansum possidebit ulterius Rodolphus de Damme ad X annos ab anno LXX *[1370]* Petri pro IIj *[2.5]* marc et Ij *[1.5]* loet argenti aut pagamento equivalenti in Traiecto et III solidis et VIII caponibus annuatim Martini et Petri solvendis aut cadet ab omni iure et cetera prout littera tenet. Per fratrem Johannem Gaude.ᵇ

ᵈJohannes Koeze et Egidiusᵈ
ᵉRodolphus de Dammeᵉ

ᵃ *cancelled.* ᵇ *in a different hand (C).* ᶜ *in another hand behind the text; the item has a long brace in the left margin.* ᵈ *in the right margin in the basic hand, cancelled.* ᵉ *in the right margin, in the same hand as* ᵇ.

fol.114v,   In Benscop
the first lines are somewhat corroded:

Item habet dicta domus in parrochia de Benscop quartale terre prout iacet/ inter terram pronunc [Nycolai van der Lane a parte] superiori et terram Arnoldi/ Screvel a parte inferiori, prout illud quondam possidebant a nobis Nycolaus Weldighe et Egidius filius eius. Modo possident ᵃJohannes Koze et Egidius Wolteri una cum ceteris terrarum iugeribus ab alio prescriptis latere, ad annos et sub eadem annua pensione superius signatos.ᵃ

ᵇUlterius possidebit dictum quartale Petrus de Muden una cum VIII iugeribus ab alio latere prescriptis, ad annos et sub eadem annua pensione superius signatos.ᵇ

ᶜJohannes Koze et Egidiusᶜ
ᵈPetrus de Mudenᵈ

Item ibidem VIII hont terre prout iacent a latere septentrionali ville in Benscop inter terram pronunc Aleydis Ysebrandi a parte orientali et terram pronunc Ermegardis Kox a parte occidentali. Modo possidet eam Wilhelmus Buchinc perpetuo pro II libris X grossis annuatim Martini et Petri solvendis.

ᵉWillem Buchinc
 perpetuoᵉ

Item ibidem II iugera terre que dedit Jutta de Hermalen baguta, iacentia inter terram pronunc dicti Lyzenzaet a parte superiori et terram domini de Egmonda a parte inferiori, prout illam modo possidet Arnoldus filius Cristine hereditarie pro XX grossis annuatim denariorum Traiectensium.
<u>ᵉArnoldus filius Cristine</u>
  <u>perpetuoᵉ</u>

ᵃ *added in different writing.* ᵇ *in a different hand (C).* ᶜ *in the left margin, cancelled.* ᵈ *in the left margin, in the same hand as* ᵇ*.* ᵉ *in the left margin, in the basic hand.*

fol.115r, <u>In Benscop</u> CXV
the first part is heavily corroded:

Item ibidem [—]/ iacent [— a parte superiori et terram]/ heredum Wilhelmi [— parte inferiori —]/ possidebat a nobis [—. Modo possidebit]/ Nycolaus [Mugge ad XVI annos ab anno LXI *[1361]* Petri pro <u>XXIII</u>]/ <u>libris [denariorum</u> -- absque defalcatione infra mensem]/ post Martini et Petri solvendis [aut cadet ab omni iure et cetera prout littera] exinde tenet./ Per commendatorem de Brunsberch. ᵃUlterius idem ad X annos ab annoᵃ
ᵇModo hanc terram possidebit ulterius Henricus de Ecke ad X annos ab anno LXXVII *[1377]* Ponciani pro XVIII antiquis scudatis auri regis Francie monete aut pro pagamento equivalenti in Traiecto et VII caponibus, VII pullis absque defalcatione solvendis infra mensem post Martini et Petri vel cadet ab omni iure et cetera prout littera tenet. Per fratrem Johannem Gaude commendatorem.ᵇ
ᶜModo hanc terram possidebit ulterius Johannes Screvel ad X annos ab anno LXXXVI *[1386]* Petri pro XVII antiquis scudatis aut pagamento equivalenti in Traiecto et VII caponibus, VII pullis absque defalcatione Martini et Petri solvendis annuatim vel cadet ab omni iure et cetera prout littera tenet. Per fratrem Johannem de Arnhem.ᶜ
<u>ᵈClaes Mugge</u>
  <u>Henricus de Eckeᵈ</u>
<u>ᵉJan Screvelᵉ</u>

Item in Goudenpoel <u>quartale terre et Ij *[1.5]* iugera</u> prout iacent a parte septentrionali ville in Benscop inter terram monialium monasterii in Oudwica a parte orientali et terram domini Johannis Wirt presbyteri et Belie Scomakers a parte occidentali, prout illa Vj *[5.5]* iugera modoᶠ possidebat a nobis Ghisebertus van der Welle. Modo possidet ea Wilhelmus de Spengen pro <u>V libris V grossis denariorum</u>

<u>Traiectensium annuatim</u> Martini et Petri solvendis hereditarie.
perpetuo^g
^hWilhelmus de Spengen^h

^a *in a different hand, cancelled.* ^b *in another hand.* ^c *in yet another hand.* ^d *in the right margin, cancelled.* ^e *in the right margin, in the same hand as* ^c. ^f *cancelled.* ^g *in the left margin, in the basic hand.* ^h *in the right margin, in the basic hand.*

fol.115v,   In Benscop
the first part is heavily corroded:

[Item ibidem VII iugera terre prout iacent — filii]/ Sanderi a parte superiori —]/ que modo [possidet Theodericus Goyer — ab anno/ LXVII *[1367]* Petri pro III [antiquis scudatis — IIj *[2.5]*] solidis/ [aut pagamento equivalenti in Traiecto —] absque/ defalcatione [infra quindenam post Martini et Petri solvendis aut cadet ab omni] iure/ et cetera prout littera exinde tenet. Per fratrem Hugonem.
^aUlterius idem Theodericus et Jacobus filius eius possidebunt ad IX annos ab anno LXXVII *[1377]* Petri pro XLIII libris XV solidis, VII pullis annuatim absque defalcatione solvendis ut superius. Per commendatorem fratrem Johannem Gaude.^a
^bDirc die Goyer^b

Item ibidem <u>quartale terre</u> prout iacet inter terram pronunc Ghise-berti dicti Vunke et Arnoldi dicti Lange a parte superiori et terram Everardi Oudeland a parte inferiori, prout illud possidebat a nobis Johannes Everocker. Modo possidet Wilhelmus filius Alberti ad VI annos ab anno LXIX *[1369]* Valentini pro XXIIII libris denariorum Traiectensium et IIII caponibus annuatim absque defalcatione infra quindenam post Martini et Petri solvendis aut cadet ab omni iure, et in fine annorum dictam terram ex toto incultam resignabit, et cetera prout littera exinde tenet. Per fratrem Hugonem. Nycolaus Mugge fideiussit.
^cModo dictam terram possidebit ulterius Conradus Buys ad X annos ab anno LXXXVI *[1386]* Petri pro XXIX libris X solidis pagamenti Traiectensis et IIII caponibus absque defalcatione Martini et Petri solvendis aut cadet ab omni iure et cetera prout littera tenet. Per fratrem Johannem de Aernhem.^c
^dWillem Alberts zoen^d
^e<u>Conradus Buys</u>^e

^a *in a different hand (C).* ^b *in the left margin, in the basic hand.* ^c *in another hand (E).* ^d *in the left margin, cancelled.* ^e *in the left margin, in the same hand as* ^c.

fol.116r,   In Benscop   CXVI
the first lines are somewhat corroded:

Item ibidem [V iugera] et II hont terre que emimus erga pro/[cura-
tores —] ibidem prout iacent inter terram pronunc ᵃJacobi Stelle a
parte orientali et terram Theoderici filii Arnoldi a parte occidentali.
Quam terram prescriptam una cum XVIj *[16.5]* iugeribus postea
scriptis nunc possidebunt ulterius heredes Jacobi Koeze ad X annos
ab anno LXXI *[1371]* Purificatione Marie, et solvent tam de hac
terra quam de aliis insimul LXXXI libras et XV solidos pagamenti
Traiectensis et XVII capones et V pullas annuatim Martini et Petri
solvendas vel cadent ab omni iure et cetera prout littera exinde tenet.
Per fratrem Thomam dispensatorem.ᵃ
ᵇCob Koezeᵇ
ᵈheredes eiusᵈ

Item ibidem V iugera terre que dederunt Aleydis [et Machteldis Tho-
me]/ prout iacent inter terram heredum Arnoldi de [Scraghen ab
utroque]/ [latere] a superiori scilicet et inferiori, prout illa [modo
possidet a nobis]/ relicta eiusdem Arnoldi de Scraghen ad X [annos
ab anno/ LXI *[1361]* Ponciani pro IX libris denariorum Traiectensium, II caponibus, II pullis annuatim absque defalcatione Martini et
Petri solvendis aut cadet ab omni iure et cetera prout littera tenet. Per
fratrem Hugonem.
ᵃModo predictam terram ulterius possidebunt Theodericus Scriver et
Aleidis filia Arnoldi Scraghen ad X annos ab anno LXXI *[1371]*
Valentini pro XXVI libris V solidis et II caponibus et II pullis annuatim Martini et Petri solvendis absque defalcatione aut cadent ab omni
iure. Per fratrem Thomam.ᵃ
ᶜrelicta Arnoldi de Scraghenᶜ
ᵈDirc Scriver ende Aleid Scraghenᵈ

ᵃ *continued in a different hand (B).* ᵇ *in the right margin, erased.* ᶜ *in the right
margin, cancelled.* ᵈ *in the right margin, in the same hand as* ᵃ.

fol.116v,   In Benscop
the whole page is somewhat corroded:

[Item ibidem VIj *[6.5]* iugera terre prout iacent inter —]/ [XIIIj
[13.5] iugeribus —]/ [iacent inter terram Florencii filii Loefs a parte
superiori et terram heredum Wilhelmi]/ [filii Hasekine a parte inferiori. Idem Gerardus Kivit modo possidet]/ ad X annos ab anno LX

[1360] Agnetis [pro XIIII libris denariorum Traiectensium et VII]/ caponibus absque defalcatione Martini et Petri solvendis aut cadet ab omni iure et cetera prout littera exinde tenet. Per fratrem Hugonem. ᵃModo predictam terram possidet Gerardus de Veno prout iacet inter terram pronunc dicti Loef filii Florencii a parte superiori et terram Henrici de Ecke a parte inferiori ad X annos ab anno LXXI *[1371]* Purificatione Marie pro XXXV libris et XV solidis pagamenti Traiectensis et VII caponibus absque defalcatione Martini et Petri aut cadet ab omni iure. Per fratrem Thomam.ᵃ
ᵇUlterius idem Gerardus possidebit modo ad X annos ab anno LXXVII *[1377]* Agnetis pro XLII libris V solidis pagamenti Traiectensis et VII caponibus absque defalcatione et cetera prout littera tenet. Per fratrem Johannem Gaude commendatorem.ᵇ
ᶜGerardus Kivitᶜ
ᵈGerardus de Venoᵈ

[Item ibidem dimidium mansum] terre prout iacet communi sulcu cum/ alio [dimidio manso terre] spectanti ad heredes Maechelmi de Busco/ [in iurisdictione domini] de Yselsteine. Cum integro manso propius iacet/ terra canonicorum in Yselsteyne a parte [superiori et terra Nicolai Vunke]/ filii Nycolai a parte inferiori, prout illum dimidium mansum posside-/[bant a nobis Grieta] relicta Hermanni Stamers, Hermannus et Bya/ [eius liberi] ad vitam eorum trium pro IX libris bonorum et VII pullis annuatim/ [per fratrem Henricum de Orscoten] eis locatum. Modo possident eundem Her/mannus Stamer et Bya eius soror ad vitam eorum <u>pro VIII cum dimidio antiquis scudatis auri aut cum</u> pagamento equivalenti <u>et VIII pullis annuatim</u> infra tres septimanas post Martini et Petri solvendis aut cadent ab omni iure et cetera prout littera exinde tenet. Per fratrem Hugonem sic renovatum.
ᵃModo dictam terram possidebit ulterius Wilhelmus filius Ghisberti ad X annos ab anno LXXIII *[1373]* Petri pro X antiquis scudatis aut pagamento equivalenti et VIII pullis annuatim absque defalcatione solvendis Martini et Petri vel cadet ab omni iure et cetera prout littera tenet. Per fratrem Thomam dispensatorem.ᵃ
ᵉUlterius idem Wilhelmus et Hermannus Stamer eius filius possident dictam terram ad X annos ab anno LXXXIII *[1383]* Petri pro XI antiquis scudatis VIII pullis absque defalcatione.ᵉ
ᶠUlterius idem Hermanus Stamer ad X annos ab anno XCII *[1392]* Petri pro XI antiquis scudatis ende VIII pullis ut supra prout littera tenet.ᶠ
obieruntᵍ
ᶜ<u>Hermannus Stamer et Bya eius uxor ad</u> vitam eorumᶜ

^hWillem Ghisbert zoen^h
ⁱWilhelmus Spengen et Hermannus Stamer eius filiusⁱ

---

^a *in a different hand (B).* ^b *in another hand.* ^c *in the left margin in the basic hand, cancelled.* ^d *in the left margin, in the same hand as* ^a. ^e *in yet another hand (D).* ^f *in yet a different hand.* ^g *in the left margin, in still a different hand.* ^h *in the left margin, like* ^d *in the same hand as* ^a, *but cancelled.* ⁱ *in the left margin, in the same hand as* ^e.

fol.117r, <u>In Benscop</u> CXVII
the first part is heavily corroded:

[Item ibidem —]/ [—]/ [— a parte meridionali —]/ die [— a parte septentrionali —]/ [— Gerardus Jonghe ad X annos ab]/ [anno LXVIII *[1368]* Valentini pro <u>XXXI antiquis scudatis auri</u>]/ aut cum pagamento equivalenti solvendis et <u>XVI caponibus</u> annuatim infra quindenam post Martini et Petri solvendis aut cadet ab omni iure. Non conburet nisi IIII iugera si volucrit semel et cetera prout littera exinde tenet. Per fratrem Hugonem.
^a[Gherardus Jonghe]^a

Item ibidem <u>quartale terre</u> prout iacet in ^btribus^b ^cIIII^{or}.^c campis distinctis a latere septentrionali ville in Benscop, inter terram pronunc Hugonis filii Theoderici a parte superiori et terram heredum Johannis Pot civis Traiectensis a parte inferiori, prout illud possidebat a nobis Wilhelmus Weldighe. Modo possidet dictum quartale Reynerus filius Hannen ad X annos ab anno LX *[1360]* [-] pro XXIX loet et quartale unius loet argenti et IIII pullis annuatim infra quindenam post Martini et Petri solvendis absque defalcatione aut cadet ab omni iure et cetera prout littera exinde tenet. Per fratrem Hugonem.
^dUlterius possidebit dictam terram ad X annos ab anno LXXVI *[1376]* Petri pro XXVII libris et IIII pullis absque defalcatione prout littera tenet. Per fratrem Johannem Gaude commendatorem.^d
^a<u>Reynerus filius Hannen</u>^a

---

^a *in the right margin.* ^b *cancelled.* ^c *written above the cancelled word.* ^d *in a different hand (C).*

fol.117v, <u>In Benscop</u>
the first part is heavily corroded:

[Item ibidem dimidium quartale prout iacet —]/ [— inter terram Alberti —]/ [—] de Yselsteyne a parte [—]/ [dominii de Yselsteyne

a parte occidentali —]/ a nobis ulterius Wilhelmus Smale. [Modo possidebit dominus de Egmonda]/ et Yselsteyne <u>pro II libris X grossis</u> [annuatim Martini et Petri solvendis perpetuo].
^a[dominus de Yselsteyne] et Egmonda
<u>perpetuo</u>^a

Item ibidem <u>dimidium quartale</u> prout iacet iacet a latere septentrionali ville de Benscop inter terram pronunc Arnoldi van den Hoeve a parte orientali et terram domini de Vianen a parte occidentali, quod modo possidet a nobis Jacobus van den Hoeve hereditarie <u>pro X grossis</u> annuatim solvendis Martini et Petri.
^b<u>Jacobus van den Hove</u>^b
<u>hereditarie</u>^a
^cHenricus van den Hove^c

Item ibidem <u>quartale terre</u> quod fuit domine Hasekine de A et filiorum eius, prout iacet communi sulcu cum XIII iugeribus spectantibus pro nunc ad relictam Wilhelmi de Snellenberch et heredes eius a parte septentrionali ville de Benscop, quibus XIII iugeribus propius iacet a superiori parte terra Reyneri Kozen et ab inferiori parte terra domine de Yselsteyne. Quod modo possidet relicta Wilhelmi de Snellenberch hereditarie <u>pro V libris V grossis</u> annuatim.
^aRelicta Wilhelmi de Snellenberch
<u>hereditarie</u>^a

---

^a *in the left margin.* ^b *in the left margin, cancelled.* ^c *in a different hand.*

on a loose leaf of paper between fol.117v. and 118r, in a 15th-century hand:

Een viertel lands dat toe plach te horen vrouwe Hasekyn vander A ende hoerre kynder, also alst gelegen is in gemengder voren mit XIII mergen lands nu tobehorende Willems wedu van Snellenberch ende synre erfgenamen aen die noertsijde des kirspels van Benscop, welke XIII mergen aen dat over eynde naest gelandt is Reyner Koze, ende an dat neder eynde die vrouwe van Yselsteyne, dat nu bruyct Willems wedu van Snellenberch erfliken voer V libris V groten jaerlix.
Item hier na haddet Peter Snyder ende Arnt van Welle,
Item hier na haddet Albert die Scillingemaker ende Heyn Wyse.

fol.118r,   In Benscop   CXVIII
the first lines are rather corroded:

[Item ibidem quartale terre quod fuit eiusdem domine Hasekine]/ [et filiorum eius prout iacet.]
[a][Aleydis Hildebrandi] Wolfs[a]
hereditarie[b]

Item ibidem X iugera terre prout iacent inter terram pronunc Jacobi Stellen a parte superiori et terram Petri Blome a parte inferiori, que possidebat a nobis Nycolaus de Troyen. Modo possidet ea Gheza relicta eiusdem Nycolai ad X annos ab anno LXIII *[1363]* Valentini pro XXVI libris denariorum Traiectensium et X caponibus annuatim absque defalcatione Martini et Petri solvendis aut cadet ab omni iure. Non conburet. Medietatem incultam resignabit et cetera prout littera exinde tenet. Per fratrem Hugonem.
[c]Ulterius eadem Gheza possidebit dictam terram ad X annos ab anno LXXIII *[1373]* Petri pro XVI antiquis scudatis aut pagamento equivalenti et X caponibus annuatim absque defalcatione solvendis Martini et Petri vel cadet ab omni iure prout littera tenet. Per fratrem Thomam dispensatorem.[c]
[d]Ulterius possidebit Henricus de Troyen ad X annos ab anno LXXXIII *[1383]* Petri pro XVj *[15.5]* antiquis scudatis et X caponibus annuatim absque defalcatione solvendis Martini et Petri vel cadet ab omni iure prout littera tenet.[d]
[e]Gheza van Troyen[e]
[f]Henric van Troyen[f]

---

[a] *in the right margin.* [b] *in the left margin.* [c] *in a different hand (B).* [d] *in another hand (D or E).* [e] *in the right margin, cancelled.* [f] *in the right margin, in the same hand as* [d].

fol.118v,   In Benscop
the first lines are heavily corroded, the second part only to some extent:

[Item ibidem — iugera terre —]/ [prout iacent inter terram domus leprosorum extra muros Traiectenses a parte su]/[periori et terram nostre domus quam pronunc possident Hermannus Stamer] et Bya/ [eius soror a parte inferiori, prout illa possidebat a nobis Wilhelmus]/ [de Snellenberch. Modo possidet] ea Nycolaus de Jutfaes ad VI annos ab anno LXIIII *[1364]* Petri pro XII libris XIII solidis et V caponibus annuatim absque defalcatione Martini et Petri solvendis aut cadet

ab omni iure et cetera prout littera exinde tenet. Per fratrem Hugonem.
ªNycolaus de [Jutfaes]ª

[Item ibidem <u>quartale terre</u> prout iacet inter terram domini] de Eg-
monda/ a parte [superiori et terram Everardi filii] Berneri a parte
inferiori, prout/ [illud possidebat a nobis Arnoldus de Scraghen.]
Modo possidet/ [illud Theodericus Scriver] ad X annos ab anno
LXVIII *[1368]* Petri/ [pro <u>II marcis et III loet argenti</u> ant.ᵇ aut cum
pagamento equi/[valenti et <u>II caponibus et II pullis</u> annuatim] absque defalcatione Martini et Petri solvendis/ aut [cadet ab omni iure.
Non conburet et cetera] prout littera exinde tenet./ Per fratrem Hugonem.
ª<u>Theodericus Scriver</u>ª

ª *in the left margin.* ᵇ *cancelled.*

fol.119r,   <u>In Benscop</u>   CXIX
the whole page is heavily corroded:

Item ibidem [-j *[-.5]* iugera terre prout iacent inter terram nostre
domus quam]/ nunc possidet [—]/ a parte orientali [et terram —
a parte occiden]/tali prout ill[—]/ [- Jacobus Koze ad X annos
ab anno LXVII *[1367]* Petri pro X]/ [libris VIII solidis − denariis et
[—] absque defalcatione Martini et Petri]/ solvendis aut cadet ab
omni iure. [Non conburet et cetera prout littera exinde tenet.]/ Per
fratrem Hugonem.
ªUlterius predictam terram possidebunt heredes Jacobi Koze adᵇ una
cum V iugeribus et II hont superius signatis ad X annos ab anno
LXXI *[1371]* Purificatione Marie sub annua pensione superius iuxta
aliam terram signata. Per fratrem Thomam.ª
ᶜ<u>Cop Koeze</u>ᶜ
<u>heredes</u>ᵈ

Item ibidem [<u>quartale terre</u> prout iacet —]/ foerde a parte [superiori
—]/ hoeve a parte [inferiori —]/ Schuerzac ad [X —]/ <u>libris I
talento</u> cere et IIII caponibus —]/ solvendis aut [cadet ab omni iure.
— Per fratrem Hugonem.]
ᵉUlterius possidebit ad X annos ab anno [—] pro/ XXVII libris, I
talento cere, IIII caponibus annuatim Martini et Petri solvendis/ aut
cadet ab omni iure. Per fratrem Johannem commendatorem.ᵉ ᶠVen-
dita est hec terra.ᶠ

^cJan Schuerzac^c
^gvendita est.^g

---

^a *in a different hand (B).* ^b *cancelled.* ^c *in the right margin, in the basic hand.* ^d *in the right margin, in the same hand as* ^a. ^e *in another hand (C).* ^f *in yet another hand.* ^g *in the right margin, in the same hand as* ^f*, but in different writing and ink.*

fol.119v,   In Benscop
the whole page is heavily corroded:

[Item ibidem II iugera et VII hont terre —] Bloc de Y/selsteyne prout iacent inter terram Johannis filii — a superiori parte]/ [et — a parte inferiori, prout illa possidebat a nobis]/ [Cristina Berinxs. Modo possidebit a nobis Nycolau]s Henrici ad/ [X annos ab anno LX *[1360]* Petri pro VII libris XIII solidis et V caponibus]/ [absque defalcatione Martini et Petri solvendis aut cadet ab omni iure. Non conburet]/ [et cetera prout littera exinde tenet. Per fratrem Hugonem.
^aUlterius possidebit dictam terram Gerardus filius Rotardi ad X annos ab anno LXXX *[1380]* Petri pro V antiquis scudatis auri et IIII caponibus, absque defalcatione solvendis Martini et Petri vel cadet ab omni iure prout littera tenet. Per commendatorem.^a
^bClaes Henrix zoen^b
^cGherid Rotard^c

[—] terram heredum domini Symo/[—] terram nostre domus quam/ [—] Theodericus Witte/ [— possidet] a nobis Gode/[—] ad X annos ab anno LXIX *[1369]*/ Petri [pro — et VII solidis denariorum Traiectensium et XVI] pullis annuatim absque/ defalcatione [Martini et Petri solvendis aut] cadet ab omni iure. Non conburet et cetera prout/ [littera exinde tenet. Per fratrem Hugonem.]
^aUlterius idem Godefridus et Ghertrudis eius uxor possidebunt dictam terram prout iacet pro nunc inter terram Magni Jacobi dicti Ver pistoris a parte superiori et terram nostre domus a parte inferiori ad X annos ab anno LXXIX *[1379]* Petri pro XXIII antiquis scudatis auri et XVI pullis annuatim absque defalcatione et cetera prout littera tenet. Per fratrem Johannem commendatorem.^a
^dModo dictam terram ulterius possidebit Henricus Hollander filius Godefridi ad X annos ab anno LXXXVI *[1386]* Petri pro XX antiquis scudatis auri monete Cesaris aut Francie vel pagamentum equivalens pro eisdem et XVI pullis absque defalcatione et cetera prout littera tenet. Per fratrem Johannem de Aernhem.^d

^bGodefridus filius Henrici Hollander^b
^eHenric Hollander <u>Goderds zoen</u>^e

---

^a *in a different hand (C).* ^b *in the left margin, cancelled.* ^c *in the left margin, in the same hand as ^a.* ^d *in another hand (E).* ^e *in the left margin, in the same hand as ^d.*

on a loose piece of paper between fol.119v. and 120r, in a 15th-century hand:

Item wy bevynden in onsen liggher in welke al onss convents rynten ende bepalynghen ghescreven staen, dat wy hebben in Benscop II merghen lants ende VII hont, daer bouwen naest ghelant was inden jaere ons Heren dusent vierhondert^a driehondert ende LX *[1365]* Jan Evertszoen ende beneden die kercke van Benscop ende bruckten op die tijt een van ons convents weghen gheheyten Kristina Berinx; daer na brucktent Claes Henrixzoen; daer nae heeft dat selver lant van ons convent gebruck Gerijt Rotertszoen.

Item daer langhe jaeren na bevynden wy om der kortheyt et cetera dat ons convent dit voerscreven lant verhuert hebben Herman Evertszoen alsoe als gheleghen is ende bouwen naest ghelant was her Lodewick van Montfort ende beneden die kerkcke in Benscop ende doe screfmen Dusent vierhondert ende XLI *[1441]*.

Item daer nae heeft dijt voerscreven lant van onss ghebruckt ende gheheuert Gerbrant Reynnerszoen inden Jaer van LIII *[1454]*.

Item daer nae heeft dijt voerscreven lant van onss ghebruckt ende gheheuert Heyn Loefzoen omme III Hollandse riders ende III honre inden jaere van LXIII *[1463]* ende daer nae ende ist dijt voerscreven lant nyet verhuert alsoe dat wy daer op des tijt nyment aen en kennen te hebben.

---

^a *cancelled.*

fol.120r, <u>In Benscop</u> CXX
the first part is heavily corroded:

Item ibidem [XIIII iugera terre —]/ [——]/ [——]/ prout illa —]/ [filius Wolteri. Modo possident ea Gherardus Jonge et Theodericus]/ Wittecouse ad X [annos ab anno LXVII *[1367]* Petri pro -]/ <u>libris X solidis et XIIII caponibus</u> [annuatim absque defalcatione Martini et Petri solvendis/ ab^a aut cadent^b ab omni iure et cetera prout littera tenet. Per fratrem Hugonem.
^cUlterius medietatem dicte terre scilicet VII iugera possidebit Gode-

fridus filius Jacobi ad X annos ab anno LXXXVI *[1386]* Petri pro
XLIIII libris VII caponibus Martini et Petri solvendis. Per fratrem
Johannem de Arnhem.^c

[———]^d

^eGodert Jacobs <u>zoen</u>^e

Item ibidem <u>II iugera terre</u> que dedit [Hasekina] de A prout iacent
communi sulcu in VII iugeribus cum bagutis in Traiecto a parte
septentrionali ville in Benscop, quibus VII iugeribus propius iacet
terra domini de Yselsteyne a parte superiori et terra canonicorum in
Yselsteyne a parte inferiori, que II iugera possidebat a nobis Ghertrudis relicta Reyneri Sculteti. Modo possidet ea Johannes Bloc filius
Gerardi Boudewini ad *X* annos ab anno LXIX *[1369]* Petri pro <u>I
marca boni argenti</u> annuatim aut pro pagamento equivalenti in
Traiecto, absque defalcatione Martini et Petri solvendis aut cadet ab
omni iure et cetera prout littera exinde tenet. Per fratrem Hugonem.
^fUlterius possidebit Johannes Nicolai Wittinx dictam terram ad X
annos ab anno LXXVI *[1376]* Petri pro XV libris denariorum
Traiectensium sub condicione ut littera tenet. Per fratrem Johannem
Gaude commendatorem.^f

^dJohannes Bloc^d
^eJohannes Wittinc^e

---

^a *cancelled.* ^b cadet *ms.* ^c *in a different hand.* ^d *in the right margin, cancelled.* ^e *in
the right margin, in the same hand as* ^f. ^f *in another hand (C).*

fol.120v,   In Benscop
the first part is heavily corroded:

Item ibidem [—] bi de/ [———]/ [———]/ [—] tribus/ [– marcis
argenti et IIII caponibus annuatim absque defalcatione infra]/ [quin-
denam post Martini et Petri solvendis aut cadet ab omni iure]/ [et
cetera prout littera exinde tenet. Per fratrem] Hugonem.
^aUlterius possidebit dictam terram ad X annos ab anno LXXVI
[1376] Petri pro XXXV libris denariorum Traiectensium et IIII caponibus, absque defalcatione solvendis Martini et Petri vel cadet ab
omni iure prout littera tenet. Per commendatorem fratrem Johannem
Gaude.^a
^bUlterius possidebit dictam terram Petrus de Vuren filius predicti
Jacobi ad X annos ab anno LXXXVI *[1386]* Petri pro XXXV libris
pagamenti Traiectensis IIII caponibus sub condicionibus ut littera
exinde tenet. Per fratrem Johannem de Aernhem.^b

^cJacobus [—]^c
^dPetrus de Vuren^d

---

^a *in a different hand (C).* ^b *in another hand (E).* ^c *in the left margin, cancelled.* ^d *in the left margin, in the same hand as* ^b.

fol.121r,   In Pulsbroec   CXXI
the whole page is highly corroded:

[Item habet domus nostra in parrochia de Pulsbroec mansum]/ terre [— prout iacet inter terram nostre]/ [domus quam nunc possident Gerardus Doure et Arnoldus eius frater a su]/periori parte [et — filii Gherardi – a parte inferiori pronunc]/ eundem mansum. Modo [possidet a nobis Wilhelmus] filius Johannis de Foreest.
^aUlterius possidebit hanc terram Gerardus uten Winckel ad X annos ab anno XIIII^c *[1400]* Petri pro XIX antiquis scudatis, VIII caponibus VIII pullis.^a
^bWilhelmus filius Johannis de Foreest^b

Item ibidem [tria quartalia terre] prout iacent inter terram domine de Yselsteyne/ a latere superiori et [terram nostre domus] quam nunc possidet Wilhelmus/ filius [Johannis de Foreest] a parte inferiori, prout illa modo possident a/ nobis Gerardus Doure et [Arnoldus frater eius] ad X annos ab anno/ LX *[1360]* pro XXVI libris denariorum Traiectensium et XII caponibus annuatim absque defalcatione Martini et Petri solvendis aut cadent ab omni iure et cetera prout littera exinde tenet. Per fratrem Hugonem.
^cModo dictam terram possidebit ulterius Matheus Saffentiin ad X annos ab anno LXXII *[1372]* Petri pro LX libris denariorum dicte monete et VI caponibus, VI pullis annuatim absque defalcatione solvendis Martini et Petri, vel cadet ab omni iure prout littera tenet. Per fratrem Thomam dispensatorem.^c
^dGerardus Doure^d
^eMatheus Saffentiin^e

---

^a *in a different hand.* ^b *in the right margin, in the basic hand.* ^c *in another hand (B).* ^d *in the right margin in the basic hand, cancelled.* ^e *in the right margin, in the same hand as* ^c.

fol.121v, <u>In Pulsbroec</u>
the whole page is somewhat corroded:

Item ibídem <u>VII iugera et II hont terre</u> prout iacent inter terram
pronunc Andrie filii Gherwardi a parte superiori et terram Regularium canonicorum in Traiecto a parte inferiori, prout illa modo possidet a nobis Kyel Aernds zoen ad X annos ab anno LXVI *[1366]* Petri
pro <u>XXII libris denariorum Traiectensium, IIII talentis cere et VII
caponibus</u> annuatim Martini et Petri solvendis, aut cadet ab omni
iure et cetera prout littera exinde tenet. Per fratrem Hugonem. ^aMo-
do possidebit dictam terram Mauritius Nycolay ad X annos ab anno
LXXVI *[1376]* Petri pro XL libris III solidis ende IIII denariis et IIII
pont cere et VII caponibus annuatim ab defalcatione Martini et Petri
solvendis aut cadet ab omni iure et cetera prout littera tenet. Per
fratrem Johannem Gaude commendatorem.^a
^b<u>Kyel Aernds zoen</u>^b
^cMouwerens Claes zoen^c

Item ibidem <u>XIIj *[12.5]* iugera et XV scacht lands</u> prout iacent/ et
nunc mensurata sunt, inter terram [-]kori filii Hermanni a/ parte
superiori et terram [Theoderici filii Gerardi] a parte inferiori, prout/
illa modo possidet a nobis idem Theodericus filius [Gerardi] ad/ X
annos ab anno LXVII *[1367]* Petri [pro] <u>XXII antiquis scudatis/
auri legalis ponderis et monete</u> aut pro pagamento equivalenti <u>in
Traiecto et IIj *[2.5]* solidis pagamenti Traiectensis et XIIII pullis</u>
annuatim absque defalcatione terminis consuetis solvendis aut cadet
ab omni iure et cetera prout littera tenet. Per fratrem Hugonem.
^aUlterius idem Gerardus possidebit hanc terram ad X annos ab anno
LXXVI *[1376]* Petri pro LXXV libris pagamenti Traiectensis et
XIIII pullis annuatim absque defalcatione Martini et Petri solvendis,
vel cadet ab omni iure et cetera prout littera tenet. Per fratrem Johannem Gaude commendatorem.^a
^dUlterius dictam terram post possidebit Arnoldus van den Hove filius
supradicti Theoderici ad XI annos ab anno LXXXV *[1385]* Petri
pro LXXV libris denariorum Traiectensium et XIIII pullis annuatim
absque defalcatione Martini et Petri solvendis. Per fratrem Johannem
de Arnhem dispensatorem.^d
^b<u>Dirc Gheridszoen</u>^b
^eAernd van den <u>Hove Dirix zoen</u>^e

---

^a *in a different hand.* ^b *in the left margin, cancelled.* ^c *in the left margin, in the same
hand as* ^a. ^d *in another hand (D).* ^e *in the left margin, in the same hand as* ^d.

fol.122r,   In Pulsbroec   CXXII
the whole page is rather corroded:

Item [ibidem <u>mansum terre</u> prout iacet inter terram Andree filii
Gher]/[wardi a parte superiori et terram Theoderici filii Gherardi a
parte in]/[feriori, prout eundem modo possidet a nobis Johannes Boc
ad X]/ annos ab anno LX *[1360]* Petri pro <u>XXXI libris denariorum
Traiectensium et [XVI pullis]</u>/ annuatim absque defalcatione solvendis Martini et Petri aut cadet ab omni iure et cetera prout littera
tenet. Per fratrem Hugonem.
[a]Ulterius dictam terram possidebit Johannes de Vliete ad X annos ab
anno LXX *[1370]* Petri pro V marcis et IX loet argenti et VII denariis et XVI caponibus annuatim absque defalcatione Martini et Petri
solvendis aut cadet ab omni iure et cetera prout littera tenet. Per
fratrem Johannem Gaude dispensatorem.[a]
[b]Jan Bocke[b]
[c]Johannes de Vliete[c]

Item ibidem <u>quartale terre</u> prout iacet inter terram ecclesie de Puls/
broec a parte superiori et terram Jacobi de Rewijc a parte inferiori,
prout illud possidebat a nobis Wilhelmus filius Takonis. Modo pos/
sidet Johannes filius Gerardi [Ghiselmaers] ad XI annos ab anno/
LXIIII *[1364]* Purificatione Marie pro <u>VIII libris denariorum Traiectensium, IIII talentis cere et IIII caponibus annuatim</u> absque defalcatione Martini et Petri solvendis aut cadet ab omni iure et cetera prout
littera tenet. Per fratrem Hugonem.
[d]Johannis filius Gerardi Ghiselmaers[d]

---

[a] *in a different hand (C).* [b] *in the right margin, cancelled.* [c] *in the right margin, in the
same hand as* [a]. [d] *in the right margin, in the basic hand.*

fol.122v,   In Pulsbroec
the first part is heavily corroded, the second part to some extent:

[Item ibidem quartale terre prout iacet —]/ [——]/ [——]/ [Modo
possidet][a] [b]vendita est[b]
[c][—]
perpetuo[c]

[Item ibidem <u>quartale terre</u> prout iacet] inter terram heredum domini Ge/[rardi de Vliete militis a parte superiori] et terram collegii
sancte/ [Marie Traiectensis a parte inferiori prout] quondam a nobis

posside/[bant Symon Rodekin et eius uxor. Modo] possidet Johannes filius/ [Wilhelmi ad X annos ab anno LXIII *[1363]* Petri pro VIII libris denariorum [Traiectensium et IIII caponibus annuatim absque defalcatione] infra quindenam post Martini/ et [Petri solvendis aut cadet ab omni iure.] Medietatem incultam resig/nabit et cetera prout littera exinde tenet. Per fratrem Hugonem.

[d]Modo dictam terram possidebit ulterius Nicolaus filius Sanderi ad X annos ab anno LXXIII *[1373]* Petri pro XVI libris, IIII caponibus annuatim absque defalcatione solvendis Martini et Petri, vel cadet ab omni iure prout littera tenet. Per Thomam dispensatorem.[d]

[e]Ulterius idem Nicolaus possidet dictam terram ad X annos ab anno LXXXIII *[1383]* Petri pro V antiquis scudatis, IIII caponibus absque defalcatione.[e]

[f]Johannes filius Wilhelmi[f]
[g]Nicolaus filius Sanderi[g]

---

[a] *not continued.* [b] *in a different hand.* [c] *in the left margin, in the basic hand.* [d] *in another hand (B).* [e] *in yet another hand.* [f] *in the left margin, cancelled.* [g] *in the left margin, in the same hand as* [d].

fol.123r,   In Pulsbroec   CXXIII
the first line is heavily corroded:

[Item ibidem —]/ iacet in dominio de Yselsteyne inter terram Johannis de Almelo a parte superiori et terram Johannis Gerardi et Arnoldi filii Theoderici communi sulcu iacentem a parte inferiori, prout idem quartale possidebat a nobis Ghisebertus filius Johannis. Modo possidebit illud Elysabet Johannis Rozemonds ad X annos ab anno LXIX *[1369]* Petri pro Ij *[1.5]* marcis argenti et IIII caponibus annuatim aut pro pagamento equivalenti infra quindenam post Martini et Petri solvendis aut cadet ab omni iure et cetera prout littera exinde tenet. Per fratrem Hugonem.

[a]Modo possidebit dictam terram Johannes filius Sanderi ad X annos ab anno LXXXIII *[1383]* Petri pro V antiquis scudatis et IIII caponibus absque defalcatione.[a]

[b]Elysabet Johannis Rozemonds[b]
[c]Johannes filius Sanderi[c]

Item ibidem Vj *[5.5]* iugera terre prout iacent inter terram heredum Wilhelmi filii Takonis a parte superiori et terram monialium monasterii sancti Servacii Traiectensis a parte inferiori, prout iacent in dominio de Yselsteyne et illa quondam possidebat a nobis Johannes

filius Arnoldi. Modo possidet ea Hildegondis filia Nycolai Wantmans
ad X annos ab anno LXVII *[1367]* Petri pro XIj *[11.5]* antiquis
scudatis auri aut pro pagamento equivalenti in Traiecto et III pullis
annuatim absque defalcatione Martini et Petri solvendis aut cadet ab
omni iure. Non conburet. Medietatem incultam resignabit et cetera
prout littera tenet. Per fratrem Hugonem.
ᵈUlterius dictam terram possidebit Jacobus de Rewijc ad X annos ab
anno LXXV *[1375]* Petri pro XXXII libris denariorum Traiectensium et VI pullis absque defalcatione et cetera prout littera tenet. Per
fratrem Johannem Gaude commendatorem.ᵈ
ᵇHildegond Claes Wantmans dochterᵇ
ᵉJacob van Rewijcᵉ

ᵃ *in a different hand (D).* ᵇ *in the right margin, cancelled.* ᶜ *in the right margin, in the
same hand as* ᵃ. ᵈ *in another hand (C).* ᵉ *in the right margin, in the same hand as* ᵈ.

fol.123v, In Lopic
the first line is heavily corroded:

[Item —]/ Nesse XXV iugera terre que fuerunt fratris Theoderici de
A et domine Hasekine uxoris sue prout iacent inter terram pronunc
Ghiseberti filii Wilhelmi de Vliete a parte superiori et terram capituli
sancte Marie Traiectensis a parte inferiori, prout illa quondam possidebat a nobis Pelegrinus filius Gerardi. Modo possidet ea Theodericus filius Nycolai ad XII annos ab anno LXVII *[1367]* Valentini pro
XCVI libris denariorum Traiectensium et XII caponibus, XII pullis
absque defalcatione Martini et Petri solvendis aut cadet ab omni iure
et cetera prout littera exinde tenet. Per fratrem Hugonem.
ᵃModo dictam terram possidebit ulterius Theodericus filius Wilhelmi
ad XII annos ab anno LXXV *[1375]* Petri pro C.XXV libris VI
solidis VIII denariis, XII caponibus, XII pullis absque defalcatione
Martini et Petri solvendis vel cadet ab omni iure et cetera prout littera
tenet. Per fratrem Johannem Gaude vicecommendatorem.ᵃ
ᵇUlterius possidebit dictam terram ad X annos ab anno LXXXVII
[1387] Petri pro C.XXX libris pachts ghelds, XII caponibus, XII
pullis absque defalcatione sub condicione prout littera tenet. Per fratrem Johannem de Arnem.ᵇ
ᶜDirc Claes zoenᶜ
ᵈDirc Willems zoenᵈ

Item ibidem VIII [iugera terre prout] iacent streckende an den

Leckedijc,/ quibus a parte orientali propius iacet die Uutwech et a parte occidentali dominus de Vianen, prout ea modo possidet domicella Ghertrudis filia Gerardi Jonghen pro X libris X grossis annuatim Martini et Petri solvendis hereditarie. ᶜModo Jonghe Willem vanden Vliet.ᶜ
ᶠGhertrudis filia Gerardi Jongen
hereditarieᶠ

ᵃ *in a different hand (C).* ᵇ *in another hand (E).* ᶜ *in the left margin, cancelled.* ᵈ *in the left margin, in the same hand as* ᵃ*.* ᵉ *in yet another hand.* ᶠ *in the left margin, in the basic hand.*

fol.124r.   In Lopic   CXXIIII

Item ibidem II iugera terre que dedit quondam Agnesa uxor quondam Petri Jonge, prout iacent inter terram pronunc Conradi filii Jacobi de Damme a parte superiori et inferius Ghisebertus filius Ecberti de Damme propius iacet cum terra quam tenet a domino de Vianen, prout illa modo possidet presbyter capelle in Lopic pro tempore existens pro XV grossis annuatim Martini et Petri solvendis perpetue.
perpetuoᵃ
ᵇpresbyter capelle in Lopicᵇ

Item ibidem XIX iugera et II hont terre data quondam per fratrem Theodericum de A et Hasekinam uxorem suam et pueros suos prout iacent et mensurata sunt inter terram curati parrochialis ecclesie in Lopic a latere orientali et terram pronunc ᶜ a parte occidentali, prout modo possidet ea Florencius die Jonge ad X annos ab anno LXIX *[1369]* Valentini et solvet annuatim exinde XII marcas argenti aut pagamentum equivalens in Traiecto et IX capones et IX pullas absque defalcatione infra quindenam post Martini et Petri aut cadet ab omni iure et cetera prout littera tenet. Per fratrem Hugonem.
ᵈUlterius possidebit idem Florens dictam terram ad decem annos ab anno LXXIII *[1373]* Petri pro C libris denariorum Traiectensium et IX caponibus et IX pullis annuatim absque defalcatione Martini et Petri solvendis aut cadet ab omni iure.ᵈ
ᵉUlterius possidet post annos Florencii predicti Rutgherus Quaetvoet ad X annos pro CXV libris denariorum Traiectensium et IX caponibus et IX pullis annuatim absque defalcatione Martini et Petri solvendis aut cadet ab omni iure et cetera prout littera tenet. Per fratrem Johannem Gaude.ᵉ

[f]Florens die Jonge[f]
[g]Ruthger Walich Quaetvoets zoen[g]

---

[a] *in the left margin.* [b] *in the right margin.* [c] *not filled in.* [d] *in a different hand (B).* [e] *in another hand.* [f] *in the right margin, cancelled.* [g] *in the left margin, in yet another hand.*

fol.124v.   In Lopic

Item ibidem <u>III iugera terre</u> prout iacent inter duo iugera nostre domus que [a]solebat colere Petrus filius Bartholomei. Modo vero possidebit ea Florentius Jonghe ad X annos ab anno LXXIII *[1373]* Petri pro XV libris denariorum Traiectensium annuatim Martini et Petri solvendis vel cadet ab omni iure et cetera prout littera tenet. Per fratrem Thomam.[a]

[b]Ulterius possidet post annos Florencii predicti Rutgherus Quaetvoet ad XX annos pro XV libris denariorum Traiectensium annuatim Martini et Petri solvendis vel cadet ab omni iure et cetera prout littera tenet. Per fratrem Johannem Gaude.[b]

[c]Peter Meus zoen[c]
[d]Florens Jonge[d]
[e]Ruthger Walich Quaetvoets zoen[e]
nota[f]

---

[a] *continued in a different hand (B).* [b] *in another hand.* [c] *in the left margin, in the basic hand, cancelled.* [d] *in the left margin, in the same hand as* [a], *cancelled.* [e] *in the left margin, in yet another hand.* [f] *in the right margin, in the basic hand.*

fol.125r.   In Lopic   CXXV

[a]Item ibidem <u>quartale terre</u> prout iacet opten Nesse inter terram relicte Petri Lamberti et puerorum eius a parte superiori et terram Machteldis filie Heynonis de Nesse a parte inferiori, prout illud quondam possidebat Yo de Nesse. Modo possidet Jacobus Lubbe <u>pro IIII grossis</u> annuatim Martini et Petri solvendis perpetuo.[a] [b]dit heeft Peter van Snellenberch qwijt ghecoft.[b]

perpetuo[c]
[d]Jacobus Lubbe[d]

Item ibidem <u>quartale terre</u> prout iacet inter terram pronunc Alphardi de Lichtenberch a parte superiori et terram Ghiseberti van den Nesse a parte inferiori, prout illud modo possidet a nobis idem Ghisebertus de Nesse ad <u>XII</u> annos ab anno <u>LXIIII</u> *[1364]* Petri <u>pro XIIII libris</u> <u>denariorum Traiectensium et IIII caponibus annuatim</u> absque defalcatione infra quindenam post Martini et Petri solvendis aut cadet ab omni iure. Medietatem incultam resignabit et cetera prout littera exinde tenet. Per fratrem Hugonem.

^eModo dictam terram possidebit ulterius Adam filius Ghiseberti ad X annos ab anno LXXV *[1375]* Agnetis pro XXVI libris denariorum Traiectensium et IIII caponibus absque defalcatione prout littera tenet. Per fratrem Johannem Gaude vicecommendatorem.^e

^fUlterius possidebit dictam terram predictus Adam ad X annos ab anno LXXXV *[1385]* Petri pro XXVII libris monete qua pactus in Traiecto persolvitur et quattuor caponibus absque defalcatione et cetera. Per fratrem Gerardum.^f

^g<u>Ghisebertus van den Nesse</u>^g
^h<u>Daem Ghisberts zoen</u>^h

---

^a *the whole item in the basic hand, crossed out by the same hand as* ^b. ^b *in a different hand.* ^c *in the left margin.* ^d *in the right margin, both in the basic hand.* ^e *in another hand (C).* ^f *in yet another hand.* ^g *in the right margin, cancelled.* ^h *in the right margin, in the same hand as* ^e.

fol.125v.   <u>In Lopic</u>

Item ibidem <u>II iugera terre</u> prout iacent inter terram nostre domus quam nunc possidet Theodericus filius Gerardi de Cattenbroec a parte orientali et terram Gherardi Schuerman et Agneze Ghiseberti Hasen communi sulcu a parte occidentali, prout illa modo possidet a nobis Gerardus Schuerman predictus hereditarie pro <u>XX grossis</u> annuatim Martini et Petri solvendis.

^aDese renten bleven inden Wael verloren ende darenboven sprake wiit aen. Ende doe dedingde Jan Gherijds soen mit ons vander helfte ende gaf ons daer voer IIII Hollandse guldens, die wi voert beleyt hebben, ende die ander helfte is ons mit recht of ghegaen dat wi daer gheen reden toe hebben.^a

^bGerid Schuerman
<u>perpetuo</u>^b

Item ibidem <u>VI iugera terre</u> prout iacent inter terram domini Johannis de Boloys domini de Schoenhoven et de Gouda, quam nunc ab ipso tenet in feodo Bertoldus filius Volquini, a parte superiori et terram heredum Ghisekini filii Andree a parte inferiori, prout illa modo possidet a nobis Gerardus^c Theodericus filius Gerardi de Cattenbroec ad X annos ab anno LXVII *[1367]* Valentini <u>pro XVj</u> *[15.5]* <u>antiquis</u>

scudatis auri aut pro pagamento equivalenti in Traiecto et VI caponibus annuatim Martini et Petri solvendis aut cadet ab omni iure. Non
conburet. Medietatem incultam resignabit et cetera prout littera exinde tenet. Per fratrem Hugonem.

ᵈ¶ Ulterius possidebit dictam terram Adam filius Ghiseberti ad X
annos ab anno LXXV *[1375]* Petri pro XXXIX libris denariorum
Traiectensium et VI caponibus annuatim Martini et Petri solvendis
absque defalcatione aut cadet ab omni iure. Non conburet etcetera
prout littera tenet. Per fratrem Johannem Gaude commendatorem.ᵈ

ᵉ¶ Ulterius possidebit Wilhelmus filius Andree ad X annos ab anno
LXXXV *[1385]* Petri pro XXXIX libris pachtghelds et VI caponibus
absque defalcatione et cetera prout littera tenet. Per fratrem Johannem de Aernhem.ᵉ

ᶠDirc Gherids zoenᶠ
ᵍAdam filius Ghisebertiᵍ
ʰWillem Andries zoenʰ

ᵃ *in a different hand.* ᵇ *in the left margin, in the basic hand.* ᶜ *cancelled.* ᵈ *in another
hand (C).* ᵉ *in yet another hand (D).* ᶠ *in the left margin in the basic hand,
cancelled.* ᵍ *in the left margin, in the same hand as* ᵈ*, cancelled.* ʰ *in the left margin, in
the same hand as* ᵉ*.*

fol.126r.   In Lopic   CXXVI

Item ibidem quartale terre quod fuit Reyneri filii Yen prout iacet
inter terram puerorum Theoderici Stuyx a parte orientali et terram
Jacobi Scoute a parte occidentali, prout illud quondam possidebat
Jutta Coppardi. Modo possidet Nycolaus Buchinc hereditarie pro VI
libris X grossis et V pullis annuatim Martini et Petri solvendis. Per
fratrem Johannem de Via Lapidea commendatorem.

perpetuoᵃ
ᵇNicolaus Buchincᵇ

Item ibidem quartale terre prout iacet inter terram Griete uxoris
Heynonis Corlen et puerorum suorum a parte superiori et terram
domini Johannis de Boloys domini de Schoenhoven a parte inferiori,
prout illud modo possident a nobis Gerardus Splinter et Gerardus
Molnar eius filius ad X annos ab anno LXII *[1362]* Petri pro XVIII
libris denariorum Traiectensium et IIII caponibus annuatim absque
defalcatione solvendis Martini et Petri aut cadent ab omni iure et
cetera prout littera exinde tenet. Per fratrem Hugonem.

ᶜ¶ Modo possidet dictam terram Bernardus Scottelvoet ad X annos
ab anno LXXII *[1372]* Petri pro XXI libris denariorum Traiecten-

sium et IIII caponibus annuatim absque defalcatione Martini et Petri solvendis vel cadet ab omni iure prout littera tenet. Per fratrem Thomam.[c]

[d]Gerardus Splinter[d]

[e]Bernardus Scottelvoet[e]

---

[a] *in the left margin.* [b] *in the right margin.* [c] *in a different hand (B).* [d] *in the right margin, cancelled.* [e] *in the right margin, in the same hand as* [c].

fol.126v.   In Lopic

Item ibidem <u>VIII iugera terre</u> que fuerunt quondam fratris Lyborii prout iacent inter terram pronunc Wilhelmi filii Jacobi a parte superiori et terram Hughemanni filii Hugonis a parte inferiori, prout illa possidebat a nobis Petrus Jonge. Modo possidet ea dominus Hugo de A presbyter ad X annos ab anno LXVIII *[1368]* Petri pro <u>XXIIj</u> *[22.5]* <u>antiquis scudatis auri vel pro pagamento</u> equivalenti in Traiecto tempore solucionis et <u>IIII caponibus et IIII pullis</u> annuatim Martini et Petri solvendis aut cadet ad omni iure et cetera prout littera exinde tenet. Per fratrem Hugonem.

[a]Modo possidebit Jacopus Frederici Scottelvoets dictam terram ad X annos ab anno LXXVI *[1376]* Petri pro LX libris et VIII pullis annuatim absque defalcatione sub condicionibus ut littera tenet solvendis Martini et Petri. Per fratrem Johannem Gaude commendatorem.[a]

[b]Ulterius possidebit predictus Jacobus dictam terram ad X annos ab anno LXXXVI *[1386]* pro LX libris et VIII pullis annuatim sub condicione predicta.[b]

[c]her Hughe van der A[c]

[d]Jacop Dirc Scottelvoets zoen[d]

Item ibidem <u>quartale terre</u> quod dedit quondam dominus Hermannus Meynard decanus sancti Johannis Traiectensis, prout iacet inter terram Johannis de Mille a parte orientali et terram Ghiseberti filii Hugonis a parte occidentali, prout illud possidebat a nobis Brunardus Nannonis. Modo possidet Johannes de Mille <u>pro V libris denariorum</u> Traiectensium annuatim.

[e]Modo her Johan die Bastart van Bloes.[e]

[c]Jan van Mille[c]

---

[a] *in a different hand.* [b] *in another hand.* [c] *in the left margin, in the basic hand.* [d] *in the left margin, in the same hand as* [a]. [e] *in yet another hand.*

fol.127r.   ¶ In Jaersvelt   ¶ In Yselmunde   CXXVII

¶ Item in parrochia de Jaersvelt quartale terre prout iacet in loco dicto Covernes in iurisdictione temporali dominorum de Arkel, de Culenborch et de Asperen, inter terram pronunc dicti Loef filii Leyden a parte superiori et terram Johannis Werneri a parte inferiori, prout illud modo possidet a nobis Lambertus filius Wilhelmi hereditarie pro IIII libris annuatim Martini et Petri solvendis et cetera prout littera exinde tenet et instrumentum quod et quam inde habemus, signatum de foris signo tali ⬦ ª Frater Johannes de Denemarken quondam dedit.
ᵇhereditarie
ᶜLambertus filius Wilhelmiᶜ

¶ Item habet domus in parrochia de Yselmunde XVI virgatas terre que fuerunt quondam Jacobi filii domini Engelberti, quarum VIII virge iacent in die Sluyswere inter terram Theoderici Tyel a parte superiori et terram heredum domine de Weterighen filie domini Symonis de Teylinghen a parte inferiori. Relique VIII virgate iacent opten Veensloet inter terram Johannis Fabri ab utroque latere prout illas possidebat Ockerus Bave. Modo possidet eas Wilhelmus Vinke hereditarie pro IIII libris annuatim Martini et Petri solvendis.
hereditarieᵇ
ᶜWilhelmus Vinkeᶜ

ª *a coat of arms with a chevron.* ᵇ *in the left margin.* ᶜ *in the right margin.*

fol.127v.   ¶ In Ammers

¶ Item in parrochia de Ammers habet domus dimidium mansum terre prout iacet in Graveland inter terram Johannis de Ammers et Wolbrandi a parte orientali et terram dictam Cromme Halve Hoeve a parte occidentali, prout eundem possidebat Jacobus Vlassenbaert. Modo possidet eum Petrus filius Griete pro II libris denariorum Traiectensium annuatim hereditarie Martini et Petri solvendis.
ªPeter Grieten zoen
perpetuoª

Item ibidem dimidium mansum prout situs est infra terram Ottonis et Graveland inter terram Laurencii filii Vrouwins ᵇa parte orientaliᵇ et ᵇterramᵇ Hanekini Kuzer communi sulcu a latere orientali et terram

Herberni de Liesvelt a latere occidentali, prout eundem possidebat Jacobus Vlassenbaert. Modo possidet Johannes Sculpe <u>pro I libra</u> parvorum denariorum Martini et Petri solvendis annuatim hereditarie.
^a<u>Johan Sculpe</u>
<u>perpetuo</u>^a

Item ibidem in Ghelekin Nesse <u>Vj *[5.5]* virgatas terre</u> prout iacent et illas quondam possidebat Arnoldus de Liesvelt. Modo possidet Herbernus de Liesvelt hereditarie <u>pro IIII solidis nigrorum</u> annuatim.
^a<u>Herbernus de Liesvelt</u>
<u>perpetuo</u>^a

---

^a *in the left margin.* ^b *cancelled.*

fol.128r.   <u>In Ammers</u>   ¶ <u>In Langerake</u>   CXXVIII

Item ibidem in <u>Ghelekin Nesse V virgatas et dimidiam partem dimidie virge</u> prout iacent inter terram pronunc domini Hackonis presbyteri a parte orientali et terram Arnoldi dicti Bonghe a parte occidentali, prout illas possidebat Flore filius Heynemanni. Modo possidet Petrus filius Wilhelmi <u>pro VIII grossis</u> annuatim Martini et Petri solvendis.
^a<u>Petrus filius Wilhelmi</u>^a

¶ Item in parrochia de Langerake habet domus <u>IIII iugera terre cum dimidio iugere</u> et dimidium hont prout iacent, que dedit domina Margareta de Langerake, quibus ab utroque latere scilicet superius et inferius propius iacet terra pronunc Margarete Theoderici Nycolai et suorum liberorum. Que modo possident procuratores ecclesie de Langerake ad usus dicte ecclesie perpetuo <u>pro Vj *[5.5]* libris et III caponibus</u> annuatim pagamenti Traiectensis Martini et Petri aut infra postea in Traiecto, dummodo guerra non impedierit, aut cadent ab omni iure et ad hoc cederent tunc domui nostre de dicta ecclesia II libras nigrorum perpetue annuatim et cetera prout littera tenet quam habemus signatam signo tali . D .
^b<u>Ipsi habent litteram et non tenetur de caponibus.</u>^b
<u>perpetuo</u>^c
^a<u>procuratores ecclesie in Langerake</u>^a

---

^a *in the right margin.* ^b *in different writing.* ^c *in the left margin.*

fol.128v.   In Langerake   ¶ in Molnersgrave

Item ibidem <u>II virgatas terre</u> quas dedit dominus Wolfardus prout iacent et illas modo possidet Theodericus Mol perpetuo <u>pro X solidis et VIII denariis</u> annuatim Martini et Petri solvendis.
ᵃTheodericus Mol
<u>perpetuo</u>ᵃ

¶ <u>Item in Molnersgrave</u> habet domus terram dictam Ziitwinde prout iacet infra Ghisenrevliet et Ofweghen et Ruggebroke cum omnibus suis, prout eandem quondam a nobis optinuit et possidebat dominus Johannes de Graveland miles et post eundem Henricus Molnar. Modo vero possident eandem <u>heredes</u> domini Danyelis de Tholoysen militis <u>pro VI libris nigrorum pagamenti Hollandensis quo tempore solucionis</u> domino comiti <u>Hollandie pactum persolvi potest</u> annuatim infra quindenam post Martini et Petri solvendis in Traiecto. Quod si non fecerint extunc mittetur nuncius nostre domus apud ecclesiam in Molnarsgrave in uno hospicio ibidem sub eorum expensis iacendus cui tunc infra triduum satisfacient. Quod si non fecerint ibit nuncius coram plebano ecclesie ibidem et aliis duobus vel tribus testibus dicendo eis quod fecerit monicionem de pacto prescripto et quod per triduum ibidem solutionem exspectaverit et eandem non sit prosecutus. Quod si sic evenerit et non per talem modum tunc satisfactum nobis fuerit, ex tunc possessor dicte terre caderit ab omni iure. et cetera secundum tenorem littere quam inde habemus signo tali querendo . E . Per fratrem Johannem de Via Lapidea commendatorem.
ᵃ<u>dominus Daniel de Tholoyse</u>
<u>hereditarie</u>ᵃ

ᵃ *in the left margin.*

fol.129r.   ¶ <u>In Ameyda</u>   CXXIX

¶ <u>Item in parrochia de Ameyda</u> habet domus <u>dimidium mansum terre</u> prout iacet supra Oesternesse vel Extervelt inter terram canonicorum regularium in Traiecto a latere superiori et terram Cosini de Schoenhoven a latere inferiori, quem quondam possidebat Theodericus Godekini. Modo possidet Elysabeth filia Winrici hereditarie <u>pro VIII libris denariorum</u> annuatim Martini et Petri solvendis in tali pagamento quale de nostro pacto receperimus in Traiecto.
<u>perpetuo</u>ᵃ
ᵇElysabeth filia Winriciᵇ

Item ibidem VIj *[6.5]* iugera terre iacentia in den Hoefslach supra Extervelt apud terram pronunc domini Loef presbyteri filii Winrici ab una parte, prout illa quondam possidebat a nobis Theodericus dictus Roede. Modo possidet Jacobus van de Ness filius eius hereditarie pro VIII libris denariorum pagamenti in Ameyda tempore solucionis dativi infra quindenam post Martini et Petri solvendis aut cadet ab omni iure et hereditario pacto. Inde habemus litteram scabinorum in Ameyda signatam signo tali . A .
perpetuo[a]
[b]Jacob de Nesse[b]

---

[a] *in the left margin.* [b] *in the right margin.*

fol.129v.   <u>In Ameyda</u>   ¶ <u>In Merkerke</u>

Item ibidem in Middelbroec <u>dimidium mansum terre</u> prout iacet in dominio terre de Ameyda prope Merkerke inter terram [a]Everardi filii Everardi a parte meridionali et terram dicti Scadeland a parte aquilonis, prout eundem a nobis possidebat Wilhelmus filius Wolteri. Modo possidet eundem Johannes filius Henrici, una cum dimidio manso subscripto, ad X annos ab anno LXX *[1370]* Petri sub annua pensione inferius signata. Per fratrem Johannem Gaude. ¶ Ulterius idem possidebit dictam terram ad X annos ab anno LXXX *[1380]* Petri pro XXXVIII libris.[a]
[b]Wilhelmus filius Wouteri[b]
[c]Jan Henrixzoen[c]

Item in Merkerke <u>dimidium mansum terre</u> prout iacet in Quakernake inter terram [d]nostre domus quam nunc possidet[d] [a]domini Herberni de Liesvelt militis a parte meridionali et terram Jacobi filii Jacobi a parte aquilonis, prout eundem modo possidet a nobis, una cum dimidio manso suprascripto, Johannes filius Henrici ad X annos ab anno LXX *[1370]* Petri et solvet de hiis duobus dimidiis mansis insimul XXVI libras denariorum Traiectensium annuatim absque omni defalcatione Martini et Petri solvendas aut cadet ab omni iure et cetera prout littera tenet. Per fratrem Johannem Gaude.
¶ Ulterius idem possidebit istam terram una cum dimidio manso suprascripto ad X annos ab anno LXXX *[1380]* pro annua pensione superius signata.[a]
[b]Ghisebertus filius Folpardi[b]
[c]Jan Henrixzoen[c]

---

[a] *continued in a different hand (C).* [b] *in the left margin, cancelled.* [c] *in the left margin, in the same hand as* [a]. [d] *cancelled.*

fol.130r.   In Merkerke   CXXX

Item ibidem apud Merkerke in Quakernake <u>dimidium mansum terre</u>
prout iacet inter terram domicelli de Meghen a parte meridionali et
terram Theoderici filii Berwoudi a parte septentrionali, prout eundem possidebat a nobis Henricus custos de Ameyde. Modo possident
Heyno de Osse, Nycolaus filius Arnoldi et Lambertus filius Grawen
Heynen, hereditarie pro <u>IIII libris bonorum denariorum, grosso
Turonensi regio pro XII denariis</u> conputato, 'et cetera prout littera
exinde tenet quam a scabinis in Merkerc habemus signata signo tali
. B .
<u>hereditarie</u>[a]
[b]Heyne van Osse[b]

Item ibidem super Quakernake <u>IIII iugera terre</u> prout iacent inter
terram Rufi Coppardi a parte meridionali et terram nostre domus
quam nunc hereditarie possidet a nobis Wilhelmus filius Johannis vel
Lize a parte septentrionali, prout illa modo possidet a nobis dictus
Roede Coppard hereditarie pro <u>II libris bonorum denariorum talis</u>
pagamenti quale de pactu nostro receperimus in Traiecto tempore
solucionis Martini et Petri solvendis annuatim et cetera prout littera
scabinorum in Merkerc quam exinde habemus tenet . ✡ .[c]
<u>hereditarie</u>[a]
[b]Roede Coppard[b]

[d]Item ibidem een hoeve lants geleghen op Bloemendaell tusschen
lande Henric Dicbier aen die oversijde ende Volpert Willamssoens
erfgenamen aen die nedersijde.[d]

---

[a] *in the left margin.* [b] *in the right margin.* [c] *a six-pointed star of David.* [d] *in a
different hand.*

fol.130v.   In Merkerc   In Gasperde
In Nyeland

Item ibidem <u>IIII iugera terre</u> prout iacent inter unum quartale terre
nostre domus quod nunc possidet Roede Coppard hereditarie a parte
meridionali et terram domini Gerardi presbyteri a parte septentrionali, prout illud modo possidet a nobis Wilhelmus filius Johannis vel
Lize hereditarie <u>pro XL grossis</u> annuatim Martini et Petri solvendis.
[a]Wilhelmus filius Johannis vel Lyze
<u>hereditarie</u>[a]

¶ Item in Gasperde unum agrum terre qui fuit Andree Fabri prout
iacet in loco dicto Bulgarie inter terram domini Johannis de Leyden-
berch militis ab utroque latere, prout eundem modo possident heredes dicti Andree hereditarie pro X solidis denariorum Traiectensium
annuatim Martini et Petri solvendis.
ᵃAndreas Faber
hereditarieᵃ

¶ In parrochia Nyelander kerke VIII iugera sita in den Nyenlande,
prout illa quondam dominus Arnoldus de Houweninghen miles et
Theodericus Corthals possidebant. Modo possidet ea ᵇ pro XL
grossis annuatim Martini et Petri solvendis. Habemus inde litteras
scabinorum in Gorichem cum signo . + .ᶜ
ᵃTheodericus Corthals
hereditarieᵃ

ᵃ *in the left margin.* ᵇ *not filled in.* ᶜ *a Greek cross.*

fol.131r.   In Nyelanderkerke   ¶ In Lederbroec   CXXXI

Item ibidem in Nyelanderkerke IX iugera et I hont que quondam
fuerunt unius dicti Quaetvoet, prout iacent inter terram heredum
Wolteri Gheylen a parte superiori et terram Mychaelis filiiᵃ Heynonis
Bruninxs a parte inferiori, prout illa possidebat a nobis Petrus Stoec.
Modo possidet ea Arnoldus Stoec ad X annos ab anno LXII *[1362]*
Circumcisio Domini pro XIX libris pagamenti Traiectensis ᵇet IX
pullisᵇ annuatim absque defalcatione Martini et Petri solvendis aut
cadet ab omni iure et cetera prout littera tenet. Per fratrem Hugonem.
ᶜ¶ Modo possidet dictam terram Theodericus Oudeleyst ad X annos
ab anno LXXII *[1372]* Petri pro XVI libris monete in Gorichem
absque omni defalcatione solvendis Martini et Petri vel cadet ab omni
iure et cetera prout littera tenet. Per fratrem Thomam.ᶜ
ᵈArnoldus Stoecᵈ
ᵉDirc Oudeleistᵉ

¶ In parrochia Lederbroec VIII iugera prout iacent apud Merkerc,
quibus a superiori parte propius iacent IIj *[2.5]* iugera terre spectancia ad Terram Sanctam et a parte inferiori terra Theoderici filii Mychaelis, prout illa possidebat a nobis quondam Theodericus
Vrouwiin, postea Bruno die Horder et modo possidet ea Nycolaus
filius Teden hereditarie pro V libris V grossis pagamenti quale de

nostro pacto receperimus in Traiecto, Martini et Petri aut infra quindenam postea solvendis annuatim aut possessor eiusdem cadet ab
omni iure sibi in dicta terra competenti. Inde habemus litteram scabinorum in Merkerke tali signo signatam . C .

perpetuo^f

^dBruno die Horder^d

^gNycolaus filius Teden^g

ᵃ *filii filii* ms. ᵇ *cancelled.* ᶜ *in a different hand (B).* ᵈ *in the right margin,
cancelled.* ᵉ *in the right margin, in the same hand as* ᶜ. ᶠ *in the left margin.* ᵍ *in the
right margin, in the basic hand.*

fol.131v.   ¶ In Nyeland   ¶ In Goudriaen

¶ <u>Item in Nyeland mansum terre</u> prout iacet inter terram domine de
Merwiic et eius pueri a parte septentrionali et terram Petri Screyer a
parte meridionali, prout eundem possidebat a nobis Alardus Goede.
Modo possidet eum Nycolaus die Lewe <u>ad X annos</u> ab anno LXVII
[1367] Petri <u>pro XXV libris</u> denariorum quibus in Traiecto pactum
persolvi potest annuatim absque defalcatione Martini et Petri solvendis aut cadet ab omni iure et cetera prout littera exinde tenet. Per
fratrem Hugonem.

ᵃ¶ Ulterius idem Nycolaus possidebit dictam terram ad X annos ab
anno LXXVII *[1377]* Petri pro XXXI libris denariorum Traiectensium. ¶ Modo ulterius possidebit dictam terram Nicolaus Witte ad X
annos ab anno LXXXVII *[1387]* Petri pro VIII antiquis scudatis
annuatim Martini et Petri solvendis vel cadet et cetera prout littera
tenet.ᵃ

ᵇClaes die Lewe^b

ᶜClaes die Witte^c

¶ <u>Item parrochia in Goudriaen</u> ex uno dimidio manso terre iacenti
Opten Oesteren Egge inter terram Gerardi filii Hermanni a parte
orientali et terram Theoderici Vrouwin a parte occidentali <u>XXX
denarios</u> nigrorum annuatim Martini solvendos. Symon filius Wilhelmi possidebat. ᵈModo possident eundem Jacobus de Buren, Petrus de
Buren et Aleydis des Goyers hereditarie.^d

ᵉJacobus de Buren etcetera
 <u>hereditarie</u>^e

ᵃ *in a different hand (D).* ᵇ *in the left margin, cancelled.* ᶜ *in the left margin, in the
same hand as* ᵃ. ᵈ *added in writing different from the basic hand.* ᵉ *in the left margin, in
the same writing as* ᵈ.

fol.132r.   In Goudriaen   ¶ In Almekerc   CXXXII

Item ibidem <u>dimidium mansum</u> terre prout iacet int Nedersteynde van Podelwijc, quem quondam dictus Teylinc, postea Gerardus Borchman, deinde Herbernus Buyscher a nobis possidebant. Modo possidet eundem Florentius Jonghe <u>ad X annos</u> ab anno LXVI *[1366]* Petri <u>pro XII libris denariorum</u> Traiectensium annuatim absque defalcatione Martini et Petri solvendis aut cadet ab omni iure et cetera prout littera exinde tenet. Per fratrem Hugonem.
^a¶ Ulterius possidebit Florencius Bennic ad IX annos ab anno LXXVII *[1377]* Petri pro XV libris denariorum Traiectensium solvendis annuatim Martini et Petri et cetera. Per commendatorem fratrem Johannem Gaude.^a
^b¶ Ulterius possidebit predictus Florencius ad X annos ab anno LXXXVII *[1387]* pro XV libris. Per fratrem Johannem Haze.^b
^cFlorens die Jonghe^c
^d<u>Florens Benne</u>^d

¶ Item in parrochia<u> de Almekerc IIj *[2.5]* iugera terre</u> nuncupata vulgariter die Bodemdrecht prout iacent in die Spiic inter terram pronunc Rodolphi^e de Riiswijc a parte orientali et terram Johannis^f filii Emondi a parte occidentali, prout illa possidebat a nobis Rodolphus de Rijswijc. Modo possidet ea Noydo de Ganswijc hereditarie <u>pro V libris</u> denariorum Traiectensium annuatim Martini et Petri solvendis.
<u>hereditarie</u>^g
^c<u>Rodolphus de Rijswijc</u>^c
^h<u>Noydo de Ganswijc</u>^h

---

^a *in a different hand (C).* ^b *in another hand.* ^c *in the right margin, cancelled.* ^d *in the right margin, in the same hand as* ^a*.* ^e *Rodolphus ms.* ^f *Johannes ms.* ^g *in the left margin.* ^h *in the right margin, in the basic hand.*

fol.132v.   ¶ In Rewijc et Slupic

¶ Item in parrochia de Rewijc <u>VII hunt terre</u> quibus a parte orientali propius iacet die Queldiic et a parte occidentali terra domini de Brederoede. Jacobus filius Sibrandi modo possidet ad X annos ab anno LXVI *[1366]* Purificatione Marie <u>pro III libris denariorum</u> Traiectensium annuatim absque defalcatione Martini et Petri solvendis aut cadet ab omni iure et cetera prout littera exinde tenet. Per fratrem Hugonem.

^aUlterius ad X annos ab anno LXXVI *[1376]* Petri pro IIII libris.^a
^bUlterius possidet Gherardus Valc ad X annos ab anno LXXXVI
[1386] Petri pro IIII libris. Per fratrem Johannem de Arnhem.^b
^cJacobus filius Sibrandi^c
^dReynout Heynriczoen^d
^eGherit Valc
  caret littera^e

Item ibidem <u>medietatem unius iugeris terre cum dimidio,</u> daer Willem Dirix zone nu die wederhelft af heeft, quibus a superiori parte
propius iacet terra Theoderici Hughen et a parte inferiori terra Johannis Nycolai. Idem Theodericus Hughe predictus modo possidet
ad X annos ab anno <u>LXVI</u> *[1366]* Purificatione Marie pro <u>II libris et
IIII solidis annuatim</u> absque defalcatione Martini et Petri solvendis
aut cadet ab omni iure et cetera prout littera exinde tenet. Per fratrem Hugonem.
^aUlterius possidet ad X annos ab anno LXXVI *[1376]* Petri Willam
Dirc Hughen soen soen.^a
^bUlterius possidet Wilhelmus ad X annos ab anno LXXXVI *[1386]*
Petri pro II libris XVIII solidis VIII denariis. Per fratrem Johannem
de Arnhem.^b
^cDirc Hughe^c
^eWillem Dirc Hughezoen zoen
  caret littera^e

---

  ^a *in a different hand.* ^b *in another hand.* ^c *in the left margin, cancelled.* ^d *in the left
margin, in the same hand as* ^a, *cancelled.* ^e *in the left margin, in yet another hand (D).*

fol.133r.   <u>In Rewijc</u>   ¶ <u>In Middelborch</u>   CXXXIII

Item ibidem <u>ex uno agro terre</u> qui fuit Walteri van der Wintmolen
<u>XII Hollandenses</u> quos contulit quondam Machteldis mater eiusdem
Walteri ex agro predicto prout iacet et eundem possidet Hermannus
filius Kerstancii, solvendos Martini annuatim.
<u>perpetuo</u>^a
^bHermannus Kerstancii^b

Item ibidem <u>ex uno agro terre</u> prout iacet et eundem modo possidet
Margareta relicta Coppardi Duven <u>XVI denarios</u> annuatim Martini
solvendos.
<u>perpetuo</u>^a
^bMargareta Coppardi Duven^b

Item in Middelborch unum iuger terre situm in loco dicto Bredenhoeve, prout illud possidebat Bekans Nichte. Modo possidet Bredekinus filius Theoderici pro XII solidis annuatim Martini et Petri solvendis, ^cad annos^c ^d

^ecaret annis^e
^bBredekinus filius Theoderici^b

---

^a *in the left margin.* ^b *in the right margin.* ^c *in a different writing.* ^d *not filled in.*
^e *in another hand (D).*

fol.133v.   ¶ In Svademerdam   ¶ In Nyencop   ¶ In Gheervliet

¶ Item in Suademerdam ex uno agro terre V solidos III denarios bonorum annuatim, quos solebat dare Zanna Conradi. Modo solvet
a

perpetuo^b

¶ In Nyencop unam virgatam terre prout iacet inter terram pronunc Arnoldi dicti Ovenmaker a parte superiori et terram Theoderici Ovenmaker eius fratris a parte inferiori. Cristianus filius Tydemanni modo possidet eandem et solvet exinde IIII solidos nigrorum annuatim hereditarie, Martini solvendos.
^bCristianus filius Tydemanni
  perpetuo^b

¶ In Gheervliet ex dominio de Putten I waghe kazen annuatim. Item ibidem ab eodem dominio I waghe kazen vel II libras pro eis annuatim. ^cEt hos caseos quondam felicis recordacionis dominus de Putten et de Gheervliet ob salutem et remedium et pro perpetua memoria animarum sue, uxoris sue, parentumque suorum, nostre domui sancte Katerine pie contulit et legavit, annuatim in Mayo per successores suos dominos dominii de Putten perpetuis temporibus persolvendos.^c
^bdominus de Putten
  perpetuo^b

---

^a *not filled in.* ^b *in the left margin.* ^c *added in different writing.*

fol.134r.

Item habet dicta domus ex pia donatione felicis recordacionis domini Wilhelmi comitis Hollandie de decimis in Reynerscop et de censu in

Oudewater XXV libras Turonenses nigrorum, et de terra in Woerden dicta Hofgoed XXV libras eiusdem monete, cum quibus quinquaginta libris idem comes duas vicarias pro memoria reverendi
patris domini Wilhelmi Traiectensis episcopi dotavit perpetuis temporibus per nostros fratres deserviendas. Et quociens easdem vicarias
per decessum nostrorum fratrum ipsas officiantium vacare contigerit
dictus comes Hollandie pro tempore existens de eis aliis nostris fratribus ydoneis providebit et nullis aliis personis. In festis beatorum Martini et Petri solvendis annuatim.
perpetuo^a
^bdominus comes Hollandie^b

^cItem bi Rotterdam op Sent Katherinen camp IIII solidos Hollanden-
ses tsiaers.

Item so is den huse an ghecomen van bovengescreven broeder Florens Claes zoen van Rotterdam VII libre hollandenses tsiaers die
staen op Dirc Ghijsbrechtszoens huus ende hofstede opten diic te
Rotterdam, daer Jan van der Aer an de oestzide naest gheleghen is
mit huse ende mit erve ende Jan Zweym Dirxzoen an de westzide.

Item van den selven broeder Florens voors VI morghen lands die
gheleghen sijn ter capellen bi Rotterdam daer Meyer Janszoen an die
oestzide naest ghelant is ende Dirc Nanne Willems zoen an de
westzide.^c

---

^a *in the left margin.* ^b *in the right margin.* ^c *in much later writing.*

fol.134v.   In Rijswijc

Item V morghen lants luttel meer of min alse gheleghen ziin inde
kerspel van Riiswijc, Floriis Doeden zoens woeninghe die beleghen
hebben an die oestside die heren van der canesie in die Haghe ende
aen die westside Mechtelt Willam Hoitemans zoens weduwe mit
horen kinderen, streckende dat zuyteynde an enen banwech is ghehe-
ten die Brede Wech ende dat noerteynde an Ghisebertus Jacobs
zoens lande. Dit lant zel besitten Oedsier Hughe Blote ten erfpachte
om V oude vrancken siaers of ander payment daer voer na hoerre
werde te betalen jaerlix tsinte Peters misse of binnen eenre maend
daer na of hi valt van allen rechte. Hier is een brief of.
^aOedzier Hughe
perpetue^a

In Haestrecht

Item achtenhalven merghen lants geleghen tot Haestrecht des die
drie merghen gheleghen siin in een weer van acht merghen daer die
vrouwen van Teylingen die vijff merghen af toebehoren, streckende
uuter Ysel aen den Bilwijcker Tiendweech, daer aen die acht merghen naest gelant sijn aen die oversijde Gherit Aernts soen ende her
Jan Pieters zoen aen die nedersijde. Ende die wijfte halven merghen
daer is naest gelant Symon Tellen zoen aen die oversijde ende Bilwijcker Gheer aen die nedersijde. Dit lant zellen besitten Jacop Poerterszoen ende Mechtelt sijn wijff tot eenen erfpacht om drie
Engelsche nobel tsiaers Martini et Petri tot eenen vers[]enden pacht.
Ende gheviel enich gebreck aen desen erve daer staet voert ander lant
tot eenen onderpande nae inhout des briefs dien wij daer aff hebben.
Hier aff zellen Willam die Roede ende Barbara sijn wijff hebben twee
nobel des jaers tot hoeren lijve, die nae hoere doet comen zellen aen
die pietantie ons goetshuys van voirs. te deylen onder den broederen.
ᵇJacop Poerterszoen perpetueᵇ

Ibidem sess merghen lands soe als die geleghen sijn in den lande van
Haestrecht in Billic strekende van Billiker Tiendwech aen Stolwijcker
Lantscheidinghe tusschen lande Hoel die Borgher ende Peter Claes
soen aen die oestzijde ende tusschen landen Hoel die Borgher voerg.
ende Jan Derfzoen aen die nederzijde. Dit lant sel besitten Gherit
Witten zoen ende sijn erfgenamen tot eenen eweliken erfpacht om
anderhalven Engelschen nobel tsiaers te betalen jaerlics op Martini
hyemalis vel infra quindenam postea vel cadet ab omni iure prout in
littera continetur inde habita.
ᵇGherit Wittenzoen perpetueᵇ

Ibidem die helfte van eenre halver hoeve lants geleghen aen die Vlist
streckende van der Vlist oestwert op aen die lantscheidinghe alse die
zuytsijde daer aff. Aen wilker halver hoeve Claes van Troien naest
gelandt is aen die zuytsijde ende Deric die Ghoyer aen die noertsijde.
Dit lant zellen besitten Borre van Tiel ende Zwanelt sijn wijff tot
eenen erfpacht om ander halven Engelschen nobel tsiaers vryes gel-
des te betalen jaerlis Martini vel infra quindenam vel cadent ab omni
iure. Inde habemus litteram.

ᵃ *in the left margin, in much later writing.* ᵇ *in the left margin, in other, later writing.*

PART C

VISITATION-ACTS AND INQUIRIES

C.1. 1373 JUNE

Visitation of the St.John's houses at Mechelen and Aachen at the request of Jan van Arkel, Bishop of Liège, and ordered by Pope Gregorius XI.
Archiva Vaticana Roma, Instrumenta miscellanea

This text has been copied from *L'Enquête Pontificale de 1373 sur l'Ordre des Hospitaliers de Saint-Jean de Jérusalem*, publiée sous la direction de Jean Glénisson, volume I, *L'Enquête dans la Prieuré de France*, par Anne-Marie Legras avec la collaboration de Robert Favreau, Editions du Centre National de la Recherche Scientifique, Paris 1987, p.158-160; formerly published by D.Ursmer Berlière O.S.B., 'Inventaire des Instrumenta miscellanea des Archives Vaticanes au point de vue de nos anciens diocèses', in: *Bulletin de l'Institut Historique Belge de Rome*, 4me fascicule, Rome-Bruxelles-Paris 1924, nr.76, p.85-103, Enquête sur les biens de l'Hôpital de S.Jean de Jérusalem dans le diocèse de Liége faite à la demande de l'évêque Jean d'Arkel, sur ordre de Grégoire XI, p.101-102.

<p.158> [fol.15 verso]
– – Reperiuntur etiam in dicta diocesi Leodiensi due alie domus satis modici valoris a principali quadam domo, quam habet dictus Ordo in diocesi Coloniensi dependentes, quarum una vocatur domus sive preceptoria in Mechghelen, et alia de Aquis que solum habent unum preceptorem infra nominatum. Sed frater Paulus de Galopia, miles inscriptus, sub se habet duodecim fratres, quorum nomina et cognomina necnon etates et redditus sequuntur, secundum ordinem punctorum predictorum:
  Primo, frater Paulus de Galopia, preceptor dictarum domorum, miles, est etatis 58 annorum vel circiter.
  Frater Johannes de Hoetkerken, qui solus residet in domo sive hospitale de Aquis, est etatis 70 annorum vel circiter et presbyter.

<p.159> Frater Willelmus de Panhuse, prior domus de Mechghelen, est etatis 62 annorum vel circiter et presbyter.
  Frater Egidius de Seurs est etatis 52 annorum et presbyter.

Frater Henricus de Wippervorde est etatis 32 annorum, presbyter.

Frater Willelmus Brant est etatis 30 annorum vel circiter, presbyter.

Frater Constantinus de Colonia est etatis 30 annorum vel circiter, presbyter.

Frater Willelmus de Coelgroven est etatis 22 annorum, subdyaconus.

Fratres milites dicti Ordinis:

Frater Henricus de Lovenich est etatis 44 annorum, miles.

Frater Meynardus de Lovenich est etatis 31 annorum, miles.

Frater Henricus de Odendorpe, celerarius, 42 annorum, miles.

[fol.16] Frater Johannes de Trajecto est etatis 67 annorum, miles.

Frater Johannes de Hoemborgh est etatis 56 annorum, miles.

Summa fratrum predictorum: 13.

Deinde sequuntur fructus, redditus et emolumenta fratrum domus de Mechghelen predictorum.

Primo, domus de Mechghelen predicta, cum capella Ordinis Hospitalis Sancti Johannis Jherosolomitani, habet bona et redditus subscriptos eidem adjacentes, videlicet in terris arabilibus, pratis, pascuis et nemoribus 200 bonnaria, et estimato bonnario in redditu pro uno floreno, valent 200 fl.

Summa: 200 fl.

Item, adjacent domui una decima que valere potest annuatim 50 florenos.

Summa: 50 fl.

Item, habet dicta domus in censu pecuniario singulis annis 6 florenos vel quasi.

Summa: 6 fl.

Item, habet dicta domus tam in caponibus quam pullis et gallinis annuatim pro vite necessariis ipsius domus 100 pecias, qui tamen vendi non solent neque consueverunt.

Valor domuncule de Aquis:

[fol.16 verso] Domus de Aquis, cui preest solus frater Johannes de Hoetkerken, cum omnibus suis appertinentiis, videlicet cum una parva boveria consistente in diocesi Coloniensi, nuncupata Elkenrode, habet seu valet annuatim 60 fl.

Summa: 60 fl.

Et dicunt dicti fratres sub prestito per ipsos juramento, quod computatis omnibus suis redditibus, exceptis caponibus et pullis, ipsi redditus vix ascendunt annuatim ad 316 fl.

Summa totalis dictarum domorum est: 316 fl.

Deinde sequuntur onera domibus predictis incombentia.

Quolibet anno tenentur et exsolvunt suo superiori ultra mare duas marchas puri argenti, que estimate sunt insimul ad 10 florenos fortis ponderis.

Item, tenentur adhuc pro trecensu domus sue unum florenum.

Item, de residuo oportet eosdem 13 fratres dicti Ordinis vivere tam in vestimentis, quam etiam pro hospitibus recipiendis ac juribus ipsarum domorum defendendis.

Asserunt etiam predicti fratres, quod nisi ipsi excolerent personaliter suas terras, non haberent nec habere possent terciam partem reddituum predictorum.

<p.160> [fol.17] In quorum omnium et singulorum testimonium huic presenti informationi sic ut premittitur diligenter et fideliter facte, et in formam publicam per notarios infrascriptos redacte, sigillum meum[1] ad causas in ejus robur et fidem apponi feci pariter et appendi; quam cum omni humilitate et reverencia destino eidem Sanctitati[2]. Recepta et facta fuit dicta informatio Leodii per dictos venerabiles commissarios meos per me auctoritate apostolica deputatos, ut prefertur, sub anno Domini millesimo trecentesimo septuagesimo tercio et de mense junii dicti anni. In cujus mensis principio litteras apostolicas supradictas recepi reverenter.

<followed by the testimonies with the signets of two public notaries of the Liège curia, i.e. Johannes, dictus de Wytven de Mierle, & Lambertus, dictus de Columpna.>

---

[1] sc. sigillum episcopi Johannis de Arkel.
[2] sc. papae Gregorio XI.

C.2 & 3.   VISITATION-ACTS OF 1495 AND 1540

The following edition of the visitation acts of 1495 and 1540 concerning the Dutch preceptories of the Order of St John is not the first one ever made, but it is the first one made after the manuscripts in the central Archives of the Order of Malta in Valletta, the AOM. The earlier edition was made after the contemporaneous copies in the Rijksarchief (RA) at Arnhem, Gelderland, which are far from complete. Sometimes entire preceptories, appendices or smaller passages that are present in the AOM text are missing. Those differences will be indicated in the footnotes. However, alternative readings of the AOM text as compared with the RA Gelderland text are not annotated.

The first edition is to be found in:
'Visitatie-verslagen van de Johanniter-kloosters in Nederland (1495, 1540, 1594)', medegedeeld door E.Wiersum en A.Le Cosquino de Bussy, in: *Bijdragen en Mededeelingen van het Historisch Genootschap (BMHG)*, 48, Utrecht 1927, pp.146-340, especially 155-232 (1495) and 233-261 (1540).

A study that is based on the same visitation acts in the AOM but does not deal with the Dutch preceptories is the following:
Walter Gerd Rödel, *Das Großpriorat Deutschland des Johanniter-Ordens im Übergang vom Mittelalter zur Reformation, an Hand der Generalvisitationsberichte von 1494/95 und 1540/41*, (Inaugural-Dissertation der Philosophischen Fakultät zu Mainz 1966), Köln 1966; 2.neubearbeitete und erweiterte Auflage, Köln 1972.

+++++++++++++++++++++++++++++++

C.2. AOM 45, VISITATION OF GERMANY, 1495

The visitation of 1495 was proclaimed by Grand Master and general chapter in a bull of 5 August, 1493:

1493, August 5 — *Frater Pierre d'Aubusson, Grand Master, and the General Chapter order the visitation of the Order's houses in all parts of Germany.*
    Chancery notice, including copy of the bull: AOM 392, libri bullarum 1494-1496, *fol.95v-97v.*

[fol.95v]   In nomine Domini Amen. Anno eiusdem millesimo quadringentesimo nonagesimo quarto, indictione tertiadecima, die vero nona mensis Decembris pontificatus sanctissime in Xpo patris et domini nostri domini Allexandri papae sexti anno tertio inceperunt

reverendi et religiosi viri domini fratres Petrus Stoltz de Banbeckeln-
heym sacri conventus Rhodi magnus baiulius et frater Johannes Antonius de Actis praeceptor Pucini prioratus Capuae ad exequendum
commissionem visitationis prioratuum, baiuliarum, praeceptoriarum
in partibus Alemaniae superioris et inferioris, Hungariae, Bohemiae,
Datiae, Suetiae, Frisiae et cetera reverendissimo in Xpo patri et domino Petro Daubusson sacro sanctae Romanae ecclesiae sancti Hadriani diacono cardinali Rhodique magno magistro et conventu
generali emanatam, cuius commissionis tenor sequitur et est talis:

Frater Petrus Daubusson miseratione divina sacro sanctae Romanae
ecclesiae sancti Hadriani diaconus cardinalis ac sacrae domus hospitalis sancti Joannis Hierosolymitani magister humilis pauperumque
Jesu Xpi custos et nos baiulivi, priores, praeceptores et fratres capitulum generale celebrantes universis et singulis huiusmodi nostras litteras visuris, audituris et lecturis salutem in Eo qui est omnivera salus.
Nuper siquidem venerabiles sexdecim capitulares auctoritate capitulari [fol.96r] fungentes intellecta petitione capitulantium facta per ro-
tulos et supplicationes eorum generali capitulo presentatas super
visitatione facienda in nostro ordine de beneficiis eiusdem, considerantes etiam quod in quolibet statu et republica convenientissimum
existit vires, proventus et facultates recognoscere quibus status manu-
tenetur, defenditur et conservatur, quodque annis triginta tribus vel
circiter exactis visitatio in nostro ordine non extitit.

Quare congruum est ut ea fiat ad recognoscendum verum valorem
beneficiorum eapropter matura deliberatione prehabita determinarunt et decreverunt quod huiusmodi visitatio omnium et singulorum prioratuum, Castellaniae Empostae, baiulivatuum,
praeceptoriarum, praediorum et beneficiorum ordinis nostri exemptorum et non exemptorum, nam exemptio merito obedientiae voto et
publice utilitati adversari non debet, tam in partibus occidentalis
quam orientalis constitutorum fiat, volentes igitur cum deliberatione
et ordinatione dictorum venerabilium sexdecim super dicta visitatione facienda debitae exequutioni demandari, cum ea fieri non possit
nisi per deliberationem presentium, serie presentium invicem maturo
et deliberato consilio auctoritate et decreto nostri presentis generalis
capituli citra revocationem aliorum visitatorum nostrorum in aliis
provintiis deputatorum omni meliori via, modo et forma quibus melius et validius fieri potest et debet, confisi de fidei probitate curaque
et diligentia venerandi et religiosorum in Xpo nobis praecharum
fratrum Petri Stoltz praeceptoris Maguntiae et Frankfordiae ac Castri
Novi et cetera nostri conventus Rhodi magni baiulivi et Joannis Antonii de Actis praeceptoriae Pucini prioratus Capuae praeceptoris,

eos eligimus, constituimus, facimus, creamus, et solemniter ordinamus visitatores, commissarios, procuratores et iconomos nostros ordinis et capituli generales et speciales in prioratibus nostris Alamanniae
Superioris et Inferioris, Ungariae, Bohemiae, Datiae, Suetiae, Frisiae,
Balliagi de Brandemburg ac praeceptoriarum Brabantiae et Leodi
praeceptoriis, beneficiis, membris, *[fol.96v]* proprietatibus exemptis et
non exemptis eorundem specialiter et expresse acceptandum, perscrutandum, perquirendum, noscendum, intelligendum et requiren-
dum verum et legittimum valorem ipsorum prioratuum, baiuliarum,
praeceptoriarum et membrorum tam in genere quam in specie des-
tincte et particulariter, et dictorum perscrutationem et inquisitionem
in scriptis authenticis per dictorum visitatorum signatam et notariorum verificatis et subscriptis redigendum et redigi faciendum. Dantes
et concedentes eiisdem visitatoribus, commissariis et procuratoribus
nostris et dicti thesauri atque religionis in hiis, super his et ratione
horum plenam auctoritatem, facultatem totaliterque vices nostras ac
huiusmodi generalis capituli ut^a pro cuiusquidem rei exequutione et
deductione praefati visitatores accedere debeant ad loca, limites, situs
et provintias huiusmodi prioratuum, praeceptoriarum et membrorum
et diligenter atque cum summa attentione visitari, perscrutari et in-
quirere verum et legittimum valorem eorundem, deductis expensis et
oneribus ordinariis et consuetis tantum. Quodque ut commodius,
melius, perfectius huiusmodi verus, liquidus et legittimus valor habeatur, intelligatur et sciatur, dicti visitatores religiosos ordinis nostri,
etiam vassallos, subditos, arrendatores cuiusvis condictionis fuerint et
alias quascumque personas tam ecclesiasticas quam seculares in vim
auctoritatis capitularis solemni iuramento praestito adigant et astringant, impellant et in periculum et dispendium animarum suarum
manifestent, revelent, notificent, declarent, dicant et notum reddant
verum liquidum et verum valorem huiusmodi prioratuum et beneficiorum exemptorum et non exemptorum super quibus et de quibus
non interrogabuntur in variis et diversis provintiis dictorum limitum,
referendo singula singulis, quod si facere recusaverint, neglexerint seu
noluerint, quod non credimus, contra eosdem *[fol.97r]* religiosos et
subditos nostros procedant tanquam contra inobedientes, rebellos et
periurios auctoritate capitulari et stabilimentorum nostrorum, invocato etiam ad hoc exequendum si necesse fuerit ecclesiastico aut seculari brachio, ne religio nostra aliquo pacto defraudetur. Amplius forma
et modus erit sciendum et dignoscendum huiusmodi verum valorem
beneficiorum pro locatione et arrendamenta quae fiunt communibus
annis, videlicet sterili, fertili et mediocri, super quo ipsi visitatores et
commissarii habeant notitiam et consulant atque interrogent testes
idoneos et fidedignos de quantitate pecuniarum pro quibus arrenda-

menta sunt facta et fiunt in patria de praefatis beneficiis tam in capite quam in membris tempore sterili, fertili et mediocri et talis dispositio in scriptis redigatur ex quibus summaretur valor qui ex mediocritate insurgit tamquam verus et legittimus. Et quia forsitan his modis de aliquibus praeceptoriis et beneficiis intelligi[b] verus valor non posset quia testes non adessent vel arrendata nunquam fuissent, expediens et necesse erit, habeant et intelligant dicti visitatores et commissarii plenariam commissionem, qualitatem, conditionem, genus et speciem fructuum et reddituum tam frumenti, grani, vini, pecudum, pecuniarium, censuum et proventuum et ceterorum emolumentorum de valore quoque eorundem, anno fertili, sterili et mediocri pro qualitate condictionis et dispositione patriae, ut inde noscatur verus, legittimus et equalis valor, non summendo tempus sterilitatis aut fertilitatis sed mediocritatis, quae in scriptis redigantur.

Ordinantes et mandantes quod visitatores cum intraverint limites dictorum prioratuum per eorum presentiam propriam vel nuntium de eorum adventu et visitatione exequutione priores et receptores seu in eorum absentia vicepriores reddant, ut visitatione praedicta consilium, auxilium et favorem praestent quatenus visitatio huiusmodi prompte fiat et exequutioni demandetur. Hortamurque et monemus igitur venerandos priores et receptores et illos qui eorum vices tenent nostraeque religionis [fol.97v] tanquam verae obedientiae filii quibus plena spes est collata ut praedictis commissariis ordinis consiliariis, ut circa praedicta omni cura intendant et pareant ut effectualis exequutio sequatur et ne ordo ipse defraudetur. Mandantes insuper et eis si opus est − praecipimus in vim obedientiae − ingiungentes tertia monitione praehabita, receptoribus, praeceptoribus et possessoribus exemptis et non exemptis huiusmodi prioratuum, baiuliarum et camerarum magistralium et priorialium, praeceptoriarum et beneficiorum, pariter et fratribus, hominibus et vassallis nostri ordinis in dictis locis constitutis sub sacramento fidelitatis et homagii quo nobis et nostrae dictae domui sunt astricti, ut dictis nostris procuratoribus, commissariis et visitatoribus pareant, obediant et intendant auxilia quoque, favorem et consilium in hiis praebeant, quatenus huiusmodi visitatio et inquisitio perfecte haberi et exequutioni demandari possit. Ordinamusque et decernimus ut quam diligentissime huiusmodi visitatio et inquisitio fiat et in scriptis redigantur et termino praefixo celebrationis capituli generalis proxime futuri quod assignatum est die prima Septembris anni millesimi quadringentesimi nonagesimi quinti nobis et dicto capitulo generali presentetur, ut secundum earum tenorem indemnitati ordinis nostri consultatur et provideatur.

In cuius rei testimonium bulla nostra communis plumbea presentibus est appensa.

Datum Rhodi durante nostro generali capitulo die quinta mensis Augusti anno ab incarnato Xpo Jesu Domino nostro millesimo quadringentesimo nonagesimo tertio.

  ᵃ ut *fails ms.* ᵇ et intelligi *ms.*

The visitation acts of 1495 are to be found in AOM 45, a volume bound in parchment on wood, in folio on paper without papermark but with the lines of the deckle edge visible, 39 to 40 cm high and 26 to 27 cm wide. The volume consists of 244 written leaves and two flyleaves. Folio 224 seems to have been torn before it was used for writing: part of it is missing, but this has not affected the text, neither recto nor verso. Some of the leaves have been pasted onto strips of paper and the quires have been sewn on ropes. Sometimes the outer margins have been cut too narrow and the sequence of the leaves has been disturbed in the binding. Moreover, the original first leaf with the largest part of the bull of 5 August 1493 has been removed in the binding process. After this confusion had taken place, a modern folio numbering was stamped on the right side at the foot of the rectos; this numbering will be followed here.

At the end of this volume a letter dated 19 August 1540 from the bailiff of Utrecht to the Grand Master has been added, concerning the visitation of 1540 (see below, under C.3.).

The text of the 1495 visitation acts has been written in clear Gothic characters and is well legible notwithstanding the fact that some leaves have acquired a brownish colour by oxidation of the ink and moist stains. All pages of the book have been marked at the bottom with *G f Not.* (G.Froren Notarius) and some of them bear the additional mark *f.P.Stolz gran b. v.f.Johannes visitatores* (frater Petrus Stoltz grandus baiulivus, venerabilis frater Johannes visitatores). Sometimes remarks have been added in a different hand, i.e. the hand that has also written the notary notice on fol.244r, which bears the name of G.Froren Notarius.

The many mistakes in the spelling of proper names in these acts have neither been corrected nor marked with footnotes in this edition. The few clerical errors or deletions in the Latin text have been corrected tacitly. This edition is confined to the preceptories in the current territory of the Netherlands with their members inside and outside the Dutch boundaries, and the members of the Westphalian preceptory of Burgsteinfurt in the Dutch province of Groningen and the German East-Frisia.

The book bears the title:
Visitatio Commendarum Superioris et Inferioris Alemaniae
Anno Domini 1495
and contains a description of the following preceptories (a contemporaneous table of contents is missing, as well as the largest part of the bull of 5 August 1493):

Obrist menbrum   *[mentioned only]*   fol.99r
Bassel menbrum preceptorie in Torleszhem   fol.102r-103v
Hagenauwe menbrum preceptorie in Torleszhem   fol.103v-105r
Franckfort preceptoria (in qua est preceptor
    reverendus dominus Petrus Stolz
    sacri conventus Rodi magnus baiulivus)   fol.105v-107v
Moiszbach menbrum   *[mentioned only]*   fol.106r
Maguncia preceptoria (magnus baiulivus preceptor) fol.108r-110v
Wyszhem menbrum preceptorie in Maguncia   fol.111r-112r
Heymbach preceptoria   fol.112v
    [wrongly bound]   & fol.92r-92v
                                            & fol.114r-117r

Wyssenburg menbrum preceptorie in Heymbach   fol.117r
Spira gransea preceptorie in Heymbach   fol.117v-118r
Bruchsal menbrum preceptorie in Heymbach   fol.118v
Mueszbach menbrum preceptorie in Heymbach   fol.119r-121r
Wurmacia preceptoria   fol.121v
Wyssensehe preceptoria   fol.122r
Erlingen preceptoria   fol.122r-125v
Ratisbona preceptoria   fol.126r-127v
Altmunster menbrum preceptorie in Ratisbona   fol.127v-130v
Mergetem preceptoria   fol.131r-133v
Halle preceptoria   fol.134r-135r
Rotenburg preceptoria   fol.135v-137v
Wirtzburgh preceptoria   fol.138r-139v
Schluyssingen preceptoria   fol.140r-141r
Rudikem preceptoria   fol.141v-144r
Nidda menbrum preceptorie in Rudikem   fol.144r-146r
Grevenauwe menbrum preceptorie in Rudikem   fol.146v-147v
Wyssel preceptoria   fol.148r-150r
Meysenheim preceptoria   fol.150v-154r
Sultzbach menbrum preceptorie in Meysenheim   fol.154v-155v
Dieffenbach menbrum preceptorie in Meysenheim fol.156r-157r
Sobernhem preceptoria   fol.157v-158v
Brisach preceptoria   fol.159r-160v
Honyngen menbrum preceptorie in Brisach   fol.161r-162v
Colonia preceptoria (camera prioralis)   fol.163r-169r
    [folio 169v is void]
Wesentfelt preceptoria   fol.170r-171r
Wyldungen preceptoria   fol.171v-173v
Pannenschel menbrum preceptorie in Wyldungen fol.174r-174v
Adenauwe preceptoria   fol.175r-175v
Mechelen preceptoria   fol.176r-177v

fol.176r Mechelen preceptoria.

Die vicesimosexto mensis Iulii 1495 existentibus dominis visitatoribus
in preceptoria Wesalie comparuit ex eorum mandato frater Ulricus
Vittel miles ordinis sancti Johannis, preceptor in Mechelen et Velden
in persona, que preceptoria Mechelen est situata in provincia Brabancie sub dominio Comitum de Schwartzberg, Leodiensis diocesis.
    Die vero eodem prestitum fuit iuramentum eidem domino precep-
tori ad informandum dominos visitatores de quesitis per eos in quantum sibi innotuerit.

Primo domus preceptorie est situata intus villam Mechelen et est
antiqua, datur ruine, habet ecclesiam non parrochialem mediocrem,
intitulatur sub vocabulo sancti Johannis, habet quatuor altaria, primum consecratum in honore sancti Johannis Baptiste, secundum
beate Marie virginis, tercium sancti Anthonii, quartum sancte Crucis.

In dicta preceptoria sunt tres presbyteri quorum nomina sunt frater
Joachim, alius frater Johannes de Breda qui sunt ordinis sancti Johannis, tercius est presbyter secularis. Dicti tres cappellani habent omni
die celebrare unam missam in ecclesia predicta.

Item dicta preceptoria habet quandam ecclesiam parrochialem in
villa Wyler in qua predictus frater Johannes habet celebrare tres missas in septimana, distat a preceptoria spacio quarte unius hore itineris.

Nota de bonis et cleynodiis ecclesiarum non fit inventarium quia laici
habent curam omnium bonorum ecclesiarum antedictarum et habent
dare oleum et ceram ad usum ecclesiarum.

Sequuntur bona et utensilia domus

Item lecti XII cum eorum necessariis. Item mensalia II. Item manutergia VI. Item cacobi erei VIIII. Item pelvia erea quinque. Item
telleria stagnea VIII. Item scutelle stagnee parve et magne XXII.
Item anfre stagnee III. Item patelle ferree V. Item candelabra tria
quorum unum est stagneum. Item lavacra II.

Item dicta preceptoria habet quoddam menbrum in civitate Aquis
quod est affictatum cuidam fratri Nicolao de Kochem omni anno pro
florenis auri quinque ultra responsionem quam eciam predictus frater

Nicolaus tenetur solvere. Dicta affictacio est facta cum consensu capituli provincialis ut ipse preceptor asserit medio iuramento.

Nota[a] Ad sciendum monetam currentem in Mechelen[b], valorem frumentorum et vini et quantitatem mensurarum.

Item XVIII obli faciunt unum album. Item albi XXXVIII faciunt unum florenum Renensem in auro.

Item VIII sommeria faciunt unum modium. Item modium [fol.176v] unum siliginis valet omnibus annis florenum unum in auro. Item modium unum avene valet omnibus annis albos XVIIII. Item XXV fertel faciunt unam amam. Item VI ame faciunt unum foderium. Item foderium unum vini valet omnibus annis florenos auri VIIII albos VIIII, ut constitit dominis visitatoribus per informacionem preceptoris predicti medio eius iuramento.

---

[a] in the left margin. [b] in a different hand corrected from Aquis.

Sequitur introitus pecuniarum

Item dicta preceptoria habet de ficto omni anno racione census super domibus, agris et aliis possessionibus in villis Mechelen, Wyler etc. florenos 2 albos 13 oblos 15   II XIII XV.

Item preceptor habet ad usum suum certas pratas qui si locarentur potest preceptoria consequi omni anno ex dictis pratis florenos 9 albos 18   VIIII XVIII.

Item dicta preceptoria habet ultra predictas pratas alias pratas que valent quando locarentur omni anno florenos 15 albos 30

XV XXX.

[a]Item dicta preceptoria potest consequi ex pascuis omnibus annis quando locarentur   VIII XVI.[a]

Item quando redituarii qui tenentur annuos census preceptorie vendunt eorum agros aut bona, tunc tenentur dare decimam partem precii vendicionis, que decima pars valet preceptorie omnibus annis albos 24   XXIIII.

Item dicta preceptoria habet omni anno racione affictacionis menbri in Aquis ut predicitur florenos 5   V.

Summa floreni XXXXI, albi XXV, obli XV.

---

[a] in a different hand.

Introitus siliginis

Item dicta preceptoria habet omni anno de ficto in locis Wyler et Mechelen racione census agrorum modia XXIII.

Item dicta preceptoria habet omni anno ex quodam molino in Mechelen modia VIIII.

Item dicta preceptoria habet omni anno ex massaria in Elkenrode modia XXVIII.

Item dictus preceptor facit cultivare bonderos agri 133 qui si locarentur posset preceptoria libere consequi omni anno ex IIII bonderis modia siliginis tria, faciunt modia LXXXXVIII.

Item dicta preceptoria habet omnibus annis racione decime in Mechelen modia XXIIII.

Summa modia CLXXXII.

Nota quodlibet modium valet omnibus annis florenum unum in auro et sic predicta modia 182 valent florenos 182   CLXXXII.

fol.177r   Introitus avene

Item dicta preceptoria habet de ficto minuto omni anno in locis Wyler et Mechelen racione census agrorum modia quatuor sommeria septem.

Item dicta preceptoria habet omnibus annis racione decime in Mechelen modia duodecim.

Summa modia XVI, sommeria VII

Nota quodlibet modium valet omnibus annis albos XVIIII. Et sic dicta modia 16 sommeria 7 valent florenos 8 albos 15 oblos 13÷
[13.5]   VIII XV XIII÷.

Introitus vini

Item dicta preceptoria habet racione trium iucharorum vinearum in villa Alffter ame III. Et quodlibet foderium valet omnibus annis florenos auri VIIII et albos VIIII. Sic predicte ame III valent florenos 4 albos 24   IIII XXIIII.

Summa summarum omnium introituum pecuniarum, frumentorum et vini reductarum in pecunias
floreni auri CCXXXVI albi XXVII obli X÷ *[10.5]*.

Sequitur exitus pecuniarum.

Item dicta preceptoria tenetur omni anno domino comiti de Schwartz-berg ab antiqua consuetudine iure defensionis florenos 20   XX.

Item duobus cappellanis pro eorum salario florenos 9 albos 33
VIIII XXXIII.

Item tercio cappellano nichil datur quia habet oblaciones ecclesie parrochialis in Wyler.

Item coco pro salario florenos 4   IIII.

Item canuario qui est pistor pro salario florenos 6   VI.

Item famulo domus qui est braxator cervisie pro salario florenos auri quatuor   IIII.

Item expenditur omnibus annis pro lignis ad usum domus floreni decem   X.

Item pro cera et oleo in ecclesia Wyler omnibus annis florenos 4   IIII.

Item in dicta preceptoria sunt sex persone ultra ipsum dominum preceptorem, videlicet cappellani tres, canuarius, cocus et famulus domus. Et quia pastor in Wyler tenetur per *[fol.177v]* totam quadragesimam et sextis feriis dare pisces racione pietancie et sabathinis, ergo taxaverunt domini visitatores pro expensis cuiuslibet persone florenos auri XIIII, faciunt floreni 84   LXXXIIII.

Summa   floreni CXXXXI   albi XXXIII.

Nota ad vitam[a]
Item dicta preceptoria tenetur dare cuidam fratri Johanni Rode ordinis sancti Johannis solum vita sua durante florenos auri quatuor.

Summa summarum omnium exituum pecuniarum
floreni auri CXXXXI   albi XXXIII.

---

[a] *in the left margin.*

Aquis menbrum in Mechelen

Die decimo mensis Iulii 1495 existentibus dominis visitatoribus in preceptoria Coloniensi comparuit vocatus coram eis frater Nicolaus

Kochemsz prior ecclesie in Adenauwe, affictator menbri in Aquisgrano quod est menbrum preceptorie in Mechelen, in qua est preceptor frater Udalricus Vittel miles ordinis sancti Johannis.

Die predicto prestitum fuit iuramentum eidem fratri Nicolao Kochemsz ad informandum dominos visitatores de vero et legittimo valore dicti menbri.

Item dicta domus est parva, antiqua, situata intus civitatem Aquisgranum et habet quandam cappellam parvam intitulatam sub vocabulo sancti Johannis Baptiste et *[fol.178r]* habet tria altaria, primum consecratum in honore sancti Johannis Baptiste, secundum consecratum in honore beate Marie virginis, tercium in honore sancte Crucis.

Sequuntur bona ecclesie

Item calices argentei deaurati cum eorum patenis duo. Item monstrancia una argentea. Item missalia duo. Item casule VIII. Item cappa una sete. Item breviarium unum. In aliis vero necessariis ecclesia est sufficienter provisa.

Sequuntur bona domus.

Item lecti cum eorum necessariis quinque. Item olle eree VIII. Item lavacra erea IIII. Item cacobi erei sex. Item pelvia erea duo. Item patelle quinque. Item candelabra erea quinque. Item mensalia III. Item manutergia duo. Item scutelle stagnee parve et magne XXXI. Item anfre et flasci stagnei XI. Item telleria stagnea septem.

In dicta domus est solum necessarius unus cappellanus qui tenetur celebrare omnibus diebus festivis missam unam.

Item dictum menbrum est affictatum predicto fratri Nicolao per presentem dominum preceptorem cum consensu reverendi domini prioris Almanie et capituli provincialis omni anno pro florenis auri quinque ultra omnes expansas. Et eciam tenetur ipse frater Nicolaus solvere responsionem et omnia onera pro iure thesauri imposita et imponenda ut constitit dominis visitatoribus medio iuramento domini Nicolai predicti. Ergo domini visitatores taxarunt dictum menbrum valere tantum florenos auri quinque.

Summa summarum omnium introituum preceptorie Mechelen floreni auri CCXXXVI, albi XXVII, obli X÷ *[10.5]*.

Summa summarum omnium exituum dicte preceptorie Mechelen floreni auri CXXXXI, albi XXXIII.

Restant preceptorie liquide una cum menbro Aquis floreni auri LXXXXIIII, albi XXXII, obli X÷ *[10.5]*.

fol. 191v Arnhem Preceptoria.

Die decimo octavo mensis Iulii 1495 intrarunt domini visitatores preceptoriam in Arnhem, in qua est preceptor frater Johannes de Hatstein, miles ordinis sancti Johannis, qui eciam est preceptor in Heymbach; in dicta preceptoria Arnhem est quidam frater Brandolffus Hoeckelum cappellanus ordinis predicti, qui est factor et locumtenens dicte preceptorie.

Dicta preceptoria est situata intus opidum Arnhem sub dominio ducis Gelrensis Traiectensis diocesis.

Die vero decimanona eiusdem domini visitatores prestarunt iuramentum eidem domino factori sive locumtenenti ad informandum eos de quesitis per ipsos inquantum sibi innotuerit.

Domus preceptorie est magna, lapidea; in longo tempore non fuit in aliquo reparata, ut apparet ex ruina.
Item dicta preceptoria habet ecclesiam non parrochialem magnam antiquam et eciam male reparatam ad latus domus, consecratam in honore sancti Johannis; habet octo altaria, primum consecratum in honore sancti Johannis Babtiste, secundum beate Marie virginis, tercium sancte Crucis, quartum sancti Nicolai, quintum sancti Egidii, sextum sancte Anne, septimum sancte Marie Magdalene, octavum sancte virginis Katherine.
In dicta preceptoria sunt quatuor cappellani ordinis sancti Johannis, quorum nomina sunt: frater Brandolffus Hoeckenhem, locumtenens predictus, frater Nicolaus de Schoten, frater Henricus de Tholl et frater Johannes Wei.
Dicti cappellani tenentur omni die legere unam missam, et cantare aliam et cantare omni die vesperas et completorium.

Sequuntur cleynodia ecclesie.

Item calices argentei deaurati quatuor cum eorum patenis. Item ciborium unum argenteum deauratum pro venerabili sacramento.

Item thuribulum unum argenteum. Item ampelle sive anfre argentee due parve pro servicio missarum. Item casule sete diversarum colorum VIIII. Item cappe sete diversarum colorum VII. Item vestes levitiace sete diversarum colorum decem. Item casule panni diversarum colorum VIII cum eorum necessariis. Item missalia VI. Item gradualia IIII. Item antiphonarii IIII. Item psalteria IIII. Item candelabra erea IIII. Item candelabra stagnea IIII. Item lavacrum unum ereum.

In dicta ecclesia est una lampas coram venerabili sacramento die noctuque ardens.

fol.192r   Sequuntur bona et utensilia domus.

Item lecti cum eorum necessariis XII. Item anfre stagnee parve et magne XIII. Item candelabra erea VI. Item lavacra erea V. Item pelvis una. Item cacobi erei VIII. Item patelle ferree V. Item stagnee parve et magne XXXV. Item telleria stagnea XII. Item olle eree VIIII. Item manutergia V. Item mensalia VIII.

Item dicta preceptoria habet quoddam menbrum in civitate Novimagio, distat a preceptoria spacio itineris quatuor horarum, sub dominio ducis Gelrie Coloniensis diocesis.
ªNovimagium membrumª

ª *in a different hand in the left margin.*

Domini visitatores fuerunt informati per fratrem Henricum Tholl conventualem presentis preceptorie et ipsum dominum factorem seu locumtenentem, quod frater Johannes Hatstein preceptor non fuit in preceptoria Arnhem in undecim annis, propter quod preceptoria passa est diversa dampna et bonorum alienaciones et inpignoraciones, ut in exitu largius declarabitur; et pro nunc temporis dominus baiulivus Traiectensis ob mortem alterius quondam factoris deputavit fratrem Randolffum predictum in factorem et locumtenentem preceptorie, qui debet solvere annuatim responsionem et iura thesauri et dare annuatim domino preceptori pro sua absencia quantum per baiulivum Coloniensem et baiulivum futuro tempore declaratum fuerit, ut apparet per litteram domini baiulivi Traiectensis in vulgari Almanico scriptam et per me notarium visitacionis in Latinum redactam, cuius tenor sequitur et est talis:ª
    Nos frater Allexander de Rey baiulivus et preceptor in Traiecto ordinis sancti Johannis sacri hospitalis Jherosolimitani notum facimus omnibus hominibus quod nos ex potestate venerabilis et religiosi do-

mini Johannis Hatstein preceptoris in Heimbach et Arnhem predicti
ordinis in nomine Domini commisimus et committimus nostro dilecto
et amato fratri Randolfo de Hoekelnhem predicti ordinis domum
predictam in Arnhem cum bonis et redditibus ubicumque constitutis
ad dictam domum pertinentibus; qui ante omnia habebit curam quod
divina servicia die noctuque secundum stabilimenta nostri ordinis
iuxta possibilitatem domus predicte exequantur et fiant tenereque
domum reparatam cum omnibus suis curiis meliorare debet et non
ruynare permittat, qui eciam non debet aliqua bona ipsius domus
vendere, inpignorare, permutare nec in emphiteosim perpetuam locare sine speciali licencia eorum qui super hoc potestatem habent.
Eciam debet bona mobilia et immobilia recipere et dare ac coram
quocumque iudicio debito tempore ubi necessarium erit defendere ac
omni tempore esse sub visitacione, obediencia et correctione nostri
domini graciosi magistri in Rhodo et domini prioris Almanie, baiulivi
Traiectensis aut eorum visitatorum iuxta bonam consuetudinem nostri ordinis et possibilitatem ipsius domus. Eciam debet annuatim solvere responsionem et imposiciones Rodianas ac ex pecunia
provincialis capituli aut aliorum, ubi necessarium fuerit comparere in
capitulo uti alii preceptores ab antiquo usi sunt sine fallo, et ultra hoc
dare domino Johanni Hatstein preceptori prenominato *[fol.192v]* annuatim et solvere pro sua absencia iuxta possibilitatem ipsius domus
ad declaracionem dominorum baiulivi Coloniensis et baiulivi Traiectensis futuro tempore declarandum. Qua propter desideramus et si
opus fuerit precipimus in virtute sancte obediencie omnibus conventualibus domus in Arnhem nostri ordinis presentibus et futuris ut
predicto domino Randolfo obediant in omnibus licitis et debitis ac
omnibus debitoribus predicte domus ut solvant predicto domino
Randolfo et ab eo quietancias recipiant. Et quicquid in premissis fiet
erit eiusdem efficacie uti si per nos factum foret sine aliqua fara[b]. In
fidem veritatis fecimus nos baiulivus predictus ex potestate domini
Johannis de Hatstein preceptoris prenominati nostrum sigillum in
fine appendi. In anno Domini millesimo quadringentesimo nonagesimo quarto die sexto Augusti.

Nota[c] Ad sciendum monetam currentem in Arnhem, valorem frumentorum et quantitatem mensurarum: Item XII ortgen faciunt
unum stuber. Item XXXIIII stuber faciunt unum florenum Renensem in auro. Item IIII scheffel faciunt unum malderium. Item malderium siliginis valet omnibus annis stuber XXV et ortgin VI. Item
malderium unum tritici valet omnibus annis florenum unum in auro,
ut constitit dominis visitatoribus per informacionem Johannis de Sa-

lant, Allexandri Tengnegel et fratris Randolffi locumtenentis.

^a *the content of the letter is missing in the RA Gelderland copy.* ^b *uncertain reading ms.* ^c *in the left margin.*

Sequitur introitus pecuniarum.

Item dicta preceptoria habet de ficto omni anno a quodam Johannis Halle in Arnhem de agris in Lymersz in ducatu Clevensi, quos ipse habet a preceptoria, florenos 25 stuber 30   XXV XXX.

Item dicta praeceptoria habet de ficto annuatim de Johannis Wichmansz et Wychmansz Bertolsen in Brummen racione census possessionum, quas habent in ducatu Gelrensi, florenos 42 stuber 12   XXXXII XII.

Item dicta preceptoria habet omni anno a quodam Gerart Jonge in Brommen racione agrorum quos habet a preceptoria in ducatu Gelrensi, florenos 7 stuber 32   VII XXXII.

Item dicta preceptoria habet de ficto omni anno a quodam Johanni Bosch racione agrorum quos habet a preceptoria in ducatu Gelrensi, florenos 13   XIII.

Item dicta preceptoria habet annuatim a quodam Wilhelmo de Delen in Arnhem de massaria Wolkenhusen propre civitatem Arnhem florenos 9 stuber 14   VIIII XIIII.

Item dicta preceptoria habet annuatim a quodam Volker de Kever in Davantria recione decime in Nybroick florenos 11   XI.
fol.193r.

Item dicta preceptoria habet omni anno a quodam Gerhardo Beyer in Elst de massaria vocata Hollenderbroick florenos 22 XXII.

Item dicta preceptoria habet annuatim a quodam Reynhart de Pande in Arnhem de pratis que tenet in Arnhemerbroick, florenos [8 stuber 8]   VIII VIII.

Item dicta preceptoria habet annuatim de quodam Godert Kistenmecher in Arnhem de pratis et agris, que habet in Velles florenos [9 stuber 24]   VIIII XXIIII.

Item dicta preceptoria habet omni anno a quodam Bercardo Nyenhusz in Arnhem de agro quem tenet a preceptoria circa Arnhem, florenos [3 stuber 8]   III VIII.

Item dicta preceptoria habet annuatim a quodam Ottoni Arnasti in Linden de agris que habet a preceptoria, florenos 4 stuber 4   IIII IIII.

Item dicta preceptoria habet omni anno a quodam Helmico Welden in Greb de agris florenos 9 stuber 14   VIIII XIIII.

Item dicta preceptoria habet annuatim de agris et pratis in Umbren que nunc possidet frater Hermannus Ewick, florenos 10   X.

Item dicta preceptoria habet omni anno a quodam Johanni Westenenge et Johanni Engelkensz de agris quos tenetur in Maltburghen, florenos 13 stuber 8   XIII VIII.

Item dicta preceptoria habet de ficto minuto omni anno de diversis personis in diversis partitis in civitate Arnhem super domibus et aliis bonis florenos 35 stuber 10   XXXV X.

Item dicta preceptoria habet quandam massariam in polde[a], quam locumtenens facit cultivare pro media parte frumentorum in ea massaria crescencium; tamen habet facere in dicta cultura aliquas expensas, sed quando dicta massaria locaretur pro censu perpetuo, tunc preceptoria posset consequi omni anno libere ex dicta massaria florenos 102 stuber 32   CII XXXII.

Summa floreni CCCXXVII, stuber XXVI.

---

[a] *probably means: polder (= massaria).*

Introitus siliginis.

Item dicta preceptoria habet de ficto omni anno a quibusdam Johanni Wychmansz et Wichmansz Bertelsen in Brommen racione census massarie, quam habent in ducatu Clevensi, malderia XXXXVIII.

Item dicta preceptoria habet omni anno a quodam Reynhart Hermessen in Beroncken de massaria in Broickhusen malderia XXXIII.

Item dicta preceptoria habet omni anno a quodam Gisberto Johannis in Ede racione massarie ibidem malderia XVII.

Item dicta preceptoria habet omni anno a quodam Hartgero Hartgeri in Arnhem ex quibusdam agris prope Arnhem malderia quinque.

Item dicta preceptoria habet omni anno a quodam Jacobo Falck in Arnhem de uno agro scheffel III.
fol.193v

Item dicta preceptoria habet omni anno ex quodam molino circa Arnhem racione census malderia XXVI.

Summa malderia CXXVIIII scheffell III.

Nota quodlibet malderium valet omnibus annis stuber XXV et ortgen VI et sic dicta malderia CXXVIIII scheffell III valent florenos auri LXXXXVII stuber X ortgin VII÷ *[7.5]*

LXXXXVII   X   VII÷.

Introitus tritici.

Item dicta preceptoria habet omni anno ex quodam molino circa Arnhem racione census malderia XVIIII scheffel II. Et quodlibet malderium valet omnibus annis florenum unum in auro, sic dicta malderia 19 scheffel 2 valent florenos 19 stuber 17   XVIIII XVII.

Summa summarum omnium introituum pecuniarum et frumentorum reductarum in pecunias
    floreni auri CCCCXXXXIIII, stuber XVIIII, ortgin VII÷ *[7.5]*.

Sequitur exitus pecuniarum.

Item dicta preceptoria tenetur dare omni anno domino duci Gelrensi racione census ab antiquo florenos 13   XIII.
    Item dicta preceptoria tenetur dare omni anno duci Clevensi et abbatisse de Elten racione census ab antiquo florenos 7   VII.
    Item pastori in Arnhem racione certarum massariarum omni anno ab antiquo florenos 2 stuber 17   II XVII.
    Item quatuor cappellanis predictis cuilibet pro suo salario florenos auri 3 et stuber XVIII, faciunt simul florenos 14 stuber 4 XIIII IIII.
    Item preceptoria tenetur dare Wilhelmo Johannis in Hoesten omni anno racione debiti facti tempore huius preceptoris fratris Johannis Hatstein florenos 4   IIII.
    Item preceptoria tenetur dare omni anno Gerhardo Hommen in Hoesden racione debiti facti per procuratorem moderni preceptoris florenum 1 stuber 26   I XXVI.
    Item preceptoria tenetur dare omni anno Cornelio Palmart in Hoesden racione debiti facti moderni preceptoris florenum 1   I.
fol.194r
Item preceptoria tenetur dare omni anno Gerhardo Schymmelpen-nynck in Sutfania racione debiti facti per procuratorem seu locumte-nentem moderni preceptoris florenos 7   VII.
    Item preceptoria tenetur dare omni anno Gotfrido Moyses apud Arnhem racione debiti facti per preceptorem defunctum florenum 1 stuber 6   I VI.
    Item preceptoria tenetur dare omni anno Hartgero Hartgeri apud Arnhem racione debiti facti per locumtenentem moderni preceptoris florenos 5   V.
    Item preceptoria tenetur dare omni anno Helwico de Wely racio-ne debiti facti tempore moderni preceptoris florenos 7   VII.
    Item preceptoria tenetur dare expensas et vestitum cuidam Theo-dorico Bisen vita sua durante racione florenorum aureorum LVIII et

stuber XXVIII, quas recepit quidam frater Johannes Holt tempore moderni preceptoris, et dicte expense valent omni anno florenos auri XV et stuber X, et quia sunt ad vitam, non sunt positi in exitu.

Item preceptoria tenetur dare omni anno duabus monialibus in monasterio in Wyck, solum vita earum durante, florenos auri viginti, et quia abbatissa dicti monasterii recepit dictas pecunias annis 48 et nescitur, an vivant ille due mulieres, et nescitur de eorum nomine, ergo domini visitatores non scribunt pro nunc dictos florenos viginti pro exitu.

Item preceptoria tenetur dare omni anno Johanni Holl in Arnhem racione debiti facti tempore huius preceptoris florenum 1 stuber 26

I XXVI.

Item preceptoria tenetur dare omni anno Hermanno Wurm in Arnhem racione debiti facti tempore moderni preceptoris stuber 30

XXX.

Item preceptoria tenetur dare omni anno menbro suo Novimagio racione census Hollanderbroick florenos 4 stuber 17   IIII XVII.

Item procuratori, qui colligit redditus, pro salario et expensis florenos XI stuber 26   XI XXVI.

Item coco pro suo salario florenos 5 stuber 10   V X.

Item famulo coci pro salario florenos 2 stuber 12   II XII.

Item sacriste pro salario florenos 2 stuber 12   II XII.

Item canuario, qui eciam est porterius, pro salario florenum 1 stuber 26   I XXVI.

Item racione olei et cere ad usum ecclesie non fit exitus, quia magistri fabrice accipiunt oblaciones, ex quibus dant oleum et ceram necessariam.

Item in dicta preceptoria est necessario unus equus pro procuratore, cum quo expenduntur omnibus annis floreni 9   VIIII.

ªItem expenduntur omnibus annis in emptione lignorum ad usum preceptorie floreni 10   X.ª

Item in dicta preceptoria sunt octo persone, videlicet quatuor cappellani, canuarius, sacristi, cocus et famulus coci; taxaverunt domini visitatores pro expensis cuiuslibet persone florenos auri XV et sic dicte persone VIII faciunt florenos 120   CXX.

Item dicta preceptoria tenetur dare omni anno Henrico de Eghmont in Sutfania racione census bonorum in Hollenderbroick ab antiquo florenos duos stuber novem   II VIIII.

Item expenditur omnibus annis in reparacione agrorum sive diches propter fluminis Reni periculum certa quantitas [fol.194v] pecuniarum, et quia locumtenens a dominis visitatoribus et me notario sepe quesitus fuit et non dixit quantitatem parvam nec magnam, ergo nichil scribi potuit pro tali reparacione.

Summa floreni CCXXXV, stuber XVII.

Nota ad vitam[b]
Item dicta preceptoria tenetur dare omni anno fratri Hermanno
Ewick ordinis sancti Johannis vita sua durante florenos auri XVII
racione debiti facti tempore preceptoris defuncti quondam fratris
Theodorici Wolff.

Item dicta preceptoria tenetur dare fratri Johanni Aldenneel ordinis sancti Johannis vita sua durante omni anno florenos auri XV
racione debiti facti tempore moderni preceptoris.

---

[a] *in a different hand.* [b] *in the left margin; the items are linked by means of a large brace.*

Exitus siliginis.

Item preceptoria tenetur dare omni anno Gerhardo de Halle in
Brommen racione debiti facti tempore moderni preceptoris malderia
VI.

Item preceptoria tenetur dare omni anno Luberto Werneri in
Brommen racione debiti facti tempore moderni preceptoris malderia
IIII.

Item preceptoria tenetur dare omni anno Gerhardo de Brynnen
racione debiti facti tempore presentis preceptoris malderia VI.

Item preceptoria tenetur dare omni anno ecclesie sancte Walburgis in Arnhem ab antiquo scheffell III.

Item cuidam in Bare omni anno ab antiquo scheffel II.

Item preceptoria tenetur dare omni anno Katherin in Gallo intus
opidum Arnhem racione debiti facti tempore moderni preceptoris
malderia IIII.

Summa malderia XXI scheffell unum.

Nota quodlibet malderium valet omnibus annis stuber 25 et ortgin 6,
et sic predicta malderia 21 scheffell 1 valent omnibus annis florenos
15, stuber 31, ortgin 10÷ *[10.5]*   XV XXXI [X÷].

Exitus avene.

Item dicta preceptoria tenetur dare omni anno domino duci Clevensi
racione census massarie in Lymersz malderia *[fol.195r]* quatuor. Et
quodlibet malderium valet omnibus annis stuber VIII et ortgin VI, sic

dicta malderia 4 valent in auro florenum unum   I.

Summa summarum omnium exituum pecuniarum et frumentorum reductarum in pecunias floreni auri CCLII, stuber XIIII, ortgin X÷ *[10.5]* sine pecuniis que dantur ad vitam.

Sequuntur debita ad que preceptoria tenetur semel ªsolvendoª.

Item preceptoria predicta tenetur in una summa Theoderico de Besen racione debiti facti moderni preceptoris florenos 21 stuber 6.

Item preceptoria tenetur dare in una summa Stuyrman in Sutfania racione debiti facti tempore moderni preceptoris florenos auri 13.

Item preceptoria tenetur dare in una summa Johanni Heubtman in Venlo racione debiti facti tempore moderni preceptoris et eciam debiti antiqui florenos CIII stuber X.

Item preceptoria tenetur dare Reynhero de Arena in Arnhem racione debiti facti tempore moderni preceptoris florenos IIII stuber IIII.

Item preceptoria tenetur in una summa Everhardo Glaszmacher in Arnhem racione debiti facti tempore moderni preceptoris florenos quinque stuber decem.

Item preceptoria tenetur in una summa Elisabet de Arnhem racione debiti facti tempore moderni preceptoris florenos IIII stuber IIII.

Item preceptoria tenetur in una summa fratri Johanni de Brynnen ordinis sancti Johannis racione debiti facti tempore moderni preceptoris florenos XXII.

Item preceptoria tenetur in una summa Goswino de Aquis racione debiti antiqui florenos CXXXVII.

Item preceptoria tenetur in una summa Ignacio Holle racione debiti facti tempore moderni preceptoris florenos VIIII stuber XIIII.

Item preceptoria tenetur cuidam Gysberto Bolch in Arnhem racione debiti facti tempore presentis preceptoris florenos III stuber XXVIII.

Item preceptoria tenetur in una summa Johanni Verber in *[fol.195v]* Arnhem racione debiti facti tempore moderni preceptoris florenos XII stuber XII.

Item preceptoria tenetur dare in una summa Gysberto de Wagenszvelt racione debiti facti tempore moderni preceptoris florenos 15 stuber 10.

Item preceptoria tenetur dare Johanni Bleick in Huyssen racione debiti facti tempore moderni preceptoris florenos XVI.

Item preceptoria tenetur cuidam Henrico N. in Novimagio racione debiti facti tempore moderni preceptoris florenos XVII.

Item preceptoria tenetur dare Hermanno Schomecher in Arnhem racione debiti antiqui florenum 1 stuber XXVI.

Item preceptoria tenetur dare Wilhelmo Bumeister racione debiti facti tempore moderni preceptoris florenos VIII stuber XXVIII.

Item preceptoria tenetur dare Gariti Henrici racione debiti facti tempore moderni preceptoris florenum 1 stuber XXVI.

Item preceptoria tenetur Hermanno Wurm in Arnhem racione debiti facti tempore moderni preceptoris florenos 4 stuber 24.

Item preceptoria tenetur Wilhelmo de Delen in Arnhem racione vini, quod bibit quondam frater Johannes Holt locumtenens preceptoris moderni in spacio trium mensium, florenos XXXVII.

Item preceptoria tenetur Adriano Hommen racione debiti facti tempore moderni preceptoris florenum 1 stuber 1.

Item preceptoria tenetur Ludowico Sutendael in Rynden racione debiti facti tempore moderni preceptoris florenos XV stuber X.

Item preceptoria tenetur Rodolffo Domseller racione debiti facti tempore moderni preceptoris stuber XX.

Item preceptoria tenetur fratri Ottoni de Hafften locumtenenti in Novimagio racione debiti facti tempore moderni preceptoris florenos LXXVIII.

Item preceptoria tenetur fratri Henrico Hoichbein ordinis sancti Johannis racione debiti facti tempore moderni preceptoris florenos X.

Item preceptoria tenetur Stephano de Furchten racione debiti facti tempore moderni preceptoris florenos V.

Item preceptoria tenetur fratri Henrico Tholle, conventuali in Arnhem, racione salarii sui tempore moderni preceptoris deserviti florenos VI stuber XVI.

Item domini visitatores informantur per fratrem Randolffum locumtenentem presentem, quod preceptoria tenetur secundum suum videre diversis personis non scriptis in presenti quaterno, ultra florenos auri centum, que debita ipse pro nunc non scit nominare, quia non fuit in preceptoria ad unum annum et est novus locumtenens [a]florenos C[a].

Item preceptoria tenetur Johanni Zurduffen in Colonia racione vini debiti facti tempore moderni preceptoris florenos XII.

Item preceptoria tenetur dare Henrico de Egkmont racione debiti facti tempore moderni preceptoris florenos IIII stuber XVIII.

Item preceptoria tenetur dare Jacobo de Malborgen racione debiti facti tempore moderni preceptoris florenos IIII stuber IIII.

Summa floreni VI [C] LXIIII, stuber XXIII.

---

[a] *in a different hand.*

fol.196r Novimagium
menbrum preceptorie in Arnhem.

Die trecesimo mensis Iulii existentibus dominis visitatoribus in preceptoria in Arnhem comparuit ex eorum mandato frater Otto de
Hafften cappellanus ordinis sancti Johannis, factor et locumtenens
membri aut domus in Novimagio, quod distat a preceptoria Arnhem
spacio itineris quatuor horarum, in qua est preceptor frater Johannes
Hattstein, qui eciam est preceptor in Heymbach, miles predicti ordinis.

Dicta domus aut Menbrum est situatum intus civitatem Novimagium
in ducatu Gelrensi Coloniensis diocesis in loco amenissimo, est lapi-
data, antiqua, sed tamen competenter bona; habet ecclesiam non
parrochialem parvam intitulatam sub vocabulo sancti Johannis, habet
sex altaria: primum consecratum in honore sancti Johannis Babtiste,
secundum sancte Crucis, tercium bcatc Marie virginis, quartum Katherine, quintum Johannes Evangeliste, sextum sancti Georgii.

Die predicto domini visitatores prestarunt iuramentum eidem locumtenenti ad informandum eos de quesitis per ipsos in quantum sibi
innotuerit.

In dicta domo sunt quatuor cappellani ordinis sancti Johannis et unus
miles ordinis sancti Johannis, quorum nomina sunt: frater Otto de
Hafften cappellanus, qui est locumtenens dicti menbri, frater Fredericus Jacobi, frater Petrus Bommel, frater Johannes de Maeshese, quintus – qui est miles – vocatur frater Rutgerus Judeus de Everdingen.
    Dicti cappellani tenentur omni die legere unam missam et cantare
unam missam et cantare vesperas et completorium; die vero festivo
tenentur legere duas missas et cantare unam.

        Sequuntur bona ecclesie.

Item calices argentei deaurati quatuor cum eorum patenis. Item tres
patene argentee ad ornamentum capparum. Item IIII anfre argentee
parve pro servicio missarum. Item ciborium unum argenteum deauratum. Item due alie monstrancie argentee deaurate, una cum ligno
sancte Crucis, altera cum digito sancte Barbare. Item una monstranciola parva argentea. Item cappe sete diversarum colorum III. Item
casule sete VI. Item casule panni diversarum colorum VI. Item vestes
levitiace IIII. Item missalia quinque. Item antiphonarios II. Item gra-

dualia III. Item psalteria III. Item candelabra erea II. Item candelabra stagnea IIII. Item duo lectionalia.

Sequuntur bona domus.

Item lecti cum eorum necessariis XI. Item de omnibus aliis necessariis ad usum domus est domus bene provisa.
fol.196v
Nota[b]   Ad sciendum monetam currentem in Novimagio, valorem
frumentorum et quantitatem mensurarum:
     Item XII ortgin faciunt unum stuber. Item XXXIIII stuber faciunt
unum florenum Renensem in auro.
     Item quatuor scheffel faciunt unum malderium. Item malderium
unum siliginis valet omnibus annis stuber XXV et ortgin VI. Item
malderium unum tritici valet omnibus annis florenum unum in auro.
Item malderium unum avenae valet omnibus annis stuber VIII et
ortgin VI. Item malderium unum ordei valet omnibus annis stuber
XV, ut constitit dominis visitatoribus per informacionem predicti fratris Ottonis medio eius iuramento.

Sequitur introitus pecuniarum.

Item dicta domus habet annuatim de ficto minuto de diversis personis
in locis Nymmagen, Oy, Loet, Valbroich, Hernelt, Nederboesz etcetera racione census super domibus, agris, pratis et aliis possessionibus
florenos 76 stuber 4   LXXVI IIII.
     Item dicta domus habet omnibus annis racione offertoriorum et
oblacionum florenos 10   X.
     Item domus habet omnibus annis ex faro florenos 18   XVIII.
     Item locumtenens habet tres massarias in Lende circa Novima-
gium, quas concessit tribus massaris pro medietate frumentorum in
eis crescencium, et tamen tenetur facere medias expensas, sed quando dicte massarie locarentur pro censu perpetuo, tunc domus posset
consequi racione dictarum massariarum omni anno ultra omnes expensas florenos 100   C.
     Item dicta domus habet unam massariam in Duffell, distat a domo
spacio duarum horarum itineris, que massaria valet domui omnibus
annis ultra omnes expensas florenos 25   XXV.
     Item dicta domus habet unam massariam in villa Horsen, distat a
Novimagio spacio itineris quatuor horarum, que massaria valent
omnibus annis domui ultra omnes expensas florenos 25   XXV.
     Item domus habet unam massariam in Gronesbeck apud Silvam

Rickes, distat a Novimagio spacio duarum horarum itineris, que massaria valent omnibus annis ultra omnes expensas florenos 8   VIII.

Summa floreni CCLXII, stuber IIII.

Introitus siliginis.

Item dicta domus habet omni anno a diversis personis de ficto minuto
in locis Novimagio et circa Novimagium racione census ex agris malderia XXXVIII et quodlibet malderium valet omnibus annis stuber
XXV et ortgin VI, sic dicta malderia 38 valent florenos 28 stuber 17
                                                      XXVIII XVII.

fol.197r, cut off in the right margin

Introitus tritici.

Item dicta domus habet omni anno de ficto minuto de diversis personis in Novimagio et circa Novimagium racione census agrorum scheffel II. Et quodlibet malderium valet omnibus annis florenum unum in
auro, sic dicti duo scheffell valent stuber 17   XVII.

Introitus avene.

Item dicta domus habet omni anno de diversis personis in Novimagio
et circa Novimagium racione census agrorum malderia IIII scheffell
III. Et quodlibet malderium valet omnibus annis stuber VIII et ortgin
VI. Sic dicta malderia quatuor scheffel tria valent florenum unum,
stuber 6, ortgin 4   I VI [IIII.]

Introitus ordii.

Item dicta domus habet omni anno a quodam Gerhardo Bruer in
Novimagio racione census certi agri malderium unum. Et quodlibet
malderium valet omnibus annis stuber XV. Sic dictum malderium
unum valet stuber 15   XV.

Summa summarum omnium introituum pecuniarum et frumentorum
reductarum in pecunias
    floreni auri CCLXXXXII, stuber XXV, ortgin IIII÷ *[4.5]*.

Sequitur exitus pecuniarum.

Item est necessarium locumtenenti tenere unum equum ad colligendum redditus, cum quo expenduntur omnibus annis in avena, feno, palea et ferratura floreni 9   VIIII.

 Item canuario pro salario florenos 7   VII.

 Item coco et famulo coci pro salario florenos 6 stuber 16 VI XVI.

 Item sacriste pro salario florenos 4 stuber 4   IIII IIII.

 Item quatuor cappellanis predictis pro salario ªeorumª simul ultra oblaciones quas habent, florenos 6 stuber 16   VI XVI.

 Item in dicta domo sunt VIIII persone, videlicet IIII cappellani, unus miles, canuarius, cocus, sacrista et famulus coci; taxaverunt domini visitatores pro expensis cuiuslibet persone florenos auri XV, faciunt florenos 135   CXXXV.
fol.197v
Item expenduntur omnibus annis pro ligno ad usum domus floreni viginti   XX.

 Item expenduntur omnibus annis pro oleo et cera ad usum ecclesie floreni 13   XIII.

 Summa floreni CCI, stuber II.

Nota ad vitam.[b]
Item dicta domus tenetur dare cuidam Joanni Rode in Novimagio omni anno vita sua durante florenos auri V et stuber XXX racione florenorum aureorum LII et stuber XXII, quos recepit quidam frater Hinricus de Basdunck, olim locumtenens dicti menbri tempore fratris Theodorici Wolff preceptoris in Arnhem. Item dicta domus tenetur dare duabus personis in Novimagio, videlicet presbitero Theodorico Besman et matri sue, eorum vita durante racione debiti facti per quondam fratrem Theodoricum Baesdung locumtenentem omni anno florenos auri quinque ªstuber X.ª

Nota[b] Dictum menbrum in Novimagio est arrendatum per ipsum fratrem Johannem de Hatstein preceptorem in Arnhem predicto fratri Ottoni de Hafften vita sua durante omni anno pro florenis aureis XV cum consensu reverendi domini prioris Almanie et capituli provincialis celebrati Spiris cum tamen pacto et condicione, quod ipse frater Otto teneatur solvere annuatim responsiones, imposiciones et alia onera imposita et imponenda dicte domui et tenere domum bene reparatam et quod divina officia exequantur iuxta ritum et statuta ordinis, et maneat et debeat esse sub visitacione, correctione et ordinacione reverendissimi domini Rhodi magistri et prioris Almanie. Et casu quo ipse frater Otto defecerit in solucione ut predicitur, eo casu sit privandus domui; et eciam advenienti alteri preceptore, cui non placuerit dicta arrenda XV florenorum, iterum possit introitus dicte domus taxari facere de novo, non tamen taxando melioracionem factam per pecunias proprias ipsius fratris Ottonis. Et si plus valeret quam arrendatum est, tunc preceptor adveniens possit eidem fratri Ottoni domum de novo arrendare. Praedicta constant dominis visitatoribus per litteram reverendi domini prioris Almanie cum sigillo priorali appendente sub dato XXIIII die Aprilis anno LXXXXIIII *[1494]*.

Nota[b] Domini visitatores fuerunt informati, quod predictus frater Otto de Hafften locumtenens vendidit annui census super possessione in Oyen omni anno florenos auri XV et predictus frater Otto vendidit perpetui census siliginis modia V foras portem Wymmoele.

Summa summarum omnium introituum preceptorie Arnhem floreni auri IIII C XXXXIIII, stuber XVIIII, ortgin VII÷ *[7.5]*.

Summa summarum omnium exituum dicte preceptorie Arnhem floreni auri CCLII, stuber XIIII, ortgin X÷ *[10.5]*.

Restant liquide floreni CLXXXXII, stuber IIII, ortgin VIIII.

Restant racione arrendacionis menbri in Novimagio florenis auri XV[c] 15[a].
Summa summarum restant preceptorie in Arnhem cum menbro Novimagio floreni CCVII, stuber IIII, ortgin VIIII.

Tamen restant liquide menbro in Novimagio ultra omnes expensas, ut particulariter in menbro annotatur,
floreni LXXXXI, stuber III, ortgin IIII÷ *[4.5]*.

---

[a] *in a different hand.* [b] *in the left margin; the items are linked by means of a large brace.* [c] *corrected from* XVIII *ms.*

fol.198r is blank.

fol.198v   Traiectum preceptoria.

Die secundo mensis Augusti 1495 intrarunt domini visitatores preceptoriam aut cameram prioralem in Traiecto, in qua est preceptor venerabilis frater Allexander de Rey, cappellanus ordinis sancti Johannis, baiulivus Traiectensis.

Die vero tercio domini visitatores visitarunt membrum in Engen et membrum in Buren.

Die quinto eiusdem domini visitatores prestarunt iuramentum predicto domino preceptori ad informandum eos de quesitis per ipsos in quantum sibi innotuerit.

Primo domus dicte preceptoriae est magna et bona, lapidea, situata intus civitatem Traiectensem cum pulcro viridario. Habet ecclesiam magnam, pulcram, intitulatam sub vocabulo sancte Katherine virginis; habet VIIII altaria, quorum sex sunt consecrata et III sunt nova non consecrata; consecratorum altarium est unum in honore sancti Johannis, secundum in honore Apostolorum, tercium sancti Bartholomei, quartum beate Marie virginis, quintum Undecim milium Virginum, sextum sancti Nicolai.

Sequntur bona ecclesie.

Item calices argentei deaurati octo cum eorum patenis. Item una monstrancia magna argentea deaurata. Item duo thuribilia argentea magna. Item patena argentea una ad dandum pacem deaurata. Item fibule tres magne argentee deaurate pro cerimonio capparum. Item due monstranciole argentee parve, quarum una est deaurata. Item ciborium unum argenteum. Item ampulle due argentee pro servicio missarum. Item cappe sete rubee et bleue sex ornate nolis argenteis. Item cappe sete diversarum colorum V. Item vestes levitiace sete diversarum colorum VII. Item casule diversarum colorum sete VII. Item casulae diversarum colorum panni et sete antique XX. Item candelabra erea VI. Item in aliis necessariis ecclesia est bene provisa. Item missalia VIII. Item gradualia quinque. Item antiphonarios V. Item psalteria V. Item lectionalia II. Item breviarium unum.

Item in dicta preceptoria sunt pro nunc temporis octo cappellani, quorum nomina sunt: frater Allexander de Roy preceptor, frater Gervasius de Someren prior ecclesie, frater Bertoldus de Salant, frater Cornelius Stael, frater Johannes de Gauda, frater Bernhardus de Duffen, frater Henricus de Arnhem, frater Goswinus de Novimagio. Dicti cappellani tenentur omni die cantare unam missam et legere quatuor missas omni die et cantare omnes horas canonicas nocte dieque.

Nota ante guerras, que inceperunt anno LXXXI° *[1481]* inter regem Romanorum et reverendum dominum dominum episcopum Traiectensem, quando ipse dominus rex obsedit civitatem Traiectensem, fuerunt in dicta preceptoria *[fol.199r]* cappellani duodecim et diaconi duo; illo anno ad mitigandum expensas fuerunt transmissi quatuor cappellani et duo diaconi in alias ordinis domus propter dampna passa in destructione bonorum et possessionum preceptorie, sic quod preceptor nichil utilitatis habuit racione bonorum preceptorie et menbrorum suorum in tribus annis. Ergo pervenit preceptoria in magnum debitum et paupertatem, et hoc quia ipse guerre durarunt annis quatuor. Informantur domini visitatores per ipsum preceptorem ad omne minus necessarium fore habere cappellanos duodecim ad divina celebranda predicta, quod tamen domini visitatores remittunt ad reverendissimum dominum cardinalem Rhodi magistrum, et non taxarunt nisi cappellanos septem, quos repereunt ultra dominum preceptorem.

Item preceptoria habet undecim menbra: unum in Buren, distat a preceptoria spacio sex horarum itineris; secundum in Aldenwater, distat a preceptoria spacio sex horarum itineris; tercium in Hermelen, distat a preceptoria spacio itineris IIII horarum; quartum in Werder, distat a preceptoria spacio VIII horarum itineris; quintum in Wemeldingen, distat a preceptoria spacio dierum trium itineris; sextum in Engen, distat a preceptoria spacio VIII horarum itineris.

Item dicta preceptoria habet tria menbra que sunt conventus: unum in Valle sancti Johannis, distat a preceptoria spacio unius diei itineris; secundum in Frisia, vocatur Schneck, distat a preceptoria spacio trium dierum itineris; tercium in Kirckwerff in Selandia in terra Walkaria, distat a preceptoria spacio dierum quatuor itineris et est conventus monialium.

Item preceptoria in Harlem etiam est membrum preceptorie aut camere, tamen separata a preceptoria per bullas Rodianas; distat a preceptoria spacio itineris unius diei.

Item aliud membrum vocatur Myddelburgh in partibus Selandie.

Sequntur bona domus.

Item in dicta preceptoria sunt lecti XXIIII cum eorum necessariis; in aliis necessariis est domus bene et optime provisa.

Sequntur cleynodia pietancie preceptorie.

Item taxie argentee XXVIIII. Item becheria argentea XVIII. Item duo becheria argentea cum coperturis argenteis. Item duo becheria argentea cum pedibus. Item becheria alia parva argentea XII. Item anfra una argentea parva. Item anfra amphora[a] una facta ex nuce Judaico ornata argento. Item ciphi IIII lignei ornati argento. Item coclearia argentea duo ad usum confectionum. Item scutella una argentea. Item cocleria argentea XXIIII. Item taxea argentea una parva. Item becherium argenteum unum parvum. Item due anfre argentee parve ad usum ministrandi aquam. Item saleria duo argentea.
fol.199v
Item dicta preceptoria habet in latere domus hospitale unum, in quo ex antiqua consuetudine acceptant infirmi, cuiuscumque eciam infirmitatis infecti sunt, preter leprosi.
Nota[b]　Ad sciendum monetam currentem in Traiecto, valorem frumentorum et quantitatem mensurarum: Item XII wytgin faciunt unum stuber. Item XXVIII stuber faciunt unum florenum Renenensem in auro. Item modium unum tritici valet omnibus annis florenum unum in auro. Item modium unum siliginis valet omnibus annis stuber XX. Hec constarunt dominis visitatoribus per informacionem domini preceptoris medio eius iuramento.

---

[a] *in a different hand in the left margin.* [b] *in the left margin.*

Sequntur introitus pecuniarum.

Item dicta preceptoria habet omni anno ex locacione septem domorum et undecim camerarum intus civitatem Traiectensem de diversis personis florenos 70 stuber 25　　　　　　　　LXX XXV.

Item preceptor fecit edificari unam domum intus civitatem Traiectensem, ex quo habebit omni anno florenos quinque stuber 2　V II.

Item dicta preceptoria habet omni anno racione census ficti minuti ex domibus intus civitatem Traiectensem florenos 5 stuber 6　V VI.

Item preceptor facit cultivare in loco Schulpen iucharos agri XVI; quando locarentur, valerent preceptorie omni anno florenos undecim stuber 12　　　　　　　　　　　　　　　XI XII.

Item dicta preceptoria habet omni anno a quodam Johanni Reyers in Schulpen racione iucharorum XII agrorum florenos 7 stuber 20　　　　　　　　　　　　　　　　VII XX.

Item dicta preceptoria habet omni anno de diversis personis in dicto loco Schulpten racione agrorum et pascuum florenos 31 stuber 12　　　　　　　　　　　　　　　　XXXI XII.

Item dicta preceptoria habet omni anno a quodam Theodorico Johannis in Westbroich racione pascuarum florenos 6 stuber 12

VI XII.

Item dicta preceptoria habet omni anno a Egidio Jacobi in Achtenhoven racione pascuarum florenos 30   XXX.

Item preceptoria habet omni anno in loco dicto Achtenhoven de diversis personis racione terrarum cespitum, id est torfflandt, florenos auri 49 stuber 3   XXXXVIIII III.

Item dicta preceptoria habet omni anno de diversis personis in dicto loco Oistween racione terrarum cespitum torff florenos 105 [stuber] 7   CV VII.

Item dicta preceptoria habet omni anno a quodam Alberto de Seist in Overlanckbroich racione agrorum florenos 4 stuber 8

IIII VIII.

Item dicta preceptoria habet omni anno in loco Cotten de diversis personis racione census agrorum florenos 56 stuber 8 wytgin 6

LVI VIII VI

fol.200r, the utmost Roman numerals in the right margin cut off

Item dicta preceptoria habet de diversis personis in villis Odick, Holten, Schalckwick et tWael racione agrorum omni anno florenos 13, stuber 6, wytgin 6   XIII VI V[I.]

Item dicta preceptoria habet omni anno in loco Tollenstige de diversis personis racione census agrorum et pascuarum florenos 48 stuber 11   XXXXVIII XI.

Item dicta preceptoria habet omni anno in parrochia Burkirck et Galenkop de diversis personis racione census agrorum et pascuum florenos 87 stuber 14   LXXXVII XIIII.

Item dicta preceptoria habet omni anno de diversis personis in Juetfaesz racione census agrorum et pratarum florenos 19 stuber 23

XVIIII XXIII.

Item dicta preceptoria habet omni anno de diversis personis in Merkirch et Juerkom racione iucharorum agri XXXXVIII florenos 34 stuber 8   XXXIIII VIII.

Item dicta preceptoria habet omni anno in locis Langenraeck et Poelwyck de diversis personis racione census agrorum florenos 5 stuber 8   V VIII.

Item dicta preceptoria habet omni anno in Aldenwater de diversis personis racione census agrorum et pascuarum florenos 54, stuber 7, witgin 9   LIIII VII VI[III.]

Item dicta preceptoria habet omni anno in Werderer de diversis personis racione census agrorum et pascuarum florenos 78 stuber 7

LXXVIII VII.

Item dicta preceptoria habet omni anno in villa Camerick de di-

versis personis racione census agrorum et pascuum florenos 15 stuber
6   XV VI.

Item dicta preceptoria habet omni anno in villa Werden de diversis personis racione census agrorum et pascuum florenos 33 stuber 11
                                         XXXIII XI.

Item dicta preceptoria habet omni anno in villa Hermelen de diversis personis racione census agrorum et pascuum florenos 184, stuber 24, witgin 6   CLXXXIIII XXIIII [VI.]

Item preceptor facit cultivare in villa Hermelen iucharos agri 103,
qui si locarentur valerent preceptorie omni anno florenos 66 stuber 6
                                              LXVI VI.

Item dicta preceptoria habet in Cattenbroick iucharos agri
XXXVI, qui si locarentur valerent omni anno preceptorie florenos
12 stuber 24   XII XXIIII.

Item dicta preceptoria habet omni anno in Lopeck de diversis
personis racione census agrorum et pascuum florenos 39, stuber 26,
witgin 6   XXXVIIII XXVI [VI.]

Item dicta preceptoria habet omni anno in villa Jarszvelt de diversis personis racione census agrorum et pascuum florenos 3, stuber 25,
witgin 6   III XXV [VI.]

Item dicta preceptoria habet omni anno in Ysselstein de diversis
personis racione census agrorum et pascuum florenos 27 stuber 13
                                           XXVII XIII.

ªItem dicta preceptoria habet omni anno in Bentzkop de diversis
personis racione iucharorum 32 agrorum libere sine interesse florenos
17 stuber 4   XVII IIII.ª

Item dicta preceptoria habet omni anno in Betzkop de diversis
personis racione census agrorum et pascuum florenos 53 stuber 21
                                           LIII XXI.

Item preceptor habet in Betzkop iucharos agri XXIII, quos culti-
vatur, sed quando locarentur valerent preceptorie omni anno florenos
12 stuber 9   XII VIIII.

Item dicta preceptoria habet omni anno in Poelszbroick de diversis
personis racione census agrorum et pascuum florenos 44, stuber 22,
witgin 6   XXXXIIII XXII [VI.]

Item dicta preceptoria habet omni anno in Monfort de diversis
personis racione census agrorum et possessionum florenos 30 stuber 8
                                           XXX VIII.

Item dicta preceptoria habet omni anno in Vleten de diversis personis racione census agrorum et pascuum florenos 95 stuber 20 wytgin 6   LXXXXV XX [VI.]

fol.200v, the utmost characters in the left margin cut off

Item dicta preceptoria habet in Vloten iucharos 159 pascuum,

valent omnibus annis florenos 159   CLVIIII.
Item dicta preceptoria habet in Marsen de diversis personis racione census agrorum et pascuum florenos 50 stuber 20   L XX.
Item dicta preceptoria habet in Broekelen de diversis personis racione census agrorum et pascuum florenos 19, stuber 24, wytgin 6
                              XVIIII XXIIII VI.
Item dicta preceptoria habet omni anno in locis Loenen, Apcau, Horst, Werde, Riswick, Hostricht de diversis personis racione census agrorum et pascuum florenos 12 stuber 9   XII VIIII.

ª *this item is missing in RA Gelderland.*

[B]uren menbrumª
Item dicta preceptoria habuit omni anno de preceptori in Buren florenos auri quinquaginta racione arrendacionis menbri in Buren, sed quia domus dicti menbri et ecclesia sunt penitus destructe, ergo preceptor in Traiecto in tribus annis nichil habuit pro dicta arrendacione, nec sperat in futuris temporibus consequi plus quam florenos 30   XXX.

[A]ldenwater menbrumª
Item preceptoria habet omni anno racione arrendacionis menbri in Aldenwater florenos 14 stuber 8   XIIII VIII.

[He]rmelen menbrumª
Item preceptoria habet omni anno racione arrendacionis menbri in Hermelen florenos 17 stuber 7   XVII VII.

Werderer menbrumª
Item dicta preceptoria habet omni anno racione menbri in Werderer pro arrendacione florenos 20 stuber 20   XX XX.

Wemeldingen menbrumª
Item dicta preceptoria habet omni anno racione arrendacionis menbri in Wemeldingen florenos 42 stuber 24   XXXXII XXIIII.

[E]ngen menbrumª
Item dicta preceptoria habet omni anno racione arrendacionis menbri in Engen florenos 100   C.

[Va]llis sancti Johannis menbrumª
Item dicta preceptoria habet omni anno racione arrendacionis menbri Vallis sancti Johannis florenos 40   XXXX.

[K]yrchdorff menbrum[a]

Item dicta preceptoria solebat habere racione arrendacionis menbri in Kirchwerff florenos auri 17 et stuber 4, sed presens preceptor et certi sui antecessores nichil habuerunt longis temporibus et modo eciam nichil habet presens preceptor in Traiecto.

Sneck menbrum[a]

Item dicta preceptoria habet omni anno racione arrendacionis menbri in Schneck florenos 50   L.

Item dicta preceptoria habet omnibus annis racione offertorii et oblacionum florenos 20   XX.

Item dicta preceptoria habet in diversis locis de diversis personis racione census libras cere XXVI, valet quelibet libra omnibus annis stuber IIII, faciunt florenos 3 stuber 20   III XX.

Summa floreni M VIIII^C XXXXIII, stuber XII, wytgin VIIII.

---

[a] *in the left margin.*

Introitus tritici.

Item dicta preceptoria habet omni anno de ficto minuto de diversis personis in Coten racione census agrorum modia XXXV et quodlibet modium valet omnibus annis florenum unum in auro, sic dicta modia 35 valent florenos 35   XXXV.

fol.201r Introitus siliginis.

Item dicta preceptoria habet omni anno de diversis personis in locis Oysterween, Ginckel et Doren racione census agrorum modia XXXXIIII÷ *[44.5]* et quodlibet modium valet omnibus annis stuber XX, sic dicta modia 44÷ valent florenos 31 stuber 22 XXXI XXII.

Summa summarum omnium introituum pecuniarum et frumentorum reductarum in pecunias floreni auri II.^{M} X, stuber VI, witgin VIIII.

Sequitur exitus pecuniarum.

Item preceptor dicte preceptorie dat omni anno reverendo domino priori Almanie racione arrendacionis dicte preceptorie aut camere Traiectensis in auro florenos 200   CC.

Item preceptor tenetur dare pietancie Traiectensi racione census unius agri florenos 10 stuber 20   X XX.

Item dicta preceptoria tenetur dare omni anno diversis personis racione census agrorum et pascuum in diversis locis situatis florenos 10   X.

Item dicta preceptoria tenetur dare omni anno Bernhardo Friesz in Renen racione debiti facti tempore reverendi quondam domini Johannis de Auwe prioris Almanie per suum locumtenentem fratrem Engelbertum Frese florenos 15   XV.

Item dicta preceptoria tenetur dare omni anno Alberto Albertstein in Traiecto racione debiti facti tempore quondam reverendi domini Johannis Auwe prioris Almanie florenos 15   XV.

Item dicta preceptoria tenetur dare omni anno Gotfrido Verber in Traiecto racione debiti facti tempore reverendi domini Johannis Auwe prioris Almanie florenos 6   VI.

Item dicta preceptoria tenetur dare cuidam Berte Johannis in Amsterdam racione debiti facti tempore quondam reverendi domini Johannis Auwe prioris Almanie florenos 5   V.

Item dicta preceptoria tenetur dare omni anno hospitali in Cusa racione census ab antiquo florenos 12 stuber 14   XII XIIII.

Item dicta preceptoria habet in Sculpen iucharos agri et pascuum LXXVIIII et omnibus annis expenditur in reparacione *[fol.201v]* [aggerorum] contra periculum maris pro quolibet iucharo stuber IIII, faciunt simul florenos auri 11 stuber 8   XI VIII.

Item dicta preceptoria habet in Westbroick certam quantitatem feni, scilicet campi ubi colliguntur cespites, qua pecia campi expenditur omnibus annis pro reparacione aggerorum[a] propter periculum maris stuber 27   XXVII.

Item dicta preceptoria habet in Achtenhoeven certam quantitatem agrorum et pascuum, ex quibus preceptoria habet omni anno racione census scuta currentis monete, et preceptoria dat omnibus annis pro angariis dictorum scutorum florenos 7 stuber 17   VII XVII.

Item dicta preceptoria habet omni anno in Oistween supra agris et pratis scuta 128 et preceptoria solvit omnibus annis pro angariis racione cuiuslibet scuti stuber 3÷ *[3.5]*, faciunt florenos 16   XVI.

Item dicta preceptoria habet omni anno racione census modia siliginis 44÷ *[44.5]* et preceptoria solvit omnibus annis racione dictorum modiorum pro angariis florenos 4, stuber 10, witgin 6   IIII X VI.

Item dicta preceptoria habet in Overlanckbroich iucharos agri XVI, racione quorum preceptoria solvit omnibus annis pro angariis florenum 1 stuber 12   I XII.

Item dicta preceptoria habet in Coten iucharos agri et pratorum

LXXXV et preceptoria solvit omnibus annis pro angariis cuiuslibet iuchari stuber 3÷ *[3.5]*, faciunt florenos 10, stuber 17, wytgin 6
X XVI VI.

Item dicta preceptoria habet certam quantitatem agrorum in Houten, Schalckwych et Twalen, racione quorum solvit preceptoria omnibus annis pro angariis stuber 24 wytgin 6   XXIIII VI.

Item dicta preceptoria habet in Tollenstegen iucharos agri et pratorum XXXXVII et preceptoria solvit omnibus annis racione cuiuslibet iuchari stuber III, faciunt florenos 5 stuber I   V I.

Item dicta preceptoria habet in Buyrkirch iucharos agri et pascuum LXXXVI et solvit omnibus annis racione angarie pro quolibet iucharo ᵇstuber 4, faciunt florenos 12 stuber 8   XII VIII.

Item dicta preceptoria habet in Juetfaesz iucharos agri et pratarum XXII et solvit omnibus annis pro conservacione cuiuslibet iuchariᵇ stuber 3÷ *[3.5]*, faciunt florenum 1 stuber 21   I XXI.

Item dicta preceptoria habet in Merkirch iucharos agri et pratarum XXXXVIII et solvit omnibus annis pro angariis cuiuslibet iuchari stuber VIII, faciunt florenos 13 stuber 20   XIII XX.

Item dicta preceptoria habet in Hermelen iucharos agri et pascuum 439 et preceptoria solvit pro reparacione cuiuslibet iuchari omnibus annis causa periculi maris stuber 6, faciunt [florenos 94 stuber 2]   LXXXXIIII II.

Item dicta preceptoria habet in Langlack iucharos agri et pascuum IIII÷ *[4.5]* et solvit omnibus annis pro reparacione cuiuslibet iugari stuber VI, faciunt stuber 27   XXVII.

fol.202r, the utmost Roman numeral in the right margin cut off

Item dicta preceptoria habet in Poelwyck iucharos agri 6 et solvit omnibus annis racione reparacionis pro quolibet iugaro stuber VI, faciunt florenum 1 stuber 8   I VIII.

Item dicta preceptoria habet in Aldenwater iucharos agri et pascuum 115÷ *[115.5]* et solvit omnibus annis pro reparacione cuiuslibet iuchari stuber IIII, faciunt florenos 16 stuber 14   XVI XIIII.

Item dicta preceptoria habet in Werder iugaros agri et pratarum 180÷ *[180.5]* et solvit omnibus annis racione cuiuslibet iuchari pro reparacione stuber V, faciunt florenos 32 stuber 6 wytgin 6
XXXII VI [VI.]

Item dicta preceptoria habet in Camerick iucharos agri et pascuum LIII et solvit omnibus annis pro reparacione cuiuslibet iuchari stuber V, faciunt florenos 9 stuber 12   VIIII XII.

Item dicta preceptoria habet in Wurden iucharas agri et pascuum 117 et solvit omnibus annis pro reparacione cuiuslibet iugari stuber V, faciunt florenos 20 stuber 25   XX XXV.

Item dicta preceptoria habet in Lopick iucharos agri et pascuum

LXV÷ *[65.5]* et solvit omnibus annis pro reparacione cuiuslibet agri stuber VI, faciunt florenos 14 stuber 1 XIIII I.

Item dicta preceptoria habet in Jaerszfelt iucharos agri et pascuum IIII÷ *[4.5]* et solvit omnibus annis pro reparacione cuiuslibet iuchari stuber 4, faciunt stuber 18 XVIII.

Item dicta preceptoria habet in Bentzkop iucharos agri et pascuum 109÷ *[109.5]* et solvit omnibus annis pro reparacione cuiuslibet iuchari stuber VIII, faciunt florenos 31 stuber 8 XXXI VIII.

Item dicta preceptoria habet in Pulzbroick iucharos agri et pratarum LXXXVI et solvit omnibus annis pro reparacione cuiuslibet agri stuber VII, faciunt florenos 21 stuber 14 XXI XIIII.

Item dicta preceptoria habet in Montfort iucharos agri et pascuum XXXXVI et solvit omnibus annis pro reparacione cuiuslibet agri stuber V, faciunt florenos 8 stuber 6 VIII VI.

Item dicta preceptoria habet in Cattenbroich iugaros agri et pascuum XXXVI et solvit omnibus annis pro reparacione cuiuslibet iuchari stuber VI, faciunt florenos 7 stuber 20 VII XX.

Item dicta preceptoria habet in Vlorten iucharos agri 295 et solvit omnibus annis pro reparacione cuiuslibet iuchari stuber IIII, faciunt florenos 42 stuber 4 XXXXII IIII.

Item dicta preceptoria habet in Broikelen iucharos agri et pascuarum LVII÷ *[57.5]* et solvit pro reparacione cuiuslibet iugari stuber IIII, faciunt florenos 8 stuber 6 VIII VI.

Item dicta preceptoria habet in Loenen iucharos agri duos et solvit omnibus annis pro reparacione cuiuslibet iugari stuber IIII, faciunt stuber 8 VIII.

fol.202v, cut off in the left margin

Item dicta preceptoria habet in Apcau iucharos agri et pascuarum VII et solvit omnibus annis pro reparacione cuiuslibet iugari stuber quatuor, faciunt florenum unum I.

Item coco pro salario florenos 9 stuber 16 VIIII XVI.

Item famulo coci pro salario florenos 3 stuber 16 III XVI.

Item canuario pro salario florenos 7 stuber 24 VII XXIIII.

Item pistori, qui eciam est braxator cervisie, pro salario florenos 9 [stuber] 3 VIIII III.

Item famulo pistoris pro salario florenos 5 V.

Item famule, que lavat et gubernat ortum, pro salario florenos 4 stuber 8 IIII VIII.

Item porterio pro salario florenos 3 stuber 16 III XVI.

Item procuratori domus pro salario florenos 10 stuber 8 X VIII.

---

a agrorum *ms.* b stuber — iuchari *fails in RA Gelderland.*

In infirmaria.

Item quatuor ancillis pro earum salario florenos 15	XV.
Item doctori medicinarum pro salario florenos 6	VI.
Item siroico pro salario florenos 3	III.
Item causidico pro salario florenos 2 stuber 4	II IIII.
Item pedello in Traiecto pro salario florenum 1 stuber 2	I II.

Item pedello in Wurden omni anno pro salario florenum 1 stuber 17   I XVII.

Item dicta preceptoria tenetur ex antiqua consuetudine dare pro encinio pedellis et officialibus civitatis Traiectensis florenos 4 stuber 8   IIII VIII.

Item preceptor dat omni anno cuilibet cappellanorum pro suis necessariis florenos auri IIII et stuber XIIII, et sunt preter preceptorem cappellani VII, faciunt florenos 31 stuber 18   XXXI XVIII.

Item preceptoria necessario habet tenere equum unum pro procuratore ad colligendum census; in ferretura et aliis necessariis, videlicet avena, expenduntur singulis annis floreni 9   VIIII.

Item expenduntur omnibus annis pro oleo et cera ad usum ecclesie florenii 30   XXX.

Item in dicta preceptoria sunt XVI persone ultra ipsum dominum preceptorem, videlicet septem cappellani, unus diaconus, procurator, cocus, famulus coci, canuarius, pistor, famulus pistoris, famula que lavat lintheamina, porterius; taxaverunt domini visitatores pro expensis cuiuslibet persone florenos 18, faciunt florenos 288

       CCLXXXVIII.

Item expenduntur omnibus annis in reparacione domorum ex quibus preceptoria habet annuos census, floreni 15   XV.

Item expenduntur omnibus annis pro carne, cervisia, pane, oleo, butiro et linteaminibus ad opus famularum et pauperum in hospitali floreni 54   LIIII.

Item expenduntur omnibus annis pro ligno et cespitibus pro preceptoria et hospitali floreni 100   C.

Summa floreni MCCLXXXIIII, stuber XVI.

[Not]a ad vitam^a
Item dicta preceptoria tenetur dare omni anno cuidam domino Eberardo Cornelii in Delfft, solum vita sua durante, est etatis circa LXX^ta annorum, florenos auri VI racione debiti facti tempore quondam domini Johannis Auwe prioris Almanie.

fol.203r

Nota ad vitam[b]

Item dicta preceptoria tenetur dare omni anno Jacobo Johannis in Traiecto racione debiti facti tempore quondam fratris Auwe prioris Almanie florenos auri duos.

Item preceptoria tenetur dare omni anno Alheide Gentersz in Traiecto, solum vita sua durante, florenos auri XII.

Item preceptoria tenetur dare omni anno Martino Jacobi in Antwerpia vita sua durante racione debiti facti tempore quondam reverendi domini prioris Almanie florenos auri XIII.

Item dicta preceptoria tenetur dare omni anno magistro Wyt in Selandia vita sua durante florenos auri XII racione debiti facti tempore quondam domini Johannis Auwe prioris Almanie.

Item preceptoria tenetur dare omni anno domicello Hermanno de Coneu vita sua durante racione debiti facti tempore quondam domini Johannis Auwe prioris Almanie florenos auri XX.

Item preceptoria tenetur dare magistro Gerhardo de Wagenyng in Traiecto vita sua durante florenos auri VI stuber XIIII racione debiti facti tempore predicti quondam prioris.

Item preceptoria tenetur dare omni anno fratri Johanni Huperti preceptori in Buren vita sua durante florenos auri XII racione debiti ut supra.

Item dicta preceptoria tenetur dare omni anno fratri Alberto Henrici preceptori in Werder vita sua durante florenos auri VI racione debiti antiqui.

Item dicta preceptoria tenetur [dare] omni anno Belie de Randwick in Traiecto vita sua durante florenos auri XIII racione debiti facti tempore predicti quondam prioris Almanie.

[c]Item preceptoria tenetur dare omni anno domicelle Johanne de Nyevelt vita sua durante florenos auri IIII racione debiti facti tempore quondam prioris Almanie vita sua durante.[c]

Item preceptoria tenetur dare omni anno fratri Gervasio de Someren vita sua durante florenos auri III, pro quibus fuerunt empti redditus perpetue ad utilitatem preceptorie.

Item preceptoria tenetur dare omni anno Jacobo Guillermi et uxori eius in Traiecto vita eorum durante florenos auri XIIII racione debiti facti tempore quondam predicti prioris Almanie.

[d]Item preceptoria tenetur dare omni anno Dewer Cornelii in Traiecto vita sua durante ratione debiti antiqui florenos X.[d]

Exitus tritici.

Item preceptoria tenetur ab antiqua consuetudine et ex fundacione expendere in elimosinis omni anno modia XIII et quodlibet modium valet omnibus annis in auro florenum unum, sic predicta modia XIII valent florenos 13   XIII.

Summa summarum omnium exituum pecuniarum et frumentorum reductarum in pecunias floreni auri MCCLXXXXVII stuber XVI, sine omnibus illis pecuniis que dantur ad vitam, quia non sunt census perpetui et in dies moriuntur.

fol.203v Sequitur introitus pietanciae in Traiecto.

Item dicta pietancia habet omni anno a preceptori in Traiecto racione agrorum quos habet preceptor de conventualibus, florenos decem stuber XX.

Item dicta pietancia habet omni anno racione domus vocate Engel in Traiecto florenos X.

Item dicta pietancia habet omni anno racione census duarum domorum in Traiecto libere florenos 2 stuber 4.

Item dicta pietancia habet omni anno a quodam Waltero Johannis in Haversau racione agrorum florenum 1 stuber 12.

Item dicta pietancia habet omni anno de castro de Worden racione unius misse perpetue fundate per dominum castri florenos 26 stuber 22.

Item dicta pietancia habet omni anno a quodam Guillermorno Gerhardi in Gallicanes racione iucherorum decem agri florenos quinque stuber X.

Item dicta pietancia habet omni anno a Mathia Henrici in Reyerszkop racione census septem iucherorum agri florenos quinque.

Item dicta pietancia habet a quodam Adriano Mathie in Heycop racione quatuor iucharorum agri florenos II stuber IIII.

Item dicta pietancia habet omni anno a quodam Petro Frit in Heycop racione duorum iucharorum agri florenum I stuber XII.

Item dicta pietancia habet omni anno a quodam Ernst Gotfridi in Aldenryn racione duorum iucharorum agri florenos II stuber IIII.

Item dicta pietancia habet omni anno a quodam Jacobo Gerhardi in Aldenryn racione duorum iucharorum agri florenum 1 stuber XII.

Item dicta pietancia habet omni anno de diversis personis in Aldenwater racione census domorum florenum 1 stuber XII.

Item dicta pietancia habet omni anno racione insule circa Rynhen ultra expenses florenos decem stuber XX.

Item dicta pietancia habet omni anno in ducatu Gelrie in locis Engen, Eck et Linden de diversis personis racione agrorum et pascuum florenos XXII stuber IIII.

^aSumma floreni CII, stuber XXIIII.^a

fol.204r Sequitur exitus pietanciae in Traiecto.

Item dicta pietancia dat omni anno cappellanis dicte preceptorie, quorum unus est dominus preceptor, pro eorum necessariis florenos auri II et stuber 16, faciunt simul florenos 24 stuber 24.

Item dicta pietancia dat procuratori pietancie et magistro coquine pro salario floreni VII stuber IIII.

Item dicta pietancia dat doctori medicinarum pro salario omni anno florenos duos stuber quatuor.

Item dicta pietancia expendit omnibus annis in medicinis florenos duos.

Item pietancia expendit omnibus annis in vino pro conventualibus florenos vigintiquinque stuber viginti.

Item pietancia expendit omnibus annis in amigdalis, zukaro et ficubus per totum annum florenos II stuber XXIIII.

Item dicta pietancia expendit omnibus annis in exactionibus quas facit dominus dux Gelrie florenos II.

Item dicta pietancia tenetur ex antiqua consuetudine dare expenses in profesto sancte Agnetis omni anno, in quibus expenditur omnibus annis floreni II.

^aItem dicta pietancia expendit omnibus annis in reparatione aggerum propter periculum fluminum florenos X.

Summa floreni LXXVIIII, stuber XXVII.^a

Nota ad vitam^b
Item dicta pietancia tenetur dare cuidam Helie Henrici in Traiecto vita sua durante racione pecuniarum quondam receptarum per pietanciam florenos auri XII.

Item dicta pietancia tenetur dare omni anno fratri Gervasio de Someren priori ecclesie, solum vita sua durante, florenos auri quatuor et stuber VIII racione florenorum auri XXXXV et stuber XVI, quos pietancia recepit ab eodem domino priori et emit locum quandam, in quo potest edificare domus.

---

^a Summa — XXIIII *and* Item — XXVII *in a different hand.* ^b *in the left margin; the items are linked by means of a large brace.*

fol.204v   Engen menbrum preceptorie in Traiecto

Die secundo Augusti 1495 intrarunt domini visitatores in Traiecto
que est camera reverendi domini prioris Almanie, in qua est preceptor venerabilis frater Allexander de Roy, baiulivus Traiectensis.

Die vero tercio domini visitatores prestarunt iuramentum fratri
Ottoni de Sevenhusen, locumtenenti menbri aut domus in Engen,
quod est menbrum camere predicte, ad informandum dominos visitatores de quesitis per eos in quantum sibi innotuerit.

Primo: dictum menbrum Engen est situatum sub dominio ducatus
Gelrensis Traiectensis diocesis in campestris; distat a preceptoria spacio unius diei itineris.

Domus dicti menbri est magna, lapidea, antiqua, tamen satis bona,
circumdata fossa aque plena; habet ecclesiam parrochialem antiquam, distat a domo spacio parvo in villa Engen, intitulatur sub
vocabulo sancti Johannis et habet tria altaria: primum consecratum
in honore sancti Johannis Baptiste, secundum in honore sancte Katherine, tertium sancte Crucis.

In dicta ecclesia est una lampas coram venerabili sacramento die
noctuque ardens.

In dicta domo sunt tres cappellani ordinis sancti Johannis, quorum
nomina sunt: frater Otto predictus, frater Anthonius Duesz, frater
Arnestus de Mertin, qui tenentur omni septimana celebrare missas
novem.

Sequuntur bona ecclesie.

De bonis ecclesie non sit inventarium, quia magistri fabrice deputati a
communitate ville habent curam bonorum ecclesie.

Sequuntur bona domus.

Item lecti novem cum eorum necessariis. Item scutelle stagnee parve
et magne XXXIIII. Item telleria stagnea XXXXVIII. Item anfre
stagnee parve et magne XVIII. Item coclearia argentea XII. [a]Item
una anfra argentea parva. Item becheria argentea XII[a]; dictum ar-
gentum valet circa florenos auri quinquaginta. Item calix unus argenteus. Item domus est bene provisa cum aliis necessariis et bonis
utensiliis ad eius usum.

Nota[b]   Ad sciendum monetam currentem in Engen: item IIII ortgen
faciunt unum stuber, item XXXVIII stuber valent florenum unum in
auro.

fol.205r   Introitus pecuniarum.

Item dicta domus habet omni anno de ficto minuto in diversis partitis
de domibus, hortis^c et aliis possessionibus in villis Engen et Umberen,
florenum unum stuber duos   I II.

Item dicta domus habet iucharos agri XXXX in Engen locatas pro
nunc Johanni Crauwell, valent domui omnibus annis libere florenos
viginti duos   XXII.

^aItem dicta domus habet in Mauerick iucharos agri XXXX, quos
habet locatos Johannes Crauwel, valent domui omnibus annis libere
florenos viginti duos   XXII.^a

Item dicta domus habet iucharos agri in Engenbroick XXXVII
locatos diversis personis, valent domui omnibus annis ultra omnes
expensas florenos 51 stuber 32   LI XXXII.

Item locumtenens in Engen facit cultivare magnis expensis
iucharos agri XXIIII in Klinckenberg, qui si locarentur valerent domui omnibus annis libere florenos 14 stuber 24   XIIII XXIIII.

Item domus habet iucharos agri quindecim in Steynkamp, Tekesz-
kamp et Scharpenkamp, quos locumtenens facit cultivare, sed quando locarentur tunc valerent domui omni anno libere florenos   XI.

Item dicta domus habet in Hogenvelt iucharos agri LII locatos
diversis personis, valent omnibus annis florenos 23   XXIII.

Item dicta domus habet in Tommeten iucharos agri XX locatos
tribus personis, valent omni anno domui florenos 14 stuber 24

XIII XXIIII.

Item dicta domus habet in Hoemeyen in Lynden iucharos agri
XIII locatos cuidam Ortsoyt, valent domui omnibus annis florenos 2
stuber 4   II IIII.

Item dicta domus habet omnibus annis racione decimarum in
Engen pro parte sua, que pars est medietas decime in Engen, alia
medietas est diversorum nobilium, florenos 80   LXXX.

Summa floreni CCXXXXII stuber X.

---

^a *missing in RA Gelderland.* ^b *in the left margin.* ^c *the 'h' has been added in a*
different hand.

fol.205v   Exitus pecuniarum

Item dictus locumtenens dat omni anno camere sive domui in Traiecto racione arrende dicti menbri Engen florenos 100   C.

Item omni anno castellanus ducis Gelrensis tenetur visitare aggera
seu dichen circa parrochiam dicti domus quatuor vicibus in anno

propter periculum fluminis Reni, cui castellano domus tenetur ex antiqua consuetudine dare expensas cum decem aut duodecim equis et famulis, in quo expenduntur omnibus annis floreni 14   XIIII.

Item domus tenetur dare pauperibus omni anno quinque modia tritici seu malderia que sunt eiusdem quantitatis, racione agri in Umbern, que modia V valent omnibus annis florenos 7 stuber 19

VII XVIIII.

Item domus dat omni anno de laudabili et bona consuetudine pauperibus tritici malderia IIII et quodlibet malderium valet omnibus annis florenum unum in auro et stuber XVIIII et sic dicta quatuor malderia valent florenos 6   VI.

Item canuario, qui est pistor et braxator cervesie, pro salario suo floreni septem   VII.

Item coco pro suo salario floreni IIII stuber VIII   IIII VIII.

Item iuveni qui servit coco et domui, pro salario floreni II   II.

Item dicta domus tenetur omnibus annis expendere racione agro-rum quos domus habet, in reparacione aggerum sive dichen propter periculum fluminis Reni florenos 12   XII.

Item expenditur omnibus annis in reparacione domus florenos 3

III.

Item locumtenens dat omni anno duobus cappellanis pro eorum salario ultra offertorium et oblaciones quas habent de trecentis com-municantibus et stola, quod non est moris in baliatu Traiectensi, florenos 9   VIIII.

Item in dicta domus sunt sex persone videlicet tres cappellani, quorum unus est locumtenens, cocus, canuarius et iuvenis qui est communis famulus; taxaverunt domini visitatores pro expensis cuius-libet persone florenos auri XV, faciunt florenos 90   LXXXX.

Summa floreni CCLIIII stuber XXVII

fol.206r Buren membrum preceptorie in Uttricht

Die tercio Augusti 1495 existentibus dominis visitatoribus in precep-toria in Uttricht comparavit coram eis frater Johannes Herberti lo-cumtenens in domo Buren, que domus est menbrum preceptorie aut camere in Traiecto sive Uttricht.

Die vero eodem prestiterunt iuramentum eidem fratri Joanni Her-berto ad informandum dominos visitatores de quesitis per eos in quantum sibi innotuerit.

Primo domus dicti menbri est et eius cappella in anno nonagesimo secundo per baronem Ysselstein dominum Fredericum militem fundi-tus destructa, qui eciam abscidit pomerium et alias arbores fructiferas

penitus et omnino devastavit propter guerram quam habuit cum domino duci Gelrensi. ᵃDictum menbrum est situatum circa opidum
Buren sub dominio Gelrensiᵃ, distat a Traiecto spacio sex horarum
itineris, Traiectensis diocesis.

Sequuntur bona que fuerunt in cappella et nunc sunt penes locumtenentem predictum.

Item calix unus argenteus deauratus cum sua patena.Item casule due.
    In dicto menbro ante devastacionem erant duo cappellani ordinis
sancti Johannis, nunc propter destructionem est solus ipse locumtenens; et quia non habet ecclesiam nec domum, habitat intus opidum
Buren et celebrat quando sibi ex devocione placet.

Sequuntur bona utensilia que fuerunt in domo et nunc sunt penes
locumtenentem.

Item lecti spoliati nudi sine necessariis VIII. Item anfre stagnee parve   ᶜ
et magne III. Item scutelle stagnee parve et magne XVIII. Item equi
VII. Item vacce IIII. Item coclearia argentea VIII. Item taxie argentee due.

Notaᵇ Ad sciendum monetam currentem in Buren: item IIII ortgen
faciunt unum stuber; item XXXIIII stuber faciunt unum florenum
renensem in auro.

        Introitus pecuniarum

Item dicta domus habet iucharos agri CXXV circa opidum Buren,
quos ipse locumtenens facit cultivare magnis expensis, quorum
[fol.206v] aliqui sunt boni, aliqui mali, sed quando locarentur boni
cum malis, tunc domus posset consequi racione locacionum a quolibet iuchero florenum unum in auro, faciunt floreni 125   CXXV.
    Item domus non habet alios redditus nec decimas nec aliquas obla-
ciones.
    ᶜSumma floreni CXXV.ᶜ

        Sequitur exitus pecuniarum

Item locumtenens dat omni anno camere sive domui in Uttricht racione arrendacionis florenos 50   L.
    Item dictum menbrum tenetur dare omni anno domino terre ab

antiquo florenos tres   III.

Item dictum menbrum tenetur dare omni anno domui in Novimagio racione census ex agris florenum 1 stuber 8 ortgin 2   I VIII II.

Item dictum menbrum tenetur dare omni anno preceptorie in Arnhem racione census ex agris florenum 1 stuber 8 ortgin 2

                                            I VIII II.

Item dictum menbrum tenetur dare omni anno sacriste ecclesie in Avensolt racione census ab antiquo florenum 1 stuber 25 ortgin 2

                                            I XXV II.

^cSumma floreni 57 stuber VIII ort II.^c

Nota ad vitam^b

Item predictum menbrum tenetur dare omni anno cuidam fratri Guillermo Sell ordinis Brigittarum, solum vita sua durante, florenos aureos VIII.

Item facto calculo introituum et exituum. uti particularitur prescribitur, manent superflui floreni auri LXVII stuber XXV÷ *[25.5]*, de quibus pecuniis est necessarium tenere tres personas, videlicet ipsum locumtenentem qui est cappellanus, cocum et famulum domus, et solvere omnibus annis florenos aureos tres in expensis capittuli provincialis, et facere ecclesiam novam a fundo, et domum novam funditus eciam, itaque in longo tempore nichil remanebit superfluum, ut sic dominis visitatoribus visum est.

fol.207r.   Vallis sancti Johannis
           menbrum in Uttricht ^csive Traiectum^c

---

  ^a *missing in RA Gelderland.* ^b *in the left margin.* ^c *in a different hand.*

Die quinto Augusti 1495 existentibus dominis visitatoribus in preceptoria Traiectensi comparuit ex eorum mandato frater Engelbertus Degeroit, preceptor domus Vallis sancti Johannis, menbri preceptorie aut camere prioralis in Traiecto, quod menbrum distat a preceptoria spacio unius diei itineris, est situatum sub dominio ducis Gelrensis, Traiectensis diocesis, in campestris in silva circa opidum Harderwijck.

Die vero predicto domini visitatores prestiterunt iuramentum eidem preceptori ad informandum eos de quesitis per ipsos in quantum sibi innotuerit.

Primo domus aut menbrum est situatum in loco ut supra, habet domum lapideam tectum palea, est antiqua circumdata fossata. Habet ecclesiam parvam non parrochialem ad latus ipsius domus, intitulatur sub vocabulo sancti Johannis Baptiste, habet tria altaria, primum consecratum in honore Johannis Babtiste, secundum in honore beatorum Petri et Pauli apostolorum, tercium Marie virginis.

In dicta domo sunt sex cappellani ordinis sancti Johannis, quorum nomina sunt: frater Engelbertus Degenroit preceptor, frater Conradus Conradi, frater Egbertus Degenroit, frater Otto de Spoeldi, frater Gerhardus Bengert, frater Gerhardus de Leysten.

Item dicti cappellani debent vivere in communi sine propriis et eligere preceptorem inter se, qui debet confirmari per priorem Almanie aut eius locumtenentem in preceptoria aut camera Traiectensi, qui preceptor Vallis sancti Johannis debet reddere compotum introituum et exituum reverendo priori Almanie seu locumtenenti aut visitatoribus, quibus non comparentibus conventualibus dicte domus, qui conventuales debent conservare illum compotum usque ad adventum domini prioris Almanie aut sui locumtenentis seu visitatorum, et illi seu illis compotum predictum manifestare, et servire Deo omnipotenti in celebrando divina et manere sub visitatione et correctione prioris Almanie, sicuti eis concessum apparuit dominis visitatoribus per quoddam vidimus aut copiam aut sigillo opidi Harderwyck et manibus et signetis duorum notariorum, videlicet Gisberti de Westrenen, clerici Traiectensis diocesis, et Gerhardi Rodolphi de Hervorde, eiusdem diocesis, sigillatam subscriptam et signatam, extractam ex quadam littera autentica quondam reverendi domini Hesse Slegelholtz prioris Almanie et preceptoris in Lango in lingua Almanica scripta cum sigillo prioratus predicti appendenti sub data anno Domini millesimo quadringentesimo tercio feria tercia ante festum Pentecosten *[29 May, 1403]*, quam litteram licencie confirmavit reverendus dominus frater Ropertus de Diana, prior Messanensis, procurator et commissarius per Almaniam, Ungariam et cetera per reverendum dominum Rhodi magistrum et capitulum generale missus et deputatus, ut apparet per copiam autenticam sigillo opidi Hardewick et manibus predictorum notariorum munitam, ut de verbo ad verbum sequitur:

Frater Robertus de Dyana, ordinis sancti Johannis Jerosolomitani per Messanam prior humilis nec non prioratuum per Almaniam, Bohemieque Ungarie regna unicus a reverendissimo *[fol.207v.]* in Christo patre et domino domino nostro domino Anthonio Fluviano sacre domus hospitalis magistro dignissimo eiusque sacro conventu Rhodi capitulum generale celebrantibus procurator, reformator, corrector et visitator specialiter deputatus, universis et singulis Christi fidelibus et presertim fratribus domus Vallis sancti Johannis baiulive Traiectensis presentibus et futuris, salutem in Domino sempiternam. Quoniam ad hoc ut firmiter credimus iubar Sancti Spiritus, qui est ignis lucens sed non consumens, corda dictorum reverendissimi magistri et suorum procerum perlustravit et docuit, ut nos ad supradictas longinquas regiones Alemaniam videlicet Ungariam et Bohemiam divina gratia, ut prava in directa et aspera in vias planas reformaremus, direxerunt et destinarunt, et quoniam ea que iuste petuntur minus iuste denegantur, idcirco volentes quantum cum Deo possimus commissionem nostre seriem exequi in hac parte previlegia sive graciam per reverendum priorem et dominum fratrem Hessonem Slegelholtz pie memorie tunc priorem prioratus Almanie ordinis pretacti et eius sigillo prioratus sigillatam supradictis fratribus domus Vallis sancti Johannis presentibus et futuris indultam, ut videlicet celebrem vitam ducere valeant secundum regulam et statuta nostre Religionis pro tunc per eos incepta, in omnibus et singulis suis punctis et articulis, prout in eisdem litteris gracie lacius continetur, conservare debeant, vobis auctoritate predicti reverendi in Christo patris et domini Antonii Fluviani magistri et sacri conventus Rodi et eorum successorum perpetue et irrevocabiliter renovamus, emulamus, laudamus, approbamus, ratificamus et confirmamus per presentes, mandantes eciam prioribus, preceptoribus et fratribus quibuscunque ut contra hanc nostram confirmacionem nullomodo faciant vel venire presumant, in virtute sancte obediencie quinymo illam studeant inviolabiliter observari. In cuius rei testimonium sigillum nostrum presentibus duximus appendendum. Datum Maguntium in domo nostre Religionis ibidem sita XX° die mensis Marcii, nostro provinciali capitulo durante, anno incarnacionis Domini millesimo quadringentesimo tricesimo *[20 March, 1431, according to Annunciation-style]*.

Sequuntur cleynodia ecclesie.

Item calices argentei deaurati quatuor cum eorum patenis. Item unus calix argenteus cum sua patena intus solum deauratus. Item thuribulum argenteum. Item patena una pro pace. Item due ampulle argentee pro servicio missarum. Item ciborium unum argenteum deauratum. Item cappe sete III. Item casule de brucata et seta II. Item vestes levitiace sete IIII. Item casule panni diversarum colorum VIII. Item missalia VI. Item antiphonarii IIII. Item gradualia IIII. Item psalteria IIII. Item candelabra erea VI.

fol.208r. Sequntur bona domus.

Item lecti cum eorum necessariis VIIII. Item coclearia argentea XVIII. Item taxie argentee IIII. Item nuces iudaice laboratu argenteo. Item dictum argenteum valet circa florenos quinquaginta. Item anfre stagnee parve et magne XXVI. In aliis domus est pro necessitate provisa, sed fuit melius provisa et tempore guerre fuerunt multi lecti et alia utensilia rapta per inimicos. Item vacce X. Item equi V.

Nota[a] Ad sciendum monetam currentem in Valle sancti Johannis, valorem frumentorum et quantitatem mensurarum: Item XII wytgin faciunt unum stuber. Item XXXXIIII stuber faciunt unum florenum in auro. Item quatuor scheppel faciunt unum malderium. Item malderium unum siliginis valet omnibus annis stuber XXXIII. Item malderium unum avene valet omnibus annis stuber XIIII et wytgin VIII, ut constitit dominis visitatoribus per informacionem predicti domini preceptoris domus medio eius iuramento.

Sequitur introitus pecuniarum.

Item dicta domus habet omni anno de ficto in diversis partitis de diversis personis in locis Dorspick, Ermel, Nuenspiet, Hardewyck et cetera super possessionibus et agris florenos 17 stuber 16

XVII XVI.

Item dicta domus habet omni anno a quodam Gerhardo Theoderici in Wytlo racione census agrorum seu massarie florenos 5 stuber 20

V XX.

Item dicta domus habet omni anno a quodam Tymanno Konyng racione census agrorum seu massarie florenos 5 stuber 30 V XXX.

Item dicta domus habet omni anno a quodam Johanne Gerhardi racione massarie in Spick florenos 10 stuber 20 X XX.

Item dicta domus habet omni anno a quodam Bartholomeo Gerhardi racione massarie in Horsterbosch florenos 6 stuber 8 VI VIII.

Item dicta domus habet omni anno a quodam Gysberto Kampfelt in Fuerick racione massarie florenos 3 stuber 28 III XXVIII.

Item dicta domus habet de diversis personis racione agrorum circa Vallem sancti Johannis situatorum omni anno florenos 40

XXXX.

Item domus habet omni anno a quodam Helwico Gisberti in Callenbroick racione massarie florenos 26 stuber 0 XXVI.

Item dicta domus habet omni anno a quodam Wyne Arnoldi in Callenbroick racione massarie florenos 13 XIII.

fol.208v.

ᵇItem dicta domus habet omni anno a quodam Gerhardo Johannis in Callenbroick racione massarie florenos 15 XV.ᵇ

Item dicta domus habet omni anno a quodam Henrico de Dorneck in Callenbroick racione massarie florenos 17 XVII.

Item dicta domus habet omni anno [a quodam] Luberto Foerman in Callenbroick racione massarie florenos 12 XII.

Item dicta domus habet omni anno a Rutgero Custodis in Callenbroick racione massarie florenos quinque V.

Item dicta domus habet omni anno a Eberhardo Bartholomei in Callenbroick racione massarie florenos 6 VI.

Item dicta domus habet omni anno a Henrico Themasii in Callenbroick racione massarie florenos 14 XIIII.

Item dicta domus habet omni anno a Johanni Rutenbeck in Callenbroick racione massarie florenos 9 VIIII.

Item dicta domus habet omni anno a Johanni Rutenbeck in Callenbroick racione massarie florenos 23 XXIII.

Item dicta domus habet omni anno de Hermanno Cristiani in Callenbroick racione massarie florenos 17 XVII.

Item dicta domus habet omni anno a Jacobo Bertoldi in Callenbroick racione massarie florenos novem VIIII.

Item dicta domus habet a quodam Jacobo Henrici in Callenbroick racione massarie florenos 30 XXX.

Item predicti massari tenentur dare ultra pecunias predictas certos stuber, et quia non sunt eiusdem monete, ergo reducti sunt in florenos et faciunt in auro simul florenos 4 stuber 36 IIII XXXVI.

Item dicta domus habet omni anno racione moline in Harderwick florenos 20 stuber 4 XX IIII.

Item preceptor dicte domus facit cultivare certam quantitatem agrorum in Callenbroick, qui si locarentur valerent domui omni anno florenos quindecim stuber 37 XV XXXVII.

Item preceptor dicte domus facit cultivare in Valle sancti Johannis certam quantitatem agrorum, qui si locarentur valerent domui omni anno florenos 13 stuber 28 XIII XXVIII.

Item domus habet omnibus annis racione offertorii florenos 6 stuber 16 VI XVI.

Summa floreni CCCXXXXV stuber XXIII.

fol.209r. Introitus siliginis.

Item dicta domus habet omni anno de ficto racione moline in Callenbroick malderia XXXXVI.

Item dicta domus habet omni anno a quodam Tymanno Konynck in Valle sancti Johannis racione agrorum malderia XXI scheppel II.

Item dicta domus habet de ficto omni anno in diversis partitis de diversis personis in Valle sancti Johannis racione agrorum malderia XXXXII scheppel III.

Item dicta domus habet omni anno a Helwico Gisberti in Callenbroick racione agri malderia II.

Summa malderia CXII scheppel I.

Nota quodlibet malderium valet omnibus annis stuber XXXIII et sic dicta malderia 112 schepel I valent florenos 84 stuber 8 wytgen 3

LXXXIIII VIII III.

Introitus avene.

Item dicta domus habet omnibus annis racione decime in Callenbroick malderia XXV, et quodlibet malderium valet omnibus annis stuber XIIII, ᶜwitgin 8ᶜ, sic predicta malderia 25 valent florenos 8 stuber 14 wytgin 8 VIII XIIII VIII.

Sequitur exitus pecuniarum.

Item dicta domus tenetur dare omni anno preceptorie aut camere Traiectensi racione arrende ipsius domus florenos 40 XXXX.

Item dicta domus tenetur dare omni anno domino duci Gelrensi racione census ex certis massariis florenos 12 XII.

Item dicta domus tenetur dare omni anno quibusdam nobilibus vocatis Bockrolle racione census agrorum stuber 33 XXXIII.

Item dicta domus tenetur dare omni anno abbacie sancti Pauli racione census ab antiquo stuber 27 wytgin 6 XXVII VI.
fol.209v.

Item dicta domus tenetur dare omni anno Jacobo Gerhardi in Valle sancti Johannis racione census agrorum stuber 8 wytgin 3

VIII III.

Item dicta domus tenetur dare omni anno Jacobo de Bernen in Harderwick racione census agrorum stuber 5 wytgin 3 V III.

Item dicta domus tenetur dare omni anno certis personis in villa Barbeldensi stuber 8 VIII.

Item dicta domus tenetur dare omni anno certis personis in Egde racione census ab antiquo stuber 22 XXII.

Item canuario pro salario, qui eciam est pistor et braxator cervisie, florenos sex VI.

^bItem coco et famulo coci pro salario florenos 6　　　　　VI.^b

Item famulo domus pro salario florenos 5　　　　　　　　V.

Item expenduntur omnibus annis in oleo et cera ad usum ecclesie floreni 12　　　　　　　　　　　　　　　　　　　　XII.

Item dicta domus tenetur dare omni anno cuidam Henrico Woeben in Harderwick racione molendine in Harderwyck stuber 20
　　　　　　　　　　　　　　　　　　　　　　　　XX.

Item in dicta preceptoria aut domo sunt ultra ipsum dominum preceptorem novem persone, videlicet quinque cappellani, canuarius, cocus, famulus coci et famulus domus, taxaverunt domini visitatores pro expensis cuiuslibet persone florenos auri quindecim, faciunt florenos 135　　　　　　　　　　　　　　　　　CXXXV.

Item pro vestitu et necessariis quinque cappellanorum florenos 25
　　　　　　　　　　　　　　　　　　　　　　　XXV.

Item expenduntur omnibus annis in reparacione massariorum floreni 20　　　　　　　　　　　　　　　　　　　　XX.

Item expenduntur omnibus annis in ligno et cespitibus colligendis floreni 20　　　　　　　　　　　　　　　　　　　XX.

Summa floreni CCLXXXIII stuber XXXVI.

Exitus siliginis.

Item dicta domus tenetur dare omni anno cuidam Wymar de Byler racione molendine in Harderwyck malderia quinque et quodlibet malderium valet omnibus annis stuber XXXIII, et sic dicta malderia quinque valent florenos 3 stuber 33　　　　　　　III XXXIII.

---

^a *in the left margin.* ^b *missing in RA Gelderland.* ^c *in the left margin, missing in RA Gelderland.*

fol.210r. Aldenwater menbrum preceptorie Traiectensis.

Die sexto Augusti 1495 existentibus dominis visitatoribus in preceptoria Traiectensi comparuit ex eorum mandato coram eis frater Henricus van der Cappel, locumtenens domus aut menbri in Aldenwater, quod est menbrum preceptorie Traiectensis camere prioralis, et distat a preceptoria spacio itineris sex horarum in provincia Hollandie sub dominio domini ducis Burgundie Traiectensis diocesis.

Die vero eodem prestitum fuit iuramentum eidem fratri Henrico locumtenenti ad informandum dominos visitatores de vero et legittimo valore dicti menbri.

Primo domus dicti menbri est situata intus opidum Aldenwater, est domus lapidea, magna, antiqua, tamen satis bona; habet cappellam intus domum parvam intitulatam sub vocabulo sancti Johannis, habet tria altaria, primum consecratum in honore sancti Johannis Baptiste, secundum sancte Katherine, tercium sancte Crucis.

In dicta domo est unus cappellanus, videlicet frater Henricus predictus, et tempore preterito ante guerras fuerunt duo cappellani, sed locumtenens dicit non sufficere redditus ad tenendum duos cappellanos. Dictus locumtenens omni die festo missam unam.

In dicta cappella est una lampas die noctuque coram venerabili sacramento ardens.

Sequuntur cleynodia ecclesie.

Item calices argentei duo deaurati cum eorum patenis. Item ciborium argenteum unum. Item missale unum. Item casule bone et male III. In aliis cappella est satis provisa.

Sequuntur bona domus.

Item lecti cum eorum necessariis novem. Item scutelle stagnee parve et magne LXX. Item anfre stagnee parve et magne XXX. Item telleria stagnea XII. Item in aliis necessariis ad usum domus est domus sufficienter provisa.

Nota[a] Ad sciendum monetam currentem in Aldenwater: XVI denarii faciunt unum stuber. Item XXVIII stuber faciunt unum florenum Renensem in auro.

fol.210v. Introitus pecuniarum.

Item dicta domus habet omni anno de diversis personis intus civitatem Aldenwater super domibus, ortis et agris florenos 37 stuber 21 denarios 7   XXXVII XXI VII.

Item dicta domus habet omni anno a quodam Hugoni Albertz in Aldenwater racione XVI iucharorum agri florenos 17 stuber 25
                                                         XVII XXV.

Item locumtenens facit cultivare circa terram Aldenwater iucharos agri XVI, qui si locarentur valerent domui racione census omni anno florenos [14 stuber 28]   XIIII XXVIII.

Item domus habet omni anno a quibusdam Bertolo Johannis et

Gysberto Egidii in Aldenwater racione census iucharorum agri XXXII florenos [10 stuber 10]   X X.

[b]Item locumtenens facit cultivare circa Aldenwater iucharos agri IIII; quando locarentur, valerent domui omni anno florenos 4 IIII.[b]

Item locumtenens facit cultivare in alia partita iucharos agri XIII; quando locarentur, tunc domus posset consequi ex dictis agris omni anno racione census florenos 8 stuber 28   VIII XXVIII.

Item domus habet omni anno a quodam Jacobo Keyser racione census iugarorum agri V÷ *[5.5]* quod locumtenens emit suis propriis pecuniis, florenos 5 stuber 9   V VIIII.

Item locumtenens facit cultivare iucharum unum agri, quem ipse locumtenens emit suis propriis pecuniis, qui si locaretur potest domus consequi ex dicto uno iucharo florenos 4 stuber 18   IIII XVIII.

Item domus habet omnibus annis racione oblacionum florenos 12   XII.

Summa floreni CXV   stuber XXXIII   [c]denar.[c]

Exitus pecuniarum.

Item dicta domus tenetur dare omni anno preceptori in Traiecto racione census XIII iucharorum agri florenos 5 stuber 19 denarios 8   V XVIIII VIII.

Item locumtenens dat omni anno preceptori in Traiecto pro arrendacione domus predicte florenos 13 stuber 23   XIII XXIII.

Item coco pro salario florenos 4 stuber 24   IIII XXIIII.

Item famulo domus pro salario florenos 4 stuber 24   IIII XXIIII.

Item in dicta domo sunt duo persone, videlicet famulus domus et cocus; taxaverunt domini visitatores pro expensis cuiuslibet persone florenos auri 14, faciunt florenos 28   XXVIII.

Item expenditur omnibus annis in reparacione aggarum propter periculum fluminis floreni 12   XII.

Item domus tenetur ex antiqua consuetudine dare duobus vicibus iudicibus, burgemagistris et scabinis opidi Aldenwater et certis presbyteris, in quo expenduntur omnibus annis floreni 12   XII.

Item expenditur omnibus annis in oleo et cera ad usum ecclesie floreni 5   V.

[d]Summa floreni LXXXVI   stuber II   den. VIII.[d]

---

[a] *in the left margin.* [b] *fails in RA Gelderland.* [c] *pasted away in the binding.* [d] *in a different hand.*

fol.211r. Werderer menbrum preceptorie Traiectensis.

Die sexto Augusti 1495 existentibus dominis visitatoribus in preceptoria Traiectensi comparuit coram eis vocatus frater Albertus de Traiecto preceptor domus in Werderer menbri preceptorie Traiectensis, quod menbrum distat a Traiecto spacio VIII horarum itineris in provincia Hollandie sub dominio ducis Burgundie Traiectensis diocesis.

Die eodem domini visitatores prestiterunt iuramentum eidem preceptori menbri predicti ad informandum eos de vero et legittimo valore dicti menbri.

Primo domus predicta est situata in campestris in villa Werderer, est antiqua, parva, tecta stramine; habet ecclesiam parrochialem, que distat a domo spacio medie hore itineris, intitulatam sub vocabulo sancti Pancracii, habet tria altaria, primum consecratum in honore sancti Pancracii, secundum beate Marie, tercium sancte Crucis.

Item dicta domus habet quandam parvam cappellam intus domum consecratam in honore sancti Johannis Baptiste.

In dicta domo sunt duo cappellani, quorum nomina sunt frater Albertus de Traiecto preceptor predictus, et frater Henricus Berenfelt ordinis sancti Johannis.

Item dicti cappellani tenentur solum celebrare festivis diebus unam missam.

Item dicta ecclesia habet circa CCLX communicantes.

Sequuntur bona cappelle domus.

Item calix unus argenteus deauratus. Item missale unum. Item casula una panni antiqua. Item duo candelabra erea.

Item bona ecclesie parrochialis non inventariantur, quia magistri fabrice deputati per communitatem ville habent curam bonorum ecclesie.

Sequuntur bona domus.

Item lecti cum eorum necessariis VIII. Item taxea una argentea. Item coclearia argentea IIII. Item scutelle stagnee parve et magne XXXXIIII. Item telleria stagnea XII. Item anfre stagnee parve VII. Item olle eree III. Item candelabra erea VIII. Item equi antiqui et iuvenes XII. Item vacce VIIII.

Nota[a] Ad sciendum monetam currentem in Werderer: Item XII denarii faciunt unum stuber. Item XXVIIII stuber faciunt unum florenum in auro.

fol.211v. Introitus pecuniarum.

Item dicta domus habet omni anno de ficto de diversis personis in Werder racione census iucharorum agri XXXXII florenos 21 stuber
5   XXI V.
Item preceptor dicti menbri facit cultivare iucharos agri LVIII, qui si locarentur possit domus consequi omni anno ex dictis agris racione census florenos 30   XXX.
Item dicta domus habet omnibus annis racione offertoriorum et oblacionum in ecclesia parrochiali et cappella florenos 19 stuber 28
                                                                                    XVIIII XXVIII.
Item dicta domus habet omnibus annis racione decime in Werderer florenos duos stuber 22   II XXII.

Summa floreni LXXIII   stuber VI.

Exitus pecuniarum.

Item preceptor menbri predicti dat omni anno preceptori in Traiecto racione arrende menbri florenos 20 stuber 20   XX XX.
Item coco pro suo salario florenos 4 stuber 24   IIII XXIIII.
Item famulo domus pro salario florenos 4 stuber 24   IIII XXIIII.
Item in dicta domo sunt due persone ultra ipsum preceptorem, videlicet cocus et famulus domus; taxaverunt domini visitatores pro expensis cuiuslibet persone florenos auri XIIII, faciunt florenos 28
                                                                                    XXVIII.
Item racione cere et olei non fit exitus, quia magistri fabrice tenentur dare sufficienciam.
Item dicta domus habet iucharos agri 100 et solvit omnibus annis racione reparacione cuiuslibet iuchari stuber V, faciunt florenos [17 stuber 24]   XVII XXIIII.

Summa floreni LXXVI   stuber V.

fol.212r. Hermelen menbrum preceptorie Traiectensis.

Die sexto Augusti 1495 existentibus dominis visitatoribus in preceptoria Traiectensi comparuit vocatus frater Gerhardus Vastardi preceptor domus in Hermelen, que est menbrum preceptorie Traiectensis;

dictum menbrum est situatum in dominio Traiectensi eiusdem diocesis, distat a preceptoria spacio duarum horarum itineris.

Primo domus dicti menbri est magna, antiqua, lapidea, tecta stramine, situata intus villam Hermelen; habet ecclesiam parrochialem mediocrem, novam, intitulatam sub vocabulo sancti Dionisii; habet duo altaria, primum consecratum in honore sancti Dionisii, secundum in honore sancti Johannis Baptiste.

Item in dicta [ecclesia] est unus cappellanus, videlicet preceptor menbri predictus. Dictus cappellanus tenetur omni die festo celebrare unam missam et celebrare duas missas in septimana.

In dicta ecclesia est una lampas die noctuque ardens.

Item in dicta ecclesia sunt circa CCL communicantes.

Sequuntur bona ecclesie.

Item non fit inventarium bonorum ecclesie, quia magistri fabrice deputati per communitatem ville habent curam.

Sequuntur bona domus.

Item lecti cum eorum necessariis quinque. Item anfre stagnee parve et magne VIII. Item scutelle parve et magne stagnee XXII. Item cum aliis bonis utensiliis est domus competenter provisa. Item equi antiqui et iuvenes VIII. Item vacce VIII.

Nota[a] Ad sciendum monetam currentem in Hermelen: Item VIII denarii faciunt unum stuber. Item XXVIIII stuber faciunt unum florenum Renensem in auro.

fol.212v. Introitus pecuniarum.

Item dicta domus habet omni anno de ficto racione census iucharorum agri VIIII locatas duabus personis florenos 6 stuber quindecim denarios quatuor   VI XV IIII.

Item dicta domus habet omnibus annis racione oblacionum florenos 2 stuber 22   II XXII.

Item preceptor dicti menbri facit cultivare iucharos agri LXXIII magnis expensis, sed quando locarentur, tunc domus posset consequi omni anno racione dictorum agrorum libere ultra expensas aggerum florenos 36 stuber 14 denarios 4   XXXVI XIIII IIII.

Item dicta domus habet omnibus annis racione decime in Hermelen stuber 25   XXV.

Summa floreni XXXXVI [stuber] XVIIII.

Exitus pecuniarum.

Item expenduntur omnibus annis in reparacione aggerum racione periculi fluminis stuber 18   XVIII.

Item preceptor menbri dat preceptori in Traiecto racione arrende dicti menbri omni anno florenos 17 stuber 7   XVII VII.

Item coco pro suo salario florenos 4 stuber 4   IIII IIII.

^bItem famulo domus pro salario florenos 4 stuber 4   IIII IIII.^b

Item racione olei et cere non fit exitus, quia magistri fabrice deputati per communitatem ville tenentur dare oleum et ceram sufficientem.

Item in dicta domo sunt due persone ultra preceptorem, videlicet cocus et famulus domus; taxaverunt domini visitatores pro expensis cuiuslibet persone florenos auri XIIII faciunt florenos 28   XXVIII.

Summa floreni LIIII   stuber IIII.

---

^a *in the left margin.* ^b *fails in RA Gelderland.*

fol.213r.   Wemenlinghen menbrum preceptorie Traiectensis.

Die nono mensis Augusti 1495 existentibus dominis visitatoribus in preceptoria Traiectensi camera priorali comparuit vocatus frater Lucas Huet cappellanus ordinis sancti Johannis, preceptor domus aut menbri in Wemenlingen, quod menbrum distat a preceptoria spacio trium dierum itineris, situatum est in provincia Selandie sub dominio domini ducis Burgundie Traiectensis diocesis.

Die eodem domini visitatores prestiterunt iuramentum eidem preceptori ad informandum eos de quesitis per eos in quantum sibi innotuerit.

Primo domus dicti menbri est situata in campestris circa villa Wemelingen, est domus antiqua, tamen non patitur ruynam; habet cappellam parvam bene reparatam ad latus domus, intitulatur sub vocabulo sancti Galli, habet solum unum altare.

Item in dicta cappella ardet die nocteque lampas una coram venerabili sacramento.

Item in dicta domo est solus ipse preceptor, qui celebrat omnibus diebus festivis et hóc ex sua devotione.

Sequuntur bona cappelle.

Item calix unus argenteus deauratus cum sua patena. Item missale unum. Item casule due. Item candelabra stagnea duo.

Sequuntur bona domus.

Item lecti cum eorum necessariis X. Item becheria argentea VI. Item coclearia argentea IIII. Item anfre stagnee parve et magne VI. Item scutelle stagnee parve et magne LXI. Item candelabra erea VI. Item de aliis necessariis est domus pro statu suo sufficienter provisa. Item equi quatuor. Item vacce sex.

Nota[a] Ad sciendum monetam currentem in Wemelinghen: Item ortgin IIII faciunt unum stuber. Item stuber XXVIII faciunt unum florenum Renensem in auro.

fol.213v. Introitus pecuniarum.

Item dicta domus habet omni anno de ficto de diversis personis in Cappellen, Wemenlinghen et Cattendyck racione agrorum stuber 17
XVII.

Item dicta domus habet omni anno a quodam Johanni Guillerini in Cattendick racione iucharorum X agri florenos 14 stuber 8
XIIII VIII.

Item dicta domus habet omni anno a quodam Johanni Balwini in Cappellen racione iucharorum agri VIIII florenos 12 stuber 24
XII XXIIII.

Item dicta domus habet omni anno a quodam Adriano Wyssen in Wemelingen racione iucharorum agri VIIII florenos 12 stuber 24
XII XXIIII.

Item dicta domus habet a quodam Fort Cornelii in Wemelyngen racione iucharorum agri quatuor florenos 5 stuber 2   V XX.

Item dicta domus habet omni anno a quodam Huperto Loy in Wemelingen racione iucharorum agri II÷ *[2.5]* florenos 3 stuber 16
III XVI.

Item dicta domus habet omni anno a quodam Johanni Henrici in Wemelingen racione iucharorum agri II florenos 2 stuber 24
II XXIIII.

Item dicta domus habet omni anno a quodam Petro Henrici in Wemelingen racione iucharorum agri II÷ *[2.5]* florenos 3 stuber 16
III XVI.

Item dicta domus habet omni anno a quodam Jacobo Deynen in Wemelingen racione iucharorum agri V florenos 7 stuber 4

VII IIII.

Item dicta domus habet omni anno a quodam Adriano Wilhelmi in Wemelynghen racione iucharorum agri III florenos 4 stuber 8

IIII VIII.

Item dicta domus habet omni anno a quodam Thomasio Bartholomei in Wemelynghen racione iucharorum agri II÷ *[2.5]* florenos 3 stuber 16

III XVI.

Item dicta domus habet omni anno a quodam Johanni Guillerini in Cappellen racione iucharorum agri III florenos 4 stuber 8

IIII VIII.

Item dicta domus habet omni anno a quodam Hadriano Petri in Cattendyck racione iucharorum agri quinque florenos 7 stuber 4

VII IIII.

Item dicta domus habet omni anno a quodam Aell Ballwini in Wemenlynghen racione iucharorum agri VII÷ *[7.5]* florenos 10 stuber 20

X XX.

Item dicta domus habet omni anno a quodam Hadriano Guillerini in Wemelynghen racione iucharorum agri V florenos 7 stuber 4

VII IIII.

*fol.214r.*Item dicta domus habet omni anno a quodam Adriano Walteri in Wemelingen racione iucharorum agri V÷ *[5.5]* florenos 7 stuber 24

VII XXIIII.

Item dictus preceptor facit cultivare iucharos agri XXXVII in Wemelingen, Cappellen et Cattendick, qui iuchari 37, si locarentur, valerent racione census domui omni anno florenos 52 stuber 24

LII XXIIII.

Item domus habet omnibus annis racione offertorii florenos 4 stuber 8

IIII VIII.

Summa floreni CLXV   stuber VI.

ᵇExitus pecuniarum.

Item locumtenens dicti membri tenetur dare omni anno preceptori in Traiecto racione arrendacionis dicti menbri florenos 42 stuber 24

XXXXII XXIIII.

Item expenditur omnibus annis in oleo et cera ad usum cappelle florenos 4 stuber 8

IIII VIII.

Item dicta domus habet in totum iucharos agri 112÷ *[112.5]*. Et constat dominis visitatoribus per iuramentum predicti locumtenentis,

quod omnibus annis expenduntur pro quolibet iucharo agri stuber
XVIII in reparacionem aggarum propter maximum periculum maris,
faciunt florenos 72 stuber 9   LXXII VIIII.
    Item coco pro salario florenos 4 stuber 24   IIII XXIIII.
    Item famulo domus pro salario florenos 4 stuber [2]4

                                               IIII XXIIII.
    Item in dicta domo sunt due persone ultra ipsum preceptorem aut
locumtenentem, taxaverunt domini visitatores pro expensis cuiuslibet
persone florenos XIIII faciunt florenos 28   XXVIIII.

    Summa floreni CLVII   stuber V.[b]

---

  [a] *in the left margin.* [b] *fails in RA Gelderland.*

fol.214v. Kirchwerff menbrum preceptorie Traiectensis.

Die decimo septimo Augusti 1495 existentibus dominis visitatoribus
in preceptoria Traiectensi fuerunt domini visitatores informati de facto, introitu et exitu dicti menbri in Kerckwerff per preceptorem
Traiectensem.
    Primo dictum menbrum est conventus monialium, situatum in
Selandia sub dominio ducis Burgundie Traiectensis diocesis, distat a
preceptoria spacio quatuor dierum itineris.
    Item domus dicti menbri est lapidea, magna, bene reparata; habet
ecclesiam non parrochialem, que intitulatur sub vocabulo sancti Johannis, habet tria altaria, primum consecratum in honore sancti Johannis Baptiste, secundum in honore beate Marie virginis, tercium
sancte Crucis.
    In dicta ecclesia seu menbro sunt duo cappellani, quorum unus est
preceptor; eorum nomina sunt frater Henricus Wilhelmi et frater
Ewaldus de Leyen, ambo ordinis sancti Johannis, qui celebrant omni
die missam unam.
    Item in dicta domus sunt moniales XII, que legunt omnes horas
canonicas.

    Sequuntur bona ecclesiae.

Item calices argentei duo deaurati cum eorum patenis. Item ciborium
unum argenteum. Item missalia duo. Item casule bone et male quinque. Item cappam unam. In ceteris necessariis est ecclesia satis provisa.

Sequuntur bona domus.

Item domus est satis provisa cum omnibus necessariis.

Nota[a] Ad sciendam monetam currentem in Kerckwerff: Item VIII duytgin faciunt unum stuber. Item XXVIII stuber faciunt unum florenum Renensem in auro.

fol.215r. Introitus pecuniarum.

Item dictum menbrum habet iucharos agri et pratorum 116÷ *[116.5]* circa Kerckwerff locatos diversis personis, ex quibus domus habet omni anno racione census florenos 257 stuber 4   CCLVII IIII.
    Item dicte moniales faciunt cultivare iucharos agri XXXIII÷ *[33.5]*, qui si locarentur valerent domui omni anno florenos 53 stuber 16   LIII XVI.
    Item dictum menbrum habet omnibus annis racione offertorii florenos 4   IIII.

Summa floreni CCCXIIII   stuber XX.

Exitus pecuniarum.

Item dicte moniales tenentur dare omni anno domino duci racione cuiuslibet iuchari agri stuber III, faciunt florenos 16 stuber 2
                                                                           XVI II.
    Item dicte moniales dant omnibus annis pro reparacione aggarum pro quolibet iucharo stuber VI et sunt iuchari 150, faciunt florenos 32 stuber 4   XXXII IIII.
    Item in dicta domo sunt tres famule, quibus datur pro salario floreni 12   XII.
    Item famulo domus pro salario florenos 4 stuber 8   IIII VIII.
    Item porterio pro salario florenos 4 stuber 8   IIII VIII.
    Item pro cespitibus ad ardendum omnibus annis florenos 24
                                                                         XXIIII.
    Item in dicta domo sunt ultra preceptorem persone XVIII, videlicet unus cappellanus, XII moniales, item tres famule, item porterius, item famulus domus; taxaverunt domini visitatores pro expensis cuiuslibet persone florenos auri XII, faciunt simul florenos 216
                                                                         CCXVI.
    Item dantur pro necessariis cuiuslibet dictarum personarum videlicet XII monialium et uni cappellano floreni auri duo et stuber XVI,

faciunt florenos 33 stuber 12   **XXXIII XII**

Summa floreni CCCXXXXI   stuber XIIII.

Nota exitus predicti menbri excedunt introitus, tamen ille moniales supplent necessitatem eorum ingenio et labore.

fol.215v. Myddelburch menbrum preceptorie Traiectensis.

Die decimo quinto Augusti 1495 existentibus dominis visitatoribus in preceptoria Traiectensi comparuit coram eis vocatus frater Johannes Clivis, cappellanus ordinis sancti Johannis, preceptor domus in Myddelburg, que est menbrum preceptorie Traiectensis; dictum menbrum est situatum in provincia Selandie sub dominio domini ducis Burgundie Traiectensis diocesis.

Die eodem domini visitatores prestiterunt iuramentum eidem fratri Johanni Cliwis preceptori ad informandum eos de quesitis per ipsos in quantum sibi innotuerit.

Primo domus dicti menbri est antiqua tamen bona, situata intus opidum Middelburg; habet ecclesiam non parrochialem ad latus domus, intitulatur sub vocabulo sancti Johannis, habet tria altaria, primum consecratum in honore sancti Johannis Baptiste, secundum beate Marie virginis, tercium sancti Sebastiani.

In dicta domo est solum unus cappellanus videlicet ipse frater Johannes preceptor, qui celebrat festivis diebus et quando sibi ex devocione placet.

In dicta ecclesia est una lampas die nocteque coram venerabili sacramento ardens.

Sequuntur bona ecclesie.

Item calix unus argenteus deauratus cum sua patena. Item missalia duo. Item casule due antique. Item candelabra quatuor erea. Item monstranciola una argentea.

Sequuntur bona domus.

Item lecti cum eorum necessariis sex. Item anfre stagnee parve et magne XII. Item scutelle stagnee parve et magne XI. Item candelabra erea quinque. Item in aliis necessariis est domus competenter provisa.

Nota[a] Ad sciendium monetam currentem in Myddelburg: Item VIII duytgen faciunt unum stuber. Item XXVIII stuber faciunt unum florenum Renensem in auro.

fol.216r. Introitus pecuniarum.

Item dicta domus habet omni anno de ficto super tribus domibus in Middelburg racione census stuber 21 duytgen 4   XXI IIII.

Item dicta domus [habet] omnibus annis racione offertorii florenos 17 stuber 24   XVII XXIIII.

Item dicta domus habet omni anno a quodam Pancracio Henrici in Bredam racione iucharorum agri V florenos 10 stuber 26   X XXVI.

Item dicta domus habet omni anno a quodam Petro Arnoldi in Bredam racione census iucharorum agri duorum cum dimidio florenos 3 stuber 24   III XXIIII.

Item dicta domus habet omni anno de diversis personis in Bredam in diversis partitis racione census iucharorum agri XVII florenos 8 stuber 22   VIII XXII.

Item dicta domus habet omnibus annis racione pascue circa domum aut Menbrum florenos 10 stuber 20   X XX.

Item dicta domus habet omni anno racione census unius curie ad usum balistariorum in Middelburg florenos 7 stuber 19 VII XVIIII.

Item dicta domus habet omni anno racione census trium ortorum parvorum in Middelburg florenos 4 stuber 1   IIII I.

Item dicta domus habet omni anno a quodam Petro Arnoldi in Myddelburg racione census unius orti florenos 5 stuber 27   V XXVII.

Item dicta domus habet omni anno de quatuor camerarum locatarum quatuor personis florenos 11 stuber 15   XI XV.

    Summa floreni LXXXII   stuber III   dutgen [IIII][b]

    Exitus pecuniarum.

Item expenditur omnibus annis in reparacione aggerum racione periculi maris floreni 3 stuber 15   III XV.

Item expenduntur omnibus annis in oleo et cera ad usum ecclesie floreni 2 stuber 24   II XXIIII.

Item coco pro salario florenos 4 stuber 8   IIII VIII.

[c]Item famulo domus pro salario florenos 4 stuber 8   IIII VIII.[c]

Item in dicta domo sunt due persone ultra ipsum preceptorem, videlicet cocus et famulus domus; taxaverunt domini visitatores pro expensis cuiuslibet persone florenos auri XIIII, faciunt florenos 28

XXVIII.

Item expenditur omnibus annis in cespitibus ad ardendum pro usu domus floreni 4 stuber 8   IIII VIII.

Summa floreni XXXXVII   stuber VII.

Restant in menbro Middelburg floreni auri XXXV stuber XXIIII denarii IIII et tamen nichil dat preceptorie Traiectensi racione absenciae aut arrendacionis.

ᵃ *in the left margin.* ᵇ *cut off ms.* ᶜ *is missing in RA Gelderland.*

fol.216v. Sneck menbrum preceptorie Traiectensis.

Dic quarto decimo Augusti 1495 existentibus dominis visitatoribus in preceptoria Traiectensi comparuit coram eis vocatus frater Johannes Elten preceptor domus in Schneck, que est menbrum preceptorie Traiectensis. Dictum menbrum est situatum in provincia Frisie sub dominio nobilium de Bock Traiectensis diocesis.

Die eodem prestitum fuit juramentum eidem domino preceptori ad informandum dominos visitatores de questis per eos inquantum sibi innotuerit.

Primo domus dicti menbri est lapidea, magna, in bona reparacione, situata extra muros opidi Schneck; habet ecclesiam non parrochialem mediocrem bene reparatam, intitulatam sub vocabulo sancti Johannis, habet sex altaria: primum consecratum in honore sancti Johannis, secundum sancte Crucis, tercium Patriarcharum, quartum beate Marie virginis, quintum Marie Magdalene, sextum est de novo erectum non consecratum.

Item communitas opidi predicti habet septem ecclesias parrochiales, vacante una earum; habet communitas providere de dictis ecclesiis tamen uni religionis sancti Johannis, videlicet in Ysbredum, Vulschar, Hummers, tWalgega, Opmehuse, Adra, Sneck.

Item preceptor habet providere una parrochiali ecclesia in Bulszwerdia, et habet conferre de duabus gransiis, una in Thosinghusen, alia in Peruswalde.

Item in dicta domo sunt septem cappellani, quorum unus est preceptor, secundus frater Gauricus Theoderici, tercius frater Nicolaus Berszdock, quartus frater Arnoldus Johannis, quintus frater Jacobus Alckmane, sextus frater Bartholomeus Amsterdammis, septimus frater Jacobus Delfft.

Item dicti cappellani tenentur omni die cantare unam missam et legere duas et cantare omnes horas canonicas.

Item in dicta ecclesia est una lampas die noctuque ardens coram venerabili sacramento.

Sequuntur bona ecclesiae.

Item calices argentei deaurati VII cum eorum patenis. Item missalis sex. Item cappe sete due. Item casule sete diversarum colorum VI. Item vestes levitiace sete IIII. Item casule panni diversarum colorum XII. Item in ceteris est ecclesia bene provisa. Item monstrancia una deaurata ad usum venerabilis sacramenti. Item crux una argentea magna. Item ampulle due de argenta.

Sequuntur bona domus.

Item lecti cum eorum necessariis XXX. Item domus est in reliquis *[fol.217r.]* necessariis bene provisa. Item vacce XXIIII. Item equi duo. Item coclearia argentea XXIIII.

Item dicta domus et eius conventuales sunt exempti a quibuscunque exactionibus, subvencionibus et oneribus impositis et imponendis, ut apparet per quandam antiquam copiam non auctenticam; tamen illius litere tenor sequitur et est talis:

Frater Conradus de Bruynsberg sacre domus hospitalis sancti Johannis Iherosolimitani parcium Almanie prior nec non frater Johannes Gaude commendator totusque conventus sancte Katherine Traiectensis hospitalis eiusdem universis et singulis ᵃpresens scriptum visuris et audituris facimus manifestum quod cum nos ex certis et legittimis causis nobis ad hoc monentibus nunc de novo nostre relegionis in Xpo nobis dilectis fratribus Ludolpho pro nunc commendatori totique conventui domus nostre in Monte sancti Johannis prope Sneke parcium Oistfrisie eorumque successoribus quasdam novas responsiones annuas quo ad summam viginti quinque antiquorum schudatorum auri Francie vel imperatoris monete iusti et recti ponderis, duarumque lagenarum butiri, omissis antiquis eorum responsionibus penitus et oblitis imposuimus, auctoritate nobis priori a domino nostro parcium ultra marinatarum magistro concessa, per dictos commendatorem et conventum eorumque successores solvendas ex nunc in antea singulis annis in festo Lamberti episcopi vel infra quindenam postea sub eorum periculis, dampnis et expensis, nostre domui sancte Katherine in Traiecto quo ad subsidium responsionis eiusdem domus ad partes ultramarinas annuatim ministrandas, cuius nove reponsionis occasione ipsis sicut predicitur per nos imposite necnon ex racione et occasione cuiusdam quantitatis certe summe pecunie ipsis pro porcione eorum a nobis indicte et attaxate ad subvencionem exactionis seu contribucionis nuper a summo pontifice nostre religioni per partes Almanie ad usus imperatoris suis litteris apostolicis imposite graviter et indicte, nos promisimus et in hiis scriptis promittimus bona fide ex nunc in antea predictos nobis in Xpo dilectos fratres commendatorem et conventum dicte nostre domus in Monte sancti Johannis prope Sneke singulosque nostre religionis fratres et personas necnon eorum domos grangias per partes Oestfrisie eis subiectas et attinentes cum racione dicte nove responsionis quam eciam racione certe summe pecunie nobis ab eisdem pro porcione et rata eos contingente ad usus dicte exactionis integraliter persoluta, quitos penitus et liberos ab omnibus exactionibus, contribucionibus, taliis, passagiis, procuracionibus aut subsidiis quibuscumque, eciam a religiosis citra vel ultra mare faciendum, de viris bellicosis ultra mare constituendum, de prediis ad usum Sancte Terre vendendum, de bonisque fratrum discedencium ad usum nostrum seu ad quemcumque alium usum tollendum ac ab omnibus aliis exactionibus eciam quibuscumque nominibus seu vocabulis ultra mare vel citra de consuetudine vel usagio proferuntur, quibus dictis commendatori et conventui in Monte sancti Johannis prope Sneck possent dampna, iniurie, vexaciones, labores et expense suboriri seu eciam presentes nostre littere diminui seu infringi valerent in parte vel in toto, ac eciam communiter nostre religioni a Romanorum pontificibus et imperatoribus aut a nostris magistratibus ultra marinatarum parcium seu Almanie parcium prioribus vel eciam commendatore et conventu domus et baiulie nostre sancte Katherine Traiectensis pervenire valentibus, quas procuraciones, exactiones, tallias, contribuciones eciam quibuscumque nominibus [fol.217v.] nuncupantur, dictus ultra marinatarum parcium magister seu nos vel commendator et conventus domus nostre Traiectensis predicti domibus et grangiis eis et nobis subiectis ulterius imponere et attaxare possent et debent, deberemusque et possemus pro nobis et successoribus nostris firmiter in perpetuum observare taliter, quod iidem ab huiusmodi exactionibus omnibus et singulis quibuscumque verbis seu vocabulis exprimuntur ammodo libere sint et immunes nec ad easdem quitquam solvere teneantur. Et si quod absit ab aliquibus huiusmodi de causis dicti commendator et conventus prope Sneke dampna, vexaciones aliquas seu obstacula paterentur, hoc seu hac nos vel nostri successores nomine et ex parte et de bonis dicte domus nostre Traiectensis ipsis refundere et pro eis exinde respondere totaliter et plenarie satisfacere deberemus ut promisimus. Et hiis presentibus promittimus bona fide, quod si tunc facere neglexerimus, extunc idem infra talem annum seu annos illos huiusmodi neglectionis ad solucionem annue responsionis predicte minime tenerentur. Et de anno seu annis sic per neglecto vel neglectis nil responsionis ab eisdem percepturi nec tunc responsiones premissas ulterius sunt daturi nisi prius per nos ipsis de premissis iuxta tenorem presencium fuit plenarie satisfactum. Sed habita satisfactione a nobis de premissis, statim responsiones premissas ulterius de annis tunc futuris modo premisso solvere teneantur. Quod si eciam a sede apostolica vel a magistro ultramarino seu a capitulo generali seu particulari dicti hospitalis seu ab aliis quibuscumque fuerit diffinitum, quod tales littere nemini debeant suffragari, nichilominus tamen iste littere in suo vigore et valore debent permanere et omnia in eis contenta firmiter ut promisimus debemus perpetuis temporibus observare. Si vere auctoritate sedis apostolice seu ipsius legati aut auctoritate ordinaria propter decimas, procuraciones seu alias imposiciones quocumque nomine censeantur, dictos domus, conventum ac fratres eciam occasione ecclesiarum parrochialium ad ipsos pertinencium specialiter atque singulariter ac aliter quam superius est expressum impeti contigerit seu vexari ab huiusmodi impeticionibus et vexacionibus, ipsos non tenebimur quolibet relevare, ipsi eciam pretextu huiusmodi impeticionum et vexacionum non poterunt nec debebunt nobis vel successori nostro subtrahere responsiones supradictas sed ad solucionem earum absque contradictione qualibet tenebuntur termino prelibato. Ceterum promisimus et in hiis scriptis promittimus bona fide premissam annuam responsionem dictis commendatori et conventui prope Sneke nunc impositam ex nunc in antea non augmentare, sed eandem in summo et valore superius signatis volumus in perpetuum permanere. Nec eciam contra presentes litteras et in eis contenta de cetero facere vel venire de iure vel de facto debemus per nos vel per alium seu alios quovis quesito colore, sed ipsas omnia et singula premissa sine contradictione quacumque firmiter ut predictum est observare, fraude et dolo penitus exclusis in omnibus premissis et quolibet premissorum.

In quorum omnium testimonium et munimen sigillum prioratus nostri fratris Conradi predicti presentibus est appensum. Nosque frater Johannes Gaude commendator et conventus domus sancte Katherine prenarrate nostra sigilla una cum sigillo prioratus dicti domini nostri prioris presentibus duximus appendenda.[a]

Datum anno Domini millesimo trecentesimo septuagesimo octavo ipso die beati Remigii episcopi et confessoris *[1 October, 1378]*.

fol.218r,   the outermost numerals cut off in the margin.

Nota[b] Ad sciendum monetam currentem in Schnek: Item schobe XV faciunt unum stuber. Item XXIII stuber et VII÷ *[7.5]* schobe faciunt unum florenum Renensem in auro.

Introitus pecuniarum.

Item dicta domus habet omni anno a quodam Oza Uperee in Ysz- brechen racione centum et LXXIIII pont maten pascuarum florenos 82 stuber 11 schoben VII÷   LXXXII XI [VII÷].

Item dictum menbrum habet omni anno a quodam Alberto Symo- nis in Iszbrecht racione LXXVIII pont maten pascuarum florenos 40
XXXX.

Item dictum menbrum habet omni anno a quodam Ababusz in Iszbrecht racione LXXX pont maten florenos 32   XXXII.

Item dictum menbrum habet omni anno a monasterio Taber in Iszbrecht racione XXXXV pont maten florenos 23   XXIII.

Item dictum menbrum habet omni anno a quodam Sicca Abbas in Iszbrecht racione LXX pont mate florenos 35 stuber 17 schobe 7÷
XXXV XVII [VII÷].

Item dicta domus habet omni anno a quodam Eynck in Yszbrecht racione V pont maten pascuarum florenos 2 stuber 13   II XIII.

Item dictum menbrum habet omni anno a quodam Yeliken Pauli in Iszbrecht racione XXXVI pont maten florenos 19 stuber 16 scho- be 7÷   XVIIII XVI [VII÷].

Item dictum menbrum habet omni anno a quodam Here Nicolai in Ternes racione LXX pont maten florenos 38 stuber 7
XXXVIII VII.

Item dictum menbrum habet omni anno a quodam Wilhelmo Jo- hannis racione LVIII pont maten pascuarum florenos 29 XXVIIII.

Item dictum menbrum habet omni anno a quodam Bruer Dudes in Ternes racione LX pont maten florenos 30 stuber 12 schoben 7÷
XXX XII [VII÷].

Item dicta domus habet omni anno a quodam Frauken Gerhardi in Ternes racione quinquaginta pont maten florenos 25 stuber 12 schobe 7÷   XXV XII [VII÷].

Item dicta domus habet omni anno a quodam Theoderico Johan- nis Anthonii in Gautum racione 75 pont maten florenos 40 stuber 20 schobe 7÷   XXXX XX [VII÷].

Item dicta domus habet omni anno a quodam Theoderico [in] Gau- tum racione XXX pont maten pascuarum florenos 15 stuber 7 scho- be 7÷   XV VII [VII÷].

Item dicta domus habet omni anno a quodam Berbent Joren in Gautum racione XX pont maten pascuarum florenos 25 stuber 12 schobe 7÷ XXV XII [VII÷].

Item dicta domus habet omni anno a quodam Meynauwe in Gautum racione XXX pont maten pascuarum florenos 17 schobe 7÷

XVII [VII÷].

fol.218v.

Item dicta domus habet omni anno a quodam Nicolao Symoni Johannis in Gautum racione LXXVIII pont maten florenos 40

XXXX.

Item dicta domus habet omni anno a quodam Gerban in Vollen racione L pont maten pascuarum florenos 24 stuber 6 XXIIII VI.

Item dicta domus habet omni anno a quodam Lolck in Twalgerga racione LXIIII pont maten florenos 15 stuber 7 schobe 7÷

XV VII VII÷.

Item dicta domus habet omni anno a quodam Heyrgin in Elst racione LXXX pont maten pascuarum florenos 17 stuber 20 schobe 7÷ XVII XX VII÷.

Item dicta domus habet omni anno a Reynero Aurifabro in Schnek racione certi pascue florenos 7 stuber 15 schobe 7÷

VII XV VII÷.

Item dicta domus habet omni anno a quodam Petro Kannen in Sneck racione pascue florenos 5 stuber 10 V X.

Item dicta domus habet omni anno a quodam Laurencio Carnificis in Sneck racione pascue florenos 4 stuber 4 IIII IIII.

Item dicta domus habet omni anno a Volquino in Schneck racione pascue florenos 4 stuber 4 IIII IIII.

Item dicta domus habet omni anno a quodam Gelmaro in Sneck racione pascue florenos 3 stuber 21 III XXI.

Item dicta domus habet omni anno a quodam Ferck Jacobi in Sneck racione pascue florenos 3 stuber 9 III VIIII.

Item dicta domus habet omni anno de diversis personis in opido Sneck racione pascue florenos 21 stuber 9 XXI VIIII.

Item dicta domus habet omni anno in Schneck a diversis personis racione pascuarum florenos 33 stuber 12 XXXIII XII.

Item dicta domus habet pascuas ad usum vaccarum suarum, que valent quando locarentur omni anno florenos 41 stuber 11

XXXXI XI.

Item racione offertorii non fit introitus, quia quando fiunt offertoria veniunt tot hospites, quod magis consumitur quam lucratur; eciam offertorium non est magnum, quia ecclesia est cappella et non parrochialis.

Summa floreni VI ^C LXXX stuber VIIII schobe V[II÷]ᶜ

fol.219r. Exitus pecuniarum.

Item dicta domus tenetur dare omni anno magistris fabrice ecclesie parrochialis in Sneck racione census qui possunt redimi, florenos 18   XVIII.

Item dicta domus tenetur dare omni anno Olfart Yeingen in Iszbrechten racione census certe pascue florenos 3   III.

Item dicta domus tenetur dare omni anno magistro fabrice ecclesie in Gautum racione census florenos 6   VI.

Item dicta domus tenetur dare omni anno Johanni Reyneri in Schneck racione census florenos 6   VI.

Item dicta domus tenetur dare omni anno cuidam Sebando Sibrandi in Schneck racione census florenos 4   IIII.

Item dicta domus tenetur dare omni anno Heyngen in Elst racione census florenos 6   VI.

Item dicta domus tenetur dare omni anno Golmero Gysberti in Schneck racione census florenos 40   XXXX.

Item dicta domus[e] tenetur dare omni anno ex certa pascua florenos 4 stuber 4   IIII IIII.

Item preceptor dicte domus dat omni anno preceptorie in Traiecto racione arrendacionis dicti menbri florenos 50   L.

Item sacriste pro salario florenos 4 stuber 4   IIII IIII.

[a]Item canuario pro salario florenos 4 stuber 4   IIII IIII.[a]

Item coco pro salario florenos 5   V.

Item porterio pro salario florenos 4 stuber 4   IIII IIII.

[a]Item famulo domus pro salario florenos 4 stuber 4   IIII IIII.[a]

Item famulo coci pro salario florenum 1 stuber 19   I XVIIII.

Item expenduntur omnibus annis pro ligno et cespitibus floreni 40   XXXX.

Item pistori pro salario florenos 6 stuber 6   VI VI.

Item in dicta domus sunt ultra ipsum preceptorem sex cappellani; dicit ipse preceptor sufficere pro expensis cuiuslibet cappellani omni anno florenos XII, faciunt florenos 72   LXXII.

Item in dicta domo sunt septem famuli, videlicet sacrista, canuarius, cocus, porterius, famulus domus, famulus coci et pistor; dicit ipse dominus preceptor sufficere pro expensis cuiuslibet famuli omni anno florenos 7, faciunt florenos 49   XXXXVIIII.

Summa floreni CCCXXVII   stuber XXI   s[chobe][d]

Nota ad vitam[b]

Item dicta domus tenetur dare omni anno cuidam fratri Guillerino pastori in Iszbrechten, vita sua durante tantum, omni anno florenos auri XII.

fol.219v. Nota ad vitam[b]
[f]Item dicta domus tenetur dare omni anno fratri Johanni Emerica vita sua durante omni anno florenos auri IIII.

[f]Item dicta domus tenetur dare omni anno fratri Nicolao Barsdorff ordinis sancti Johannis vita sua durante florenos auri XII stuber XII.

[f]Item dicta domus tenetur dare omni anno Gaurico conventuali in Sneck vita sua durante florenos auri VIII stuber VIII.

Restant menbro Sneck ultra florenos L, quos preceptor menbri tenetur dare omni anno preceptorie Traiectensi, et ultra omnes expensas liquide floreni CCCLII stuber XI schobe VII÷ *[7.5]*.

Summa summarum omni introituum preceptorie Traiectensis
floreni auri II.^M.X   stuber VI   ortgen VIIII.

Summa summarum omnium exituum dicte preceptorie Traiectensis floreni auri MCCLXXXXVII stuber XVI, sine omnibus illis pecuniis que dantur ad vitam, quia non sunt census perpetui et in dies moriuntur.

Summa summarum restant liquide preceptorie Traiectensi cum arrendacionibus, quas habet a menbris Buren, Aldewater, Hermelen, Werderer, Wemelingen, Engen, Vallis sancti Johannis, Kirckwerff et Sneck, ultra omnes expensas floreni VII.^C.XII stuber XVIII ortgen VIIII. Et racione pietancie floreni XXXXI stuber XXV, [g]faciunt florenos   754   15   9.[g]

Summa restant floreni VII.^C.LIIII stuber XV ortgen VIIII [h]cum pietantia[h].

Nota menbrum aut conventus Vallis sancti Johannis habet liquide ultra illam summam quadraginta florenorum, quam tenetur dare preceptorie Traiectensi, et ultra omnes expensas florenos auri CL stuber XX witgin XI.

[g]Restant menbro Myddelburch ultra omnes expensas floreni XXXV stuber XXIIII denarii IIII ut in loco suo scriptum est, et tamen hoc menbrum nichil absentie dat preceptorie Traiectensi.[g]

---

[a] *is missing in RA Gelderland.* [b] *in the left margin.* [c] *illegible because of the binding.* [d] *cut off ms.* [e] domus *in a different hand corrected from* preceptoria. [f] *the items are linked by means of a large brace.* [g] *in a different hand.* [h] *in a different hand in the right margin.*

fol.220r. Harlem preceptoria subiecta priori Almanie.

Die undecimo mensis Augusti 1495 intrarunt domini visitatores preceptoriam in Harlem, que est menbrum camere prioralis in Traiecto,
tamen est privilegiata per litteras Rodianas, quod inter se conventuales possunt eligere preceptorem; et pro nunc temporis est preceptor
venerabilis frater Johannes Guillerini Johannis cappellanus ordinis
sancti Johannis. Dicta preceptoria est situata intus civitatem Harlem
sub dominio domini ducis Burgundie Traiectensis diocesis.

Die duodecimo eiusdem fuit prestitum iuramentum eidem domino
preceptori ad informandum dominos visitatores de quesitis per eos
inquantum sibi innotuerit.

Primo domus preceptorie est magna et spaciosa, bona, lapidea;
habet ecclesiam mediocrem pulcram ad latus ipsius domus, non parrochialem, intitulatur sub vocabulo sancti Johannis Baptiste, habet
sex altaria: primum consecratum in honore sancti Johannis Baptiste,
secundum sancti Andree, tercium sancte Crucis, quartum Katherine,
quintum Marie virginis, sextum in honore nominis Ihesu.

In dicta preceptoria sunt quinque cappellani ordinis sancti Johannis, quorum nomina sunt frater Johannes Guillerini Johannis preceptor, frater Nicolaus Bartolomei de Delfft prior ecclesie, frater Jacobus
Gerhardi, frater Jacobus Martini, frater Johannes de Bermen.

Dicti cappellani cantant die noctuque horas canonicas et omni die
cantant unam missam et legunt tres, ad quas tenentur. Et ad hoc
tenent duos cappellanos seculares, et tenentur ad unam aliam missam. Et quia bona vendita sunt per quondam preceptores, antecessores huius vendiderunt bona et reditus, ergo non legunt quintam
missam.

Item dicta preceptoria habet conferre quatuor ecclesias parrochiales: unam in Beverwyck, quam possidet frater Jacobus Nicolai de
Delfft, et distat a preceptoria specio trium horarum itineris; super
collacione dicte ecclesie pendet lis in curia Romana.

Item habet preceptoria providere de ecclesia parrochiali in
Heymszburck, quam possidet frater Petrus de Harlem; distat a preceptoria spacio quatuor horarum itineris.

Item habet preceptoria providere de ecclesia parrochiali in Sutter-
wau, quam tenet dominus preceptor preceptorie incorporatam; distat
a preceptoria spacio septem horarum itineris.

Item habet preceptoria providere de ecclesia parrochiali in Hu-
sersauwe, quam possidet frater Laurencius Adriani; distat a preceptoria spacio unius diei itineris.

Sequuntur bona ecclesie.

Item calices argentei deaurati cum eorum patenis IIII. Item monstrancie due argentee, quarum una est magna. Item ciborium *[fol.220v.]* unum argenteum. Item crux una argentea. Item thuribulum unum argenteum. Item ampule due argentee. Item patena una argentea pro pace. Item fibule tres argentee ad usum capparum. Item missalia tria. Item antiphonarii duo. Item gradualia duo. Item psalteria II. Item cappe sete bone et male VII. Item casule sete bone et male VI. Item vestes levitiace bone et male VI. Item casule panni diversarum colorum bone et male XII. Item ecclesia est cum candelabris et aliis necessariis bene provisa.

Sequuntur bona domus.

Item lecti cum eorum necessariis XIII. Item de aliis necessariis ad usum domus est domus bene et sufficienter provisa.

Item dicta preceptoria habet quoddam hospitale circa domum, in quo preceptor tenetur tenere sex personas antiquas, et pro nunc temporis sunt sex persone in eo.

Item dicti conventuales preceptorie Harlamensis possunt decedente preceptori semper in perpetuum eligere alium preceptorem, quem dominus prior Almanie confirmare habet sine aliqua contradictione, tamen quod preceptor in Harlem teneatur omni futuro tempore dare omni anno reverendo domino priori Almanie florenos auri Renenses centum et eciam solvere iura thesauri imposita et imponenda et manere sub visitacione reverendissimi magistri de Rodo et prioris Almanie, ut apparuit dominis visitatoribus per bullam reverendissimi domini Baptisti de Ursinis magistri de Rodo, cuius bulle tenor sequitur et est talis:

Frater Baptista de Ursinis Dei gracia sacre domus hospitalis sancti Johannis Iherosolimitani magister humilis, pauperumque Ihesu Xpi custos, ᵃet nos conventus Rhodi domus eiusdem, religiosis in Xpo nobis carissimis fratribus Petro de Schoten dicte domus nostre cappellano ceterisque fratribus cappellanis religionem nostram professis in claustro sive domo nostra de Harlem, constitutis et commorantibus presentibus et futuris salutem in Domino sempiternam. ᵇHis queᵇ decus, honorem et commodum religionis nostre ac fratrum nostrorum concordiam et animorum tranquillitatem concernunt, libenti animo nostram auctoritatem addicimus et gracias atque libertates elargimur. Cum itaque paucis elapsis annis nonnullis occasionibus et causis, nobis satis notis et manifestis, certe differencie, dessensiones et contraversie orte sint, racione et causa administracionis dicti claustri sive domus de Harlem loci dicte nostre religionis in prioratu nostro Almanie et camere priorali ipsius prioratus spectantis; quibus de causis non parva scandula atque detrimenta dicto claustro sive domo fratribusque eiusdem in nostri ordinis dedecus et incommodum non mediocre contigerunt, videbanturque maiora secutura nisi de remedio oportuno provideretur. Nuper autem litteris patentibus sigillo pendenti munitis venerandi religiosi in Xpo nobis precarissimi fratris Johannis de Ors, dicti nostri prioratus Almanie prioris, accepimus huiusmodi rebus pro honore et commodo dicte nostre ordinis formis et modis inferius annotatis providendum atque consulendum. Quibusquidem visis, intellectis, discussis *[fol.221r.]* diligenterque examinatis pro honore et evidenti utilitate nostre dicte religionis invicem maturo et deliberato consilio de nostra certa sciencia, deliberamus, instituimus et ordinamus cum consensu, voluntate pariter et assensu dicti venerandi prioris et preceptoris dicti prioratus ac fratrum in assembleam Coloniensem congregatorum fratrum quoque venerande lingue Almanie, hic Rodi ad Dei et religionis obsequia residencium ut infra continetur. Itaque consideratis meritis, ydoneitate et sufficiencia vestri fratris Petri ᶜde Schotenᶜ et quod sub vestro utili regimine atque administracione dictum claustrum sive domus de Harlem decus et augmentum suscipiet; ideo gubernatorem, rectorem et administratorem dicti claustri sive domus de Harlem cum suis pertinenciis, attinenciis et dependenciis, cum omni honore, onere et emolumentis consuetis, vita vestra durante, serie presencium vos declaramus et ordinamus ad ipsum claustrum sive domum, gubernandum, regendum et administrandum tam in spiritualibus quam temporalibus ac suis pertinenciis et iuribus committentes vobis fiducialiter circa curam et regimen et administracionem accomodam dicti claustri sive domus de Harlem iuriumque ac bonorum eius, tam in agendo quam defendendo harum serie vices nostras. Ita tamen quod vos et qui pro tempore rector et gubernator, modo inferius annotato, eligetur in dicto claustro sive domo, teneamini supportari, ultra iura prioris et communis thesauri inferius declarato ex fructibus et proventibus dicti claustri sive domus onera et expensas solitas et consuetas in dicto claustro sive domo eiusque pertinenciis et subvenire victui, vestitui et rebus necessariis fratrum cappellanorum in eodem existencium et pro tempore commoriancium, dantes et concedentes vobis potestatem et auctoritatem fructus, redditus et emolimenta eiusdem claustri sive domus ac pertinenciarum suarum, petendum, exigendum, recuperandum, recipiendum et habendum, dictum quoque claustrum sive domum de Harlem cum suis pertinenciis ad honorem et divini cultus

augmentum amplioribus graciis prosequentes per inperpetuum constituimus et stabilimus, quod cedente vel decedente vobis fratre Petro
de Schoten rectore, gubernatore et administratore dicti claustri sive
domus et futuris per inperpetuum rectoribus, gubernatoribus et admi-
nistratoribus ipsius claustri qui pro^c tempore fuerint instituti et modo
infrascripto electi et confirmati pariformiter decendentes aut ceden-
tes, eo in casu fratres cappellani nostrum dictum ordinem professi et
in ipso claustro sive domo constituti atque pro tempore commorantes
insimul dicto in loco sollempniter congregati, possint et valeant creare, eligere et nostra auctoritate deputare ad regimen et administracionem dicti claustri sive domus de Harlem, cum pari et simili potestate
vobis prefato fratri Petro concessa, unum virum religiosum cappellanum dicti nostri ordinis ydoneum, sufficientem et aptum ex suo gre-
mio, si ydoneum invenerint, sin minus alium ex nostra religione
sufficientem et ipsum rectorem, gubernatorem et administratorem
dicti claustri ordinare ipsamque creacionem et electionem, sic factam,
venerabili priori dicti nostri prioratus Almanie presenti et futuro presentare debeant et teneantur, qui prior presens et futuri postea talem
electum administratorem, seclusa contradictione, confirmare teneantur; super quibus facultatem et auctoritatem predictis serie presencium, concedimus et donamus. Ut eciam religionis zelus et odor
fragrantissimus morumque honestas in vobis prefulgeat, ordinamus et
consensu quo supra stabilimus, ut omnes et singuli fratres cappellani
tam rector quam alii in dicto claustro sive domo degentes et Deo
omnipotenti, beate Marie virgini et sancto Johanni Baptiste servientes, secundum regulam, stabilimenta et consuetudines et usus dicte
domus et religionis nostre, honeste rite^d et moraliter vivere et Deo
obsequi firmiter teneantur et sint obligati. Et ne propter has nostras
instituciones et ordinaciones, que potissime in honorem et utilitatem
ipsius ordinis nostri facte censentur, dampnum aut dispendium aliquod cuiquam afferre videatur, declaramus, instituimus *[fol.221v.]* ^{c}et
ordinamus^c quod rector, gubernator atque administrator dicti claustri
sive domus presens et qui pro tempore erit, teneatur, debeat et obligatus sit cum effectu solvere annuatim in festo sancti Johannis Baptiste de mense Iunii, florenos Renenses centum tantum in civitate
Coloniensi aut alibi ubi per priores fuerit ordinatum, venerabili priori
dicti prioratus moderno et futuris, de fructibus et redditibus dicti
claustri sive domus, pro pensione annua et nomine vere pensionis
annue. Preter quoque et ultra dictam annuam pensionem florenorum
Renensium centum, rector et gubernator prefatus modernus et futuri
infallibiliter et absque ulla contradictione aut excusacione teneatur et
sit obligatus solvere nostro communi thesauro Rhodi sive receptori
aut commissario dicti communis thesauri, per nos aut per nostros

successores deputato aut deputandum responsionem ordinariam fructuum omnium dicti claustri sive domus de Harlem pertinenciumque
eiusdem et cetera onera imposita et imponenda per religionem nostram, secundum rerum et temporum exigenciam pro ut pro rata dicto
claustro sive domui de Harlem eiusque pertinenciis pertinebit et spec-
tabit secundum eius valorem et estimacionem. Et ut auctoritas prioralis conservetur, statuimus quod cedente aut decedente rectore et
gubernatore dicti claustri sive domus presente et futuro pro omni iure
mortuarii et vacantis ac eciam pro confirmacione noviter instituti
rectoris, prior Almanie qui presens est et qui pro tempore erit, habeat
et recipiat florenos Renenses ducentos quinquaginte dumtaxat et non
plures. Verum quia racioni consonum et decentissimum censeri debet, quod, quibus onera imposita sunt, libertates et immunitates a
nobis recipiant, quo melius exequi iniuncta possint et valeant, ea
propter de consensu quo supra, dictum claustrum sive domum ᶜde
Harlemᶜ cum suis pertinenciis et iuribus ac rectorem, gubernatorem
ac administratorem, fratres quoque cappellanos et subditus ipsius, ab
obediencia, subiectione, preeminencia, superioritate, correctione, visitacione et administracione preceptoris sive administratoris presentis
et futurorum preceptorie Traiectensis camere prioralis dicti prioratus
et ipsius preceptoris Traiectensis, liberamus, eximimus, absolvimus et
separamus per inperpetuum, correctioni quoque superioritati, obediencie, subiectioni et visitacioni prioris presentis et pro temporeᶜ
existentis ac nostri magistri et conventus Rodi submittimus et constituimus. Quodque ut hec commodius adimpleri valeant gubernator et
administrator predictus, teneatur et sit obligatus cum effectu infra
decennium a die date presencium reluere, redimere et liberare dictum claustrum sive domum de Harlem cum suis attinenciis et pertinenciis, ab omnibus et singulis obligacionibus, inpignoracionibus et
ypotecacionibus suarum pertinenciarum, hactenus quovismodo factis
et obligata sive ypoteticata ipsi claustro sive domui reintegrare et
unire. Postremo quia quod in honorem et commodum ipsius ordinis
institutum censetur nemini certe detrimento cedere debet, ideo decernimus de consensu quo supra declaramus, quod venerabilis prior
modernus tantum dicti prioratus, frater Johannes de Ors predictus,
qui hiis rebus consentit bono zelo et pro utilitate religionis, pro ut
litteris suis auten[ti]cis apparuit, propter has nostras instituciones aut
ordinaciones nullomodo directe vel indirecte habere aut querere possit vel valeat sua vita durante aliam cameram prioralem in commuta-
cionem et cambium ipsius preceptorie Traiectensis aut claustri de
Harlem, nec eciam possit dictus prior modernus tantum aliquam
aliam recompensacionem occasione predicta querere aut habere.
Omnia autem et singula que preter presentes nostras litteras pro dicto

claustro sive domo de Harlem eiusque pertinenciis constituta et quovismodo predictis de causis ordinata essent, quequidam hiis in nostris
litteris expressa non fuissent abolimus et revocamus. Verum cuncta et
singula supradicta dumtaxat secundum quod supra declarata et ordinata fuere sanximus, decernimus et de consensu predicto instituimus,
mandantes et precipientes universis et singulis dicte domus nostre
fratribus quacumque auctoritate, dignitate[c] officioque fungentibus in
virtute sancte obediencie et presertim dicti prioratus [fol.222r.]
Almanie presentibus et futuris ne contra presentes nostras litteras
institucionis, declaracionis, ordinacionis, decreti et mandati aliquatenus facere vel venire presumant quinymo inviolabiliter observare studeant. In cuius rei testimonium bulla nostra communis plumbea
presentibus est appensa.[a]

Datum Rodi in nostro conventu die quinta mensis Octobris anno
ab incarnacione Domini millesimo quadringentesimo sexagesimo
nono [5 October, 1469].

---

[a] *is missing in RA Gelderland; collated from AOM 45 with the original bull in
Stadsarchief Haarlem, Inventaris Enschede I nr.1789; cf. the edition by* Mario de
Visser, *La Commenda di S.Giovanni in Haarlem e le chiese dipendenti. Notizie e
Documenti,* Amsterdam, 1938, pp.30-37. *An abbreviated registration of the bull is to
be found in AOM 378, libri bullarum 1469, fol.144r-145v. Cf.elsewhere in this
edition, A.nrs.71 and 76.* [b] *according to the original bull; AOM 45 has:* hiiszque.
[c] *added from the original bull.* [d] *according to the original bull; AOM 45 has:* vite.

Nota[a]   Ad sciendum monetam currentem in Harlem, valorem frumentorum et quantitatem mensurarum:

Item XVI denarii faciunt unum stuber. Item XXVIIII stuber faciunt unum florenum Renensem in auro. Item IIII quartalia faciunt
unum octale. Item octale unum siliginis valet omnibus annis stuber
VIII. Item octale unum tritici valet omnibus annis stuber X, ut constitit dominis visitatoribus per informacionem ipsius domini preceptoris predicti medio eius iuramento.

Sequitur introitus pecuniarum.

Item dicta preceptoria habet omni anno racione ficti minuti de diversis personis intus opidum Harlem super domibus, ortis et aliis possessionibus florenos 8 stuber 10 denarios 11   VIII X X[I].[b]

Item dicta preceptoria habet omni anno a quodam Johanni Bartholomei in Molen racione duorum iucharorum agri florenos 6 stuber
26   VI XXVI.

Item dicta preceptoria habet omni anno a Theoderico Hagen in

Harlemerlehe racione iucharorum septem agri florenos 18 stuber 28
XVIII XXVIII.

Item dicta preceptoria habet omni anno de diversis personis in villis Rick et Nukirck racione agrorum florenos 19 stuber 9 denarios 4
XVIIII VIIII [IIII].[b]

Item dicta preceptoria habet omni anno a quodam Theoderico Guillerini in Eymszkirck racione census agrorum florenos 20 stuber 20
XX XX.

Item dicta preceptoria habet omni anno a quodam Nicolao Pariden in Casticom racione census agrorum florenos 9 stuber 19
VIIII XVIIII.

Item dicta preceptoria habet omni anno a quodam Theoderico Laurencii in Casticom racione census agrorum florenos 13 stuber 3
XIII III.

Item dicta domus habet omni anno in ficto minuto de diversis personis in locis Heymskerck racione agrorum florenos 22 stuber 2 denarios 8
XXII II [VIII].[b]

*fol.222v.*Item dicta domus habet omni anno in villis Ackerschlot et Hilligum de diversis personis racione agrorum florenos 4 stuber 21 denarios 8
IIII XXI VIII.

Item dicta preceptoria habet omnibus annis racione decimarum in Eynskirch et Velsen florenos 48 stuber 28   XXXXVIII XXVIII.

Item dicta preceptoria habet omni anno de ficto in diversis partitis de diversis personis in villa Naebwick racione census agrorum et pratarum florenos 30 stuber 10 denarios 4   XXX X IIII.

Item dicta praeceptoria habet omni anno in Monster de diversis personis racione census agrorum et pratarum florenos 31 stuber 10
XXXI X.

Item dicta preceptoria habet omni anno in villa Waeringen de diversis personis racione census agrorum florenos 22 stuber 12
XXII XII.

Item dicta preceptoria habet omni anno de diversis personis in villis Rijswick et Lice racione agrorum florenos 65 stuber 7 denarios 8
LXV VII VIII.

Item dicta preceptoria habet omni anno de ficto de diversis personis in villa Maeszlant racione agrorum et pratarum florenos 14 stuber 14
XIIII XIIII.

Item dicta preceptoris habet omni anno in villis Delff et Oistgest de diversis personis racione agrorum et pratarum florenos 8 stuber 8
VIII VIII.

Item dicta preceptoria habet omni anni in villa Renszberg et Kaldenberck de diversis personis racione agrorum florenos 9 stuber 7
VIIII VII.

Item dicta preceptoria habet omni anno de diversis personis in villis Wassener, Wortich, Vorschoten racione agrorum et pratarum florenos 7 stuber 17 denarios 8   VII XVII VIII.

Item preceptor facit cultivare in tribus locis circa opidum Harlem iucharos agri VII, qui [si] locarentur, posset preceptoria consequi omni anno recione census dictorum agrorum florenos 12 stuber 2

XII II.

Item dicta preceptoria habet omnibus annis racione offertorii et oblacionum florenos 31 stuber 1   XXXI I.

Item dicta preceptoria habet omni anno racione census pertinentis ad hospitale in diversis partitis de diversis personis in villa de Heyle racione agrorum florenos 18 stuber 18   XVIII XVIII.

Nota preceptoria habet pietanciam, racione cuius habet introitus sequentes:

Item preceptoria habet omni anno racione pietancie super domibus intus opidum Harlem de diversis personis florenos 20 stuber 17

XX XVII.

Item dicta preceptoria habet racione pietancie in villa Beverwick de diversis personis super domibus et agris florenos 10 stuber 12

X XII.

Item preceptoria habet omni anno racione missarum fundatarum in ecclesia in villis Heymskirck, Castricom, Ackerszschlot, Hillicem, Oistorp, Lysz, Sacdam de diversis personis super diversis possessionibus florenos 43 stuber 17   XXXXIII XVII.
fol.223r.

Item dicta preceptoria habet omni anno racione pietancie in villa Maeszlant de diversis personis super agris et pratis florenos 16 stuber 16   XVI XVI.

Summa floreni V.^{C}.XIIII   stuber XVI   denarii [III].[b]

Introitus tritici

Item dicta preceptoria habet omni anno in Wateringen in Henztlerdick et Monster de diversis personis racione agrorum octalia CLX. Et quodlibet octale valet omnibus annis stuber X, sic dicta octalia 160 valent florenos 55 stuber 5   LV V.

Introitus siliginis.

Item dicta preceptoria habet omni anno ex decima in Heymszkirck ad distribuendum pauperibus octalia 96. Et quodlibet octale valet

omnibus [annis] stuber VIII, sic dicta LXXXXVI valent florenos 26
stuber 14   XXVI XIIII.

Summa summarum omni introituum pecuniarum et frumentorum
reductarum in pecunias
floreni auri V.^C.LXXXXVI   stuber VI   denarii III.

Sequitur exitus pecuniarum.

Item dicta preceptoria tenetur dare omni anno conventui Carmelitarum in Harlem racione census unius domus et alterius census stuber
11 denarios 8   XI VIII.
   Item dicta preceptoria tenetur dare omni anno comiti Hollandie
racione census stuber 2   II.
   ^cItem dicta preceptoria tenetur dare omni anno balisteriis in Harlem stuber 2   II.^c
   Item dicta preceptoria tenetur dare omni anno Ade filie Henrici
de Colonia florenos auri XXIIII et stuber XXIIII racione debiti facti
per fratrem Nicolaum [de] Schoten preceptorem preteritum, et possunt redimi   XXIIII XXIIII.
fol.223v.
   Item dicta preceptoria tenetur dare omni anno cuidam Theoderico mercatori in Harlem racione debiti facti per quendam fratrem
Petrum [de] Schotten, possunt redimi, florenos 12 stuber 12
                                                    XII XII.
   Item preceptoria tenetur dare omni anno relicte Arnoldi Rolandi
in Harlem, et possunt redimi, florenos 6 stuber 26   VI XXVI.
   Item procuratori pro salario florenos 12   XII.
   Item pro necessitate IIII cappellanorum florenos   XVI XVI.
   Item predicatori, qui predicat omni die festo per totum annum
florenos 10   X.
   Item custodi ecclesie pro salario florenos 6   VI.
   Item organiste et famulo suo pro salario florenos 7 stuber 17
                                                       VII XVII.
   Item barbetonsori pro salario florenos 2 stuber 22   II XXII.
   Item canuario pro salario florenos 6 stuber 6   VI VI.
   Item porterio pro salario florenos 2 stuber 2   II II.
   Item coco pro salario florenos 6 stuber 26   VI XXVI.
   Item expenduntur omnibus annis in reparacione aggerum floreni
10   X.
   Item collectori oblacionum in ecclesia pro salario et expensis quan-
do venit florenos 6 stuber 21   VI XXI.
   Item famulo coci pro salario florenos 2   II.

In dicta preceptoria sunt XII persone ultra dominum preceptorem, videlicet sex cappellani, quorum duo sunt seculares, qui habent solum expensas, procurator, canuarius, cocus et famulus coci, sacrista et porterius; taxaverunt domini visitatores pro expensis cuiuslibet persone florenos auri XVI, faciunt florenos 192   CLXXXXII.

Item expenduntur omnibus annis in ligno et cespitibus ad usum domus floreni 35   XXXV.

Summa floreni CCCLVIIII   stuber XXVI   denarii VIII.

Nota ad vitam[d]

[e]Item preceptoria tenetur dare relicte magistri Guillerini in Hagen Comitis, vita sua durante tantum, omni anno florenos auri VIII et stuber VIII racione debiti facti per quendam fratrem Petrum de Schotten, et est circa sexaginta annorum.

[e]Item preceptoria tenetur dare cuidam Johanni Hugonis Buscart in Delfft, solum vita sua durante, et eciam uxori sue vita sua durante omni anno florenos auri XIII et stuber XXIII.

[e]Item preceptoria tenetur dare omni anno domino Johanni Bertoldi in Hagen Comitis, solum vita sua durante omni anno florenos auri IIII.

[e]Item dicta preceptoria tenetur dare omni anno magistro Thome pensi[o]nario opidi Harlemensis vita sua durante florenos auri VIII stuber VIII.

Exitus siliginis.

Item preceptoria tenetur dare omni anno pauperibus omnem siliginem predictum, videlicet octalia 96, ex legato quorundam nobilium et quodlibet octale valet omnibus annis stuber VIII, sic dicta octalia 96 valent florenos [26 stuber 14]   XXVI XIIII.

Summa summarum omni[um] introituum preceptorie Harlem floreni auri V.[C].LXXXXVI   stuber VI   denarii III.

Summa summarum omnium exituum dicte preceptorie Harlem floreni auri IIII.[C].LXXXVI   stuber XI   denarii VIII.

Restant liquide floreni CCVIIII   stuber XXIII   denarii XI.

---

[a] *in the left margin.* [b] *cut off ms.* [c] *is missing in RA Gelderland.* [d] *in the left margin, in a different hand.* [e] *the items are linked by means of a large brace.*

fol.233v. Steinfort preceptoria[a]

Die vicesimo tercio mensis Augusti 1495 intrarunt domini visitatores in preceptoriam in Steinfordia, in qua est preceptor venerabilis frater Herbertus Schnetloch miles ordinis sancti Johannis baiulivus Westphalie. Dicta preceptoria est situata in provincia Westphalie sub dominio reverendi domini episcopi Monasteriensis eiusdem diocesis.

Die vero vicesimo quarto eiusdem domini visitatores visitarunt preceptoriam in Borckhem.

Die vero vicesimo quinto eiusdem mensis domini visitatores visitarunt preceptoriam in Laech.

Die vero vicesimo quinto eiusdem mensis prestitum fuit iuramentum eidem domino preceptori predicte preceptorie in Steinfort ad informandum eos de quesitis per ipsos inquantum sibi innotuerit.

Dicta preceptoria est situata circa opidum Steinfort, habet domum magnam et bonam bene reparatam, habet ecclesiam magnam parrochialem intitulatam sub vocabulo sancti Johannis, habet octo altaria, primum consecratum in honore sancte et individue Trinitatis, secundum in honore beate Marie virginis, tercium sancti Johannis Baptiste, quartum Angelorum, quintum apostolorum Petri et Pauli, sextum sancte Crucis, septimum Anthonii, octavum Redempcionis beate Marie.

In dicta preceptoria sunt VIIII cappellani ordinis sancti Johannis quorum nomina sunt frater Nicolaus de Rine prior ecclesie, frater Theodericus Holthusen, frater Hermannus Overhagen, frater Hinricus Weren, frater Hinricus Bispinch, frater Johannes Monster, frater Hinricus Ebekinck, frater Hinricus de Resz, frater Walterus Marcolff.

Item in dicta preceptoria est unus diaconus cuius nomen est frater Johannes Borckem[b].

Item in dicta preceptoria sunt quinque milites ordinis sancti Johannis quorum nomina sunt frater Johannes Geysteren, frater Gotfridus Graesz, frater Ludolphus Scheven[c], frater Herbertus de Lotten, frater Wylprant de Dinckelhich[d].

Item [in] dicta preceptoria ab antiquo sunt XVI persone ordinis sancti Johannis cum preceptore quorum nomina sunt prescripta.

Item dicti cappellani tenentur omni die cantare missam unam et omnes horas canonicas et tenentur legere tres missas. Ultra missas quatuor predictas tenentur omni septimana legere tres alias missas.

In dicta ecclesia est una lampas et una candela de sevo, id est sepia, coram venerabili sacramento die nocteque ardentes.

Sequuntur bona ecclesie.

Item calices argentei deaurati cum eorum patenis XII. Item monstrancia una argentea magna. Item caput sancti Johannis in *[fol.234r.]* disco argentea, valet circa florenos XXXX. Item ymago sancti Johannis argenteum, valet iuxta videre florenos —*[e]*. Item ymago beate Marie virginis argenteum. Item quatuor ampulle argentee. Item thuribila duo argentea. Item duo libri, unum evangeliare, aliud exemplare, ornati argento. Item cappe sete diversarum colorum bone et male XII. Item vestes levitiace sete diversarum colorum bone et male X. Item casule sete diversarum colorum bone et male IIII. Item casule sete et panni diversarum colorum bone et male XX. Item in ceteris necessariis est ecclesia bene provisa.

Item dicta preceptoria habet circa mille quadringentos communicantes.

Sequuntur bona domus.

Item in dicta preceptoria sunt lecti boni et mali cum eorum necessariis LI. Item domus est in aliis necessariis ad usum suum competenter provisa. Item coclearia argentea VI. Item equi domestici. Item equi silvacie XII. Item vacce XVIII.

Item dicta preceptoria habet conferre unam ecclesiam parrochialem in Laer, distat a preceptoria spacio duarum horarum itineris, quam possidet frater Hermannus Senen ordinis sancti Johannis.

[Mona]sterium membrum*[f]*

Item dicta preceptoria habet duo menbra in episcopatu Monasteriensi, unum intus civitatem Monasteriensem quod possidet frater Theodericus de Campis cappellanus ordinis sancti Johannis; dictum menbrum distat a preceptoria spacio quinque horarum itineris.

[Horst] menbrum*[f]*

Dicta preceptoria habet aliud menbrum in Horst quod possidet frater Henricus Drost miles ordinis sancti Johannis. Dictum menbrum distat a preceptoria spacio itineris unius diei.

XIIII*[f]*

Item dicta preceptoria habet in partibus Frisie menbra XIIII, que omnia eligunt inter se preceptores quos preceptor in Steinfort habet confirmare, qui baiulivus et preceptor in Steinfort non potest eligere preceptorem nec conventuales dare nec tollere. Super hec omnia menbra sequencia habent privilegia a preceptoria in Steinfort ab antiquis temporibus ultra memoriam hominum ut informantur domini visitatores per ipsum iam modernum baiulivum Westphalie, sed super hoc non viderunt litteras nec exempciones nec indultum sed solum ex relatu hec sciunt, que privilegia dicit esse conservata in Monasterio et propter pestem non audet pro nunc temporis accedere ut ea portet ad videndum.

Sequuntur nomina menbrorum.

[Werffun]g membrum[f]

Primum menbrum est situatam in Werffung, in quo est preceptor frater Rodulphus de Laege qui habet secum duos cappellanos ordinis sancti Johannis et circa sexaginta moniales ordinis sancti Johannis, que legunt et cantant omnes horas canonicas; distat a preceptoria *[fol.234v.]* spacio trium dierum itineris, Monasteriensis diocesis.

Wytwart membrum[f]

Secundum menbrum in Wytwart in qua est preceptor frater Rodolfus Horngin, qui habet secum unum cappellanum ordinis sancti Johannis et quindecim mulieres ordinis sancti Johannis que eciam legunt et cantant omnes horas canonicas; distat a preceptoria spacio uti primum, sub dominio civitatis Gronyngen, predicti diocesis.

Oesterwerung membrum[f]

Tercium menbrum in Oesterwerung in qua est preceptor frater Johannes Hergrae, habet secum quinque fratres ordinis sancti Johannis, sub dominio civitatis Gronyngen, eiusdem distancie, predicti diocesis.

Obingwere membrum[f]

Quartum in Obingwere in qua est preceptor frater Habo Hey, habet quatuor cappellanos ordinis sancti Johannis, sub dominio comitis Frise, distat a preceptoria spacio quinque dierum itineris, Monasteriensis diocesis.

Dunbroick membrum[f]

Quintum in Dunbroick in qua est preceptor frater Johannes ex Brabancia, distat a preceptoria spacio quinque dierum itineris Osnaburgensis diocesis, sub dominio comitum Frisie.

Yemegon membrum[f]

Sextum in Yemegon in qua est preceptor frater Hey Friso cappellanus ordinis sancti Johannis, habet secum quatuor cappellanos ordinis predicti, sub dominio comitum de Frisia, distat a preceptoria ut supra, Monasteriensis diocesis.

Herselen membrum[f]

Septimum in Herselen in qua est preceptor frater Henricus de Brabancia cappellanus ordinis sancti Johannis, distat a preceptoria spacio quinque dierum itineris, sub dominio comitum de Frisia, Monasteriensis diocesis.

Boccasael membrum[f]

Octavum in Boccasael in qua est preceptor frater Hermannus N. cappellanus ordinis sancti Johannis, distat a preceptoria ut supra, sub dominio comitum de Frisie, Monasteriensis diocesis.

Buschmonichem membrum[f]

Nonum in Buschmonichem in qua est preceptor frater Gerhardus Friso cappellanus ordinis sancti Johannis, sub dominio comitum de Frisia, distat a preceptoria ut supra, Bremensis diocesis.

Hofen membrum[f]

Decimum in Hofen in qua est preceptor frater Sibertus de Assendau cappellanus ordinis sancti Johannis, sub dominio nobilium de Erich, distat a preceptoria sex dierum spacio itineris, Bremensis diocesis.

Moda membrum[f]

Undecimum in Moda in qua est preceptor frater Goesman cappellanus ordinis sancti Johannis, habet secum duos cappellanos ordinis predicti, distat a preceptoria spacio quatuor dierum itineris sub dominio comitum de Frisia Monasteriensis diocesis.

Breydhorn membrum[f]

Duodecimum in Breydhorn in qua est preceptor frater Spilwynck laycus, nullum habet cappellanum, distat a preceptoria spacio quinque dierum itineris sub dominio comitum de Aldenborch Bremensis diocesis.

Bocalische membrum[f]

Tercium decimum in Bocalische in qua est preceptor frater Hermannus Wolff cappellanus ordinis sancti Johannis, distat a preceptoria spacio quatuor dierum itineris sub dominio comitum de Frisia, Osnaburgensis diocesis.

Langholt membrum^f

Quartum decimum in Langholt in qua est preceptor frater Herher cappellanus ordinis sancti Johannis sub dominio comitum de Frisia, distat a preceptoria spacio trium dierum itineris Monasteriensis diocesis.

fol.235r.
Circa Frisiam est situata una insula circumdata mari vocata Butgarnerlant, habet Frisiam linguam. In dicta insula sunt due preceptorie, non respondent aliquid nec obediunt alicui.

Item predicta preceptoria habet vasallos centum qui tenentur ad certa servicia, que servicia valent preceptorie tantum quantum expenditur. In empcione lignorum et cespitum id est turff ad usum preceptorie ergo non fit mencio in exitu racione lignorum.

Ad sciendium monctam currentem in Steinfort, valorem frumentorum et quantitatem mensurarum.

Item XII denarii faciunt unum solidum. Item XVIII solidi faciunt unum florenum Renensem in auro.

Item quatuor scheppel faciunt unum malderium.

Item malderium unum tritici valet omnibus annis solidos VIIII et denarios IIII. Item malderium unum siliginis valet omnibus annis solidos sex et denarios decem. Item malderium unum ordii valet omnibus annis solidos sex et denarios duos. Item malderium unum avene valet omnibus annis solidos duos, denarios IIII. Hec constarunt dominis visitatoribus per informacionem domini preceptoris et fratris Hermanni Overhagen granatarii preceptorie medio eorum iuramento.

Sequitur introitus et primo pecuniarum.

Item preceptoria habet omni anno racione arrendacionis menbri in Werffung florenos 6   VI.

Item preceptoria habet omni anno racione menbri in Wytwart florenos 12 solidos 9   XII VIIII.

Item preceptoria habet omni anno racione menbri in Oisterwerung florenos 15   XV.

Item preceptoria habet omni anno racione menbri in Abinckwer florenos 12 solidos 9   XII VIIII.

Item preceptoria habet omni anno racione menbri in Dunbroick florenos 2   II.

Item preceptoria habet omni anno racione menbri in Yenegem florenos 5   V.

Item preceptoria habet omni anno racione menbri in Herselen florenos 14   XIIII.

Item preceptoria habet omni anno racione menbri in Bockasael florenos 4   IIII.

Item preceptoria habet omni anno racione menbri in Boszmonichem florenos 5 solidos 9   V VIIII.

Item preceptoria habet omni anno racione menbri in Hofen florenos 3   III.

Item preceptoria habet omni anno racione menbri Moda florenos 7 solidos 9   VII VIIII.

Item preceptoria habet omni anno racione menbri in Breythem florenos 12   XII.

fol.235v.

Item preceptoria habet omni anno racione menbri in Bocalische florenos 6 solidos 9   VI VIIII.

Item preceptoria habet omni anno racione menbri in Langholt florenos 6   VI.

Item preceptoria habet omni anno racione menbri in Horst florenum unum solidos 9   I VIIII.

Item dicta preceptoria habet omni anno de ficto minuto de diversis personis in locis Steinfort, Laer, Notlen, Leyer, Horstmar et cetera racione census domorum, agrorum et aliarum possessionum florenos 72 solidos 16 [denarios 6]   LXXII XVI VI.

Item dicta preceptoria habet omnibus annis racione iogalium sive salmatico suorum vasallorum florenos 40   XXXX.

Item dicta preceptoria habet omni anno de ficto de diversis personis in Steinfort et aliis villis circum iacentibus porcellos centum viginti et quilibet porcellus valet omnibus annis solidos IIII et denarios sex, faciunt florenos 30   XXX.

Item preceptor facit cultivare certam quantitatem agrorum qui si locarentur pro censu perpetuo valerent preceptorie omni anno racione census florenos 21 solidos 6   XXI VI.

Item dicta preceptoria habet omnibus annis racione parvarum decimarum in diversis suis massariis florenos 3 solidos 2   III II.

Item dicta preceptoria habet omnibus annis racione glandium florenos 10   X.

Item preceptoria utitur cum suis vaccis certas pratas qui valent omnibus [annis] florenos 3   III.

Item dicta preceptoria habet omnibus annis racione oblacionum florenos 58 solidos 2 denarios 6   LVIII II VI.

Item dicta preceptoria habet omni anno racione prioratus racione census ficti florenum unum solidos quinque denarios sex   I V VI.

Item dicta preceptoria habet omni anno de ficto racione census in Steinfort libras cere IIII, valent omnibus annis solidos 12   XII.

Summa   floreni CCCLIII   solidi VIII   denarii [VI][g].

Introitus tritici.

Item dicta preceptoria habet omni anno de ficto minuto in parrochia Laer, Borchhorst et Billerbeck de diversis personis racione census agrorum malderia 47 scheppel 3. Et quodlibet malderium valet omnibus annis solidos VIIII et denarios IIII. Sic dicta malderia XXXXVII scheppel III valent florenos 24 solidos 13 denarios 5 XXIIII XIII V.

Introitus siliginis.

Item dicta preceptoria habet omni anno de ficto de diversis personis in parrochia Steinfort racione census agrorum malderia XXIII scheppel I.
fol.236r.
Item[h]

Summa summarum omnium introituum pecuniarum et frumentorum reductarum in pecunias
floreni auri VII.^{C}.XXVII   solidi XII   denarii VIII.

Sequitur exitus pecuniarum.

Item dicta preceptoria tenetur dare omni anno Burdewyck in Borchorst racione census ab antiquo solidos 10   X.
Item dicta preceptoria tenetur dare omni anno monasterio sancti Egidii in civitate Monasteriensi racione census solidos 5   V.
Item expenditur omnibus annis in oleo et cera, hostiis, vino ad usum ecclesie floreni 17 solidi 6   XVII VI.
Item barbetonsori pro salario solidos 12   XII.
Item preceptor dat priori ecclesie pro labore suo florenos 4   IIII.
Item preceptor dat omni anno ex consuetudine conventualibus certis diebus vinum et agnellos scolaribus, magistro scolarium, decano synodi pro sancta crismate et aliis certis festivitatibus florenos 19 solidos 11 denarius 3   XVIIII XI [III]^g.
Item procuratori pro salario florenos 3   III.
Item canuario pro salario florenos 3   III.
Item scriptori domus Henrico Zysendorff qui est prebendarius domus pro suo salario florenos 2   II.
Item pistori qui est braxator pro salario florenos 5   V.
Item molendario pro salario florenos 5   V.
Item coco pro salario florenos 5   V.
Item secundo coco pro salario florenos 2   II.
Item porterio pro salario florenos 2   II.

fol.236v.

Item famulo pistoris pro salario florenos 3   III.

Item famulo coci pro salario florenos 2   II.

Item famulo domus pro salario florenos 5   V.

Item racione ligni et cespitum id est turff ad usum domus non fit exitus quia vasalli proprii preceptorie tenentur portare ligna et turff ad usum domus et quia servicia ad que tenentur magis valent quam solum portare ligna, ergo non fit exitus racione certe quantitatis lignorum quam emit preceptor ultra ligna et cespites que ex propriis silvis habet.

Item [in] dicta preceptoria sunt ultra dominum preceptorem quinque milites ordinis sancti Johannis, novem cappellani et unus diaconus quorum nomina sunt prescripta. Taxaverunt domini visitatores pro expensis cuiuslibet persone florenos auri XVI. Et hoc propter subvencionem quam habet preceptoria racione pietancie faciunt dicte persone florenos 240   CCXXXX.

Item in dicte preceptoria sunt undecima famuli qui sunt prescripti. Taxaverunt domini visitatores pro expensis cuiuslibet persone florenos auri XII, faciunt simul florenos 132   CXXXII.

Item dicta preceptoria tenetur ab antiqua consuetudine omni die XIIII pauperibus dare expensas in prandio et cena per totum annum et dare quartodecimo certam quantitatem cibi supermanentis et panis ac cervisie. Taxaverunt domini visitatores pro expensis pauperis cuiuslibet dictorum XIIII quolibet anno florenos auri VIII faciunt florenos 112   CXII.

Item preceptor expendit omnibus annis ut dicit in reparacione molendine florenos 11   XI.

Summa floreni V.C.LXXIIII   solidi VIII   denarii [III]g.

[Nota ad vitam]i

Item dicta preceptoria tenetur dare omni anno Druytgin de Senden sua vita durante tantum racione debiti antiqui florenos 2 solidos XII.

Item dicta preceptoria tenetur dare omni anno fratri Gotfrido Graesz militi conventuali in dicta preceptoria vita sua durante florenos auri IIII et solidos III racione debiti facti tempore preteriti preceptoris.

Item dicta preceptoria tenetur dare omni anno fratri Rodolpho Schefenc conventuali dicte preceptorie vita sua durante florenos auri quatuor et solidos tres racione debiti facti tempore preteriti preceptoris.

Item dicta preceptoria tenetur dare omni anno fratri Hermanno Senden pastori in Lare vita sua durante florenos auri quinque racione debiti facti tempore preteriti preceptoris.

Item dicta preceptoria tenetur dare omni anno fratri Henrico Horngin locumtenenti in Borckem vita sua durante florenos auri IIII et solidos III racione debiti facti tempore defuncti preceptoris.

Item in dicta preceptoria est quidam Alart Drost prebendatus laycus vita sua durante. Taxaverunt domini visitatores pro expensis illius florenos auri XVI.

In dicta preceptoria sunt quatuor prebendati eorum vita durante quorum duo emerunt mensam aut expensas a preceptori defuncto et duo emerunt mensam et expensas tempore moderni domini preceptoris, quorum nomina *[fol.237r.]* sunt Hermannus Quendorp, Bernhardus Parvus, Henricus Heymhoff, Johannes Langenhorst. Taxaverunt domini visitatores pro expensis cuiuslibet persone florenos auri XIIII, faciunt florenos LVI.

     Exitus siliginis.

Item dicta preceptoria tenetur omni sexta feria dare stipendias pauperibus cum quibus expenduntur omni septimana scheppel tria, faciunt simul malderia XXXVIIII. Et quodlibet malderium valet omnibus annis solidos sex, denarios decem. Sic dicta malderia 39 valent florenos 14, solidos 14, denarios 6   XIIII XIIII VI.

Summa summarum omnium exituum pecuniarum et frumentorum reductarum in pecuniis sine pecuniis que dantur ad vitam
     floreni auri V.C.LXXXVIIII   solidi IIII   denarii VIIII.

     Sequitur pietancia conventualium in Steinfort.

Die vicesimoseptimo mensis Augusti 1495 prestitum fuit iuramentum fratri Johanni de Geysteren militi et cappellano ordinis sancti Johannis, magistro sive collectori pietanciarum, ad informandum dominos visitatores de introitibus et exitibus pietancie conventualium in Steinfort.

     Introitus pecuniarum.

Item dicta pietancia habet omni anno in Steinfort et diversis aliis locis de diversis personis racione census et anniversariorum super domibus, agris et aliis possessionibus florenos L, solidos VII, denarios III.

Item dicti conventuales habent omni anno certos redditus in diversis locis de diversis personis quos redditus dicunt esse pro eorum vestitu.

ʲFaciunt dicti census florenos 49, solidos X, denarios VI.ʲ
  Summa floreni LXXXXVIIII   solidi XVII   denarii VIIII.

fol.237v. Introitus tritici.

Item dicta pietancia habet omni anno in diversis locis de diversis
personis racione census agrorum, domorum et aliarum possessionum
et racione anniversariorum malderia XVIIII. Et quodlibet malderium
valet omnibus annis solidos VIIII denarios IIII. Sic predicta malderia
valent florenos VIIII solidos XV, denarios IIII.

         Introitus siliginis.

Item dicta pietancia habet omni anno in diversis partitis, diversis locis
et de diversis personis racione census ficti anniversariorum malderia
LXXV scheppel III.
  Item dicti conventuales habent omni anno de ficto in diversis locis
racione census agrorum et aliarum possessionum pro eorum vestitu
malderia LXX.
  Item dicti conventuales habent omnibus annis racione quarte partis frumentorum massarie in Boekel florenos XVII.

    Summa malderia CLXII   scheppel III.

Nota quodlibet malderium valet omnibus annis solidos sex et denarios decem. Et sic predicta malderia 162 scheppel 3 valent florenos
LXI solidos XIIII denarios I÷ *[1.5]*.

         Introitus ordii.

Item dicta pietancia habet omni anno racione census in diversis locis
de diversis personis et racione anniversariorum malderia CXXI,
scheppel ÷ *[0.5]*.
  Item dicti conventuales habent omni anno racione census in diversis locis pro eorum vestitu malderia LXII, scheppel I÷ *[1.5]*.
  Item dicti conventuales habent omnibus annis racione quarte partis frumentorum massarie in Boekel malderia V scheppel II.

    Summa malderia CLXXXVIIII.

Nota quodlibet malderium valet omnibus annis solidos sex denarios duos et sic predicta malderia 189 valent florenos LXIIII, solidos XIII, denarios VI.

fol.238r. Introitus avene.

Item dicta pietancia habet omni anno de ficto minuto in diversis partitis in Steinfort et aliis locis racione census ficti et anniversariorum malderia LXXII scheppel III.

Item dicti conventuales habent omni anno racione census in diversis locis pro eorum vestitu malderia VIII.

Item dicti conventuales habent omnibus annis racione quarte partis frumentorum massarie in Boeckel malderia III.

Summa malderia LXXXIII   scheppel III.

Nota quodlibet malderium valet omnibus annis solidos II denarios IIII. Et sic predicta malderia LXXXIII scheffel III valent florenos X, solidos XV, denarios V.

Exitus pietancie.

Item dicti domini conventuales tenentur omnibus sextis feriis, sabatinis diebus et per totam quadragesimam dare pisces, buttirum et certis temporibus vinum et presencias, species, oleum ad usum coquine in subvencionem expensarum domini preceptoris et in diversis aliis communibus utilitatibus, in quibus expendunt omnibus annis florenos auri CLXX.

fol.238v.
Nota domini visitatores ex informacione domini preceptoris et eciam ex parte domini comitis in Steinfort fuerunt informati de dissoluta vita et inhonestate cappellanorum preceptorie Steinfort propter continuas inebrietates et alia vicia. Volentes igitur de remediis ad hoc oportunis providere fecerunt certas ordinaciones in modum sequentem quarum tenor sequitur et est talis:

Die vicesimo octavo Augusti 1495 existentibus in preceptoria Steinfort reverendo domino fratri Petro Stoltz de Gaubicklnhem sacri conventus Rhodi magno baiulivo et venerabili fratri Johanni Oisterwick preceptori in Wesalia baiulivo Coloniensi in locum venerandi fratris Johannis Anthonii de Actis preceptoris Pucini prioratus Capue visitatoribus per reverendissimum in Xpo patrem et dominum dominum Petrum Daubuson sacro sancte Romane ecclesie tituli sancti Hadriani diaconum cardinalem Rodique magnum magistrum et capitulum generale in Almaniam, Ungariam, Bohemiam, Poloniam, Daciam et cetera destinatis et ordinatis et volentes exequi seriem et tenorem eorum commissionum visitacionis faciunt et ordinant ordinaciones infrascriptas quas mandant conventualibus in Steinfort, cappellanis, militibus ordinis sancti Johannis in virtute sancte obediencie firmiter et inviolabiliter omni futuro tempore observari.

Primo et ante omnia boni et veri religiosi ad laudem omnipotentis Dei ad celebracionem divinorum officiorum devote et cum summa reverencia inclinati esse debent. Qua propter domini visitatores ordinant et mandant ut infra quod cappellani preceptorie in Steinfort debeant cantare et legere missas cum reverencia, honore et devocione iuxta morem et consuetudinem ac stabilimenta ordinis.

Item iuxta stabilimentum et statutum religionis Johannis ubi sunt sex cappellani in una domo ordinis sancti Johannis debent cantare omnes horas canonicas. Ergo domini visitatores ordinant et mandant quod conventuales cappellani in Steinfort debitis horis debeant et teneantur cantare omnes horas canonicas cum devocione reverenter, attente et pausatim moderatis vocibus in eorum mantellis conventualibus et non alias, accensis candelis iuxta morem ordinis predicti.

Item mandant domini visitatores quod conventuales milites qui non sunt prepediti officiis debeant intrare chorum ad omnes horas canonicas cum eorum mantellis conventualibus.

Item domini visitatores mandant et volunt quod omnes conventuales debeant sedere in mensa induti mantellis conventualibus et legere in mensa iuxta statuta et laudabilem consuetudinem ordinis sancti Johannis uti in aliis conventibus.

Item domini visitatores volunt et mandant quod nemo conventualium debeat exire domum sine licentia et voluntate domini preceptoris aut domini prioris ut decet bonos et religiosos obedientes.

Item domini visitatores volunt et mandant quod conventualis qui habet officium cellerarii debeat semper facta collacione serotina accipere claves a suo kemenario et tenere penes se per totum noctem.
fol.239r.

Item domini visitatores volunt et mandant dominis conventualibus quod incontinenti post completorium debeant intrare quivis cameram suam et ibi quiescere et non post completorium ultro bibere et crapulose ac ebriose vivere, quia stabilimenta ordinis hoc prohibent.

Item domini visitatores iuxta stabilimenta ordinis precipiunt et mandant dominis conventualibus ne sine licencia domini preceptoris aliquis conventualium fiat patrinus.

Item domini visitatores mandant quod domini conventuales debeant vivere iuxta tria vota substancialia et decenter et honeste incedere cum decenti corona et abbreviatis crinibus ac habitu secundum approbatam et laudabilem consuetudinem religionis sancti Johannis.

Summa summarum omnium introituum preceptorie Steinfort
floreni auri VII.^C.XXVII solidi XII denarii VIII.

Summa summarum omnium exituum dicte preceptorie Steinfort
floreni auri V.^C.LXXXVIIII solidi IIII denarii VIIII.

Restant preceptorie liquide compotatis omnibus utilitatibus preceptorie et menbrorum suorum omnium floreni CXXXVIII, solidi VII, denarii XI, non tamen compotatis quantitatibus exituum et expensarum que dantur ad vitam personarum in exitu scriptarum, quia non sunt census nec exitus perpetui.

---

^a *this entire preceptory with its members is missing in RA Gelderland.* ^b *corrected from* Worckem. ^c Ludolphus Scheven *or* Rudolphus Schefen; *cf.fol.233v.and 236v.* ^d *uncertain reading ms.* ^e *unspecified.* ^f *in a different hand in the left margin; on the recto-side of fol.234 partly illegible because of the binding.* ^g *illegible because of the binding.* ^h *this is a cancelled item about 426* malderia *and 1* scheppel *from the parishes* Meteler, Lere *and* Wuller *with a value of 55 florins, 4 shillings and 7 pennies.* ⁱ *rendered illegible by pasting in the left margin, together with a large brace until the end of the verso-side.* ^j *in a different hand, i.e. the hand of the notary public.*

fol.244r., notice of the notary public (missing in RA Gelderland):

Et ego Gaspar Froren de Rensz clericus Treverensis diocesis publicus Apostolica Imperialique auctoritate Notarius atque presentis visitationis scriba, quia arduis meis de causis reverendis dominis visitatoribus bene cognitis et manifestis Romam perrexi, quapropter presentem visitationem ex prothocollo meo ipsemet copiare sive extrahere non valui, ordinatus fuit per dominos visitatores quidam iuvenis virtuosus et probus ad copiandum et exemplandum ex prothocollo meo presentem visitationem, cuius manu in foliis seu cartis ducentis quinquaginta scripta est, quam in reditu meo ex Roma fideliter scriptam et copiatam cum prothocollo meo collationavi et auscultavi. Omnesque et singulos preceptoriarum et membrorum valores in fine cuiuslibet preceptorie et membrorum, deductis tamen deducendis, per dominos visitatores limitatis limitandis, defalcatis defalcandis oneribus et expensis annualibus licitis, solitis et consuetis iuxta uniuscuiuslibet preceptorie et menbrorum exigentiam et dominorum visitatorum ordinationem bene exemplatos reperi et inveni ideoque presentem visitationem in forma publici instrumenti manu mea propria in fine

cuiuslibet folii subscripsi et in hanc publicam et auctenticam formam
redegi signoque nomine et cognomine meis solitis et consuetis unacum eorundem dominorum visitatorum et commissariorum manuum
et signorum apposicione et subscripsione signavi in fidem, robur et
testimonium omnium et singulorum premissorum requisitus pariter
atque rogatus.

*This text is marked at the bottom with the notary hallmark, consisting of an
octagonal star, bearing a three-pointed crown on the upper star point, and two keys
that are placed diagonally alongside the upper star point. The emblem is based on
a lying trunk, supported by two of its branches that extend toward each other. In
the trunk are the letters G – froren –*

C.3. AOM 6340, VISITATION OF GERMANY, 1540

A volume in folio on paper, sewn on ropes and bound in sheets of thick paper, 173 folia plus a title page, a contemporaneous table of contents at the back and two flyleaves. The folia are an average 30.5 cm high and 20.5 cm wide. Many but not all the leaves bear paper-marks: up to fol.88 'Basler Stab' (C.M.Briquet, *Les filigranes*, nr.1275, appearing in Basel since 1538), and from fol.93 'Bern Bear' (Briquet, nr.12267, to be found in Bern between 1507 and 1553). The leaves are a bit wormeaten, especially the flyleaves.

The text has been written in clear Italian handwriting, but in a Latin that probably was influenced by German, characterized among others by on the one hand the omission and on the other hand the repetition of characters in words like *comendator* or *anotantur* and *generossus* or *religiossus*. In this edition these peculiarities are neither corrected nor marked with footnotes. The numerous mistakes in the spelling of proper names have also been left untouched. Only in case of incomprehensibility a single character or a better reading has been added between [–]. As was the practice in the edition of the other visitation acts, the few doublings or deletions of words in the Latin text have been corrected tacitly. This edition is confined to the preceptories that reside in the current territory of the Netherlands with their members inside and outside the Dutch boundaries, and the members of the Westphalian preceptory of Burgsteinfurt in the Dutch province of Groningen and the German East-Frisia.

The visitation acts of a small number of these preceptories have been edited earlier after a copy in the Rijksarchief (RA) in Gelderland at Arnhem. They can be found in: 'Visitatie-verslagen van de Johanniter-kloosters in Nederland (1495, 1540, 1594)', medegedeeld door E.Wiersum en A.Le Cosquino de Bussy, in: *Bijdragen en Mededeelingen van het Historisch Genootschap (BMHG)*, 48, Utrecht 1927, pp.146-340, especially 233-261. The passages and entire preceptories that are missing in RA Gelderland are marked with footnotes.

The AOM-volume has the title:
Descriptio visitationis preceptoriarum, beneficiorum et domorum ordinis sancti Johannis Hierosolomitani per Germaniam, facte per reverendum et generossum dominum fratrem Josephum de Cambianis cumdominum Roffie militem Italicum, et per fratrem Anastasium Smals comendatorem in Weissense et Schleusingen, ad hoc specialiter electos et deputatos; in qua expresse anotantur census, reditus et situs dictarum domorum et beneficiorum prout in presenti libro describitur.

The table of contents at the end of the volume is out of sequence with the contents of the book and dispenses with folio numbers. The sequence of the volume itself is as follows:

Stronden preceptoria in ducatu Montensi   fol.131r-132r
Duessberg preceptoria in ducatu Montensi
 membrum de Borch   fol.132v-133v
Valsum membrum dependens a Borch et Stronden fol.134r-134v
Vesalia in ducatu Clivensi   fol.135r-137v
Borchen preceptoria sacerdotalis in Westfalia fol.138r-139r
Steinfordt preceptoria in Westfalia   fol.139v-142r
Munster membrum dependens a Steinforde   fol.142v-143v
Horst membrum dependens a Steinfordia   fol.144r-145v
Herford preceptoria in Wesfalia   fol.146r-146v
Werffen preceptoria virginum in Frisia   fol.147r-148r
Witwert preceptoria virginum in Frisia   fol.148v-149v
Osterverum preceptoria virginum in Frisia   fol.150r-152r
Frisia orientalis [privilegia]   fol.152v-154v
Dunbroch preceptoria in Frisia orientali   fol.155r
Mude preceptoria in Frisia orientali   fol.155v-156v
Gemingum preceptoria in Frisia orientali   fol.156v-157r
Langolt preceptoria in Frisia orientali   fol.157r-157v
Haselt preceptoria in Frisia orientali   fol.157v-158r
De domibus existentibus in comitatu Aldemburg fol.158v
 Supradicte quatuor preceptorie Breorn, Rodense, Inede et
 Struchosen erant sub protectione et obediencia baiulivi Vesfalie et
 singulis annis ab ipso visitabantur sibi reservata annuali pencione,
 videlicet a Breorn ff XIIᴛ *[12.5]*, a Rodense ff 2/9/3, a Inede ff 2,
 a Stuchosen ff 2. Sed a decem annis citra dicti comites omnes
 fructus recipiunt et in proprios usus exponunt.
Arnem preceptoria in ducatu Geldrie   fol.158v-160v
Numingen preceptoria conioncta cum Arnhem   fol.161r-162v
Buren preceptoria dependens a baiulivatu
 Traiectensi   fol.162v-163v
Ingen preceptoria in Betavia Geldrie dependens a
 Traiecto   fol.163v-164r
Int Loe preceptoria prope Hardwick in Geldria fol.164v-165v
Aldemvater preceptoria dependens a baiulivatu
 Traiectensi   fol.166r-166v
Werder preceptoria dependens a baiulivatu
 Traiectensi   fol.167r-167v
Hermelen preceptoria dependens a baiulivatu
 Traiectensi   fol.168r-168v
Wemellingen preceptoria in Zellandia dependens a
 baiulivatu Traiectensi   fol.169r-169v
Middelburg preceptoria in Zellandia dependens a
 baiulivatu Traiectensi   fol.170r-170v

Chercherff preceptoria virginum in Zellandia fol. 171r[a]-171v
Seneick preceptoria in Frisia dependens a baiulivatu Traiectensi fol. 172r[a]-173r[a]
Numerus preceptoriarum et membrorum per ordinem secundum provincias, divissus et descriptus [fol. 174r-175r][b]

[a] *A different hand later changed the originally correct foliation of these leaves into 170, 171 and 172.* [b] *These leaves have no foliation.*

fol. 1r [a]Copia bullarum visitationis

Frater Johannes de Homedes, Dei gracia sacre domus hospitalis santi Johannis Hierosolomitani magister humilis, pauperumque Jesu Christi custos, et nos baiulivi, priores, preceptores et fratres domus eiusdem consilium completum retentionum in vim generalis capituli Melite in Domino celebrantes, universis et singulis presentes nostras literas visuris, lecturis et audituris salutem in Eo qui est omnium vera salus. Nobis ex officio incumbit circa ea tota mente intendere, que nostre religioni commodo honori, et utilitate conducere videntur, et presertim circa statum preceptoriarum nostrarum quibus ordo noster alitur et sustinetur, omni vigilancia et studio statuere, ordinare et providere.

Itaque cum reverendi sexdecim capitulares de statu religionis nostre in proxime preterito generali capitulo consultantes et deliberantes, animadvertissent et cogitavissent in qualibet re publica fore rem admodum iustam et necessariam omni conatu ac studio cognossere et inteligere census, reditus, et proventus quibus huiusmodi respublica conservatur et sustinetur, preterea considerantes iam circiter annos sex et quadraginta elapsos esse a tempore quo omnes et singuli prioratus, castellania Emposte, baiulivatus, preceptorie et cetera ordinis nostri beneficia visitata et recognita fuerunt, quapropter valde veritati sit consonum valorem, reditus et proventus eorundem partim incrementum, partim diminutionem suscepisse; idcirco deliberavunt, ordinaverunt et decreverunt quod per nos autoritate dicti generalis capituli eligerentur et deputarentur tot commissarii sive visitatores qui prefatos prioratus, castellaniam Emposte, baiulivatus et preceptorias ac reliqua ordinis nostri beneficia tam exempta quam non exempta in oriente ac in partibus occiduis constituta viderent, recognosserent et visitarent. Nos igitur premissorum contemplacione suassi prefatam deliberationem sive ordinationem executioni demandare cupientes et confisi de fide, probitate, cura, solertia et diligencia religiossi in Cristo nobis carissimi fratris Josephi Cambiani venerande nostre lingue *[fol. 1v]* Italie militis ac cuiuspiam alterius nostri ordinis fratris una

cum prefato de Cambianis ad infrascriptam comissionem exequendam per venerandum religiossum in Xpo nobis precarissimum fratrem Johannem Hatstain prioratus nostri Alemanie priorem eligendi
et deputandi tenore presentium de nostra certa scientia adinvicem
maturo et deliberato consilio, autoritate et decreto prelibati generalis
capituli facimus, creamus, constituimus ac solemniter ordinamus nostros commissarios, visitatores, procuratores, actores, factores, sindi-
cos, nonciosque nostros speciales et generales; ita quod specialitas
generalitati non deroget nec econtra ad infrascripta videlicet quod
prestito prius per eosdem comissarios solemni iuramento super quatuor santis evangeliis, unus videlicet iurando in manibus alterius, de
bene rite et fideliter remoto omni amore, spe, odio ac timore exequendo infrascriptam commissionem; de quo quidem iuramentum in
libro visitationum manu publici notarii constare volumus, specialiter
et expresse nomine et vice eiusdem generalis capituli accedant personaliter ad visitandum, videndum et recognoscendum prioratum
nostrum Alemanie cum eiusdem camara magistrali et cameris prioralibus, preceptoriis, membris ac ceteris nostri ordinis beneficiis tam
exemptis quam non exemptis infra limites dicti prioratus Alemanie
positis et constitutis, iuraque et bona earundem spiritualia et tempo-
ralia, informationemque veram et distinctam, universalem et particu-
larem faciendam et habendam de vero valore fructuum, redituum et
proventuum censuum et emolumentorum eiusdem prioratus ac preceptoriarum et ceterorum nostri ordinis beneficiorum in prenominato
prioratu sitorum et positorum, et ad veram noticiam prefati valoris
habendam et consequendam super omnibus et singulis dictum valorem concernentibus, priores ac preceptores sive eorum procuratores
ac factores sive locatenentes et testes fide dignos locorum vicinos et
habitatores quos ad hoc idoneos reperietis medio iuramento exami-
nandum, interogandum ac scripturas, *[fol.2r]* arendamenta, libros
censuales, cabrenaciones sive apeamenta ac omnia alia denique docu-
menta quibus valor eiusdem prioratus et preceptoriarum ac reliquo-
rum beneficiorum aparet et continetur, diligenter videndi, legendi et
visitandi ac aliter omnia et singula ad prefatam visitationem con-
cernencia, spectancia et pertinencia faciendi et agendi, ac informacionem et noticiam predictas postea quam de vero valore et legitimo
dictarum preceptoriarum et beneficiorum informati fuerint et omnia
et singula distincte et particulariter liquide et pure in scriptis autenti-
cis redigendi, ordinandi sive redigi faciendi per notarium publicum et
legalem, que quidem informacio et visitacio ad nos deferatur ut verum, certum et legitimum valorem dicti prioratus et preceptoriarum
ceterorumque beneficiorum in eorum limitibus constitutorum, scia-

mus, cognoscamus, taxemus, estimemus et verificemus. Nichilominus tamen precipimus et mandamus quod prenominati visitatores et commissarii a nobis deputati alterius ex ipsis gravi infirmitate sive alia iusta et legitima causa impediti, ita quod predictam comissionem et visitationem personaliter exequi aut adimplere non valeret, ponant et substituant fratrem nostri ordinis idoneum et suficientem ad prefatam comissionem exequendam qui preceptoriam obtineat, qui quidem comissarius sive visitator premisso modo substitutus in manibus dictorum comissariorum et visitatorum idem iuramentum prestare teneatur quo ipsi ab inicio astricti fuerunt. Dantes et concedentes dictis comissariis, visitatoribus, procuratoribus et sindicis nostris ac substitutis ab eisdem in premissis et circa premissa autoritate dicti generalis capituli amplissimam facultatem et autoritatem totaliter vices nostras, habentes ratum, gratum et firmum quicquid ocasione huiusmodi visitationis fecerint et executioni demandaverint, mandantes et precipientes omnibus et singulis dicte domus nostre fratribus quacumque autoritate, dignitate officioque fongentibus in virtute sante obediencie, ac universis et singulis hominibus, subditis et vasalis nostris in limitibus dicti prioratus existentibus, residentibus, *[fol.2v]* habitantibus et constitutis sub sacramento fidelitatis et homagii que nobis religionique nostre sunt astricti, ut prefatis comissariis et visitatoribus ac nostris procuratoribus in omnibus et singulis prefatam eorum comissionem et mandatum concernentibus pareant, obediant et intendant, prebeantque et prestent auxilium et favorem quemadmodum ex voto obedientie et sacramento fidelitatis tenentur et sunt astricti. In cuius rei testimonium bulla nostra comunis plombea presentibus est apenssa. Datum Melite in conventu nostro die XVI mensis octobris anni millessimi quingentessimi trigessimi noni *[1539, October 16]*.

Subscriptiones

Registrata in Canzellaria.
frater Gullielmus Benedictus Vicecanzellarius.[a]

Below follows the information, missing in RA Gelderland, that frater Josephus de Cambianis left Malta on 1 January 1540, received a papal letter of recommendation in Rome on 13 February, and arrived at Speyer and Heimbach, where the prior of Germany then resided, on 17 March. On 11 April a provincial chapter was held where the visitation bull was read. Amongst those present was frater Philipus Schilling, comendator in Rottborg, in Arnem et Numigen.

fol. 7r

ᵃSequitur forma iuramenti per dictos dominos visitatores prestiti secundum instructionem sibi commissam.

Anno domini milessimo quingentessimo quadringentessimo die vero decima quinta mensis Iunii *[1540, June 15]*, cum sit quod in provisionibus et bullis reverendissimi magni magistri et consilii completi in vim generalis capitulli circa visitationem preceptoriarum Germanie concessum et ordinatum fuerit quod reverendus et strenuus prior Allemanie frater Johannes de Hatstein eligeret et deputaret alium fratrem eiusdem ordinis una cum strenuo fratre Josepho de Cambianis comissario et visitatore deputato a reverendissimo magno magistro pro supradicta visitatione et comissione exequenda, ipseque reverendus dominus prior cum concensu et voluntate totius capituli provincialis elegerit et deputaverit venerabilem fratrem Anastasium Smalcz comendatorem in Weissensse et Scheleusingen, ideo ipsi domini comissarii et visitatores prout supra dictum est ellecti et deputati, fuerunt conionti in hac civitate Traiectensi Inferioris in domo ordinis santi Johannis Baptiste et intrantes ecclesiam audiverunt missam Santi Spiritus, deinde intrarunt in aula nova dicte domus unanimes et prompti mandatis et preceptis reverendissimi magni magistri et superiorum suorum parere et obedire. Ibi primo fuit revisa bulla visitationis, fuerunt lecte et revise instructiones et mandata de forma et modo visitationis, unde omnibus mature perpenssis et consideratis, tamquam veri et obedientes religiossi promisserunt et super sacro santa quatuor Dei evangelia cum invocatione domini nostri Jesu Cristi, beate Marie virginis et santi Johannis Baptiste iurarunt tactis corporaliter scripturis, unus videlicet iurando in manibus alterius de bene rite et fideliter remoto omni amore, spe, odio ac timore, exequendo infrascriptam visitationem, de quo quidem iuramento et promissione mihi notario publico et in hac visitatione promotto iniontum fuit quod particularis fieret descripcio. Hec omnia facta fuerunt in civitate iam *[fol. 7v]* dicta Traiectensi presentibus reverendo domino fratre Bernardo de Duven comendatore et baiulivo Traiectensi et domino fratre Gulliermo de Winbergen coadiutore Traiectensi et comendatore in Verder, ambobus de ordine sancti Johannis.

ᵃᵇHec omnia extracta fuerunt ab originalibus auctenticis Johannis de Haltren, Notarii publici, et per me Theodoricum Nolden Notarium apostolicum collationata et perlecta, in cuius rei testimonium hic me manu propria subscripsi et auctenticavi die nona Augusti 1542.

 Theodoricus Nolden de Creveltᵃᵇ

Notandum est quod in hoc libro describuntur visitationes secundum formam comissionis et bulle et non secondum formam visitationis. Quia prius fuerunt visitate domus et preceptorie Inferioris Germanie per Ollandiam, Sellandiam, Frisiam, Geldriam, Frisiam [orientalem] et Vesfaliam ac ceteras circumstantes partes, que licet prime visitate fuerint propter comoditatem vie et temporis, tamen in hoc libro non prime descripte sunt. Describentur ergo prius camare magistrales et priorales cum suis membris et dependenciis, postea successive ponentur preceptorie secundum regiones et provincias in quibus concistunt, nulla tamen mutata forma vel substantia dictarum visitationum.[a]

---

[a] *the copy of the bull, the oath and the notices of the notaries public are missing in RA Gelderland.* [b] *in a different hand.*

fol.8v

Traiectum camara prioralis et civitas episcopalis inter Geldriam et Ollandiam.[a]

Anno domini MVcXXXX die veneris XVI Iulii *[1540, July 16]* dicti domini visitatores frater Josephus de Cambianis et frater Anastasius Smalcz in comissione sua procedentes visitarunt preceptoriam sive baiulivatum Traiectensem que est una ex quinque camaris prioralibus et pro vera informatione habenda, dominum fratrem Bernardum de Duven[b] baiulivum et comendatorem vocarunt, coram quo fuit lecta bulla visitationis: deinde sibi inionxerunt et comisserunt quod omnes libros, apeamenta, cabrenationes et scripturas suas circa reditus et proventus dicte preceptorie coram ipsis et me notario *[fol.9r]* stipullante presentaret, qui incontinenti preceptis paruit, deinde dato sibi iuramento super sacro santis evangeliis de veritate declaranda circa informationes redituum et emolumentorum respondit et iuravit se esse paratum puram et meram veritatem exponere, et sic supradictis registris et libris particulares informationes extracte sunt.

Primo notandum est quod bona et proventus dicte preceptorie sive baiulivatus in tres dividuntur partes, habet enim multa bona que a diversis epischopis Traiectensibus, a comitibus Ollandie, et a dominis de Verden aliisque bonis fautoribus priscis temporibus collata sunt in usum et sustentationem hospitalitatis pro omnibus miserabilibus ut vocant personis illic advenientibus. Secondo habet diversa bona et proventus a predictis comitibus Hollandie et dominis de Werden collata et collatos pro observatione quotannis et perpetue certarum cirimoniarum exequiarum, missarum et vigiliarum certis constitutis temporibus in ecclesia. Tercio eciam habet certa bona ex parte ordi-

nis provenientia pleraque etiam successive per baiulivos comendatores illorumque procuratores diligenti cura, solercia ac providencia
illorum administratione empta et aquisita; et omnia huiusmodi bona
sunt adeo commista et conioncta ut in presentiarum pro certo sciri
nequeat unde hec vel illa pro maiori parte proveniant, salvo quod
presumi et extimari potest quod maior pars eorundem pro sustentatione zenodochii sit collata et deputata. Racio commistionis ilius est
quia prius per conflagracionem domus que brevi tempore combusta
fuerat *[1518, February 17]*,[1] et post diversa bella, item per subitam
translacionem eiusdem domus in absencia dicti baiulivi tunc ad curiam Brebancie accersiti et vocati, multe imo maior pars literarum et
registrorum de predictis bonis huiusmodi loquencium, concremata,
intercepta et deperdita est. Et omnia et singula huiusmodi bona spectancia vel ad domum vel ad ecclesiam vel ad hospitale, rursus sunt
divisa in duplices reditus, silicet census *[fol.9v]* ex domorum locatione
et secondo proventus ex agrorum arrendatione.

---

[1] *GA Utrecht*, Buurspraakboek anno 1518, *fol.194v, 1518 February 19*: "Alsoe
overmits den brant eergisteren lestleden tot Sunte Katrijnen – God betert –
geweest, veel goets uuten convent gevlucht ende vertogen is, dat nyet weder
gebracht en wert, soe laet die rait weten ende gebiet, dat een yegelick de
enich goet dairaff heeft, dat selve goet wederbrenge in den convent
voirscreven bynnen een atmael oft men selt rechten ende houden voer
dieverije."

Primo census sive reditus domorum in civitate Traiectensi sitarum
extendunt se quotanis ad sommam centum et viginti septem florenorum et scutiferorum quatuordecim cum quarta parte unius scutiferi.
Unde pro reparatione eorundem deducta quarta parte ad minus restant liquide circiter LXXXXVI ff. qui faciunt in auro florenos Renenses sexaginta et octo cum dimidio   ff LXVIII т *[68.5]*.
   Secondo quo ad proventum agrorum colonis arendatorum in provincia Traiectensi sitorum videlicet in Vloten ubi sita est collonia ther
Weiden,   Marsen,   Camerick,   Brokelelonen,   Abekardoren,
Amer[o]ngen, Intvell, Schalvilck, Hermelen, una cum agricultura
domus que anno elapso primum incepta est, continens iugera
CXXXIII, extendunt se ad sommam duorum millium et sex centum
et quadraginta duos florenos Carolinos et duodecim scutiferos; numerus autem iugerorum extendit se circiter ad sommam novem centum
iugerorum.
   Somma florenorum   ff IIm VIc XXXXII.
Inde deducto onere cuiusdam nove exactionis quod vocatur onus
antiqui scutati, quod est quod quisque habeat scutatum annue tocies
habeat de singulis scutatis conferre quatuor scutiferos cum dimidio

qui asendunt ad sommam ducentum octuaginta duorum florenorum Carolinorum et decem septem scutiferorum.

Item sunt onera circa ageres reficiendos et circa molendina que aquam a pocessionibus eiciunt aliisque extraordinariis oneribus quotannis ad singula statuta taxantur quinque scutiferi, faciunt in somma florenos Carolinos trecentum et decem septem floreni, sic deductis oneribus restant liquide aduc floreni aurei Renenses circa mile quatuor centum et quinquaginta et octo cum dimidio

ff Im IIIIc LVIII τ [1458.5].

Preterea habet predicta preceptoria sive baiulivatus quasdam comendarias que membra ipsius domus vocantur, que fratribus conventualibus ad decennium committi solent pro certis pensionibus sive responsionibus, cuius quidem arendationis racione comendarie vocantur, que pro maiori parte ab eisdem comen-*[fol.10r]*datoribus sive pensionariis tamen non solvuntur nec solvi possunt, adeo quod huiusmodi proventus quasi incerti sunt et ultra expensas circa extorssum eorundem atque capitullo similiumque expensarum interdum parum supermanet, prout ex visitatione eorundem comendatorum et membrorum elucessere poterit ad quos se refert; tamen extimat huiusmodi proventus comunibus annis ad sommam centum septuaginta quinque florenorum

ff Ic LXXV auri.

Item reditus et proventus de agris et terris extra dominium sive provinciam Traiectensem sitis videlicet in Hollandia Iselstein et Vianden extendunt se quotannis ad sommam mille et viginti quatuor florenorum Carolinorum et duodecim scutiferos   ff Im XXIIII s.XII.

De quibus reditibus deductis expensis ad vetera et cateracterum sive aqueductus, novis operibus, aliisque impensis id est circa agerum et molendinorum reparationem una cum redituariorum stipendiis extendunt se ad sommam ducentum octuaginta quinque florenorum Carolinorum.

Sic deductis expensis restant liquide floreni aurei Renenses quinque centum et viginti et octo et octo scutiferi   ff Vc XXVIII s.VIII.

Item ultra premissa habet hec preceptoria duplices redituum porciones a statibus dominii Traiectensis videlicet a statu ecclesiastico et a statu militum civitatum, qui se extendunt ad sommam florenorum Philipencium quadraginta unum qui non solvuntur nec intra annos duodecim soluti sunt   ff XXXXI.

Sic modo liquide constat quod dicta preceptoria non decimas neque census alios nisi superius declarati; nulam habet iurisdictionem vel vasalos; preterea petiit comendator quod scriberetur quod certis annis et temporibus propter bella, propter inondaciones aquarum maris et Rheni atque agerorum ruinam, quod furmenta et seminata corroduntur et damnificantur et predicti reditus et introitus interdum vix pro media parte quandoque minus medietatem valent, quod facile credendum est propter vicinitatem Reni.

Interogatus an sint alia bona proventus vel reditus huic preceptorie spectantes *[fol.10v]* respondit quod non nisi ea que superius declarata fuerunt.

Interogatus an ab ecclesia reditus, emolumenta aut aliam utilitatem habeat respondit quod nihil habet, presertim his temporibus tam perverssis.

Sequuntur onera et expense necesarie.

Ex predicto introitu et proventu solvuntur annui reditus in censibus perpetuis et aliis redimi[bi]libus ac vitalicii ad sommam ducentum et quadraginta novem florenorum aureorum, quos comunibus annis diversis personis solvere tenetur [ff 249].

Item fratribus conventualibus duodecim loco competencie et necesitatis eorum singulorum sex florenos et officiantibus decem faciunt in somma circa florenos sexagintaquinque et ultra [ff 65]

somma ff IIIc XIIII.

Item administratur et datur pauperibus ex eisdem proventibus in elimosinam singulis mensibus duo modia tritici, similiter eciam consueverunt pauperes accedere ad colloniam quibus distributio indies fit cum pane, caseo et butiro que elimosina as[c]endit ad tres modios tritici singulis mensibus et quolibet modium computatur ad duos florenos aureos, somma ff Ic XX.

Ulterius ex predictis reditibus oportet intertenere zenodochium sive hospitale pro omnibus miserabilibus advenientibus una cum quinque prefectis ministris quod quidem constat annuatim cum salario ministrorum qui omnibus infirmis et pestilenciosis servire coguntur florenos quinque centum ff Vc.

Item pro lineis pannis pro medicis cirugicis et similibus extraordinariis expensis circa hospitale ultra florenos quinquaginta ff L.

Preterea ex supradicto introitu solvuntur ordini et thesauro de antiqua consuetudine floreni aurei septuaginta quinque ff LXXV.

Item pro restante antique reponsionis non solute tenetur comendator ad certos annos solvere viginti quinque florenos ff XXV.

NB Item reverendo domino magistro Allemanie quia ipsa preceptoria dicitur esse una ex camaris prioralibus ideo sibi comunibus annis solvuntur pro eius pensione floreni ducentum aurei ff IIc.

Item pro sustentatione et alimentatione XII vel XIII fratrum conventualium *[fol.11r]* ac certo numero famulorum ministrancium videlicet custodis ecclesie, celerarii, braxatoris cum famulo, coci cum famulo, ancile cum adiutrice, et lectoris, et aliorum duorum baiulivi famulorum, similiter duorum agricolarum in curia sive domo agriculture in Traiecto site, preterea eciam unius extraordinarii ministri qui in conventu et extra pro noncio et in laborando usurpatur et servit, quarum quidem personarum viginti et sex numeris est.

Preter hos aduch [=adhuc] foris in curia agriculture Therveiden noncupate sunt undecim servientes persone, sic illorum numerus est XXXVII persone et extimantur eorum expense uni plus alteri secundum cuiuscumque condicione pro qualibet persona decem et octo floreni, in somma sunt sex centum et sexaginta sex floreni aurei vel circa ff 666.

Item cogitur commendator habere quasi continue propriam mensam pro captando favore nobilium dominorum et optimatum precipue eorum sub quorum dominio sunt bona ordinis sita pro qua annualiter exponuntur circa trecentum floreni aurei singulis computatis ff IIIc.

Item pro salario famulorum baiulivi et conventus et ceteris ff L.

Item reipublice Traiectensi pro cervisia que in predicta domo et in hospitali bibitur pro accisia annuali ff XVII.

Item pro ornamentis, cereis, lampadibus ceterisque requisitis in ecclesia ff XL.

Item ad processus litium et causarum coram alto Cesaree maiestatis consilio racione collacionum ecclesiarum previlegiorum exemptionumque ff [- -].

Item pro reparatione domus et edificiorum, pro emendis tellis lineis, pro diversis aliis expensis necesariis que extimari non possunt, pro vestibus comendatoris et similibus florenos ducentum aureos

  ff IIc.

Hac deposicione habita dominus baiulivus petiit et requisivit quod hoc proemium inferius descriptum ad longum extenderetur, quodquidem ad ipsius requisitionem ipsi domini comissarii admisserunt.

Premissorum omnium et singulorum onerum et impensarum occasione domus predicta procul dubio singulis annis debita contraheret ad minus trium vel [fol.11v] quatuor centum florenorum nisi Deo dante ac diligenti solicitaque cura dicti comendatoris rebus consuleretur atque impensis ordinariis circa ipsum et conventum interdum abstraheretur, alioquin tamen fieri et preferiri non potuit quin debitis aliquot non oneraretur. Ex lesione conflagrationis quam passus est maximo suo damno de anno 1518, ex maxima inondatione aquarum, ac subinde bellorum procellus in anno XXVII et XXVIII [1527 et 1528], demum quoque ratione ireparabilis atque inestimabilis iacture ex subita et inopinata translatione edium perpesse, nempe diruptionis ac oblationis domus egregit una cum ecclesia, hospitali, totaque here-

ditate per imperatorem vel ab eius ministris perpetrate anno XXIX
[1529], pro qua [n]ullam comparabilem aut equalem recompensationem fecerit aut restituerit; licet policitationes desuper facte fuerint,
quinimo coactus fuit baiulivus de novo construere et restaurare domum, ecclesiam ac hospitale et plerasque sibi comparare domos pro
ipso et conventu comoditate et statione maximo quidem precio, inte-
rimque ex frequentibus et continuis exactionibus quibus premitur
adversus exemptionem et privilegia ordinis, quibus nulus respectus ab
officialibus imperatoris habetur, imo quod magis est iam alie infinite
exactiones et contributiones imminent. Ultima etiam ruina ecclesie ut
aparet et constat, maximum damnum intullit.

Concludens imposibile esse ullam esse domum in toto ordine
tantopere pressam et molestatam, nec est in civitate et provincia
Traiectensi ulla religiosorum domus sive collegium eciam cui vel quibus tanta seu similia onera imponantur indiferenter prout promiscuo-
rum religiossorum monasteriis per decanos et canonicos quinque
collegiorum in hac civitate sitorum pro eorum libitu et beneplacito,
licet ipse comendator ad hoc nunquam vocetur ut concentiat, in vilipendium imo et specialem immunitatis ac exemptionis militaris nostri
ordinis; que quidem ipsorum collegiorum presumpta tacxacio durius
et iniquius omnibus aliis urget, adversus quam nula unquam privilegia locum sorciuntur, et duravit ista afflictio ad multos annos circa
quam sucurssus quam humilime et devote petit, datum Traiecti die et
anno ut supra.

Dicti domini visitatores audita et intelecta tali suplicatione et informatione *[fol.12r]* pro servicio totius ordinis et pro exemptione dicti
domini baiulivi decreverunt ad Cesaream maiestatem accedere, et
secundum informationem de remediis oportunis inquantum ad ipsos
atinet providere; quod quidem cum summa diligencia executioni de-
mandarunt; et pro parte dicto domino comendatori satisfactum fuit,
sed quia similia non conveniunt in hoc libro visitationis conscribi,
ideo talia permitemus et ad residuum visitationis revertemur.[2]

---

[2] *At the end of AOM 45, Visitation of 1495, a letter has been inserted, directed to (at
the backside):*

Illustrissimo et Reverendissimo domino domino Magno Magistro ordinis
sancti Joannis Iherosolymitani etc.

with the following contents:

Illustrissime et reverendissime magne magister. Ego me amplitudini tue
omni cum subiectione summa tui reverentiam plurimum commendo.

Illustrissime magne magister, fuit apud me nobilis et imprimis vir prudens
frater Josephus de Cambianis ordinis et lingue Italice eques auratus, gratia
visitandi me et baliviam Traiectensem una cum membris ad eam pertinentibus, quod et fecit, ac summa cum diligentia perfecit, cuius ego visitationi ut

spero sic me cum membris meis obtuli ut parentem et subiectum ordinis fratrem decet, veluti id iuxta mandatum sibi commissum fieri par erat, quod tua quoque celsitudo illo ex visitatione redeunte latius congnoscere et explorare poterit. Preterea quum idem ille tue celsitudinis commissarius omni diligentia apud Cesaream maiestati omnem moverit lapidem ut mihi pro hac balivia sive membris eius liceret privilegiis ordinis uti (a quibus ipsa iam dudum abhinc propter bella diversa, tumultus aliaque incomoda decidit) quemadmodum et relique ordinis domus in alias regionibus iisdem privilegiis utuntur et gaudent, eo per summam eius tum diligentiam tum prudentiam res perducta est, ut bonam hoc presertim tempore spem conceperim. Quod si rem fortasse progressum sortiri non contingerit per alios malevolos qui ordini non admodum favere videntur, et maxime quia ipse tuus commissarius propter alias occupationes coram addesse nequeat, propterea quod temporis ulterius visitandi brevitate excluditur, oro celsitudinem tuam suppliciter eam rem tibi commendatam habere velis et Cesarie maiestatis legatos si qui interea temporis ad tuam celsitudinem forte venerint, diligenter instruere et docere, ne velit Cesarea maiestas hisce membris Traiectensibus minus favere minusve permittere quam soleat aliis omnibus ordinis membris in universis Christianitatis regionibus sitis. Nihilominus si rem ut spero assequor eo videlicet fretus promisso quo me Cesarea maiestas ex commissarii tue celsitudinis procuratione bene sperare iussit, faciam celsitudinem tuam certiorem. Amplitudinem tuam precor ut supplicem me ac benevolum ministrum et ordinis fratrem commendatum habere dignetur quam amplitudinem Christus diu servet incolumen. Datum Traiecti XIX° Augusti anno et cetera XL *[1540, August 19]*.

Illustrissime dominacionis predicte humillimus et obedientissimus servus et ordinis frater frater Bernardus de Duven balivus et commendator Traiectensis.
so far the letter that has been inserted at the end of AOM 45.

Deposicio et examinacio testium circa reditus et onera.

Pro verficatione et certitudine supradicte deposicionis habenda dicti domini visitatores examinarunt et interrogarunt egregios viros magistrum Theodoricum Sassen, Gotfridum Waszman, et Jacobum Stelle testes vere et indubitate fidei et locorum vicinos qui de his generalitatibus et particularitatibus cognitionem et noticiam certam habent, a quibus separatim et particulariter intelexerunt nec plus nec minus esse quam supra dictum sit, et hoc mediante solemni iuramento super santis evangeliis adiongentes quod secundum fertilitatem et penuriam annorum reditus interdum crescunt et discrescunt.

Valores monetarum
 scutiferi XXXVII faciunt coronam Francie
 scutiferi XXXVI faciunt coronam novam
 scutiferi XXXX faciunt ducatum largum
 scutiferi XXVIII faciunt florenum aureum

scutiferi **XXIIII** faciunt florenum Carolinum.

Valor mensure furmentorum
Quatuor quartalia faciunt unum modium. Modium est pondus unius hominis, venditur ff 2.

> ^cHec omnia extracta fuerunt ab originalibus scripturis manu Johannis de Haltren Notarii publici scriptis et per Theodoricum Nolden publicum apostolicum auctoritate Notarium, collationata et revisa sunt, in cuius rei testimonium hic me manu propria subscripsi.
> Theodoricus Nolden de Crevelt^c

[fol.12v] Est supradicta preceptoria in civitate Traie[c]ti inferioris que est civitas epischopalis inter Geldriam et Hollandiam et olim fuit collonia Romanorum, non multum distans a flumine Rheni. Vocatur domus ordinis ad santam Caterinam et annis preteritis fuit comendator expulsus a domo propria et antiqua ordinis ab officialibus Imperatoris, in qua domo construcxerunt arcem et in recompensam dederunt conventum ordinis Carmelitarum in quo nunc residet dictus comendator cum cumfratribus; domus est satis ampla cum hortis et aliis rebus necesariis pro quibus reficiendis multe expense facte sunt, precipue pro restauratione domus et ecclesie prout supra dictum est. Habet hec preceptoria sive baiulivatus circa duodecim comendarias in quibus resident comendatores qui ipsum dominum baiulivum reconoscunt per superiorem et per ipsum vel elliguntur vel confirmantur prout in suis visitationibus declarabitur, et dicuntur membra baiulivatus.

---

^a *the entire preceptory of Utrecht is missing in RA Gelderland.* ^b *or Dunen, because the scribe does not make a clear difference between* n *and* v. *The name of this bailiff really was* Bernard van Duven. ^c *in a different hand.*

fol.31r, cut off in the right margin
Arlem^a quinta camara prioralis in Hollandia.

Anno domini **MVcXXXX** die **XXVI** Iunii dicti domini visitatores in sua comissione procedentes visitarunt preceptoriam sive domum santi Johannis in Arnem sive Arlem civitate Ollandie et pro vera informatione habenda vocarunt religiossum fratrem Simeonem de Zanen ipsius domus comendatorem cum aliis sacerdotibus capitulariter congregatis coram quibus fuit lecta bula visitationis, deinde dicto comendatori comisserunt et inioncxerunt quod omnes libros et scripturas suas circa informationes redituum et emollumentorum coram ipsis presentaret, tandem dato sibi iuramento de veritate decclaranda circa requisita, iuravit et dicxit eum esse paratum puram et meram veritatem exponere; et sic ex supradictis registris et libris sequentes informationes extracte sunt.

Introitus peccuniarum in censibus.

Primo habet hec preceptoria diversas domos in platea sive in vico sante Sicilie que sunt locate diversis personis pro annuali censu sive locagio florenorum triginta duo et solidorum quinque in somma
ff 32 [s 5].

Item in platea sive vico monialium habet solidos quinque cum dimidio in censu   ff – [s 5 τ *[5.5]*.

Item ex aliis domibus in civitate habet solidos quinque cum dimidio in censu   ff – s [5 τ *[5.5]*.

Item ex aliis domibus in plateis matageorgii in latere santi Bavonis, in Zille et in platea regis habet singulis annis in diversis censibus in somma   ff 1 s [?].

Item in aliis diversis censibus ex domibus in dic[t]a civitate existentibus et a diversis personis singulis annis florenos quatuor et solidos decem   ff 4 s [10].

Item ex loco dicto Heemstede ex diversis censibus et personis singulis annis habet in somma florenos circa quinquaginta et duos Carolinos   ff 52.

Item ex loco dicto Bennebrorch singulis annis sex florenos Carolinos   ff 6.

fol.31v

Item habet in diversis minutis censibus ex pocessionibus circumcirca opidum Arllem et in aliis censibus florenos triginta et quatuor Carolinos   ff 34.

Item habet ex aliis diversis locis et pocessionibus locatis pro annuali censu peccuniario singulis annis florenos quinquaginta Carolinos
ff 50.

Item ex aliis censibus in diversis locis et a diversis personis prout in libris et registris declaratur florenos sex vel circa Carolinos   ff 6.

Item ex loco Beverwick habet ex diversis pocessionibus et pratis diversis personis locatis singulis annis florenos quadraginta et novem cum dimidio   ff 49 τ *[49.5]*.

Item ex loco dicto Heemschirke habet ex diversis pocessionibus et pratis diversis personis locatis et ex aliis diversis censibus prout constat in libris et registris singulis annis florenos centum et triginta tres et solidos sex   ff 133 s 6.

Item habet ex loco dicto Castricom ex diversis pocessionibus et

pratis diversis personis locatis singulis annis florenos quadraginta Carolinos   ff 40.

Item habet ex loco dicto Heylo ex diversis pocessionibus et pratis
diversis personis locatis singulis annis florenos triginta et quatuor cum
dimidio   ff 34   *[34.5]*.

Item habet ex loco dicto Akerszsloet ex diversis pocessionibus et
pratis diversis personis locatis singulis annis florenos undecim et solidos XV   ff 11 s 15.

Item habet ex loco Illegon et Aelszmeer ex diversis pocessionibus
et pratis diversis personis locatis in solucione peccuniaria prout constat in libris et registris singulis annis florenos tres vel circa Carolinos
         ff 3.

Item habet ex loco Ruderstrate in censibus circa florenum unum
Carolinum   ff 1.

Item habet ex loco Soterwouda ex diversis censibus pocessionibus
et pratis diversis personis locatis prout constat in registris in solucione
et censu peccuniario singulis annis florenos ducentum et septuaginta
et duos cum dimidio Carolinos, hoc est aureos Renenses et de iusto
pondere   ff 272 т *[272.5]*.

Item habet ex locis Autdorp, Warmenheus, Sanpancraci, Indem-
broiche, *[fol.32r, cut off in the right margin]* Erstiwonda et Hoctiwonda ex
diversis censibus in pocessionibus agris et pratis diversis personis locatis pro solutione peccuniaria singulis annis florenos viginti et tres et
solidos quatuor cum dimidio   ff 23 s 4 [т *[4.5]*.

Item ex locis Schiermer, Wegenem, Nierdorp, et in civitate Arllem
pro agris et pratis locatis singulis annis florenos viginti et tres et solidos XVI   ff 23 s 16.

Item habet ex decimis in locis Bredesape, Velsen, et Heem-
schircken que comunibus annis locantur in peccuniis: florenos trecentum et duos Carolinos   ff 302.

     Sequuntur reditus in Delflandia et Rinlandia de pascuis in
     peccuniis locatis.

Habet hec preceptoria multa pascua padulossa in Naldtwick et in
loco dic[t]o Naldtwicem que locata sunt pro florenis quatuordecim
Carolinis   ff 14.

Item ex pascuis in locis Honselredick et Munster habet singulis
annis in locatione florenos centum et septem et solidos viginti et sex
         ff 107 s [26].

Item habet ex locis Watteringe et Riswick pro pascuis locatis singulis annis in peccuniis florenos centum et triginta et octo et solidos
duodecim   ff 138 s [12].

Item habet ex locis Lier et Maeslant pro pascuis locatis singulis annis in peccuniis numeratis florenos sexaginta et quatuor et solidos XXVI   ff 64 s [26].

Item habet ex loco Delff super Kragemburg pro pascuis locatis singulis annis in peccuniis numeratis florenos tres et solidos duodecim

ff 3 s [12].

Item habet ex locis Oestgeist, Rinszburg, Couckirche, Vorschoten et Wassenes pro pocessionibus locatis: florenos quinquaginta cum solidis sex   ff 50 s [6].

Item habet ex loco Leiderdorp in censibus pro pocessionibus locatis annis singulis florenos sexaginta et quatuor Carolinos prout sunt supradicti   ff 64.

Sequ[u]ntur reditus pitancie.

Habet hec preceptoria quosdam proventus pro pitancia qui a diversis *[fol.32v]* personis solvu[n]tur pro pocessionibus et agris in locis Riswick, Voorschotten et Maeslant qui in somma faciunt florenos viginti quinque et solidos XXI   ff 25 s 21.

Sequuntur alii diversi reditus.

Habet hec domus plures pocessiones et agros qui diversis personis locantur pro solutione peccuniaria prout supra declaratum est, sed in furmentis habet tantummodo quinquaginta et quinque saccos tritici; residuum opus est propriis peccuniis emere prout inferius describetur solidos 55.

Item habet alios parvos census in caponibus, in caseis et in butiro que omnia consumantur in coquina et ideo non existimantur.

Habet preterea aliqua legumina in fabis et pizis que eciam comeduntur in domo.

Sequitur generalis deposicio comendatoris.

Hac deposicione prout superius describitur sic particulariter habita dictus dominus comendator producxit quandam scripturam manibus suis propriis scriptam et extractam ac sommatam ab originalibus suis libris et registris per quam fideliter confessus est, dictam domum sive preceptoriam habere singulis annis in firmis et stabilibus censibus ex locatione domorum, pocess[i]onum, agrorum et pascuorum ac eciam ex aliquot oblacionibus ecclesie omnibus computatis et calcullatis circumcirca florenos mille et quinque centum monette currentis, qui floreni mille et quinque centum faciunt florenos aureos Rhenenses circa mille et centum, nam floreni centum Rhenenses faciu[n]t florenos centum et quadraginta istius monette Arnensis; cum quibus quidem reditibus tenetur sustentare domum in expenssis, in serviciis ecclesiasticis, et in reparatione edificiorum, pro quibus omnibus intertenendis quasi non suficiu[n]t supradicti reditus, prout inferius particulariter describetur, nisi providencia comendatoris supleretur.

fol.33r

Exponuntur singulis annis pro pensione reverendi domini prioris Allemanie floreni centum Rhenenses quia est camara prioralis ff 100.

Item dantur recepitori pro annuali responcione ordinis floreni Rhenenses viginti et quinque qui faciunt circa florenos triginta quinque currentes ff 35.

Item distribuuntur octo sacerdotibus ordinis ibi continue residentibus pro quolibet ipsorum floreni sex, floreni aurei, qui in somma faciunt quadraginta et octo florenos, vel quinquaginta et duos currentes ff 52.

Item in ipsa domo est hospitale in quo continue sustentantur sex persone pauperes pro quorum sustentatione computantur floreni triginta quinque ff 35.

Item tenetur comendator in diebus festibus et in quadragessima habere predicatorem cui dantur pro stipendio floreni duodecim currentes ff 12.

Item habent organistam cui dant singulis annis novem florenos ff 9.

Item dantur adiutori sive famullo organiste duo floreni ff 2.

Item sepe accidit quod veniunt sacerdotes alieni qui celebrant et ipsis datur panis et vinum pro quibus computantur floreni sex currentes ff 6.

Item pro servicio ecclesie in luminaribus et aliis rebus necesariis quia est conventum et ecclesia magnifica exponuntur circa floreni quadraginta ff 40.

Item ex legato matris comendatoris mortui tenetur domus vel sacerdotes omni feria quinta cantare missam et laudes ad honorem sacratissimi corporis Cristi cum septem candelis cereis; et pro tali servicio quilibet sacerdos ultra supradictum stipendium recipit florenum unum aureum; in somma exponuntur ff 40.

Item dantur singulis annis pauperibus hospitalis in peccuniis numeratis ff 2.

Item singulis annis fiunt quatuor generales ellimosine omnibus pauperibus advenientibus pro quibus exponuntur in furmentis quadraginta floreni ff 40.

Item exponuntur singulis annis in carnibus, pissibus et aliis rebus

[fol.33v] necesariis pro coquina circa floreni ducentum istius monette
ff 200.

Item pro carnibus salcis et pissibus exponuntur circa centum floreni
ff 100.

Item exponuntur pro lignis, carbonibus et cespitibus singulis annis
circa centum et viginti floreni quia est maxima penuria lignarum
ff 120.

Item pro conficienda cervisia exponuntur ultra centum floreni
ff 100.

Item pro aromatibus et sale singulis annis exponuntur viginti floreni
ff 20.

Item pro servitoribus domus videlicet camerario, custodi et duobus
cocis exponuntur singulis annis circa quadraginta floreni curentes
ff 40.

Item pro redituario in partibus Delflandie et Rinlandie cui datur
pro labore decima pars proventuum exponuntur floreni triginta et
quatuor
ff 34.

Item pro officialibus domus s[c]ilicet medico, advocato, barbiton-
sore et aliis similibus singulis annis exponuntur circa triginta quinque
floreni
ff 35.

Item pro reparatione agrarum *[=aggerum]* propter continuas inondationes maris et Rheni singulis exponuntur circa sexaginta floreni
curentes
ff 60.

Item pro annuali censu cuiusdam domini de Heemstede singulis
annis solvuntur viginti et unum florenum et non possunt redimi
ff 21.

Item dantur curato in Arnem racione canonice portionis floreni
duo
ff 2.

Item dantur pastori in Heenstrech singulis annis viginti floreni et
est ordinis santi Johannis sed residet in ipsa perochia pro pastore
ff 20.

Item dantur cellerario qui recuperat census pro salario viginti floreni
ff 20.

Item exponuntur singulis annis pro emendo vino et aliis generibus
cervisiarum pro comendatore et hospitibus circa quinquaginta floreni
ff 50.

Item ordinarie computando ipsum comendatorum cum octo fratribus et aliis servitoribus, continue sunt in domo sexdecim persone,
preterea sepe adveniunt hospites et fautores domus quibus denegare
non possunt victum.

fol.34r

Sunt preterea alie plures expensse que particulariter et specialiter
describi non possunt; que tamen sunt maximi detrimenti et preiudicii,
videlicet exactiones civitatis in reficiendis menibus et fortaliciis, exac-

tiones imperatoris, reparationes domus et ecclesie pro quibus omnibus non suficiunt singulis annis centum floreni quia ligna sunt in caro precio ff 100.

Sequitur numerus iugerorum et pocessionum.

Visis reditibus et oneribus domini comendatores sive visitatores interogarunt supradictum comendatorem si particulariter declarare et specificare posset numerum iugerorum et pocessionum dicte preceptorie spectancium, qui respondidit quod tempore suo numquam iugera mensurata fuerunt; tamen quia omnes pocessiones locantur, secundum descriptionem registri numerus ipsorum dinumerari potest, et sic numeratum fuit.

In loco dicto Bennenbroch sunt duo iornalia cum dimidio terre cultivate I 2 т *[2.5]*.

Item extra maiorem portam lignorum habet unum iornale cum dimidio I 1 т *[1.5]*.

Item extra portam Schaltvvich habet sex iornalia et duo honden terre I 6.

Item extra portam Zille habet duo iornalia terre cultivate I 2.

Item in loco dicto Sparnewalt habet circa unum iugerum cum dimidio I 1 т *[1.5]*.

Item in Overveenn habet circa quinque iugera prati et pascua I 5.

Item in Waerdt habet circa quatuor iugera pascuorum pro vaccis domus I 4.

Item in Harlemer Liedt habet circa septem iugera terre cultivate I 7.

Item in eodem loco habet unum iugerum cum dimidio prati I 1 т *[1.5]*.

Item in Niemwerchirche habet circa sex iugera agri et prati I 6.

Item in Bevervick habet circa sex iugera agri et prati indiferenter I 6.

Item in Heemschircke habet circa quadraginta et quatuor iugera I 44.

Item in loco dicto Castricom habet circa duodecim iugera terre I 12.

fol.34v

Item ex loco Heilo habet circa quindecim iugera terre cultivate et prati I 15.

Item in Akerszsloet habet circa quatuor iugera terre cultivate I 4.

Item in Hillegom habet circa unum iugerum cum dimidio terre cultivate I 1 т *[1.5]*.

Item in Aelszmeer habet circa unum iugerum terre cultivate in
ortis tribus   I 1.

Item in Soterwouda habet circa septuaginta et tria iugera terre
                                                                                                                      I 73.

Item in Varmenheus habet circa duo iugera terre cultivate   I 2.

Item in San Pancracio habet circa unum iugerum cum dimidio
terre cultivate   I 1 т *[1.5]*.

Item in Dembroiche palude habet quinque germas agri cultivati
                                                                                                                 I – g.5.

Item in Schermer habet trecentum florenos aureos depositos et
sicuratos super quandam peciam terre de qua certam mensuram non
habet   I –.

Item in Wegenen habet duo iugera terre cultivate   I 2.

Item in Nierdorp habet circa unum iugerum cum dimidio terre
cultivate   I 1 т *[1.5]*.

Item in Nardtwick et circumcirca sunt iugera novem pascuorum
                                                                                                                      I 9.

Item in Honselredick habet circa septem iugera terre cultivate
                                                                                                                      I 7.

Item in dicto loco sunt alia sexdecim iugera eciam terre cultivate
                                                                                                                     I 16.

Item in Munster habet in diversis locis viginti et quinque iugera
agri   I 25.

Item in Watteringe habet viginti et septem iugera terre cultivate
                                                                                                                     I 27.

Item in Riszvick in diversis locis habet iugera quadraginta et qua-
tuor   I 44.

Item in Lier habet duodecim iugera cum dimidio terre cultivate
                                                                                                       I 12 т *[12.5]*.

Item in Maeszlant habet octo iugera terre cultivate vel circa   I 8.

Item in Delff supra Kragemburg habet iugera duo vel circa   I 2.

Item in Oestgeit habet duo iugera terre cultivate   I 2.

Item in Rinszburg habet quatuor honden quorum tria faciunt ior-
nale   I 1 h.1.

Item in Coukirche habet circa novem iugera terre cultivate et prati
                                                                                                                      I 9.

Item in Voorschoten habet septem iugera terre cultivate et prati
                                                                                                                      I 7.

fol.35r

Item in loco dicto Leiderdorp habet iugera sexdecim agri et prati
I 16.

Item in Maeszlant pro pitancia habet decem et octo iugera terre
cultivate   I 18.

Interogatus quot furmenta recipiat comunibus annis a dictis pocessionibus sive agris, respondidit quod habet quinquaginta et quinque sacos tritici tantummodo in furmentis, quia residuum locatur rusticis in peccuniis prout supra dictum est, et opus est quod comendatur emat furmenta pro servicio domus, pro quibus comunibus annis solvit circa florenum aureum pro quolibet modio interdum plus et minus secundum fertilitatem annorum.

Interogatus ubi sint domus ex quibus habet census superius descriptos, respondidit quod maior pars est in civitate de Arnem et alique sunt in pagis et vilis circumstantibus, quorum nomina in registro annotantur.

Interogatus an dicta domus sive preceptoria habeat aliqua membra sibi subposita vel alias preceptorias conionctas, respondit quod non quia antiquo tempore dicta domus de Arnem erat subpostia baiulivo Traiectensi et comendator eligebatur et confirmabatur a dicto baiulivo, sed tempore fratris Baptiste de Orsinis magni magistri tocius ordinis de concessu capituli generalis et venerande lingue Allemanie fuit hec preceptoria liberata et exempta a subiectione baiulivi et fuit vocata et dicta quinta camara prioralis et prior Allemanie contentus fuit hanc per suam quintam camaram acceptare; unde pro tali convencione tenetur comendator solvere reverendo domino priori singulis annis centum florenos aureos; et moriente comendatore sacerdotes conventuales faciunt et elligunt alium comendatorem ex suis conventualibus, quem reverendus dominus magister sive prior Alemanie reconfirmare tenetur, et pro tali confirmatione solvit comendator ellectus ducentum florenos aureos domino priori sive magistro.

fol.35v   Sequitur deposicio testium.

Pro verificatione et certitudine supradicte deposicionis habenda supradicta visitatores examinarunt et interogarunt religiossos fratres Johannem Delffte et Cornelium de Schoten conventuales sacerdotes et seniores eiusdem domus qui de omnibus particularitatibus supradictis cognitionem et noticiam certam habent, a quibus particulariter et separatim intelecxerunt sic esse prout supra dictum est et hoc affirmarunt mediante solemni iuramento.

Situs preceptorie sive domus.

Domus ordinis est in civitate Arlem[a] in provincia vel comitatu Ollandie, satis ampla cum suis hortis et aliis rebus necesariis, habet ecclesiam conionctam ad honorem santi Johannis pro servicio cuius resident octo vel novem sacerdotes; in regione illa non nascuntur vina, ideo caro precio venduntur.

[b]Hec omnia extracta fuerunt ab originalibus scripturis et auctenticis manu Johannis Halteren publici Notarii scriptis, et per me Theodoricum Nolden publicum apostolica auctoritate Notarium visa, recognita et auctenticata fuerunt, in quorum fidem hic me manu propria subscripsi. Die quarta mensis Octobris anno domini 1542.

Theodericus Nolden de Crevelt[b]

Valores monettarum
Unus solidus valet duodecim denarios.
Viginti solidi valent florenum Carolinum.
Viginti et octo solidi faciunt florenum aureum.
Triginta et septem solidi faciunt coronam solis.
Quadraginta solidi faciunt ducatum largum.

Valores furmentorum
Saccus tritici venditur pro floreno aureo.
Saccus ordei venditur pro floreno Carolino.
Sac[c]us siliginis venditur pro floreno aureo.
Saccus havene venditur media corona.
Vina venduntur pro duobus solidis mensura.

---

[a] *corrected from* Arnem; *the entire preceptory of Haarlem is missing in RA Gelderland.*
[b] *in a different hand.*

fol.126r Mechlin preceptoria prope Aquisgranum[a]

Anno domini MVcXXXX die XVIII Octobris dicti domini visitatores in sua comissione procedentes visitarunt domum sive preceptoriam ordinis santi Johannis prope Aquisgranum dictam Mechlin, et pro vera informatione habenda vocari fecerunt religiossum fratrem Leonardum Kremer de Herll ipsius domus procuratorem pro parte comendatoris fratris Johannis Cerich dicti ordinis servientis, coram quo fuit lecta bulla visitationis, deinde sibi comisserunt et inioncxerunt quod omnes libros et scripturas circa informationes reddituum et emollumentorum dicte domus coram ipsis presentaret; tandem dato sibi iuramento de veritate declaranda circa requisita, iuravit et dicxit eum esse paratum puram et meram veritatem exponere; et sic ex supradictis registris et libris sequentes informationes sunt extracte.

Introitus pecuniarum.

Primo habet hec domus in minutis censibus in Mechlin duas marcas
Collonienses ff marcas 2.
Item habet ex quodam prato locato colloni pro viginti florenis
aureis ff 20.
Item sunt circa ducentum oves intra comendatorem et collonum
ex quibus accipitur lana, et pro parte comendatoris perveniunt circa
decem et octo floreni aurei ff 18.
Item habet ex iuribus temporalibus cormedia sive electionem me-
lioris bestie quando moritur subditus aliquis domus, ex quibus proveniunt circa floreni decem annuatim ff 10.
Item habet ex domo santi Johannis in Aquisgrano decem florenos
singulis annis ff 10.

Sequuntur furmenta.

Habet in censibus firmis singulis annis ex pago sive bonis in Mechlin
modia viginti et unum cum dimidio siliginis a diversis personis in
censu M 21 т [21.5].
Item in havena in firmis censibus singulis annis tria modia havene
in Mechlin M 3.
Item habet dicta domus mollendinum in quo omnes subditi domus
molere tenentur et proveniunt singulis annis sex modia siliginis interdum plus et minus M 6.
Item habet hec domus decimas in Mechlin ex quibus comunibus
annis proveniunt secundum fertilitatem annorum circa triginta duo
modia siliginis M 32.
fol.126v
Item ex dictis decimis in Mechlin perveniunt circa septem modia
tritici M 7.
Item ex dictis decimis perveniunt singulis annis circa sex modia
spelte immondate M 6.
Item ex decimis in ordeo perveniunt circa duo modia hordei
M 2.
Item habet hec preceptoria quandam curtem sive grangiam prope
Aquisgranum que vocatur Elchenrot, locata cuidam collono pro an-
nuali pencione quadraginta modiorum siliginis, que solvere tenetur
circa diem santi Martini M 40.
Item habet ex predicta grangia sex modia havene singulis annis
M 6.
Preterea habet dicta preceptoria unam grangiam domui conionc-
tam quam colonus ibidem colit pro medietate fructuum, que quidem

grangia habet in terris arabilibus centum et tringinta tres burnalia terre cum dimidio, et omne burnale continet quatuor iornalia terre, et comunibus annis habet ex ipsa grangia circumcirca sexaginta modia siliginis, interdum plus et minus secundum annos   M 60.

Item habet ex eadem curia circa quatuordecim modia tritici annuatim   M 14.

Item in havena ex eadem curia habet circa quadraginta et sex modia   M 46.

Item habet ex dicta curia in ordeo et havena mixtum octo modia in toto   M 8.

Item habet ex dicta curia singulis annis circa duodecim modia spelte immondate   M 12.

Item ex dicta curia habet singulis annis circa sex modia ordei

    M 6.

Item habet ex dicta curia in semine raparum circa duo modia pro oleo   M 2.

Item habet in leguminibus ex dicta curia circa duo modia pro coquina   M 2.

Preterea habet hec domus quasdam terras que olim steriles erant, nu[n]c ad culturam redacte sunt et diversis personis sunt locate et dant circa decem modia siliginis   M 10.

Item in minutis censibus habet sexaginta quinque capones et quinque galinas.

Item habet membrum cum domo in civitate Aquisgrani de quo inferius describetur.

Item habet vaccas cum quibus fit butirum et casei pro servicio domus.

Item collonus tenetur dare medietatem omnium bestiarum suarum pro parte comendatoris.

Alii non sunt reditus sive proventus quam supradicti.

fol.127r

Circa onera tenetur comendator providere et intertenere ecclesiam perochialem in Wilre cum edificiis et fenestris, cum calicis, libris et vestibus ecclesiasticis, nec non cum campanis funibus et similibus in quibus exponuntur singulis annis   ff 6.

Item tenetur providere quod in omni hebdemoda celebrentur quatuor misse; tenetur solvere proprium custudem ecclesie, pro quibus omnibus exponentur   ff 5.

Item tenetur comendator providere et intertenere ecclesiam in Mechlin ut quotidie celebretur ad minus una missa, cum uno custode ecclesie, et similiter reparare corum ecclesie cum finestris et aliis rebus necesariis pro quibus exponuntur   ff X.

Item tenetur dare reverendissimo epischopo Leodiensi annuatim 31 albos rotatos   ff /.

Item tenetur comendator alere et solvere unum plebanum pro servicio perochie de Wilre cum uno equo, pro quibus expenssis et salario exponuntur   ff 40.

Item tenetur habere alios duos sacerdotes pro servicio ecclesie de Mechlin, quibus dantur ultra expensas septem floreni aurei pro quolibet, faciunt   ff 14.

Item tenetur dare in triginta et septem diebus festivis singulis annis vinum pro sacerdotibus, pro quo computantur annuatim sex floreni aurei   ff 6.

Item tenetur in festibus Pasche, Pentecostes, Nativitate Domini et carnisplivio dare vinum, pro quo exponuntur circa tres floreni aurei
ff 3.

Item dantur pro salario dispensatoris singulis annis septem floreni aurei   ff 7.

Item dantur duobus servitoribus continuis floreni octo pro salario
ff 8.

Item dantur ancile pro coquina et famule pro bestiis floreni sex aurei   ff 6.

Item tempore estivo opus est habere alium laboratorem, cui dantur quatuor floreni   ff 4.

Item pro vino quod emitur quando veniunt hospites et domini singulis annis   ff 7.

Item pro confectione instrumentorum cervisie exponuntur floreni tres annuatim   ff 3.

Item pro fabro ferrario et aliis operariis annuatim circa quatuor floreni   ff 4.

Item pro telis et lineamentis domus exponuntur octo floreni annuatim   ff 8.

fol.127v

Item pro carnibus recentibus singulis annis exponuntur quindecim floreni   ff 15.

Item pro pissibus recentibus et salsis exponuntur quatuor floreni
ff 4.

Item singulis annis occiditur unus bos pro quo exponuntur quatuordecim floreni   ff 14.

Item pro carbonibus quia non semper habent ligna, duodecim floreni   ff 12.

Item pro sale et pro quadam pitancia sacerdotum circa sex floreni
ff 6.

Item tenetur solvere pro responcione ordinis decem et septem florenos   ff 17.

Item pro expensis capitularibus et viaticis solvuntur quinque floreni   ff 5.

Item pro salario pastoris ovium solvuntur singulis annis duo floreni
aurei   ff 2.

Item tenetur collonus omnes carbones et ligna ac alia necesaria
pro igne vehere et viceversa tenetur comendator famulis et equis
expenssas dare. Item tenetur collonus omnia furmenta comendatoris
ad civitatem Aquensem vehere et tunc comendator expenssas dat
famulis et equis, pro quibus computantur decem floreni   ff 10.

Item tenetur comendator solvere singulis annis domino de Vetten
in cuius dominio est domus de Mechlin pro reconocensia florenos
viginti aureos   ff 20.

Consumontur in domo pro pane et pro ellemosina que datur ter in
hebdemoda omnibus advenientibus triginta et octo modia siliginis
annuatim   M 38.

Item in tritico consumontur singulis annis quatuor modia tritici
                                                                        M 4.

Item pro facienda cervisia consumontur quadraginta tria modia
siliginis   M 43.

     Sequitur deposicio testium.

Pro verificatione et certitudine supradicte deposicionis habenda dicti
domini visitatores examinarunt et interogarunt dominum fratrem
Michaelem de Endovia et dominum Johannem Kei sacerdotes et
conventuales dicte domus et ordinis, qui de omnibus et singulis supradictis cognitionem et noticiam certam habent, a quibus particulariter
et separatim intelecxerunt sic esse prout supra dictum est et hoc affirmarunt mediante solemni iuramento posita manu super crucem.

fol.128r
Domus ordinis est in pago quod vocatur Mechlin in dominio domini
de Wetten de progenie Pallant, inter Aquisgranum et Traiectum superius vel Mastrich; est dicta domus antiqua et ruinossa cum ecclesia
conioncta ad honorem santi Johannis. Comendator habet iurisdictionem temporalem in minoribus rebus super quosdam subditos et elligit
scultetum et septem scabinos; habet eciam dicta domus membrum in
civitate Aquisgrani distans per spacium duarum horarum, de quo
inferius describetur.

Modium siliginis et tritici venditur comunibus annis pro uno floreno aureo; modium spelte et havene venditur pro novem vel decem
baciis.

Curssus et valores monettarum conveniunt cum supradictis
visitationibus.[b]

^cHec visitatio recepta fuit per eundem notarium prout in Mechelen.^c

---

^a *the preceptory Mechelen with member Aachen fails in RA Gelderland.* ^b*cf. Nideggen, member of Velden, AOM 6340 fol.124r:*
Valores monetarum: XXIIII albi faciunt unam marcam; quatuor marche faciunt florenum Colloniensem et septem marche faciunt florenum aureum Rhenense. ^c*with a different hand; because this is the visitation of Mechelen, this notice probably refers to Velden and Nideggen.*

Aquisgranum membrum de Mechlin.

Anno domini MVcXXXX die decima nona octobris dicti domini visitatores in sua comissione procedentes visitarunt domum santi Johannis in Aquisgrano et pro vera informatione habenda vocari fecerunt fratrem Leonardum de Kremer procuratorem dicte domus, coram quo fuit lecta bulla visitationis; deinde sibi comisserunt et inioncxerunt quod omnes libros et scripturas circa informationes redituum et emollumentorum dicte domus coram ipsis presentaret; tandem dato sibi iuramento de veritate decclaranda circa requisita iuravit et dicxit eum esse paratum puram et meram veritatem exponere; et sic ex supradictis registris et libris sequentes informationes extracte sunt presente notario.

In peccuniis.

Habet hec domus in diversis minutis censibus a diversis personis in civitate Aquensi singulis annis circa unum florenum aureum   fl 1.

Sunt preterea aliqui minuti census qui denegantur a debitoribus quos iuridice compelere necesse esset, asendentes ad sommam duorum florenorum   ff 2.

Item sunt alii census per procuratorem preteritum venditi prout inferius describetur.
fol.128v

Item sunt diversi census in furmentis, videlicet in siligine prout constat in registro qui a diversis personis recuperantur in somma modia tredecim siliginis   M 13.

Item habet in censibus ex dominio Schoinfurst prope Aquisgranum singulis annis tredecim modia havene que non possunt augeri neque diminui   M 13.

Ulterius habet dicta domus curiam unam sive grangiam locatam cuidam rustico pro annuali censu triginta et octo modiorum siliginis et dicitur curia Zer Cullen   M 38.

Item ex eadem curia et a dicto collono habet triginta et octo modia
havene   M 38.

Item dat minutos census in caseis, butiro et oleo, que omnia ionta
extimantur pro sex florenis comunibus annis et omnia consumantur
in coquina cum 5 caponibus.

Alii non sunt reditus sive proventus quam supradicti nec ab ecclesia aliquid habet.

Sequuntur bona alienata per procuratorem preteritum

Primo vendidit et alienavit unum modium siliginis annui reditus
quem dicta domus habebat ex pago zer Viden, pro quo nescitur quid
receperit.

Item impignoravit alium modium siliginis annualem, quem domus
habebat in pago dem Paffenbroich, pro quo recepit circa decem et
octo florenos aureos.

Item impignoravit tria vasa cum dimidio siliginis que habebat in
annuali reditu ex quodam domino de Pontoff pro quo recepit decem
florenos aureos.

Item vendidit quatuor mensuras havene quas habebat ex pago
Haerten, nescitur quanti.

Item habebat hec domus septem florenos monette Aquensis super
balnea Cornelisbad singulis annis, quos impignoravit pro quindecim
florenis eiusdem monette.

Item habebat hec domus singulis annis de domo santi Spiritus in
Aquisgrano unum modium siliginis et quatuor capones in censibus
redimi[bi]libus, qui census fuerunt redempti pro florenis aureis circa
viginti et novem, quos idem procurator recepit nec denuo revertit ad
usum dicte domus, sed omnia consompsit.

Ulterius vendidit lapides et ferramenta edificii domus in Aquisgrano.

fol.129r

Interogatus circa onera necessaria dicxit quod comendator tenetur
habere in ipsa domo proprium sacerdotem, qui omnibus diebus festivis et ter in hebdemoda missas celebret; et lumen sive lucernam in
ecclesia continue ardentem teneat, pro quibus omnibus exponuntur
singulis annis quinquaginta floreni aurei   ff 50.

Item pro restauratione domus exponuntur singulis annis sex floreni
                                                            ff 6.

Item solvit in censibus singulis annis unam marcam Aquensem
                                                      ff marcam 1.

Aprobatio circa deposita.

Pro verificatione et certitudine supradicte deposicionis habenda dicti domini visitatores inioncxerant dicto procuratori quod testes fide dignos produceret, qui de supradictis cognitionem et noticiam certam haberent; sed quia non potuerunt reperiri persone alique qui pre-scriptorum omnium plenam noticiam habuissent, ideo de hac deposi-cione ipsos contentos esse oportuit.

Domus ordinis est in imperiali civitate Aquisgrani, antiqua et rui-nossa domus cum parva ecclesia conioncta ad honorem santi Johan-nis Baptiste, prope claustrum sive monasterium santi Dominici, et tam distructa est domus quod comendator non posset in ea habitare, nisi plures peccunias exponeret pro reparatione.

Mensure et precia furmentorum conveniunt cum supradicta visita-tione. Vina in illis partibus non crescunt sed portantur a partibus Collonie.

Valores et precia monetarum concordant cum aliis visitationibus, et licet in Aquisgrano sint alia genera monetarum, tamen per domi-nos visitatores fuerunt tacxata et compensata cum baciis et florenis supradescriptis in visitatione de Nideck.[a]

> [b]Hec omnia extracta fuerunt ab originalibus scripturis et auctenti-cis manu Johannis de Vivario publici Notarii scriptis et per me Theodoricum Nolden publicum apostolica auctoritate Notarium, visa, recognita et auctenticata fuerunt, in quorum fidem hec me manu propria subscripsi, die 15 mensis Octobris, anno domini 1542.
> Theodoricus Nolden de Crevelt[b]

---

[a] *cf. Nideggen, AOM 6340 fol.124r:*
Malterum triticie et siliginis venditur comunibus annis pro uno floreno aureo; et malterum havene venditur pro decem vel duodecim baciis. Valores monetarum: XXIIII albi faciunt unam marcam; quatuor marche faciunt florenum Colloniensem et septem marche faciunt florenum aureum Rhenense.
[b] *in a different hand.*

fol.147r Werffen preceptoria virginum in Frisia.

Anno Domini MVcXXXX die tertia mensis Iulii prenominati domini visitatores in sua comissione procedentes visitarunt [a]domum sive[a] pre-ceptoriam de Vorffen, ubi resident virgines moniales ordinis santi Johannis sub protectione et obediencia reverendi baiulivi Wesfalie, et pro vera informatione habenda vocari fecerunt religiosam dominam

Geburgiam priorissam dicte preceptorie cum toto capitullo virginum monialium in numero circa octuaginta, portantes mantellum et crucem dicti ordinis santi Johannis, coram quibus fuit lecta bulla visitationis; deinde dicte priorisse comisserunt, quod omnes libros et scripturas suas circa informationes redituum et emolumentorum dicte preceptorie coram ipsis presentaret, que immediate commissit religiosso capellano et sacerdoti fratri Hermanno de Davendria, quod precepta exequeretur, cui sacerdoti dato solemni iuramento de veritate declaranda circa requisita iuravit et dixit eum esse paratum puram et meram veritatem exponere; et sic ex supradictis libris et registris sequentes informationes extracte sunt presente notario stipullante.

Somma omnium redituum.

Primo dicxit, quod omnes introitus sive proventus se extendere possunt usque ad summam octo centum florenorum aureorum iuxta communem extimationem, qui concistunt in censibus et pensionibus annualibus prout inferius specificatum erit.

Sequuntur particulares reditus.

Particulariter specificarunt, quod fundi de quibus predicti census capiuntur, sunt agri, prata et pascua sita partim circumcirca ipsam domum et partim in diversis locis et perochiis circunstantibus, videlicet in perochia Oserverdt, Brede, Amdeel, Enalingum, Baffelt, Ranum, Obergum, Wissum, Stemswert et Nordick.

Requisitus fuit, quod declararet numerum et quantitatem agrorum et pocessionum; dicxit hoc fieri non posse nisi presencialiter et de novo mensurarentur, quia suis temporibus non mensurata fuerunt neque in registris vel libris talis numerus aut quantitas aparet *[fol.147v]* vel describitur, sed pleraque sunt fosatis distincta, alie vero in communi adiacencia et sita, in quibus sunt termini vel distenciones interposite.

Dicxit quod habent predia, prata et pascua pro sustentatione domus, que partim collunt et partim dimittunt pro vaccis et peccoribus pas[c]endis et nutriendis, que in summa esse possunt circa septem centum iugera terre.

Item ex propria agricultura possunt habere comunibus annis circa quinque centum modia ordei, que consumuntur pro conficienda cervisia pro monialibus et domo et pro nutriendis bestiis tempore hiemali, quia interdum non suficit fenum.

Item est propria agricultura habere possunt circa quatuor vel quinque centum modia havene, ex quibus furmentis nihil venditur, quia omnia consumuntur in domo.

Circa alios reditus et census et quibus proveniunt supradicti octo centum floreni, dicxit quod comuniter locantur et arendantur ad sex annos.

Interogatus an habeant alia frumenta in tritico et siligine, dicxit quod omnino nichil, sed coguntur emere, quia terra est nimis arenossa et padulossa.

Dixit preterea quod habent circa centum vaccas, a quibus bona emolumenta recipiunt in butiro et caseis, sed omnia sunt necesaria pro sustentatione domus.

Dicxit eciam pro quando recipiuntur virgines, parentes earum solvunt dotem secundum posibilitatem et quod peccunie exponuntur in censibus vel in aliis reditibus.

Item quod ab ecclesia aliquas oblationes recipiunt, sed postquam venit hec secta Luterana deficiunt oblationes et fere suficiunt pro illuminaribus ecclesie.

Interogatus an habeant iurisdictionem, subditos et vasalos, dicxit quod non.

Interogatus an habeant decimas, membra vel grangias, dicxit, quod nisi supradicta.

Sequuntur onera.

Primo tenentur solvere singulis annis in censibus centum et quatuor florenos aureos racione et pro causa bellorum, quia coacte fuerunt peccunias accipere cum preiudicio, ut solverent imposiciones sibi factas tempore ducis Caroli Geldiensis et *[fol.148r]* ducis Sacxonie; alias coacte fuissent vel locum dimittere aut fame mori.

Item pro sustentatione domus cum circa octuaginta virginibus et quatuor sacerdotibus multa exponuntur, quia necessarium est fere omnia furmenta emere et caro precio.

Item pro salario servitorum et ancilarum pro agricultura et vaccis singulis annis exponuntur circa centum et quinquaginta floreni aurei Rhenenses   ff 150.

Item dantur cappellanis pro eorum stipendiis singulis annis quadraginta floreni   ff 40.

Item pro advenientibus hospitibus et affinibus monialium multe fiunt expense.

Deposicio testium circa supradicta.

Pro verificatione et certitudine supradicte deposicionis habenda dicti visitatores examinarunt et interogarunt venerabilem sacerdotem fratrem Henricum Rosendal et religiossas sorores Wisielman, Kareportingen et Bellamfuestes, moniales seniores que de omnibus supradictis cognitionem et noticiam certam habebant, a quibus particulariter et separatim intelecxerunt sic esse prout supra dictum est mediante iuramento.

Situs preceptorie.

Domus ordinis est in loco campestri prope flumen Amasi, a quo interdum multa damna eveniunt propter inondationem aquarum. Distat a civitate Gruningen per spacium quatuor horarum. Domus est bene structa cum fossis latissimis circumcirca, que pertransiri non possunt nisi naviculla. Omnes virgines literis attendunt adeo quod plures linguam latinam calent. Moriente priorissa cetere virgines aliam priorissam elligunt, quam baiulivus Vesfalie reconfirmat. Et ipsas singulis annis visitare tenetur, cui dant expenssas et sex florenos aureos singulis annis. Fertur quod dicta preceptoria cum aliis duabus Wittwert et Ostorverum fuerint fondate et ᵃdotate a quodam comitte Frisie in quibus priorissam preposuit filiam suam; tamen dictaᵃ domus his temporibus nulam habet superioritatem in aliis domibus, sed unaqueque habet propriam priorissam.

> ᵇHec omnia extracta fuerunt ab originalibus scripturis et auctenticis manu Johannis Halteren publici Notarii scriptis et per me Theodoricum Nolden publicum apostolica auctoritate Notarium visa, recognita et auctenticata fuerunt, in quorum fidem hic me manu propria subscripsi die 16 mensis Octobris anno Domini 1542.
> Theodoricum Nolden de Crevelt.ᵇ

fol.148v Witwert preceptoria virginum in Frisia.

Anno Domini MVcXXXX die quinta mensis Iullii supradicti visitatores in sua comissione procedentes visitarunt domum sive preceptoriam de Witwert in Frisia et pro vera informacione habenda vocari fecerunt venerabilem riligiossam dominam priorissam cum ceteris virginibus et venerabilem fratrem Wolterum de Gruningen ipsius domus sacerdotem et administratorem, coram quibus fuit lecta bulla visitationis; deinde ipsis comisserunt et inioncxerunt, quod omnes libros et scripturas suas circa informationes redituum et emolumentorum dicte domus coram ipsis presentaret; tandem dato sacerdoti iuramento de veritate declaranda circa requisita iuravit et dicxit eum esse paratum puram et meram veritatem exponere, et sic ex dictis registris et libris sequentes informationes extracte sunt presente notario stipullante.

Sequuntur reditus et numera agrorum.

Circumcirca preceptoriam sunt sexaginta graminata[a] seu iugera terre, que propriis expenssis cultivantur, ex quibus habentur furmenta inferius descripta　　　　　　　　　　　　　　　　60.

 Item in perochia Maerhusen habet ducentum et quinque graminata sive iugera terre　　　　　　　　　　　　　　205.

 Item in perochia Erenstchem habet trecentum graminata seu iugera terre　　　　　　　　　　　　　　　　300.

 Item in perochia Saecxum habent tantummodo quinque [a]graminata vel[a] iugera terre　　　　　　　　　　　　　　5.

 Item in perochia Petersburen habent tredecim graminata pro sacerdotibus in Witwert　　　　　　　　　　　　13.

 Item in Wattwert et in Uisquat habent quatuordecim graminata terre　　　　　　　　　　　　　　　　14.

 Item in perochia Oldorp habent octo graminata et unum quod sante Cruci datum est　　　　　　　　　　　　　8.

 Item in perochia Uuthus habent quadraginta et septem cum dimidio graminata　　　　　　　　　　47т *[47.5].*

 Item in Perochia Meedt habent sex graminata sive iugera terre
　　　　　　　　　　　　　　　　　　6.

 Item sunt quatuor principales colloni, qui corpus conventus nominantur; cetera sunt exigua et concurrencia. Ideo omnibus computatis domus de Wittwert habet circa sexcenta et quinquaginta et octo graminata [a]sive iugera terre[a] quibus utuntur colloni. Ulterius habet alia graminata et pascua iuxta litus fluminis Amasi et maris, que vento flante inundantur aquis; ideo nichil certi habet ex iis　　　650.

 Haec preceptoria habere potest comunibus annis ex reditibus dictarum pocessionum circa quatuorcentum florenos aureos interdum plus et interdum minus　　　　　　　　　　ff 400.
fol.149r

Iugera sive graminata quibus domus de Witwert fruitur cum sua masaria, sunt trecenta graminata ultra ea que sunt subposita inundationibus maris　　　　　　　　　　　　　300.

 Item circa reditus furmentorum dicxit, quod comunibus annis factis omnibus expenssis vendere possunt circa trecentum modia havene et ducentum modia hordei; tamen interdum accidit, quod anni sunt steriles et omnia consumuntur in domo, quia sunt continue quindecim virgines et tres sacerdotes cum multis servitoribus et ancilis.

Habet preterea plures vaccas, boves et equos et comunibus annis ex eis vendunt pro triginta vel quadraginta florenis, et interdum alios emunt   ff 35.

Vendunt eciam butirum et alia lacticinia comunibus annis pro viginti quinque florenis   [ff 25].

Interogatus an habeat decimas, subditos et vasalos, respondidit quod non.

Interogatus an ab ecclesia emolumenta recipiat, dicxit, quod his temporibus nichil habet et si aliquid recepit, quasi non suficit pro illuminaribus ecclesie.

Conclusive dicxit alios non esse reditus vel proventus quam supradicti et quod, si omnia furmenta venderentur, cum ceteris reditibus comunibus annis vix habere posset mille et ducentum florenos aureos in somma, cum quibus sustentaretur preceptoria   [ff] 1200.

Sequuntur onera.

De supradictis reditibus sunt sexaginta persone quotidie comedentes in domo demptis hospitibus et armigeris continue transeuntibus; ulterius sunt pauperes et laborantes tempore estivo in furmentis et feno, et tempore hiemalis pro purgandis et extra[h]endis furmentis a spicis, que omnia sunt onera necesaria.

De supradictis reditibus singulis annis oportet emere circa centum modia siliginis pro faciendo pane et emitur modium pro uno floreno Emdensi vel circa.

Item emuntur singulis annis circa viginti quinque modia tritici pro uno floreno aureo pro quolibet modio, interdum plus et minus, ᵃsecundum fertilitatem annorumᵃ.

Item in lupullis pro conficienda cervisia exponuntur circa octo floreni aurei.

Item pro sale et pissibus salcis et pro aromatibus circa triginta quinque floreni.

Item pro carnibus recentibus et aliis rebus pro coquina ultra ducentum floreni.

fol.149v

Item pro reparatione edificiorum exponuntur comunibus annis ultra quindecim floreni.

Item pro vestibus virginum et lineamentis domus annuatim ultra quinquaginta floreni.

Item pro salario et mercede sacerdotum et servitorum quinquaginta sex floreni.

Item pro continuis exactionibus imperatoris extimari non potest, nam a decem annis citra coacti fuerunt solvere ultra mille florenos demptis aliis oneribus.

De supradictis reditibus tenentur dare singulis annis baiulivo Wesfalie florenos duodecim, quos accipit prout dicit pro ordinaria responcione ordinis, unde conqueritur administrator quod hec domus plus ceteris gravetur et petit liberari, quia dictus baiulivus neque alii defendunt domum a continuis gravaminibus.

Sunt preterea multa alia onera, que describi non possunt, precipue ex continuis undationibus aquarum pro reficiendis ageribus, in iudiciis, pro defencione iurium et privilegiorum ordinis et in aliis similibus inconcideratis accidentibus.

Deposicio testium.

Pro verificatione et certitudine supradicte deposicionis habenda dicti domini visitatores examinarunt et interogarunt fratrem Gerlacum Rain, sacerdotem ordinis santi Johannis, et dominum Henricum Gloe, qui de omnibus supradictis cognitionem et noticiam certam habebant, a quibus particulariter et separatim intelecxerunt sic esse prout supra dictum est et hoc affirmarunt mediante solemni iuramento ªprestito in manibus notarii infrascriptiª.

Situs preceptorie.

Domus ordinis est in loco campestri distans a preceptoria de Vorffen per spacium unius hore, eciam prope flumen Amasi. Vita et mores istarum virginum est talis pr[o]ut in domo Vorffen, sed non sunt in tanto numero; portant mantellum et crucem ordinis santi Johannis et caste ac religiosissime vivunt, prout est fama.

bcHec omnia extracta fuerunt ab originalibus scripturis et auctenticis manu Johannis Haltren publici Notarii scriptis et per me Theodoricum Nolden publicum apostolica auctoritate Notarium visa, recognita et auctenticata fuerunt, in quorum fidem hic me manu propria subscripsi die 16 mensis Octobris anno Domini 1542.
Theodericus Nolden de Creveltbc

fol.150r Osterverum preceptoria virginum in Frisia.

Anno Domini MVcXXXX die nona mensis Iuliid supradicti visitato-

res in sua comissione procendentes visitarunt domum sive preceptoriam de Osterverum in Frisia, ubi residet comendator sacerdos cum
duodecim virginibus monialibus laicis, quia non tenentur divina officia cantare vel horas canonicas, nam sunt indocte. Et pro vera informatione habenda vocari fecerunt religiossum fratrem Egebertum
Levinck comandatorem, coram quo fuit lecta bulla visitationis; deinde sibi comisserunt et inioncxerunt quod omnes libros et scripturas
suas circa informationes emollumentorum et redituum dicte domus
coram ipsis presentaret; tandem dato sibi iuramento de veritate declaranda circa requisita iuravit et dicit eum esse paratum puram et
meram veritatem exponere et sic ex supradictis registris et libris sequentes informationes extracte sunt ªpresente notario subscripto sti-
pullanteª.

Sequuntur reditus et proventus.

In primis habet a quodam colono pro fictu sive locatione centum et
viginti iugerum sive graminatorum terre cultivate florenos sexaginta
Emdenses, quia comunibus annis solvitur pro quolibet graminato
medium florenum; tamen interdum accidit quod propter inondationes maris terre steriles et salse remanent in preiudicium domusff 60.

Item habet ab alio collono pro fictu sive locatione sexaginta iugerum terre annis comunibus triginta florenos Emdenses, et interdum
minus pro inundatione   ff 30.

Item habet ab alio collono pro locatione decem iugerum quinque
florenos Emdenses   ff 5.

Item ab alio colono pro locatione quadraginta iugerum viginti
florenos Emdenses   ff 20.

Item ab alio colono pro locatione viginti iugerum habet decem
florenos Emdenses   ff 10.

Item ab alio colono pro locatione centum iugerum quinquaginta
florenos Emdenses   ff 50.

Item ab alio colono pro fictu viginti iugerum habet decem florenos
Emdenses   ff 10.

Item ab alio collono pro locatione triginta iugerum quindecim
florenos Emdenses   ff 15.

Item ab alio colono pro fictu septuaginta iugerum habet triginta
quinque florenos Emdenses   ff 35.
fol.150v

Item ab alio collono pro locatione viginti iugerum habet decem
florenos Emdensses   ff 10.

Item ab alio collono pro locatione quadraginta iugerum viginti
florenos Emdensses   ff 20.

Item in loco dicto Nuenhaus habet septuaginta graminata ^asive iugera terre^a locata cuidam rustico, pro quibus recipit triginta quinque florenos Emdenses ff 35.

Item in eodem loco habet alia septuaginta graminata locata alio rustico, pro quibus singulis annis eciam recipit triginta et quinque florenos Emdensses ff 35.

Item ab alio rustico pro locatione quadraginta iugerum viginti florenos Emdensses ff 20.

Item prope ageres pro locatione quadraginta iugerum viginti florenos Emdenses ff 20.

Item in Otterdum pro locatione triginta quinque iugerum XVII florenos Emdenses ff 17т [17.5].

Item in Meedhusen pro fictu quadraginta iugerum viginti florenos Emdensses ff 20.

Item in Meedhusen pro ficta quadraginta iugerum alios XX florenos Emdenses ff 20.

Item pro locatione sexaginta iugerum habet XXX florenos Emdenses ff 30.

Item in Duerswalt pro fictu quindecim iugerum habet XII florenos Emdenses ff 12.

Item pro locatione quadraginta iugerum habet XX florenos Emdenses ff 20.

Item pro locatione decem iugerum habet quinque florenos Emdensses ff 5.

Item in Buchsel pro locatione viginti iugerum habet X florenos Emdensses ff 10.

Sommatis supradictis reditibus habet hec preceptoria in somma florenos Emdensses quinque centum et quinquaginta et duos ^asive ff VcLII^a ff 552.

Habet preterea proprias pocessiones, in quibus alit uno anno quadraginta vaccas, alio anno quadraginta et quinque, et tercio anno quinquaginta secundum fertilitatem annorum; item alit decem, undecim et interdum duodecim iuga vel paria bovum et decem vel duodecim equos, interdum plus et minus; et numerus agrorum sive pascuorum se extendit ad sommam trecentum iugerum sive graminatorum, que si locarentur, reciperet singulis annis circa centum et quinquaginta florenos Emdenses ff 150.

Preterea sacerdotes in Osterwerum habent proprias pocessiones prout sequitur.

fol.151r

Primo in Ostrowerum ex locatione quadraginta iugerum XX florenos Emdenses ff 20.

Item in Weivert ex locatione quadraginta iugerum XX florenos Emdensses ff 20.

Item in propria agricultura collunt quadraginta graminata ᵃsive iugera terreᵃ, ex quibus habent comunibus annis ducentum modia ordei et havene simul M 200.

Ultra predictos reditus dicxit quod sint multa pascua domui spectancia, quorum numerum specificare non potest, quia non sunt ultra quinque anni quod istorum bonorum est administrator; libri et registri antiqui perditi sunt tempore quo dux Carolus Geldrienssis Frisiam obcessit et opidum Dam expugnavit.

ᶜInterogatus an sint alia membra hinc preceptorie spectancia dicxit quod non.ᶜ

ᶜInterogatus an habeant decimas, iurisdictionem et subditos, respondidit quod non.ᶜ

ᶜInterogatus an ab ecclesia emollumenta recipiat respondidit quod saltim minima.ᶜ

Sequuntur onera.

Consumuntur singulis annis pro faciendo pane in domo circa trecentum modia siliginis, quia plures sunt persone ordinarie et pauperes advenientes M 300.

Item pro pane albo in tritico consumuntur circa quadraginta modia tritici M 40.

Item pro conficienda cervisia consumuntur circa sexcentum modia havene et ordei et pro nutriendis equis, porcis et aliis animalibus tempore hiemali M 600.

Item occiduntur singulis annis pro servicio domus circa triginta boves, vacce et tauri, quadraginta vel quinquaginta sues, et circa centum et quinquaginta vel sexaginta oves et agni, que omnia consumuntur pro servicio domus.

Item indigent quotannis centum florenis Emdensis pro pissibus emendis ff 100.

Item exponuntur in sale singulis annis circa quinquaginta floreni Emdenses ff 50.

Item pro emendis diversis generibus cervisiarumᵉ circa XXXX florenos ff 40.

Item tenentur et coguntur singulis annis dare et solvere officialibus imperatoris [fol.151v] triginta florenos aureos Rhenensses pro liberatione et deffencione patrie; tamen hec domus nullam habet defencionem, quia est in via eundia a civitate Gruningen ad civitatem Emdenssem et plures milites et alii negociatoresᶠ pertranciunt in grave preiudicium preceptorie, adeo quod singulis annis preiudicant ultra centum florenos Emdensses ff 130.

Item gravantur ex continuis inundationibus aquarum et exponuntur comunibus annis ultra centum floreni in reparationibus riparum et agerorum, et non sufficiunt   ff 100.

Preterea solvit singulis annis domino baiulivo Vesfalienssi pro visitatione et reconocensia quindecim florenos Rhenenses et servitoribus unum florenum   ff 16.

Item coacti fuerunt dare comiti Frisie Orientalis florenos mille et quinque centum pro adiutorio belli, quod habuit contra ducem Geldrienssem a decem annis citra.

Item exponunt pro salario servitorum et ancilarum singulis annis pro gubernandis vaccis et aliis bestiis florenos centum Emdensses et interdum plus   ff 100.

Item habent ecclesiam prope opidum Dam, ubi nuli sunt reditus; tamen tenetur propriis expenssis edificare et restaurare edificia et coperturam dicte ecclesie, et pro dicta ecclesia eciam tenentur dare baiulivo Vesfaliensi duos florenos annuatim   ff 2.

Item dant de alia grangia in Golchoren dicto baiulivo singulis annis tres aureos florenos, et propter inondationes aquarum petunt absolvi a tali solutione   ff 3.

Ulterius pro restauracione domorum et grangiarum comunibus annis exponuntur ultra centum floreni, quia ligna caro precio venduntur   ff 100.

De expenssis et salario sacerdotum nulla fit mencio, quia prout supra dictum est, habent proprios particulares reditus, cum quibus se sustenant.

Deposicio testium.

Pro verificatione et certitudine supradicte deposicionis habenda dicti visitatores examinarunt et interogarunt venerabiles fratrem Theodoricum Luens et fratrem Johannem Piscatoris conventuales dicte domus testes idoneos et fide dignos, qui de omnibus supradictis cognitionem et noticiam certam habent, a quibus particulariter et separatim [fol.152r] intelecxerunt sic esse prout supra dictum est et hoc affirmarunt mediante solemni iuramento, ex eo quod comendator tenetur omnibus annis ipsis conventualibus computum dare de receptis et expositis prout in presenti anno fideliter dedit.

Situs preceptorie ᵃsive domusᵃ.

Domus ordinis est in loco campestri non multum distans a flumine Amaso inter Gruningen et Emdem; est satis ampla domus, sed quia est in communi via multa gravamina patitur presertim tempore belli. In ipsa domo sunt duodecim moniales laice et quatuor sacerdotes, est sub protectione et visitatione baiulivi Wesfalie et moriente comendatore sacerdotes conventuales alium eligunt, quem baiulivus confirmat.

Mensure et precia furmentorum [a]cum valore et curssu monettarum.
Mensure furmentorum:[a]
Modium est mensura continens pondus unius hominis.
Venditur modium siliginis pro uno floreno aureo.
Modium tritici pro una corona Francie.
Modium havene et ordei pro floreno Emdensi.

Curssus monettarum:
Viginti et quatuor scutifferi faciunt florenum Emdensem.
Viginti et novem schutiferi faciunt florenum aureum.
Triginta et octo schutiferi faciunt coronam Francie.

Mensure pocessionum:
Graminatum et iugerum idem est et continet laborem unius hominis per totam diem in laborando cum uno arato. Idem est per domos de Worffen et Wittwert, tamen in Wittwert graminata sunt paulo maiora.

[b]Hec omnia extracta fuerunt ab originalibus scripturis et auctenticis manu Johannis Haltren publici Notarii scriptis et per me Theodoricum Nolden publicum apostolica auctoritate Notarium visa, recognita et auctenticata fuerunt, in quorum fidem hic me manu propria subscripsi, die 16 mensis Octobris anno Domini 1542.
Theodoricus Nolden de Crevelt.[b]

---

[a] *is missing in RA Gelderland.* [b] *in a different hand.* [c] *summarized in RA Gelderland.* [d] *the ms.has* Iunii. [e] *the following specification in the RA Gelderland copy is missing in AOM (edited by Wiersum and Le Cosquino de Bussy, in: BMHG 48, 1927, p.259):* sc. Hambu(r)gerbier, Rostokerbier, Lubickerbier, Bremerbier sc. Nottbier, Brounswycker Mumme und Hanover Breihau etc. [f] *the following addition in the RA Gelderland copy is missing in AOM (ibidem, p.259):* scilicet kauffleute mit ihren ossen von Dennemercke.

fol.158v Arnem preceptoria in ducatu Geldrie[a]

Anno domini MVcXXXX die XXIII Augusti dicti visitatores in sua comissione procedentes visitarunt domum sive preceptoriam ordinis santi Johannis in opido de Arnem in Geldria et pro vera informatione habenda vocari fecerunt religiossum fratrem Johannem Beltg sacerdotem et procuratorem pro parte reverendi domini fratris Philipi Schilling militis et comendatoris dicte domus, coram quo fuit lecta bulla visitationis, deinde dato sibi iuramento de veritate declaranda circa requisita iuravit et dicxit eum esse paratum puram et meram veritatem exponere et in sue deposicionis fidem presentavit registra sive libros ex quibus sequentes informationes extracte sunt.

fol.159r, cut off in the right margin
Primo habet in quodam pago dicto Apeldorn singulis annis racione agrorum ad sex annos arendatorum florenos duodecim aureos Rhenenses   ff 12.

Item habet prope opidum de Arnem sex iugera agri in loco dicto Ad Paludem pro quibus recipit singulis annis circa viginti et unum florenos aureos Rhenenses   ff 21.

Item habet propriam curiam in Brummen cum agris circumstantibus, pro quibus singulis annis recipit florenos aureos viginti et sex et scutiferos tredecim   ff 26 s [13].

Item habet in supradicto loco ex agris florenos viginti et octo aureos   ff 28.

Item habet in eodem loco ex agris florenos tredecim et scutiferos XXVII Brebantinos   ff 13 s 2[7].

Item habet in Batavia superiore in quodam pago dicto Elst domum sive curiam cum agris et pascuis ex quibus recipit singulis annis circa florenos LIIII sive   ff 54.

Item habet in pago Malburgen agros et pascua ex quibus recipit singulis annis circa florenos triginta et septem aureos Rhenenses

     ff 37.

Item habet in Elden ex parvo agro circa florenos duos aureosff 2.

Item habet in Betavia inferiori in pago Hoeshdem ex quibusdam agris et pascuis circa sexaginta et octo florenos aureos singulis annis

     ff 68.

Item in eodem loco habet propriam curiam cum agris et pascuis adiacentibus ex quibus singulis annis recipit florenos octuaginta et duos et scutiferos quinque   ff 82 s [5].

Item habet quedam parva agra in Ucten, Omern, Ingen et Amerung ex quibus singulis annis recipit in somma florenos aureos triginta et octo   ff 38.

Item habet aliqua parva agra circum opidum Wagening in diversis locis, ex quibus singulis annis recipit triginta et duos florenos aureos

     ff 32.

Item in loco dicto Velope prope Arnem ex quibusdam agris habet singulis annis circa florenos undecim cum dimidio   ff 11 т *[11.5]*.

Item habet in loco dicto Kattempoil prope Arnem quedam agra arenossa et quasi sterilia, ex quibus recipit singulis annis circa florenos decem, tamen plura sustinentur incommoda adeo quod parva utilitas superest.

fol.159v

Item habet a monialibus in Arnem racione unius agri annuatim florenos duos aureos ff 2.

Item habet in ducatu Clivensi in pagis Groesshem, Vestervort et Sevener ex agris et pocessionibus diversis florenos quinquaginta et quinque cum dimidio ff 55 т *[55.5]*.

Item habet hec domus in minutis censibus in opido et extra opidum de Arnhem circiter florenos duodecim quos fratres conventuales ab olim susceperunt in usum pitancie et aduc in presenti recipiunt

ff 12.

Item habet ex oblationibus et emollumentis ecclesie circa florenos duodecim ff 12.

Sequuntur reditus furmentorum.

Habet hec domus in pago Brumen ex agris singulis annis triginta et tria modia sive maltera siliginis que nomine census agrorum recipiuntur M 33.

Item habet in eodem pago ex aliis agris racione arrendationis singulis annis viginti et sex maltera sive modia siliginis M 26.

Item habet in pago Bernchem ex agris ratione census arrendationis singulis annis triginta et unum maltera sive modia siliginis M 31.

Item prope Arnem habet a Carthusianis unum malterum siliginis annuatim M 1.

Item habet in pago Eede ex agris racione census arendationis singulis annis decem et novem maltera siliginis M 19.

Item habet prope Arnhem in loco dicto Valkenhussen coloniam unam cum agris arenosis ex quibus proveniunt comunibus annis circa decem maltera siliginis M 10.

Item habet molendinum prope Arnhem ex quo proveniunt singulis annis viginti et tria maltera tritici M 49.

Item habet in ordeo a diversis locis in opido et circumcirca opidum singulis annis viginti et duo maltera hordei et tria maltera siliginis M 25.

Dicxit ulterius quod dicta domus habet unam ecclesiam perochialem in pago Spanckern intra Arnem et Sutphaniam in qua residet unus sacerdos ordinis qui se ex emolumentis vix sustentare potest, igitur nihil inde provenit sed anno XXXVIII *[1538]* pro reparatione domus in tectura exposuerunt ultra florenos decem et octo.

fol.160r

Dicxit preterea quod est alia preceptoria conioncta et incorporata cum Arnhem que vocatur Numingen de qua inferius largius describetur.

Interogatus an habeat iurisdictionem, decimas, vel alios proventus dicxit quod non.

Interogatus an reditus olim fuerint maiores quam nunc sint, dicxit quod non, sed citius sit meliorata quam deteriorata, quod quidem autentice probabit, et quod tempore presentis comendatoris redemerit censum trium florenorum annualium in Malburgen, et prope opidum duo iugera terre a monialibus sante Agnetis.

Sequuntur onera.

In domo continue residere debent quatuor sacerdotes pro divinis officiis celebrandis, quibus dantur sex floreni pro quolibet, sunt in somma ff 24.

Item dant procuratori pro suo salario viginti et quinque florenos ff 25.

Item pro sacrista sive custode ecclesie exponuntur duo floreniff 2.

Item dantur coquo cum subcoquo singulis annis septem floreni ff 7.

Item portario, barbitonsori, pistori et bracxatori floreni XII cum dimidio ff 12 т *[12.5]*.

Item pro supelectilibus domus in telis et vasis coquinariis et aliis rebus similibus singulis annis exponuntur circa decem floreni interdum plus ff 10.

Item in quibusdam diebus festivis emitur vinum pro sacerdotibus, constat ff 8.

Item exponuntur in lignis et cespitibus pro faciendo igne floreni duodecim ff 12.

Item pro resentibus carnibus et pissibus per totum annum floreni XXXX ff 40.

Butirum habent pro necesitate domus a colonis et aliis rusticis.

Item singulis annis occidunt duos boves pro quibus solvunt florenos XXX ff 30.

Item habent a colonis singulis annis quinque porcos macros pro quibus impinguendis exponuntur singulis annis circa decem maltera ordei M 10.

Preterea singulis annis comsumuntur pro faciendo pane XVIII maltera siliginis M 18.

Item dantur pro ellemosina singulis annis tria maltera siliginis M 3.

Item coguntur emere singulis annis pro conficienda cervisia triginta et sex maltera *[fol.160v]* avene et emitur pro medio floreno aureo unum malterum, esset in somma ff 18.

Item consumuntur pro cervisia quatuordecim maltera ordei singulis annis [M 14].

Item dantur predicatori qui in quibusdam diebus deputatis predicat quinque floreni ff 5.

Item pro sale et pissibus salsis exponuntur annuatim quinque floreni ff 5.

Item pro necessariis in ecclesia in illuminaribus et reparatione decem floreni ff 10.

Item solvuntur pro ordinaria responcione ordinis floreni XXXII
ff 32.

Item dantur domui de Numingen de agris in Elst quatuor floreni
cum dimidio ff 4 т *[4.5]*.

Item solvuntur in censu redimibili singulis annis circa undecim
floreni diversis personis ff 11.

Item pro reparatione curiarum et edificiorum et pro intertenendis
ageribus ff 50.

Item pro expenssis equi procuratoris et pro hospitibus advenientibus ff 15.

Deposicio testium circa supradicta.

Pro verificatione et certitudine supradicte deposicionis habenda prenominati visitatores examinarunt et interogarunt fratres Henricum de
Kalcker priorem et Cornelium Rampert conventuales dicte domus,
qui de omnibus supradictis cognitionem et noticiam certam habebant, a quibus particulariter et separatim intelecxerunt sic esse prout
supra dictum est et hoc affirmarunt mediante solmni iuramento.

Situs preceptorie sive domus.

Domus ordinis est in opido Arnhem in loco satis amplo cum ecclesia
conioncta ad honorem santi Johannis, in qua omnibus diebus cele-
brantur divina officia per quatuor sacerdotes. Circa domus sunt orti
et pomaria domui pertinencia, et non sunt vina.

Malterum siliginis venditur comunibus annis pro uno floreno aureo;
malterum tritici pro una corona, maltera ordei pro media corona.

Triginta et duo scutiferi Brebantini faciunt florenum aureum Rhenense.

[b]Hec omnia extracta fuerunt ab originalibus scripturis et auctenticis manu Johannis Haltren publici Notarii scriptis et per me Theodoricum Nolden publicum apostolica auctoritate Notarium visa,
recognita et autenticata fuerunt, in quorum fidem hic me manu

propria subscripsi, die 29 mensis Octobris anno 1542.
Theodoricus Nolden a Crevelt[b]

fol.161r, cut off in the right margin
Numingen preceptoria conioncta cum Arnhem[a]

Anno domini MVcXXXX die XXV Augusti dicti visitatores in sua
comissione procedentes visitarunt domum ordinis santi Johannis in
civitate Novemmagenssi et pro vera informatione habenda vocari fecerunt religiossum fratrem Johannem de Beltg ibidem procuratorem
pro parte reverendi domini fratris Philipi Schilling comendatoris, coram quo fuit lecta bulla visitationis, deinde sibi inioncxerunt et comisserunt quod omnes libros et scripturas suas circa informationes
redituum et emollumentorum dicte domus coram ipsis presentaret.
Tandem dato sibi iuramento de veritate declaranda circa requisita
iuravit et dicxit eum esse paratum puram et meram veritatem exponere et sic ex supradictis registris et libris sequentes informationes
extracte sunt presente infrascripto notario stipullante.

Sequuntur reditus.

Habet hec domus in Betavia superiori prope fluvium Valium in vila
Lenndt unam colloniam cum agris circunstantibus arendatis ad sex
annos, pro quibus recipit singulis annis florenos quinquaginta et duos
et scutiferos **XXVI**   ff 32 s 2[6].

    Item in eodem loco habet aliam colloniam eciam arendatam per
sex annos, pro qua singulis annis recipit quadraginta florenos aureos
                                         ff 40.

    Item ibidem habet aliam colloniam eciam arendatam per sex an-
nos, pro qua singulis annis recipit quadraginta et quatuor florenos
aureos   ff 44.

    Item habet aliam colloniam sub dominio de Batemburg in vila
dicta Horsszen ex qua singulis annis recipit quinquaginta et octo
florenos aureos et scutiferos **V**   ff 58 s 5.

    Item habet aliam colloniam in villa Niell ex qua recipit florenos
XXX et scutiferos **XIIII**   ff 30 s 1[4].

    Item habet in villa Loet duas pecias agri arendati pro novem flo-
renis et decem et novem scutiferis Brebantinis singulis annisff 9 s 19.

    Item habet octavam partem navigii sive transitus in flumine Valli
ex quo singulis annis proveniunt circa undecim floreni aurei pro sua
parte   ff 11.

Item dicta preceptoria habet in civitate Numingen quinque parvas domos locatas diversis *[fol.161v]* personis a quibus recipit singulis annis circa undecim florenos aureos   ff 11.

Item habet in diversis minutis censibus in Numingen, Arnhem, Bueren, in Oij, in Lendt, Hervelt, Valburg, Nederbusch, Wichen, Boning, Heese, Erwick et Horssen a diversis personis singulis annis in somma florenos triginta et septem   ff 37.

Sequuntur reditus furmentorum.

Habet in pago dicto Grosbecke curiam cum agris ex quibus proveniunt singulis annis in censu decem et septem malteria cum dimidio siliginis   M 17 т *[17.5]*.

Item ibidem de quodam agro proveniunt circa duo maltera siliginis   M 2.

Item habet circumcirca opidum Numingen agros locatos diversis personis ex quibus singulis annis proveniunt triginta et septem maltera siliginis   M 37.

Item habet in Horssen in arendatione viginti et sex maltera havene   M 26.

Item habet in Lendt triginta maltera ordei singulis annis   M 30.

Item ibidem et in Bemmel habet singulis annis tria maltera havene   M 3.

Item ibidem habet medium malterum tritici   M т *[0.5]*.

Interogatus an ab ecclesia emolumenta recipiat, respondit quod non, quia non est perochia sed tantummodo capella, et oblationes non suficiunt ad illuminaria.

Interogatus an reditus dicte domus olim fuerint meliores quam nunc sint, respondit quod non in multis annis; sed quod comendator modernus diligenti administratione per se et suos procuratores melioravit, videlicet in extinctione et solutione debitorum per predecessorem suum contractorum ad sommam florenorum aureorum trecentum et triginta.

Item redemit annualem censum unius floreni et quarte partis floreni in hac civitate.

Item exposuit pro reparatione domus viginti florenos aureos.

Alios dicxit non esse reditus, alie non sunt curie, quam superius descripte.

Sequuntur onera.

Solvit singulis annis pro ordinaria responcione ordinis XX florenos
     ff 20.

     Item solvit in censibus canonicis civitatis et abatisse Novi Monaste-
rii   ff 2 s 14.

     Item sunt quatuor sacerdotes ordinis quibus dantur viginti et qua-
tuor floreni   ff 24.

fol.162r

     Item dantur procuratori pro suo salario et labore singulis annis
viginti floreni   ff 20.

     Item dantur custodi ecclesie et predicatori singulis annis octo flor-
enis in somma   ff 8.

     Item dantur bracxatori, barbitonsori et pistori in somma decem
floreni   ff 10.

     Item pro supelectilibus domus in camaris et coquina annuatim sex
floreni   ff 6.

     Item occiduntur singulis annis in domo duo boves qui emuntur
pro florenis XXVII   ff 27.

     Item habent porcos a collonis pro quibus impinguendis exponun-
tur floreni V   ff 5.

     Item pro carnibus recentibus et pissibus et similibus quadraginta
floreni   ff 40.

     Item pro butiro et caseis et aromatibus singulis annis decem et
octo floreni   ff 18.

     Item pro lignis et carbonibus singulis annis exponuntur XXV flo-
reni   ff 25.

     Item pro necesariis in ecclesia per totum annum octo floreni ff 8.

     Item pro faciendo pane in domo et pro ellemosina decem et sep-
tem maltera siliginis   M 17.

     Item pro pane et pro conficienda cervisia consumuntur quatuorde-
cim maltera tritici   M 14.

     Item pro reparatione navigii et domorum arendatarum annuatim
quinque floreni   ff 5.

     Item pro vino sacerdotum et hospitum singulis annis tres floreni
     ff 3.

     Item pro reparatione edificiorum et ecclesie ac grangiarum XXV
floreni   ff 25.

Deposicio testium.

Pro verificatione et certitudine supradicte deposicionis habenda dicti
domini visitatores examinarunt et interogarunt religiossum fratrem

Henricum Kalcker priorem in Arnhem qui in Noumagensi domo religionem professus est et conventualis fuit, qui de his supradictis cognitionem et noticiam certam habet et medio iuramento affirmavit sic esse prout supradictum est. Similiter affirmavit superius deposita circa melioramenta, et ulterius dictus procurator exibuit instrumenta et scripturas circa solutionem dictorum trecentum et triginta florenorum per notarium subscriptas. Superius descripta eciam testificavit et medio iuramento affirmavit frater Adam de Horst conventualis.

Domus ordinis est in civitate sive opido de Numingen in ducatu Geldrie distans *[fol.162v]* a preceptoria de Arnhem per spacium quatuor miliarum. Est hec civitas in ripa fluminis Rheni in satis ampla civitate olim imperiali. Habet parvam ecclesiam conionctam, in qua omnibus diebus cantantur divina officia per quatuor sacerdotes ordinis.

Mensure furmentorum sunt parum maiores quam in Arnhem, sed quasi eodem precio venduntur. Valores et curssus monettarum omnino concordant.

[b]Hec omnia extracta fuerunt ab originalibus scripturis et auctenticis manu Johannis Haltren publici Notarii scriptis et per me Theodoricum Nolden publicum apostolica auctoritate Notarium visa, recognita et auctenticata fuerunt in quorum fidem hic me manu propria subscripsi die 29 mensis octobris anno 1542.

Theodericus Nolden a Crevelt[b]

---

[a] *the preceptories Arnhem and Nimwegen are missing in RA Gelderland. An authentic copy of the visitation of Arnhem, made by the chancery at Malta dd. 7 March 1713, with the black seal of Grand Master frater Ramon Perellos, is to be found in GLA Karlsruhe, 90/337 fol.55r-57v.* [b] *in a different hand.*

fol.162v Buren preceptoria dependens a baiulivatu Traiectensi[a]

Anno domini MVcXXXX die XXVIII Iulii dicti visitatores in sua comissione procedentes visitarunt domum ordinis santi Johannis in opido de Bueren et pro vera informatione habenda vocari fecerunt religiossum fratrem Johannem Guliermum de Endovia ibidem comendatorem, coram quo fuit lecta bulla visitationis; deinde sibi comisserunt et inioncxerunt quod omnes libros et scripturas suas circa informationes redituum et emollumentorum dicte domus coram ipsis presentaret. Tandem dato sibi iuramento de veritate dicenda circa requisita, iuravit et dicxit eum esse paratum puram et meram verita-

tem exponere, et sic ex supradictis registris et libris sequentes informationes extracte sunt.

Sequuntur reditus.

Habet dicta domus circumcirca opidum de Bueren et cuiusdam vile
dicte Erckum in diversis peciis et locis iugera octuaginta et septem
locata diversis personis ad sex annos et recipit pro quolibet iugero
duos florenos cum dimidio secundum comunem extimationem et essent in somma floreni ducentum et decem et septem cum dimidio
ff 217 т *[217.5]*.

Item comendator colit propria agricultura tredecim iugera agri, ex
quibus potest habere comunibus annis valorem quadraginta florenorum vel circa ff 40.

Item dimissit cuidam colono viginti et quatuor iugera agri pro
medietate fructuum et ex eis habere potest comunibus annis circa
septuaginta et duos florenis ff 72.

Habet preterea prata et pascua pro servicio equorum et vacarum
in domo existencium.

fol.163r

Interogatus an habeat alias curias, grangias, vel alios reditus, respondidit quod non.

Interogatus an ab ecclesia emollumenta recipiat, respondit quod
his temporibus non.

Sequuntur onera.

Tenetur dare domino baiulivo Traiectensi pro annuali pencione
quinquaginta florenos ff 50.

Item dat in censu domino de Buren et domino de Palant et custodi
in Aversat in Geldria et hospitali in opido Buren in somma florenos
quatuor et scutiferos decem ff 4 s 10.

Item dat thesaurario sante Marie Traiectensis in censu florenos
tres cum dimidio á./. *[?]* ff 3 т *[3.5]*.

Item dat comendatori in Arnhem et Numigen duodecim libras
Geldrienses in censu ff L 12.

Item dat in domo Traiectensi pro pitancia et pro conventu et
familia florenos V cum dimidio ff 5 s 16.

Dicxit ulterius quod anno elapso combusta est domus cum omnibus furmentis et fructibus et cum omnibus rebus domesticis et mobilibus ac eciam equis et vaccis, pro qua et quibus reficiendis exposuit
ultra florenos mille et hos habuit a bonis amicis et precipue a reverendo domino baiulivo Traiectensi.

Consumuntur in domo pro pane quinque modia tritici et venditur modium pro octo florenis aureis, quia modium est mensura continens octo maltera ff 40.

Item consumuntur duo modia havene que extimantur ad octo florenos aureos ff 8.

Item consumuntur circa sexaginta vasa cervisie, extimantur quadraginta florenos ff 40.

Item pro duobus bovibus pinguis pro servicio coquine qui extimantur pro ff 26.

Item pro porcis et ovibus pro servicio domus, qui extimantur in somma pro ff 20.

Item pro butiro, sale, pissibus, carnibus et similibus triginta floreni ff 30.

Item pro cespitibus et carbonibus quia non habent ligna pro coquina ff 20.

Item pro lineamentis et aliis similibus per totum annum quatuor floreni ff 4.

Item pro mercede servitorum et ancilarum singulis annis viginti et quatuor floreni ff 24.

Item pro reparatione edificiorum et pro quibusdam conviviis annualibus ff 15.

Item pro vestibus comendatoris et pro expensis viaticis quindecim floreni ff 15.

Pro verificatione et certitudine supradicte deposicionis habenda dicti visitatores *[fol.163v]* examinarunt et interrogarunt Jacobum Stelle redituarium et Godfredum Wasman, qui de omnibus supradictis cognitionem et noticiam certam habebant, a quibus particulariter et separatim intelecxerunt sic esse prout supra dictum est et hoc affirmarunt mediante solemni iuramento.

Domus ordinis est in opido Bueren intra Traiectum et Geldriam et est comitatus cuidam comiti pertinens de sanguine de Aigmont. Domus est noviter edificata cum curia et orto conioncto. Comendatur eligitur a baiulivo Traiectensi cui dantur pro pencione quinquaginta floreni singulis annis prout supra dictum est.

bHec omnia extracta fuerunt ab originalibus scripturis et auctenticis Johannis Haltren publici Notarii scriptis et per me Theodoricum Nolden publicum apostolica auctoritate Notarium visa, recognita et auctenticata fuerunt in quorum fidem hic me manu propria subscripsi die 29 mensis Octobris anno 1542.

Theodoricus Nolden a Creveltb

Ingen preceptoria in Betavia Geldrie dependens a Traiecto[a]

Anno domini MVcXXXX die XIIII Iulii dicti domini visitatores in
sua comissione procedentes visitarunt domum ordinis santi Johannis
de Ingen in Betovia et pro vera informatione habenda vocari fecerunt
religiossum dominum fratrem Bernardum de Duven baiulivum
Traiectensem cui frater Guliermus comendator in Ingen extrema infirmitate gravatus declarationem hanc sequentem commisserat circa
reditus et exitus dicte domus, quam ante infirmitatem suam presentaret. Dato ergo iuramento dicto domino baiulivo de veritate declaranda circa requisita iuravit et deposuit prout sequitur presente notario
stipullante.

Sequuntur reditus.

Habet hec domus in territorio perochie de Ingen et perochie Ommeren diversas pocessiones et agros, qui in somma se extendunt ad
numerum centum et sexaginta trium iugerum, ex quibus singulis annis proveniunt pro quolibet iugero duo cum dimidio floreni aurei
Rhenenses, faciunt in somma florenos quatuor centum et septem cum
dimidio   ff 407 т [407.5].
   Item comendator habet propriam curiam sive colloniam in perochia Maurick cum quibusdam agris, quorum numerum specificare
non scit, et propria agricultura cultivare facit, unde comunibus annis
proveniunt circa centum floreni   ff 100.
fol.164r
   Item habet in perochia de Ingen terciam partem omnium decimarum que annis comunibus cedunt pro eorum parte centum et
quinquaginta florenos   ff 150.
   Alios dicxit non esse reditus vel proventus quam supradicti.

Sequuntur onera.

Tenetur dare singulis annis pro pencione comendatori sive baiulivo
Traiectensi, quem pro colatorem et superiorem recognoscunt, florenos centum aureos   ff 100.
   Item tenetur intertenere et reparare centum et quadraginta et septem virgas sive rotas ageris et omnis virga continet decem pedes pro
quibus exponuntur   ff 20.
   Residuum consumitur pro servicio domus in pane, cervisia et carnibus et ceteris rebus necesariis et eciam pro servicio ecclesie in qua
residet comendator sacerdos cum alio sacerdote, et in pluribus servitoribus et ancilis.

Deposicio testium.

Pro verificatione et certitudine supradicte deposicionis habenda dicti
visitatores examinarunt et interrogarunt providum virum Theodoricum Sassen et Gedefridum de Washman, qui de omnibus predictis
cognitionem et noticiam certam habebant, a quibus particulariter et
separatim intelecxerunt sic esse prout supra dictum est et hoc affirmarunt mediante solemni iuramento, adeo quod in ipsis dubitandum
non est.

Situs preceptorie sive domus.

Domus ordinis est in pago dicto Ingen in insula Betavie et in ducatu
Geldrie, que insula fit ex flumine Rheni; est satis bona domus cum
ecclesia parva et curiis ac ortis conionctis; distat a civitate Traiecti per
spacium sex horarum, et est subposita baiulivo Traiectensi quia comendator per ipsum eligitur et sibi reservat annualem pensionem
cum spolio comendatorum, a quibus non parum utilitatis recipit.

[b]Hec omnia extracta fuerunt ab originalis scripturis et auctenticis
manu Johannis Haltren publici Notarii scriptis et per me Theodoricum Nolden publicum apostolica auctoritate Notarium visa, recognita et auctenticata fuerunt, in quorum fidem hic me manu
propria subscripsi die 29 mensis Octobris anno domini 1542.
   Theodoricus Nolden a Crevelt[b]

---

[a] *the preceptories Buren and Ingen are missing in RA Gelderland.* [b] *in a different hand.*

fol.164v   Int Loe preceptoria prope Hardwick in Geldria

Anno Domini MVcXXXX die XIIII Iulii dicti visitatores in sua comissione procedentes visitarunt domum sive preceptoriam de Int Loe
vel in Valle santi Johannis prope opidum de Hardwick, que domus
dependet a baiulivatu Traiectensi, et pro vera informatione habenda
vocari fecerunt religiossum fratrem Bernardum Thenstert comendatorem, coram quo fuit lecta bulla visitationis; tandem dato sibi iuramento de veritate declaranda circa requisita sibi inioncxerunt et
comisserunt, quod omnes libros et scripturas suas circa informationes
redituum et emolumentorum coram ipsis presentaret, ex quibus sequentes informationes extracte sunt.

Sequitur introitus.

Habet hec domus parvas decimas in Kaldembroick in territorio Bern-
felt prope Amsfordiam, ex quibus recipit circa sex maltera siliginis et
havene M 6.
Item ibidem habet maiores decimas, quarum tamen proprietas
spectat ad principem terre, sub titullo et beneficio redemptionis pro
florenis quatuor centum aureis, que decime simul cum manso predicto reddunt comunibus annis sex maltera siliginis M 6.
Item ex dictis decimis habentur circa octuaginta maltera havene
M 80.
Item ex dictis decimis habentur circa sex vel septem maltera pani-
cii M 7.
Item habet proventus et reditus in Kaldembroick, qui locantur
rusticis pro annuali censu, a quibus comunibus annis habent florenos
trecentum et triginta et duos, sed tempore belli multo minus et interdum nihil habent ff 332.
Item ibidem habet molendinum, quod vento agitatur, ex quo comunibus annis habet et recipit nomine locationis maltera quadraginta
et octo siliginis M 48.
Item habet propre opidum de Hardwick et villam Nunspeet census
et reditus, ex quibus singulis annis recipit circa duodecim florenos
aureos ff 12.
Item habet hereditates et mansiones circumcirca Loe et in territorio de Ermell, ex quibus habet singulis annis florenos centum et decem aureos ff 110.
Item habet proprium molendinum prope Hardwick, pro cuius
proprietate est diferencia et lis; tamen ex eo recipiunt singulis annis
circa florenos viginti et quinque aureos ff 25.
fol.165r
Item habet pascua et prata sub perochiis Niekirken et Puten, que
modo sunt arrendata pro florenis Filipensibus septuaginta et septem
singulis annis ff 77.
Item habet circumcirca domum pocessiones, quas olim propria
agricultura colebat, nunc autem arrendate sunt pro sexaginta et duobus florenis Filipensibus ff 62.
Item habet ex dictis agris tercium manipullum fructuum, sed specificare non potest valorem, quia non semper equaliter seminantur;
tamen extimatur pro ff 30.
Item habet unam peciam agri continens undecim iugera; fructus
consumuntur in domo.
Item habet silvam prope domum et singulis annis venduntur ligna

et nemora pro centum florenis Emdensibus, interdum plus et interdum minus   ff 100.

Preterea habet prata et pascua pro sex vaccis et quinque equis,
cum quibus conficitur butirum et reponuntur furmenta et alii reditus.

Circa arendamenta et locationes dicxit, quod tempore quieto et
pacifico fiunt ei florenis aureis Rhenensibus, sed tempore belicosso vel
pestifero fiunt in florenis Philipensibus vel Emdensibus, quod quidem
notandum est.

Interogatus an sint alie curie vel reditus quam supradicti [a]respon-
didit quod non.

Interogatus[a] an ab ecclesia emollumenta recipit, respondidit quod
his temporibus non.

      Sequuntur onera.

Tenentur dare domino baiulivo Traiectensi eorum superiori singulis
annis pro pencione quadraginta florenos aureos, quos interdum tempore belli remittit   ff 40.

Tenentur solvere principi terre de predictis bonis tredecim florenos
cum dimidio   ff 13 т *[13.5]*.

Item solvunt in minutis censibus abati santi Pauli, comunitati in
Eede, comunitati in Herseler et alibi in somma florenos duos vel circa
singulis annis in censibus   ff 2.

Item tenentur solvere de molendino in Hardwick quinque maltera
siliginis annuatim   ff 5.

Item fuerunt coacti alienare et impignorare aliquos census propter
bellum et incendium, quod passi sunt a Burgondionibus, qui census
singulis annis se extendunt ad sommam florenorum viginti et trium,
et sunt redimibiles ad quinque pro centum   ff 23.

Et ex dicto incendio domus passa est damnum quinque millium
florenorum et ultra.

fol.165v

Item resident in dicta preceptoria sex sacerdotes conventuales,
quibus dantur pro competencia cuilibet viginti floreni Carolini, faciunt in somma florenos CXX   ff 120.

Multe preterea imposiciones et gravamina sibi imponuntur a duce
Geldrie et ab officialibus suis, que singulis annis excedunt summam
centum florenorum   ff 100.

[a]Residuum exponitur pro expenssis et allimentatione domus, pro
salario et mercede servitorum, pro reparatione edificiorum et pro
hospitibus continue advenientibus, adeo quod interdum reditus non
suficiunt.[a]

Deposicio testium.

Pro verificatione et certitudine supradicte deposicionis habenda dicti domini visitatores examinarunt et interogarunt religiossos fratrem Anthonium de Kotte et fratrem Joachinum de Spoelde, qui de omnibus supradictis cognitionem et noticiam certam habebant, a quibus particulariter et separatim intelecxerunt sic esse prout supra dictum est, et hoc ᵃaffirmarunt medianteᵃ solemni iuramento ᵃtacta cruce more ordinisᵃ.

Situs preceptorie.

Domus ordinis est in loco campestri in ducatu Geldrie distans ab opido Hardwick per spacium duarum horarum; est satis ampla et bene edificata domus sive conventus cum suis curiis, ortis et silvis circumstantibus; habet ecclesiam conionctam ad honorem santi Johannis; et comendator est sub protectione baiulivatus Traiectensis et dicitur esse membrum, quia solvit annualem pencionem quadraginta florenorum.

Circa valores monettarum: scutiferi 32 Brebantini faciunt florenum aureum Rhenense; scutiferi XXVIII faciunt florenum Philipinum; scutiferi XXV faciunt florenum Emdense et scutiferi XXIIII faciunt florenum Carolinum Geldriense.

Venditur malterum siliginis pro floreno aureo et havene pro medio floreno.

ᵇHec omnia extracta fuerunt ab originalibus scripturis et auctenticis manu Johannis Haltren publici Notarii scriptis et per me Theodoricum Nolden publicum apostolica auctoritate Notarium visa, recognita et auctenticata fuerunt, in quorum fidem hic me manu propria subscripsi die 29 mensis Octobris anno 1542.

Theodoricus Nolden a Creveltᵇ

ᵃ *is missing in RA Gelderland.* ᵇ *in a different hand.*

fol.166r
Aldemvater preceptoria dependens a baiulivatu Traiectenssiᵃ

Anno Domini MVcXXXX die XX Augusti dicti domini visitatores in sua comissione procedentes visitarunt domum sive preceptoriam de Aldemvater in dominio Traiectensi, et pro vera informatione haben-

da vocari fecerunt fratrem Gerardum de Amesfordia ibidem comendatorem, cui comisserunt quod omnes libros et scripturas suas circa
informationes redituum et emollumentorum dicte domus coram ipsis
presentaret. Tandem dato iuramento de veritate declaranda circa
requisita iuravit et dicxit eum esse paratum puram et meram veritatem exponere et sic ex supradicta registris et libris sequentes informationes extracte sunt, presente notario stipullante.

Sequuntur reditus.

Primo hec domus habet diversos minutos census provenientes ex domibus, domistadiis, pomeriis, hortis et terris intra et extra opidum de
Aldemvater, ex quibus omnibus in somma habet singulis annis florenos quadraginta aureos   ff 40.

Item habet in quadam villa nomine Papemckop quindecem vel
sexdecim iugera terre cum manso, ex quibus habet singulis annis
quatuordecim florenos aureos   ff 14.

Item habet in eadem villa aliam curiam ex qua habet alios quatuordecim florenos   ff 14.

Item habet partem unius curie in Heckendorff, sed his temporibus
nihil recipit quia pendet lis et diferencia coram iudicio comitatus
Ollandie.

Item habet viginti et duo iugera prati et pascui que comendator
reservat pro vaccis et bestiis suis, sed quando loquarentur habere
posset ex quolibet iugero duos florenos Filipenses vel aureos; essent in
somma florenis quadraginta quatuor   ff 44.

Item habet quatuordecim iugera pascuorum prope pagum Lin-
schotten et pro quolibet iugero recipit duos florenos aureos, essent in
somma floreni viginti et octo   ff 28.

Item habet in eodem loco quinque iugera cum dimidio pro quibus
recipit annuatim   ff 12.

Item habet ibidem alia quatuor iugera que locantur pro octo florenis   ff 8.

Item habet alia octo iugera que locantur singulis annis pro decem
et septem florenis   ff 17.

Item habet alia quatuor iugera que locantur annuatim pro XII
florenis   ff 12.

Item habet alia sexdecim iugera que locantur pro quadraginta
florenis   ff 40.
fol.166v

Habet preterea caseos, butirum et cetera lactitinia pro servicio
domus et interdum ex eis vendit pro decem florenis singulis annis vel
circa   ff 10.

Sequuntur onera necesaria.

Solvit singulis annis baiulivo Traiectensi pro pensione XXIIII florenos aureos   ff 24.

Item solvit pro intertenendis ageribus et pro molendinis
extra[h]entibus aquam a pocessionibus et pro aliis similibus oneribus
annuatim XV florenos aureos   ff 15.

Item dat capellano adiuvanti singulis annis quinque florenos pro
salario   ff 5.

Residuum exponit pro allimentatione domus in carnibus, pissibus,
sale et aliis similibus, et pro reparatione edificiorum et ecclesie, pro
advenientibus hospitibus et pro intertenenda domo in omnibus rebus
necessariis.

Interogatus an sint alii reditus quam supradicti et si ab ecclesia
aliquid recipit, respondit non.

Deposicio testium.

Pro verificatione et certitudine supradicte deposicionis habenda dicti
domini visitatores examinarunt et interogarunt probos viros Theodoricum Sassen et Godfridum Washman, qui de omnibus supradictis
cognitionem et noticiam certam habebant, quia singulis annis a comendatore computum recipiunt pro parte domini baiulivi, a quibus
particulariter et separatim intelecxerunt sic esse prout supra dictum
est, et hoc affirmarunt mediante solemni iuramento super sacris santis
evangeliis.

Domus ordinis est in opido dicto Aldemvater in dominio Traiectensi
distans a dicta civitate per spacium quatuor horarum. Habet ecclesiam conionctam et baiulivus Traiectensis eligit comendatorem,
sibi reservata pencione quadraginta florenorum.

Valores et cursus monettarum concordant cum supradicta visitatione.
Etiam concordant mensure et precia furmentorum. Vina non crescunt.

[b]Hec omnia extracta fuerunt ab originalibus scripturis et auctenticis manu Johannis Haltren publici Notarii scriptis et per me Theodoricum Nolden publicum apostolica auctoritate Notarium visa,
recognita et auctenticata fuerunt, in quorum fidem hic me manu
propria subscripsi die 29 mensis Octobris anno 1542.
Theodoricus Nolden a Crevelt[b]

fol.167r
Werder preceptoria dependens a baiulivatu Traiectenssi[a]

Anno Domini MVcXXXX die XVII Augusti dicti domini visitatores
in sua comissione procedentes visitarunt domum sive preceptoriam
ordinis santi Johannis de Werder et pro vera informatione habenda
vocari fecerunt religiossum fratrem Guliermum de Winbergen comendatorem in Werder et coadiutorem baiulivatus Traiectenssis, coram quo fuit lecta bulla visitationis; deinde sibi comisserunt et
inioncxerunt quod omnes libros et scripturas suas circa informationes
redituum et emollumentorum coram ipsis presentaret; tandem dato
sibi iuramento de veritate declaranda circa requisita, iuravit et dicxit
eum esse paratum puram et meram veritatem exponere, et sic ex
supradictis registris et libris sequentes informationes extracte sunt.

Habet hec domus ecclesiam perochialem sibi anexam, que tamen
non est subposita baiulivo Traiectensi sed preposito sante Marie; tamen comendator emollumenta recipit et habet in reditibus et terrarum pensionibus florenos XII et scutiferos XII   ff 12 s 12.
    Habet eciam aliquas decimas quas comunibus annis dat pro XI
florenis   ff 11.
    Sunt eciam alique oblationes minime que quasi non suficiunt pro
illuminariis.
    Habet preterea ex reditibus preceptorie singulis annis in pencione
florenos XXX   ff 30.
    Item habet circumcirca domum centum et undecim iugera agro-
rum, quorum maior pars, videlicet iugera centum et quinque, ipse
comendator propriis expenssis cultivare facit et declarare non posset
qualem proventum ex ipsis accipiat. Tamen ad comunem extimationem habere potest circa duos florenos aureos pro quolibet iugero,
essent in somma ducentum et decem floreni aurei singulis annis vel
circa   ff 210.
    Item habet ex aliis sex iugeribus locatis pro decem et septem flo-
renis aureis   ff 17.
    Item habet plura prata et pascua circa domum in quibus tenet et
passit vacas et equas suas; sed quia talis proventus evenit ex propria
industria, sibi videtur quod in continuis reditibus computari non debet, quia plus habet ex dicta industria quam ex certis reditibus, et pro
coroboratione verborum suorum dicxit quod alii duo sacerdotes fuerunt provisi de hac preceptoria et propter exiguos reditus coacti fuerunt ipsam restituere baiulivo Traiectensi; nunc autem ipsam pro
bona administracione *[fol.167v]* non tantummodo se sustentat sed
domum edificat et omnia bona restaurat et bonificat.

Sequuntur onera.

Tenetur dare baiulivo Traiectensi pro pencione singulis annis triginta florenos quos postquam ellectus fuit coadiutor ex gracia sibi remissit
ff 30.

Item exponit racione molendinorum aquam extra[h]encium, racione agerorum et reparationum continue inondationis singulis annis viginti et duos florenos et scutiferos XVII ff 22 s 17.

Tenetur habere sacerdotem cui dat singulis annis sex florenos aureos ff 6.

Residuum exponit pro servicio et allimentatione domus, pro fabrica et pro reparatione edificiorum. Accidit eciam quod plures veniunt hospites quia hec domus est in recta via eundi a Traiecto in Ollandiam et ideo maxime gravatur.

Circa generales interogationes an sint alii reditus et cetera respondidit quod non.

Deposicio testium.

Pro verificatione et certitudine supradicte deposicionis habenda dicti domini visitatores examinarunt et interogarunt providos viros Theodoricum de Sassen et Godfridum Vashman qui de omnibus supradictis cognitionem et noticiam certam habebant, quia singulis annis pro parte domini baiulivi computum de comendatore accipiunt, a quibus particulariter et separatim intelecxerunt sic esse prout supra dictum est et hoc affirmarunt mediante solemni iuramento super sacrosantis Dei evangeliis.

Scitus preceptorie.

Domus ordinis est in loco campestri inter Ollandiam et civitatem Traiectensem. Est satis bene edificata domus et restaurata per presentem comendatorem; non multum distat ab opido Leiden^c; habet dicta domus duas eclesias videlicet perochialem et aliam capellam conionctam cum preceptoria; et comendator eligitur per baiulivum Traiectensem.

^bHec omnia extracta fuerunt ab originalibus scripturis et auctenticis manu Johannis Haltren publici Notarii scriptis et per me Theodoricum Nolden publicum apostolica auctoritate Notarium visa, recognita et auctenticata fuerunt, in quorum fidem hic me manu propria subscripsi die 29 mensis Octobris anno domini 1542.

Theodoricus Nolden a Crevelt[b]

---

[a] *the preceptories Oudewater and Werder are missing in RA Gelderland.* [b] *in a different hand.* [c] *in the margin corrected from* Laida.

fol.168r
Hermelen preceptoria dependens a baiulivatu Traiectensi

Anno Domini MVcXXXX die XVIII Augusti dicti domini visitatores in sua comissione procedentes visitarunt domum [a]sive preceptoriam[a] de Hermelen ordinis santi Johannis et pro vera informatione habenda vocari fecerunt providum virum Jacobum Stelle redituarium preceptorie Traiectensis et administratorem dicte domus, quia comendator ex nimia senectute puerescit, cui redituario comisserunt [a]et inioncxerunt[a] quod omnes libros et scripturas suas circa informationes redituum et emollumentorum coram ipsis presentaret; tandem dato sibi iuramento de veritate declaranda circa requisita iuravit et dicxit eum esse paratum puram et meram veritatem exponere; et sic ex supradictis registris et libris sequentes informationes extracte sunt.

Sequuntur reditus.

Habet hec domus in diversis locis septuaginta et novem iugera terre, que comendator propriis expenssis cultivare facit, et calcullatis fructibus in peccuniis secundum communem extimationem habet de quolibet iugero duos florenos aureos, in somma   ff 158.
    Item habet ecclesiam perochialem, que habet suos census divisos a preceptoria, et primo habet quandam peciam terre, ex qua annuatim proveniunt pro locatione   ff 4 s 10.
    Item habet in diversis aliis minutis reditibus in somma florenos XII cum dimidio   ff 12 т *[12.5]*.
    Item de alia pecia terre recipit singulis annis novem florenos et X scutiferos   ff 9 s 10.
    Item habet ex oblationibus ecclesie annuatim circa triginta et sex florenos   ff 36.
    Circa generales interogationes an habeat alios reditus vel proventus, dicxit quod non.

Sequuntur onera.

Tenetur comendator dare in annuali censu sex florenos aureos cuidam seculari, qui redimi possent pro centum florenis aureis et comendator impignoravit   ff 6.

Item dat alios sex florenos Carolinos pro annuali censu alio seculari, qui eciam sunt redimibiles pro centum florenis Carolinis, quos comendator impignoravit   ff 6.

Item dat alios sex florenos Carolinos pro annuali censu cuidam seculari, qui eciam sunt redimibiles pro centum florenis Carolinis, quos comendator eciam impignoravit   ff 6.

Item dat quatuor florenos Carolinos pro annuali censu alio seculari, qui eciam sunt *[fol. 168v]* redimibiles pro septuaginta florenis Carolinis, quos comendator impignoravit   ff 4.

Item solvit florenos tres Carolinos impignoratos pro quinquaginta florenis   ff 3.

Item solvit alios tres florenos eciam impignoratos pro quinquaginta florenis   ff 3.

Item habet alium sacerdotem pro servicio ecclesie, quia comendator est decrepitus, et dat pro salario et expenssis suis singulis annis viginti et quatuor florenos   ff 24.

Item dat baiulivo pro pensione singulis annis viginti et quinque aureos florenos   ff 25.

Item exponit pro reparatione agerorum et aqueductium ultra tredecim florenos   ff 13.

Residuum exponit pro allimentatione domus, pro restauratione edeficiorum et pro hospitibus et pauperibus advenientibus et pro sustentacione senectutis comendatoris et pro solvendis imposicionibus et gravaminibus inpositis et que continue imponuntur per officiales imperatoris quasi incomportabiles.

Deposicio testium.

Pro verificatione et certitudine supradicte deposicionis habenda dicti domini visitatores examinarunt et interrogarunt dominum baiulivum Traiectensem ibidem presentem et Theodoricum Sassen ac Godefridum Washman, qui de omnibus predictis cognitionem et noticiam certam habebant, a quibus particulariter et separatim intelecxerunt sic esse prout supra dictum est ^aet hoc affirmarunt^a mediante solemni^a iuramento.

Situs preceptorie.

Domus ordinis est in territorio Traiectensi distans a dicta civitate per spacium quatuor horarum et habet ecclesiam perochialem et principalem illius loci, pro servicio cuius sunt duo sacerdotes. Comendator elligitur per baiulivum Traiectensem, cui singulis annis dantur viginti et quinque floreni pro pencione ut supra dictum est.

Scutiferi XXXII faciunt florenum aureum; scutiferi XXVI faciunt florenum Filipense et XXIIII faciunt florenum Carolinum.

bcHec omnia extracta fuerunt ab originalibus scripturis et auctenticis manu Johannis Haltren publici Notarii scriptis et per me Theodoricum Nolden publicum apostolica auctoritate Notarium visa, recognita et auctenticata fuerunt, in quorum fidem hic me manu propria subscripsi die 29 mensis Octobris anno 1542.
Theodericus Nolden a Creveltbc

ᵃ *is missing in RA Gelderland.* ᵇ *in a different hand.* ᶜ *summarized in RA Gelderland.*

fol.169r Wemellingen preceptoria in Zellandia dependens a baiulivatu Traiectenssiᵃ

Anno Domini MVcXXXX die XVIII Iunii dicti domini visitatores suam primam visitationem incipientes visitarunt domum sive preceptoriam ordinis santi Johannis de Wemlingen in Zellandia et pro vera informatione habenda vocari fecerunt religiossum comendatorum et fratrem Simeonem de Confluencia, coram quo fuit lecta bulla visitationis, deinde sibi comisserunt et inioncxerunt quod omnes libros et scripturas suas circa informationes redituum et emollumentorum coram ipsis presentaret; tandem dato sibi iuramento de veritate declaranda circa requisita, iuravit et dicxit eum esse paratum puram et meram veritatem exponere, et sic ex registris sequentes informationes extracte sunt.

Sequuntur reditus.

Primo dicxit quod omnes reditus et proventus concistunt in agris et pocessionibus in quibus nascuntur et crescunt furmenta et alii fructus cum quibus alit domum. Numerus autem agrorum se extendit ad sommam centum et duodecim iugerum, quorum septuaginta et sex arendavit rusticis et collonis, et de illis recipit singulis annis duos florenos Carolinos pro quolibet iugero; essent in somma CLII florenos   ff 152.

Preterea ipse comendator propriis expenssis cultivare facit triginta et sex iugera terre ex quibus comunibus annis recipit circa centum mensuras furmenti, tritici et siliginis, que mensura vocatur achtoill et est fere pondus unius hominis. Venditur comunibus annis mensura pro uno floreno aureo vel circa   ff 100.

Item colit alia tria iugera terre in quibus seminat ordeum et havenam pro facienda cervisia et pro nutriendis animalibus, ad quod ex eis nihil venditur.

Habet preterea pascua et prata pro nutriendis vaccis, ex quibus recipit butirum et caseos pro servicio domus; nutrit eciam equos pro agricultura.

Super generalibus interogatus an sint alii reditus respondidit quod non.

Interogatus si ab ecclesia emollumenta recipit, dicxit quod non quia solum est capella.

Sequuntur onera.

Tenetur dare domino baiulivo Traiectenssi pro annuali pensione triginta et sex florenos aureos, de quibus petit si posibile esset relevari et absolvi   ff 36.
fol.169v

Item exponit pro reficiendis et intertenendis ageribus circumcirca insulam ne absorbeatur a mari prout interdum accidit, singulis annis pro parte sua LVI florenos Carolinos   ff 56.

Item dat singulis annis pro censu cuidam civi in Gosa florenos decem et octo Carolinos quos impignoravit comendator predecessor suus sub ti[tu]lo redemptionis   ff 18.

Residuum exponit pro allimentatione domus, pro restauratione edificiorum et pro ecclesia ac aliis rebus necessariis, pro servitoribus et ancilis.

Deposicio testium.

Pro verificatione et certitudine supradicte deposicionis habenda dicti domini visitatores examinarunt et interogarunt honestos viros magistrum Jacobum Cornelii plebanum in Wemlingen, et Oliverium Wolvortis scultetum predicti pagi, qui de omnibus supradictis cognitionem et noticiam certam habebant, a quibus particulariter et separatim intelecxerunt sic esse prout supra dictum est, mediante iuramento.

Situs preceptorie.

Domus ordinis est prope pagum quod dicitur Wemlingen in provincia Zellandie et in quadam insulla ubi est opidum principale nomine Tregoz *[=ter Goes]*, distans ab opido de Midelburg per spacium quatuor horarum navigationis. Dicta insulla est circumdata periculosso mari; nam bis in die crescit in tantum quod est multo altior insulla et nisi repararetur cum ageribus, totam insullam innondaret et absorberet; tota illa regio est divisa in quindecim insulis, quarum octo sunt principales, et multa damna et periculla patiuntur ex inundationibus aquarum, et nisi maximis expenssis et laboribus construerent agera circumcirca insullas, iam omnes perdite essent, quia non obstantibus ageribus iam alie insulle perdite sunt, quorum vestigia et sommitates turrium iterum aparent; et de anno 1532 tres insulle perdite sunt et omnes insullarum habitatores, vel sunt submerssi, vel navibus salvati, omnibus suis bonis spoliati, que omnia per dictos visitatores personaliter vissa fuerunt.
[in the left margin:] NB

[b]Hec omnia extracta fuerunt ab originalibus scripturis et auctenticis manu Johannis Haltren publici Notarii scriptis et per me Theodoricum Nolden publicum apostolica auctoritate Notarium visa, recognita et auctenticata fuerunt, in quorum fidem hic me manu propria subscripsi die 29 mensis Octobris anno domini 1542.
  Theodoricus Nolden a Crevelt[b]

---

  [a] *the preceptory of Wemeldinge is missing in RA Gelderland.* [b] *in a different hand.*

[fol.170r] Middelbug preceptoria in Zellandia dependens a baiulivatu Traiectensi

Anno Domini MVcXXXX die XIX Iunii dicti domini visitatores in sua comissione procedentes visitarunt domum ordinis santi Johannis in civitate Midelburg et pro vera informatione habenda vocari fecerunt religiossum fratrem Johannem de Eick comendatorem, coram quo fuit lecta bulla visitationis; deinde sibi commisserunt et inioncxerunt quod omnes libros et scripturas suas circa informationes redituum et emollumentorum coram ipsis presentaret; tandem dato sibi iuramento de veritate declaranda circa requisita iuravit et dicxit eum esse paratum puram et meram veritatem exponere; et sic ex supradictis registris et libris sequentes informationes extracte sunt.

Sequuntur reditus.

Primo habet ªhec preceptoriaª quandam domum in civitate Middelburg que domus dicitur Browrie, que locatur singulis annis pro quinquaginta et quatuor florenis Carolinis   ff 54.

Item habet quendam hortum prope menia civitatis, in quo conveniunt cives sagittarii, et dant singulis annis pro locatione duodecim
florenos Carolinos   ff 12.

Item habet pomerium intus civitatem, ex cuius fructibus recipit
annuatim circa viginti ªvel viginti etª quinque florenos Carolinos, interdum plus et minus   ff 25.

Item habet tres parvas domos prope cimiterium, ex quibus recipit
annuatim   ff 17.

Item habet in minutis censibus ex conventu sororum et ex quibusdam domibus in civitate in somma circa duos florenos Carolinos
singulis annis   ff 2.

Item habet ex alio pomerio sive orto conioncto cum illo ubi stant
sagitarii   ff 24.

Item habet quindecim iugera terre prope civitatem, que locantur
singulis annis pro quinquaginta et duobus florenis Carolinis   ff 52.

Item habet ex oblationibus ecclesie fere tantum quantum exponit
pro illuminaribus.

Super generalibus interogatus an sint alii reditus vel proventus,
dicxit quod non.

Sequuntur onera.

Tenetur solvere singulis annis ex parte domus pro reficiendis et intertenendis ageribus circumcirca insulam pro defencione inundationis
florenos **XXIIII** Carolinos   ff 24.
fol.170v

Item tenebatur dare baiulivo Traiectensi annualem pencionem viginti florenorum, sed attenta paupertate domus ex gracia singulari
hanc pencionem remissit.

Item tenetur comendator omni hebdemoda legere tres missas; et
quia interdum est aliis negociis occupatus vel infirmus, alium sacerdotem admitit.

Residuum exponit pro allimentatione domus, pro salario unius
servitoris et ancile, pro reparatione edificiorum et pro aliis rebus necessariis; accidit eciam quod interdum veniunt hospites et cives, pro
quibus necessarium est emere vinum, quod caro precio venditur, quia
in illa regione non nascitur.

Deposicio testium.

Pro verificatione et certitudine supradicte deposicionis habenda dicti domini visitatores examinarunt ᵃet interrogaruntᵃ honorabiles dominos Gulliermum de Malenstein et Martinum de Adriani ecclesiarum collegiarum canonicos et comendatoris intrinsecos, qui de omnibus supradictis cognitionem et noticiam certamᵃ habebant, a quibus particulariter et separatim intelecxerunt sic esse prout supra dictum est et hoc affirmarunt in eorum concientia omni suspicione carentes.

Situs preceptorie.

Domus ordinis est in civitate principali totius regionis Zellandie, que dicitur Middelburg, et est prope menia in loco satis ameno cum suis hortis et aliis rebus necessariis. Habet parvam ecclesiam conionctam ad honorem santi Johannis, sed non est perochia. Hec civitas est in insulla maiori Zellandie, sed eciam multa damna patitur ex inundationibus aquarum et in reficiendis ageribus.

Valores et cursus monettarum concordant cum aliis visitationibus et eciam mensure et precia furmentorum, que furmenta portantur a regno Dacie et Norvegie.

ᵇHec omnia extracta fuerunt ab originalibus scripturis et auctenticis manu Johannis Haltren publici Notarii scriptis et per me Theodoricum Nolden publicum apostolica auctoritate Notarium visa, recognita et auctenticata fuerunt, in quorum fidem hic me manu propria subscripsi die 29 Octobris anno 1542.
Theodoricus Nolden a Creveltᵇ

fol.171r, changed later into 170 in a different hand
Chercherff preceptoria virginum in Zellandia

Anno Domini MVcXXXX die XX Iunii dicti domini visitatores in sua comissione procedentes visitarunt domum ordinis ᵃsanti Johannisᵃ in Chercherff, in qua resident virgines moniales dicti ordinis, et pro vera informatione habenda vocari fecerunt venerabilem dominam sororem Sottam Wilhelmi priorissam necnon Guliermam Petri procuratricem, quibus comisserunt ᵃet inioncxeruntᵃ, quod omnes libros et scripturas suas circa informationes redituum et emollumentorum dicte domus coram ipsis presentarent; tandem dato sibi iuramento de veritate declaranda circa requirenda posita manu super crucem more ordinis iurarunt et dicxerunt eas esse paratas puram et meram veritatem exponere, quod fecerunt prout sequitur.

Sequuntur reditus.

Habet hec domus circumcirca preceptoriam in diversis locis ducentum et sexdecim iugera terre, quorum in arendam nomine locationis dimisserunt iugera centum et sexdecim, ex quibus singulis annis recipiunt quatuor centum et quinquaginta florenos Carrolinos; et isti agri sunt remotiores a domo situati ff 450.

Reliqua centum iugera viciniora propriis expenssis cultivare faciunt et recipiunt comunibus annis circa ducentum et quinquaginta mensuras tritici M 250.

Item habent in havena ex dictis agris circa centum et quadraginta mensuras M 140.

Item habent in ordeo ex dictis agris circa centum et quadraginta mensuras M 140.

Item habent ex dictis agris fabas, pissa et alia legumina et canapam et linum, que omnia consumuntur in domo pro coquina et bestiis et nichil venditur.

Item singulis annis vendunt boves pingues pro centum florenis Carolinis ff 100.

Item vendunt semina raparum cum quibus conficitur oleum pro LXXX florenis Carolinis ff 80.

Item habent silvam novem iugerum, in qua accipiunt ligna pro servicio domus et coquine.

Ex ecclesia emollumenta non habent nec alios reditus sive proventus, salvo quod finitis divinis officiis atque orationibus manuum honesto muliebri labore aliquid interdum questuant, unde comodius se sustentent et vestiant. Alia bona non habent.

[fol.171v] Sequuntur onera.

Tenetur dare comendatori Traiectensi pro annuali pencione XX florenos aureos ff 20.

Item dant duobus sacerdotibus ordinis pro salario XXXX florenos Carolinos ff 40.

Item habent plures servitores et ancilas, quibus dant pro eorum salario ff 173.

Item tempore laboris accipiunt mercenarios, quibus dant annuatim ff 50.

Item dant ecclesie perochiali in Soutenlande in censu redimibili annuatim   ff 9.

Item dant cuidam mulieri pro denariis expositis in reparatione agerorum   ff 24.

Item coguntur dare terciam partem omnium redituum pro reparatione agerorum, que tercia pars tacxatur pro trecentum florenis Carolinis singulis annis   ff 300.

Item solvunt pro continuis exactionibus singulis annis XXIIII florenos Carolinos   ff 24.

Item dant pro reconocensia nemoris ᵃsive silveᵃ annuatim tres florenos   ff 3.

Residuum exponitur pro allimentatione domus; nam continue esse debent duodecim sorores cum priorissa, quibus antiquo tempore dare solebant pro competencia in peccuniis duo floreni pro qualibet sorore et quatuor floreni pro priorissa; sed nunc propter inopiam nihil habent et manuali labore se sustentant.

Sequitur deposicio testium.

Pro verificatione et certitudine supradicte deposicionis habenda dicti domini visitatores examinarunt ᵃet interrogaruntᵃ fratrem Jodocum de Coistveldia comendatorem sive capellanum dicte domus et fratrem N. sacellanum, qui de omnibus supradictis noticiam et cognitionem certam habent, a quibus particulariter et separatim intelecxerunt sic esse prout supra dictum est, et hoc affirmarunt mediante solemni iuramento.

Situs preceptorie.

Domus ordinis est in loco campestri distans a civitate de Midelborg per spacium trium horarum; in ea sunt virgines religiossissime viventes, portantes crucem in vestibus secularibus, et sunt sub protectione baiulivi Traiectensis.

Venditur mensura siliginis et tritici pro medio floreno aureo vel circa.

ᵇᶜHec omnia extracta fuerunt ab originalibus scripturis et auctenticis manu Johannis Haltren publici Notarii scriptis et per me Theodoricum Nolden publicum apostolica auctoritate Notarium visa, recognita et auctenticata fuerunt, in quorum fidem hic me manu propria subscripsi die 29 Octobris anno 1542.

Theodericus Nolden a Creveltᵇᶜ

fol.172r, changed later into 171 in a different hand
Seneick preceptoria in Frisia dependens a baiulivatu Traiectensi

Anno Domini MVcXXXX die ultima Iunii dicti domini visitatores in sua comissione procedentes visitarunt domum sive preceptoriam ordinis santi Johannis prope opidum de Senick et pro vera informatione habenda vocari fecerunt religiossum fratrem Reinerum Sibrandi comendatorem, coram quo fuit lecta bulla visitationis; deinde sibi inioncxerunt ᵃet comisseruntᵃ quod omnes libros et scripturas suas circa informationes redituum et emollumentorum dicte domus coram ipsis presentaret; tandem dato sibi iuramento de veritate declaranda circa requisita iuravit et dicxit eum esse paratum puram et meram veritatem exponere, et sic ex dictis registris et libris sequentes informationes extracte sunt.

Sequuntur reditus.

Primo declaravit quod omnes reditus et proventus dicte preceptorie sunt in censibus agrorum, pratorum et pascuorum circumcirca domum et in perochiis et pagis circumstantibus, quorum nomina inferius specificentur, tamen dicxit quod numerum agrorum particulariter declarare non potest, quia in registris et libris non specificatur, sed pleraque ipsorum agrorum et pascuorum sunt fossatis et terminis sive signis distincta et separata ab aliorum pocessionibus.

Habet in quadam villa nomineᵃ Isbrachten prata et pascua que diversis personis locantur pro annuali censu centum et septuaginta quatuor florenorum aureorum ff 174.

Item in alia villa nomine Terns sunt prata et pascua que diversis personis locantur pro annuali censu centum et viginti trium florenorum aureorum ff 123.

Item in alia villa que dicitur Gouten sunt prata et pascua que diversis personis loquantur pro annuali censu centum et quadraginta florenorum aureorum ff 140.

Item in alia villa dicta Loengen sunt prata et pascua que diversis personis locantur pro annuali censu quinquaginta et octo florenorum aureorum ff 58.

Item ex alia villa dicta Tralinger habet ex locatione pratorum et pascuorum singulis annis a diversis personis decem et octo florenos aureos Renenses ff 18.

fol.172v

Item in alia villa dicta In der Ilst sunt pascua et prata que locantur diversis personis pro annuali censu ᵃsive solutioneᵃ tredecim florenorum aureorum Rhenencium ff 13.

Item in alia[a] villa dicta[a] Dersum sunt pascua et prata que locantur
[a]singulis annis[a] pro [a]censu sive[a] solutione octo florenorum aureorum
Rhenensium   ff 8.

Item prope opidum de Sneick sunt prata et pascua que locantur
singulis annis diversis personis pro solutione quinquaginta et septem
florenorum aureorum   ff 57.

Item habet quedam prata et pascua circumcirca preceptoriam que
servantur pro vaccis et bestiis domus, quia continue habent circa
triginta vaccas et cum earum fructibus sustentant domum cum caseis
et butiro ac aliis lacticiniis.

Dicxit preterea quod habent undecim ecclesias perochiales que
administrantur per fratres conventuales, ex quibus domus nullum
habet emollumentum, nisi quod comendator post obitum pastorum
capit spolia in usum domus, que extimare non potest, quia interdum
sacerdotes contracxerunt debita ultra quam comperiatur in spoliis.

[c]Super generalibus interogatus an sint alii reditus vel proventus et
an habeant aliqua furmenta, an ab ecclesia emollumenta recipiat,
respondidit quod nihil aliud habet nisi id quod superius specificatum
est et quod oblationes ecclesie his temporibus vix suficiant pro illuminaribus ordinariis.[c]

Sequuntur onera.

Primo tenentur singulis annis dare et solvere pro pensione domini
baiulivi Traiectensis quinquaginta florenos aureos Rhenensses ff 50.

Item cogitur comendator singulis annis solvere imposiciones et
exactiones per officiales imperatoris impositas nullo habito respectu
previlegiis [a]vel exemptionibus[a] ordinis, que gravamina sunt incom-
portabilia, unde requirit sublevari.

Residuum exponitur pro allimentatione domus, in qua continue
resident octo vel novem sacerdotes ordinis exceptis aliis advenientibus; habent eciam plures servitores et ancilas pro campo et pro bestiis; coguntur emere omnia furmenta [fol.173r, changed later into 172 in
a different hand] pro pane et pro conficienda cervisia, qae furmenta ex
Dacia et Norvegia veuntur; consumuntur preterea plures peccunie in
carnibus, pissibus et similibus et in vestibus sacerdotum conventualium, in mercede et salario servitorum et ancilarum, que omnia si
bene calcullantur, excedunt summam redituum predictorum.

Patiuntur eciam inundationes aquarum et tenentur reparare et
restaurare agera pro quibus reficiendis plures peccunie consumuntur.
Accidit eciam interdum quod rompuntur agera et aque innundant et
submergent prata et pascua, et tunc tenentur defalcare annualem
censum ad iudicium et arbitrium proborum virorum.

Deposicio testium.

Pro verificatione et certitudine supradicte deposicionis habenda dicti domini visitatores examinarunt et interrogarunt religiossos fratres Petrum de Bolsiert, pastorem in Tralinger, et Sirderum de Dotenkemper, pastorem in Folsgaer, conventuales seniores in dicta preceptoria, qui de omnibus supradictis cognitionem et noticiam certam habebant, a quibus particulariter et separatim intelecxerunt sic esse prout supra dictum est, quia singulis annis computum a comendatore recipiunt, et hoc affirmarunt cum iuramento.

Situs preceptorie

Domus ordinis est in provincia Frisie non multum distans ab opido de Snick et est amplum monasterium [a](ut vulgo loquar)[a] in quo residet comendator cum octo sacerdotibus. Moriente comendatore conventuales elligunt alium comendatorem, quem baiulivus Traiectensis confirmat, [a]et sunt omnes sub protectione dicti baiulivi[a].

Valores monettarum concordant cum aliis visitationibus et sunt omnes floreni aurei Rhenenses, computando scutifferos XXXII pro floreno.

> [b]Hec omnia extracta fuerunt ab originalibus scripturis et auctenticis manu Johannis Haltren publici Notarii scriptis et per me Theodoricum Nolden publicum apostolica auctoritate Notarium visa, recognita et auctenticata fuerunt, in quorum fidem hic me manu propria subscripsi die 29 mensis Octobris anno 1542.
> Theodoricus Nolten a Crevelt[b]

---

[a] *is missing in RA Gelderland.* [b] *in a different hand.* [c] *summarized in RA Gelderland.*

C.4. VISITATION-ACTS OF 1594

The following visitation acts have been included in this edition for reasons of comparison only. They have been edited already in: 'Visitatie-verslagen van de Johanniter-kloosters in Nederland (1495, 1540, 1594)', medegedeeld door E.Wiersum en A.Le Cosquino de Bussy, in: *Bijdragen en Mededeelingen van het Historisch Genootschap (BMHG)*, 48, Utrecht 1927, pp.146-340, especially 262-339.

Probably a contemporaneous document existed in the central archives of the Order or the archives of the Priorate of Germany, but none has turned up, neither in the AOM nor in the GLA.[1] So the late 16th-century copy in the Rijksarchief (RA) at Arnhem, Gelderland, after which this edition has been made, is the only available one. It is to be found in the Inventory by J.Loeff, *Het archief der Commanderij van St Jan te Arnhem*, Rijksarchief in Gelderland, 's-Gravenhage 1950, no.523; written on sheets of paper of more or less the same size, c.33x22 cm., folded into four quires, three of which are kept together in the upper left corner of the recto-sides, without a jacket; the paper has no clear papermark. At the end the notary public has undersigned the text, which he probably had written himself as well. German and Latin passages have been written in a different hand by the same person, as was the custom at the time.

In dorso, in a hand of not much later date, has been written:

Acta visitationis et commissionis de A° 95 quibus accedunt diversae designationes omnium commendarum in Provintiis unitis sitarum et cathalogus bonorum ad eas spectantium.

Here the text of the *BMHG* has been followed with only a few exceptions, due to our own interpretation of some queer words in that older edition as compared with the copy in the RA Gelderland. These differences have been marked with notes. Without further marking the 'j' in Latin words has been changed into 'i' (e.g., iuramentum instead of juramentum). Some missing letters or words had already been added in brackets by the editors in the *BMHG* and have been placed in [ ] in this edition.

---

[1] *Only a report of the address to vice-chancellor and councellors of the province of Guelders, delivered during the visitation of Arnhem on 12 August 1594, erroneously dated 2 August 1594, is to be found in the GLA; see A.nr.135 above, dd. 4 November 1594. From the covering letter with this report it seems evident that the prioral headquarters at Heitersheim must have received a copy of the visitation acts as well.*

[fol. 1r]

Acta visitationis et commissionis de mandato dess hochwürdigen Fürsten unnd Herrn Philipsen Riedessell von Camberg, des ritterlichen St.Johans Ordens Meistern in Teütschlanden, Röm.Kays.Mayestäts Rath und General uber deroselben Armada des Thonawstroms etc., Durch die ehrwürdige wollgebornen gestrenge unnd edle Herrn Augustin Freyhern zu Mörssberg und Beffort, Commenthur zue St.Johan Pasell, Dorlessheim unnd Hemmendorff, und Herrn Arnolden von Lülstorff, Commenthurn zu Strunden, Burgk, Dussburg und Velden etc., ahn hochgemeltes Ordens Personen, Heüssern, Commenden undt Güthern in niderländischen Provincien, zu Arnheim, Neümagen, Utrecht undt Harlheim etc., gelegen, vorgenohmmen und verichtet anno etc. MDLXXXX4.

Dem Hochwürdigen Fürsten undt Herrn Herrn Philipsen Riedessel von Camberg, St.Johans Ordens Mäistern in Teütschlanden, Röm. Kays. Mayestäts Rath und General über deroselben Armada des Thonawstroms etc., unsserm gnedigen Fürsten und Herrn.

Hochwürdiger Fürst etc.

Ew.fürstl.Gn. seyen unsser underthänig Gehorsamb unnd willige Dienste jederzeit bevorahn.

Gnediger Fürst unnd Herr. Derselben sollen wir underthänig nit verhalten, welchermassen in afgelauffenem vierundtneünzigsten Jahren, under dato des letsten Maij, eine Ew.fr.Gn. Commission, auch dabey under selbigem Dato ein Vollgwaldt mit zugelegten sonderbahrer Instruction, alle mit Ew.fr.Gn. Insiegell uff offenem Spacio besigellt, praesentirt und zugestelt, inhaltende wir in Krafft solcher Befelchen uns gesambt uff ehest zu den Niderländischen Uniirten Provincien, und daselbsten zue des Ordens Haüssern, Commenden und Güthern zu Arnheim, Neümagen, Utrecht und Harlheim *[fol. 1v]* und dero angehörigen Membren solten ergeben, dero Gelegenheit und jetziger Zeit Gestalnussen umbstendtlichen zu visitiren, zu lustriren, die weldtliche Obrigkeiten eines jeden designirten Orths uff sonderliche mitgetheilte Credentz in Ew.fr.Gn. Nahmmen zu besuechen, alles fernern Inhalts derselben Commission, Gwaldts und Instruction hernegst mit den litt. A, B. und C wörttlichen inserirt. Solche Befelen wir sambt und sonder mit gebüerlicher Reverentz underthäniglichen auff und angenohmmen, auch denselben durchauss mit eüssersten Vermögen zu gelieben und nachzusetzen uns gantz underthänige Pflichtige und Schüldigen erkennet.

Demnach, alss ich Augustin Freyherr zue Mörssberg etc., in Julio vorgemeltes vierundneünzigsten Jahrs gehn Cöllen ankhommen, mein zugeordneten lieben Mitordensbruders Gelegenheit genahmett, haben wir unss am 14ten selbigen Monatts Julii in Gotts Nahmen uff die Räise begeben, also unse ahnbefohlene Geschefft und Werbung underthäniglichs moeglichs Fleiss verichten.

Und wann Ew.fr.Gn. gnediglichen befolehen alle unsse Verichtung in scriptis zu redigiren, darnach under unssern jedes Handtschrift und Insiegel relationsweise underthänigen zuzufüegen, – also haben wir alle vorgefallene Händel und Sachen, sambt wass wir nach Gelegenheit deroendts erfahren und inquireren konnen – dan die Zeiten und Mores bey schwebendem Kriegswesen nit erleiden wollen, das wir der Gepühr in omnibus ad speciem etwas genawer gehen mögen –, durch den ehrnhafften unnd wollgelehrten Adolphen Six von Eller etc. vors erst prothocolliren, demnach in diese Geschrifft bringen lassen, die wir zu Ende mit unssern jedes Handtschrifften und uffgedruckhten Insieglen bezeüget und befestiget. Und thuen selbige anjetzo Ew.fr.Gen. mit underthäniger Reverentz praesentieren, gleich samblichen pittende Ew.fr.Gen. geruhen solches in Gnaden anzunehmmen. Unsser gnediger Fürst und Herr, der Allmechtiger Gott wolle Sie in Irem fürstlichen Stande, uns zue gebieten, langwihrig gefristen. Geben zue Speyr im 1595ten Jahren am 24ten des Monats Aprillis.

Sein und pleiben Ew. fürstl.Gen. underthänig willige

Augustin Freyheer zu Morsperg, Ritter und Commenthur.
Arnold von Lulstorff, Ritter und Commenthur.

[fol.2r]   Volgt Ew. fürstlichen Gnade in Latin beschribene commissio visitationis mit A, diesses Inhalts.

Nos Philipus Riedesell a Camberg, Ordinis Sancti Johannis Hierosolymitany per Germaniam magister, universis et singulis presentes nostras litteras visuris et audituris salutem in Domino sempiternam. Ratio officii nostri, quod nobis incumbit et potissimum circa curam et regimen Alemaniae prioratus dicti Ordinis nostri versatur, deposcit adeoque nos monet, ut ad ea, per quae in genere quidem Ordini seu Religioni nostrae, in specie autem eiusdem domibus, rebus et personis sub dicti prioratus nostri limitibus constitutis consulitur, quanta maxima cura et vigilantia possumus animum nostrum intendamus.

Cum igitur post tot intestina et exitiosa bella in partibus Inferioris Germaniae per plurimos annos commota de statu quarundarum domorum sive commendarum ibidem sitarum valde dubitemus nec eundem commodiori quam diligenti visitationis via cognoscere possimus, nostrarum autem virium non sit, ut ipsi ad pretacta loca nos conferamus et dictam visitationem, quodquidem velimus, personaliter faciamus, idcirco iuxta Ordinis nostri laudatissima statuta alios eam ad rem aptos et idoneos eligere et deputare decrevimus. Confidentes itaque de fidei probitate, industria atque etiam in rebus agendis prudentia venerandorum atque religiosorum in Christo nobis charissimorum fratrum Augustini baronis de Mörssberg commendatarii in Passel et Hemmendorff etc., tum etiam Arnoldi de Lulsdorff commendatarii in Strunden, de nostra certa scientia – citra tamen revocationem quorumcunque procuratorum nostrorum ubilibet constitutorum – tenore presentium omnibus melioribus modo, via, iure, causa et forma, quibus melius, firmius et efficacius possumus et debemus, eosdem fratres Augustinum baronem de Mörssberg et Arnoldum de Lulsdorff etc., illum presentem, hunc vero absentem, omnes tamen hoc instrumentum acceptantes, fecimus creavimus et constituimus, facimus creamus constituimus solenniterque ordinamus et deputamus in nostros nostrique prioratus praeceptoriarum, domorum, personarum, rerum et bonorum, sub prioratus nostri Alemaniae limitibus, presertim vero in Germania Bassa sive Inferiori, constitutorum, visitatores, reformatores, correctores, commissarios, procuratores, syndicos ac nuncios nostros speciales et generales, ita quod specialitas generalitati non deroget nec econtra. Videlicet specialiter et expresse ad domos sive praeceptorias Ordinis nostri in Arnheim et Novimagio, item ad cameras nostras [fol.2v] magistrales in Traiecto et Harleim necnon omnia et singula dictarum domorum sive camerarum omnia et singula dictarum domorum sive camerarum priorialium membra et ab iisdem dependentes praeceptorias sive commendas exemptas et non exemptas accedendum atque earum [?] iuxta Ordinis nostri statuta visitationem faciendam diligenter et cum summa attentione visitandum perscrutandum inquirendum ac intelligendum verum valorem et legitimum dictarum nostrarum camerarum atque et commendarum, deductis oneribus et expensis ordinariis solitis et consuetis tantum. Ut autem huiusmodi verus et legitimus valor commodius, melius et perfectius habeatur, intelligatur et sciatur, dicti visitatores religiosos Ordinis nostri cuiuscunque status aut dignitatis sint, item vasallos, subditos, arrendatorios, cuiusvis conditionis fuerint, et alias quascunque personas tam ecclesiasticas quam seculares solenni sacramento et iuramento prius adactos cogant, astringant et compellant, ut manifestent, notificent, revelent et dicant verum et legitimum valorem dictarum camerarum, praeceptoriarum, domorum et beneficiorum membrorumque et pertinentiarum earundem, quod si facere renuerint aut in eorum depositionibus a veritate discesserint, per censuram ecclesiasticam, etiam via ordinaria, cogantur, si fuerint religiosi aut Religionis nostrae vasalli et contra eos tanquam periuros vel rebelles iuxta Ordinis nostri stabilimenta procedatur, si mandatis dictorum visitatorum, imo verius nostris, obedire recusaverint, invocato ad hoc etiam, si opus fuerit, brachio seculari vel ecclesiastico, ne Religio nostra ab alicuius contumatiam aut mendacium damnum patiatur et suis iuribus defraudetur. Modus etiam et forma sciendi et cognoscendi verum et legitimum valorem antedictum erit per locationes et arrendamenta, quae fiunt communibus annis, videlicet fertili, sterili et mediocri, super quo dicti visitatores et commissarii nostri habebunt notitiam et consulent et interrogabunt testes fidedignos, sacramento coa[c]tos, de quantitate pecuniarum, pro qua arrendamenta sunt facta in patria seu territorio praefatarum camerarum et praeceptoriarum tam in capite quam in suis membris, iuribus et pertinentiis tempore fertili, sterili et mediocri, et talis depositio in scriptis redigatur. Ex quibus quidem arrendamentorum depositionibus sumatur valor, qui erit medius inter fertilem et sterilem annum. Et quia forsitan hoc modo de aliquibus praeceptoriis et beneficiis huiusmodi liquidus et verus valor haberi non *[fol.3r]* posset vel quia testes non adessent, vel quia nunquam fuissent arrendata, expediens imo necesse erit, quod dicti commissarii nostri habeant veram et indubitatam notitiam a colonis, habitatoribus et vicinis dictarum commendarum et beneficiorum; ut puta de pecunia numerata proveniente ex censibus, pascuis et locationibus proprietatum Religionis, etiam de quantitate frumenti, ordei, speltae, siliginis et aliarum frugum, item et vini si in illa patria crescit, et aliorum quorumcunque fructuum, qui ex possessionibus dictarum praeceptoriarum proveniunt; similiter et pecudum et aliorum animalium, cuiusvis generis existant, et aliorum quorumcunque emolumentorum, quae secundum morem patriae in qualibet praeceptoria capi consueverunt; et pariformiter se informabunt de pretio dictarum frugum et fructuum ac animalium, pro quo tempore sterili prefata omnia vendi consueverunt, quod nos mediocre apellamus; quod quidem mediocritatis pretium pro vero ac iusto valore accipiatur et in scriptis redigatur, a quo expensae ordinariae, solitae et consuetae, prout superius expressum est, subtrahantur, et restans liquidum pretium remaneat.

Mandamus insuper atque committimus dictis visitatoribus et commissariis nostris, ut in qualibet camera, praeceptoria et domo atque membris praedictis et sub nostri magistratus limitibus constitutis faciant diligentem inquisitionem super vita et moribus tam commendatarii quam aliorum fratrum nostrorum, quocunque officio seu dignitate praefulgeant; et si aliquid absonum et ab honestate discrepans invenerint, authoritate et vice nostra corrigant, castigent et emendent, ac mores malos elim[in]ando, bonas inducant.

Similiter ecclesias et pia loca Ordinis nostri visitent, quando divina ibi tractentur, inquirant reliquias, porro iocalia[a] et ornamenta ecclesiarum et oratoriorum caeteramque suppellectilem div[in]o cultui dicatem *[fol.3v]* describant, et quae ad divinum cultum spectant, allimpleri [faciant]. In ipso quoque visitationis processu camerarum nostrarum et commendarum predictarum libros censuales, iurisdictiones, praeeminentias et privilegia, tam in capite quam in membris, notabunt; item onera, lites motas et pendentes. Res etiam Ordinis nostri occupatas, alienatas et deterioratas, quae vero reparandae fuerint, statim aut ad certum tempus reparari mandent et procurent, prout rei qualitas postulabit. Generaliter omnia et singula agant, exerceant et procurent, quae in huiusmodi visitatione et aliis premissis et circa ea necessaria fuerint, seu etiam quomodolibet oportuna, et quae nos faceremus et facere possemus si premissis omnibus et singulis personaliter interessemus, etiamsi talia forent, quod mandatum exigerent magis speciale quam presentibus est expressum. Damus quoque praefatis nostris visitatoribus, commissariis et procuratoribus authoritatem, facultatem et potestatem audiendi et cognoscendi et determinandi causas et lites, quae vertantur inter fratres Ordinis nostri in prefatis nostris cameris prioralibus[b] aliisque commendis visitandis degentibus, et illas per eorum sententias definitivas decidendi, quibus stetur acsi a nobis emanatae essent. Caeterum mandamus, et si opus fuerit, in vim verae obedientiae strictius iniungimus omnibus et singulis praeceptoribus, procuratoribus et fratribus infra limites nostri magistratus et prioratus constitutis ac beneficiorum nostrorum possessoribus exemtis et non exemptis, etiam vasallis et subditis nostris in supradictis beneficiis existentibus, sub sacramento fidelitatis et homagii, quo nobis, Ordini et Religioni nostrae sunt adstricti, ut dictis nostris visitatoribus commissariis et procuratoribus pareant, obediant et intendant, auxilium quoque et favorem prebeant in his, super quibus a dictis nostris visitatoribus et procuratoribus fuerint requisiti. Et ad hoc, ut huiusmodi visitatio et inquisitio suum debitum sortiatur effectum, volumus ut visitatio huiusmodi diligenter fiat et ad nos in scriptis manibus visitatorum nostrorum subsignatis et eorundem si-*[fol.4r]*gilis confirmatis remittatur, ut bonorum Ordinis nostri status cognoscatur et, quae fuerint convenientia, provideri possint. In quorum omnium et singulorum fidem et testimonium premissorum prioratus nostri sigillum presentibus est impressum. Datum ex castro nostro Heitterssheimiano ultima mensis Maij a° 1594.

---

[a] *the editors in BMHG p.267, note 1, read* jotalia *but do not understand it properly;* iocalia *means jewels.* [b] *BMHG p.268:* prioratibus.

Volgt jetzt des gemeinen Gewalts Inhalt, mit B.

Wir Philips Riedessell von Camberg, des ritterlichen St. Johan Ordens Meister in Teütschlanden etc., Röm. Kays. May. Rath und General uber deroselben Armada dess Thonawstroms, erpieten den würdigen wollgebornen und gestrengen unsern besonders lieben Augustin Freyherrn zue Mörsperg unnd Befortt, Commenthurn zue S^t.Johan Pasell, Darlissheim und Hemmendorff etc., und Arnolden von Lulstorff, Commenthurn zue Strunden, unsern günstigen Gruess. Und dabey zue wissen, demnach uns alss Mäistern ermeltes unssers Ordens in Teütschlanden unsers tragenden Ambts halben in allwege obligt und gepührt die fleissige und ernstliche Vorschung zue thuen, dass alle und jede unssers Ordens Balleyen, Commenthureyen und Heüsser, auch deroselben zugehörige Güther allenthalben under unsserm des teütschen Prioraths Limiten und Begrieff gelegen, in gutem Wesen, Ehren und Auffnehmen erhalten und vor Nachtheill, Schaden und Abgang verhüetet pleiben, – wir aber dessen besser nit dan durch eine ordentliche Visitation Wissens haben möegen, dass wir derowegen uns unsser zustehender Praeminentz und Gerechtsamt halben ein gebiehrliche Visitation vermittels Göttlicher Gnaden zu thuen endtschlossen, – und dieweill uns selbsten in der Persohn solche zu verichten vast unmöglich, Eüch beyde ahn unsser Statt hierzue und zue solchen Werckh verordnet haben, verordnen, constituiren und setzen Eüch auch hiemit und in Crafft diess Brieffs in bester und bestendigster Form, alss es von Rechtsgewonheit, auch unssers ritterlichen *[fol.4v]* Ordens Stabilimenten wegen immer beschehen soll, kan oder mag, zue unsern Visitatorn, Procuratorn und Gewaldtshabern, Eüch bey heilger Gehorsamb und den Pflichten, damit Ihr und Ewer jeder unssern Orden und unss zuegethaen und verwandt sein, befehlend und gepietent, dass Ir alssbalden, ohn langes Verziehen, und zue Ewer ehesten Gelegenheit zue nachgesezten und specificirten unssers Ordens und unsser Camer Magisträl-Häüsser unnd Commenthureyen, nemblich unnd zum ersten gehn Arnheim und Newmägen unnd dan gehn Utrecht und Harlheim, wie auch zue allen und jeden deren zugehörigen Glidern, Preceptoreyen und Heüssern Eüch verfügen, gepürende Visitation und Inquisition aller und jeder derselbigen und ihren jedes Gelegenheit in gäistlichen und weltlichen Sachen und Händlen des Hausshaltens, derselben Auff- und Abnehmens, Einkhomen und Gefällen, Schulden und Gegenschulden vor die Hant nehmmen, auch Notturfftlichen, nachdeme Ir die Sachen beschaffen findet, befehlet, schaffet, gebiettet unnd verbietet; auch sonsten gemeinlich und sonderlich alles unnd jedes handlet und thuet, das – zue Ehr, Nutz und Aufgang unssers Ordens unnd berürter Heüsser, auch Verrichtung einer rechtmessigen und bey unssern Orden gepreüchlichen Visitation – die gelegenheit unnd Notturft erforderen wirdt, aller Gestalt undt Mass wirselbs eigner Persohn zeügen thuen sollten und mögten.

Und was sich unssers Ordens Brauch und Stabilimenten nach zue solchen Visitationen zijmmen und gebühren thuet, auch von alter Herkhommen ist, damit Ihr auch diesen unsern Befelch desto stattlichen verichten und zue wahrer und bestendiger Erkändtnus und Erkündigung der Wahrheit und aller der Heüsser Gelegenheit und Notturfften destobass khomen mögen, – so geben wir Eüch hiemitt Gewaldt, Macht und Befelch, das Ir die Commenthur selbsten, auch alle andere Ordenspersohnen, so uff vorgeschriebenen Heüssern befunden, in gepiehrliche Pflicht uff ihr Creütz, nach Ordens Gebrauch, zu deme auch alle und jede der Heüsser Schaffner, Dienstverwalten, Ehehalten, Underthanen und Angehörigen, und wah von Nöthen, auch ausslendische frembde Persohnen [fol.5r] durch Mittell derselben Obrigkeit in Geliebte bey Trewen an rechten Ayds Statt oder selbs geschwohrnen Aide nehmen und empfangen möget und sollen auff alle und jede vorfahlene Sachen zu der Visitation gehörig inquiriren und fragen Eüch die lautter Warheit zue sagnen und was sie und iro jeder von der Haushaltung, Regiment, Einnehmen und Aussgeben, Zue und Abnehmmen der Haüsser Wissens tragen, zu eröffnen. Gebietendt und befehlent auch daruff benanten Commenthurn und andern Ordenspersohnen, so vorgeschriebener Massen hierunder ersuecht werden, bey heiliger Gehorsame, und den andern der Heüser Schaffenern, Dienstverwalten, Ehehalten, Angehören unnd Underthanen bey ihren Pflichten und Verwandtnussen, dass sye uff obbenanter unser verordneten Commissarien unnd Visitatorn Ersuechen, Inquirieren und Befragen gehorsamb seyndt die lautter Warheit zue sagen und zu eröffnen, und dass umb keinerley Sachen willen zu verschweigen noch zue underlassen, also lieb inen den Commenthurn und Ordenspersohnen seyen, die Pöen und Straffen in unssers Ordens Stabilimenten begrieffen und den andern unsser Ungnad und die Pöen der Ungehorsambe und dero Rechten zu vermeiden, ohn alle Widerrede und Geverde.

Und wass Ihr also in solcher Visitation vernehmen und erfahren und erkünden werden, das alles wollent eigentlichen beschreiben und unss demnach underscheidtlicher relationsweise in Geschriefften under Eüren Handtschrifften und Sigelen zukhommen lassen, darnach ferner haben zue richten und zu verordenen. Ahn deme allen thuet Ihr unssern Befelch unnd ernstliche Mäinung uns in Gnaden hinwiderumb gegen Eüch zu erkhennen. In Urkundt dieser Commission, die mit unssern zu Endt uffgetruckhten Secret bewarth unnd geben ist den letzten Tag Maii Anno 1594.

Verner volgt special Instruction, Befelch undt Gewalt mit C, dieses Inhalts.

Unser Philipsen St.Johan Ordens Meister in Teütschlanden special Instruction und Befelch, wessen sich unsser verordnete Commissarii unnd Visitatores, die würdige wollge-*[fol.5v]*bohrne und gestrenge unssere liebe besondere Augustin Freyherr zue Mörssberg undt Beffortt, Commenthur zue St.Johan Basell, Dorlissheim und Hemmendorff etc., und Arnold von Lulstorff, Commenthur zue Strunden etc., bey der Visitation beeder Heüsser Arnheim unnd Neümägen zu verhalten.

Demnach wir in Erfahrung gebracht, dass beide Stätte Arnheim und Neümägen mit itziger Administration unnd Bestellung unssers Ordens beider bey inen gelegene Heüsseren übell zuefrieden und vieleicht lieber einen ordenlichen Commenthurn, so ein Ritter und von Adell, dan Priester alda sehen möchten, so sollen unsser Visitatores, Commissarii undt Gewalthaber nit underlassen die Obrigkeit beederseiths Orthen persöhnlichen anzusprechen, denselben unssern Gruess undt alles Gutts, wie sichs dieser Orthen am besten gezimbt unnd inen unssern Commissarien Wissens sein wirdt, zu vermelten, und dan weiters vor- und anzubringen, dass uns nit weniger alss inen diese Administration missfählig und zuewider, und derowegen, dass solche vor diesser Zeit hett mögen geёndtert und gebessert werden, wünschen mögen, – dass aber biss anhehro keine Mutation erfolgt, seyen allerhandt Verhinderung und vornehmlichen die schwärliche und immerdar dieser Örther erregende Krieg; auch Philips von Rosenbach, der Commenthur selbsten, deme diesse Heüsser von unsserm Orden zue administriren ubergeben und anbefohlen, welcher aber die Administration derselben gleichwohl verlassen, jedoch vor diesser Zeit darvon niet allerdings abtretten und sye einem andern einrauhmen wollen. Wan aber vor einem Jahr, uff den damahlen gehaltenen Capitull, an inen Philipsen von Rosenbach solche Heüsser zue resigniren und dem Orden zue uberlassen alles Ernst begehrt worden, er daruff solche resignirt und ein solches alss baldt gehn Maltha berichtet, so zweifflen wir nit, wo nit albereith einem andern Ritterbruder solche Heüsser conferirt und verlihen, das doch solchs noch beschehen werde, wie wir dan zu geschehen an fleissiger Anmahnung diss Orths nicht ermanglen lassen wolten.

[fol.6r] Unnd sollen daruff unsere Commissarii sye die beede Stette von unsertwegen, auch vor sich selbsten, ansprechen und pitten, dass sy fürters, wie biss dahehro, unsern Orden und dessen bey ihnen gelegenen Heüssern günstig pleiben, biss uff andere Verordnung mit

jetziger derselben Administration Gedult tragen, auch alles unnach-
bahrlichen thadtlichen Eingrieffs sich inmittels enthalten wolten, und
beneben diesse gewisse Vertröstung thuen, dass ohn lange verzehen
ein anderer Commenthur verordnet werden solte, so des Adels, und
ohne Zweiffel also qualificirt sein werde, zue dem sie selbsten Gefallens haben und tragen werden.

Wass dan etliche unssers Ordenshausses zue Arnheim Erbgüether
belangen thuet, ob wir gleichwohl äigentlichen nit wissen, wie es damit eine Gelegenheit, ob und auss wass Ursachen, dessgleichen zu
wass Intent und Meinung solche von dem Rath daselbsten in Verbott
gelegt und verpachet worden; auch nit hoffen, dass hiedurch solche
unssern Orden gentzlichen entzogen und genohmen sein solten, – so
sollen mehrgedachte unser Commenthur bey dem Rath daselbsten
zue Arnheim ein solches vernehmen und dahin alles Fleisses hande-
len, wa ir, wie wir bericht werden, etliche specificirte Güeter arrestirt
und in Verbott gelegt, dass doch solche wider der Gepiehr relaxirt
und dess Arests entschlagen. Item da auch solche Güther verpachtet
und andern verlihen, dass entweder solche Verpachtung und Verly-
hung wider retractirt, oder wo solches nit zu erhalten, die Sachen
doch dahin gerichtet werden, alss wan solche Verpachtung vonn unssers Ordensweegen beschehen und ime derowegen inkünfftig der järlich Canon endtricht unnd gelieffert werde. Unnd weill nit woll
möglich uff alle und jede Fähl offtbesagte unssere Commissarios diss
Orths zue instruiren und inen Bevelch zue geben, so setzen wir es in
Ubrigen zue ihrer Discretion und deren beywohnenden Verstandt
und wohlen unss dabey getrösten, sie werden allem unsserm Orden
besorgenden Nachtheil vorzuekhommen weissen ahn irem möglichen
Fleiss, und was unsser Orden sy zum Besten verrichten khonten,
nichts underlassen. Dessen wir inen dan volkhommen Gewalt geben
unnd hiemit gegeben *[fol. 6v]* haben wollen in bester undt bestendigster Form, es von Rechts- oder Gewonheitwegen immer beschehen
solle, kan oder mag. Unnd da sie mehrers Gewaldts dan hierinn
begrieffen nottürfftig, den wöllen wir inen hiemit auch zugestelt haben. Wass sie dan von unssertwegen und unsserm Orden zu Guthen
handlen, schaffen und verrichten werden, dass wöllen wir ratum,
gratum, angenehm und vest halten, Geverde aussgeschlossen. Und
dessen zue Urkundt haben wir diese Instruction, Befelch und Gwalt
eignerhandt underschrieben undt mit unsserm Secret zue Ende ver-
wahren lassen. Geben den letzten Tag Maij Anno etc. 94 *[1594]*.

Philips Meister etc.

Neümägen.

Also am 16en vorgerürts Monaths Julii mit Gottes Hilff zue Neümägen ankhommen, und wiewoll wir unss erinnert, das dess Ordens Hauss daselbsten nur ein Membrum undt Gleidt, das Corpus aber zue Arnheim ist, und derowegen der Ordnung nach unss billig dahin zum ersten Zeitten ergeben und nachfolgens Neümägen besuechen sollen, so hatts doch die Reise, die sonst uff Arnheim den Rhein strombab mit etwas mer Gefahr geschüet, nit ander erleiden wollen, auch von wegen ein Ordenspriester Frater Heinrich von Rechen alss Administrator beeder Häüsser zue Arnheim unnd Neümägen, alda zue Neümägen in Residentz gesessen, darab wir der Gelegenheit uns etlichermassen mögen erkündigen, und aber sonsten zue Arnheim alss unbekante Fremblin keine Anweisung oder Nachrichtung gehaben können, derowegen und uffs ehrste zue Neümägen einstellen muessen.

Sontags den 17ten Julii.
Nachdem wir bey dem Magistrath der Statt Neümägen unssere Ankunfft vermelten lassen, seint selbiges Tags die sechs Herren Burgermeistere sambt iren Syndicis und Secretarien zue uns ins Ordenshauss gratulandi et salutandi gratia eingekehrt, von wegen Ew.fr.Gen. unss alss deroselben Abgesandten *[fol.7r]* mit ihrem Wein und aller Erpietung stattlichen verehret, die Mallzeit unnd alle gute Conversation bey unss genohmmen, mit der Gelegenheit wir inen sembtlichen Ew.fr.Gen. Credentzschreiben gepierlichermassen presentirt und dabey unssere auffhabende Werbungen kurtzlichen vermeldet, freündtlich piettende, sie unss zue irer bester Gelegenheit bey sich und ihren ahnsehenlichen löblichen Rathstande Audienz machen und alda unssere weitere Werbungen undt Geschefft günstlichen anhören wollen. Deruff sie zwaren gantz reverenter Ew.fr.Gen. Credentz zu Handen genohmmen und uns zu fehrner Audientz morgenstags den 18ten Julii die achte Stunde Vormittags bestimbt, mit Angelobnus, dass sie in iren gesessenen Rath die Credentz eröffnen und uns dernach alles unsres Vertragens und Werbens gehrn hören unnd vernehmmen wollen.

Montags den 18 Julii.
Do die sechs Herren Burgermeister sambt den gantzen Rathstande der löblichen Statt Neümägen ihn iren Zimmer ordentlichen gesessen, haben wir durch unsseren darzu uffgenohmmen Redner nachfolgendermassen vortragen lassen.
Es hetten Ew.fr.Gen. uns zu dem löblichen Magistrath etc. gnediglichen abgeferttiget etc., welche Ihren freundtlichen Gruss, gnedigen

Willen und alles Liebs ihnen sambt und anders theten erpieten. Und
dass Ew.fr.Gen. in Erfahrung gebracht, wie derselbigen löblichen
Magistrath und Gemeine mit jetziger Administration des Ordens-
haüsser und Güther zue Neümägen ufs Best nit seinen zuefriden,
undt filleicht lieber einen ordenlich Commenthuren, so ein Ritter
und des Adels, dan Priestere alda sehen möchten etc. So wehre
Ew.fr.Gen. nit weniger alss inen dise Administration missfellig und
zuwider und derrowegen, dass solche vor dieser Zeit hett mögen
geёndert und gebessert werden, offt gewünschet. Das aber biss anhehro keine Mutation ervolgt, wehren allerhandt Verhinderung und
vornehmlichen die beschwerlichen und immerdar dero Orther erregende Kriege; auch Philips vonn Rosenbach, *[fol.7v]* der Commenthur selbsten, deme diesses Hauss neben der Commend zu
Arnheim von unsseren Orden zue administriren ubergeben und anbefohlen, welcher doch die Administration daselbsten verlassen, aber
gleichwohl vor diser Zeit davon nicht allerdings abtretten und sye
einem andern einrauhmmem wollen. Es wehre aber vor einem Jar uff
dem damahls gehaltenen provincial Capitul an gemelten Philipsen
von Rosenbach solche Heüsser [zu] resigniren und dem Orden abzu-
tretten alles Ernsts begehrt worden, er doruf solche resignirt hette,
und das alles also gehn Malta berichtet. So wollen Ew.fr.Gen. noch
wir nit zweiflen, wohnit bereith einem andern Ritterbruder solche
Heüsser conferirt und verlijhen, dass es doch geschehen werde, dorzu
Ew.fr.Gen. mit fleissiger Beforderung immer würden anhalten lassen.

Dass aber, dissen Verdruss unangeshen, sy die Herren vom Magistrath und gemeiner Burgerschafft daselbsten, bey allen einfallenen
beschwärlichen Kriegen, Verenderungen und ledigen Weesen, des
Ordens Hauss, Gütter und Persohnen so getreülichen und nachparlichen, wie uns solchs von gedachten Herrn Heinrichen von Rechen
gerühmet wehre, alsoviel Zeit und Gelegenheit erleiden wollen, beschonet, gehandthabt undt mit ihren mercklichen Beistandt geholffen
hetten, unnd noch uf diese gegenwertige Stunde, wie wirs in der
Thaet selber erführen, spürten und vernehmmen, solches nit nachlas-
sen, – darab und von allen dem Orden erzeigten Diensten und Gefallen thaten von Ew.fr.Gen., auch wir vor uns selbsten und alle
ritterliche Ordensbrüder, uns gahr freündt- und dienstlichen bedancken; dabey gleichmessig pittende, sie wollen also vorthin unsseren
Orden, dessen Persohnen und bey ihnen gelegenen Heüssern günstig
beygethan pleiben, biss uff andere Verordnung mit jetziger deselben
Administration Gedult tragen und alles unnachparlichen thattlichen
Eingrieffs inmittels sich enthalten, vaster Zuversicht, es werde un-
lengst ein ander Commenthur angestelt, so ein Ritter und des Adels
und also qualificirt, auch sich gen menniglich dermassen verhalten
werde, dass sie ein Gefal-*[fol.8r]*lens daran haben und tragen mögen.

Dass wolten wir bey Ew.fr.Gen. undt sambtlich Mitordensbrüdern hochrühmen, die es neben uns gegen sie mit danckhbarlichen Gemüdt und Hertzen erkhennen und willfferlichen beschulden sollen etc.

Heruff sye — nach gehabter irer Communication — anfenglichen durch ihren altern Burgermeister dess zugewünscheten freündtlichen Gruss unnd gnedigen Willens sich gegen Ew.fr.Gen. theten underthänig fleissig bedanckhen, lessen vorter angeben: wass sie sampt und sonders vor disem biss anhehro des Ordens Persohnen undt Güthern nach Getrage und Gelegenheit der Zeitten und ledigen Fellen Gutts und Behilffs erzeiget, dass hetten sie, alss dem Orden sonderlichen wollwillende, gern gethaen; wanss aber dermassen nit allemahl geschehen wie sie gewilt und sich gepürtt hette, dass wehre nit in ihrer Macht gestanden, sondern müst dem nun so viel Jahren beharrlichen Kriegsempörungen und wechsellweisse inen zugestandenen Verhergungen zugeschrieben werden. Unnd wie sie dan bis daher den Orden bey seinen Heüssern, Renten und Güthern, in ihrem Gepieth und Bezirckh gelegen, so viel möglichen gehrn gehandthabt und verdedingt, also wollen sie vorohin dasselbige mehr und nit minder schaffen und geschehen lassen; pätten iren underthänigen Dienst und Erpiettung an Ew.fr.Gen. zue gelangen.

Betreffent die Administration, und das sie etwach damit nit solten zum Bestem zufriden sein etc., hetten sie biss hieher niemahlen sich understanden dem ritterlichen Orden einige Mass oder Ziell vorzusetzen, wie und durch wasserley Persohnen derselbig seine daselbsten gelegene Güter administriren lassen wolte; begehrten auch uff gegenwertige Zeit ires Theils dem Orden in deme nit einzureden noch ichtwas vorzuschreiben, hiltens ihnen auch nit zimblichen. In Specie jetzigen Administratoren, Herrn Heinrichen von Rechen, anlangent, wehren sie mit dessen Persohn und seinem Thuen und Lassen wohl [fol.8v] zufriden, der sich bey ihnen und iren Mittbrudern sollchermassen verhielte und erzeigte, dass sy inen rühmen und loben müesten; jedoch, wie vorerklertt, sie dem Orden dessfals vorgreiffen wolten etc. Hierab und von erstatten günstigen Audientz, mit repetirter voriger Pitt, theten wir unss abermahls bedanckhen und alles Guten getrösten etc.

Darnach, wie wir gesehen und Herr Heinrich uns beklagt, dass etliche Soldaten vor und nach ins Ordenshauss gelosiertt würden, mit mercklichen Beschwert und Kosten des Ordenshausse und dero Einwöhner etc., haben wir etliche Herren vom Rath appart desswegen angesprochen, die uns verheissen, so viel ohn Verweiss der gemeiner Burgerschafft zu geschehen möglichen, dass sy darzo helffen und gedenckhen wollen, womit des Ordens Hauss hierin möge verschonet pleiben.

Von der Kirchen Gebäw und Gelegenheit.

Vorbass haben wir die Kirchengebäw des Ordens visitirt. Ist gelegen binnen Neümägen nehst bey des Ordens Hausse an S^t.Johans Marckt, Sancto Johanni Baptistae consecrirt. Alle Altaria nider- und aussgerissen; hatt vorhin eingehabtt sex Altaria, darvon Summum altare in honorem S^{ti}.Johannis, noch eines in honorem D.Mariae Virginis, 3 S^{tae}.Crucis, 4 Johannis Evangelistae, 5 S^t.Cathrine unnd dass 6te in honorem D^i.Anthonii Confessoris consecrirt gewesen, nun alle funditus aussgerottet.

Es haben aber an jetzo die Magistrath von der Statt ihre offene gemeine Fleischscharr in die Kirche gelegt und am einwendigen Gebewe gantz verwüstet. Geschehen darin keine Sacra. Seint etliche Pfeiler und Gewölbe nidergefallen gewest, welche Herr Heinrich der Administrator auss Zwang der Statt Obrigkeit – die sich sonsten doran massen wollen – anno etc. 87 *[1587]* widder erbawett. In negster Belegerung anno etc. 90 *[1590]* so am Dach sehr zerbrochen unnd beschädiget.

[fol.9r]   De Bonis ecclesiae.

Dem volgendes ehegemelten Herrn Heinrichen von Rechen persöhnlichen vorgenohmmen, welcher zu forderst facto signo crucis einen Ayd zu Gott würckhlichen aussgeschwohren bey der Pflicht, damit er dem Orden verwandt, uff alles wass wir in Krafft eröffeneter Commission und Befelchs von ihme fragen werden, so viel ihme wissig und er sich endsinnen könne, Antworth und wahren Bericht zu geben, und dass nit underlassen weder umb Geldt, Gutt, Gunst und Vergunst, Nutz oder Schaden, noch umb ichtwas so des Menschen Hertz erdenckhen kan etc., trewlichen und ungefehrlichen.

Sagt von den Kirchengüttern, das er in seiner Ahnkunfft keine Ornamenta oder Gewandt befunden, allein etliche gar schlechte und geringschetzige, so in einer alten Kisten gestanden, doch vor Jahrsfrist durch die Kriegeslaüth hingenohmen worden. So seye aber noch eine schwartze sambete Chorkap vorhanden, die bey dem Parochien zue Huisen in Fürstenthumb Cleve verwahrsamblichen verhalten werde.

Ahn sielbern Kleinoten und Geschier zue der Kirchen gehörich waren vorhanden: Ein silbern vergülte Monstranz, dabey eine vergülte Custodia darin gehörig, in qua conservatur hostia. Item ein sielbern Oelfass. Item zwe sielbern unden und oben vergülte Polluln. Ein sielbern Rauchfass. Zwee sielbern vergülte Platten an Cohrkappen, eine mit S^t.Johannes, die ander mit S^t.Cathrinen Bildt aussgestochen. Vier silberen vergülte Kelche sambt ihren Platten und Zugehör. Item zwo sielberne vergülte Monstrantzen, darin Reliquiae verhalten werden. Item noch eine kleine sylberne Monstrantz unvergüldet. Item ein vergülter Chorkappe, ser klein. Item ein Osculum pacis mit sylberen Moschelen. Diesse Stückh hat obgemelter Herr Heinrich von Rechen vor Einahm und Belegerung der Statt zue seinem ersten Antritt binnen eine Clevische Catholische Statt, genant Huissen, bey einer Burgerin daselbsten, Wittiben Johans Baumeisters, gefleühet und also mit grosser Mühe und Gefahr dem Orden erhalten.

[fol.9v]　　Vons Ordenshausse daselbsten.

Dass Hauss ist von Steinen erbawet, zimblicher Weitte, negst bey des Ordens Kirchen an S^t.Johans Marckt gelegen, etliche umbligende Heusser anhabent, die ehetzeits vor sichere Zijnssen verpachet gewesen, jetzo vast alle oede, wüest und gar zerbrochen gestanden. Zue einer Seiten des Hausses ein klein Baumgarten, zur ander Seiten ein Mössgarten, auch mit einer Porten uff die Schnitzstrass aussgehendt. Dass Hauss aber, dieweill es widder Bergs, etwas in der Höhe über andere Heüsser gelegen, ist durchs grosse Geschüss in vergangenen Belägerungen gar bescheidiget und nemblichen – referente fratre predicto – in der erster Belegerung anno etc.85 *[1585]* mit 36, darnach anno etc.86 *[1586]* mit 3 Kugelen, letzlichen anno etc.90 *[1590]* ungefehr mit 400 und etlichen groben Kugelen beschossen und an viellen Orthern in dem Maurwerckh und an denn Zymmern, auch am Dach, ser zerbrochen, deren etliche bereiths durch Herrn Heinrichen widder gebessert, etliche auch noch ungebessert wüst gelegen, welches ohn grossen Unkosten in Vorigen nit zu bringen. Diss Hauss in Continentz hats beniden an der Erden ein grossen Sall, ein Kuechen, ein Stuben, drey Cammeren und ein gross Gezymer, welches vormals dass Refectorium gewesen, aber an viellen underschiedtlichen Örthen durchs grobe Geschütz ser verwüstet.

In selbigem Hausse an Persohnen gäistlichen Standes befonden offgemelten Herrn Heinrichen von Rechen, ein Priester des Ordens und Administrator beeder Heüsser zu Arnheim und Neümägen begeben und durch seine Gegenwarth so viel möglichen dasselbig auss weltlichen Händen erhalten. Er hatt bey ime zwo alte Mägte und einen Jungen, seiner Schwestrin Söhen, und kein Gesindtlin mehr; selbiges Gesindlin aber von des Ordens Güethern und Gelegenheit nichts Wissens geben können. Herr Heinrich zeigt verner ahn, dass in diessem Hausse, so ein Membrum gehn Arnheim gehörig, von alters etwah acht, etwan sechs, und vor ihme vier Priester gehalten; er seye aber jetzo allein; und doch nit uff diss, sonder ufs Hauss Arnheim sein Orden und Creütz von dem Herrn Philipsen von Rosenbach empfangen. Hatt sich bey vorangelobter Pflicht *[fol.10r]* durchauss Catholisch bekennet und alle Zeit also getragen und gehalten; verhoffen auch durch Gottes Gnaden – wie er sagte – die Zeit seines Lebens bey solcher Bekandtnussen zu verpleiben.

Von Eigethumb des Hausses.

Nach dem Eigenthum dess Hausses gefragt sagt Herr Heinrich, das er in seiner Ankunfft alhie ins Ordenshausse an Eigenthum und Haussgeraht mehr nit befonden dan erstlichen drey alte Bethe, auss welchen er zwey Bethe, zwien Pullen und zwey Haubtküssen machen lassen, die jetzo durch die eingelegte Reütter gebraucht wärden. An Leynwath überall nichts; er habe aber ins Hauss Nottürfftig haufft, einmahls vor 50 Gulden 5 1/2 Stuber Br., darnach 30 Ellen, item nachmals 63 Ellen leinen Tuechs; heraussgemacht und sonsten erkaufft 7 Per Schlafflin, sechs Fuessziechen, item drey Tischlackhen, 20 Handtzwielen, item 40 Servieten, etliche gebildt etlich ohngebilt, auch theils numehr ser verschliessen; item zwey Kochbanckstüecher, 9 Kuechendüecher.

Von dem Herrn Rosenbach seye ime kein Inventarium, sondern anno etc.87 *[1587]* am 30ten Maij auss rechtlichem Zwang und Befelch eines ersamen Raths von weylandt Heinrichen von Pollwickh, gewesenen Renthmeisters Herrn Philipsen von Rosenbach, offterlassenen Wittiben nachfolgende Haussgeraht empfangen.

Zynenwerckh.

Erstlichen an engelisch Zinnen, an Schüsselen klein und gross, an Tellern, an Kannen und Kimpgen, zusamen 76 lb. 12 Loth.

Item an gemeinen schlechten Zynen von allerhandt, sonsten wegent zusammen 26 1/2 Loth.

Küpfferwerckh.

Item 4 kupfferen Töpffe zu der Kuechen gehörig, dero zwien nit zu gebrauchen. Noch einen ser alten kupfferen Topff. Item 6 alte Bekkehrn, 2 kupffern Handtfass, dero eines gar nichts tugnet. Item ein alten Schöpfkessell und ein alt zerlapts Spüllkessell. Item ein alten roten Kessell und zween alte Kesselltöpff, alle nichts tugende. Item ein alten zerlapten Schulderkessell. Item ein grossen rothen Pletzkessel. Item 4 alten kupfferen gebrochen Lavorkanden. Item ein alt zerbrochen Feürpfänlin. Item ein alt zerbrochen kupffern Sprütz und im Bawhausse ein *[fol.10v]* halber Kessel, obich mit Holtzwerckh ufgelegt.

Holtzwerckh.

Item in der Stuben ein ser alt Cantoir. In der Kuechen weiters nit dan ein alt zerbrochen Trittsoir und eine alte Hawbanckh, Hoenerkawe. In der Mägt Cammer einen alten Betladen mit einer kleinen Kastlin in der Mauren. Item in der Herren Refectorio eine grosse lange Taffell und ein alt Sytzwerckh; darinen auch gehangen eine alte eisene Cron. Item in der Gast Cammern einen alten Bethladen, item ein alte zerbrochene vierkäntige Taffell und ein zerbrogens Kästgen in der Mauhren. Item in des Commenthurs Cammeren zwey oder drey Stückh von alten Betladen, ein alt Cantoir, drey alte Kästlin in der Mauren. Alles vermög damahl ufgerichten und uns jetzo gezeigten underschrieben Inventarii. Hierzu noch allerhandt Holtzenwerckh machen lassen; wirdt zue seiner Rechnung sich finden.

Brieff undt Sygell und ander Monumenta.

Es hat Herr Heinrich die Brieffe und Sygell, Register und Rollen in merckhlicher Anzahl in andern gütern Bürger Heüssern verborgen müssen halten, unnd dieweill derselben ser viel, und ohne alle Registrathur, in Fässern und Kasten verpackhet, auch die Zeit unnd Gelegenheit selbige zu lustrieren, registriren und verzeichnen nit leiden mögen, haben wir Herrn Heinrichen uffgeben unnd befohlen solche zue seiner bester Fugen zu inventarissiren unnd die Verzeichnus davon uffs Capitull verschaffen, welches er so viel zu geschehen möglichen angelobt.

Von eingehörigen Güthern, Renthen und Gefellen.

Alhie zu Underrichtung der Müntz und Mass ist fleissig anzumerckhen, dass ein Thaler in numero thuet zu Neümägen 30 Stüfer. Item ein Goltgülden in Golde thuet 55 Stüffer. Ein Philips-gülden 28 Stüfer. Een brabendischen 20 Stüfer. Item ein Malter holt 4 Schepfel. Ein Schepffell halt 4 Spynnt. Es wirdt aber ein Malder Roggen diser

Zeit zu Neümägen gemeintlich zu gelt angeschlagen uff 3 1/2 [Gl.]
brab. Ein Malter Havern 2 Gl. brab. Ein Malter Gersten 3 Gl. Ein
Malter Waitzen 5 Gl.brab.

[fol.11r] Einkömpst an Roggen.

Dess Ordens Hauss zu Neümägen hat ein Erbgutt im Fürstenthumb
Geldern gelegen uff die Graffwegen, ungefehr haltent 15 oder 16
Morgen Ardtlandts, darzu viel Häidtlandts, welchs nit zu bawen ist,
ostwarth an des Hochwaldt, sudewart Johan Valkenberg, westwarth
an St.Johannislandt, nortwarth an die Capelle und gemeine Strass
streckende. Disses Hoffs hat Herr Heinrich, wie er sagt, bey seinen
Zeiten nichts genossen, in Vorthin aber lauth einer alten Rechnung,
die uns gezäigt, hatt jarlichs gethan an Roggen 20 Malter 3 Schepffel.
Wie es der Herr Rosenbach verpachtet, ist kein Bericht gefonden, die
Pechtere verstorben, und möge kriegshalben jetzund nit cultivirt werden.

Item ein ander Erbgutt, gnant Uff Graffwegen, in der Herrligkeit
Graussbeckh gelegen, hatt von alters in Jahrpacht gethan an Roggen
15 Malter. Item dass klein Guth daselbsten 8 Malter, der Zehend am
selben Orth 2 Malter 1 Schepffell. Bey jetziger Zeit aber kan diss
Gutt von Krigswesen nit gebawt werden, ligt wüst und öede, und sagt
Herr Heinrich, dass er auch dorab bey seiner Administration mehr
nicht genossen.

Item noch 15 holländische Morgen, jeden ad 600 Voten, mit Nahmen der Kirchoff, gelegen an gehn Wessbroickh, ehezeits in Erbpacht aussgethan gewesen vor 7 Malter Roggen 2 Reinsch Gulden,
jetzo aber der Erbgewihn durch Herrn Heinrichen mit Recht abgethan, und also dominium utile cum directo consolidirt, wie uns
dorab ein besiegelter Brieff mit zweyen Siglen gezäigt undt vorgelegt,
in welchen sich die Erpechtere des Erbgewyns adeoque iuris sui em-
phyteuseos erblichen verziegen. Gleichwoll mag noch zue Zeit nit
gebawet oder genossen werden.

Item ettliche Lenderey, so umb und bey der Statt gelegen und in
Erbpacht an sichere Persohnen vor langen Jahren aussgeleihen, ver-
möge eines gezeigten Hebregisters, thuet jarlichs zusamen an Roggen
28 Malter 1 1/2 Schepffel. Solche Erbpechte wehren alle in gutem
Gebrauch und Recognition, aber des Kriegswesens halben möegen
sie nit alle, sondern zumweillen halb, zumweillen weniger genossen
werden.

Summa summarum thuet diss Hauss von alters und in Fri-
*[fol.11v]*dens Zeiten an Roggen 81 Malter 1 1/2 Schepffel, jetzo un-

gefehr 14 Malter, jedes bey disser Zeit gerechent uff 3 1/2 Gl.brab., thuet 49 Gl.brab., macht unsser Müntzen 17 Goltgl. 45 Stüfer.

Einkhomens an Wäitzen.

Item Fraw von Reisswickh, nun dero Erben, geben in Erbpacht an Weitz 1 Schepffell, Reiner Vayck 1 Schepffell. Item der Hoff Roy zu Lenth in seiner newer Pachtung jarlichs 1 Schepffell.

Summa Weitzen 1 1/2 Malter, thuet in Gelde 2 Goltgulden 40 Stüfer.

Gersten.

Item uff der Bethaw gegen der Statt Neümägen zu Lenth drey Baw-höfe, dero einer, gnant die Roy, thuet vom alters in Pachtung ahn Gersten 10 Malter; ist aber jetzo unverpachtet; wirdt darvon in der Geltrenthen weiter Meltung geschehen. Der ander Hoff, Lawickh gnant, thuet von alters an Gersten 10 Malter; nun im Grunde ver-brandt; ufs new aussgepachtet thuet an Gersten 6 Malter. Der dritte Hoff daselbsten, gnant Vijssfelde, thuet vom alters an Gersten 10 Malter, jetzo nur 4 Malter.

Summa an Gersten von alters 30 Malter, jetzo 10 Malter, jedes ad 3 Gl.brab., macht unsser Müntzen 10 Goltgl. 50 Stüfer.

Haver.

Item vermög Hebregisters an zweyen Persohne järlichs in Erbpacht an Havern 3 Malter 1 1/2 Schepffell.

Item ein Hoff zu Hörssen, im Lande vonn Gelder zwischen Möss und Wäll gelegen, pflag von alters an Havern zu thuen 25 Malter, wirdt jetz nit genossen.

Summa Havern von alters 28 Malter 1 1/2 Schepffell, bey diesser Zeit im Geniess mehr nit dan 3 Malter 1 1/2 Schepffell, jedes 2 Gl. brab., facit 2 Goltgl. 25 Stüfer.

Einkhomens an Gelde.

Item dass Hauss Neümägen hat jarlichs an dieverssen Persohnen bin-nen der Statt an Hausszynssen und Er[b]pächten einfallent zuesah-men gerechent, vermög Hebregisters, uff 84 Gl. 15 Stüfer. Hiervon etlichs verlassen, davon in gravatis et alienatis zue finden; die übrige seint etlichermassen in Esse, aber von wegen *[fol.12r]* Krigesverderbs und Verarmung der Burger werden sie wenig zalt. Die Heüsser aber, welcher syben in Antzall, ligen alle öede und unbewohnt, darzu in der Belegerung mit den groben Geschütz gar zerbrochen und dachloss gemacht, inmassen wie solches in Augenschein befunden.

Item ein Hoff, gelegen und geheissen zu Nijell im Fürstenthumb Cleve, hatt vorzeiten in Jahrpacht aussgebracht 88 Gl. brab., noch zwey Schwein, 8 Hüener und vier Kranenberger Käiss. Solchen Hoff seine nachgehends durch den Herrn Rosenbach verpachtet an einen Derickh Janssen seines Nahmens, jarlichs vor 50 Thaler brab., item 2 Schwein, 8 Hüener, 4 Kranenberger Käiss, und hatt der Herr Rosenbach zu einem Vorpacht darvon genohmen 25 Thaler.

So zeigen Herr Heinrich dabey ahn, das der Pechter bey daurenden leidigen Kriegswesen nit rühlichen bawen noch winnen mögen, seine Pferde, Kühe und alles genohmen, derowegen in sechs oder siben Jahren wenig genossen, und muess mahn ohn dass darab schwärliche Contributions verichten. Waruff am 19 Julii den Pachtern Dirickh Janssen persöhnlichen vor uns bescheiden, des Hofs Gelegenheit – semoto fratre Heinricho – abgefragt, zeügt und sagt bey leiblichen aussgeschworen Ayde, der Hoff habe an Wäide und Bawlandt ungefehr 42 Morgen hollendisch, welcher ime vor 15 Jahren umbtrent von dem Herrn Rosenbach verpachtet ad 24 Jare, jarlichs zu geben wie oben verzeichnet. Er habe aber bey diessen Krigesempöhrung und gezwinden verderbten Zeiten seinen Pacht nit völlig zahlen können, desswegen er sich mit Herrn Heinrichen Administratorem verglichen vor alle verlauffne Jahren zu geben 100 Gl. brab., deren er etliche zahlt, etlich auch noch schüldig stehe.

Zugleich inen de administratione, moribus et vita fratris Heinrichi underfraget, zeügt seines Wissens, könne anders nit sagen dan das Herr Heinrich sich woll gehalten und noch auch des Ordens Güthern so viel möglichen fleissig und mit guthen Eiffer vorgestanden.

Item ein Hoff geheissen tho Loeth, gelegen im Lande von Cleve und der Dinckhbang Duiffel im Kurspell Loeth, ehezeits in *[fol.12v]* Erbpacht aussgethaen jarlichs vor 10 Goltgulden; nunmehr aber, da die Erbpechter in Zahlung seümig worden, durch Herr Heinrich mit Recht eingenohmen und dem Orden in utroque dominio angebracht; ist aber des Kriges halben noch zur Zeit nit verpachtet.

Item ein Hoff tho Hoessen zwischen Mass und Wall im Lande von Geller gelegen, thuet von alters järlichs in Gelde 75 Philipsgld., jeden pro 28 Stüfer; nachfolgends durch den Herrn Rosenbach vonn newen verpachtet, wie hoch war Herrn Heinrichen unbewüsst. Er habe auch bey seine Zeiten nichts davon genossen, liege wüst und unbewohnt. Noch thuet der Hoff von alters etliche Haver wie bey den Früchten angezogen.

Item gegen die Statt Neümägen in Betaw tho Lenth drey Bawhöffe, zu welchen zusamen gehörig mehr dan 170 hollendische Morgen, Weide undt Ackherlandt. Dero ersten Hoff, geheissen die Roye, thuet von alters zu Pacht jarlichs 58 Philipsgld., jeden pro 28 Stüfer, facit 81 Gl. 4 Stüfer brab.; von Gendtgheins Lande 17 Philipsgld., jede pro 26 Stüfer, facit 22 Gl. 2 Stüfer brab.; item ein Viertel Vass Butteren, 8 Cappohnen, 6 Hüner, 2 Schwein, undt Gerst wie oben vermeltet. Dissen Hoff ist bey dem Krigeswesen zu Grundt nidergebrandt und etliche Jahren wüst und ungebawt gelegen, und abersonsten in Handen Meister Johans von den Höfe von wegen des Herrn Rosenbachs bey ihme gemachter Schulden gestanden, nunmehr durch Herrn Heinrichen uff seine Unkosten mit Recht eingewohnen. Wirdt an jetzo durch Gerdt Vermer zur Halbscheidt gebawet; wass darab kommen sol, seye noch ungewiss und nit versucht. Gibt ferner zur Küchen 50 lb. Buttern, jedoch diss erste Jahr nur 25 lb., und etliche Weitzen wie bey den Früchten gemelt.

Der ander Hoff, ᵃdie Lawickh genant, thuet von alters an Gelde 140 Gl. brab. und etlich Gerst wie oben; item 1 Vass Buttern, item 2 Schwein, 2 Lemmer, 1 Hamel, 2 Genss, 8 Caponen und 12 Hüner.ᵃ Derselbig ist gleichfalss durch Herrn Heinrichen auss Handen Meister Johans von den Hofe, welcher solchen von Schulds wegen, von Herrn Rosenbach herkhommenden, eingehabt, dem Orden mit Recht angewohnnen, nunmehr an Allert Gerds von newen verpachtet ad 6 Jahren, jedes Jahrs zu geben in Gelte 80 Gülden brab., jedoch das erste Jahr [fol.13r] nur 40 Gülden; item etliche Gersten, alss in den Früchten angezeigt; dorzu an Buttern 75 lb.; item ein järig Verckhen oder darvor 6 Gl.; unnd wannehr der Pechter Schaff angehen mag, alssdan alle Jahr ein Hammel.

Der dritter Hoff, Wissfelt gnant, thete von alters 100 Gl. 16 Stüber; item Gerst wie bey den Früchten angezogen; item ein Viertell Vass Buttern; item 2 Verckhen, 2 Lammer, 2 Gensse, 8 Capponen, 12 Hüner. Ist auch vorgemeltermassen in Handen Meister Hanss von Höfe schuldenhalben gestanden, aber durch Herrn Heinrichen recuperirt. Nunmehr verpachtet ad 6 Jahren, dass erste Jahr zu geben 10 Thaler, die folgende Jahren alle Jars 60 Gl. brab.; an Buttern 50 lb.; item ein järich Verckhen oder darvor 6 Gl. brab.; noch etliche Gerst, wie in der Fruchtrenth verzeichnet.

Unnd es seyen uff allen dreyen Höfen die Geheugter gantz ab- und niddergebrandt, die auch biss hieher allerding dessert und wüst gelegen.

Ferner hatt Stʲ Johanshauss an dem Vhär zu Neümägen einen achten Theill; dieweil man aber alle Jahren zu Bawung und Erhaltung der Vährschüffknecht mehr müssen anwenden dan darvon aussgetragen, hat nunmehr ein erbar Rath der Statt solchen achten Theill und aller Consorten Antheille zu sich gezogen, jarlichs doraus an St.Johans zu bezahlen 6 Gl.brab.

Summa das Hauss St.Johans binnen Neümägen hatt järlichs von alters und in Fridenszeiten in Gelterenthen 649 Gl. 7 3/4 Stüfer brab. Bey diessen leidigen und doch uff etwas gebesserten Zeitten mögen sich die Geltrenthen desselbigen Hauss eines- mehr, andersmahls weniger, nach Gelegenheit des Krigsschaden und Leüffen, jarlichs ungefähr ertragen uff 221 Gülden brab.

Doch wolt gedachter Herr Heinrich sich bezeügt und dienstlich gebetten haben, da hernacher auss den Brieffen, Registern unnd Rollen ichtwas weiter möcht [fol.13v] befonden werden, dieweill er deroselben biss dahin krigesverstörnussenhalben nit vollauss mechtig sein konnen, inen desswegen nit zu bedenckhen, will ers in Erfahrung zu bringen und auss zu kundtschafften an seinen getrewen Fleiss nit manglen lassen.

Summarum dass Hauss Neümägen thuet järlichs von alters an Früchten: inn Korn 81 Malter 1 1/2 Schepffell, in Weitzen 1 1/2 Malter, in Gersten 30 Malter, in Havern 28 Malter 1 1/2 Schepffell, in baren Gelde 649 Gl. 1 3/4 Stüber brab.; item an Schweinen 8, an Genssen 4, an S[ch]affen 5 Stückh; item an Hünern 38, an Capponen 24, an Buttern ein Thon oder Vass, an Käissen 4 Stückh. Nun zur Zeit und solang sich die Krigsleüffe nit ärgern, thuts ungefehr in Roggen 14 Malter, in Weitzen anderhalb Malter, in Gersten zehen Malter, in Havern 3 Malter 1 1/2 Schepfell, in Gelde 80 Goltgulden 20 Stüfer, an Schweinen 4, jedes 6 Gl., an Hühern 8 Stück, jedes 6 Stüfer, an Cappon nichts, an Käissen 4 ungerechnet. Summa alles zu Gelt angeschlagen ertragt sich das Einkohmen dess Hauss Neümägen bey dieser Zeit und Gelegenheit in rheinischer Müntzen 136 Goltgulden 38 Stüfer.

ᵃ *written on fol.13r, with reference mark on fol.12v, as indicated in BMHG 48 (1927) p.287.*

Aussgulden.

Hiervon gehen jarlichs erblichen und continue: Item die Fraw von Neü Closter 3 Gl. brab. Item ratione antique pensionis auss einem Stückh Landes, gnant Velburgerbroich jarlichen ablosslichen 14 Phil. Gl., jeden Gulden pro 25 Stüfer brab., thut 17 1/2 Gl. brab. Item noch etliche kleine Erbzinnssen und Aussgulden, welche, dweill bey

jetziger Zeit die Gueter, davon sie geben werden, niet im Prauch, ime deme Administratoren darab die Registern nit gelieffert, vor dissmahl nit mögen specificirt werden.
Summa continuorum exituum 20 1/2 Gl. brab.

Unköst zur Hausshaltung.

Item vor zwey Mägte und einen Jongen jarliche Besoldung 48 Gl. brab. Item vor die Hausshaltung jarlichs ungefehr 500 Gulden brab., jedoch hernechtst davon special Rechnung uffzulegen.

Summa a[n]nuorum exituum pro tempore 568 1/2 [Gl.] brab., thuet Reinischer Müntzen 206 Goltgulden 40 Stuefer.
[fol.14r] Also gegen die järliche Aussgulten wolt bey gegenwartigen Zeitten an dem Einkomens ermangelen 70 Goldgulden 7 Stüfer.

De alienatis et gravatis.

Auss obspecificirten Ordensgüetern, zu angezwungenen Uffbawe des Ordens Kirchen und Hausses daselbsten, hat Herr Heinrich verkaufft und alienirt ein Hauss binnen der Statt Neümägen uf der Nonnenstrassen[a] gelegen, so ein Teill wahr von dem grossen Hausse, auch daselbsten dem Orden zustendig, gnant Brabandt, an Gerhardten die Boess vor zweyhundert Thaler jeden pro 30 Stüfer, davon abgezogen 10 Thaler seint in der Erbung, Cession, Proclamation und sonsten an Unkost uffgangen; verpleiben 190 Thalers. Jedoch sey der Kauff mit dissen Vorbehalt gededingt, dass nemblich die Keüffer und ire Erben von nun vortmehr alle Jahren uf das Fest Victoris erblichen an St. Johanshauss zu einer Ausszinse und Recognition geben und zahlen sollen ein gülden Schylt ad 15 Stüfer brab.; auch da selbigs Hauss immermehr wider verkaufft werden, sollte alssdan der Orden daran den Vorkauff et iuris retractus seu prothimiseos zugehaben. Waruff wir weiter Nachkündigung gethan, den Geldern Gerhardt de Boss vorschrieben persöhnlichen zur Handt gefordert, welcher den Kauff in aller Massen vorerklirt bekennet, ferner bezeügent, dass gerürter Herr Heinrich von den Kauffpfenig kein Heller von ime in seine Hände empfangen, sondern er gestracks Werckhern, alss Steinhawern und Zimmerleüthen, vor ihre gethane Bawkosten und Arbeidt gelieffert.
Weiter [bezeugt] jetzigen Herrn Heinrichen das er, alles zu Reparation der Kirchen und Ordenshausse, bey einem Burgern zu Neümägen, Johann Vermoelen seines Nahmens, anno etc.86 [1586]

endtleihet und uffgenohmmen die Summa von 600 Gl. brab., thuet
Reinischer Müntzen 218 Goltgulden 10 Stüfer, darvon demselben
zue Underpfande gesetz und verschrieben auss des Ordens Güethern
uff der Betaw 4 Morgen Weidt- und 5 Morgen Bawlandt, solche zue
geniessen und zu gbrauchen, mit vorbehaltener Widerlassen. Gemelten Johan Vermoelen haben wir gleichfals zue unss kommen lassen
und die Gelegenheit erfragt; sagt er habe uff genente Underpfande
die Summa von 600 Gulden dem Administratorn vorgestreckt, dass
Gelt aber seye nit in Handt *[fol.14v]* des Administrators, sondern den
Arbeittern und Zimmerleüthen gelieffert worden, so habe er darvor
die Underpfende in Brauch nehmen sollen biss zu dem Widerkauff;
dieweill er aber jetzo nicht darvon geniessen könne, patt er gantz
dienstlich die Versehung zu thuen oder machen, damit er sein auss-
gelegtes Gelt wider bekhommen möge.

Demnach den Baw und Reperation so an der Kirchen alss an des
Ordens Hausse, daran vorgemelten Summen gewendet sein solten, in
Augenschein eingenohmmen, auch bey Benachbarten darüber nach-
gefragt, gesehen und erfahren, dass in der Kirchen obich dem Chor
ein gantz new Gewölb geschlagen, auch zwo neüe Seüllen darin gesetz und mit eisse[r]n Anckhern allenthalben gevestet; an dem
Orden[s Hausse] ahn vielen underschidtlichen Örthern gebewet, gebessert und reparirt, unnd solches alles anno etc.86 *[1586]* geschehen, damahls die Statt Neümägen mit Co.Wür. von Hispanien wider
vereiniget und alle Geistlichen, so vordeme verwichen wesen, widder
einkhommen und ihrer Güter Besitz angenohmmen, wehre die Or-
denskirch St.Johan, zusambt des Ordens Hausse, gar nidergewohnt,
abgefallen undt wüst gestanden; also durch zwanglichen Befelch eines
erbahren Raths bey Poen bedrawter Confiscation wider erbawet werden müssen.

Von solchen Bawkosten hatt Herr Heinrich uns special Rechnun-
gen vorbracht unnd ufgelegt, die alle durch die zeitliche Obrigkeit
daselbsten oder sonsten durch Scheffen und gude erbahre Burger mit
deren Handtunderschrifften urkundet und bezeügt worden, welche
sich in Summa ertragen ungefehr 1872 Gl. 19 1/2 Stüfer brab., thuet
Reinischer Müntzen 681 Goltgulden 4 1/2 Stüfer.

Hiervon die Pfennonge, so von verkaufften Hausse undt beschwör-
tem Lande herkhommen, nemblich 321 Goltgulden, abgezogen, hatt
Herr Heinrich ahn die Reparation weiter verwendet unnd angelegt
350 Goltgulden 14 1/2 Stüfer.

Noch hatt Herr Heinrich am 19 July anno etc.94 *[1594]* uns eine
Rechnung ubergeben von allem, wass er ausserthalben obengewente
Kosten in Zeit seiner Administration zu Erhaltung des Ordens Güe-
theren und sonsten zu dero Besserung extraordinarie aussgeben, welche sich in Summa ertragen und er in Capitulo ferner uflegen wirdt,

852 Gl. 12 1/2 Stüfer brab., thuet Rheinischer Müntz 310 Goltgulden 2 1/2 Stüfer.

[fol.15r] Summa summarum der uffgenohmmer Lasten und wass sonsten ahn das Herr Heinrich vermög seiner obgenanten Rechnung uf diesse Guether angewendt und verschossen zu haben vorgibt, thuet zusammen 991 Goltgulden 7 Stüfer.

Item die drey Höfe zu Lenth haben vorgemeltermassen in Handen Meister Johan von dem Hoefe lenger dan 6 Jahren gestanden, welcher doruff 2000 Gl. brab. an Herrn Rosenbach affterselbigen Schulden pretendirte, waruff der Herr Rosenbach ime 900 Gl. anpieten lassen, aber er nit gewilt; zuletz durch Herrn Heinrichen uff dessen eigen Unkosten, wie er sagte, mit Recht recuperirt und erhalten. Ausserthalben dass bezeügt Herr Heinrich bey geleister Pflicht, dass seines Wissens von dess Ordens Güthern des Hausses Neümägen bey allen diessen leidigen Zeitten und aussgestandenen Kriegstraubelen nichts sei verkaufft, versetz noch beschwähret.

---

a *BMGH 48 (1927) p. 289 has* Monnenstrassen.

Arnheim.

Nach verrichten Sachen, so viel möglichen, zue Neümägen haben wir uns am 20 July uff die Reissen gehn Utrecht begeben; dieweill aber dass Hauss Arnheim dass rechte Corpus von Neümägen ist, also füglicher geachtet desselben Geschefft, Visitation und Verrichtung, so in der Widderkunfft von Utrecht allererst verhandlet, alhie negst der Visitation von Neümägen zu referiren. Seint also in dem Uffkhommen von Utrecht am 10 Augusti zu Arnheim angelangt; den 11en bey den Herren Cantzler und Räthen der Regierung des Fürstenthumbs Geller und Graveschafft Zutphen, gleichfalss bey einem erbahren Rath derselben Statt Arnheim, negst Praesentirung habender verschlossenen Credentz umb Audientz unsser ferner Werbung fleissig angehalten, die uns auch auff folgenden Morgen den 12 Augusti verstattet und angesezt.

De templo atque eius immunitate.

Inmittelss wir die Kirchen und Ordenshauss etlichermassen aussen umbher lustrit und besichtiget. Ist die Kirch und Ordenshauss beyde bey einander an einem Orthe in der Statt Arnheim gelegen; die Kirche gar nidergefallen, dass Dachwerck, *[fol.15v]* ausserthalben ein gerings Stückh, so noch ahn einer Mauhren gehangen, alles abe[r] der Einbaw, Gwölbe und Mauhrwerck gantz verfallen und verwüstet, welchs mit einer mercklichen Summa Gelts nit mögt in vörigen Standt gebracht werden. Die Immunitet darumbher alles nidergeworffen und defastirt.

De bonis et ornamentis templi.

Von Kirchengeschierden und Ornamenten hat Herr Heinrich von Rechen Administrator diesse nachfolgende Stückhe bey allen aussgestandenen Leüffen, Rauben und Devastatione wunderbahrlichen und mit grosser Muehe und Gefahr, nit alle Zeit bey sich noch in der statt Arnheim, sondern zumweillen ann underschidtlichen Orthern durch Behülff und guthertziger catholischer Leüthe und benachbarten Clevischen und sonsten wie er best gekannt, bisshehre erhalten und unss gezäigt. Zum ersten ein silberne Munstrantz. Item ein sielberen Rauchfass. 4 sielbern vergulte Kelch cum patenis; wehren vorhin 5 Kelch gewesen, aber einer im Kriegstraubel abkhommen, doch verhofften selbigen noch etwah auszukundtschafften und wider beyzubringen. Item ein silberne vergulte Blatt an Chorcap. Item ein ser groess und schön silbernen vergulten Chorknop. Item ein sylbernen osculum pacis. Item 2 silbern Ampullen, so Herr Heinrich wie er sagt selbst machen lassen. Item es seye auch gewesen ein silbern Öelfass, aber in ipsa devastatione wegkhommen. Item ein klein silbernen Cibori, so vors Ablass pflag gebraucht zu werden. Item seye noch ein silbern Creütz hinder einer Wittiben weylandt Jacob then Over in Bewahrung.

Kirchengewanth.

Nachfolgende Kirchengewandt seint zu dem Hauss Arnheimb gehörig, aber durch Herrn Heinrichen mit grossen Fleiss, Mühe, auch mit Gefahr seines Lebens — wie ime guthe erbahre Burger Zeügnus gaben und die Sach an ihme selbs erscheine — auss der Statt Arnheim in die Statt Neümägen gebracht und daselbsten sehr heimblichen bey einem schlechten Burgersmahn, welcher sie in Kisten obich in seinem Hausse under einem Hauffen Holtz und [fol.16r] anderm Gepeckhe bisshehro an erhalten; undt seindt uns zu inventarisiren stücklichen gezeigt und vorgezeunet, wabey gemelts Herrn Heinrichs trewer Fleiss mercklichen gespörth worden.

Zum ersten ein blauw Carsufell von Semmett. Item ein Vorhang vors Sacrament von verblomt Sammet. Item ein Carsufell von gülden Stückh in rott Sambet gewirckht. Item 2 Chorröckh aschfarbich

Sammet mit Golt eingewärckt. Item ein Carsüfel von selbiger Arth und Wö[r]th und mit etlichen Perlen verstickt. Item noch Carsüfel von rotten Sammet mit ubermachten eingewürckten gülden Creütz. Item ein roth attlass Carsüfell, ein Carsüfel weiss attlass mit etwas eingewürckten gülden Dratt. Item ein roten frawenbildt Rockh von Sammet mit umbgehenden lassen Leisten. Noch ein bilden Rockh von lautern gülden Stückh mit lassen Leisten. Item ein kleines bilden Rocklin von gülden Stückh mit lassen Leisten. Item 11 leinen Corporalduecher, 2 bilden Haubttuecher. Item ein schwartz sammeten Thoidtlachen mit einem weissen attlass Creütz. Item ein schwartz sammeten Carsüfell miten rotem sambeten Creütz. Item ein rote attlass Chorkap, der Uberhang an der Kappen von gulden Stuckh, sonder Knopf. Item ein Carsüfell von blaw Sammet mit eingewürckten gülden Creütz. Item von rotwüllen Lachen ein Carsüfel mit einen gelben Creütz. Item ein Carsüfel von danneten Lachen mit eim fallroten Creütz. Item ein Carsüfell von grün Sammet mit rot und weiss verblümbt. Item ein schwartz Carsüfell von Sammet mit einem weissen Creütz. Item ein alt Carsüfell und zwey Chorröckhe von Leinen mit eingewürckten falschen Golde. Item ein Carsüfell von dunet Sammet mit gülden Creütz, vast alt. Item noch eines von phall dunet Sambet und 2 Chorrockhe von gleicher Wörth. Item noch 2 Rockhe dunet Sammet mit gelben Creützen. Item ein Alba mit weissen attlas Lappen. Item ein Alba mit roten sameten Lappen. Item am guden und bössen Lachen unnd Twellen uf Altaren 12 Stück. Item noch an Alben guth und quad 12 Stückhe. Item zwo Gardinen von Leinewath vorhanden gewest; sagt Herr Heinrich, dass es des Herr Rosenbachs Kuchin zu ihrem Nutz verschnidten.

[fol.16v] Von des Ordens Hausze.

Dess Ordens [Hauss] ist in einem zimblichen weiten Befange gelegen. Der Magistrath von der Statt hatts seithehr der Kriegsverstörrung in ihren Gewalt genohmmen und an etliche underschiedliche Burgere und Haussgesessen verliehett; war doch zimblichermassen inen Dach und Nothbaw erhalten, welches sonsten, da es obgemelter Gestalt in Gewalt des Magistraths nit gestanden, weniger nit dan auch die Kürch und viele andere Heüsser ohngezweiffelt wehre verwüstet, woh nit gahr zu Boden gerissen worden.
    Dass Eingethumbe und Haussgerath alles verkhommen.

Von eingehörigen Güttern, Renthen und Gefellen und dero Alienation, wie volgt.

Von den Güttern, Höffen, Renthen unnd Gefellen diesses Hausses hatt der Orden bey jetziger Zeit nichts in seinem Gewalt, konten auch darab weder Register noch Rechnung oder rollen gezeigt werden. Sondern negst vor der Statt sampt etlichen Bleichplätzen guthen Weiden,Kempfen, Ackherlandt undt Holtzwachs gelegen, welche die Regierung von Gelderlandt in Gebrauch genohmmen. Viele andere Güther und Gefehle seindt durch den Herrn von Rosenbach in seinem Zeiten an diversse Persohnen verpfendet, verkaufft und sonsten durch dessen Creditoren mit Recht besprochen, ausserfolgt und verwonnen, wie uns Herr Heinrich Administrator darab special Verzeichnus ubergeben, auch uns ohne dass durch andern bezeüget worden, alss nachfolgt:

Special ahnzeig dero Gütheren und Renthen, so von der Commenden zue Arnheim St.Johansordens durch den Herrn Rosenbach verpfendet, verkaufft oder sonsten dessen Schulden halben et ob eiusdem contumaciam, am Rechten sein erwonnen und jetzo in wercklichen Privathanden verhalten werden.

Zum ersten in Kirspell und Dorff Brummen, under Velwezoem gelegen, hat der ritterliche Orden viele schöne Güther an Baw- und Weidtlandt und pflegen doruff zu stehen drey Bawheüsser, von dero einen, genant Klein Everdingen, seint etliche Lenderey verkaufft, verpfendet und *[fol.17r]* in Erbpacht ausgethan durch Herr Rosenbach an diverse Persohnen, nentlich an einem Edelman Grissbreth von Mackhern, Ottho Voetz, Johan und Dirickh tho Hoender etc.; wie viel aber Pfennung daruffgenohmmen, war Herrn Heinrichen unbewüst, doch seeliger Herr Jochim Crab Prior zue Arnheim und er hetten [von] Evert Minderfoit, Pechtern zur Zeit desselben Hoffs, verstanden anno etc.78 *[1578]*, das dassjenig, so allein von dem einen Hoffe alienirt wehre, woll mögt jarlichs 40 Thahlers in Pachtung ausspringen.
    Item zu Brummen durch Otto Voetz lassen verkauffen und abhowen viele junge Aichbaume.
    Item zu Spanckheren, ein Dorff also genant, auch in Velwezoem gelegen, ein Holtzwachs von jungen Aichen zusamen lassen abhauwen und verkauffen an Ottho Voetz, den Gront in Erbpacht ausgethaen an St.Anthonis Bruderschafft binnen die Statt Zutpfen.
    Item Gerhardt Custer, ein gewessener Renthener des Herrn Rosenbachs, ahn obgemelten Orth auch grossen Schaden gethan mit Holtz abhawen und zu verkauffen umb kleinen Preiss.
    Item zu Apeldorn, uf Velwen gelegen, hat der Orden etliche Lenderey, welcke pflegen Pacht zu geben jarlichs 40 Thahler frey Gelt;

seint nun ungefehr vor 12 Jahren ob contumaciam von die Haussmeistern St.Cathrinen Gottshauss binnen Arnheim verwonnen.

Item vor Arnheim uf St.Johanns Müllen alle Pöppellbäume lassen abhowen und verkauffen an Johan von Welij.

Item ein Stückh von dess Ordens Müllenbleich erblichen verkaufft an einen Burger binnen Arnheim, Wilhelmen Veeren gnant; wie theür, ist Herr Heinrich nit wissig.

Item ein Stückh Bawlands gelegen uf den Arnheimischen Enck; noch ein Werthgen in dem Kirspell Malbrugen; item ein Kampf Weidtlands haltende 4 holländische Morgen, die Speltwertt gnant, gelegen in die Liemerss, – alle drey Stück an Reiner Kempink verpfendet vor die Summa – wie sagt wirdt – von 400 Thaler ohn Beschwernus und Ohnsratzgelt, so weiter daruf gangen, mit dem anklebenden Pacto, wannehr gleich die Summe restituirt, das dannach der Pfandtherr der Underpfande 12 Jahren zu seinen Besten *[fol.17v]* soll haben zu gebrauchen.

Item noch ein Stücklin Lands, ungefehr 1/2 hollendischen Morgen, in Liemerss gelegen, verpfendet ahn Gossen Smullingk, ein Edelman; weiss nit wie hoch.

Item alle andere Ordensguether zu Liemerss gelegen, so vormahls järlichs in Pachtung zu geben pflegen 140 Thalers, seint zusammen verpfendet, eins Theils von den Commenthur Herrn Johan Schmiesinck, anders Theils von Herr Rosenbach, wie man sagt vor die Summa von 800 Gl. brab. aussgescheiden Ohnratzgelt; so mehr daruff gelauffen, mögt alles klärlichen auss den Pfandtzetulen, welche der Herr Rosenbach in Bewahr gehabt, erlernet werden; die Güter stehen in Geprauch Steven Reynerssen.

Item under Malburgen vier Hondt Landen gelegen, so an den Licentiaten Friderich von Boymer verpfendet vor 100 Philips Thaler.

Item noch etliche Lenderey, uf Malburgen gelegen, hatt Burgermeister Arendt von Brienen in Pfandtschafft vor 200 Carolusgulden, aussgenohmmen Ohnratzpfenning, und alls die Pfennige in sorte restituirt, mag der Pfandtherr der Lendereyen noch 12 Jahren geprauchen.

Item an Joachim von Hoemen stehet ein schöner Kampf verschrieben in Niderbetaw under dem Kirspel von Oichten gelegen, mit angehenckten Pacto, nach restituirten Haubtgelt des Pfandts noch 12 Jahren zu gebrauchen; wie hoch der Haubtschilling, müssen dess Herren Rosenbachs Pfandtzetulen nachweissen.

Item in Niderbetaw in den Kirspeln Ingen und Oemeren hat des Ordens Hauss Arnheim viele guthe Baw- und Weidtlandt, welche pflagt in Pachtung zu haben Thonius von Hattem und jarlichs gaben zu Pacht – uber groesse Accidentz – in baren Gelte 60 Jachimsthaler

frey Gelt, unt seint anno etc.79 *[1579]* verpfendet an einem Edel-
mahn, genant Johan Ingehen Neulandt, vor vie[f]- oder sechshondert
hollendische Thalern, alles lauth der Pfandtzetlen bey dem Herrn
Rosenbach zu gesinnen.

Item zu Oberbetuw zu Elst hat des Ordens Hauss ein Bawhoff,
gnant Hollanderbrockh, pflagt in die Regierung seeligen Joachim
Craben Prior und Schaffner gewesen, anno etc. 59 *[1559]* jarlichs in
[fol.18r] Pacht zu gelten − ausserthalben Rubsaet, Butter, Schwein,
Korn, Hüener und Specerei zur Kuechen und ander Accidentz − 110
Thaler frey Gelt etc. Diesser Bawhoff ist in Zeit von 12 Jahren durch
die Haussmeister von S\t.Cathrinen Gottshauss per contumacia[m]
verwonnen und also vons Ordenshausse abkhommen.

Item alle dass Eichenholtzgewachs jong und alt, welches der Orden ligent gehabt im Kirspell von Bennekhem uf Velwen, ist zusamen
verhawen undt verkaufft an Heinrich Wilhelmssen und Johan Bon-
gart.

Item noch uf Veluwe in einer Baurschafft gnant Doesburg under
dem Kirspell von Eede, hat das Hauss Arnheim ein schön Turffveen
umb so viel Brantz dorauss zu hohlen, alss zu der Hausshaltung
nöthig; ist nun zusahmen häill aussgegraben und dieversse Haussleü-
the verkaufft.

Haec dictante et referente predicto domino Heinrico a Rechen
etc.

Hiebey hatt Herr Heinrich mündtlich adrevertirt, dafehrn mahn zu
einigen Zeiten gedenckhen wolte die vorspecificirte und andere vera-
lienirte, verpfendte und beschwerte Güther deroendts zu recuperiren
und unserm Orden widder anzubringen, dass vor allen Dingen nöetig
seye von dem Herrn Rosenbach umbstendtliche Gelegenheit zu erfragen, darzu alle Pfandbrieffe, Zetulen, Register und Rechnung ab-
fordern, umb auss denselben zu ersehen und zu lernen, wie es uff ein
jedes Stückh eigentliche Gelegnus habe, und die Sachen uffs Beste
anzugreiffen. Wan solches vorhanden und Herrn Heinrichen ichtwas
Beystandts geleistet würde, wollt er seinen gehorsamben pflichtigen
Dienst gehren dahin versprechen und sich trewlichen erzeigen, wie
dan auch wir nach allen befundenen Umbstenden es vor eine solche
Notturfft müssen erachten.

12 Augusti.

Alss wir Morgens umb 8 Uhren, in Abwessens des Herren Cantzlers
von Gelderlandt, von dem Herrn Vicecancellario unnd zweyen andern Landträthen und Rechtsgelehrten Audientz erhalten, haben wir

denselben, nach Ew. fl. Gen. inen angewünscheten Gruess und allen
Wollstandts etc., ungeferlicher folgender-*[fol.18v]*massen vortragen
lassen. Dass Ew. fl. Gen. mit leittmüttigen Hertzen deroendes Landen
j[a]mmerlichen Zustands, derin sie eine Zeit hehro gelegen, ver-
nohmmen, dabey in der That erfahren, wie der ehrwürdig gestrenger
und edler Herr Philips von Rosenbach, ein Ritter unssers Ordens,
deme die Administration selbigen Ordens Hausses alda zu Arnheim
durch den Herrn Grossmeistern zu Mallta gnedigst zugelegt und befohlen, solche vor etlichen Jahren ohn Geheiss und Belieben seiner
Obern verlassen. Waruff leider erfolgt, dass nachgehends bey an-
wachssenden und zunehmmenden Kriegswessen, dah die Policei nit
der Gepiehr geübt und in Achtung genohmmen werden können, des
Ordens Kirch daselbsten verwüstet und nidergefallen, dass Hauss,
alle umligende angehörige Höffe, Gütter, Müllin, Renthe und Gefelle
in ander secular Privatthende verkommen, dem Orden aber darauss
nichts gefolget noch gelieffert worden, wie wir auch solches uff unssr
Ankunfft und uff Erkündigung theils augenscheinlichen, theils auss
Bericht erfahren und eingenohmmen. Welchen so viel möglichen
zu remediren unssr ritterlicher Orden und dessen Vorsteher lengst
gesinnet gewesen ire Bottschafften an die Haubter und Regierung
deroends Landen abzuferdigen, doch alles biss dahin kriegesunwe-
senshalben offerplieben. Nunmehr aber die Landen und Provincien
Unijrt in besseren Standt gerathen und lobseelige vielgewünschete
Policei restaurirt und wider erbawet, hetten Ew. fl. Gn. uns gnediglichen abgeordenet unnd wollen also ire Edel unnd L.L. freündtlichen
erinnern, welchermassen der ritterlicher Orden St.Johans von Hierusalem, in Malte residirent, von allen innerlichen und civil Krieg in
der Christenheit gantz unparteisch und neutral seyen, auch sich jederzeit also gehalten und noch dan ire Provession allein wider denen
Erbfeindt christlichen Nahmens der allingen Christenheit – alles Un-
derschiedts iro Religionen ungeachtet – zum Schutz *[fol.19r]* und
Besten gerichtet stehe, darwider sie sich immerzu und ohne Underlass mit Ansetzung Leibs, Guts und Bludts dapfer ufhielten. Deroweg
von römischen Kayssern und Königen und Potentaten des Reichs
Teütscher Nation hoch privilegirt und begnadet wehren, auch noch
biss an hehro in allen christlichen Lendern, wo guthe Policei verhan-
den, under andern beim Teütschen Reich und dessen Chur- und
Fürsten, Graven und Herrschafften, Stenden und Stetten, von wass
Religion sie seyen, darzu eben in den Niderteütschen Uniirten Provintien, bey ufgerichter und anietzo Gottlob restaurirter vigirender
Policei, vermög und nach Verfolg underschiedlichen Pacificationen
und derselben Landschafften Abscheiden und Reverssen zu allem
Guten respectirt, und so viel die Zeiten erleiden können, beschonet

und verdedingt worden. Und das unsers Bedünckhens umb desto mehr, sijtemahl Ew. fl. Gn. alss St Johans Ordens Meister in Teütschlanden daselbsten ein ungemittelt Gliedt des Reichs seyen und darvor gehalten würden, under dessen Magisterio de Güther zue Arnheim mit andern gehörig, demnach von Ew. fürstl.Gn. und unssers Ordenswegen wir alss Abgesante freündtlich und fleissig patten, ir Ed. L. und Gestr. wolten dem ritterlichen Orden seine alde gelegenes Ritterhauss mit dessen Pertinentien und angehörigen Gütern günstlichen restituiren und einantwurten, oder dass solchs geschehe bey anderen, schaffen und helffen etc.

Wass dan die Administration uf künfftige Zeit anlangte, solte dorthin ufs allerehest ein ander Commenthur und Ritterbruder verordnet werden, so des Adels und verhöffentlichen also qualificirt sein, auch dermassen sich nachparlichen verhalten, dass ire L.L. und Gest. menniglichen Gefallens tragen werden. Daran geschehe wass an ihme selbsten recht und billig und zu Erhaltung des hochwürdigen ritterlichen Ordens, auch der Landen daselbsten löblicher Ritterschafft, erschiesslichen. So würdens uber dass Ew.fl.Gen. mit Gunst, Freündschafft und allen zimblichen Diensten *[fol.19v]* beschulden, und wir wöltens bey unssern Ritterbrudern unnd gantzen Orden stattlichen rühmmen etc.[1]

Daruff der Herr Vicecanceler und seine mitanwesende Räthe, mit dienstlicher Dancksage des angewünscheten Wollstandts, folgendermassen uns beantwurten lassen. Es seye nit ohn nachdem vorgenannter Herr Rosenbach aussgewichen, dass dessen Creditoren uff des Ordens Güter hin und wider mit Recht gesprochen unnd auch selbige ob contumaciam Rosenbachs viele an sich geworben und verwunnen; gleichfals war dieweill die uffgelegte Contribution und Servitten von etlichen Ordensgüttern, so theils ungebawet und ungewohnt gelegen, nit geleistet, dass die Regierunge dero Landen selbige angeschlagen und ahn andere Hände aussgethan und verpachtet, und solches seye durch Rath und Verordnung der gemeiner Landtstende geschehen. Ob dan sie, die gegenwertige Räthe, nit zweiffelten, dan dem ritterlichen Orden würdt uf Anhalten und Ersuechen alle Gepiehr widerfahren, so wolt es doch ihnen vor diss Pass, alss die in kleiner Anzahl gegenwertig, nit gezymmen noch schicklich sein widder die allgemeine Ordnung ichtwas ohn derselben Vorerklerung zu verenderen und den Landtstenden vorzugreiffen; sie wahren aber urbietig diesse unsse Werbung ufs trewlichst an ihren Herren Cantzler und Mitträthe, gleichfalss an sembtliche Stende des Fürstenthumbs Geller, zu referiren, auch an ihren geneigten Willen nichts ermangelen zu lassen; thetten sich zu Ew. fürstl. Gen. und unsserm Orden alles Diensts, Liebs und Guts erpieten etc.

Nun haben wir woll mit disem Bescheide uns ungehrn willen lassen abweissen und derowegen ihnen allerhandt Bewegnussen zugemuthet, und dabey die Exempta der General Stadten belangent die Commenthorey zu Harlheim in den Teütschen Orden, die alle restituirt, eingebracht, aber ubers vörige nichts oblang mögen.

Uff vast gleiche Form haben wir bey Burgermeister, Scheffen und Rath zu Arnheim angesuecht, die *[fol.20r]* unss ebenmessig auss irem gesambten Räthe beantwortet, dass sie sambt und sonder unsserm Orden gern beygethan und bewogen zu allem Guten, aber ihnen nit gebühren wolte den Regierung undt Landtstenden in diessen Fall vorzugreiffen; wass bey denen künfftiglichen erhalten werden mögte, des soll mahn ahn und bey inen zumahl und nit weinigers haben zu gewarten.

Wan nun aber die Landtstende uff dass Mahl nit zusamzubringen, wir auch sonsten an dieselbe sonders nit recommendirt noch mit Credentz versehen, und also weiter daselbsten nichts verrichten konnen, sondern alle ferner Gelegenheit vonn dem von Rosenbach albereith werden müesse, also haben wir in Krafft unsser Commission, des Ordens Geschefften zum Besten, vorgenannten Herrn Heinrichen von Rechen Ordenspriestern die Administration und Ufsicht des Hausses zu Arnheim und zu Neümägen biss uf Ew. fürstl. Gen. fernern gnedigen Bescheit befohlen und neben ihme alss volmächtigte Anwelde, alles biss uf Ew. fürstl. Gen. gnedige Verordnung, constituirt und angesetzt die ehreveste hochgelehrten und erbahre Gebhardum Poctow, dero Rechten Doctorn, und Heinrichen de Jong, Burgern zu Tijll, dergestalt führohin denjenigen, so etwan weiter uf des Ordens Güther Ansprach thuen würden, in Rechten und Gerichten zu begegenen, auch mit Gelegenheit bey den Landtstenden und Burgermeisteren der Statt die Sachen uf forderlichst zu dirigihren, vorzustellen und sonsten des Ordens Nutz zu werben und Schaden so viel moeglichen verhüeten zu helffen, wie die sambt und sonder unss versprochen und vor den Herren Scheffen sich mit belasten und befehlen lassen.

---

[1] *cf. A.nr.135 above, dd. 4 November 1594.*

Visitation und Verrichtung zue Utrecht.

Im vorgemelten fünffzehenhondert und vierundneüntzigsten Jahren den 21 Julii seint mir von Neümägen ab gen Utrecht ankhommen. Wir haben uns aber erinnert, dass vermöeg unsser Stabilimenten in visitationibus neben den abge-*[fol.20v]*ordneten Ritterbrudern ein Priester des Ordens propter sacra visitanda etc. gemeinlichen zugeben werde. Nun das nit beschehen, haben wir offtgemelten Herrn Heinrichen von Rechen alss ein Priester des Ordens herzugezogen, ime per sanctam obedientiam vigore commissionis eiusque clausulorum generalis befohlen allen folgenden Actibus sich beyzufügen, wie er gehorsamblichen gethan.

Zu [Ut]recht des Ordens Hauss ist camera prioralis et bauilivatus, hat under sich eilff commendas minores. Jetziger Baiulivus, der erwürdiger Herr Heinrich Bärck seines Nahmmens, ex nobili familia patriciorum Traiectensium, welcher 41 Jahren im Orden gewesen unnd nunmehr 33 Jahren Baiulivus gewesen, demselben in coetu suorum conventualium wir unssere habende Commission und Befelch eröffent, vorgelegt und gezeigt, solche sie sambt und sonder mit underthäniger gehorsamber Reverentz agnoscirt, ufgenohmen und deren sich als Ordensbrüdern woll anstehet, zu undergeben allerdings willig und bereith erklehret.

Von der Kirchengebewen.

Daruff wir die Kirchengebewe in Augenschein gesehen und visitirt. Ist gelegen binnen Utrecht intra emunitatem conventus uff der Newen Grafft; auswendig an Maur und Dachwerckh woll gebawet, zimblicher Grösse und Weitte, einwendig aber durch den Krigsvolckh bey den viel aussgestandenen Empörungen devastirt, verwüstet und alle Bildtwerckh daraus- und abgerissen. Consecratum est templum in honorem S^{ti}.Joannis Baptistae et Catharinae^a Virginis; non est parochialis; habet altaria septem, quorum summum S^{to}.Joanni Baptistae, 2. dominae^b Annae et 11000 Virginibus, 3. S^{tae}. Cruci, 4. dominae^b Catharinae, 5. Tribus Regibus sunt sacra, 6. vero et 7. sine singulari dedicatione. Dabey haths einen ser schönen verwölbten Creützgang. Es werden bey diessen Zeiten in selbigem Templo keine Sacra verrichtet, dan solchs bey Leibstraff und uff Verluss und Confiscation aller Güther durch den Magistrath verbotten. Aber intra eandem emunitatem Bauilivatus ist ein Oratorium mit einstehenden [fol.21r] Altar noch unverstörth, darin zumweilen, doch gar heimblichen und mit Gefahr, mehrtheils alle Wochen Sacra peragirt würden, auch in unsser Gegenwerth geschehen.

De bonis ecclesiae.

Demnach hat der Herr Balier tacta cruce bey der Pflicht damit er seinem Orden verwandt, angelobt uff unsse Fragen und Vorstellen die lauther ungefarbte Warheit, so viel ime wissig etc., ausszusagen, zu bekhennen und unss zu berichten und dass nit underlassen weder umb Gelt, Guth, Ehr, Gunst und Vergunst, Nutz oder Schaden etc., alles trewlichen und ohngefehrlichen. Also uf unsser Abforderung hat uns gezeigt und vor Augen gestelt nachfolgende Kirchenkleinoden, die er durch Gottes Hilff mit seinen hochsten Fleiss, grosser Mühe und Gefahr, wunderbarlich versteckt unnd bey allem Krigswesen noch biss hehro erhalten:

Erstlichen zwey silbern ubergülte Ciboria. Item zwey schöne vergülte Büecher, eines Evangeliorum, anders Epistolarum. Item 3 schöne silbern vergülte Platten an Chorkappen. Item ein ser schön vergultes Osculum pacis mitten S^t.Johannshaubt in einer perlenmutter Antlich eingeschmidet. Item 2 schöne vergülte Ampullas. Item ein schön silbern Rauchfass. Item 2 silbern Schüsselen eine darin Agnus Dei, die ander caput S^{ti}.Johannis in figurirt. Item zwein Kelch mit hohen schmalen Stengeten und ufgelegten Decklen. Item drey silbern vergulte Kelche, so vorhanden mit Platen und Zugehör. Item noch zwey vergülte Kelch hatt der Herr Balier der Krigsgefahr halben – wie auch alle andere Stückhe – an ausswendige Örthe gepflogen, aber ungewiss, ob sie wider zu erlangen. Item 6 silberne vergülte plate Chorknöpfe.

Von Kirchengewanth und Ornamenten.

Zum ersten ein Messgewanth mit 6 Chorknöpfen von rot verblumbten Sammet mit eingewirckten Golde, ser schöen, und mit klar guldenen verwerckten Kappen [fol.21v] und abgehenden Leisten, das Gewandt aber mit eine von steiff verwerckten Golte ubergehendt Creütz. Item noch drey Chorkappen von bruen Attlass mit eingewerckten und verblümten Golde, mit versticken goltenen Kappen und gehenden Leisten. Item 2 Chorröcke sambt ihren Carsüfell von blaw Sammet mit güldenen Blommen und steiff guldenem Bordiersell. Item 3 Chorkappenn von weissen Tammast mit gülden Blommen, die Kappen aber hinden abgehendt, wie auch die vordere Leisten von roten Sammet und eingewirckten Golte, verblomet, mit abhangenden Knopfen vonn Kupffer, vergültet. Item ein Carsüfel sambt zwey Chorrockhen von weiss Tammast mit gulden Blomen, auch mit breiden rot Sammet und gülden Leisten bordirth. Item 3 Chorkappen von grünen Sammet mit gülden Leisten rondtumb und vorherab bordirt, dero eine ad oculum gezäigt, die ander zwo nach ausswendig geflohen und gefahrshalben nit zu Handt zu bringen. Item zu allen obgenannten Stückhen die zugehörige Alben. Item etliche Vorhenge an die Altaren mit Tapeten und dergleichen Chrorornamenten, die noch vorhanden, aber ausswendig geflihet und jetzo nit bey der Handt seyen.

De xenodochio eiusque bonis.

Es ist verner in dissem Balivat, auch intra emunitatem, negst bey der Kirchen ein Hospital gelegen, seye schön auss- und einwendig, mit zweyen steinen Gezymmer, negst neben einander gebawet. In dem ersten und grossern Zimmer, welches ser hoch mit holtzenen Gwölb und grossen schönen Fenstern gemacht, ist vorzeiten ein Altar gestanden, daruff Sacra geschehen pflegen, aber jetzmehr durch den Magistrath de facto nidergerissen und abgethan. Hierin seint befunden 19 Bethe ser guth, sauber und frisch, sambt Bethlacken, ein jedes vom andern abgesondert, mit iren rothen Decken, alle gleicher Farben; item jedes mit zwey Par Leinlachen, darzu Küssen und ander Notturfft; item ein jedes besonder mit seinen zinnen Drinkh-*[fol.22r]* und Bethgeschir bestellet und gleich sauber gehalten. Dass ander Zimmer hat jetziger regirender Balivus von newen gebawet, nit weniger schön und sauber dan dass erste; darin gestanden 7 Bethe, ebenmessig schön, mit Bethladen, Vorhengen, roten Deckhen, Leinlachen, Drinckh- und Betgeschier versehen. Noch ein ander Zimmer darbey, auch von jetzigen Herrn Bärck ordinirt und erbawet, darin die Kranckhen ire Feührung und Erwermung besonder haben. Item vor den Hossspitahlmeistern und dessen Gesindt ein Kuchen und Cammern, darin drey Bethladen mit Bethen und allem Zugehörn. In solchem Hospitahl würden eingenohmmen und uf des Ordens Costen in Speiss und Dranck, wie auch mit Aboteck und Arzney und aller nothürfftiger Artzung verpflögen alle arme Kranckhen, Verwünten und Gebrechliche, so die welche in der Statt gebohren und wonhafft alss andere ausswendig einkommende. Zue welcher Verpflegung wirdt bestelt und erhalten ein Hospitalmeister den Kranckhen und allen Notturff ufzusehen; war jetziger Zeit darzu bestellet Herr Gerhardt von Kuik, ein Priester, aber nit unssers Ordens. Denselben wir bey aussgeschworen Aide umb ferner Beschaffenheit des Hospitals erfraget und gibt dissen Bericht, welchermassen zu dem Hospithall und dessen Verpflegung uff Kosten des Herren Baleir bestellet seyen:

Ein Doctor medicus, järlichs vor 59 Gl.brab.; item ein Wundtartz, jarlichs 100 Gl.brab. und 4 Mudt Wäitzen. Seye des Hospitahlsmeisters Besoldung jarlichs 25 Gl.brab. Neben ihme vier Mägte uff die Kranckhen und dero Verpflegung bescheiden; ihre Belohnung jarlichs 60 Gl.brab. Und da von wegen Viele der Kranckhen weiter Hilff von Nötthen, möge ers zu aller Nothurfft uff des Herren Bailivi

Unkosten versehen. Zeigt dabey ahn, das der Herr Balier alle Tage in eigner Persohn und das Hospital und die Kranckhen visitire, dieselben mit guten Speissen woll zugerust versorgen lasse, *[fol.22v]* und ob jemandt zu enigen andern Speissen Lust hette, dass sold der Herr Balier von seiner Taffeln unwegerlich mittheillen. Und in aller Massen wir dass Hospitahl anjetzo bestelt und zauber gesehen, da es also ohn Underlass gehalten werde. De sumtibus ordinariis zeügt und sagt er^c, das zu der Hospitahlskuchen gehalten würden vier Melchekühe, und dass uber solches auch onsserthalben Butter, Käiss, Bier undt Brodt und gesalzten Fleisch nog täglichen uf dem Marckt aussgeben und verthan ungefehr 3 Gl.brab., doch thue der Herr Balier an disser Abspeissung keinen Kosten erspahren. Es wehre uff genwertige Zeit der einligender Kranckhen 15, und wen einer stürbe, müste der Herr Balier von jeder Persohn zu vergraben geben 10 Stüfer.

De domo Balivatus eiusque bonis mobilibus.

Dass von der Balley, wie gleichfals Conventus, ist gelegen in der Statt Utrecht uff der Newen Grafft, daselbsten anno 1529 erbawet. Vorhin aber des Ordens Hauss und Kirch an einem Ende von der Statt an St.Catrinenpfordt gelegen, uff welchen Plan durch den grossmechtigen Kayssern Herr Carl den 5ten ein Castiel, Freüdenberg genant, gebawet, dass selbig nachfolgendes anno 79 *[1579]* durch die Burgerschafft wider abgebrochen. Es ligt dass Hauss und alle angehörige Gebewe, sambt dem Hospitahl, in einer vermaurter Emunitet in vierkandt zwischen vier gemeinen Strassen. Darnzwischen drey verschiedene Baum- und Mosgarten. Hat noch folgende Zimmer: ein gross Salet neben der Kuechen mit zwey Tischen, ein Trittsoir, new und wohl gezirt; darin 6 Stüll und Küssen. Item nechst dabey ein Buttelrey, darin dass Kuchengeschier wirdt verhalten. Item ein klein Salet mit Tisch, Schencktisch und Trittsoir, 6 Stüllen und Küssen, auch mit Tabeten zu einer Seithen behangen. Item zwo Kuchen mit allen eingehörigen Schanckhen, Geschier und dorgleichen. Darhinden ein Spüll- und Waschhauss. Item ein gross Salet, dass Hochsalet genant, mit einem Tisch, *[fol.23r]* vier Stuelen, Küssen und ein Trittsoir. Item ein gross Sall, im Mittel ein Schencktrisoir. Item ein Camerlin hinder der alten Kuechen, gnant im Stuben, ein Trittsoir, Beth, Bethladen, Püllen, Decken und Zubehoir. Item nechst dabey des Herren Balier Cammer met Beth, Bethladen und allen Zugehör. Item darhinden noch ein Zimmer mit Bethladen, Beth, Decken und ein Tisch. Item nebich dem grossen Sall ein Camer mit Bett, Bettladen, Küssen und Deckhen, ein Tisch, 2 Stüll und Küssen. Item dabey ein kleines Cä-

merlin, ein Beth und Bethladen. Item obenuff ein Cämerlin obich
einer gewölbten Gellerey, daruff ein Bethladen, Küssen, Trittsoir und
zwey Stüll. Item darneben ein Cämerlin, daruff ein Bethladen sonder
Beth. Item ein Cammer vor den Herrn Commentorn von Wyemelen
mit 1 Tisch, 2 Stuelen, ein Trittsoir, Beth und Bethladen. Item oben
des Herren Balley Cammer ein Cämerlin mit Betladen, Beth, Küssen, Deck und Tisch. Darneben allernechst eine schöne Cammer mit
ein Tisch, Trietsoir, Bethladen und schönen Vorhengen, Beth, Küssen und Deckhen sambt zweyn kupfern Brandtvüssen. Item nechst
dabey zur ander Seithen zur Strassen war eine Camer mit einen
Tisch, Bethladen und Vorhängen, Beth, Küssen, auch Deckhen,
zween Stüllen und Küssen. Item bey den Convent in Ambitu eine
Cammer mit ein Beth, Bethladen, ein Tisch, zwey Stüllen. Item daselbsten in Ambitu ein Zimmer, die Mittelcammer, mit ein Beth,
Bethleden, ein Tisch und ein grosser Stull, 4 Küssen. Noch vor Diener und Gesinde zwo Cammer sambt vier Bethladen, Deckhen und
Zubehör. Item neben des Hospitallsmeisters Behaussung ein gross
B[r]awhauss mit einem grossen B[r]awkessel, Büdden und allen nöt-
tigen Gereidtschafft; obenuf ein gross Zimmer umb dass Maltz zu
drückhen, mit einer Oefen. Item hat intra emunitatem eine Rossmül-
le, daruff zu der Haushaltung alle Getreide wirt gemahlen, vor auss-
wendigen aber nichts.

Kuchengeschier, Zynnenwerck, Tisch- und Betgewandt.

Mit diesem allen ist dass Hauss zu guther Notturfft versehen, und
dieweil selbigs mehrentheils durch jetzigen Herrn Balier new gemacht – dan dass alte durch den Krieg wegkommen – auch *[fol.23v]*
taglichen führo gebessert wirdt, ist es stündtlichen zu inventarisieren
offerplieben.

ᵃ *ms. and BMHG p.303 have* Cathatrinae. ᵇ *BMHG p.303 has* dᶜ, *ms.* dᵒ.
ᶜ *BMHG p.306 has* E., *ms.* E:.

De proventibus Baiulivatus.

Zu Underrichtung der Müntzen und der Mass zu Utrecht is zu wis-
sen: daterus numeralis hat 30 Stüfer, ein Gulden brab. 20 Stüfer, ein
Goltgulden 54 Stüfer; ein Malter holt 4 S[ch]epfel, aber vast umb ein
fünfften Theill geringer dan zu Neümägen; ein Schepfel 4 Spinnt. Ein
Malter Roggen communiter geästimirt uff 2 1/2 Gl.brab., ein Malter
Weitzen 3 1/2 Gl., ein Malter [Gersten] 2 Gl. 1 Orth, ein Malter
Buchweitz 30 Stüfer.

Nachfolgende Gütter, Gülte und Renthen haben beide der Herr Balier, dan auch neben seiner wir, deroselben Diener und Schaffner, auss aufgesuchten Registern, Rollen und Rechenbüchern verzeichnet und bey verpflicht und respective wahren Wortten attestirt und bezeüget.

Einkhomen in Gelde.

Zum ersten uff Schulpen im Stifft Utrecht 69 Morgen, davon wirdt jarlichs zu Pacht geben 203 Gülden. Item Westbroich, im Stifft Utrecht gelegen, ein Viertel Landes, thut in Gelde 35 Gl., auch etlich Korn wie bey den Fruchtrenten. Item uff Meirrifelt in der Lorssdrecht 6 Morgen vor 16 Gl. Item uff Achtienhofen 7 1/2 viertel Lands unnd 22 Morgen jarlichs im Gelde 250 Gl., auch etliche Früchten. Item im Dorff Ost[v]äin 3 Vertel und 6 Stückh von Vertels mit 112 Morgen, thun jarlichs 410 Gl. sambt etliche Früchten. Item uff Lambroich und zu Darthuissen von etlichen Lendereyen an diverssen Percellen jarlichs 19 Gl. und etlich Roggen, de quo post[e]a. Item zu Kothen 45 Morgen, thun in Gelde jarlichs ahn etlichen Weitzen 130 Gl. Item zu Hauten, zu Odich, in Twoll, uff Schalckweick an Erb- und Jahrpachten 66 Gl. 12 St.

   Summa lateris 1123 Gulden 12 Stüfer.

Item vor der Statt Utrecht an Zollstegspfortt 44 Morgen, jarlichs 121 Gl. Item Juthväss 7 Morgen, 14 Gl. Item uff Galekopen 5 Morgen, 23 Gulden. Item uff Buirkirchen, Hochweiden, uff den Rhein und Mehren 79 1/2 Morgen, 193 Gl. Item zum Merekert in Landt von Vianen 48 Morgen, thuen 150 Gl. Item uff Buirwink 6 Morgen, 15 Gld. Item uff Langerack Deich- und *[fol.24r]* Erbpachlands 9 Morgen vor 20 Gl. Item uff Hermelen ein Bawhoff umbtrint 29 Morgen mit noch 325 Morgen, so an diversse Persohnen verpachtet vor 1500 Gl. Item uff Lobeck und zu Cappellen 203 Gl. Item ein Erbpacht daselbsten 4 Gl. 4 St. Item uff Jarfelt 13 1/2 Morgen, 28 Gl. Item uff Floeten 143 Morgen, 450 Gl. und etliche Früchten. Item daselbsten ein Erbrenth 3 Gl. 7 St. Item uff Ma[r]ssen 75 Morgen, 226 Gl. Item am selben Orth ein Erbpacht 2 Gl. Item zu Bruekelen 67 Morgen, 170 Gl. Item Abtkaw 4 Morgen, 18 Gl. Item uff Lonen an Jahr- und Erbrenth 9 Gl. 4 St. Item zue Reissweickh in Hollandt Erbpacht 6 Gl. 15 St.

   Summa lateris 3169 Gl. 10 St.

Item zu Camerick 52 Morgen, jarlichs in Pachtung an Gelte 150 Gl. Item in der Statt Utrecht de diversis personis an Erbrenthen vermög

der Register 37 Gl. 15 St. Item auss Hausspacht jarlichs, ausserhalben die Reparation, 70 Gl. Item in den Lande Monforth, Oldenwater, Werder und Wo[er]den von underschiedtlichen Parcelen 1350 Gl. Item Iselstein, Benschafft unnd Pulssbr[o]ich 290 Morgen, jarlichs 714 Gl. Item noch ein Bawhoff, gnant zur Weide, negst vor der Statt Utrecht, wirdt durch des Herren Baliers äigen Pferdt und Kösten erbawet, mag jarlichs communiter aussbringen 800 Gl.
Summa huius 3121 Gl. 15 St.

Summa reddituum annuorum in prompta pecunia
7414 Gl.brab. 17 Stuefer.

Einkhomens an Früchten und Getreide.

Item Westbroich, im Stifft Utrecht gelegen, ein Viertel Lands, 5 Malter Roggen. Item uff Achtenhofen an Roggen 10 Malter. Item uff Dorf Ost[v]äin an Roggen 14 Malter. Item uff Lambroich und zu Dorsthuissen 5 Malter. Item zu Dorn Erbpacht 6 Malter. Item daselbsten in Jahrpacht und underschiedtlichen Lendereyen 14 Malter.
Summa in Roggen 54 Malter − [=0] Schepfell, jeder Malter pro 2 1/2 Gl.brab., thut in Gelde 135 Gl.brab.

[fol.24v] Weitzen.

Item zu Kothen vom Bawhofe an Weitzen 35 Malter. Item noch daselbsten 20 Malter. Item zu Werckhofen von 12 Morgen 10 Malter. Item uff Buirkirchen, Hochweiden etc. 13 Malter. Item uff Floeten 30 Malter.
Summa Weitzrenthen 108 Malter, jedes Malter pro 3 1/2 Gl., thuet in Gelde 378 Gl.brab.

Gerst und Buechweitz.

Item von etlicher Lendereyen vor Tollstegspforten zu Utrecht an Gersten 38 Malter. Item uff Buirkirchen, Hochweiden etc. ahn Gersten jarlichs 6 Malter. Item uff Floeten 36 Malter.
Summa Gersten 80 Malter.
Buechweitzen. − Item Antenhoffen an Bueckweitz 11 Malter. Item im Dorff Ost[v]ein 10 Malter. Item zu Gynckell 13 Ackern vor 4 Malter.
Summa 25 Malter.
Jeder Malter Gersten gerechtnet uff zwey Gülden 1 Orth, jeder Mal-

ter Bueckweitz uff 30 Stüfer, thuet zusammen in Gelde 217 1/2
Gl.brab.

Summa alles Einkhommen in Gelt undt in Früchten thuet zusamen
8145 Gl. 7 St. brab., macht Rheinischer Müntzen, den Goltgulden
pro 54 Stüfer, summa 3016 1/2 Goltgulden 16 Stüfer.

De exitibus.

Dass Hauss zu Utrecht zalt jarlichs vor Respons ordinariae ans Trie-
sor in Malta 75 Goltgulden, dan noch dem Herrn Meistern ad Cameram 200 Goltgulden, jeden Goltgulden sie von alters gerechtnet
uff 30 Stüfer, facit 412 Gl. 10 St. Item gehen jarlichs auss an Erb-
pachten und Zinsen 82 Gl. 12 St. Item uff Underhalt des Hospitals
eines weniger des ander Jar mehr, communiter geschlagen ungefehr
1800 Gl. Item gibt dass Hauss järlichs 13 Spenden den Armen, jedes-
mahl ungefehr an Roggen und Weitzen 6 Malter, wirdt angeschlagen
jarlichs uff 200 Gl. Item zu Lohn dess Haussgesindts, alss Renthmeis-
ter, Diener, Mägte, Portier, Beckher und Brawer, Garttnier, Botten-
lohn, jarlichs 500 Gl. Item jarlichs pro reparatione domus 800 Gl.
Item jarlichs vor Freyheit der Wachte 60 Gl. Item vor Impost, Ac-
cinss und Contri-*[fol.25r]*bution von Bier 500 Gl. Item vor Brandt
undt Torff und ander Brandt 50 Gl.
    Summa lateris 4855 Gl.

Exitus.

Item [zu] Underhaltung der Predicanten werden des Ordens Hauss
abgetrungen jarlichs 226 Gl. Item alss bey diessen langwürigen
Kriegswesen der Herr Balivus von des Ordens Güthern nit geniessen
mögen, gleichwohl seine Persohn mit den Herren Conventualen, darzu des Hospitall mit zwärlichen Unkosten erhalten und versehen
müssen, hetten iro wir noth- und drangnusshalben uffgenohmmen
undt entleihett die Summa ungefehr vonn 3500 Reichsthaler; darvon
müssen noch zur Zeit biss zur Ablössung in Pension zalt und aussgeben werden 420 Gülden. Solche Sumben aber hat Herr Baiulif versprochen und zugesagt, dafern Gott Friden und Lebent verlehen
würde, ungefehr in wenig sechs oder sieben Jahren dennechst volgent
abzulössen und des Ordens Gütern zu verfreyen. Sonsten und ausserhalb dissen sei bey Lebzeiten seines, des Herrn Baiulivus, von des
Ordens Gütern nichts alienirt, gravirt oder veringert worden.
    Summa huius 646 Gl.

Summarum exituum 5501 Gl. 2 St.brab.

Summarum Rheinischer Müntzen 2037 Goltgulden 24 Stüfer, demnach die Aussgülden und järlich Beschwarnussen von den einkom-
menden Renthen abgezogen, pleibt uberig 979 Goltgulden 19 Stüfer,
davon sich der Herr Baiulivus zusambt den Herren Conventualen
mitt Hauss- und Hoffgesinde, nemblich zweyen Dienern, 3 Mägten,
ein Portirer, Beckher und Bawer und Garthnier zu underhalten.

De Commendis Balivatus in Utrecht et commendatariis membrorum.

Under den Baiulivat zu Utrecht gehören elff Commendae, die ahn
underschiedtliche Örthern gelegen und beschaffen wie folgt.

1.   Die erste Commenda: Schnieck

In Frieschlandt eine gelegen vor der Statt Schnieck, gnant S^t. Johan
Dall, welche ufm Bodem gantz nidergerissen; die Güter wüst. Der
Commendatarius hat etliche Conventualen und *[fol.25v]* Pastoreyen
under ihme, aber jetzo gantz verstrewet; man khönne auch nit erfah-
ren, wie oder wah sie vor dissmahl anzutreffen. Ist Membrum in
Utrecht.

2.   Kirchwerff.

In Zeelandt ein Jungfferenconvent zu Kirchwerff, davon die Jungfra-
wen verstorben, die Gebew verbrandt und nidergerissen, die zugehörige Güther und Gefelle durch den Magistrath verkaufft und alienirt
worden.

3.   Harderwick.

Im Fürstenthum Geller bey der Statt Harderwick ein Convent, darin
von alters ein Comendatarius von Utrecht dahin commendirt, mit
etlichen Conventualen, jetzo alle abgestorben, ausserthalben einer,
welcher apostahirt; die Gebew nidergerissen, ein angehörigen Busch
und Holtzgewachs abgehawen, die andere Güter von der Regierung
zu Arnheim eingenohmmen, die sie auch noch verhalten.

4.   Meidelbürgk.

Item Zeelandt in der Statt Middelbürgk eine kleine Commenda, davon die Güther durch den Magistrath confiscirt seyen.

5.   Harmelen.

In Stifft Utrecht zu Harmelen eine Commenda, die Kirch abgebrandt, dass Hauss zum Theill auch nidergerissen. Ist ledig und vacirt, aber also mit Schulten belastet und beschwerth, dass sie der Herr Balier in Henden verhaltet, administirt und die Schulden darauss abzahlen lasset.

6.   Engen.

Im Fürstenthum Geller in der Niderbetaw im Kirspell Engen gelegen; dass Hauss seye [von] die Kriegsleüth vor achtzehen Jahren nidergerissen und abgebrandt; ist daselbsten Commendatarius modernus der würdiger Herr Heinrich Reüsch, ein vast alter betagter Herr von 76 Jahren, thete sich anjetzo binnen der Statt Utrecht in des Ordens [fol.26r] Hausse, zu der Balley gehörig, mit günstigen Willen des Herrn Balivus wonhafft verhalten, welcher sich der Visitation williglichen ergeben und bey gewonlicher Pflicht uf die abgefertigte Gelegenheit seiner Commenden folgendermassen geantwortet.

De ecclesia eiusque bonis.

Des Ordens Kirch daselbsten seie parochialis, und pflegen uf Kosten der Commenden zwen Cappellani erhalten zu werden; die Ornamenta aber und wass zu der Kirchen gehörig, seye nit in Handen und Gewalt des Ordens, sondern zweyer darzu bestelten Kirchenmeistern gestanden; derowegen darüber zu inquiriren unnötig erachtet. Von Hauss und Haussgerädt zeügt und sagt, dass Hauss seye lengst devestirt, Hausgräide, Beth, Kisten, Kasten und alles wegkgeraubet, unnd er gnaw mit blosser Persohn davon khommen.

De proventibus.

Es habe die Commenda einen Bawhoff, gelegen zu Engen im Dorff Maurick, gnant Osterwerst, anhaltent 70 hollendische Morgen, und weill die Lenderey nit vast Guth, ist von alters verpachtet vor jarlichs

300 Gl., aber jetziger Zeit vor 250 Gl. Item uff Ummerfelde 7 Morgen Ardtlands, so vor disem Orde gelegen, thue nun jarlichs zu Pacht 14 Gl. Item im Dorff von Engen, Maurick, Ummeren und Lijnden ungefehr 100 Morgen theils Ardtlandt theils Weidelant, zusambt einem Zehenden zu Engen, thuen von alters und noch 986 Gl.

Summa proventuum in Engen 1250 Gl., thuet Rheinischer Müntzen 481 Goldgulden 26 Stüfer.

De exitibus.

In Vorzeiten pflegen uff disser Commenden gehalten zu werden zween Cappellani; an dern Statt würdt der Commendatarius gezwungen dem Predicanten daselbsten jarlichs zu geben 250 Gl. Item von alters halt die Commenda drey Persohnen, welche die Deich beschawen, darvor jarlichs 100 Gl. Item in Fridenszeiten pflag ein Commenda des Endts in der Hausshaltung zu haben zween Capellanos, drey Mägte, vier Bawknecht, und *[fol.26v]* zween Diener; hat zu disser Zeit in seiner Haussaltung mehr nit dan zwo Mägte und einen Jungen, gibt einer zu Lohn 24 Gulden, der ander 12 Gl.brab., facit 36 Gl.

Exitus non continui.

Item vor Contribution an dem Ambtmahn von Tyell bey dissen Krigszeiten jedes Jahrs 100 Gl. Item vor monathliche Contribution in diessen Krigsweessen alle Jahr geben müssen 100 Thaler pro 30 Stüfer, facit 150 Gl. Item an einen Nebendeich zu machen negstlitten dreyen Jahren alle Jahr aussgeben 400 Gl., fellet aber nicht alle Jahr zu machen.

Summa exituum 1036 Gl., thuen in Rheinischer Müntzen 383 1/2 Goltgulden 11 Stüfer.

Wan dan die Aussgulden dieser Zeit von den Uffkünfften abgezogen, pleibt in der Commenda Engen zu des Commendatarii und seines Gesindes Haussaltung ubrig 96 1/2 Goltgulden 15 Stüfer.

Und hat endtlichen attestirt, dass bey allen aussgestandenen Benawungen und leidigen Verderben, dannoch von des Ordens Güthern durch ihnen nichts verkaufft noch umb ichtwas verpfendet oder beschwehret.

[7.]   Büren, Membrum in Utrecht.

In der Graveschafft undt Statt Bühren gelegen, daselbsten Commendatarius Herr Gijssbertus Abass. Uffm Wege von Tyell gen Utrecht
seint wir am selben Orth zugezogen. Der Orden hat daselbsten kein
Kirchen; dass Hauss ist nunmehr in der Statt uf einer Strassen, gnant
der Seüllendall, gelegen, von Steinen fein auffgebawet, unverwüstet,
in guter Qualitet erhalten; hat einen feinen beygelegenen Garten; bey
der Erden zwo Kuechen, ein Salett, eine Cammer unnd ein cleines
Cämmerlin, mit nöthürfftigen Haussgeräide versehen. Die Kirche ist
ehezeits sambt dem Hausse vor der Statt gelegen, aber vor langst
nidergelegt.

De proventibus.

Vorgemelter Commendatarius modernus, nach abgenohmener
Pflicht wie gewonlichen, gab von allen Einkommens nach- *[fol.27r]*
geschrieben Bericht. Es habe die Commenda ein Hoffgut der Jordan,
davon dass Gebaw abgebrochen; halt 40 Morgen Landts, dero fünff
Weidt- und die ubrige Ardtlandt seyen; item dem Graven von Bühren mit einem Wagen zu dienen verpflicht, und neben solche Diensten zusammen verpachtet vor 162 Gl. Item noch 12 Morgen, thuen
28 Gl. Item uff Erikum 8 Morgen, 32 Gl. Uff Grassbroch 10 Morgen,
70 Gl. Item in die Polder 4 Morgen, 26 Gl. Item noch in die Polder
underschiedtlichen 15 Morgen, thuen 90 Gl. Item uff Tricht 11 Morgen, 28 Gl. Item uff Bürenmalsen 6 Morgen, 13 Gl. Item uff Ass
underschiedtlichen 14 Morgen, 66 Gl. Item in die Polder 20 Morgen,
werden umb halbschiedt gebawen; davon zur Abkunffts geschetz 150
Gl.
     Summarum proventuum in Büren 665 Gl., in Rheinischer Münt-
zen 246 Goltgulden 16 Stüfer.

De exitibus et oneribus.

Item zu Erhaltung der Gebew jarlichs 25 Gl. Item hat in der Hausshaltung zwo Mägte, dero eine verdient jarlichs 30 Gl., die ander 10
Gl., facit 40 Gl. Item ist die Comende beschwert und müssen an
dieversse Persohnen zalt werden jarlichs 36 Gl. 5 st. Contribution von
der Le[n]dereyen 140 Gl. Item es hat weylandt Herr Gerhardt vor
der Kettel, huius antecessor, zu Ufbringung seines Ransoins, da er
gefangen gewesen, uf des Ordens Güthern zu ablösen verschrieben
Haubtgelts 500 Goltgulden brab., jarlichs zu verzinssen mit 31 Gl. 5

St. Item noch hat jetziger Commendatarius zu notthürfftiger Erbawung eines newen Deichs in der Betaw mit Consens des Herrn Balivi
ufgenohmen Haub[t]gelt 200 Gl., davon jarlichs 12 1/2 Gl. Ausserthalben jetzgemelter Beschwernus seye von und aus diessen Güthern
nichts veralienirt noch verpfendet. Er hatt restlichen in Beywesen des
Herrn Baiulivi angelobt die vorgemelte 200 Gl., so zu Erbawung des
Deichs uffgenohmmen, uffs allerehest alss moeglichen wider abzulössen und des Ordens Güter darvon zu befridigen 285 Gl.

   Summa facit der Auss-*[fol.27v]*gülden 285 Gl., thuet Rheinischer
Müntze 105 Goltgulden 30 Stüfer.

   Solche Aussgülde von dem Einkhomens abgezogen pleibt Uber-
schüss 140 Goltgulden 40 Stüfer; wird vor die täglichen Hausshaltung
geacht.

[8.]   Oldewater, Membrum in Utrecht.

Item in Hollandt in der Statt Oldenwater hat diss Hauss gelegen und
umb sich her einen zimblichen Plan gehabt, aber anno 1575 gar
abgebrochen und durch den Plan die Graben vor der Statt gemacht.
Daselbsten Commendatarius der würdig Herr Jacobus Weynen, alt
und wolbetagt. Nach abgenohmmenen Pflicht attestirt er von Gelegenheit der Commenden, dass der Orden alda ein Cappellen gehabt,
aber von den Kriegesleüthen abgebrochen und verbrandt, und durch
den Plan die Stattgrafften gemacht. Die Güther und Ornamenta sey-
en alle wegkgeraubet, nichts ubrigs plieben, allein in Persohna dar-
vonkhommen.

   De proventibus.

Zu disser Commenden gehören erstlich an der Nortseithen von
Lindtschoten 63 1/2 Morgen Weidtlandt, thuet jeder Morgen jetz
jarlichs 5 Gl., facit 327 Gl. Item an die Südeseith von Lindtschoten
16 Morgen Weidtlandt, thuet jeder 4 Gl., facit 64 Gl. Item in einer
Baurschafft, gnant Papenkop, gelegen 28 Morgen Weidtlandt vor 50
Gl. Item in Grott Heckendorff 8 Morgen, 32 Gl. Item 2 Morgen
Hochlandt, jeder in Pachtung jarlichs 20 Gl., facit 40 Gl.

   Summa proventuum Oldewater 513 Gl., thuet Reinisch 190 Goltgulden.

De exitibus et oneribus.

Der Commendatarius, inn Anwesen dess Herrn Baliers attestiert unnd bezeuget, dass er bei seiner Zeit von Ordensgütern nichts versetzt noch verkaufft oder, dass solches geschehen seye, Wissens hab, ausserthalben bei dem langwirigen Kriegsswesen und Verhergung, allein zu seines Leibssunnderhalt, hab er uffnehmen *[fol.28r]* unnd auff die Ordensgüter verschreiben müssen 900 Gl.brab., dero vor Jhars abgelöst 300 Gl., also restiert Haubtgeldts 600 Gl.; wurden verpensioniert jedes Hundert mit 6 Gl. – 36. So pflege mann daselbsten zu unnderhalten ein Capellanum, zwo Mägd, einenn Knecht: ietzo halt er keine Diener noch Dienerin, sonndern seie bei seiner Schwester in der Statt Utrecht inn der Kost; also könne er auch von denn ordinari Aussgulden jetzt nichts eigentlichs definieren.

9.   Werder.

Ist gelegen inn Hollandt in einem Dorff, Werder genant; jetziger Commendatarius Herr Arnoldus Hieren, seines Alters – wie gesagt – omtrent 78. Dennselben wir durch den Herrn Baleir zu unss gen Utrecht fordern lassen – dann sonsten in locum zu reisen, wie auch ann die anndere, keine Gelegenheit gewesen – hat er sich seines Aussbleibens von wegen schweren Alters und Unvermögenheit schrifftlichen entschuldigt, sonnsten zu allem gehorsamlich willig erklärt, nicht minder in selbiger Missiven gemeltter Commenden Gelegenheit nachfolgendergestalt erklärt und aussgesetzt.

Es seyen die Capell unnd Behausung daselbsten in den vorigen Kriegsempörungen lengst gantz verbrandt unnd nidergeworffen, alle Kirchenornamenta und Haussgeräth wegkgeraubet, er allein bloss mit dem Leib darvonkommen.

De proventibus annuis.

Es seien zu dieser Commenden gehörig ann Weide- und Saatlandt 100 Morgen, thaten järlichs 450 Gl. Nun wären ferner noch 10 Morgen ann der Pastorei, wurden aber durch die Obrigkeit zu Erhaltung ihres Predicanten verwendet. Also ertragt sich die Summa der Einkumbsten ut supra 450, thun Reinische Müntzen –.

De exitibus et gravaminibus.

Er habe hie bevoren, da er von diverssen Kriegssobristen und Soldaten überfallen, zu dero abgenöttigten Underhaltung, da er auch der
Einkombsten nicht geniessen können, cum consensu d.Baiulivi uffgenommen die Summa von 416 Gl.brab., jhärlichss davon zu verzinsen
26. In Nachmals cum consensu ut supra zu Uffbawung eines Bau-
hoffs uff die Commenda beschwerth 640 Gl. Haubtgeldts, järlichs zu
ablosen, zu verzinsen mit 40. *[fol.28v]* Item er müsse alle Jahr von
allen Ländereien Schatzung und Contribution geben allermassen wie
anndere hollänndische Underthanen – sich hoch bezeugende, dass
ihme jhärlichs zu seines Leibs Unnderhaltung mehr nicht dann ungefähr 100 Daler, jeden zu 30 Stüfer, uberschiesse, thut 150 Gl.

Hierab und sonnderlichen wegen der uffgenommenen Pfenningen
und desshalben verleiheten Consens wir bei dem Hernn Balier unnd
anndern anwesenden Commendatarios Nachfrag gethan, so habe
wol der Herr Balier in angezogenen Nöthen seinen Consensum zu
der Ufnahm gegeben, aber mit diesem Geding, wie auch der Com-
mendat vestlich versprochen, alle Jars folgends 100 Gl. biss zu völli-
ger Ablöss zu quitieren. Weil er dann deme also noch keines Jhars
nachkommen, haben wir ihme schrifftlichen befohlen solcher seiner
Gelöbnuss fürter Volg zu thuen, womit dess Ordens Güter wieder
gefreiet werden mögen.

10.   Wemelingk.

Inn Zud-Bevelandt in einem Dorff, Wemelingk genandt, ist noch ein
annder Membrum gelegen, unnd weil es übel dahin zu reisen, darzu
am selbigen Orth der Orden kein Residentzhauss hat, also den jetzigen Commendaturn durch den Herrn Balier gen Utrecht verschreiben lassen, welcher, mit Nahmen Herr Heinrich Vochss, dahin
gehorsamblichen erschienen unnd uf gelaiste Aydsspflicht seiner
Commenden Beschaffenheit nachgesetztermassen bericht geben.

De ecclesia [et] eiusdem ornamentis.

Die Commenda hab von alters gehabt ein sehr kleines Sacellum,
welches bei diesem Kriegswesenn, ehe dann er dahin commendirt,
gar verwüstet, dass Dach nidergefallen, die Klocken aussgenommen;
doch hätten auch bei von alters die Commendatarii keinen, sonndern
nur auff S\.Johannis Midtsommer unnd in der Creutzwochen der
Kurspelsspastor, daselbsten Dienst gehalten. Von Ornamenta der

Kirchen sey ihme nichts vorkommen; es hab auch einwendig 30 Ja-
ren [kein] frater Ordinis daselbsten von wegen böser Lufft residiret.

De domo et eius bonis mobilibus.

Hab kein Residentzhauss, dann allein zu Wemelingk ein Bawers-
hauss, darin er kein Haussrath überall gefunden, angesehen so lange
Zeit, alss obgemelt, keiner von Ordenspersonen da haussgehalten.
[fol.29r] Er aber hab sich vor diesem siben Jhar lang in einem Stätt-
lein nechst darbey, genant Gouss, jetziger Zeit in Hollandt in der
Statt Leyden verhalten.

De proventibus.

Zu Wemlingk einen Bawrenhoff, halt an Ländereien, gut und böss,
220 Mätten, je zwo Mätten machen einen holländischen Morgen;
seie zusammen verpacht mit allen Lasten jhärlichss für 823 Gl. brab.,
unnd habe weiter keine Einkommen; thut Reinisch 304 Goltgulden
44 Stüfer.

De exitibus.

Item vor Hausshewer jhärlichss, weil uf der Commenden keinss gewesen, 72 Gl. Item einem Diener, so die Gefäll jährlichss erhebt und
verrechent, jhärlich 36 Gl. Item vor Wasserpfeningk, Deickgeldt,
Schatzung und anndere Beschwernussen jährlichss 297 Gl.
     Summa exituum in Wemeling 405 Gl., thut Reinisch 150 Goltgul-
den.

Von denn Einkombsten abgezogen verbleibt dem Herrn zu sein und
der seinigen Underhaltung 154 Goltgulden 44 Stüfer.
Zeugt expresslichen, dass keine Güter oder Einkommen von der
Commenden versetzt, verkaufft oder einigergestalt alienirt seien.

11.   Montfort, Membrum in Utrecht.

Ist gelegen in Stifft Utrecht in der Statt Monfort, ethwa 20 Meil wegss
von der Statt Utrecht; von dem gewesenen Baiulivo zu Utrecht Bern-
hardt von Duven anno 1544 erst fundiert und erbawet. Darin ist
Commendatarius modernus Herr Johannes Ridder, dess Ordens gewesen 35 Jahr; durch Erfordern des Herren Baiulivi uf Utrecht er-

schienen, der Visitation sich gehorsamblichen unndergeben und folgende Gelegenheit seiner Commenda mittes leiblichen Aidss angezeiget.

De ecclesia et eius ornamentis.

Es habe in der Statt uf der Hoffstrat ein klein Sacellum mit einem Altar in honorem S^{ti}.Joannis Baptistae consecratum, welches noch seie in Esse, alleine aber alle darufgestandene Ornamenta und Bildtwerck abgerissen. In selbigem Sacello thue er noch zur Zeit Sacrum, aber heimblichen. Darin gehörig ein kupffern vergulten Kelch und sonsten keine Kleinoden mehr gefunden. An Messgewandt seie vorhanden ein Carsufel von rotem Sammet verb[l]üemt mit eingewercktem Goldt, mit seiner Alben und Zugehör. Item ein Carsufel von rotem Treipe. Item zween Chorröck von schwartzem Lacken sonder Atinentien. Item zwei Behängselss umb groiss Gestuel von rotem Treipfen. Item zwei alte Antependia vor Altaren.

[fol.29v] De domo et eius utensilibus.

Item bei der Capellen intra Emunitatem eine Behausung von Steinen uffgebawet, zimblicher Weitte in seinem Bezirck gelegen, mit Haussgeräth, Leinwandt, Zinen und anderm Kuchengeschirr; item Beth, Bethladen und allem Zugehör nottürfftiglichen versehen, welches er verbessert häte, auch ferner zu verbessern angelobt.

De proventibus.

Hab in Willeskop 11 Morgen Weid- unnd Sehelandt, verpacht jährlichs vor 54 Gulden. Noch daselbst 4 Morgen, järlichss 20 Gulden. Item inn Kortte Blocklandt 4 Morgen, 22 Gulden. Item int Blocklandt 16 Morgen, 100 Gulden. Item uf Isefeldt 3 Morgen, 12 Gulden. Item im Kattenbroich 6 Morgen 4 Hont, 40 Gulden. Item in Pulssbroich 7 Morgen 40 Gulden.

Erbgeltrenten uff Widerloss.

Item auss dem Bailivat zu Utrecht lossbar Renthen järlichss 50 Gulden.
Summa lateris 338 Gulden.

Item bei dem Erbgenamen Wilhelms von Houff lossbar 50 Gulden.
Item an Maximillian von Baxenn 60 Gulden. Item an Dederich De-
richsssohn zu Worden 60 Gulden. Item ann Frantz von Schnick 62
1/2 Gulden. Item ein Renth auss einem alten Stall 11 Gulden.

Summa summarum der Einkombsten zu Monfort 581 1/2 Gulden, thuet Reinischen Müntzen 215 Goltgulden 20 Stüfer.

De exitibus.

Vor Reparation der Kirchen un dess Hauses, den zu Ablösung einer
Leibrenthen von 13 Gl.brab., jährlich, uffgenommen an Haubtgeldt
100 Dhaler jeden pro 30 Stüfer, davon gibt man järlichss 9 Gl. 7 1/
2 Stüfer. Item von einer Kuchenmagd Belohnung järlich 16 Gl. Item
vor einen Jungen, Kleidung unnd Lohn, 25 Gulden. Item obgemelten
Renthen durch Ordinantien von Herren Statten werden järlich ge-
kürtzet 30 Gulden.

Summa exituum 80 Gulden 7 1/2 Stüfer, thut Reinisch 29 Goltgulden 41 1/2 Stüfer.

Von dem Einkombsten abgezogen bleibt dem Herrn vor Hausshaltung unnd anndere extraordinari Kriegssuncosten 185 Goltgulden
32 1/2 Stüfer.

Pastorat Ommeren.

Im Fürstenthumb Geldern inn der Nider-Battaw im Kirspell Ummeren ein Pastorat gelegen, pflag durch ein Ordensconventual zu
Utrecht bedienet zu werden, nunmehr aber ibidem mutata religione
pro sola conservatione iuris durch den Herrn Balier durch einen auss-
wendigen Person ad literarum revocationem conferirt, welcher der
Ennden die Predigen versehen thuet.

[fol.30r] De conventu et conventualibus [Traiectensi].

Dass Convent is neben und bei der Balei intra eandem emunitatem
ann der Ordenskirche und Creutzgang gelegen; ein schön, hohes,
vonn Steinen erbawtes Hauss, unnden und oben mit herrlichen Saa-
len, Refectorien unnd anndern Schlaffzimmern und darin gehöriger
Notturfft reichlichen versehen. Von alters mit so viel Conventualen
unnd Ordensbrüdern bestellet zu werden alss einem Balier gefallig
unnd Einkommens ertragen können. Waren aber uf gegenwärttige
Zeit darin siben in Anzal, mit Nahmen:

Andreas Schimmelpfenning, Prior.
Bernhardus Schönhoffen.
Petrus von dem Berge.
Frater Alexander Bärck.
Johannes Winndt.
Johannes de Huen.
Stephanus ab Harttenfeldt.

Von obgemelten Conventualen ist Petrus von dem Berg sine licentia abwesendt gewesen unnd frater Johannes de Huen studii gratia cum licentia et beneplacito huius d.Baiulivi verzogen; die anndere waren alle gegenwerttig.

Examen conventualium.

1.   Frater Andreas Schimmelpfenning Prior zuu Aidt ufgenommen, underfragt, zeugt ad interrogata alss nach folgt. Er seie dess Ordens gewest 31 Jahr.

De sacrificiis sagt, dass sie jetzo in ihrer grossen Kirchen keinen Dienst thuen mögen auss Verbott dess Magistrats, nichts destoweniger sacrificirten sie wechssellweiss alle Sontag unnd fornehmen Festtag in dess Herrn Balivi Oratorio.

De vita et moribus d.Baiulivi et conventualium anndtwortt, dass er uber Person oder Regierung des Herrn Baliers nicht klagen könne, so wurden sie durch dennselben in conventu suo wol und reichlichen unnderhalten. Die Conventualen betreffendt, seien dero uf diese Zeit, mit seiner Person, in Anzahl siben, dero sechss in gutenn fridlichen Chatolischen Wesen sich vertragen, der sibende aber, Petrus von dem Berge, seie rebellis und von dem Convent ohn Erlaubnuss abgetreten, so bei ihnen in Conventu seither dem Monat Januario nit gegessen ausserthalben ein Monatzeit, da er an seiner Hanndt verbrandt gewesen. *[fol.30v]* Ihrer seien fünff Priester, zween, nemblich Johannes de Huen und Stephanus de Hartenfeldt, allererst binnen Jahrs dass Creutz empfangen. De bonis ecclesiae et domus sagt, ihme seie nicht kundig, dass durch denn Herrn Balier ichtwass in Gereiden oder Ungereiden verkaufft oder versetzt stehe.

De membris vacantibus sagt, dass zu dieser Zeit drey commenden vacirten: eine zu Kirchwerff inn Seelandt, hatten die Magistrat von Staten confiscirt und verkaufft; – die anndere in der Statt Middelburg, het eine Renth an selbiger Statt järlich 17 lb. grott, wurdden zelt unnd dem Herrn Balivo geliffert; umb die übrige Güter hätt er keine Wissenschaft; – die dritte gelegen im Stifft Utrecht zu Hermelen, seie noch in Esse, vorhin aber also mit Schulden betastet, dass

sich ein Ordensperson daselbsten nicht erhalten mögen; wurde derowegen in Handen dess Herrn Baliers erhalten, biss sie auss iren Uff-
kumbsten sich selber eingelöset.

De commendatariorum bonis, vita et moribus andtwortt, er wiste
keines Person zu verklagen, weren auch seines Wissens keine Ordensgüter versetzt oder in welttliche Hännde transferirt; allein were ime
vorkommen, dass der Commendatarius zu Oldenwater seine Commenden und Güter an seinen Schwagern, eine weltliche Person, verpachtet habe, welcher hinwiederumb uff seinen unnd nicht dess
Ordens Nahmen selbige verlihen thäte; ob daer einige Gefahr zu
besorgen, wolle er zu unsern Bedencken gestellett haben.

De prestantia conventus interogatus respondebat, dass die Conventualen eigener Renthen jetztmehr fast an die 350 Gl. Einkommens hätte, welche durch ihren Prioren jhärlich eingenommen und
den Conventualen verrechnet wurden. Damit erlassen.

[2,3,4]   Demnach gleichermassen erfraget fr.Johannes Windt, dess
Ordens 33 Jahr, fr.Bernhardt Schönhofen, dess Ordens 24 Jahr,
fr.Alexander Bärck, 22 Jahr, alle und ein jeder sonderlichen, mit Aid
ufgenommen, gaben diesen einmüthigen Bericht.

De sacrificiis, das inen offentliche Exercitia von dem Magistrath
nit [fol.31r] werde gestattet; heimblichen theten sie Dienst in Oratorio
uff alle Son- und Vesttage.

De vita et moribus d.Balivi wissen nichts dan alles guths unnd
werde inen nach aller Gebihr in Conventu irr Notturfft subministrirt.

De bonis ecclesiae, de membris vacantibus, de commendatariis, de
suis conventualibus, quilibet de aliis, attestiren sie und ein jeder sonderlich in effectu, wie der Herr Prior fr.Andreas Schimmelpfenningk.

De pre[s]tantia conventus. Soviel die Speiss betreffe, werdt inen
durch den Herrn Balier subministrirt und gereichet. Zu irer Kleidung
hetten sie jarlichs ungefehr 350 Gl., die der Herr Prior zu guder
Rechnung einnehme und ausstheille.

[5]   Fr.Stephanus ab Hartenfelt, ut caeteri iuratus, sagt, das er allererst negstlitten 2 Februarii das Creütz empfangen, noch nit Priester
worden. De sacrificiis zeüget, wie die andern alle sonsten; uff die
andere Fragen, dieweill er so newlich einkommen, ausserthalben das
er under seinen Herrn mit Conventualen, so viel deren gegenwertig,
ein züchtig fridlich Lebens erfführe, wüst er nichts sonders zu berichten, et sic dimissus.

Anno quo supra 8 Augusti.

Nachdem wir vor und nach im Gesprech, auch in examine conventualium fratrum verstanden, dass etliche Gebrechen zwischen denselben Conventualen sich erreüget und verhielten, auch sie contra
d.Jacobum Weinen Commendatarium [in] Oldenwater ichtwas zu
klagen hetten, haben wir inen darzu heüth dato sonderliche Audientz
gemacht und verstattet, dabey beruffen d.Heinricum Bärck Baiulivum,   d.Heinrichum   Reüsch   Commendatarium   in   Engen,
d.Gijsbertum ab Ass Conmmendatarium in Bühren, d.Heinrichen
Vochss Commendatarium [in] Wemelingk, d.Johannem Ridder
Commendatarium in Monfortt.

Processus contra fratrem Petrum von den Berg.

[fol.31v] Fr. Peter von dem Berge wardt verklagt, das er auss seinem
Conventu ohn Licentz und Verlaubnus abgetretten, daraussen sich
ein lange Zeit biss noch verhalten, des Ordens Güthern, ohn Befelch
und Commission, eigner Thadt und unzimblicherweisse bey ausslen-
dischen secular Persohnen, nemblichen der Graffen von Leycester,
einem Engelschen Obristen, sich de Commenda herralso providiren
lassen, darzu seines Lebens nit religios erzeigte etc. Waruff ihnen gen
heüt Datum vorbescheiden, er aber in Persohn aussplieben und
zween von seinen Blutfreunden und Verwanten zu unss abgefertiget
die Klag und —, wie sie sagten, anzuhöhren, welchen wir obgemelte
Stücke verstündtlichen vorgehalten unnd alssbaldt, nach erholten
Raths bey dem Beklagten, sie zu dessen vermeinter Defension antra-
gen lassen. Zum ersten: seines [Abwesens] Ursach wehren die Creditoren, welche inen dermassen verfolgten, das er sich [in] Utrecht nit
verhalten dörffte. Zum andern: die Commenda zu des Herrn Lho
hab er bey Graven von Leycester impetrirt, dan er bericht gewest,
alss solte selbig von alters in Collatione des Herrn baiulivi nit, sondern weldtlicher Obrigkeit stehen. Paten umb Gnad und Verzeihung,
darzu umb Hilff und Securs seine Creditoren abzurichten, mit Erpieten führo sich in allen Gehorsamb [zu] erzeigen. Alss nun in weitere
Verkündung befonden, das beklagter Peter von dem Berge solche
seine Schulden eben in Zeiten seiner Rebellion und wan er sich aussen dem Conventu verhalten, gemacht habe und also vitium ex vitio
seye, die dem Orden uffzuweissen unzimblich et res mali exempli sein
werde, so haben wir doch auss allerhandt bewegenden Ursachen, mit
reiffen Bedacht und Rath vorgemelter Herren unssers Ordens, uf
fleissige Inte[r]cession gerürts Beklagtens Bludtverwandten, darüber
decretirt, recessirt und verabscheidet dissermassen: wofernn gedach-

ter Peter von den Berge vor seinnen Herrn Balier undt *[fol.32r]*
sembtlichen Conventualen in Capitulo erscheinen, sich demütigen
und umb Nachlass bitten, die Ordensgüter so ungepiehrlicherweisse
impetrirt ad manus d.Balivi libere resignieren und abtretten, auch
ohn Schaden und Zuthuen des Ordens seyne privat gemachte Schulden abrichten, und sich führo nach Religion und Ordenspflicht verhalten wolte, soll damit aller Verlauff ufgehoben und verziehen sein.
Jedoch also, dass er die Zeit von acht Jahren das Convent vermeiden,
dessen nit gaudiren, auch ᵃ sonderlichen Beruf nit einkhommen zwischen deme alle, und jedes Jars zu seinem Underhalt auss Henden
des Herrn Balivi die Summa von 150 Gl.brab. zu zweyen Terminen
empfangen [und] haben solle, − jedoch nach seinen Verhalten die
Zeit des Ausswesens uf Wolgefallen und Belieben des Herrn Baliers
und Conventualen zu vermindern. Mit angehenckter ausstrücklicher
Declaration, da diese erzeigte Gratia und Ordinatio ime Peter von
Berge nit ahnnemlich seyen, sondern er in seinen Ungehorsamb und
unzimblicher Occupation beharren würde, dass er, dan alss jetzo und
jetzo alss dan, seines Ordens Dignitet Beneficium und Freyheiten
gentzlichen endtsetz und privirt sein solle, wie wir ihnen uff den Un-
verhofften in Krafft habender Commission entsetzen, abthuen und
priviren gegenwürdtglichen sole[m]niter et cum effectu etc.

> Processus contra d.Jacobum Weinen,
> Commenthur in Aldenwater.

Ferner wordt unss vorbracht, welchergestalt der erwürdig Herr Heinrich Bärck, Balier, vor etlichen Jahren dem würdigen Herrn Jacob
Weinen die Commenda Aldenwater und darzu noch eine andere
Commenda zu Harderwickh conferirt mit dem ausstrücklichen Vor-
bedinge, dass er einwendig einer darzu assignirter Zeit eine von beiden Commenden an Hände obgemelts Herren Baliers wider
resigniren und abstehen solte, und aber er deme alssnit nachkhom-
men, sondern ungefehr 8 Jahren Zeits beide Commenden titulotenus
an sich behalten, unnd solchs contra Ordinis nostri stabilimenta et in
preiudicium fratrum conventualium expectantium etc. Hergegen beklagten [von] Oldewater, nach Nottürfft gehördt: tehte *[fol.32v]* er der
conditional Collation gestandt, allein sich beduncken lassen wollen,
dieweill er die eine Commenden zu Ha[r]derwick ex manibus secularibus noch nit recuperiren können, sollt die Resignation biss zu dero
Verrichtung in seinem Gefahlen stehen. Econtra gaben die Conventualen vor, dass er zu resigniren vermögt Ordens Stablimenten schüldig seye; moege eine auss beiden zu seinem Chur behalten; sonsten
was er nit recuperiren könne, mögt ein ander volgender negster Con-

ventual versuechen, die sust ires Rechtens unbillig suspendirt wirdt.

Nach lang Verschlagenen, alss gedachter von Aldewater nit eine aus zweyen Commenden resigniren wollen oder darzu in Güthe zu berichten gewest, haben wir communicato consilio omnium fratrum ibidem praesentium votis collectis endtlichen decretirt und verabscheiden, das gerürter Herr Jacob Weinen nit gezimbt wider Besage und Ordnung unsser Stabilementen, zu Nachtheil und Behindernus nechstvolgender Conventualen und wider aussgedrückte beleidigte Condition collationis factae beide Commenden zugleich und vor sich zu behalten, derowegen schüldig seye einwendig eines halben Jahrs Frist eine deroselben abzutreten und ad manus d.Balivi zu resigniren, wie wir ihnen darzu schüldig sprechen und erkennen, sub poena privationis commendarum utriusque etc.

Nach dissen Verrichtungen haben die vorgemelter Herr Balier unnd sembtlichen Commendatarii und Ordensbrüder daselbsten uns vermerckt unnd an Ew. fürstl. Gn. underthänig zu referiren gebetten, wassgestalt ein Ro. Pabst Pius quintus[1] Pontifex Maximus in Bestifftung des Ertzbischoffthum zu Utrecht an dasselbig auss den Commenden Oldewater und Werder alle Jars zu lieffern die Summa van 500 Gl.br.; bey jetziger Ihrer Pabstlichen Heilligkeit zu versuechen, ob solche angemuthe Beschwernus ab- und zurückzubringen würden, sonsten beide Commenden, da es ins Werck ginge, dermassen aussgemattet und verschwacht, dass ein Ordensbruder sich daruff nit moegen erhalten.

---

^a *BMHG p.328 puts the word* (sonder) *between the words* auch *and* sonderlichen *which is not in the ms. and in our opinion does not make sense here.*

[1] *It was not Pope Pius V but Pius IV (1559-1565) who in his bull of 11 March 1561 granted the new Archbishop of Utrecht 500 golden ducats from the revenues of the St John's houses at Oudewater and Waarder. In 1563 or 1564 the Grand Master protested against this decision, but on 29 December 1564 he cancelled his protest because of the many favours the Order enjoyed from King Philip II of Spain, lord of the Netherlands. See M.Dierickx, De oprichting der nieuwe bisdommen in de Nederlanden onder Filips II 1559-1570 (Antwerpen-Utrecht 1950), pp.245-246 and Truus van Bueren, Macht en onderhorigheid binnen de Ridderlijke Orde van Sint Jan. De commandeursportretten uit het Sint Jansklooster te Haarlem (Haarlem 1991), pp.68-69 with note 205 on p.108. The papal bull of 11 March 1561 has been edited by G.Brom & A.H.L.Hensen, Romeinsche bronnen voor den kerkelijk-staatkundigen toestand der Nederlanden in de 16de eeuw ('s-Gravenhage 1922, Rijks Geschiedkundige Publicatiën 52), nr.84, pp.84-87.*

[fol.33r] Visitation und Verrichtung zu Harlhem.

Vorgemelt 94en Jahrs *[1594]* den 29 Julij sein wir uf Harlheim zuge-
langt. Dess Ordens Hausse und Commenda daselbsten mit ihren At-
tinantien ist Camera magistralis. Jetzigerzeit Commendator, der
ehrwürdig und andechtiger Herr Timanus de Wou, hat sich sambt
seinen Conventualen, nach eröffneter Commission unnd Befelch, der
Visitation gern underworffen. Demnach der Ordens Kirch mit bey-
gelegenem Hospitall visitirt, so ist die Kirch bey des Ordens Hausse
gelegen, von Steinen schön uffgebawet. Wordt gesagt und bezeügt,
dass darzu gestanden ehezeits sechs Altaria; dieselbe anno etc.72
[1572] durchs Krigesvolckh nidergerissen; folgents anno etc.73
[1573] die Statt durch Kon. Wür. von Hispanien wider eröbert, hab
der Herr die Kirch repariren und vier Altaria darin bawen und richten lassen, welche nunmehr bey abermaliger erfolgter Verenderung
auch gantz umbgeworffen. Magistratus von der Statt haben die Kirch
in ihren Gewalt und ire Predicanten darin gestellet; des Ordens Persohnen mögen daselbsten keine Sacrificia verbringen.

De bonis et ornamentis ecclesiae.

Folgents den Herren Commendatoren, mittelss abgenohmmener
Aydspflicht, umb dero Kirchen Ornamenten und sonsten derselben
Gesteltnussen underfraget. Bezeüget, das er nach Einehmung der
Statt in seiner Widerkunfft von Ornamenten der Kirchen nichts gefonden, sondern alles vom Feint weckgeraubt gewesen. Hett von newen lassen machen, die uns auch gezeiget: zum ersten Casüfel von
rot Scharlachen mit verstickten gülden Blommen, sambt seiner Alben
und Zugehör. Item uff ihrem Oratorio am Altar ein Antependium
von roth Chambeloth. Item ein roth Carsüfel von Cambelott sambt
Zugehör. Item ein Carsüfel von roden Sambet mit eingewerckten
Golt verblumet, mit einem gölden verstickten Creütz. Item ein Cohr-
kapp von roten Sambet mit Golt eingewirckt. Reliquien,
Monst[r]antzen, Kelch *[fol.33v]* und dergleichen wahren keine ver-
handen, alle in den Krigleüffen verkommen und geraubet.

De xenodochio eiusque situ.

Ein Hospital an des Ordens Hausse gehörig ist gelegen nechst an der
Ordenskirchen, war in der Belegerung ser beschediget und alle zugehörige Eigenthumb weckgeraubt; nunmehr durch den Herrn Commendatorn wider erbawet, reparirt und mit Notturfft bestellet. Darin

befonden sechs arme Weibspersohnen, die mit sicheren Portionen auss des Ordens Hausse erhalten und gespeiset werden.

De domo praeceptoriae et eiusdem bonis mobilibus etc.

Des Ordens Hauss ist gelegen gewest in Harlhem uf S^t.Johansstrassen nit weit von S^t.Jo. Porte; aber in den Belegerungen anno 72 und 77 *[1572 & 1577]* gantz nidergeschossen, abgebrochen und devastirt, davon mehr nichts ubrig plieben dan etliche alte Maurwerck ohn Dach. Uff selbigen Plan durch jetzigen Herrn Commendatorn uff Andringen dero Statt Obrigkeit widerumb zwey schönen steinen Gebaw, eines von 155 Werckschue in die Lengte und in seiner Breite 35 Werckschueh, das ander in der Lenge 95, in der Breide 21 S[ch]ueh holtente, von Zieglen und schönen Hawsteinen, mit etlichen uffgehenden Gebellen, erbawen lassen, mit schönen Zimmer verordenet, doch noch zur Zeit nit völlig aussgebawet. Hatt einen sehr lüstigen beyligenden Garthen, welcher in der Belegerung gar verwüstet und aussgegraben, dieweill dass Kriegsvolck sich darin beschantzet, jetzmehr durch den Herrn Commenthuren mit allerhandt guten Obsbaümen artlichen verpostet. Hauss-, Kuechen- und Bethgeräide hette der Herr in seinen Antritt nichts befonden, seidher aber soviel die Gelegenheit erleiden wollen, die Nottürfft wider einkaufft, nemblichen zehen fetteren Bethe mit ihren Bethladen, Pullen, Küssen, Dekken und Zubehoir; item 80 Servieten, 11 Tischtüecher; item an Leinwath, Kuechengeschier und dergleichen nach zimblicher *[fol.34r]* Notturfft, alles bezahlt mit 800 Thaler. In disem Hauss pflegen von alters zu residiren neben einem Commendatorn vier oder fünff Priestern, bey jetziger Zeit vünff, benentlich: frater Jodocus Winck senior Pitantzenmeister, fr.Cornelius Gaudamus Hospitalmeister, fr.Theodorus de Vrije, Pastor inn Hasserswou, frater Andreas Petri Hortolanus, fr.Franco Doobius, welcher apostahirt unnd vom Convent aussgetretten auswendig sich verhielte, deme gleichwohl der Herr Commendator auss zwanglichen Befelch der Obrigkeit jarlichs zue seinem Underhalt liefern und geben muss 200 Thaler. Die andere alle und ein jeder von inen erzeigten sich gehorsamb, züchtig und gantz religioss; unnd dieweillen inen nit zugelassen in irer Kirchen publice Sacra zu peragieren, verrichteten sie dennoch taglichen alterius vicibus iren Dienst einwendigs Hauss privatim.

De membris commendae in Harlemo.

Zue diessem Hausse gehören alss Membra vier Pastoraten, die erste
gelegen in Hollandt zue Bieverwijckh, die ander zue Hemsskirck, die
dritte Suderwau, die vierte Hausserwau. Hat jede ungefehr järlichen
Einkhomens 200 Gl.brab., werden jetzo in Gewalt und Handen dero
Herren Statten verhalten, welche die Renthen zu Besoldung irer Predicanten verwenden. Pflegen sonsten vor mutirt Religion durch dess
Ordens Persohnen auss der Commenda Harlem bedient zu werden.

Alss dan der Herr Comenthur sambt seinen Conventualbrudern, nit
ins Ordenshausse – welches noch ungefertiget -, sondern nit weit von
dannen extramenten emunitatem Ordinis in einem andern Burger-
hausse sich wonhafft gehalten, seint wir geursacht zu erfragen und
zue inquiriren, wie es [da]mit eine Gelegenheit hette. Daruff hat unss
mit Zustimmung semtblicher Conventualen diessen Bericht [erstat-
tet].

Nachdem des Ordens Hauss niddergrissen und verwüstet, hetten
sie eine zeithero zu irer Notturfft eins Burgers Behaussung in Standt
nehmmen müssen; endtlichen aber, womit sie nit immer zu vortruk-
ken dürffen, iro jetziges Wohnhaus *[fol.34v]* dermassen durch Contract an sich geworben, das es in electione commendatoris seye
selbiges Hauss entweder in Jahrpachtung oder in Eigenthumb vor
einen abgedingten Pfenningk zu behalten. Doch seye solcher Contracten nit vollezogen, auch dan hinc inde respective nec precium
solutum nec traditio facta, vermög uns vorbrachter versigelter Urkundt de dato 6 Septembris 1593. Nun aber der Magistrath der Statt
Harlem den Commendatorn darzu vermöget und angehalten, das er
dass Hauss uff St.Johansstrassen mit uberschwören Kösten auss dem
Grunde new ufbawen müssen, auch bereits den Baw uffgesetz und in
Maur und Dachwerck gebracht, also bey inen endtschlossen und
rathsamb erachtet das gegenwärtigen Wohnhausses wider abzuste-
hen, – welchs wir ime nach gestalten Sachen nit bewüst zu behin-
dern.[1]

De introitu pecuniarum.

Nota   Des Ordens Hauss zu Harlem hatt keine Fruchtenrenthen, in
Gelte aber hatts zu Vormanhüsse ungefehr 10 Gars Weidelandt an
underschiedtliche Persohnen verpachtet, jahrlichs thuen 30 Gl. Item
zue Heylo 17 Morgen, thuen 125 Gl. Item Ackherslott von 5 1/2
Mat Lands 9 Gl.

Summa lateris 164 Gl.

Item Kasterkum 1 1/2 Morgen, 9 Gl. Item Hemsskercke 32 Morgen, 200 Gl. Item Beürweick 7 Morgen, 17 Gl. Item Zehent daselbsten, 40 Gl. Item Velsen ein Zehende, 200 Gl. Item zu Bresarp ein Zehende, 32 Gl. Item bey Harlem uber Spari in die Wardt ungefehr 10 1/2 Mat Lands, 89 Gl. Item Harleymerleye 20 Morgen, 115 Gl. Item baussen Zeelportt 1 1/2 Morgen, 14 Gl. Item Overveno 7 1/2 Morgen, 60 Gl. Item Salckweick 30 Morgen, 138 Gl. Item baussen die Holltporte 9 1/2 Morgen, 100 Gl. Item Neuerkercke 6 Mat Lands, 11 Gl. Item zue Ostgeist 2 Morgen, 22 Gl. Item Rijnssbrack 4 Hont Landes, 5 Gl. Item Leyerdorff 16 Morgen, 100 Gl. Item zue Coukercke an Erbpacht 15 Gl. Item zue Hasserwau 5 Morgen, 20 Gl. Item Zuterwau ungefehr 112 Morgen, 507 Gl. *[fol.35r]* Item zu Vorschoten 7 Morgen, 31 Gl. Item zu Reissweick gelegen 44 Morgen, thuen jarlichs 206 Gl. Item zu Vateringe 27 Morgen, 112 Gl.

Summa lateris 2307 Gl.

Item zu Monster 39 Morgen, noch daselbsten 6 Morgen, 273 Gl. Item Honsslerdicke 20 Morgen, 65 Gl. Item Lijer 13 Morgen, 82 Gl. Item Maesslandt 34 Morgen, 147 Gl.

Summa huius 727 Gl.

Summa summarum introituum domus Harlemensis 3198 Gl., thuet in Reinischer Müntzen, den Goltgulden pro 54 Stüfer wie zu Utrecht gerechnet, 1184 Goltgulden 34 Stüfer.

Von Aussgülden und Beschwernussen.

Diss Hauss wirdt jarlichs dem Herrn Maister vor Respons ad Cameram schüldig 100 Goltgulden; item den Triesoir zu Malta 25 Goltgulden; dieselbe weren vor altshin zalt mit 212 Gl. 10 Stüfer. Item vor die Conventualen jede Persohn, dero jetz drey residiren, jarlichs 100 Gl.brab., thuet 300 Gl. Item vor noch einen Conventual, so sich cum consensu zu Utrecht ex causis verhelt, 200 Gl.

Summa huius 712 Gl. 10 Stüfer.

Item dem Apostaten jahrlichs auss Zwang der Obrigkeit 300 Gl. Item vor zwey Mägte jarliche Besoldung 70 Gl. Item zu Erhaltung dess Hospitals und sonsten taglichen den Armen vor die Porte jarlichs ungefehr 600 Gl. Item muss mahn alle Jahrs der Stattmagistrath zu Underhaltung der Schulden geben 200 Gl. [a]Seint newe uffgesezte.[a] Item bey diessen langewerten Kriegsweesen, item zu Einkauffung nottürfftigen Haussgeräide und sonst zu Uffbaw und Reparation seint uff des Ordens Güeter uffgenohmen an Haubtgelden 4000 Gl., davon jahrlichs an Pension 300 Gl.

Summa huius 1470 Gl.

Summa summarum aller Aussgulden vorschrieben kumpt uff 2182 1/
2 Gl., thuet in Reinischer Müntzen 808 Goltgulden 18 Stüfer.

Wan diese von den Einkunfften dess Hauss abgezogen, verpleibt
dem Herrn Commendatori pro sui suaeque familiae sustentatione
376 Goltgulden 16 Stüfer.

_____

ᵃ *in the left margin.*

[fol.35v]   De alienatis et gravaminibus.

Zu Uffbawung des Hausses, Kirchen und Hospitals hatt der Commendator unnd Conventualen erblichen verkaufft 10 hollandische
Morgen vor 6481 Gl. 5 Stüfer;[1] dieweil aber bereits solche Pfenningk daran gelegt und die Behaussung beyweiten noch nit aussgebawet, will er nach vollendigten Bawe darab gute bestendige Rechnung
aller Kosten uflegen. Item es hetten die Stadten von Holland auss des
Ordens Gütern de facto genohmmen 4 Morgen Weidtlandts, dieselbe
in Hände von Cornelis Petersum Boemondt versezt vor 360 Gl. Item
noch in gemelts Cornelius Hände versetzet 15 Gl.brab. und vier
Goltgulden Erbrenthen vor 229 Gl. Und obwohl St.Johannishausse
und einem Comenthur die Loss selbiger Stuck vorbehalten, hett doch
gerürter Pfender gegen Anpietung des Haubtgelz noch zur Zeit nit
abstehen wollen.

Summa alienatorum 7070 Gl. 5 St.

Ausserthalben diesse Stück seyen von des Ordens Güthern bey Zeit
sein des Commendatoris Regierung nichts weiter veralienirt oder
abkhommen ipso attestante firmiter. Weites underfragt ob auch der
Commendator sich mit dem Herrn Stadten oder Magistratu von der
Statt in einige sonderbahre Verträge, Contracten und Vergleichnus-
sen gegeben, antwurtt: nachdem die Landen von Königs Seithen an
die Regierung der Stadten durch Kriegesweesen ubergegangen, sey-
en alle geistliche Gütter, zusambt den Güthern St.Johans Ordens in
Harlem, durch die Stadten von Hollandt angeschlagen, confiscirt und
zu Händen gefasset anno 1572. Folgends wie anno 1576 zu Gent eine
Pacification und Landtregierung uffgericht, also hett der Commenthur in Krafft dero anno 1577 bey den General Stadten von wegen
St.Johans Ordens Güthern zue Harleim underthänig supplicirt und
damit so viel *[fol.36r]* erhalten, das ime St.Johans Ordens Güther,
wass dero bereiths nit verkaufft oder alienirt, aus andern gemeinen
geistlichen Standts Güthern eximirt und ime zu geniessen restituirt,
auch desswegen so an die Magistrath der Statt Harlem alss andere

Rentmeister der Landtschafft mandata restitutionis et evacuationis mitgetheilt worden. In welcher Massen er sie allnoch in seinem Gebrauch und Besitz gehalten biss ungefehr anno 1581, dass die Stat Harlem von den General Stadten von Hollandt den Eigenthumb alle geistlichen Güter in Harlem gelegen an sich geworben, cum pacto de evincendo etc. So hetten die von Harlem Sᵗ.Johans Ordens Güter mit in solchem Kauff unnd also nach sich ziehen wollen, auch desswegen de evictione die Herren General Statten versprochen, seyen doch die General Statten bey der Exemption bestanden, biss noch und diesser Güeter halben evictionem nit praestiren wollen. Immittellss und dessen unangesehen, hett die Statt Harlem dem Commenthurn mit underschiedtlichen Manieren und Vorschlegen angesuecht umb die Güeter an ire Hände zu bekhommen; under andern vorschlegen, dass der Commenthur und dessen jetzige Conventualen die Zeit ires Lebens die Güter sollen moegen geprauchen, keine Conventualen weiter an sich nehmen, undt entlichen der Eigenthumb an der Statt zu verpleiben; auch bereiths zu dem Ende Register und Rollen abgefordert etc. So hette aber der Commenthur in solche An- und Vorschlege nit khonnen noch wollen verstehen, sondern dieselbe mit redelichen Argumenten widerlegt, und in denselben Terminis stehe es gegenwuertiglichen. Demnach wir nit underlassen, die Herren Schultheiss und Burgermeistern der Statt angesprochen, inen E. fürstl. Gn. freündtlichen Gruess und beygethanen Willen und ferner etlichermassen, soviel wir an dem Orth dienlichen erachtet, die Befelch unsser Commission vermeltet, inen auch Danck gesagt, dass sie unsser Mittordensbruder alda in allem ausgestandenen leidigen Kriegsweesen so nachparlichen geduldet, ge-*[fol.36v]*fordert und mit iren trewlichen Vorstande geholffen. Zäigten dabey an unssers Ordens gemeinen Beruff und Intentionem, die allein widder den algemeinen Erbfeint gerichtet und sonsten von allen inerlichen Civilkriegen neütral und unparteisch were etc. Patten sie Eüro, unssern Orden und dessen bey inen gelegenen Haüssern, Güetern und Persohnen beygethaen sein und pleiben wollen etc. Hergegen sie uns gedanckt und alles Gutten versprochen.

Examen et depositiones conventualium.

Uff das wir alles Berichts, der unns von den Comenthurn beschehen, desto gewisser würden, haben wir die sämbtliche Conventualen, so viel deren ine Conventu gegenwürtig, nemblichen fratrem Jodocum Vijnck seniorem, welcher des Ordens geweesen 34 Jahren, fr.Cornelium Gaudanum, so des Ordens gewesen 33 Jar, fr.Andraeum Petri, des Ordens 24 Jahre, gleichfals fr.Theodoricum

de Vrije pastorem in Hasserwau, so sich zu Utrecht verhalten in
unsser Uffreissen daselbsten, alle und einen jeden sonderlichen vorge-
fordert, den gewönlichen Ordensayd von jedem abgenohmmen und
also einem jeglichen ad partem besonder uber alle Posten, die unss
der Commenthur berichtet, underscheidtlichen underfraget. Sagten
dieselbe durchauss also wahr sein, hoc de persona et moribus sui
commendatoris singuli addentes, das er sich religios und mit inen
sonderlichen friedsamblichen verhielte, auch inen alle Notturfft sub-
ministrirte, dass sie durchauss content und wollzufrieden weren. So
stünden alle Gütter und Renthen unverschiedentlichen in Gewalt
und Administration des Herrn Commendatoris, welcher sie alss Conventualen darab erhielte und alles seiner Verwaltung gute richtige
Rechnung zu geben wüste. Auch die Conventualen under sich sagt
ein jeder von dem andern alles Guths, allein fr.Franco Dobbius seye
von inen ungeursachet aussgetretten, welcher nun apostasirt und
doch auss des Ordens Güthern erhalten werden müste. De bonis
ecclesiae addebat fr.Jodocus Vijnck senior, das er in Zeit der Belegerung binnen *[fol.37r]* der Statt gewesen, damahls grosse Hungersnot
eingefallen, also das die bed[r]angte Menschen viele abscheüliche
Sachen gegessen; gleichwohl ins Ordenshauss etliche Kriegsknecht
eingelegt, die er underhalten müssen. Hab er auss Zwang und Befelch der Obrigkeit in Mangel des Underhalts drey oder 4 Kelch
verkaufft; uber selbige where ein ciborium vorhanden gewest, welchs
die Kriegsleüth sambt allen Messgewanth wegkgenohmmen. Die
Bawkosten und wass daruff genohmmen konten sie noch zur Zeit nit
bescheidentlichen wissen, angesehen der Baw nit volnzogen und der
Commendator seine Rechnung davon noch nit einbracht; wan aber
der Baw aussgeübt, er richtige Rechnung darvon einbringen würdt.
Sonsten aber habe der Commendator ohn iro Belieben und Willen
nichts verkaufft, versetz noch beschwärdt. Religiositatem et obedientiam debitam pollicentes.
  Deo aeterno gloria.

---

[1] *afterwards, the preceptor Timan van Wou asked for the Order's consent, which appears from the following copy in GLA Karlsruhe 90/345, fol.2r-6v, dd. 1 May 1595:*
[fol.2r-3r] Supplicatio, Ad Illustrissimum, Nobilissimumque Dominum,
D.Philippum A Ryetesel, Imperii principem; ac dignissimum S^{ti} Johannis
Hierosolimitani, per Almaniam Magistrum, et ad strenuos Equites,
Nobilesque proceres eiusdem ordinis Spira Capitulum celebrantes,
  fratris Timanni a Wou Praeceptoris humilis domus in Haerlem, ac
confratrum suorum supranominati ordinis. —
[fol.3r] Primo, ut pensiones vobis his fatalibus ac funestis annis debitae,
remittantur, et immunitas earum quinque annis sequentibus permittatur.
  Secundo, ut alienatio circa undecim iugerum, quorum dimidium
Akersloti, duo Woggenomi, reliqua Castercomi sunt posita, sumptibus

ferendis, venditioque domus sitae in platea vulgo die Smeestrate, (quae habitationi nostrae a privato cive comparata, sed necdum tradita erat), necnon et traditio illius per venditoris haeredes Ottoni Vogelio, saepe repetis de more fratrum nostrorum consiliis, facta, vestra quoque authoritate, ac tabulis, confirmentur, sicuti ob utilitatem, ac necessitatem rei, a prudentissimis visitatoribus, cum in rem presentem venissent, fuere comprobata.

Tertio ut liceat vobis comprobantibus, areolas aliquot exiguas, ad publicam plateam sitas, alienare, aut in emphyteusim tradere, quo iam diu si nostris eas substructionibus ornare nolimus, compellimur.

followed on fol.4r-6v by a
Demonstratio, Ad Illustrissimum [etc.]
F.Timanni van Wou Praeceptoris humilis [etc.]

Primum, ut pensiones superiorum annorum, et quinque sequentium nobis remitterentur, ut ex tanta rerum calamitate nobis recolligendis spatium esset.

Deinde ut alienatio atque oppigneratio paucorum agri iugerum, et venditio domus in platea vulgo die Smeestrate, quae a privato cive ad commorandum comparata, sed nondum tradita erat, necnon et traditio illius per venditorem Ottoni Vogelio facta, vestra quoque authoritate, ne tabulis confirmenturi sicuti generosorum visitatorum calculo fuere comprobatae.

Tertio ut ratum firmumque a vobis haberetur, si quae areola ad publicam viam positae, (ne ipsi in iis struere cogeremur) *[fol.4v]* vel in emphyteusim praeberentur, vel alieno aere solvendo venderentur. Quibus illud colophonis loco adiiciebatur, ut nimirum ratio iniretur, qua bona, quae magnis laboribus, periculis, ac sumptibus recuperata sunt, in posterum nostro ordini, divinoque honori, conservari possent.

[so far the Supplicatio and Demonstratio of frater Timan van Wou.]

In Urkundt, das vorinserirte Geschichten vor unss also ergangen, wir es allenthalben solcher und keiner andern Gestalt erfonden und unsse wahre Verrichtung seint, haben wir nach Befelch Ew. fürstl. Gen. gegenwertige Acta mit eignen Händen underschrieben und mit unssen jedes Insijgel uffin Spacio besigellt, Ew. fürstl. Gen. unss underthänig befehlende.

    locus sigilli.   locus sigilli.

Augustin Freyherr zu Mörssperg,   Arnoldt von Lulstorff,
Ritter und Commenthur etc.   Ritter und Commenthur.

Dieweill dan ich Adolph Fix von Eller, von Römischen Kayserlichen Maiestät gemeiner Notarius, von den ehrwürdigen wollgebornen gestrengen unnd edlen Herrn, Herrn Augustin Freyherrn zu Mörsperg und Beffortt, Commenthurn zue Basell, Darlessheim unnd Hemmendorff etc., und Herrn Arnolden von Lulstorff, Commenthur zu Strunden, Burgk, Dussburg unnd Velden etc., zu den vorinserirten Visitation, Examination, Geschichten unnd Handlungen beruffen, denselben persöhnlichen beygewohnt, sellbs gesehen, gehörtt und in Notam genohmmen, so hab ich sie diessermassen mit eigner Handt geschrieben[a], auch au mehrern Zeügnus underschrieben, alles trewlichen unnd ungefehrlichen.

Adolph Fix von Eller scripsit.

---

[a] underschrieben *ms.; BMHG p.339 supposes:* geschrieben.

C.5. VISITATION OF UTRECHT, 1603

GLA Karlsruhe 90/345, fol.8r-11r, dd.8 & 9 November 1603.

These acts have been written in contemporaneous Dutch handwriting on some sheets of paper, inserted in a larger volume, which also contains (in a different handwriting) the *Supplicatio* and *Demonstratio* of frater Timan van Wou, preceptor of Haarlem, dd. 1 May 1595 (see above, C.4. pp. 625-626 as note 1 to the visitation of Haarlem, 1594). They are probably a copy of a (no longer extant?) original document. The visitation took place after the death of the bailiff frater Hendrik Berck on 12 October 1602 and after the Estates of the Province of Utrecht decided on 23 October 1602 to take over the administration of the bailiwick's goods and to prohibit the election of a new bailiff. On 18 August 1603 the Prior of Germany, frater Weypert, wrote a letter of protest against this decision, which was presented to the Estates during their meeting of 26 October 1603 by two delegates of the Order, the same who subscribed to the visitation at hand; however, it was in vain. Cf. P.Q.Brondgeest, *Bijdragen tot de geschiedenis van het Gasthuis, het Klooster en de Balije van St.Catharina der Johanniter-ridders en van het Driekoningengasthuis te Utrecht*, Hilversum 1901, pp.32-35 and Bijlage VII on pp.105-109; see also A.nr.136 above, dd. 28 December 1603, and D.nr.8 below, printed pamphlet.

fol.8r

Eerstlijck vrag stucken soo van ons onderges. den Heeren Conventualen des huijs Utrecht voorgehouden den 8 & 9 Novembris anno 1603.

Eerstlijck gevraegt hoe veel Ordens personen die Commanderij Utrecht heeft daer op sij gelijck geantwoort hebben van derthien & met namen als volcht daeronder 11 Ordens personen & 2 novitij die sub anno probationis staen.

Naemen der Commandeurs
1   1. Heer Berent van Schoonhoven Prior & Commandeur te Veer-
       der
    2. Hr Andreas Schimmelpenninck Commandeur tot Ingen
    3. Hr Jacobus Winandi Commandeur tot Oudewater
    4. Hr Hendrick Vos Commandeur in Wemelinge in Zeelandt
    5. Hr Johan Ridder Commandeur in Montfört
    6. Hr Alexander Berck Commandeur in Buren
    7. Hr Johan Quint Commandeur in Hermelen
    8. Hr Petrus Montanus Commandeur in s Heeren Lohe Conven-
       tuales

Hr Johan Heun Conventual & priester
Hr Stephan Hartevelt   { Conventualen
Hr Anthonius Vrieswijck   & geen priester
Everhardus Preis   { Novitij
Wilhelmus Neuhoef

Twede Articul

2 Weil die godtsdienst door dese neuwe religion bij hun afgeschaft of
sij dan niet tot de restitutie vande Catholysche relege bij de overi-
cheyt ofte Generale Staeten angehouden hebben

Daer op der Prior geantwoort heeft, neen uijt dese oorsaecke
dat sij sulcx uijt furcht naegelaeten hebben & heeft daer bij gesegt
dat sij de Godts dienst heimlyck bij haer in huijs gedaen hebbe, &
also noch doen mit groot gefaer.

Andreas Schimmelpenninck Commandeur in Ingen, geantwoort, dat sulx niet hebben doen mogen uijt forcht & gefaer halve,
het werde doch sulcke Godts dienst heimlijck bij haer gehouden.

Jacobus Weinand Commandeur in Oudewaeter, ist tegenwoor-
dich in de stadt Utrecht gewesen, heeft doch niet erscheinen willen.

Hendrick Vos Commandeur in Wemelinge in Zeelant fuit ab-
sens ergo non examinatus.

Heer Johan Ridder Commandeur in Montfort, heeft geantwort
dat het uijt forcht naegelaeten worden, geschiede doch heimlijck
doch bij de Staeten pro restitutione niet aenhouden dorfen.

Hr Alexander Berck Commandeur in Buren geantwoort die
catholischen hebben wel int gemeen daer om aengehouden maer
niet verkregen.

fol.8v

Heer Johan Quint Commandeur in Hermelen geantwoort dat sulcke Godts dienst heimlijck in huijs bij haer gehouden worden doch
uijt forcht bij de Staeten niet daerom dorfde aenhouden.

Petrus Montanus Commandeur in s' Heeren Loo heeft geantwoort alsde voorsz.

H. Johan Heun priester
Conventualen { Hr Stephan Hartevelt
              Hr Anthonius Vrieswijck seggen van dese
point als de voorsz.

3 Of oock alle Ornamente van de kercken voorhanden & wel be-
waert syn.

Hr Bernhart van Schoonhove Prior, heeft geantwoort het is
veel gerooft. Wat noch in weese is weet hij & is op heymlijcke
plaetse in goede bewaring.

Andreas Schimmelpennig Commandeur segt hij weet daer niet af, den Prior heeft hier van goede wetenschap, also seggen alle de andere opden Priors seggen & soude voorhande syn een St Jans hooft in silver; Item 2 grooten silveren beekers daer uijt man op St Jans dage den wein te schencken pleegt & eenige kelcke soo de Commandeur van Oudewater bij hem heeft.

Heer Jan Heun segt, den Prior heeft dat werck in bewaring, doch die Staeten hebben haer in voortyden gedrongen de kercken met synre toebehoore over te geven ofte een somma gelts daer voor te geven.

Item Heun hat melding gedaen van 2 silvere schottelen, in dat eene een St Jans hooft, in dat ander een Agnus Dei; Item twee monstrantztien die noch voor handen sijn.

4 Oft Hospitael wel bedient & de armen krancken wel op gewart wort & wie het nu gehouden wort
Daer op alle geantwoort hebbe, dat t selve altyt wel gehouden wort & nu beeter als te vooren & getuijcht dort eene vande heeren i[n]der tyt tot een hospetalier is geweest, nu een vremde vande Staeten daer tot geset.

5 Of in anfang der regering Her Hendrick van Berck saliger dat huijs Utrecht ofte syn membra met eenige schulden beladen is geweest oft dat by syn tyt bij dat huys Utrecht ofte membra schulde gemaeckt syn geworde & hoe veel de selvege syn & uijt wat oorsaecken.

fol.9r

Prior daer op geantwoort hij weet wel dat daer schulden sijn geweest maer weet niet hoe veel. Item den Prior segt den leste gestorve Balij oock schulde gemaeck heeft weet niet hoe veel, vermeent doch den verstorven Commandeur soo veel bewecheliche goederen uijt haere uijthove voor de stadt verlaeten dat de schulden konnen daer mede betaelt werden.

Andreas Schimmelpenninck, het syn in syn aenkomst weynich schulden gevonden maer veel schulden van Berck saliger gemaeckt wegen veel scattinge vande Staeten.

Johan Ridder & alle die anderen op den Montanus hebben geantwoort gelyc Schimmelpenninck.

Montanus segt het war bij de 9000 gulden opgenomen & schulden gemaeckt van de overleden Commandeur sonder consout vant Conve[nt]; weet oock niet waer de selvige gelaeten sijn.

Johan Heun segt daer waeren etlijcke schulden maer daer tegen soo veel naegelaeten dat die schulden konnen betaelt werden.

Item Heun daer was eenig onfruchtbaer lant, fruchtbaer gemaeckt & dat selvige op twee ofte drie luijden leven lang verheurt.

Item heeft den verstorven Baiulivij begraffenis twee ofte drie duysent gulden gekost.

Stephan Hartevelt & Anthonius Vrieswyck seggen dat sij vande voorsz. niet weeten maer bij Bercken tyden waeren etlijcke duijsent gulden opgenomen; weet niet waer aen sulckx is besteet geworden & gene van haer daer toe consent gegeven.

6 Of bij die tijt eenige goederen als landerije, garden soo dit huijs ofte membre toebehoort verkoft ofte erflijck versets sijn geworden.

Prior refereert dat den saliger Balier bruder heeft een huijs & garde oock etlijcke landern om & bij de stadt gelegen in besitz; weet niet eygentlijck hoe veel dat huijs & garden syn in circuitus ofte bij der Commanderij gelegen & begrepen, weet niet met wat tutul die selve sulcx besit, oft hij daerin beleent is ofte etlijcke penningen daer op gedaen weet hij niet.

Andreas Schimmelpenningh antwoort als de voorsz. Prior.

Johan Ridder geantwoort als de voorgaende.

Alexander Berck een broeder des verstorven Baliers segt hij weet niet daer van.

Johan Quint refereert sich op de voorsz.

fol.9v

Petrus Montanus dat den overleden Baliers broeder 41 morgen landts soo beij tijden vande heeren visitatoren Mersbach & Lulsdorf voor heur gehouden, negen doch voor leen goet geschatz geworden & sich derhalve op seekere leenbrieve refereerden.

Item Montanus soo heeft den Berck dat artielerter *[?]* huijs soo meest alle dingen vervallen met sijnne eygen kosten op gerepareert tot behoef van hem & sijnne huijsvrouwe te genieten & te bewonen.

Item segt Montanus dat den broeder vande overleden Commandeur over die 41 morgen lands, item twee hove landts doen in alles 31 morgen landts, in heur *[besitz]* heeft & soude noch veel vande selve heur schuldich syn. Item noch 8 morgen lants & een boomgaert liggende ande meer, noch 7 morgen lants liggende tot Schalckwijck.

Johan Heun segt den saliger Baliers Broeder eenig lant in besitz heeft daer[a] op hij eenige penningen gedaen heeft. Weet niet hoe veel.

Item Heun dat des saliger Baliers bruder dat huijs met synne eygen kosten gerepareert heeft sijn leven lang met sijnne huijsvrouwe tselve te bewonen.

Hartevelt & Vrieswijck den bruder, des verstorven Baliers bruder, gebruijckt etlijck lant om de stadt gelegen, weet niet met wat titul; soo veel die reparation des huijs aengaet bekennen sy als de vurige.

7 Of oock bij den regering van den verstorven Balier etlijck huijse ofte goederen aengekoft heeft.

Prior segt dat den Balier saliger ses huijsen & den halve deel des gardens gelegen aen de syde van tConvent tot behoef vant selve gekoft, om dat selvige af te breeken & in tummerage te brengen & segt den Prior dat sulcke huijse ontrent voor 6 ofte 7 hondert gulden gekoft syn.

Andreas Schimmelpenninck & alle de anderen behalven Vrieswijck refereren sich aende voorsz. Vrieswijck segt dat sulcke huijsen gekoft sijn, maer daer tegen van saliger Balier wederom in de Stat Utrecht een groot huijs is verkoft geworden.

8 Hoe vele huijsen soo dat huijs Utrecht toebehoort daer syn, voor wie & met welcke condition die selvege bewoont worden.

Prior segt daer syn ses huijsen & werden van etlijcke oude dienaren bewoont, weet doch niet met wat titul.

Ridder hij weet niet hoe vele huijsen daer syn doch den Baliers saliger broeder besitz een huijs, weduwe van saliger Rentmeester dat ander huys, van wie die ander bewoont worde weet hij niet.

Alexander Berck daer sijn etlijcken huijsen aen der straeten gelegen; ontrent 7 ofte 8 werden van oude dienaren bewoont, deel om niet, een deel om etlijcke heur.

Quint Montanus segt het syn 6 of 7 huijsen werden vande oude dienaren bewoont, een deel om gelt & een deel om niet wegen haere trouwen diensten.

fol. 10r

Heun segt van 10 & een out clein gardeners huijs doch de principaelste woont den afgestorven Baliers bruder die tselve met sijne eijgen onkosten gerepareert heeft waer voor hij & sijnne huijsvrouwe haer leven lang in sullen wonen;

Int ander woont den weduwe vande overleden Rentemeester om niet.

Diederick Cornelis den overleden Baliers diener woont int drieden huijs int lesten van den Baliers leven in agone mortis Baiulivi dat selve syn leven lang te besitten soo den Heun vande voorsz. diener heeft verstaan.

Anna Wijnberg int vierde huijs een dienstmaegt ofte kockinne des Convents dat selve vande overleden Balij gegeven haer leven lang daer in te wonen.

Meester Cornelis Steenmetseler int vijfde huijs met sijnne huijs-

vrouwe dat selve te bewonen wegen etlijcke arbeytsloon ontrent 200 gulden & daer en boven noch jaerlijcks te geven 12 gulden.
Het sesten besit Oesteren genoemt, heeft jaerlijcks seekere heur.
Arent Hoedemaker woont in dat sevende huijs met sijnne huys-vrouwen haer leven lang in te wonnen, op dat selve eenig gelt gesetz, geven daer en boven noch eenige heur.
Int 8 huijs wert door een predicant bewoont uijt ordre vande Magistraet der stadt Utrecht.
Jan Timmerman int 9 huijs om seekere heur jaerlijcks.
Juffer van Kuijlenberg wedue int 10 huys om eenige huer jaer-lijcks.

9 Wat voor desen & bij leven vande overleden heer Bercke soo wel desen huijs als sijnne membris vande Heeren Staeten voor oplagen ofte beswaernis op gelegt is.

Prior segt dat met veele ontellijcke schattinge vande Heeren Staeten tot onderhoudinge der predicanten & arme huijsen & son-der de burger schattinge onbillich sijn geschats geworden, also oock alle de anderen seggen behalven de Heun seggen dat veel ontellijcke schattinge haer opgelegt syn.

Heun segt dat tot onderhouding van een predicant jaerlijcks moet geven 300 gulden behalve de particuliere burgerschattinge. Item het gedenckt Heun dat op eenmael erlegt syn geworden vijf-tien hondert gulden.

Hartevelt dat huijs wert in alle ordinarie & extraordinarien schattingen overvallen doch sollen des Ordens hospitael in elecs [= alles?] extimeert sijn.

Vrieswijck sij moeten gemeene burgelijcke last helpen dragen.

10 Of int afsterven vanden heer Hendrick Berck saliger geen gelde ofte gout ofte silver werck is gevonden & waer sulcx gebleven is.

Prior segt dat ontrent 1600 gulden in saliger Baliers gemach is gevonden welcken den Rentemeester vande Staeten aenbevolen is geworden te ontfangen & te bereekenen.

fol.10v

Wat dat silver werck aenlangt is weynich voorhanden & is over twee jaer voort afsterven vande Balier door seynnen diener bestol-len geworden, sijn noch voorhande 2 ofte 3 silvere sout vaeten & een silvere beeker & een lampet.

Schimmelpenningh hij en heeft niet gesien oft gehoort uijt oor-saeken hij niet daer is geweest, etlijck silver heeft hij gesien, dat ander is door den Baliers diener gestolen geworden.

Ridder segt als die voorsz. het is silver werck gestolen gewor-den, weet niet hoe veel.

Item Ridder deposuit hij heeft gehoort dat 1600 gulden aen gelt geweest is.

Berck, Quint & Montanus seggen als de voors.

Heun segt het is 1600 gulden gevonden geworden & den Staeten Rentmeester bevolen te ontvangen & te berekenen. Item het sij aen achterstaende renten ontrent 25000 gulden oock den Rentemeester te ontfangen & te bereekene bevolen. Item het is aen hove & weije ontrent voor 4000 gulden verkoft, beisters & kooren vanden saliger Balier daer selfs gebracht, oock voorraet geweest is, oock aende voorsz. Rentemeester te ontfangen & te bereeken bevolen is geworden. Item dat huys tot Woerden verkoft voor 1200 gulden oock den Rentemeester geweesen te ontfangen & te bereekenen bevolen. Wat dat silver werck aengaet & gevonden is ontrent op 1000 gulden geschats geworden daer mede in gerekent een goude cruijs, item tande stooker, silveren beeker, signet, silveren glas schroeven, lepels, sout vaeten, silveren lampet & geet kan.

Hartevelt segt het is eenig silver werck daer geweest, dat ander is vanden diener gestolen geworden, hij heeft gehoort daer is geweest 1600 gulden.

Vrieswijck segt het is 1625 gulden op den saliger Baliers gemack gevonden welcke oock den Rentemeester ontfangen bevolen.

11 Of sijn eerweerdigen voor sijn afsterven een testament gemaeckt & wel sijn verwansschap vertestert.

Prior segt hij heeft geen testament gemaeckt maer int uijtersten van sijn leven in agone mortis het Convent tot gedachtenis 400 gulden geschenkt.

Also hebben alle de anderen gerefereert.

12 Of sij selven oorsaecken hebben gegeven dat de Staeten eenige ingrep in haer huijs gedaen hebben.

Prior segt hij heeft daervan geen wetenschap, hebben haer oock geen oorsaecke gegeven om eenige ingrep te doen; alsoo oock alle de anderen behalven Montanus refereren als den Prior.

Montanus hij vermeint de Staeten hebben daer uijt oorsaecken geschept de weil Berck des verstorven Baliers bruder als een secularis des Ordens goederen aen hem genomen heeft.

Heun hij weet niet eygentlijck doch sij hem & anderen Conventualen vanden Commandeur tot Oudewater aengesegt alle haere secreten brieven & movementen des Ordens de Staeten te overleveren by haere *[fol.11r]* eet, sulcken vermoedingh hem daermede eene gunste bij de Staeten te scheppen, daermede hij sijnne pension van 300 gulden bij den overleden Commandeur naestende hinvorder mochte seeker becommen & ontfangen, alles tot syne voordeel also met den Staeten als een groot sengior des Convents gedirigeert.

Item uijt getuijgen des Hartevelts die vermoet dat den Prior met dese veranderinge vande stat die deur heeft op gedaen daer mede hij dat huijs & toebehoren aen hem mochte brengen & de heere Staeten daer voor bedancken.

Hartevelt & Vrieswijck seggen sij weeten niet daer van & hebben de Staten deshalven oock geen oorsaecke gegeven.

13 Onder wat titul de heeren Staeten sulcx te doen sich eerst onderstanden hebben.

Prior & alle de anderen seggen sij hebben niet anders gehoort dan dat die Staeten sulx doen tot conservatie des Ordens & dat hospitael in welstant te houden.

14 Hoe veel nu de heeren Conventualen daer sijn & hoe veel priester, hoe out de selvege soo niet priester sijn & hoe lang die selvege in huijs gewesen sijn.

Daerop sij alle geantwoort daer syn 11 Conventuales daer onder syn 8 Commandeurs, 2 novitii, daeronder 9 priester.

Hartevelt & Vrieswijck sijn geen priester.
Hartevelt is ontrent sijns ouders 26 jaer.
Vrieswijck sijns ouders 30 jaer.
Hartevelt in huijs geweest 11 jaer.
Vrieswijck — — 8 jaer.

Eenige seggen sij haere ouderdom niet weeten of het bij haer manqueert ofte bij den saliger Balier geweest sij dat sij geen priester geworden syn.

Hartevelt segt hij quam dagelijcks bij sijnne vrienden & verwanten & werden van haer dagelijcks deshalven bespot.

Vrieswijck hij ist altijt willig geweest, het is hem van saliger Balier geen gelegentheijt sulcx te doen voorgestelt geworden.

15 Waerom sij haer niet en becleden gelijck de priesters behooren te gaen ghelijck die van adel & soldaeten.

Daer op de novitij geantwort hebben sij worden van een ider belaght & bespot.

[b]Eberhart van Galen Ridder
Commandeur te Steinfort

Johan Nolt Sint Johans Commandeur
te Falkenstein.[b]

---

[a] daer daer *ms.*   [b] *in a different hand by a clerk, not by the subscribers themselves.*

C.6. SPECIFICATION OF THE NIMWEGEN PRECEPTORY GOODS OUTSIDE THE TOWN, 1700

GLA Karlsruhe 90/337, fol.51r-54v, undated draft of a treaty [18 May 1700]. Cf. A.nr.198 above, dd.7 January 1698, some claims concerning the revenues of the house at Nimwegen, and A.nr.199, c.1700, the full text of the other parts of this treaty.

[dorsal note on fol.54v:]
Proiect van Accoort door sijn Hooghvorstelijcke Genade van Heitersheim en t'Illustre Capittel gemaeckt aengaende de restitutie der goederen gehoorende tot de Commendeurie van St.Jans binnen Nijmegen, en sulcx naer het proiect van deselve stadt deswegen overgelevert.

fol.51r —

2º. Volght hier naer de specificatie der Bouwhoven, Renten, en Effecten soo de Stadt Nijmegen bij dese restitueert, en overgeeft
fol.51v
Eerstelijck eenen bouwhoff tot Lent den Broodtkorff genoemt, verpacht aen de Weduwe van Bartholomeus Goossens jaerlijcx voor
            − 300 − . − . −

Eenen Hoff tot Lent den Lauwijck genoemt verpacht aen Frans Broesterhuijsen iaerlijcx voor   − 400 − . − . −

Eenen Bouwhoff tot Lent het Visveldt genoemt verpacht aen Jan van den Pavort iaerlijcx voor   − 300 − . − . −

Eenen Hoff tot Horssen gelegen den Vlootsen hoff genoemt is verpacht aen Roeloff de Ruijter iaerlijcx voor   − 200 − . − .−

Eenen hoff tot Niel in de Duiffel, genoemt Wolfswijck verpacht aen Daem Heinen jaerlijcx voor   − 200 − . − . −

Eenen Hoff tot Groesbeeck gelegen, is verpacht aen Thonis Simons jaerlijcx voor dartien malder rogge, ende seven malder boeckweit, heeft 1697 gedaen   − 172 − 10 −. −

Het holtgewas tot Groesbeeck St.Jans Heijde genoemt ende noch een kampken elsenholt mede aldaer gelegen en sijn op den 30 Decembris 1697 in massa verpacht aen Derck Winants Wijers voor 260 gulden.

Eenen kamp weijlandts groot vier mergen tot Valburgh gelegen is verpacht aen Jan Aernts voor   − 30 − . − . −

Den Heere Grave van Bijlandt betaelt jaerlijcx uijt een stuck landts in d'Oij gelegen eene rente van   − 16 − 15 − 13−

Henrich Janssen gelt jaerlijcx uijt een hofstadt tot Lent

$$- . - 10 - . -$$

Ruth Goossens gelt jaerlijcx uijt een stuck landts tot Lent

$$- . - 5 - . -$$

Ditmar de Raet gelt jaerlijcx uijt eenen bouwhoff tot Ressen, de Locht genoemt, anderhalff malder haver, ende een schepel terwe en 1697 bedraegen $- 6 - 15 - . -$

Jan Vos tot Böningen jaerlijcx twee hoenders

D'Erfgenamen van Laurents Palmers negen hoenderen jaerlijcx.

fol.52r

Volgen St.Jans coorn Renten in het Schependom van Nijmegen en gestelt naer de politie van het jaer 1697.

Op het Hooge Veldt, en elders

Nicolaes van Hervelts Erfgenamen twee malder, en een schepel rogge

$$- 21 - 7 - 8 -.$$

Deselve noch uijt een ander parceel drie schepel rogge.

Deselve noch uijt een parceel drie schepel rogge.

De Weduwe van Girrit Koenders vier malder rogge.

Claes Cruiff een halff malder rogh.

Herman den Ram een halff malder rogh.

De Erffgenamen van Derck Thonissen drie malder rogge.

De Weduwe van Herman Tros anderhalff malder rogge, dit land is 1694 voor de rent overgegeven en wort verpacht, mits dat den pachter selfs de verpondinge moet betalen jaerlijcx voor 14 gulden. [a]Dit voor de stadt[a] Deselve Weduwe Tros alnoch een halff malder rogge.

Henrich Becker twee malder rogge.

Willem Aecker anderhalff malder rogge.

Girrit Girrits[b] een malder rogge.

Adriaen Daenen drie schepel rogge.

Jan Pauwels drie schepel rogge.

Heer Flemminghs Erffgenamen drie schepel rogge.

Jan Claessen een halff malder rogge.

Den Heer van Heumen twee, en een halff malder rogge.

De Weduwe van Girrit Janssen vijff spint rog, en een schepel wintergarst.

Den Drost van der Heijden uijt een parceel tot Hees vijff spint rogge.

Catharina van Zeller uijt haer landt tot Nederbosch seven malder rogge.

Marten Peters uijt een parceel op het Hooge Veldt een halff malder rogge.

D'Erffgenamen van de Heer Schepen Henrick Heijsen een halff
malder rogge en vier quarten olie.

Samen aller roggen inkomsten 31 malder 2 spint

Weijt 1 schepel
Garst 1 schepel
Haver 1 1/2 malder

---

^a *in the left margin.* ^b *uncertain reading ms.*

C.7. TAXATION OF THE FARM AT NIEL, BELONGING TO THE PRECEPTORY AT NIMWEGEN

GLA Karlsruhe, 90/462, fol.1r, original document on paper,
1719, December 7

Anno 1719 in Decembri[a] hebben wij ondergeschreven Schepenen van Niell, door versoeck des Hern Doctoris N.Marcker een taxatie naer onse kennisse gemaackt, von den 8. Johanniter hoff in Niell alwaer Phil[i]ps Philipsen op woent, welcke in morgentaell groot ist 39 morgens 486 roeden. Wat die in erffcoop weert soude sijn; So hebben wij den morgen durch ein ander getaxiret op vijftien Hollanse gulden ofte Cleefse dalers jaerlix ofte een jaer in pacht, wan deese dan soo taxiret weere dan soele den hoff in erffcoop weert weesen 12000 Hollanse gulden ofte dalers Cleefs [b]teegen 5 per Cent gere-kent[b]. Dan muste men afftrecken die conincklicke schattingen, welike jaerlix daer op loopen, den morgen ordinaris op 3 dalers. Unt dan noch jaerlix 4 dalers aen morgengeldt unt biswilen noch andre din-sten ofte castjens, dan solte die summa naer onsen tax noch bliben pro domino te proffutiren eens voor all 6400 gulden. Edoch omni meliori modo ad quemcunque meer kennisse daer van hebbende. Sic actum Niell in der Duiffelt den 7. Decembris[c] 1719.

Henrig Gabriels schepen in Niel
Hendrick Sanders schepen

---

[a] Xbri *ms.*   [b] *in the right margin.*   [c] Xbris *ms.*

Cf. [J.in de Betouw], *Kerken en godsdienstige gestichten te Nymegen* [Nijme-gen, c.1787], pp.25-26:
"— De overeenkomst *[of 18 May 1700]* wierdt eerlang bekrachtigd door den Groot-Prior in Duitschland, en door den Grootmeester der Orde te Maltha, maar niet gestendigd door zijn Heiligheid. Door welk gebrek van ratificatie van den Paus, het Verdrag geacht wierdt te zijn vervallen. — De Orde deedt, hier na, eene procedure tegens de Stad voor het Hof-Gericht van Cleve entameren, om in possessie gesteld te worden van den Bouwhof Wolfswijck, te Niel in de Duffelt gelegen, en vervolgens om te erlangen het accomplissement van de transactie van den 18 Mai 1700. Doch die eisch wierdt bij sententie van *[p.26]* den 10 Januarii 1714 gerejecteert: Men appelleerde van dit Vonnis aan het Keiserlijke Camer-Gericht te Wetzlar."

C.8. STATE OF THE NIMWEGEN PRECEPTORY GOODS

GLA Karlsruhe, 90/337, fol.60r-61r, copy of a nameless inquiry, undated, perhaps c.1704 or perhaps after 1746. Cf. the permission to sell some Nimwegen goods in A.nr.200 dd. 4 March 1704 and the unsuccessful attempts to get the treaty of 18 May 1700 executed, described in A.nr.204, dd. 26 May 1746.

Moreover, GLA Karlsruhe, 90/83, fol.1-51, contains numerous remonstrances of the Order of St John to the town government of Nimwegen, dated from 1703 to 1736, about the restitution of these goods, especially to abandon the stipulation of papal consent in the treaty of 18 May 1700.

Cf. also the pamphlet *Memoriale Iuris* from 1732 in GLA Karlsruhe, 90/352, fol.9r-12v (D.nr.58. below).

The folio sheets of paper have been divided into two columns, the right one containing the questions and the left one the answers.

[fol.60r, right column]
Quaeritur 1mo: An bona existentia Neomagii et spectantia ad magnum Prioratum Allemanniae, Ordinis Hierosolymitani consistant in una grancia, prout multas habent similes prioratus Melitenses et, an dicta grancia habeat ecclesias eidem Prioratui subiectas?

[left] Ad 1mum respondit: Bona Equestris Ordinis Sancti Joannis Hierosolymitani vulgo Melitensis, tam intra quam extra urbem Neomagensem situata non in una grancia, sed in diversis sub ducatu Superioris Geldriae et Cliviae situatis rusticis praediis, pratis aliisque censiticis et emphyteutecis bonis in Transactione anno 1700 decima octava Maii inita, et hic in copia, pro celeriori informatione sub littera A. adjacenta, consistere, Ecclesiam vero, quam benefatus Ordo ante dominatum introducti Calvinianismi in urbe praedicta habuit, circa annum 1638, tempore ultimi commendatoris Melitensis, dicti à Golstein per hereticum magistratum funditus esse destructam, ita, ut ex loco, in quo destructa ecclesia steterat, publicum forum capidibus stratum reperiatur, in quo grana publice venduntur.

[right] 2do: an bona alienanda possint esse mansum assignatum in erectione dictae ecclesiae, ideoque considceranda sint tanquam bona ecclesiae in exstructione, aut praedicta bona sint absque ecclesia, sed mere acquisita seu empta a magnis Prioribus.

[left] Ad 2^{dum} respondit: Bona, vigore adjacentis Transactionis inclyto Ordini Melitensi restituenda non fuisse praecise ad usum illius
destructae ecclesiae sed sustentationem temporalis domini commendatoris Melitensis, ibidemque pro divino cultu peragendo sub huius
gubernio alimentatorum capellanorum de obedientia praefati Ordinis
destinata.

[right] 3^{tio}: Quatenus adsit ecclesia praedictis bonis annexa, quaeritur
an fuerit efficiata ab ecclesiasticis religionis Melitensis? Quomodo in
praesens servetur? et an sit cura animarum Catholicorum, ibi forsan
existentium?

[left] Ad 3^{tium} respondit: Ecclesiam Melitensis Ordinis (ut praefertur)
a saeculo fere funditus destructam non ab ecclesiasticis, sed Ordinis
Melitensis capellanis officiatam, nunquam tamen huic ecclesiae curam animarum Catholicorum ante introductum Calvinianismum
fuisse annexam.

[fol.60v, right column]
4to an dicta bona vendenda habeant iurisdictionem, et subditos Catholicos, aut haereticos, et an eisdem adiunctum sit aliquod onus
missarum seu alterius pii operis?

[left] Ad 4^{tum} respondit: Bona Melitensia, vigore praememoratae
Transactionis restituenda non habere iurisdictionem, neque imprae-
sentiarum subditos Catholicos, sed horum bonorum, quae iam a centum fere annis haereticus magistratus Neomagensis Equestri Ordini
Melitensi per vim majorem praedetinuit et usurpavit, praesentaneos
pachtarios sive colonos omnes esse haereticos.

[right] 5to an mediante alienatione dictorum bonorum ecclesiasticorum permaneret ecclesia absque reditibus, unde promanaret praeiu-
dicium exercitio Catholicae religionis pro Catholicis ibi existentibus.

[left] Ad 5^{tum} respondit: primam particulam esse evacuatam per
praecedentes responsiones, quoad q[ui]dam autem exercitium Catholicae religionis in urbe Neomagensi non publice sed per diversos regu-
lares Catholicos missionarios scilicet patres Augustinianos Eremitas,
Franciscanos recollectos strictioris observantiae, et Jesuitas in privatis
ad hoc erga certum annuum locagium conductis aedibus et politica
conniventia magistratus Neomagensis clanculario peragi.

[right] 6to an per concordata (prout in aliis Hollandiae partibus prac-
ticatur) regularibus permittatur, suas abbatias aut grancias retinere,
cum possessione bonorum aut exercitio religionis Catholicae, sicuti
permissum esse creditur Praemonstratensibus in multis partibus Hollandiae, et etiam in Germania vigore concordatorum, quapropter
[fol.61r, right] cognosci debet, an magistratus Neomagii iniuste occu-
pando praefata bona Religionis Melitensis cogi possit? et a quo? ad
cessandum ab huiusmodi usurpatione, et a vulnerando concordata.

[fol.60v,left] Ad 6^tum neque in partibus Geldriae Superioris, neque
aliis Foederatis haereticae reipublicae Hollandicae Provinciis, regularibus monasteriis, conventibus, aliisque collegiatis capitulis aut corpo-
ribus Catholicis in dictis provinciis ante dominatum haereseos
Calvinianae fundatis, aut existere repertis, bona et reditus, quae possidebant, relicta, sed cum expulsione omnium quotquot fuerunt, tam
regularium religiosorum quam ecclesiasticorum Catholicorum ab
haereticis confiscata et vi ablata esse, e contra Catholicorum regularium, ordinum monasteriis et ecclesiasticorum collegiis extra territoria
Unitarum haereticarum Hollandicarum Provinciarum situatis, bona
sua et reditus *[fol.61r, left]* taliter, qualiter, cum impositione gravissi-
morum onerum tamen, permissa esse, cumque nunc domus Ordinis
Melitensis et ecclesia in urbe Neomagensi, et sic sub iurisdictione
haeritici magistratus situata exstiterint, mentionatus magistratus ex
primo allegato principio illam cum ecclesia, aliisque bonis ad
Equestrem Ordinem spectantibus, confiscavit, invasit, et usque modo
usurpavit.

[right] 7mo: Denique requiritur (si fieri possit) informatio pretii, ad
quod ascendere possunt bona alienanda, et an adsint exempla, in
quibus concessa sint Beneplacita Apostolica pro venditione bonorum
ecclesiasticorum, magistratibus haereticis?

[left] Ad 7^mum: Bona vigore supra allegatae Transactionis restituenda
in reditibus annuis plus minus importare posse ad mille quingentos
florenos Hollandicos; quod vero ultimum punctum concernit, appo-
nitur extractus sub littera B: ex annotationibus abbatiae Veteri Campi Ordinis Cisterciensis, ex quo patet, consensum Sanctae Sedis
praedictae abbatiae anno 1633 impertitum fuisse super alienatione
suorum bonorum in manus haereticas facta, notandumque singulariter, quod bona, de quibus in extractu fit mentio, situata fuerint prope
urbem Neomagensem Mosam inter et Vahalim, in quo districtu situata quoque Nota Bene reperiuntur bona, Ordini Melitensi, vigore
Transactionis sub littera A. appositae, abs haeretico magistratu Neomagensi restituenda.

C.9. VISITATION OF ARNHEM 1732

AOM 6339, Priorato d'Alemagna, Visite 1733

This volume contains a number of quires of unmarked paper in folio, c.35 x 22.5 cm, sewn on ropes and bound with flyleaves in a jacket of three thick pieces of paper on top of each other; the pages lack folio or page numbers, and only the visitation reports themselves have been numbered. The volume has no title on the front or inside, but only on the spine: *Priorato d'Alemagna, Visite*; a different hand has later written in pencil on the first flyleaf: *1733*. The German texts have been written in German (gothic) characters, the Latin passages in Roman characters, covering both sides of the paper with ink that left strong marks of oxidation afterwards.

The following visitation of Arnhem from 9 October 1732 takes 13 leaves of 33.5 x 22.7 cm, with a blank leaf at the end and flyleaves on both sides. Small writing errors have tacitly been corrected in this edition.

The book contains:
Nr. 1 Visitatio Prioralis Grosz Priorats
Nr. 2 Visitatio prioralis der Commenden Rotenburg
Nr. 3 Visitatio prioralis der Commenden Wirzburg
Nr. 4 Visitatio prioralis der Commenden Tobel
Nr. 5 Visitatio prioralis der Commenden Rottweil
Nr. 6 Visitatio prioralis der Commenden St.Johan Bassell et Dorlis-
heim
Nr. 7 Visitatio prioralis der Commenden Hemmendorf
Nr. 8 Visitatio prioralis der Commenden Mainz
Nr. 9 Visitatio prioralis der Commenden Franckfort
Nr.10 *has no title but concerns* Rhordorf & membrum Dezingen
Nr.11 Visitatio prioralis der Commenden Hohenrhein
Nr.12 Visitatio prioralis der Commenden Sulz, Colmar und Mulle-
hausen
Nr.13 *has no title but concerns* Basel & Rheinfelden
Nr.14 *is missing*
Nr.15 *has no title but concerns* Schwäbisch Hall, Affeltrag & Schleusin-
gen, *only* Affeltrag *was visited;*
Nr.16 Visitatio prioralis der Commenden Klein Erdtlingen
Nr.17 Visitatio prioralis der Commenden Leuggeren
Nr.18 Visitatio prioralis der Commenden Brussall und Cronweissen-
burg
Nr.19 Visitatio prioralis der Commenden Überlingen

Nr.20 Visitatio prioralis der Commenden Schleusingen *is a supplement to nr.15*

Nr.21 Visitatio prioralis der Commenden Strasburg und Schlettstatt

Nr.22 Visitatio prioralis der Commenden Regensburg

nr.23 Visitatio prioralis der Commenden Wormbs

Nr.24 Visitatio prioralis der Commenden Ss.Joannis et Cordula binnen Cöllen

Nr.25 Visitatio prioralis der Commenden Arnheim

Nr.26 *has no title and contains only one leaf with the notice of the notary public to the visitation of Steinfurt and Münster, with the remark that the administrator of this preceptory refused entry to the visitators on 10 October 1732, because he was ordered by his lord Freiherr von Schade not to accept orders from the Prior of Germany;*

Nr.27 Visitatio prioralis der Commenden Wesel

Nr.28 Visitatio prioralis der Commenden Lagen

Nr.29 *fails*

Nr.30 Visitatio prioralis der Commenden Trier

Nr.31 Visitatio prioralis der Commenden Hasselt.

Nr.25 Visitatio prioralis der Commenden Arnheim

[fol.1r] In nomine Domini amen.

Kundt seije das demnach der Hochwurdigste fürst und herr Philip Wilhelm des hochritterlichen Sankt Joannis Malteser ordens obrist meister in teutschen Landen, des Heiligen Römischen Reichs fürst zu Heitersheim, Seiner hochwürden und gnaden Herrn von Cappell Commendeuren zu Rottweil, Schleusingen und Weissensee nebst Herrn Johan Baptist Kenzinger Prioren der Commenden Strasbourg und Schlettstatt, nachgesezte Commission aufgetragen videlicet:

Nos Philippus Wilhelm Dei gratia sacri Romani Imperii princeps in Heitersheim, ordinis Sancti Joannis Hierosolimitani supremus per Alemaniam magister, dilectis nobis in Christo fratribus Bernardo Mauritio baroni de Cappel prioratus nostri Alemania[e] militi ac commendatario in Rottweil, Schleusingen et Weissensee, nec non Joanni Baptistae Kenzinger commendarum Argentinensis et Schlett-stadiensis priori, salutem in Eo qui est omnium vera salus, et diligentiam in commissis; cum iuxta formam statutorum seu stabilimentorum sacri militaris ordinis praedicti quolibet quinquennio praeceptorias seu commendas, membra, domos, conventus, hospitalia

ac quaecunque alia bona et loca praetacti ordinis infra limites prioratus nostri *[fol.1v]* Alemaniae existentia sive per nos sive per alios a
nobis deputandos visitare teneamur, hinc est quod cum propter alia
negotia visitationi huiusmodi personaliter vacare nequeamus, vos iuxta indultum venerandi concilii nobis sub die XVII mensis Februarii
anni 1731 ultimo praeteriti impartitum, deputandos et nominandos
duximus prout harum serie vos deputamus, et eligimus in nostros
vicarios et visitatores, adhoc ut servata forma statutorum praedictorum ad visitationem commendarum in Lagen, Münster, Hasselt et in
Arnheim eorumque bonorum quorumcunque ad quae commode accedere poteritis, procedatis ibique eademmet iurisdictione ad nos
spectante utentes si quae restauranda, ordinanda et corrigenda seu
qualitercunque adimplenda sint, ordinetis et praecipiatis ac restaura-
ri, corrigi et adimpleri curetis, eaque omnia tam in spiritualibus quam
temporalibus exerceatis, quae nosmet facere possemus si personaliter
adessemus atque ideo omnibus et quibuscunque vasallis et subditis
nec non personis memorato sacro ordini subjectis infra limites prae-
dictos constitutis praecipimus et stricte mandamus ut vos tanquam
veros et legitimos visitatores admittant, vobisque obediant et quod-
cunque opportunum auxilium desuper praebeant; taliter igitur in
praemissis et circa ea vos geratis quatenus *[fol.2r]* in primis divino
cultui ac bonorum ordinis nostri praedicti conservationi atque regimini sit satisfactum et opinio quam de vobis concepimus, nos minime
fallat; in quorum fidem has praesentes manu nostra subscriptas nostroque quo in similibus utimur sigillo impressas et munitas dedimus.
Herten 28va Septembris 1732.

L[oco] S[igilli]   Philippus Wilhelmus O[rdinis] S[acri] Magister
M[anu] P[ropria]

Dahero beijde vorgenante herren visitations Commissarii hochedelen
und gnaden mit zuziehung mein zu und benenten notarii sich in die
statt Arnheim im hällandischen und die daheselbst ahn der Sankt
Joannis stras gelegene Commende Sankt Johan genant begeben, forth
darinnen heuth montags den 6^t. Octobris 1732 die aufgetragen prioral visitation nach vorhm tacta cruce gewöhnlicher äydts praestirung
mittels befestigung genanter Commendrie gebawer ahngefangen.

Jeztgemelte Commende begreifet in sich zimmlich vielle und grose
gebäw ahs primo gleich ahn der einfarth oder porten rechter hands
ein portners hauss und pferdts stallung welche aber grosten theils zu
einem oratorio oder capellen gemacht worden worinnen *[fol.2v]* für
die dahier wohnende Catholische der Gottes dienst celebrirt, von
diessen Catholischen auch solches oratorium in allem erhalten wie

nicht weniger der geistliche so den gottes dienst celebriret, salarijrt wird, vor diessem oratario liggen noch zehn kleine zu hiesiger Commenden gehörige zins häuser in uno consigno; die Sankt Joannis stras hinauf gegen der Commenderie einfahrt oder garten über ligget das haubt Commende wohnhausz so von dem verwalteren bewohnet wird, rechter hand von diessem Commende wohnhauss ligget noch ein anderes jedoch kleineres haus sambt einer stallung, worinnen der Catholischer geistlicher jeder gegen zins wohnen thut, lincker hands stehet die ehemahlige Commende kirch so ein sehr gros und schönes gebaw ist, hat ahn sich zweij grose und schöne thürne, einen zimlich grosen kirch hoff, so fast rings umb mit einigen darahn stosenden häuseren umbgeben ist, jeztgemelte kirch wird von denen anatholischen gebraucht, mus gleichwohlen von der *[fol.3r]* Commenden in tach und sach unterhalten werden, immasen dan dieselbe auch noch in perfect guthem stand sich befindet, hingegen aber ein anderer zwischen der kirchen und dem Commenderie wohnhausz stehendes bäwlein so dermahlen zu legung des holzes etc. gebrauchet wird, vormahls aber ein gang zu der kirchen gewesen zu sein scheinet, ahn tach und boden dergestalt baufallig dasz solches nothwendig reparirt werden musz; etwahe 10 schritt von diessem Commende wohnhausz ahn dem kirchhoff ligget noch ein anderes kleines hausz so ebenfals gegen zinsz bewohnet wird; alle diese häuser und wohung so ins gesambt von stein aufgeführet seint, befinden sich zwaren in tach und sach erhalten, jedoch ziemlich alt und in dem principal Commende wohnhaus auff dem oberen stock das gepliester abgefallen, auch der hindere boden oder so genante grose soller id est die frücht schutte der kirchen zu, wie auch das söllergen und gang *[fol.3v]* ober der kuchen zerlöcheret und zerschlissen, dahero auffs new mit dillen zu belegen, forth das tach ober dem Cantor so baufällig ist, widder zu erneweren, so dan auch im unterem stockwerck die so genante thurn cammer mit newen dillen zu belegen, ferners der ahn der porten gelegener von dem capitain gegen zinsz bewohnende bau ahn tach und dem söllern so schadhaft dasz wie diesser klagte der regen durch tringet, und er nicht einmahl auff dem bett davon trücken liggen könte, einfolglich solches ebenfals zu repariren; mit allen vorspecificierten gebäwer wird eines theilsz, und anderen theils mit einer mauren die Commende beschlossen, worinnen neben solchen gebäwer auch noch 3 wohl unterhaltene garthen liggen, als einer und zwarm der gröste ahn dene zehn zinszhäuser, der anderte zwischen dem vom pfarrherren bewohnendem hausz und dem principal Commende wohnhausz, und der 3te ahn der grosen Commende kirch *[fol.4r]* übrigens obgleich wie erwehnt die Commende weder zu erhaltung des oratorii weder des geistlichen so von dem nuntio Apostolico ahn

und abgesezet wird, mithin vom orden gar keine dependence hat,
weder zu ahnschaffung der paramenten obligiret ist, so seint doch
zufolg von weyland Seiner hochfürstlichen gnaden Goswin Herman
Otto als letzteren Commendariu[s] dem verwalteren uberliefferte[n]
und producirten inventarii nachbeschriebene paramenten vorhanden
so in einer kisten aufbehalten werden, als
ein silber übergoldeter kelch sambt paten,
ein silbernes Creuz
zweij silberne meskäntlein
ein viereckige silberne platte worauf Sankt Joannis haubt bildnus
ein silbernes wirauchs fass
    ahn Chor cappen
eine weise damastene mit goldenen bluhmen
zweij dunckel rothe von sammet
eine rothe von satin
    leviten röck
zweij purpere von seijden mor
zweij grüne von sammet
zweij schwarze mit blumen
noch 3 bahnen und eine halbe
[fol. 4v] bahn von einem dunckelen sammaten leviten rock.
    ahn mesgewand
ein grünes mit kleinen blumen
ein rothes von trip
ein schwarzes von wand mit einem dunckel rothem sammeten Creuz
ein schwarz sammetes mit einem rothen Creuz
ein blaues
ein vaales mit einem Creuz
    manipul und stolen
eine dunckell rothe stola und eine manipel von sammet
eine rothe stol und manipul von triep
eine schwarze stol von wand
eine rothe stol, eine grune stola, eine bunthe schlechte stola
eine purpure manipel
eine leinene alb mit 3 alten und schlechten altar tücher
ein schwarz altes sammetes toden kleid
ein roth sammet küssen
ein fouderal vor den kelch worinnen 2 kelchteckelen von seijd
noch schlecht blau unterfutter für 3 meszgewand oder leviten rock,
wobey zu notiren dasz obige *[fol. 5r]* parimenta zwaren alt jedoch ahn
sich kostbahr und zu bedauren seye dasz solche nicht gebraucht werden und so forth wegen beständigem liggen in sich verderben.
    Ferners seint vorhanden ahn hausz mobilien

12 stühl von brumbaumen holz und 2 sesselen
24 telleren von blockzinn
2 grose schüsselen von solchem zinn
eine haal auff dem hert
eine grose roster
ein haw oder fleischmesser
2 nachtsgeschirs von zinn
6 Englische zinnerne löffelen
2 zinnerne leuchteren
ein praesentir teller
eine eijserne platt in der kuchen
      herren tischzeug
3 touzend *[=dutzend]* servietten die rose genant
2 tafel lacken von 3 und 3/8 ehlen lang
4 kleine tafel lacken
6 handücher alle von selbiger blum
2 tuzend und ein serviett das grosz Creuz genant
2 tafel lacken von selbiger blum 4 1/8 ehlen lang.
      leinen
ein paar von 2 1/2ª bahn feine bettlacken
[fol.5v] 3 paar von 2 bahnen feine bettlacken
4 paar küssenziechen worunter ein paar mit kanten.
      fur das gesind
ein paar flaxene lacken
2 paar grobe lacken
ein paar kussen ziechen von flax
3 grose tafel lacken
3 handücher
      bettwerck
2 grose cataunene decken mit watte
ein herren bett mit einem püll und zweij küssen
ein bett mit einem püll
2 bett fur bedienten aber schlecht mit 2 püllen
ein lidicant von eichenholz mit inlagen und einem holzenen deckell
und einem umbhängsell von weisz und roth cataun
eine nuszbaumene rüstbanck mit kupffernen schrauben
eine darzu gehörige matrass und püll
eine bettstätte im hintersten zimmer
eine bettstette in der kuchen
3 wullene decken fur die bedienten
[fol.6r] noch ander hauszrath
ein spiegell mit schwarzen rahmen incirca 2 schuhe hoch
ein schwarz und gelb ahngestrichene tafell

ein parsch fur das tischzeug drein zu legen
ein alter nachtsstuhl
ein grosz und ein klein kuffer alt und schlecht
ein kästgen oder schrein
ein längliches kistgen oder schrein
3 kleine täfeltgen
ein oval tisch
ein klein verlacktes täfeltgen
ein kupfferne feurschüp mit einer zang
ein eijserne pfann auff den hert mit zweij darahn fast gemachten
brand ruthen mit kupffernen knöpffen
ein bratpfann mit einem spisz
ein wasser eymer
ein papier scheere
eine brand cupe mit 3 eysernen banden und eine stelle darunter mit
4 hacken und 2 bolten von eysen
ein brandleijder
2 brandhackens
12 brand eymer
eine schneidbanck mit messer und zubehör umb hexell zu schneiden.
[fol. 6v] Sönsten weilen keine cabraeen vorhanden so hat man von
der Commenderie recht und gerechtigkeiten wie auch deren gütheren und rhenten keine andere nachrichten haben können als welche
vom verwalteren Henrick van Wanray ahngegeben worden, welcher
nachdene er seiner aijd und pflichten gegen seinen herren Comman-
deuren quoad hunc actum entlasen worden umb alles beij gegenwärtig visitation getrewlich ahn zu zeigen, referirte das hiesige
Commende von der wacht und das Commende hausz von der einquartirung (es séije dan dasz ein solcher casus necessitatis wäre wobeij
die herren bürgermeistere selbsten einquartirung nehmen müsten)
exempt seije; sonsten aber wüste er von keiner anderen exemption,
und seije mehrgenante hiesige Commende von seiner hochfürstlichen
gnaden Goswin Herman Otto herrn von Mervelt recuperirt worden,
das darzu gehöriges membrum [Nimwegen][b] aber wäre annoch
[fol. 7r] von den herren Holländeren oder dem magistrat zu Nimwegen occupirt, und obgleich des herrn Ballij Ambassadeuren herr von
Schade hochedeler Excellenz alsz dermahliger Commandeur umb
desselben recuperirung instanz gemacht auch voriges jahr darumb
beij genantem magistrat münd- und schriftlich sich gemeldet mithin
nachgehents noch durch ihnen verwalteren ahnerrinnerung thuen
lasen, so seije doch bisz dahin von genantem magistrat die verspro-
chene resolution nnoch[c] nicht erfolget; sönsten aber hätte die Commende nebst denen vorbenanten in hiesiger statt Arnheim gelegenen

zinszhäuseren auch ausser der statt eine papier mülle gleich ausser
der statt ahm Sankt Joannis thor gelegen, item zweij bauhöff etwahe
eine stund von hier, Falckenhoff und die Cleuse genant: item noch 4
bauren häuszer im ambt Brümmen, item einen bauhoff zu Ben-
nickum, item einen auff der Hull, item einen in der baurschafft Dusburg, item im Abeldornschen bruckland einen bauren *[fol.7v]* hoff,·
ferners einen im Holderbruck, zweij bauhöfe zu Heusen, item 36
morgen landereijen zu Umbren, 6 morgen unter Engen, incirca 8
morgen unter Elden, incirca 6 molder sath unter Wagenen, noch 6
morgen unter Wagenen, noch 8 morgen, in der Nue unter Ameron
incirca 6 morgen. Item einige floch landereijen in der Limmers, item
umb hiesige statt einige landereyen wovon er verwalter die aigentli-
che morgen zahl nicht wiste, von welchen gutheren die Commende
welche durch genanten Herrn Henrick van Wanray administriret
wird und sönsten jahrlichs zu beziehen hat wie folgt.

	gulden	hollendisch	st.	d.
ahn grunszinszen	gl.	18	13	12
von den zehn hauseren in der statt und noch 3 häuser umb die Commende gelegen jährlichs hauszzinsz	gl.	600	–	–
die Commende papier mülle, bau- und weijd-land in dem scheffenthumb von Arnheim nebens zweij bauhöff *[fol.8r]* Falckenhausen und die Cleus genant, Item dreij weyden in dem Velpsenbruch	gl.	1184	10	–
die Häuser und landereijen in dem ambt Brummen	gl.	85	8	–
die landereijen unter Wagen	gl.	85	–	–
der bauhoff unter Benicken	gl.	275	–	–
ein plazlein auff der Hull	gl.	38	–	–
ein bauhoff in der baurschafft Dusburg	gl.	242	–	–
der bauhoff in der Apelldunisch brouch	gl.	95	–	–
die landereijen unter Malburg und Hüssen	gl.	196	14	–
die landereijen unter Elden	gl.	68	–	–
ein hausz und landereijen unter Els und Houmuth	gl.	358	13	–
2 bauhöf unter Heusen die Poller genant	gl.	1460	–	–
das land unter Engen	gl.	39	18	–
die landereijen unter Ummeren	gl.	170	–	–
die Commende Beuren	gl.	4	–	–
das land unter Ameringen	gl.	38	–	–
die landereijen in der Limmers	gl.	680	–	–

ferners beziehet die Commende von einigen

landereijen die halbe früchten oder so genante
  garben korn so sich jahrlichs incirca betragen gl.   300   –   –
ferners hat die Commende einiges schlagholz so
  incirca jährlichs rendiren kan   gl.   130   –   –

——————————

Summa   gl.   6745   13   12

[fol.8v] Hingegen seint von solchen gefällen
    nachstehende jährliche onera zu bestreithen
    ahn die statt Arnheim   gülden   1200   –   –
so der praedicant und schullmeister beziehen ^d
die verpondungen oder contributiones ordinar
    und extraordinar von den landereijen in dem
    scheffenthumb Arnheim   284   9   8
das hertstätten gelt so wegen dem camin oder feur
    gerechtigkeit zahlt werden musz   26   5   –
pompen, kleper und latern gelt   11   18   –
ordinar und extraordinari verpondung in dem
    ambt Brummen   262   15   4
die schazung von 17 morgen unter Malburg und
    deich und wasserungs gelt   160   –   –
die schazung in der Limmers incirca   230   –   –
das erbegelt aldahe   15   –   –
der gelt zinsz alldage   13   4   8
die ordinar und extraordinare verpondungen von
    dem guth in dem ambt Elst   69   16   8
ambtslasten   46   –   –
dorffslasten   10   –   –
die ordinar und extraordinare verpondungen und
    dorffslasten zu Elden   29   1   4

——————————

Summa   2358   10   –

[fol.9r] p[er] transport   gulden   2358   10   –
die verpondung und dichgelt von zweij weijden
    unter Velp   52   16   4
die ordinar und extraordinare dichpfennigen in
    dem Arnheimische brouch   37   16   –
die ordinar und extraordinar verpondung von
    dem guth unter Bennickum und die extra-
    ordinar auszsezung   113   6   8

die ordinar verpondung von der bauung unter Eide burschafft Dusburg und die auszsezung	80	–	–
die ordinar und extraordinar verpondung von dem land in dem Wagenheimschen Enck	4	9	–
die ordinar und extraordinar verpondung von 2 bauhofen zu Heusen	330	–	–
die extraordinar ambtslasten und dichpfennig	50	–	–
die ordinar und extraordinar verpondung unter Ummeren und ambtslasten	139	–	–
die verpondung von dem guth in dem Apeldonser bruchland	32	–	–
ahn den rathsherren [zu] Hasselt interesse von 2000 gulden ad 5%	100	–	–
ahn Sankt Peters gasthausz	1	10	–
ahn die vicari S.Walburg jährlichs 3 scheffell roggen	4	–	–
ahn das Convent von Bittanie	14	16	–
	3336	3	8

[fol.9v] p[er] transport gl.	3336	3	8
ahn den Kattepol	–	15	–
ahn die kirch zu Elten	–	10	–
ahn sandig zins	1	10	–
ordinar und extra[ordinar] verpondung von einer weijde unter Westervelt	8	3	4
salaria ahs dem rhentmeistren seint zugeleyt vom empfang 5% incirca	337	–	–
dem portner	60	–	–
dem obsichter im ambt Brumen	60	–	–
ahn die wittib Scherer wegen abstand vom erbpfacht und einiger zimmeren im ambt Brummen jährlichs	70	–	–
dem leijendecker sein jahrgehalt umb die Sankt Joannis kirch und die in der statt gelegene häuser in ordinare reparation zu halten	50	–	–
dem glaszmacher fur den ordinari unterhalt der gläser in Sankt Joannis kirch	20	–	–
dem urmachers steller	24	–	–
fur extraordinari reparation des urwercks und weisser, auch auszstauben der Sankt Joannis kirchen	20	–	–

fur machen und unterhalten der strasen fur der
    Commende   30   –   –
deserviten ahn procuratoren und advocaten
    jähr[lichs] incirca   150   –   –
ahn ordinares und extraordinares reparationes
    jähr[lichs] incirca   1000   –   –
reys und zehrungskosten wegen beijtreibung der
    gefällen incirca   80   –   –

                                          f. 5248   11   10

[fol.10r]   p[er] transport gl. 5248   11   10
brief porto incirca   15   –   –
die ordens lasten ahs resp. imposit. herbergs und
    capitelskosten betrag sich jahrlichs reichs
    gulden 66 . 3 X *[=kreuzer]* . 3 3/4 den. oder   88   –   –

Summa   5351   11   10

Wan nun solche auszgaab vom empfang abgezogen wird so pleiben
vorräthig gülden hollandisch 1394 . 2 st. & 2 den. oder reichsgulden
1045 . 35 X *[=kreuzer]*.

NB. 20 steuber machen einen gulden hollandisch und 16 den.
einen steuber.

    ᵃ *unknown abbreviation ms., looking like* ≐, *by me interpreted as 1/2.* ᵇ *Arnheim ms.* ᶜ *nnoch cancelled ms.* ᵈ *not filled in.*

Die zu dieser Commenden gehorige brieffschafften und documenten
werden in 2 kasten wohl registrirter auffbehalten und ahs man die-
semnach sich von gegenwärtigen visitations wegen zu besichtigung
der ausser der statt gelegenen höfen und häuser und zwaren nach der
vor Sankt Joannis thor gelegenen papier müllen (so wegen den exten-
dirten statt Arnheimischen fortificationen etwahe *[fol.10v]* weiters hin-
ausz hat transferirt und dahero anno 1728 newgebawet werden
müsen) wie auch zu den beijden in hiesiger statt Arnheim scheffen-
thum etwahe eine stund weith von der statt gelegenen bauhöfen
begeben und solche wie auch die papier müll in perfect guthem stand
befunden und ubrigens den verwalteren über nachgesezte puncten
aydlich vernohmen

1° ob die übrige von hiesigen Commende zu unterhaltende gebäwer
in gutem stand oder welche baufallig seyen

2º ob die Commenderie iura fleisig manutenirt

3º die rhenten und gefälle fleisig beygetrieben

4º nichts davon in untergang gekommen, deteriorirt, versezet oder alienirt worden

5º ob auch processen vorhanden und solche fleisig getrieben etc., worüber dieser geantworthet wie folgt

ad 1. R[esponsit] es fielen zwaren alljährlichs ein und andere reparationes vor, welche auch gethan und die häuser in wesentlichem stand unterhalten würden.

ad 2. affirmative

ad 3. affirmative so viell möglich

ad 4. negative

[fol.11r] ad 5. affirmative, es wäre ein process vorhanden wegen zweij malter korn und 2 malter gersten so von der Commenden der burgemeister Schlot zu Suttphen praetendirte, von seithen der Commenden aber man diese praetension diffitirte und den titulum solcher praetension von gegneren wissen wolte, in welcher sachen zwaren die Commende ahm landgericht condemnirt, von solcher urthell aber ahn hiesigen hof nacher Arnheim appellirt die sache auch so weith poussiret hatte, dasz solche auff die decision alleinig beruhete.

Weilen man nun wegen weither entlegenheit, auch eingefallenen wasserfluthen, nicht füglich auff die übrige guether kommen können so hat man gleichwohlen umb über eins und anderes mehrere sicherheith zu haben etwelche Commenderie hoffbauren ahnhero berufen und solche gleichfals über nachgesezte articulen vernohmen

1º ob ihre güther noch in guthem stand, davon nichts alienirt oder verkommen

2º ob sie auch was widder den verwalteren zu klagen oder

3º wasz ahnzuzeigen wisten wasz zu nachtheill der Commenden gereichete

[fol.11v] worauf der hoffbaur Wilhelm Willems auff Sutenthal geantworthet dasz ihr hausz zimmlich baufällig und wan solches bewohnet werden solte astan widder zu repariren seije; dan hätte der voriger verwalter ihm noch einige über 2 stund davon gelegenen güthere zu cultiviren auffgetrungen, welche er wegen allzu weither entlegenheit und allzu schlechten ländereijen nicht bauen könten sonderen viell eher das hoff guth verlassen müsten.

Sönsten wisten sie nichts zu klagen, weder auch wasz zu nachtheill der Commenden geschehen zu sein.

Ahs nun auch hierüber der verwalter befraget wurde so sagte derselbe dasz dieser hoff der schlechste im gebäw und zu repariren ahm nöthichsten wäre, nicht weniger seye des bauren klagt wegen solcher gar zu schlecht, und des cultivirens nicht wohl meritirenden allzu weith entlegenen ländereyen gegründet; mithin vielleicht dienlicher wan diese mit holz besezet und boschage darauf gemacht würde *[fol.12r]* masen man darzu keinen pfachter bekommen könte wan dieser solche quittiren würde.

Ferners erschiene Jost Willems hoffbaur zu Hull und contestirte dasz sein hausz zwaren annoch im stand, der kühe und viehe stall aber höchst nöthig zu repariren seije, und auch die frucht nicht lasen könte, mithin obgleich ihme die verfügung nothiger reparation schon lang versprochen, so wäre solche bis dahin noch nicht geschehen, bathe also umb deren bewerckstelligung, übrigens seye davon nichts abgekommen, hätte sönsten auch nichts zu klagen, wüste mithin nichts zu nachtheill der Commenden geschehen zu sein.

Weithers wurde der hoffbaur zu Dusburg Peter Rese vernohmen, und sagte dasz sein hausz noch in zimmlichen guthem stand seije, wäre auch nichts davon alienirt, wüste sonsten auch nichts zu klagen, ausser dasz der pfacht wasz hoch seije. Weilen nun auch der über die beschaffenheith der vom hoffbauren zu Hull verlangten *[fol.12v]* reparation befragter verwalter auszsagte dasz solches hausz so wohl schutten ahs auch die reparation der stallungen nöthig hätte, auch solche nothwendigkeiten ihme hoffbauren in contractu versprochen wären, ahs haltet man von gegenwartig visitations wegen dafur dasz diese zu verfügen seije, und dahe man sich auch secrete absonderlich beij dem Herrn Caplanen über eins und andere informirt mithin man weithers nicht in erfahrung bringen können ahs wasz vorhero beschrieben ist, so hat man damit die visitation beschlossen, so geschehen Arnheim den 9ten Octobris 1732.

In quorum omnium fidem praesens instrumentum desuper feci, scripsi et subscripsi solitoque meo sigillo roboravi
[super impressed paper seal   Johannes Frembzen
with legend:]   notarius Caesareus
                                                    et Apostolicus publicus
Progredior recta via   et iuratus manu propria

[fol.13r] Wir ends unterschriebene von unseres herren Obristmeistren in teutschen landen Philip Wilhelm hochfürstlichen gnaden zu verrichtung ihro prioral visitation specialiter deputirte commissarii haben uns mit notario und gezeugen auff die Commende Arnheim persönlich begeben und nach abgelegten gewöhnlichen aijd hausz und andere von dieser Commende zu unterhaltende gebäwer, und alles übriges nach auszweisz unseres ordens statuten fleisig visitirt und besichtiget, und auch tam secrete quam publice informirt, und also

besag vorstehenden visitations instrument befunden dasz über hiesiger Commenden guethere und revenues ordentliche cabraeen zu machen, dan ahn dem zwischen der Commende wohnhausz und der kirchen stehendem bäwlein tach und boden ganz verfault einfolglich new zu machen, und in dem wohnhausz das abgefallene pflaster, desgleichens die schutte nach gemelter kirchen zu, oder auff dem so genantem grosen soller, wie auch das sollergen *[fol.13v]* und gang oben der kuchen, item die thurn cammer, mit dillen new zu belegen, auch das tach oben dem cantor, ahnbeij ferners auff dem ahn der porten gelegenem bau das tach zu repariren, dan auff dem hoff Sutenthal das hausz, und auff dem Hull der S[it] V[enia] kuhe und viehe stall zu repariren, mithin auff das hausz fruchtschütten zu machen seijen, worzu wir dan des herren Ambassadeuren Balli Herrn von Schade hochwürden Excellence, und dasz es beschehen in zweij jahren à die huius communicationis, zu douren *[?]* schüldig erkennen, urkund eigen hand unterschrifft und beijgetrückten pittschafften.

	B.M. von Cappell
[seal in red wax]	Commendator
	manu propria

	Fr. J.B Kentzinger
[seal in read wax]	manu propria
	Ir.Gen.il.Allem.

LIST OF PAMPHLETS

Titles of pamphlets, memories, propositions, deductions etc. in printed or written form. Only such items are included that are found to be
or to have been really existing in libraries and archives all over Europe. Items that are only referred to without exact data have been left
aside.

Abbreviations used:

AOM   = Archives of the Order of Malta, in Valletta, Malta.
ARA   = Algemeen Rijksarchief, 's-Gravenhage, the Nether-
     lands.
GA   = Gemeente-archief or Stadsarchief, in every Dutch
     town.
GLA   = Generallandesarchiv, Karlsruhe, Germany.
RA   = Rijksarchief, in every Dutch province.

Allan   = F.Allan, *Geschiedenis en beschrijving van Haarlem, van de
     vroegste tijden tot op onze dagen*, 4 vols (Haarlem 1874-
     1888); especially vol.II (Haarlem 1877) pp.249-386:
     C.J.Gonnet, 'De commanderij van St.Jan'.

Bethonica   = *Bethonica Ende Bethoninge, Van saecken aengaende het Recht
     't welcke den Ridderlijcken Orden van S.Johan tot Hierusalem
     int Eylandt van Malta residerende, competeert tot der selver
     Goederen ghelegen alomme inde Vereenighde Nederlandtsche
     Provincien.* in quarto, VIII+96 pp., 1642; the 'Stucken
     ende Munimenten tot dese Bethoninghe ghehooren-
     de' are to be found on pp. 39-96. Printed pamphlet,
     Knuttel nr.4882 (nr.12 below).

Describuntur   = *Describuntur hic breviter quae, quot, & in quo Statu sint
     Commendae Ordinis Sancti Joannis Hierosolymitani Sitae in
     Regionibus Dominatui Provinciarum Confoederatarum sub-
     jectis,* quae Commendae etsi à Magno Prioratu
     Alemanniae dependent, eas tamen Confoederatae
     Provinciae occupant. In folio, 32 pp., sine loco et
     anno, c.1668. Printed pamphlet, Loeff nr.632 (nr.52
     below).

Heinemann = Otto von Heinemann, *Die Handschriften der herzoglichen Bibliothek zu Wolfenbüttel*, 2.Abteilung, Die Augustei-schen Handschriften, II (Wolfenbüttel 1895).

Huiskamp = M.W.Huiskamp, P.J.Boon, R.L.M.M.Camps, *Catalo-gus van de pamfletten aanwezig in de Bibliotheek Arnhem 1537-1795* (Hilversum 1995).

Klein = Michael Klein, *Die Handschriften 65/1 – 1200 im Gene-rallandesarchiv Karlsruhe* (Wiesbaden 1987; Die Hand-schriften der Staatsarchive in Baden-Württemberg, Band 2).

Knuttel = W.P.C.Knuttel, *Catalogus van de pamfletten-verzameling berustende in de Koninklijke Bibliotheek*, I/2, 1621-1648 ('s Gravenhage 1889); and II/1, 1649-1667 ('s Gra-venhage 1892).

Loeff = *Het Archief der Commanderij van St Jan te Arnhem*, Rijks-archief in Gelderland, Inventaris J.Loeff ('s-Graven-hage 1950).

Maris = A.Johanna Maris, *De reformatie der geestelijke en kerkelijke goederen in Gelderland*, in het bijzonder in het Kwartier van Nijmegen ('s-Gravenhage 1939).

Petit = Louis D. Petit, *Bibliotheek van Nederlandsche Pamfletten*, I, 1500-1648 ('s-Gravenhage 1882).

Recueil 1750 = *Recueil de pieces justificatives du droit de l'Ordre de Malte, pour la recuperation de ses biens situés dans les Provinces Unies des Pays-Bas.* [at the end:] De l'Imprimerie de la Veuve d'Houry, Imprimeur de l'Ordre, 1750. In fo-lio, 40 pp. Printed pamphlet in the Rijksarchief Gelderland at Arnhem, Huisarchief Rossum / fami-liearchief van Randwijk, inv.nr.229 (henceforth nr.59).

Suir = *Inventaris van het archief van de Balije van Utrecht der Johanniterorde 1251-1851* by G.C.M.van Dijck, sec-ond, fully revised edition by E.T.Suir. Rijksarchief Utrecht, Inventaris 1 (Utrecht 1985).

Van Schevichaven

= H.D.J.van Schevichaven, *Repertorium Noviomagense. Proeve van een register van boekwerken en geschriften betrekking hebbende op de stad en het Rijk van Nijmegen* (Nijmegen 1906).

1. c.1561 — Suir nr.32;
written copy, in folio, 11 pp.
Printed as 'Bijlage VI' in P.Q.Brondgeest, *Bijdragen tot de geschiedenis van het Gasthuis, het Klooster en de Balije van St.Catharina der Johanniter-ridders en van het Driekoningengasthuis te Utrecht* (Hilversum 1901), pp.101-105.

Memorie inder zaecken vanden Elect vander Balijen t'Utrecht.
'Gehoert bij Heeren Heijnrick Barck Elect vander Balijen van Sanct Johans oerdens tUtrecht, het gheene hem uuijt den naem ende van weghen de Hoocheijt vande Hertoghinne van Parma gouvernante aengegeven is, beroerende zeeckere drije poincten daer inne de zelve zoude consenteeren, mets obtinerende zijne versochte brijeven van placet ende aggreatie hem bij Co: Mat. op die voorschreven zijne electie te verleenen, heeft onder alle onderdanicheijt Hair Hoicheijt wel willen tkennen geven, tgene hier nae volcht:'

[This memorandum of the elect-bailiff of St John in Utrecht, frater Hendrik Berck, to the Duchess of Parma, Governess of the Netherlands on behalf of her brother King Philip II, concerns three points, 1st the privilege of free election of a new bailiff without prior royal consent; 2nd the enlargement of the hospital of St Catherine's Convent, which the elect will try to perform to the Governess's pleasure; and 3rd the payment of taxes, to which he is neither able nor authorized because of his dependance on the Grand Master at Malta and the Prior of Germany, in combination with his obligations for the renewal of his house and hospital and the distribution of bread to the poor.]

2. 1577, August 9 — *Bethonica*, pp.40-42, nrs. 3 & 4;
resolution and letter, included as proofs in a printed pamphlet.

[Resolution of the Estates of the provinces Holland and Zeeland, in which they grant the head and brethren of the St John's preceptory at Haarlem the right to recover their confiscated goods, insofar as they are not sold or alienated; followed by a letter of the Estates to the town government of Haarlem to part with these goods.
Both resolution and letter are also included as proofs 1 & 2 in the printed pamphlet *Insichten van de publijcque Rechten ende redenen* from 1652, Knuttel nr.7337 (nr.31 below); and in French translation in *Recueil* 1750, pp.1-2, No.2. Cf. Allan II p.366 with reference to Inv. Arch. Haarlem, I^e Afd. No.1821. Nowadays, the letter remains in GA Haarlem, Stads Archief grote lade 7-1-f-2.]

3. 1582, August 6 – *Describuntur*, fol.BIIr-Cv (pp.7-10); notarial act, included as proof in a printed pamphlet.

Coactio Consulum Harlemensium, eorumque deliberatio circa Commendam dicti loci cum responsione Commendatoris.

[This notarial act gives an extensive Latin report of the negotiations between the town government of Haarlem and the head of the St John's preceptory frater Timan van Wou, resulting in an agreement on 6 August 1582, pending the consent of the Grand Master and the Prior of Germany; cf. Allan II pp.369-370.]

4. 1582, August 16 – GLA Karlsruhe 90/82, fol.8r-10v, & GA Haarlem, Stads Archief loketkas 7-7-1-1, without foliation; written copy, in folio, 3 leaves.

Conditiones super Administratione bonorum Conventus Ordinis D.Johannis à Magistratu Harlemeo propositae et Domini Commendatoris Responsio.

[With respect to the previous pamphlet, this copy gives a different Latin translation of a collated copy dd. 16 August 1582, made by the town secretary of Haarlem, of the notarial act dd. 6 August 1582.]

5. undated – GLA Karlsruhe 90/82, fol.5r-6v, & GA Haarlem, Stads Archief loketkas 7-7-1-1, without foliation; written copy, in folio; cf. *Describuntur* p.8, where a shorter version of this text can be found. This text is an enlarged version of a part of the above items 3 & 4.

Demonstratio Domini Commendatoris D.Johannis continens rationes quibus movori [sic] *Senatus Harlemaus debeat ut manus à sui Ordinis bonis abstineat.*

6. undated, but shortly after 6 August 1582 – GA Haarlem, Stads Archief loketkas 7.7.2 nr.3b; compilation of written copies, in folio, 41 pp.

Memoriael van diligentie moeijte ende anders met zyn appendenten om weder te geraecken in Actuale possessie perceptie vande vruchten van alle goederen in Hollant gelegen toecomende die Commandurie van St.Ian Heeren binnen Haerlem die wellycke nae die belegeringe van die stadt Haerlem eerst aengeslaegen ende geanno-

tijert worden gelyck alle andere Burgers ende inwoonders goederen doen ter tyt in Haerlem residerende.

[This is a compilation of acts from the years 1577-1582 regarding the confiscation of the goods of the St John's preceptory at Haarlem and the agreement of 6 August 1582, made on order of frater Timan van Wou and complemented with comments by him.]

7. 1594 August 2 – GLA Karlsruhe 90/82, fol.12r-13r; written report, in folio; see full text before under A.nr.135, dd.4 November 1594, and cf. C.4., Visitation of 1594, especially Arnhem, 12 August 1594.

Propositio des Herrn Maisters St.Johans Orden in teutschen Landen abgefertigten Commissarius an die Herren des Gubernammts in Gellerlandt. Anno 94 2. Augusti.

8. without address and date, between 1594 and 1614 – Loeff nr.527, & Suir nr.4; printed pamphlet, in quarto, 8 pp.

Copye van eenige Missiven Van de Commandeurs van de Ordre van Malthe tot Utrecht aenden Meester vande selve Ordre in Duytsland.

[This pamphlet contains letters of the Utrecht bailiff frater Hendrik Berck dd. 3 April 1594 and 3 April 1601, both in old style, to the Prior of Germany, stating that his old age prevents him from appearing at the Provincial Chapter and that he cannot fulfil his contributary obligations because of continuous war taxation; and a letter written after his death on 12 October 1602 by the Prior of the St Catherine's Convent in Utrecht, frater Berndt van Schoonhoven, and the heads of the houses at Oudewater, Harmelen, s'Heerenloo, Montfoort and Buren, dd. 14 April 1603, conveying a petition for help on behalf of the bailiwick Utrecht and the management of its goods; and a letter by frater Berndt van Schoonhoven dd. 10 March 1614, that he cannot appear at the Provincial Chapter and pay his responsions. Cf. before, A.nr.120, dd. 3 March 1573, and C.5., Visitation of Utrecht, 1603.]

9. 1639 – Knuttel nr.4642a;
printed pamphlet, in quarto, 30 pp.
a shorter version of this pamphlet with the same title that has not
been described by Knuttel can be found in the Koninklijke Bibliotheek in 's-Gravenhage, nr.4642b, in quarto, 22 pp.

*Verantwoordinghe Voor Burgermeisteren Schepenen ende Raet der Stadt Nymegen,
Dienende soo tot Justificatie van 't aenveerden der Commandurie van St.Jan
binnen de voorsz. Stadt met die goederen daer toe gehoorende, als mede tot weder-
legginge van 't geene daer teghens soude mogen gemoveert worden.* Tot Nymegen,
.... by N.van Hervelt, ... 1639.

[This pamphlet is the reaction of the town government of Nimwegen
to a petition of sir Walraven Scheiffart van Merode, receptor-general
of the Order of St John in the Netherlands. The petition was offered
to the Estates of Guelders on 17 November 1638 and purported that
sir Walraven should take over the preceptories Arnhem and Nimwegen after the death of their last head frater Bernhard von Goltstein in
January 1638. Cf. Van Schevichaven pp.42-43, Loeff nr.538 and
Maris pp.337-342, where a *Bericht* from the town of Arnhem is mentioned as well, using the same arguments as the *Verantwoordinghe* van
Nimwegen.]

10. 1641 – Knuttel nr.4786;
printed pamphlet, in quarto, 12 pp.

*Iteratae Vindiciae Noviomagensium. Copie Van sekere Missive des Eerw. Classis
van Nymegen aen de Eed.Mog. Heeren Staten des Furstendoms Gelre ende Graefschaps Zutphen in Majo 1641 op eenen Landtdagh binnen de stadt Zutphen
vergadert.* [without address] 1641.

[This message from the church government of the 'classis' Nimwegen
to the Estates of Guelders contains a piece from 5 May 1641, followed by an 'Extract uyt de resolutien des Quartiers van Nijmegen
vanden Jare 1641, in Junio' and an 'Extract uyt de Acten des Synodi
Provinciael van Gelrelandt van den jaere 1641, tot Zutphen in Jul.',
advocating the confiscation of the Nimwegen St John's preceptory
properties; cf. Van Schevichaven p.43 and Maris p.344-346.]

11. 1641, December 12 – Heinemann, p.19, Kat.Nr.2137 sub 152, fol.386r-387r.
written copy, in folio, 2 leaves.

'Heere Walraven Scheiffert van Merode, der Ridderlicke Ordre van Maltha Commandeur tot Meijins, Steinfurt ende Munster, ende Receptor Generalis vande selve Ordre in Neerlant' [requests]
Aen de Ed.Gr.Mo. Heeren Staten van Hollant ende West Vrieslant

[that some reply be given to his petitions, referring to his earlier petitions from October 1640 and March 1641 and the resolution from 9 August 1577 about the restitution of the Haarlem St John's properties. Apart from that he has been informed that the lord major and town government of Haarlem]

'bij affixie van billietten seecke[re] notabele huysinge ende Erve de voors. Ordre toecomende en binnen Haerlem staende te vercoopen hebben gestelt tegens Donderdach den 12 deser Maent Decembris',

[and states that this public auction of a mansion and area of the Order in the town of Haarlem thwarts the decision-making about the restitution of these goods. Therefore he calls upon the Estates of Holland to suspend the auction until the matter is settled. Cf. Allan II pp.381-382.]

12. 1642 – Knuttel nr.4882;
printed pamphlet, in quarto, VIII+96 pp.; the 'Stucken ende Munimenten tot dese Bethoninghe ghehoorende' are on pp.39-96.

Bethonica Ende Bethoninge, Van saecken aengaende het Recht 't welcke den Ridderlijcken Orden van S.Johan tot Hierusalem int Eylandt van Malta residerende, competeert tot der selver Goederen ghelegen alomme inde Vereenighde Nederlandtsche Provincien... Ghestelt tot dienst van... den Heer Grootmeester ende de samentlijcke Ridderlijcke Orden tot Malta. Anno M.DC.XLII. [without address].

[This piece is in part a reaction to the pamphlets *Verantwoordinghe* (above, nr.9) and *Iteratae Vindiciae Noviomagensium* (nr.10); cf. Van Schevichaven p.43 and Maris p.346-350. For the largest part it deals with the preceptories Arnhem and Nimwegen as described under nr.13.]

13. 1642 – GLA Karlsruhe 65/266;
composite manuscript volume, containing pamphlets from 1642, 1651, 1652 and 1647, translated into a rather clumsy German; in folio. Cf. Klein, p.106. The pamphlet of 1642 is on pp.1-92. For the other ones see nrs.18 (1647), 27 (1651) and 32 (1652) below.

Bethonica und Bezeigung von sachen angehend dasz Recht welches den Ritter Orden von St. Johan zu Jerusalem in die Insel von Malta residirend, competirt zu der selben Gütteren gelegen hin, und wieder in die Vereinigten Niederländische Provincien.

'Conservirt durch
Natur der vorgemelden Gütteren.
Neutralität des Ordens Ritteren.
Concordaten der Vereinigten Provincen.
Gestellt hinn Dienst von seiner fürstlichen Altesse den Herrn Grossmeister und den sämbtlichen Ritterlichen Orden zu Malta. Anno MDCXLII.'

[On pp.49-92 German translations of 31 proofs are to be found, mostly concerning the preceptories Arnhem and Nimwegen. Exceptions are the nrs.3 and 4, wrongly dated 19 August 1577 instead of 9 August 1577 (above, nr.2), nr.28 dd. 12 December 1641 pertaining to Haarlem, and the nrs.8 and 9 concerning the preceptory Ter Brake near Alphen. The nrs.8 and 9 are resolutions of the Estates General dd. 19 November 1611 and 23 June 1612 (see *Resolutiën der Staten Generaal, nieuwe reeks 1610-1670*, I, 1610-1612, ed. A.Th.van Deursen, 's-Gravenhage 1971, Rijks Geschiedkundige Publicatiën, large series 135, p.516 nr.1239 and p.678 nr.720). Both in the Dutch and the German versions of the *Bethonica*, these pieces are wrongly dated 19 October 1611 and 23 July 1612. Finally, some proofs deal with general decisions concerning the restitution of church property (nrs.2 and 5), whereas nr.10 pertains to some Westphalian preceptories. The rest concerns Arnhem and Nimwegen.]

14. 1643 – Petit nr.2204;
printed pamphlet, in quarto, 16 pp.

Remonstrantie, Van wegen de Ghedeputeerde des Provincialen Synodi/ aende Ed: M: Heeren de Staten des Vorstendoms Gelre ende Graefschaps Zutphen. Rakende de uyt ghegevene Betonica vande Iohanniters. Waerinne dat aengewesen word/ de onwetlickheyt van der Johanniters versoeck/ ende de nieticheyt van haere be-

schuldinge/ tegen de Leeraren vande Gereformeerde Religie. – – Gedruckt in't
Jaer onses Heeren, 1643 [without address].

[This remonstrance of the provincial synod of the reformed church in
the province of Guelders to the Estates of Guelders is a reaction to
the *Bethonica* of the Order of St John concerning the confiscated goods
of the preceptories Arnhem and Nimwegen. According to Van
Schevichaven p.44 it was written by J.Smetius Sr. Cf. Maris pp.344-
345, note 3.]

15. 1643, September 2 – GLA Karlsruhe 90/474, fol.8r-16v
& Loeff nr.544;
written document, in folio, 9 leaves, in 2 copies.

*Memorie oft Verbael van het geene op den 2 Septembris 1643 door interpositie van
Mijn Heeren vanden Hove van Gelderland aande[a] Gecommittierde vanden Magistraat van Nijmegen om alle disputen met die Ridderlicke Ordre, nopende die
goederen vande Commandurije van Nijmegen in der vrientschap bij te leggen,
geproponiert is geworden, als mede wat die Ed: Heeren Raaden tot dien eijnde
mede aen ons voorgestelt hebben.*
[followed by:] *Poincten ende Conditien soo van zijde van die Hochloffeliche
Ordre aen die heeren Gecommitteerde vande magistraat van Nijmegen den 2.
Septembris 1643 gepresenteert sijn geworden op naeder aggreatie van onsen Heeren
Principalen.* [8 points, undersigned:] R.Kempinck

---

[a] *vande* ms.

[report by the Order's agent Reynier Kempinck about his meeting,
mediated by the Court of Guelders, with representatives of the town
government of Nimwegen in order to reach a compromise about the
confiscated preceptory goods, and the eight points or conditions that
he presented at that occasion on behalf of the Order.]

16. 1646, May 14 – Heinemann p.19, Kat.Nr.2137 sub 154,
fol.392r-v;
written copy, in folio, 1 leaf.

'Heere Jacob de Souvré Ridder vande Ordre van St.Jan van Jerusalem tot Maltha Bailly vant Groot Cruys vande selve Ordre, Commandeur van Valleure ende Haarlem, Gemachtichde van de selve
Ordre tot aenvaerdinge en regeringe van alle haere goederen in de

Geunieerde Provincien, in plaetse vanden Heeren Ridder Walrave Scheyffert van Merode die overleden is' [requests] *Aen de Ed.Gr.Mo. Heeren de Heeren Staten van Hollant ende West Vrieslant*

[to press the town government of Haarlem to return the confiscated properties to the Order of St John, referring to former requests, to the Order's efforts for the safety of trading-vessels on the Mediterranean that would otherwise be menaced by the Turks, and to the resolution dd. 9 August 1577 concerning the restitution of the Haarlem preceptory goods.

    Cf. A nr.158 above, dd. 28 July 1644, in which frater Jacques de Souvré gets the right to regain the Dutch preceptories, A.nr.159, dd. 27 December 1647, in which he announces his intention to negotiate with the Estates of Holland about their restitution, and A.nr.160, dd. 31 January 1648, in which Grand Master and Convent grant him the authority to do so. This request of 14 May 1646 to the Estates of Holland and West-Frisia therefore cannot be considered a first step into actual negotiations.]

17. 1647 – Knuttel nr.5583;
printed pamphlet, in quarto, 8 pp.

Remonstrantie Aen De... Staeten des Furstendoms Gelre ende Graefschaps Zutphen, Raeckende Het aenveerden van de Commandurije van St.Johan tot Nymeghen, met der selver goederen ende gevolgh van dien etc. 1647 [without address].

[Remonstrance of the elders and deacons of the reformed church at Nimwegen to the Estates of Guelders about the legitimacy of their use of the goods of the former St John's preceptory at Nimwegen, located not only inside but also outside the town and the sheriff's district of Nimwegen. Cf. Maris pp.353-354.]

18. 1647 – GLA Karlsruhe 65/266, pp. 181-186;
composite manuscript volume, in folio; cf.Klein p.106 and before, nr.13.

Remonstration an die Edle Mogende Herren Staaten des fürstenthumb Gelre, und Graffschaffts Zütphen; Angehend, dasz annehmen der commanderie von St. Johan zu Nimegen, mit derselben Güteren, und gefolgen von selbigen. Getrückt im Jahr unseres Herren 1647.

[German translation of the previous item.]

19. 1647 = Petit nr.2387, & RA Gelderland, catalogue of the library nr.III 144B, & Huiskamp nr.100;
printed pamphlet, in quarto, IV+88 pp.

Anacrisis ofte Ondersoeck van seeckere sententie, by den Hove provinciael van Gelrelandt ende pretense geadjungeerde heeren teghen die stadt Nymegen, tot merckelijcke nadeel van des selves hebbende privilegien ende gherechtigheyden, vermeyntlijck in contumaciam uytgesproocken op den 19. Decembris 1646. Tot Nieumegen, by Nicolaes van Hervelt, 1647.

[Cf. about this pamphlet by the Order's adversaries, Van Schevichaven p.44 and Maris p.353. The sentence of the Court of Guelders dd. 19 December 1646 stated that the head or the receptor of the preceptory Nimwegen should be maintained in the possession of the preceptory's goods as far as they were outside the town and the sheriff's district ('schependom') of Nimwegen; see Maris pp.351-353; the Dutch text and several translations are to be found in Loeff nr.550, GLA Karlsruhe 90/349, fol.2-3 and 90/457, fol.4-7, and *Recueil* 1750 p.5 No.12.]

20. 1648 – Knuttel nr.5806, & Petit nr.2443;
printed pamphlet, in quarto, IV+44 pp.

Anaclisis ofte Weerschyn vande cracht der Sententie by den Hove, mitsgaders de Heeren den selven gheadjungeert uyt de Landtschap des Furstendoms Gelre ende Graeffschaps Zutphen, op het Intendit, bewijs, schijn ende bescheyt over-ghegeven door ende van wegens de Volmachtiger vande Heere Walraven Scheiffart van Merode, St.Jans Ordens Ridder, Commandeur ende Receptor Generael van des Ordens goederen in Nederlandt, Impetrant. Tegens de Heeren van de Magistraet der Stadt Nymegen, Gedaegde, uytgeroepene, ende niet erschenene, op den 19. Decem. 1646. uytgesproken. Waer inne, neffens verhandelinge der Impertinentien van seeckeren Anacrisis ofte Ondersoeck Aengewesen wordt de wettelijckheyt van de voorsz. Sententie. ... Ghedruckt in 't jaer 1648 [without address].

[The Order's refutation of the *Anacrisis*, nr.19 above, cf. Van Schevichaven pp.44-45 and Maris p.354.]

21. 1648 – GLA Karlsruhe, 90/475, fol.42r-70v;
written German translation of the previous item, in folio, 29 leaves.

Anaclisis oder Wiederschein.

22. 1648, September 23 – Heinemann p.19, Kat.Nr.2137 sub 150, fol.383r-v;
written copy, in folio, 1 leaf.

Protestation de M. le Commandeur de Souvré --- Fait a Delft le 23 iour de Septembre 1648.

[Frater Jacques de Souvré, ambassador of the Order of Malta in the Netherlands, sends a letter to the Estates General that he finishes his embassy with nothing achieved, because he has not been treated with the honours his Order deserves.]

23. 1648, September 23 – bound with Knuttel nr.6921 (nr.25 below);
printed pamphlet, in quarto, 2 pp.

Translaet van de Protestatie van den Heer Ambassador Souvré --- Ghedaen tot Delff den 23.dagh van September 1648.

[Dutch translation of the previous item, bound with the *Korte Deductie* from 1650, Knuttel nr.6921 (nr.25 below).

On 24 September 1648 the Estates General declared to dismiss this letter of protest and to return it to the sender. Notwithstanding their resolution dd. 19 September 1648 not to restitute the Order's goods in the Dutch provinces (see Heinemann, p.19 sub 156, fol.394r-v), they were willing to grant ambassador De Souvré an audience if he should ask for one.]

24. 1648, after September 23 – Heinemann p.19, Kat.Nr.2137 sub 155, fol.393r-v;
written copy, in folio, 1 leaf.

'Mr.Cornelis Boeij Advocaet voor den Hove van Hollant, als Gemachtichde ende Procuratie hebbende van Heere Jacob de Souvré Ridder ende Groot Bailly vande Ordre van St.Jan van Jerusalem ende van Maltha', [sent after the departure of De Souvré as one more attempt, requests]
Aen de Grootmogende Heeren Staten van Holland ende West Vrieslandt
[to press the town government of Haarlem to restitute the goods of St John, referring to the Order's role in safeguarding Dutch vessels in the Mediterranean and the Levant:]

'ten eynde alle inconvenienten ende onheylen over de Schepen van desen Staet ende voornaamentlyck van die van U.Ho.Mo. Provintie, die welcke de Levant ende Midlandsche zee sijn frequenterende by tyts mogen werden verhoet, ende voorcomen.'

25. 1650 – Knuttel nr.6921;
printed pamphlet, in quarto, 28 pp.

Korte Deductie, over de gheleghentheydt van de Ridderlijcke Orden van St.Iohan van Ierusalem, Nu in 't Eylant Malta residerende. Aengaende desselfs Fundatie ende Gouvernement ... In specie desselven Ordens wel ghefondeert recht over de Commanderie, Huysinghe, ende Goederen, in ende ontrent de Stadt Haerlem, in Hollandt gheleghen: Soo in 't jaer 1625, ... den selven zijn ontrocken, ende tot noch toe van de voorsz. Stadt de facto worden gheusurpeert ende ghenoten. Ghedruckt tot Haerlem, door de Ordre van St.Johan. M.DC.L.

[Short deduction concerning the lawful rights of the Order of Malta to the buildings and goods of the St John's preceptory at Haarlem in the province of Holland, that were usurped by the town in 1625.]

26. 1651 – Knuttel nr.7084;
printed pamphlet, in quarto, 82 pp.

Verkondinghe van de Rechtveerdighe Pretensie des Ridderlycken Ordens van S.Ian van Ierusalem, residerende tot Malta, Teghen Eenighe Onderdanen der... Staeten van de Vereenighde Provincien in Neder-landt,... M.DC.LI.

[Declaration of the lawful pretensions of the Order of St John of Malta to some subjects of the Estates General of the Netherlands, who have usurped the Order's goods.]

27. 1651 – GLA Karlsruhe 65/266, pp.93-156;
composite manuscript volume, in folio; cf.Klein p.106 and nr.13 above.

Verkündigung von die Rechtfertige Pretension des Ritterlichen Ordens von St. Johan von Jerusalem, residirend zu Maltha.
Gegen einige unterthanen der Hoch Mögenden Herren Staaten von die Vereinigte Provintzen in Niederland, welche des vorbesagten Ordens Güter unter die jurisdiction der vorbesagten Staaten gelegen, inhalten, und usurpiren.

Gedruckt im Jahr 1651.

[German translation of the previous item.]

28. 1651 – Knuttel nr.7085;
printed pamphlet, in plano, 1 leaf.

*Propositie Gedaen aen de ... Staten van Hollant ende West-Vrieslandt, Van den
E: Gecommitteerde van ... Fredrick, Land-Grave van Hessen d'Arm-stadt, der
Ridderlycke S.Ians Ordens van Jerusalem, Overste Meester in Duytslandt, ... in
Decembri 1651.* [without address].

[Proposition to the Estates of Holland and West-Frisia by the agent of
frater Friedrich Landgraf von Hessen, Prior of Germany, about the
confiscated goods of the Order. Prince Friedrich had been given the
right to regain the Dutch commanderies on 26 May 1649; see above,
A.nr.163. Cf. the correspondence of the Grand Master with Prince
Friedrich about future negotiations with the Estates of Holland in this
matter, A.nr.164 above, dd. 4 August and 4 September 1650.]

29. 1652 – AOM 2198, Alemagna, fol.138r-516v, dossier about the
confiscated goods of the Order in the Dutch Republic, 17th century,
especially fol.464r-478r;
printed pamphlet, in quarto, I+29 pp.

*Brevis ac solida Deductio iuris et facti, super indultis, privilegiis, immunitatibus,
ac reliquo jure Sacri Ordinis S.Joannis Hierosolymitani. Cum subnexa Conclu-
sione Quod eorum, & adductarum rationum intuitu, superioritas Territorialis in
ditione Heitersheimiana, Illustrissimo ac Supremo Joannitarum per Alemaniam
Priori pro tempore existenti, indubitate, neutiquam vero Serenissimae Domui Aus-
triacae, eiusdemve Regimini Ensi heimiano, nuper Friburgum translato, competat,
pro aris & focis in possessario & petitorio, modis omnibus manutenenda, sicut hoc
Illustrissimo Magno Priori per Alemaniam, Praecepto Apostolico, sub poena excommunicationis impositum repetitur. Anno M.DC.LII.* [without address].

[This pamphlet does not deal especially with the confiscated Dutch
goods, but with the position of the Prior of Germany at Heitersheim
as a territorial prince of the Empire.]

30. 1652 – Knuttel nr.7336, & Huiskamp nr.187;
printed pamphlet, in quarto, 38 pp.

*Considerable Insichten van de Publycque Regten en redenen, Noopende 't
Geduyrigh profyt vande ... Ordre van St.Ian tot Hierusalem ... die Restitutie ende
Redintegratie van der selver Baliagien, Commandeurien, Huysen ende goederen, die
binnen 't gebiedt van de ... Staten Generael ... gelegen, ..., behoort geconsenteert te
werden.* Tot Vytrecht, By Jacob vander Poel..., 1652.

[arguments in favour of the restitution of the Order's confiscated
properties in the territories of the Estates General.]

31. 1652 – Knuttel nr.7337, & Loeff nr.611a, & Suir nr.33;
printed pamphlet, in quarto, 60 pp.

*Insichten van de publijcque Rechten ende redenen, waerom tot geduyrich profijt
vande ... Ordre van St.Jan tot Hierusalem, ... die Restitutie ende Redintegratie van
der selver Baliagien, Commandeurien, Huysen ende goederen, die binnen 't gebiedt
van de ... Staten Generael ... gelegen, ..., behoort gheconsenteert te werden.* Gedruckt in den Jare 1652. [without address].

[the same arguments as before, only more extensive.]

32. 1652 – GLA Karlsruhe 65/266, pp.156-180;
composite manuscript volume, in folio; cf. Klein p.106 and before,
nr.13.

*Insigten deren Publicken Rechten und ursachen, warumb zum beständigen Nutzen
von dem Militaire, und Ritterlichen Orden, von St. Johan von Jerusalem und
derselben Republique von Maltha; forth zum zeitlichen Nutzen von dem durch-
lauchten Hochgeboren Herren Friedrich Prinz Cardinal, und landgraff von Hessen, Grosz prior deszselben ordens in Teutschland, fürst des Heyligen Römischen
Reichs etc. im Nahmen von den hoch gemelten orden bereithwillig, und thätlich, die
restitution, und Redinteregratia von derselben Baliagien, Commanderieren, Häuser,
und Güter, welche in dem gebied von die Hoch. Mögende Herren Staaten General
der Vereinigten Niederländischen Provintzen, und im gebied von die Edel grosz
Mögende Herren Staaten derselben provintzen gelegen, und in dem eijgenthumb von
dem hochgemelten orden herumb conservirt geblieben [p.157] seind, beij Ihre
Hoch, Grosz, und Edel Mogenden behöhrt consentirt zu werden.*

[German translation of the previous item, finishing on p.180 with the words:]
'sICVt erant In prInCIpIo sIC sInt, erIt ILLIs, aC hIs greX paCIs VnIVs VnVs. aMen.'
Gedruckt im Jahr 1652.

33. 1652 – GLA Karlsruhe 90/86, fol.113;
written notice, in folio, 1 leaf.

Memoriael voor den Heer Canseler tot bevorderinge van de restitutie van de goede-ren van Synne H.V. Eminentie wegen de ordre van Malta gelegen inde Provincie van Hollant
[beginning with:]
'Dat seer nodig is copie te hebben vande visite door die vande ordre van Malta gedaen A° 1624 wegen de commanderie tot Haerlem om daermede te connen weten ende des nodig synde bewijsen wat goedren datter syn geweest, waer in die bestaen hebben, te connen weten wat restitutie te vordren is, alsmede uyt de ander visite wat goedren vande twee commanderyen als Woerden ende Ouwater synde membres van Utrecht ende nochtans inde Provintie van Hol-lant gelegen te vordren is.'

[Notice for the Order's chancellor to obtain a copy of the visitation of Haarlem from 1624 in order to learn and see evidence of the rights and goods of that preceptory, and also those of the Utrecht members Woerden and Oudewater in the province of Holland.

One visitation of Haarlem from 1624 has not been kept in the archives. On 9 January 1625 the last head of that preceptory, frater Andries Pietersz. van Souwen, died, after which the town government sequestered the moveables and immoveables of the preceptory and ordered an inventory of the letters, furniture, paintings etc. of the St John's house. This inventory can be found in GA Haarlem, Stads Archief grote lade 5-1-III letter vvv; cf. Truus van Bueren, *Macht en onderhorigheid binnen de Ridderlijke Orde van Sint Jan, De commandeursportret-ten uit het Sint Jansklooster te Haarlem* (Haarlem 1991) pp.80-81.]

34. 1652 – Knuttel 7338;
printed pamphlet, in quarto, 20 pp., with several appendices from May-August 1652.

Propositie Gedaen Aen d'... Staten van Hollant ende West-Vrieslandt, den 10

*August. 1652. van den ... Heere Jan Jacob van Pallant, der Ridderlijcke St.
Iohans Ordens van Hierusalem tot Malta Ridder, ... Om te hebben by die beste
ende vriendlicxste wegen, een Catagorische Resolutie, tot die herstellinge van den
Illustr. Ordens Goederen der Commandurie van Haerlem, ende inde Provintie van
Hollandt gelegen.* Tot Amsterdam, Gedruct by Brvyn Cornelisz. van
VVageninge, ... 1652.

[Proposition of frater Jan Jacob van Pallandt, Maltese knight, to the
Estates of Holland and West-Frisia, to get a categorical resolution
about the restitution of the Order's goods belonging to the preceptory
of Haarlem and other goods in the province of Holland.]

35. c.1660 – GLA Karlsruhe 90/476, fol.60;
written copy in French, in folio, 1 leaf;
a written copy of the Dutch original letter is to be found in
Loeff nr.604.

A Messieurs les Bourguemaistres et Regents de la Ville d'Hoorn.
'Remonstrent tres humblement les Marchands soubsignéz de-
meurants dans ceste ville, qu'ils ont appris de bonne main, que ceux
de Malthe renouvellent leurs devoirs et instances aupres de Messieurs
les Estats Generaux pour obtenir restitution et satisfaction des biens
et Commanderies, qui appartiennent a ceux de Malthe dans les Provinces Unies, comme aussii leurs biens situez dans la ville d'Haerlem
et dans la iurisdiction d'icelle, affin que par une amiable convention
et satisfaction l'on pourroit eviter les actes d'hostilité qu'autrement ils
en pourroient entreprendre, —.'

[French translation of a petition by 31 merchants (whose names are
mentioned) from Hoorn to the magistrate of that town to reach a
compromise with the Order of Malta to prevent further detriment to
the Mediterranean trade.]

36. 1660, September 27 – *Recueil* 1750, p.15-16, No.19;
appendix to a treaty, included as proof in a printed pamphlet; written
copies and translations of this declaration of the King of France,
given in Paris dd. 27 September 1660, and of a similar one, given by
the King of Spain in Madrid, dd. 12 November 1660, are to be found
in GLA Karlsruhe 90/281 fol.7, & GLA Karlsruhe 90/462 fol.32, &
RA Gelderland, Loeff nr.601.

Inclusion de la part de Sa Majesté très-Chrétienne du S. Prince Cardinal Frederic Landgrave de Hesse, Grand-Prieur d'Allemagne de l'Ordre de S.Jean de Jérusalem, dit de Malte, dans le Traité de Paix fait entre la France et l'Espagne le septiéme jour de Novembre 1659.
Fait à Paris le vingt-septiéme jour de Septembre 1660. Signé LOUIS, & plus bas, De Loménie.

[The King of France declares that the Prior of Germany, Prince-Cardinal Friedrich Landgraf von Hessen, will be included in the peace treaty between France and Spain from 7 November 1659.]

37. before 1660, November 12 – Loeff nr.633;
printed pamphlet, without title, address nor year, in folio, 10 pp.

Don Pedro Geronimo de Sessè, Gentilhombre, y Secretario de Embaxada del Cardenal Principe Friderico Lançtgraue de Asia [= Hessen], *en su nombre*
[tells the King of Spain that many goods of the Order of St John of Jerusalem are laying in the United Provinces,]
'dependientes del Gran Priorado, que su Eminencia tiene en Germania, el qual se llama la Baylia de Vtrehs, en la qual ay muchas Encomiendas, y Conuentos, y fuera de la dicha Baylia, le toca a su Eminencia otra Encomienda, que se llama Harlem, que todas rentaràn en cada vn año ochenta mil escudos de plata,'
[but that all efforts to get them back have been unsuccessful, just like the letters concerning this matter by the King of Denmark, the Emperor and the College of Electors (dd. 12 and 13 May 1652 and 5 December 1653; cf. *Recueil* 1750 No.15 and 17). Therefore he asks if the Spanish ambassador in 's-Gravenhage can get permission to appeal to the Estates General in this matter and if his Eminence the Prince-Cardinal can be included in the Spanish-French peace treaty.
The margins of pp.2-8 state the purposes and deeds of the Order in Latin and also several attempts at recovery of the goods.]

38. 1660, December 8 – *Recueil* 1750, p.16-20, No.20;
18th-century (re?)print of a 17th-century pamphlet, in folio, 5 pp.

Proposition de Monsieur de Thou, Comte de Meslay, Ambassadeur de Sa Majesté très-Chrétienne, faite en l'Assemblée de Messieurs les Etas Généraux des Provinces Unies des Pays-Bas le 8 Décembre 1660.

[Proposition of Monsieur de Thou, ambassador of the King of

France, to the Estates General about the restitution of the Order's confiscated goods. His credential dd. 12 November 1660 is to be found in *Recueil* 1750 p.16.

A written instruction for Monsieur de Thou comte de Meslay, ambassador of the King of France to the Estates General on behalf of the Prince-Cardinal Landgraf von Hessen as Prior of Germany, dd. 12 November 1660, is to be found in GLA Karlsruhe 90/349, fol.21-24.]

39. 1661, November 25 – AOM 2198, Alemagna, fol.440r-443v & 448r-451v (2 copies);
printed pamphlet, in octavo, 8 pp., reprinted in *Recueil* 1750, pp.21-24, No.22.

Proposition présentée a Messieurs les Estats Generaux des Provinces Unies des Pays-Bas par Monsieur Friquet, Conseiller de S.M.Imperiale & son Député Extraordinaire vers lesdits Seigneurs Estats Generaux: Touchante la Restitution des Commanderies de l'Ordre de Malthe situees en les dits Provinces, pretendue par Monsieur le Cardinal Prince de Darmstat, comme Grand-Prieur dudit Ordre en Allemagne. Le 25. Nov. 1661. [without address].

[Proposition of Monsieur Friquet, deputy of the Emperor to the Estates General, about the restitution of the Order's confiscated goods on behalf of the Prince-Cardinal Landgraf von Hessen, Prior of Germany.]

40. 1661, November 25 – Knuttel nr.8526;
printed pamphlet, in quarto, 12 pp.

Memoire Presenté à Messieurs les Estats Generaux des Provinces Unies des Pays-Bas Par Monsieur Friquet, [etc.]. *Le 25 Nov.1661. Memorie Overgelevert aende ... Staten Generael.* [without address].

[Memorandum to the Estates General about the Order's rights in French, followed by a Dutch translation.]

41. undated, but probably 1661 – GLA Karlsruhe 90/340, fol.18r-20v, & ARA 's-Gravenhage, Archief van de Staten Generaal, Loket-kas Lopende (undated) nr.12549.10, 4 leaves without foliation, double-sided;

written copies, in folio, the copy in ARA is about 1 page longer than the one in GLA as it has a more extensive text.

Instruction fait par Mons. Friquet et par luij rendu a Mess. les Commissaires de Commis pour les Estats pour l'affaire de l'Ordre de Malta.

[On the ARA copy has been written, probably by the receiver:]
Pointen nopende de pretensien der Maltheser goederen.

42. 1661, December 14 – AOM 2198, Alemagna, fol.444r-445v & 446r-447v (2 copies);
printed pamphlet, in octavo, 4 pp., reprinted in *Recueil* 1750, p.24-25, No.23.

Proposition présentée a Messieurs les Estats Generaux des Provinces Unies des Pays-Bas par Monsieur Don Estevan de Gamarra & Contreras Ambassadeur de sa Majesté Catholique vers les dits Seigneurs Estats Generaux, Touchante la Restitution des Commanderies & biens de l'Ordre de Malthe situees dans les dictes Provinces, pretendue par Monsieur le Cardinal Prince de Hesse, comme Grand-Prieur dudit Ordre en Allemagne. Le 14.me dubre [sic] 1661. [without address].

[Proposition of Don Estevan de Gamarra, deputy of the King of Spain to the Estates General, about the restitution of the Order's confiscated goods on behalf of the Prince-Cardinal Landgraf von Hessen, Prior of Germany.]

43. 1662 – Knuttel nr.8612, & GLA Karlruhe, 90/342, fol.5, 6 & 7 (3 copies);
printed pamphlet, in plano, 1 leaf.

Ontsegh-brief vande Ho: Mog: Heeren Staten Generael, aenden Heer Cardinael Lant-graef Van Hessen ende de ridders van Malta. Ter oorsaecke van t'arrest van hare Onderdanen, Schepen gedaen doen in Engelant, door d'Admiraliteyt aldaer. Actum den ... Iuny 1662. Tot Rotterdan [sic] voor Carel vande Mander inde korte Bree-straet.

[Letter of protest by the Estates General to the Prior of Germany about the sequestration of some Dutch vessels in England.]

44. 1662 – GLA Karlsruhe, 90/347, fol.1-12;
written copy, in folio, 12 leaves, not described in any Dutch catalogue
of pamphlets.

Raisons evidentes par droict et in facto, par quoy Messieurs les Estats generaux des
Pays bas sont obligez de rendre les Commandes, Biens et Maisons que quelques
villes ou particuliers detiennent a l'ordre des Chevaliers de Malte et a
l'eminentissime et serenissime Seigneur le Prince Frideric Cardinal et Landgrave
d'Hessen comme Grand Prieur dudit Ordre en Allemagne.

[The following arguments are given to motivate the restitution of the
Order's confiscated goods by the Estates General:]
1e Raison, leur propres constitutions, decrets et conclusions;
2e Raison, poursuitte desdits biens de l'ordre de Malte;
3e Raison, nullité des procédures et possession iniuste;
4e Raison, iustification de l'arrest en l'Angleterre des vaisseaux de
Holande.
[concerning the last argument, cf. nr.43 above, *Ontsegh-brief.*]

45. 1663, March 3 & 5, Knuttel nr.8736, reprinted in *Recueil* 1750,
p.25-31, No.24; written copy in AOM 2198, Alemagna, fol.198r-
205v, followed by a shortened Italian translation;
printed pamphlet, in quarto, II+16 pp.

Memoires et Deduction des Raisons qui justifient le droit, que l'Ordre de Malthe
a sur les Commanderies situés dans les Provinces Unies, presentés par Monsieur le
Comte d'Estrades, Ambassadeur Extraordinaire de France. [without address].

[Memorandum of the Comte d'Estrades, ambassador of France,
about the lawful rights of the Order of Malta to its preceptories in the
United Provinces; with two letters as appendices: 1st. dd. 19 September 1662, from the Grand Master to the Comte d'Estrades, and 2nd.
dd. 14 July 1662 from the Prince- Cardinal Landgraf von Hessen to
the Estates General.]

46. 1663 – Knuttel nr.8737;
printed pamphlet with Dutch translation of the previous item, in
quarto, II+20 pp.

Memorien ende Deductie, Justificerende het recht, het welcke d'Ordre van Maltha heeft op de Commanderien, gelegen in de Geuniëerde Provintien, gepresenteert door den Grave d'Estrades. M. DC.LXIII. [without address].

47. 1664, May 16 – AOM 2198, Alemagna, fol.428r-433v;
printed pamphlet, N.6- [60 ? illegible] with page-numbers 457-468, in octavo, 12 pp.

La Continuation des instances faites aupres des Estats Généraux, par le Comte d'Estrades, Ambassadeur de France, pour la restitution des Biens de la Religion de Malthe. Paris, le 16e Mai 1664.

48. 1664, May 30 – AOM 2198, Alemagna, fol.434r-439v;
printed pamphlet, N.63 with page-numbers 509-520, in octavo, 12 pp.

La Suite des Instances du Roy, aupres des Estats Généraux des Provinces-Unies des Païs-Bas, pour la restitution des Biens de l'Ordre de Malthe. Paris, le 30e Mai 1664.

49. 1664, March 15 – ARA 's-Gravenhage, Archief van de Staten Generaal, Loketkas Malta, nr.12578.47, & RA Utrecht, Suir nr.34; written copies, in folio, 25 pp.

Deductie van de Staten van Utrecht wegens het different met de Ridders van Maltha.

[The Estates of the province of Utrecht persist in their resolution not to restitute the confiscated Maltese goods; cf. the Estates' resolution dd. 15 March 1664 (RA Utrecht, Archief Staten van Utrecht no.232-31, 1662, December 10 – 1665, October 4), in which a summary of this *Deductie* has been included. It has been fully edited without title or date in Antonius Matthaeus, *Veteris aevi analecta* (editio secunda, Hagae-Comitum 1738), V pp.952-974, as part of his *Libellus de Equestri Ordine Melitensi*, pp.935-974; cf. also Maris p.355 note 2.]

50. 1664, October 21 – ARA 's-Gravenhage, Archief van de Staten Generaal, nr.3270, Resoluties 1664, fol.800v, & GLA Karlsruhe 90/462, fol.14;
written copies, in folio, 1 leaf.

Extract uijttet register der resolutie van de Hoog Mogende Heeren Staten Generael der Vereenichde Nederlanden. Martis den 21 October 1664.

[The Estates General want to reach a compromise with the Estates of Utrecht about the Maltese goods, because the most powerful princes of Europe are engaged in this matter. Therefore, they write a letter] *Aende Provincie van Uttrecht,* den 21. October 1664 [requesting her to authorize her deputies to visit a meeting with deputies of other provinces]

'— over het subject raeckende de versochte restitutie der goederen ende commanderijen vande Ridderlijcke Ordre van Malta, hier te lande gelegen, ende die saecke tot een goet eijnde te helpen beleijden, op dat die questie niet eijntelijck een quaden uuttslag tott naedeel van desen staet, ende de goede ingesetenen van dien en come te nemen, te meer alsoo haer de machtigste princen van Europa al t'sedert eenigen tijt herwarts daer mede gemoeijt, ende sich daer aen gelegen hebben laeten sijn, —.'

[A copy of this letter is to be found in GLA Karlsruhe, 90/462, immediately following the *Extract* on fol.14; the draft is in ARA 's-Gravenhage, Archief van de Staten Generaal nr.5035, Lias Lopende September-December 1664, Minuten Oktober.]

51. 1667, October – Knuttel nr.9574, & Loeff nr.614, mentioned under N.B.;
printed pamphlet, in quarto, 8 pp.; the appendices A, B, C and D that are referred to in the text, fail.

Memoriael versoeck van den Lant-Graef van Hessen, Wegens de Maltesche Goederen. Gedruckt in 't Jaer ons Heeren, 1667. [at the back:] Was geteyckent R.Kempinck. Hage den ... October, 1667.

[Petition to the Estates General by Reynier Kempinck on behalf of the Landgraf von Hessen, Prior of Germany, about the restitution of the confiscated Maltese goods in the Netherlands.]

52. 1668 [?] – AOM 2198, Alemagna, fol.480r-494r, & Loeff nr.632, with written copy in GLA Karlsruhe, 90/466;
printed pamphlet, in folio, 32 pp.

Describuntur hic breviter quae, quot, & in quo Statu sint Commendae Ordinis Sancti Joannis Hierosolymitani Sitae in Regionibus Dominatui Provinciarum

Confoederatarum subjectis, quae Commendae etsi à Magno Prioratu Alemanniae dependent, eas tamen Confoederatae Provinciae occupant. [without date nor address].

[This pamphlet has not been described in any Dutch catalogue of pamphlets. It deals with all the Dutch preceptories in different stages of their attempts to recover the goods, including the redemption of the preceptory Haarlem for 150,000 florins on 5 December 1667 (cf. Allan II p.385 and GA Haarlem, Stads Archief loketkas 7-12-5-7, letter p-2, and above, A.nr.187, dd. 8 December 1668.]

53. after 1674 – GLA karlsruhe 90/84, fol.3r-16r (18 pp.+ 4 scribbling-papers), & Loeff nr.600, in folio, 13 leaves (25 pp.);
written drafts of an instruction on behalf of the Prince-Cardinal Landgraf von Hessen to be offered to the peace negotiators in Cologne and Nimwegen.

Libellus cum Adiunctis Illustrissimis Excellentissimis ad tractatus Pacis pleno cum potestate Legatis

&

54. 1674 or after – GLA Karlsruhe 90/352, fol.29r-32r, & Loeff nr.600;
written instruction & draft, 6 pp.

Breve compendium ad Reverendissimos, Illustrissimos et Excellentissimos pacis componenda dominos legatos, et plenipotentiarios, in quo consistit summa orationis et petitionis Illustrissimi Equestris Melitensis Ordinis et Serenissimi et Eminentissimi Principis Cardinalis Lantgravii Hassiae, utpote per Germaniam praedicti Ordinis Magni Magistri, baiulivas, commendas, domos, bona --- in Unito Belgio sita et iure proprietatis ac dominii ad eundem inclijtum Ordinem Melitensem spectantia --- usurpata, praeter ius avulsa et detenta, denuo cedenda, restituenda, et tradenda esse.

55. 1712 [?] – GLA Karlsruhe 90/340, fol.2r-11v;
written draft, undated, in folio, 10 leaves.

Memoriale commendarum et bonorum Illustrissimo Ordini equestri S.Joannis Hijerosolimitani in Belgio foederato recuperandum, ex parte -- Raijmundi de Perellos -- Magni Magistri -- exhibitum per Illustrissimum D. Goswinum Her-

mannum Ottonem Baronem de Mervelt fati Equestri Ordinis per Germaniam magnum Baiulivium.

[summing-up of the confiscated Dutch commanderies.]

56. 1712, August 16 – GLA Karlsruhe 90/461, fol.1r-13r;
written draft of a pamphlet, in folio, 13 leaves;

Memoriale, restitutionem commendarum et bonorum inclyto ordini militari Sancti Joannis Baptistae Hierosolymitani in Belgio Foederato violenter ablatorum concernens.

[cf. the reference in the next item to a printed pamphlet in Latin from 1712; this may be the written draft of that pamphlet, composed on behalf of 'M. le Baron de Merweldt, grand Bailli d'Allemagne', and meant for the negotiators of the Peace of Utrecht, who must be stimulated to find a solution for the confiscated Maltese goods. Frater Goswin Herman baron van Merveldt was given the right to regain the Dutch preceptories, because he wanted to make some efforts to that purpose at the peace negotiations at Utrecht; see before, A.nr.201, dd. 16 March 1709, and A.nr.202, his letter of credence dd. 16 March 1712.]

57. 1713, June 27 – *Recueil* 1750, p.37-38, No.36
act of a notary public, included as proof in a later printed pamphlet.

Continuation des poursuites du Bailli, Baron de Merweldt. Il fut au Congrès d'Utrecht, en qualité d'Envoyé extraordinaire, & Ministre Plénipotentiaire de l'Ordre pour négocier la récupération desdits Biens; & après avoir fait ce qui dépendoit de lui, sans espérance d'aucun succès, il en partit, & laissa au Chevalier de Rossi le soin de veiller aux intérêts de l'Ordre: celui-ci n' ayant pas été plus heureux, prit le parti de rendre publique la protestation ci-après, qui lui fut adressée par le vénérable Chapitre de l'Ordre du Grand-Prieuré d'Allemagne.

[Act from 17 May 1713, collated on 27 June 1713 by G.Marthens, Notaire. This act of protestation refers to a Latin pamphlet, composed on order of the Baron van Merveldt, 'imprimé à la Haye en 1712', in which the Maltese Order's goods in the United Provinces are summed up; cf. nrs.55 and 56 above.]

58. 1732 – GLA Karlsruhe, 90/352, fol.9r-12v;
printed pamphlet, in quarto, 8 pp.

Sacra Congregatione S.Officii Melevitana Beneplaciti pro Baiulivo Barone de Schade Oratore Religionis Hierosolymitanae. Memoriale Iuris. Typis Leone, & Mainardi 1732.

[This pamphlet has not been described in any Dutch catalogue of pamphlets. It deals with the arguments of the lawyer Jacobus Lamius Advocatus to consider the papal consent for the redemption of the Order's goods in Nimwegen as being granted implicitly, a consent that until then had been asked for in vain. The main point is that the transaction of 1668 regarding Haarlem, for which no explicit papal consent had been given, had nonetheless been accepted by the papal court and had even become, as appears from a papal letter dd. 23 July 1678, the financial basis for the redemption of the Commenda Vratislaviensis in the priorate of Bohemia; with the text of this papal letter by Innocentius Papa XI.

On 18 May 1700 a treaty with the Nimwegen magistrate was concluded about the restitution of part of the preceptory goods of St John on the condition (posed by the magistrate) that papal consent was given. As this consent was postponed by war circumstances in Italy, the Order's agents repeatedly pressed upon the magistrate to abandon the condition; this was in vain, however. Cf. the remonstrances to this purpose in GLA Karlsruhe, 90/83, fol.1-51, 1703-1736, and [J.in de Betouw], *Kerken en godsdienstige gestichten te Nymegen* [Nijmegen, c.1787], pp.25-26. See also above, A.nr.199, c.1700, A.nr.204, dd. 26 May 1746, and C.8., c.1704 or after 1746.]

59. 1750 – RA Gelderland at Arnhem, Huisarchief Rossum / familiearchief van Randwijk, inv.nr.229;
printed pamphlet, in folio, 40 pp.

Recueil de pieces justificatives du droit de l'Ordre de Malte, pour la recuperation de ses biens situés dans les Provinces Unies des Pays-Bas. [at the back:] De l'Imprimerie de la Veuve d'Houry, Imprimeur de l'Ordre, 1750.

[This pamphlet has not been described in any Dutch catalogue of pamphlets. It contains 37 (French translations of) proofs concerning the Order's rights to its goods in the United Provinces of the Netherlands, followed by a short 'Spécification des Commanderies de l'Ordre de S.Jean de Jérusalem dit de Malte, situées dans les Provinces Unies des Pays Bas.' The pieces date from 1576 to 1749 and contain treaties, letters, juridical sentences and reprints of earlier pamphlets.]

60. 1788 – GLA Karlsruhe 90/339, fol.6r-12v;
written pamphlet, in folio, 7 leaves.

Pro Memoria

[Memorandum about the claims of the Maltese Order pertaining to its goods in the United Provinces, with a list of these goods. This Memorandum has been added to a letter dd. 17 June 1788 to the Prior of Germany at Heitersheim, in which the difficulties of the recovery are explained.]

61. [1788] – GLA Karlsruhe 90/337, fol.24r-31;
written pamphlet with French translation of the previous item, in folio, 8 leaves.

Memoire sur la Recuperation des biens de l'ordre de Malthe situés dans les Païs Bas.

GENERAL BIBLIOGRAPHY

F.Allan, *Geschiedenis en beschrijving van Haarlem, van de vroegste tijden tot op onze dagen*. 4 vols, Haarlem 1874-1888; especially vol.II, Haarlem (J.J.van Brederode) 1877, pp.249-386: C.J.Gonnet, 'De commanderij van St.Jan'

D.F.Allen, 'Anti-Jesuit rioting by knights of St John during the Malta carnival of 1639', in: *Archivum Historicum Societatis Jesu*, 65 (1996) pp.3-30

Udo Arnold, 'Entstehung und Frühzeit des Deutschen Ordens', in: Josef Fleckenstein & Manfred Hellmann (eds), *Die geistlichen Ritterorden Europas*. Sigmaringen (Thorbecke Verlag) 1980; (Vorträge und Forschungen, Bd.26), pp.81-108

U.Arnold & G.Bott (eds), *800 Jahre Deutscher Orden*. Ausstellungskatalog des Germanischen Nationalmuseums Nürnberg in Zusammenarbeit mit der Internationalen Kommission zur Erforschung des Deutschen Ordens. Gütersloh-München (Bertelsmann Lexicon Verlag) 1990

U.Arnold (ed.) *Kreuz und Schwert. Der Deutsche Orden in Südwestdeutschland, in der Schweiz und im Elsaß*. Ausstellungskatalog in Zusammenarbeit mit der Internationalen Kommission zur Erforschung des Deutschen Ordens, Mainau (Blumeninsel Mainau GmbH) 1991

U.Arnold e.a. (eds), *Ritter und Priester. Acht Jahrhunderte Deutscher Orden in Nordwesteuropa / Ridders en Priesters. Acht eeuwen Duitse Orde in Noordwest-Europa*. Ausstellungskatalog / Tentoonstelling van de Landcommanderij Alden Biesen 1992; [Turnhout] (Brepols) 1992

Malcolm Barber (ed.), *The Military Orders. Fighting for the faith and caring for the sick*. The papers from the International Conference on Military Orders held at Clerkenwell, September 1992, Aldershot (Variorum, Ashgate Publishing Ltd.) 1994

E.A.van Beresteyn, *Geschiedenis der Johanniter-Orde in Nederland tot 1795*. Assen 1934 (Van Gorcum's Historische Bibliotheek, deel 8)

D.Ursmer Berlière O.S.B. (ed.), 'Inventaire des Instrumenta miscellanea des Archives Vaticanes au point de vue de nos anciens diocèses', in: *Bulletin de l'Institut Historique Belge de Rome*, 4me fascicule, Rome-Bruxelles-Paris 1924, nr.76, p.85-103, Enquête sur les biens de l'Hôpital de S.Jean de Jérusalem dans le diocèse de Liége faite à la demande de l'évêque Jean d'Arkel, sur ordre de Grégoire XI

S.Bernardi abbatis Clarae-Vallensis, De laude novae militiae, ad milites Templi liber, in: J.P.Migne (ed.), *Patrologia Latina* tomus 182, Parisiis (Garnier) 1854, column 921-939

[J.in de Betouw], *Kerken en godsdienstige gestichten te Nymegen*. [Nijmegen, c.1787]

Hartmut Boockmann, *Der Deutsche Orden. Zwölf Kapitel aus seiner Geschichte*. München (Beck Verlag) 1981

G.Brom & A.H.L.Hensen (eds), *Romeinsche bronnen voor den kerkelijk-staatkundigen toestand der Nederlanden in de 16de eeuw*. 's-Gravenhage (Martinus Nijhoff) 1922 (Rijks Geschiedkundige Publicatiën 52)

P.Q. Brondgeest, *Bijdragen tot de geschiedenis van het gasthuis, het klooster en de balije van St.Catharina der Johanniter-ridders en van het Driekoningengasthuis te Utrecht*. Hilversum (Nonhebel & Co.) 1901

Truus van Bueren, *Macht en onderhorigheid binnen de Ridderlijke Orde van Sint Jan. De commandeursportretten uit het Sint Jansklooster te Haarlem*. Haarlem (Schuyt & Co) 1991

Donald Campbell, *Arabian Medicine and its influence on the Middle Ages. Origin and development of Arab medical science and its subsequent cultivation among the Arabistae of the Latin West*. 2 vols, London (Kegan Paul) 1926; reprint in 1 vol., Amsterdam (Philo Press) 1974

Corpus sigillorum Neerlandicorum, [H.Brugmans & K.Heeringa (eds)]. 3 vols, 's-Gravenhage (Martinus Nijhoff) 1937-1940

C.Dekker, *Het Kromme Rijngebied in de Middeleeuwen. Een institutioneel-geografische studie*. [Zutphen] (De Walburg Pers) 1983 (Stichtse Historische Reeks, 9)

Joseph Delaville le Roulx, *Cartulaire général de l'Ordre des Hospitaliers de St. Jean de Jerusalem*. 4 volumes, Paris (Ernest Leroux) 1894-1906

Joseph Delaville le Roulx, *Les Hospitaliers à Rhodes, 1310-1425*. Paris (Ernest Leroux) 1913, London (Variorum Reprints) 1974

A.Th.van Deursen (ed.), *Resolutiën der Staten Generaal, nieuwe reeks 1610-1670*, I, 1610-1612, 's-Gravenhage (Martinus Nijhoff) 1971 (Rijks Geschiedkundige Publicatiën, large series 135)

Leopold Devillers, *Inventaire analytique des archives des commanderies belges de l'Ordre de Saint-Jean de Jérusalem ou de Malte*. Mons (Manceaux) 1876

M.Dierickx, *De oprichting der nieuwe bisdommen in de Nederlanden onder Filips II 1559-1570*. Antwerpen-Utrecht (Standaard-Boekhandel / Het Spectrum) 1950

F.Rofail Farag, 'Why Europe responded to the Muslims' medical achievements in the Middle Ages' in: *Arabica, Revue d'Etudes Arabes*, 25 (1978) pp.292-309

Jean Flori, *L'Essor de la chevalerie, XIe-XIIe siècles*. Genève (Librairie Droz), 1986

Jean Flori, *La première croisade. L'Occident chrétien contre l'Islam*. Bruxelles (Editions Complexe), 1992

Jean Flori, *La chevalerie en France au Moyen Age*. Paris (Presses Universitaires de France) 1995 (Que sais-je?)

C.H.C.Flugi van Aspermont, *De Johanniter-Orde in het Heilige Land (1100-1292)*. Assen 1957 (Van Gorcum's Historische Bibliotheek, deel 54)

C.J.Gonnet, 'De commanderij van St.Jan', see: F.Allan

Otto von Heinemann, *Die Handschriften der herzoglichen Bibliothek zu Wolfenbüttel*, 2.Abteilung, Die Augusteischen Handschriften, II, Wolfenbüttel (Julius Zwissler) 1895

S. Hiddema and C. Tromp, *Inventaris van archieven van kloosters in de provincie Groningen*. Publikaties van het Rijksarchief in Groningen nr.7, Groningen 1989

Rudolf Hiestand, 'Die Anfänge der Johanniter', in: Josef Fleckenstein & Manfred Hellmann (eds), *Die geistlichen Ritterorden Europas*. Sigmaringen (Thorbecke Verlag) 1980 (Vorträge und Forschungen, Bd.26), pp.31-80

P.J.C.G. van Hinsbergen, *Inventaris van het archief van de Ridderlijke Duitsche Orde Balije van Utrecht 1200-1811*. Utrecht (Oud Archief Ridderlijke Duitsche Orde Balije van Utrecht) 1955-1982

F.A.Hoefer en J.S.van Veen, 'De commanderieën der orde van St.Jan in Gelderland', in: *Bijdragen en Mededeelingen van Gelre*, 13 (1910) pp.277-332

T.J. Hoekstra, 'Vredenburg, Archeologische Kroniek van de gemeente Utrecht over 1967-1977', *Maandblad Oud-Utrecht*, 53 (1980), 24-31

T.J. Hoekstra, 'Utrecht, Vredenburg', *Bulletin Koninklijke Nederlandse Oudheidkundige Bond (KNOB)* (1977), pp.39-45

M.W.Huiskamp, P.J.Boon, R.L.M.M.Camps, *Catalogus van de pamfletten aanwezig in de Bibliotheek Arnhem 1537-1795*. Hilversum (Verloren) 1995

Michael Klein, *Die Handschriften 65/1 – 1200 im Generallandesarchiv Karlsruhe*. Wiesbaden (Otto Harrassowitz) 1987 (Die Handschriften der Staatsarchive in Baden-Württemberg, Band 2)

W.P.C.Knuttel, *Catalogus van de pamfletten-verzameling berustende in de Koninklijke Bibliotheek*, I/2, 1621-1648, and II/1, 1649-1667, 's Gravenhage (Algemeene Landsdrukkerij) 1889-1892

M. Krebs, *Gesamtübersicht der Bestände des Generallandesarchivs Karlsruhe*, Veröffentlichungen der Staatlichen Archivverwaltung Baden-Württemberg, Hefte 1-2, Stuttgart (Kohlhammer) 1954-1957

Anne-Marie Legras & Robert Favreau (eds), *L'Enquête Pontificale de 1373 sur l'Ordre des Hospitaliers de Saint-Jean de Jérusalem*, publiée sous la direction de Jean Glénisson, volume I, *L'Enquête dans la Prieuré de France*. Paris (Editions du Centre National de la Recherche Scientifique) 1987

J. Loeff, *Het archief der Commanderij van St Jan te Arnhem*, Rijksarchief in Gelderland, 's-Gravenhage (Ministerie van Onderwijs, Kunsten en Wetenschappen) 1950

Anthony Luttrell, *The Hospitallers in Cyprus, Rhodes, Greece and the West (1291-1440)*. London (Variorum Reprints) 1978 (Collected Studies 77)

Anthony Luttrell, *Latin Greece, The Hospitallers and the Crusades, 1291-1440*. London (Variorum Reprints) 1982 (Collected Studies 158)

Anthony Luttrell, *The Hospitallers of Rhodes and their Mediterranean World*. Aldershot, Hampshire (Variorum Reprints) 1992 (Collected Studies 360)

A. Maisch, U. Nieß, C. Rehm, U. Schäfer (eds), *Bestand 90, Akten Heitersheim. Reichs- und Kreissachen*. Karlsruhe (Generallandesarchiv) 1991

E. Mannier, *Ordre de Malte. Les commanderies du Grand-Prieuré de France d'après les documents inédits conservés aux Archives Nationales à Paris*. Paris, 1872

A.Johanna Maris, *De reformatie der geestelijke en kerkelijke goederen in Gelderland, in het bijzonder in het Kwartier van Nijmegen*. 's-Gravenhage (N.V. Drukkerij "De Residentie") 1939

Antonius Matthaeus, *Veteris aevi analecta*. editio secunda, Hagae-Comitum (apud Gerardum Block) 1738

Max Meyerhof, *Studies in medieval Arabic Medicine: Theory and Practice*, ed. by Penelope Johnstone, London (Variorum Reprints) 1984 (Collected Studies 204)

J.A.Mol, 'De Johannieter Commanderij van Wemeldinge', in: *Historia. Jaarboek van Zuid- en Noord-Beveland* 10 (1984), pp.35-56

S.Muller & A.C.Bouman (eds), *Oorkondenboek van het Sticht Utrecht tot 1301*, I, Utrecht (Oosthoek), 1920; K. Heeringa (ed.), *item*, II, 's-Gravenhage (Rijksuitgeverij), 1940

Louis D. Petit, *Bibliotheek van Nederlandsche Pamfletten*, I, 1500-1648, 's-Gravenhage (Martinus Nijhoff) 1882

Jonathan Riley-Smith, *The Knights of St John in Jerusalem and Cyprus, 1050-1310*. London (Macmillan) 1967

Walter Gerd Rödel, *Das Großpriorat Deutschland des Johanniter-Ordens im Übergang vom Mittelalter zur Reformation, an Hand der Generalvisitations-berichte von 1494/95 und 1540/41.* Inaugural-Dissertation der Philosophischen Fakultät zu Mainz 1966, Köln (Wienand Verlag) 1966; 2.neubearbeitete und erweiterte Auflage, Köln (Wienand Verlag) 1972

Franz Rosenthal, *Science and Medicine in Islam. A collection of essays.* Aldershot, Hampshire (Variorum Reprints) 1991 (Collected Studies 330)

H.D.J.van Schevichaven, *Repertorium Noviomagense. Proeve van een register van boekwerken en geschriften betrekking hebbende op de stad en het Rijk van Nijmegen.* Nijmegen (F.E.Macdonald) 1906

Heinrich Schipperges, *Die Assimilation der arabischen Medizin durch das lateinische Mittelalter.* Wiesbaden (Steiner Verlag) 1964 (Sudhoffs Archiv, Beiheft 3)

Andrée Scufflaire, 'Les archives de l'Ordre de Saint-Jean de Jérusalem à la Royal Malta Library, La Valette. Rapport de mission', in: *Bulletin de la Commission Royale d'Histoire*, 129 (1963), pp.lxix-lxxiv and pp.cccxxxii-ccclxxii

Andrée Scufflaire, 'De Hospitaalbroeders op Malta belicht vanuit hun archief', in: Marleen Forrier (ed.), *De Orde van Malta in de Zuidelijke Nederlanden (12de-18de eeuw).* Brussel 1993 (Algemeen Rijksarchief en Rijksarchief in de Provinciën, Educatieve Dienst, Dossiers 2e reeks 7); (Dossier with the exhibition of the same name in the General State Archive in Brussels), pp.41-48

H.J.A.Sire, *The Knights of Malta.* New Haven and London (Yale University Press) 1994.

L.A.J.W.Sloet (ed.), *Oorkondenboek der graafschappen Gelre en Zutfen.* 's Gravenhage (Martinus Nijhoff) 1872-1876

Suir, *Balije*: G.C.M. van Dijck, *Inventaris van het archief van de Balije van Utrecht der Johanniterorde 1251-1851*, second, completely revised edition by E.T. Suir, Rijksarchief Utrecht, Inventaris I, Utrecht 1985

Marjan Tumler, *Der Deutsche Orden in Werden, Wachsen und Wirken bis 1400.* Wien (Panorama) 1955

Manfred Ullmann, *Die Medizin im Islam*. Handbuch der Orientalistik, I.Abteilung, Ergänzungsband VI, 1.Abschnitt, Leiden (Brill) 1970

M.Ullmann, *Islamic Medicine*. Edinburgh (Edinburgh University Press) 1978

L'Abbé De Vertot, *Histoire des Chevaliers Hospitaliers de S.Jean de Jerusalem, appellez depuis les Chevaliers de Rhodes, et aujourd'hui les Chevaliers de Malte.* 4 vols., Paris (chez Rollin, et Quillau, et Desaint) 1726

Mario de Visser, *La Commenda di S.Giovanni in Haarlem e le chiese dipendenti. Notizie e Documenti.* Amsterdam (without publisher) 1938

Mario de Visser, *I sigilli del Sovrano Militare Ordine di Malta.* Milano (Mario Sejmand) 1942

Berthold Waldstein-Wartenberg, 'Beiträge zur mittelalterlichen Liturgie des Johanniterordens, II, Das Totengedächtnis', in: *Annales de l'Ordre souverain militaire de Malte*, 30 (1972), pp.84-91

A. Wauters, 'Exploration des chartes et des cartulaires belges existants à la Bibliothèque Nationale à Paris', in: *Compte rendu des séances de la Commission Royale d'Histoire, ou Recueil de ses Bulletins*, 4e série tome II, Bruxelles (F.Hayez, Imprimeur de la CRH) 1875, pp.78-198, especially pp.155-177

E. Wiersum and A. Le Cosquino de Bussy (eds), 'Visitatie-verslagen van de Johanniter-kloosters in Nederland (1495, 1540, 1594)', in: *Bijdragen en Mededeelingen van het Historisch Genootschap*, 48 (1927) pp.146-340

Johanna Maria van Winter, *Ridderschap, ideaal en werkelijkheid*. Bussum (Van Dishoeck) 1965 (Fibulareeks 11); 4th edition, Haarlem (Fibula-Van Dishoeck) 1982; German translation: *Rittertum, Ideal und Wirklichkeit*, München (Beck Verlag) 1969; 2nd edition, München (Deutscher Taschenbuch Verlag) 1979

Johanna Maria van Winter, "Uxorem de militari ordine, sibi imparem", in: *Miscellanea Mediaevalia in memoriam Jan Frederik Niermeyer*, Groningen (Wolters) 1967, pp.113-124 (in French)

Johanna Maria van Winter, "Cingulum Militiae', Schwertleite en 'miles'-terminologie als spiegel van veranderend menselijk gedrag' (avec résumé français), in: *Tijdschrift voor Rechtsgeschiedenis / Revue d'Histoire du Droit* 44 (1976), pp.1-92

Johanna Maria van Winter, 'Knighthood and nobility in the Netherlands', in: Michel Jones (ed.) *Gentry and lesser nobility in late medieval Europe*. Gloucester-New York (Alan Sutton / St.Martin's Press) 1986, pp.81-94

Johanna Maria van Winter, 'De heren van Sint-Catharijne te Utrecht', in: *Bewogen en bewegen. Liber amicorum aangeboden aan Prof. dr. H.F.J.M. van den Eerenbeemt*, Tilburg (Gianotten) 1986, pp.349-364, and in French translation: Johanna Maria van Winter, 'Les seigneurs de Sainte-Catherine à Utrecht, les premiers Hospitaliers au Nord des Alpes', in: Michel Balard (ed.), *Autour de la Première Croisade*. Actes du Colloque de la Society for the Study of the Crusades and the Latin East (Clermont-Ferrand, 22-25 juin 1995), Paris 1996 (Série Byzantina Sorbonensia, 14), pp.239-246.

INDICES

CONTENTS TO THE INDICES

INTRODUCTION TO THE INDICES

The six indices that follow hereafter, of Persons, Places, Coins, Weights and Measures, Patron Saints, and Concepts, have for the largest part been derived from a data-base that was made with Dbase IV under MS-DOS. Because this data-base was started long before the printer's proofs of this book were available, the references to Parts A and C are not to the pages but to the numbers of Bulls and Letters (Part A) or the numbers and folia of the Visitation Acts (Part C). So now you will find the references to the Introduction as pages of this book; to Part A as numbers of A; to Part B, the Rent-roll of St Catherine's, as pages; to Part C as numbers and folia of the Visitation Acts and Inquiries; and to Part D, the List of Pamphlets, to the pages of this book. Hopefully, because the relevant data are given on top of the pages, you will find your way easily. Data that are only to be found in the notes, are marked with *.

J.M.v.W.

INDEX OF PERSONS

Chancellor & Councillers at Heitersheim; Canzler & Räthen; 1652/12/20, A.167

Chancellor & Councillors of Priorate/Germany; 1664/01/28, A.174

Chaplain [Mechelen]; 1495, C.2, f.177

Chaplain, 1 [Wytwerd]; 1495, C.2, f.234

Chaplain, assistant [Oudewater]; 1540, C.3, f.166

Chaplains, 4 [Abbingwehr]; 1495, C.2, f.234

Chaplains, 4 [Arnhem]; 1495, C.2, f.193

Chaplains, 9 [Burgsteinfurt]; 1495, C.2, f.236, 238, 239

Chaplains [Haarlem]; 1469/10/05, C.2, f.221

Chaplains, 4 [Haarlem]; 1495, C.2, f.223

Chaplains, 3 incl.commander [Ingen]; 1495, C.2, f.205

Chaplains, 2 [Ingen]; 1594, C.4, f.26

Chaplains, 4 [Jemgum]; 1495, C.2, f.234

Chaplains, 2 [Muhde, Frisia]; 1495, C.2, f.234

Chaplains, 4 [Nimwegen]; 1495, C.2, f.197

Chaplains [Nimwegen]; capellani de obedientia; 1704 or 1746? C.8

Chaplains, 2 incl.commander [Oudewater]; 1495, C.2, f.210

Chaplains, 5 excl.commander [Sint Jansdal]; 1495, C.2, f.209

Chaplains, 6, excl. commander [Sneek]; 1495, C.2, f.219

Chaplains, 7 [Utrecht]; 1495, C.2, f.202, 204

Chaplains, 2 [Warffum]; 1495, C.2, f.234

Chaplains, 2 incl. commander before 1492 [Buren]; 1495, C.2, f.206

Chaplains, 2 secular [Haarlem]; 1495, C.2, f.220, 223

Charles V (1519-1556); German emperor, king of Spain; Intro p.17

Charles V; Emperor; 1594, C.4, f.22

Chigi, [Fabio] (later: Pope Alexander VII*); apostolic nuncio; 1648/08/31, A.161

Cicero, [Marcus Tullius]; Roman writer; 1588/12/01, A.133

Cistercians; order under Benedictine Rule; Intro p.6

Cistercians; Cistercian abbey Camp; 1704 or 1746? C.8

Citizens of Haarlem; get letter from Grand Master; 1603/12/28, A.139

Citizens of Utrecht; get letter from Grand Master; 1603/12/28, A.136

Claes zoen, Peter; landowner at Haastrecht; 1367+, B.p.387

Claessen, Jan; tenant of Nimwegen; 1700, C.6, f.52

Clairvaux, Bernard of; head of Cistercian Order, protector of Knights Templar; Intro p.6, 8

Clarenborgh, Johan van; landowner in Utrecht; 1367+, B.p.209

Classis of Nimwegen; church government; 1641, D.p.664

Cleyne, Johan; landowner at Loosdrecht; 1367+, B.p.283

Cleyninx, Arnold son of; former tenant at Oudewater; 1367+, B.p.332

Cliis, Johan; landowner at Loosdrecht; 1367+, B.p.283

Clivis/Cliwis, Johannes; chaplain, commander of Middelburg; 1495, C.2, f.215

Clotinx, Hendrik, see Rijn, Johan van

Cloyer, Jacob; landowner in Utrecht; 1367+, B.p.206

Cluze, Ghisekin van der; landowner at Loenen; 1367+, B.p.282

Coeldou, —; tenant in Utrecht; 1367+, B.p.205

Coelgroven, Willelmus von; resident in Mechelen; 1373, C.1

Coesfeld, Jodocus van (de Coistveldia); commander/capellanus at Kerkwerve; 1540, C.3, f.171

Colen, Wouter van; landowner near Utrecht; 1367+, B.p.214

Colentyer van Jutfaes, Hubert son of Ghisbert; vasal of Zuylen at Maarssen; 1367+, B.p.274

Coliin, Gerard; tenant at Vleuten; 1367+, B.p.267-269

Colonia, Ada daughter of Henricus de; inhabitant of Haarlem[?]; 1495, C.2, f.223; cf. Keulen, van

Colonia, Constantinus de; resident at Mechelen; 1373, C.1

Columpna, Lambertus dictus de; notary public of Liege curia; 1373, C.1

Coman, Gerard; landowner in Utrecht; 1367+, B.p.206

Goldstein, Bernard von (à Golstein); [Bernard]; late commander of Nimwegen; 1704 or 1746? C.8

Goltstein, Bernard von; last commander of Arnhem/Nimwegen; 1639, D.p.664

Golen, heirs of Jacob; landowners at Montfoort; 1367+, B.p.349

Göms [?], Guilelmus; has a debenture from J.Krab; 1572/05/09, A.119

Goossens, Ruth widow of Bartolomeus; tenant of Nimwegen; 1700, C.6, f.51

Gotfridi, Ernst; inhabitant of Oudenrijn; 1495, C.2, f.203

Gouda (Gaude), frater Johan van; administrator/ vicecommander/ commander of St Catherine's, Utrecht; 1367+, B.p.200, 220, 222, 251, 252, 259, 265, 266, 268, 276, 289, 296, 306, 312, 319, 325, 332, 340, 341, 350, 353, 355, 356, 358, 359, 365, 367, 368, 370, 372, 373, 375, 379, 383

Gouda (Gaude), Johannes; commendator of St Catherine's, Utrecht; 1378/ 10/01, C.2, f.217

Gouda (Gauda) Johannes van; cappellanus of St Catherine's; 1495, C.2, f.198

Gouda, —; tenant in Utrecht; 1367+, B.p.203

Gouda, Dirk van; vasal of Holland at Oudewater; 1367+, B.p.337

Gouda, Johan son of, tenant near Utrecht; 1367+, B.p.224;

Government of Low Austria; Statthalter, Regenten & Räthe; 1652, A.165, 167

Goyer, Dirc die, & son Jacob; tenants at Benschop; 1367+, B.p.356

Goyers, Aleydis des; tenant at Goudriaan; 1367+, B.p.382

Graesz, Gotfridus; convents knight at Burgsteinfurt; 1495, C.2, f.233, 236

Grand Bailiff; magnus baiulivus Alamanie; 1501, 1510, 1572, A.88, 89, 95, 119

Grand Bailiff, lieutenant of; 1543, 1613, A.105, 143

Grand Commander, lieutenant of; locumtenens magni preceptoris; 1510/06/22, A.95

Grand Master; head of the Order, resides at headquarters; Intro p.17, 18, 21, 23, 25, 26

Grand Master; head of the Order; 1700/[05/18], A.199

Grand Master; magister parcium ultramarinatarum; 1378/10/01, C.2, f.217

Grand Master; magister Rhodi; 1494, 1495, C.2, f.192, 197, 220

Grand Master; dominus magister; 1540, C.3, f.35

Grand Master; head of the Order; 1594, C.4, f.18, 32*

Grand Master*; head of the Order; 1719/12/07, C.7, f.1*

Grand Master; head of the Order; 1561, 1582, 1642, 1646, 1651, 1663, D.p.661, 662, 665, 666, 668, 672, 679

Grauwert (Grawert), Ghisbert; landowner near Utrecht; 1367+, B.p.222, 225

Graveland, dominus Johan van, knight; former tenant at Molenaarsgraaf; 1367+, B.p.378

Grawen Heynen zoon, Lambert; tenant at Meerkerk; 1367+, B.p.380

Grieten zoen, Peter; tenant at Groot Ammers; 1367+, B.p.376

Groenewoud*, Arnoldus; treasurer of Utrecht, chaplain; Intro p.10*

Groenewoud, Arnold van (Groenhem, de); commander of Arnhem; 1421/ 07/04, A.24

Groenewoude, Johan van; landowner near Utrecht; 1367+, B.p.252

Groner, Otto, vicecommander of St Catherine's, Utrecht; 1367+, B.p.233;

Grote (Magnus), Reyner & wife Aleydis Dogheden; tenants at Harmelen; 1367+, B.p.306

Grotenhuys [?], Willem son of Hase [van der]; landowner at Vleuten; 1367+, B.p.269

Grotenhuys, Ghisbert van den; late tenant at Maarssen; 1367+, B.p.275

Grotenhuys, Hasa van der, widow of Spiker Benscop; landowner at Maarssen; 1367+, B.p.273, 275

Grunbach, Johannes von; commendator in Würzburg; 1323^1324/01/11, A.2

Gruningen, Wolterus van; priest, administrator of Wijtwerd; 1540, C.3, f.148

Gruter, Frederik; former tenant at Oudewater; 1367+, B.p.339

Gruter, Hendrik & Johan; tenants at Oudewater; 1367+, B.p.339

Gruuthusen, van*; Steven; commander of Arnhem, chaplain; Intro p.10*

Hasen, Agnes daughter of Ghisbert; landowner at Lopik; 1367+, B.p.373

Hatstein*, Johann von; commander of Arnhem, knight; Intro p.10*

Hatstein, Johann von (Atsteyn); commander of Arnhem/Nimwegen; 1496/10/10, A.83

Hatstein*, Johann von; commander of Heimbach; 1503/11/24, A.83*

Hatstein, Johann von (Haisten); magnus baiulivus conventualis, becomes prior Alemanie; 1512/07/03, A.97

Hatstein, Johann von (de Hatsteyn); prior Alemanie, Maister in Teutsch Landen; 1534, 1542, 1546, A.102, 103, 107, 109

Hatstein, Johann von (Hastent); late prior Alamanie; 1547/02/28, A.112

Hatstein, Johann von; knight, commander of Heimbach & Arnhem/ Nimwegen; 1494, 1495, C.2, f.191-193, 196, 197

Hatstein, Johann von; Prior of Germany; 1539, 1540, C.3, f.1, 7

Hattem, Thonius van; tenant of Arnhem; 1594, C.4, f.17

Hawe, Jacob; tenant in Utrecht; 1367+, B.p.202, 203

Haze/ Haeze/ Hase, frater Johan; administrator of St Catherine's, Utrecht; 1367+, B.p.218, 244, 260, 285, 295, 299, 312, 314, 315, 322, 338, 351, 383

Hechtenberg, Betz von; locumtenens magni baiullivi; 1462/07/06, A.67

Heemstede, lord of; gets census from Haarlem; 1540, C.3, f.33

Heggenzer, Joannes; magnus baiulius conventualis; 1506/02/10, A.94

Heggezer, Johannes; prior Alemanie; 1512/07/03, A.97

Heijden, van der, Drost; tenant of Nimwegen; 1700, C.6, f.52

Heijsen, Henrick; alderman, tenant of Nimwegen; 1700, C.6, f.52

Heinen, Daem; tenant of Nimwegen; 1700, C.6, f.51

Helenburgis, Hendrik; tenant at Harmelen; 1367+, B.p.301

Hellinc, Nicolaus; tenant at Loenen; 1367+, B.p.282

Hellinx, Elisabeth daughter of Peter, wife of Johan Everardi; tenant near Utrecht; 1367+, B.p.219

Helwick, Zander van; ballivus domus Traiecti; 1422/05/31, A.28

Henrici, Albertus; commander of Waarder; 1495, C.2, f.203

Henrici, Garitis; ? [Arnhem]; 1495, C.2, f.195

Henrici, Helias; inhabitant of Utrecht; 1495, C.2, f.204

Henrici, Jacobus; tenant of Sint Jansdal; 1495, C.2, f.208

Henrici, Johannes; inhabitant of Wemeldinge; 1495, C.2, f.213

Henrici, Mathias; inhabitant of Reierskop; 1495, C.2, f.203

Henrici, Pancracius; inhabitant of Breda; 1495, C.2, f.216

Henrici, Petrus; inhabitant of Wemeldinge; 1495, C.2, f.213

Henrici, Johan; tenant at Ameide; 1367+, B.p.379

Henrixzoen, Claes; tenant at Benschop; 1367+, B.p.363, 364

Henry V; German king/emperor (1106-1125); Intro p.14

Herberti, Johannes; chaplain, locumtenens of Utrecht at Buren; 1495, C.2, f.206

Herbord, Herman; landowner at Breukelen; 1367+, B.p.278

Herbord, Loef; landowner in Utrecht; 1367+, B.p.210

Heredia, Juan Fernandez d'; Grand Master (1377-1396); A.4, 6, 7

Hergrae, Johannes; commander of Oosterwierum; 1495, C.2, f.234

Heringen, Echardus/ Erhardus von; proxy of lingua Alamanie; 1466, A.70, 71

Hermanni, Dirk; tenant at Horstweerde; 1367+, B.p.286

Hermanni, Gerard; landowner at Goudriaan; 1367+, B.p.382

Hermanni, Gerard & wife Wendelmodis; tenants at Maarssen; 1367+, B.p.273

Hermanni, Jacob; tenant at Maarssen; 1367+, B.p.275

Hermanni, Johan; tenant near Utrecht; 1367+, B.p.228, 295

Hermanni, Johan son of Johan; tenant at Maarssen; 1367+, B.p.274

Hermessen, Reynhart; inhabitant of Bennekom [?]; 1495, C.2, f.193

Herte, heirs of Jacob van den; landowners in Utrecht; 1367+, B.p.213

N.N.servant of organ player [Haarlem]; 1540, C.3, f.33

N.N.servant, boy [Nimwegen]; nephew of administrator; 1594, C.4, f.9

N.N.servants [Utrecht]; Hauss- und Hoffgesinde; 1594, C.4, f.24, 25

N.N.servants [bailiff Westfalia]; 1540, C.3, f.151

N.N.servants [Haarlem]; 1540, C.3, f.33

N.N.servants [Ingen]; 2 maids + 1 boy; 1594, C.4, f.26

N.N.servants [Mechelen]; 2 servitores; 1540, C.3, f.127

N.N.servants [Montfoort]; kitchenmaid, boy; 1594, C.4, f.29

N.N.servants [Nimwegen]; domesticques; 1700/[05/18], A.199

N.N.servants [Utrecht]; 14 famuli ministrantes; 1540, C.3, f.11

N.N.servants [Vleuten, Hof ter Weide]; 11 servientes; 1540, C.3, f.11

N.N.servants and guests [Sint Jansdal]; servitores et hospites; 1540, C.3, f.165

N.N.servants and maids [Buren]; servitores et ancille; 1540, C.3, f.163

N.N.servants and maids [Ingen]; servitores et ancille; 1540, C.3, f.164

N.N.servants and maids [Kerkwerve; servitores et ancille; 1540, C.3, f.171

N.N.servants and maids [Oosterwierum]; servitores et ancille; 1540, C.3, f.151

N.N.servants and maids [Sneek]; servitores et ancille; 1540, C.3, f.172

N.N.servants and maids [Warffum]; servitores et ancille; 1540, C.3, f.148

N.N.servants and maids [Wemeldinge]; servitores et ancille; 1540, C.3, f.169

N.N.servants and maids [Wijtwerd]; c.40 servitores et ancille; 1540, C.3, f.149

N.N.servants, old [Utrecht]; oude dienaren; 1603, C.5, f.9

N.N.shepherd [Mechelen]; pastor ovium; 1540, C.3, f.127

N.N.sheriff [Mechelen]; scultetus; 1540, C.3, f.128

N.N.sick people in the Holy Land and elsewhere; Intro p.17

N.N.sick people laying in Jerusalem Hospital; Intro p.4

N.N.sick people, not mentioned in Templar Rule; Intro p.6

N.N.sick people in Jerusalem, living outside the Hospital; Intro p.5

N.N.sick poor people [Utrecht]; arme Kranckhen); 1594, C.4, f.22

N.N.slater [Arnhem]; leijendecker; 1732, C.9, f.9

N.N.smith [Mechelen]; faber ferrarius; 1540, C.3, f.127

N.N.soldiers [Haarlem]; Kriegsknecht, Kriegsleüth; 1594, C.4, f.37

N.N.steward of town Nimwegen; rentmeester; 1700/[05/18], A.199

N.N.subordinates [Mechelen]; subditi domus; 1540, C.3, f.126

N.N.supervisor at Brummen [Arnhem]; 1732, C.9, f.9

N.N.surgeons [Jerusalem]; 4 surgeons in Jerusalem Hospital; Intro p.5

N.N.surgeon [Utrecht]; syroicus; 1495, C.2, f.202

N.N.surgeons [Utrecht]; medici cirurgici; 1540, C.3, f.10

N.N.surgeon [Utrecht]; Wundtartz; 1594, C.4, f.22

N.N.treasurer of St Mary's, Utrecht; 1540, C.3, f.163

Nagelsoen/ Negelszoen, Peter Jan; former tenant at Bodegraven (1447); 1367+, B.p.329, 330

Naillac, Philibert de; Grand Master (1396-1421); 1400, 1408, 1410, 1414, 1415, 1419, 1420, A.8, 9, 10, 15, 16, 17, 18, 19, 21, 22

Nanne Willems zoen, Dirk; landowner at Rotterdam; 1367+, B.p.386

Nannonis, Brunard; former tenant at Lopik; 1367+, B.p.375

Nassau, Maurits* van; stadtholder; 1603/12/28, A.136*

Ness, Jacob van de; tenant at Ameide; 1367+, B.p.379

Nesse, Ghisbert van den; tenant at Lopik; 1367+, B.p.372, 373

Nesse, Machteldis daughter of Heyno van; landowner at Lopik; 1367+, B.p.372

Nesse, Yo van; former tenant at Lopik; 1367+, B.p.372

Neuhoef, Wilhelmus; novice of St Catherine's, Utrecht; 1603, C.5, f.8, 11

Nicolai, Here; inhabitant of Tirns; 1495, C.2, f.218

Nicolai, Johan; landowner at Oudewater; 1367+, B.p.339

Nicolai, Martin; landowner at Kamerik; 1367+, B.p.313

Nicolai, Nicolaus; tenant at Kamerik; 1367+, B.p.314

Nicolas, Jean; seaman from Edam; 1629/02/03, A.153

Nijenvelt, dominus Stephan van; landowner at Harmelen; 1367+, B.p.289

Noddert, Willem; tenant near Utrecht; 1367+, B.p.251, 252

Nolden a Crevelt, Theodoricus; publicus apostolica auctoritate notarius; 1540, C.3, passim

Nolt, Johan; commander of Falkenstein; 1603, C.5, f.11

Norchg, Ricardus van; frater; 1428/06/01, A.29

Novimagio, Goswinus de; cappellanus of St Catherine's, Utrecht; 1495, C.2 f.198

Noyden, Ghertrudis daughter of Arnold, wife of Willem Passard; tenant in Utrecht; 1367+, B.p.208

Nycolai, Dirk; tenant at Lopik; 1367+, B.p.370

Nycolai, Johannes; landowner at Reeuwijk; 1367+, B.p.384

Nycolai, Margareta daughter of Dirk, & children; landowners at Langerak; 1367+, B.p.377

Nycolai, Tideman; tenant at Weesp; 1367+, B.p.287

Nycolay, Mauritius; tenant at Polsbroek; 1367+, B.p.367

Nyendael, Jacob & Alphard van; late leasers near Utrecht; 1367+, B.p.228

Nyenhusz, Bercardus; inhabitant of Arnhem; 1495, C.2, f.193

Nyenrode, dominus Ghisbert van, knight; landowner at Breukelen & Oudewater; 1367+, B.p.278, 279, 343

Nyevelt, Johanna domicella de; ? [Utrecht]; 1495, C.2, f.203

Odendorp, Henricus von; cellerarius in Mechelen; 1373, C.1

Oerde, Elias van den; tenant at Doorn & Langbroek; 1367+, B.p.236, 239

Oesterzel, Henricus; cappellanus prioratus Alamanie; 1449/12/29, A.47

Oesterzel, Henricus; commander of Kattendijke; 1449, 1450, A.48, 49, 51, 52

Oestrum, Nicolaus van; tenant at Houten; 1367+, B.p.246

Officialis Traiectensis; made sealed letter about 't Waal; 1367+, B.p.249

Oisterwick, Johannes; commander of Wesel, bailiff of Cologne; 1495, C.2, f.238; cf. Usterwich

Oldenburg, counts of; East-Frisia [Burgsteinfurt]; 1495, C.2, f.234

Olislagher, Johan; landowner at Oudewater; 1367+, B.p.348

Olislagher, Nicolaus; tenant at IJsselstein; 1367+, B.p.353

Oliverius, Michael; capellanus linguae Alemaniae; 1575/03/05, A.122

Oliverius, Michael; chaplain, commander of Mechelen; 1579/08/19, A.125

Oliverius, Michael; commander of Mechelen & Kieringen; 1586/05/13, A.126

Oliverius, Michael; commander of Mechelen, resigns; 1587/03/20, A.128

Oliverius, Michael; commander of Worms; 1587/03/20, A.129

Ommeren, van, c.s.*; deputies of Estates General; 1665/02/11, A.181*

Oorschot (Oerschoten), frater Willem van; administrator of St Catherine's, Utrecht, provisor curtis Reijerscop; 1367+, B.p.216, 219, 298-300

Oorschot (Oerscoten), Hendrik van; tenant at Harmelen; 1367+, B.p.293, 294

Oorschot (Orscoten), frater Hendrik; located tenants at Benschop; 1367+, B.p.358

Opburen, Willem van; tenant at Maarssen; 1367+, B.p.275

Opburen, Zweder van, son of Willem x Hasa van den Grotenhuys; tenant at Maarssen; 1367+, B.p.275

[Opburen], Hendrik son of Zweder [van]; tenant at Maarssen; 1367+, B.p.275

Orange (princeps Auraniae), [Maurits, stadtholder]; 1622/02/13, A.149

Orange, Frederick Henry, prince of; stadholder; Intro p.22

[Orange], Frederic Henderic [of]; prince-stadtholder; 1626, 1629, A.152, 153, 154

Orange, Philip William, prince of; had goods in Burgundy; Intro p.25

Orsbach, Gualtherus von (de Orspach); knight, without knight's commandery; 1587/03/20, A.129

Orsbach, Gualtherus von; knight, commander of Kieringen; 1589/03/23, A.134

Put (de Puteo), Jacob van de, father of Ghisbert van Ruwiel; house-owner in Utrecht; 1367+, B.p.258

Put (de Puteo), Nicolaus van de; landowner at Vleuten; 1367+, B.p.265

Putten & Geervliet, lord of; founded a yearly gift of cheeses from Geervliet; 1367+, B.p.385

Puy, Raymond du; Grand Master (1125-1153); Intro p.4

Quaedvoet, — ; former tenant at Nieuwlanderkerk; 1367+, B.p.381

Quaetvoet, Rutger son of Walich; tenant at Lopik; 1367+, B.p.371, 372

Quattelar, dominus Gerard; former tenant at Oudewater; 1367+, B.p.346

Quendorp, Hermannus; prebendatus at Burgsteinfurt; 1495, C.2, f.237

Quinon, Guillelmus; elemosinarius of Grand Master; 1510, A.95, 96

Quinon, Guillermus; commander of Arnhem; 1527/01/19, A.98

Quinon, Johannes; commander of Du Burgault, France; 1527/01/19, A.98

Quinon, Johannes; commander of Arnhem; 1530/03/18, A.99

Quint, Johan; convents brother Utrecht, commander of Harmelen; 1603, C.5, f.8-10

Quint, Machteldis widow of; late tenant at Harmelen; 1367+, B.p.302

Racht, Anton; commander of Wesel; 1458/08/01, A.58

Raet, Ditmar de; tenant of Nimwegen; 1700, C.6, f.51

Raffini, Petrus; Grand Commander (magnus preceptor conventus Rhodi); 1460/11/02, A.61

Raffini, Petrus; locumtenens of Grand Master [?]; 1462/05/29, A.65

Rain, Gerlacus; priest of St John, Wijtwerd; 1540, C.3, f.149

Ralof, Hendrik; see Witte (Albus), Johan

Ram, Herman den; tenant of Nimwegen; 1700, C.6, f.52

Ramkin, Hendrik; tenant in Utrecht; 1367+, B.p.207

Rampe, Gerard; tenant at Waarder; 1367+, B.p.326, 327, 328

Rampert, Cornelius; conventualis at Arnhem; 1540, C.3, f.160

Rampoys [?] (Pampoys), Tideman; land-owner in Utrecht; 1367+, B.p.206

Rampoys, Albert; tenant at Oudewater; 1367+, B,p.349

Rampoys, Gerard; tenant at Oudewater; 1367+, B.p.332

Rampoys, Hendrik; tenant at Nigtevecht; 1367+, B.p.285

Rampoys, Nicolaus & Copitte; tenants at Oudewater; 1367+, B.p.332, 345

Rampoyse, Dirk; landowner at Oudewater; 1367+, B.p.346

Randwick, Belia van; inhabitant of Utrecht; 1495, C.2, f.203

Rattenau*, Johann Werner von; frater [of German tongue]; 1626/08/24, A.151*

Ravenswade, Alard van; late tenant at Ravenswaaij; 1367+, B.p.238

Reccrot, Johannes; chaplain, commander of Hohenrein; 1493/08/05, A.82

Receiver of Delfland & Rijnland [Haarlem]; 1540, C.3, f.33

Receiver of King of Spain in Low Germany; 1572/05/09, A.119

Receiver of the Order; receiver of yearly responsions; 1540, C.3, f.33

Receivers of the Order; 1606/01/20, A.142

Receivers of Priorate Germany; 1432/ 07/03, A.33

Receivers of provincial chapter; 1606/ 01/20, A.142

Rechberc, Ulricus de; commander of Colmar; 1319/04/12, A.1

Rechen, Heinrich von; Order's priest, administrator Arnhem & Nimwegen; 1594, C.4, f.6-18, 20

Rechtenstein/ Rechenstein, Heinrich Ferdinand Freiherr von Stain a R.; commander of Sulz; 1695/06/18, A.195, 196

Reede, Bernardus Ernestus Freiherr von; late Prior of Germany; 1721/ 11/06, A.203

Reiffenberg*, Philips von; knight, commander of Arnhem; Intro p.10*

Reiffenberg, Philippus von (de Riffenberg); commander in Rüdigheim; 1449, 1451, A.53

Reiffenberg, Philippus von (de Riffenberg); frater prioratus Alamanie; 1462/07/06, A.66

Reiffenberg, Philippus von (de Riffenberch); commander of Arnhem &

ers at Oudewater; 1367+, B.p.344

Rodolphi, Leyda widow of Constant, & her children; tenants at Oudewater; 1367+, B.p.338

Roede, Dirk; former tenant at Ameide; 1367+, B.p.379

Roede, Hugo die; tenant at Harmelen; 1367+, B.p.288-290, 295, 296

Roede/ die Rode, Willem son of Johan; tenant near Utrecht & annuitant at Haastrecht; 1367+, B.p.226, 387

Roeden, Gijsbert van; tenant near Utrecht; 1367+, B.p.256, 260

Roeloffs, Henrij; citizen of Hoorn, galley-slave; 1629/02/05, A.154

Roemst, Gijsbert van; late tenant at Cothen; 1367+, B.p.243

Rohan, Emmanuel de; Grand Master (1775-1797); 1777/08/21, A.206

Rol, Johannes; commander of Hohenrein, Boux & Bassel; 1695/06/18, A.195, 196

Rolandi, widow of Arnold; inhabitant of Haarlem; 1495, C.2, f.223

Rosenbach, Philips von; commander of Arnhem/Nimwegen; 1572, 1575, 1594, A.119, 123, 135

Rosenbach, Philips von; commander of Arnhem/Nimwegen; 1594, C.4, f.5, 7, 9-12, 15-20

Rosenbach, Wipert von; commander of Basel & Hohenrein; 1586/09/20, A.127

Rosendal, Henricus; priest at Warffum; 1540, C.3, f.148

Rossi, Chevalier de; delegate of Grand Bailiff; 1713, D.p.683

Rotardi, Gerard; tenant at Benschop; 1367+, B.p.363, 364

Rotardi, Herman; tenant at Woerden; 1367+, B.p.317

Rotardi, Peter; landowner at Oudewater; 1367+, B.p.345

Rothusen*, Thomas van; commander of Arnhem, knight; Intro p.10*

Rothusen, Thomas van; knight, commander of Arnhem/Nimwegen; 1496, 1500, 1501, 1503, A.83, 84, 85, 86, 87, 90

Rotterdam, broeder Florens Claes zoen van; benefactor of St Catherine's, Utrecht; 1367+, B.p.386

Rouvière, de la; envoy of the Order to Münster; 1647/12/27, A.159

Rozemond, Elisabeth daughter of Johan; tenant at Polsbroek; 1367+, B.p.369

Ruijter, Roeloff de; tenant of Nimwegen; 1700, C.6, f.51

Ruisch (Reüsch), Hendrik; commander at Ingen; 1594, C.4, f.25, 31

Rutenbec, Johannes; tenant of Sint Jansdal; 1495, C.2, f.208

Ruter, frater Frederik; administrator [?] of St Catherine's, Utrecht, 1354; 1367+, B.p.350

Rutgheri, Aleydis widow; late tenant at Oudewater; 1367+, B.p.340

Ruthgeri, Speyard; tenant at Oudewater; 1367+, B.p.340, 343

Ruwiel (Ruweel), Ghisbert van, son of Jacob van de Put (de Putco); house-owner in, & landowner near Utrecht; 1367+, B.p.202, 258-259

Ruys, Huych; surveyor of Utrecht, 16th/17th century; 1367+, B.p.234

Ruysche, Gerard; tenant at Oudewater; 1367+, B.p.331

Ruyschen, Aleydis, wife of Johan Bernardi; tenant in Utrecht; 1367+, B.p.200

Ruyter, [Michiel de]; vice admiral; 1664/11/24, A.181

Ryqwiinssoen, Jan; former tenant at Horstweerde; 1367+, B.p.286

Saffentiin, Matheus; tenant at Polsbroek; 1367+, B.p.366

Salant, Bertold van; cappellanus of St Catherine's, Utrecht; 1495, C.2 f.198

Salant, Johan van; ? [Arnhem]; 1495, C.2, f.193

Sammels, Heyno; tenant at Wijk bij Duurstede; 1367+, B.p.241

Sanderi, — ; landowner at Benschop; 1367+, B.p.356

Sanderi, Johan; tenant at Polsbroek; 1367+, B.p.369

Sanderi, Nicolaus; tenant at Polsbroek; 1367+, B.p.369

Sanders, Hendrick; alderman (schepen) at Niel; 1719/12/07, C.7, f.1

Sassen, Theodoricus; magister, account manager of Bailiff of Utrecht; 1540, C.3, f.12, 164, 166-168

Sayn, Oliuerius von (de Seina); commendator in Arnhem; 1323^1324/ 01/11, A.2

Scade van Kweekhoven (de Quedinc-

Wolfard, Johan, & wife, daughter of Florens Vischer; landowners at Oudewater; 1367+, B.p.343

Wolff, Herman; chaplain, commander of Bockelesch; 1495, C.2, f.234

Wolfortis, Oliverius; sheriff (scultetus) at Wemeldinge; 1540, C.3, f.169

Wolter, Dirk; tenant at Oudewater; 1367+, B.p.346

Wolteri, Egidius; tenant at IJsselstein & Benschop; 1367+, B.p.353, 354

Wolteri, Nicolaus; tenant at Oudewater; 1367+, B.p.334

Wolteri, Willem; former tenant at Ameide; 1367+, B.p.379

Wou, Timan van; commander of Haarlem; 1594, 1595*, C.4, f.33-36, 37*

Wou, Timan van; commander of Haarlem, 1594/1595; 1603, C.5, f.8

Wou, Timan van; commander of Haarlem; 1582, D.p.662, 663

Woude, Engelbert van der; landowner at Oudewater; 1367+, B.p.340

Wouteri, Albert; tenant at Breukelen; 1367+, B.p.278

Wulven (Uulven), Hubert van; landowner near Utrecht; 1367+, B.p.230, 263

Wurm, Herman; inhabitant of Arnhem; 1495, C.2, f.194, 195

Wurze, Barbara daughter of Gerard van, wife of Willem Roede; tenant near Utrecht & annuitant at Haastrecht; 1367+, B.p.226, 387

Wyse, Heyn; tenant at Benschop; 1367+, B.p.360

Wyssen, Adrianus; inhabitant of Wemeldinge; 1495, C.2, f.213

Wyt, magister; inhabitant of Zeeland; 1495, C.2, f.203

Wytven de Mierle, Johannes dictus de; notary public of Liege curia; 1373, C.1

Xanten (de Zanctis), Lodewijk van; tenant in Utrecht; 1367+, B.p.206

Ydenszoon, Peter; house-owner in Utrecht; 1367+, B.p.202

Yeingen, Olfart; inhabitant of IJsbrechtum; 1495, C.2, f.219

Yen zoen, Rover; landowner at Linschoten, 1367+, B.p.312;

Yen, Johan son of Herman; tenant at Breukelen; 1367+, B.p.278, 279

Yen, Reyner son of; former tenant at Lopik; 1367+, B.p.374

Ymme, Nicolaus son of Hendrik, & son Nicolaus jr.; landowners near Utrecht; 1367+, B.p.231

Yoie, Johan son of Lubbert; tenant at Harmelen; 1367+, B.p.293

Yoie, Johan son of Peter; tenant at Harmelen; 1367+, B.p.292, 293, 300, 302, 311

Ysebrandi, Aleydis; landowner at Benschop; 1367+, B.p.354

Ysebrandi, Johan; tenant at Harmelen; 1367+, B.p.305, 307

Ysendoern, domina Beerta van; usufructuary at Cothen; 1367+, B.p.242

IJsselstein & Egmond (Egmonda et Yselsteine), — lord of; landowner/tenant at Benschop; 1367+, B.p.360, 362

IJsselstein (Yselsteine), — lady of; landowner at Benschop & Polsbroek; 1367+, B.p.360, 366

IJsselstein (Yselsteyne), — lord of; lord of justice at Jutphaas &c., landowner at Woerden; 1367+, B.p. 255, 315, 316, 358, 360, 365, 369

IJsselstein (Yselsteyne), Ghisbert van; landowner at Vleuten; 1367+, B.p.268

IJsselstein (Yselsteyne), Otto van; landowner in Utrecht; 1367+, B.p.205

IJsselstein, Frederic van; knight, lord of IJsselstein; 1495, C.2, f.206

Ysselt, Cosinus van; landowner at IJsselstein; 1367+, B.p.353

Zacosta, Petrus Raymundus; Grand Master (1461-1467); 1462, 1465, A.66, 68, 69

Zalen, Heynekin Heynekini; tenant at Kamerik; 1367+, B.p.314

Zalen, Johan son of Hendrik, & children; landowners at Waarder; 1367+, B.p.326

Zand, Rheynher van 't (de Arena); inhabitant of Arnhem; 1495, C.2, f.195

Zanen, Simeon van; priest, commander of Haarlem; 1540, C.3, f.31, 32, 34, 35

Zasse, Dirk; tenant near Utrecht; 1367+, B.p.223

Zeller, Catharina van; tenant of Nimwegen; 1700, C.6, f.52

Zeuwelkin, Arnt; priest, prior conventus domus Traiecti, locumtenens during

INDEX OF PLACES

half farm Utrecht; 1367+, B.p.379

Meerkerk, op Bloemendaell; location with farm Utrecht; 1367+, B.p.380

Meerkerk, Quakernake; location with half farm Utrecht; 1367+, B.p.379, 380

Meerkerk, Scadeland; land next to half farm Utrecht; 1367+, B.p.379

Meerkerk (Merkirch); village with fields Utrecht; 1495, C.2, f.200, 201

Meerkerk (Merekert); village in Land van Vianen; 1594, C.4, f.23

Meern (Merna, Meerne); stream next to fields Utrecht; 1367+, B.p.259, 264

Meerndijk (Marendiic, Maernediic); dike next to fields Utrecht, 1367+, B.p.288, 289, 290

Meisenheim (Meyfenbeym); preceptoria in Alta Alemania; 1501/10/01, A.88

Meisenheim (Meysenheim); preceptoria; 1495, C.2 contents

Mereveld [?] (Mehren); fields near Utrecht; 1594, C.4, f.23

Mergenheim; membrum of Niederbreisig, preceptoria pro capellano/serviente; 1493/08/05, A.82

Mergenheim; [membrum of Niederbreisig], preceptoria in Bassa Alemania; 1501/10/01, A.89

Mergentheim (Mergetheim); preceptoria pro fratre milite; 1493/08/05, A.82

Mergentheim (Mengetheim); preceptoria in Bassa Alemania; 1501/10/01, A.89

Mergentheim (Mergetem); commandery; 1495, C.2 contents

Mergenthcim (Mergtthen); preceptoria conioncta cum Hall; 1540, C.3 contents

Messina; town with early hospital; Intro p.5

Messina (Messana); priorate; 1431/03/20, C.2, f.207

Messina (Messanensis); priorate; 1495, C.2, f.207

Meteler* [?]; parish near Burgsteinfurt; 1495, C.2, f.(236)> 239*

Middelburg*; commandery in Zeeland; Intro p.16, 23

Middelburg (Midelburg); domus sive preceptoria, commandery under Utrecht; 1450, 1588, c.1652, A.51, 131, 168

Middelburg (Middelborgh); parish with fields Utrecht; 1367+, B.p.196, 384, 385

Middelburg, Bredenhoeve; location with field Utrecht; 1367+, B.p.385

Middelburg (Myddelburgh, Myddelburch); membrum of Utrecht; 1495, C.2 contents, f.199, 215, 216

Middelburg (Middelbug, Midelborg, Midelburg); town in Zeeland, with membrum of Utrecht; 1540, C.3 contents, f.169-171

Middelburg, Brouwerij (Browrie); house, located; 1540, C.3, f.170

Middelburg, conventus sororum; Tertiaris convent, Grauwzusters; 1540, C.3, f.170

Middelburg (Meidelbürgk); town in Zeeland with commandery, vacant; 1594, C.4, f.3, 25

Molen [?]; hamlet with fields Haarlem; 1495, C.2, f.222

Molenaarsgraaf (Molnersgrave); parish with fields Utrecht; 1367+, B.p.196, 378

Molenaarsgraaf, Ghisenrevliet et Ofweghen et Ruggebroke; locations next to field Utrecht; 1367+, B.p.378

Molenaarsgraaf, Ziitwinde; field Utrecht; 1367+, B.p.378

Mons, Belgium*; town with State archives; Intro p.25*

Monster; village with fields Haarlem; 1495, C.2, f.222, 223

Monster (Munster); village in Delfland with fields Haarlem; 1540, C.3, f.32, 34

Monster; village with fields Haarlem; 1594, C.4, f.35

Montbrison*; commenda; 1663/06/05, A.173*

Montfoort*; membrum of Utrecht; Intro p.23*

Montfoort (Montforth); commandery; c.1652, A.168

Montfoort (Montfoerde); parish with fields Utrecht; 1367+, B.p.196, 340, 349-352

Montfoort, an den Tiendwech; location with field Utrecht; 1367+, B.p.352

Montfoort, in den Achtersloet; location with field Utrecht; 1367+, B.P.352

Montfoort, Kaeviertel; field Utrecht; 1367+, B.p.350

Montfoort (Monfort, Montfort); town

INDEX OF COINS

ward for Kempinck & Pallandt; 1667/12/09, A.189*

marca Aquensis*; 7 = 1 florenus aureus Renensis; 1540, C.3, f.129

marca argenti; 1367+, B.p.224, 244, 276, 278, 291, 298, 304, 315, 322, 365, 369, 371

marca Coloniensis; 2, part of income Mechelen; 1540, C.3, f.126

marca*; 7 = 1 florenus aureus; 1540, C.3, f.128*

marca, marc; 1367+, B.p.243, 245, 251, 256, 257, 273, 277, 289, 290, 292, 295, 301, 303, 305, 307, 309, 317, 331, 333, 335, 338, 353, 354, 362, 368

marcha puri argenti; 2 marc = 10 f fortis ponderis; 1373, C.1

nobel, Engelsche; 1367+, B.p.387

oblus; 18 obli = 1 albus, Mechelen; 1495, C.2, f.176, 177, 178

ortgen, ortgin; 12 = 1 stuber, Arnhem, Nimwegen; 1495, C.2, f.193, 195-197

ortgen; 4 = 1 stuber, Ingen, Buren, Wemeldinge; 1495, C.2, f.204, 206, 213

ortgen; 9, part of stuber, Utrecht; 1495, C.2, f.219

ortgin; 6 +st.8 for 1 malder of oats, Nimwegen; 1495, C.2, f.197

orth; Br.f2 + 1 Orth for 1 Malter barley; 1594, C.4, f.23, 24

penninc; 1367+, B.p.242

Philips Thaler; 100, borrowed by house Arnhem; 1594, C.4, f.17

Philipsgulden; 1 = 28 Stüfer, Nimwegen; 1594, C.4, f.10

Philipsgulden; 75, rent from Huissen; 1594, C.4, f.12

Philipsgulden; 14, to pay for debt, Nimwegen; 1594, C.4, f.13

plagga, plak; 24 anetas (ducks) vel 24 plaggas, 1 plak pro 1 pulla; 1367+, B.p.313, 314, 351

plastrum; 40,000, minimum prize for house Nimwegen; 1704, A.200

postulaets gulden; 4 postulaets = 3 Rijnse, Waarder (1447); 1367+, B.p.330

quartier; 1/4 of oud scilde; 1367+, B.p.351

reichs gulden; 66+ = f88, chapter costs Arnhem; 1732, C.9, f.10

reichsdahler; 8000, against Dutch merchants [?]; 1652/11/14, A.166

reichsthaler/ Reichswärung; 8 yearly, chapter costs Utrecht + 2468, debts in anti-Turktax; 1606/01/20, A.142

reichsthaler; 3500, borrowed by house Utrecht; 1594, C.4, f.25

rider, Hollandse; 1367+, B.p.364

schild, oud scilt, scilde; 1367+, B.p.218, 270, 271, 280, 351

schild, see also: scutum

schild, golden (gülden Schylt); 1, recognition house Nimwegen; 1594, C.4, f.14

schobe; 15 = 1 stuber, Sneek; 1495, C.2, f.218, 219

scudatus auri moncte Cesaris aut Francie, antiquus; 1367+, B.p.197, 214, 227, 363

scudatus auri regis Francie moncte, antiquus; 1367+, B.p.[322], 355

scudatus auri, antiquus; 1367+, B.p.244, 249, 255, 275, 279, 282, 303, 332, 352, 353, 358, 359, 363, 367, 370, 373-374, 375

scudatus, antiquus; 1367+, B.p.202, 215, 240, 246, 248, 306, 316, 331, 342, 356, 361, 366, 369, 382

schudatus antiquus auri Francie; 25, responsio of Sneek; 1378/10/01, C.2, f.217

scudo aureo; 50, annual rent from Erlingen; 1587, 1589*, A.130

scudo; 30,000, due from Dutch houses; c.1652, A.169

scudo in moneta di Malta; 6550 = 7205 fiorini imperiali; 1777-1796, A.210

scutifer Brebantinus; 32 = 1 florenus aureus Rhenensis, Arnhem, St Jansdal; 1540, C.3, f.160, 165

scutifer Brebantinus; part of florenus, Nimwegen; 1540, C.3, f.161

scutifer; part of florenus (not Renensis), Utrecht; 1540, C.3, f.9

scutifer; 37 = 1 corona Francie, Utrecht; 1540, C.3, f.12

scutifer; 24 = 1 florenus Emdensis, Oosterwierum; 1540, C.3, f.152

scutifer; part of f aureus Renensis, Arn-

INDEX OF WEIGHTS AND MEASURES

INDEX OF PATRON SAINTS

INDEX OF CONCEPTS

Studies in the History of Christian Thought

EDITED BY HEIKO A. OBERMAN

50. HOENEN, M. J. F. M. *Marsilius of Inghen.* Divine Knowledge in Late Medieval Thought. 1993
51. O'MALLEY, J. W., IZBICKI, T. M. and CHRISTIANSON, G. (eds.). *Humanity and Divinity in Renaissance and Reformation.* Essays in Honor of Charles Trinkaus. 1993
52. REEVE, A. (ed.) and SCREECH, M. A. (introd.). *Erasmus' Annotations on the New Testament.* Galatians to the Apocalypse. 1993
53. STUMP, Ph. H. *The Reforms of the Council of Constance (1414-1418).* 1994
54. GIAKALIS, A. *Images of the Divine.* The Theology of Icons at the Seventh Ecumenical Council. With a Foreword by Henry Chadwick. 1994
55. NELLEN, H. J. M. and RABBIE, E. (eds.). *Hugo Grotius – Theologian.* Essays in Honour of G. H. M. Posthumus Meyjes. 1994
56. TRIGG, J. D. *Baptism in the Theology of Martin Luther.* 1994
57. JANSE, W. *Albert Hardenberg als Theologe.* Profil eines Bucer-Schülers. 1994
59. SCHOOR, R.J.M. VAN DE. *The Irenical Theology of Théophile Brachet de La Milletière (1588-1665).* 1995
60. STREHLE, S. *The Catholic Roots of the Protestant Gospel.* Encounter between the Middle Ages and the Reformation. 1995
61. BROWN, M.L. *Donne and the Politics of Conscience in Early Modern England.* 1995
62. SCREECH, M.A. (ed.). *Richard Mocket, Warden of All Souls College, Oxford, Doctrina et Politia Ecclesiae Anglicanae.* An Anglican Summa. Facsimile with Variants of the Text of 1617. Edited with an Introduction. 1995
63. SNOEK, G.J.C. *Medieval Piety from Relics to the Eucharist.* A Process of Mutual Interaction. 1995
64. PIXTON, P.B. *The German Episcopacy and the Implementation of the Decrees of the Fourth Lateran Council, 1216-1245.* Watchmen on the Tower. 1995
65. DOLNIKOWSKI, E.W. *Thomas Bradwardine: A View of Time and a Vision of Eternity in Fourteenth-Century Thought.* 1995
66. RABBIE, E. (ed.). *Hugo Grotius, Ordinum Hollandiae ac Westfrisiae Pietas (1613).* Critical Edition with Translation and Commentary. 1995
67. HIRSH, J.C. *The Boundaries of Faith.* The Development and Transmission of Medieval Spirituality. 1996
68. BURNETT, S.G. *From Christian Hebraism to Jewish Studies.* Johannes Buxtorf (1564-1629) and Hebrew Learning in the Seventeenth Century. 1996
69. BOLAND O.P., V. *Ideas in God according to Saint Thomas Aquinas.* Sources and Synthesis. 1996
70. LANGE, M.E. *Telling Tears in the English Renaissance.* 1996
71. CHRISTIANSON, G. and T.M. IZBICKI (eds.). *Nicholas of Cusa on Christ and the Church.* Essays in Memory of Chandler McCuskey Brooks for the American Cusanus Society. 1996
72. MALI, A. *Mystic in the New World.* Marie de l'Incarnation (1599-1672). 1996
73. VISSER, D. *Apocalypse as Utopian Expectation (800-1500).* The Apocalypse Commentary of Berengaudus of Ferrières and the Relationship between Exegesis, Liturgy and Iconography. 1996
74. O'ROURKE BOYLE, M. *Divine Domesticity.* Augustine of Thagaste to Teresa of Avila. 1997
75. PFIZENMAIER, T.C. *The Trinitarian Theology of Dr. Samuel Clarke (1675-1729).* Context, Sources, and Controversy. 1997
76. BERKVENS-STEVELINCK, C., J. ISRAEL and G.H.M. POSTHUMUS MEYJES (eds.). *The Emergence of Tolerance in the Dutch Republic.* 1997
77. HAYKIN, M.A.G. (ed.). *The Life and Thought of John Gill (1697-1771).* A Tercentennial Appreciation. 1997
78. KAISER, C.B. *Creational Theology and the History of Physical Science.* The Creationist Tradition from Basil to Bohr. 1997
79. LEES, J.T. *Anselm of Havelberg.* Deeds into Words in the Twelfth Century. 1997
80. WINTER, J.M. VAN. *Sources Concerning the Hospitallers of St John in the Netherlands, 14th-18th Centuries.* 1998
81. TIERNEY, B. *Foundations of the Conciliar Theory.* The Contribution of the Medieval Canonists from Gratian to the Great Schism. Enlarged New Edition. 1998
82. MIERNOWSKI, J. *Le Dieu Néant.* Théologies négatives à l'aube des temps modernes. 1998

Prospectus available on request

KONINKLIJKE BRILL — P.O.B. 9000 — 2300 PA LEIDEN — THE NETHERLANDS